Jeff Herman's
GUIDE TO
BOOK
PUBLISHERS,
EDITORS,
& LITERARY
AGENTS
2011

Who they are!
What they want!
How to
win them
over!

21ST EDITION

JEFF HERMAN

sourcebooks

Published by Sourcebooks, Inc.
P.O. Box 4410, Naperville, Illinois 60567-4410
(630) 961-3900
Fax: (630) 961-2168
www.sourcebooks.com

Printed and bound in the United States of America.
DR 10 9 8 7 6 5 4 3 2 1

ACKNOWLEDGMENTS

Me

Deborah Herman

Caleb Plakun. Frankly, I still find the sound of his name to be odd. But he's a good guy and does a very fine job. He can be found in my office, until the day that he can't be.

Cassie Lynch. I've always liked the sound of her name and the super professionalism of her work. Try her out, cassielynch@gmail.com.

Peter Lynch. He's my editor at Sourcebooks. If he didn't actually exist, I would have to pray that he would.

People who use this book. If you weren't using it, I'd stop generating it.

To everyone I forgot. You probably don't know who you are, but that doesn't negate the fact that you made a difference.

DEDICATION

In some ways these few words might be the most crucial part of this book. In that spirit, I want writers to remind themselves that they are at the heart of creation whenever they write.

PUBLISHERS, EDITORS, AND LITERARY AGENTS

ADVICE FOR WRITERS

THE INDEPENDENT EDITORS

RESOURCES FOR WRITERS

INTRODUCTION

Dear Writer,

Welcome to the 2011 (21st) edition of this book. Generating it each year for so many years gives me a unique sense of pride and purpose.

As someone who was young and is presently less young, I will confirm that nothing beats lessons learned from direct experience, especially those instances that carve humility into our know-it-all hides. But being a newbie at anything, including writing for publication, has crucial advantages that veterans can only reminisce about.

Not knowing that there's a lot you don't know is empowering. Being ignorant won't hold you back from entering the contest, but feeling ignorant can be paralyzing. Many people achieve the biggest strides, and experience the greatest satisfaction of their lives, when engaged in something completely new. Ignorance is an opportunity for innovation, because you haven't been corrupted with a litany of dissuasions about what "can't be done," or how it "must be done." You're a clean vessel with the power to recreate reality. Inadvertently, you might even change the rules.

If you're a rookie in the contest of getting published, celebrate. Don't approach the venture with the mindset you don't know what to do, or that the odds are too daunting. Accept that you're capable of discovering what you need to know along the way, and perhaps you'll stumble upon new methods that others dismissed or failed to consider. It helps to soak up information from self-help books like the one in your hands, to attend classes, and to listen to others who have previously arrived. Beaten paths have worked before and are likely to work again, but nothing will compare to the firsthand experiences waiting specifically for you. Whatever happens to you belongs to you.

Originality is rarely deliberate; it's more likely to result from errors, unintended consequences, or from people who are organically different. The better we become at a particular task, the less likely we are to be original. It's a mistake to compare yourself to other people's apparent abilities and accomplishments. Many gifted people fail to act, lack passion, or have simply moved on, whereas many "ordinary" people make valuable contributions because they show up, do the best they can, and are true to themselves.

True writers are disciplined enough to be free; sane enough to knowingly risk pain and disappointment; generous enough to give themselves time to think and write; and compassionate enough to carry themselves through the burn when no one else will. Writing demands isolation while delivering unification. Anything you want can be manifested in thought and on paper. Writers are creators.

Use this book as a friendly tool. Nothing herein is meant to constrain you; everything is conveyed in the spirit of promoting your possibilities and choices. None of us can dictate nor absolutely predict outcomes, but any of us can choose what we want to achieve. Books and lives will come and go, but not without rippling into the future.

Stay in touch,
Jeff Herman
jeff@jeffherman.com; 413-298-0077; PO Box 1522, Stockbridge, MA 01262

ABOUT THE AUTHOR

Jeff Herman is the founder of The Jeff Herman Literary Agency, LLC, based in Stockbridge, Massachussetts. One of the most innovative agents in the book business, he represents more than 100 writers and has sold more than 500 titles in the United States and internationally. Herman has been extensively written and talked about in numerous print publications and broadcast programs, and he speaks at writers' conferences around the country. He is the coauthor with Deborah Levine Herman of *Write the Perfect Book Proposal*. Be sure to visit his high-content website at www.jeffherman.com.

CONTRIBUTORS

Deborah Levine Herman, Chairman of the Board, The Jeff Herman Literary Agency, Stockbridge, Massachusetts, deborah@jeffherman.com, blog: www.spiritualwritingagent.com

William Hamilton, Publisher, University of Hawaii Press

Greg Ioannou, Editorial Director, Colborne Communications, Toronto, Ontario, gregg@colcomm.ca

Jerry Gross, Freelance Editor and Book Doctor, Croton-on-Hudson, NY, GrosAssoc@aol.com

Mr. Jamie Forbes, 212-924-0657

Toni Robino, President, With Flying Colours Literary Services, Conifer, Colorado, ToniRobino@yahoo.com

Gerald Sindell, Independent Publishing Consultant, ThoughtLeadersINTL., www. thoughtleadersintl.com, 415-789-9040

OPPORTUNITY AT A GLANCE

It's all about fit. Just because you've written the perfect book doesn't mean every publisher will want to buy it. McGraw-Hill develops nonfiction—they're not interested in a romance, even a super-steamy one. Likewise Simon Spotlight, a children's imprint, doesn't want to read your memoir. However, there are dozens (perhaps hundreds) of publishers who might be interested in your book, and we've made it easier to find them.

At the top of every listing, there are images noting the publisher's priority genres. These are the categories of books that they have specifically mentioned as having an interest in acquiring or have demonstrated great success in promoting. As you skim through the front half of the book, you'll get a rough idea of whom you or your agent should approach (especially for a niche like poetry, science fiction, or craft). Then go back and be sure to read the full listings for details about submission guidelines and to learn more about the individual publishers.

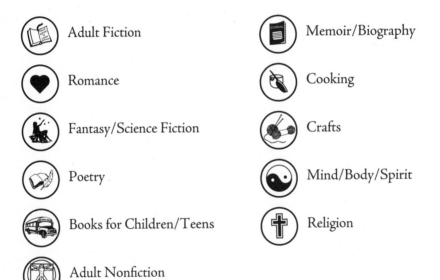

Adult Fiction

Romance

Fantasy/Science Fiction

Poetry

Books for Children/Teens

Adult Nonfiction

Memoir/Biography

Cooking

Crafts

Mind/Body/Spirit

Religion

SECTION ONE

PUBLISHING
CONGLOMERATES

THE MULTINATIONAL CONGLOMERATED PUBLISHING ENTITIES

JEFF HERMAN

A long time ago, the U.S. book publishing business consisted of hundreds of mom-and-pop companies. Each was generally named for the individual(s) who founded the firm, and their respective catalogues reflected their own special tastes and sensibilities. Separately, none of these entities or individuals had the power to dictate the contemporary status or future direction of publishing. They were a thriving community of several hundred distinct pieces. Collectively, they comprised our nation's entire book publishing structure.

The revolution came and happened quickly. Some of us complained, but it didn't make any difference. It was a funny revolution in that it reversed the usual dynamic. Unlike the breaking away of exploited tribes from masters of conquest, which is revolution in its most romantic form, we watched as faceless and formless conquerors wrapped themselves around most of our precious tribes and soundlessly absorbed them into a small number of obese oceans. Perhaps those who might have cared the most saw gold before they saw the cost. Can we blame them? Should we even judge the result? Perhaps it is wiser to simply adjust.

We have consolidated the largest multinational publishing properties into their own section. It seemed right to do so, since consolidation has been their most striking feature. These companies possess the brand names of the firms they have acquired over the past three decades. While some of the firms may be led by high-profile individuals or greatly influenced by multigenerational families that control large blocks of non-traded stock, it is also safe to say that these firms are greater than any one person or any unified collection of people. At the end of the day, it is the various pension funds and institutional investment firms that must be satisfied.

There are two other key features of multinational publishers. 1) Most of them are controlled by foreign interests. 2) The book publishing programs are an extremely small part of a much larger agenda, which includes movies, magazines, broadcast and cable channels, newspapers, music, and the Internet.

Do not let my irreverent or ominous tone chase you away. At all of these firms you will find hardworking, dedicated editors who want nothing more than the ability to publish good books. And they manage to achieve that. So join with them and adjust to the system as it is. The best thing you can do is get your book published.

This section is followed by a large number of independent and small houses, each of which is capable of doing as much, or more, than the big houses. The independent houses are not vestiges from a dead past. To the contrary, they keep the current publishing climate vibrant, and help create the future with their entrepreneurial and innovative ways. Don't ever think twice about joining them.

I have asserted my discretionary powers to place a few houses in the Independent Section that could also fit into the Conglomerates Section. Obviously, not all corporations are the same. Some are the equivalent of Jupiter, while others are more like Mercury (I'm actually referring to size, not "personalities"). When the book division is not a mere asterisk within its corporate envelope, but is instead a crucial piece, you will find it with the independents.

BERTELSMANN AG

A global media firm based in Germany, Bertelsmann AG is comprised of publishing, music, and broadcasting operations in nearly 60 countries; these include Random House, the world's largest English-language general trade book publisher. Bertelsmann is a privately held company, owned by the Mohn family and their foundation.

Recent Bertelsmann acquisitions—including BBC Books, Multnomah, and Triumph Books—helped Bertelsmann in 2006 achieve their "most successful year in history" with record sales of 19.3 billion euros. CEO Thomas Rabe said they plan to start shopping for more corporate acquisitions in 2008, fueling even more growth and opportunity within this media leviathan.

RANDOM HOUSE, INC.

CROWN PUBLISHING GROUP

KNOPF DOUBLEDAY PUBLISHING GROUP

RANDOM HOUSE CHILDREN'S BOOKS

RANDOM HOUSE INFORMATION GROUP

RANDOM HOUSE PUBLISHING GROUP

1745 Broadway, New York, NY 10019

212-782-9000

www.randomhouse.com

Founded in 1925 and acquired by Bertelsmann in 1998, Random House has grown into an intricate web of divisions, publishing groups, and imprints. The years 2008 and 2009 have been witness to a massive reorganization and the consolidation of Random House's many components. The Bantam Dell, WaterBrook Multnomah, Doubleday, and Knopf divisions have all been combined or have had their imprints shifted around, leading to the creation of the Knopf Doubleday Publishing Group and the expansion of the Crown Publishing Group and Random House divisions.

The span of this house's titles runs both wide and deep, including a broad array of categories in fiction and nonfiction. Random House publishes in hardcover, trade paperback, mass-market paperback, audio, electronic, and digital, for adults, young adults, and children.

The company was founded when Bennett Cerf and Donald Klopfer purchased The Modern Library, an imprint that reprinted classic works of literature, from publisher Horace Liveright. Two years later, in 1927, the publisher decided to broaden its publishing activities, and the Random House colophon made its debut.

In recent years, Random House revenues have continued to grow, despite a sluggish international marketplace. Random House steadily produces a stellar number of *New York Times* bestsellers—thirty-seven at number one in 2006 alone. The international nature of the company tends to attract a global audience, with operations in Asia, South Africa, South America, and the UK, to name a few. In 2007, Random House launched Insight, a U.S. book and audio search and browse service that operates as a widget inside Web browsers. If you have online access, be sure to explore the Random House website; it's chock full of information, including blogs, podcasts, and newsletters.

Random House editors prefer to accept manuscripts submitted by literary agents. They do not accept unsolicited submissions, proposals, manuscripts, or submission queries via email at this time.

Markus Dohle, CEO, Random House

CROWN PUBLISHING GROUP

BROADWAY BOOKS

CLARKSON POTTER

CROWN

CROWN BUSINESS

CROWN FORUM

DOUBLEDAY RELIGION

HARMONY BOOKS

SHAYE AREHEART BOOKS

TEN SPEED PRESS

THREE RIVERS PRESS

WATERBROOK MULTNOMAH

WATSON-GUPTILL PUBLICATIONS

The Crown Publishing Group originated in 1933 and is known today for the broad scope of its publishing program and its singular market responsiveness, qualities that are reflected in its savvy selection of authors and books and in its aggressive efforts to market them.

Acquired by Random House in 1988, Crown incorporates a number of Random House imprints and acquisitions that together make up the Crown Publishing Group. Random House has restructured its organization to incorporate Broadway, Doubleday Religion, and Waterbrook Multnomah into the Crown Group. Random House has also purchased and incorporated the previously independent Ten Speed Press and Watson-Guptill under the Crown umbrella.

Jenny Frost, Publisher

BROADWAY BOOKS

Broadway generates a variety of nonfiction, including celebrity autobiography and biography; historical, political, and cultural biography and memoirs; politics and current affairs; multicultural topics; popular culture; cookbooks, diet, and nutrition; consumer reference; business; personal finance; and popular psychology, spirituality, and women's issues. The house also provides selective commercial/literary frontlist fiction, primarily by established or highly promotable authors. Broadway's emporium strategy involves publishing unique, marketable books of the highest editorial quality by authors who are authorities in their field and who use their credibility and expertise to promote their work.

Broadway has established many long-running bestsellers, including *Saving Graces: Finding Solace and Strength from Friends and Strangers* by Elizabeth Edwards; Frances Mayes's *Bella Tuscany* and *Under the Tuscan Sun*; Bill Bryson's *In a Sunburned Country*, *A Walk in the Woods*, and *I'm a Stranger Here Myself*; Bob Costas's *Fair Ball*; and Bill O'Reilly's *Who's Looking Out for You?*

In addition to narrative nonfiction, Broadway publishes a highly successful range of self-help, mind/body/spirit, business, and cooking books.

Recent Broadway titles include *Jasmine and Fire* by Salma Abdelnour; *Wise as Serpents, Harmless as Doves* by Alethea Black; *Exes and Ohs* by Shallon Lester; *The Break-Up Bible* by Rachel Sussman; and *Black Fire: The True Biography of the Original Tom Sawyer* by Robert Graysmith.

Broadway does not accept unsolicited manuscripts; only agented works are considered.

Jenny Frost, President and Publisher

Charles Conrad, Deputy Editorial Director—New nonfiction projects; popular culture, social history, humor, biography, and literary nonfiction; contemporary literary and quality fiction

Stacey Creamer, Editor-in-Chief

Gerald Howard, Vice President and Editorial Director—Narrative nonfiction, unusual literary fiction

Christine Pride, Editor—Narrative nonfiction, fiction

Lorraine Glennon, Editor—Memoir, general nonfiction

Jenna Ciongoli, Editor—Nonfiction narrative, reference, current affairs, politics, history

Vanessa Mobley, Editor—History, politics, current affairs

Talia Krohn, Editor—Humor, business and financial investing, science

Hallie Falquet, Editor—Humor, relationship and advice

Roger Scholl, Editor—Nonfiction narrative, business, current affairs

Laura Swerdloff, Editor—Humor, politics, reference

CLARKSON POTTER
POTTER CRAFT
POTTER STYLE

Clarkson Potter is a leader in beautifully illustrated nonfiction books on cooking, parenting, pets, crafts and hobbies, decorating, self-help, and other lifestyle topics. Clarkson Potter authors include Martha Stewart, Mario Batali, Chris Casson Madden, and Ina Garten.

In 2006, Clarkson Potter hired a new editorial director, Doris Cooper, who came on board to explore new options in lifestyle publishing. The house also hired its first editorial director for the Potter Style imprint, Chris Navratil.

Recent titles include *The By Hand Kitchen* by Alana Chernila; *Fresh American Style* by Annie Selke; *Pretty Delicious* by Gayla Trail; *Hammered* by Thom Filicia; *Lost and Found* by Tereasa; and *A New Turn in the South* by Hugh Acheson.

Direct query and SASE to:

Lauren Shakely, Senior Vice President, Publisher

Doris Cooper, Editor-in-Chief—Lifestyle, narrative

Emily Takoudes, Senior Editor—Cooking, nonfiction narrative

Judy Pray, Senior Editor

Rica Allannic, Senior Editor—Cookbooks

Aliza Fogelson, Editor—Decorating, cooking, food, how-to, biography, life-style

Rosy Ngo, Editor—Memoir, lifestyle, cooking

Ashley Phillips, Editor—Cooking

POTTER CRAFT

Potter Craft publishes books in the areas of crocheting, jewelry making, knitting, paper crafts, sewing, embroidery, and general crafts. Some recent titles include *Knitting and Tea: 25 Classic Knits and the Teas That Inspired Them* by Jane and Patrick Gotellier; *Martha Stewart's Encyclopedia of Crafts* by Martha Stewart; and *Born-Again Vintage: 25 Ways to Deconstruct, Reinvent, and Recycle Your Wardrobe* by Bridgett Artiste.

Victoria Craven, Editorial Director

Rosy Ngo, Editor

Thom O'Hearn, Editor

POTTER STYLE

Potter Style publishes books on crafts, etiquette, journals, cards, and gift books. Some recent titles include *The Art of Correspondence: An Etiquette Book and Complete Set of Stationery* by Florence Isaacs; *The Bronte Sisters Mini Journal*; and *Create Your Own Paper Quilt Cards: Everything You Need to Make 16 Designs Without Scissors or Glue* by Sandra Lounsbury Foose.

Chris Navratil, Editorial Director

Karrie Witkin, Editor

CROWN

The Crown Group's eponymous imprint's nonfiction encompasses popular titles in biography, history, art, pop culture, contemporary culture, crime, sports, travel, popular and literary science, languages, spirituality, cookbooks, self-help, how-to, and antiques and collectibles, as well as popular reference works. Fiction titles focus on literary and popular works in hardcover.

Recent bestsellers include *The Audacity of Hope: Thoughts on Reclaiming the American Dream* by Barack Obama; *World War Z* by Max Brooks; and *Thunderstruck* by Erik Larson.

Other recent Crown titles include *The Charleston Consul: How Great Britain Changed the Course of the American Civil War* by Christopher Dickey; *The Land of Painted Caves* by Jean M. Auel; *The Cardturner* by Louis Sachar; *Genius Is Not a Plan* by Jason Fagone; *The New Industrial Revolution* by Chris Anderson; and *Fixed: China, the U.S., and the Pitfalls of a Mispriced World* by Michael Casey.

Direct queries and SASEs to:

Rick Horgan, Executive Editor—Nonfiction, business, politics, current affairs, pop culture, historical narratives, humor

Heather Jackson, Executive Editor—Nonfiction, memoir, humor, pop culture

Brett Valley, Editor

Suzanne O'Neill, Senior Editor—Humor, pop culture, fiction

Rachel Klayman, Executive Editor—Pop culture, politics, memoir

Allison McCabe, Senior Editor—Nonfiction, memoir, debut and historical fiction

Sean Desmond, Senior Editor—Politics, history, political thrillers, reference

Lucinda Bartley, Associate Editor—Social and cultural studies, science, narrative nonfiction

Julian Pavia, Associate Editor—Fiction, mysteries, horror, sports, narrative

Mary Choteborsky, Assistant Editor—Politics, pop culture, memoir

Heather Proulx, Assistant Editor

John Mahaney, Editor—Business and investing, current affairs, history

John Glusman, Editor—Politics, history, current affairs, fiction, memoir, thriller

CROWN BUSINESS

Crown Business is one of the leading publishers of business books, producing titles by authors such as Charles Schwab, Suze Orman, Ram Charan, and Michael Hammer. Crown Business looks to publish both traditional and cutting-edge business books. Crown Business recently incorporated the Doubleday Business imprint.

Recent titles include *Good Strategy/Bad Strategy* by Richard Rumelt; *Grow* by Jim Stengel; and *Crash of the Titans* by Greg Farrell.

Direct queries and SASEs to:

Tina Constable, Vice President and Publisher

John Mahaney, Executive Editor—Business and investing, current affairs

CROWN FORUM

Crown Forum is the newest addition to Crown's growing family of targeted imprints. Serving a conservative readership, it includes several bestselling titles from Ann Coulter, Tammy Bruce, Kenneth Timmerman, the writers at NewsMax.com, and more.

Recent titles include *Teaching the Pig to Dance* by Fred Thompson; *The 5 Big Lies About American Business* by Michael Medved; *We Are Doomed* by John Derbyshire; *The Age of Reagan: The Conservative Counterrevolution* by Steven Hayward; and *The Last Best Hope* by Joe Scarborough.

Tina Constable, Vice President and Publisher

DOUBLEDAY RELIGION

Doubleday Religion was recently moved to the Crown Publishing Group. It produces select titles in hardcover, as well as makes some books available as e-books. Categories cover spirituality and religion, including Christianity, Buddhism, and Judaism.

Recent titles include *Grace Before Meals: Recipes for Family Life* by Leo Patalinghug; *Home Tonight: Further Reflections on the Parable of the Prodigal Son* by Henri J.M. Nouwen; *The Rite: The Making of a Modern Exorcist* by Matt Baglio; and *Say Yes to No: Using the Power of No to Create the Best in Life, Work, and Love* by Greg Cootsona.

Trace Murphy, Editor-in-Chief, Associate Publisher

Gary Jansen, Editor

Darya Porat, Assistant Editor

HARMONY BOOKS

Harmony Books is a market leader in the area of mind, body, and spirit, as well as biography/memoir, science, and general narrative nonfiction. Its critically acclaimed and bestselling authors include Cesar Millan, Stephen Jay Gould, Caroline Myss, Deepak Chopra, and Suzanne Finstad.

Harmony's bestsellers include *Anatomy of the Spirit: The Seven Stages of Power and Healing* by Caroline Myss; *Life After Death: The Burden of Proof* by Deepak Chopra; *Emotional Alchemy* by Tara Bennett-Goleman; *Bhagavad Gita* translated by Stephen Mitchell; *Loving What Is: Four Questions That Can Change Your Life* by Byron Katie and Stephen Mitchell.

Recent titles include *Discover the Gift* by Shajen Joy Aziz and Demian Lichtenstein; *It's All Relative* by Wade Rouse; *A Man in Uniform* by Kate Taylor; *My Happy Days* by Garry Marshall; *In My Father's Country* by Saima Wahab; and *Return to Treasure Island* by Sir Andrew Motion.

Harmony Books does not accept manuscripts without agent representation. Direct queries with SASEs to:

John Glusman, Executive Editor—Fiction and nonfiction, including memoir, debut fiction, coming-of-age novels, how-to

Sarah Knight, Senior Editor

Julia Pastore, Editor—Nonfiction, memoir, religion, spirituality

Kate Kennedy, Associate Editor—Narrative nonfiction, biography, memoir, spirituality, self-help

Anne Berry, Assistant Editor

SHAYE AREHEART BOOKS

(Note: Shaye Areheart's imprint was closed at press time.)

Shaye Areheart Books is devoted to contemporary literary and commercial fiction. Authors include Chris Bohjalian, Craig Nova, Jeanne Ray, John Smolens, Sheri Reynolds, and Maggie Estep. Shaye Areheart Books embraces a typically vanguard literary tone.

Recent titles include *The Birthday Present* by Barbara Vine; *Angels of Destruction* by Keith Donohue; *Fidel's Last Days* by Roland Merullo; *The Sweet In-Between* by Sheri Reynolds; and *Kissing Games of the World* by Sandi Kahn Shelton.

Shaye Areheart Books does not accept manuscripts without agent representation. Direct queries with SASEs to:

Shaye Areheart, Publisher

Sarah Knight, Senior Editor

TEN SPEED PRESS

    CELESTIAL ARTS

    CROSSING PRESS

    TRICYCLE PRESS

P.O. Box 7123, Berkeley, CA 94707

510-559-1600   fax: 510-559-1629

www.tenspeed.com

Founder Philip Wood began the Ten Speed Press in 1971 with *Anybody's Bike Book*, still in print with more than a million copies sold. Ten Speed went on to build its reputation with titles including *What Color Is Your Parachute?*, *Moosewood Cookbook*, *White Trash Cooking*, *Why Cats Paint*, and *Flattened Fauna*. Ten Speed Press publishes 150 books per year under its four imprints: Ten Speed Press, Celestial Arts, Crossing Press, and Tricycle Press.

Random House recently acquired Ten Speed Press and incorporated it into the Crown Publishing Group. However, the editorial offices will stay in Berkeley, California. Jenny Frost, president and publisher of Crown, says "They have a lot of eclectic and quirky books, and I think maybe the soil in Berkeley helps grow that. I wouldn't want to take that away."

Julie Bennett, an acquiring editor at Ten Speed, said recently that the press is in the process of expanding its list in the area of "quirky" or "alternative" crafts. "We're hoping it's where the cookbook world was ten to 15 years ago," she said. As the design elements of the books are improved, consumers will buy crafts books as they do cookbooks, for inspiration, whether they make the crafts in them or not, Bennett predicted. Other Ten Speed categories include how-to, cooking, business/career, relationships, gardening, gift, humor, and pop culture.

Recent titles from Ten Speed include *The Gluten-Free Asian Kitchen* by Laura Russell; *The Omnivore's Recipe Keeper* by Celia Sack; *You Can Tutor Your Own Child: The Fun, Easy Way to Help Any Student Succeed in Any Subject* by Koestler Ruben; *Study Your Brains Out (Without Losing Your Mind)* by Anne Crossman; and *Who Moved My Mouse* by Dena Harris.

For all Ten Speed imprints, direct queries, proposals, and SASEs to the attention of "Acquisition Editors" for the specific imprint. No unsolicited email submissions.

Aaron Wehner, Editorial Director—Cooking

Lisa Westmoreland, Editor—Parenting, humor, health, finance

Julie Bennett, Editor—Cooking, various areas of nonfiction

CELESTIAL ARTS

Celestial Arts was founded by poster printer Hal Kramer in San Francisco in 1963. During the Human Potential Movement of the seventies, Celestial Arts blossomed

into a book publisher and made a name for itself with bestsellers like *Loving Someone Gay* and Virginia Satir's inspirational poem-book *Self-Esteem*.

The Celestial Arts imprint was acquired by Ten Speed Press in 1983 and continues to publish a diverse list of alternative medicine, health, nutrition, parenting, inspiration, self-help, and spirituality titles.

Recent titles include *The Accidental Vegan* by Devra Gartenstein; *The Ethical Slut: A Practical Guide to Polyamory, Open Relationships, and Other Adventures* by Dossie Easton and Janet Hardy; and *Simple Food for Busy Families: The Whole Life Nutritional Approach* by Jeannette Bessinger and Tracee Yablon-Brenner.

CROSSING PRESS

Crossing Press (originally called New Books) began as a small poetry publisher founded by poet John Gill in the village of Trumansburg, New York, just outside of Ithaca, in 1963. He changed the press's name to the Crossing Press in 1969 (after consulting the I Ching, as legend has it) and began branching out into literature, feminist and political works, and cookbooks. Early landmarks include *The Male Muse* (1974), a pioneering collection of gay poetry, and unique cookbooks like *Moog's Musical Eatery* (1978). In 1986, the company relocated to northern California and, in 2002, it was acquired by Ten Speed Press.

The Crossing Press publishes a wide range of hardcover and trade paperback editions of books, videos, and audios on natural healing, spirituality, alternative healing practices, and, occasionally, cooking. Dedicated to social and spiritual change, Crossing Press focuses on metaphysics, alternative therapies, mysticism, feminism, herbal medicine, and chakra and color healing.

Recent titles include *Planetary Apothecary: An Astrological Approach to Health and Wellness* by Stephanie Gailing; *Healing Herbs A to Z: A Handy Reference to Healing Plants* by Diane Stein; and *Aromatherapy: A Complete Guide to the Healing Art* by Kathi Keville and Mindy Green.

TRICYCLE PRESS

Tricycle Press is the children's imprint for Ten Speed. They focus on board books, picture books, young-adult novels, and real-life books to help kids understand themselves and the world. Recent titles from Tricycle include *A Curious Collection of Cats* by Betsy Franco; *Little Goose* by David Mraz and Margot Apple; *Temple of the Sun* by Moyra Caldecott; and *What Can You Do with a Paleta?* by Carmen Tafolla and Magaly Morales.

Nicole Geiger, Publisher

THREE RIVERS PRESS

Three Rivers Press publishes trade paperbacks and hardcovers as well as reprints of books issued initially in hardcover by the other Crown imprints. Categories include humor, popular culture, music, and other nonfiction.

Titles representative of the list include *Waiting for the Biblioburro* by Monica Brown; *May B* by Caroline Rose; *Double Play* by Betsy Franco; *Buglette, the Messy Sleeper* by Bethanie Murguia; *Sylvia and Aki* by Winifred Conkling; and *Fiesta Babies* by Carmen Tafolla and Amy Cordova.

Brett Valley, Editor

Julian Pavia, Editor

Heather Proulx, Assistant Editor

Lindsay Orman, Editor

Nicole Geiger, Editor—Children's literature

WATERBROOK MULTNOMAH

12265 Oracle Boulevard, Suite 200, Colorado Springs, CO 80921

719-590-4999 fax: 719-590-8977

www.randomhouse.com/waterbrook email: info@waterbrookmultnomah.com

The WaterBrook Multnomah Publishing Group was formed in 2006 when Random House purchased Multnomah from founder Don Jacobson and integrated it with WaterBrook Press. Waterbrook Press and Multnomah operated as distinct imprints before they were restructured into the Crown Publishing Group in 2009 as a single imprint: WaterBrook Multnomah.

WaterBrook Multnomah is committed to creating products that both intensify and satisfy the elemental thirst for a deeper relationship with God. Their publishing list includes books for Christian living and spiritual growth, Bible studies, tips on parenting, inspiring works of fiction for adults and youth, engaging books for children, series for men, and titles on marriage, love, finances, and prophecy.

Recent titles include *Departures* by Robin Jones Gunn; *Praying for my Future Husband* by Robin Jones Gunn and Tricia Goyer; *Deserter: How I Went from Warrior to AWOL in the Culture Wars* by Alisa Harris; *Sparrow* by Meg Moseley; *Average Joe* by Troy Meeder; and *Touched by a Vampire* by Beth Felker Jones.

WaterBrook Multnomah accepts unsolicited manuscripts only from literary agents. Direct queries and SASEs to:

Jenny Frost, President

Steve Cobb, Publisher

David Kopp, Executive Editor

Ron Lee, Editor

Shannon Hill, Editor—Inspirational fiction

Jeanette Thomason, Editor—Nonfiction

Shannon Marchese, Editor—Religion, science fiction, fantasy, romance

Alice Crider, Editor—Young-adult fiction

Ken Petersen, Editor—Business, general nonfiction

WATSON-GUPTILL PUBLICATIONS

AMPHOTO BOOKS

BACK STAGE BOOKS

BILLBOARD BOOKS

LONE EAGLE

www.watsonguptill.com   email: info@watsonguptill.com

Watson-Guptill's name is synonymous with design and art instruction. One of America's foremost publishers of lavishly illustrated art and art instruction titles and reference books on performing and visual arts, Watson-Guptill was founded in 1937. Nielsen is a global media and information company based in New York.

The house publishes under five imprints: Watson-Guptill, Amphoto Books, Back Stage Books, Billboard Books, and Lone Eagle. Watson-Guptill offers a cutting-edge frontlist combined with a solid and successful backlist of over 700 titles; the house publishes about 80 new titles each year.

The Watson-Guptill imprint focuses on technique books for drawing and painting in all media, sculpture, cartooning, animation, crafts, and graphic design. They also publish illustrated young-adult and tween nonfiction in the crafts category. Amphoto Books covers all aspects of photography technique. Back Stage, Billboard, and Lone Eagle concentrate on reference titles for theater, music, and film respectively.

Recent titles from Watson-Guptill include *Creating Animated Cartoons with Character: A Guide to Developing and Producing Your Own Series for TV, the Web, and Short Film* by Joe Murray; *The New Face of Jazz* by Cicily Janus; and *The Artist's Guide to Grant Writing* by Gigi Rosenberg.

Email submissions and phone calls will not be accepted. Send a proposal and cover letter in writing via regular mail. Address queries and SASEs to the Editors.

Jenny Frost, President

Victoria Craven, Editorial Director—Photography, lifestyle

Candace Raney, Executive Editor—Art, illustrated books, technique, cartooning

Joy Aquilino, Executive Editor—Crafts

Julie Mazur, Senior Editor—Crafts, lifestyle, hobbies, juvenile nonfiction

Abigail Wilentz, Senior Editor—Photography, lifestyle, graphic design

Amy Vinchesi, Editor—Nonfiction, reference, pop culture

AMPHOTO BOOKS

A leading publisher of photography, Amphoto Books is at the forefront in publishing for professionals and amateurs on such vital topics as digital, lighting, nature, glamour, wedding, and the business of photography. Some recent titles

include *The BetterPhoto Guide to Exposure* by Sean Arbabi; *Wedding Photography Unveiled: Inspiration and Insight from 20 Top Photographers* by Jacqueline Tobin; and *Understanding Close-Up Photography: Creative Close Encounters with or without a Macro Lens* by Bryan Peterson.

BACK STAGE BOOKS

Synonymous with the performing arts, Back Stage Books publishes titles for professionals, students, and enthusiasts on acting, theater, and dance as well as the history and business of theater and its leading performers. Some titles include *How I Lost 10 Pounds in 53 Years: A Memoir* by Kaye Ballard and Jim Hesselman; *500 Episodes and No Commercials: The Ultimate Guide to TV Shows on DVD* by David Hofstede; *The Back Stage Guide to Working in Regional Theater: Jobs for Actors* by Jim Volz; and *Ask an Agent: Everything Actors Need to Know about Agents* by Margaret Emory.

BILLBOARD BOOKS

A leading publisher of music and entertainment, titles range from rock, pop, classical, and jazz to biography, business, and professional reference how-to and chart books created from the database of *Billboard* magazine. Some titles are *Special Effects: The History and Technique* by Richard Rickitt; *The Film Director Prepares: A Complete Guide to Directing for Film and TV* by Myrl A. Schreibman; and *I Could Have Sung All Night* by Marni Nixon and Stephen Cole.

LONE EAGLE

Lone Eagle publishes books for entertainment industry professionals as well as those aspiring to enter the industry as screenwriters, television writers, directors, producers, actors, video game creators, and musicians. Some titles are *This Business of Film: A Practical Guide to Achieving Success in the Film Industry* by Paula Landry and Stephen G. Greenwald and *What I Really Want to Do On Set in Hollywood: A Guide to Real Jobs in the Film Industry* by Brian Dzyak.

KNOPF DOUBLEDAY PUBLISHING GROUP

ALFRED A. KNOPF
ANCHOR BOOKS
DOUBLEDAY
EVERYMAN'S LIBRARY

FLYING DOLPHIN PRESS

NAN A. TALESE

PANTHEON BOOKS

SCHOCKEN BOOKS

VINTAGE

In 2009, Random House created the Knopf Doubleday Publishing Group, reorganizing and combining the previously separate divisions and many imprints of Knopf and Doubleday Broadway.

Sonny Mehta, Publisher

ALFRED A. KNOPF

Knopf nonfiction categories include biography, history, nature, travel, cooking, and select poetry. The house also publishes nature guides and travel guides including *National Audubon Society Field Guides, Sibley Field Guides, Knopf MapGuides,* and *Knopf City Guides.* The Harlem Moon and Morgan Road imprints were recently incorporated into Knopf.

Recent Knopf titles include *The Arsonist* by Sue Miller; *The Redeemer* by Jo Nesbo; *The Smitten Kitchen Cookbook* by Deb Perelman; *Daughters of the Revolution* by Carolyn Cooke; and *Maine* by J. Courtney Sullivan.

Send query letters and SASEs to:

Sonny Mehta, Chairman and Editor-in-Chief—Fiction

Pat Johnson, Publishing Director

Robin Desser, Senior Editor—Fiction

Ann Close, Senior Editor—Literary fiction, geography, social and cultural history

Jonathan Segal, Vice President and Senior Editor—Twentieth-century history, contemporary events, biography, health

Jennifer Jackson, Senior Editor

George Andreou, Senior Editor—Nonfiction

Victoria Wilson, Senior Editor—Fiction, current affairs, memoir

Marty Asher, Editor-at-Large

Jordan Pavlin, Editor—Fiction, health

Andrew Miller, Editor—Nonfiction, history, current affairs

Lexy Bloom, Editor—Biography, cooking

ANCHOR BOOKS

Anchor Books is the oldest trade paperback publisher in America. It was founded in 1953 by Jason Epstein with the goal of making inexpensive editions of modern classics widely available to college students and the adult reading public. Today, Anchor's list includes award-winning history, science, women's studies, sociology, and quality fiction.

Authors published by Anchor Books include Susan Sontag, Natalie Angier, Thomas Cahill, Ian McEwan, Anne Lamott, and Margaret Atwood.

New titles include *Christ the Lord: The Road to Cana* by Anne Rice; *City of the Sun* by David Levien; *The Miracle at Speedy Motors* by Alexander McCall Smith; *Knockemstiff* by Donald Ray Pollock; *Morning and Evening Talk* by Naguib Mahfouz; and *Panama Fever* by Matthew Parker.

Direct queries with SASEs to:

Anne Messitte, Publisher, Vintage/Anchor

LuAnn Walther, Senior Vice President, Editorial Director—Literary fiction

Edward Kastenmeier, Vice President, Executive Editor

Lexy Bloom, Senior Editor—Fiction, memoir

Jennifer Jackson, Senior Editor—Fiction, debuts

DOUBLEDAY

Doubleday, with more than a century in the publishing business, remains one of the world's most renowned houses. Perhaps best known for its strong commercial list in fiction and nonfiction, Doubleday continues to be a dominating force in mainstream popular nonfiction, in addition to books of literary note.

Recent titles from Doubleday fiction include *Sag Harbor* by Colson Whitehead; *Waveland* by Frederick Barthelme; *The House of Wittgenstein: A Family at War* by Alexander Waugh; and *The Glister* by John Burnside.

Doubleday nonfiction categories include biography and autobiography, art and photography, current affairs, political science, public affairs, philosophy, ethics, family, marriage, sports and recreation, health, history, home and garden, and self-help.

Recent nonfiction titles include *The Straight Razor Cure* by Daniel Polansky; *Khost* by Joby Warrick; *Disaster Was My God* by Bruce Duffy; *King Peggy* by Peggielene Bartels and Eleanor Herman; *The Anniversary Clock* by Pam Jenoff; *A Whole New Beast* by Monte Reel; and *The Lady's Handbook for Her Mysterious Illness* by Sarah Ramey.

Direct query letters and SASEs to:

Bill Thomas, Senior Vice President, Editor-in-Chief, Publisher—Memoir, nonfiction science

Jason Kaufman, Vice President and Executive Editor—Thrillers, action adventure, true crime, narrative nonfiction

Phyllis Grann, Senior Editor—Nonfiction

Kristine Puopolo, Senior Editor—Literary nonfiction, self-help, spirituality, health, fitness, memoir, current affairs

Gerry Howard, Editor-at-Large—Fiction, memoir, nonfiction narrative

Andrew Corbin, Senior Editor—Biography, nonfiction, fiction

Alison Callahan, Executive Editor—Fiction, including fantasy and debut

Dan Feder, Associate Editor—Science, popular culture, narrative nonfiction

Darya Porat, Assistant Editor—Nonfiction, religion, spirituality

Melissa Danaczko, Associate Editor—Fiction

Robert Bloom, Editor—Fiction

Jackie Montalvo, Editor—Fiction, nonfiction narrative

EVERYMAN'S LIBRARY

Everyman's Library was founded in 1906 by London Publisher Joseph Malaby Dent, who sought to put out literature that would appeal to "every kind of reader: the worker, the student, the cultured man, the child, the man and the woman." These beautiful editions feature original introductions, up-to-date bibliographies, and complete chronologies of the authors' lives and works. The series has grown to hundreds of volumes and includes sets such as *100 Essentials*, *Children's Classics*, *Contemporary Classics*, and *The Great Poets*.

Titles include *Music's Spell: Poems About Music and Musicians* edited by Emily Fragos; *Three Hundred Tang Poems* edited by Peter Harris; *The Bascombe Novels* by Richard Ford; and *Poems About Horses* by Carmela Ciuraru.

FLYING DOLPHIN PRESS

Flying Dolphin Press focuses on popular culture and fiction titles. Great emphasis is placed on the quality of the writing as well as finding subject matter that examines people and ideas central to contemporary culture. A new imprint, it will release six new titles per year to start.

Recent titles include *BORAT: Touristic Guidings to Minor Nation of U.S. and A. and Touristic Guidings to Glorious Nation of Kazakhstan* by Borat Sagdiyev; *The Alphabet from A to Y With Bonus Letter Z* by Steve Martin and Roz Chast; and *Mosaic: Pieces of My Life So Far* by Amy Grant.

Phyllis Grann, Senior Editor

NAN A. TALESE

Formed in 1990, Nan A. Talese is committed to publishing quality fiction and nonfiction, both in terms of its authors and the production of its books. This literary trade paperback imprint is known for its new authors of fiction and nonfiction, as well as for the authors Nan Talese has published for many years.

Among its writers are Peter Ackroyd, Margaret Atwood, Pinckney Benedict, Thomas Cahill, Kevin Canty, Lorene Cary, Pat Conroy, Jennifer Egan, Mia Farrow, Antonia Fraser, David Grand, Nicola Griffith, Aleksandar Hemon, Thomas Keneally, Alex Kotlowitz, Robert MacNeil, Ian McEwan, Gita Mehta, George Plimpton, Edvard Radzinsky, Mark Richard, Nicholas Shakespeare, Barry Unsworth, and Gus Van Sant. Nan A. Talese is also well known as the publisher of the controversial memoir, *A Million Little Pieces*, by James Frey.

Recent titles include *The Fat Years* by Chan Koon-Chung; *Isabella* by Kirstin Downey; *My Life in Books* by Pat Conroy; *The Blind Astronomer's Note-book* by John Pipkin; and *Everything* by Kevin Canty.

This imprint does not accept unagented or unsolicited submissions.

Nan Talese, Senior Vice President, Publisher, and Editorial Director; ntalese@randomhouse.com—Fiction, biography, nonfiction

Luke Epplin, Editor; lepplin@randomhouse.com

PANTHEON BOOKS

Pantheon handles nonfiction books in categories such as current events, international affairs, contemporary culture, literary criticism and the arts, popular business, psychology, travel, nature, science, and history. The house has a strong list in contemporary fiction, poetry, and drama. Pantheon also offers the Fairytale and Folktale Library.

Pantheon was founded in 1942 by Helen and Kurt Wolff, refugees from Nazi Germany. "Building on its tradition of publishing important works of international fiction in translation and groundbreaking works of social policy, Pantheon now publishes quality fiction and nonfiction in a wide range of areas."

Representative titles include *Corduroy Mansions* by Alexander McCall Smith; *The Newhate* by Arthur Godwag; *Offspeed* by Terry McDermott; *Borrow: A Brief History of Debt in Modern America* by Louis Hyman; *The Flame Alphabet* by Ben Marcus; *The Pirates of Puntland* by Jay Bahadur; and *Bad Dog: A Love Story* by Martin Kihn.

Recent titles include *Netherland* by Joseph O'Neill; *Brothers* by Yu Hua; *Elsewhere U.S.A.* by Dalton Conley; *The First Person* by Ali Smith; and *Down at the Docks* by Rory Nugent.

Direct query letters and SASEs to:

Pat Johnson, Publishing Director

Tim O'Connell, Associate Editor

Dan Frank, Editorial Director

Deborah Garrison, Senior Editor

Edward Kastenmeier, Editor—Fiction, mystery; nonfiction narrative, sports

Marty Asher, Editor—Fiction, memoir

SCHOCKEN BOOKS

Schocken publishes books of Jewish interest in the following areas: history, biography, memoir, current affairs, spirituality, religion, philosophy, politics, sociology, and fiction.

Founded in Berlin in 1931 by Salman Schocken, a department store magnate, bibliophile, and ardent Zionist, Schocken Verlag was closed down by the Nazis in 1938. Salman Schocken founded Schocken Books in the U.S. in 1942. The company became a division of Random House in 1987.

Recently published books include *The Murmuring Deep* by Avivah Gottlieb Zornberg; *Laish* by Aharon Applefeld; *Zohar: The Book of Splendor* by Gershom Scholem; and *Betraying Spinoza* by Rebecca Goldstein.

Direct queries with SASEs to:

Altie Karper, Editorial Director

VINTAGE

Vintage is the trade paperback arm of the Knopf Publishing Group and consists of Vintage Books and Anchor Books.

The Vintage Books publishing list includes a wide range, from world literature to contemporary fiction and distinguished nonfiction, featuring such writers as William Faulkner, Vladimir Nabokov, Albert Camus, Ralph Ellison, Dashiell Hammett, William Styron, A. S. Byatt, Philip Roth, Richard Ford, Cormac McCarthy, Alice Munro, David Guterson, and Arthur Golden. Vintage Crime/Black Lizard titles focus on crime and suspense.

Representative titles include *A Wonderful Sight from the Air* by Sarah Gardner Borden; *A Ladder of Rain and the Roof Beyond* by Jesse Ball; *Machine Man* by Max Barry; and *Here Comes Tomorrow* by Alex Pappademas.

Send query letters and SASEs to:

Edward Kastenmeier, Vice President, Executive Editor

Lexy Bloom, Senior Editor

Jennifer Jackson, Senior Editor—Fiction

Tim O'Connell, Senior Editor

Andrew Miller, Editor

Zack Wagman, Editor—Science fiction, fantasy, pop culture

RANDOM HOUSE CHILDREN'S BOOKS

ALFRED A. KNOPF BOOKS FOR YOUNG READERS

DELACORTE PRESS BOOKS FOR YOUNG READERS

DISNEY BOOKS FOR YOUNG READERS

DRAGONFLY

GOLDEN BOOKS

RANDOM HOUSE BOOKS FOR YOUNG READERS

ROBIN COREY BOOKS

SCHWARTZ & WADE BOOKS

WENDY LAMB BOOKS

YEARLING BOOKS

Random House Children's Books publishes Dr. Seuss and other well-known licenses, such as Arthur, the Berenstain Bears, Disney, Sesame Workshop, and Thomas the Tank Engine. The house also publishes many of children's favorite authors, including Judy Blume, Robert Cormier, Madeleine L'Engle, Leo Lionni, Mary Pope Osborne, Gary Paulsen, Tamora Pierce, Philip Pullman, Faith Ringgold, and Jerry Spinelli. Random House is the publisher of Christopher Paul Curtis's novel *Bud, Not Buddy*, winner of the 2000 John Newberry Medal and the Coretta Scott King Author Award, and David Almond's novel *Kit's Wilderness*, winner of the 2001 Michael L. Printz Award.

Random House has a number of book series specifically designed for young readers, including the *Stepping Stones* first chapter book series: *Marvin Redpost*; *A to Z Mysteries*; *The Magic Tree House*; *Junie B. Jones*; *Replica*; *Dinoverse*; and Francine Pascal's *Sweet Valley High Senior Year*, a popular series aimed at middle-grade and young-adult readers.

In addition to series, Random House Children's Books publishes popular fiction including *Anne of Green Gables, Where the Red Fern Grows*, and *The Phantom Tollbooth*, as well as Newbery Honor and Medal-winning books such as *The Watsons Go to Birmingham 1963, Lily's Crossing, Holes, A Wrinkle in Time, The Giver, The Dark-Thirty*, and *Shabanu*. The Random House list also features Caldecott Honor- and Medal-winning books, including *Tar Beach, Time Flies, Song and Dance Man*, and the late Leo Lionni's *Frederick, Swimmy*, and *Alexander and the Wind-Up Mouse*.

Recent releases include *Pajama Mamas* by Kate Spohn; *Sneezy Louise* by Irene Brznak and Janet Pedersen; *Babe Ruth and the Baseball Curse* by David A. Kelly and Tim Jessell; *The Princess and the Unicorn* by Carol Hughes; *Baby Nose to Baby Toes* by Vicky Ceelen; and *Bones of Faerie* by Janni Lee Simner.

Random House Children's accepts unsolicited manuscripts only through their contests, The Delacorte Press Contest for a First Young Adult Novel and the Delacorte Dell Yearling Contest for a First Middle-Grade Novel. You may request the rules and guidelines at the Random House address, attention Contests, or view them online. All other submissions should come via a literary agent.

Chip Gibson, Publisher

Michelle Poploff, Vice President and Editorial Director—Children's paperbacks

Mallory Loehr, Vice President and Associate Publisher

Schuyler Hooke, Senior Editor

Jennifer Arena, Executive Editor

Diane Landolf, Editor

Hilary Kilgras, Editor—Picture books

ALFRED A. KNOPF BOOKS FOR YOUNG READERS

Alfred A. Knopf Books for Young Readers (BFYR) publishes quality books for children of all ages, toddlers to young adults. The imprint publishes between 60–70 new hardcover books each year, ranging from board books to picture books to novels to nonfiction. Known for both the caliber of its authors and artists and the high quality of its book design and production, Alfred A. Knopf BFYR publishes books intended to entertain, inspire, and endure. The imprint is deeply committed to its authors and illustrators, and believes that by working closely with them, they can create books that children, and adults who read to children, will love for years to come. Authors and illustrators published by Alfred A. Knopf BFYR include Marc Brown, Robert Cormier, Leo and Diane Dillon, Carl Hiaasen, Leo Lionni, Christopher Paolini, Philip Pullman, Eric Rohmann, Judy Sierra, and Jerry Spinelli.

Some recent titles from Alfred A. Knopf BFYR include *Sing a Song of Murder* by Dandi Daley Mackall; *Pigeon-Shot* by Amy Timberlake; *Super Love* by Charise Harper; *The Wednesdays* by Julie Bourbeau; *The Running Dream* by Wendelin Van Draanen; *The Book of Blood and Shadow* by Robin Wasserman.

Nancy Hinkel, Publishing Director

Nancy Siscoe, Executive Editor—Middle-grade children's literature

Michelle Frey, Executive Editor—Young adult, picture books

Erin Clarke, Editor—Young adult, children's fantasy

Allison Wortche, Editor—Young adult, picture books

DELACORTE PRESS BOOKS FOR YOUNG READERS

Delacorte Press Books for Young Readers publishes literary and commercial novels for middle-grade and young-adult readers, as well as nonfiction that crosses both educational and general interest categories. Among the many bestselling authors published by Delacorte Press Books for Young Readers are David Almond, Ann Brashares,

Libba Bray, Caroline Cooney, Robert Cormier, Lurlene McDaniel, Phyllis Reynolds Naylor, Joan Lowery Nixon, Louis Sachar, Zilpha Keatley Snyder, and R.L. Stine.

Some recent Delacorte BFYR titles are *Paper Covers Rock* by Marilyn Shank; *Gossip from the Girls' Room* by Rose Cooper; *The Way Boys Read* by Jenny Hubbard; *Someone Else's Footprints* by Katie Dale; *Teenage Waistland* by Lynn Biederman and Lisa Pazer; *Vixen* by Lila Fine; and *Sandinista* by Mary O'Connell.

Beverly Horowitz, Vice President and Publisher—Young adult

Francoise Bui, Executive Editor—Young adult

Wendy Loggia, Publishing Director—Young adult, middle-grade children's literature, graphic novel

Krista Marino, Senior Editor

Stephanie Lane, Senior Editor

Claudia Gabel, Editor

Michelle Poploff, Editor—Young adult

Stephanie Elliott, Editor—Young adult, middle-grade children's literature, fiction

DISNEY BOOKS FOR YOUNG READERS

Disney Books for Young Readers features a wide array of books based on Walt Disney live-action and animated films; titles include coloring and activity books, storybooks, novelty books, and early readers. Some titles are *The Wild Read-Aloud Storybook* by Ahmet Zappa; *Playground Pile-Up*; *Banana Hunt* by Andrea Alvin; and *Pooh Gets Stuck* by Isabel Gaines and Nancy Stevenson.

DRAGONFLY

Dragonfly introduces children to talented and award-winning artists and writers through affordable paperback picture books. These inspiring and imaginative full-color books range from first concept books to read-together stories to books for newly independent readers. Through the variety of writing and illustration styles, children reap the rich rewards that Dragonfly's paperback picture books offer. Authors and illustrators include Leo and Diane Dillon, Jarrett J. Krosoczka, Grace Lin, Leo Lionni, Anita Lobel, Jack Prelutsky, Raffi, Faith Ringgold, Lizzy Rockwell, Eric Rohmann, Judy Sierra, Peter Spier, Meilo So, Nancy Van Laan, and more.

Some Dragonfly books are *Hurry and the Monarch* by Antoine O Flatharta and Meilo So; *Transparencies* by Robert Edwards; *The Extended Words: An Imaginary Dictionary* by Sid Gershgoren; and *Read a Rhyme, Write a Rhyme* by Jack Prelutsky and Meilo So.

GOLDEN BOOKS

In August 2001, Random House acquired all the book-publishing properties of Golden Books Family Entertainment, which produces storybooks, coloring and

activity books, puzzle books, educational workbooks, reference books, novelty books, and chapter books. The Golden Books publishing program features Blue's Clues, Rugrats, Bob the Builder, and Barbie; and the Little Golden Books series publishes classic favorites such as *Pat the Bunny* and *The Poky Little Puppy*.

Chris Angelilli, Editor-in-Chief

ROBIN COREY BOOKS

In Fall 2007, Robin Corey Books, Random House Children's newest original imprint, launched its inaugural list. They publish board books and interactive books for ages 4–8. Some of their titles include *My Dance Recital* by Maryann Cocca-Leffler; *Mommy Calls Me Monkeypants* by J.D. Lester and Hiroe Nakata; *Nick Jr.'s Pop-Up Songs* by Sarah Albee and Bruce E. Faster; and *Sammy's Suitcase* by Lisa Buccieri et al.

Robin Corey, Vice President and Publisher

SCHWARTZ & WADE BOOKS

Established in March 2005, Schwartz & Wade Books is co-directed by Anne Schwartz and Lee Wade, who take a unique approach to the creative process and believe that the best books for children grow from a seamless collaboration between editorial and design. The imprint launched its first list in spring 2006 with four picture books and continues to publish approximately 20 hardcover books a year. Authors and illustrators include Tad Hills, Deborah Hopkinson, James E. Ransome, Ronnie Shotter, Giselle Potter, and Valorie Fisher.

Recent titles include *The Apple Riddle* by Margaret McNamara; *The Girl in the Park* by Mariah Frederick; *Cecil, The Pet Glacier* by Matthea Harvey; and *A Boy Called Dickens* by Deborah Hopkinson.

Anne Schwartz, Editorial Director—Young adult, picture book

WENDY LAMB BOOKS

Wendy Lamb Books, established in 2002, focuses on innovative middle-grade and young-adult fiction by award-winning writers such as Christopher Paul Curtis, Peter Dickinson, Patricia Reilly Giff, Gary Paulsen, and Graham Salisbury. The imprint also seeks new talent and publishes many first novels. Recent titles include *Now It Begins* by Beth Ann Bauman; *Flip* by Martyn Bedford; *What They Found: Love on 145th Street* by Walter Dean Myers; and *No Cream Puffs* by Karen Day.

Wendy Lamb, Publisher—Young adult

YEARLING BOOKS

Yearling Books is celebrating 40 years of providing parents, teachers, and children ages 8–12 with distinguished paperback books in an affordable digest format.

The Yearling imprint features a wide variety of books: beloved classics, Newbery-award winners, first-rate contemporary and historical fiction, fantasy, mystery, and adventure. The Yearling brand is recognized by generations of readers as representing quality. Yearling is the middle-reader paperback home of such beloved authors as Judy Blume, Christopher Paul Curtis, Patricia Reilly Giff, Norton Juster, Madeleine L'Engle, Lois Lowry, Gary Paulsen, Philip Pullman, and Louis Sachar, and classic characters such as Encyclopedia Brown, Harriet the Spy, Nate the Great, and Sammy Keyes. Recent titles include *The Elevator Family* by Douglas Evans; *Corydon and the Island of Monsters* by Tobias Druitt; *Following Fake Men* by Barbara Ware Holmes; and *Space Race* by Sylvia Waugh.

RANDOM HOUSE INFORMATION GROUP

FODOR'S TRAVEL PUBLICATIONS

LIVING LANGUAGE

PRIMA GAMES

THE PRINCETON REVIEW

RANDOM HOUSE PUZZLES & GAMES

RANDOM HOUSE REFERENCE PUBLISHING

SYLVAN LEARNING BOOKS

1745 Broadway, New York, NY 10019

212-782-9000

www.randomhouse.com

A division of Random House, the Information Group publishes a well-developed list of consumer reference and dictionary titles, language study courses, and academic test preparation titles. The newest imprint is Sylvan Learning Books, with titles focusing on building academic skills for elementary through high school students.

Tom Russell, Vice President and Publisher

FODOR'S TRAVEL PUBLICATIONS

www.fodors.com

Fodor's Travel Publications is a unit of Fodor's LLC, a subsidiary of Random House. It is the world's largest English-language travel information publisher, with more than 440 titles to destinations worldwide. Fodor's publishes niche market travel guidebooks, as well as more traditional guides that offer practical information on popular destinations. Fodor's publishes over 14 different series to address every type of travel experience. These series include the flagship *Gold Guides Series, Fodor's FYI, Escape, Around the City with Kids, To Go,* and *Fodor's Road Guides USA.*

Recent titles include *Fodor's Greece, 9th Edition with Great Cruises and the Best Island Getaways; Fodor's Edinburgh's 25 Best, 2nd Edition; Las Vegas' 25 Best, 3rd Edition; Lisbon's 25 Best, 4th Edition; Los Angeles' 25 Best, 6th Edition.*

Send book proposals or queries to the attention of the Editorial Director. For more information about Fodor's, visit its website at www.fodors.com. Information on researcher-writer positions is also available online.

Linda Cabasin, Editorial Director

Kelly Lack, Associate Editor

LIVING LANGUAGE

Living Language is one of the most well-known names in both foreign-language and English-language instruction, and publishes courses that meet a variety of needs. Living Language offers a wide range of programs, including *Complete Basic Courses; the All-Audio, Ultimate, In-Flight,* and *English for New Americans* series; and the popular *Daily Phrase & Culture Calendars.* The Living Language line includes books, cassettes, CDs, and DVDs in 23 languages including sign language.

Chris Warnasch, Publishing Director

PRIMA GAMES

3000 Lava Ridge Court, Suite 100, Roseville, CA 95661

www.primagames.com

Prima Games publishes strategy guides for PC and console games and has more than 90 million strategy guides in print. Located near Sacramento, California, Prima Games continues to dominate the niche it created in 1990. They publish about 140 new titles per year.

Recent titles include *Street Fighter IV: Prima Official Game Guide* by Bryan Dawson; *Fire Emblem: Shadow Dragon* by Stephen Stratton; *F.E.A.R. 2: Project Origin* by Catherine Browne; and *Rise of the Argonauts* by Ron Dulin.

Prima Games welcomes submissions from experienced strategy guide authors or expert gamers who love to write. Send a query letter with résumé and writing samples to:

Debra Kempker, President

THE PRINCETON REVIEW

The Princeton Review imprint publishes books that help students sharpen their academic skills, prepare for standardized tests, and gain entrance into college and graduate school. Representative titles include *Cracking the SAT*, *The Best 331 Colleges*, and *Word Smart*, the flagship title of The Princeton Review's "Smart" series. A new series, *Ahead of the Curve*, focuses on K–12 education.

Recent titles include *Paying for College Without Going Broke, 2010 Edition* by Princeton Review; *Best 168 Medical Schools: 2010*; *5 GED Practice Tests*; *Cracking the AP Biology Exam*; and *Essential SAT Vocabulary*.

Tom Russell, Vice President and Publisher

RANDOM HOUSE PUZZLES & GAMES

Random House Puzzles & Games publishes crossword puzzle books, including those drawn from the pages of the *Los Angeles Times*, the *Boston Globe*, and the *New York Times*. The imprint also has a line of Dell Crossword puzzle books, as well as trivia books on baseball by Jeffrey and Doug Lyons.

Recent titles include *Jane Austen Puzzle* by Potter Style; *Alice in Wonderland Puzzle* by Linda Sunshine; *Quotable Cryptograms* by Terry Stickels and Sam Bellotto, Jr.; *Extreme Sudoku* by Carol Vorderman; *The Puzzlemaster Presents* by Will Shortz; and *The Los Angeles Times Sunday Crossword Omnibus, Volume 3* edited by Sylvia Bursztyn and Barry Tunick.

Helena Santini, Editor

RANDOM HOUSE REFERENCE PUBLISHING

Random House Reference Publishing is a leading publisher of reference works in both print and electronic formats. Its lexicography program is highly regarded for its inclusion of new words in the English language earlier than most other reference publishers.

The house also publishes the works of Ralph and Terry Kovel, including the most popular price guide for collectors, dealers, and appraisers: *Kovel's American Collectibles 1900–2000*.

Other classic titles include *Random House Webster's College Dictionary*; *Random House Webster's Unabridged Dictionary*; *Random House Roget's College Thesaurus*; and *Random House Historical Dictionary of American Slang*.

Random House Reference also publishes a line of trade reference titles including, most recently, *Bryson's Dictionary for Writers and Editors* by Bill Bryson; *The Best of Emerge Magazine* by George Curry; and *The Virginia Woolf Writers' Workshop: Seven Lessons to Inspire Great Writing* by Danell Jones.

Helena Santini, Editor

SYLVAN LEARNING BOOKS

Sylvan Learning Books is a publishing partnership established in 2007 by Random House and Sylvan Learning, Inc. Initial titles focus on supplemental learning for elementary school-aged children, with an eventual expansion into titles for children in grades K–12, and their parents.

Recent titles include *Fifth Grade Reading Comprehension Success*; *Fifth Grade Writing Success*; *Fourth Grade Spelling Success*; and *Sylvan Learning SAT/PSAT Math Skills and Verbal Skills*.

Tom Russell, Vice President and Publisher

THE RANDOM HOUSE PUBLISHING GROUP

BALLANTINE BOOKS

BANTAM DELL

DEL REY

THE DIAL PRESS

ESPN BOOKS

THE MODERN LIBRARY

ONE WORLD

PRESIDIO PRESS

RANDOM HOUSE

RANDOM HOUSE TRADE PAPERBACKS

SPECTRA

SPIEGEL & GRAU

STRIVERS ROW

TRIUMPH BOOKS

VILLARD BOOKS

The Random House Publishing Group was formed in 2003, uniting the two divisions formerly known as the Random House Trade Group and the Ballantine Books Group. Publishing in all formats—hardcover, trade paperback, and mass-market—The Random House Publishing Group recently absorbed many of the imprints of the former Bantam Dell division, including Bantam Dell, Delta, Dial Press, and Spectra.

Gina Centrello, President and Publisher

Kate Medina, Executive Vice President, Associate Publisher, and Executive Editorial Director

Susan Kamil, Senior Vice President and Editor-in-Chief

Jennifer Hershey, Senior Vice President, Editorial Director

BALLANTINE BOOKS

Ballantine Books publishes commercial fiction and general nonfiction, including health, diet, psychology, history, and biography. The mass-market list includes such bestselling authors as John Case, Robert Crais, Fannie Flagg, Sue Grafton, Kristin Hannah, John Irving, Jonathan Kellerman, Richard North Patterson, Anne Perry, Anne Rice, Edward Rutherfurd, and Anne Tyler.

Recent titles include *Maximum Brainwidth* by Collins Hemingway; *Recipe for Style: A Cookbook for Your Closet* by Jessica Schroeder; *I Do… Now What?: Stories and Advice from America's Favorite Couple* by Giuliana Rancic and Bill Rancic; *The Last Great Game* by Gene Wojciechowski; *Friendship Bread* by Darien Gee; *How to Build a Fire* by Erin Bried; and *Homesick and Happy* by Michael Thompson.

Libby McGuire, Publisher

Luke Dempsey, Editorial Director—Nonfiction, memoir, parenting, finance

Marnie Cochran, Executive Editor—Nonfiction lifestyle, parenting, advice, diet, memoir

Linda Marrow, Vice President and Editorial Director—Women's fiction, thrillers and suspense, paranormal fiction, inspirational fiction

Bruce Tracy, Executive Editor—Nonfiction, sports

Susanna Porter, Executive Editor—Fiction, nonfiction, current affairs, business

Anika Streitfeld, Senior Editor—Fiction

Mark Tavani, Senior Editor—Thrillers, memoirs, true crime

Kate Collins, Senior Editor—Women's fiction, romance, suspense

Rebecca Shapiro, Editor—Nonfiction

Charlotte Herscher, Editor—Women's fiction, romance

Laura Ford, Editor—Fiction

Christina Duffy, Editor—Nonfiction

Paul Taunton, Editor—Thrillers, sports

Tricia Narwani, Editor—Fiction, including graphic novels and short stories, memoir

Ryan Doherty, Associate Editor

Jill Schwartzman, Editor—How-to, humor

Caitlin Alexander, Editor—Fiction

Christopher Schluep, Editor—Science fiction, fantasy, young adult

Pamela Cannon, Editor—Memoir, cooking

BANTAM DELL

Established in 1945, Bantam was one of the most successful publishers of adult fiction and nonfiction, and Dell was one of the biggest publishers of paperbacks for more than seven decades. As a part of massive Random House reorganizations, both houses were merged to become Bantam Dell and incorporated into the Random House Publishing Group in 2009. Their fiction list includes commercial novels, mysteries, thrillers, suspense, science fiction and fantasy, romance, women's fiction, and select literary works, and their diverse nonfiction lists cover genres from memoir to current events to history.

Titles include *Can't Buy Me Love* by Molly O'Keefe; *A Lady Awakened* by Cecilia Grey; *The Book of Bright Ideas* by Sandra Kring; *The Stranger You Seek* by Amanda Kyle Williams; *The Bread of Life* by Barbara O'Neal; *Beautiful Malice* by Rebecca James; *The Vanishing of Katharina Linden* by Helen Grant; and *Churchill's Secretary* by Susan Elia.

Gina Centrello, President and Publisher

Nita Taublib, Executive Vice President, Publisher, and Editor-in-Chief

Gina Wachtel, Associate Publisher

Toni Burbank, Vice President and Executive Editor—Self-help, spirituality, health

Kate Miciak, Editorial Director—Mysteries, thrillers, other fiction, narrative nonfiction

Juliet Ulman, Senior Editor—General fiction, science fiction, fantasy

Shauna Summers, Senior Editor—Women's fiction, romance, erotica

John Flicker, Editor—Nonfiction, including history, politics, war, current events, historical; time-travel fiction

Caitlin Alexander, Editor—Fiction including debut fiction, mysteries

Molly Boyle, Assistant Editor—Commercial fiction, mysteries, particularly for women; memoir; narrative; pop culture nonfiction

DEL REY

DEL REY MANGA

Del Rey publishes manga, science fiction, fantasy, speculative fiction, and alternate history in hardcover, trade paperback, and mass-market paperback formats. Its founders were the late Judy-Lynn and Lester del Rey, legendary publishers who catapulted science-fiction/fantasy titles onto the national bestsellers lists for the first time. Del Rey is also home to LucasBooks, publishing *Star Wars* novelizations, spin-off novels, and nonfiction books.

Recent titles include *Little Women and Werewolves* by Porter Grand and Louisa

May Alcott; *Rivers of London* by Ben Aaronovitch; *The Children of Hurin* by J.R.R. Tolkien; and *Hounded, Hexed, and Hammered* by Kevin Hearne.

Scott Shannon, Vice President

Betsy Mitchell, Editor-in-Chief—Paranormal fiction, horror, science fiction, fantasy

DEL REY MANGA

Del Rey Manga launched its first titles in May 2004 when Random House and Kodansha entered into a large-scale cross-publishing relationship. As a result, Kodansha, the largest publisher in Japan, brought their strongest properties to the Del Rey Manga Line. With just eleven manga releases that year, Del Rey's success resulted in its becoming the number four manga publisher in the United States, quickly establishing the company as a powerhouse in the fastest-growing field in American publishing. Del Rey Manga has continued to expand and release new mangas.

Some new titles include *Orange Planet 1* by Haruka Fukushima; *The Wallflower* by Womoko Hayakawa; *Parasyte 7* by Hiroshi Iwaaki; and *Wolverine 1* by Antony Johnston and Wilson Tortosa.

THE DIAL PRESS

The Dial Press publishes literary fiction and nonfiction. This imprint includes works by Sophie Kinsella, Allegra Goodman, Justin Cronin, Marie Arana, Patrick Ryan, Elizabeth McCracken, Ian Caldwell, Dustin Thomason, and Sting.

Recent titles include *Bright's Passage* by Josh Ritter; *Vaclav and Lena* by Haley Tanner; *The Slide* by Kyle Beachy; *When Skateboards Will Be Free: A Memoir of a Political Childhood* by Said Sayrafiezadeh; and *Confessions of a Shopaholic* by Sophie Kinsella.

Direct queries and SASEs to:

Susan Kamil, Vice President and Editorial Director

ESPN BOOKS

ESPN Books began in 2008 when Ballantine and ESPN announced a publishing alliance and a plan to release 10–12 books a year.

Recent titles include *Al: An Unauthorized Biography of Raiders Owner Al Davis* by Shelley Smith; *The Great Last Game* by Gene Wojciechowski; *Lefty: An American Odyssey* by Lawrence Goldstone; and *Kiss 'Em Goodbye: A Treasury of Failed, Forgotten, and Departed Franchises* by Dennis Purdy.

Steve Wulf, Editor—Sports

THE MODERN LIBRARY

The Modern Library, one of the most beloved lines of American classics, celebrated its 75th anniversary at Random House in 2000 and has continued to thrive. In 1999 it generated spirited debate with its published lists of the 100 Best Novels and the 100 Best Nonfiction Books published in English in the 20th century. The year 2000 saw the introduction of *Modern Library Chronicles*, short histories by the world's great historians, including *Islam* by Karen Armstrong and *The Age of Shakespeare* by Frank Kermode. That same year the Modern Library introduced its first line of paperback classics, a list that has grown to more than 300 titles. Twenty-two leading writers and intellectuals, including A. S. Byatt, Joyce Carol Oates, Edmund Morris, Shelby Foote, and Maya Angelou, make up the Modern Library Editorial Board, which continues its unique role of providing editorial counsel to the Modern Library and its editors.

Recent titles include *Nonviolence: The History of a Dangerous Idea* by Mark Kurlansky; *The First Americans: In Pursuit of Archaeology's Greatest Mystery* by Jake Page and James Adovasio; *The Christian World* by Martin Marty; *The Gambler* by Fyodor Dostoevsky; and *Baseball: A History of America's Favorite Game* by George Vecsey.

John Flicker, Executive Editor

David Ebershoff, Editor-at-Large

Judy Sternlight, Editor

ONE WORLD

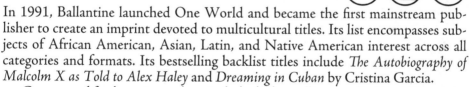

In 1991, Ballantine launched One World and became the first mainstream publisher to create an imprint devoted to multicultural titles. Its list encompasses subjects of African American, Asian, Latin, and Native American interest across all categories and formats. Its bestselling backlist titles include *The Autobiography of Malcolm X as Told to Alex Haley* and *Dreaming in Cuban* by Cristina Garcia.

Current and forthcoming authors include the bestselling novelist Pearl Cleage, the film historian Donald Bogle, and one of the rising stars of "street lit," Nikki Turner.

Recent titles include *Stay in Your Lane: Judge Karen's Navigational Guide to Living Your Best Life* by Judge Karen Mills-Francis; *Growing Up Bin Laden* by Jean Sasson; *Lemon City: A Novel* by Elaine Meryl Brown; *Numbers* by Dana Dane; *Seen It All and Done the Rest* by Pearl Cleage; *Root Shock: How Tearing Up City Neighborhoods Hurts America, and What We Can Do About It* by Mindy Fullilove; and *A One Woman Man* by Travis Hunter.

Melody Guy, Editor

PRESIDIO PRESS

The military history publisher Presidio Press was acquired by Ballantine in 2002.

Presidio Press publishes about 25 new titles per year, under the supervision of Ron Doering. Formats include mass-market, paperback, and hardcover.

Most recent titles include *Xin Loi, Viet Nam: Thirty-One Months of War: A Soldier's Memoir* by Al Sever; *The Art of Maneuver: Maneuver Warfare Theory and Airland Battle* by Robert Leonhard; and *Black Sheep One: The Life of Gregory Pappy Boyington* by Bruce Gamble.

Direct queries and SASEs to:

Ron Doering, Senior Editor

RANDOM HOUSE

Random House publishes distinguished trade fiction and nonfiction covering a broad scope of literary and commercial appeal. Since 1995, it has published four of the bestselling books of all time: *My American Journey* by Colin Powell; *Midnight in the Garden of Good and Evil* by John Berendt; *The Greatest Generation* by Tom Brokaw; and *Seabiscuit* by Laura Hillenbrand.

This group has also become a showcase for fiction and nonfiction authors publishing for the first time. Particularly notable titles include *The Dante Club* by Matthew Pearl; *Reading Lolita in Tehran* by Azar Nafisi; *Shadow Divers* by Rob Kuraon; and *The God of Small Things* by Arundhati Roy.

Recent titles include *Salt, Sugar, Fat* by Michael Moss; *Partial History of Lost Causes* by Jennifer duBois; *The Siege* by Arturo Perez-Reverte; *Enon* by Paul Harding; *Thirteen Ways of Looking* by Colum McCann; and *Antigone in Vogue* by Lincoln Rhonda Garelick.

Direct queries and SASEs to:

Kate Medina, Executive Vice President, Executive Editor

Bob Loomis, Executive Vice President, Executive Editor

Jennifer Hershey, Editorial Director—Fiction, biography

Susan Mercandetti, Senior Editor

Susanna Porter, Senior Editor

Tim Bartlett, Senior Editor

Jonathan Jao, Editor—Biography

Will Murphy, Editor

David Ebershoff, Editor-at-Large—Fiction

Andy Ward, Editor—Current affairs, humor, science nonfiction

Susan Kamil, Editor—Fiction, memoir

RANDOM HOUSE TRADE PAPERBACKS

First launched in 2001, Random House Trade Paperbacks is the paperback imprint of Random House, with an emphasis on serious nonfiction and literary fiction.

The nonfiction list includes the bestseller *Reading Lolita in Tehran* by Azar Nafisi; *The Crisis of Islam* by Bernard Lewis; *PARIS 1919* by Margaret McMillan; and *Mountains Beyond Mountains* by Tracy Kidder. E. L. Doctorow, Sarah Dunant, David Mitchell, Matthew Pearl, and Arthur Phillips are among its many award-winning fiction writers.

Random House Trade Paperbacks also has a line of mysteries and thrillers called Mortalis, comprising both originals and reprints. Recent Mortalis titles include *Red Square* by Martin Cruz Smith; *From Doon with Death: The First Inspector Wexford Novel* by Ruth Rendell; and *The Last Nightingale: A Novel of Suspense* by Anthony Flacco.

Other recent titles include *Coming Home* by Melanie Rose; *Undateable: 311 Things Men Do That Guarantee They Won't Be Dating or Having Sex.*

Jane Von Mehren, Senior Vice President, Publisher

Jill Schwartzman, Senior Editor

Lea Beresford, Editor

SPECTRA

For more than twenty years, Bantam Spectra has been publishing the finest science-fiction, fantasy, horror, and speculative novels from recognizable authors including Isaac Asimov, Ray Bradbury, Arthur C. Clarke, George R. R. Martin, Kim Stanley Robinson, and M. John Harrison.

Recent titles include *Nightrunner # 7* by Lynn Flewelling; *Black and White* by Jackie Kessler and Caitlin Kittredge; *The Burning Skies* by David J. Williams; *Norse Code* by Greg Van Eekhout; and *The Island* by Tim Lebbon.

SPIEGEL & GRAU

Spiegel & Grau publishes books that help us make sense of our lives in a world besieged by conflict, rapid change, ideology, and constant pressures. They aim to create a list of books that share the potential to unite people in a common experience, whether it be through fiction, memoir, narrative journalism, or works on current issues.

Some Spiegel & Grau books include *The Nature of the Beast* by Cary Groner; *They Call Me Baba Booey* by Gary Dell'Abate; *Stand by Me* by Susan Pinker; *Infidels: In Search of the First Evolutionists* by Rebecca Stott; and *Decoded* by Jay-Z.

Julie Grau, Senior Vice President and Publisher

Celina Spiegel, Senior Vice President and Publisher—Fiction, science nonfiction

Christopher Jackson, Executive Editor

Michael Mezzo, Editor

STRIVERS ROW

Strivers Row, founded in 2001 to showcase African American fiction, was named after the street in Harlem which was largely inhabited by first-generation African American professionals during the time of the Harlem Renaissance. Its authors include Parry "Ebony Satin" Brown, Tajuana Butler, Travis Hunter, and Nichelle Tramble.

Some titles from Strivers Row include *Candy Licker* by Noire; *The Apostles* by Y. Blak Moore; *The Night Before Thirty* by Tajuana Butler; *G-Spot: An Urban Erotic Tale* by Noire; and *Every Shut Eye* by Collen Dixon.

Melody Guy, Editor—Fiction, relationship advice

TRIUMPH BOOKS

542 S. Dearborn St., Suite 750, Chicago, IL 60605

Triumph Books, a leading publisher of sports books, became an imprint of the Random House Publishing Group in May 2006. Triumph has had success with the *New York Times* bestseller *Dale Earnhardt: Remembering the Intimidator* and has published such sports figures and authors as Dan Marino, Jerome Bettis, Whitey Ford, Brett Favre, Mario Lemieux, and more. Recent titles include *Conquering a Continent: The Astonishing Story of Triumph, Suffering, and the Most Extreme Endurance Race in the World* by Amy Snyder; *Learning to Play* by Mark Schlereth and Mark Preisler; *Summers in the Bronx: Atilla the Hun and Other Yankee Stories* by Ira Berkow; and *What Happens When the Cheering Stops* by William Bendetson.

Tom Best, Editor—Sports

VILLARD BOOKS

Villard Books was founded in 1983 and named after the Stanford White brownstone mansion on Madison Avenue that was the home of Random House for 20 years. It publishes a general nonfiction and fiction list that has positioned itself on the leading edge of popular culture. Among the bestselling authors it has published are Jon Krakauer, Eve Ensler, former Governor Jesse Ventura, and the "Travel Detective," Peter Greenberg. Villard is also known for its titles in the areas of humor, personal narrative, and new-voice fiction, including the books of Laurie Notaro and Jon Katz.

Recent titles include *My Parents Were Awesome* by Eliot Glazer; *Regretsy* by April Winchell; *Historical Tweets* by Alan Beard and Alec McNayr; and *Old Jews Telling Jokes* by Sam Hoffman and Eric Spiegelman.

Jill Schwartzman, Senior Editor—How-to, cooking

Ryan Doherty, Editor—Nonfiction anthology, humor

CBS CORPORATION

The CBS Corporation was formed in 2005, when Viacom, Inc., split into two publicly traded companies: Viacom and CBS Corporation. Based in New York, CBS Corporation holds assets in television, radio, digital media, outdoor advertising, and publishing, including Simon & Schuster.

SIMON & SCHUSTER

SIMON & SCHUSTER ADULT PUBLISHING GROUP

SIMON & SCHUSTER CHILDREN'S PUBLISHING

1230 Avenue of the Americas, New York, NY 10020

212-698-7000

www.simonsays.com

Simon & Schuster was founded in 1924 by Richard L. Simon and M. Lincoln Schuster. Their initial project was a crossword puzzle book, the first ever produced, and it was a runaway bestseller. From that, the company has grown to become a global, multifaceted publishing house releasing more than 1,800 titles annually. Simon & Schuster titles have won 54 Pulitzer Prizes, 15 National Book Awards, 14 Caldecott, and 18 Newbery Medals.

Simon & Schuster today is wholly focused on consumer publishing. Its seven divisions—the Simon & Schuster Adult Publishing Group, Simon & Schuster Children's Publishing, Simon & Schuster Audio, Simon & Schuster Online, Simon & Schuster UK, Simon & Schuster Canada, and Simon & Schuster Australia—are home to many distinguished imprints and recognizable brand names, including Simon & Schuster, Scribner, Pocket Books, The Free Press, Atria, Fireside, Touchstone, Atheneum, Margaret K. McElderry, Aladdin Paperbacks, Little Simon, and Simon Spotlight.

The newest Simon and Schuster imprints are Howard Books, a religious and inspirational publisher; Threshold Editions, a Pocket imprint for conservative readers; a Hispanic/Latino publishing line in its Atria imprint; and Simon Scribbles, a coloring and activity imprint for children. An exciting moment at Simon & Schuster in 2007 was their largest ever reprint order, two million copies of blockbuster *The Secret* by Rhonda Byrne.

Simon & Schuster does not accept unsolicited manuscripts and recommends working with an agent.

SIMON & SCHUSTER ADULT PUBLISHING GROUP

ATRIA BOOKS

THE FREE PRESS

POCKET BOOKS

SCRIBNER

SIMON & SCHUSTER

SIMON SPOTLIGHT ENTERTAINMENT

TOUCHSTONE FIRESIDE

1230 Avenue of the Americas, New York, NY 10020

212-698-7000

www.simonsays.com

The Simon & Schuster Adult Publishing Group includes a number of publishing units that offer books in several formats. Each unit has its own publisher, editorial group, and publicity department. Common sales and business departments support all the units.

ATRIA BOOKS

BEYOND WORDS

STREBOR BOOKS

WASHINGTON SQUARE PRESS

The Atria imprint, established in 2001, publishes a mix of fiction and nonfiction—especially biography and celebrity memoirs. It is the hardcover imprint for Pocket Books, a commercial publishing house pledged to bring the world a wealth of timely, important, and entertaining publications. Atria Books is the home of several bestselling authors including Jennifer Weiner, Jodi Picoult, Judith McNaught, Vince Flynn, and Jude Deveraux.

In recent years, Atria has placed an emphasis on publishing for diverse audiences and has launched a Hispanic/Latino line, acquired Strebor Books, and entered a co-publishing deal with Beyond Words that gives Atria world rights to that company's titles. Atria releases trade paperbacks under the Washington Square Press imprint.

Recent Atria titles include *The Couturiere* by Maria Duenas; *Because of You* by Sarah Pekkanen; *The Very Thought of You* by Rosie Alison; *Josefina's Sin* by Claudia H. Long; *The Woman I Was Born to Be* by Susan Boyle; and *Kitchen on Fire* by Aaron Sanchez.

Direct query letters and SASEs to:

Judith Curr, Publisher

Emily Bestler, Vice President and Executive Editorial Director—Commercial fiction and nonfiction, thriller, mystery

Greer Hendricks, Vice President and Senior Editor—Literary and commercial fiction, narrative nonfiction, memoir, lifestyle

Malaika Adero, Senior Editor—Literary fiction, narrative nonfiction, health and fitness, spirituality, memoir, biography, African American interests, art and culture

Peter Borland, Senior Editor—Narrative nonfiction, pop culture, sports, memoir, "quality" commercial fiction

Johanna V. Castillo, Senior Editor—Hispanic-Latino and Spanish language publishing program

Amy Tannenbaum, Editor—Fiction

Krishan Trotman, Associate Editor—Nonfiction

Sarah Branham, Editor—Fiction, cooking, mystery

Sarah Durand, Editor—Health, memoir

BEYOND WORDS

Beyond Words, founded in 1983 as a publisher of coffee table books, currently releases around 15 new titles a year in the Mind/Body/Spirit category. They entered into a co-publishing agreement with Atria Books in 2006. See the listing for Beyond Words in the Independent Publishers section for more information.

Richard Cohn, Publisher

Cynthia Black, Editor

STREBOR BOOKS

Strebor Books is the company originally founded in 1999 by author Zane to publish her first three books. The imprint's editors now focus on popular fiction and nonfiction by African American writers and are on the lookout for the next big thing. It releases 48 new titles per year in hardcover and paperback.

Recent titles from Strebor include *Nothing Stays the Same* by Suzetta Perkins and *Scared Silent* by Mildred Muhammad.

Zane, Publisher

WASHINGTON SQUARE PRESS

Atria imprint Washington Square Press publishes literary fiction and topical non-fiction in trade paperback format.

Recent titles from Washington Square Press include *Certain Girls* by Jennifer Weiner; *Girls Like Us: Carole King, Joni Mitchell, Carly Simon—and the Journey of a Generation* by Sheila Weller; *Mother of the Believers: A Novel of the Birth of Islam* by Kamran Pasha; and *The Glamorous Double Life of Isabel Bookbinder* by Holly McQueen.

THE FREE PRESS

For more than 50 years, The Free Press has published cutting-edge nonfiction works in social thought, politics, current affairs, history, science, psychology, religion and spirituality, music, and a broad business list. It also produces college textbooks. Titles are produced in hardcover format.

Recent releases include *I Wore the Ocean in the Shape of a Girl* by Kelle Groom; *Cake Boss: Stories and Recipes from Mia Famiglia* by Buddy Valastro; *Game Face: Unlocking the Power of Game Mechanics in Everyday Life* by Aaron Dignan; *Do Skinny Chicks Have More Daughters?* by Jena Pincott; *The Butterfly Cabinet* by Bernie McGill; *Make the Bread, Buy the Butter* by Jennifer Reese; and *Horses Never Lie* by Jana Harris.

Direct query letters and SASEs to:

Martha K. Levin, Vice President, Publisher

Dominick Anfuso, Editor-in-Chief—General nonfiction, history, politics, business and careers

Amber Qureshi, Senior Editor—Narrative nonfiction, fiction

Hilary Redmon, Senior Editor

Emily Loose, Senior Editor—Nonfiction

Martin Beiser, Senior Editor—Nonfiction, sports, history, current affairs

Leslie Meredith, Editor—Animals, spirituality, health, pop science

Wylie O'Sullivan, Editor—Fiction, narrative nonfiction

Leah Miller, Assistant Editor

Priscilla Gilman, Editor—Mystery, science, health

Jackie Kaiser, Editor—Health, memoir, nonfiction

George Lucas, Editor—Thriller, biography, current affairs

POCKET BOOKS

DOWNTOWN PRESS

G-UNIT

JUNO

MTV BOOKS

THRESHOLD

Pocket Books, founded in 1939, was America's first publisher of paperback books. Today, Pocket is producing general-interest fiction and nonfiction books in mass-market and trade paperback formats. Pocket Books is also the publisher of the Star Trek novels.

Pocket Books only accepts agented submissions. Guidelines for Star Trek novels are available on the Simon & Schuster website, www.simonsays.com.

Louise Burke, Publisher

Anthony Ziccardi, Associate Publisher

Margaret Clark, Executive Editor

Jennifer Heddle, Senior Editor—Fiction, including young adult and manga; paranormal; fantasy

Micki Nuding, Senior Editor—Women's fiction, chick lit

Lauren McKenna, Editor—Fiction, romance, pop culture, music, fantasy

Abby Zidle, Senior Editor—Fiction

Brigitte Smith, Editor—Fiction, including young adult

DOWNTOWN PRESS

Downtown Press publishes chick lit and women's fiction. Some recent titles include *Every Demon Has His Day* by Cara Lockwood; *Chasing Harry Winston* by Lauren Weisberger; *As Sure as the Sun* by Anna McPartlin; *The Love of Her Life* by Harriet Evans; and *Lessons in Heartbreak* by Cathy Kelly.

G-UNIT BOOKS

A message from 50 Cent: Just like I rounded up some of the top rappers in the game, I'm rounding up some of the top writers working today to form G-Unit Books. The stories in the G-Unit series are the kinds of dramas me and my crew have been dealing with our whole lives: death, deceit, double-crosses, ultimate loyalty, and total betrayal. It's about our life on the streets and no one knows it better than us. You know I don't do anything halfway, and I'm going to take this street lit thing to a whole other level. Are you ready?

Some titles include *Blow* by K'wan and 50 Cent; *The Diamond District* by Derrick Pledger; *Heaven's Fury* by Meta Smith; and *Harlem Heat* by Mark Anthony.

JUNO

Juno became an imprint of Pocket Books on January 1, 2009, moving from Prime Books/Wildside Press. They specialize in fantasy featuring strong female characters in richly imagined contexts. As they move into a new era with Pocket, the concentration will still be on female protagonists and high imagination, but the general direction will shift towards contemporary/urban fantasy.

Some upcoming titles include *Silver Zombie* by Carole Nelson Douglas; *Concrete Savior* by Yvonne Navarro; and *Dark Oracle* by Alayna William.

Paula Guran, Editor-in-Chief—Science fiction, fantasy

Jennifer Heddle, Senior Editor

MTV BOOKS

MTV Books captures the real-life stories of today's hottest artists, goes behind-the-scenes of hit shows, and brings you fresh and entertaining fiction. Some titles include *Forget You* by Jennifer Echol; *Hollywood Ending* by Kathy Charles; *The Fairest of Them All* by Jan Blazanin; *Shrinking Violet* by Danielle Joseph; and *The Rose That Grew from Concrete* by Tupac Shakur.

THRESHOLD

Threshold publishes titles for a conservative audience. Recent titles from Threshold include *Grass Roots: How 100 People Just Like You Are Saving America* by Scott Hennen; *Won by One* by Laura Ingraham; *A Nightmare's Prayer: A Marine Harrier Pilot's War in Afghanistan* by Michael Franzak; *You Know I'm Right* by Michelle Caruso-Cabrera; *The Post-American Presidency* by Robert Spencer; *The Race in Middle Earth: Between the Caliphate and Democratic Revolution* by Walid Phares; and *Obama Zombies* by Jason Matera.

Anthony Ziccardi, Editor—Current affairs, fiction

Mitchell Ivers, Editor—History, politics

SCRIBNER

Scribner was founded in 1846 by Charles Scribner and Isaac Baker, and initially focused on religious books. As Charles Scribner's Sons, and under legendary editors such as Maxwell Perkins and John Hall Wheelock, the house published many of the giants of nineteenth and twentieth-century American literature, including Henry James, Edith Wharton, Ring Lardner, Ernest Hemingway, F. Scott Fitzgerald, Thomas Wolfe, and Marjorie Kinnan Rawlings. Many of these authors and their classic works remain in print today as a mainstay of the Scribner list.

Today, Scribner produces fiction and nonfiction titles in hardcover format. Categories include general fiction, history, military, social science, popular culture, and self-help. Scribner authors include Annie Proulx, whose novel *The Shipping News* (1993) won both the Pulitzer Prize and the National Book Award; Frank McCourt, whose memoir *Angela's Ashes* (1996) became a mainstay of the *New York Times* bestseller list, was awarded the Pulitzer Prize and the National Book Critics Circle Award, and was followed by the bestselling *'Tis* and *Teacher Man*; and Don DeLillo's *Underworld* (1997). Scribner is also the home of bestselling authors Stephen King, Kathy Reichs, and Linda Fairstein, and to the *Joy of Cooking*, revised in 2006 for a 75th Anniversary edition.

Recent releases include *Insanity: An American Psychiatrist, a Japanese Nationalist, and an Unsolved Mystery of World War II* by Eric Jaffe; *Bed* by

David Whitehouse; *The Death of Cool* by Gavin McInnes; *The Priest* by Gerard O'Donovan; *Sinclair* by Kitty Pilgrim; *Eleven* by Mark Watson; and *One Last, Green Home* by Mark Harris.

Send query letters with SASEs to:

Nan Graham, Vice President, Editor-in-Chief—Fiction

Beth Wareham, Director of Lifestyle Publishing

Colin Harrison, Executive Editor—True crime, narrative nonfiction, thrillers, current affairs, history

Brant Rumble, Senior Editor—Biography, memoir, sports, current events, pop culture, fiction

Samantha Martin, Associate Editor—Nonfiction

Alexis Gargagliano, Editor—Fiction

Anna deVries, Editor—Fiction, crime and mystery

SIMON & SCHUSTER

Simon & Schuster was founded in April 1924 when Richard L. Simon and M. Lincoln Schuster pooled their resources and published *The Cross Word Puzzle Book,* capitalizing on the crossword craze of the time and packaged with a pencil to aid readers in solving the puzzles. In its early years, S&S achieved commercial success from such groundbreaking mega-sellers as Will and Ariel Duran's *The Story of Philosophy* and Dale Carnegie's *How to Win Friends and Influence People.*

Over the years, the name Simon & Schuster has also grown to signify the much larger publishing enterprise of Simon & Schuster, Inc., but the Simon & Schuster trade imprint has remained a cornerstone to the business and one of the most venerated brand names in the world of publishing. It is widely known as a powerhouse publisher of general fiction and nonfiction for readers of all tastes.

Titles representative of this list include *I, Too, Am America* by Langston Hughes and Bryan Collier; *Spy School* by Stuart Gibbs; *A Young Wife* by Pam Lewis; *Darkside* by Belinda Bauer; *The Case of the Deadly Butter Chicken* by Tarquin Hall; *From Betrayal to Trust* by John Gottman and Nan Silver; *Better Off Without 'Em* by Chuch Thompson; *Ghost Boy* by Martin Pistorius; and *How the People Rule America* by Bill Schneider.

Send query letters and SASEs to:

David Rosenthal, Publisher

Robert Bender, Vice President, Senior Editor—Nonfiction, history, science nonfiction, fiction

Liesa Abrahms, Executive Editor

Amanda Murray, Senior Editor—Hardcover nonfiction, both narrative and practical; memoir, women's issues, popular reference, beauty, inspiration, entertainment, mind/body/health

Dedi Felman, Senior Editor—Nonfiction

Colin Fox, Senior Editor—Fiction, nonfiction

Roger Labrie, Editor—Nonfiction, history, military, current affairs

Priscilla Painton, Editor—Current affairs, biography, memoir, relationship advice, religion and spirituality, science, politics

Kerri Kolen, Editor—Fiction

Sarah Hochman, Editor—Parenting, memoir, thriller

Courtney Bongiolatti, Editor—Young adult, children's picture book

Marysue Rucci, Editor—Sports, fiction

SIMON SPOTLIGHT ENTERTAINMENT

Simon Spotlight Entertainment (SSE) launched in September 2004 with *He's Just Not That Into You: The No-Excuses Truth to Understanding Guys* by Greg Behrendt and Liz Tuccillo, which became an instant national bestseller, hitting the number one spot on the *New York Times, USA Today, Publishers Weekly*, and *Wall Street Journal* bestseller lists. The imprint continues to publish original nonfiction, fiction, and media tie-ins, including *Angelina's Bachelors* by Brian O'Reilly; *The White Lie* by Pamela Redmond Satran; *Flawless* by Carrie Lofty; *In Stitches* by Alan Eisenstock; *Can You Survive the Zombie Apocalypse* by Max Brallier; *Paradise Rules* by Jimmy Gleacher; *The Laws of Motion* by Laurel Corona; and *Extracurricular* by Josie Brown.

Direct query letters and SASEs to:

Jennifer Bergstrom, Vice President, Publisher

Tricia Boczkowski, Senior Editor

Patrick Price, Senior Editor

Jeremie Ruby-Strauss, Senior Editor

Sarah Sper, Editor

Terra Chalberg, Editor

TOUCHSTONE FIRESIDE

TOUCHSTONE

FIRESIDE

HOWARD BOOKS

Touchstone Fireside was created at Simon and Schuster in 1970 to publish books in trade paperback, although the changing marketplace resulted in the addition of hardcover books in 2003. The two imprints share an editorial staff and have separate small, focused lists. The Touchstone Fireside group of imprints incorporated Howard Books in February 2006.

TOUCHSTONE

Touchstone publishes fiction and serious nonfiction books in all categories of history, politics, military, political science, biography, and autobiography. They publish almost exclusively original trade paperbacks and hardcovers as well as reprints from other houses in the industry. In 2007, the imprint launched Touchstone Faith, to release religious and spiritual titles, like *God Wants You to Be Rich: How and Why Everyone Can Enjoy Material and Spiritual Wealth in Our Abundant World* by Paul Zane Pilzer.

Titles representative of Touchstone's list include *The Autoimmune Epidemic* by Donna Jackson Nakazawa and Douglas Kerr; *Bound South* by Susan Rebecca White; *Bloodprint: A Novel of Psychological Suspense* by Kitty Sewell; *Mr. Darcy's Dream* by Elizabeth Aston; and *Mother in the Middle: A Biologist's Story of Caring for Parent and Child* by Sybil Lockhart.

FIRESIDE

The Fireside imprint has traditionally published practical and inspirational books on subjects such as self-help, parenting and childcare, popular psychology, and health and medicine. The list includes how-to titles on just about any topic including games, sports, cooking, gardening, finding a job, and running a business. Among its bestselling authors are Sean Covey, Danny Dryer, Rick Lavoie, and Jay McGraw. Under its current mission, Fireside has also embraced popular culture with bestsellers from celebrities such as Fantasia, Allison DuBois, Carolyn Kepcher, and Paris Hilton. Fireside publishes nonfiction titles in hardcover and trade paperback format, and reissues paperback books previously published in hardcover format.

Recent releases include *The Rise and Fall of WaMu* by Kirsten Grind; *The Secret Lives of Sisters* by Gabrielle Donnelly; *The Cougar* by Victoria Christopher Murray; *Off Balance* by Dominique Moceanu; *JFK and the Unspeakable: Why He Died and Why It Matters* by James Douglass; *Long May You Run* by Chris Cooper; *The Pathfinder* by Nick Lore; and *How to Start a Conversation and Make Friends* by Don Gabor.

Direct query letters and SASEs to:

Trish Todd, Editor-in-Chief—Humor, celebrity memoir, education, history, pop culture, fiction; especially historical fiction and commercial women's fiction

Michelle Howry, Senior Editor—Nonfiction, including health, relationships, self-help, food, memoir, investing; especially practical nonfiction and compelling narrative nonfiction

Zachary Schisgal, Senior Editor—Nonfiction, including pop culture, sports, relationships, exercise, fiction, business and investing

Trish Lande Grader, Senior Editor—Fiction, especially mystery, suspense, crime, inspirational, debut novels

Sulay Hernandez, Editor—Fiction and nonfiction, especially narrative nonfiction, humor, pop culture, urban stories, women's fiction, erotica. She loves dark novels, books that aren't easily categorized, and acquiring new voices in Latin and African American markets.

Stacy Creamer, Editor—Fiction, thriller, memoir

Lauren Spiegel, Editor—Fiction, thriller

HOWARD BOOKS

Howard Books was founded in 1969 and has grown into an award-winning publisher of more than 45 titles per year in Christian living, inspirational, gift, fiction, devotional, and youth books. Howard Publishing was acquired by Simon & Schuster in 2006 and renamed Howard Books.

Not affiliated with any religious group or denomination, Howard Books maintains a distinctly objective editorial independence, which allows for a broad base of authors and subject matter. Its titles promote biblical principles for godly living as expressed by qualified writers whose lives and messages reflect the heart of Christ. Howard authors include Point of Grace, Andy Stanley, Sandi Patty, Big Idea's VeggieTales, Ed Young, David and Claudia Arp, Tony Campolo, Dr. Ken Canfield, Calvin Miller, and Bill Bright.

Recent titles include *You'll Lose that Baby Weight (And Other Lies About Pregnancy and Childbirth)* by Dawn Meehan; *The Uprising of Christ: Resurrection as Insurrection* by Peter Rollins; *Far From Here* by Nicole Baart; *Called to Coach: The Life, Faith, and Career of College Football's Most Popular Coach* by Bobby Bowden; and *To Die For* by Sandra Byrd.

Howard Books is open to unsolicited queries; do not send manuscripts until invited to do so.

Jonathan Merkh, Vice President and Publisher

Denny Boultinghouse, Executive Editor

David Lambert, Senior Editor

Cindy Lambert, Senior Editor

Becky Nesbitt, Editor—Religion and spirituality, fiction, women's reference, sports

SIMON & SCHUSTER CHILDREN'S PUBLISHING

ALADDIN/PULSE

LITTLE SIMON/LITTLE SIMON INSPIRATIONS

SIMON & SCHUSTER CHILDREN'S PUBLISHING

1230 Avenue of the Americas, New York, NY 10020

212-698-7000

www.simonsays.com

Simon & Schuster Children's Publishing is one of the world's leading children's book publishers. In 2008 Simon & Schuster Children's announced a restructuring of the division that created three distinct units to handle both hardcover and paperback editions: Aladdin/Pulse, the Little Simon/Little Simon Inspirations novelty and interactive division, and Simon and Schuster Children's Publishing.

Jon Anderson, Executive Vice President, Publisher

ALADDIN/PULSE

ALADDIN PAPERBACKS

SIMON PULSE

Aladdin/Pulse was created in 2008 when Simon & Schuster's combined into one division the previously separate Aladdin Paperbacks and Simon Pulse imprints.

Bethany Buck, Vice President, Publisher

ALADDIN PAPERBACKS

Aladdin Paperbacks publishes juvenile fiction and nonfiction early readers, chapter books, and middle-grade books, for ages 4–12. The imprint includes a line for beginning readers; Ready-to-Read books (including the *Henry & Mudge* series by Cynthia Rylant and Suçie Stevenson); and the Ready-for-Chapters line for newly independent readers (including *The Bears on Hemlock Mountain* by Alice Dalgliesh and *The Unicorn's Secret* series by Kathleen Duey). The backbone of the Aladdin list is reprints from the hardcover imprints, including some of the most enduring children's books of the modern era, such as classic picture books like *Chicka Chicka Boom Boom* by Bill Martin, Jr., John Archambault, and Lois Ehlert and *Strega Nona* by Tomie DePaola; honored fiction like *From the Mixed-Up Files of Mrs. Basil E. Frankweiler* by E.L. Konigsburg; *Hatchet* by Gary Paulsen; *Frindle* by Andrew Clements; the *Shiloh* trilogy by Phyllis Reynolds Naylor; and the *Bunnicula* books by James Howe. Aladdin's strong reprint list also is supplemented by a limited number of original series and single titles.

Recent titles include *Lysander Singleton* by Ariel Winter; *Traitor* by Julia Platt

Leonard; *The Monstore* by Tara Lazar; *Presenting… Tallulah* by Tori Spelling; *Dead to You* by Lisa McMann; and *The Go-See Chronicles* by PG Kain.

Send query letters with SASEs to:

Liesa Abrams, Senior Editor

Emily Lawrence, Associate Editor—Children's literature, illustrated books

Kate Angelella, Assistant Editor

Alyson Heller, Editor—Children's middle grade

SIMON PULSE

Simon Pulse is a hardcover and paperback imprint for late tweens to older teens with a focus on contemporary, commercial fiction. Pulse publishes and markets directly to its readership, and addresses topical, edgy, and trend-driven subjects that are prevalent in the teen world today.

Included in Pulse are series like R.L. Stine's *Fear Street*; Cathy Hopkin's *Mates, Dates*; Scott Westerfeld's *Specials*; and *The Au Pairs* by Melissa de la Cruz; contemporary classics like *Go Ask Alice*; National Book Award winners *The House of the Scorpion* by Nancy Farmer and *True Believer* by Virginia Euwer Wolff; and literary titles such as *The Dark Is Rising* sequence by Susan Cooper and *The Tillerman Series* by Cynthia Voigt.

Recent titles include *Friend Me: Mates, Dates, and Inflatable Bras* by Cathy Hopkins; *Night World: Huntress, Black Dawn, Witchlight* by L.J. Smith; *The Fortunes of Indigo Skye* by Deb Caletti; *Pure* by Terra Elan McVoy; and *When the Black Girl Sings* by Bil Wright.

Direct query letters and SASEs to:

Jennifer Klonsky, Editorial Director

Anica Rissi, Editor

Michael Del Rosario, Associate Editor

Annette Pollert, Assistant Editor

LITTLE SIMON/LITTLE SIMON INSPIRATION

LITTLE SIMON

LITTLE SIMON INSPIRATION

SIMON SCRIBBLES

SIMON SPOTLIGHT

Little Simon/Little Simon Inspiration was created with the integration of Little Simon, Simon Inspirations, and Simon Scribbles in 2008. The division primarily produces activity, novelty, and media tie-in books for children.

Alyson Grubard, Vice President and Associate Publisher

LITTLE SIMON

Little Simon specializes in the most innovative novelty books for children, including pop-ups, lift-the-flap books, board books, sticker books, interactive e-books, and other specialty formats.

Recent titles include *Karate Pig* by Alan Katz; *Peek-a-Baby: A Lift-the-Flap Book* by Karen Katz; *My Mom and Me* by Alyssa Satin Capucilli and Susan Mitchell; *My Mother Is Mine* by Marion Dane Bauer and Peter Elwell; and *The Foolish Tortoise* by Richard Buckley and Eric Carle.

Direct query letters and SASEs to:

Sonali Fry, Editorial Director

Brooke Linder, Editor

LITTLE SIMON INSPIRATION

Little Simon Inspiration publishes faith-based books that celebrate a child's relationship with God and reaffirm a belief in faith-based family values. This exciting line of children's books goes beyond Bible stories and presents an appreciation for God and God's gifts through a mix of charming, relevant picture and novelty books from inspiring role models who present positive messages to children.

Some recent titles include *You Can Do It* by Tony Dungy; *Momma Loves Her Little Son* by John Carter Cash and Marc Burckhardt; *Thank You, God!: A Year of Blessings and Prayers for Little Ones* by Sophie Allsopp; and *Unexpected Treasures* by Victoria Osteen and Diane Palmisciano.

SIMON SCRIBBLES

Simon Scribbles was launched in 2006 to produce coloring and activity books. It releases 60 titles per year, including, most recently, *Dancey Dance* by Maggie Testa; *Let's Explore* by Tina Gallo; *Mission Accomplished* by Orli Zuravicky; and *Go, Go, Go, Wubbzy!* by Rudy Ovrero.

Send queries with SASEs to:

Siobhan Ciminera, Senior Editor

Lisa Rao, Editor

SIMON SPOTLIGHT

Simon Spotlight publishes hardcover and mass-market paperback fiction books tied to media properties such as Rugrats and The Busy World of Richard Scarry. Launched in the fall of 1997, this imprint has since become one of the fastest-growing imprints in the children's book industry—releasing titles for preschool through middle-grade children.

Other titles indicative of Simon Spotlight's list include *We Love a Luau (The*

Backyardigans) by Jodie Shepherd, illustrated by Carlo Lo Raso; *The Deathless (Buffy the Vampire Slayer)* by Keith R.A. DeCandido; *High Spirits (Charmed)* by Scott Ciencin; and *Hooray for Dads! (SpongeBob Squarepants)* by Erica Pass, illustrated by The Artifact Group.

Recent Spotlight titles include *Sleep and Dream of Happy Things* by Veronica Paz and Mike Lee Giles; *Friends Are Fun!* by Lauryn Silverhardt; *Foofa's Happy Book* by Irene Kilpatrick; and *G.I. JOE Movie Sticker Book* by Edgar Echeverria, Jr., and Dan Panosian.

Direct query letters and SASEs to:

Valerie Garfield, Publisher

Jennifer Bergstrom, Publisher

Karen Sargent, Executive Editor

SIMON & SCHUSTER CHILDREN'S PUBLISHING

ATHENEUM BOOKS FOR YOUNG READERS

MARGARET K. MCELDERRY BOOKS

PAULA WISEMAN BOOKS

RICHARD JACKSON BOOKS

SIMON & SCHUSTER BOOKS FOR YOUNG READERS

The Simon & Schuster Children's Publishing Trade Division was expanded in 2008 with the addition of Atheneum Books and the consolidation of other imprints.

Anne Zafian, Deputy Publisher

ATHENEUM BOOKS FOR YOUNG READERS

Atheneum Books for Young Readers is a hardcover imprint with a focus on literary fiction and fine picture books for children and young adults. The imprint, founded in 1961 by legendary editor Jean Karl (1928–2000), has garnered awards and prizes for such books as *The View from Saturday* by E.L. Konigsburg; *Alexander and the Terrible, Horrible, No Good, Very Bad Day* by Judith Viorst and Ray Cruz; *Shiloh* by Phyllis Reynolds Naylor; the *Bunnicula* books by James Howe; Doreen Cronin and Betsy Lewin's *Duck* series; and Sharon Draper's *Ziggy and the Black Dinosaurs* series.

Recently Atheneum has begun to publish novelty books, the first being the *New York Times* #1 bestseller *Pirates* by John Matthews, to be followed by *Santa Claus* and others.

Recent titles include *Crafty Chloe* by Heather Ross; *The Witchlanders* by Lena Coakley; *Olivia Goes to Venice* by Ian Falconer; *Eva of the Farm* by Dia Calhoun; *Good God Bird* by John Corey Whaley; *Young Malcolm X* by Ilyasah Shabazz; and *If Eyes Had No Tears* by Laura Lascarso.

Emma Dryden, Vice President and Publisher

Caitlyn Dlouhy, Editorial Director

Namrata Tripathi, Executive Editor

Kiley Frank, Editor—Young adult, children's

MARGARET K. MCELDERRY BOOKS

Founded by legendary editor Margaret K. McElderry in 1972, the imprint publishes in hardcover with an emphasis on picture books, poetry, middle-grade and teen fiction. Recent lists include the first-ever authorized sequel to J. M. Barrie's *Peter Pan*, Geraldine McCaughrean's *Peter Pan in Scarlet*; *Ironside* by Holly Black; and *Skin* by Adrienne Maria Vrettos.

Other recent titles include *City of Glass* by Cassandra Clare; *Solving Zoe* by Barbara Dee; *A Whiff of Pine, a Hint of Skunk: A Forest of Poems* by Deborah Ruddell and Joan Rankin; *The Genie Scheme* by Kimberly K. Jones; *Shine, Coconut Moon* by Neesha Meminger; and *What's the Weather Inside?* by Karma Wilson and Barry Blitt.

Send query letters with SASEs to:

Emma Dryden, Vice President and Publisher

Karen Wojtyla, Editorial Director

PAULA WISEMAN BOOKS

Paula Wiseman, formerly an editorial director at Harcourt, launched her eponymous children's imprint at Simon & Schuster in 2002. Some Paula Wiseman titles include *Legacy* by Molly Cochran; *The Secret Ingredient* by Laura Schaefer; *Poindexter* by Mike Twohy; *Superhero Joe: The Creature in the Hood* by Jacqueline Preiss; and *Spike* by Susan Hood.

Paula Wiseman, Vice President and Publisher

Alexandra Penfold, Associate Editor

RICHARD JACKSON BOOKS

This is the Simon & Schuster imprint of veteran children's book editor Richard Jackson. Some recent titles include *The Man Who Lived in a Hollow Tree* by Anne Shelby and Cor Hazelaar; *Sleepsong* by George Ella Lyon and Peter Catalanotto; and *The Hinky-Pink: An Old Tale* by Megan McDonald and Brian Floca.

SIMON & SCHUSTER BOOKS FOR YOUNG READERS

Simon & Schuster Books for Young Readers publishes fiction and nonfiction titles for children of all ages, from preschool through teens, in hardcover format. Titles in this house span the spectrum from social situations and self-esteem, to animals and pets, action and adventure, holidays and festivals, science fiction, fantasy, African American, and other ethnic stories.

This list includes the classic *Eloise* books by Kay Thompson and Hilary Knight; *Sylvester and the Magic Pebble* by William Steig; *Frindle* by Andrew Clements; *Chicka Chicka Boom Boom* by Bill Martin, Jr., John Archambault, and Lois Ehlert; and *Click, Clack Moo: Cows That Type* by Doreen Cronin and Betsy Lewin. SSBFYR includes among its authors and illustrators Loren Long, John Lithgow, Derek Anderson, Kate Brian, and Rachel Cohn. Recent notable Simon & Schuster Books for Young Readers titles include *The Spiderwick Chronicles* by Tony DiTerlizzi and Holly Black; *Ellington Was Not a Street* by Ntzoke Shange, illustrated by Kadir Nelson; the *Pendragon* series by D.J. McHale; *Room One* by Andrew Clements; *Gideon the Cutpurse* by Linda Buckley-Archer; and the *Shadow Children* series by Margaret Peterson Haddix.

Other recent titles include *Crazy Hot* by Melissa de la Cruz; *The Monsters of Otherness* by Kaza Kingsley and Melvyn Grant; *Great Balls of Fire* by Loren Long and Phil Bildner; *Anything But Typical* by Nora Raleigh Baskin; *Found* by Margaret Peterson Haddix; and *When Papa Comes Home Tonight* by Eileen Spinelli and David McPhail.

Send query letters with SASEs to:

David Gale, Editorial Director—Middle-grade and young-adult novels; looks for sharp writing and fresh voices. Does not want to consider standard young-adult problem novels or romances, but is interested in more unusual, hard-hitting, and literary young-adult novels, also interested in fantasy.

Kevin Lewis, Editorial Director

Alexandra Cooper, Senior Editor

HACHETTE LIVRE

Hachette Livre, France's largest publishing company, is a wholly-owned subsidiary of Lagardère, a French company that is active on the worldwide stage in the areas of aerospace, defense, and media.

HACHETTE BOOK GROUP USA

CENTER STREET

FAITHWORDS

GRAND CENTRAL PUBLISHING

LITTLE, BROWN AND COMPANY

LITTLE, BROWN BOOKS FOR YOUNG READERS

OCTOPUS USA

ORBIT

WINDBLOWN MEDIA

237 Park Avenue, New York, NY 10017

212-364-1200

www.hachette-bookgroupusa.com

In 2006, Hachette Livre acquired Time Warner Book Group from Time Warner, and renamed it Hachette Book Group USA. The terms of the sale stipulated that Warner Books must shed its name, and the publisher lost little time in rechristening as Grand Central Publishing. In April 2007, Hachette Book Group moved to new offices on Park Avenue, just north of Grand Central Terminal.

Hachette Book Group USA (HBG) is comprised of the following groups: Grand Central Publishing; Little, Brown and Company; Little, Brown Books for Young Readers; FaithWords; Center Street; Orbit; Octopus USA; and Yen Press.

Publishers in the Hachette Book Group USA do not consider unsolicited manuscript submissions and unsolicited queries. The publisher recommends working with a literary agent.

CENTER STREET

Two Creekside Crossing, Ten Cadillac Drive, Suite 220, Brentwood, TN 37027
615-221-0996   fax: 615-221-0962

Center Street is a general market imprint based near Nashville that was launched in 2005 to publish wholesome entertainment, helpful encouragement, and books of traditional values that appeal to readers in America's heartland. Unlike FaithWords, which publishes specifically for the Christian market, Center Street books are intended for a broad audience.

Recent titles include *God and Dog* by Wendy Francisco; *Dare to Take Charge* by Glenda Hatchet; *The Four Pillars of Success* by Don Yaeger; *Unsaid* by Neil Abramson; *The Five Levels of Leadership* by John Maxwell; *Kiss of Night* by Debbie Viguie; *What Is He Thinking* by Rebecca St. James; and *Swing Your Sword* by Mike Leach and Bruce Feldman.

Rolf Zettersten, Publisher

Michelle Rapkin, Executive Editor—High-profile authors and notable current events titles

Christina Boys, Editor—Fiction and nonfiction, including lifestyle, business, memoir

Meredith Pharaoh, Editor—Nonfiction, especially lifestyle, advice

Harry Helm, Editor—Nonfiction, sports, relationship advice

FAITHWORDS

Two Creekside Crossing, Ten Cadillac Drive, Suite 220, Brentwood, TN 37027
615-221-0996   fax: 615-221-0962

From its headquarters in Tennessee, FaithWords is an imprint that deals with Christian faith, inspiration, spirituality, and religion, with fiction and nonfiction titles. The imprint publishes books for the broad Christian market reflecting a range of denominations and perspectives. Formerly known as Warner Faith, FaithWords titles include Christian chick lit by Lisa Samson and inspirational fiction by T.D. Jakes, as well as traditional nonfiction religious titles. FaithWords is the publisher of the bestselling books *Your Best Life Now* by Joel Osteen and *The Confident Woman: Start Today Living Boldly & Without Fear* by Joyce Meyer.

Recent titles include *Angels All Around Them: A Journey of Love, Loss and Hope* by Abby Rike; *Angel Harp* by Michael Phillips; *Surviving the Financial Future:*

Prophetic Warnings About the New Global Economy by David Jeremiah; and *Snow Day* by Billy Coffey.

Rolf Zettersten, Publisher

Anne Horch, Editor

GRAND CENTRAL PUBLISHING

5-SPOT

BUSINESS PLUS

FOREVER

SPRINGBOARD PRESS

TWELVE

VISION

WELLNESS CENTRAL

237 Park Avenue, New York, NY 10017

212-364-1200

www.hachette-bookgroupusa.com

As Warner Books, Grand Central Publishing was esteemed for publishing mass-market commercial fiction from authors like Nicholas Sparks and James Patterson. Known as Grand Central Publishing since April 2007, it still publishes a lot of commercial fiction, but has also started imprints that move in other directions and expects to become equally well known for those.

As for the name, Grand Central Publishing, publisher Jamie Raab dissects this way: Grand because they are big and impressive, Central because they embrace a larger audience of readers, and Publishing because emerging forms of publishing go beyond books and paper.

Grand Central produces hardcover, mass market, and trade paperback originals, as well as reprints. Nonfiction categories include biography, business, cooking, current affairs, history, house and home, humor, popular culture, psychology, self-help, sports, games books, and general reference; fiction titles include commercial novels and works in the categories of mystery and suspense, fantasy and science fiction, action thrillers, horror, and contemporary and historical romance. The Grand Central imprints are 5-Spot, Business Plus, Forever, Springboard Press, Twelve, Vision, and Wellness Central. Altogether, Grand Central publishes about three hundred books per year.

Recent titles include *Ticket to Last Chance* by Hope Ramsay; *The Two Mrs.*

Stones by Candace Bushnell; *The Bed Bug Survival Guide* by Jeff Eisenberg; *Sins of the Innocent* by Caridad Pineiro; *The Orchard* by Theresa Weir; and *Another Touch of Venus* by Sherrill Bodine.

Jamie Raab, Senior Vice President and Publisher, oversees the publication of all Grand Central titles. She has a particular fondness for fiction, narrative nonfiction, and current affairs, and the authors she has edited include Nicholas Delblanco, Nelson DeMille, Henry Louis Gates, Jr., Jane Goodall, Olivia Goldsmith, Billie Letts, Brad Meltzer, Michael Moore, Rosie O'Donnell, Nicholas Sparks, Jon Stewart, and Lalita Tademy.

Les Pockell, Associate Publisher, has held editorial positions at St. Martin's Press, Doubleday, Kodansha International, and the Book-of-the-Month Club in addition to Grand Central. He is generally involved in acquiring and editing backlist nonfiction titles, though he has been known to dabble in fiction, especially mysteries. In his spare time, he is an anthologist, having edited, among other titles, *The 100 Best Poems of All Time*.

Beth de Guzman, Editorial Director of Mass Market, has spent 20 years in publishing and has held positions at Berkley Books, Silhouette Books, and Bantam Books. She has edited over 30 *New York Times* bestsellers. At Grand Central, she oversees the mass-market program and acquires commercial fiction and nonfiction.

Karen Kosztolnyik, Executive Editor, acquires fiction and nonfiction for all divisions including mass market, trade paperback, and hardcover. Her acquisition interests are romance, women's fiction, chick lit, suspense, and nonfiction concerning women's issues and pop culture. She is the editor of bestselling authors Carly Phillips and Wendy Corsi Straub writing as Wendy Markham, *How to Meet Cute Boys* novelist Deanne Kizis, romantic suspense author Karen Rose, historical romance author Claire Delacroix, and Megan Crane, author of the chick-lit novel *English as a Second Language*. She also edited the personal biography *My Father, My President: A Personal Account of the Life of George H.W. Bush* by Doro Bush Koch.

Caryn Karmatz Rudy, Executive Editor, has been at Grand Central/Warner for 15 years. Her areas of interest are women's commercial fiction and women's interest nonfiction. Her nonfiction focus is on lifestyle, relationships, parenting, women's issues, and memoir, while in fiction she looks for a strong narrative voice and topical subjects. Some of the bestsellers she has worked on include *AmandaBright@Home* by Danielle Crittenden; *Swell: A Girl's Guide to the Good Life* by Ilene Rosenzweig and Cynthia Rowley; and *Jewtopia: The Chosen Book for the Chosen People* by Bryan Fogel and Sam Wolfson.

Jaime Levine, Executive Editor, works with such authors as David and Leigh Eddings, Walter Mosley, Nalo Hopkinson, and Gregory Benford. Her interests lie with science fiction, fantasy, thrillers, and dark fiction. Past acquisitions include Thomas Monteleone's *Borderlands* trilogy and novels by Douglas Preston and Lincoln Child.

Mitch Hoffman, Executive Editor, acquires fiction, especially thrillers, mystery, and crime. He was previously at Dutton.

Karen Thomas, Executive Editor, formerly at Kensington and Dafina, acquires and edits street novels, erotica, and other fiction for Grand Central. A recent purchase was Pink's erotic novels.

Amy Pierpont, Senior Editor

Ben Greenberg, Editor, acquires in nonfiction, primarily pop culture, humor, memoir

Emily Griffin, Associate Editor

Alex Logan, Editor—Romance, thriller, women's fiction

Michele Bidelspach, Editor—Fiction, romance

Deb Futter, Editor—Fiction, humor, memoir

Selina McLemore, Editor—Fiction, how-to, women's romance

Diana Baroni, Editor—Diet, how-to nonfiction

Rick Wolff, Editor—Sports, general nonfiction, business

Celia Johnson, Editor—Humor, fiction

5-SPOT

5-Spot is a list of books for women who want entertainment but refuse to leave their brains at the door. The imprint releases about 15 new fiction and nonfiction titles per year. Recent acquisitions have been primarily in the women's fiction and romance categories.

Recent titles include *I Couldn't Love You More* by Jillian Medoff; *Eight Months on Emmer Street* by Roisin Meaney; *Your Roots Are Showing* by Elise Chidley; *The Smart One and the Pretty One* by Claire LaZebnik; *Live a Little* by Kim Green; and *I'm With Stupid* by Elaine Szewcyk.

Caryn Karmatz Rudy, Editorial Director

Karen Kosztolnyik, Executive Editor

BUSINESS PLUS

Business Plus represents the international outgrowth of Warner Business Books, which was founded in 2000 and has enjoyed great success. Their books aim to give voice to innovative leaders and thinkers in the business world.

Recent titles include *Management Secrets of the Grateful Dead* by Barry Barnes; *18 Minutes* by Peter Bregman; *The Wallstrip Edge: Using Trends to Make Money—Find Them, Ride Them, and Get Off* by Howard Lindzon; and *Game Over: How You Can Prosper in a Shattered Economy* by Stephen Leeb.

Rick Wolff, Publisher and Editor-in-Chief

FOREVER

Forever publishes every kind of romance for every romantic reader, in mass-market format. Recent titles include *Passion Unleashed* by Larissa Ione; *Seducing a Scottish Bride* by Sue-Ellen Welfonder; *Trouble in High Heels* by Leanne Banks; and *Flirting with Temptation* by Kelley St. John.

Amy Pierpont, Editorial Director

SPRINGBOARD PRESS

Springboard Press focuses on titles for and about baby boomers, with books to improve their lives, themselves, and their relationships. The categories of these books range from memoir and popular culture to beauty, well-being, inspiration, relationships, and career.

Recent titles include *A Million Is Not Enough: How to Retire with the Money You'll Need* by Michael Farr and Gary Brozek; *Throw Out Fifty Things: Clear the Clutter, Find Your Life* by Gail Blanke; and *Send Yourself Roses: Thoughts on My Life, Love, and Leading Roles* by Kathleen Turner and Gloria Feldt.

Karen Murgolo, Editorial Director—Strong narrative nonfiction on subjects that will resonate with readers, and prescriptive nonfiction books by authoritative experts in well-being, beauty, relationships, lifestyle, career, self-help

TWELVE

(Note: The Twelve imprint was closed at press time.)

Because Twelve publishes only 12 new books a year, this imprint looks for books that matter, books that enliven the national conversation, books that will sell at least 50,000 copies. The editors at Twelve look for meaningful stories, true and fictional, and singular books that will entertain and illuminate. A recent purchase was Senator Ted Kennedy's autobiography.

Each book receives the marketing focus of the entire imprint for the month of its release, and is promoted well into its paperback life. This imprint is known to put great marketing and editorial muscle behind each and every title.

Recent titles include *Race Against Time* by Jerry Mitchell; *The Evolution of Bruno Littlemore* by Benjamin Hale; *The ORG* by Tim Sullivan; *The Legacy of Brown v. Board of Education* by Jack Greenberg; and *The Geography of Bliss: One Grump's Search for the Happiest Places in the World* by Eric Weiner.

Jonathan Karp, Publisher and Editor-in-Chief

WELLNESS CENTRAL

The Wellness Central list focuses on health, fitness, and self-help. Recent titles include *Brain Surgeon: A Doctor's Inspiring Encounters with Mortality and Miracles* by Keith Black and Arnold Mann; *Where Did I Leave My Glasses? The What, When, and Why of Normal Memory Loss* by Martha Weinman Lear; and *Dr. Gott's No Flour, No Sugar Cookbook* by Peter H. Gott.

Diana Baroni, Editorial Director—With Grand Central/Warner for 14 years, acquires fiction and nonfiction titles with a focus on health, self-help, diet, child care, women's issues.

LITTLE, BROWN AND COMPANY

BACK BAY BOOKS

REAGAN ARTHUR BOOKS

237 Park Avenue, New York, NY 10017

212-364-1100

www.hachette-bookgroupusa.com

Founded in 1837, Little, Brown originated as an independent house with a Boston home base, but joined Warner Books in Manhattan in 2002. A former Little, Brown imprint, Bulfinch Press, was dissolved by parent HBG late in 2006. However, the imprimatur "a Bulfinch Press book" is added to traditional art books (photography, art, and museum-related titles) published as Little, Brown titles.

Little, Brown and Company is home to noted debut novelists like Eduardo Santiago and masters of the trade like Herman Wouk. The house publishes David Sedaris's essays and Holly Hobbie's pigs, Walter Mosley's mysteries and James Patterson's thrillers.

Recent titles from Little, Brown include *Dark Justice* edited by Lee Child; *One Hundred and One Nights* by Benjamin Buchholz; *Hold Me Tight: Seven Conversations for a Lifetime of Love* by Sue Johnson; *90 Days* by Bill Clegg; and *Fed Up* by Rick Perry.

Michael Pietsch, Senior Vice President and Publisher, has worked with the novelists Martin Amis, Peter Blauner, Michael Connelly, Martha Cooley, Tony Earley, Janet Fitch, Mark Leyrier, Rick Moody, Walter Mosley, James Patterson, George Pelecanos, Alice Sebold, Anita Shreve, Nick Tosches, David Foster Wallace, and

Stephen Wright; the nonfiction writers John Feinstein, Peter Guralnick, and David Sedaris; and the cartoonist R. Crumb. Prior to joining Little, Brown in 1991, Michael worked at Harmony Books and before that at Scribner, where he edited a posthumous memoir by Ernest Hemingway, *The Dangerous Summer*.

Geoff Shandler, Editor-in-Chief, primarily acquires histories, biographies, and journalism. Among the many authors he has worked with are James Bradley, John LeCarré, Robert Dallek, Tom Shales, Ann Blackman, Robert Wright, William Least Heat-Moon, Gary Giddins, James Miller, Doug Stanton, Elaine Shannon, Elizabeth Royte, Eileen Welsome, and Luis Urrea. His numerous bestsellers and award winners include *An Unfinished Life*, *Flyboys*, *Blind Man's Bluff*, *Black Mass*, *Paris in the Fifties*, and *In Retrospect*.

Tracy Behar, Executive Editor, joined Little, Brown in 2004 after serving as Editorial Director at Atria and Washington Square Press. At Little, Brown she has edited authors Arianna Huffington and Dr. Mark Liponis from Canyon Ranch. Her editing interests include life-improvement categories such as psychology, parenting, health, creativity, and empowerment.

Pat Strachan, Senior Editor, joined Little, Brown in September 2002. She is acquiring literary fiction and general nonfiction. Most recently at Houghton Mifflin, she began her career at Farrar, Straus & Giroux, where she worked as an editor for 17 years. She was then a fiction editor at *The New Yorker*, returning to book publishing in 1991. She received the PEN/Roger Klein Award for Editing. Among the prose writers she has edited are Elizabeth Benedict, Harold Bloom, Ian Frazier, James Kelman, Jamaica Kincaid, Wendy Lesser, Rosemary Mahoney, John McPhee, David Nasaw, Edna O'Brien, Peter Orner, Padgett Powell, Marilynne Robinson, Jim Shepard, Tatyana Tolstaya, and Tom Wolfe. Her Little, Brown books include fiction by Christina Adam, Kathryn Davis, Michelle de Kretser, Lucia Nevai, and Michael Redhill.

Judy Clain, Senior Editor, joined Little Brown in 1998. She began her career as a film agent and was a Sony executive on *Deep End of the Ocean* and *Donnie Brasco*. She has edited novelists including Jody Shields (*The Fig Eater*), Simon Mawer (*The Fall*), Elisabeth Robinson (*The True and Outstanding Adventures of the Hunt Sisters*), and Robb Forman Dew (*The Evidence Against Her*). She has also edited narrative nonfiction by Kien Nguyen (*The Unwanted*) and Daphne de Marneffe (*Maternal Desire*), among others.

Asya Muchnick, Editor, joined Little, Brown in 2001, and has edited novelists Alice Sebold (*The Lovely Bones*), Carolyn Parkhurst (*The Dogs of Babel*), and Elise Blackwell (*Hunger*), and nonfiction by Lisa Hilton (*Athénaïs: The Life of Louis XIV's Mistress*), William Poundstone (*How Would You Move Mount Fuji?*), and Asne Seierstad (*The Bookseller of Kabul*). Recent acquisitions include a look at how rulers through the ages have collected rare and exotic animals by art historian Marina Belozerskaya; a meditation on the meaning of suffering by *New Yorker* and *Harper's* contributor Peter Trachtenberg; and first novels by Jardine Libaire and Thomas O'Malley. Previously, she was at Knopf.

John Parsley, Senior Editor, joined Little, Brown in 2007. His acquisitions focus on serious and narrative nonfiction including popular and natural science, history, ideas books, music, sports, food, and humor. He was previously at Thomas Dunne/St. Martin's.

Michael Sand, Editor—Biography, cooking, illustrated nonfiction

Junie Dahn, Editor—History, current affairs

BACK BAY BOOKS

In 1993, Little, Brown created a new trade paperback imprint, Back Bay Books, to focus on long-term publication of the company's best fiction and nonfiction. Recent titles from Back Bay include *The Animal Dialogues: Uncommon Encounters in the Wild* by Craig Childs; *Endgame, 1945: The Missing Final Chapter of World War II* by David Stafford; *Sway* by Zachary Lazar; and *The Italian Lover* by Robert Hellenga.

REAGAN ARTHUR BOOKS

Reagan Arthur Books is the imprint of Reagan Arthur, a Little, Brown editor who is noted for signing Tina Fey for a $6 million deal in 2008. The first list was published in Fall 2009 and they plan on growing the line to 15 to 20 books a year. Acquisitions include a new historical novel from Kathleen Kent, the author of *The Heretic's Daughter*; the U.S. rights to *The Rehearsal*, a debut novel from New Zealand's 23-year-old Eleanor Catton; and a new novel by Sherman Alexie.

Reagan Arthur, Vice President, Editorial Director

LITTLE, BROWN BOOKS FOR YOUNG READERS

LB KIDS

POPPY

237 Park Avenue, New York, NY 10017

212-364-1100

www.hachette-bookgroupusa.com

Little, Brown's children's books division produces picture books, board books, pop-up and lift-the-flap editions, chapter books, manga, and general fiction and nonfiction titles for middle-grade and young-adult readers. This division also issues resource guides and reference titles in careers, social issues, and intellectual topics for higher grade levels and the college-bound.

The house offers volumes in Spanish language and in dual Spanish/English editions and is on the lookout for multicultural titles. The LB Kids imprint features original novelty books as well as TV, brand, and licensed tie-in publishing programs. Poppy publishes books for teens.

Representative Little, Brown Books for Young Readers titles include Caldecott winner *Saint George and the Dragon* illustrated by Trina Schart Hyman; Newbery winner *Maniac Magee* by Jerry Spinelli; *Toot & Puddle* by Holly Hobbie; *Daisy and the Egg* by Jane Simmons; *Kevin and His Dad* by Irene Smalls; *47* by Walter Mosley; *Maximum Ride: The Angel Experiment* by James Patterson; *The Jolly Pocket Postman* by Janet and Allen Ahlberg.

Recent releases include *She Loves You, She Loves You Not…* by Julie Anne Peters; *Rock On* by Denise Vega; *You Read to Me, I'll Read to You* by Mary Ann Hoberman; *Winter Town* by Stephen Emond; *Everybody Sees the Ants* by A.S. King; *Snowflake Baby* by Elise Broach; *Boy 21* by Matthew Quick; *If All of the Animals Came Inside* by Eric Pinder; *Monster High* by Lisi Harrison; and *All Kinds of Kisses* by Nancy Tafuri.

LB KIDS

LB Kids publishes novelty and licensed books and focuses primarily on interactive formats, licensed properties, media tie-ins, and baby and toddler focused projects.

Liza Baker, Editorial Director

POPPY

Poppy publishes paperback original series for teen girls. They have launched several bestselling series, including *Gossip Girl* and *The It Girl* by Cecily von Ziegesar; *The Clique* by Lisi Harrison; and *The A-List* by Zoey Dean. Some titles include *Bunheads* by Sophie Flack; *Ricki Jo* by Alecia Whitaker; *How to Rock Braces and Glasses* by Meg Haston; *The Traveling Fashionista* by Bianca Turetsky; *Arrivals and Departures* by Jennifer Smith; *Spoiled* by Heather Cocks and Jessica Morgan; *Ophelia Live* by Michelle Ray; and *The Magnolia League* by Katie Crouch.

Megan Tingley, Publisher

Andrea Spooner, Editorial Director—Trade hardcover and paperback lists

Cindy Eagan, Editorial Director—Teen chick-lit paperbacks

Jennifer Hunt, Editor

Nancy Conescu, Associate Editor

Alvina Ling, Editor—Young adult, children's fantasy

Liza Baker, Editor—Picture book, children's fiction

Julie Scheina, Editor—Young adult

Lauren Hodge, Editor—Picture book

Elizabeth Bewley, Editor—Young adult

OCTOPUS USA

HAMLYN

MITCHELL BEAZLEY

CONRAN OCTOPUS

ASSEL

GAIA

GODSFIELD

SPRUCE

4680 Calle Norte, Newbury Park, CA 91320

805-498-2484   fax: 805-499-4260

Launched in 2009, this new-for-the-USA imprint is a leading publisher in the UK of illustrated adult nonfiction, with particular strengths in art, reference, design, cooking, mind/body/spirit, and pop culture. Previously distributed by Sterling Publishing in the U.S., this Hachette USA imprint now allows Octopus to publish internationally. All of the Octopus imprints will publish as part of the U.S. operation as well.

Recent titles include *Tuned Droves* by Eric Baus; *How to Taste* by Jancis Robinson; *Leon: Ingredients and Recipes* by Allegra McEvedy; and *The Interior World of Tom Dixon* by Tom Dixon.

Jonathan Stolper, Vice President, Associate Publisher

ORBIT

YEN PRESS

237 Park Avenue, 16th Floor, New York, NY 10017

212-364-1100

www.hachette-bookgroupusa.com   email: orbit@hbgusa.com

Orbit is the new science fiction and fantasy imprint at Hachette Book Group. Orbit publishes across the spectrum of science fiction and fantasy—from action-packed urban fantasy to widescreen space opera, from sweeping epic adventures to near-future thrillers. They publish approximately 40 titles each year from both established and debut authors.

In 2008, Orbit and Yen Press, Hachette's manga imprint, were combined into the same division. They will continue to develop titles independently.

Some Orbit titles are *Heartless and Timeless* by Gail Carriger; *The Troupe* by Robert Jackson Bennett; *Catching the Moon* by A. Lee Martinez; *The Wall of Night*

Quartet by Helen Lowe; *Shadowheart* by Tad Williams; *The Tarnished Crown* by Karen Miller; and *Married with Zombies* by Jesse Peterson.

Tim Holman, Vice President, Publisher—Across the spectrum of fantasy, science fiction

Darren Nash, Editorial Director

Devi Pillai, Senior Editor—Science fiction, paranormal

DongWon Song, Associate Editor

YEN PRESS

Yen Press is dedicated to publishing graphic novels and manga in all formats and for all ages. It was founded in 2006 by former Borders Group, Inc., buyer Kurt Hassler and former DC Comics Vice President Rich Johnson. Yen Press is devoted to publishing a diverse line of books that will reflect what is happening in the growing graphic novel and manga markets.

Some recent Yen Press titles include *Nightschool* by Svetlana Chmakova; *Oninagi* by Akira Ishida; *Pig Bride* by KookHwa Huh and SuJin Kim; *Croquis Pop* by KwangHyun Sea and JinHo Ko; *One Thousand and One Nights* by JinSeok Jeon and SeungHee Han; and *Spiral* by Hyo Shirodaira and Eita Mizuno.

Kurt Hassler, Publishing Director

VERLAGSGRUPPE GEORG VON HOLTZBRINCK

Verlagsgruppe Georg von Holtzbrinck, Germany's second-largest publisher, owns more than 80 companies in 20 different countries; holdings include Macmillan in the UK and Die Zeit in Germany. The American division is based in New York City.

MACMILLAN

BEDFORD, FREEMAN & WORTH PUBLISHING GROUP

FARRAR, STRAUS & GIROUX

HENRY HOLT AND COMPANY

MACMILLAN CHILDREN'S BOOK PUBLISHING GROUP

PALGRAVE MACMILLAN

PICADOR USA

ST. MARTIN'S PRESS

TOR/FORGE

175 Fifth Avenue, New York, NY 10010

212-674-5151

http://us.macmillan.com

Macmillan (formerly Holtzbrinck Publishers) is a group of publishing companies, including renowned houses like Farrar, Straus & Giroux; St. Martin's; and Henry Holt; the companies include trade and educational imprints, and the *Scientific American* magazine.

Former Scholastic publisher Jean Feiwel joined Macmillan in 2006 to start a broadly defined children's effort and to guide strategy within the group. As well as creating new children's imprints, like Feiwel & Friends and Square Fish, she is publishing into paperback and other formats.

John Sargent, CEO

Jean Feiwel, Senior Vice President and Publisher of Children's Books

BEDFORD, FREEMAN & WORTH PUBLISHING GROUP

BEDFORD/ST. MARTIN'S

W.H. FREEMAN

WORTH PUBLISHERS

41 Madison Avenue, New York, NY 10010

212-576-9422   fax: 212-545-8318

www.bfwpub.com

Holtzbrinck merged their three college and university publishing houses, Bedford/St. Martin's, W.H. Freeman, and Worth Publishers, to become the Bedford, Freeman & Worth Publishing Group. Each of the three publishers has its own separate subject area focus. Bedford/St. Martin's focuses on liberal arts and humanities; W.H. Freeman focuses on the sciences; Worth's areas of focus are psychology, economics, and sociology.

BEDFORD/ST. MARTIN'S

33 Irving Place, New York, NY 10003

212-375-7000   fax: 212-614-1885

Boston office:

75 Arlington Street, Boston, MA 02116

617-399-4000   fax: 617-426-8582

www.bedfordstmartins.com

Bedford/St. Martin's creates textbooks that end up on college desks worldwide, titles that will seem familiar to anyone who has faced the first day of *Intro to Public Speaking* or *English 101*. Bedford's titles include the bestselling textbook ever: *A Writer's Reference* by Diana Hacker. The list focuses on the disciplines of business and technical writing, communication, English, history, music, philosophy, and religion.

Recent titles include *The Anatomy of Film* by Bernard F. Dick; *Style in Rhetoric and Composition* by Paul Butler; *California Dreams and Realities* by Sonia Maasik et al; *Media and Culture: An Introduction to Mass Communication* by Richard Campbell et al; and *Model for Writers* by Alfred Rosa and Paul Eschholz.

This publisher's preferred method of receiving unagented and unsolicited submissions is via email by subject:

Music: music@bedfordstmartins.com

Communication: communication@bedfordstmartins.com

History: history@bedfordstmartins.com

Business and Technical Writing: bus&tech@bedfordstmartins.com

Literature and Linguistics: lit&linguistics@bedfordstmartins.com

Developmental Reading and Writing: developmental@bedfordstmartins.com

Composition: composition@bedfordstmartins.com

W.H. FREEMAN

41 Madison Avenue, 37th Floor, New York, NY 10010

212-576-9400   fax: 212-689-2383

www.whfreeman.com

Founded in 1946, W.H. Freeman publishes college and high school science textbooks written by scientists and teachers. Freeman's first book was *General Chemistry* by the late Nobel laureate Linus Pauling. That pioneering text revolutionized the chemistry curriculum and set the high standard of book production that established Freeman as a premier science publisher.

Recent titles include *The Human Mosaic* by Mona Domosh et al; *Psychology* by David G. Myers; *Mathematics: A Human Endeavor* by Harold R. Jacobs; *Abnormal Psychology* by Ronald J. Comer; *The Development of Children* by Michael Cole et al; and *What Is Life? A Guide to Biology* by Jay Phelan.

This publisher's preferred method of receiving unagented and unsolicited submissions is via email by subject:

Astronomy: Astronomymkt@whfreeman.com

Biology: Biology@whfreeman.com

Chemistry: Chemistrymktg@whfreeman.com

Geography: Geography@whfreeman.com

Mathematics: Mathmktg@whfreeman.com

Physics: Physics@whfreeman.com

WORTH PUBLISHERS

41 Madison Avenue, 35th Floor, New York, NY 10010

212-576-9400   fax: 212-561-8281

www.worthpublishers.com

Since 1998, Worth has focused its efforts on publishing textbooks specifically in the social sciences of psychology, economics, and sociology. Among its global bestsellers are David Myers's *Psychology* (the world's most popular introduction to psychology); Myers's *Exploring Psychology*; Kathleen Berger's *The Developing Person Through Childhood and Adolescence*; Elliot Aronson's *The Social Animal*; and N. Gregory Mankiw's *Macroeconomics*. In 2003, Worth expanded into the high school market with its new text, Blair-Broeker and Ernst's *Thinking About Psychology*.

Recent titles include *Economics* by Paul Krugman and Robin Wells; *Psychology Study Guide* by Don H. Hockenbury; and *Games Strategies and Decision Making* by Joseph Harrington and N. Gregory Mankiw.

This publisher's preferred method of receiving unagented and unsolicited submissions is via email by subject:

Economics: Economics@worthpublishers.com

Psychology: Psychology@ worthpublishers.com

FARRAR, STRAUS & GIROUX

FABER AND FABER, INC.

HILL AND WANG

NORTH POINT PRESS

18 West 18th Street, New York, NY 10011

212-741-6900

www.fsgbooks.com   email: fsg.editorial@fsgbooks.com

blog: www.fsgpoetry.com

Farrar, Straus & Giroux (FSG) was founded in New York City in 1946 by Roger Straus and John Farrar; Robert Giroux joined the company in 1955. The firm is widely acclaimed for its international list of literary fiction, nonfiction, poetry, and children's books. FSG is also known for building authors over time through strong editorial relationships. This was the way Roger Straus built the company, and it continues so under current publisher Jonathan Galassi.

FSG authors have won extraordinary acclaim over the years, including numerous National Book Awards, Pulitzer Prizes, and 21 Nobel Prizes in literature. Nobel Prize winners include Knut Hamsun, Hermann Hesse, T. S. Eliot, Par Lagerkvist, Francois Mauriac, Juan Ramon Jimenez, Salvatore Quasimodo, Nelly Sachs, Czeslaw Milosz, Elias Canetti, William Golding, Wole Soyinka, Joseph Brodsky, Camilo Jose Cela, Nadine Gordimer, Derek Walcott, and Seamus Heaney.

Today's Farrar, Straus & Giroux list includes some of the most renowned names in poetry and fiction, including Elizabeth Bishop, Marilynne Robinson, Ted Hughes, Phillip Larkin, Michael Cunningham, Jonathan Franzen, Alice McDermott, Scott Turow, and Tom Wolfe.

History, art history, natural history, current affairs, and science round out the list in nonfiction, represented by Thomas Friedman, Philip Gourevitch, Roy Jenkins, Gina Kolata, Ben Macintyre, Louis Menaud, Giles Milton, and John McPhee.

Recent titles include *Lowboy* by John Wray; *Dead Aid: Why Aid Is Not Working and How There Is a Better Way for Africa* by Dambisa Moyo; *Our Life in Gardens* by Joe Eck and Wayne Winterrowd; and *Important Artifacts and Personal Property from the Collection of Lenor Doolan and Harold Morris* by Leanne Shapton.

FSG does accept unsolicited and unagented manuscripts. All editorial inquiries should be emailed to the editorial department at fsg.editorial@fsgbooks.com. FSG does not accept manuscript submissions via email. Queries may be sent via mail with SASEs to:

Jonathan Galassi, Publisher—Fiction, nonfiction, art history, belles lettres, business, poetry

Eric Chinski, Editor-in-Chief—Science, history, business, general nonfiction

Courtney Hodell, Executive Editor

Paul Elie, Senior Editor—Nonfiction

Lorin Stein, Editor—Fiction

Sarah Crichton, Publisher, Sarah Crichton Books

FABER AND FABER, INC.

Faber and Faber specializes in books on the arts and entertainment, pop culture, cultural criticism, and the media with a special emphasis on music. Among its authors are Courtney Love and Billy Corgan, as well as Pulitzer Prize–winning playwrights David Auburn, Margaret Edson, and Doug Wright; Pulitzer finalist Richard Greenberg; British dramatists Tom Stoppard and David Hare; and filmmaker and playwright Neil LaBute.

Faber and Faber also publishes books designed to reach a younger readership, one it feels loves and understands itself through popular culture.

Recent titles include *The Backwards Law: How Failure, Uncertainty & Death Can Save Your Life*; *The Reel Truth: Everything You Didn't Know You Need to Know About Making an Independent Film* by Reed Martin; *The God of Carnage* by Yasmina Reza; and *An Elegy for Easterly* by Petina Gappah.

All editorial inquiries should be emailed to the editorial department at fsg .editorial@fsgbooks.com. FSG does not accept manuscript submissions via email. Queries may be sent via mail with SASEs to:

Mitzi Angel, Publisher

Sarah Savitt, Editor

HILL AND WANG

Hill and Wang focuses on books of academic interest for both the trade and college markets, in both hard and soft cover. The list is strong in American history, world history, politics, and graphic nonfiction. Among its authors are Roland Barthes, Michael Burleigh, William Cronon, Langston Hughes, Robert Wiebe, and Elie Wiesel.

Recent titles include *Mr. George & Mr. John: How Two Secretive Brothers*

Built the A&P and Unleashed the Consumer Revolution by Marc Levinson; *Climate Capitalism: Natural Capitalism in the Age of Change* by Hunter Lovins and Boyd Cohen; and *Students for a Democratic Society: A Graphic History* by Harvey Pekar and Gary Drumm.

Query letters and SASEs may be directed to:

Thomas LeBien, Publisher—History, politics, current affairs

NORTH POINT PRESS

North Point Press specializes in hard and soft cover literary nonfiction, with an emphasis on natural history, travel, ecology, music, food, and cultural criticism. Past and present authors include Peter Matthiessen, Evan Connell, Beryl Markham, A. J. Liebling, Margaret Visser, Wendell Berry, and M. F. K. Fisher.

Recent titles include *Trespass: Living at the Edge of the Promised Land* by Amy Irvine; *Mouth Wide Open: A Cook and His Appetite* by John Thorne and Matt Lewis Thorne; *The Dirt on Clean: An Unsanitized History* by Katherine Ashenburg; and *The Bhagavad Gita: A New Translation* by George Thompson.

Eric Chinski, Editor-in-Chief

HENRY HOLT AND COMPANY

METROPOLITAN BOOKS

TIMES BOOKS

175 Fifth Avenue, New York, NY 10010

646-307-5095

www.henryholt.com

Founded in 1866 by Henry Holt and Frederick Leypoldt, Henry Holt is one of the oldest publishers in the U.S. Henry Holt is known for publishing high quality books, including those by authors such as Erich Fromm, Robert Frost, Hermann Hesse, Norman Mailer, Robert Louis Stevenson, Ivan Turgenev, and H. G. Wells. Today the company continues to build upon its illustrious history by publishing bestselling, award-winning books in the areas of literary fiction, mysteries and thrillers, history, biography, politics, current events, science, psychology, and books for children and young adults.

Recent titles include *Fifty Grand: A Novel of Suspense* by Adrian McKinty; *This Land Is Their Land: Reports from a Divided Nation* by Barbara Ehrenreich; *No Such Creature* by Giles Blunt; and *Do Polar Bears Get Lonely? And Answers to 100 Other Weird and Wacky Questions About How the World Works* from the team behind *New Scientist*.

Henry Holt and its adult imprints do not accept or read any unsolicited manuscripts or queries.

Marjorie Braman, Vice President and Editor-in-Chief—Fiction, memoir, biography

David Patterson, Senior Editor

Webster Younce, Senior Editor

Sarah Knight, Editor

Jack MacRae, Editor

Gillian Blake, Editor—Nonfiction, science, nonfiction narrative

Stephen Rubin, Editor—Fiction, mystery, crime

METROPOLITAN BOOKS

Metropolitan Books, established in 1995, publishes American and international fiction and nonfiction. With a mission to introduce unconventional, uncompromising, and sometimes controversial voices, Metropolitan publishes titles in categories ranging from world history to American politics, foreign fiction to graphic novels, and social science to current affairs.

Authors published by Metropolitan Books include Ann Crittenden, Mike Davis, Barbara Ehrenreich, Susan Faludi, Orlando Figes, Michael Frayn, Eduardo Galeano, Atul Gawande, Todd Gitlin, Arlie Russell Hochschild, Michael Ignatieff, Orville Schell, and Tom Segev.

Titles representative of Metropolitan's nonfiction list include *Failed States: The Abuse of Power and the Assault on Democracy* by Noam Chomsky; *What's the Matter with Kansas? How Conservatives Won the Heart of America* by Thomas Frank; *Dancing in the Streets: A History of Collective Joy* by Barbara Ehrenreich; and *Complications: A Surgeon's Notes on an Imperfect Science* by Atul Gawande.

Titles indicative of Metropolitan fiction include *All for Love: A Novel* by Dan Jacobeon; *The Nubian Prince* by Juan Bonilla, translated by Esther Allen; *The Beholder* by Thomas Farber; and *Spies* by Michael Frayn.

Recent titles include *Partitions* by Amit Majmudar; *Junk: How the 1980s Changed Everything* by Stephen Metcalf; *Crawling Away from Armageddon* by Mohamed El Baradei; *Haiti: The Aftershocks of History* by Laurent Dubois; *Everything I Possess, I Carry With Me* by Herta Müller; and *A Thousand Moves: The Uncharted World of Freight* by Rose George.

Henry Holt and its adult imprints do not accept or read any unsolicited manuscripts or queries.

Sara Bershtel, Associate Publisher—Nonfiction, nonfiction narrative, history, current events, general fiction

Riva Hocherman, Editor—Fiction, nonfiction narrative, history

TIMES BOOKS

Times Books, launched in 2001, is the result of a co-publishing agreement between Holt and the *New York Times*; its nonfiction list focuses on politics, current events, international relations, history, science, business, and American society and culture. About half of the imprint's books are written by *New York Times* reporters and the rest are written by other American intellectuals, journalists, and public figures.

Titles representative of this list include *Overthrow: America's Century of Regime Change from Hawaii to Iraq* by Stephen Kinzer; *Key Management Solutions: 50 Leading Edge Solutions to Executive Problems* by Tom Lambert; *The Supreme Court: The Personalities and Rivalries That Defined America* by Jeffrey Rosen; and *Imagination Engineering: How to Generate and Implement Great Ideas* by Paul Birch.

Recent releases include *Boiling Mad* by Kate Zernike; *The Teacher* by Seth Davis; and *Invisible Men* by Michael Addis.

Direct queries and SASEs to:

Paul Golob, Editorial Director—Nonfiction, sports, politics, current events

Robin Dennis, Senior Editor

MACMILLAN CHILDREN'S BOOK PUBLISHING GROUP

FARRAR, STRAUS & GIROUX BOOKS FOR YOUNG READERS

FEIWEL & FRIENDS

FIRST SECOND

HENRY HOLT AND COMPANY BOOKS FOR YOUNG READERS

PRIDDY BOOKS

ROARING BROOK PRESS

SQUARE FISH

STARSCAPE

TOR TEEN

175 Fifth Avenue, New York, NY 10010

212-982-3900

The Macmillan Children's Book Publishing Group was created in late 2008 with the consolidation of Macmillan's far-flung children's imprints. Jean Feiwel, senior vice president and co-director of the new division, sees the move as harnessing separate assets to work in tandem and compared the new infrastructure to a "Star Wars federation" of imprints. Each editorial team will be able to pursue its own agenda while drawing upon the shared resources of other departments.

Dan Farley, Director

Jean Feiwel, Senior Vice President, Co-Director

Simon Boughton, Senior Vice President

FARRAR, STRAUS & GIROUX BOOKS FOR YOUNG READERS

www.fsgkidsbooks.com   email: childrens.editorial@fsgbooks.com

The FSG juvenile program publishes fiction and nonfiction books for toddlers to young adults. This list includes many Caldecott, Newbery, and National Book Award winners. Award-winning authors include Jack Gantos, Madeleine L'Engle, Louis Sachar, Uri Shulevitz, Peter Sis, David Small, William Steig, and Sarah Stewart. Newer FSG authors include Kate Banks, Claudia Mills, Jack Gantos, Suzanne Fisher Staples, and Tim Wynne-Jones.

Recent titles include *Sea Rose Red* by Cat Hellisen; *If You Were a Dog* by Jamie Swenson; *Struck* by Jennifer Bosworth; *Spunky Tells All* by Ann Cameron; *Nine Rules of Flirting* by Laura Bowers; *Dot: A Book of Contrasts* by Patricia Intriago; and *The Pumpkin Princess* by Kristina Springer.

All children's book editorial inquiries should be emailed to the editorial department at childrens.editorial@fsgbooks.com. Direct all submissions with SASEs to the Children's Editorial Department.

Margaret Ferguson, Associate Publisher and Editorial Director—Middle-grade children's literature, young adult, graphic novel

Wes Adams, Senior Editor

Janine O'Malley, Editor—Children's picture books, young adult

Beverly Reingold, Editor

Frances Foster, Publisher—Middle-grade children's literature, children's picture books, young adult

Beth Potter, Editor—Young adult

FEIWEL & FRIENDS

646-307-5151

Feiwel & Friends is a new imprint developed by former Scholastic publisher Jean Feiwel, who joined Macmillan in 2006. They publish innovative children's fiction and nonfiction literature including hardcover, paperback series, and individual titles. The list is eclectic and combines quality and commercial appeal for readers ages 0–16. The imprint is dedicated to "book by book" publishing, bringing the work of distinctive and outstanding authors, illustrators, and ideas to the marketplace. Feiwel & Friends is defined and guided by their principal: Our Books Are Friends for Life.

Titles from Feiwel & Friends include *Peep! A Little Book About Taking a Leap* by Maria van Lieshout; *Top of the Order* by John Coy; *Ava Tree and the Wishes Three* by Jeanne Betancourt; and *Mighty Casey* by James Preller and Matthew Cordell.

Direct queries and SASEs to:

Jean Feiwel, Publisher

Liz Szabla, Editor-in-Chief

FIRST SECOND

In 2006, Roaring Brook launched First Second, an imprint devoted to graphic novels. First Second editors seek to acquire titles that attract a diverse audience of readers by working on many different levels. First Second titles include *The Strange Crimes of Red Wheelbarrow* by Matt Kindt; *Voted Most Likely* by Prudence Shen; and *Foiled II: Curses, Foiled Again* by Mike Cavallaro.

Mark Siegel, Editorial Director

Calista Brill, Editor—Graphic novel

HENRY HOLT AND COMPANY BOOKS FOR YOUNG READERS

CHRISTY OTTAVIANO BOOKS

www.henryholtchildrensbooks.com

Henry Holt and Company Books for Young Readers publishes a wide range of children's books, from picture books for preschoolers to fiction for young adults. Their titles cover a wide variety of genres, featuring imaginative authors and illustrators who inspire young readers.

Their list includes classic picture books like *Panda Bear, Panda Bear, What Do You See?* by Bill Martin, Jr., illustrated by Eric Carle; *Tikki Tikki Tembo* by Arlene Mosel, illustrated by Blair Lent; *The Book of Three (The Chronicles of Prydain)* by Lloyd Alexander; *Whirligig* by Paul Fleischman; *My First Chinese New Year* by Karen Katz; *Frog in Love* by Max Velthuijs; *My Thirteenth Season* by Kristi Robert; and *Beach Patrol* by John O'Brien, illustrated by Max Bilkins.

Recent titles include *Brother Minotaur* by Tracy Barrett; *Bad For You* by Kevin Pyle and Scott Cunningham; *Dead Lines* by Jennifer Salvato Doktorski; *37 Things I Love* by Kekla Magoon; *Circus Galacticus* by Deva Fagan; and *C-Side Tales* by Tara Kelly.

When submitting to Henry Holt and Company Books for Young Readers, send a manuscript and cover letter to: Submissions. Do not send an SASE; the editors will respond only to those manuscripts they wish to pursue. All other submissions will be recycled. No multiple submissions. Full guidelines are available at www.henryholtchildrensbooks.com.

Laura Godwin, Vice President and Associate Publisher

Sally Doherty, Executive Editor

Reka Simonsen, Editor—Picture books, middle grade, young adult

Robin Tordini, Editor—Young adult

Noa Wheeler, Editor—Young adult, children's picture book

Kate Farrell, Associate Editor—Graphic novel, young adult

CHRISTY OTTAVIANO BOOKS

After 15 years in the editorial department at Henry Holt Books for Young Readers, Christy Ottaviano launched her own eponymous imprint. Christy Ottaviano Books acquires and edits both fiction and nonfiction for the full range of the children's audience, from preschool through teens, and will publish roughly 20 titles annually. 50 percent of titles will be picture books, 45 percent middle grade and YA, and 5 percent nonfiction.

Recent titles include *The Witch's Guide to Hunting with Children* by Keith McGowan; *Skipped* by Janci Patterson; *Village Greenmarket* by G. Brian Karas; *You're a Crab* by Jenny Whitehead; and *Beresford* by Whitlet Strieber.

Christy Ottaviano, Executive Editor—Middle-grade children's literature, young adult

ROARING BROOK PRESS

212-674-5151

Roaring Brook Press published its debut list of children's books in Spring 2002 and less than a year later one of its picture books, Eric Rohmann's *My Friend Rabbit*, won the Caldecott Medal. Another Roaring Brook picture book, Mordicai Gerstein's *The Man Who Walked Between the Towers*, won the Caldecott Medal in January 2004. This was the first time in 30 years that the Caldecott had been awarded to the same publisher two years in a row (in 1976 and 1977, Dial Press won for *Why Mosquitoes Buzz in People's Ears* by Verna Aardema, illustrated by Leo and Diane Dillon, and *Ashanti to Zulu* by Margaret Musgrove, again illustrated by Leo and Diane Dillon).

Macmillan acquired the Connecticut-based publisher in 2004. Roaring Brook publishes 40 books per year, half picture books and half novels for middle-grade and young-adult readers, and is in the midst of a growth pattern.

Roaring Brook Press is an author-centered publisher with a small but eclectic list. They are seeking long-term relationships with their authors; they don't do series; they don't do merchandise. What they do is edgy teen fiction, middle-grade fiction with humor, and high-quality picture books with an individual approach to art and format.

Recent Roaring Brook titles include *Hero Dogs* by Chris Demarest; *The Canticle of Whispers* by David Whitley; *The Other Felix* by Keir Graff; *The Children of the Lost* by David Whitley; and *Stop Thief!* by Adam Lane.

Direct queries and SASEs to:

Simon Boughton, Publisher—Middle-grade children's literature

Nancy Mercado, Editor—Middle grade, picture books

Katherine Jacobs, Editor

Neal Porter, Editorial Director—Children's picture book

SQUARE FISH

Square Fish is a paperback imprint that reprints hardcover children's books from all of the Macmillan publishers. The imprint launched in summer 2007 with Madeleine L'Engle's Time Quintet, which includes the classic *A Wrinkle in Time*. They do not accept submissions.

More recent titles from Square Fish include *One-Handed Catch* by MJ Auch; *Dreamhunter* by Elizabeth Knox; *We Are Witnesses: Five Diaries of Teenagers Who Died in the Holocaust* by Jacob Boas; and *Dodger and Me* by Jordan Sonnenblick.

STARSCAPE

Starscape publishes science fiction and fantasy for middle-grade readers ages 10 and up, in hardcover and paperback. All titles are age- and theme-appropriate. Some titles include *Down the Mysterly River* by Bill Willingham; *The Battle of the Red Hot Pepper Weenies* by David Lubar; and *Keyholders #2: The Other Side of Magic* by Debbie Dadey and Marcia Thornton Jones.

Susan Chang, Senior Editor

TOR TEEN

Tor Teen publishes science fiction and fantasy for young-adult readers ages 13 and up, in hardcover and paperback. All titles are age- and theme-appropriate. Some titles are *Truancy Origins* by Isamu Fukui; *The Comet's Curse* by Dom Testa; and *In Exile* by Orson Scott Card.

Susan Chang, Senior Editor

PALGRAVE MACMILLAN

175 Fifth Avenue, New York, NY 10010

212-982-3900

www.palgrave-usa.com

Formerly the Scholarly and Reference division of St. Martin's Press, Palgrave

Macmillan is a global cross-market publisher specializing in quality nonfiction and cutting-edge academic books. They publish general interest books as well as textbooks, journals, monographs, professional, and reference works in subjects ranging from political science, economics, and history, to literature, linguistics, and business.

Recent titles include *Was Jesus Born on Christmas?* by Greg Tobin; *Conversations with Power: Lessons on Leadership from Presidents and Prime Ministers* by Brian Till; *Stealing Rembrandt* by Tom Mashberg; *The Retail Revolution: Transformation of the World's Biggest Industry* by Robin Lewis and Michael Dart; *The Bully Action Guide* by Edward Dragan; and *George Eliot in Love* by Brenda Maddox.

Direct query letters and SASEs to:

Airié Stuart, Senior Vice President—Trade, current affairs, business

Farideh Koohi-Kamali, Executive Editor—Academic, literature, film, media, religion, anthropology, cultural studies, theater, gender studies

Laurie Harting, Executive Editor—Academic and professional, economics, business and management

Alessandra Bastagli, Senior Editor—History, biography, current affairs

Luba Ostashevsky, Editor—Latin American studies, African studies, parenting, psychology, science

Julia Cohen, Editor—Education

Jake Klisivitch, Editor—Business, politics, finance

Emily Carleton, Editor—Economics

PICADOR USA

175 Fifth Avenue, 19th Floor, New York, NY 10010

212-674-5151   fax: 212-253-9627

www.picadorusa.com

Picador USA was founded by St. Martin's Press and is now the reprint house for Farrar, Straus & Giroux; Henry Holt; and other Macmillan publishers. With an international list of world-class authors, Picador has rapidly established itself as one of the country's literary trade paperback imprints.

Representative titles include *Winter Under Water* by James Hopkin; *Bridget Jones's Diary* by Helen Fielding; *The Ice Soldier* by Paul Watkins; *Physical: An American Checkup* by James McManus; *A Taxonomy of Barnacles: A Novel* by Galt Niederhoffer; *Deep Water: The Epic Struggle over Dams, Displaced People, and the Environment* by Jacques Leslie; *Golden Boy: Memories of a Hong Kong Childhood* by Martin Booth; and *Limitations* by Scott Turow.

Recent titles include *Seven Pleasures: Essays on Ordinary Happiness* by Willard

Spiegelman; *Wolf Hall: A Novel* by Hilary Mantel; *The Philosophical Baby: What Children's Minds Tell Us About Truth, Love, and the Meaning of Life* by Alison Gopnik; *It's Beginning to Hurt* by James Lasdun; and *The Good Soldiers* by David Finkel.

Frances Coady, Publisher

David Rogers, Editor

Sam Douglas, Editor

ST. MARTIN'S PRESS

GRIFFIN

MINOTAUR

THOMAS DUNNE BOOKS

TRUMAN TALLEY BOOKS

175 Fifth Avenue, New York, NY 10010

212-674-5151

www.stmartins.com

Founded in 1952 by Macmillan Publishers of England, St. Martin's Press is now one of the largest publishers in America. Together, their imprints produce over 700 books a year, and their editors are as equally committed to establishing new and innovative authors, as to maintaining a strong backlist of titles. Publishing in hardcover, trade paperback, and mass-market formats enables St. Martin's Press to offer a diverse assortment of titles with wide-ranging appeal. St. Martin's is looking for new authors to discover, to build, and to support.

The house is particularly strong in a number of specialty areas, some with associated lines and imprints (including popular culture, international arts and letters, relationships, multicultural topics, science, business, and professional topics). St. Martin's publishes across the spectrum of trade nonfiction and hosts a wide range of popular and literary fiction.

Representative titles include *Twelve Sharp* by Janet Evanovich; *Running with Scissors: A Memoir* by Augusten Burroughs; *Big Papi: The Story of How My Baseball Dreams Came True* by David Ortiz and Tony Massoroti; *Brendan Wolf* by Brian Malloy; *How Not to Be Afraid of Your Own Life: Opening Your Heart to Confidence, Intimacy, and Joy* by Susan Piver; *10 Things Your Minister Wants to Tell You (But Can't Because He Needs the Job)* by Oliver Thomas; *Cat O'Nine Tales* by Jeffrey Archer; *Friends in High Places* by Marne Davis Kellogg; and *Vicente Minnelli: Hollywood's Dark Dreamer* by Emanuel Levy.

Recent titles include *Hex Symbols* by P.N. Elrod; *Insanewiches: 101 Ways to*

Think Outside the Lunchbox by Adrian Fiorino; *The Forever Fix: The Rise. Fall and Rebirth of Gene Therapy and the Boy Who Saved It* by Ricki Lewis; *Blown Sky High: The Murder of Gary Triano* by Kerrie Droban; *Survival Cannot Be Expected* by John Wukovits; *Groove Interrupted* by Keith Spera; and *Baby Squared* by Jane Roper.

Queries and SASEs may be directed to:

George Witte, Editor-in-Chief—Quality literary and commercial fiction, current affairs and issues, and narrative nonfiction; "During my twenty-two years here, I've taken particular pleasure in the number of first books we've published—many of those authors are now writing their fifth, tenth, fifteenth, or even twentieth book for us. Discovery, energy, and commitment to authors are the driving forces of our house."

Lisa Senz, Vice President, Associate Publisher, Reference Group—"We actively seek out titles that inform, educate, and amuse: both branded titles and titles that can become brands. Self-help, health, business, pop-culture, science/technology, and reference are all fair game."

Charles Spicer, Executive Editor—Commercial fiction: crime, suspense, mysteries, and historical fiction; nonfiction: true crime, biography and history; "I also oversee the True Crime Library Imprint, which has long been the most successful publisher of nonfiction crime, with many *New York Times* bestsellers and Edgar winners to its credit."

Elizabeth Beier, Executive Editor—"I couldn't be more enthusiastic about the kinds of books I work on—they span a generous variety of categories, from issues-oriented books to pop-culture, cookbooks to fiction, celebrity memoir to biography. Especially exciting is to work with first-time authors—I love introducing a writer to the process, trying to smooth the bumps along the way, and watching them take leaps as we pull the book together."

Hope Dellon, Executive Editor—Mysteries, serious contemporary and historical novels; "In nonfiction, my interests include biography, social history, and psychological memoirs. As the wife of a psychiatrist and mother of two daughters, I also find myself drawn to books on parenting, education, women's issues, and medicine."

Jennifer Enderlin, Editor—Fiction, thriller, cooking, women's romance

Jennifer Weis, Executive Editor and Manager, Concept Development—Commercial fiction: women's, thrillers, romance; commercial, YA; nonfiction: people books, narrative nonfiction, cookbooks, self-help, health and parenting, humor and popular culture; "The common theme of the novels I acquire is that they tell a story. From the most boldly commercial, to the quieter, what we call literary commercial crossover titles, they must make me keep turning the pages—usually, far into the night!" She is also looking, from a content/book perspective, to tie in with opportunities in areas of new media, branding, and Hollywood.

Philip Revzin, Senior Editor—Business, international subjects, memoir; "Since I came to St. Martin's in 2005 after having worked for the *Wall Street Journal* for more than thirty years, I have a natural interest in business titles. Having lived in Europe and Asia, I also like international subjects. But most of all, as a journalist, I like well-reported books of general interest."

Keith Kahla, Senior Editor—Thrillers, crime fiction, historical, literary fiction, Asian fiction (domestic and translated), new age works, divination systems, biography and history; "What draws me to a particular book is the quality of the writing, and a distinct, compelling authorial voice. Editorially, I believe it isn't the topic, story, or 'hook' that is the determining factor for interesting and successful books—it's the execution of the work by a uniquely talented author."

B. J. Berti, Senior Editor—She started at St. Martin's in 2005 with a mandate to reinvigorate the line of craft, style, and home books and develop a range of new titles in this area. In addition to practical nonfiction titles like *Easy Knitted Socks*, she is also interested in considering books that are not specifically craft but have a strong practical "how-to" component, like *The Art of Friendship*. She writes, "An attractively designed book with unique projects of information and something new to teach is what appeals to me most."

Marc Resnick, Senior Editor—Outdoor adventure, sports, military, popular culture, memoirs, thrillers, commercial fiction; "I have been working at St. Martin's Press since 1996—my first job in publishing."

Michael Flamini, Executive Editor—He acquires in history, politics, current affairs, memoirs, and cookbooks. He says, "It's an eclectic list, but why be boring? Life's too short and I hope my publishing reflects that philosophy."

Monique Patterson, Senior Editor—She joined St. Martin's in 2000 and acquires for all parts of the list and with wide variety; "The nonfiction that I like to do is mostly commercial and in fiction my tastes run from fun to suspenseful, from dark to breezy, from emotional to sexy—preferably a delicious combination of any of these."

Nichole Argyres, Senior Editor—"The search for a good story drives me both as a reader and as an editor. I love discovering stories with strong voices, beautiful language, and mysterious secrets. In nonfiction, I acquire idea books, memoirs, and platform-driven nonfiction of all kinds. I have a special interest in women's issues, current events, mental health, and medicine, as well as popular science and anything Greek."

Rose Hilliard, Associate Editor—Women's fiction and romance; "I'm on the lookout for exciting new romance authors in every subgenre, from romantic suspense to romantic comedy." She looks for stories with a great hook, an appealing voice, and winning characters that have her rooting for them from page one—and bonus points is a story that makes her laugh aloud or tear up. She is also considering branching out in the direction of pop-culture books.

Michael Homler, Editor—Biographies, history, pop science, crime fiction, sophisticated thrillers, and literary novels; "I'm really fascinated by material that breaks convention. At the same time, I look for solid voice-driven writing—something that makes the book and the author stand out from the pack. A sense of humor doesn't hurt either. In addition, I'm looking for more sports books, with a particular interest in baseball, which I can never get enough of."

Daniela Rapp, Editor—Humor, pets, biography, food/travel/wine, pop science, mysteries, thrillers, historical fiction, literary fiction; "I am actively looking for young Native American writers, as well as fiction in translation (I read German, French, and Italian) and am intrigued by literary references and anything to do with sword fights."

Hilary Rubin Teeman, Associate Editor—Social and cultural history, narrative nonfiction, popular sociology, playful self-help, memoirs, up-market women's fiction, romantic suspense, chick lit, literate commercial fiction, thrillers, and edgy YA novels; "I'm particularly interested in anything geared toward the twenty-to-thirty-something market."

Kathy Huck, Executive Editor—Cooking, parenting

Ruth Cavin, Senior Editor—Fiction, mystery and crime

Michelle Richter, Editor

Regina Scarpa, Editor

Alyse Diamond, Editor

Sarah Goodman, Associate Editor—Young adult

Yaniv Soha, Associate Editor—Nonfiction, pop culture, health, humor

Rob Kirkpatrick, Editor—True crime nonfiction, sports, memoir, history, current affairs

Lindsay Sagnette, Editor—Fiction, humor

Allison Caplin, Editor—Fiction, mystery, true crime nonfiction

GRIFFIN

The Griffin List features a wide range of contemporary paperbacks and includes hundreds of bestselling works of fiction—from commercial, literary, and graphic novels to titles of African American and young-adult interest. The hallmarks of Griffin's varied nonfiction publishing program extend to such categories as biography, memoir, pop-culture, politics, business, self-help, humor, reference, gay, health and fitness, home and travel, crafts, hobbies, nature, medicine, crossword puzzles, sudoku, and more.

Recent releases include *Never Fall in Love at the Jersey Shore* by Jenni Farley and Ronnie Ortiz-Magro; *Let's Panic About Babies!* by Alice Bradley and Eden Kennedy; *Birthright* by Ellie James; *The Pink Locker Society* by Debra Moffitt; *Great on the Job* by Jodi Glickman-Brown; and *Outside Wonderland* by Lorna Cook.

Jennifer Enderlin, Vice President and Associate Publisher, St. Martin's Paperbacks, Executive Editor—"I grew up reading commercial women's fiction—haunting, romantic novels; sexy, hilarious novels; and three-hankie reads." She also writes, "And commercial nonfiction is another pleasure of mine: popular psychology, self-help, relationships, and memoir. I also love collections of humorous observational essays."

Alyse Diamond, Editor—Nonfiction, pop culture, lifestyle, parenting, middle-grade children's literature; business and finance

MINOTAUR

www.minotaurbooks.com

Minotaur publishes mystery and all its sub-genres, but doesn't kill itself with gravity. A comic crime novel is not an oxymoron at this imprint. The position at Minotaur is that a good mystery is any good novel that has a crime as the foundation of the story. St. Martin's Press began releasing mystery novels in the 1950s—publishing classics like *Enter a Murderer* by Ngaio Marsh—and created Minotaur in 1999 to recognize the importance of the genre to the list.

Andy Martin, formerly of Crown and Sterling, became Minotaur publisher in 2006; he has said that the fun in his job is discovering, launching, and marketing major new talent, like John Hart, Marcus Sakey, Chelsea Cain, and Louise Penny. Minotaur publishes about 135 books per year.

Recent Minotaur titles include *Purgatory Chasm* by Steve Ulfelder; *Hideout* by Kathleen George; *Play Dead* by Gemma Halliday; *Death Watch* by Jim Kelly; *Maledictus* by Kelli Stanley; and *The Four Stages of Cruelty* by Keith Hollihan.

Minotaur/SMP co-sponsor two best first mystery novel contests; the winners are awarded publication prizes. Details are available on the Minotaur website (www.minotaurbooks.com/contests.html) or by sending an SASE to Contests/St. Martin's Press, Thomas Dunne Books, 175 5th Avenue, NY, NY 10010.

Direct queries with SASEs to:

Andrew Martin, Vice President and Publisher, Minotaur—Mysteries and crime fiction; everything from cozies and international thrillers to police procedurals and amateur sleuths

Ms. Kelley Ragland, Executive Editor, Minotaur—Mystery, suspense fiction, crime; "My taste in crime runs the gamut from cozy to hardboiled but is becoming increasingly dark and more serious."

Marcia Markland, Senior Editor—Nonfiction, biography, crime fiction, memoir

Keith Kahla, Senior Editor

Hope Dellon, Editor—Young-adult fiction, crime fiction, general fiction

THOMAS DUNNE BOOKS

www.thomasdunnebooks.com

The Thomas Dunne imprint produces roughly 175 titles per year—about 50/50 fiction/nonfiction—and covers a wide array of interests that include commercial fiction, literary fiction, thrillers, biography, politics, sports, popular science, and more.

Thomas Dunne editors have a wide range of tastes, backgrounds, even ages—from mid-twenties to late eighties. They believe that almost any book of commercial or literary merit will find a good home in their house.

Recent releases include *Things the Grandchildren Should Know* by Mark Oliver Everett; *Urban's Way: Urban Meyer, The Florida Gators and His Plan to Win* by Buddy Martin; *Artisan Bread in Five Minutes a Day: The Discovery that Revolutionizes Home Baking* by Jeff Hertzberg and Zoe Francois; and *Let the Right One In* by John Ajvide Lindqvist.

The Tony Hillerman Prize for first mysteries set in the Southwest was announced in 2007. For details on the competition guidelines see the website.

Queries and SASEs should be directed to:

Thomas L. Dunne, Vice President, Executive Editor, Publisher—Eclectic interests, commercial women's fiction, mysteries, military histories, biographies, divination systems, politics, philosophy, humor, literary fiction, and current events; he says that many of the biggest authors he has personally edited have been British—Rosamunde Pilcher, Frederick Forsyth, Wilbur Smith, Michael Palin—but also he has edited first books by Americans Dan Brown and Madeleine Wickham (aka Sophie Kinsella). In nonfiction, he has a particular interest in politics, history, biography, and current events.

Peter Wolverton, Senior Editor and Associate Publisher—Fiction: commercial and popular literature, genre mysteries; and a wide range of nonfiction consistent with the Thomas Dunne list; he says, "During my seventeen years in the business, I've published a wide variety of titles, but inevitably I find myself drawn to sports books (of all kinds), explosive thrillers and mysteries, outdoor literature (a particular passion—I'm always looking for the next Stegner or Mosher), the early years of NASA and the Apollo missions, and I occasionally journey into every genre."

Ruth Cavin, Senior Editor and Associate Publisher—crime fiction, contemporary fiction, anecdotal science and medicine, novelties (quotation books); "Although people in publishing who know me at all think I publish only mystery novels, they're wrong." Although she does love good mysteries, she is free to pick out anything she likes as long as it's well written, interesting, and she thinks it will sell.

Erin Brown, Editor—Acquires women's fiction, ranging from commercial women's fiction to more literary novels, all featuring strong female characters. She writes that she is partial to mysteries with smart and sassy female sleuths.

Mark LaFlaur, Senior Editor—Politics, current affairs, and other nonfiction; "I am interested in political biography, foreign affairs, social and economic policy, intelligence, national security (military and environmental), and the intersection of politics and religion, politics and psychology, etc. I also welcome works on cultural history, literary biography, global warming, hurricanes (or anything related to New Orleans), etc."

Rob Kirkpatrick, Senior Editor—Pop culture, sports, politics, current events; "I'm on the lookout for strong, platform-friendly nonfiction titles in sports, pop culture, history, and politics, as well as (on a very, very select basis) fiction."

Marcia Markland, Editor—Fiction and nonfiction; "As a former editor of The Mystery Guild, my taste naturally leans toward suspense fiction. My favorite category right now is what I think of as the semi-literary thriller. I also like police procedurals and legal thrillers. International suspense writing fascinates me. I devour disaster novels of any stripe, so if any given topic will make me lose sleep, that's the project for me." In nonfiction, she likes issue books, nature, and animals. She likes reading manuscripts that are a bit offbeat, and is most likely to request a manuscript that reflects a passionate belief on the part of the author, regardless of subject matter.

Karyn Marcus, Editor—Nonfiction with a focus on science, music, food, and humor; "I'm looking to acquire fiction projects which combine quality prose with clever plotting, particularly those with strong female protagonists. I'm also interested in writers working on a series of thrillers or historicals who are prolific enough to do a book a year. In nonfiction, my interests range from layman's science, psychology, and sociology to memoir and contemporary biography. Books about dogs, and animals in general, always make the top of my list."

Kathleen Gilligan, Associate Editor—Women's fiction and memoirs; "Whether it's a narrative of motherhood, or a quirky 24-year-old with an aversion to lipstick, I'm acquiring works with curious, genuine narrators—writing of a profound and well-crafted voice."

Peter Joseph, Editor—History, biography/autobiography, narrative nonfiction, travel, humor, pop-culture, film, music, social history, mysteries, thrillers, historical, and literary fiction. He also manages the Tony Hillerman Prize for first mysteries set in the Southwest.

Joel Ariaratnam, Editor—History, memoir, literary nonfiction, politics, social and cultural studies, memoir, and international fiction."

Toni Plummer, Associate Editor—Fiction and nonfiction, including sassy relationship advice, humor, and mysteries; "My nonfiction interests include memoir, narrative, advice/relationships, and social issues. My taste in mysteries runs the gamut, from gritty police procedurals to eloquent historicals to hilarious cozies."

Diana Szu, Associate Editor—Chick lit, reference and lifestyle, mysteries, fiction with Asian hooks; "When I first arrived at Thomas Dunne Books, my reading list primarily consisted of literary and ethnic fiction—particularly anything Asian—as well as religious and sociological nonfiction on modern-day issues. While these genres continue to be my favorites, I also do enjoy well-crafted women's fiction, mysteries, and narrative nonfiction with a compelling voice, in addition to cookbooks, crafting guides, and memoirs/biographies.

John Schoenfelder, Editorial Assistant—Fiction, science fiction, mysteries, crime; "I look for clarity of content that immediately grabs my attention and simply makes me want to turn to the next page."

Brendan Deneen, Editor—Fiction, paranormal fiction, young adult, thriller, science fiction, fantasy

TRUMAN TALLEY BOOKS

The Truman Talley imprint was run by Truman "Mac" Talley, who had been one of New York's most respected editors over the past 40 years. He retired in 2008. The list focuses on law, business, and leadership.

Recent titles include *The Time of Their Lives: The Golden Age of Great American Book Publishers, Their Editors, and Authors* by Al Silverman; *The Iranian Time Bomb: The Mullah Zealots' Quest for Destruction* by Michael A. Ledeen; *The Swordless Samurai: Leadership Wisdom of Japan's Sixteenth-Century Legend—Toyotomi Hideyoshi* by Kitami Masao and Tim Clark; and *Taste: Acquiring What Money Can't Buy* by Letitia Baldridge.

TOR/FORGE

TOR

FORGE

ORB

175 Fifth Avenue, New York, NY 10010

212-388-0100

www.tor-forge.com

Tor was created in 1981 at Tom Doherty and Associates, an independent publishing company known for its science fiction and fantasy list, including the bestselling *Sword of Truth* series by Terry Goodkind.

Today, Tor publishes science fiction and fantasy in both paperback and hardcover formats. Forge Books, an imprint of Tor, publishes nonfiction, thrillers, suspense, mysteries, historicals, and Westerns, targeted to the mainstream audience.

Recent Tor titles include *All Men of Genius* by Lev A.C. Rosen; *Ganymede* by Cherie Priest; *Sailor* by Tom Epperson; *Cold Glory* by B. Kent Anderson; *The Rapture of the Nerds* by Cory Doctrow and Charles Stross; *The Osteomancer's Son* by Greg van Eekhout; and *Lost Everything* by Brian Francis Slattery.

Direct query letters and SASEs to:

Bob Gleason, Editor—Fiction, thriller, mystery and crime fiction, fantasy

Liz Gorinsky, Editor—Sci-fi and fantasy, graphic novel

Eric Raab, Editor—Fiction, thriller, nonfiction anthology

Paul Stevens, Editor—Science fiction, fantasy, mystery and crime fiction

Kristin Sevick, Editor—General fiction, thriller, mystery and crime fiction

Melissa Frain, Editor—Young adult

Heather Osborn, Editor—Paranormal fiction, women's romance

David Hartwell, Editor—Science fiction, fantasy, general fiction

Stacy Hague-Hill, Editor—Paranormal fiction, thriller

Jim Frenkel, Editor—Paranormal fiction, thriller

Beth Meacham, Editor—Science fiction, fantasy

FORGE

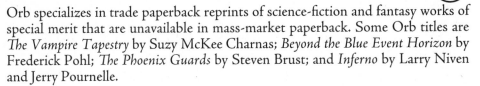

The Forge imprint publishes a wide range of fiction, including a strong line of historical novels and thrillers, plus mysteries, women's fiction, and a variety of nonfiction titles. Forge has also become a leading modern publisher of American Westerns.

Recent Forge titles include *The Zodiac Deception* by Gary Kriss; *Cosmic Electricity* by James Hogan; *A Game of Lies* by Rebecca Cantrell; and *The Damage Done* by Hilary Davidson.

ORB

Orb specializes in trade paperback reprints of science-fiction and fantasy works of special merit that are unavailable in mass-market paperback. Some Orb titles are *The Vampire Tapestry* by Suzy McKee Charnas; *Beyond the Blue Event Horizon* by Frederick Pohl; *The Phoenix Guards* by Steven Brust; and *Inferno* by Larry Niven and Jerry Pournelle.

NEWS CORPORATION

News Corporation is a worldwide media and entertainment corporation with subsidiaries that include HarperCollins, one of the world's largest English-language publishers. News Corp. chairman and major shareholder Rupert Murdoch turned his family's business into a multinational media corporation, which now has 40,000 employees and annual revenues in excess of $24 billion.

News Corp.'s $55 billion in assets include MySpace.com, Fox Broadcasting, Twentieth Century Fox, Blue Sky Studios, the *New York Post*, many radio stations, newspapers, magazines, the Los Angeles Lakers, and the National Rugby League.

HARPERCOLLINS PUBLISHERS

HARPERCOLLINS GENERAL BOOKS GROUP

HARPERCOLLINS CHILDREN'S BOOKS GROUP

HARPERONE

ZONDERVAN

HarperCollins publishes a diverse list of commercial, trade, professional, academic, and mass-market books in hardcover, paperback, and multimedia editions—fiction, nonfiction, poetry, history, reference, business, children's books, cookbooks, romance, mystery, art, and style. If the subject exists, there's likely a HarperCollins title representing it, or will be very soon.

Recent changes at HarperCollins include the renaming of the HarperSanFrancisco imprint to HarperOne. In 2007, HarperCollins created a new position of Senior Vice President and Director of Creative Development, hiring Lisa Sharkey, a former television producer. She and her team acquire current events and personality-driven books and work to position authors for maximum media exposure. She acquires books for all the general imprints and is listed below under HarperCollins.

Recent HarperCollins bestsellers include *The Dangerous Book for Boys* by Conn Iggulden and Hall Iggulden; *Deceptively Delicious* by Jessica Seinfeld; and *The Daring Book for Girls* by Andrea Buchanan and Miriam Peskowitz.

In 2006, HarperCollins began partnering formally with their corporate siblings at Fox Television Studios, developing programming intended for television, DVD, and digital media. The initial agreement covers mystery and romance titles including thrillers by Lisa Scottoline and *The Reading Group* by Elizabeth Noble. TV producer Karen Glass is working out of Harper's New York offices to facilitate projects and serve as liaison between Fox and the publisher.

Harper and Row (founded in 1817) was an early publisher of Mark Twain, the Brontë sisters, and Charles Dickens. In the U.K., William Collins and Sons, founded in 1819, published H. G. Wells, C. S. Lewis, and Agatha Christie.

HarperCollins formed when News Corp. acquired both of these publishers in 1987 and 1990. The publisher has continued to expand with subsequent acquisitions including Fourth Estate, Avon Books, William Morrow, and Amistad.

HarperCollins has publishing groups in the U.S., Canada, the UK, Australia/New Zealand, and India. The company has revenues that top $1 billion annually. With more than 30 imprints, HarperCollins serves an enormous audience and provides a home for hundreds of authors, from debut novelists like Bryan Charles (*Grab On to Me Tightly as if I Knew the Way*) to former Secretary of State Madeleine Albright (*The Mighty and the Almighty*).

For submissions to all imprints, please note that HarperCollins Publishers prefers material submitted by literary agents and previously published authors.

HARPERCOLLINS GENERAL BOOKS GROUP

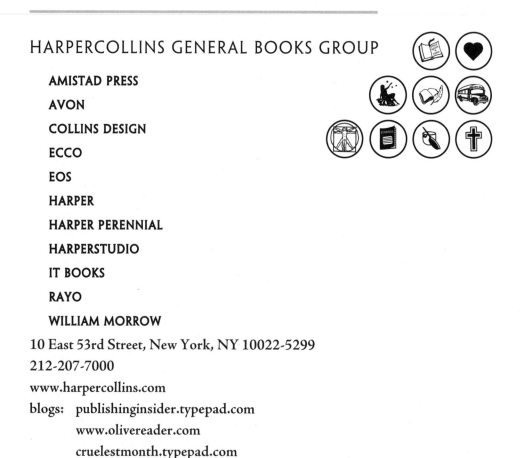

AMISTAD PRESS

AVON

COLLINS DESIGN

ECCO

EOS

HARPER

HARPER PERENNIAL

HARPERSTUDIO

IT BOOKS

RAYO

WILLIAM MORROW

10 East 53rd Street, New York, NY 10022-5299

212-207-7000

www.harpercollins.com

blogs: publishinginsider.typepad.com

www.olivereader.com

cruelestmonth.typepad.com

HarperCollins is a broad-based publisher with strengths in literary and commercial fiction, business books, cookbooks, mystery, romance, reference, religious, and spiritual books. The company has revenues that top $1 billion annually.

In 2009, the Collins imprint was closed and integrated its operations with the rest of the company. The Collins general nonfiction list is now published under Harper, Collins Reference and Collins Design remain intact, and Collins Business is now published as Harper Business. Collins trade paperbacks have been folded into Harper Perennial and Harper paperbacks.

HarperCollins has three blogs, which will be useful to check for insider tips and information. One of the blogs, called Publishing Insider, is from marketing guru Carl Lennertz and is at http://publishinginsider.typepad.com. The Harper Perennial blog, named after their oval-shaped logo, is The Olive Reader, at http://www.olive reader.com. The HarperCollins poetry blog, called Cruelest Month, is at http://cruelest month.typepad.com. Many of the imprints also have pages on MySpace.com.

AMISTAD PRESS

Amistad Press publishes works by and about people of African descent and on subjects and themes that have significant influence on the intellectual, cultural, and historical perspectives of a world audience. The house published Edward P. Jones's Pulitzer Prize-winning novel, *The Known World*.

This imprint is named for the 1839 slave rebellion on board a Spanish schooner, *Amistad*, and the resulting 1841 Supreme Court case that found the rebels to be free people. The Africans traveled home in 1842.

Newest releases from Amistad include *Marshalling Justice: The Early Civil Rights Letters of Thurgood Marshall* edited by Michael Long; *From Harvey River* by Lorna Goodison; *Ida: A Sword Among Lions* by Paula J. Giddings; and *Act Like a Lady, Think Like a Man* by Steve Harvey.

Direct query letters and SASEs to:

Christina Morgan, Editor—All categories including biography

Dawn Davis, Editor—Nonfiction biography, history, politics

AVON

Founded in 1941, Avon Books is the second-oldest paperback publishing house in the U.S. Acquired by HarperCollins in 1999, Avon publishes titles for adults and young readers. It is recognized for pioneering the historical romance category and continues to produce commercial literature for the broadest possible audience in mass-market paperback format. In trade paperback, Avon Trade focuses on contemporary romance and other chick-lit titles. An imprint called Avon Red publishes steamy erotic romance. A new imprint, Avon Inspire, moves into Christian fiction for women, and is run from HarperOne in San Francisco. You may read more about Avon Inspire in the HarperOne section.

Recent Avon titles include *Blood of the Wicked* by Karina Cooper; *Tainted by Temptation* by Katy Madison; *The Butterfly's Protector* by Anna Clevenger; *The Rose Notes* by Emily Arsenault; *His Darkest Salvation* by Juliana Stone; and *I'll Find You in Mansfield Park* by Cindy Jones.

Avon Books is actively seeking imaginative stories that can establish new voices in historical and contemporary romance, romantic suspense, and African American romance. Detailed manuscript and submission guidelines are available online or by written request with SASE.

Send a brief query with no more than a two-page description of the book. Avon editors prefer email queries with the word Query in the subject area. You will receive a response one way or another within approximately two weeks. The email address is: avonromance@harpercollins.com. To query by mail, be sure to include an SASE.

Liate Stehlik, Senior Vice President, Publisher

Carrie Feron, Vice President and Executive Editor—General fiction

Lucia Macro, Executive Editor—General fiction, women's romance

Lyssa Keusch, Executive Editor

Erika Tsang, Executive Editor—Women's romance

May Chen, Editor

Keshini Naidoo, Editor

Esi Sogah, Editor—Women's romance

Tessa Woodward, Editor—Women's Romance

COLLINS DESIGN

Collins Design books focus on all areas of design including architecture, interior design, graphic design, animation, art, style, and popular culture. They seek to publish stunning, visual books that capture and illuminate trends.

Recent Collins Design books include *Hip Girl's Guide to Homemaking*; *Minimalism and Color DesignSource* by Aitana Lleonart; *Sci-Fi Art: A Graphic History* by Steve Holland and Alex Summersby; *High Voltage Tattoo* by Kat Von D; and *Views* by Roger Dean, Donny Hamilton, and Carla Capalbo.

Direct queries and SASEs to:

Marta Schooler, Vice President and Publisher, Collins Design

Elizabeth Sullivan, Senior Editor—Pop culture, fashion, style

ECCO

Ecco publishes approximately 60 titles per year by such critically acclaimed authors as John Ashbery, Paul Bowles, Italo Calvino, Gerald Early, Louise Glück, Robert Hass, Zbigniew Herbert, Erica Jong, Cormac McCarthy, Czeslaw Milosz, Joyce Carol Oates, Josef Skvorecky, Mark Strand, and Tobias Wolff. The imprint has also created a number of literary series that enjoy a special celebrity in the world of book publishing.

Recent titles include *Ten Thousand Saints* by Eleanor Henderson; *An Oral History of London* by Craig Taylor; *I'm Your Man* by Sylvie Simmons; *The Fates*

Will Find Their Way by Hannah Pittard; *Tubes: A Physical Journey to Our Virtual World* by Andrew Blum; *Proust's Overcoat* by Lorenza Foschini; and *Dear Mrs. Kennedy* by Ellen Fitzpatrick.

Query letters and SASEs should be directed to:

Daniel Halpern, Editor-in-Chief—Narrative nonfiction, biography

Lee Boudreaux, Editorial Director—Fiction

Matt Weiland, Senior Editor—Narrative nonfiction, pop culture

Ginny Smith, Editor

EOS

A science-fiction and fantasy imprint, Eos has gained a positive reputation for its progressive editorial style, bold packaging, and innovative promotional campaigns. Named for the Greek goddess of the dawn, Eos looks for work that "transcends the ordinary in science fiction and fantasy." Best-selling Eos authors include Raymond E. Feist, Anne McCaffrey, and Gregory Benford.

Recent Eos books include *Despair* by Dakota Banks; *Fresh Start* by Merrie Destefano; and *Z Is for Zombie* by Johnny Atomic.

Direct query letters and SASEs to:

Liate Stehlik, Senior Vice President, Publisher

Jennifer Brehl, Editorial Director

Diana Gill, Executive Editor—Fantasy, thriller, science fiction

Emily Krump, Editor—Science fiction

HARPER

COLLINS REFERENCE

HARPER BUSINESS

SMITHSONIAN BOOKS

Harper produces adult hardcover books, trade paperbacks, and mass-market paperback editions that cover the breadth of trade publishing categories, including feature biographies (celebrities, sports, and historical), business, mysteries and thrillers, popular culture, humor, inspiration, and how-to (including cookbooks and health), in addition to works in most reference categories. The editors strive to find books that come from the heart of our literary, popular, and intellectual culture.

Best-selling authors include Milan Kundera, Michael Chabon, Barbara Kingsolver, Michael Crichton, Dr. Laura Schlessinger, Emeril Lagasse, Tony Hillerman, Barbara Taylor Bradford, Louise Erdrich, Anne Rivers Siddons, and Ursula K. Le Guin.

Recent fiction books include *Keeping Mum* by Kate Lawson; *The White Raven* by Robert Low; *Once in a Lifetime* by Cathy Kelly; *Showbiz Sensation (Coleen Style Queen)* by Coleen McLoughlin; and *Sorted! (Agent Alfie)* by Justin Richards.

Recent nonfiction titles include *Filthy Lucre: Economics for People Who Hate Capitalism* by Joseph Heath; *Gordon Ramsay's Great British Pub Food* by Gordon Ramsay and Mark Sargeant; *Riding: Expert Instruction for All Ages and Abilities* by The British Horse Society; and *Digital SLR Photography: Expert Advice on Getting the Best from Your Camera* by John Freeman.

Direct queries and SASEs to:

Jonathan Burnham, Publisher

David Hirshey, Executive Editor—Pop culture, celebrity books, politics, current affairs

Tim Duggan, Executive Editor—Serious nonfiction, literary fiction

Carolyn Marino, Executive Editor, William Morrow—Thrillers, fiction, mysteries, crime

Claire Wachtel, Executive Editor—Fiction, memoirs, narrative nonfiction

Cal Morgan, Executive Editor

Kate Hamill, Editor—Fiction, memoir, sports

Matthew Benjamin, Editor—Sports, pop culture, lifestyle, how-to, reference

Lisa Sharkey, Senior Vice President

Maureen O'Brien, Executive Editor

Doug Grad, Senior Editor

Matt Harper, Editor

Stephanie Fraser, Associate Editor

Terry Karten, Editor

Rob Crawford, Editor

Stephanie Meyers, Editor—Nonfiction, health and lifestyle, pop culture, how-to and reference, humor

COLLINS REFERENCE

Collins Reference has been moved under the Harper family of imprints following the closing of Collins in early 2009. Collins Reference has incorporated Harper Information and Harper Resource.

Bruce Nichols, Vice President and Publisher

HARPER BUSINESS

Harper Business titles formerly were published under the Collins Business name. Following the dissolution of Collins, Harper Business has incorporated Collins Business. Some incoming titles include *Digital Mom$: Motherhood + Internet = A Dream Career at Home* by Audrey McClelland and Colleen Padilla; *How*

Companies Win: Capturing Profitable Demand by David Calhoun; *Brainsteering: The Breakthrough Approach to Developing More and Better Ideas of Any Kind* by Kevin and Shawn Coyne; *Talespin* by Larry Kramer; and *Beta* by Jeff Jarvis.

Hollis Heimbouch, Vice President and Publisher

SMITHSONIAN BOOKS

Smithsonian Books is an imprint of HarperCollins in collaboration with the Smithsonian Institution that publishes a select list of narrative nonfiction books. Their publishing program includes categories where the Smithsonian's authority is unparalleled, such as history, science, technology, art, museums, collections, and artifacts. Among the distinguished list of Smithsonian Books authors are Deborah Cramer, Ken Davis, Thomas Fleming, Joy Hakim, and Robert Remini.

Some recent titles include *Clean Living Is Bad for You* by Robert Dunn; *Indomitable Grit* by Edward Achorn; and *Theodore Roosevelt's History of the United States* by Daniel Ruddy.

HARPER PERENNIAL

HARPER PERENNIAL MODERN CLASSICS

Home of such esteemed and award-winning authors as Barbara Kingsolver, Ann Patchett, Howard Zinn, and Harper Lee, Harper Perennial has been publishing fiction, nonfiction, and the classics for nearly 50 years. Perennial's broad range varies from Matt Groening's *The Simpsons* to Thomas Moore's *Care of the Soul*. A trade paperback format imprint, Harper Perennial publishes fiction and nonfiction originals and reprints.

Titles representative of Perennial's list include *Coming of Age on Zoloft: Notes on My Generation on Drugs* by Katherine Sharpe; *How the French Invented Love* by Marilyn Yalom; *The Call* by Yannick Murphy; *You Don't Love This Man* by Dan DeWeese; *When We Danced on Water* by Evan Fallenberg; *Fante* by Dan Fante; and *Far to Go* by Alison Pick.

Direct queries and SASEs to:

Carrie Kania, Publisher—Commercial and literary fiction

Cal Morgan, Vice President, Editorial Director—History, general fiction, pop culture reference

Jeanette Perez, Editor—Fiction, including coming of age, debuts, crime books

John Williams, Editor—Fiction, humor

Michael Signorelli, Editor—Fiction, crime

Allison Lorentzen, Editor—General fiction, memoir

Rakesh Satyal, Editor—Fiction

Amy Baker, Editor—Fiction, nonfiction narrative, memoir

HARPER PERENNIAL MODERN CLASSICS

The Harper Perennial Modern Classics imprint is home to many great writers and their most significant works. Featuring classic books from writers as diverse as Richard Wright, Harper Lee, Thomas Pynchon, Aldous Huxley, Sylvia Plath, and Thornton Wilder, Harper Perennial Modern Classics is the foundation stone for Harper Perennial itself. The newly redesigned Harper Perennial Modern Classics line is being expanded to include more contemporary classics.

Recent titles include *Major Works: Selected Philosophical Writings* by Ludwig Wittgenstein; *On Creativity and Consciousness: The Psychology of Art, Literature, Love and Religion* by Sigmund Freud; *Works of Love* by Soren Kierkegaard; and *The Prime of Miss Jean Brodie: A Novel* by Muriel Spark.

HARPERSTUDIO

(Note: The Studio imprint was closed at press time.)

HarperStudio is a new imprint started by Bob Miller, former president and founder of Hyperion. Frustrated and feeling straitjacketed by many of the publishing industry's conventions, Bob started HarperStudio with the intention of using a different business model than most publishers. HarperStudio wants to change distribution arrangements to improve efficiency, prevent bookstore returns, and pay smaller advances but with 50/50 royalties.

Some announced titles include *One to One Million* by Kevin Rose; *Cara & Phoebe's Quarter-Life Kitchen* by Cara Eisenpress and Phoebe Lapine; *Tolstoy and the Purple Chair* by Nina Sankovitch; *Till I End My Song* edited by Harold Bloom; and *The Mad Men Files* by Natasha Vargas-Cooper.

Bob Miller, Publisher

Debbie Stier, Senior Vice President, Associate Publisher

Julia Cheiffetz, Senior Editor

IT BOOKS

It Books, founded in March 2009 and led by Harper Perennial publisher Carrie Kania, focuses on pop culture, sports, style, and entertainment. HarperEntertainment's pending titles have been merged into the new imprint. Some upcoming titles include *Menagerie* by Sharon Montrose; *A Life Revealed* by Carre Otis; *This Outlaw Bit: How Waylon, Willie and the Boys Shook Up the Nashville Scene* by Michael Streissguth; *A Is for Armageddon* by Richard Horne; and *My First Dictionary* by Ross Horsley.

Carrie Kania, Publisher

Mario DiPrenta, Editorial Director

Cal Morgan, Editorial Director

Michael Signorelli, Editor

Kate Hamill, Editor—Humor, pop culture

RAYO

Rayo publishes hardcover and paperback books that exemplify the diversity within Hispanic communities, in both English- and Spanish-language editions. Rayo strives to connect culture with thought and to invigorate tradition with spirit. The imprint's eclectic publishing list has included titles in both nonfiction and fiction since it was founded in 2000. Because of the line's continual success, it has expanded to include more bilingual children's books, spiritual, self-help, and general reference titles. Rayo publishes 75 titles per year.

Recent titles include *Book Fiesta!: Celebrate Children's Day/Book Day; Celebremos El día de los niños/El día de los libros* by Pat Mora and Rafael Lopez; *Cómo lidiar con lo sex: Hombres, mujeres y fantasmas del pasado* by María Antonieta; *El infinito en la palma de la mano: Novela* by Gioconda Belli; *La fortuna en tus manos: Cambia tu vida financiera y alcanza la veradera felicidad (Adelante)* by Brent Kessel; and *La ultima niebla: Novela (Esenciales)* by Maria Luisa Bombal.

Direct queries and SASEs to:

Rene Alegria, Publisher

WILLIAM MORROW

MORROW COOKBOOKS

William Morrow, acquired in 1999 by HarperCollins Publishing, is one of the nation's leading publishers of general trade books, including bestselling fiction, nonfiction, and cookbooks.

William Morrow has an 80-year legacy of bringing fiction and nonfiction to the broadest possible audience, including works from bestselling authors Bruce Feiler, Neil Gaiman, Dennis Lehane, Neal Stephenson, John Grogan, Elmore Leonard, Ray Bradbury, Steven Levitt and Stephen J. Dubner, Susan Elizabeth Phillips, Christopher Moore, Sena Jeter Naslund, James Rollins, and Cokie Roberts.

Recent nonfiction titles include *Ultimate Volumetrics* by Barbara Rolls; *Bloom* by Kelle Hampton; *The Lady and Her Monsters* by Roseanne Montillo; *Agorafabulous!* by Sara Benincasa; *Undisputed* by Brock Lesnar; and *Bringing Metal to the Children: The Complete Berserker's Guide to World Tour Domination* by Zakk Wylde.

Recent fiction includes *Sanctus* by Simon Toyne; *The Art of Saying Goodbye* by Ellyn Bache; *White Picket Fences and Other Crimes Against Humanity* by Liza Palmer; *Cannibal Reign* by Thomas Koloniar; and *Life on Earth* by Joyce Maynard.

Direct query letters and SASEs to:

Jennifer Brehl, Senior Vice President—General fiction, thriller

Carolyn Marino, Executive Editor—Commercial fiction, mysteries, suspense, women's fiction

Marjorie Braman, Vice President, Executive Editor—Thrillers, fiction, mysteries

Laurie Chittenden, Executive Editor—Commercial nonfiction

Lyssa Keusch, Executive Editor

Diana Gill, Executive Editor

Henry Ferris, Executive Editor—Nonfiction narrative

David Highfill, Executive Editor—Fiction, thriller

Cassie Jones, Executive Editor—Diet, memoir, nonfiction

David Sweeney, Cookbook Director, Editor

Jennifer Pooley, Editor—Commercial nonfiction and fiction

Sarah Durand, Editor—Commercial nonfiction and fiction

Katherine Nintzel, Editor

Matthew Benjamin, Editor—Fiction, thriller, sports, current affairs

Lynn Grady, Editor—Biography, politics

Peter Hubbard, Editor—General nonfiction, science, politics, current affairs

MORROW COOKBOOKS

Morrow has a long-standing history of publishing some of the finest cookbooks in the industry, including *The Cake Bible* by Rose Levy Beranbaum; *Cookwise: The Secrets of Cooking Revealed* by Shirley Corriher; *Authentic Mexican* by Rick Bayless and Deann Groen Bayless; and *Chez Panisse Vegetables* by Alice L. Waters.

Recent books include *The Pleasure Is All Mine: Selfish Food for Modern Life* by Suzanne Pirret and *Wheat-Free Cook: Gluten-Free Recipes for Everyone* by Jacqueline Mallory.

David Sweeney, Editor

HARPERCOLLINS CHILDREN'S BOOKS GROUP

AMISTAD KIDS

BALZER AND BRAY

EOS

GREENWILLOW BOOKS

HARPER CHILDREN'S

HARPERFESTIVAL

HARPERTEEN

HARPERTROPHY

JOANNA COTLER BOOKS

KATHERINE TEGEN BOOKS

LAURA GERINGER BOOKS

RAYO

1350 Avenue of the Americas, New York, NY 10019

212-261-6500

www.harpercollinschildrens.com

www.harperteen.com

The broad range of imprints within HarperCollins Children's Group reflects the strength of the house as it both embraces new markets and values traditional literature for children. This group is impressively successful and has been cited by HarperCollins CEO Jane Friedman as being responsible for much of the publishing house's recent growth.

AMISTAD KIDS

Amistad publishes works by and about people of African descent on subjects and themes that have significant influence on the intellectual, cultural, and historical perspectives of a world audience. Amistad Kids is the home of Nina Crews, David Diaz, Julius Lester, Jerry Pinkney, Joyce Carol Thomas, and Donna L. Washington.

Recent titles include *From Havery River: A Memoir of My Mother and Her Island* by Lorna Goodison; *Ida: A Sword Among Lions: Ida B. Wells and the Campaign Against Lynching* by Paula J. Giddings; and *Jumped* by Rita Williams-Garcia.

Direct queries and SASEs to:

Dawn Davis, Editorial Director

BALZER AND BRAY

Balzer and Bray is the eponymous imprint of Donna Bray and Alessandra Balzer, who were formerly editorial director and executive editor respectively at Hyperion. The imprint is scheduled to debut in Autumn 2009 and will publish across the spectrum of children's literature, from picture books to YA.

Some upcoming titles include *Now I Know Me* by Charise Harper; *Lucky Human* by Emily Danforth; *Wildwood* by Colin Meloy; *For Darkness Shows the Stars* by Diana Peterfreund; *A Need So Beautiful* by Suzanne Young; *I Am Shark!* by Bob Shea; *The Death and Life of Emily Cooke* by Jeff Sampson; *The Doubting* by Heidi Ayarbe; and *Fox Heart* by Tricia Springstubb.

Donna Bray, Co-Publisher—Middle-grade children's literature, young adult, children's picture books

Alessandra Balzer, Co-Publisher—Middle-grade children's literature, young adult

Kristin Daly, Editor—Young adult

EOS

Eos offers exciting and innovative titles for the young-adult science-fiction and fantasy reader. The books are intended to be engaging enough to appeal to adults and include *Fire-us Trilogy* by Jennifer Armstrong and Nancy Butche; *The Books of Magic* by Hillari Bell; and *Sacred Sacrament* by Sherryl Jordan, author of several critically acclaimed and award-winning books including *The Raging Quiet*, a School Library Journal Best Book and ALA Best Books for Young Adults.

Recent Eos books include *Despair* by Dakota Banks; *Fresh Start* by Merrie Destefano; and *Z Is for Zombie* by Johnny Atomic.

Direct query letters and SASEs to:

Diana Gill, Executive Editor—Thriller, science fiction, fantasy

GREENWILLOW BOOKS

Greenwillow, founded in 1974, publishes books in hardcover and library bindings for children of all ages. They strive for books filled with emotion, honesty, and depth, books that have something to say to children and an artful way of saying it.

Recent titles that are representative of the Greenwillow list include *Counting Cars* by Christina Meredith; *The Princess and the Godstone* by Rae Carson; *Wintercraft* by Jenna Burtenshaw; *A Touch Mortal* by Leah Clifford; *The Ivy* by Lauren Kunze and Rina Onur; and *The Secret Zoo* by Bryan Chick.

Virginia Duncan, Vice-President, Publisher—Young adult, children's picture books

Steve Geck, Executive Editor—Young adult

Martha Mihalick, Editor—Young adult

HARPER CHILDREN'S

HarperCollins Children's Books is known worldwide for its tradition of publishing quality books in hardcover, library binding, and paperback for children, from toddlers through teens. This imprint also releases several successful series, such as *I Can Read*, *Math Start*, and *Let's Read and Find Out*, plus seemingly non-stop titles from authors Meg Cabot and Lemony Snicket.

Titles representative of this list are *A Hat Full of Sky* by Terry Pratchett; *Two Times the Fun* by Beverly Cleary, illustrated by Carol Thompson; *Ten Go Tango* by Arthur Dorros; *I'm Not Going to Chase the Cat Today!* by Jessica Harper; *The Princess Diaries, Volume VIII: Princess on the Brink* by Meg Cabot; *Arabat: Days of Magic, Nights of War* by Clive Barker; and *A Series of Unfortunate Events Box: The Complete Wreck (Books 1–13)* by Lemony Snicket, illustrated by Brett Helquist.

Recent releases include *The Selection* by Kiera Cass; *Casper Candlewacks in Death by Pigeon* by Ivan Brett; *The Vengekeep Prophecies* by Brian Farrey; *Shift* by Nicole Maggi; *Life Happens Next* by Terry Trueman; and *Hereafter* by Tara Hudson.

Send query letters and SASEs to:

Kate Jackson, Editor-in-Chief

Maria Modugno, Editorial Director—Middle-grade children's literature

Rosemary Brosnan, Executive Editor—Middle-grade children's literature, young adult

Susan Rich, Executive Editor—Young adult

Farrin Jacobs, Executive Editor—Teen fiction

Tara Weikum, Executive Editor—Young adult, middle-grade fiction

Anne Hoppe, Executive Editor—Manga, fantasy, fiction

Melanie Donovan, Senior Editor

Kelly Smith, Senior Editor

Barbara Lalicki, Editor

Clarissa Hutton, Editor

Kristin Daly, Editor—Young adult

Phoebe Yeh, Editor—Middle grade

Brenda Bowen, Publisher—Graphic novels, international titles, pop culture

Erica Sussman, Editor—Young adult

Laura Arnold, Editor

Zareen Jaffery, Editor—Young adult, lifestyle

Catherine Onder, Editor—Young adult

Sarah Sevier, Editor—Fantasy

HARPERFESTIVAL

HarperFestival is home to books, novelties, and merchandise for the very young: children up to six years of age. Classic board books, such as *Goodnight Moon* and *Runaway Bunny* established the list over ten years ago. Today, Festival produces a wide range of novelty and holiday titles as well as character-based programs such as Biscuit, Little Critter, and the Berenstain Bears.

Recent books include *Bella Sara: Fiery Fiona* by Felicity Brown and Jennifer L. Meyer; *Little Critter: Happy Mother's Day!* by Mercer Mayer; *Monsters vs. Aliens: Meet the Monsters* by N.T. Raymond; and *Easter Bunny in Training* by Maryann Cocca-Leffler.

Jodi Harris, Editorial Director

HARPERTEEN

HarperTeen produces original titles and previously published books in both hardcover and paperback formats, as well as original titles for young adults. In addition to typical teen fare, HarperTeen imprint regularly publishes fiction that deals with difficult personal and social issues like the death of a parent or senseless violence.

Recent titles include *Firelight* by Sophie Jordan; *Cold Kiss* by Amy Garvey; *Freaked* by J.T. Dutton; *In Mike We Trust* by P.E. Ryan; *Jo-Jo and the Fiendish Lot* by Andrew Auseon; and *Serendipity Market* by Penny Blubaugh.

Farrin Jacobs, Executive Editor

HARPERTROPHY

HarperTrophy is a leading paperback imprint for children, producing original fiction and nonfiction, as well as paperback reprints of previously published titles. From picture books by Maurice Sendak to novels by Laura Ingalls Wilder, E. B. White, Katherine Paterson, and Beverly Cleary, Trophy continues its tradition of offering a broad list of the old and the new.

Recent titles include *The Tiara Club at Pearl Palace: Princess Lucy and the Runaway Puppy* by Vivian French; *Dark River* by Erin Hunter; *Queen of Hearts* by Mary Engelbreit; *Battle of the Brain-Sucking Robots* by Peter Hannan; and *Crystal the Snow Pony* by Poppy and Rob Berg.

JOANNA COTLER BOOKS

Joanna Cotler Books publishes literary and commercial picture books and fiction for all ages. Authors and illustrators include award winners, bestsellers, and luminaries such as Clive Barker, Francesca Lia Block, Sharon Creech, Jamie Lee Curtis, Laura Cornell, Patricia MacLachlan, Barbara Robinson, Art Spiegelman, Jerry Spinelli, and William Steig.

Joanna Colter has stepped down from her position as publisher to focus on her sideline passion—painting. She will continue to acquire books and act as editor-at-large; however, it is unclear how many books she will do (previously JC Books was issuing 15 books a year).

Joanna Cotler, Editor-at-Large

Alyson Day, Associate Editor

KATHERINE TEGEN BOOKS

This imprint is looking for books made from stories that entertain, inform, and capture the excitement and emotions of children's lives. Katherine Tegen is a publisher who believes that "narratives created through memorable characters and original voices are the most powerful way to connect the reader with the experience of growing up in our world." The editors buy fantasy, middle grade, and young adult, as well as picture books.

Recent titles include *Divergent* by Veronica Roth; *Love and Leftovers* by Sarah Tregay; *My Soul to Reap* by Courtney Allison Moulton; *Summer Jackson: Grown Up* by Teresa Harris; and *Once in a Full Moon* by Ellen Schreiber.

Direct queries and SASEs to:

Katherine Tegen, Publisher

Sarah Shumway, Editor—Young adult

Molly O'Neill, Editor—Young adult, middle-grade children's literature

LAURA GERINGER BOOKS

Laura Geringer Books strives to provide children with award-winning, bestselling, and innovative authors and artists who continually set new standards of excellence. The list includes authors William Joyce, Laura Numeroff, Felicia Bond, Bruce Brooks, Richard Egielski, and Sarah Weeks.

Recent titles include *If You Give a Cat a Cupcake* by Laura Joffe and Felicia Bond; *Sword* by Da Chen; *13* by Jason Robert Brown; *Mildred and Sam Go to School* by Sharleen Collicott; and *The Mystery of Martello Tower* by Jennifer Lanthier.

Direct query letters and SASEs to:

Laura Geringer, Senior Vice President, Publisher

Jill Santopolo, Editor

RAYO

Rayo publishes books that embody the diversity within the Latino community, in both English- and Spanish-language editions. This imprint strives to publish titles that connect culture with thought and invigorate tradition with spirit, and does so with a reliably award-winning flair.

Recent titles include *Ana's Story, or La historia de Ana: Un camino Ileno de esperanza* by Jenna Bush and Mia Baxter; *Chasing the Jaguar* by Michele Greene; and *Sammy and Juliana in Hollywood* by Benjamin Alire Saenz.

Direct queries and SASEs to:

Rene Alegria, Publisher

HARPERONE

353 Sacramento Street, Suite 500, San Francisco, CA 94111

415-477-4400

In 2007, HarperSanFrancisco changed its name to HarperOne to completely dispel the idea that it is a regional publisher. This imprint publishes books important and subtle, large and small, titles that explore the full range of spiritual and religious literature. It releases about 85 titles annually, with a backlist of some 800 titles.

HarperOne strives to be the preeminent publisher of the most important books across the spectrum of religion, spirituality, and personal growth, with authors who are the world's leading voices of wisdom, learning, faith, change, hope, and healing.

By respecting all spiritual traditions, the editors strive to offer their readers paths leading to personal growth and well-being. In addition to traditional religious titles, HarperOne publishes inspirational fiction including their classic titles *The Alchemist* by Paulo Coehlo; *The Heart of Christianity: Rediscovering a Life of Faith* by Marcus J. Borg; *God's Politics: Why the Right Gets It Wrong and the Left Doesn't Get It* by Jim Wallis; *The Essential Rumi* by Coleman Banks; *The Right Questions: Ten Essential Questions to Guide You to an Extraordinary Life* by Debbie Ford; and *The World's Religions* by Huston Smith.

HarperOne started a new line of Christian romance fiction for women in 2007 under the Avon Inspire imprint; it is edited by Cynthia DiTiberio. She said, "Avon Inspire is gentle reading, safe reading. They end with a kiss and a proposal…It's *Sex & the City* without the sex." This imprint will publish one historical and one contemporary romance per season.

Also in 2007, HarperOne initiated an annual award, the Huston Smith Publishing Prize, for previously unpublished writers who complete manuscripts that are effective in promoting religious understanding. Details are available from the editors.

Recent titles representative of this list include *Route to Christianity* by Jonathan Phillip; *All Things Sacred: A Memoir of the Holy Land*; *Sexual Intelligence: What We Really Want from Sex and How to Get It* by Marty Klein; *Growing Up in Heaven* by James Van Praagh; *Furious and Bewildered* by Barbara Brown Taylor; and *Families of Honor* by Shelly Shepard Gray.

Query letters and SASEs should be directed to:

Mark Tauber, Senior Vice President, Publisher—Books on hybrid topics, such as the intersection of religion and politics, parenting and spirituality, and the Christian green movement

Michael Maudlin, Vice President, Editorial Director

Gideon Weil, Executive Editor—Religion and spirituality, general nonfiction

Eric Brandt, Senior Editor—Science, world religions, finance, lifestyle, narrative nonfiction

Roger Freet, Senior Editor—Memoir, music, history, Christianity, fiction

Cynthia DiTiberio, Assistant Editor—Avon Inspire, nonfiction for HarperOne

Jan Weed, Assistant Editor—Lifestyle

Jan Baumer, Editor

Nancy Heacock, Editor—Memoir, health, nonfiction

ZONDERVAN

INSPIRIO

ZONDERKIDZ

5300 Patterson Avenue SE, Grand Rapids, MI 49530

616-698-6900   fax: 616-698-3454

www.zondervan.com   email: submissions@zondervan.com

Zondervan Publishing House (founded in 1931) became a division of HarperCollins in 1988. Zondervan publishes both fiction and nonfiction Christian-oriented books and has held at least five (and as many as ten) out of the top ten positions on the Christian Booksellers bestseller lists since 1995.

Zondervan is publisher of the 20-million-copy bestseller, *The Purpose-Driven Life: What on Earth Am I Here For?* by Rick Warren, as well as other notable titles like *The Myth of a Christian Nation: How the Quest for Political Power Is Destroying the Church* by Gregory A. Boyd; *Boundaries* by Dr. Henry Cloud and Dr. John Townsend; and *The Case for Christ: A Journalist's Personal Investigation of Evidence for Jesus* by Lee Strobel.

Zondervan also publishes faith-based fiction for adults and children including *Faithgirlz* series for 9–12-year-olds and the *Kanner Lake* series for adults.

Although Zondervan specializes in publishing Bibles and books, the house also produces a wide variety of resources, including audio books, e-books, videos, CD ROMs, and inspirational gifts. Zondervan has six primary product-group departments: Bibles; Books; New Media, which publishes electronic format books, Bibles, and software products; Zonderkidz; Inspirio; and Vida Publishers, Zondervan's multilingual publishing and distribution unit.

Zonderkidz was formed in 1998 to represent the children's and juvenile division at Zondervan. Zonderkidz is now the leading publisher of children's Bibles, children's Christian books, and other related products. In 2000, Zondervan launched its gift program, Inspirio.

As the world's largest Bible publisher, Zondervan holds exclusive publishing rights to the New International Version of the Bible—the most popular translation of the Bible—and has distributed more than 150 million copies worldwide. Zondervan publishes approximately 50 Bible products, 150 books, 80 gifts, and 50 new media products each year.

Recent titles include *North of the Morning Calm* by Don Brown; *Insight* by Diana Greenwood; *Throw It Down: Leaving Behind the Behaviors and Dependencies That Hold You Back* by Jud Wilhite; *Veneer: Living Deeply in a Surface Society* by Timothy Willard and R. Jason Locy; *Everyone Overcome* by Brady Boyd and Ashley Wiersma; *Prisoner of Conscience* by Frank Wolf; and *Start: Becoming a Good Samaritan*.

Currently Zondervan is only seeking manuscripts in academic, reference, and ministry resources categories. Zonderkidz is not currently accepting unsolicited manuscripts.

Direct queries and SASEs to:

Dudley Delffs, Vice President and Publisher—Looking for fresh voices and new authors

Paul Engle, Executive Editor—Memoirs, inspirationals

Jay Howver, Editor—Inspirationals, YA

Andy Meisenheimer, Editor—Current events

Angela Scheff, Editor—Media tie-ins, current events, lifestyle, religion and spirituality, sports

Sue Brower, Editor—Romance, mystery, religious fiction, inspirational books, thrillers

Barbara Scott, Editor, Zonderkidz—Picture books, YA, fantasies

Debra Durham, Editor—Religion and spirituality

PEARSON

Pearson is an international media company based in the United Kingdom with businesses in education, business information, and consumer publishing. Pearson's 29,000 employees are in 60 countries, connecting a family of businesses that draws on common assets and shares a common purpose: to help customers live and learn. In addition to the Penguin Group, Pearson divisions include Pearson Education and the Financial Times Group.

The Penguin Group, with primary operations in the UK, Australia, the U.S., and Canada, and smaller operations in South Africa and India, is led by CEO and Chairman, John Makinson. The Penguin Group is the world's second-largest English-language trade book publisher.

PENGUIN GROUP (USA), INC.

PENGUIN PUTNAM ADULT DIVISION

PENGUIN PUTNAM YOUNG READERS DIVISION

DORLING KINDERSLEY/DK PUBLISHING

Penguin Group (USA), Inc., is the U.S. affiliate of the Penguin Group. Formed in 1996 as a result of the merger between Penguin Books USA and the Putnam Berkley Group, Penguin Group (USA), under the stewardship of Chief Executive Officer David Shanks, is a leading U. S. adult and children's trade book publisher.

Penguin Group (USA) publishes under a wide range of prominent imprints and trademarks, among them Berkley Books, Dutton, Grosset & Dunlap, New American Library, Penguin, Philomel, G. P. Putnam's Sons, Riverhead Books, Viking, and Frederick Warne. The Penguin Group's roster of bestselling authors includes, among hundreds of others, Dorothy Allison, Nevada Barr, Saul Bellow, A. Scott Berg, Maeve Binchy, Harold Bloom, Sylvia Browne, Tom Clancy, Robin Cook, Patricia Cornwell, Catherine Coulter, Clive Cussler, Eric Jerome Dickey, Richard Paul Evans, Helen Fielding, Ken Follett, Sue Grafton, W. E. B. Griffin, Nick Hornby, Spencer Johnson, Jan Karon, Anne Lamott, James McBride, Terry McMillan, Arthur Miller, Jacqueline Mitchard, Toni Morrison, Kathleen Norris, Joyce Carol Oates, Robert B. Parker, Nora Roberts, John Sandford, Carol Shields, John Steinbeck, Amy Tan, Kurt Vonnegut, and the Dalai Lama.

Penguin Group (USA), Inc., is a global leader in children's publishing, through its Books for Young Readers, with preeminent imprints such as Dial Books, Dutton, Grosset & Dunlap, Philomel, Puffin, Speak, Firebird, G. P. Putnam's Sons, Viking, and Frederick Warne. These imprints are home to acclaimed authors Ludwig Bemelmans, Judy Blume, Jan Brett, Eric Carle, Roald Dahl, Tomie dePaola, Don Freeman, Hardie Gramatky, Eric Hill, Brian Jacques, Robert McCloskey, A. A. Milne, Richard Peck, Patricia Polacco, and dozens of other popular authors.

Dorling Kindersley/DK Publishing has been a part of the Penguin Group since 2000. In 2007, DK in New York largely ceased acquiring books for U. S. readers, focusing instead on the international market.

PENGUIN PUTNAM ADULT DIVISION

ALPHA BOOKS

AMY EINHORN BOOKS

AVERY GROUP

BERKLEY BOOKS

DUTTON

HP BOOKS

HUDSON STREET PRESS

NEW AMERICAN LIBRARY/NAL

PENGUIN PRESS

PERIGEE BOOKS

PLUME

PORTFOLIO

PRENTICE HALL PRESS

G.P. PUTNAM'S SONS

RIVERHEAD BOOKS

SENTINEL

JEREMY P. TARCHER

VIKING PRESS

375 Hudson Street, New York, NY 10014

212-366-2000   fax: 212-366-2666

us.penguingroup.com

blog: http://thepenguinblog.typepad.com

The Adult Division of Penguin Putnam has been a strong performer for many years. Penguin USA President Susan Petersen Kennedy said recently, "It's very nice when both the economic side and the artistic side coincide."

In spite of the economic recession, Penguin USA reported a record year, with 13 of its imprints having #1 *New York Times* bestsellers last year, and gains posted throughout the company's divisions. Penguin has not made any major acquisitions in several years, but it has added a few new imprints, including Amy Einhorn Books, which in 2009 released its first title, *The Help*; Celebra, which releases titles by or about Hispanic and Latin American celebrities; and Pamela Dorman Books

Authors should definitely check out the Penguin blog, where editors post the latest news from the company: new acquisitions, sneak previews from works in progress, industry gossip, and advice on how to get published. Although it comes from the UK editorial office, the blog offers insight into the day-to-day running of the company and how books are made.

Penguin Putnam houses PenguinClassics.com, an online community devoted to classic titles. The company also launched Penguin Lives, a series of short biographies about well-known historical and cultural figures, written by some of today's most respected authors. In addition, Penguin Putnam resumed its Pelican Shakespeare series, which has remained one of the bestselling series of Shakespeare's plays since the line was introduced in the mid-1960s.

Kathryn Court, Publisher

Stephen Morrison, Editor-in-Chief and Associate Publisher

ALPHA BOOKS

800 E. 96th Street, Indianapolis, IN 46240

fax: 317-428-3504

375 Hudson Street, New York, NY 10014

212-366-2000

www.idiotsguides.com   submissions@idiotsguides.com

With the slogan "knowledge for life," Alpha Books publishes original nonfiction and how-to titles for adults who seek to learn new skills or otherwise enrich their lives. Alpha publishes the very popular series, *The Complete Idiot's Guides*.

With more than 400 titles already in print, *The Complete Idiot's Guides* is one of the world's most easily recognizable title series. Despite the dizzying success of the series, ideas and manuscripts are continually welcomed. Best-selling topics include personal finance, business, health/fitness, foreign language, New Age, and relationships.

A random selection of recent titles is *New Résumé New Career: Get the Job You Want With the Skills and Experience You Already Have* by Catherine Jewell; *The Quizzical Bride's Wedding Guide* by Jessica Horvath; and *The Wealthy Freelancer: 12 Secrets to a Great Income and an Enviable Lifestyle* by Steven Slaunwhite, Ed Gandia, and Peter Savage.

Send electronic submissions with proposals as an email attachment. Submit to the attention of the Editorial Coordinator in the Indianapolis office or at submissions@idiotsguides.com. Detailed submission guidelines are available on the website.

Mike Sanders, Editorial Director (IN office)—Finance, investing

Ms. Randy Ladenheim-Gil, Senior Acquisitions Editor (NY office)

Paul Dinas, Senior Acquisitions Editor (NY office)

Tom Stevens, Acquisitions Editor (IN office)

AMY EINHORN BOOKS

Amy Einhorn Books was founded in 2007 by Amy Einhorn and launched in February of 2009. The imprint publishes fiction, narrative nonfiction, and commercial nonfiction. The overarching tenet of Amy Einhorn Books is intelligent writing with a strong narrative, always with great storytelling at its core. They seek the perfect blend of literary and commercial.

Some new titles include *Let's Pretend This Never Happened: a Mostly True Memoir* by Jenny Lawson; *The Weird Sisters* by Eleanor Brown; *You Know When the Men Are Gone* by Siobhan Fallon; *High at the Bottom* by Stephen Wetta; *Next Stop* by Glen Finland; and *This Is Not the Story You Think It Is: A Season of Unlikely Happiness* by Laura Munson.

Amy Einhorn, Vice President and Publisher—Memoir, fiction

AVERY GROUP

AVERY BOOKS

GOTHAM BOOKS

In late 2008, The Penguin Group put together Gotham Books and Avery Books under the direction of Bill Shinker, who is now president and publisher of both lines. The two imprints will work through a joint publicity and marketing department.

Bill Shinker, President and Publisher

Lisa Johnson, Vice President, Publicity and Marketing Director

AVERY BOOKS

Avery's publishing program is dedicated primarily to complementary medicine, nutrition, and healthful cooking. It was established in 1976 as a college textbook publisher specializing in niche areas. Through a series of alliances, most notably with Hippocrates Health Institute, Avery began a program of health books by such authors as Ann Wigmore and Michio Kushi, whose work on macrobiotics helped propel the Avery list in the health food and alternative markets. The firm was acquired by the Penguin Group in 1999 and currently publishes 30 new titles per year. Avery's scope of titles has broadened to include psychology, inspirational memoir, and sociology.

In addition to producing original titles in hardcover and paperback formats, Avery has a backlist of several hundred titles in trade and mass-market formats that include works by pioneers in alternative healing, scientists, and health care professionals involved in cutting-edge research.

Titles representative of the Avery list are *Zombie Economics: The Undead Guide to Personal Finance* by Lisa Desjardins and Rick Emerson; *To Life: A Physician's Quest to Transform the Way We Die* by Ira Byock; *The Science of Willpower* by Kelly McGonigal; *A Child's Writing Life* by Pam Allyn; *Letting Go With Love and Confidence* by Kenneth Ginsburg and Susan FitzGerald; and *Alissa Cohen's Raw Food for Everybody: The Ultimate Essentials Cookbook* by Alissa Cohen and Leah Dubois.

Direct your query letter and SASE to:

Megan Newman, Vice President, Editorial Director—High-profile memoir, health, diet

Lucia Watson, Editor—Parenting, cooking, relationships

Rachel Holtzman, Editor—Business, science, general nonfiction

GOTHAM BOOKS

The Gotham Books imprint strives for both commercial and literary success in its titles. This nonfiction imprint publishes 35 books per year. Its emphasis is on self-help, spirituality, business, sports, travel writing, biography, food, current affairs, health, humor, and narrative nonfiction

Representative titles include *Eats, Shoots & Leaves: The Zero Tolerance Approach to Punctuation* by Lynne Truss; *The Man Who Heard Voices: Or, How M. Night Shyamalan Risked His Career on a Fairy Tale* by Michael Bamberger; *Me and a Guy Named Elvis* by Jerry Schilling with Chuck Crisafulli; *Curb Your Enthusiasm: The Book* by Deirdre Dolan; *Only Joking* by Jimmy Carr and Lucy Greeves; *Real Love in Marriage* by Greg Baer, MD; *The Ode Less Traveled* by Stephen Fry; *Roll the Bones* by David G. Schwartz; *The Kitchen Diaries* by Nigel Slater; and *War Made New* by Max Boot.

Recent releases include *The Good Food Revolution* by Will Allen; *Wine to Water* by Doc Hendley; *Big Day Coming: Yo La Tengo and the Rise of Indie Rock* by Jesse Jarnow; *I Beat the Odds: My Amazing Journey from Foster Care to the NFL and Beyond* by Michael Oher and Don Yeager; and *Just My Type* by Simon Garfield.

Direct query letters and SASEs to:

Lauren Marino, Vice President, Editorial Director

Patrick Mulligan, Editor—Narrative nonfiction, history, sports, music, pop culture, humor

Megan Newman, Editor—General nonfiction, parenting, memoir, current affairs, sports, nonfiction narrative

Bill Shinker, Editor—Memoir, sports, general nonfiction

Jessica Sindler, Editor—General nonfiction, health

BERKLEY BOOKS
ACE BOOKS
JOVE BOOKS
BERKLEY PRIME CRIME

Berkley Books was founded in 1955 by a group of independent investors. The company performed quietly but profitably for ten years, and in 1965 was bought by G.P. Putnam's Sons, which in turn was bought by MCA ten years later. In 1982, Putnam bought Grosset & Dunlap and Playboy Press, and the Ace and Playboy lists were added to Berkley. The Playboy list was eventually absorbed into Berkley, while the Jove and Ace Lists have continued as distinct imprints.

Under the leadership of President and Publisher Leslie Gelbman, Berkley publishes more than 500 titles per year under their imprints, in mass-market paperback, trade paperback, hardcover, and multimedia formats.

Recent titles include *Demon Marked* by Meljean Brook; *Totally Together* by Stephanie O'Dea; *Heart Search* by Robin Owen; *Vampire's Keeper* by Joey Hill; *Enchanting Lily* by Anjali Banerjee; *Lilli's Garden* by Katharine Fisher Britton; *No Way Out* by Kevin Maurer; and *Connor's Story* by Pamela Clare.

Direct query letters and SASEs to:

Leslie Gelbman, President, Publisher, Editor-in-Chief—Wide range of projects in fiction and nonfiction

Susan Allison, Vice President and Editorial Director—Fiction, including fantasy, women's fiction

Tom Colgan, Executive Editor—Wide range of commercial fiction and nonfiction, including history, business, inspiration, biography, military, thrillers, adventure, suspense

Natalee Rosenstein, Vice President, Senior Executive Editor—General fiction and mystery, thrillers, history, politics

Cindy Hwang, Senior Editor—Women's fiction, popular culture, young adult, paranormal romance, historical romance, contemporary romance

Denise Silvestro, Executive Editor—Lifestyle, memoir, parenting, health, humor, business, leadership

Kate Seaver, Senior Editor—Fiction including paranormal romance, erotica, Berkley Heat

Jackie Cantor, Editor—Narrative nonfiction, memoir, fiction, historical fiction

Leis Pederson, Editor—Women's fiction, romance, Berkley Heat, Berkley Sensation

Andie Avila, Editor—Narrative nonfiction, memoir, parenting

Carolyn Morrisroe, Editor—Mystery, fiction

Emily Rapoport, Assistant Editor—Nonfiction including parenting, business, blogs

Katie Day, Assistant Editor—Fiction, mystery, thrillers, true crime

Wendy McCurdy, Editor—General fiction, women's romance, mystery

Shannon Jamieson Vazquez, Editor—Mystery, true crime nonfiction

Faith Black, Editor—General fiction, mystery and crime fiction

Danielle Stockley, Editor—Pop culture, science fiction and fantasy

Ginjer Buchanan, Editor—Science fiction, fantasy, horror, mystery and crime fiction

ACE BOOKS

Ace Books, founded in 1953 by A. A. Wyn, is the oldest continuously operating science-fiction publisher in the U.S. Ace released some of the most outstanding science-fiction writers of the 1950s and 1960s, including Samuel R. Delany, Philip K. Dick, Ursula K. Le Guin, and Robert Silverberg.

Ace produces original titles in hardcover and mass-market paperback, as well as reprints previously published in hardcover and trade paperback fiction.

Recent titles include *Hunter Kiss* by Marjorie Liu; *The Doomsday Vault* by Steven Harper; *Heaven's Shadow* by David Goyer and Michael Cassutt; *Dust* by Joan Frances Turner; and *Aftermath* by Ann Aguirre.

Direct query letters and SASEs to:

Ginjer Buchanan, Editor-in-Chief

Anne Sowards, Editor—Science fiction and fantasy, young adult, paranormal fiction

JOVE BOOKS

Jove is the mass-market paperback imprint of the Berkley group. It originated as Pyramid Books, which was founded in 1949 by Alfred R. Plaine and Matthew Huttner, and was sold to the Walter Reade Organization in the late 1960s. In the early 1970s, Pyramid published the first four titles in John Jakes's *Kent Family Chronicles*. These popular titles, among others, drew the attention of Harcourt Brace Jovanovich, which was looking for a paperback division, and in 1975, Pyramid was bought by HBJ and its name changed to Jove.

The Jove imprint is known for such significant bestselling authors as Nora Roberts, Catherine Coulter, Steve Martini, Jayne Ann Krentz, Dick Francis, and W. E. B. Griffin.

Recent titles include *Diabolical* by Hank Schwaeble; *The Genius* by Jesse Kellerman; *The Gunsmith 328: East of the River* by J.R. Roberts; *The Orpheus Deception* by David Stone; *The Third Circle* by Amanda Quick; *Tribute* by Nora Roberts; and *Nutcase* by Charlotte Hughes.

Direct query letters and SASEs to:

Leslie Gelbman, Publisher

BERKLEY PRIME CRIME

Berkley Prime Crime publishes mystery and crime fiction. Some recent titles include *From Dead to Worse* by Charlaine Harris; *Wormwood* by Susan Wittig Albert; *Grand Cayman Slam* by Randy Wayne White; *Murder She Wrote: Madison Avenue Shoot* by Donald Bain and Jessica Fletcher; and *Never Say Sty* by Linda O. Johnston.

Shannon Jamieson Vazquez, Editor

Ginjer Buchanan, Editor

Allison Brandau, Editorial Assistant

Michelle Vega, Editor—Paranormal fiction, mystery and crime fiction

Emily Beth Rapoport, Editor—Mystery and crime fiction

DUTTON

Dutton dates back to 1852, when Edward Payson Dutton founded a bookselling firm, E. P. Dutton, in Boston. Dutton currently publishes about 50 hardcover titles per year, fiction and nonfiction.

Dutton authors include Ken Follett, Eckhart Tolle, Harlan Coben, Al Franken, Raymond Khoury, Eric Jerome Dickey, John Hodgman, John Lescroart, John Jakes, and Jenny McCarthy.

Recent titles include *The Moral Molecule: Vampire Economics and the New Science of Good and Evil* by Paul Zak; *I Want My MTV* by Craig Marks and Rob Tannenbaum; *Hopper: A Savage Journey to the Heart of the American Dream* by Tom Folsom; *Queen of Kings* by Maria Dahvana Headley; *Children of Paranoia* by Trevor Wiessmann; and *The Fat Man: A Tale of North Pole Noir* by Kenneth Harmon.

Direct query letters and SASEs to:

Brian Tart, President and Publisher

Carrie Thornton, Executive Editor—Pop culture, biography, science non-fiction, memoir

Stephen Morrow, Executive Editor—Entertaining books on serious subjects, popular science

Amy Hertz, Editor-at-Large

Ben Sevier, Senior Editor—Fiction, mystery and crime fiction

Erike Imranyi, Editor—General fiction

Denise Roy, Editor—Fiction

HP BOOKS

HP Books originated in Tucson, Arizona, as publishers of nonfiction books in the categories of cooking, automotive, photography, gardening, health, and child care. HP now specializes in cooking and automotive titles, publishing about 20 books per year in trade paperback and a few in hardcover. Among the stars of the list, Mable Hoffman's *Crockery Cookery* recently celebrated its 20th year in print with more than 5 million copies sold.

As of 2009, new acquisitions for HP will be exclusively in the automotive category, as cooking and craft titles move to HP's sister imprint, Perigee.

Recent titles representative of this list include *The Classic Chevy Truck Handbook: How to Rod, Rebuild, Restore, Repair, and Upgrade Classic Chevy Trucks 1955–1960* by Jim Richardson.

Direct query letters and SASEs to:

John Duff, Publisher

Marian Lizzi, Editor-in-Chief

Meg Leder, Editor

Maria Gagliano, Associate Editor

HUDSON STREET PRESS

Hudson Street Press's list was launched in the winter of 2005. Hudson Street focuses on narrative and practical nonfiction: memoirs, biography, sex, self-help, relationships, money, women's issues, health/diet, science, and popular history.

Hudson Street Press looks for books exploring issues that keep people up at night and for voice-driven narratives with emotional resonance. Their mission is to publish authors who bring a new perspective or a unique voice to the traditionally successful nonfiction categories. They publish approximately 30 books per year.

Recent titles include *Am I a Jew: Lost Jews, Former Jews, Crypto-Jews, Hipster Jews, and One Man's Search for Himself; How to Make a Self* by Hazel Markus et al; *The Last Best Cure* by Jackson Nakazawa; *The Myth of the Middle Child* by Catherine Salmon and Katrin Schumann; *Why Women Need Fat* by William Lassek and Steven Gaulin; and *From Emotional Chaos to Clarity* by Phillip Moffitt.

Claire Ferraro, Publisher

Caroline Sutton, Editor-in-Chief—Science nonfiction, health, parenting, religion and spirituality, business and investing, relationship advice

Meghan Stevenson, Editor

Anna Sternoff, Editor

NEW AMERICAN LIBRARY/NAL

ACCENT

CALIBER

OBSIDIAN MYSTERIES

ONYX

ROC

SIGNET

Kurt Enoch and Victor Weybright, two former Penguin editors, started the New American Library in 1948. Introducing Signet and Mentor as leading imprints, NAL began with titles such as William Faulkner's *Sanctuary*, D.H. Lawrence's *Lady Chatterly's Lover*, and John Steinbeck's *Tortilla Flat*. After selling at least 3 million copies of James Jones's *From Here to Eternity* in its first year of publication, NAL was quick to publish the popular fiction of Ian Fleming and Mickey Spillane.

New American Library—popularly known as NAL—publishes a diverse and exciting range of paperback books, including *New York Times* bestsellers by Maeve Binchy, Stuart Woods, John Lescroart, Ken Follett, Sylvia Browne, Catherine Coulter, Stuart Woods, Greg Iles, and John Jakes. Under the Signet, Onyx, and Roc imprints, NAL publishes both fiction and nonfiction and has recently expanded its trade paperback and hardcover programs in addition to the core mass-market format. As part of NAL's ongoing efforts to initiate new developments in areas of commercial fiction and nonfiction, its editors are looking for strong, innovative authors who offer distinctive voices and original ideas.

For all of NAL, direct queries and SASEs to:

Kara Welsh, Publisher, NAL—Fiction, romance

Claire Zion, Editorial Director—Fiction, including Accent and Eclipse titles

Ellen Edwards, Executive Editor—Fiction, romance, mystery

Tracy Bernstein, Executive Editor—Mystery, romance, nonfiction

Laura Cifelli, Senior Editor—Fiction, thrillers, romance, supernaturals

Mark Chait, Senior Editor—History, politics, humor, health, sports, nonfiction

Kristen Weber, Senior Editor—Crime novels—traditional, noir, thrillers, private eye—and dark chick-lit mysteries

Anne Bohner, Editor—Chick lit, young-adult romance

Becky Vinter, Editor—Romance, including historical and contemporary

Kerry Donovan, Associate Editor—Romance

Brent Howard, Associate Editor—Mystery, thrillers, history, military

Danielle Perez, Editor—Fiction, nonfiction anthology, memoir, humor

Sandy Harding, Editor—Mystery and crime fiction

Jhanteigh Kupihea, Editor—General fiction, women's romance

ACCENT

Accent publishes quality fiction. Some titles include *Rooftops of Tehran* by Mahbod Seraji; *East Hope* by Katharine Davis; *Echoes* by Maeve Binchy; *Nights of Rain and Stars* by Maeve Binchy; and *You Made Me Love You* by Joanna Goodman.

CALIBER

Caliber publishes war memoirs and other military-related material. Some titles include *Shifty Powers: The Band of Brothers Quiet Warrior* by Marcus Brotherton; *With All Thy Might: Life Lessons from My Father, His Father & Our Personal Heroes* by Benjamin Patton; *Gone but Not Forgotten* by Marcus Brotherton; *Shadows in the Jungle: The Alamo Scouts behind Japanese Lines in World War II* by Larry Alexander; and *Alamo in the Ardennes: The Untold Story of the American Soldiers Who Made the Day* by John C. McManus.

OBSIDIAN MYSTERIES

Obsidian Mysteries publishes mystery novels of all kinds. Some titles include *Cool Cache* by Patricia Smiley; *Dial Emmy for Murder* by Eileen Davidson; *Mr. Monk Is Miserable* by Lee Goldberg; *Clubbed to Death* by Elaine Viets; and *The Cat, the Quilt, and the Corpse* by Leann Sweeney.

ONYX

Onyx produces mass-market and trade paperbacks, both reprints and originals. Titles representative of the list include *Lover Revealed: A Novel of the Black Dagger Brotherhood* by J. R. Ward; *Dead Past: A Diane Fallon Forensic Investigation* by Beverly Connor; *A Garden of Vipers* by Jack Kerley; *Unwound* by Jonathan Baine; *Nothing but Trouble* by Michael McGarrity; *The Tooth of Time: A Maxine and Stretch Mystery* by Sue Henry; and *Final Sins* by Michael Prescott.

Recent titles include *Trashed* by Alison Gaylin; *Silent Fall* by Barbara Freethy; *Garden of Darkness* by Anne Frasier; and *The Perfect Fake* by Barbara Parker.

ROC

Roc publishes science fiction and fantasy, reprints and originals, in hardcover, trade paperback, and mass-market formats.

Recent releases include *Chimera* by Rob Thurman; *Prince of Thorns* by Mark Lawrence; *Supervolcano* by Harry Turtledove; *Dead Man's Moon* by Devon Monk; *Grave Witch* by Kalayna Price; *Dead Sexy* by Rachel Caine; and *A Thousand Doors* by Rob Thurman.

SIGNET

This imprint produces mass-market paperback reprints, as well as some original titles in mass-market paperback format.

Recent Signet titles include *The Border Lord's Bride* by Beatrice Small, *Comanche Heart* by Catharine Anderson; *Bound by Honor* by Colette Gale; *The Secret Wedding* by Jo Beverly; and *An Indecent Proposition* by Emma Wildes.

PENGUIN PRESS

Dedicated to publishing literary nonfiction and select fiction, this is an imprint that embraces new writers. Penguin Press publishes 40 titles a year, including those by authors Alan Greenspan, Al Gore, Thomas Pynchon, Ruth Reigl, and Nicholas Wade. In 2005, the Penguin Press introduced The Penguin History of American Life, a series of 50 books that range across all of American history.

Recent titles that are indicative of this list include *Eruption: A Portrait of 21st Century Delhi* by Rana Dasgupta; *The Quantum Universe* by Brian Cox and Jeff Forshaw; *The Thirteenth Step* by David Sheff; *Battle Hymn of the Tiger Mother* by Amy Chua; and *An Ocean Apart* by Terrie Williams.

Direct query letters and SASEs to:

Ann Godoff, President, Publisher

Vanessa Mobley, Editor

Nick Trautwein, Editor—Nonfiction

Jane Fleming, Editor—General fiction

Laura Stickney, Editor—Narrative nonfiction; politics

Eamon Dolan, Editor—Relationship advice, narrative nonfiction, history

PERIGEE BOOKS

Perigee Books, originally created as the trade paperback imprint for G. P. Putnam's Sons, has expanded into hardcover as well as original paperback publishing. This imprint features an eclectic range of nonfiction titles including careers, decorating, cookbooks, parenting, health, fitness, relationships, self-help, humor, puzzles, and memoirs. This house also publishes the *52 Brilliant Ideas* how-to series with recent titles: *Discover Your Roots, Raising Pre-Teens, Land Your Dream Job, Defeat Depression*, and *Boost Your Heart Health.*

Other recent titles include *The Idealist.org Handbook to Building a Better World: How to Turn Your Good Intentions into Actions that Make a Difference* by Stephanie Land; *Petit Appetit: Eat, Drink, and Be Merry: Easy Organic Snacks, Beverages, and Party Foods for Kids of All Ages* by Lisa Barnes; and *POP! Create the Perfect Pitch, Title, and Tagline for Anything* by Sam Horn.

Direct query letters and SASEs to:

John Duff, Publisher

Marian Lizzi, Editor-in-Chief—Prescriptive nonfiction, health/fitness, parenting, relationships and communication

Meg Leder, Editor—Pop culture, lifestyle, communications, fashion

Maria Gagliano, Associate Editor—Lifestyle, health, fashion, cooking, pop culture, craft, business, reference, communications

Jeanette Shaw, Editor—Humor, biography, business and investing

PLUME

Plume, founded in 1970 as the trade paperback imprint of New American Library, is now recognized as one of the preeminent trade paperback imprints. By the 1990s, Plume was publishing 100–120 titles a year, and its backlist currently encompasses approximately 700 titles.

Throughout its history, Plume has been dedicated to giving an opportunity to voices previously neglected by mainstream publishing. The pioneering program in multicultural literature, which began with Toni Morrison and Jamaica Kincaid, has expanded to include groundbreaking works by Latino, African American, and Asian American authors. Plume was also a pioneer in gay publishing, with such classics as Edmund White's *A Boy's Own Story* and Andrew Holleran's *Dancer from the Dance*, which built the foundation for an exceptional gay and lesbian publishing program.

Recent Plume titles include *Confessions of a Teenage Accomplice: Insider Strategies, Advice and Secrets on How to Deal with What Your Kids Won't Tell You* by Vanessa Van Petten; *I'll Be Dead by the Time You Read This: The Evolution of Despair* by Romeo Alaeff; *That's What She Said: 1,001 Uses for the World's Most Versatile Joke* by Justin Wishne and Bryan Nicolas; *Missing Persons* by Clare O'Donohue; and *San Andreas Fault* by James Stinson.

Direct query letters and SASEs to:

Cherise Davis, Editor-in-Chief

Becky Cole, Senior Editor—Health, mystery and crime fiction, pop culture

Ms. Signe Pike, Editor—Literary, historical, commercial fiction; romance; narrative nonfiction, especially pop culture, food, memoir

Nadia Kashpaer, Editor—Humor, pop culture

PORTFOLIO

Portfolio is an imprint that publishes business and career books exclusively. It publishes books in the fields of management, leadership, marketing, business narrative, investing, personal finance, economics, and career advice.

Recent titles include *Purple Cow* by Seth Godin; *The Smartest Guys in the Room* by Bethany McLean and Peter Elkind; *Tough Choices* by Carly Fiorina; *Small Is the*

New Big by Seth Godin; *Andy Grove* by Richard S. Tedlow; and *The Starfish and the Spider* by Ori Brafman and Rod Beckstrom.

Direct queries and SASEs to:

Adrian Zackheim, President and Publisher—Leadership, high-profile memoirs, investing

David Moldawer, Editor—Sports, science, business and investing, finance

Courtney Young, Editor—Relationship advice, history, narrative nonfiction, finance, science nonfiction

Adrienne Schultz, Editor—Business and investing

PRENTICE HALL PRESS

Prentice Hall Press, formerly the trade imprint of Pearson's Prentice Hall Direct Division, was moved to Penguin Group USA in 2002. The list comprises business, health, and self-help/popular reference titles. Acquisitions currently focus on popular reference for career, education, and business communications.

Some titles are *The Language of Trust: Selling Ideas in a World of Skeptics*; *Putting the Power of Your Subconscious Mind to Work: Reach New Levels of Career Success Using the Power of Your Subconscious Mind* by Joseph Murphy, PhD; and *How to Say It on Your Résumé: A Top Recruiting Director's Guide to Writing the Perfect Résumé for Every Job* by Brad Karsh with Courtney Pike.

Amanda Moran, Editor

G.P. PUTNAM'S SONS

For the past fifteen consecutive years, G.P. Putnam's Sons has led the publishing industry with more hardcover fiction and nonfiction *New York Times* bestsellers than any other imprint in the publishing industry. The company began in 1838 when 24-year-old George Putnam joined with John Wiley in the firm Wiley & Putnam. Ten years later, when the two men parted ways, George went into business under his own name where he published such luminaries as William Cullen Bryant, Thomas Carlyle, Samuel Taylor Coleridge, James Fenimore Cooper, Nathaniel Hawthorne, Washington Irving, and Edgar Allan Poe.

Recent titles include *Pursuit* by Karen Robards; *Grave Goods* by Arianna Franklin; *A Quiet Flame* by Philip Kerr; *Corsair* by Clive Cussler and Jack Du Brul; *Dead Silence* by Randy Wayne White; *Just One Wish* by Janette Rallison; and *I'm Sorry You Feel That Way* by Diana Joseph.

Direct query letters with SASEs to:

Neil Nyren, Editor-in-Chief—Serious and commercial fiction and nonfiction

Peternelle van Arsdale, Executive Editor—Fiction and memoir

Christine Pepe, Senior Editor—Women's fiction, mysteries, thrillers, suspense, general nonfiction, parenting

Rachel Kahan, Senior Editor—Fiction, narrative nonfiction

Rachel Holtzman, Assistant Editor—Narrative nonfiction, memoir

RIVERHEAD BOOKS

Founded in 1994 by Susan Petersen Kennedy, Riverhead Books is now well established as a publisher of bestselling literary fiction and quality nonfiction.

Recent titles include *No One Is Here Except All of Us* by Ramona Ausubel; *The Neruda Case* by Roberto Ampuero; *The Great Noodle Bazaar* by Jen Lin-Liu; *A Teaspoon of Earth and Sea* by Dina Viergutz; *The Man With No Money* by Mark Sundeen; and *A Purpose More Obscure* by Gideon Lewis-Kraus.

Direct query letters and SASEs to:

Geoffrey Kloske, Publisher—Narrative nonfiction, biography, fiction

Sean McDonald, Vice President and Executive Editor—Fiction, narrative nonfiction, memoir

Rebecca Saletan, Editorial Director—Cooking, narrative nonfiction, general nonfiction

Jake Morrissey, Executive Editor

Sarah McGrath, Senior Editor—Fiction

Megan Lynch, Senior Editor

Laura Perciasepe, Associate Editor

Sarah Bowlin, Assistant Editor—Fiction

SENTINEL

Sentinel is a politically conservative imprint of Penguin, established in 2003. It has a mandate to publish right-of-center books on politics, history, public policy, culture, and religion. The imprint publishes 10–15 new titles per year, in both hardcover and paperback. The name Sentinel symbolizes a tough-minded defense of America's fundamental values and national interests.

Recent titles include *A Patriot's History of the Modern World* by Larry Schweikart; *Bought and Paid For* by Charlie Gasparino; and *The Tyranny of Cliches* by Jonah Goldberg.

Direct queries and SASEs to:

Adrian Zackheim, President and Publisher

Tim Sullivan, Senior Editor

JEREMY P. TARCHER

Jeremy P. Tarcher publishes some 50 titles annually in both hardcover and paperback, covering a broad spectrum of topics that range from current affairs, social commentary, literary nonfiction, and creativity to spirituality/religion, health, psychology, parenting, business, and other topics. It has had numerous national bestsellers including *Drawing on the Right Side of the Brain* and *Seven Years in Tibet*. Recent bestsellers include *Quarterlife Crisis; Trust Us, We're Experts; and The Hard Questions*. Tarcher also produces paperback reprints of previously published titles.

Recent titles include *The Key* by Whitley Strieber and *Food Fight: How Parents Can Start a School Food Revolution* by Amy Kalafa.

Direct query letters and SASEs to:

Joel Fotinos, Publisher

Mitch Horowitz, Editor-in-Chief—Focuses on new trends in spirituality, science, social thought, personal growth

Sara Carder, Editor—Practical nonfiction, narrative nonfiction

Gabrielle Moss, Editor—How-to nonfiction, relationship advice

VIKING PRESS

PAMELA DORMAN BOOKS

VIKING STUDIO

The Viking Press, founded in 1925 by Harold K. Guinzburg and George S. Oppenheim, swears by the creed "To publish a strictly limited list of good nonfiction, such as biography, history, and works on contemporary affairs, and distinguished fiction with some claim to permanent importance rather than ephemeral popular interest." The firm's name and logo, a Viking ship drawn by Rockwell Kent, were chosen as symbols of enterprise, adventure, and exploration in publishing.

Titles representative of Viking's list include *Eat, Pray, Love: One Woman's Search for Everything Across Italy, India and Indonesia* by Elizabeth Gilbert; *Julia Child* by Laura Shapiro; *The Mistress's Daughter* by A. M. Homes; *Kindness Goes Unpunished: A Walt Longmire Mystery* by Craig Johnson; *Shades of Difference: Mac Maharaj and the Struggle for South Africa* by Padraig O'Malley; *The Friendship: Wordsworth and Coleridge* by Adam Sisman; and *Reading Judas: The Gospel of Judas and the Shaping of Christianity* by Elaine Pagels and Karen King.

Recent releases include *Wake* by Robert J. Sawyer; *Babe Ruth* by Wilborn Hampton; *Before You Were Here, Mi Amor* by Samantha Vamos and Santiago Cohen; *Excellent Emma* by Sally Warner and Jamie Harper; and *Growing Up on the Spectrum: A Guide to Life, Love, and Learning for Teens and Young Adults with Autism and Asperger's* by Lyn Kern Koegel and Claire LaZebnik.

Paul Slovak, Publisher—poetry, literary fiction, beat work (Kerouac and the like), intellectual nonfiction

Wendy Wolf, Executive Editor, Editorial Director for Nonfiction

Molly Stern, Executive Editor, Editorial Director for Fiction

Rick Kot, Executive Editor—Commercial works in nonfiction, current affairs

Carolyn Carlson, Executive Editor—Fiction, memoir

Joy de Menil, Executive Editor

David Cashion, Senior Editor—Nonfiction

Joshua Kendall, Senior Editor—Fiction, nonfiction

Sabila Khan, Editor—Nonfiction

Kendra Harpster, Editor—Fiction

Alessandra Lusardi, Editor—Nonfiction: memoirs, journalism, social science, pop science, pop culture

Kevin Doughten, Associate Editor

PAMELA DORMAN BOOKS

An editor at Viking for more than 19 years, Pamela Dorman has a reputation for spotting debut novels that sell millions of copies. Some of her titles include *Bridget Jones's Diary, The Secret Life of Bees, The Memory Keeper's Daughter,* and *The Deep End of the Ocean.* She has returned to Viking after a brief hiatus at Hyperion to head her own imprint.

Some upcoming titles include *The Thinking Woman's Guide to Real Magic* by Emily Croy Barker; *22 Britannia Road* by Amanda Hodgkinson; *The Last Letter from Your Lover* by Jojo Moyes; *The Poison Tree* by Erin Kelly; *The Age of Ardor* by Jennie Fields.

Pamela Dorman, Director—Fiction

VIKING STUDIO

Viking produces illustrated titles through its imprint, Studio. Titles on Viking Studio's list include *Eric Clapton* by Mark Roberty; *Mr. Marshal's Flower Book: The Royal Collection* by Alexander Marshal; *Sweet Melissa Baking Book* by Melissa Murphy; and *X-Ray: See the World Around You* by Nick Veasey.

Direct query letters and SASEs to:

Megan Newman, Publisher

Lucia Watson, Senior Editor

Jeff Galas, Editor

PENGUIN PUTNAM YOUNG READERS DIVISION

DIAL BOOKS FOR YOUNG READERS

DUTTON CHILDREN'S BOOKS

FIREBIRD

GROSSET & DUNLAP

PHILOMEL BOOKS

PRICE STERN SLOAN

PUFFIN BOOKS

G. P. PUTNAM'S SONS BOOKS FOR YOUNG READERS

RAZORBILL

VIKING CHILDREN'S BOOKS

FREDERICK WARNE

345 Hudson Street, New York, NY 10014

212-414-3600

us.penguingroup.com

Penguin Putnam Books for Young Readers produces titles for children of all ages. This house offers an array of distinctive divisions, imprints, and affiliates of Penguin Putnam's component houses, including Dial Books for Young Readers, Dutton, Firebird, Frederick Warne, Grosset & Dunlap, Philomel, Price Stern Sloan, Puffin Books, and Viking Children's Books, and their newest imprint, Speak. Together, these imprints produce a broad range of titles serving every market in children's book publishing.

DIAL BOOKS FOR YOUNG READERS

Dial Books for Young Readers is a hardcover trade children's book division publishing around 50 titles per year for children from preschool age through young adult, fiction and nonfiction titles. This Penguin Group (USA), Inc., imprint traces its roots to 1880 and the founding of *The Dial*, a monthly literary magazine that published such literary giants as e. e. cummings, T. S. Eliot, D. H. Lawrence, and Gertrude Stein.

Since the children's list was launched in 1961, Dial has been known for books of high literary merit and fine design for readers of all ages. It has pioneered books for the young, including the first quality board books published in the U.S. Dial introduced its Easy-to-Read series in 1979 to publish full-color early readers with popular children's book authors and artists, including James Marshall, creator of the Fox series.

Recent titles include *Moving with the Sun* by Sheila Turnage; *May Queen* by Ruth Long; *Big Bad Baby* by Bruce Hale; *Peanut and Fifi* by Randall de Seve; *Extraordinary* by Nancy Werlin; and *Octopus and Squid* by Tao Nyeu.

Dial Books for Young Readers accepts unsolicited manuscripts of entire picture books or the first ten pages of longer works, with cover letters. Do not include SASEs as they will only contact within four months those authors they want to publish. All other submissions will be recycled without comment. Send submissions through the mail only to:

Lauri Hornik, Vice President and Publisher—Young adult, children's picture books

Susan Kamil, Editorial Director—Memoir, general fiction

Kathy Dawson, Associate Editorial Director

Kate Harrison, Senior Editor—Middle grade, young adult

Robyn Meshulam, Editor—Picture books, middle grade, young adult

Alisha Niehaus, Editor—Picture books

Liz Waniewski, Editor—Picture books

Jessica Garrison, Editor

DUTTON CHILDREN'S BOOKS

Dutton Children's Books is one of the oldest continually operating children's publishers in the U.S. Edward Payson Dutton opened the doors of his Boston bookshop in 1852 and shortly thereafter began to release "fresh and entertaining" books for young readers.

More than 150 years later, Dutton's tagline, "Every book a promise," reflects the imprint's mission to create high-quality books that will transport young readers. Today, the Dutton list looks very different, but its commitment to excellence, freshness, and entertainment has not changed.

The recent list includes *Reversible Verse* by Marilyn Singer; *The Last Christmas Tree* by Stephen Krensky; *Digger's Story* by Priscilla Cummings; *Marvin Makes Music* by Marvin Hamlisch; *Anna and the Boy Masterpiece* by Stephanie Perkins; *The Slayer Journals* by Heather Brewer; and *Antsy Goes on a Cruise* by Neal Shusterman.

Direct query letters and SASEs to:

Julie Strauss-Gabel, Associate Publisher—Middle-grade children's literature, young adult

Maureen Sullivan, Executive Editor—Young adult

Carrie Thornton, Executive Editor

Erika Imranyi, Editor

Steve Meltzer, Editor—Children's picture books

FIREBIRD

Firebird is a paperback science-fiction and fantasy imprint specifically designed to appeal to both teenagers and adults. Launched in January 2002, Firebird books are all reprints, drawn from a variety of sources: the children's imprints at PPI; adult genre imprints (Ace and Roc); outside hardcover houses; and the authors themselves. All have covers by adult genre artists and feature a short essay or autobiography written by their authors. The imprint publishes between 12 and 18 books each year. More information is available at the website: www.firebirdbooks.com.

Some recent titles include *Spirits that Walk in Shadow* by Nina Kirki Hoffman; *Changeling* by Delia Sherman; *High Whulain: A Tale from Redwall* by Brian Jacques; *Dingo* by Charles de Lint; and *Piratica II* by Tanith Lee.

Sharyn November, Editorial Director

GROSSET & DUNLAP

Grosset & Dunlap produces about 125 mass-market children's books each year in hardcover, paperback, library binding, and other formats. Since the 1940s, in addition to the original Nancy Drew and Hardy Boys series, Grosset has published the Illustrated Junior Library. This collection of hardcover editions of *Little Women*, *Tom Sawyer*, and more than 20 other classics is a mainstay of practically every bookstore selling children's books.

Other series include Smart About Art (all about art for kids 5–9); Katie Kazoo; Strawberry Shortcake; Spot; Miss Spider; The Wiggles; The Weebles; and Who Was…? (a biography series for kids 8–11).

Recent titles include *Hello, Gorgeous!* by Taylor Morris; *Splurch Academy for Disruptive Boys* by Julie Berry and Sally Gardner; and *Dinkin Dings and the Frightening Things* by Guy Bass.

Direct query letters and SASEs to:

Francesco Sedita, Vice President and Publisher

Judy Goldschmidy, Editor—Children's middle grade

PHILOMEL BOOKS

Philomel Books was created in the early 1980s from World Publishing Books for Young People, by Editor and Publisher Ann Beneduce. Ms. Beneduce was a pioneer as far as books that would sell to both trade and institutional markets, so for the new list she chose the name Philomel, a term for an English nightingale that means literally "love of learning." The name implied that these books would be distinguished, beautiful in concept and form, fine enough to be sought as gifts, and original and handsome enough to be bought by libraries and schools.

Headed these days by President and Publisher Michael Green, who joined the imprint in 1991 as an editorial assistant and never left, Philomel still looks toward fostering a love of reading in children and young adults.

Some recent titles from Philomel include *The Theory of Everything* by Kari Luna; *Big Hug, Little Hugs* by Felicia Bond; *Ollie and Claire* by Tiffany Strelitz; *The Crayon Chronicles* by Drew Daywalt; and *Andrew Henry's Meadow* by Doris Burn.

Michael Green, President and Publisher—Children's picture books

Patricia Lee Gauch, Editor-at-Large

Kiffin Steuer, Editor

Jill Santopolo, Editor—Young adult, middle-grade children's literature

Tamra Tuller, Editor—Middle-grade children's literature

PRICE STERN SLOAN

Price Stern Sloan (PSS) was founded in Los Angeles in the 1960s to publish the Mad Libs series that Roger Price and Leonard Stern had concocted during their stint as writers for Steve Allen's *Tonight Show*. Along with their partner Larry Sloan, they expanded the company into a wide variety of publishing categories, especially children's books, novelty formats, and humor. The company's proprietary brands include Mad Libs, Wee Sing, Mr. Men & Little Miss, Serendipity, Crazy Games, and Doodle Art.

With about 75 titles per year, PSS continues to publish successfully its proprietary brands, as well as titles that fall into the preschool children's mass merchandise categories. PSS also produces a successful annual list of desk calendars and occasional humor titles for the adult market. In addition to producing original titles, this imprint reissues previously published books.

Recent titles include *Mad Art: At the Beach* by Salina Yoon; *Mommy Loves Me* by John and Wendy; *More Mad for Miley: An Unauthorized Biography* by Lauren Alexander; *Peace, Love and Mad Libs* by Roger Price and Leonard Stern; *Hide and Squeak* by Ed Heck; and *Easter at Grandma's* by Emily Bolam.

Direct query letters and SASEs to:

Francesco Sedita, Vice President and Publisher

PUFFIN BOOKS

Puffin Books was founded on a strong literary tradition and a commitment to publishing a successful mix of classic children's fiction and brand new literature for children. Over the years, Puffin has transformed from a small, yet distinguished paperback house into one of the largest and most diverse children's publishers in the business, publishing everything from picture books to groundbreaking middle-grade and teen fiction. In addition to publishing new editions of quality literary fiction, Puffin has started several original series with broad commercial appeal.

Puffin produces titles for young readers in every age group: lift-the-flaps and picture books for young children, Puffin Easy-to-Reads for first-time readers, Puffin Chapters and historical and contemporary fiction for middle-graders, and critically acclaimed novels for older readers under the Speak imprint. The house has a backlist packed with award-winning children's literature, including Robert McCloskey's

Caldecott Medal winner *Make Way for Ducklings*; Ludwig Bemelmans's Caldecott Honor book *Madeline*; and Don Freeman's classic *Corduroy*.

Classic Puffin picture book titles include *The Gingerbread Boy* by Ludwig Bemelmans, illustrated by Jan Brett; *The Very Hungry Caterpillar* by Eric Carle; *Strega Nona* by Tomie dePaola; *The Snowy Day* by Ezra Jack Keats; and *Max and Ruby* by Rosemary Wells.

Middle-graders and teen readers titles include *Time Cat* and *The Chronicles of Prydain* by Lloyd Alexander; *Charlie and the Chocolate Factory* by Roald Dahl; *Amber Brown* by Paula Danziger; *The Outsiders* by S.E. Hinton; *Pippi Longstocking* by Astrid Lindgren; *Roll of Thunder, Hear My Cry* by Mildred D. Taylor; and *Miracle's Boys* by Jacqueline Woodson.

Recent titles include *Virtual Kombat* by Chris Bradford; *Alice à Paris* by Robin Palmer; *Young Samurai: The Book of Rings* by Chris Bradford; *Wereworld* by Curtis Jobling; *Cass Around the World* by Linda Gerber; and *Casey Collier, Snoop for Hire* by John Madormo.

Direct query letters and manuscripts with SASEs to:

Eileen Bishop Kreit, President and Publisher

Jennifer Bonnell, Editor

Angelle Pilkington, Editor

Karen Chaplin, Editor—Middle-grade children's literature

Shannon Park, Editor—Young adult

G. P. PUTNAM'S SONS BOOKS FOR YOUNG READERS

G. P. Putnam's Sons Books for Young Readers publishes about 60 trade hardcover books for children per year. It publishes popular novels and picture books for toddlers to middle-readers, aged 9–12.

G. P. Putnam's Sons is the home of celebrated picture-book creators Tomie dePaola, Jan Brett, Eric Hill, Rachael Isadora, Maira Kalman, Keiko Kasza, and Peggy Rathmann. Award-winning authors for older readers include Joan Bauer, Paula Danziger, Jean Fritz, Vicki Grove, Suzy Kline, Robin McKinley, Jacqueline Woodson, and Laurence Yep.

Recent titles include *Sensible Hare and the Case of the Carrots* by Daren King and David Roberts; *The Song of Francis* by Tomie dePaola; *Thank You, God, For Everything* by August Gold and Wendy Halperin; and *Uh-oh, Cleo: Underpants on My Head* by Jessica Harper and Jon Berkeley.

Direct queries and SASEs to:

Stacey Barney, Director

Susan Kochan, Editorial Director

RAZORBILL

Razorbill, which launched in Fall 2004, is dedicated to publishing teen and tween books for "kids who love to read, hate to read, want to read, need to read." A typical Razorbill book is contemporary commercial fiction, with a high-concept plot hook and a fresh, eye-catching package—a book that a young reader will pick up on his or her own. The imprint publishes between 30 and 40 new titles a year, both stand-alone titles and limited series (3–6 books.) Formats range from paperback to hardcover, with an emphasis on alternative formats and trim sizes. Hardcovers and trade paperbacks appear in mass-market formats 12–18 months after initial publication.

Recent titles include *Giant Man-Eating Frogs with Hideous Fangs!* by Richard Farr; *Ripple* by Mandy Hubbard; *Across the Universe* by Beth Revis; *Department 19* by William Hill; *Firecracker* by David Iserson; *The Probability of Miracles* by Wendy Wunder; and *Karma* by Cathy Ostlere.

Ben Schrank, President and Publisher—Young adult

Kristen Pettit, Editor

Jessica Rothenberg, Associate Editor—General fiction, young adult

Lexa Hillyer, Editor

Brianne Mulligan, Editor—Young adult

VIKING CHILDREN'S BOOKS

Viking Children's Books, founded in 1933, publishes approximately 60 titles per year, ranging from books for very young children, such as board and lift-the-flap books, to sophisticated fiction and nonfiction for teens. The current Viking list is known for classic characters such as Madeline, Corduroy, Pippi Longstocking, Roald Dahl's Matilda, Rosemary Wells's Max and Ruby, The Stinky Cheese Man, Cam Jansen, and Froggy.

Among the groundbreaking titles published by Viking are *The Outsiders* (1969), still the bestselling young-adult book ever published; *The Snowy Day* (1963), which brought multicultural books mainstream recognition; and *The Stinky Cheese Man* (1992), widely hailed for its innovative design.

Recent titles include *Audition* by Stasia Ward Kehoe; *The Edge of Nowhere* by Elizabeth George; *A Diamond in the Desert* by Kathryn Fitzmaurice; *In a Mood* by Tameka Brown; *Sophie's Fish* by A.E. Cannon; and *The Slave Next Door* by Kim Purcell.

Direct query letters and SASEs to:

Regina Hayes, Publisher

Joy Peskin, Editor—Children's picture books, young adult

Tracy Gates, Editor

Catherine Frank, Associate Editor—Middle-grade children's literature, children's picture books

Kendra Levin, Editor—Young adult

FREDERICK WARNE

Frederick Warne was founded in 1865 by a bookseller turned publisher. The hallmarks of the publishing program are spin-offs of historic original works, such as books by authors Beatrix Potter and Cicely Mary Barker.

Recent titles include *Return to Fairyopolis* by Cicely Mary Barker; *Miss Potter: The Novel* by Richard Maltby, Jr.; *The Miniature World of Peter Rabbit*; and *Quack Quack with Peter Rabbit* by Beatrix Potter.

Sally Floyer, Managing Director

SECTION TWO

INDEPENDENT U.S. PRESSES

INDEPENDENT U.S. PRESSES

JEFF HERMAN

I get to see things a bit differently as an agent than I would as a writer. As discussed elsewhere, publishing houses have more or less fallen into two huge categories: the "globalized" conglomerates, and everyone else. The former can be counted on the fingers of one hand, yet they constitute at least half of all trade book revenues. The latter are countless in number and always expanding like an unseen universe.

Some of these players—the "micro-presses" not included here—have revenues that could be rivaled by a nine-year-old's lemonade stand. Whereas others are eight-figure operations.

Together the "independents" are the other half of the game. As a unified force, they are smaller than they were a decade ago, and are likely to keep getting smaller. But as their market-share shrinks, their indispensability only grows.

The choice of the word "independent" reflects the best word I could come up with, but it's not a perfect description. There are shades of gray, as in all things. Here you will find a few imprints of major houses that I felt operate in a particularly independent fashion. There are also cases where an independent house is distributed by one of the large mega-publishers, and it is listed here rather than with its large umbrella house.

In the end, it's quality that counts, not quantity. And the long-term consequences of the growing consolidation in the industry are not clear yet. Dominance leads to comfort, which leads to inertia. When the asteroids return, it's the ponderous dominators who will be the first to fall.

But it wasn't me who predicted that the meek will inherit the Earth.

So welcome to the world of the independent publisher. Rest assured, we have been very careful not to include any vanity publishers or "fly-by-nights" who will take your money and promise the world without any intention of delivering. The publishing houses we have included are established and reputable.

Independent publishers tend to be more open to direct queries and proposals from authors, rather than requiring that work be submitted through agents.

For some, an independent press might be a stepping-stone to a mega-press. For others, the right independent house is exactly the place to be. Often, a smaller press is able to offer more editorial attention, more authorial involvement throughout the process, and a more focused, long-term involvement with specialized audiences of readers and their communities.

It all depends—on you, your work, and on the methods of the publisher involved. So study each listing that seems of possible interest and look closely at their books.

In all cases, be sure to scrutinize their guidelines and prepare your material carefully. You want to put your best foot forward, and a clear query, followed by a well-written, well-organized proposal, is just as important for a small house as for a large one.

ABBEVILLE PUBLISHING GROUP

ABBEVILLE PRESS

ABBEVILLE FAMILY

ARTABRAS

137 Varick Street, 5th Floor, New York, NY 10013

212-366-5585   fax: 212-366-6966

www.abbeville.com   email: abbeville@abbeville.com

Since 1977, Abbeville has published a wide variety of distinctive art, photographic, and illustrated books. With an active backlist of over 700 titles, Abbeville Publishing Group releases approximately 40 new titles annually in subjects ranging from the arts, gardening, fashion, and food and wine to travel and history. Titles are published in hardcover and trade paperback editions, with close attention given to production standards. Abbeville also produces printed gift items.

ABBEVILLE PRESS

The Abbeville Press imprint publishes fine art and illustrated books for an international readership. Their Tiny Folio and miniSeries lines include palm-sized volumes popular in the gift shop sections of museums and bookstores.

Recent titles from Abbeville Press include *Caravaggio* by John T. Spike; *Discovering the Arts of Japan: A Historical Overview* by Tsuneko S. Sadeo and Stephanie Wada; *The Horse: From Cave Paintings to Modern Art* by Jean-Louis Gouraud, Michel Woronoff, and Henri-Paul Francfort; *The Human Figure and Jewish Culture* by Eliane Strosberg; and *Turkish Art and Architecture* by Giovanni Curatola.

ABBEVILLE FAMILY

Abbeville Family is an imprint for high-quality illustrated books that appeal to the youth market, especially designed to teach children about ways of seeing the world by interacting with art. Recent titles from Abbeville Family include *T. Rex and the Great Extinction* by Matteo Bacchin and Marco Signore; *Sometimes It's Grandmas and Grandpas: Not Mommies and Daddies* by Gayle Byrne and Mary Haverfield; *123 Caterpillar* by Calino; *Animal Fables* by Aesop Charles Perrault, Marie-France Floury, and Jacob and Wilhelm Grimm; *Giant vs. Giant: Argentinosaurus* by Matteo Bacchin and Marco Signore.

ARTABRAS

The Artabras imprint makes select Abbeville titles available at bargain prices. Some titles include *Ansel Adams: The National Park Service Photographs* by Ansel

Adams and Alice Gray; *The Art of Florence* by Glenn M. Andrews et al; and *Hot Rods and Cool Customs* by Pat Ganahl.

Abbeville Press is not currently accepting unsolicited book proposals. Should they decide to expand their list in the future, they'll post a notice on their website. Abbeville Kids is accepting submissions in parenting subjects and illustrated books for all ages of children.

Cynthia Vance, Editor

ABC-CLIO

P.O. Box 1911, Santa Barbara, CA 93116-1911

805-968-1911/800-368-6868   fax: 866-270-3856

www.abc-clio.com

GREENWOOD PUBLISHING GROUP

88 Post Road West, Box 5007, Westport, CT 06881-5007

203-226-3571   fax: 203-222-1502

www.greenwood.com   email: editorial@greenwood.com

HEINEMANN USA

361 Hanover Street, Portsmouth, NH 03801

603-431-7894

www.heinemann.com   email: proposals@heinemann.com

Established in 1953, ABC-CLIO is a family-owned business specializing in history reference. It annually publishes approximately 80 encyclopedias, guides, and handbooks for teachers, students, and scholars. Its best-known reference works are the annotated *Historical Abstracts* and *America: History and Life*, both accessible online, which together represent the largest bibliographic history database in the world. Since 1961, ABC-CLIO has won over 80 best-reference awards from the American Library Association and Library Journal. They also have a large e-book program, with all reference book titles published in both print and electronic formats.

The company's corporate headquarters are in Santa Barbara, California, with offices in Denver, Colorado, and Oxford, England. ABC-CLIO was founded by Eric Boehm and is headed today by Ron Boehm.

ABC-CLIO recently became the publisher for Greenwood Books and all associated imprints.

ABC-CLIO's publishing focus is on American and world history, politics, law, government, geography, popular and traditional culture, current issues, and history of religion, science, technology, and medicine. They generally accept single volume titles of approximately 80,000 to 150,000 words.

Recent ABC-CLIO titles include *The 21st Century Elementary Library Media Program* by Carl A. Harvey II; *Abolition and John Brown's Raid* by Lee W. Eysturlid, Jeremy Gypton, Chris Mullin, and Brett Peirsma; *Climate Change: A Reference Handbook* by David L. Downie et al; *Gangs: A Reference Handbook* by Karen L. Kinnear; and *Mormonism: A Historical Encyclopedia* by E. Paul Reeve and Ardis E. Parshall.

Query letters or proposals with CVs and SASEs should be addressed to the attention of the Editorial Director, Books.

GREENWOOD PUBLISHING GROUP

GREENWOOD PRESS

PRAEGER PUBLISHERS

LIBRARIES UNLIMITED

The Greenwood Publishing Group is one of the world's leading publishers of reference titles, academic and general interest books, texts, books for librarians and other professionals, and electronic resources. With over 18,000 titles in print, GPG publishes some 1,000 books each year, many of which are recognized with annual awards from Choice, Library Journal, the American Library Association, and other scholarly and professional organizations.

For submissions to Praeger and Greenwood, please classify your project as either reference (Greenwood Press) or non-reference (Praeger), and send your proposal to the appropriate editor. If you cannot identify the appropriate editor, or if you are writing on an interdisciplinary topic such as women's studies, send an email outlining your proposal to editorial@greenwood.com or send via mail to the Acquisitions Department. Send proposals or queries via email or regular mail with SASEs.

GREENWOOD PRESS

GPG imprint Greenwood Press publishes reference books in all subject areas taught in middle schools, high schools, and colleges, as well as on topics of general interest. Their many award-winning titles in the social sciences and humanities range from in-depth multivolume encyclopedias to more concise handbooks, guides, and even biographies.

Recent titles from Greenwood include *Documenting Steppe Empires and Silk Roads: Historical Sources on the World of Genghis Khan* by George Lane; *America's Service Meltdown: Restoring Service Excellence in the Age of the Customer* by Raul Pupo; *Boy Culture* by Shirley Steinberg et al; *Contesting History: The Bush Counterinsurgency Legacy in Iraq* by Matthew Flynn; and *The Cultural Context of Medieval Music* by Nancy Van Deusen.

Jeff Olsen—Business and economics; jeff.olsen@greenwood.com

Kristi Ward—Contemporary music, popular culture and media, sports; kristi .ward@greenwood.com

Sandy Towers—Current events, media literacy; sandy.towers@greenwood.com

Wendi Schnaufer—Food, social issues, world cultures, multicultural/African American/Latino American/Asian American/Native American issues; wendi .schnaufer@greenwood.com

Debby Adams—Health and medicine, high school reference, young-adult literature, arts; debra.adams@greenwood.com

Kevin Downing—Health and medicine; kevin.downing@greenwood.com

George Butler—Literature/college reference; gbutler@greenwood.com

PRAEGER PUBLISHERS

GPG Imprint Praeger Publishers has a distinguished history (since 1949) of producing scholarly and professional books in the social sciences and humanities, with special strengths in modern history, military studies, psychology, business, current events and social issues, international affairs, politics, visual and performing arts, and literature. Praeger books serve the needs of scholars and general readers alike by providing the best of contemporary scholarship to the widest possible audience.

Recent titles from Praeger include *Diversity in Mind and in Action* by Jean Lau Chin; *Religious Myths and Visions of America* by Christopher Buck; *Women in India* by Sita Raman; *Light, Bright, and Damned Near White* by Stephanie Bird; and *Gender and Violence in the Middle East* by David Ghanim.

Suzanne Staszak-Silva—Crime, literature, religion; sstaszak@greenwood.com

Daniel Harmon—Contemporary music, popular culture and media, sports, arts; daniel.harmon@greenwood.com

Robert Hutchinson—Interdisciplinary; robert.hutchinson@greenwood.com

Debora Carvalko—Psychology, social work; dcarvalk@greenwood.com

Adam Kane—Military history; adam.kane@greenwood.com

LIBRARIES UNLIMITED

Libraries Unlimited serves the needs of the library profession through quality publications for library and information science students and faculty, practicing librarians, media specialists, and teachers. Titles include *100+ Literacy Lifesavers: A Survival Guide for Librarians and Teachers K–12* by Pamela S. Bacon and Tammy K. Bacon; *American Reference Books Annual: 2009* by Shannon Graff Hysell; and *Best Books for High School Readers, Grades 9–12* by Catherine Barr and John T. Gillespie.

For Libraries Unlimited submissions, please query one of the editors listed below via email prior to sending a proposal.

Barbara Ittner—Public library and high school reference books; barbara .ittner@lu.com

Sharon Coatney—School library books; sharon.coatney@lu.com

Sue Easun—Textbooks and reference books; sue.easun@lu.com

HEINEMANN USA

Heinemann USA is a national leader in the publishing of professional books for teachers of language arts K–12, and has growing lists in math, science, social studies, and art education. In 1987, Boynton/Cook, the leading publisher of professional books for English teachers at the middle and high school levels and for college English teachers, joined Heinemann. The company also has an active presence in several niche markets, most notably in theater and arts, and Third World writing, with literature lists in the Caribbean, Asia, Middle East, and Africa.

Recent Heinemann titles include *Classroom Reading Assessments* by Frank Serafini; *Code-Switching Lessons* by Rebecca Wheeler and Rachel Swords; *What's the Big Idea?* by Jim Burke; *Reading Ladders* by Teri Lesesne; and *The Drama of AIDS* by Michael Kearns.

To submit to Heinemann, email proposals@heinemann.com or send your proposal or query via regular mail with SASE to the Acquisitions Editor.

ABINGDON PRESS

DIMENSIONS FOR LIVING

KINGSWOOD BOOKS

201 Eighth Avenue South, P.O. Box 801, Nashville, TN 37202-0801

615-749-6000

www.abingdonpress.com

Abingdon Press is one of the oldest houses in religious publishing. It has been in existence since 1789 and began as an imprint of the United Methodist Publishing House. Its efforts expanded in the 1920s with books in many different subject areas such as academics, inspirational, and materials for church communities. In the early 1920s, Abingdon began publishing a wide array of academic, professional, inspirational, and life-affirming religious literature with the goal of enriching church communities across the globe.

Abingdon is open to a wide range of subject matter, which provides opportunity for writers who do not fit within the more narrow guidelines of other houses. Abingdon looks to include popular material as long as it has contemporary spiritual and ethical themes that influence the lives of its readership. For example, in *50 Ways to Pray: Practices from Many Traditions and Times*, Teresa A. Blythe considers a wide variety of prayer types, gleaned from centuries-old practices of Christian spiritual leaders, including the Christian mystics.

Abingdon publishes hardback and paperback editions, covering religious specialty, religious trade, and popular markets. They also publish professional reference and resources for the clergy, as well as academic and scholarly works in the fields of religious and biblical history and theory. One new example of an adult Bible study book is *Hurry Less, Worry Less at Christmastime* by Judy Christie. This book helps busy people learn to celebrate more joyfully, peacefully, and deeply during the "holiday season" between Thanksgiving and New Year's Day.

Abingdon also issues several series of books for children and resources for Sunday school and general Christian education.

Recent Abingdon titles include *Faith Beyond Borders: Doing Justice in a Dangerous World* by Don Mosley; *Introduction to World Religions* by Jacob Neusner; *Hurry Less, Worry Less for Families* by Judy Christie; *The Gifts of the Small Church* by Jason Byassee; *Lord, Give Me Patience, and Give It to Me Right Now!* by James Moore; and *This We Believe: The Core of Wesleyan Faith and Practice* by William Willimon.

Dimensions for Living Books help Christian apply their faith to daily life. Recognizing that living faithfully in today's world isn't easy, Dimensions for Living offers daily mediations, inspiration, practical suggestions, faith-filled advice, and other helps for Christian living.

Kingswood Books is an academic imprint devoted the scholarly works in all periods and areas of Methodist and Wesleyan studies. This imprint honors John Wesley's lifelong commitment to an informed and reflective Christian life.

DIMENSIONS FOR LIVING

Dimensions for Living is an imprint of Abingdon devoted to general-interest religious trade books on practical Christian living. It publishes inspiration, devotion, self-help, home and family, as well as gift volumes. The editorial approach is to combine contemporary themes with mainstream Christian theology. "Quality books that celebrate life and affirm the Christian faith."

Dimensions for Living titles include *Lessons I Learned From My Grandchildren* by Delia Halverson; *Healing Where It Hurts* by James W. Moore; *Goodbye, Murphy's Law: Whatever Can Go Wrong, God Can Make Right* by Judy Pace Christie; *My Tummy Talked in Church Today* by Christy Colby Heno; and *The Wide Open Spaces of God: A Journey with God through the Landscapes of Life* by Beth Booram.

KINGSWOOD BOOKS

Kingswood Books is an Abingdon imprint that publishes scholarly works in all areas of Methodist and Wesleyan studies. The imprint honors John Wesley's lifelong commitment to the Christian lifestyle. This commitment, which found expression in his extensive writing and publishing, took form in his establishment of the Kingswood School, near Bristol, England.

Recent Kingswood titles include *Doctrine in Experience: A Methodist Theology of Church and Ministry* by Russell E. Richey; *The Manuscript Journal of the Rev. Charles Wesley, M.A., Vol. 1* by S. T. Kimbrough, Jr. and Kenneth G. C. Newport; and *Early Methodist Spirituality* by Paul W. Chilcote.

In addition to distributing its own books, Abingdon Press handles the lists of several other smaller religious publishers. Dimensions for Living is currently no longer producing new titles. No multiple submissions. Query letters and SASEs should be directed to:

Shirley Briese, Submissions Editor

Gary Alan Smith, Music Resources Senior Development Editor

HARRY N. ABRAMS, INC.

ABRAMS BOOKS

ABRAMS BOOKS FOR YOUNG READERS

ABRAMS IMAGE

AMULET BOOKS

STEWART, TABORI & CHANG

115 West 18th Street, 6th Floor, New York, NY 10011

212-206-7715   fax: 212-519-1210

www.hnabooks.com

Harry N. Abrams, Inc. (HNA), is a prominent publisher of high-quality art and illustrated books. This house publishes and distributes approximately 250 titles annually and currently has more than 2,000 titles in print. HNA encompasses Abrams Books, Stewart, Tabori & Chang, Abrams Books for Young Readers, Amulet Books for Middle Grade and Young Adult, and Abrams Image.

Abrams is a specialist house and acquires nonfiction projects on a selective basis, giving particular weight to the national or international renown and credentials of artists, photographers, and writers. Their illustrated volumes (mainly in hardcover, with some trade paperback editions and series, as well as works in electronic formats) focus primarily on the fields of fine art, architecture, design, anthropology, archaeology, ethnology and culture, gardening and the home, crafts especially knitting, literary and art criticism, world history, travel, the natural sciences, and the creative use of technology and new media.

Abrams Books titles include *(un)Fashion* by Tibor Kalman and Maira Kalman; *1,000 Ways to Be a Slightly Better Woman* by Pamela Redmond Satran; *1000 Years of English Literature* by Chris Fletcher; *1900* by Robert Rosenblum and Maryanne Stevens; and *20000 Years of Fashion* by Francois Boucher.

Eric Himmel, Editor-in-Chief, Abrams

Deborah Aaronson, Editorial Director, Abrams

ABRAMS BOOKS FOR YOUNG READERS

Authors of middle-grade and young-adult fiction should not overlook Abrams Books for Young Readers. Abrams Books for Young Readers include *Library Mouse: A Friend's Tale* by Daniel Kirk; *All in a Day* by Cynthia Rylant; *Beyond* by Michael Benson; *My First Nursery Book* by Franciszka Themerson; *Good Night, Baby Ruby* by Rohan Henry.

Susan Van Metre, Senior Editor

ABRAMS IMAGE

The Abrams Image imprint focuses on edgy pop culture books, but also had a best-seller with the 2007 book about philosophy, *Plato and a Platypus Walk into a Bar: Understanding Philosophy Through Jokes* by Thomas Cathcart and Daniel Klein.

Abrams Image titles include *11,002 Things to Be Miserable About* by Lia Romeo and Nick Romeo; *Poem in Your Pocket* edited by Elaine Bleakney; *Spott's Canine Miscellany* by Mike Darton; and *Itty Bitty Kitty Ditties* by Alex Boies and Tim Hodapp.

Leslie Stoker, Publisher

David Cashion, Editorial Director

AMULET BOOKS

Amulet has a bestselling series, *The Sisters Grimm* by Michael Buckley, and publishes books for teens. Some other titles are *Diary of a Wimpy Kid* by Jeff Kinney; *My Life in Pink & Green* by Lisa Greenwald; and *Escape the Mask* by David Ward.

Susan Van Metre, Senior Editor

STEWART, TABORI & CHANG

Stewart, Tabori & Chang editor Melanie Falick is one of the most respected publishing professionals focusing on crafts, especially knitting. This imprint also releases bestselling lifestyle, environmental, and food titles.

Stewart, Tabori & Chang titles include *1,000 Ways to Be a Slightly Better Woman* by Pamela Redmond Satran; *1,001 Reasons to Love Dogs* by Christine Miele and Mary Tiegreen; and *100 Years of Oz* by Willard Carroll and John Fricke.

Leslie Stoker, Publisher

Melanie Falick, Editorial Director—Knitting, crafts

Dervla Kelly, Editor—Style, lifestyle

Luisa Weiss, Senior Editor—Cookbooks, food narratives
Abrams distributes its own books in the U. S. and Canada.

Query letters and SASEs should be directed to the Editorial Department of the specific imprint to which you are submitting. If you are a nonfiction author, proposals may be sent directly to Abrams Books for Young Readers and Amulet Books and to Abrams Books only. Due to heavy volume, Stewart, Tabori, & Chang cannot accept unsolicited book proposals at this time, and Abrams Books for Young Readers and Amulet Books cannot accept unsolicited works of fiction (picture books, novels, or related formats).

ACADEMY CHICAGO PUBLISHERS

363 West Erie Street, 7E, Chicago, IL 60654

312-751-7300/800-248-READ   fax: 312-751-7306

www.academychicago.com   email: info@academychicago.com

A small press with a noteworthy list, Academy Chicago publishes general nonfiction, art, history, and cultural studies, as well as fiction (including mysteries). The house also offers a line of classic reprints. Academy Chicago makes notable contributions to American letters.

Nonfiction from Academy Chicago includes popular works with an emphasis on contemporary culture, current events, and historical interpretation. The house does not publish science fiction, thrillers, cookbooks, self-help, books dealing with the supernatural, horror, books of photography, children's books, or books with explicit, gratuitous sex and violence.

Recent Academy Chicago titles include *Backstabbers: The Reality of Politics* by Rickey Hendon; *Who Shall Live: The Wilhelm Bachner Story* by Samuel Oliner and Kathleen Lee; *Prisoners: A Novel* by Burt Zollo; *The Lodger* by Marie Belloc Lowndes; and *Lady Molly of Scotland Yard* by Baroness Orczy.

Academy Chicago handles its own distribution. All submissions must be by regular mail, not by email or by fax. Send the first three to four chapters, synopsis, cover letter and SASE to the Editorial Department.

Anita Miller, Editorial Director

ACCESS MED BOOKS [SEE THE MCGRAW-HILL COMPANIES]

ADAMS MEDIA

Owned by F+W Publications

POLKA DOT PRESS

PLATINUM PRESS

PROVENANCE PRESS

57 Littlefield Street, Avon, MA 02322

508-427-7100   fax: 800-872-5628

www.adamsmedia.com

This midsize trade house has long been known for specific, high-quality content and impressive design. Primary areas of interest covered are business, leadership, parenting, pets, personal finance, motivational guidance, travel, weddings, and writing. Adams publishes both single-title breakouts and signature series, and releases under three imprints: Platinum Press, Polka Dot Press, and Provenance Press.

With their motto, "Value looks good," Adams Media particularly innovates in the fields of business, self-help, and New Age how-to books. Since being acquired by F + W Publications in 2003, Adams has been extending its reach and now has a list with over 300 books in 25 categories.

National bestsellers in the single-title category include *A Beginner's Guide to Day Trading Online* by Toni Turner; *Why Men Love Bitches* by Sherry Argov; *Please Stop Laughing at Me* by Jodee Blanco; *The Verbally Abusive Relationship* by Patricia Evans; and the teen hit, *Mean Chicks, Cliques and Dirty Tricks* by Erika V. Shearin Karres. Career and business bestsellers like Martin Yate's *Knock 'Em Dead* and Stephan Schiffman's *Closing Techniques* are also popular.

Perhaps the best known of Adams Media's output is the Everything series. This is the ubiquitous user-friendly how-to series with titles like *The Everything Father's First Year Book* and *The Everything Dog Book*. The Streetwise line is dedicated specifically to the small businessperson. The Cup of Comfort and Small Miracles series are meant to inspire readers with anthologies of true stories. Many of these anthologies have regular calls for submissions on the Adams Media website.

Recent Adams Media titles include *Dream So Big* by Christopher B. Pearman with Ian Blake Newhem; *Size Sexy* by Stella Ellis; *The Everything Father-to-Be Book* by Kevin Nelson; and *The Everything Kids' Easy Science Experiments Book* by J. Elizabeth Mills.

Paula Munier, Director of Acquisitions and Innovation—New brands, new series, inspiration, trends, self-help, women's interest, general trade

Meredith O'Hayre, Associate Project Manager—General interest

Peter Archer, Associate Editor—Business, personal finance, reference

Brendan O'Neill, Assistant Editor—Business, humor reference, general trade

Lisa Laing, Managing Editor—Everything Series

POLKA DOT PRESS

The Polka Dot Press imprint specializes in nonfiction for female readers ages 18–35. Polka Dot Press aims to bring the witty energy of chick lit to the self-help shelf. Recent titles include *The 10 Women You'll Be Before You're 35* by Alison James; *28 Days* by Gabrielle Lichterman; *Tales from the Scale* by Erin J. Shea; and *The Dating Cure* by Rhonda Findling.

Chelsea King, Associate Editor

PLATINUM PRESS

Platinum Press publishes prescriptive books on emerging trends in management, leadership, and investing for businesspeople. Platinum titles include *Get Them on Your Side* by Sam Bacharach; *Creating We* by Judith Glaser; and *Done Deal* by Michael Benoliel.

PROVENANCE PRESS

The Provenance Press imprint adds to the New Age shelf with "sophisticated books for the intermediate practitioner." Titles include *Power Spellcraft for Life* by Arin Murphy-Hiscock; *The Way of the Hedge Witch: Rituals and Spells for Hearth and Home* by Arin-Murphy-Hiscock; and *The Healing Power of Faery: Working with Elementals and Nature Spirits to Soothe the Body and Soul* by Edain McCoy.

Andrea Norville, Assistant Editor

Adams does its own distribution in the U.S., also operating through wholesales and jobbers. In the UK and elsewhere, Adams distributes via overseas distributors.

Adams Media welcomes book proposal submissions, including those from first-time authors. Mail your proposals with SASEs to "Book Proposals."

Karen Cooper, Publisher

A. K. PETERS, LTD.

5 Commonwealth Rd., Suite 2C, Natick, MA

508-651-0887   fax: 508-651-0889

www.akpeters.com   email: editorial@akpeters.com

A. K. Peters, founded in 1992 by Alice Peters and Klaus Peters, is a leading independent scientific technical publisher that specializes in computer science, mathematics, computer graphics, game development, history of science, and physics. The list ranges from textbooks to advanced professional publications, a range of specialist trade titles, and scholarly monographs. A. K. Peters publishes around 20 new titles annually, and has over 200 titles in print. The guiding principle behind the company is its philosophy of working in service to the scientific community.

Recent titles from A. K. Peters include *Bright Boys: The Making of Information Technology* by Tom Green; *Computational Photography: Mastering New Techniques for Lenses, Lighting, and Sensors* by Ramesh Raskar and Jack Tumblin; *Computer Graphics: Theory and Practice* by Jonas Gomes, Luis Velho, and Mario Costa Sousa; and *Differential Geometry of Curves and Surfaces* by Thomas Banchoff and Stephen Lovett.

Send queries and SASEs to:

Alice Peters, Publisher

Klaus Peters, Publisher

ALLWORTH PRESS

10 East 23rd Street, Suite 510, New York, NY, 10010

212-777-8395   fax: 212-777-8261

www.allworth.com

Allworth specializes in practical business and self-help books for creative professionals—artists, designers, photographers, writers, filmmakers, and performers, as well as books about business, law, and personal finance for the general public. Founded in 1989 by author, attorney, and artists' rights advocate Tad Crawford, the press first published a revised edition of *Crawford's Legal Guide for the Visual Artist*. Later titles offered helpful advice to both artists and to the general public on marketing, promotion, pricing, copyright, contracts, safety on the job, personal finance, and more. Today, Allworth Press publishes 40 titles annually and has a full-time staff of ten. The press has also published books of contemporary and classic critical writings on the visual arts.

Recent noteworthy titles from Allworth include *Interior Design Clients: The Designer's Guide to Building and Keeping a Great Clientale* by Thomas L. Williams; and *Interior Design Practice* edited by Cindy Coleman.

Allworth Press enjoys excellent relationships with a number of publishing partners including the School of Visual Arts, the American Institute of Graphic Arts, the American Society of Media Photographers, the Authors Guild, *Communication Arts* magazine, the Direct Marketing Institute, and the Graphic Artists Guild.

With over 250 titles in print, Allworth Press continues to publish practical guidance for creative people. Suggestions and insights are welcomed as an aid in determining the best projects and authors for the future.

Query letters and SASEs should be directed to:

Tad Crawford, Publisher

Robert A. Porter, Associate Publisher

ALPHA BOOKS [SEE PEARSON/PENGUIN GROUP]

ALYSON PUBLICATIONS

245 West 18th Street, Floor 12, New York, NY 10011

212-209-5175

www.alyson.com

Alyson Publications is the leading publisher of books by, for, and about lesbians, gay men, bisexuals, and transgender people from all economic and social segments of society and all ages. In fiction and nonfiction format, Alyson books explore the political, financial, medical, spiritual, social, and sexual aspects of gay, lesbian, bisexual, and transgender people and their contributions to and experiences of society.

Recent titles include *Persistent Voices: An Anthology of Poets Lost to AIDS* edited by Philip Clark and David Groff; *Holy Terror* by Mel White; *Once a Marine* by Eric Alva with Sam Gellegos; *The Weaklings* by Dennis Cooper; and *Crossfire* by Staceyann China.

Direct queries and SASEs to:

Don Weise, Publisher; publisher@alyson.com

AMACOM (AMERICAN MANAGEMENT ASSOCIATION)

1601 Broadway, New York, NY 10019-7420

212-586-8100   fax: 212-903-8168

www.amanet.org

AMACOM is the book publishing division of the American Management Association. AMACOM's titles focus on business and professional leadership issues. They explore the changing workplace, the old and new concerns of managers of all kinds, and the means of improving team performance.

AMACOM trade nonfiction lines include works that cover the fields of accounting and finance, customer service, human resources, international business, manufacturing, organization development, strategy, information and communication technology, personal finance, marketing, advertising and public relations, personal development, small business, supervision, sales, management, and training. AMACOM Books is now publishing books in health, parenting, emerging sciences, current events, and public policy.

AMACOM seeks world-class educators, successful executives, business owners, trainers, consultants, and journalists—all eager to share their insights and techniques with a broad audience. The primary audience is managers in large and small companies looking to improve their effectiveness, make their organizations more competitive, keep up with current trends and thinking, energize their staff, and inspire employees at all levels. AMACOM readers are definitely not mass-market consumers. They want specialized materials and information on business issues that concern them most. AMACOM book buyers want more than a quick fix. They crave in-depth ideas and practical approaches they can try out on the job. They like to be on the leading edge and get a jump on the competition. They do not want secondhand information. They want to go straight to the source.

Noteworthy titles from AMACOM's list include *Transnational Leadership Development* by Beth Fisher-Yoshida and Kathy D. Geller; *A Class with Drucker* by William A. Cohen; *Freeing Tibet* by John Roberts II and Elizabeth Roberts; *Want It, See It, Get It!* by Gini Graham Scott; *The ROI of Human Capital* by Jac Fitzenz; *Identifying and Managing Project Risk* by Rom Kendrick; and *Managing Your Government Career* by Stewart Liff.

AMACOM distributes its own products through multiple marketing channels, including retail trade, direct marketing, special sales, and international sales (through McGraw-Hill).

Proposals and SASEs should be directed to the appropriate editor:

Ellen Kadin, Executive Editor—Marketing, career, communication skills, parenting, biography/memoirs, current events, pop psychology; Ekadin@amanet.org

Bob Nirkind, Senior Editor—Real estate, sales, customer service, parenting, biography/memoirs, current events; Rnirkind@amanet.org

Christina M. Parisi, Executive Editor—Management, human resources, leadership, parenting, biography/memoirs, current events; cparisi@amanet.org

AMERICAN PSYCHIATRIC PUBLISHING, INC.

1000 Wilson Boulevard, Suite 1825, Arlington, VA 22209-3901

703-907-7322   fax: 703-907-1091

www.appi.org   email: appi@psych.org

American Psychiatric Publishing, Inc. (APPI), is one of the most respected publishers of books, journals, and multimedia on psychiatry, mental health, and behavioral science. The house releases professional, reference, and trade books, as well as college textbooks. APPI publishes a midsize booklist in hardcover and trade paper and also produces a number of professional journals. Selected reference works are issued in electronic formats.

APPI is a wholly owned subsidary of the American Psychiatric Association. Its purpose is twofold: to serve as the distributor of publications of the Association and to publish books independent of the policies and procedures of the American Psychiatric Association. APPI has grown since its founding in 1981 into a full-service publishing house, including a staff of editorial, production, marketing, and business experts devoted to publishing for the field of psychiatry and mental health.

Under the direction of Robert E. Hales, MD, and John McDuffie, editorial acquisition and development have the highest priority at APPI. APPI is unique in the extent to which it uses peer review in both the selection and final approval of publishing projects. Proposals are reviewed and developed at the earliest stages by an Editorial Board that brings psychiatric expertise from a diverse spectrum of the field. Full manuscripts are then peer-reviewed in their entirety, with final acceptance of the manuscript dependent on appropriate response to the peer reviews. Each year more than 200 projects are reviewed by as many as 750 specialist reviewers, and fewer than 30 are accepted in the typical year.

Although by far the major portion of the American Psychiatric list is geared toward the professional and academic markets, the house catalogs a small number of books in the areas of patient information and books for the general public, among which are selected titles marketed through trade channels.

Recent noteworthy titles from APPI include *Clinical Manual of Psychopharmacology in the Medically Ill* edited by Stephen Ferrando et al; *Introductory Textbook of Psychiatry* by Donald Black, MD et al; *Obsessive-Compulsive Spectrum Disorders: Refining the Research Agenda for DSM-V* by Eric Hollander, MD et al; and *Religious and Spiritual Issues in Psychiatric Diagnosis: A Research Agenda for DSM-V* by John Peteet, MD et al.

American Psychiatric Publishing is also the publisher of the profession's acknowledged clinical guide-book, *Diagnostic and Statistical Manual of Mental Disorders (4th edition, text revision)*, also known as *DSM-IVTR*.

American Psychiatric Publishing distributes through several regional distribution services.

To receive full consideration, prospective authors must submit a completed Author Questionnaire, found on the APPI website. Query letters and SASEs should be directed to:

John McDuffie, Editorial Director

Kourtney Skinner, Manager, Editorial Support Services

AMERICAN PSYCHOLOGICAL ASSOCIATION, INC.

MAGINATION PRESS

750 First Street, NE, Washington, DC 20002-4242

800-374-2721/202-336-5792   fax: 202-336-5502

www.apa.org   email: books@apa.org

Based in Washington, D.C., and founded in 1892, the American Psychological Association (APA) is a scientific and professional organization that represents psychology in the United States. With 150,000 members, APA is the largest association of psychologists worldwide. In their publications, the APA aims to promote psychological knowledge and the usefulness of psychologists through high standards of ethics, conduct, education, and achievement. They hope to advance scientific interests and inquiry, and the application of research findings to the promotion of health, education, and the public welfare.

Virtually all aspects of psychology are examined in APA publications: methodology, history, student aids, teaching, health, business strategies, violence, personality, and clinical issues. APA produces books, journals, publishing resources, continuing-education/home-study programs, audiocassettes, videotapes, and databases. Life Tools is a special series of APA books written to help the general public find the best advice that psychology can offer.

Recent entries in the APA list include *Prevention of Treatment Failure: The Use of Measuring, Monitoring, and Feedback in Clinical Practice* by Michael Lambert; *Individual Pathways of Change: Statistical Models for Analyzing Learning and Development* edited by Peter Molenaar et al; *Elusive Alliance: Treatment Engagement Strategies with High-Risk Adolescents* by David Casto-Blanco and Marc Karver; and *Earning a Living Outside of Managed Health Care: 50 Ways to Expand Your Practice* edited by Steven Walfish.

MAGINATION PRESS

Magination Press is an APA children's imprint that publishes innovative books to help children ages 4–18 deal with the challenges and problems they face growing up. Topics include everyday situations, such as starting school and the growing family, as well as more serious psychological, clinical, or medical problems, such as divorce, depression, anxiety, asthma, attention disorders, bullying, death, and more. Formats include picture books, illustrated readers, interactive books, and nonfiction.

Examples of recent Magination titles are *Take the Time: Mindfulness for Kids* by Maud Roegiers; *Phileas's Fortune: A Story About Self-Expression* by Agnes de Lestrade; *Black Jack Jetty: A Boy's Journey Through Grief* by Michael Carestio; and *Eli's Lie-O-Meter: A Story About Telling the Truth* by Sandra Levins.

Query letters and SASEs should be directed to:

Edward Porter, Editorial Assistant (APA Books)

Julia Frank-McNeil, Director (APA Books)

Shenny Wu, Editorial Assistant (Magination Press)

Becky Shaw, Editor (Magination Press)

AMERICAN SOCIETY FOR TRAINING AND DEVELOPMENT (ASTD) BOOKS

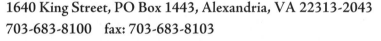

1640 King Street, PO Box 1443, Alexandria, VA 22313-2043

703-683-8100   fax: 703-683-8103

www.astd.org   email: customercare@astd.org

ASTD Books is a business-information specialist providing guides on workplace learning and performance, HR development, management, career building, consulting, teamwork, IT issues, and creative problem solving. In addition to books, ASTD offers training kits, diagnostic tools, presentation materials, games and simulations, videos, audiocassettes, and computer software.

Founded in 1944, ASTD Books is the publishing wing of the American Society for Training and Development, a nonprofit membership organization. ASTD aims to address the most current workplace topics, the most innovative techniques, and the most experienced authors in the field. Books listed in the ASTD catalog are reviewed and selected by a distinguished and professional peer group.

Recent titles from ASTD include *Riding the Tiger: Leading Through Learning in Turbulent Times* by Priscilla Nelson and Ed Cohen; *The New Social Learning* by Tony Bingham and Marcia Conner; and *Evidence-Based Training Methods: A Guide for Training Professionals.*

ASTD Books distributes its own list via a catalog, easy ordering and an online store. Some ASTD books are available through other publishing houses. ASTD also distributes and co-publishes books from a variety of other business-oriented publishers, including McGraw-Hill, Jossey-Bass, Berrett-Koehler, and others. ASTD also distributes through Amazon.com.

If you are writing on a book targeted to trainers that you think ASTD might like to publish, please contact ASTD at 703-683-9205. Guidelines for submitting a book proposal are available upon request. Query letters and SASEs should be directed to:

Mark Morrow, Senior Acquisitions Editor; mmorrow@astd.org

AMG PUBLISHERS

GOD AND COUNTRY PRESS

LIVING INK BOOKS

6915 Shallowford Road, Chattanooga, TN 37421

800-266-4977/423-894-6060   fax: 800-265-6690/423-894-9511

www.amgpublishers.com   email: info@amgpublishers.com

AMG Publishers was created by AMG International in the 1960s with the sole purpose of teaching the Word of God as a beacon to a lost world. AMG has a broad interest in biblically oriented books including biblical reference, applied theology and apologetics, Christian ministry, Bible study books in the Following God series format, Christian living, women/men/family issues, single/divorce issues, contemporary issues, (unique) devotionals, inspirational, prayer, gift books, and young-adult fantasy fiction. AMG produces about 30 books per year.

AMG Publishers' focus is on books that help the reader get into the Bible, facilitate interaction with Scripture, encourage and facilitate a reader's personal growth in areas such as personal devotion and skillful use of the Bible, and encourage studying, understanding, and applying Scripture.

Recent examples include *The Ark, the Reed, & the Fire Cloud* by Jenny Cote; *Battlefield Blessings* by Larkin Spivey; *Life Principles from the Women of Acts* by Xavia Arndt Sheffield; *Making Disciples in Your Community* by Barbara Henry; *Second Corinthians: Grace Under Siege* by Dan Mitchell; and *First & Second Thessalonians: Watching and Waiting* by Mike Stallard.

GOD AND COUNTRY PRESS

God and Country Press is a new imprint that publishes books dealing with themes of Christianity and war, patriotism, history, faith, and politics. Some titles from God and Country Press include *The Faith of America's First Ladies* by Jane Hampton Cook; *The Faith of America's Presidents* by Daniel Mount; *The Pledge: One Nation Under God* by William J. Murray; *Stories of Faith and Courage from World War II* by Larkin Spivey; and *Stories of Faith and Courage from the War in Iraq & Afghanistan* by Jane Hampton Cook.

LIVING INK BOOKS

Living Ink Books is an imprint of AMG Publishers that focuses on subjects like Christian living, fiction, inspirational and devotional, and specialty gift book products. This imprint also publishes several series, including Matterhon the Brave, Oracles of Fire, Angel Light, Dragons in Our Midst, Made Simple, and Twenty-third Psalm.

Recent Living Ink titles include *The Bones of Makaidos* by Bryan Davis; *The Ark, the Reed, and the Fire Cloud* by Jenny Cote; *Last of the Nephilim* by Bryan Davis; *The Believer's Guide to Legal Issues* by Stephan Bloom; *Not My Child: Contemporary Paganism and the New Spirituality* by Linda Harvey; *Angela's Answer* by Pat Matuszak; and *Prayer: The Timeless Secret of High-Impact Leaders* by Dave Earley.

Query by email or regular mail with SASE to:

Rick Steele, Editor, Acquisitions, Bible study, Christian living

---

AMULET BOOKS [SEE HARRY N. ABRAMS, INC.]

ANDREWS MCMEEL PUBLISHING

ACCORD

1130 Walnut Street, Kansas City, MO 64106

800-851-8923   fax: 816-932-6684

www.andrewsmcmeel.com

Andrews McMeel Publishing (AMP), a division of Andrews McMeel Universal, is a leading publisher of general nonfiction trade books, gift and humor books, and calendars, publishing as many as 300 new works annually. Its titles—such as *The Complete Far Side* by Gary Larson and *The Blue Day Book* by Bradley Trevor—have enjoyed long stays on the *New York Times* bestseller lists. In recent years, Andrews McMeel Publishing has expanded its scope and now offers books on a wide range of subjects (popular culture and lifestyles, popular psychology, self-help, and women's issues) appealing to readers of all ages and interests.

Recent titles are *All Wound Up: The Yarn Harlot Writes for a Spin* by Stephanie Pearl-McPhee; *The Good Neighbor Cookbook: 125 Easy and Delicious Recipes to Surprise and Satisfy the New Moms, New Neighbors...* by Sara Quessenberry and Suzanne Schlosberg; *Love Bugs: A Bug-Eyed View of Romance* by Maryjo Koch;

Shapes and Colors: A Cul de Sac Collection by Richard Thompson; and *Tastes Like Chicken: An Argyle Sweater Treasury* by Scott Hilburn.

ACCORD

AMP publishes children's books under the Accord imprint. Recent titles include *Bee & Me* by Elle J. McGuinness and Heather Brown; *Silly Dogs* by Gandee Vasan; *Here's Looking at You: In Your Dreams* by Leslie Jomath and Jana Christy; and *Eyeball Animation Drawing Book: African Safari Edition* by Jeff Cole.

AMP is also the country's premier calendar publisher, annually publishing calendars based on many top-selling properties such as The Far Side, Dilbert, Disney, Mary Engelbreit, and Jeopardy! Gift books, such as those from the Tiny Tomes series, are also a specialty of this house.

Agents, please query. No unsolicited manuscripts are accepted. Query letters should be addressed: Attn. Book Submissions.

JuJu Johnson, Acquisitions—All categories

Kirsty Melville, Publisher—Cooking

Christine Schillig, Editor-in-Chief—General nonfiction

Dorothy O'Brien, Vice President and Managing Director—Humor, general nonfiction

Patty Rice, Senior Editor, Book Division/Editorial Director, Gift Books—General nonfiction, gift books

Jean Lucas, Senior Editor—General nonfiction, illustrated books, humor, New Age

Lane Butler, Editor—Humor

THE APEX PRESS

THE BOOTSTRAP PRESS

Council on International and Public Affairs

777 United Nations Plaza, Suite 3C, New York, NY 10017

800-316-2739/212-972-9877   fax: 212-972-9878

Branch office:

P.O. Box 337, Croton-on-Hudson, NY 10520

www.cipa-apex.org   email: cipa@cipa-apex.org

Introduced in 1990, the Apex Press is an imprint of the nonprofit research, education, and publishing group the Council on International and Public Affairs (CIPA).

Apex publishes books to build a better world: hardcover and paperback titles offering critical analyses of and new approaches to economic, social, and political issues in the United States, other industrialized nations, and the Third World. Subjects include corporate accountability, grassroots and worker organization, and intercultural understanding. The primary focus is on justice, human rights, and the impact of technology on contemporary society.

The Council on International and Public Affairs was founded in 1954 and is a nonprofit research, education, and publishing group. The Council seeks to further the study and public understanding of problems and affairs of the peoples of the United States and other nations of the world through conferences, research, seminars and workshops, publications, and other means.

The Apex Press is the official publisher of books for POCLAD (the Program on Corporations, Law, and Democracy). POCLAD is a group dedicated to instigating conversations and actions to contest the authority of corporations to define culture, control governments, and to plunder the earth.

Titles from Apex Press include *Gaveling Down the Rabble: How "Free Trade" Is Stealing Our Democracy* by Jane Anne Morris; *Through Japanese Eyes, 4th Edition* by Richard H. Minear; *The Rule of Property* by Karen Coulter; *Through Indian Eyes, 5th Edition* by Donald J. Johnson and Jean E. Johnson; and *Through Chinese Eyes, 3rd Edition: Tradition, Revolution, and Transformation* by Edward Vernoff and Peter J. Seybolt.

The Apex Press handles its own distribution. The house catalog includes books and additional resources (including videos) from a number of publishers worldwide.

THE BOOTSTRAP PRESS

The Bootstrap Press (inaugurated in 1988) is an imprint of the Intermediate Technology Development Group of North America (ITDG/North America) in cooperation with the Council on International and Public Affairs. Bootstrap's publishing interest focuses on social economics and community economic change; the house covers small-scale and intermediate-scale or appropriate technology in both industrialized and emerging countries, with an aim to promote more just and sustainable societies. Its books explore business and industry theory and how-to, gardening and agriculture, building and construction, and communications.

Representative titles from Bootstrap include *Chicken Little, Tomato Sauce, and Agriculture: Who Will Produce Tomorrow's Food?* by Joan Dye Gussow; *A World That Works: Building Blocks for a Just and Sustainable Society* edited by Trent Schroyer; and *Greening Cities: Building Just and Sustainable Communities* by Joan Roelofs.

Bootstrap publications are distributed with those of sibling operation the Apex Press.

For both Apex and Bootstrap, email queries are preferred: cipa@cipa-apex.org. Letters and SASEs should be directed to:

Ward Morehouse, Publisher

APPLAUSE [SEE HAL LEONARD CORPORATION]

ARCADE PUBLISHING

116 John Street, #2810, New York, NY 10038

212-475-2633   fax: 212-353-8148

www.arcadepub.com   email: info@arcadepub.com

Arcade Publishing (founded in 1988 by Jeannette and Richard Seaver) produces commercial and literary nonfiction, as well as selected poetry. Nonfiction standouts include issue-oriented titles, contemporary human-interest stories, and cultural historical works. Arcade's fiction list includes entrants in such categories as mystery, suspense, and thrillers. Arcade's program leans toward learned and enlightened reading. They have brought to the North American reading public works by 252 authors from 31 different countries.

Recent titles include *Urban Animals: A Comic Field Guide* by Mireille Silcoff; *The Templars: The Secret History Revealed* by Barbara Frale; *A Brief History of the Future* by Jacques Attali; *Capital Punishment: An Indictment by a Death-Row Survivor* by Billy Sinclair and Jodie Sinclair; *Promised Virgins: A Novel of Jihad* by Jeffrey Fleishman; and *The Johns: Sex for Sale and the Men Who Buy It* by Victor Malarek.

Arcade Publishing is distributed by Hachette Book Group USA.

Arcade Publishing accepts submissions and queries only from agents. Query letters and SASEs should be directed to:

Jeannette Seaver, Publisher

Calvert Barksdale, Executive Editor

Casey Ebro, Editor

JASON ARONSON, INC., PUBLISHERS [SEE ROWMAN & LITTLEFIELD PUBLISHING GROUP]

ATLANTIC BOOKS [SEE GROVE/ATLANTIC, INC.]

AUGSBURG FORTRESS BOOKS

FORTRESS PRESS

100 South Fifth Street, Suite 600, Minneapolis, MN 55402-1222

Mailing address:

P.O. Box 1209, Minneapolis, MN 55440-1209

612-330-3300/800-426-0115 fax: 612-330-3455

www.augsburgfortress.org email: booksub@augsburgfortress.org

Augsburg Fortress, the publishing house of the Evangelical Lutheran Church in America, publishes titles in popular and professional religious categories. The publishing house produces about 100 books each year. The Augsburg Fortress list accents works of interest to general readers, in addition to books that appeal primarily to a mainstream religious readership and a solid selection of works geared to professional clergy and practitioners of pastoral counseling.

Categories include theology and pastoral care, biblical and historical academic studies, the life and tradition of Martin Luther, self-improvement and recovery, and books for younger readers from nursery to young adults.

Recent titles include *A Field Guide to Contemporary Worship: How to Begin and Lead Band-Based Worship* by Andrew Boesenecker and James Graeser; *The Dialogue Comes of Age: Christian Encounters with Other Traditions* edited by John Cobb, Jr., and Ward McAfee; *The Emergence of Christianity: Classical Traditions in Contemporary Perspective* by Cynthia White; *The Emergence of Buddhism* by Jacob Kinnard; and *Anatomy of the New Testament* by Robert Spivey et al.

Authors should note: Augsburg Fortress prefers to receive a proposal rather than a completed manuscript.

FORTRESS PRESS

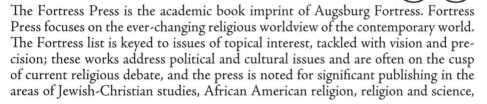

The Fortress Press is the academic book imprint of Augsburg Fortress. Fortress Press focuses on the ever-changing religious worldview of the contemporary world. The Fortress list is keyed to issues of topical interest, tackled with vision and precision; these works address political and cultural issues and are often on the cusp of current religious debate, and the press is noted for significant publishing in the areas of Jewish-Christian studies, African American religion, religion and science, and feminist theology. The Fortress market orientation tilts toward both the general trade and the religious trade.

Titles from Fortress Press include *Christians and War: A History of Practices and Teachings* by A. James Reimer; *Green Christianity: Five Ways to a Sustainable Future* by Mark I. Wallace; *New Proclamation: Year C, 2010, Easter to Christ the King* by David B. Lott; *The Bible: An Introduction* by Jerry L. Sumney; and *The Priestly Vision of Genesis I* by Mark S. Smith.

Query letters and SASEs should be directed to Book Submissions via regular mail or email: booksub@augsburgfortress.org.

Beth Lewis, President and CEO

AVALON BOOKS

160 Madison Avenue, 5th Floor, New York, NY 10016

212-598-0222   fax: 212-979-1862

www.avalonbooks.com   email: editorial@avalonbooks.com

Established as an imprint of Thomas Bouregy & Company, Inc., in 1950, the aim of the Avalon Books (not to be confused with the Avalon Publishing Group) is to provide readers with quality fiction in a variety of genres. The emphasis has always been on good and wholesome entertainment primarily for distribution to library and institutional markets on a subscriber basis. The specialties are mystery, mainstream romance, historical romance, and traditional genre Westerns. Avalon also produces a line of literary classics in reprint (on the Airmont Classics imprint).

The house emphasis on new original novels caters to the tastes and preferences of the all-important library readership. Stories should consist of those likely to be of high interest to the patrons of this wholesome core market. The house publishes 60 books per year.

Recent titles from Avalon Books include *Love 'em or Leave 'em* by Angie Stanton; *On the Crest of a Wave* by Fran McNabb; *Island Intrigue* by Marty Ambrose; and *Denim Ryder* by Stone Wallace.

Submit a two to three page synopsis and the first three chapters of a manuscript, along with SASE to the editors. Physical queries are preferred for now, but email submissions are acceptable: editorial@avalonbooks.com.

Face Black, Editor

Chelsea Gilmore, Associate Editor

AVALON TRAVEL PUBLISHING [SEE PERSEUS BOOKS GROUP]

B&H PUBLISHING GROUP

127 9th Avenue, North, MSN 114, Nashville, TN 37234-0115

1-800-448-8032   fax: 1-615-251-3914

www.bhpublishinggroup.com

B&H is the trade publishing division of LifeWay Christian resources, owned by the Southern Baptist Convention. Formerly Broadman & Holman, this house began as a producer of Bibles, textbooks and reference books. It is now a major publisher of Christian living, fiction, youth, and history for the Christian market. The B&H Español imprint focuses on Spanish-language titles.

B&H bestsellers include *Praying God's World* by Beth Moore, and *Experiencing God* by Dr. Henry Blackaby, as well as Oliver North's novels and Chuck Norris's autobiography.

In 2004, the company's Holman Bible division introduced the new *Holman Christian Standard Bible (HCSB)* translation. It is also the largest publisher of Spanish language Bibles in the United States.

Recent titles include *Double Cross* by James Jordan; *The Power of Prayer and Fasting* by Ronnie Floyd; *Simple Life* by Thom and Art Rainer; *Black Belt Patriotism* by Chuck Norris.

Submit query with SASE to:

David Shepherd, Publisher

Thomas Walters, Senior Acquisitions Editor

BAEN PUBLISHING ENTERPRISES

P.O. Box 1108, Wake Forest, NC 27587

919-570-1640

www.baen.com   email: info@baen.com

Baen publishes science-fiction and fantasy writing. The house's new releases are generally published in mass-market paperback format with targeted lead titles produced in trade paper and hardcover editions. Baen is also a prominent publisher of fiction series, collections, and anthologies geared to various subgenre traditions in science fiction and fantasy.

Founded in 1984, Baen concentrates its concise list on its proven categories of publishing strength. Baen's roster of writers includes John Ringo, Harry Turtledove, Martin Scott, Mercedes Lackey, Murray Leinster, Andre Norton, Lois McMaster Bujold, and Eric Flint.

Writers are encouraged to familiarize themselves with the house output. For science fiction, solid plot-work with scientific and philosophical undercurrents is a must. For fantasy, magical systems must be coherent and integral to the plot. For any Baen title, style need never call attention to itself.

Recent titles from the Baen catalog are *Belisarius II: Storm at Noontide* by Eric Flint and David Drake; *The Rolling Stones* by Robert A. Heinlein; *Duainfey* by Sharon Lee and Steve Miller; *Better to Beg Forgiveness* by Michael Z. Williamson; and *One Day on Mars* by Travis S. Taylor.

Electronic submissions are strongly preferred. Due to spam, submissions are no longer accepted by email. Send manuscripts using the submission form at http://ftp.baen.com/Slush/submit.aspx. Only Rich Text Format (.rtf) files are accepted. Further details are available on the website. No multiple submissions. Query letters and SASEs may be directed to:

Toni Weisskopf, Publisher

BAKER PUBLISHING GROUP

BAKER ACADEMIC

BAKER BOOKS

BETHANY HOUSE

BRAZOS PRESS

CHOSEN BOOKS

FLEMING H. REVELL

SPIRE BOOKS

Baker Publishing Group, 6030 East Fulton Road, Ada, MI 49301

Mailing address:

P.O. Box 6287, Grand Rapids, MI 49516-6287

616-676-9185   fax: 616-676-9573

www.bakerpublishinggroup.com

Baker Publishing Group is a major player in the Christian book market. Their mission is to publish writings that promote historic Christianity, irenically express the concerns of evangelism, and reflect the diversity of this movement. At the 2006 Christianity Today Book Awards, Baker Publishing Group won six, more than any other single publisher. Taking top honors in the Christian Living category was Ron Sider's *The Scandal of the Evangelical Conscience* (Baker Books). *Dictionary for the Interpretation of the Bible* by Kevin Vanhoozer (Baker Academic) took the top award in the Biblical Studies category. Awards of Merit went to *Real Sex: The Naked Truth About Chastity* (Brazos Press); *Startling Joy* (fiction, Fleming H. Revell); *The Changing Face of World Missions* (Baker Academic); and *Is the Reformation Over?* (Baker Academic).

BAKER ACADEMIC

As a Christian academic publisher, Baker Academic seeks thoughtful and scholarly works that enhance the pursuit of knowledge within the context of the Christian faith. Baker Academic publishes textbooks, reference books, and scholarly works.

The main areas of specialty are biblical studies, theology (biblical, systematic, and historical), and church history. They also publish works in the areas of Christian education, Christian mission, and integrative works in a variety of liberal arts disciplines (e.g., literature, communication, ethics, psychology).

Recent Baker Academic titles include *The Temple in the Gospel of Mark* by

Timothy Gray; *Jesus and the Land* by Gary Burge; *When God Shows Up: A History of Protestant Youth Ministry in America* by Mark Senter; *The Worship Architect* by Constance Cherry; and *Magnifying God in Christ* by Thomas Schreiner.

Baker Academic welcomes submissions from authors with academic credentials. Send a proposal by post or email (submissions@bakeracademic.com)

BAKER BOOKS

The primary focus of the Baker trade division is the church. It publishes for pastors and church leaders, concentrating on topics such as preaching, worship, pastoral ministries, counseling, and leadership. Topics include the intersection of Christianity and culture, discipleship, spirituality, encouragement, relationships, marriage, and parenting. In addition, Baker trade publishes books that enable parents to pass their faith to their children.

Highlighting the Baker program: *Christless Christianity: The Alternative Gospel of the American Church* by Michael Horton; *A Great and Terrible Love: A Spiritual Journey into the Attributes of God* by Mark Galli; *The Great Emergence* by Phyllis Tickle; *Heaven's Calling: A Memoir of One Soul's Steep Ascent* by Leanne Payne; and *Holy Questions: Encountering Jesus' Provocative Questions* by Winn Collier.

Baker Books accepts manuscripts only through literary agents. All unsolicited manuscripts received will be returned to the sender without review.

BETHANY HOUSE

www.bethanyhouse.com   fax: 952-996-1304

Recognized as a pioneer and leader in Christian fiction, Bethany House publishes nearly 120 titles annually in subjects including historical and contemporary fiction, Christian living, family, health, devotional, children's, classics, and theology. Bethany House titles are often found on the Christian bestseller lists.

Recent titles include *A Dream to Follow* by Lauraine Snelling; *Flight to Heaven* by Capt. Dale Black and Ken Gire; *No More Christian Nice Girl* by Phil Coughlin and Jennifer Degler; *Once Upon a Summer* by Janette Oke; and *The Winds of Autumn* by Janette Oke.

Bethany House only accepts one-page facsimile proposals directed to Adult Nonfiction, Adult Fiction, or YA/children editors. Detailed tips for writing a successful query are on the Bethany House website; in general, familiarize yourself with the Bethany House list and read their books, tell the editor why you chose to query them, and deliver a fantastic one-paragraph description of your manuscript. Fax to 952-996-1304.

BRAZOS PRESS

P.O. Box 4287, Wheaton, IL 60189

www.brazospress.com   email: rclapp@brazospress.com

Brazos Press is a publisher of theology and theologically-based cultural criticism, grounded in and growing out of the Great Tradition common to Roman Catholic, Eastern Orthodox, Anabaptist, Protestant, and Protestant evangelical Christianity.

Recent titles include *Apocalypse and Allegiance* by J. Nelson Kraybill; *Claiming Abraham: Reading the Bible and the Qur'an Side by Side* by Michael Lodahl; *Revelation* by Joseph Mangina; *Unlearning Protestantism* by Gerald Schlabach; *Death and Afterlife* by Terence Nichols.

Send a short proposal, CV, and one or two sample chapters via email with attachment or by regular mail to:

Rodney Clapp, Editorial Director

CHOSEN BOOKS

Chosen is the division of Bethany that explores the ministry of the Holy Spirit in areas like intercessory prayer, spiritual warfare, evangelism, prophecy, healing, and general charismatic interest. Several hundred titles over more than 30 years, from Charles Colson's *Born Again* to Cindy Jacobs's *Possessing the Gates of the Enemy*, reflect the publishing mandate of Chosen Books to publish well-crafted books that recognize the gifts and ministry of the Holy Spirit and help readers live more empowered and effective lives for Jesus Christ.

Recent titles include *This Day We Fight!* by Francis Frangipane; *Unbound* by Neal Lozano; *Crushing the Spirits of Greed and Poverty* by Sandie Freed; *Discerning and Defeating the Ahab Spirit* by Steve Sampson; and *Money and the Prosperous Soul* by Stephen DeSilva.

Chosen Books accepts manuscripts only through literary agents. All unsolicited manuscripts received will be returned to the sender without review.

FLEMING H. REVELL

Revell looks for practical books that help bring the Christian faith to everyday life. The list includes fiction, Christian living, self-help, marriage, family, and youth books.

Recent titles include *My Middle Child, There's No One Like You* by Dr. Kevin Leman; *3 Things Kids Need the Most* by Fred Hartley III; *Finding Hope When Life's Not Fair* by Lee Ezell; *Journey to the Well* by Diana Wallis Taylor; *Michal: A Novel* by Jill Eileen Smith; *100 Amazing Answers to Prayer* by William J. Petersen; and *Against All Odds* by Irene Hannon.

Revell accepts manuscripts only through literary agents. All unsolicited manuscripts received will be returned to the sender without review.

BARRICADE BOOKS, INC.

185 Bridge Plaza North, Suite 308-A, Fort Lee, NJ 07024

201-944-7600   fax: 201-944-6363

www.barricadebooks.com   email: customerservice@barricadebooks.com

Barricade publishes nonfiction and welcomes provocative material; its mission is to publish books that preserve, protect, and extend the First Amendment. House interests include arts and entertainment, pop culture, cultural studies, biography, history, politics and current events, true crime, Jewish interest, New Age, psychology, health and sexuality, and how-to/self-help.

Barricade Books was founded in 1991 by veteran publisher Lyle Stuart, who had previously founded Lyle Stuart, Inc. (Lyle Stuart, Inc., was sold and eventually became the Carol Publishing Group before Carol closed its doors in late 1999.) Barricade was launched in order to continue the tradition begun in 1956, when Lyle Stuart left his career as a newspaper reporter to become a publisher. That tradition is to specialize in books other publishers might hesitate to publish because the books are too controversial.

Recent titles from Barricade include *Terrorist Cop* by Mordecai Dzikansky and Robert Slater; *Jailing the Johnston Gang* by Bruce Mowday; *Gaming the Game* by Sean Patrick Griffin; *The Mafia and The Machine* by Frank Hayde; and *Battle of the Two Talmuds* by Leon Charney and Saul Mayzlish.

Complete proposals (including author bio, marketing plan, comparative titles, and sample chapters) and SASEs should be directed to:

Carole Stuart, Publisher

Allan Wilson, Senior Editor

BARRON'S/BARRON'S EDUCATIONAL SERIES, INC.

250 Wireless Boulevard, Hauppauge, NY 11788

800-645-3476   fax: 631-434-3723

www.barronseduc.com   email: barrons@barronseduc.com

Founded in 1941, Barron's Educational Series, Inc., rapidly became a leading publisher of test preparation manuals and school directories. Among the most widely recognized of Barron's many titles in these areas are its SAT I and ACT test prep books, Regents Exams books, and Profiles of American Colleges. In recent years,

Barron's has expanded into many other publishing fields, introducing extensive lines of children's books, foreign language learning books and cassettes, pet care manuals, New Age books, cookbooks, business and financial advice books, parenting advice books, and art instruction books, as well as learning materials on audiocassette, VCR, Compact Disc, and CD-ROM. On average, Barron's publishes up to 300 new titles a year and maintains an extensive backlist of well over 2,000 titles. The focus remains educational.

The house offers a number of practical business series, retirement and parenting keys, programs on skills development in foreign languages (as well as in English), healthy cooking, arts and crafts techniques, biographies of well-known artists, and home and garden titles. Books on pets and pet care include numerous titles keyed to particular breeds and species of birds, fish, dogs, and cats.

Children's and young-adult books and books of family interest include series on pets, nature and the environment, dinosaurs, sports, fantasy, adventure, and humor. Many of these are picture storybooks, illustrated works, and popular reference titles of general interest.

Barron's offers an extensive general-interest series lineup for students and educators: the Masters of Music series, the Megascope series, the Bravo series, the History series, the Natural World series, and the Literature Made Easy series.

Recent titles from Barron's are *The Golden Book of Desserts* by Carla Bardi and Rachel Lane; *Baby's Books* by Francesca Ferri; *Magic Bath Books* by Moira Butterfield; and *E-Z Calculus* by Douglas Downing, PhD.

Barron's handles its own distribution. Send query letters with SASEs to the Acquisitions Manager.

Wayne Barr, Acquisitions Manager

Anna Damaskos, Senior Editor

Robert O'Sullivan, Managing Editor

BASIC BOOKS [SEE PERSEUS BOOKS GROUP]

BASKERVILLE PUBLISHERS

7105 Golf Club Drive, Suite 1102, #112, Fort Worth, TX 76179

817-923-1064/866-526-2312   fax: 817-886-8713

www.baskervillepublishers.com   email: authors@baskervillepublishers.com

Baskerville Publishers is a publisher of literary fiction and nonfiction, particularly books of interest to lovers of serious music and opera.

Baskerville titles include *Samuel Ramey: American Bass* by Jane Scovell; *Mario Lanza: An American Tragedy* by Armando Cesari; *Tebaldi: The Voice of an Angel* by Carlamaria Casanova; *Corelli: A Man, A Voice* by Marina Boagno; and *George London: Of Gods and Demons* by Nora London.

Send queries and SASEs to:

F. Ann Whitaker, Controller

BEACON PRESS

25 Beacon Street, Boston, MA 02108

617-742-2110   fax: 617-723-3097

www.beacon.org

Beacon Press celebrated its 150th anniversary in 2004. The Press has been a light of independent American publishing since 1854, when the house was established by the Unitarian Universalist Church. This is an independent publisher of serious nonfiction and fiction. The output is meant to change the way readers think about fundamental issues; they promote such values as freedom of speech and thought; diversity, religious pluralism, and anti-racism; and respect for diversity in all areas of life.

Beacon has published many groundbreaking classics, including James Baldwin's *Notes of a Native Son*; Herbert Marcuse's *One-Dimensional Man*; Jean Baker Miller's *Toward a New Psychology of Women*; and Mary Daly's *Gyn/Ecology*. In 1971, Beacon printed the Senator Gravel Edition of *The Pentagon Papers* in five volumes. This groundbreaking achievement marked the first time those papers had appeared in book form. Beacon is also the publisher of Marian Wright Edelman's bestselling book, *The Measure of Our Success: A Letter to My Children and Yours*, and Cornel West's acclaimed *Race Matters*.

Beacon's current publishing program emphasizes African American studies, anthropology, essays, gay/lesbian/gender studies, education, children and family issues, nature and the environment, religion, science and society, and women's studies. Beacon's continuing commitment to diversity is reflected in their Bluestreak books, which feature innovative literary writing by women. The series includes many acclaimed books, including the bestsellers *Kindred* by Octavia Butler; *The Healing* by Gayl Jones; and *A Thousand Pieces of Gold* by Ruthann Lum McCunn.

Recent publications include *Medicine in Translation: Journey with My Patients* by Danielle Ofri; *Illegal People: How Globalization Creates Migration and Criminalizes Immigrants* by David Bacon; *"They Take Our Jobs!": And 20 Other Myths about Immigration* by Aviva Choomsky; *The Coming Population Crash and Our Planet's Surprising Future* by Fred Pearce; and *The Death of Josseline* by Margaret Regan.

Beacon is an associate member of the Association of American University Presses and a department of the Unitarian Universalist Association.

Beacon Press is distributed to the trade by Houghton Mifflin.

Query letters, proposals, CVs, and SASEs should be sent by regular mail to the Editorial Department.

Amy Caldwell, Executive Editor

Gayatri Patnaik, Executive Editor

Allison Trzop, Assistant Editor

BEAR AND COMPANY [SEE INNER TRADITIONS/BEAR AND COMPANY]

BENBELLA BOOKS

6440 N. Central Expressway, Suite 617, Dallas, TX 75206

214-750-3600

www.benbellabooks.com   email: feedback@benbellabooks.com

BenBella is an independent publishing house based in Dallas, Texas. Founded by Glenn Yeffeth in 2001, BenBella specializes in nonfiction books on popular culture, health, and nutrition, along with books on science, politics, psychology, and other topics.

BenBella publishes the acclaimed Smart Pop series, a series of anthologies on the best of pop culture. The Smart Pop series is where the world's smartest philosophers, scientists, psychologists, and religious scholars write—in clear English—about pop culture, and take television and movies seriously—but not too seriously.

Recent titles from BenBella Books include *Surviving the Coming Tax Disaster* by Roni Deutch; *Inside Joss' Dollhouse* edited by Jane Espenson; *The Safe and Sane Guide to Teenage Plastic Surgery* by Frederick N. Lukash, MD; *The Five-Year Party:*

How Colleges Have Given Up on Educating Your Child and What You Can Do About It by Craig Brandon; and *the Vision Revolution* by Mark Changizi.

BenBella is looking for nonfiction only. Email queries are accepted. Address queries and SASEs to Editorial Submissions.

Glenn Yeffeth, Publisher; glenn@benbellabooks.com

MATTHEW BENDER & COMPANY, INC.

125 Park Avenue 23rd Floor, New York, NY 10017

212-309-8100   fax: 212-309-8187

www.reed-elsevier.com/OurBusiness/LexisNexis/Pages/MatthewBender.aspx

Founded in 1887, Matthew Bender is a member of the Reed Elsevier plc group and a leading provider of analytical legal research information (general references as well as state-specific works) in print, CD-ROM, and via the Internet. Their comprehensive legal information covers every major practice area and is authored by the leading experts in the legal community.

Matthew Bender & Co, Inc., produces works in the fields of law, accounting, banking, insurance, and related professions. Areas of Bender concentration include general accounting, administrative law, admiralty, bankruptcy, civil rights law, computer law, elder law, employment/labor, environmental, estate and financial planning, federal practice and procedure, government, health care, immigration, insurance, intellectual property, law-office management, personal injury/medico-legal, products liability, real estate, securities, taxation, and worker's compensation.

Matthew Bender works in print include authoritative treatises and expert legal analysis such as *Collier on Bankruptcy*, *Moore's Federal Practice*, *Nimmer on Copyright*, and much more. Bender produces treatises, textbooks, manuals, and form books, as well as newsletters and periodicals. Many Matthew Bender publications are available in the CD-ROM format on the Internet and on LexisNexis.

Practicing attorneys often serve as contributing legal writers in their areas of expertise. Bender considers itself an essential partner with law professionals, providing integrated information, resources, and tools, and delivering that information in formats that help its customers reach solutions with confidence.

Representative titles from Bender include *Tax Controversies: Practice and Procedure* by Leandra Lederman; *Understanding Antitrust and Its Economic Implications* by Thomas Sullivan; *Business Enterprises: Legal Structures, Governance, and Policy* by Douglas Branson; and *Law and Public Education: Cases and Materials* by E. Gordon Gee.

Matthew Bender is not currently accepting unsolicited submissions.

BERRETT-KOEHLER PUBLISHERS

235 Montgomery Street, Suite 650, San Francisco, CA 94104-2916

415-288-0260   fax: 425-362-2512

www.bkconnection.com   email: bkpub@bkpub.com

Founded in 1992, Berrett-Koehler Publishers is committed to supporting the movement toward a more enlightened work world. The house specializes in nonfiction titles that help integrate our values with our work and work lives in the hope of creating more humane and effective organizations. More specifically, the books focus on business, management, leadership, career development, entrepreneurship, human resources, and global sustainability.

The work world is going through tumultuous changes, from the decline of job security to the rise of new structures for organizing people and work. BK believes that change is needed at all levels—individual, organizational, community, and global. Their titles address each of these levels whether applying new scientific models to leadership, reclaiming spiritual values in the workplace, or using humor to cast light on the business world.

Just as BK publications are redefining the boundaries of business literature, the house is also "opening up new space" in the design and operation of their own business. Partnering with authors, suppliers, subcontractors, employees, customers, and societal and environmental communities, BK makes all involved in the creation of their books "stakeholders." They are striving to create a more equitable, open, and participative environment than is typically the case in the increasingly "lean and mean" world of corporate publishing.

Berrett-Koehler's current affairs line is called BK Currents. These titles explore the critical intersections between business and society with an eye on social and economic justice. The BK Life series helps people to create positive change, BK Business delivers pioneering socially responsible and effective approaches to managing organizations, and Fast Fundamentals provides practical expertise in article-length format for busy professionals.

Recent titles include *Leaders as Teachers* by Edward Betof; *Glow: How You Can Radiate Energy, Innovation, and Success* by Linda Gratton; *Making the Good Life Last: Four Keys to Sustainable Living* by Michael Schuler; *The Introverted Leader: Building on Your Quiet Strength* by Jennifer Kahnweiler; and *The Hamster Revolution: How to Manage Your Email Before It Manages You* by Mike Song et al.

Berrett-Koehler tends its own multichanneled distribution, through bookstores, direct-mail brochures, catalogs, a toll-free telephone-order number, book clubs, association book services, e-books, and special sales to business, government, and nonprofit organizations. The house is distributed to the trade via Publishers Group West.

Query letters and SASEs should be directed to:

Jeevan Sivasubramaniam, Acquisitions; bkpub@bkpub.com
Steven Piersanti, President and Publisher
Johanna Vondeling, Editorial Director
Kate Piersanti, Copyright Editor

BETHANY HOUSE [SEE BAKER PUBLISHING GROUP]

BEYOND WORDS

20827 N.W. Cornell Road, Suite 500, Hillsboro, OR 97124-9808

503-531-8700   fax: 503-531-8773

www.beyondword.com   email: info@beyondword.com

Beyond Words is a publishing company for artists, authors, and readers who share a love of words and images that inspire, delight, and educate. Founded in 1984 by Cynthia Black and Richard Cohen, Beyond Words is a boutique publisher that has published over 250 titles and has nearly 10 million books in print. In 2006, Beyond Words formed a co-publishing deal with Simon and Schuster's Atria imprint; while Beyond Words continues to publish around 15 titles per year, Atria handles the marketing, publication design, and production for all Beyond Words titles.

Subjects include mind, body, and spirit, global native wisdom, spiritual lifestyles, spiritual parenting, holistic health, and science and spirituality. Beyond Words is the publisher of our own Deborah Herman's *Spiritual Writing from Inspiration to Publication*.

Other recent titles include *Partnering with Nature* by Catriona MacGregor; *Intuitive Parenting* by Debra Snyder; *Your Every Word Has Power* by Yvonne Oswald; *Thriving after Divorce* by Tonja Evetts Weimer; and *Elemental Love Styles* by Craig Martin.

Beyond Words looks for authors who have passion for their books and want to work in a collaborative way. Most of their titles are by first-time authors. The editors seek to discover new authors and develop bestselling book projects.

Beyond Words no longer publishes children's, cooking, or photography books. Due to the high volume of submissions, they are unable to accept unsolicited manuscripts; however, they are accepting submissions from literary agents or trusted advisers.

Cynthia Black, President, Editor-in-Chief

Lindsay Brown, Managing Editor
Richard Cohn, Publisher

BLOOMBERG PRESS

731 Lexington Avenue, New York, NY 10022
212-617-8585   fax: 917-369-5000
www.bloomberg.com/books   email: press@bloomberg.com

(Note: Bloomberg and its backlist catalogue was acquired by John Wiley & Sons at press time.)

Bloomberg Press publishes practical books for financial professionals as well as books of general interest on investing, economics, law, and current affairs. More than 130 titles have been released since 1996. The books are written by leading practitioners and specialists, including Bloomberg News reporters and columnists, and are published in more than 20 languages. The Press also publishes cartoon collections with *The New Yorker* and distributes the *Economist* line of books in the U.S.

Bloomberg Press is part of Bloomberg LP, the global, multimedia information service that provides news, data, and analysis to financial markets and businesses. The parent company's core product is the Bloomberg Professional service, the real-time financial-information network often referred to on Wall Street as "the Bloomberg." Bloomberg LP is the parent of Bloomberg News, which provides instantaneous electronic news to clients of the Bloomberg Professional service, to newspapers, and to other electronic media. Bloomberg News operates its own radio, Web, and television enterprises (Bloomberg Radio, Bloomberg.com, Bloomberg Television) in multiple languages 24/7 worldwide, and has been the source of a number of award-winning public-affairs books published by Bloomberg Press.

The goal at Bloomberg Press is to deliver a useful picture of how the capital markets work. Bloomberg Press books emphasize clear explanations and practical information. Authors are either prominent authorities or financial journalists. Target readers are brokers, traders, money managers, CEOs, CFOs, bankers, other professionals, and sophisticated investors. Subjects include investment intelligence, portfolio management, markets, financial instruments (equities, bonds, derivatives, real estate, alternative investments), financial analytics, risk management, financial planning, and economic analysis of use to traders, hedge fund managers, businesses, and policymakers.

Bloomberg Press titles include *Confidence Game: How a Hedge Fund Manager Called Wall Street's Bluff* by Christine Richard; *Complicit: How Greed and Collusion Made the Credit Crisis Unstoppable* by Mark Gilbert; *Market Indicators: The Best-Kept*

Secret to More Effective Trading and Investing by Richard Sipley; *Aqua Shock: The Water Crisis in America* by Susan Marks; and *Chart Patterns* by Bruce Kamich.

Bloomberg Press is distributed by Ingram Publisher Services in North America and by Kogan Page outside the Americas. Bloomberg Press also markets its books and subsidiary rights to corporations and selling partners internationally through a variety of direct outlets, including traditional print venues and electronic distribution.

Bloomberg Press typically does not publish management, strategy, leadership, professional development, entrepreneurship, personal finance, or general consumer books. Query first by email at press@bloomberg.com. Submissions and SASEs should be directed to the Editorial Acquisitions Department.

Mary Ann McGuigan, Publisher

BLOOMSBURY USA

BLOOMSBURY PRESS

BLOOMSBURY CHILDREN'S BOOKS USA

175 Fifth Avenue, 8th Floor, New York, NY 10010

212-674-5151   fax: 212-780-0015

www.bloomsburyusa.com   email: info@bloomsburyusa.com

WALKER PUBLISHING COMPANY

WALKER BOOKS FOR YOUNG READERS

646-307-5151   fax: 212-727-0984

www.walkerbooks.com

Bloomsbury USA, launched in 1998 by Bloomsbury Publishing plc, is an independent publisher of high-quality fiction and nonfiction for adults and children. Bloomsbury Publishing plc is a London-based publisher best known for literary novels and for being the original *Harry Potter* publisher. In 2004, Bloomsbury purchased U.S.-based Walker Publishing (see the separate entry). The acquisition and integration of Walker enabled Bloomsbury to broaden its presence in the U.S. market, especially in adult narrative nonfiction and children's nonfiction. In 2008, Bloomsbury debuted a new imprint, Bloomsbury Press, devoted to serious nonfiction and headed by Peter Ginna, former editorial director of Oxford University Press.

Bloomsbury USA adult titles include works in fiction, arts, memoir, science, travel, history, biography, food, humor, sports, gardening, relationships and self-help, crime, women's studies, reference, and current affairs.

Recent releases include *The Father of Us All: War and History, Ancient and Modern* by Victor Davis Hanson; *Merchants of Doubt* by Naomi Oreskes and Erik Conway; *Apocalypse Noun: Grammar Grumps, Comma Cops, and the Greatly Exaggerated Death of the English Language* by Evan Morris; *Marie-Therese, Child of Terror: The Fate of Marie Antoinette's Daughter* by Susan Nagel; *Troubadour* by Mary Hoffman; *The Speech: Race and Barack Obama's "A More Perfect Union"* by T. Denean Sharpley-Whiting; *Caught in the Middle: America's Heartland in the Age of Globalism* by Richard C. Longworth; and *Daphne: A Novel* by Justine Picardie.

BLOOMSBURY PRESS

Titles from Bloomsbury Press include *After Tamerlane: The Global History of Empire Since 1405* by John Darwin; *Bozo Sapiens: Why to Err Is Human* by Michael Kaplan and Ellen Kaplan; *Family of Secrets: The Bush Dynasty* by Russ Baker; *Mrs. Woolf and the Servants: An Intimate History of Domestic Life in Bloomsbury* by Alison Light; *The Great Warming: Climate Change and the Rise and Fall of Civilizations* by Brian Fagan; and *The Last Thousand Days of the British Empire: Churchill, Roosevelt, and the Birth of the Pax Americana* by Peter Clarke.

BLOOMSBURY CHILDREN'S BOOKS USA

Bloomsbury Children's Books welcomes picture book manuscripts and queries for longer works, whether fiction or nonfiction. They publish picture books, chapter books, easy readers, middle-grade and YA novels, fantasy, and some nonfiction. With queries, please include a synopsis of the book and the first ten pages or first chapter to the Children's Book Acquisitions Department. Please do not send originals or only copies, because Bloomsbury Children's Books no longer respond to unsolicited submissions, and will only contact authors if they are interested in acquiring the work.

Recent children's titles from Bloomsbury USA include *Pickle Impossible* by Eli Stutz; *My Invisible Sister* by Beatrice Colin and Sara Pinto; *Darkwood* by M.E. Breen; *Poser* by Sue Wyshynski; *Princess of Glass* by Jessica Day George; and *Demon Princess: Reign Check*.

Bloomsbury USA does not accept unsolicited submissions, and does not assume responsibility for unsolicited manuscripts they receive. They consider manuscripts represented by established literary agents.

Because of new postal weight regulations, Bloomsbury cannot return any manuscripts, art, or other materials. Please only include recyclable materials with your submission, and send a letter-sized stamped envelope for their response only.

Karen Rinaldi, Publisher, Bloomsbury, USA

Melanie Cecka, Executive Editor, Bloomsbury Children's USA

Peter Ginna, Director, Bloomsbury Press

WALKER PUBLISHING COMPANY

Walker Publishing Company became an imprint of Bloomsbury USA when it was acquired by Bloomsbury in 2004. During the course of its 47-year history as an independent, Walker has published bestsellers in its adult and children's lists; recently they have published Dava Sobel's bestsellers, *Longitude* and *Galileo's Daughter*; Mark Kurlansky's *Cod and Salt*; Ross King's *Michelangelo and the Pope's Ceiling*; and Judith Finchler's children's classic, *Testing Miss Malarkey*, illustrated by Kevin O'Malley.

Walker currently publishes three lists a year, each consisting of around 10 picture books and 4–5 middle-grade and/or young-adult works, for a total of 40–45 titles annually.

Walker has been credited in *Business Week* as "a pioneer of a now-ubiquitous book genre—stories about forgotten people or offbeat things that changed the world." Sometimes called microhistories, these books are biographies of inanimate objects—like salt or longitude. Walker publisher, George Gibson, said recently that he looks to acquire manuscripts with great storytelling and fine writing. He publishes books for "thoughtful folks."

The prolific Isaac Asimov published more books with Walker than with any other publisher, and now David Bodanis (*E=mc2*); Simon Singh (*Fermat's Enigma*); Chet Raymo (*Climbing Brandon* and *An Intimate Look at the Night Sky*); and, most recently, Harvard astronomer Owen Gingerich (*The Book Nobody Read*), have published with Walker.

While mystery/thriller publishing is somewhat less the focus of the house, it has published John Le Carré. Please note that Walker does not publish adult fiction outside of the mystery category. The house no longer publishes Westerns, thrillers, or Regency romance novels.

Recent Walker titles include *Ambrose Bierce's Write It Right* by Ambrose Bierce and Jan Freeman; *An Artist in Treason* by Andro Linklater; *The Astronomer* by Lawrence Goldstone; *Beyond Walden* by Robert Thorson; and *Blood Count: An Artie Cohen Mystery* by Reggie Nadelson.

WALKER BOOKS FOR YOUNG READERS

Beth Walker started the children's division, which has now been a central part of the company for some 40 years, featuring authors such as Barbara Cooney, Tomie de Paola, Michael McCurdy, and Pat and Fred McKissack, whose *Long Hard Journey* won the Coretta Scott King Award.

Walker Young Readers is actively seeking middle-grade and YA novels and well-paced picture book manuscripts for the preschool and early elementary age levels. They do not publish folk tales, fairy tales, textbooks, myths, legends, series, novelties, science fiction, fantasy, or horror.

Recent Walker Young Readers titles include *Bedtime for Mommy* by Amy Krouse; *The Wide-Awake Princess* by E.D. Baker; *Little Blog on the Prairie* by

Cathleen Davitt Bell; *My Circus* by Xavier Deneux; *Poop Happened!* by Sarah Albee; and *Rules of Attraction* by Simone Elkeles.

Submit your manuscript—or the first 75 pages of it—with SASE for a response only to (they recycle all submissions and return only their response):

George Gibson, Publisher, Walker

Emily Easton, Publisher, Walker Children's

Jacqueline Johnson, Editor, Walker—Adult nonfiction as per house interests.

BLUEBRIDGE BOOKS

240 West 35th Street, Suite 500, New York, NY 10001

212-244-4166   fax: 212-279-0927

www.bluebridgebooks.com   email: janguerth@bluebridgebooks.com

BlueBridge is an independent publisher of international nonfiction based in New York City. BlueBridge, with subjects ranging from culture, history, biography, travel, and current affairs to spirituality, self-help, and inspiration, is a press focusing on books about spirituality. Publisher and founder, Jan-Erik Guerth, started BlueBridge after four years directing the Hidden Spring imprint of Paulist Press. Guerth left Hidden Spring in 2003 and spent a year preparing for the launch of BlueBridge, which he founded with his own money and investments from friends and family. BlueBridge is currently publishing six to eight books a year.

Recent titles from BlueBridge include *The Angelic Way: Angels Through the Ages and Their Meaning for Us* by Rami Shapiro; *Mr. Langshaw's Square Piano: The Story of the First Pianos and How They Caused a Cultural Revolution* by Madelin Goold; *The Frozen Ship: The Histories and Tales of Polar Exploration* by Sarah Moss; and *The Door of No Return: The History of Cape Coast Castle and the Atlantic Slave Trade* by William St. Clair.

BlueBridge is distributed by IPG. Send queries and SASEs to:

Jan-Erik Guerth, Publisher

THE BOOTSTRAP PRESS [SEE THE APEX PRESS]

BOYDS MILLS PRESS

A Subsidiary of Highlights for Children

CALKINS CREEK BOOKS

FRONT STREET

LEMINSCAAT

WORDSONG

815 Church Street, Honesdale, PA 18431

570-253-1164/800-490-5111

www.boydsmillspress.com email: contact@boydsmillspress.com

Boyds Mills Press, the trade division of Highlights for Children, Inc., was launched in 1990. Publishing books was a logical step for Highlights, which has a long tradition of helping children develop a love of reading. Boyds Mills produces books for children, picture books, novels, nonfiction, and poetry—nonsensical verse, as well as more serious fare. The press promotes a solid seasonal list of new titles and hosts a hefty backlist of titles that challenge, inspire, and entertain.

Boyds Mills Press reaches children primarily through bookstores, libraries, and schools. The list runs about 50 books per year. Poetry, published under the Wordsong imprint, is the only imprint of its kind devoted exclusively to poetry for children.

Respect for children is among the highest priorities when Boyds Mills Press acquires a manuscript. They aim to publish good stories with lasting value, avoid the trendy, and never publish a book simply to fill a market need. Whether pure entertainment or more challenging subject matter, the story always comes first.

Recent Boyds Mills titles include *A Beach Tail* by Karen Lynn Williams; *Planet Hunter* by Vicki Wittenstein; *My School in the Rain Forest* by Margriet Ruurs; and *Mama, Will It Snow Tonight?* by Nancy White Carlstrom.

CALKINS CREEK BOOKS

The Calkins Creek Books imprint introduces children to the people, places, and events that shaped American history. Through picture books, chapter books, and novels for ages eight and up, combining original and extensive research with creative energetic writing, Calkins authors transport their readers back in time to recognizable places with living and breathing people. Recent books from Calkins Creek include *Birmingham Sunday* by Larry Dane Brimner; *For Liberty* by Timothy Decker; *Birchbark Brigade* by Cris Peterson; and *Upon Secrecy* by Selene Castrovilla.

FRONT STREET

Front Street publishes young-adult fiction that deals with children in crisis or children at risk, and offers hope and comfort no matter how difficult the subject matter. Their picture books emphasize art and design. Recent titles from Front Street include *The Dog in the Wood* by Minoka Schröder; *Planet Pregnancy* by Linda High; and *Wild Things* by Clay Carmichael.

LEMINSCAAT

Leminscaat is a highly esteemed publishing house located in Rotterdam, The Netherlands. Their list represents the broad traditions of European picture books and incorporates the best contemporary art, design, and story. Some titles from Leminscaat include *Cold Skin* by Steven Herrick; *Loserville* by Peter Johnson; and *Markus and the Girls* by Klaus Hagerup.

WORDSONG

Wordsong is the only imprint in children's publishing in America that is dedicated to poetry. Their books range from the silly to the serious and are infused with the wordplay and imagery that lets readers view the world in new and thoughtful ways. Latest from Wordsong include *Well Defined* by Michael Salinger; *Rules of the Game* by Marjorie Maddox; *A Mirror to Nature* by Jane Yolen; and *Becoming Billie Holiday* by Carole Weatherford.

Boyds Mills Press handles its own distribution.

This publisher is actively seeking picture books, middle-grade and young-adult novels, and nonfiction and poetry for all ages. For all imprints, send manuscripts, query letters, and SASEs to the Manuscript Coordinator.

Larry Rosler, Editorial Director (Boyds Mill)

Carolyn P. Yoder, Editor (Calkins Creek)

Andy Boyles, Editor—Science and Natural History

Joan Hyman, Editor—Wordsong

GEORGE BRAZILLER, INC.

171 Madison Avenue, New York, NY 10016

212-889-0909   fax: 212-689-5405

www.georgebraziller.com   email: info@georgebraziller.com

Founded in 1955 and celebrating more than half a century in business, George Braziller, Inc., is a small, independent publishing house based in New York City. The house publishes international literature and beautiful books on art and design, architecture, and art movements and history. The house also publishes selected literary titles, as well as philosophy, science, history, criticism, and biographical works.

Much of Braziller's fiction and poetry is foreign literature in translation, although the publisher does publish original literary novels (such as works by Janet Frame) and works in the English language that have received initial publication elsewhere. The house aims to be consistently discovering new writers and exploring new areas in the world of art.

Braziller also has a strong interest in literary criticism and writing relating to the arts, in addition to a small selection of contemporary and modern poetry. Essential Readings in Black Literature is a Braziller series that features world-class writers from around the globe. Other Braziller series include Library of Far Eastern Art and New Directions in Architecture.

Braziller recently introduced a Young Adult series with titles including *Figs and Fate: Stories about Growing Up in the Arab World Today* by Elsa Marston; and *Changing, Changing* by Aracelis Girmay.

Other recent titles include *The Art of American Book Covers: 1875–1930* by Richard Minsky; *Charles Dickens: His Journal* adapted by Vincent Torre; *Sexuality and Catholicism* by Thomas Fox; and *Montaillou: The Promised Land of Error* by Le Roy Ladurie.

Braziller titles are distributed by W.W. Norton & Co.

Submissions with manuscript (nothing in excess of 50 pages) and CV should be directed to:

George Braziller, Publisher

BRAZOS PRESS [SEE BAKER PUBLISHING GROUP]

BROADMAN & HOLMAN [SEE B & H PUBLISHING GROUP]

BURNS & OATES [SEE CONTINUUM INTERNATIONAL PUBLISHING GROUP]

CANONGATE BOOKS [SEE GROVE/ATLANTIC, INC.]

CAREER PRESS

NEW PAGE BOOKS

220 West Parkway Unit 12, Pompton Plains, NJ 07444

201-848-0310/800-227-3371

www.careerpress.com

www.newpagebooks.com

With their motto "Enriching Your Life One Book at a Time," Career Press publishes general nonfiction that addresses real, practical needs. Their useful, accessible "how-to" books reach a broad market of average Americans—people grappling with issues relating to job-hunting, career management, education, money management, and personal goals.

Career Press was launched in 1985 with a commitment to publish quality books on careers, business, reference, motivation, sales, personal finance, real estate, and more. Career Press publishes quality books on topics most needed in the marketplace, written by established, credentialed, media-savvy professionals, and then promotes and publicizes them full force. They are seeking books in the categories of business, career, job search, college preparation, small business, entrepreneurship, motivation, sales, negotiation, study aids, and reference. This list is not comprehensive, and other categories are published based on the project's tone, approach, and sales potential.

Recent titles from Career Press include *Business Reports for Busy People* by Greg Holden; *100 Ways to Boost Your Self-Confidence* by Barton Goldsmith; and *Your Virtual Success* by Alan Blume.

NEW PAGE BOOKS

In 2000 Career Press created a new imprint, New Page Books, to expand the category list to include New Age, supernatural/paranormal, ancient mysteries, Wicca, mythology, alternative health, nutrition/wellness, pop history, and weddings.

Recent titles from New Page include *Tell Me What to Eat If I Have to Suffer from Heart Disease* by Elaine Magee; *The Déjà Vu Enigma* by Marie Jones and Larry Flaxman; and *Dark Fairies* by Bob Curran.

Career Press/New Page Books distributes its own list.

Query letters, proposals, and SASEs should be directed to the Acquisitions Department.

Michael Pye, Acquisitions Editor; mpye@careerpress.com
Adam Schwartz, Acquistions Editor; aschwartz@careerpress.com
Gina Hoogerhyde, Editorial Director; ghoogerhyde@careerpress.com

CCC PUBLICATIONS

9725 Lurline Avenue, Chatsworth, CA 91311

818-718-0507   fax: 818-718-0655

Founded in 1983, CCC Publications accents nonfiction trade books in crisply targeted categories: relationships, self-help and how-to, humor, inspiration, humorous inspirational titles, age-related and over-the-hill titles, gift books, and a series catalogued as On the Edge. CCC has published a number of books by bestselling author Jan King.

Recent CCC titles include *The Poetry Oracle* by Amber Guetebier and Brenda Knight and *Sacred Places North America: 108 Destinations* by Brad Olsen.

Best-selling CCC titles have included *Hormones from Hell: The Ultimate Women's Humor Book* by Jan King; *Farting: Gas Past, Present, and Future* by Desmond Mullan; and *50 Ways to Hustle Your Friends* by Jim Karol.

From the On the Edge series: *Men are Pigs, Women are Bitches* by Jerry King; *The Very, Very Sexy Adult Dot to Dot Book* by Tony Goffe; and *The Complete Wimp's Guide to Sex* by Jed Pascoe.

CCC handles its own distribution.

Query and SASEs should be directed to the Editorial Staff.

CEDAR FORT, INC.

CFI BOOKS

BONNEVILLE BOOKS

COUNCIL PRESS

SWEETWATER BOOKS

2373 West 700 South, Springville, UT 84663

801-489-4084/800-SKYBOOK fax: 801-489-1097/800-388-3727

www.cedarfort.com   email: submissions@cedarfort.com

HORIZON PUBLISHERS

191 N. 560 East, Bountiful, UT 84010-3628

801-295-9451/866-818-6277   fax: 801-298-1305

www.horizonpublishersbooks.com

email: service07@horizonpublishersbookstore.com

Cedar Fort was founded in May 1896 and initially produced Latter-day Saints (LDS) books for other publishers as an LDS book printer broker. Founder Lyle Mortimer began distributing LDS books and other items until in September 1987 the company released its first publication, *Beyond the Veil* by Lee Nelson, which became an immediate bestseller.

CFI BOOKS

CFI searches for life-enriching, edifying, and enhancing LDS books geared to the Latter-day Saint marker in any form. In recent years the company has published several highly acclaimed novels and continues to branch out into the world beyond the LDS books market, both in the traditional manner and on the Internet and alternative markets.

CFI Books publishes LDS doctrinal books, scriptural commentaries, self-help, cookbooks, and some fiction. Recent titles from CFI Books include *The Hoarders* by Jean Stringham; *The Biblical Roots of Mormonism* by Eric Shuster and Charles Sale; *The Rhea Jensen Series Book 1: City of Angels*; *The Widower's Wife* by Prudence Bice; and *The Road Show* by Braden Bell.

BONNEVILLE BOOKS

Bonneville Books mainly publishes LDS fiction. Titles from Bonneville Books include *The Canticle Kingdom* by Michael D. Young; *The Adventures of Hashbrown Winters* by Frank Cole; *Deadly Treasure* by Jillayne Clements; *Torn Apart* by Diony George; *Where Hearts Prosper* by Suzanne V. Reese; and *Against the Giant* by Christy Hardman.

COUNCIL PRESS

Council Press mostly publishes historical fiction and nonfiction. Titles include *Storm Testament III* by Lee Nelson; *The White Bedouin* by George Potter; *The Bearded White God of Ancient America: The Legend of Quetzalcoatl* by Donald Hemingway and W. David Hemmingway; and *Jumping Off Places* by Laura Stratton Friel.

SWEETWATER BOOKS

Sweetwater Books produces books intended primarily for the national market.

Titles include *The Santa Letters* by Stacy Gooch Anderson; *Trust in the Lord: Reflections of Jesus Christ* by Deen Kemsley; and *The Shell Game* by Steve Alten.

Email submissions are accepted, but hard copies are preferred. Send a query letter and SASE to the Acquisitions Editor:

Jennifer Fielding, Acquisitions Editor; submissions@cedarfort.com

Jeffrey Marsh, Acquisitions Editor

HORIZON PUBLISHERS

Horizon Publishers is a family-run corporation that publishes wholesome, informative books and tapes for a variety of marketplaces. In 2004, Horizon was acquired by Cedar Fort, Inc. (CFI), a leading publisher of LDS (Latter-day Saints) fiction and nonfiction titles since its founding in 1986; CFI now publishes 100 titles per year, roughly 25 percent of the Utah book market. In a unique arrangement, CFI is slowly acquiring Horizon's assets; Horizon continues its editorial operations while CFI picks up production and distribution.

Established in 1971, Horizon Publishers has various product lines in which it has "distinctive competencies"—publishing areas in which it is noted for having a strong offering of products of noteworthy quality. In the general trade market, these areas include such topics as outdoor life, camping, Dutch-oven and outdoor cooking, cookbooks, outdoor survival skills, food storage, gardening, emergency preparedness, life-after-death and near-death experiences, marriage and family life, and counted cross-stitch designs.

Many of Horizon Publishers' books are written for readers in the general religious marketplace. Numerous books the firm produces are for the general Christian marketplace, including those on marriage, family life, raising and teaching children, Bible studies, and comparative religions.

Recent titles include *They Walked with God* by Duane Crowther; *Enjoying the Journey* by Jaime Theler and Deborah Talmadge; *Decoding Ancient America: A Guide to the Archaeology of the Book of Mormon* by Diane Wirth; *Lost for Christmas* by Ted and Shirlene Hindmarsh; and *Now, What Do You Believe?* by Gregory Wille.

Horizon Publishers is distributed by Cedar Fort.

The editorial board of Horizon Publishers seeks products that will lift, inspire, inform, and entertain its readers. Horizon publishes 20–30 new titles per year, selecting its new releases from the 2,000-plus queries and manuscripts it receives annually. Email queries are not accepted. Direct queries, proposals, and SASEs to the Editorial Board.

Duane S. Crowther, Founder and CEO

CELESTIAL ARTS [SEE TEN SPEED PRESS]

CHELSEA GREEN PUBLISHING COMPANY

P.O. Box 428, 85 North Main Street, Suite 120, White River Junction, VT 05001

802-295-6300   fax: 802-295-6444

www.chelseagreen.com   email: info@chelseagreen.com

Chelsea Green publishes trade nonfiction on sustainable living, organic gardening and food, renewable energy and green building, nature and the environment, and books on political and social issues. Founded in 1984, Chelsea Green Publishing is an independent and individualistic firm; the house continues to grow its list with about 15 new releases each year (in hardcover and trade paper formats) and a hardy backlist with well over 400 titles in print. Chelsea Green sees publishing as a tool for effecting cultural change. Their purpose is "to stop the destruction of the natural world by challenging the beliefs and practices that are enabling this destruction and by providing inspirational and practical alternatives that promote sustainable living."

Some areas of particular interest for Chelsea Green include organic gardening and market farming, local agricultural movements and healthy food supplies, environmentally friendly building techniques, renewable energy sources and energy conservation, simpler lifestyles, economic systems that account for environmental and social needs, political activism that promotes sustainable economies, philosophical writing that promotes sustainable living, and natural science with a cross-disciplinary and ecological perspective.

Recent Chelsea Green titles are *Inquiries into the Nature of Slow Money* by Woody Tasch; *The Systems Thinking Playbook* by Linda Booth Sweeney and Dennis Meadow; *The Farmstead Creamery Advisor* by Gianaclis Caldwell; *Poisoned for Profit: How Toxins Are Making Our Children Chronically Ill with New Information on What We Can Do* by Philip Shabecoff and Alice Shabecoff; *Up Tunket Road: The Education of a Modern Homesteader* by Philip Ackerman-Leist.

Chelsea Green handles its own distribution and distributes for a number of other small, innovative independent presses such as Green Books, Ltd.; Otto Graphics; Ecological Design Press; Harmonious Press; and Seed Savers Exchange.

An electronic query may be addressed to submissions@chelseagreen.com. Proposals with SASEs should be directed via regular mail to:

Margo Baldwin, President and Publisher; mbaldwin@chelseagreen.com

Joni Praded, Editor-in-Chief; jpraded@chelseagreen.com

Amy Burton, Editorial Assistant; editorial@chelseagreen.com

INDEPENDENT U.S. PRESSES

CHOCKSTONE [SEE THE GLOBE PEQUOT PRESS]

CHOSEN BOOKS [SEE BAKER PUBLISHING GROUP]

CHRONICLE BOOKS

680 Second Street, San Francisco, CA 94107

415-537-4200/800-722-6657   fax: 415-537-4460

www.chroniclebooks.com   email: frontdesk@chroniclebooks.com

Chronicle Books was founded in 1967 and over the years has developed a reputation for award-winning, innovative books. The company continues to challenge conventional publishing wisdom, setting trends in both subject and format. Chronicle titles include cookbooks, fine art, design, photography, architecture titles, nature books, poetry and literary fiction, travel guides, and gift items. Chronicle publishes about 175 books per year.

Titles of note include Martha Zamora's *Frida Kahlo: The Brush of Anguish* (1990), and Nick Bantock's *Griffin & Sabine* (1991). Originally slated for an edition of 10,000, this interactive book became the most talked-about title of the year and a *New York Times* bestseller for 50 weeks. The two subsequent volumes in the trilogy, *Sabine's Note-book* and *The Golden Mean*, were also *Times* bestsellers. A more recent monster hit was the *Worst-Case Scenario* franchise.

The company brought the same innovative philosophy to cookbooks with its four-color release of *Sushi* (1981), which sold 90,000 copies and is still in print. Chronicle Books also publishes James McNair's eye-catching cookbooks, all perennial bestsellers having sold over one million copies.

The Children's list was launched in 1988 and has published the bestselling *Mama, Do You Love Me?* (over one million copies in hardcover); *Ten Little Rabbits* (450,000 copies); and N.C. Wyeth's *Pilgrims* (100,000 copies). The list has grown to include not only traditional picture books but also affordable paperbacks, board books, plush toys, and novelty merchandise.

In 1992, Chronicle Books launched its gift division to develop ancillary products such as the Griffin & Sabine address book and writing box, the bestselling 52 Deck series, and a motorcycle journal and address book based on the Harley-Davidson image archives.

Recent Chronicle titles are *30 Postcards* by David Choe; *Beach: A Book of Treasure* by Josie Iselin; *Bears! Bears! Bears!* by Bob Barner; *Curious Cats* by Mitsuaki Iwago; and *Designer's Note-book* by Andrerw Schapiro and Brad Mead.

Recent Chronicle Children's books include *A Long Piece of String* by William Wondriska; *Chicken Big* by Keith Graves; *Classic Horse Stories* by Christina Darling; *Day & Night* by Teddy Newton; and *Feelings Flash Cards* by Todd Parr.

For adult titles, query letters, proposals, and SASEs should be directed via regular mail only to the Adult Trade Editorial Staff. Chronicle Books is no longer accepting fiction.

With children's titles, projects for older children should be submitted by a query letter, synopsis, and three sample chapters, with SASE. Projects for younger children may be sent in their entirety. Send via regular mail to the Children's Division.

Sarah Malarkey, Publishing Director

Jodi Warshaw, Senior Editor

Victoria Rock, Editor-at-Large—Children's

Bill LeBlond, Editorial Director—Cookbooks

CITADEL [SEE KENSINGTON PUBLISHING CORP.]

CITY LIGHTS PUBLISHERS

261 Columbus Avenue, San Francisco, CA 94133

415-362-8193   fax: 415-362-4921

www.citylights.com   email: staff@citylights.com

City Lights publishes literary essays and criticism, biography, philosophy, literary fiction (including first novels), poetry, books on political and social issues, and ecumenical volumes featuring both words and visual images.

City Lights Booksellers and Publishers is a renowned American institution. Founded in 1953 by Beat poet Lawrence Ferlinghetti, its San Francisco bookstore is a North Beach landmark and, above all else, a resolute cultural tradition.

City Lights initially featured the Pocket Poets series, which introduced such writers as Gregory Corso, Allen Ginsberg, Jack Kerouac, and other Beats to a wider audience. Since then, as successive literary generations have commenced and terminated, City Lights continues to flourish. Today, it has nearly 200 titles in print and puts out a dozen new titles each year.

Recent City Lights titles include *Colorblind* by Tim Wise; *New World of Indigenous Resistance* by Noam Chomsky et al; *Absence of the Hero* by Charles Bukowski and David Calonne; *Prison/Culture* by Sharon Bliss et al; *Islanders* by Ammiel Alcalay; and *Trance Archive: New and Selected Poems* by Andrew Joron.

City Lights is distributed by Consortium Book Sales and Distribution and has its own in-house mail-order fulfillment department.

City Lights no longer accepts unsolicited submissions.

Elaine Katzenberger, Acquisitions Editor—Latin American literature, women's studies, fiction

Nancy J. Peters, Publisher

Robert Sharrard, Acquisitions Editor—Poetry, literature

CLARION BOOKS [SEE HOUGHTON MIFFLIN]

CLEIS PRESS

2246 Sixth Street, Berkeley CA 94710

510-845-8000/800-780-2279   fax: 415-575-4705

www.cleispress.com   email: cleis@cleispress.com

Founded in 1980, Cleis Press publishes 34 new books a year on sexual politics and self-help, lesbian and gay studies and culture, sex guides, feminism, fiction, erotica, humor, and translations of world-class literature. Cleis titles cross markets from niches of gender and sexuality to reach the widest possible audiences.

Projects from Cleis Press garner numerous awards and reviews—and include many bestselling books. The house is committed to publishing the most original, creative, and provocative works by women and men in the U.S. and Canada.

Recent titles from the Cleis list include *Biker Boys: Gay Erotic Stories* edited by Christopher Pierce; *College Boys: Gay Erotic Stories* edited by Shane Allison; *Girl Crush: Women's Erotic Fantasies* edited by R. Gay; *Making the Hook-Up: Edgy Sex with Soul* edited by Cole Riley; and *A Sticky End: A Mitch Mitchell Mystery* by James Lear.

Cleis Press is represented to the book trade by Publishers Group West.

Please do not send submissions via USPS or any other delivery service. Email queries only are accepted. Book proposals and sample chapters with SASEs should be directed to:

Frédérique Delacoste, Publisher and Acquisitions Editor; fdelacoste@cleispress.com

Felice Newman, Publisher; fnewman@cleispress.com

Brenda Knight, Associate Publisher; bknight@cleispress.com

CLEVELAND STATE UNIVERSITY POETRY CENTER

2121 Euclid Avenue, RT 1841, Cleveland, Ohio 44115-2214

216-687-3986/888-278-6473   fax: 216-687-6943

www.csuohio.edu/poetrycenter   email: poetrycenter@csuohio.edu

The Cleveland State University Poetry Center was founded in 1962 to offer encouragement to poets and writers and to further the public's knowledge of and appreciation for contemporary poetry. The Series Editor and Director is Michael Dumanis. The Poetry Center Manager is Rita Grabowski.

The Poetry Center began publishing in 1971 and since that time has developed a list of over 150 nationally distributed titles. The press publishes poets of local, regional, and international reach, generally under the aegis of one or another of the center's ongoing series. Under its flying-unicorn logo, CSU Poetry Center most often publishes trade paper editions, but has also offered some titles in hardbound. Its publications include the national CSU Poetry Series, the Cleveland Poets Series for Ohio writers, as well as other titles of interest, including the Imagination series. CSU Poetry Center presents a variety of styles and viewpoints—some with evident sociopolitical bent, others with broadly inspirational themes, and others notable for their strong individualistic inflections.

The current editorial board consists of Kazim Ali, Mary Bettinger, Michael Dumanis, and Sarah Gridley. The Cleveland State University Poetry Center Prize of $1,000 is awarded for the best book-length manuscript in two categories submitted annually from November 1 through April 15. There is a $25.00 reader's fee. The "Open" Competition is limited to poets who have published at least one book-length collection of their poems. The "First Book" Competition is for poets who have not previously published a full-length collection. Send a business-sized, self-addressed, stamped envelope for complete contest guidelines, or check the "Contest Guidelines" link on their website.

Some titles from the Cleveland State University Poetry Center are *You Don't Know What You Don't Know* by John Bradley; *Clamor* by Elyse Fenton; *Brazil* by Jesse Lee Kercheval; and *Snaketown* by Kathleen Wakefield.

Poetry Center books are distributed through Partners Book Distributing, Ingram, and Spring Church Book Company.

The Poetry Center only accepts manuscripts submitted between November 1 and February 1 ($25 entry fee; full manuscripts only). For complete guidelines on the Center's annual competitions, visit the website or send request plus SASE to:

Michael Dumanis, Director

Rita Grabowski, Manager

COFFEE HOUSE PRESS

79 Thirteenth Avenue NE, Suite 110, Minneapolis, MN 55413

612-338-0125   fax: 612-338-4004

www.coffeehousepress.org

Coffee House Press was founded in 1984, and took its name from the long tradition of coffee houses as places for the free exchange of ideas, where each individual had equal time for expression, regardless of station or background. The press is an award-winning, nonprofit literary publisher dedicated to innovation in the craft of writing and preservation of the tradition of book arts. Coffee House produces books that present the dreams and ambitions of people who have been underrepresented in published literature, books that shape our national consciousness while strengthening a larger sense of community. The house produces contemporary poetry, short fiction, and novels. Contemporary writing that is challenging, thought-provoking, daring, vibrant, funny, or lyrical is the key.

Coffee House Press aims to enrich our literary heritage, and to contribute to the cultural life of our community. Coffee House Press publishes books that advance the craft of writing; the house colophon is a steaming book that lets the reader know (as the Coffee House motto runs) "where good books are brewing."

Recent titles from Coffee House include *I Hotel* by Karen Tei Yamashita; *Drowning Tucson* by Aaron Michael Morales; *Off We Go Into the Wild Blue Yonder* by Travis Nichols; *Shoulder Season* by Ange Mlinko; and *Find the Girl* by Lightsey Darst.

Coffee House Press oversees its own marketing and sales network with the assistance of regional representatives; trade distribution is handled by Consortium.

Coffee House Press accepts manuscripts on an ongoing basis. For fiction, query letters with 20- to 30-page samples and SASEs should be directed to:

Christopher Fischbach, Senior Editor; fish@coffeehousepress.org

COLLECTOR BOOKS

A Division of the Schroeder Publishing Company

5801 Kentucky Dam Road, Paducah, KY 42003-9323

Mailing address:

P.O. Box 3009, Paducah, KY 42002-3009

270-898-6211   fax: 270-898-8890

www.collectorbooks.com   email: editor@collectorbooks.com

Collector Books was founded in 1969 and is a division of Schroeder Publishing Company. The house is dedicated to bringing the most up-to-date information and values to collectors in an attractive high-quality format. Their books are designed to be practical, easy-to-use tools to assist collectors in their pursuit of antiques and collectibles. The range of collectibles covered is always growing and now includes fields such as Depression-era glass, pottery and porcelain, china and dinnerware, cookie jars and salt shakers, stoneware, paper collectibles, Barbie dolls, dolls, toys, quilts, tools and weapons, jewelry, and accessories, furniture, advertising memorabilia, bottles, Christmas collectibles, cigarette lighters, decoys, doorstops, and gas station memorabilia.

Collector's publications are liberally illustrated editions, generally filled with histories, production facts and lore, research sources, and identification information. Collector Books also produces inventory ledgers for professional dealers and avid collectors. The house produces a midsize list of new offerings each year and maintains a sizable backlist of nearly 400 titles.

Every August, Collector publishes *Schroeder's Antiques Price Guide*, which features more than 50,000 listings and hundreds of photographs for identification and current values, as well as background and historical information.

Recent Collector Book's titles are *Collecting Costume Jewelry 202* by Julia Carroll; *B.J. Summers Guide to Coca-Cola* by B.J. Summers; *The Official Precious Moments Collector's Guide to Figurines 4th Edition* by John and Malinda Bomm; *Madame Alexander 2010 Collector's Dolls Price Guide #35* by Linda Crowsey; *Quilt Art Engagement Calendar 2011* by Klaudeen Hansen; and *Barbie Doll Photo Album 1959 to 2009* by J. Michael Augustyniak.

Collector Books looks for its authors to be knowledgeable people who are considered experts within their fields. Writers who feel there is a real need for a book on their collectible subject and have available a large comprehensive collection are invited to contact the publisher at the house's mailing address.

Collector Books distributes its own list, targeting particularly bookstore buyers and antiques-trade professionals. Collector Books operates an especially strong mail-order program and purveys selected works from other publishers, including out-of-print titles in the collectibles and antiques field. Query letters and SASEs should be directed to:

Bill Schroeder, Publisher

CONARI PRESS [SEE RED WHEEL/WEISER, LLC]

CONTINUUM INTERNATIONAL PUBLISHING GROUP

BURNS & OATES

T&T CLARK, USA

THOEMMES PRESS

80 Maiden Lane, Suite 704, New York, NY 10038

212-953-5858   fax: 212-953-5944

www.continuumbooks.com   email: info@continuumbooks.com

Continuum is the trade and academic imprint of the Continuum International Publishing Group, a growing family of religious, trade, and academic publishers headquartered in London, with offices in New York, Harrisburg, Denver, Bristol, and Poole. Continuum publishes high-quality nonfiction in the humanities, including theology and religious studies, spirituality, philosophy, education, linguistics, literature, performing arts, the social sciences, women's studies, and popular culture. With a wide range of books from their popular music series, 33 1/3, to works by the great Jewish theologian Abraham Joshua Heschel, Jonathan Sacks, Chief Rabbi of Britain and the Commonwealth, and philosopher Roger Scruton, Continuum's books are read by academics, educators, librarians, students, and the intellectually curious around the world. Its output consists of trade books, texts, scholarly monographs, and reference works. Continuum offers about 500 new publications a year, as well as nearly 6,000 established backlist titles.

From the Continuum list are *Brian Eno's Another Green World* by Geeta Dayal; *A Cultural Dictionary of Punk* by Nicholas Rombes; *Bedside, Bathtub & Armchair Companion to Dickens* by Brian Murray; *Wesley: A Guide for the Perplexed* by Jason E. Vickers; *The Power of Comics* by Randy Duncan; *Sin Bravely* by Mark Ellingsen; *Between Heaven and Charing Cross* by Martin Warner; and *The Secret Temple* by Peter Levenda.

BURNS & OATES

Burns & Oates is the premier Roman Catholic publishing imprint in Great Britain, and a leading imprint throughout the English-speaking world. Authors include Timothy Radcliffe OP, Joseph Ratzinger (now Pope Benedict XVI), Cardinal Daneels, Eamon Duffy, Cardinal Walter Kasper, and Anselm Grün. Recent titles include *St. John of the Cross* by Peter Tyler; *Excellent Mrs. Fry* by Anne Isba; *Islam Today* by Ron Geaves; and *Tudor Queens of England* by David Loades.

T&T CLARK, USA

T&T Clark's tradition of publishing works by world-class scholars in both Europe and North America stretches back to 1821, when it was founded in Edinburgh by Thomas Clark (he was joined in 1846 by his nephew, also named Thomas). T&T Clark became part of Continuum in 2000. In 2003, the three religious academic imprints of Sheffield Academic Press, Trinity Press International, and T&T Clark were united under one imprint.

The list includes past and present biblical scholars such as James D. G. Dunn, Richard Hays, Martin Hengel, and Gerd Theissen, and theologians such as Karl Barth, Wolfhart Pannenberg, Karl Rahner, and T.F. Torrance. Recent T&T Clark titles include *Constructions of Space II: The Biblical City and Other Imagined Spaces* by Jon Berquist and Claudia Camp; *The Non-Canonical Gospels* by Paul Foster; *Calvin: A Guide for the Perplexed* by Paul Helm; *Nietzsche and Theology* by Craig Hovey; and *The Theology of Death* by Douglas Davies.

THOEMMES PRESS

Thoemmes Press began in 1989 as an adjunct to Thoemmes Antiquarian Books. Subsequently Thoemmes Press became independent. The press rapidly established an international reputation for scholarly reference publishing. In particular, it published primary source material (often in facsimile form, but sometimes re-set) and Biographical Dictionaries in Philosophy and allied areas of intellectual history. Recent Thoemmes Press titles include *The Bibliography of Modern British Philosophy* by John G. Slater; *The Biographical Dictionary of British Economists* by Donald Rutherford; *British Education: Or, The Source of the Disorders of Great Britain* by Thomas Sheridan; *The Dictionary of Seventeenth-Century French Philosophers* by Luc Foisneau.

Continuum is distributed through Books International. Continuum also distributes the publishing programs of Chiron Publications, Daimon Publications, Spring Publications, and Paragon House.

Query letters via email are preferred, or send via regular mail with SASEs, to the appropriate editor:

David Barker, PhD, Editorial Director (Continuum)—Film, music, popular culture, politics; david@continuumbooks.com

Katie Gallof, Assistant Editor (Continuum/T&T Clark)—Media studies; kgallof@continuum-book.com

Marie-Claire Antoine, Acquisitions Editor—Politics and international relations; mantoine@continuumbooks.com

Robin Baird-Smith—Publishing Director (Burns & Oates)

INDEPENDENT U.S. PRESSES

COOL SPRING PRESS [SEE THOMAS NELSON, INC.]

COPPER CANYON PRESS

P.O. Box 271, Building 313, Fort Worden State Park, Port Townsend, WA 98368

360-385-4925/877-501-1393   fax: 360-385-4985

www.coppercanyonpress.org   email: poetry@coppercanyonpress.org

Copper Canyon Press was founded in 1972 in the belief that good poetry is essential to the individual spirit and a necessary element in a thriving culture. The press publishes poetry exclusively and has established an international reputation for its commitment to its authors, editorial acumen, and dedication to expanding the audience of poetry. The Copper Canyon mission is to publish poetry distinguished in both content and design, within the context of belief that the publisher's art—like the poet's—is sacramental. The press publishes in hardcover and paperback.

Copper Canyon Press publishes new collections of poetry by both revered and emerging American poets, anthologies, prose books about poetry, translations of classical and contemporary work from many of the world's cultures, and re-issues of out-of-print poetry classics. Within its ambitious vision, there are limitations; Copper Canyon generally does not sign many new writers. The house assigns its resources to furthering its established roster. The publisher's success in its aim is proven through abundant and continuing recognition of its authors via honors, awards, grants, and fellowships.

Copper Canyon has published more than 300 books and CDs, including works by Nobel Laureates Pablo Neruda, Odysseas Elytis, Octavio Paz, Vincente Aleixandre, and Czeslaw Milosz; Pulitzer Prize-winners Carolyn Kizer, Maxine Kumin, and W.S. Merwin; and National Book Award winners Hayden Carruth and Lucille Clifton.

Recent titles from Copper Canyon are *Upgraded to Serious* by Heather McHugh; *Rising, Falling, Hovering* by C.D. Wright; *Lao-Tzu's Taoteching* translated by Red Pine; *Mister Skylight* by Ed Skoog; *Flood Song* by Sherwin Bitsui; and *The Dance of No Hard Feelings* by Mark Bibbins.

Copper Canyon distributes to the trade via Consortium.

Copper Canyon Press has suspended its annual Hayden Carruth Award while exploring other options for considering the work of new and emerging poets. For now, unsolicited manuscripts will not be accepted; however, queries will be read from poets who have previously published a book.

All queries must include an SASE, a one-page cover letter, and a biographical vitae. Query letters and SASEs should be directed to:

Michael Wiegers, Executive Editor

Alison Lockhart, Assistant Editor

COUNCIL OAKS BOOKS

WILDCAT CANYON PRESS

2015 E. 15th Street, Suite B, Tulsa, OK 74104

918-743-BOOK/800-247-8850   fax: 918-743-4288

www.counciloakbooks.com

Council Oaks Books, founded in 1984, is a publisher of nonfiction books based in personal, intimate history (memoirs, letters, diaries); nature, animals, and wildlife; Native American history and spiritual teachings; African American history and contemporary experience; small illustrated inspirational gift books; and unique vintage photo books and Americana. Bestsellers include *The Four Agreements* by Don Miguel Ruiz and *Wise Talk, Wild Women* by Gwen Mazer.

Recent Council Oaks titles include *The Second Life of John Wilkes Booth* by Barnaby Conrad; *The Microbe Factor* by Hiromi Shinya; *The Art of Navigation* by Felix Wolf; *Enzyme Factor* by Hiromi Shinya; *Sound* by Joseph Rael; and *Tibet: 100,000 Prayers of Compassion* by Ken Ballard.

WILDCAT CANYON PRESS

Wildcat Canyon Press publishes books about relationships, women's issues, and home and family, with a focus on personal growth. The editors at this imprint strive to create books that inspire reflection and improve the quality of life. Council Oaks and Wildcat Canyon Press categories include body/mind/spirit, cookbooks, environment/natural world, history, multicultural, and women's studies/feminist.

Wildcat Canyon titles include *Teen Girlfriends* by Julia DeVillers; *Celebrating the Good Times, Getting Through the Hard Times* by Julia DeVillers; *Urban Etiquette* by Charles Purdy; *40 over 40* by Brenda Kinsel; *Hip Girls' Handbook for the Working World* by Jennifer Musselman and Patty Fletcher; and *Taming Your Inner Brat: A Guide for Transforming Self-Defeating Behavior* by Pauline Wallin.

At present, Council Oaks Books is not accepting proposals. Query and SASEs to:

Sally Dennison, PhD, Editor

J. COUNTRYMAN [SEE THOMAS NELSON, INC.]

THE COUNTRYMAN PRESS [SEE W.W. NORTON & COMPANY]

COUNTRYSPORT PRESS [SEE DOWN EAST BOOKS]

CROSSING PRESS [SEE TEN SPEED PRESS]

CROSSROAD PUBLISHING COMPANY

HERDER & HERDER

831 Chestnut Ridge Road, Chestnut Ridge, NY 10977

845-517-0180

www.crossroadpublishing.com   email: ask@crossroadpublishing.com

Crossroad Publishing Company (founded in 1980) publishes general interest and scholarly titles in religion, Catholicism, spirituality, and personal improvement. Its books include spirituality, religion, mind/body/spirit, and counseling for general and popular religious markets.

Crossroad and sibling imprint Herder & Herder is a U.S.-based wing of the international firm Verlag Herder (founded in 1798). The programs of Crossroad and Herder & Herder offer books by some of the most distinguished authors in the U.S. and abroad in the fields of theology, spirituality, religious education, women's studies, world religions, psychology, and counseling. Crossroad looks for authors who can form long-term and personal publishing relationships.

Titles from Crossroad include *The Complete Mystical Works of Meister Eckhart* translated by Maurice O'C Walshe; *Discerning the Will of God* by Timothy Gallagher, OMV; *The Naked Now* by Richard Rohr, OFM; *In the Name of Jesus* by Henri Nouwen; and *The Difference God Makes* by Francis Cardinal George, OMI.

HERDER & HERDER

Herder & Herder publishes books in theology, Christian mysticism, religious studies, and religious education for professionals and active members of Catholic and mainstream Protestant churches. Titles from Herder & Herder include *The Harvest of Mysticism in Medieval Germany* by Bernard McGinn; *Leadership in the Church* by Walter Cardinal Kasper; *The Church Women Want: Catholic Women in Dialogue* edited by Elizabeth A. Johnson; *The Local Church* by Christopher Ruddy; *The Systematic Thought of Hans Urs von Balthasar* by Kevin Mongrain; and *Anti-Catholicism in America* by Mark S. Massa.

Email submissions are preferred and should be sent to info@crossroad publishing.com with the word "submission" in the subject line. Query letters and SASE should be directed to:

John Jones, Editorial Director (Herder & Herder queries)

CROSSWAY BOOKS

1300 Crescent Street, Wheaton, IL 60187-5883

630-682-4300   fax: 630-682-4785

www.gnpcb.org

Crossway Books (founded in 1938) is a division of Good News Publishers. Crossway produces a small list of books with an evangelical Christian perspective aimed at both the religious and general audience, including issue-oriented nonfiction, evangelical works, inspiration, and fiction.

Crossway Books is interested in acquiring nonfiction areas of books on the deeper Christian life, issue-oriented books, and a select number of academic and professional volumes. It feels called to publish fiction works that fall into these categories: historical, youth/juvenile, adventure, action, intrigue, thriller, and contemporary and Christian realism.

From the Crossway list: *Evangelicalism: What Is It and Is It Worth Keeping?* by D. A. Carson; *The Gospel and the Mind: Recovering and Shaping the Intellectual Life* by Bradley G. Green; *God's Glory in Salvation Through Judgment* by James

Hamilton; *Apologetics for the Twenty-First Century* by Louis Markos; and *Redeeming Singleness: How the Storyline of Scripture Affirms the Single Life* by Barry Danylak.

Sample children's books: *The Toddler's 1-2-3 Bible Storybook* by Carolyn Larsen, illustrated by Caron Turk; *Keeping Holiday* by Starr Meade; *ESV Illustrated Family Bible: 270 Selections from the Holy Bible* by Zbigniew Freus; *Kindness Counts* by Debbie Anderson; *Tell Me About Heaven* by Randy Alcorn, illustrated by Ron DiCianni; and *The Big Picture Story Bible* by David Helm, illustrated by Gail Schoonmaker.

No unsolicited manuscripts will be accepted. Send query letters and SASEs to:

Jill Carter, Editorial Administrator

DA CAPO PRESS [SEE PERSEUS BOOKS GROUP]

DALKEY ARCHIVE PRESS

University of Illinois, 1805 S. Wright Street, MC-011, Champaign, IL 61820
217-244-5700 fax: 217-244-9142
www.dalkeyarchive.com email: contact@dalkeyarchive.com

The aim of Dalkey Archive, a division of the Center for Book Culture, is to bring under one roof the best of modern and contemporary literature and to create a space where this literature is protected from the whims of the marketplace. At the heart of the house's mission is a dedication to breakthrough artistic expression in fiction and an educational, interpretive function that goes beyond what most publishers are doing.

Unlike many small presses, and certainly unlike commercial presses, Dalkey has always been rooted in critical inquiry, most evident in the *Review of Contemporary Fiction*, the periodical from which the book publisher is an offshoot and more recently in the new periodical, *CONTEXT*. When the press first started operations in 1984, the *Review* was providing criticism on overlooked writers, and the press was in many cases publishing those same writers, or writers who belonged to a similar subversive aesthetic tradition. Since its founding, the press has published over 250 works of world literature and criticism. Dalkey Archive Press is currently seeking book-length scholarly works.

Recent Dalkey Archive Press titles include *Witz* by Joshua Cohen; *Self-Portrait*

Abroad by Jean-Philippe Toussaint; *Homesick* by Eshkol Nevo and Sondra Silverston; *The Golden Age* by Michal Ajvaz and Andrew Oakland; and *The Collaborators* by Pierre Siniac and Jordan Stump.

Dalkey Archive handles its own distribution.

Dalkey prefers submissions sent by email, directed to submissions@dalkeyarchive.com. Query letters and SASEs should be directed to the "Acquisitions Editor."

John O'Brien, Director

Jeremy Davies, Editor

IVAN R. DEE, PUBLISHER [SEE ROWMAN & LITTLEFIELD PUBLISHING GROUP]

DEVORSS & COMPANY

P.O. Box 1389, Camarillo, CA 93011-1389

805-322-9010/800-843-5743   fax: 805-322-9011

www.devorss.com   email: service@devorss.com

Devorss & Company has been publishing metaphysical and spiritual books since 1929. The house was founded in Los Angeles by Douglas Kimball DeVorss, who set up as a publisher of what today would be called Body/Mind/Spirit books. At that time, the term was New Thought, and Los Angeles was already home to many centers, institutes, and churches that taught a new, "metaphysical," brand of philosophy and spirituality.

Recent Devorss titles include *The Magic Story: Updated and Revised* by Frederic Van Rensselaer Dey; *The Neville Reader: A Collection of Spiritual Writings and Thoughts on Your Inner Power to Create an Abundant Life* by Neville Goddard; *Your Weight or Your Life? Balancing the Scale for a Healthy Life from Within* by Barbara McCalmon; *Fitzpatrick Lane: A Book of Prayers* by Dianne Edleman; and *Communing with Music: Practicing the Art of Conscious Listening* by Matthew Cantello.

Submit queries, proposals, and SASEs via regular mail to Editorial Submissions. Queries only may be sent to editorial@devorss.com.

Gary Peattie, Submissions Editor

DIMENSIONS FOR LIVING [SEE ABINGDON PRESS]

DISNEY PRESS [SEE HYPERION]

DORCHESTER PUBLISHING COMPANY

HARD CASE CRIME
LEISURE
LOVE SPELL
MAKING IT
SMOOCH

200 Madison Avenue, Suite 2000, New York, NY 10016

800-481-9191

www.dorchesterpub.com

WILDSIDE PRESS

9710 Traville Gateway Dr., #234, Rockville, MD 20850

301-762-1305

www.wildsidepress.com   email: editorial@wildsidepress.com

Dorchester is the oldest independent mass-market publisher in America. From its founding in 1971, Dorchester editors have strived to bring the freshest authors to millions of fans. Although mostly known for romance, Dorchester also publishes horror, Westerns, and thrillers under its Leisure Books imprint. Dorchester has recently added science-fiction and fantasy titles from the Wildside press imprint, and has begun distributing the bestselling Family Doctor series of health guides in the U.S. and Canada.

Dorchester has given a start to hundreds of first-time authors. Authors like Madeline Baker, Norah Hess, Cassie Edwards, Patricia Gaffney, Catherine Hart, Shirl Henke, Dara Joy, Jayne Ann Krentz, Christine Feehan, and Connie Mason all began their publishing careers with Dorchester.

Dorchester is the leader in consistently publishing romances in specialty genres like time-travel, paranormal, futuristic, faerie tale, and heartspell (which involves a little magic in the affairs of the heart).

HARD CASE CRIME

Hard Case Crime is an award-winning line of pulp-style mysteries. Recent titles from Hard Case Crime include *Choke Hold* by Christa Faust; *Quarry's Ex* by Max Allan Collins; *Murder Is My Business* by Brett Halliday; and *Nobody's Angel* by Jack Clark.

LEISURE

Leisure is Dorchester's flagship imprint that publishes romances, Westerns, fantasy, science fiction, horror, thrillers, and more. Recent titles from Leisure include *The Fox Run* by David Robbins; *Queen of Song and Souls* by C. L. Wilson; *Runaway* by Bobbi Smith; *The Shore* by Robert Dunbar; *Beauty and the Bounty* by Robert J. Randisi; *Cold Cache* by Tim Champlin; and *The Coptic Secret* by Gregg Loomis.

LOVE SPELL

In 1994 Dorchester created the Love Spell imprint to react to the market for newer types of romance. Recent titles from Love Spell include *In the Midnight Hour* by Kimberly Raye; *A Stroke of Magic* by Tracy Madison; *Beneath Bone Lake* by Colleen Thompson; *Ice* by Stephanie Rowe; *When Sparks Fly* by Autumn Dawn; *Gotcha!* by Christie Craig; and *The Dangerous Book for Demon Slayers* by Angie Fox.

MAKING IT

Making It Press was launched in 2004 for trade paperback chick-lit novels. Recent titles from Making It include *I Shot You Babe* by Leslie Langtry; *Mayhem in High Heels* by Gemma Halliday; *Denim: The Fabric of Our Lives* by Phil Cosker et al; *Alibi in High Heels* by Gemma Halliday; and *Guns Will Keep Us Together* by Leslie Langtry.

SMOOCH

The Smooch imprint is for young-adult readers. Recent titles from Smooch include *Finding the Forger* by Libby Sternberg; *I Am So Jinxed!* by Naomi Marsh; and *Circus of the Darned* by Katie Maxwell.

WILDSIDE PRESS

COSMOS BOOKS

POINT BLANK

PRIME BOOKS

Since 1989, Wildside Press has become one of the industry's leading publishers of science fiction and fantasy. Wildside also runs the Cosmos Books, Point Blank, and Prime Books imprints. Talent includes award-winner Robert Silverberg, bestseller Alan Dean Foster, and Robert E. Howard, creator of Conan the Barbarian. Wildside press has been nominated six times for the World Fantasy Award for Publishing Excellence.

Recent titles from Wildside include *The Devil's Party: A Brief History of Satanic Abuse* by Brian Stableford; *Cleek the Master Detective* by Thomas W. Hanshew; *All White Girls* by Michael Bracken; *Lord of the Triple Moons* by Ardath Mayhar; *Shambleau: A Northwest Smith Adventure* by C. L. Moore; *Dream; or, The Simian Maid: A Fantasy of Prehistory* by S. Fowler Wright; and *The People of the Crater* by Andre Norton.

COSMOS BOOKS

Cosmos was originally established in 1979 by Philip Harbottle and was acquired by John Gregory Betancourt of Wildside in July 1999. Since then they have released over a hundred titles spanning science fiction, fantasy, and horror. New titles from Cosmos Books include *A Mouthful of Tongues* by Paul di Filippo; *If Lions Could Speak* by Paul Park; *Toast* by Charles Stross; *Harry Harrison: An Annotated Bibliography* by Paul Tomlinson; and *The Villages* by Dave Hutchinson.

POINT BLANK

Point Blank was established in early 2004 by JT Lindroos and John Betancourt. They specialize in publishing cutting edge fiction and nonfiction: crime, mystery, and otherwise. At this time they are not accepting unsolicited submissions; check their website to see if this has changed. Some titles from Point Blank include *The Big Blind* by Ray Banks; *Street Raised* by Pearche Hansen; *Families Are Murder* by Philip Lawson; and *New Orleans Confidential* by O'Neil De Noux.

PRIME BOOKS

Prime was established in late 2001 by Sean Wallace and specializes in publishing dark horror, science fiction, and fantasy in trade, hardcover, and mass-market paperback. Some recent titles from Prime include *Mr. Gaunt and Other Uneasy Encounters* by John Langan; *Seeds of Change* by John Joseph Adams; *Fantasy: The Best of the Year* by Rich Horton; *The Alchemy of Stone* by Ekaterina Sedia; and *Secret Lives* by Jeff Vandermeer.

Dorchester is currently acquiring the following: romance, horror, Westerns, and thrillers. Wildside Press is not currently accepting submissions. Detailed guidelines are available on their website. Submit query with first three chapters and SASE to the editorial staff.

Alicia Condon, Editorial Director—Romance all genres

Don D'Auria, Editorial Director—Horrors, thrillers, new Westerns

Chris Keeslar, Senior Editor—Romance all genres, fantasy

Leah Hultenschmidt, Editor—Romance all genres, Westerns

John Gregory Betancourt, Publisher, Wildside

DOWN EAST BOOKS

COUNTRYSPORT PRESS

P.O. Box 679, Camden, ME 04843

680 Commercial Street (US Route 1), Rockport, ME 04856

207-594-9544   fax: 207-594-0147

www.downeastbooks.com   email: info@downeastbooks.com

Down East Enterprise began at a kitchen table in 1954 with the creation of *Down East* magazine. In 1967, *Leroy the Lobster* was published and Down East Books was born. Today, Down East Books is the largest book publisher in the state of Maine and has published over 750 books. With the Countrysport Press imprint, Down East has a backlist of many hundreds of titles that grows by dozens of new books every year.

Although Down East Books is the largest book publisher in Maine, it is still a relatively small, regional publisher specializing in books with a strong Maine or New England theme. Current subject areas include general interest nonfiction, art and photography, regional attractions and travel guides, biography and memoir, gardening, cooking, crafts, history, nature and ecology, nautical books, and fiction. A fully developed regional connection is critical in Down East fiction titles, too.

Down East also publishes children's books, and here also the regional subject and setting are highly desirable. Note that the New England setting must be integral to the work; a story that with little or no change could be set in another region would not meet their requirements.

Recent Down East titles include *Atlantic Seafood: Recipes from Chef Michael Howell; Becoming Teddy Roosevelt: How a Maine Guide Inspired America's 26th President* by Andrew Vietze; *Chosen Faith, Chosen Land: The Untold Story of America's 21st Century Shakers* by Jeannine Lauber; *Damaged Goods: A Jack McMorrow Mystery* by Gerry Boyle; *Hit & Mrs.* By Lesley Crewe; and *Looking Astern: An Artist's View of Maine's Historic Waterfronts* by Loretta Krupinski.

Mark your package "Book Proposal" and direct queries and SASEs to:

John Viehman, Publisher; jviehman@downeast.com

Paul Doiron, Editor-in-Chief; editorial@downeast.com

INDEPENDENT U.S. PRESSES

WILLIAM B. EERDMANS PUBLISHING COMPANY

EERDMANS BOOKS FOR YOUNG READERS

2140 Oak Industrial Dr. NE, Grand Rapids, MI 49505

616-459-4591/800-253-7521   fax: 616-459-6540

www.eerdmans.com   email: info@eerdmans.com

William B. Eerdmans Publishing Company (founded in 1911) is one of the largest independent nondenominational Christian religious publishers in the U.S. Founded in 1911 and still independently owned, Eerdmans Publishing Company has long been known for publishing a wide range of religious books, from academic works in theology, biblical studies, religious history, and reference to popular titles in spirituality, social and cultural criticism, and literature.

Eerdmans publishes titles of general interest; religious, academic, and theological works; books for young readers; regional histories; and American religious history. The house offers a Christian handle on such areas as anthropology, biblical studies, and religious approaches to biography, African American studies, church administration, music, philosophy, psychology, science, social issues, current and historical theology, and women's interests.

New on the Eerdmans list: *Neither Calender Nor Clock: Perspectives on the Belhar Confession* by Piet Naude; *Building Cultures of Trust* by Martin Marty; *Christian Ethics in a Technological Age* by Brian Brock; *Christology and Ethics* edited by F. LeRon Shults and Brent Waters; and *Reconciled Humanity: Karl Barth in Dialogue* by Hans Vium Mikkelsen.

EERDMANS BOOKS FOR YOUNG READERS

Eerdmans Books for Young Readers, founded in 1995 as an imprint of William B. Eerdmans Publishing Company, seeks to publish beautifully written and illustrated books that nurture children's faith in God and help young people to explore and understand the wonder, joy, and challenges of life.

Eerdmans Books for Young Readers publishes picture books and middle-reader and young-adult fiction and nonfiction. They seek manuscripts that are honest, wise, and hopeful, but also publish stories that simply delight the editors with their story line, characters, or good humor. Stories that celebrate diversity, stories of historical significance, and stories that relate to current issues are of special interest to them at this time. The house considers manuscripts that address spiritual themes in authentic and imaginative ways without being didactic. They currently publish 12–18 books a year.

Some recent titles include *Do You Have a Cat?* By Eileen Spinelli; *Animals of the Bible* by Marie-Helene Delval; *Sivu's Six Wishes* by Jude Daly; *The Wild Man* by Mark Barratt; *The Nativity* by Ruth Sanderson; and *The Middle Sheep* by Frances Watts.

Eerdmans Books for Young Readers will only consider exclusive submissions that are clearly marked as such on the outside of the envelope. They do not accept simultaneous submissions and those sent will be discarded. Query letters with proposal or sample chapters and SASEs should be directed to:

Jon Pott, Editor-in-Chief (Eerdmans)

Editor, Young Readers

ENTREPRENEUR PRESS

2445 McCabe Way, Suite 400, Irvine, CA 92614

949-261-2325/800-864-6864   fax: 949-261-7729

www.entrepreneurpress.com   email: press@entrepreneur.com

Entrepreneur Press, a division of Entrepreneur Media, Inc. (publishers of *Entrepreneur* magazine), publishes trade books offering practical advice and inspirational success stories for business owners and aspiring entrepreneurs. The goal of the house is to provide essential business information to help plan, run, and grow small businesses. Areas of expertise include instructional business books, and motivational, management, marketing, new economy, e-commerce, and personal finance titles that appeal to a broad spectrum of the business book-buying audience.

Titles include *Flashpoint* by J.K. Harris; *Starting Green* by Glenn Croston, PhD; *Get Connected* by Starr Hall and Chadd Rosenberg; *Taxpertise* by Bonnie Lee, E.A.; and *Design and Launch an Online Gift Business in a Week* by Cheryl Kimball.

Entrepreneur Press books are distributed to the trade by National Book Network. Query letters and SASEs should be directed to:

Jere L. Calmes, Editor; jcalmes@entrepreneur.com

ESPN BOOKS [SEE HYPERION]

M. EVANS AND COMPANY [SEE ROWMAN & LITTLEFIELD PUBLISHING GROUP]

FACTS ON FILE

CHECKMARK BOOKS

132 West 31st Street, 17th Floor, New York, NY 10001

212-967-8800/800-322-8755   fax: 212-967-9196/800-678-3633

www.factsonfile.com   email: editorial@factsonfile.com

Facts On File (founded in 1940) is a dynamic popular-reference publisher. The house has many award-winning titles to its credit, and many Facts On File publications feature an innovative production approach. The publisher is extremely well tuned to specific category markets, which it targets with marked commercial consistency.

Facts On File is one of the nation's top providers of resources for teaching and learning. They produce high-quality reproducible handouts, online databases, CD-ROMS, and print reference and information titles in a broad popular range, including literature, science, geography, nature, technology, world history, American history, business, popular culture, fashion, design, sports, health, current affairs and politics, and the environment. Facts on File is also the first place that many teachers, students, librarians, and parents turn for general reference works. They offer a broad selection of historical and cultural atlases, dictionaries, and encyclopedias geared toward professional as well as popular interests, and are one of the pioneers of the electronic multimedia-publishing frontier.

Facts On File has made a renewed commitment to its goal of becoming the premier print and electronic reference publisher in the industry. It is striving to be the beacon and a guide for librarians, teachers, students, parents, and researchers to look to for award-winning materials, cutting-edge trends, and innovative products. This is the publisher to be sought when the requirements are nebulous and the transitions are turbulent.

Recent Facts On File books include *Justices of the United States Supreme Court* by Leon Friedman Israel; *Earth Science Experiments* by Pamela Walker and Elaine Wood; *Jupiter and Saturn* by Linda Elkins-Tanton; *The Truth About Alcohol* by Barry Youngerman et al; and *A Brief History of Afghanistan* by Shaista Wahab and Barry Youngerman.

CHECKMARK BOOKS

The year 1998 brought the launch of the trade imprint Checkmark Books. It was created to provide booksellers and consumers with quality resources focused on topics such as business, careers, fitness, health and nutrition, history, nature, parenting, pop culture, and self-help.

Examples of Checkmark Books are *Field Guide to Finding a New Career in Internet and Media* by Amanda Kirk; *The New Complete Book of Food* by Carol Ann

Rinzler et al; *The Student-Athlete's College Recruitment Guide* by Ashley Benjamin et al; *Tae Kwon Do: My Life and Philosophy* by Yeon Hwan Park; and *Virtual Apprentice! Fashion Designer* by Don Rauf and Monique Vescia.

Facts On File utilizes individualized marketing and distribution programs that are particularly strong in the areas of corporate, institutional, and library sales.

Query letters, proposals, and SASEs should be directed to:

Laurie Likoff, Editorial Director

Frank Darmstadt, Editor—Science and math

FAIRVIEW PRESS

2450 Riverside Avenue, Minneapolis, MN 55454

612-672- 4180/800-544-8207   fax: 612-672-4980

www.fairviewpress.org   email: press@fairview.org

Fairview Press publishes books dedicated to the physical, emotional, and spiritual health of children, adults, and seniors—specializing in books on aging and eldercare, grief and bereavement, health and wellness, inspiration, and parenting and childcare.

The house is a division of Fairview Health Services, a regional health care provider affiliated with the University of Minnesota. This affiliation, combined with their award-winning books, has caused industry experts to name Fairview Press as one of the "Top 50 Independent Publishers" in the U.S. Fairview authors have been featured on CNN, CBS, NBC's *Today* show, National Public Radio, and in hundreds of other local, national, and international media outlets.

At this time, Fairview is particularly interested in acquiring manuscripts that deal with the following topics: pregnancy and childbirth, health issues for young adults, complementary/holistic/integrative medicine, diet and exercise, and inspiration and mindfulness. They are de-emphasizing their previous focus on end-of-life issues, but will consider proposals on any topic pertaining to physical, emotional, or spiritual wellness.

Recent Fairview Press titles include *Daily Comforts for Caregivers* by Pat Samples; *Help Me Say Goodbye* by Janis Silverman; *Out of the Ashes* by Peter and Peggy Holmes; *Raising Strong Daughters* by Jeanette Gadeberg; and *Remembering with Love* by Elizabeth Levang, PhD, and Sherokee Isle.

Fairview Press operates through a variety of sales venues; the press is distributed to the trade through National Book Network.

Query letters, proposals, and SASEs should be addressed to:

Steve Deger, Acquisitions Manager

FAITH COMMUNICATIONS [SEE HEALTH COMMUNICATIONS, INC.]

FALCON GUIDES [SEE THE GLOBE PEQUOT PRESS]

FANTAGRAPHICS BOOKS

7563 Lake City Way NE, Seattle, WA 98115

206-524-1967/800-657-1100   fax: 206-524-2104

www.fantagraphics.com   email: fbicomix@fantagraphics.com

blog: www.fantagraphics.com/blog

Fantagraphics publishes comics and comic art. The house features a list of mainstream, classic, and underground offerings and also purveys a strong line of erotic comics and comics-related books. Fantagraphics Books (inaugurated in 1976) produces trade paperbacks, hardbound editions, and quality fine-art album editions of graphic productions, in addition to comic books, comics-related magazines, and a line of gift items dedicated to this most accessible literary form.

Comics creators cataloged by Fantagraphics include Peter Bagge, Vaughn Bode, Daniel Clowes, Guido Crepax, Robert Crumb, Dame Darcy, Kim Deitch, Julie Doucet, Jules Feiffer, Frank Frazetta, Drew Friedman, Rick Geary, Los Bros. Hernandez, Peter Kuper, Terry LeBan, Douglas Michael, Joe Sacco, Gilbert Shelton, Art Spiegelman, Ralph Steadman, Basil Wolverton, and Wallace Wood.

Recent Fantagraphics titles include *The Best American Comics Criticism* edited by Ben Schwartz; *The Search for Smilin' Ed* by Kim Deitch; *Dungeon Quest, Book One* by Joe Daly; *Tales Designed to Thrizzle # 6*; and *Wally Gropius* by Tim Hensley.

Take note of the originality and diversity of the themes and approaches to drawing in such Fantagraphics titles as *Love & Rockets* (stories of life in Latin America and Chicano L.A. which draw on influences as diverse as Luis Buñuel, Frida Kahlo, and Hank Ketcham); *Palestine* (journalistic autobiography in the Middle East); *Eightball* (surrealism mixed with kitsch culture in stories alternately humorous and painfully personal); and *Naughty Bits* (feminist humor and short stories which both attack and commiserate). Prior to submitting, try to develop your own, equally individual voice; originality, aesthetic maturity, and graphic storytelling skill are the signs by which Fantagraphics judges whether or not your submission is ripe for publication. Query letters should be accompanied by short, carefully selected samples and an SASE.

FELDHEIM PUBLISHERS

208 Airport Executive Park, Nanuet, NY 10954

845-356-2282/800-237-7149   fax: 845-425-1908

www.feldheim.com

Feldheim Publishers (founded in 1954) is among the leading houses in areas of Jewish thought, translations from Hebrew of classical works, dictionaries and general reference works, textbooks, and guides for Sabbaths and festivals, as well as literature for readers ages three and up. The Feldheim publishing program is expanding and the house releases an increasing number of titles each season. Feldheim retains a comprehensive backlist.

Recent titles include *The Miracle of the Golden Dove and Other Stories: Timeless Tales from the Lives of Our Sages* by Genendel Krohn; *Where Am I* by Ruchy Schon; *Remarkable Park* by Bracha Goetz; *Dollhouse: A Novel* by Miri Sonnenfeld; and *Women's Wisdom: The Garden of Peace for Women* by Rabbi Shalom Arush.

Feldheim handles its own distribution and offers the books of additional publishers such as American Yisroel Chai Press and Targum Press.

Query letters and SASEs should be directed to:

Yitzchak Feldheim, President

FLUX [SEE LLEWELLYN WORLDWIDE]

FORTRESS PRESS [SEE AUGSBURG FORTRESS BOOKS]

FREE SPIRIT PUBLISHING

217 Fifth Avenue North, Suite 200, Minneapolis, MN 55401-1299

612-338-2068/800-735-7323   fax: 612-337-5050

www.freespirit.com   email: help4kids@freespirit.com

For over 25 years, Free Spirit's mission has been to provide children and teens—and the adults who care for and about them—the tools they need to succeed in life and to make a positive difference in the world.

Based in Minneapolis, Minnesota, Free Spirit Publishing is known for its unique understanding of what kids want (and need) to know to navigate life successfully. The house built its reputation as the leading publisher of self-help books for teens and kids. Their books and other learning materials are practical, positive, pro-kid, and solution focused. Free Spirit is not afraid to tackle tough topics such as teen depression, kids and anxiety, grief and loss, juvenile justice, and conflict resolution. Free Spirit also offers sound advice with a sense of humor on relevant issues including stress management, character building, puberty, school success, self-esteem, and more. The house aims to meet all kids—toddlers, teens, and in-betweens—where they are (not where we wish they were), and support them to develop their talents, build resiliency, and foster a positive outlook on life so they can reach their goals.

Founded by Judy Galbraith, a former classroom teacher and education specialist, Free Spirit pushes boundaries on behalf of young people. For example, they pioneered use of the term "learning differences" to replace "learning disabilities" because they know that kids with LD are eager and able to learn—just in a different way. Free Spirit is also a recognized leader in meeting the needs of another special population—gifted and talented youth. Judy Galbraith's groundbreaking *The Gifted Kids' Survival Guides*, first published in 1984, have remained perennial bestsellers (300,000 copies in print) through several updates and revisions. One of Free Spirit's newest ventures is in expanding early childhood offerings, with titles such as *Hands Are Not for Hitting* (100,000 copies in print).

Recent titles include *Going Blue* by Cathryn Berger Kaye, MA et al; *Don't Behave Like You Live in a Cave* by Elizabeth Verdick; *Your Life in Comics* by Bill Zimmerman; and *Real Kids, Real Stories, Real Change* by Garth Sundem.

Free Spirit's distribution is through the trade market, as well as direct to schools and other youth-serving venues.

Query letters and SASEs should be directed to:

Heidi Stier, Acquisitions Editor

Judy Galbraith, Founder and President

FULCRUM PUBLISHING

4690 Table Mountain Drive, Suite 100, Golden, CO 80403

303-277-1623/800-992-2908   fax: 303-279-7111

www.fulcrum-books.com   email: info@fulcrum-books.com

SPECK PRESS

P.O. Box 102004, Denver, CO 80222

303-277-1623/800-992-2908   fax: 800-726-7112

www.speckpress.com   email: books@speckpress.com

Fulcrum is a trade publisher focusing on books that inspire readers to live life to the fullest and learn something new each day. In fiction and nonfiction, subjects include lifestyle, health and wellness, Western culture, outdoor and travel, Native American, memoirs and literature, gardening, environment and nature, and children's titles.

Fulcrum has published books from prominent politicians (Gov. Richard Lamm, Sen. Gary Hart, Sen. Eugene McCarthy), leading Native Americans (Wilma Mankiller, Vine Deloria, Jr., Joseph Bruchac), master gardeners (Lauren Springer, Tom Peace, Richard Hartlage), and important organizations in the environmental community (Campaign for America's Wilderness, World Wilderness Congress, Defenders of Wildlife).

Recent Fulcrum releases are *Awakening Spirits: Wolves in the Southern Rockeis* edited by Richard Reading et al; *Buffalo Bill: Scout Showman, Visionary* by Steve Friesen; *Endangered: Biodiversity on the Brink* by Mitch Tobin; *In the Courts of the Conqueror: The 10 Worst Indian Law Cases Ever Decided* by Walter Echo-Hawk; and *Native Plants for High-Elevation Western Gardens* by Janic Busco and Nancy Morin.

SPECK PRESS

Speck Press is an imprint that explores cultures and subcultures through nonfiction and crime fiction books—revealing scenes that are typically invisible to the casual observer. They currently publish around ten new titles a year, in the areas of subculture, music, environment issues, art, politics, travel, and gift books. New titles from Speck include *The Tattoed Lady: A History* by Amelia Klem Osterud; *The Birth (And Death) of the Cool* by Ted Gioia; *Road Show: Art Cars and the Museum of the Streets* by Eric Dregni and Ruthann Godollei; and *DeKok and the Dead Harlequin* by A. C. Baantjer.

Fulcrum handles its own distribution. Query letters and SASEs should be directed to:

Bob Baron, President and Publisher, Fulcrum

Derek Lawrence, Publisher (Speck Press)
Susan Hill-Newton, Editor (Speck Press)

GENEVA PRESS [SEE PRESBYTERIAN PUBLISHING CORPORATION]

THE GLOBE PEQUOT PRESS

INSIDERS' GUIDES

FALCON GUIDES

FOOTPRINT BOOKS

KNACK BOOKS

LYONS PRESS

SKIRT! BOOKS

246 Goose Lane, P.O. Box 480, Guilford, CT 06437
203-458-4500/800-820-2329   fax: 800-508-8938
www.globepequot.com   email: info@globepequot.com

The Pequot Press, whose name was adapted from a local Indian tribe, was founded in 1947 as an adjunct to the Stonington Printing Company in Stonington, Connecticut. The Boston Globe Newspaper Company purchased the press in February, 1981, formalizing an association that had begun in 1978. Today, more than 60 years after the publication of its first monograph, The Globe Pequot Press has established an international reputation for publication of regional guides to a myriad of travel destinations in this country and around the world and is among the top three sources for travel books in the U.S. Globe Pequot is owned by Georgia-based Morris Communications, a privately held media company with diversified holdings that include newspaper and magazine publishing, outdoor advertising, radio broadcasting, book publishing, and distribution.

Globe Pequot publishes approximately 600 new books each year. In addition to publishing its own imprint, it offers marketing and fulfillment services to client publishers whose combined annual output currently exceeds 200 new titles. Its 75,000-square-foot warehouse holds well over one million units representing approximately 4,000 titles in print, comprising books on domestic and international travel, outdoor recreation, sports, how-to, history, fiction, health and fitness, cooking, and nature.

The Globe Pequot line primarily publishes travel guides, with some select nature titles, cookbooks, and home-based business books. Insiders' Guides are travel and relocation guides written by local authors. Falcon Guides specialize in outdoor recreation, both how-to and where-to, with hiking, biking, climbing, and other specialized lines, including regional history. Footprint Guides publishes guides for experienced independent travelers looking to get off the beaten track. The Lyons Press is primarily a publisher of practical and literary books, as well as being the most distinguished publisher of fishing books in the world (see below for Lyons Press).

In the travel arena, Globe Pequot is well regarded for several bestselling series and also distributes for a number of travel-specialist houses. Among Globe Pequot lines: Quick Escapes (weekend and day trips keyed to metropolitan areas or regions); Romantic Days and Nights; Recommended Bed & Breakfasts; Fun with the Family Guides; Cadogan Guides to destinations worldwide for the discriminating traveler; and the popular Off-the-Beaten-Path series. Globe Pequot also updates a variety of annuals, among them Europe by Eurorail. Globe Pequot's regionally keyed books also cover such interest areas as biking, hiking, mountaineering, skiing, and family activities in the wilderness and on the beach.

Globe Pequot titles include *Growing Up Mary* by Melissa Sue Anderson; *The Long Walk* by Peter Wier; *Forbidden Creatures* by Peter Laufer; and *The Dangerous World of Butterflies* by Peter Laufer.

Query letters and SASEs should be directed to the Submissions Editor with a note on the envelope as to the subject category.

Laura Strom, Executive Editor

INSIDERS' GUIDES

The Insiders' Guide series began with one local guide-book to North Carolina's Outer Banks. Today the series has grown to encompass more than 60 cities and regional destinations in the United States and Bermuda. Written by local authors with years of experience writing about their community, the Insiders' Guides provide newcomers, visitors, and business travelers with a native's perspective of the area. Each guide details hotels, restaurants, annual events, attractions, nightlife, parks and recreation, real estate, and more.

Some titles from Insiders' Guides include *Insiders' Guide to Denver* by Linda Castrone; *Insiders' Guide to North Carolina's Outer Banks* by Julia Kingsley; *Insiders' Guide to Portland, Maine* by Sara Donnelly and Meredith Goad; and *Insiders' Guide to Boulder and Rocky Mountain National Park* by Ann Alexander Leggett.

FALCON GUIDES

Falcon Guides aspires to be the leading publisher of information for non-consumptive, human-powered outdoor recreation, conservation, and natural history. Their guides compel readers to move: to strap on their boots, to mount a bike, to climb a mountain, to slip into a kayak, to commandeer a yak!—in short to ignite the passion for hands-on discovery. Their guidebooks are designed to be highly visual and easily referenced for maximum ease-of-use.

Some titles from Falcon Guides include *Best Rail Trails New England: More Than 40 Rail Trails from Maine to Connecticut* by Cynthia Mascott; *Expedition Kayaking* by Derek C. Hutchinson; *Hiking Utah* by Bill Schneider; *Best Easy Day Hikes: Salt Lake City* by Brian Brinkerhoff; and *Death in the Grizzly Maze: The Timothy Treadwell Story* by Mike Lapinski.

FOOTPRINT BOOKS

The passion for travel and discovery at Footprint has been reflected in guidebooks dating back to the first edition of *The South American Handbook* in 1924: the longest established travel guide in the English language market. Each book is written by authors with firsthand knowledge of the areas they write about, written for independent travelers looking to get off the beaten track and escape the tourist crowds.

Titles include *St. Lucia* by Sarah Cameron; *The Kenya Handbook* by Lizzie Williams; *Diving Southeast Asia* by Beth and Shaun Tierney; *Britain with Kids* by William Gray; and *Scotland Highlands and Islands* by Colin Hutchinson and Alan Murphy.

KNACK BOOKS

Knack is the how-to and reference imprint of Globe Pequot. It includes both stand-alone lead titles featuring authors with visibility on television, radio, education, or the Internet. Some titles from Knack include *Sign Language: A Step by Step Guide to Singing* by Suzie Chafin; *Baby's First Year: A Complete Illustrated Guide to Your Child's First Twelve Months* by Robin McClure and Vince Iannelli; *Bartending Basics: More than 400 Classic and Contemporary Cocktails for Any Occasion* by Cheryl Charming; and *Canoeing for Everyone: A Step-by-Step Guide to Selecting the Gear, Learning the Strokes, and Planning Your Trip* by Daniel A. Gray.

LYONS PRESS

Now an imprint of Globe Pequot, Lyons Press was founded by Nick Lyons in 1984 and has established an international reputation for publishing outstanding titles in its core categories of fishing, hunting, horses, sports, pets, history, adventure, the outdoors, self-reliant living, and reference.

Recent Lyons purchases include a book of ghostly cat tales, the story of a puppy befriending U.S. soldiers in Iraq, a history of the U.S. Space Program, and an exploration of the world of modern-day shipping, indicating an expansion from their core editorial direction.

Titles include *Dead Pet: Send Your Best Little Buddy Off in Style* by Andrew Kirk and Jane Mosely; *Fishing Florida: An Angler's Guide to More than 600 Prime Fishing Spots* by Kris Thoemke; *Newshounds: The Wackiest Dog Stories from Around the World* by Ryan O'Meara; *Fight or Die: The Vinny Paz Story* by Tommy Jon Caduto and Bert Sugar; and *The Bear Almanac: A Comprehensive Guide to the Bears of the World* by Gary Brown.

Direct proposals with SASEs to the Submissions Editor.

Tom McCarthy, Executive Editor—Sports

Holly Rubino, Editor—Animals and pets

Kaleena Cote, Editor

Keith Wallman, Editor

DAVID R. GODINE, PUBLISHER

BLACK SPARROW BOOKS

9 Hamilton Place, Boston, MA 02108-4715

617-451-9600   fax: 617-350-0250

www.godine.com   email: info@godine.com

David R. Godine, Publisher, founded in 1970, is a small publishing house located in Boston, producing between 20 and 30 titles per year and maintaining an active reprint program. The company is independent and its list tends to reflect the individual tastes and interests of its president and founder, David Godine.

At Godine, quality has remained foremost. All of their hardcover and softcover books are printed on acid-free paper. Many hardcovers are still bound in full cloth. The list is deliberately eclectic and features works that many other publishers can't or won't support, books that won't necessarily become bestsellers but that still deserve publication. In a world of spinoffs and commercial product, Godine's list stands apart by offering original fiction and nonfiction of the highest rank, rediscovered masterworks, translations of outstanding world literature, poetry, art, photography, and beautifully designed books for children.

Recently, Godine launched two new series: Imago Mundi, a line of original books devoted to photography and the graphic arts; and Verba Mundi, featuring the most notable contemporary world literature in translation. Volumes in the Imago Mundi series, which has received praise from reviewers and book-sellers alike, include *Jean Cocteau: The Mirror and the Mask* by Julie Saul and *Small Rooms & Hidden Places* by Ronald W. Wohlauer. Verba Mundi has so far published works by world-renowned authors Georges Perec, José Donoso, Isaac Babel, and Anna Seghers, and has introduced new voices such as Sylvie Germain (whose *Book of Nights* was named a Notable Book of the Year by the *New York Times*) and the acclaimed Swedish novelist Goran Tunstrom, author of *The Christmas Oratorio.*

Recent titles from Godine include *Arctic Circle* by Robert Leonard Reid; *Lovers of the Lost* by Wesley McNair; *Swimmer in the Secret Sea* by William Kotzwinkle; *Genius of Common Sense* by Glenna Lang and Marjory Wunsch; and *Desert* by J.M.G. Le Clezio.

BLACK SPARROW BOOKS

On July 1, 2002, John Martin, the founder and for 36 years the publisher of Black Sparrow Press, closed down his shop in Santa Rosa, California. After finding new homes for four of his authors—Charles Bukowski, Paul Bowles, John Fante, and Wyndham Lewis—he entrusted the rest of his backlist to a fellow publisher, David R. Godine. The agreement was simple: Godine would keep Black Sparrow's offerings available to the trade, keep the bestselling titles in print, and keep the house's spirit alive through judicious acquisitions. In short, Black Sparrow Press would be reborn—as Black Sparrow Books at David R. Godine, Publisher.

Recent titles from Black Sparrow Books include *Door to the River* by Aram Saroyan; *By the Waters of Manhattan* by Charles Reznikoff; *Jazz and Twelve O'Clock Tales* by Wanda Coleman; *Holocaust* by Charles Reznikoff; and *Metropolitan Tang* by Linda Bamber.

David R. Godine, Publisher and Black Sparrow Books do not accept unagented unsolicited manuscripts. Authors are advised to have their agents establish contact if they would like their manuscripts to be considered. Do not telephone the office or submit anything via email. Query letters and SASEs should be directed to:

David R. Godine, Publisher

GOSPEL LIGHT PUBLICATIONS

REGAL BOOKS

1957 Eastmen Avenue, Ventura, CA 93003

800-446-7735

www.gospellight.com

Founded in 1933 by Dr. Henrietta Mears, Gospel Light is committed to providing effective resources for evangelism, discipleship, and Christian education through Sunday school and Vacation Bible school curricula, videos, and children's music.

Gospel Light highlights include *Clergy Tax* by J. David Epstein; *A New Kind of Conservative* by Joel Hunter; *Fusion* by Nelson Searcy with Jennifer Henson; *I Want to Believe* by Mel Lawrenz; *Raising Fit Kids in a Fat World* by Judy Halliday, RN and Joanie Jack, MD; *The Relief of Imperfection* by Joan C. Webb; *Yes, Lord* by Harold Bredesen with Pat King; and *The Big Book of Create-Your-Own Bible Lessons* by Sharon Short.

REGAL BOOKS

The Regal Book Division (founded in 1965) specializes in needs-oriented books and building efforts aimed at church leadership and families. Recent Regal titles include *A Woman After God's Heart* by Eadie Goodboy; *A Year of Blind Dates* by Megan Carson; *And He Dwelt Among Us* by A.W. Tozer; *As Long as We Both Shall Live* by Gary Smalley and Ted Cunningham; and *The Beginner's Guide to Fasting* by Elmer Towns.

Queries, proposals, and SASEs should be directed to Acquisitions Editor.

GRAYWOLF PRESS

250 Third Avenue North, Suite 600, Minneapolis, MN 55401

651-641-0077   fax: 651-641-0036

www.graywolfpress.org

Since 1974, Graywolf has been an important outlet for American poetry and helped keep fine literature off the extinction list. Their list also includes novels, short stories, memoirs, and essays, and features such writers as Elizabeth Alexander, Charles Baxter, Sven Birkerts, Linda Gregg, Eamon Grennan, Tony Hoagland, Jane Kenyon, William Kittredge, Carl Phillips, William Stafford, David Treuer, and Brenda Ueland. A commitment to quality, and a willingness to embrace or invent new models, has kept Graywolf at the forefront of the small press movement. Today, Graywolf is considered one of the nation's leading nonprofit literary publishers. The house publishes about 27 new books per year.

Representative of the Graywolf list are *Rainy Lake* by Mary Rockcastle; *I Am Not Sidney Poitier* by Percival Everett; *How to Escape from a Leper Colony* by Tiphanie Yanique; *The Best Short Stories of William Kittredge* by William Kittredge; and *The Art of Description*.

Graywolf Press accepts submissions in the months of January, May, and

September. Submissions received outside of these months will not be considered. Send one hard copy of the finished, book-length manuscript with cover letter to:

Ethan Nosowsky, Editor-at-Large

Katie Dublinski, Editorial Director

Jeff Shotts, Senior Editor

Steve Woodward, Editorial Assistant

GREAT SOURCE EDUCATION GROUP [SEE HOUGHTON MIFFLIN]

GREENWOOD PUBLISHING GROUP [SEE ABC-CLIO]

GROVE/ATLANTIC, INC.

GROVE PRESS

ATLANTIC MONTHLY PRESS

841 Broadway, 4th Floor, New York, NY 10003

212-614-7850   fax: 212-614-7886

www.groveatlantic.com   email: info@groveatlantic.com

Grove/Atlantic publishes trade nonfiction and fiction; these works often display a contemporary cultural bent or an issue-oriented edge. Grove Press and Atlantic Monthly Press, two formerly independent houses, were united under the Grove/Atlantic corporate crest in 1993. Grove/Atlantic operates from the former Grove headquarters on Broadway (with Atlantic having relocated from its pervious digs at nearby Union Square West). The publisher operates essentially as one house, while maintaining the distinction of two major imprints.

GROVE PRESS

Grove Press was founded in 1951 by literary trailblazer Barney Rosset, who established a tradition of enterprising lists that featured some of the finest and most fearless writing from around the globe. This literary institution was purchased by Ann Getty in 1985, in league with the UK-based publisher Weidenfeld & Nicholson; the publisher operated briefly under the sobriquet Grove Weidenfeld. With the early retreat of the Weidenfeld interests, the fate of Grove was a popular topic of publishing tattle rumored to be perpetually on the block, both prior and subsequent to the house's merger with Atlantic Monthly.

ATLANTIC MONTHLY PRESS

Atlantic Monthly Press was founded in 1917 as an imprint of Little, Brown. During the next 16 years, the press's books won more than 16 Pulitzer Prizes and National Book Awards. Among the press's bestselling award-winning titles published during those years were *Mutiny on the Bounty, Goodbye Mr. Chips, Drums Along the Mohawk, Ship of Fools, Fire in the Lake, The Soul of the New Machine,* and *Blue Highways.* In 1985, the press was spun off from the magazine and became independent.

In February 1993, Grove Press and Atlantic Monthly Press merged to form Grove/Atlantic, Inc. Publishing under these two imprints, Grove/Atlantic, Inc., continues to publish books that have been in the forefront of the American literary and publishing scene for more than 75 years. Imprints Canongate Books and Atlantic Books are based in the UK and may be reached via email at enquireies@ groveatlantic.co.uk.

Recent Grove/Atlantic titles include *Now or Never* by Tim Flannery; *The Bell Ringers* by Henry Porter; *Galileo* by Bertolt Brecht; *Wildlife* by Richard Ford; *What the Buddha Taught* by Walpola Rahula; *An Introduction to Zen Buddhism*; and *Oranges Are Not the Only Fruit* by Jeanette Winterson.

Grove/Atlantic books are distributed by Perseus.

Grove/Atlantic accepts unsolicited manuscripts only from literary agents. Direct queries and SASEs to:

Morgan Entrekin, Publisher

Virginia Barber, Editor-at-Large

Elisabeth Schmitz, Executive Editor—Fiction, narrative nonfiction

Joan Bingham, Editor—History

HAL LEONARD CORPORATION

APPLAUSE THEATRE & CINEMA BOOKS

AMADEUS PRESS

LIMELIGHT EDITIONS

19 West 21st Street, Suite 201, New York, NY 10010

212-575-9265   fax: 212-575-9270

www.halleonard.com

BACKBEAT BOOKS

600 Harrison Street, San Francisco, CA 94107

415-947-6615   fax: 415-947-6015

www.backbeatbooks.com   email: books@musicplayer.com

The Hal Leonard Corporation has its roots in brothers Harold "Hal" Edstrom and Everett "Leonard" Edstrom's traveling band. The print publishing company was founded in 1947 when the band broke up and the brothers began to arrange "popular" music for school bands. Since then it has continued to grow, becoming a world presence in music publishing. It has recently acquired several independent publishers of trade music and entertainment books, such as Applause Theatre and Cinema Books, Amadeus Press, Limelight Editions, and Backbeat Books.

APPLAUSE THEATRE & CINEMA BOOKS

Now in its third decade, Applause is well established as one of the country's most important publishers of theater and cinema books. The house is now owned and operated by Hal Leonard Corporation, the world's largest music print publisher.

The catalog covers everything from books on acting to biographies of theater luminaries, reference books on music and film, screenplays, play scripts, anthologies, and many other topics all for seasoned pros, rookies, and aficionados of the entertainment arts. The Applause program covers hardback and paperback editions, among them a number of generously illustrated works.

Applause issues stage plays and screenplays (many in translation and many in professional working-script format) that run the gamut from the classical repertory to contemporary works in drama, comedy, and musicals. Applause also offers audio works and a video library. The publisher's backlist is comprehensive. Special-production volumes encompass works that detail the background and history behind the creation of works for stage and screen, in addition to containing complete scripts.

Recent titles of interest are *The Miles Davis Reader* edited by Frank Alkyer; *I Hate New Music: The Classic Rock Manifesto* by Dave Thompson; *In the Studio with Michael Jackson* by Bruce Swedien; and *Broadway: The American Musical* by Laurence Maslon and Michael Kantor.

Michael Messina, Managing Director

AMADEUS PRESS

Amadeus Press was founded by Richard Abel in 1987 as an imprint of Timber Press. A music lover, Abel recognized a gap between popular music titles of somewhat dubious quality issued by large commercial houses and the narrowly specialized scholarly publications of the university presses. Amadeus Press was started with the mission of publishing books that would appeal to a wide audience of discerning music lovers yet maintain their scholarly integrity.

In 1990, the press received major attention with the publication of *Enrico Caruso: My Father and My Family* by Andrew Farkas and Enrico Caruso, Jr. The company found new acclaim in the early 2000s with its book/CD series called *Unlocking the Masters* which brings both experienced and new listeners to the world of classical music and opera. In 2006 the imprint was sold to the Hal Leonard Corporation. The mission of Amadeus is focused mainly on creating books that bring new listeners into the exciting world of classical music and opera.

Amadeus Press Books include *Schubert's Instrumental Music: A Listener's Guide* by John Bell Young; *Playing the Beethoven Piano Sonatas* by Robert Taub; *Worlds of Johann Sebastian Bach* by Raymond Erickson; *Zubin Mehta: The Score of My Life* by Zubin Mehta; and *Elisabeth Schwarzkopf: From Flower Maiden to Marschallin* by Kirsten Liese.

John Cerullo, Publisher

Carol Flannery, Editorial Director

LIMELIGHT EDITIONS

Limelight Editions is one of the world's leading small presses of books on the performing arts, theater, cinema, music, and dance. It has recently become a part of the Hal Leonard Performing Arts Publishing Group. Titles from Limelight include *Warren Oates: A Wild Life* by Susan A. Compo; *Collaboration in Theatre: A Practical Guide for Designers and Directors* by Kirk Bomer; and *Fifty Classic American Films* by John White.

John Cerullo, Publisher

Carol Flannery, Editorial Director

BACKBEAT BOOKS

Backbeat Books specializes in music books in rock, jazz, blues, country, classical, and everything in between. Titles shed light on music and its makers. Since 1991, Backbeat Books (originally Miller Freeman Books) has published books for readers who are passionate about music, whether as performers or fans.

Recent titles include *The Guitar Pick-Up Handbook* by Dave Hunter; *Waiting for the Sun: A Rock & Roll History of Los Angeles* by Barney Hoskyns; *Sonic Boom! The History of Northwest Rock, from Louie, Louie to Smells Like Teen Spirit* by Peter Blecha; *A Pure Drop: The Life of Jeff Buckley* by Jeff Apter; and *I Hate New Music: The Classic Rock Manifesto* by Dave Thompson.

Dorothy Cox, Publisher

HAMPTON ROADS PUBLISHING

500 Third Street, Suite 230, San Francisco, CA 94107

978-465-0504

www.hamptonroadspub.com   email: submissions@hrpub.com

Hampton Roads is a nonfiction publisher that describes its titles as messages for the evolving human spirit. The catalog consists of spiritual self-help from the mystical to the practical; subjects include body/mind/spirit, astrology and divination, dreams and dreaming, past lives, reincarnation, the animal world, psychics, remote viewing, business and leadership, visionary fiction, natural solutions for health problems, self-care health advice, the political dimensions of medicine, new science, studies in consciousness, out-of-body experiences, near-death experiences, exploring the afterlife, earth energies, crop circles, and shamanism. Hampton Roads publishes bestselling authors such as Richard Bach, Neal Donald Walsch, and Mary Summer Rain. The Young Spirit line focuses on New Age titles for children.

Recent titles include *The Extraterrestrial Answer Book: UFOs, Alien Abductions, and the Coming ET Presence* by Jim Moroney; *Healing God: Wake Up and Heal Yourself* by Marie Levit; *Jesus: The Explosive Story of the 30 Lost Years and the Ancient Mystery Religions* by Tricia McCannon; *Why I Am a Buddhist* by Stephen T. Asma, PhD; and *Every Moment Matters: Savoring the Stuff of Life* by John St. Augustine.

Hampton Roads editors prefer electronic submissions sent as Word attachments via email to submissions@hrpub.com. Effective January 15, 2009, they are no longer accepting hard-copy submissions.

Jack Jennings, Chief Editor

HARCOURT [SEE HOUGHTON MIFFLIN HARCOURT]

HARLEQUIN ENTERPRISES, LTD.

HARLEQUIN BOOKS

HARLEQUIN NONFICTION

HQN BOOKS

LUNA BOOKS

KIMANI PRESS

RED DRESS INK

SILHOUETTE BOOKS

STEEPLE HILL BOOKS

233 Broadway, Suite 1001, New York, NY 10279

212-553-4200

www.EHarlequin.com

Harlequin Enterprises, Ltd., is the world's leading publisher of romance fiction and women's fiction. The Toronto-based company publishes some 115 titles a month in 25 languages in 95 international markets on six continents. Harlequin is unique in the publishing industry, developing more new authors than any other publisher, and currently publishes over 1,300 authors from around the world. Harlequin is a division of the Torstar Corporation, a Toronto-based media company that also owns over 100 newspapers, a TV station, and various online ventures.

The Harlequin Enterprises home base in Ontario, Canada, issues the greater portion of Harlequin Books series (please see listing for Harlequin Books in the directory of Canadian Presses), while the New York office issues several Harlequin series, as well as the HQN, LUNA, Kimani, Red Dress Ink, Silhouette, and Steeple Hill lists. The editorial acquisitions departments for Mills & Boon, Harlequin Romance, and Harlequin Presents are located at the operation's U.K. offices (listed with Canada).

Each of the various lines within the Harlequin series of romance novels stakes out particular market-niche segments of reader interest within the overall categories of romance fiction and women's fiction. The best way to learn which imprint is appropriate for your manuscript is to read books already in print. There are many different Harlequin lines and each has its own submission and editorial guidelines. These guidelines are explored in great detail on the Harlequin website or may be requested via regular mail (with SASE) from the editors.

HARLEQUIN BOOKS

Harlequin Books in New York is home to Harlequin Intrigue. The Harlequin NEXT line has been cancelled.

Harlequin Intrigue features taut, edge-of-the-seat contemporary romantic suspense tales of intrigue and desire. Kidnappings, stalkings, and women in jeopardy coupled with bestselling romantic themes are examples of story lines the editors love most. Whether a murder mystery, psychological suspense or thriller, the love story must be inextricably bound to the mystery where all loose ends are tied up neatly and shared dangers lead right to shared passions. As long as they're in jeopardy and falling in love, the heroes and heroines may traverse a landscape as wide as the world itself.

Recent Harlequin Intrigue titles are *The Baby's Bodyguard* by Alice Sharpe; *Twelve-Gauge Guardian* by B.J. Daniels; *Daddy Devastating* by Delores Fossen; and *Royal Captive* by Dana Marton.

Harlequin invites submissions from both published and unpublished writers. They prefer a query with synopsis and one to three chapters. Make sure your query is clear as to which line it is intended for. See writing guidelines on website.

Margaret Marbury, Director of Harlequin Single Titles

HARLEQUIN NONFICTION

Harlequin Nonfiction is a new division that publishes across a diverse list of categories, such as companion pieces, original memoirs, health, fitness, self-help, relationships, and more. Some recent titles include *What I Would Tell Her* by Andrea Richesin; *Eat and Beat Diabetes with Picture Weight Loss* by Franklin Becker and Howard Shapiro; and *The Happy Stepmother* by Rachelle Katz.

Sarah Pelz, Editor

HQN BOOKS

HQN Books publishes mainstream romance fiction for readers around the world. Because HQN Books is a mainstream imprint, there are no tip sheets, although manuscripts are expected to range between 100,000–150,000 words. Recent titles include *How to Beguile a Beauty* by Kasey Michaels; *McKettricks of Texas: Garret* by Linda Lael Miller; and *The Darkest Passion* by Gena Showalter.

Direct your query letter to:

Tracy Farrell, Executive Editor—HQN Books

LUNA BOOKS

LUNA titles deliver a compelling, female-focused fantasy with vivid characters, rich worlds, strong, sympathetic women, and romantic subplots. LUNA Books editors want emotionally complex, sweeping stories that highlight the inner female power.

Whether the heroine is on a quest to save the world—or someone or something important to her—discover her past or develop her own abilities, these stories are involving, gripping, and sweep the reader away into a detailed, convincing world. They also contain romantic subplots that enhance the main story but don't become the focus of the novel.

Titles include *Bring It On* by Laura Anne Gilman; *The Snow Queen* by Mercedes Lackey; *Echoes in the Dark* by Robin D. Owens; and *The Reawakened* by Jeri Smith-Ready.

Query with synopsis and one to three chapters:

Tracey Farrell, Executive Editor, LUNA

KIMANI PRESS

Kimani Press, a new division of Harlequin, is home to four of the industry's leading imprints targeting the African American reader including Arabesque, Sepia, TRU, and Kimani Romance, which is the industry's only African American series romance program. As with the other Harlequin divisions, Kimani has different lines, each with its own guidelines available online or by querying the editors via regular mail.

Arabesque offers uplifting, contemporary love stories featuring realistic African American characters that resolve relationship conflicts through the perspective of strong moral beliefs. Arabesque titles may include several points of view, and offer classic contemporary settings.

Arabesque Romances offer contemporary, sophisticated, and entertaining love stories featuring realistic African American characters that resolve natural relationship conflicts such as issues of trust, compatibility, and outlook on life, with satisfying endings. Arabesque Romances may reflect several points of view and can include a wide variety of story subgenres including classic romance, contemporary romance, romantic comedy, and romantic suspense or romantic thriller.

Arabesque titles include *Love Takes Time* by Adrianne Byrd; *Surrender* by Branda Jackson; *Seduced by Moonlight* by Janice Sims; and *First Crush* by Marcia King-Gamble.

The newly introduced Kimani TRU is a new fiction imprint targeted to a younger audience of African American readers. This imprint is aimed at illustrating real-life situations young African American readers encounter without being preachy or naïve. The stories will reflect current trends in pop culture as well as story lines taken straight from the headlines. Recent titles are *Chasing Romeo* by A.J. Byrd; *Lesson Learned* by Earl Sewell; and *Fast Forward* by Celeste O. Norfleet.

Kimani Romance offers sexy, dramatic, sophisticated, and entertaining love stories featuring realistic African American characters that work through compelling emotional conflicts on their way to committed and satisfying relationships. Told primarily from the heroine's point of view, Kimani Romances will keep it real with true-to-life African American characters that turn up the heat and sizzle with passion. Recent titles are *Hidden Pleasures* by Brenda Jackson; *First Class Seduction* by Anita Bunkley; *Promises to Keep* by Linda Hudson-Smith; and *Recipe for Temptation* by Maureen Smith.

The Sepia imprint publishes mainstream fiction titles that predominately feature African American characters. Sepia releases a broad range of books that entertain, inform, and enrich the lives of readers. Sepia editors will review both contemporary and historical novels with subgenre plots, such as suspense-driven thrillers, paranormal and mystery, and novels that focus on social and relationship issues, as well as those that offer a realistic display of urban life. Sepia titles include *Counterfeit Wives* by Philip Thomas Duck; *Love, Lies, and Scandal* by Earl Sewell; and *Pleasure Seekers* by Rochelle Alers.

For all Kimani imprints and lines, send a detailed synopsis and three sample chapters (published authors) or a detailed synopsis and a complete manuscript (unpublished authors).

Evette Porter, Editor—Kimani TRU, Arabesque Inspirational Romance, Arabesque Romances

Glenda Howard, Senior Editor—Kimani Press, New Spirit, Sepia

Kelli Martin, Senior Editor—Kimani Press, Kimani Romance

RED DRESS INK

Red Dress Ink continues to define, as well as offer books relevant to the 21st-century woman. But they're not just about leading the chick-lit revolution; they're about leading women's fiction with attitude. The Red Dress Ink editors are looking for novels that really set themselves apart from the average chick-lit book, from young and crazy tales to contemplative and witty narratives and anything in between. RDI titles include *Eye to Eye* by Grace Carol; *Magic and the Modern Girl* by Mindy Klasky; and *Baby Needs a New Pair of Shoes* by Lauren Baratz-Logsted.

RDI has its own website: www.RedDressInk.com.

Red Dress Ink does not accept unsolicited manuscripts or proposals.

SILHOUETTE BOOKS

Silhouette Books are intense thrillers, mysteries, and even werewolf stories—but always also romances. Each imprint has its own guidelines for length, plot, and characters. We recommend writing to the appropriate editor for guidelines or reading them online prior to writing your manuscript.

Silhouette Desire books are filled to the brim with strong, intense story lines. These sensual love stories immediately involve the reader in the romantic conflict and the quest for a happily-ever-after resolution. The novels should be fast-paced reads, and present the hero and heroine's conflict by the end of chapter one in order for the reader to understand what obstacles will impact the characters for the remainder of the novel. Recent titles include *Dante's Ultimate Gamble* by Day Leclaire; *CEO's Expectant Secretary* by Leanne Banks; *Secrets, Lies… and Seductions* by Katherine Garbera and Yvonne Lindsay; and *The Billionaire Baby Bombshell* by Paula Roe.

Silhouette Romantic Suspense books offer an escape read where true-to-life heroines find themselves in the throes of extraordinary circumstances, and in the arms of powerful heroes. These books combine all the elements of category novels with the excitement of romantic suspense, creating big, sweeping romances amid dangerous and suspenseful settings. Recent titles include *Protector of One* by Rachel Lee; *The Heiress's 2-Week Affair* by Marie Ferrarella; and *The Perfect Soldier* by Karen Whiddon.

Launched at the end of 2006, Silhouette Nocturne is looking for stories that deliver a dark, very sexy read that will entertain readers and take them from everyday life to an atmospheric, complex, paranormal world filled with characters struggling with life and death issues. These stories will be fast-paced, action-packed, and mission-oriented, with a strong level of sensuality. The hero is a key figure—powerful, mysterious, and totally attractive to the heroine. In fact, both main characters are very powerful, and their conflict is based on this element. The author must be able to set up a unique existence for the characters, with its own set of rules and mythologies; these are stories of vampires, shape-shifters, werewolves, psychic powers, etc., set in contemporary times. Recent titles include *Demon Kissed* by Patti O'Shea and *Marked* by Lydia Parks.

Silhouette Special Edition books are sophisticated, substantial stories packed with emotion. Special Edition demands writers eager to probe characters deeply, to explore issues that heighten the drama of living and loving, to create compelling romantic plots. Whether the sensuality is sizzling or subtle, whether the plot is wildly innovative or satisfyingly traditional, the novel's emotional vividness, its depth and dimension, should clearly label it a very special contemporary romance. Subplots are welcome, but must further or parallel the developing romantic relationship in a meaningful way. Recent titles include *A Bride After All* by Kasey Michaels and *The Billionaire's Baby Plan*.

Krista Stroever, Senior Editor—Silhouette Suspense

Melissa Jeglinski, Senior Editor—Silhouette Desire

Patience Smith, Associate Senior Editor—Silhouette Romantic Suspense

Keyren Gerlach, Associate Editor—Silhouette Romantic Suspense

Tara Gavin, Editorial Director—Silhouette Nocturne

Gail Chasan, Senior Editor—Silhouette Special Edition

STEEPLE HILL

Steeple Hill's inspiring fiction features wholesome Christian entertainment that will help women to better guide themselves, their families, and other women in their communities toward purposeful, faith-driven lives. All Steeple Hill editors are looking for authors writing from a Christian worldview and conveying their personal faith and ministry values in entertaining fiction that will touch the hearts of believers and seekers everywhere.

This Harlequin imprint is comprised of the following lines: Love Inspired, Love Inspired Historical, Love Inspired Suspense, and Steeple Hill Women's Fiction. Steeple Hill Café is for the hip, modern woman of faith.

The Love Inspired line is a series of contemporary, inspirational romances that feature Christian characters facing the many challenges of life and love in today's world. Recent titles include *The Carpenter's Wife* and *Heart of Stone* by Lenora Worth and *A Time to Forgive* and *Promise Forever* by Marta Perry.

Love Inspired Historical is a series of historical romances launched October 2007 featuring Christian characters facing the many challenges of life and love in a variety of historical time periods. Recent titles include *The Doctor's Newfound Family* by Valerie Hansen and *the Rocky Mountain Match* by Pamela Nissen.

Steeple Hill Love Inspired Suspense is a series of edge-of-your-seat, contemporary romantic suspense tales of intrigue and romance featuring Christian characters facing challenges to their faith and to their lives. Recent titles include *End Game* by Roxanne Rustand and *Risky Reunion* by Lenora Worth.

The Steeple Hill Women's Fiction program is dedicated to publishing inspirational Christian women's fiction that depicts the struggles the characters encounter as they learn important lessons about trust and the power of faith. Recent titles include *Journey* by Angela Hunt and *Mother and Daughters: An Anthology* by Linda Bedford.

As with many programs developed for the Christian market, the Steeple Hill books have very specific guidelines, which may be requested from the editors or read online at eHarlequin.com.

To submit your work, send a detailed synopsis, three sample chapters, and SASE to:

Joan Marlow Golan, Executive Editor—Steeple Hill Café and Steeple Hill Women's Fiction

Krista Stroever, Associate Senior Editor—Steeple Hill Love Inspired and Love Inspired Suspense

Melissa Endlich, Editor—Love Inspired Historical

THE HARVARD COMMON PRESS

535 Albany Street, Boston, MA 02118

617-423-5803   fax: 617-695-9794

www.harvardcommonpress.com   email: editorial@harvardcommonpress.com

Founded in 1976, the Harvard Common Press publishes a wide variety of award-winning books on cooking, parenting, childbirth, and home gardening. The house is devoted to the home and home living.

Bestsellers from Harvard Common include *The Nursing Mother's Companion* by Kathleen Huggins; *Vegan Planet: 400 Irresistible Recipes with Fantastic Flavors from Home and Around the World* by Robin Robertson; and *Not Your Mother's Slow Cooker Cookbook* by Beth Hensperger and Julie Kaufmann.

Titles include *Not Your Mother's Fondue!* by Hallie Harron; *Techniques for Planking* by Karen Adler and Judith Fertig; *Techniques for Grilling Fish* by Karen Adler and Judith Fertig; and *Bourbon* by Fred Thompson.

Email queries are accepted; please no full manuscripts. Query letters and SASEs should be directed to the Editorial Department:

Valerie Cimino, Executive Editor

Jane Dornbusch, Managing Editor

HARVEST BOOKS [SEE HARCOURT TRADE PUBLISHERS]

HARVEST HOUSE PUBLISHERS

990 Owen Loop North, Eugene, OR 97402

541-343-0123   fax: 541-342-6410

www.harvesthousepublishers.com

Harvest House is one of the largest American publishers of Christian literature with more than 160 new books per year and a backlist of more than 700 titles. The house was founded in 1974 by Bob Hawkins, Sr., and has been run for the past 15 years by current president Bob Hawkins, Jr. Harvest House publishes in three main subject areas: self-help (relationships, family, money, Christian living), Bible help (Bibles, Bible studies, topical studies), and full-color gift books featuring name-brand artists. Recent releases include fiction and nonfiction for children and adults. Subjects include humor, Christian history, media, technology, politics, parenting, youth, relationships, family, Christian living, contemporary values, cults and the occult, personal awareness, inspiration, and spiritual growth.

Harvest House bestsellers include *Cassidy and Sabrina* by Lori Wick; *My Beautiful Broken Shell* by Carol Hamblet Adams and D. Morgan; *Grandma, Do You Remember When?* by Jim Daly; *The Power of a Praying Wife* by Stormie Omartian; and *30 Days to Taming Your Tongue* by Deborah Smith Pegues.

Recent titles include *The 10 Best Decisions a Woman Can Make* by Pam Farrel; *52 Things Kids Need from a Dad* by Jay Payleitner; *The Amazing Claims of Bible*

Prophecy by Mark Hitchcock; *Beside Still Waters* by Darrell Bush; and *Becoming Spiritually Beautiful* by Sharon Jaynes.

Harvest House is currently not accepting any unsolicited manuscripts or queries, even from agents.

Nick Harrison, Senior Editor

Steve Miller, Senior Editor

HAY HOUSE

NEW BEGINNINGS PRESS

PRINCESS BOOKS

SMILEY BOOKS

P.O. Box 5100, Carlsbad, CA 92018-5100

1-800-654-5126

www.hayhouse.com   email: editorial@hayhouse.com

Hay House was founded in 1984 by Louise L. Hay to self-publish her first two books, *Heal Your Body* and *You Can Heal Your Life*, both of which became bestsellers and established Ms. Hay as a leader in the New Age movement.

Now full-scale, Hay House publishes nonfiction only in the areas of self-help, New Age, sociology, philosophy, psychology, health, business, finance, men's/women's issues, inspirational memoirs, and celebrity biographies. Subjects include social issues, current events, ecology, business, food and nutrition, education, the environment, alternative health/medicine, money and finance, nature, recreation, religion, men's and women's issues, spiritual growth, and fitness. All titles have a positive self-help slant to them.

Hay House currently publishes approximately 300 books and 350 audio programs by more than 130 authors, and employs a full-time staff of 100-plus. They average 50 new titles per year. Imprints include Princess Books (titles from author John Edward of *Crossing Over* fame), Smiley Books (titles from Hay House author Tavis Smiley), and New Beginnings Press (financial titles).

Best-selling titles from Hay House are *Secrets and Mysteries of the World* by Sylvia Browne; *The Power of Intention* by Dr. Wayne W. Dyer; and *Yes, You Can Be a Successful Income Investor* by Ben Stein and Phil DeMuth.

Hay House titles include *Mystery of the White Lions* by Linda Tucker; *The Three Sisters of the Tao* by Terah Kathryn Collins; and *Women's Bodies, Women's Wisdom* by Dr. Christiane Northrup.

NEW BEGINNINGS PRESS

Recent titles from New Beginnings Press include *How You Can Sell Anyone Anything* by Ben Stein and Barron Thomas; *How to Ruin the United States of America*; and *Yes, You Can Get a Financial Life! Your Lifetime Guide to Financial Planning* by Ben Stein and Phil DeMuth.

PRINCESS BOOKS

Princess Books titles include *Final Beginnings: The Tunnel* by John Edward and Natasha Stoynoff; *Practical Praying* by John Edward; and *Cracking the Coconut Code* by Mary Jo McCabe.

SMILEY BOOKS

Smiley Books' latest releases are *Hope on a Tightrope: Words and Wisdom* by Dr. Cornel West; *Brainwashed: Erasing the Myth of Black Inferiority* by Tom Burrell; *America I Am: Legends, Rare Moments and Inspiring Words* by Cheryll Y. and Tavis Smiley; and *The Covenant in Action* by Tavis Smiley.

Hay House only accepts submissions from agents. See the website for details or submit hard-copy proposals by mail only to Editorial Department Submissions.

Reid Tracy, President

Patty Gift, Acquisitions Editor

HAZELDEN PUBLISHING AND EDUCATIONAL SERVICES

15251 Pleasant Valley Road, P.O. Box 176, RD15, Center City, MN 55012-0176

800-328-9000/651-213-4200   fax: 651-213-4590

www.hazelden.org/bookplace   email: customersupport@hazelden.org

Hazelden Publishing and Educational Services (established 1954) specializes in trade books that address issues relevant to alcoholism, drug addiction, and closely related psychology issues. Related topics include eating disorders, family and relationship issues, spirituality, codependency, compulsive gambling, sex addiction, depression, grief, treatment, and recovery. On the non-trade side of the publishing operation, the house publishes curricula, videos, pamphlets, and other publications for treatment programs, hospitals, schools, churches, correctional facilities, government and military agencies, as well as mental health and counseling agencies.

Hazelden Publishing and Educational Services is a division of the Hazelden Foundation, which also operates a network of addiction recovery centers. The publisher has a concentration in materials related to the Twelve-Step approach.

Hazelden publishes information that helps build recovery in the lives of individuals, families and communities affected by alcoholism, drug dependency, and related diseases. Hazelden publications and services are intended to meet a full range of issues for alcoholics, drug addicts, families, counselors, educators, doctors, and other professionals. Hazelden publications support Twelve-Step philosophy and a holistic approach that addresses the needs of the mind, body, and spirit.

Hazelden editors look for innovative materials that address issues relevant to substance abuse, prevention, treatment, and recovery. Topics include alcoholism, nicotine, and drug addictions; family and relationship issues; spirituality; eating disorders, gambling, and other addictive and compulsive behaviors; mental health; and historical information on the Twelve Steps.

Recent titles include *A Restful Mind* by Mark Zabawa; *Sane* by Marya Hornbacher; *Shock Waves* by Cynthia Orange; and *The Lois Wilson Story* by William Borchert.

Hazelden Books are distributed exclusively by Health Communications, Inc.

Physical submissions are strongly preferred. Submit proposals with sample chapters and SASEs to:

Cathy Anderson, Submissions

Nick Motu, Publisher and Vice President

Richard Solly, Senior Editor

HEALTH COMMUNICATIONS, INC.

HCI TEENS

3201 Southwest 15th Street, Deerfield Beach, FL 33442

954-360-0909/800-441-5569   fax: 954-360-0034

www.hcibooks.com

Health Communications, Inc. (HCI), has been publishing books that change lives since 1977. HCI: The Life Issues Publisher has the goal of creating personal abundance for readers and customers, one book at a time.

In 1994, HCI published the first *Chicken Soup for the Soul* book, which not only became a bestseller, but continues to be an international publishing phenomena. Books in the series have sold nearly 100 million copies.

Originally operating as a publisher of informational pamphlets for the recovery community, HCI moved into mainstream publishing in the 1980s with its first *New York Times* bestseller, the 1983 *Adult Children of Alcoholics* by Dr. Janet Woititz, a veritable "bible" of the ACOA movement. This first bestseller was followed by *Bradshaw On: The Family*, and *Healing the Shame That Binds You* both by John Bradshaw.

Aware of the significant shifts in the recovery movement, HCI actively expanded its book list to include a broader selection of titles. Now regarded as The Life Issues Publisher, HCI continues a tradition of providing readers with inspiring and motivating personal growth and self-help books.

Publisher of quality books on life issues, HCI's broad base of over 900 titles encompasses self-help, spirituality, addictions and recovery, psychology, parenting, relationships, religion, inspiration, health and wellness, and more.

Recent HCI titles include *The Power of Hope* by Henry Biller, PhD, and Anthony Scioli, PhD; *Erotic Intelligence* by Alexandra Katehakis, MFT; *The Pursuit of Nobility* by Tim Daniel; *Mindfulness and 12 Steps* by Therese Jacobs-Stewart; and *Shock Waves: A Practical Guide to Living with a Loved One's PTSD* by Cynthia Orange.

HCI TEENS

HCI Teens delivers the facts and fiction teens are asking for. HCI's commitment to teens is firm, up front, and to the point: Give teens what they want, what they need, and most important give teens a variety of quality content from which they can learn, grow, and enjoy all life has to offer now and in the future. The backbone for the imprint include the bestselling titles from Chicken Soup for the Teenage Soul series, Taste Berries for Teens series by Bettie and Jennifer Youngs, and the Teen Love series by Kimberly Kirberger.

Recent titles include *Feed Your Head: Some Excellent Stuff on Being Yourself* by Earl Hipp and L.K. Hanson; *Our Best Days* by Sally Coleman and Nancy Hull-Mast; *Mentors, Masters, and Mrs. MacGregor: Stories of Teachers Making a Difference* by Jane Bluestein; *Help for the Hard Times* by Earl Hipp; and *A Child Called It: One Child's Courage to Survive* by Dave Pelzer.

Health Communications distributes its own list. In addition, HCI is the exclusive trade distributor for Hazelden Publishing.

Due to new postal regulations, HCI can no longer use an SASE to return parcels weighing 16 ounces or more. Therefore, they no longer return any submissions weighing 16 ounces or more even if an SASE is included. See their website for more detailed submission guidelines. Query letters, proposals, and SASEs should be directed to the editorial staff.

Michele Matrisciani, Editorial Director

HEBREW PUBLISHING COMPANY

P.O. Box 222, Spencertown, NY 12165

518-392-3322   fax: 518-392-4280

Hebrew Publishing Company (established in 1901) offers a wide range of titles in such categories as reference materials and dictionaries; religions, law, and thought; Rabbinic literature; literature, history, and biography; children's books; Hebrew-language texts and Hebrew culture; Yiddish; the Bible in English and in Hebrew/English; prayers and liturgy, including daily (Hebrew only and Hebrew/English), Sabbath, high holidays, festivals, memorials, and Purim; Hanukkah; educational materials; sermons and aids of the rabbi; and calendars. The house publishes a limited number of new titles and maintains an established backlist.

On the HPC list: *Yom Kippur* by Philip Birnbaum; *Judaism as a Civilization* by Mordecai Kaplan; *Acharon Hamohikanim (The Last of the Mohicans)* by James Fenimore Cooper; *Business Ethics in Jewish Law* by Leo Jung; *Encyclopedia of Jewish Concepts* by Philip Birnbaum; and *Jewish Tales and Legends* by Menachem Glen.

Hebrew Publishing Company oversees its own distribution, utilizing the services of independent fulfillment and distribution firms.

Query letters and SASEs should be directed to:

Charles Lieber, President

HEBREW UNION COLLEGE PRESS

A Division of the Hebrew Union College-Jewish Institute of Religion

3101 Clifton Avenue, Cincinnati, OH 45220-2488

513-221-1875, extension 3292

www.huc.edu/newspubs/press   email: hucpress@huc.edu

As part of the Hebrew Union College-Jewish Institute of Religion, the Hebrew Union College Press (founded 1921) publishes scholarly Judaica for an international academic readership.

Always concerned with quality of scholarship rather than sales potential, the Hebrew Union College Press has from its inception devoted its resources and efforts to the publication of works of the highest caliber for its niche audience. HUCP has co-publishing projects with other institutions, including Harvard University Press,

KTAV Publishing House, University of Alabama Press, Yale University Press, Klau Library, Skirball Museum, and Kunstresim.

Titles include *Remnant Stones: The Jewish Cemeteries of Suriname: Epitaphs* by Aviva Ben-Ur and Rachel Frankel; *A Great Voice that Did Not Cease* by Michael Chernick; *Jewish Law in Transition* by Hillel Gamoran; *My Dear Daughter: Rabbi Benjamin Slonik and the Education of Jewish Women in Sixteenth-Century Poland* by Edward Fram; and *The New Tradition: Essays on Modern Hebrew Literature* by Gerson Shaked.

Hebrew Union College Press is distributed by Wayne State University Press.

HUCP welcomes the submission of scholarly manuscripts in all areas of Judaica. Address all editorial inquiries to:

Michael A. Meyer, Chair, Publications, Committee

Barbara Selya, Managing Editor

HEINEMANN USA [SEE ABC-CLIO]

HELIOS PRESS [SEE ALLWORTH PRESS]

HERDER & HERDER [SEE CROSSROAD PUBLISHING COMPANY]

HILL STREET PRESS

BROAD STREET BOOKS

COLLEGE TRIVIA BOOKS

GRAPHEDIA BOOKS

HOT CROSS BOOKS

191 East Broad Street, Suite 216, Athens, GA 30601

706-613-7200   fax: 866-621-1654

www.hillstreetpress.com   email: editorial@hillstreetpress.com

Hill Street Press (founded 1998) publishes approximately 20 titles annually in, current events, history, politics, fiction, memoir, African American studies, gender/women's studies, gay/lesbian interest, nature/gardening, music, business, and sports. Although many of Hill Street's books spring from the American South, the house seeks to publish books that transcend regionalism and appeal to the reader of any region.

HSP seeks to serve as incubator and archive for both the most promising and the most established writers, to offer an extraordinary range of perspectives on a multitude of subjects, while always avoiding the hackneyed notions of the South as the exclusive province of the gothic or the sentimental dominion of moonlight and magnolias.

Recent Hill Street Press titles include *The Baseball Crossword: A Hot Cross Book* by J.P. Caillault; *Dixie Dining* by Gary Saunders; *Literary Washington, D.C.* by Patrick Allen; *Space Age Santa* by Kevin O'Donnell; and *We Let the Dawgs Out* by Linda Ford and Julie Walters.

BROAD STREET BOOKS

Broad Street Books publishes traditional children's fiction and nonfiction. Some titles from Broad Street include *The Green Snake: A Fairy Tale* by Margaret Mitchell; *Tim & Sally's Vegetable Garden* by Grady Thrasher; and *Tim & Sally's Beach Adventure* by Grady Thrasher.

COLLEGE TRIVIA BOOKS

College Trivia Books publishes college or university specific trivia books. Some titles include *The Georgia Tech Trivia Book* by Tim Darnell; *The Ohio State University Trivia Book* by Raimund Goerler and Tamar Chute; *The University of Alabama Trivia Book* by Jessica Lacher-Feldman; *The University of Tennessee Trivia Book* by Tim Mattingly; and *The University of Florida Trivia Book* by Carl Van Ness.

GRAPHEDIA BOOKS

Graphedia Books publishes graphic format fiction (graphic novels) and nonfiction for children from ages six to eight. Some titles include *Stone Age Santa* by Kevin O'Donnell and *Space Age Santa* by Kevin O'Donnell.

HOT CROSS BOOKS

Hot Cross Books publishes 100 percent thematic crossword puzzle books. Some titles include *The 60s Crossword* by Karlene Allen; *The 70s Crossword* by Mike Musgrove; *The Civil War Crossword* by Jennifer L. Gross; *The Golf Crossword* by Al Clarke and Robert Carson; *The New York Crossword* by Andrew Smith; *The Presidents and First Ladies Crossword* by Andrew Smith; and *The Southern Crossword* by Al Dixon.

HSP is accepting nonfiction submissions; they are not accepting unsolicited fiction queries or manuscripts. All puzzles and games are developed in-house; they do not accept submissions for these games. See website for detailed submission guidelines. All query letters, proposals, and SASEs should be directed to:

Tom Payton, President and Publisher, payton@hillstreetpress.com

Judy Long, Vice President and Editor-in-Chief, long@hillstreetpress.com

HIPPOCRENE BOOKS

171 Madison Avenue, New York, NY 10016

212-685-4371   fax: 212-779-9338

www.hippocrenebooks.com   email: info@hippocrenebooks.com

Over more than 35 years, Hippocrene Books has become one of America's foremost publishers of foreign-language reference books and ethnic cookbooks. As a small publishing house in a marketplace dominated by conglomerates, Hippocrene has succeeded by continually reinventing its list while maintaining a strong international and ethnic orientation. In addition to cookbooks and foreign-language reference books, Hippocrene publishes on the subjects of history, Judaica, leisure, love poetry, militaria, Polish interest, proverbs, travel, and weddings.

George Blagowidow founded the company in 1970. The name Hippocrene comes from Greek mythology and refers to the sacred fountain of the Muses that was the source of their inspiration. Hippocrene's international focus derives from Blagowidow's passion for travel and his personal history.

Currently, Hippocrene features over 64 cuisines in its cookbook program. In addition to its conventional history list, the company launched a series of Illustrated

Histories in 1998. Each book features the political and cultural history of a region, accompanied by black-and-white pictures. Leading titles include *Spain: An Illustrated History* and *The Celtic World: An Illustrated History*. New publishing areas also comprise international editions of poetry, short stories, proverbs, and folk tales. *Classic French Love Poems* edited by Lisa Neal and *Pakistani Folk Tales: Toontoony Pie and Other Stories* by Ashraf Siddiqui and Marilyn Lerch are representative titles.

Recent titles include *Dari-English/ English-Dari Practical Dictionary* by Carleton Bulkin; *Chinese-English/ English-Chinese Practical Dictionary* by Yong Ho; *Afghan Food & Cookery* by Helen Saberi; *The Best of Scandinavian Cooking* by Shirly Sarvis and Barbara Scott O'Neill; and *Ancient Rome in So Many Words* by Christopher Francese.

Query letters and SASEs should be directed to the editorial staff.

Anne McBride, Editor-in-Chief

HOUGHTON MIFFLIN HARCOURT

HOUGHTON MIFFLIN HARCOURT

HOUGHTON MIFFLIN HARCOURT CHILDREN'S BOOK GROUP

HOUGHTON MIFFLIN HARCOURT SCHOOL PUBLISHERS

HOLT MCDOUGAL

Boston office:

222 Berkeley Street, Boston, MA 02116-3764

617-351-5000

New York office:

215 Park Avenue South, New York, NY 10003

212-420-5800

www.hmhco.com

Boston-based Houghton Mifflin Harcourt is one of the leading educational publishers in the U.S., publishing textbooks, instructional technology, assessments, and other educational materials for teachers and students of every age. The company also publishes an extensive line of reference works and award-winning trade fiction and nonfiction for adults and young readers.

In December 2006, Houghton Mifflin was acquired by HM Rivergroup, an Irish holding company led by Riverdeep Chief Executive Barry O'Callaghan; the combined group was renamed Houghton Mifflin Riverdeep Group. In 2007, Houghton Mifflin Company acquired Harcourt Education, Harcourt Trade, and

Greenwood-Heinemann divisions of Reed Elsevier, and became the largest educational publisher in the world. Houghton Mifflin and Harcourt combined forces to become the Houghton Mifflin Harcourt Trade and Reference Publishing Group. The children's divisions followed suit, leading to the creation of Houghton Mifflin Harcourt Children's.

With its origins dating back to 1832, Houghton Mifflin Harcourt combines its tradition of excellence with a commitment to innovation in order to satisfy the lifelong need to learn and be entertained.

HOUGHTON MIFFLIN HARCOURT

Houghton Mifflin Harcourt launched its first combined trade list in Winter 2009. Under the Houghton Mifflin Harcourt imprint, the adult group will publish approximately 80 new hardcover books each year, and under the Mariner Books imprint (incorporating the Harvest backlist), approximately 90 trade paperbacks, including paperback originals and books acquired from other publishers. The reference division continues to publish the American Heritage dictionaries and other authoritative and popular books about language, for adults and children. In addition, Houghton Mifflin Harcourt distributes books for Beacon Press, The Old Farmer's Almanac, Larousse, and Chambers.

The Houghton Mifflin nonfiction roster has included fine writers in such categories as history, natural history, biography and memoir, science, and economics, including such preeminent figures as Winston Churchill, Arthur M. Schlesinger, Jr., and John Kenneth Galbraith. They also have a proud tradition of publishing works of social criticism that have spoken with great power through the generations, including Rachel Carson's *Silent Spring*, James Agee and Walker Evans's *Let Us Now Praise Famous Men*, the works of Jane Goodall and, recently, the bestselling *Constantine's Sword* by James Carroll, and *Fast Food Nation* by Eric Schlosser.

On the literary side, Houghton Mifflin launched the careers of such writers as Willa Cather, A. B. Guthrie, Jr., Robert Penn Warren, Ann Petry, Elizabeth Bishop, Philip Roth, Willie Morris, and Robert Stone. Their fiction list today also includes such distinguished names as Tim O'Brien, John Edgar Wideman, and Edna O'Brien.

Houghton Mifflin's commitment to poetry has spanned well over 100 years. The current roster of poets includes Donald Hall, a poet laureate; Natasha Trethewey, the 2007 Winner of the Pulitzer Prize in Poetry; and Galway Kinnell, Grace Schulman, Alan Shapiro, Michael Collier, and Glyn Maxwell, among others.

Harcourt Trade Publishers was established when Alfred Harcourt and Donald Brace left Henry Holt and Company in 1919 to form a new publishing enterprise. Early Harcourt lists featured Sinclair Lewis, Carl Sandburg, and John Maynard Keynes, joined over the decades by Virginia Woolf, George Orwell, C.S. Lewis, Antoine de Saint-Exupéry, Thomas Merton, Robert Lowell, T. S. Eliot, and Robert Penn Warren. In 1961, Helen and Kurt Wolff, cofounders of Pantheon Books, became Harcourt's copublishers and brought with them their eponymous list, which included the luminaries Günter Grass, Hannah Arendt, and Konrad Lorenz. A mainstay of literature in translation, Harcourt has published celebrated international authors such as Italo Calvino, Umberto Eco, and Amos Oz, as well as the Nobel Prize winners Octavio Paz, José Saramago, and A. B. Yehoshua.

The adult trade group does not accept unsolicited manuscript submissions for fiction, nonfiction, or poetry, except through a literary agent. Send lexical submissions to the Dictionary Department at the Boston address.

Ken Carpenter, Vice President, Director of Trade Paperbacks (Boston)— Fiction, nonfiction

Andrea Schulz, Vice President, Editor-in-Chief

Susan Canavan, Executive Editor (Boston)—Nonfiction, culture

Amanda Cook, Executive Editor (Boston)—Serious nonfiction, current issues, business/finance

HOUGHTON MIFFLIN HARCOURT CHILDREN'S BOOK GROUP

CLARION BOOKS

Houghton Mifflin Harcourt Children's Book Group encompasses three award-winning imprints as well as the Graphia and Sandpaper paperback lines. Houghton Mifflin introduced its list of books for young readers in 1937. Houghton Mifflin Books for Children publishes luminaries such as H. A. and Margret Rey, Virginia Lee Burton, Bill Peet, Holling C. Holling, Scott O'Dell, and James Marshall; its contemporary authors and illustrators include Steve Jenkins, D. B. Johnson, Toni Morrison, Marilyn Nelson, Eric Schlosser, Brian Lies, Chris Van Allsburg, Allen Say, Lois Lowry, and David Macaulay. Houghton Mifflin is also home to some of the best-loved children's book characters: Curious George, Lyle the Crocodile, George and Martha, Martha of Martha Speaks, and Tacky the Penguin.

Harcourt Children's Books, known for classics such as *The Little Red Lighthouse and the Great Gray Bridge* and *The Little Prince*, features notable authors and illustrators such as Avi, Janell Cannon, Margaret Chodos-Irvine, Lois Ehlert, Mem Fox, Han Nolan, Gennifer Choldenko, David Shannon, Janet Stevens, Susan Stevens Crummel, and Helen Oxenbury.

Houghton Mifflin Harcourt Children's Books does not respond to any unsolicited submission unless they are interested in publishing it. Please do not include a self-addressed stamped envelope. Submissions will be recycled, and you will not hear from them regarding the status of your submission unless they are interested, in which case you can expect to hear back within 12 weeks. Send to Submissions at the Boston address.

Mary Ann Wilcox, Vice President, Franchise Director

Julia Richardson, Editorial Director

CLARION BOOKS

Clarion Books began publishing children's fiction and picture books in 1965 with a list of six titles. In 1979 it was bought by and became an imprint of Houghton Mifflin. The list has expanded to nearly 60 titles a year and includes nonfiction as well as fiction and picture books. In 1987 Clarion received its first Newbery Honor Medal, for *On My Honor* by Marion Dane Bauer, and in 1988 it had its first Newbery Medal winner, *Lincoln: A Photobiography* by Russell Freedman. Since then Clarion books have received children's book honors and awards nearly every year. Clarion's award-winning titles include *The Three Pigs* (2002 Caldecott Medal), *Tuesday* (Caldecott Medal), and *Sector 7* (Caldecott Honor), all written and illustrated by David Wiesner; *A Single Shard* (2002 Newbery Medal) by Linda Sue Park; *The Midwife's Apprentice* (Newbery Medal) and *Catherine Called Birdy* (Newbery Honor), both by Karen Cushman; *Sir Walter Raleigh and The Quest for El Dorado* (the inaugural Sibert Medal) by Marc Aronson; and *My Rows and Piles of Coins* (Coretta Scott King Honor for illustration) by Tololwa M. Mollel, illustrated by E. B. Lewis.

Recent titles include *Change Up: Baseball Poems* by Gene Fehler and Donald Wu; *How to Scratch a Wombat: Where to Find It...What to Feed It...Why It Sleeps All Day* by Jackie French and Bruce Whatley; and *Rabbit's Good News* by Ruth Bornstein.

In the picture books area, the editors are looking for active picture book stories with a beginning, middle, and end—stories that deal fully and honestly with children's emotions. You do not need to provide illustrations or find an illustrator; if your manuscript is accepted, the publisher will handle this. No query letter is necessary for picture book manuscripts and/or dummies.

In the nonfiction area, the editors are interested in hearing about social studies, science, concept, wordplay, holiday, historical, and biography ideas for all age levels. Send a query letter or proposal with a sample chapter(s) on all nonfiction projects.

In the fiction area, the editors are seeking lively stories for ages 8–12 and ages 10–14. They are also looking for transitional chapter books (12–20 manuscript pages) for ages 6–9 and for short novels of 40–80 manuscript pages suitable for ages 7–10. Clarion is highly selective in the areas of historical fiction, fantasy, and science fiction. A novel must be superlatively written in order to find a place on the list. The editors prefer to see complete manuscripts.

Address all submissions with SASEs to the attention of the Editorial Department in New York.

Dinah Stevenson, Publisher

Jennifer Green, Senior Editor

Lynne Polvino, Associate Editor

HOUGHTON MIFFLIN HARCOURT SCHOOL PUBLISHERS

Houghton Mifflin Harcourt School Publishers publishes resources for teachers, students, and parents for pre-K through grade 8. The School Division's renowned author teams rely on extensive market and independent research to inform the pedagogical structure of each program. Ancillary products such as workbooks, teacher guides, audio-visual guides, and computer software provide additional support for students and teachers at each grade level. The school division is headquartered in Boston.

Authors may learn more at www.hmhschool.com.

HOLT MCDOUGAL

Holt McDougal was formed with the combination of the Holt, Rinehart, and Winston division and McDougal Littell. Holt McDougal publishes an extensive offering of print and technology materials for language arts, mathematics, social studies, world languages, and science for grades 6–12.

More information is available at holtmcdougal.hmhco.com.

HQN BOOKS [SEE HARLEQUIN ENTERPRISES, LTD.]

HUMAN KINETICS

P.O. Box 5076, Champaign, IL 61825-5076

800-747-4457   fax: 217-351-1549

www.humankinetics.com   email: webmaster@hkusa.com

Human Kinetics aims to convert all information about physical activity into knowledge—information that people can use to make a positive difference in their lives. In today's world, survival of the fittest means survival of the best informed. Building that knowledge is the role of Human Kinetics (HK).

Human Kinetics published its first book in 1974. Today, HK produces textbooks and their ancillaries, consumer books, software, videos, audiocassettes, journals, and distance education courses. The world headquarters are located in Champaign, Illinois, with offices in the U.K., Canada, Australia, and New Zealand to bolster their international efforts. Their annual sales, including international operations, surpass $37 million.

A privately held company, Human Kinetics publishes more than 100 books and 20 journals annually. They have expanded operations to that of an "information packager," utilizing whatever media source can best deliver the information to the consumer. Their objective is to make a positive difference in the quality of life of all people by promoting physical activity, by seeking out the foremost experts in a particular field and assisting them in delivering the most current information in the best format.

HK's two academic book divisions—the Scientific, Technical, and Medical (STM) Division; and the Health, Physical Education, Recreation, and Dance (HPERD) Division—publish textbooks and reference books for students, scholars, and professionals in the company's fields of interest.

HK's Trade Book Division (formerly called Leisure Press) publishes expertly written books for the general public and for such groups as coaches, athletes, and fitness enthusiasts.

Recent titles include *Soccer Practice Games* by Joseph Luxbacher; *Cycling Fast* by Robert Panzera; *Fitness Professional's Guide to Strength Training Older Adults* by Thomas Baechle and Wayne Westcott; and *Golf Anatomy* by Craig Davies and Vince DiSaia.

Query letters, proposals, and SASEs should be directed to the Editorial Department of the division to which you are submitting. Detailed guidelines are available on the website.

Rainer Martens, President and Publisher

Julie Marx Goodreau, Director, Trade Division

HYPERION

HYPERION BOOKS FOR CHILDREN

VOICE

114 Fifth Avenue, New York, NY 10011

212-456-0100

www.hyperionbooks.com

www.hyperionbooksforchildren.com

Hyperion, which was founded by The Walt Disney Company in 1991, publishes general-interest fiction, literary works, and nonfiction in the areas of popular culture, health and wellness, business, current topical interest, popular psychology, self-help, and humor. The house publishes books in hardcover, trade paperback, and mass-market paperback formats. Hyperion also operates a very strong children's program. Imprint ESPN focuses on sports titles.

Recent adult titles from Hyperion include *Always Looking Up* by Michael J. Fox; *Climate Wars* by Eric Pooley; *Day I Shot Cupid* by Jennifer Love Hewitt; *Getting In* by Karen Stabiner; and *Impatient with Desire* by Gabrielle Burton.

Gretchen Young, Executive Editor

Ms. Leslie Wells, Executive Editor

HYPERION BOOKS FOR CHILDREN

Hyperion Books for Children published its first book in August 1991: *See Squares*, a paperback counting book by Joy N. Hulme, illustrated by Carol Schwartz. Since then, Hyperion Books for Children and its imprints have published books by Julie Andrews, Rosemary Wells, Louise Erdrich, William Nicholson, Michael Dorris, Jules Feiffer, Toni Morrison, Jon Agee, Paul Zindel, and William Wegman, among others. Hyperion Books for Children's imprints include *Jump at the Sun*, the first children's book imprint to celebrate black culture for all children, and *Volo*, a paperback original series.

Recent children's titles include *The Enemy* by Charlie Higson; *The Kane Chronicles Book One: The Red Pyramid* by Rick Riordan; *For the Love of Soccer* by Pelé; *A Field Guide for Heartbreakers* by Kristen Tracy; and *Passing Strange: A Generation Dead Novel* by Daniel Waters.

Jennifer Besser, Editor

VOICE

Voice is a new imprint of books for women at the center of life—fiction and nonfiction for smart, educated, busy, curious, seasoned women for whom reading is a passion. Some books from Voice include *Summer Blowout* by Claire Cook; *37* by Maria Beaumont; *Irreplaceable* by Stephen Lovely; and *The Middle Place* by Kelly Corrigan.

Hyperion accepts unsolicited manuscripts only from literary agents. Query letters and SASEs should be directed to the editorial staff.

IDEALS BOOKS

CANDYCANE PRESS

SMART KIDS PUBLISHING

WILLIAMSON BOOKS

535 Metroplex Drive, Nashville, TN 37211

800-586-2572

www.idealspublications.com   email: atyourservice@guideposts.org

Ideals Books has been publishing book and magazine products since 1944. Ideals is owned by Guideposts in Carmel, New York. Ideals Books publishes over 70 new products annually for the adult and children's markets.

CANDYCANE PRESS

Candycane Press publishes children's books and board books. Some of their titles include *My First Day of School* by P.K. Hallinan; *The Price of Fame* by Carolyne Aarsen; and *Today Is Halloween!* by P.K. Hallinan.

SMART KIDS PUBLISHING

Smart Kids Publishing publishes illustrated books and photo books for children. Some of their titles include *Busy Busy Butterfly* by Molly Carroll and Damon Taylor; *Down in the Deep, Deep Ocean!* by Joann Cleland; *It's Potty Time: Boys* by Chris Sharp and Garry Currant; and *Ladybug, Ladybug, What Are You Doing* by Jo Cleland.

WILLIAMSON BOOKS

Williamson publishes nonfiction books that encourage children to succeed by helping them to discover their creative capacity. Kids Can!, Little Hands, Kaleidoscope Kids, Quick Starts for Kids, and Good Times books encourage curiosity and exploration with irresistible graphics and open-ended instruction. The house publishes hands-on learning books in science and nature, arts and crafts, math and history, cooking, social studies, and more, featuring new Kaleidoscope Kids and Kids Can! titles. Its publishing program is committed to maintaining excellent quality while providing good value for parents, teachers, and children.

Recent titles from Williamson include *Crafts Across America* by Cindy A. Littlefield; *The Little Hands Art Book* by Judy Press; *China: Kaleidoscope Kids* by Debbi Michiko Florence and Jim Caputo; *Leap into Space* by Nancy Castaldo and Patrick McRae; and *Super Science Concoctions: 50 Mysterious Mixtures for Fabulous Fun* by Jill Frankel Hauser and Michael Kline.

Ideals Publications does not accept submissions by email or fax. Send an SASE to "Guidelines" to receive writers' guidelines. Please address queries and SASEs to "The Editors."

INDUSTRIAL PRESS

989 Avenue of the Americas, 19th Floor, New York, NY 10018

212-889-6330/888-528-7852   fax: 212-545-8327

www.industrialpress.com   email: info@industrialpress.com

Founded in 1883, Industrial Press is the leading technical and reference publisher for engineering, technology, manufacturing and education.

The house's flagship title, *Machinery's Handbook*, now in its 90th year, remains unchallenged as "The Bible" in its field, the most popular engineering title of all time. The new 28th edition remains true to the Handbook's original design as an extraordinary, comprehensive yet practical and easy-to-use reference for mechanical and manufacturing engineers, designers, draftsmen, toolmakers, and machinists.

Recent titles include *Programmable Automation Technologies: An Introduction to CNC, Robotics, and PLCs* by Daniel Kandray; *Maintenance Planning, Scheduling, and Coordination* by Don Nyman; *Interpretation of Geometric Dimensioning and Tolerancing* by Daniel Puncochar and Ken Evans; and *SolidWorks for Technology and Engineering* by James Valentino.

Industrial Press handles its own distribution.

Industrial Press is expanding its list of professional and educational titles in addition to starting a new program in electronic publishing. Additional information is available in the Authors section of the website. Email proposals are accepted at info@industrialpress.com. Contact with proposals or queries:

John F. Carleo, Editorial Director; jcarleo@industrialpress.com

INNER TRADITIONS/BEAR & COMPANY

BEAR & COMPANY

BEAR CUB BOOKS

BINDU BOOKS

DESTINY BOOKS

HEALING ARTS PRESS

INNER TRADITIONS

PARK STREET PRESS

PO Box 388, One Park Street, Rochester, VT 05767-0388

802-767-3174/800-246-8648   fax: 802-767-3726

www.innertraditions.com   email: submissions@innertraditions.com

Inner Traditions, Bear & Company is one of the largest publishers of books on spiritual and healing traditions of the world. Their titles focus on ancient mysteries, alternative health, indigenous cultures, religion, sexuality, tarot, and divination. With over 1,000 books in print, Inner Traditions has eleven imprints: Inner Traditions, Bear & Co., Bear Cub Books, Bindu Books, Destiny Books, Destiny Recordings, Destiny Audio Editions, Inner Traditions en Español, Healing Arts Press, Park Street Press, and Inner Traditions India.

BEAR & COMPANY

Bear & Company's focus is on ancient wisdom, new science, visionary fiction, Western thought, indigenous traditions, Maya studies, extraterrestrial consciousness, and complementary medicine. Titles from Bear & Company include *Animal Voices, Animal Guides: Discover Yourself through Communication with Animals* by Dawn Baumann Brunke; *The Earth Chronicles Handbook: A Comprehensive Guide to the Seven Books of the Earth Chronicles* by Zecharia Sitchin; and *The Ecstatic Experience: Healing Postures for Spirit Journeys* by Belinda Gore.

BEAR CUB BOOKS

Bear Cub Books are books for kids that feed the growing mind, body, and spirit. Titles include *The Magical Adventures of Krishna: How a Mischief Maker Saved the World* by Vatsala Sperling and Pieter Welteverde; *Ganga: The River that Flows from Heaven to Earth* by Vatsala Sperling, Harish Johari, and Pierter Weltevrede; and *Karna: The Greatest Archer in the World* by Vatsala Sperling and Sandeep Johari.

BINDU BOOKS

Bindu Books publishes books on spirituality and self-transformation for young adults and teens. Some titles are *Spiritual Journaling: Writing Your Way to Independence* by Julie Tallard Johnson; *Awakening to Animal Voices: A Teen Guide to Telepathic Communication with All Life* by Dawn Baumann Brunke; and *Teen Psychic: Exploring Your Intuitive Spiritual Powers* by Julie Tallard Johnson.

DESTINY BOOKS

Destiny Books publishes New Age and metaphysical titles with special emphasis

on self-transformation, the occult, and psychological well-being. Some titles include *The Alchemy of Sexual Energy: Connecting to the Universe from Within* by Mantak Chia; *The Way of Tarot: The Spiritual Teacher in the Cards* by Alejandro Jodorowsky and Marianne Costa; *Kalaripayat: The Martial Arts Tradition of India* by Patrick Denaud and Marie-Claire Restoux; and *Living in the Tao: The Effortless Path to Self-Discovery* by Mantak Chia and William U. Wei.

HEALING ARTS PRESS

Healing Arts Press produces works on alternative medicine and holistic health that combine contemporary thought and innovative research with the accumulated knowledge of the world's great healing traditions. Some titles include *Himalayan Salt Crystal Lamps: For Healing, Harmony, and Purification* by Clemence Lefèvre; *Bach Flowers for Crisis Care: Remedies for Emotional and Psychological Well-Being* by Mechthild Scheffer; and *Radical Medicine: Cutting-Edge Natural Therapies for a Toxic Age* by Louisa L. Williams.

INNER TRADITIONS

Inner Traditions publishes works representing the spiritual, cultural, and mythic traditions of the world, focusing on inner wisdom and perennial philosophies. Some titles include *The Elixir of Immortality: A Modern-Day Alchemist's Discovery of the Philosopher's Stone* by Robert E. Cox; *How the World Is Made: The Story of Creation According to Sacred Geometry* by John Mitchell and Allan Brown; and *The Way of Beauty: Five Meditations for Spiritual Transformation* by François Cheng.

PARK STREET PRESS

Park Street Press puts its focus on travel books, psychology, consumer and environmental issues, archaeology, women's and men's studies, and fine art. Some titles include *Morphic Resonance: The Nature of Formative Causation* by Rupert Sheldrake and *The Spiritual Anatomy of Emotion: How Feelings Link the Brain, the Body, and the Sixth Sense* by Michael A. Jawer et al.

Query via email or regular mail with SASE. Send cover letter with manuscript or proposal by regular mail with SASE to the acquisitions editor:

Jon Graham, Acquisitions Editor

Jeanie Levitan, Vice President of Editorial

INSIDERS' GUIDES [SEE GLOBE PEQUOT PRESS]

INSPIRIO [SEE ZONDERVAN]

INTERNATIONAL MARINE [SEE MCGRAW-HILL COMPANIES, INC.]

INTERVARSITY PRESS

A Division of InterVarsity Christian Fellowship/USA

FORMATIO

Letters: P.O. Box 1400, Downers Grove, IL 60515

Packages: 430 Plaza Dr., Westmont IL 60559

630-734-4000   fax: 630-734-4200

www.ivpress.com   email: submissions@ivpress.com

InterVarsity Press is the publishing arm of InterVarsity Christian Fellowship campus ministry and has been publishing Christian books for more than 50 years. Their program is comprised of three imprints: IVP Books (general interest), IVP Academic (research and classroom use), and IVP Connect (study guides for churches and small groups). A new imprint, Formatio, was launched in 2006.

As an extension of InterVarsity Christian Fellowship, InterVarsity Press serves those in the university, the church and the world by publishing resources that equip and encourage people to follow Jesus as Savior and Lord in all of Life.

Recent titles include *Closing the Window* by Tim Chester; *1 Corinthians* by Alan Johnson; *Defending Constantine* by Peter Leithart; and *The Drama of Ephesians* by Timothy Gombis.

FORMATIO

Andy Le Peau, IVP's editorial director, appealed to tradition to describe their new Formatio imprint: "People are looking for a spirituality that is rooted in the history of the church and in Scripture." Formatio books follow the rich tradition of the church in the journey of spiritual formation. These books are not merely about being informed, but about being transformed by Christ and conformed to his image.

Some new titles from Formatio include *Wisdom Chaser* by Nathan Foster; *The Good and Beautiful Life: Putting on the Character of Christ* by James Bryan Smith; *Scripture by Heart: Devotional Practices for Memorizing God's Word* by Joshua Choonmin Kang; and *The Leadership Ellipse: Sharing How We Lead by Who We Are* by Robert Fryling.

Current interests are listed on the website. IVP is particularly interested in authors with diverse backgrounds and experiences, especially non-Anglos, women, and "knowledgeable and experienced people more than writers." If you are associated with a college or seminary and have an academic manuscript, you may submit it to the attention of the Academic Editor. If you are a pastor or a previously published author, you may submit it to the attention of the General Books Editor. Their preference is to receive a chapter-by-chapter summary, two complete sample chapters, and your résumé.

Address queries with SASEs to:

Dave Zimmerman, Assistant Editor

ISLAND PRESS

1718 Connecticut Avenue, NW, Suite 300, Washington, DC 20009
202-232-7933   fax: 202-234-1328
www.islandpress.org   email: info@islandpress.org

Island Press was established in 1984 to meet the need for reliable, peer-reviewed information to help solve environmental problems. The house identifies innovative thinkers and emerging trends in the environmental field. They work with world-renowned experts and aspiring authors to develop cross-disciplinary solutions to environmental challenges, making sure this information is communicated effectively to the widest possible audience.

Island Press publishes approximately 40 new titles per year on such topics as conservation biology, marine science, land conservation, green building, sustainable agriculture, climate change, and ecological restoration. In addition, Island Press is engaged in several collaborative partnerships designed to help facilitate the stimulation of new ideas, new information products, and targeted outreach to specific audiences. Their Communication Partnership for Science and the Sea (COMPASS) is one such example.

Recent titles include *Tigerland and Other Unintended Destinations* by Eric Dinerstein; *A Guide for Desert and Dryland Restoration* by David Bainbridge; *Aldo Leopold's Odyssey* by Julianne Newton; and *Revolution on the Range* by Courtney White.

Query letters and SASEs should be directed to the Editorial Department.

Todd Baldwin, Vice President and Associate Publisher

Barbara Dean, Executive Editor

Heather Boyer, Senior Editor

Erin Johnson, Assistant Editor

Courtney Lix, Editorial Assistant

JEWISH LIGHTS PUBLISHING

Sunset Farm Offices, Route 4, P.O. Box 237, Woodstock, VT 05091

802-457-4000   fax: 802-457-4004

www.jewishlights.com   email: editorial@jewishlights.com

Jewish Lights publishes books that reflect the Jewish wisdom tradition for people of all faiths and backgrounds. Stuart Matlins, founder and publisher of Jewish Lights Publishing, was presented with the 2006 American Jewish Distinguished Service Award for engaging people of all faiths and backgrounds to help them learn about who Jewish people are, where they come from, and what the future can be made to hold.

Jewish Lights' authors draw on the Jewish wisdom tradition to deal with the quest for the self and for finding meaning in life. Jewish Lights books are non-fiction almost exclusively, covering topics including religion, Jewish life cycle, theology, philosophy, history, and spirituality. They also publish two books for children annually.

Recent titles include *I'm God; You're Not: Observations on Organized Religion & Other Disguises of the Ego* by Lawrence Kushner; *Jewish Mysticism and the Spiritual Life* edited by Lawrence Fine et al; *Sacred Treasure—The Cairo Genizah* by Rabbi Mark Glickman; *Confronting Scandal: How Jews Can Respond When Jews Do Bad Things* by Dr. Erica Brown; *How to Be a Perfect Stranger: The Essential Religious Etiquette Handbook* edited by Stuart Matlins and Arthur Magida; and *Healing from Despair: Choosing Wholeness in a Broken World* by Rabbi Elie Kaplan Spitz with Erica Shapiro Taylor.

Direct proposals and SASEs via regular mail to the Submissions Editor. No digital or email submissions. Jewish Lights does not publish biography, haggadot, or poetry.

Stuart Matlins, Publisher

THE JEWISH PUBLICATION SOCIETY

2100 Arch Street, 2nd Floor, Philadelphia, PA 19103

215-832-0600/800-234-3151   fax: 215-568-2017

www.jewishpub.org   email: jewishbook@jewishpub.org

The Jewish Publication Society (JPS) specializes in books of Jewish interest, especially traditional religious works (including the Torah), folktales, and commentaries and resources for Jewish life. JPS is over a century old, and is a non-profit publisher.

The JPS collection *Legends of the Jews* first appeared in 1909. Lately, JPS has undertaken documenting Jewish tales and legends from the around the world in a series of six massive volumes. The first, *Folktales of the Jews: Tales from the Sephardic Dispersion*, released late in 2006, also contains a detailed commentary by University of Pennsylvania folklorist Dan Ben-Amos.

Recent titles include *20th Century Jewish Religious Thought* by Arthur A. Cohen and Paul Mendes-Flohr; *American Jewish Fiction* by Josh Lambert; *A Heart Afire: Stories and Teachings of the Early Hasidic Masters* by Zalman Schachter Shalomi and Netanel Miles-Yepez; *Elvina's Mirror* by Sylvie Weil; and *Celebrating the Jewish Year: The Spring and Summer Holidays* by Paul Steinberg.

For children's titles, JPS is most interested in manuscripts for short story and folktale collections and for young adult novels—all with strong Jewish themes—and for new titles in their Kids' Catalog series. They generally do not acquire stories on immigrant themes, picture books, catalogs, or the Holocaust. For adult titles, they are not seeking fiction, poetry, memoirs, spirituality, inspiration, monographs, or books about the Holocaust. Please see the website for further details.

Direct queries with résumés and SASEs to Acquisitions.

Carol Hupping, Interim Director

Ellen Frankel, Editor Emerita

Julia Oestreich, Assistant Editor

Janet L. Liss, Managing Editor

JOSSEY-BASS [SEE JOHN WILEY & SONS]

JUDSON PRESS

A Division of the American Baptist Churches, USA

P.O. Box 851, Valley Forge, PA 19482-0851

via UPS/FedEx: 558 N Gulph Rd., King of Prussia, PA 19406

800-458-3766 fax: 610-768-2107

www.judsonpress.com   email: acquisitions@judsonpress.com

Judson Press is the publishing arm of the American Baptist Churches, USA, a Protestant denomination that includes 1.5 million members. Judson Press is a religious book publisher specializing in books on African American and multicultural issues, practical resources for churches, Baptist history, self-help, and inspirational titles for adults and children. It puts out 12–14 books a year, with more than 300 titles in print, ranging from the classic bestseller for pastors, *The Star Book for Ministers*, to the latest inspirational volume, *Before the Thunder Rolls: Devotions for NASCAR Fans*.

Judson Press's primary niches are the following: Baptist history and identity, pastoral and sermon helps, small-group studies, discipleship, Christian education (not curriculum), seasonal program resources, African American resources, sermons, inspiration, and self-help.

Titles include *Autism & Alleluias* by Kathleen Deyer Bolduc; *Tending to Eden: Environmental Stewardship for God's People* by Scott Sabin; *Reboot: Refreshing Your Faith in an High-tech World* by Peggy Kendall; *I'm a Piece of Work: Sisters Shaped by God* by Cynthia Hale; and *Coming Together in the 21st Century: The Bible's Message in an Age of Diversity* by Curtiss Paul DeYoung.

Query with SASE to:

Laura Alden, Publisher

Rebecca Irwin-Diehl, Editor

Marcia Jessen, Curriculum/Production Editor

KAPLAN PUBLISHING

New York Offices:

1 Liberty Plaza, 24th Floor, New York, NY 10006

212-313-4700

Chicago Offices:

30 South Wacker Drive, Ste. 2500, Chicago, IL 60606

www.kaplanpublishing.com   email: KaplanEditorial@kaplan.com

Kaplan Publishing is one of the nation's leading education, career and business publishers, with offices in New York and Chicago. Kaplan produces more than 150 books a year on test preparation, admissions, academic and professional development, general business, management, sales, marketing, real estate, finance, and investing. Imprints include Dearborn Home Inspection Education, Dearborn Real Estate Education, Kaplan AEC Education, Kaplan Business, Kaplan CPA Education, Kaplan Financial, Kaplan Education. The press is in the process of reorganizing the Chicago-based Dearborn imprints.

Kaplan titles are *Kaplan Catholic High School Entrance Exams*; *Kaplan PSAT/NMSQT 2011 Premier*; *Kaplan ACT 2011*; and *Kaplan LSAT 180*.

There are two divisions of Kaplan: test-prep and trade. Currently, acquisitions for both divisions are being handled out of the New York office. Query letters, proposals, and SASEs should be directed to:

Jennifer Farthing, Editorial Director (NY); jennifer.farthing@kaplan.com

KAR-BEN PUBLISHING [SEE LERNER PUBLISHING GROUP]

KENSINGTON PUBLISHING

APHRODISIA

BRAVA

CITADEL

DAFINA

KENSINGTON BOOKS

PINNACLE BOOKS

ZEBRA BOOKS

850 Third Avenue, New York, NY 10022

877-422-3665

www.kensingtonbooks.com

Kensington Publishing (founded 1974) is an independent U.S. publisher of hardcover, trade and mass-market paperback books. From the time their first book became a bestseller (*Appointment in Dallas* by Hugh McDonald), Kensington has been known as a David-vs.-Goliath publisher of titles in the full spectrum of categories, from fiction and romance to health and nonfiction. Kensington now accounts for about 7 percent of all mass-market paperback sales in the U.S. Through the Kensington, Zebra, Pinnacle, and Citadel press imprints, the company releases close to 600 new books per year and has a backlist of more than 3,000 titles.

Kensington continues to be a full-range publisher large enough to command respect in the market, yet small enough to maintain author, reader, and retailer loyalty. The company is able to respond quickly to trends, put books into the hands of readers faster than larger publishers can, and support them with targeted promotional and marketing programs to generate reader excitement.

APHRODISIA

Aphrodisia, launched in January 2006, is Kensington's popular line of erotica. New titles include *A Taste of Honey* by Jami Alden; *Addicted* by Lydia Parks; *All Night Long* by Melissa MacNeal; *Barenaked June* by Deanna Lee; and *Behind the Red Door* by Jacie Barbosa.

BRAVA

Brava publishes three erotic romances in trade paperback each month. Some Brava releases include *I Only Have Fangs for You* by Kathy Love; *Pride and Passion* by

Sylvia Day; *Wicked* by Noelle Mack; *The Stranger I Married* by Sylvia Day; and *The Bad Boys Guide to the Galaxy* by Karen Kelley.

Kate Duffy, Editorial Director—Romance, historical romance, contemporary romance, Brava erotic romance, fiction, mysteries, and thrillers; kduffy@kensingtonbooks.com

CITADEL

Citadel is Kensington's nonfiction imprint. They publish works of history, biography, military history, self-help, and humor. Citadel is also home to their line of poker titles, Lyle Stuart Books. Some titles are *Choosing Faith Against the Odds* by Evona Frink; *Everybody Must Get Stoned* by R. U. Sirius; *Jungle Breezes: From Amish Farm Boy to Jungle Doctor* by Dara Stoltzfus; *Pregnant Pause* by Carrie Friedman; and *French Women Don't Sleep Alone* by Jamie Cat Callan.

Michaela Hamilton, Editor-in-Chief, Citadel—Nonfiction including popular culture, current events, narrative nonfiction, true crime, business, biography, law enforcement, military; selected fiction including thrillers, mainstream novels; mhamilton@kensingtonbooks.com

Richard Ember, Editor, Citadel Press—general nonfiction, biography, history, narrative nonfiction, memoirs, gambling, sports, popular culture, and fratire; rember@kensingtonbooks.com

Mike Shohl, Editor, Citadel—Pop culture, entertainment, music, male interest, fratire, sports, popular science/popular psychology, humor, martial arts, mshohl@kensingtonbooks.com

DAFINA

Dafina brings the very best in African American fiction, nonfiction, and young adult titles. Some examples include *It Is What It Is: A So For Real Novel* by Nikki Carter; *Sex in the Sanctuary* by Lutishia Lovely; *Keep It Movin'* by L. Divine; *Who's Loving You* by Mary B. Morrison; and *The Way We Roll* by Stephanie Perry Moore.

Selena James, Executive Editor—General fiction, nonfiction, African-American fiction, pop culture, inspirational, young adult, and romance; sjames@kensingtonbooks.com

Rakia A. Clark, Editor—Literary and contemporary mulicultural fiction, especially African American; nonfiction interest, including memoir, history, pop culture, and entertainment; rclark@kensingtonbooks.com

KENSINGTON BOOKS

Kensington Books is the imprint for the hardcover and trade paperback line. The line is currently made up of five to eight titles each month. The typical genres are alternative health, mysteries (Partners In Crime), romance, erotica, and self-help. Kensington Mass Market features paperback titles with an emphasis on mysteries and fiction. Traditionally these titles are first published in hardcover. Alternative health titles also are published in this format for sale in the mass retailers.

Recent Kensington titles include *Between Boyfriends* by Michael Salvatore; *Blood Orange* by Drusilla Campbell; and *Blood, Guts, and Whiskey* edited by Todd Robinson.

John Scognamiglio, Editor-in-Chief, Kensington—Fiction including chick lit, historical romance, women's contemporary fiction, gay fiction and non-fiction, mysteries, suspense, horror, mainstream fiction, memoirs, erotica; jscognamiglio@kensingtonbooks.com

Audrey LaFehr, Editorial Director—Women's fiction, romance, romantic suspense, thrillers, erotica, multicultural fiction; alafehr@kensingtonbooks.com

Gary Goldstein, Senior Editor—True crime, Westerns, thrillers, military fiction and nonfiction, sports, how-to, science, world and American history, narrative nonfiction; ggoldstein@kensingtonbooks.com

PINNACLE BOOKS

Pinnacle is the imprint that features bestselling commercial fiction, including thrillers and true crime. Some titles are *Cornered* by Brandon Massey; *Enter Evil* by Linda Ladd; *A Cold Place in Hell* by William Blinn; *Cruel Death* by M. William Phelps; *No Mercy* by John Gilstrap; *Revenge of the Dog Team* by William W. Johnstone and J.A. Johnstone; *The Bike Path Killer* by Michael Beebe and Maki Becker; and *Killing Red* by Henry Perez.

ZEBRA BOOKS

Zebra, the company's flagship imprint, is primarily made up of a large number of historical romance titles, but the list also generally includes one or two lead contemporary romances, Westerns, horror, and humor. Some Zebra titles are *Navajo Night* by Carol Ann Didier; *Never Love a Lawman* by Jo Goodman; *Pleasure: The Shadowdwellers* by Jacquelyn Frank; *Seduced by a Stranger* by Eve Silver; *Silent Killer* by Beverly Barton; *What a Dragon Should Know* by G. A. Aiken; and *Lord of Pleasure* by Delilah Marvelle.

Kensington is open to submissions. Submit completed work or synopsis with the first three chapters to whichever editor you feel is the best person to review your work. No email submissions, only regular mail with SASE.

KIMANI PRESS [SEE HARLEQUIN ENTERPRISES, LTD.]

KINGFISHER BOOKS [SEE HOUGHTON MIFFLIN]

KINGSWOOD BOOKS [SEE ABINGDON PRESS]

KLUTZ [SEE SCHOLASTIC, INC.]

H. J. KRAMER [SEE NEW WORLD LIBRARY]

KRAUSE PUBLICATIONS

700 East State Street, Iola, WI 54990-0001

800-258-0929/715-445-2214   fax: 715-445-4087

www.krause.com

Krause Publications, a division of F+W Publications, is the world's largest publisher of leisure-time periodicals and books on collectibles, arts and crafts, hunting, and fishing. A special interest publisher targeting hobbyists and enthusiasts, Krause imprints cover writing; crafts; scrapbooking; graphic design; fine art; comics, fantasy art and manga; antiques and collectibles; coins; and the outdoors. The book division publishes over 125 titles annually and currently has 750 titles available.

Recent titles include *Standard Catalog of World Paper Money Modern Issues* edited by George Cuhaj; *Horror Movie Freak* by Don Sumner; *Modern Commemorative Coins* by Eric Jordan and Debbie Bradley; *Collecting Rocks, Gems and Minerals* by Patti Polk; and *Survive!: The Disaster, Crisis, and Emergency Handbook* by Jerry Ahern.

Query letters and SASEs should be directed to the Editorial Department.

Dianne Wheeler, Publishing Director—Antiques and Collectibles Division

Candy Wiza, Editor—Green and Simple Living

LARK BOOKS

67 Broadway, Asheville, NC 28801

828-253-0467 fax: 828-253-7952

www.larkbooks.com email: info@larkbooks.com

Lark Books published their first book 20 years ago, and since then their list has grown to more than 300 books, with 60 to 70 new titles now appearing every year. President and Publisher Carol Taylor calls Lark Books "a destination for do-it-yourselfers looking for information, inspiration, source materials, and a lively exchange of ideas." The Lark Books list is composed primarily of reference and how-to books with step-by-step instructions of practical subjects including ceramics, crafts, pets, and other lifestyle topics. Lark Books has published how-to books teaching basketry, weaving, woodworking, ceramics, knitting, jewelry, paper, needlework, sewing, and general crafts from wreath making to rug hooking. They do not publish fiction, and only rarely publish non-illustrated books. The children's list focuses on nonfiction, including crafts and hobbies, games, science experiments, sports, and illustrated board books. Lark Books also publishes a variety of camera manuals and how-to reference books on photography and digital imaging techniques.

Recent titles from Lark Books include *Immersed in Verse: An Informative, Slightly Irreverent & Totally Tremendous Guide to Living the Poet's Life* by Allan Wolf; *Digital Photo Madness!: 50 Weird & Wacky Things to Do with Your Digital Camera* by Thom Gaines; *Hip Handbags: Creating & Embellishing 40 Great-Looking Bags* by Valerie Van Arsdale Shrader; *Smash It! Crash It! Launch It!: 50 Mind-Blowing, Eye-Popping Science Experiments* by Bobby Mercer and Rain Newcomb; and *101 Ways You Can Help Save the Planet Before You're 12!* by Joanne O'Sullivan.

Send queries to the attention of the category editor; e.g., material on a ceramics books should be addressed to the Ceramics Editor, a craft book proposal should be addressed to the Craft Acquisitions Editor, and so on. All children's book submissions should be sent to the attention of the Children's Acquisitions Editor.

LATIN AMERICAN LITERARY REVIEW PRESS

P.O. Box 17660, Pittsburgh, PA 15235

412-824-7903   fax: 412-351-0770

www.lalrp.org   email: editor@lalrp.org

Latin American Literary Review Press was established in 1980 with the principal objective of familiarizing readers outside the field with Latin American literature. LALRP's emphasis has been on publishing translations of creative writing (Discovery series) and literary criticism (Exploration series). These initial titles were followed by bilingual Spanish/English editions of poetry, books of Spanish music, and young adult titles. Currently, LALRP publishes fewer than five new books per year.

The house has always aimed for excellence in publishing, and has relied on a prestigious body of academic editors and distinguished and accomplished translators. The press receives financial support from the National Endowment for the Arts, the Pennsylvania Council on the Arts, and from various other institutions and private foundations.

Titles include *Welcome to Miami, Doctor Leal* by Rene Vazquez Diaz; *My Heart Flooded with Water: Translations from the Poetry of Alfonsina Storni* translated by Orlando Menes; *And What Have You Done?* by José Castro Urioste; *Of My Real Life I Know Nothing* by Ana Maria Moix; and *The Imposter* by Rodolfo Usigli.

Query letters and SASEs should be directed to the editorial staff.

Yvette Miller, President

LEARNINGEXPRESS, LLC

Two Rector Street, 26th Floor, New York, NY 10006

212-995-2566   fax: 212-995-5512

www.learningexpressllc.com   email: customerservice@learningexpressllc.com

LearningExpress is a leading publisher of print and online study guides, test preparation, career guidance, and practical skills materials. LearnATest.com/Library, its online interactive resource, offers practice tests and exercises for academic and career exams. Founded in 1995 in affiliation with Random House, LearningExpress emerged as an industry leader in customized test-preparation publishing and as an expert source for information on targeted careers, vocational professions, and academic exams. In August 1999, Allen & Company, Inc., and a select group of private investors purchased a significant equity interest in the company.

LearningExpress offers more than 300 online, interactive practice exams and course series, as well as over 200 titles in print and more than 150 e-books. All LearningExpress materials are developed by leading educators and industry experts. LearningExpress was named the finalist for two 2008 Codie Awards.

Titles include *California Highway Patrol Exam*; *EMT-Basic Exam for Firefighters*; *Health Occupations Entrance Exams*; *Algebra Success in 20 Minutes a Day*; *Grammar Success in 20 Minutes a Day*; and *Reasoning Skills Success in 20 Minutes a Day*.

Query letters and SASEs should be directed to the editorial staff.

Karen Wolny, Editorial Director

LERNER PUBLISHING GROUP

CAROLRHODA BOOKS

EDICIONES LERNER

GRAPHIC UNIVERSE

KAR-BEN PUBLISHING

LERNER CLASSROOM

LERNER PUBLICATIONS

TWENTY-FIRST CENTURY BOOKS

241 1st Avenue N., Minneapolis, MN 55401

800-328-4929   fax: 800-332-1132

www.lernerbooks.com   email: info@lernerbooks.com

Kar-Ben editorial offices:

800-328-4929 x229   fax: 612-332-7615

www.karben.com   email: editorial@karben.com

Founded in 1959, Lerner Publishing Group is a large independent children's book publisher. With more than 3,500 titles in print, Lerner Publishing Group creates high-quality children's books for schools, libraries, and bookstores on a variety of subjects including biographies, social studies, science, language-arts curriculum, geography, sports, vehicles, picture books, activity books, multicultural issues, and fiction.

Lerner is proud to have published the 2006 Robert F. Silbert Informational Book Medal winner *Secrets of a Civil War Submarine: Solving the Mysteries of the H. L. Hunley* by Sally M. Walker. This important award, established by the Association for Library Service to Children, honors the most distinguished informational book published in English during the preceding year.

Lerner Publishing Group publishes distinctive books for children of all ages including picture books, fiction, and nonfiction. Imprints include Twenty-First Century Books, Carolrhoda Books, Millbrook Press, First Avenue Editions, Ediciones Lerner, LernerClassroom, Graphic Universe, and Kar-Ben Publishing.

CAROLRHODA BOOKS

Carolrhoda Books publishes grades K–12 picture books, intermediate and young-adult fiction, and nonfiction titles that inspire readers' imaginations. Some titles from Carolrhoda include *Monkey with a Tool Belt and the Noisy Problem* by Chris Monroe; *Red, White, and True Blue Mallory* by Laurie Friedman and Jennifer Kalis; *Think Happy!* by Nancy L. Carlson; *Camp Alien* by Pamela F. Service and Mike Gorman; and *The Rule of Claw* by John Brindley.

EDICIONES LERNER

Ediciones Lerner publishes grades K–4 Spanish translations of curriculum-related and fiction titles. Each title has a corresponding English edition for dual-language teaching strategies. Some titles include *Adivina que esta creciendo dentro de este huevo* by Mia Posada; *Adonde van las personas cuando mueren* by Mindy Avra Portnoy and Shelly O. Haas; and *A clases orta vez, Mallory* by Laurie Friedman and Tamara Schmitz.

GRAPHIC UNIVERSE

Graphic Universe publishes grades 4–8 nonfiction and fiction topics boosted to extreme interest through supreme graphic novel artwork created by experienced artists of the genre. Some titles include *Pigling: A Cinderella Story* by Dan Jolley and Anne Timmons; *Psyche and Eros: The Lady and the Monster* by Marie P. Croall and Ron Randall; and *The Smoking Mountain: The Story of Popocatepetl and Iztaccihuatl* by Dan Jolley and David Witt.

KAR-BEN PUBLISHING

Kar-Ben Publishing offers an expansive Jewish library for children, families, and teachers. The Kar-Ben list encompasses presentations keyed to high holidays, the Sabbath, culture and tradition, and general interest concepts. Kar-Ben was founded in 1975 by two friends to publish the children's Passover Haggadah they had created. *My Very Own Haggadah*, now in its 30th anniversary printing, went on to sell over 2 million copies. Kar-Ben continues to publish 10–12 new titles each year.

In 2001, Kar-Ben was purchased by Lerner Publishing Group in Minneapolis, although editorial operations have remained in Maryland. Under Lerner's leadership, Kar-Ben Publishing now publishes over a dozen new titles of Jewish content each year, developing a growing Jewish library for children and branching out from pre-school and young children's works into pre-teen and young-adult fiction and nonfiction. Kar-Ben has created many award-winning children's titles on such subjects as Jewish holidays, crafts, folktales, and contemporary stories.

Kar-Ben considers fiction and nonfiction for preschool through high school, including holiday books, life-cycle stories, Bible tales, folktales, board books, and activity books. In particular, they look for stories that reflect the ethnic and cultural diversity of today's Jewish family. They do not publish games, textbooks, or books in Hebrew.

Recent titles include *Annie Shapiro and the Clothing Workers' Strike* by Marlene Targ Brill; *Before We Eat* by Jacqueline Jules; *Benno and the Night of Broken Glass* by Meg Wiviott; and *Engineer Ari and the Sukkah Express* by Deborah Bodin Cohen.

LERNER CLASSROOM

Lerner Classroom provides books and teaching guides for grades K–8 in the areas of reading, math, social studies, science, biographies, and high-interest topics. They also offer fiction books, picture books, early readers, and chapter books. Some titles include *Addition* by Kristen Sterling; *Clinic* by Sheila Anderson; *Cone* by Jennifer Boothroyd; and *Count Your Way through Afghanistan* by Jim Haskins and Kathleen Benson.

LERNER PUBLICATIONS

Lerner Publications provides educational, photo-driven titles that support key curriculum topics and engage young minds for Grades K–5. Some Lerner titles are *Barack Obama: President for a New Era* by Marlene Targ Brill; *Tyra Banks: From Supermodel to Role Model* by Anne E. Hill; *An Australian Outback Food Chain: A Who-Eats-What Adventure* by Rebecca Hogue Wojahn and Donald Wojahn; and *Air Show Jets* by Matt Doeden.

TWENTY-FIRST CENTURY BOOKS

Twenty-First Century Books publishes curriculum-oriented and high-interest titles that make challenging subjects easy to digest for middle and high school students Grades 6–12. Some title are *Outbreak: Disease Detectives at Work* by Mark P. Friedlander; *Chad in Pictures* by Christine Zuchora-Walske; *Strange but True: The World's Weirdest Wonders* by Robert Sullivan; and *The Aftermath of the Wars against the Barbary Pirates* by Brendan January.

Lerner Publishing Group no longer accepts unsolicited submissions as of 2007.

Joanna Sussman, Director

LIBRARIES UNLIMITED [SEE GREENWOOD PUBLISHING GROUP]

LIFT EVERY VOICE [SEE MOODY PUBLISHERS]

LIGUORI PUBLICATIONS

One Liguori Drive, Liguori, MO 63057-9999

800-325-9521   fax: 636-464-8449

www.liguori.org

Located near St. Louis, Liguori Publications is a midsize Catholic publishing house that produces books, pamphlets, educational materials, *Liguorian* magazine, and software. The purpose of Liguori Publications is to effectively communicate the word of God in the Catholic tradition by growing and expanding their outreach to Catholics of all ages through print and electronic media. They provide English- and Spanish-language (Libros Liguori) products. Imprint Liguori Triumph Books emphasizes an ecumenical perspective in the religious trade market.

Titles include *110 Fun Facts About God's Creation: Is It Animal, Vegetable, or Mineral?* by Bernadette McCarver Snyder; *40 Simple Ways to Keep Lent Meaningful* by Victor Parachin; *7 Steps to Peace with St. Alphonsus Liguori* by Paul Coury C.Ss.R.; *A Christian Response to World Hunger* by Stephen Rehrauer C.Ss.R.; and *Advent and Christmas Wisdom from St. Thomas Aquinas* by Father Andrew Carl Wisdom O.P.

Submit proposals with SASEs to the Editorial Department or via email to manuscript_submission@liguori.org.

LIVING INK BOOKS [SEE AMG PUBLISHERS]

LLEWELLYN WORLDWIDE

FLUX

MIDNIGHT INK

2143 Wooddale Drive, Woodbury, MN 55125

651-291-1970/800-THE-MOON   fax: 651-291-1908

www.llewellyn.com   email: billk@llewellyn.com

Llewellyn Worldwide is one of the oldest and largest independent New Age publishers in the U.S., with over a century of leadership in the industry on such subjects as self-help, metaphysical studies, mysticism, alternative health, divination, astrology, tarot, the paranormal, witchcraft, paganism, Wicca, magick, goddess lore, and garden witchery. They are seeking new authors.

In the past few years, Llewellyn has expanded into fiction for adults and young adults. Midnight Ink, a new imprint of Llewellyn, offers paperback mystery novels. Llewellyn's new imprint of young-adult fiction, Flux, debuted in 2006. Llewellyn Español, their Spanish-language imprint, boasts over 50 titles.

The Llewellyn emphasis is on the practical: how it works, how it is done, and self-help material. The book should appeal to readers with basic skills and knowledge and the information presented should be well within the reach of the average reader.

Recent publications from Llewellyn include *The Case for Reincarnation: Unraveling the Mysteries of the Soul* by J. Allan Danelek; *Cosmic Energy: How to Harness the Invisible Power Around You to Transform Your Life* by Anne Jirsch; *Love and Intuition: A Psychic's Guide to Creating Lasting Love* by Sherrie Dillard; and *Magical Housekeeping: Simple Charms and Practical Tips for Creating a Harmonious Home* by Tess Whitehurst.

Llewellyn accepts submissions directly from authors (including first-time authors) and from literary agents. Submit proposals or complete manuscripts through regular mail only with an SASE to:

Elysia Gallo, Acquisitions Editor

Ms. Carrie Obly, Editor

FLUX

Flux is an imprint dedicated to fiction for teens, where young adult is a point of view, not a reading level. Their fiction avoids condescension and simplification, instead exploring the comedy, tragedy, ecstasy, pain, and discovery that's a part of every teen's life. Some recent releases from Flux include *Shadows of the Redwood* by Gillian Summers; *The Sorcerer of Sainte Felice* by Ann Finnin; *A Blue So Dark* by Holly Schindler; *Gigged* by Heath Gibson; and *Choppy Socky Blues* by Ed Briant.

Andrew Karre, Acquisitions Editor—Flux

MIDNIGHT INK

Midnight Ink is committed to publishing suspenseful tales of all types: hard-boiled thrillers, cozies, historical mysteries, amateur sleuth novels, and more. Some recent releases include *Black Moonlight: The Marjorie McClelland Mysteries #4* by Amy Patricia Meade; *Dead Sleeping Shaman: An Emily Kincaid Mystery #3* by Elizabeth Kane Buzzell; *Photo, Snap, Shot: A Kiki Lowenstein Scrap-N-Craft Mystery #3* by Joanna Campbell Slan; *The Tavernier Stones* by Stephen Parrish; *A House to Die For: A Darby Farr Mystery #1* by Vicki Doudera; and *Diamonds for the Dead* by Alan Orioff.

Barbara Moore, Editor—Midnight Ink

LONELY PLANET PUBLICATIONS

50 Linden Street, Oakland, CA 94607

800-275-8555/510-250-6400   fax: 510-893-8572

www.lonelyplanet.com   email: info@lonelyplanet.com

blog: www.lonelyplanet.com/tonywheeler

Lonely Planet began in the early 1970s after founders Tony and Maureen Wheeler completed an overland journey from London through Asia and on to Australia. That trip resulted in the first Lonely Planet guide-book—*Across Asia on the Cheap*—and laid the foundations of the world's leading independent travel publisher. Tony and Maureen are still the proud owners, still on the road, and still finding the time to continually push the boundaries of travel publishing.

Lonely Planet's head office is in Australia; the crew in Oakland publishes books for the Americas.

Lonely Planet creates and delivers the world's most compelling and comprehensive travel content, giving travelers trustworthy information, engaging opinions, powerful images, and informed perspectives on destinations around the globe. They have over 600 guidebooks and products in print. The house's titles cover every corner of the planet with guidebooks published in languages including French, Italian, Spanish, Korean, and Japanese.

Recent titles include *Discover Australia Travel Guide* by Lindsay Brown et al; *Beijing Encounter Guide* by David Eimer; *Berlin Encounter Guide* by Andrea Schulte-Peevers; and *Bolivia Travel Guide* by Anja Mutic et al.

They have a pool of 200 authors from over 20 countries. No matter how obscure the query or specialized the topic, Lonely Planet can usually find an in-house expert. In the U.S., Lonely Planet distributes its own publications. See their website for detailed submission guidelines and tips.

Query letters and SASEs should be directed to:

Tony Wheeler, Co-owner

Maureen Wheeler, Co-owner

LOTUS PRESS

P.O. Box 325/Twin Lakes, WI 53181

Shipping address:

1100 Lotus Drive, Building 3, Silver Lake, WI 53170

262-889-8561   fax: 262-889-2461

www.lotuspress.com   email: lotuspress@lotuspress.com

Lotus Press is one of the leading publishers in its field of alternative health and wellness. Of particular interest is the Lotus Press list of titles in the field of Ayurveda, which are considered to be the standard works in the field and have been reprinted in many different languages worldwide. Lotus Press titles appear in more than 23 languages thanks to an active foreign rights translation program.

Lotus Press was founded in 1981 by Santosh and Karuna Krinsky. Since that time, the house has grown its list of publications to more than 300 titles, and is currently publishing about 20–25 new titles per year.

In addition to Ayurveda, Lotus Press has actively sought out titles on traditional healing modalities as well as energetic healing. This includes herbalism, Native American health, Chinese traditional herbal medicine, aromatherapy, Reiki and much more.

On the Lotus Press list: *Inner Tantric Yoga: Working with the Universal Shakti: Secrets of Mantras Deities, and Meditation* by David Frawley; *The Way of Ayurvedic Herbs: A Contemporary Introduction and Useful Manual for the World's Oldest Healing System* by Karta Purkh Khalsa; *Troubled Tongues* by Crystal Williams; and *Ayurvedic Yoga Therapy* by Mukunda Stiles.

Direct query letters, proposals, and SASEs to:

Cathy Hoselton, Assistant to the President

LUNA BOOKS [SEE HARLEQUIN ENTERPRISES, LTD.]

LYONS PRESS [SEE THE GLOBE PEQUOT PRESS]

MACADAM/CAGE PUBLISHING

155 Sansome Street, Suite 550, San Francisco, CA 94104

415-986-7502   fax: 415-968-7414

www.macadamcage.com

MacAdam/Cage Publishing was founded as an independent trade publisher in 1998 by David Poindexter with the aim of publishing books of quality fiction and nonfiction. Publishers of *The Time Traveler's Wife* by Audrey Niffenegger, a debut novel that became a publishing phenomenon in Fall 2003, this house is committed to bringing new and talented voices to the literary marketplace.

In 1999 MacAdam/Cage Publishing acquired the independent press MacMurray & Beck, well known in the industry for launching authors such as Patricia Henley (*Hummingbird House*), William Gay (*The Long Home*), and Susan Vreeland (*Girl in Hyacinth Blue*) and heavily supported by the bookselling trade with many BookSense 76 picks as well as appearances in chain-store fiction programs that highlight new authors. MacAdam/Cage Publishing represents independent publishing at its best.

Recent titles include *The Prayer Room* by Shanthi Sekaran; *Little Book of the Sea: Food and Drink* by Lorenz Schroter; *Stray Dog Winter* by David Francis; *The Lost Country* by William Gay; and *Our Lady of Pain* by Elena Forbes.

MacAdam/Cage will not accept submissions in these categories: romance, science fiction, fantasy, supernatural, self-help, poetry, thrillers, religion, spirituality, children's, young adult, cookbooks, parenting, family, military science, or medical. They also do not accept one-page proposals, complete manuscripts, submissions on disk, or email submissions. Send a cover letter, brief synopsis, author biography, 30-page sample, and SASE to Manuscript Submissions.

Pat Walsh, Editor-in-Chief

David Poindexter, Publisher

MAGINATION PRESS [SEE AMERICAN PSYCHOLOGICAL ASSOCIATION, INC.]

MANIC D PRESS

P.O. Box 410804, San Francisco, CA 94141

415-648-8288

www.manicdpress.com   email: info@manicdpress.com

Manic D Press was founded by Jennifer Joseph in 1984 as an alternative outlet for young writers seeking to bring their work into print. Manic D Press publishes unusual fiction, narrative poetry, contemporary art, rock photography, comix, cultural studies, GLBT, and alternative travel trade paperbacks and hardcovers by new and established authors.

Recent titles include *Bang Ditto* by Amber Tamblyn; *Lynnee Breedlove's One Freak Show* by Lynn Breedlove; *Lilac Mines* by Cheryl Klein; and *Open Letter to Quiet Light* by Francesca Lia Block.

Before submitting your work to Manic D, the publisher requests that you read at least one book they have already published to familiarize yourself with their line. In your cover letter, tell them which book you have read and what you thought about it. Be specific.

Email submissions are preferred. Send submissions to subs@manicdpress.com. Manuscripts are read twice a year, during the months of January and July only. Send five to ten poems, three to five short stories, or a synopsis and first chapter of a novel with your cover letter and SASE to the attention of the editors.

Jennifer Joseph, Publisher

MARLOWE & COMPANY [SEE PERSEUS]

MCDOUGAL-LITTELL [SEE HOUGHTON MIFFLIN HARCOURT]

MCFARLAND & COMPANY

960 NC Highway 88 West, Jefferson, NC 28640

Mailing address:

Box 611, Jefferson, NC 28640

336-246-4460   fax: 336-246-5018

www.mcfarlandpub.com   email: info@mcfarlandpub.com

McFarland & Company, Inc., Publishers, founded in 1979, is located in Jefferson, North Carolina, a small town nestled in the northwestern corner of the state. The company is now one of the leading publishers of scholarly and reference books in the U.S., with 4,000 titles published to date, including nearly 2,400 in print. McFarland publishes 325 new titles each year for a worldwide market; many of them have received awards as outstanding reference or academic titles. McFarland is recognized for its serious works in a variety of fields, including performing arts (especially film), sport and leisure (especially baseball and chess), military history, popular culture, and automotive history, among other topics.

Recent titles include *Waging The War of the Worlds* by Howard Koch; *Ford in the Service of America* by Timothy J. O'Callaghan; *Black Baseball Players in Canada* by Tom Hawthorn; and *Masculinity in Vietnam War Narratives* by Brenda M. Boyle.

Authors may contact the house with a query letter, a full proposal, or a finished manuscript with cover letter. See the website for more details.

Queries may be directed to:

Gary Mitchem, Acquisitions Editor; gmitchem@mcfarlandpub.com

Steve Wilson, Editor Director; swilson@mcfarlandpub.com

David Alff, Editor; dalff@mcfarlandpub.com

THE MCGRAW-HILL COMPANIES, INC.

MCGRAW-HILL BUSINESS (FINANCE AND MANAGEMENT)

MCGRAW-HILL CONSUMER

MCGRAW-HILL HIGHER EDUCATION

MCGRAW-HILL MEDICAL/ACCESS MED

MCGRAW-HILL PROFESSIONAL (SCIENCE, ENGINEERING, TECHNICAL)

Two Penn Plaza, New York, NY 10121-2298

212-512-2000   fax: 212-904-6096

Burr Ridge address:

1333 Burr Ridge Parkway, Burr Ridge, IL 60527

www.mhprofessional.com

INTERNATIONAL MARINE/RAGGED MOUNTAIN

P.O. Box 235, Thomaston, Maine, 04861

www.internationalmarine.com

MCGRAW-HILL/OSBORNE MEDIA

160 Spear Street, Suite 700, San Francisco, CA 94105

www.osborne.com

The McGraw-Hill Companies, Inc., is a publicly traded corporation headquartered in New York City, focused on education, publishing, and financial services for a global market. It publishes numerous textbooks and magazines, including BusinessWeek and Aviation Week, and is the parent company of Standard & Poor's and J.D. Power and Associates.

The myriad of McGraw-Hill book publishing divisions and imprints may be explored in depth at www.mhprofessional.com and www.mcgraw-hill.com.

Gary Krebs, Group Publisher; gary_krebs@mcgraw-hill.com

MCGRAW-HILL BUSINESS (FINANCE AND MANAGEMENT)

McGraw-Hill Business subjects include accounting, marketing and sales, careers, communication, e-business, economics, finance and investing, general business, human resources and training, international business, management and leadership, personal finance, quality, real estate, and small business and entrepreneurship.

Mary Glenn, Editorial Director—Business management and leadership

Leah Spiro, Senior Editor—Business acquisitions

Donya Dickerson, Editor—Business and management

Leila Porteous, Editor—Business

Knox Huston, Editor—Business and management

Sophia Efthimiatou, Editor—Finance and investing

MCGRAW-HILL CONSUMER

The McGraw-Hill Consumer broad list includes titles in business, economics, computers, education, family and relationships, foreign language study, health and fitness, history, language arts and disciplines, mathematics, medical, nature, psychology and psychiatry, science, self-help, social science, sports and recreation, technology, engineering, transportation, travel, hobbies, gardening, house and home, humor, music, performing arts, and photography.

Titles include *Annual Editions: American Government 09/10* by Bruce Stinebrickner; *The Discovery of Society* by Randall Collins and Michael Makowsky; *Relationship Selling* by Mark Johnston and Greg Marshall; *THiNK: Why Do You Think the Way You Do* by Judith Boss; and *Relax and Learn Portuguese.*

MCGRAW-HILL HIGHER EDUCATION

McGraw-Hill Higher Education publishes textbooks and home study guides for adults and young adults, some of which manage to get the words "easy" and "quantum mechanics" into the same title.

Titles include *Schaum's Quick Guide to Writing Great Research Papers* by Laurie Rozakis; *Bob Miller's Algebra for the Clueless, 2nd Edition* by Bob Miller; *Schaum's Easy Outline of Quantum Mechanics* by Eliahu Zaarur and Phinik Peuven; *Schaum's Outline of Italian Grammar* by Joseph Germano; and 5 *Steps to a 5 on the Advanced Placement Exams.*

Direct queries and SASEs to:

Chuck Wall, Senior Editor—Test-prep, study guides; charles_wall@ mcgraw-hill.com

Anya Kozorez, Editor (NY)

Kimberly Easton, Editor (NY)

Christopher Brown, Publisher (Chicago)—Foreign language dictionaries, Schaum's Test-Prep and Study Guides

Karen Young, Editor (Chicago)—Foreign language, reference

Kathyrn Keil, Associate Editor (Chicago)—Chase's Foreign Language, teacher reference

Garret Lemoi, Editor (Chicago)—ESL

MCGRAW-HILL MEDICAL/ACCESS MED

Part of McGraw-Hill Professional Division, Access Med provides books for medical professionals on subjects including basic science, clinical medicine, nursing, pharmacy, allied health, and test prep and review.

Titles include *Williams Gynecology* by John O. Schorge et al; *Fishman's Pulmonary Diseases and Disorders* by Alfred P. Fishman et al; *First Aid for Family Medicine Boards* by Tao Le; and *Pharmacy Law: Textbook and Review* by Debra B. Feinberg.

If you are a medical, nursing, or health-related professional or instructor with a book project or a well-established course syllabus, McGraw-Hill Medical/Access Med would like to hear from you.

Direct query with SASE to:

Scott Grillo, Vice President and Publisher

Anne Sydor, Executive Editor (NY)—Dermatology, OB/GYN, neurology, neuroscience, pediatrics, emergency medicine, psychiatry; anne_sydor@mcgraw-hill.com

Marsha Loeb, Editor—Surgery, anesthesia

James F. Shanahan, Executive Editor (Burr Ridge, IL)—internal medicine; james_shanahan@mcgraw-hill.com

MCGRAW-HILL PROFESSIONAL (SCIENTIFIC AND TECHNICAL)

The McGraw-Hill Professional division focuses on professional, reference, and trade publishing in technical and scientific fields.

Titles include *Highway Engineering Handbook* by Roger Brockenbrough; *Harrison Manual of Medicine* by Anthony Fauci et al; *Peripheral Arterial Disease* by Robert Dieter, Jr. et al; *Adams and Victor's Principles of Neurology* by Allan Ropper and Martin Samuels; and *Thermodynamics Demystified* by Merle Potter.

Direct queries and SASEs to:

Steve Chapman, Publisher (NY)—Aviation, electrical engineering; steve_chapman@mcgraw-hill.com

Judy Bass, Senior Editor (NY)—TAB Electronics, Demystified series; judy_bass@mcgraw-hill.com

Brian Foster, Associate Editor (NY)

Joy Bramble, Senior Editor (NY)—Architecture, construction; joy_bramble@mcgraw-hill.com

Taisuke Soda, Senior Editor—Engineering; taisuke_soda@mcgraw-hill.com

Larry Hager, Senior Editor (NY)—Civil engineering, construction, technical trades, hydro-engineering; larry_hager@mcgraw-hill.com

INTERNATIONAL MARINE/RAGGED MOUNTAIN PRESS

Part of the McGraw-Hill Trade Division, International Marine has been publishing books about boats since 1970. Located near the Rockport and Camden harbors of mid-coast Maine, IM has published more than 200 titles covering everything from knots to sailboat racing, plus an impressive lineup of nautical adventure books. Ragged Mountain Press publishes nautical sports books. International Marine is always seeking new authors and has extensive guidelines online at www.internationalmarine.com or by request from the editors.

Titles representative of the list include *Canoe and Kayak Building the Light and Easy Way* by Sam Rizetta; *This Old Boat* by Don Casey; *Building Strip-Planked Boats* by Nick Schade; and *Where the Fish Are: A Science-Based Guide to Stalking Freshwater Fish* by Daniel Bagur.

Direct query letters and SASEs to:

Jonathon Eaton, Editorial Director—Boating, outdoors; jonathan_eaton@mcgraw-hill.com

MCGRAW-HILL/OSBORNE MEDIA

McGraw-Hill/Osborne Media, a unit of McGraw-Hill Education, is a leading publisher of self-paced computer training materials, including user and reference guides, bestselling series on computer certification, titles on business and technology, and high-level but practical titles on networking, programming, and Web development tools. McGraw-Hill/Osborne Media is the official press of Oracle, Corel, and Intuit. From its home base across the east bay from San Francisco, McGraw-Hill/Osborne Media is seeking proposals from computer-savvy authors.

Titles include *How to Do Everything: Adobe Illustrator CS4* by Sue Jenkins; *Software and Systems Requirements Engineering: In Practice* by Brian Berenbach et al; *Databases: A Beginner's Guide* by Andy Oppel; and *Microsoft Visual Studio 2008 Programming* by Jamie Plenderleith and Steve Bunn.

Direct proposals with SASEs to Manuscript Proposal. See the website for detailed proposal tips and guidelines.

Steve Chapman, Publisher

Roger Stewart, Editorial Director, Consumer Computing; roger_stewart@mcgraw-hill.com

Wendy Rinaldi, Editorial Director, Programming and Web Development; wendy_rinaldi@mcgraw-hill.com

Jane Brownlow, Executive Editor, Networking and Communications; jane_brownlow@mcgraw-hill.com

Timothy Green, Senior Acquisitions Editor, Certification & Career; timothy_green@mcgraw-hill.com

Elizabeth McClain, Acquisitions Editor, Databases & ERP, Oracle Press; Elizabeth_mcclain@mcgraw-hill.com

Margaret Morin, Acquisitions Editor, Consumer Computing; margaret_morin@mcgraw-hill.com

MCSWEENEY'S

McSweeney's West:

849 Valencia Street, San Francisco, CA 94110

McSweeney's East:

826 NYC, 372 Fifth Ave., Brooklyn, NY 11215

www.mcsweeneys.net   email: booksubmissions@mcsweeneys.net

Founded by author Dave Eggers, McSweeney's is a small, independent press based in San Francisco that is committed to helping find new voices—Neal Pollack, Amy Fusselman, and Paul Collins—to publishing works of gifted but under-appreciated writers, such as Lydia Davis and Stephen Dixon—and to always push the literary form forward. One also finds here bestselling authors like Dave Eggers and Nick Hornby.

McSweeney's has a very active website and an amazing quarterly; it is a place to find and share interesting, quirky, and/or brilliant fiction, essays, memoirs, children's titles, and humor.

Recent titles include *Citrus County* by John Brandon; *There Are Many of Us* by Spike Jonze; *Half a Life* by Darin Strauss; *It Is Right to Draw Their Fur* by Dave Eggers; and *I Found This Funny* edited by Judd Apatow.

Send complete manuscript or sample chapters via email or regular mail.

Barb Bersche, Publisher

MEADOWBROOK PRESS

5451 Smetana Drive, Minnetonka, MN 55343

800-338-2232   fax: 952-930-1940

www.meadowbrookpress.com   email: editorial@meadowbrookpress.com

Meadowbrook Press (founded 1975) specializes in books about parenting, pregnancy, baby care, child care, humorous poetry for children, party planning, and children's activities. Meadowbrook is also the country's No. 1 publisher of baby name books, with eight baby-naming books in print and total sales of over 6 million copies.

Recent titles include *1 Little, 2 Little, 3 Little Elephants* by Bruce Lansky and Tamara Peterson; *5 Little Monkeys Jumpin' on the Bed* by Bruce Lansky and Tamara Peterson; *Old MacDonald Had a Farm* by Bruce Lansky and Tamara Peterson; and *Grandma Knows Best, But No One Ever Listens!* by Mary McBride.

The Meadowbrook editorial staff develops and writes books as well as acquires and edits titles written by outside authors. The house is not currently accepting unsolicited manuscripts or queries for the following genres: adult fiction, adult poetry, humor, and children's fiction. Also, they do not currently publish picture books for children, travel titles, scholarly, or literary works.

See the website for submission guidelines and send all appropriate queries and SASEs to Submissions Editor.

Bruce Lansky, Publisher

MESORAH PUBLICATIONS

4401 Second Avenue, Brooklyn, NY 11232

718-921-9000/800-637-6724   fax: 718-680-1875

www.artscroll.com   email: info@artscroll.com

Mesorah Publications produces books of contemporary Jewish interest written by authors with sophisticated firsthand knowledge of Orthodox religious practices, history, and culture. It is also noted for its works in traditional Judaica, Bible study, Talmud, liturgical materials, Jewish history, and juvenile literature. Founded in 1976, Mesorah Publications remains true to tradition in all of its publications, as expressed in the motto: Mesorah Publications . . .helping to preserve the heritage, one book at a time.

Recent titles include *The Betrayal* by M. Kenan; *Stories that Warm the Heart* by Rabbi Binyomin Pruzansky; *Shiras Devorah* by Rabbi Yisroel Reisman; *Women Talk* by Debbie Shapiro; and *Aleinu L'Shabei'ach—Vayikra: Wisdom, Stories, and Inspiration* by Rabbi Yitzchok Zilberstein and Rabbi Moshe Zoren.

Address queries and SASEs to Acquisitions Editor.

MIDNIGHT INK [SEE LLEWELLYN WORLDWIDE]

MILKWEED EDITIONS

1011 Washington Avenue South, Suite 300, Minneapolis, MN 55415-1246

612-332-3192/800-520-6455   fax: 612-215-2550

www.milkweed.org   email: editor@milkweed.org

Milkweed Editions is a nonprofit literary press, publishing 15–20 books a year. Founded in 1979, the house publishes literary fiction, nonfiction about the natural world, poetry, and novels for young readers. They have published over 200 titles. The editors at Milkweed Editions believe that literature is a transformative art, and that each book bears a responsibility to convey the essential experiences of the human heart and spirit.

Although a small press, Milkweed also offers prizes for adult fiction and children's literature in their prestigious literary awards. Guidelines for the prizes are available online or by request through regular mail. The World As Home is a Milkweed website that fosters ecological literacy and renewal by linking literary writing about the natural world to specific ecoregions and to organizations active in preserving natural landscapes or focused on the art of writing.

Milkweed authors include Ken Kalfus, Susan Straight, Marilyn Chin, Larry Watson, Bill Holm, Paul Gruchow, Janisse Ray, Pattiann Rogers, and many others, including emerging and mid-career authors.

Titles include *Thirst* by Ken Kalfus; *Orion You Came and You Took All My Marbles* by Kira Henehan; *The Last Fair Deal Going Down* by David Rhodes; *Vestments* by John Reimringer; and *Extra Indians* by Eric Gansworth.

Milkweed does not accept submissions on disk or via email. Send the complete manuscript or a proposal with sample chapters, outline, and cover letter. Direct submissions to the Fiction Reader (or Nonfiction, Poetry, or Children's, as appropriate); include an SASE.

Daniel Slager, Editor-in-Chief

Jim Cihlar, Managing Editor

MIRA BOOKS [SEE HARLEQUIN ENTERPRISES, LTD., CANADA]

MIRAMAX BOOKS [SEE HYPERION]

MOODY PUBLISHERS

LIFT EVERY VOICE

A Division of the Moody Bible Institute

820 North LaSalle Boulevard, Chicago, IL 60610-3284

312-329-2101

www.moodypublishers.org   email: acquisitions@moody.edu

Moody Publishers was founded in 1894 by D.L. Moody eight years after he had founded the Moody Bible Institute, which continues to be a well-known evangelical institution. The house publishes fiction, nonfiction, and children's titles for the Christian markets.

The Moody Publishers' mission is to educate and edify the Christian and to evangelize the non-Christian by ethically publishing conservative, evangelical Christian literature and other media for all ages around the world; and to help provide resources for Moody Bible Institute in its training of future Christian leaders.

Moody titles include *Between a Rock and a Hard Place* by Tony Evans; *Marriage Matters* by Tony Evans; *Things I Wish I'd Known Before We Got Married* by Gary Chapman; *Fair Fight!* by Tim and Joy Downs; and *Pearl in the Sand* by Tessa Afshar.

LIFT EVERY VOICE

Moody Publishers partners with the Institute for Black Family Development in the creation of a joint imprint, Lift Every Voice. The vision for this endeavor is to see African American Christians encouraged in their faith in Jesus Christ through quality books written by African Americans. While Moody Publishers had already published several African American authors, such as Tony Evans, Clarence Schuler, Lois Evans, and Crawford Loritts, Lift Every Voice products will be targeted almost exclusively to African Americans.

Lift Every Voice titles include *Seven Reasons Why God Created Marriage* by James Ford; *Our Voices: Issues Facing Black Women in America* by Amanda Johnson; *The Last Woman Standing* by Tia McCollors; *Learning to Love* by Stephanie Perry Moore; *Coming Across Jordan* by Mabel Elizabeth Singletary; and *Out of the Box: Building Robots, Transforming Lives* by Andrew Williams and Edward Gilbreath.

Moody Publishers currently is not reviewing manuscripts, except from literary agents.

Paul Santhouse, Director of Acquisitions

THE MOUNTAINEERS BOOKS

SKIPSTONE

A Division of The Mountaineers Club

1001 SW Klickitat Way, Suite 201, Seattle, WA 98134

206-223-6303   fax: 206-223-6306

www.mountaineersbooks.org   email: mbooks@mountaineersbooks.org

The Mountaineers Books specializes in outdoor titles by experts. Born from the hand-scribbled trail maps and wilderness passion of its members, Washington's nearly 100-year-old Mountaineers Club established the nonprofit Mountaineers Books in 1960 to express and share its love of the natural outdoors. The house produces guidebooks, instructional texts, historical works, adventure narratives, natural history guides, and works on environmental conservation.

Today, with more than 500 titles in print, The Mountaineers Books is a leading publisher of quality outdoor books, including many award winners. For those hiking with the family, cycling over a country road, clinging to a big wall or dreaming of a trek in Nepal, The Mountaineers Books has the guidance for creating the next journey in confidence and safety. The house focuses on non-competitive, non-motorized, self-propelled sports such as mountain climbing, hiking, walking, skiing, snowshoeing, and adventure travel. They also publish works on environmental and conservation subjects, narratives of mountaineering expeditions and adventure travel, outdoor guidebooks to specific areas, mountaineering history, safety/first aid, and books on skills and techniques for the above sports. The house does not publish fiction, general tourist guides, or guides dealing with hunting, fishing, snowmobiling, RV travel, horseback riding, or team sports.

Mountaineers Press titles include *Urban Pantry: Tips & Recipes for a Thrifty, Sustainable & Seasonal Kitchen* by Amy Pennington; *Babes in the Woods: Hiking, Camping & Boating with Babies & Young Children* by Jennifer Aist; and *Eco-Chic Home: Rethink, Reuse & Remake Your Way to Sustainable Style* by Emily Anderson.

SKIPSTONE

The Skipstone imprint, launched in 2007, publishes nonfiction books on eco-conscious lifestyle topics, including sustainable home care, food/cooking, pet care, gardening, crafts, humor, and entertaining with a green focus.

Skipstone titles include *Backcountry Better Crafting with Style: 50 Nature-Inspired Projects* by Jennifer Worick and Kate Quinby; *Barking Buddha: Simple Soul Stretches for Yogi and Dogi* by Brenda Bryan and Bev Sparks; *The Zen of Mountains & Climbing: Wit, Wisdom, and Inspiration* by Katherine Wroth; and *The Salvage Studio: Sustainable Home Comforts to Organize, Entertain, and Inspire* by Amy Duncan et al.

If you plan to submit an adventure narrative, please request information about the Barbara Savage Miles From Nowhere Memorial Award. The Mountaineers Books does not publish fiction, general tourist guides, or guides dealing with hunting, fishing, snowmobiling, RV travel, horseback riding, or team sports.

Submit query letters, manuscripts, and/or proposals by regular mail only to Acquisitions.

Kate Rogers, Editor-in-Chief

MULTNOMAH PUBLISHERS, INC. [SEE BERTELSMANN AG/ RANDOM HOUSE/WATERBROOK MULTNOMAH]

MUSEUM OF NEW MEXICO PRESS

725 Camino Lejo, Santa Fe, NM 87505

Mailing address:

P.O. Box 2087, Santa Fe, NM 87504

505-476-1155   fax: 505-476-1156

www.mnmpress.org

Founded in 1951, the Museum of New Mexico Press is an award-winning publisher of finely designed and crafted books that reflect the collections of the Museum of New Mexico and explore the culture of the Southwest. Specializations include fine art and folk art, photography, Native Americana, the Hispanic Southwest, nature and gardening, and architecture and style.

Recent titles include *Richard Diebenkorn in New Mexico* by Mark Lavatelli et al; *Filipino Cuisine: Recipes from the Islands* by Gerry Gelle; *Healing the West: Voices, Culture, and Habitat* by Jack Loeffler; *Before Santa Fe* by Jason S. Shapiro; and *New Mexico Colcha Club* by Nancy C. Benson.

The house requests that authors submit book proposals rather than full manuscripts for review. For proposal guidelines, see the website. Send proposals with cover letters, CVs, and SASEs to:

Mary Wachs, Editorial Director, mary.wachs@state.nm.us

NAKED INK [SEE THOMAS NELSON PUBLISHERS]

NATARAJ PUBLISHING [SEE NEW WORLD LIBRARY]

NATION BOOKS [SEE PERSEUS]

NATIONAL GEOGRAPHIC SOCIETY

National Geographic Books (General Audience):

P.O. Box 10543, Des Moines, IA 50340

888-647-6733/515-362-3345

National Geographic Children's Books

P.O. Box 4002864, Des Moines, IA 50340

877-873-6846

www.nationalgeographic.com   email: askngs@nationalgeographic.com

Founded in 1888, the National Geographic Society is one of the world's largest nonprofit scientific and educational organizations. Their mission is to increase and diffuse geographic knowledge while promoting the conservation of the world's cultural, historical, and natural resources. National Geographic has funded over 7,000 scientific research projects, supports an education program combating geography illiteracy and reflects the world through magazines, television programs, books, videos, maps, interactive media, and merchandise.

The Press publishes quality, illustrated nonfiction books, including reference books, photography books, and travel guides. Subjects of focus are adventure and exploration, animals and nature, culture and history, geography and reference, photography, science and space, and educational materials for kids.

Recent titles include *True Food* by Annie Bond et al; *Receding Tide: Vicksburg* and Gettysburg, *The Battles that Changed the Civil War* by Edwin C. Bearss; *Green Guide Families: The Complete Guide for Eco-Friendly Parents* by Catherine Zandonella; *What Does It Mean to Be Human?* by Chris Sloan and Richard Potts; and *Vampire Forensics: Uncovering the Origins of an Enduring Legend* by Mark Jenkins.

Query letters and SASEs should be directed to the editorial staff of the Book Division.

Stephen Mico, Senior Vice President, Publisher, Children's and educational titles

Kevin Mulroy, Senior Vice President, Publisher, Books

Virginia Koeth, Editor—Children's books

Lisa Thomas, Senior Editor

NAVAL INSTITUTE PRESS

An imprint of the United States Naval Institute

291 Wood Road, Annapolis, MD 21402

410-224-3378   fax: 410-269-7940

www.usni.org/navalinstitutepress/index.asp

Naval Institute Press, situated on the grounds of the U.S. Naval Academy, is the book-publishing imprint of the U.S. Naval Institute, a private, independent, non-profit professional society for members of the military services and civilians who share an interest in naval and maritime affairs. USNI was established in 1873 at the Naval Academy in Annapolis; the press inaugurated its publishing program in 1898 with a series of basic guides to U.S. naval practice.

Naval Institute Press features trade books, in addition to the house's targeted professional and reference titles. Areas of NIP interest include how-to books on boating, navigation, battle histories, and biographies, as well as occasional selected titles in fiction (typically with a nautical adventure orientation). Specific categories encompass such fields as seamanship, naval history and literature, the Age of Sail, aviation, aircraft, World War II naval history, ships and aircraft, current naval affairs, naval science, and general naval resources and guidebooks.

The Press produces more than 70 titles each year. With its long-established tradition of publishing excellence in the fields of naval, military, and maritime history, the NIP provides the serious reader with an invaluable resource. Categories include history and reference.

Recent titles include *Beneath the Waves: The Life and Navy of Capt. Edward L. Beach, Jr.* by Edward Finch; *Shepherds of the Sea: Destroyer Escorts in World War II* by Robert F. Cross; *Guiding Lights: United States Naval Academy Monuments and*

Memorials by Nancy Prothro Arbuthnot; and *A Tactical Ethic: Moral Conduct in the Insurgent Battlespace* by Dick Couch.

Submit a proposal or the entire manuscript (paper copy) via regular mail. Send all queries and SASEs to the Acquisitions Editors.

Thomas Cutler, Director of Professional Publishing; tcutler@usni.org

Susan Todd Brook, Acquisitions Editor; sbrook@usni.org

Adam Kane, Acquisitions Editor; akane@usni.org

THOMAS NELSON PUBLISHERS

501 Nelson Place, P.O. Box 141000, Nashville, TN 37214-1000

800-251-4000

www.thomasnelson.com

Blog: www.michaelhyatt.com/fromwhereisit

Thomas Nelson Publishers is the world's largest Christian publishing company and the ninth-largest publishing company of any kind. Recently purchased by InterMedia Partners, Thomas Nelson continues with Michael Hyatt as president of this religious publishing company. The company was founded in 1798 by Scotsman Thomas Nelson, who sought to make Christian works and classic literature affordable for the common folk. Today, categories include spiritual growth and Christian thought, fiction, people and culture, Bibles, practical living, children's, gift books, general interest and lifestyle, business, small group curriculum, biblical reference, and Spanish.

Thomas Nelson formerly worked with 18 imprints, but has reorganized itself in a move called the One Company initiative. Thomas Nelson has eliminated all of its imprints and has reorganized its publishing functions around units keyed to BISAC category codes.

Some recent titles from Thomas Nelson include *Henry Blackaby Essential Bible Study* by Henry Blackaby; *Outlive Your Life* by Max Lucado; *Permission to Speak Freely* by Anne Jackson; *The Grace of God* by Andy Stanley; and *the Gospel According to Jesus* by Andy Stanley.

Thomas Nelson, Inc., does not accept or review any unsolicited queries, proposals, or manuscripts.

David Moberg, Group Publisher—Practical living, spiritual growth and Christian thought; dmoberg@thomasnelson.com

Joey Paul, Publisher—Practical living; jpaul@thomasnelson.com

Matt Baugher, Publisher—Spiritual growth and Christian thought; mbaugher@thomasnelson.com

Debbie Wickwire, Acquisitions Editor—Practical living; dwickwire@thomasnelson.com

John Mason, Vice President of Acquisitions—Spiritual growth and Christian thought; jmason@thomasnelson.com

Allen Arnold, Publisher—Fiction; aarnold@thomasnelson.com

Ami McConnell, Senior Acquisitions Editor—Fiction; amcconnell@thomasnelson.com

Amanda Bostic, Associate Acquisitions Editor—Fiction; abostic@thomasnelson.com

Wayne Hastings, Group Publisher—Bible reference and curriculum; whastings@thomasnelson.com

Karen Artl, Sr. Acquisitions Editor—Bible reference and curriculum; kartl@thomasnelson.com

Bob Sanford, Publisher—Bible Study; bsanford@thomasnelson.com

Frank Couch, Publisher—Curriculum and translation development; fcouch@thomasnelson.com

Todd Shuttleworth, Group Publisher—Specialty and global publishing; tshuttleworth@thomasnelson.com

Larry Downs, Publisher—Spanish; ldowns@thomasnelson.com

Laura Minchew, Publisher—Children's books and education; lminchew@thomasnelson.com

Dan Lynch, Publisher—Family entertainment; dlynch@thomasnelson.com

Mark Gilroy, Publisher—Gift books; mgilroy@thomasnelson.com

David Dunham, Group Publisher—General interest and lifestyle, business and culture; ddunham@thomasnelson.com

Joel Miller, Publisher—Business and culture; joel.miller@thomasnelson.com

Pamela Clements, Publisher—General interest and lifestyle; pclements@thomasnelson.com

Geoff Stone, Editor-in-Chief—General interest and lifestyle; gstone@thomasnelson.com

Victor Oliver, Senior Acquisitions Editor—General interest and lifestyle, business and culture; voliver@thomasnelson.com

NEW HORIZON PRESS

SMALL HORIZONS

Mailing address:

P.O. Box 669, Far Hills, NJ 07931

908-604-6311/800-533-7978   fax: 908-604-6330

www.newhorizonpressbooks.com   email: nhp@newhorizonpressbooks.com

New Horizon Press (established 1982) publishes 12–14 books a year examining the everyday hero among us, and social concerns. The company focuses on true crime, battles for justice, current events with a journalistic stance, as well as psychological and social problems, women's and men's issues, and parenting advice written by experts with credentials in their fields. The house develops three primary lines of titles: hardcover, trade paper, and children's books.

Titles include *Suicidal Veterans: Recognizing, Supporting, and Answering Their Pleas for Help* by Victor Montgomery III; *Your Sexually Addicted Spouse: How Partners Can Cope and Heal* by Barbara Steffens and Marsha Means; and *Invisible Scars: How to Stop, Change, or End Psychological Abuse* by Catherine Dowda.

SMALL HORIZONS

Introduced in 1992, Small Horizons teaches crisis, coping, tolerance, and service skills to children. Expanding the scope and success of NHP's books are targeted promotions and publicity via local and national print, TV shows, and strong subsidiary rights.

Small Horizons titles include *Pretty Plus: How to Look Sexy, Sensational and Successful, No Matter What You Weigh* by Babe Hope; *Troubled Childhood, Triumphant Life: Healing from the Battle Scars of Youth* by James P. Krehbiel; *The Digital Pandemic: Reestablishing Face-to-Face Contact in the Electronic Age* by Mark Hicks, PhD; *Betrayal, Murder and Greed: The True Story of a Bounty Hunter and a Bail Bond Agent* by Pam Phree and Mike "Darkside" Beakley; and *Sun Struck: 16 Infamous Murders in the Sunshine State* by Robert A. Waters and John T. Waters, Jr.

See the website for submission guidelines. Query letters and SASEs should be directed to Ms. P. Patty. To send an email inquiry, put "Attn: Ms. P. Patty" in the subject line and send to nhp@newhorizonpressbooks.com.

NEW LEAF PUBLISHING GROUP

BALFOUR BOOKS

MASTER BOOKS

3142 Highway 103 North, Green Forest, AR 72638

Mailing address:

P.O. Box 726, Green Forest, AR 72638

800-999-3777   fax: 870-438-5120

www.newleafpublishinggroup.com   email: nlp@newleafpress.com

New Leaf Publishing (established 1975) is a non-denominational Christian publishing house located in Arkansas. Subjects covered include Christian living, prophecy and eschatology, theology, applied Christianity, Bible study, family/home/marriage, friendship, love, education, evangelism, devotional works, and humor.

In 1996, New Leaf Press bought Master Books, the only publishing house in the world that publishes creation-based material exclusively, including evolution-free homeschool products. In 2003, a third imprint, Balfour Books, was launched to publish books on the importance of Israel and the Middle East, as well their relevance to America.

Recent titles include *10 Things Every Minister's Wife Needs to Know* by Jeana Floyd; *Transforming Church in Rural America* by Shannon O'Dell; and *Success Kills: Sidestep the Snares that Will Steal Your Soul* by Wayde Goodall.

BALFOUR BOOKS

Balfour Books publishes books that highlight Israel's global relevance and celebrate its unique position in world history. Some titles include *Smart Dating: How to Find Your Man* by Mary Balfour and Nick Roberts; *Nations United: How the United Nations Undermines Israel and the West* by Alex Grobman; *The Case for Democracy: The Power of Freedom to Overcome Tyranny and Terror* by Natan Sharansky and Ron Dermer; and *God's Covenant with Israel* by Binyamin Elon.

MASTER BOOKS

Master Books publishes Creation-based materials for all ages that defend the Bible from the very first verse. Recent titles from Master Books include *Deadly Disclosures* by Julie Cave; *Dinosaurs for Kids* by Ken Ham; *Discovery of Design* by Donald DeYoung and Derrik Hobbs; and *God Made the World & Me* by David and Helen Haidle and Susan Laurita.

See the website or write the house to request a proposal guideline document. Email submissions should be directed to Craig. Send proposal with SASE to:

Craig Froman, Assistant Editor, Acquisitions; craig@newleafpress.com
Tim Dudley, President and Publisher
Laura Welsh, Senior Editor

NEWMARKET PRESS

A Division of Newmarket Publishing and Communications Company

18 East 48th Street, New York, NY 10017

212-832-3575   fax: 212-832-3629

www.newmarketpress.com   email: mailbox@newmarketpress.com

Newmarket Publishing and Communications Company, and its publishing arm Newmarket Press, were founded in 1981 by President and Publisher Esther Margolis. Now in its 27th year with more than 300 books published, Newmarket Press is one of the few mainstream trade publishing houses in New York City under independent, entrepreneurial ownership. With W.W. Norton contracted as its distributor, Newmarket now publishes about 20–30 mainly nonfiction books a year, primarily in the areas of child care and parenting, film and performing arts, psychology, health and nutrition, biography, history, business and personal finance, and popular self-help and reference.

In addition, Newmarket has created a successful niche in publishing books in film, theater, and performing arts, and is especially noted for the illustrated movie books published on such films as *The Matrix; Dreamgirls; Planet of the Apes; Moulin Rouge; Crouching Tiger, Hidden Dragon; Magnolia; Cradle Will Rock; Sense and Sensibility; Saving Private Ryan;* and more.

Recent titles include *The Words of Extraordinary Women* edited by Carolyn Warner; *Everything Is Possible: Life and Business Lessons from a Self-Made Billionaire and the Founder of Slim-Fast* by S. Daniel Abraham; *The Last Station: The Shooting Script* by Michael Hoffman; *A Glorious Way to Die: The Kamikaze Mission of the Battleship Yamato* by Russell Spurr; and *A Special Mother: Getting Through the Early Days of a Child's Diagnosis of Learning Disabilities and Related Disorders* by Anne Ford.

See the website for submissions suggestions. No email queries are accepted. Queries, proposals, and SASEs may be directed to the Editorial Department.

Keith Hollaman, Executive Editor, Acquisitions

Esther Margolis, President and Publisher

NEW PAGE BOOKS [SEE CAREER PRESS]

NEW WORLD LIBRARY

H.J. KRAMER

NATARAJ PUBLISHING

STARSEED PRESS

14 Pamaron Way, Novato, CA 94949

415-884-2100   fax: 415-884-2199

www.newworldlibrary.com

New World Library has been an independent publisher of mind/body/spirit and related titles for over 30 years, located just north of San Francisco. Some of their bestsellers include *The Power of Now* by Eckhart Tolle; *The Seven Spiritual Laws of Success* by Deepak Chopra; and *Creative Visualization* by Shakti Gawain. New World Library publishes about 35–40 new titles annually, with a backlist of 250 books.

New World seeks manuscripts in the following subject areas: spirituality, personal growth, women's interest, religion, sustainable business, the human-animal relationship, Native American interest, and the environment. Their works appeal to a large, general audience.

Recent titles include *101 Exercises for the Soul* by Dr. Bernie Siegel; *Brainstorm* by Eric Maisel; *Bridge Between Worlds* by Dan Millman and Doug Childers; *Dreamgates* by Robert Moss; and *Laughter, Tears, Silence* by Pragito Dove.

H.J. KRAMER

In 2000, New World Library entered into a joint venture with H.J. Kramer, the publisher of such authors as Dan Millman, Sanaya Roman, and John Robbins. New World Library assumed responsibility for many functional areas of H.J. Kramer, including sales, marketing, subsidiary rights, fulfillment, production, and accounting. H.J. Kramer has continued to focus on author relationships and acquiring and developing new books, particularly new children's titles from Holly Bea.

NATARAJ PUBLISHING

The Nataraj imprint primarily publishes titles by New World founder, Shakti Gawain. Some of his titles include *Creative Visualization: Use the Power of Your Imagination to Create What You Want in Your Life* and *Developing Intuition: Practical Guidance for Daily Life*.

STARSEED PRESS

Starseed Press focuses on titles for younger readers (ages 4–8). Some Starseed titles include *The Fires of Shalsha* by John Michael Greer and Deva Berg; *The 8 Master Keys to Healing What Hurts* by Rue Anne Hass and Angela Treat Lyon; and *A Voyage to the Moon* by Guy Swanson.

Email submissions are preferred and can be sent to submit@newworldlibrary .com. Direct physical submissions with SASEs to Submissions Editor.

Jonathan Wichmann, Acquisitions Editor

Georgia Hughes, Editorial Director

Munro Magruder, Associate Publisher

Jason Gardner, Senior Editor

Linda Kramer, H. J. Kramer President

NOLO

950 Parker Street, Berkeley, CA 94710-2524

800-728-3555   fax: 800-645-0895

www.nolo.com   email: cs@nolo.com

Nolo is one of the nation's leading providers of do-it-yourself legal solutions for consumers and small businesses. The house goal is to help people handle their own everyday legal matters—or learn enough about them to make working with a lawyer a more satisfying experience. According to Nolo, "Americans who are armed with solid legal knowledge are confident, active participants in their legal system—and slowly but inevitably, their participation makes that system more open and democratic. Nolo is proud to be part of that process."

Since 1971, Nolo has offered affordable, plain-English books, forms, and software on a wide range of legal issues, including wills, estate planning, retirement, elder care, personal finance, taxes, housing, real estate, divorce, and child custody. They also offer materials on human resources, employment, intellectual property, and starting and running a small business.

With a staff of lawyer-editors, the house pays attention not only to changes in the law, but to feedback from customers, lawyers, judges, and court staffers. Nolo publishes legal self-help books and software for consumers, small businesses, and nonprofit organizations. They specialize in helping people handle their own legal tasks—for example, write a will, file a small claims court lawsuit, start a small business or nonprofit, or apply for a patent. Nolo does not publish fiction, first-person accounts, biographies, or any other material that strays too far from its step-by-step approach to helping individuals, businesses, and nonprofits solve specific legal problems.

Titles include *The Craft Artist's Legal Guide*; *Nannies & Au Pairs: Hiring In-Home Child Care*; *Chapter 13 Bankruptcy: Keep Your Property & Repay Debts Over Time* by Stephen Elias et al; and *Everybody's Guide to Small Claims Court* by Ralph Warner.

Queries and SASEs should be directed to the Acquisitions Editors.

Marcia Stewart, Acquisitions Editor

W. W. NORTON & COMPANY

THE COUNTRYMAN PRESS

NORTON PROFESSIONAL BOOKS

500 Fifth Avenue, New York, NY 10110

212-354-5500   fax 212-869-0856

www.wwnorton.com   email: manuscripts@wwnorton.com

The Countryman Press:

802-457-4826   fax: 802-457-1678

P.O. Box 748, Woodstock, VT 05091

www.countrymanpress.com   email: countrymanpress@wwnorton.com

Publishers of adult trade fiction, nonfiction, professional psychology, and architecture books, W.W. Norton & Company is the oldest and largest publishing house owned wholly by its employees. Norton strives to carry out the imperative of its founder to publish books not for a single season, but for the years—in fiction, nonfiction, poetry, college textbooks, cookbooks, art books and professional books. W.W. Norton & Company now publishes about 400 books annually in hardcover and paperback.

The roots of the company date back to 1923, when William Warder Norton and his wife, Mary D. Herter Norton, began publishing lectures delivered at the People's Institute, the adult education division of New York City's Cooper Union.

The Nortons soon expanded their program beyond the Institute, acquiring manuscripts by celebrated academics from America and abroad.

In 1996, Norton acquired the distinguished Vermont firm The Countryman Press and added well-respected nature, history, and outdoor recreation titles to the Norton list. In 2003, Berkshire House Press joined Norton, becoming part of the Vermont operation.

For years, Norton has been known for its distinguished publishing programs in both the trade and the college textbook areas. Early in its history Norton entered the fields of philosophy, music, and psychology, publishing acclaimed works by Bertrand Russell, Paul Henry Lang, and Sigmund Freud (as his principal American publisher).

In the past few decades, the firm has published bestselling books by such authors as economists Paul Krugman and Joseph Stiglitz; paleontologist Stephen Jay Gould; physicist Richard Feynman; and historians Peter Gay, Jonathan Spence, Christopher Lasch, and George F. Kennan. Norton has also developed a more eclectic list, with prominent titles including *Helter Skelter* by Vincent Bugliosi and Curt Gentry; Jared Diamond's Pulitzer Prize–winning bestseller *Guns, Germs, and Steel*; Judy Rogers's *The Zuni Café Cookbook*; Patrick O'Brian's critically acclaimed naval adventures; the works of National Book Award-winning fiction author Andrea Barrett; *Liar's Poker* and *Moneyball* by Michael Lewis; Fareed Zakaria's *The Future of Freedom*; and Sebastian Junger's *The Perfect Storm*.

Recent titles include *American Heroes* by Edmun S. Morgan; *Forget Sorrow* by Belle Yang; *Macroeconomics* by Chalres I. Jones; *Yvon's Paris* by Robert Stevens; and *The Earth Moves: Galileo and the Roman Inquisition* by Dan Hofstadter.

THE COUNTRYMAN PRESS

As Vermont's oldest name in publishing, The Countryman Press maintains a tradition of producing books of substance and quality. The company began in Taftsville, Vermont, in 1973, in Peter and Jane Jennison's farmhouse kitchen. In 1996 the press became a division of W.W. Norton & Company, Inc. Countryman retains its own identity, however, with editorial and production offices in Woodstock, Vermont.

Countryman publishes about 50 books per year with more than 250 books in print. Subjects include travel, food, gardening, country living, nature, New England history, and crafts. The Explorer's Guide travel series has sold over half a million copies.

The Backcountry Guides imprint features where-to books on outdoor sports activities, including fishing, cycling, walking, and paddling. The bestselling 50 Hikes series has sold more than one million copies.

Some titles from The Countryman Press include *The Best of Relish Cookbook: Celebrating America's Love of Food* by Jill Melton; *Out of Gas: Pumps and Pickups from the Golden Age of Gas* by Jeffrey E. Blackman; *Volunteer Vacations Across America* by Sheryl Kayne; *The Farmer's Market Cookbook* by Jessie Price; and *101 Best Outdoor Towns: Unspoiled Places to Visit, Live, & Play* by Sarah Tuff and Greg Melville.

NORTON PROFESSIONAL BOOKS

In 1985, Norton expanded its publishing program with Norton Professional Books, specializing in books on psychotherapy and, more recently, neuroscience. The Professional Books program has also moved into the fields of architecture and design.

Recent titles from Norton Professional Books includes *Michael Taylor: Interior Design* by Steven M. Salny; *Historic Preservation: Second Edition* by Norman Tyler et al; *The Healthy Aging Brain: Sustaining Attachment, Attaining Wisdom* by Louis Cozolino; and *How to Use Herbs, Nutrients, and Yoga in Mental Health Care* by Richard P. Brown, MD et al.

W.W. Norton does consider books from the following categories: juvenile or young adult, religious, occult or paranormal, genre fiction such as formula romances, sci-fi or Westerns, arts and crafts, and inspirational poetry.

Due to the workload of the editorial staff, Norton is no longer able to accept unsolicited submissions except from literary agents.

Alane Mason, Senior Editor—Cultural and intellectual history, literary fiction

Amy Cherry, Senior Editor—African American issues, contemporary biographies, social issues

Jill Bialosky, Vice President—Literary fiction and nonfiction, biographies

Robert Weil, Executive Editor—Translations, intellectual history, social sciences, German and Jewish subjects

Drake McFeely, President—Science, social sciences

Maria Guarnaschelli, Senior Editor—Science, food, fiction

Kermit Hummel, Editorial Director (The Countryman Press)

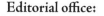

O'REILLY MEDIA

Editorial office:

10 Fawcett Street, Cambridge, MA 01238

Headquarters:

1005 Gravenstein Highway North, Sebastopol, CA 95472

707-827-7000/800-998-9938   fax: 707-829-0104

www.oreilly.com

O'Reilly Media is a premier information source for leading-edge computer technologies. Smart books written for smart people—with animals sketched on the front covers—O'Reilly titles are not for dummies. Some of their subjects include business and culture, databases, digital audio and video, digital photography, hardware, home and office, networking, sys admin, operating systems, programming, science, math, security, software engineering, and the Web.

This house is vastly interested in the newest technologies, thus it's best to check the Author section of their website for the evolving list of what they're looking for right now; you'll find it here: oreilly.com/oreilly/author/intro.csp.

Recent titles from O'Reilly include *iPad: The Missing Manual* by J. D. Biersdorfer; *Hackers & Painters: Big Ideas from the Computer Age* by Paul Graham; *Window 7 Annoyances: Tips, Secrets, and Solutions* by David Karp; *The Guild Leader's Handbook: Strategies and Guidance from a Battle-Scarred MMO Veteran* by Scott F. Andrews; and *Zen and the Magic of Photography: Learning to See and to Be Through Photography* by Wayne Rowe.

Send your proposal via email to proposals@oreilly.com with a descriptive subject line. Physical proposals should be sent to the Cambridge editorial office.

Mike Hendrickson, Associate Publisher

Simon St. Laurent, Senior Editor—Systems, programming

Brian Sawyer, Editor—Hacks

OSBORNE MEDIA [SEE MCGRAW-HILL]

THE OVERLOOK PRESS

ARDIS PUBLISHING

THE ROOKERY PRESS

141 Wooster Street, 4B, New York, NY 10012

212-673-2210   fax: 212-673-2296

www.overlookpress.com

blog: theoverlookpress.blogspot.com

DUCKWORTH

90-93 Cowcross Street, London, EC1M 6BF

+44 (0) 207-490-7300   fax: +44 (0) 207-490-0080

www.ducknet.co.uk   email: info@duckworth-publishers.co.uk

The Overlook Press (founded 1971) is an independent, general interest publisher. The publishing program consists of some 100 new books per year, evenly divided between hardcovers and trade paperbacks. The list is eclectic, but areas of strength include interesting fiction, history, biography, drama, and design.

The house was launched by owner Peter Mayer as a home for distinguished books that had been "overlooked" by larger houses. The publishing formula proved reliable, and now Overlook has nearly 1,000 titles in print. Their fiction includes novels by solidly commercial authors including espionage novelist Robert Littell (*The Company*, 90,000 sold) and international phenomenon Penny Vincenzi, whose Edwardian era family saga *No Angel* is widely acclaimed as stunning entertainment. More success came in April 2004 with *Dragon's Eye* by Andy Oakes, a thriller set in modern Shanghai. In a more literary vein, there is *Hash* by top Swedish novelist Torgny Lindgren, and Michele Slung's anthology of garden writing, *The Garden of Reading*.

History is the mainstay of the house's nonfiction list and notable books include Paul Cartledge's *The Spartans*, basis of a PBS documentary on this civilization, and Adrienne Mayor's *Greek Fire, Poison Arrows and Scorpion Bombs: Biochemical Warfare in the Ancient World*.

Recent titles from Overlook include *2017* by Olga Slavnikova; *AD 381* by Charles Freeman; *Anything Goes* by Lucy Moore; *An Appeal to Reason* by Nigel Lawson; and *Barmy in Wonderland* by P.G. Wodehouse.

ARDIS PUBLISHING

In 2002 Overlook acquired Ardis, the premier publisher of Russian literature in English. They have given that program new presence with handsome new paperback editions of titles long unavailable. Some books include *Selected Poems* by Anna Akhmatova; *A Captive Spirit* by Marina Tsvetaeva; *Envy* by Yury Olesha; *Poor Folk* by Fyodor Dostoevsky; and *Eugene Onegin* by Alexander Pushkin.

DUCKWORTH

Recently Overlook acquired the 106-year-old UK publisher Duckworth. Duckworth publishes literary and commercial fiction and nonfiction, including history, biography, and memoir. Their academic list features important new scholarly monographs in archaeology, classics, ancient history, and ancient philosophy.

Some titles from Duckworth include *The Tin-Kin* by Eleanor Thom; *Love & Sex with Robots: The Evolution of Human-Robot Relationships* by David Levy; *Go With Me* by Castle Freeman; *Becoming Female: The Male Body in Greek Tragedy* by Katrina Cawthorn; and *The Atheist's Bible: An Illustrious Collection of Irreverent Thought* by Joan Konner.

THE ROOKERY PRESS

The Rookery Press is a new imprint launched in 2006. Rookery focuses on serious nonfiction and some literary fiction, reprints, a drama list, plus illustrated books on fashion, interiors, design, art, theater, and film. Rookery plans to release 20 titles annually.

Some titles from The Rookery Press include *Ma Gastronomie* by Fernand Point and Thomas Keller; *Paradise with Serpents* by Richard Carver; *The Truth about Sascha Knisch* by Aris Fioretos; *Ten Bad Dates with De Niro: A Book of Alternative Movie Lists* by Richard T. Kelly and Andrew Rae; *Young Pushkin: A Novel* by Yury Tynyanov and Anna Rush; and *St. Trinians: The Entire Appalling Business* by Ronald Searle.

Overlook Press titles distributed to the trade by Penguin Putnam.

The house currently only accepts submissions from literary agents.

Peter Mayer, President and Publisher

Aaron Schlechter, Editor

Juliet Grames, Editor

PALADIN PRESS

Gunbarrel Tech Center

7077 Winchester Circle, Boulder, CO 80301

303-443-7250   fax: 303-442-8741

www.paladin-press.com   email: editorial@paladin-press.com

Controversial even before a 1999 multimillion dollar settlement related to the use of a murder how-to manual *Hit Man*—no longer available—Paladin Press publishes books and DVDs on personal and financial freedom, survival and preparedness, firearms and shooting, martial arts and self-defense, military and police tactics, knives and knife fighting, and more.

The company came into existence in September 1970 when Peder Lund joined Robert K. Brown as a partner in a book publishing venture previously known as Panther Publications. As former military men and adventurers, Lund and Brown were convinced there was a market for books on specialized military and action/adventure topics. Both men also firmly believed that the First Amendment guaranteed Americans the right to read about whatever subjects they desired, and this became the cornerstone of Paladin's publishing philosophy.

Recent titles include *Black Medicine Set* by N. Mashiro, PhD; *Spook School Set* by James Coats; *James Ballou's Survival Set* by James Ballou; *Home Workshop Guns for Defense and Resistance Set* by Bill Holmes; and *Ragnar's Action Encyclopedia* by Ragnar Benson.

Email queries are not accepted. Submit a proposal and SASE to the Editorial Department.

Donna Duvall, Editor Director

Cathy Wirtes, Senior Editor

PATHFINDER PRESS

4794 Clark Howell Highway, Suite B-5, College Park, GA 30349

Mailing address:

P.O. Box 162767, Atlanta, GA 30321-2767

404-669-0600   fax: 707-667-1141

www.pathfinderpress.com   email: pathfinder@pathfinderpress.com

Since 1940, Pathfinder Press has published books, booklets, pamphlets, posters, and postcards focusing on issues affecting working people worldwide. The house produces titles in English, Spanish, French, Swedish, Farsi, Greek, Icelandic, and Russian. Pathfinder also distributes the journal New International.

Subjects include black and African studies; women's rights; the Cuban revolution in world politics; revolutionaries and working-class fighters; fascism, big business, and the labor movement; Russia, Eastern Europe, and the Balkans; scientific views of politics and economics; trade unions: past, present, and future; U.S. history and politics; Latin America and the Caribbean; the Middle East and China; and art, culture, and politics. Pathfinder is usually associated with schools of thought such as populism, internationalism, utopianism, socialism, and communism.

The Pathfinder mural that once adorned the company's original editorial digs in Manhattan's Far West Village featured a depiction of a gargantuan printing press in action, as well as portraits of revolutionary leaders whose writings and speeches were published by Pathfinder; this community cultural icon represented the work of more than 80 artists from 20 countries.

Pathfinder titles include *Malcolm X, Black Liberation and the Road to Workers Power* by Jack Barnes; *The Inevitable Battle: From the Bay of Pigs to Playa Giron* by Juan Carlos Rodriguez; *Our History Is Still Being Written: The Story of Three Chinese-Cuban Generals in the Cuban Revolution* by Armando Choy et al; and *Capitalism's Long Hot Winter Has Begun* by Jack Barnes.

Direct queries and SASEs to:

Mary-Alice Waters, President

Elizabeth Stone, Managing Editor

PAULIST PRESS

997 Macarthur Boulevard, Mahwah, NJ 07430-9990

201-825-7300/800-218-1903   fax: 800-836-3161

www.paulistpress.com   email: info@paulistpress.com

Founded in 1866 by the Paulist Fathers as the Catholic Publication Society, Paulist Press publishes hardcover and trade originals for general readers, and distinguished scholarly books, in the areas of religion, spirituality, and theology. Paulist Press publishes ecumenical theology, Roman Catholic studies and books on scripture, liturgy, spirituality, church history, and philosophy, as well as works on faith and culture. Their list is oriented toward adult-level nonfiction, although they do offer a growing selection of children's stories and activity books. Children's categories include picture books, prayer books, chapter books, young-adult biographies, Catholic guidebooks, and gift books.

Titles from Paulist Press include *Doing Theology* by Jared Wicks, SJ; *Mythological Traditions of Liturgical Drama* by Christine C. Schnusenberg; *Abu al-Hasan al Shushtari: Songs of Love and Devotion* translated by Lourdes Maria Alvarez; and *Evangelization for the Third Millennium* by Avery Cardinal Dulles, SJ.

Query letters and SASEs should be directed to:

Rev. Lawrence Boadt, C.S.P., Publisher and President

Susan O'Keefe, Children's Book Editor

PEACHPIT PRESS

ADOBE PRESS

APPLE CERTIFIED

LYNDA.COM

NEW RIDERS

NEW RIDERS GAMES

1249 Eighth Street, Berkeley, CA 94710

510-524-2178

www.peachpit.com   email: proposals@peachpit.com

Peachpit Press has been publishing top-notch books on the latest in graphic design, desktop publishing, multimedia, Web publishing, and general computing since

1986. Their titles feature step-by-step explanations, timesaving techniques, savvy insider tips, and expert advice for computer users of all sorts. Peachpit is a part of Pearson Education, the world's largest integrated educational publisher.

Imprints include Peachpit Press, New Riders Press, New Riders Games, Adobe Press, Apple Certified, Lynda.com, and other imprints and series for creative computer users.

Recent titles from Peachpit include *Adobe Flash Professional CS5 Classroom in a Book* by Adobe Creative Team; *InterACT with Web Standards: A Holistic Approach to Web Design* by Erin Anderson et al; *Adobe Flash Catalyst CS5 Classroom in a Book* by Adobe Creative Team; *Nikon D3000: From Snapshots to Great Shots, Adobe Reader* by Jeff Revell; and *Adobe Flex 4: Training from the Source, Volume 1* by Michael Labriola et al.

ADOBE PRESS

Adobe Press is the official source of training materials for Adobe software and inspiration for digital communicators. Titles from Adobe Press include *Adobe Flash Professional CS5 Classroom in a Book* by Adobe Creative Team; *Adobe Flash Catalyst CS5 Classroom in a Book* by Adobe Creative Team; and *Adobe Flex 4: Training from the Source, Volume 1* by Michael Labriola et al.

APPLE CERTIFIED

Books from Apple Certified come with Apple's seal of approval and contain complete courses designed to help users master Mac apps. New titles include *Apple Pro Training Series: Aperture 3* by Dion Scoppettuolo; *Cocoa Recipes for Mac OS X* by Bill Cheeseman; and *Apple Training Series: Mac OS X Security and Mobility v10.6: A Guide to Providing Secure Mobile Access to Intranet Services Using Mac OS X Server v10.6 Snow Leopard* by Robert Kite et al.

LYNDA.COM

Lynda.com is an award-winning education provider of Hands-On Training instructional books, video training on CD and DVD, self-paced online learning, and events for creative designers, developers, instructors, students, hobbyists, and anyone who wants to learn. Titles from Lynda include *Photoshop CS4 Extended for 3D* by Chad Perkins; *Photoshop CS4 Portrait Retouching Essential Training* by Chris Orwig; *Illustrator CS4 One-on-One: Fundamentals* by Deke McClelland; and *Flash CS4 Professional: Object Oriented Programming* by Todd Perkins.

NEW RIDERS

New Riders produces beautiful instruction books that provide a forum for the leading voices in creative and information technologies. New Riders includes the Voices That Matter series and the AIGA Design Press. New titles include *Talent Is Not Enough: Business Secrets for Designers* by Shel Perkins; *The CSS Detective Guide* by

Denise Jacobs; and *From Still to Motion: A Photographer's Guide to Creating Video With Your DSLR* by James Ball et al.

NEW RIDERS GAMES

New Riders Games takes game books where they've never gone before. As the game resource, NRG touches every category: programming, design, art, and celebrity savvy. Titles include *Creating Games in C++: A Step-by-Step Guide* by David Conger and Ron Little; *Level Design for Games: Creating Compelling Game Experiences* by Phil Co; *3ds max 7 Fundamentals* by Ted Boardman; *Game Character Development with Maya* by Anthony Ward; and *Audio for Games: Planning, Process, and Production* by Alexander Brandon.

Peachpit is always looking for new authors and innovative book ideas. Mail your completed proposal to Book Proposals or email it to proposals@peachpit.com.

Marjorie Baer, Executive Editor

Keasley Jones, Associate Publisher

PEACHTREE PUBLISHERS

1700 Chattahoochee Avenue, Atlanta, GA 30318

404-876-8761/800-241-0113   fax: 404-875-2578/800-875-8909

www.peachtree-online.com   email: hello@peachtree-online.com

Peachtree is an award-winning trade publisher featuring children's picture books and chapter books for the very young child through young adult. Other categories include health and parenting, and the best of the South, including fiction, high quality gift, and regional guides. They publish about 20 books per year.

Recent titles include *About Habitats: Mountains* by Cathryn Sill and John Sill; *Flying* by Kevin Luthardt; *I Can Do It Myself!* by Diane Adams and Nancy Hayashi; *Larabee* by Kevin Luthardt; *A Place for Birds* by Melissa Stewart and Higgins Bond; and *The Printer* by Myron Uhlberg and Henri Sorensen.

Direct submissions and SASEs to Helen Harris.

Helen Harris, Acquisitions Editor

Margaret Quinlin, Publisher

Kathy Landwehr, Associate Publisher

PELICAN PUBLISHING COMPANY

1000 Burmaster Street, Gretna, LA 70053-2246

800-843-1724   fax: 504-368-1195

www.pelicanpub.com   email: editorial@pelicanpub.com

Called "innovative" by the *New York Times*, Pelican Publishing is the largest independent trade book publisher in the South. Once the publisher of William Faulkner, Pelican is now owned by the Calhouns, a family of self-professed bibliophiles.

The house publishes an average of 70 titles a year and has over 1,500 currently in print. Specialties are art/architecture books, cooking/cookbooks, motivational, travel guides, history (especially Louisiana/regional), nonfiction, children's books (illustrated and otherwise), social commentary, folklore, and textbooks. For fiction, only historical works are considered for publication.

Recent titles include *Dinosaur's Night Before Christmas* by Jim Harris; *Houston Classic Desserts* by Erin Hicks Miller; *Los Angeles Classic Desserts* by Grace Bauer; *Savannah Celebrations: Simple Southern Party Menus* by Martha Nesbit; and *Erin Brockovich and the Beverly Hills Greenscam* by Norma Zager.

The editors seek writers on the cutting edge of ideas.

To submit, send a query letter with SASE to the editors. Short children's manuscripts may be sent in their entirety at the initial contact. Direct queries and SASEs to:

Milburn Calhoun, Publisher

Nina Kooij, Editor-in-Chief

PERMANENT PRESS

SECOND CHANCE PRESS

4170 Noyac Road, Sag Harbor, NY 11963

631-725-1101

www.thepermanentpress.com   email: info@thepermanentpress.com

The Permanent Press (founded 1978 by Martin and Judith Shepard) committed itself to publishing works of social and literary merit and has, over the years, gained a reputation as one of the finest small independent presses in America. The Permanent Press is a publisher of literary fiction—and occasionally nonfiction. They publish books that are artfully written, about 12 per year.

Recent titles include *A Theory of All Things* by Peggy Leon; *Drake's Bay* by T. A.

Roberts; *Elysiana* by Chris Knopf; *Giving It All Away: The Doris Buffett Story* by Michael Zitz; and *Pretend All Your Life* by Joseph Mackin.

SECOND CHANCE PRESS

The imprint Second Chance Press reprints books of merit that had been out-of-print for at least 20 years. The Second Chance mission is to find literary fiction gems worth republishing; they have published Berry Fleming, Halldor Laxness, Richard Lortz, William Herrick, and Joseph Stanley Pennell.

Email queries are not accepted. Send the first 20 pages or so with query letter and SASE. Direct physical submissions to Judith Shepard.

Judith Shepard, Publisher, Acquisitions

Martin Shepard, Publisher

PERSEA BOOKS

853 Broadway, Suite 601, New York, NY 10003

212-260-9256   fax: 212-260-1902

www.perseabooks.com   email: info@perseabooks.com

Founded in 1975 by Karen and Michael Braziller, Persea is a small literary press of books for adults and young adults. Their titles cover a wide range of themes, styles, and genres. They have published poetry, fiction, essays, memoir, biography, titles of Jewish and Middle Eastern interest, women's studies, American Indian folklore, and revived classics, as well as a notable selection of works in translation.

They have been expanding their Young Adult list, with intelligent books by authors such as Anne Mazer, Gary Soto, and Marie Raphael. These works complement their acclaimed series of literary anthologies for youths, which include *America Street: A Multicultural Anthology of Stories; Imagining America: Stories from the Promised Land; A Walk in My World: International Short Stories About Youth; Starting With "I": Personal Essays by Teenagers;* and many more.

Recent Persea titles include *Lovely, Raspberry* by Aaron Belz; *Approaching Ice* by Elizabeth Bradfield; *Mistaken for Song* by Tara Bray; *Apocalyptic Swing* by Gabrielle Calvocoressi; *From the Fishouse: An Anthology of Poems that Sing, Rhyme, Resound, Syncopate, Alliterate, and Just Plain Sound Great* by Camille T. Dungy et al; and *Delivered* by Sarah Gambito.

Direct queries and SASEs to the attention of the Fiction Editor (or nonfiction or poetry, as appropriate).

Michael Braziller, Publisher

Karen Braziller, Editorial Director

PERSEUS BOOKS GROUP

BASIC BOOKS
BASIC CIVITAS
VANGUARD PRESS

387 Park Avenue South, New York, NY 10016

212-340-8100

www.basicbooks.com   email: perseus-promos@perseusbooks.com

www.basiccivitasbooks.com

www.vanguardpressbooks.com

AVALON TRAVEL PUBLISHING
SEAL PRESS

1700 4th Street, Berkeley, CA 94710

510-528-1444

www.travelmatters.com   email: acquisitions@avalonpub.com

www.sealpress.com

DA CAPO PRESS
DA CAPO LIFELONG BOOKS

Eleven Cambridge Center, Cambridge, MA 02142

617-252-5200

www.dacapopress.com

NATION BOOKS
PUBLICAFFAIRS

250 West 57th Street, Suite 1321, New York, NY 10107

212-397-6666   fax: 212-397-4277

www.nationbooks.com

www.publicaffairsbooks.com   email: publicaffairs@perseusbooks.com

RUNNING PRESS

2300 Chestnut Street, Suite 200, Philadelphia, PA 19103

215-567-5080

www.perseusbooksgroup.com/runningpress   email: perseus.promos@perseus
books.com

WESTVIEW PRESS

2465 Central Avenue, Boulder, CO 80301

303-444-3541   fax: 720-406-7336

www.westviewpress.com

The Perseus Books Group was founded with the belief that insightful books of quality are both necessary and desirable, that an innovative model is possible, that authors, readers, booksellers—and books—matter. That innovative model includes Perseus' mission to empower independent publishers to reach their potential whether those publishers are owned by Perseus Books, joint venture partnerships, or clients for whom they provide services. Perseus very recently acquired both distributor Consortium and publisher Avalon Publishing Group, and in doing so has greatly expanded its depth and breadth in the publishing world.

In the process of combining Avalon Publishing Group with Perseus operations, several imprints were closed or sold; these include Counterpoint, Shoemaker & Hoard, Thunder's Mouth Press, and Carroll & Graf.

Each of the remaining Perseus and former Avalon imprints is editorially independent and individually focused, with offices from California to Massachusetts. As a whole, Perseus' publishing spans the breakthroughs in science to the great public issues, from military history to modern maternity, from African American scholars to novelists just breaking out, from choosing a great wine or a great president, from gift giving to required reading.

BASIC BOOKS

Since its founding in 1952, Basic Books has helped shape public debate by publishing award-winning books in psychology, science, politics, sociology, current affairs, and history. Basic seeks to publish serious nonfiction by leading intellectuals, scholars, and journalists; to create books that change the way people think.

Recent titles include *1848: Year of Revolution* by Mike Rapport; *Keepers of the Keys of Heaven: A History of the Papacy* by Roger Collins; *Beyond the Revolution: A History of American Thought from Paine to Pragmatism* by William H. Goetzmann; *Finding Our Tongues: Mothers, Infants, and the Origins of Language* by Dean Falk; *The Bloody White Baron* by James Palmer; and *The Ego Tunnel: The Science of the Mind and the Myth of the Self* by Thomas Metzinger.

Basic does not accept unsolicited proposals or manuscripts.

John Sherer, Publisher

Lara Heimert, Executive Editor—Religion, history

Jo Ann Miller, Editor—Psychology, law, women's studies, current affairs

BASIC CIVITAS

Basic Civitas Books is devoted to publishing the best new work in African and African American studies. With authors that include Michael Eric Dyson, Cornel West, Stanley Crouch, Vernon Jordan, and Henry Louis Gates, Jr., Basic Civitas has greatly advanced the influence and presence of African American works in the marketplace.

Titles include *Triangular Road* by Paule Marshall; *Book of Rhymes: The Poetics of Hip-Hop* by Adam Bradley; *The Execution of Willie Francis: Race, Murder, and the Search for Justice in the American South* by Gilbert King; *Party Crashing: How the Hip-Hop Generation Declared Political Independence* by Keli Goff; and *The Right Mistake: The Further Philosophical Investigations of Socrates Fortlow* by Walter Mosley.

Basic Civitas does not accept unsolicited proposals or manuscripts. Direct queries with SASEs to:

John Sherer, Publisher

Chris Greenberg, Associate Editor

VANGUARD PRESS

When Perseus acquired CDS Distribution in 2005, part of that acquisition was a small publishing program that CDS had started called CDS Books. Based in New York and now called Vanguard Press, this publisher provides its authors innovative financial and creative partnerships. The Vanguard mission is to have a selective publishing list, and to look at every book as an event. The editors strive to craft substantial, focused, and energetic marketing campaigns that will reach the widest possible audience. This publisher reportedly offers substantial marketing budgets and higher than standard royalties, but does not offer advances.

In just a short time, Vanguard has built a striking list including *Scavenger* by *New York Times* bestselling author David Morrell; *Quantico* by Hugo and Nebula Award-winning author Greg Bear; and the 30th anniversary edition of *Roots* by Alex Haley, winner of the Pulitzer Prize.

New titles from Vanguard Press include *Lords of Corruption* by Kyle Mills; *Banquo's Ghosts* by Richard Lowry and Keith Korman; *Strategic Acceleration: Succeed at the Speed of Life* by Tony Leary; *Think Like a Champion: An Informal Education in Business and Life* by Donald J. Trump; and *Put Your Money Where Your Heart Is: Investment Strategies for Lifetime Wealth* by Natalie Pace.

Vanguard Press does not accept unsolicited manuscripts or book proposals.

Roger Cooper, Vice President, Publisher

AVALON TRAVEL PUBLISHING

Based in Berkeley, California, Avalon Travel Publishing was formed in 1999 with the merger of three independent travel publishers—Moon Publications, John Muir

Publications, and Foghorn Press—creating the largest independent travel publisher based in the United States.

Avalon publishes several major travel guide-book series: Rick Steves, Moon, Moon Handbooks, Moon Metro, Moon Outdoors, Moon Living Abroad, The Dog Lover's Companion, and Road Trip USA.

Recent titles include *Moon Philadelphia* by Karrie Gavin; *Rick Steves' Athens and the Peloponnese* by Rick Steves; *Queens in the Kingdom* by Jeffrey Epstein and Eddie Shapiro; *The Dog Lover's Companion to Chicago* by Margaret Littman; and *The Practical Nomad* by Edward Hasbrouck.

Send proposal by email with attachment or by regular mail with SASE to the Acquisitions Editor, acquisitions@avalonpub.com.

Bill Newlin, Publisher, Avalon Travel

Sabrina Young, Editor

SEAL PRESS

Seal Press was founded in 1976 to provide a forum for women writers and feminist issues. Since then, Seal has published groundbreaking books that represent the diverse voices and interests of women—their lives, literature, and concerns. Seal's list includes books on women's health, parenting, outdoor adventure and travel, popular culture, gender and women's studies, and current affairs.

Seal publishes books by and for women, with an emphasis on original, lively, radical, empowering, and culturally diverse nonfiction that addresses contemporary issues from a women's perspective.

Recent Seal titles include *The Purity Myth: How America's Obsession with Virginity Is Hurting Young Women* by Jessica Valenti; *Yes Means Yes: Visions of Female Sexual Power and a World without Rape* by Jaclyn Riedman and Jessica Valenti; and *Open: Love, Sex, and Life in an Open Marriage* by Jenny Block.

Seal Press is not acquiring fiction at this time. Send proposal with SASE to the Acquisitions Editor.

Krista Lyons-Gould, Publisher

Jill Rothenberg, Senior Editor

Brooke Warner, Acquisitions Editor

DA CAPO PRESS

Da Capo is an Italian musical term meaning from the beginning and Da Capo Press was once known primarily as a publisher of music and culture titles. Da Capo is an imprint of Perseus, where a reorganization in 2004 expanded Da Capo when it absorbed the Perseus health, parenting, and reference/how-to program. This means titles such as *Third Coast: OutKast, Timbaland and the Rise of Dirty South Hip Hop*, by Roni Sarig, and *Muscle Your Way Through Menopause*, by Judith Sherman-Wolin, all find a home at Da Capo.

With editorial offices in both New York and Massachusetts, Da Capo Press publishes hardcover and paperback editions in American and world history, biography, music, film, art, photography, sports, humor, and popular culture.

A Da Capo imprint launched in 2004, Lifelong Books, consolidated Da Capo titles on pregnancy, parenting, health, fitness, and relationships. New titles from Lifelong include the Staying Sane series edited by Pam Brodowsky and Evelyn Fazio; Mari Winsor's *Pilates* bestsellers; and Dr. Mike Riera's *Field Guide to the American Teenager*. The Marlowe & Company brand from Da Capo also focuses on health and wellness titles.

Most recent Da Capo titles include *An American Trilogy: Death, Slavery, and Dominion on the Banks of Cape Fear River* by Steven M. Wise; *Growing Up Dead: The Hallucinated Confessions of a Teenage Deadhead* by Peter Conners; *When I Married My Mother: A Daughter's Search for What Really Matters* by Jo Arden Maeder.

Da Capo Press does not accept unsolicited manuscripts or proposals.

Ben Schafer, Editor (NY)

Robert Pigeon, Senior Editor (Philadelphia)

Katie McHugh, Senior Editor, Lifelong (NY)

Renee Sedliar, Senior Editor, Lifelong (Emeryville)

Wendy Holt Francis, Senior Editor, Lifelong (NY)

NATION BOOKS

Nation Books, a co-publishing venture with The Nation Institute, publishes works from a progressive perspective. Nation Books is dedicated to continuing the long tradition of progressive, critical thought in America, publishing new nonfiction works on politics, current events, human rights, feminism, race, gay and lesbian issues, history, art and culture, popular science, and the environment.

Recent titles include *Rogue Nation* by Clyde Prestowitz; *Backstabbing for Beginners: My Crash Course in International Diplomacy* by Michael Soussan; *The Future's So Bright, I Can't Bear to Look* by Tom Tomorrow; *The American Dream* by Harmon Leon; and *Meltdown* by Katrina Vanden Heuvel.

No unsolicited manuscripts or proposals. Direct queries with SASEs to:

Carl Bromley, Editorial Director

Ruth Baldwin, Associate Editor

PUBLICAFFAIRS

PublicAffairs is one of the nation's primary providers of good books about things that matter. The house specializes in current events, recent history, and other pressing issues affecting contemporary society. PublicAffairs publishes original nonfiction works by field experts from journalists to politicians, from political dissidents to leaders in the arts. PublicAffairs specializes in journalism, history, biography, and memoir.

Recent titles include *Last Wish* by Betty Rollin; *Liberty Under Attack* by Gregory

Anrig and Richard Leone; *Out of My Mind* by Andy Rooney; *To What End?* by Ward Just; and *Others Unknown: Timothy McVeigh and The Oklahoma Bombing Conspiracy* by Stephen Jones.

No email submissions. Direct proposals and SASEs to PublicAffairs Submissions.

Susan Weinberg, Publisher

Peter Osnos, Editor-at-Large

Clive Priddle, Executive Editor

RUNNING PRESS

One of the country's largest independent trade publishers, Running Press Publishers has been providing consumers with an innovative list of quality books and book-related kits since 1972.

Running Press creates more than 200 new titles a year under four imprints: Running Press, Running Press Miniature Editions, Running Press Kids, and Courage Books. Titles cover a broad range of categories, including general nonfiction, science, history, children's fiction and nonfiction, food and wine, pop culture, lifestyle, photo-essay, and illustrated gift books.

Recent titles include *The Big Lebowski Kit; Desktop Aquarium; Write Starts: Creative Prompts to Get You Writing!* and *the Big Bad-Ass Book of Cocktails.*

For children's titles, to submit a proposal for interactive nonfiction, basic concepts books (such as letters, numbers, opposites, or shapes), or beginning reading projects, send a query letter accompanied by a brief outline or table of contents. When submitting a picture-book proposal, send the entire manuscript. Note that at this time Running Press Kids is not publishing novels or any fiction longer than picture-book length.

For their general interest lists (Running Press and Courage Books), they specialize in publishing illustrated nonfiction. They very rarely publish any new fiction or poetry and are not seeking submissions in those categories at this time. They also do not accept proposals for Miniature Editions of any kind. To submit a proposal for an appropriate work of nonfiction, please send a query letter accompanied by a brief outline or table of contents.

Direct all Running Press submissions to the Philadelphia office, to the attention of the Submissions Editor at Running Press Kids, or the Assistant of the Editorial Director at Running Press Book Publishers for adult titles.

Lisa Clancy, Associate Editorial Director

Jennifer Kasius, Senior Editor

Greg Jones, Editorial Director

Kelli Chipponeri, Editor—Running Press Kids

Diana von Glahn, Editor—Cookbooks

WESTVIEW PRESS

For over 30 years, Westview Press has been a leading publisher of bestselling undergraduate and graduate textbooks, including classics like Jay MacLeod's *Ain't No Makin' It*; Arthur Goldschmidt's *A Concise History of the Middle East*; *Social Theory* by Charles Lemert; Rosemarie Putnam Tong's *Feminist Thought*; William Cleveland's *A History of the Modern Middle East*; Leland Roth's *Understanding Architecture*; and *Philosophy of Mind* by Jaeg-won Kim.

The house was founded in Boulder, Colorado, as a scholarly press of social science textbooks, monographs, and general interest books. Today, Westview focuses on textbooks in core disciplines such as American politics, anthropology, area studies, art history, history, international relations, philosophy, and sociology.

Recent titles include *Contemporary Middle East: A Westview Reader* by Karl Yambert; *Elephant Destiny* by Alan Tarr and Ralph Rassum; *Understanding Words That Wound* by Richard Delgado and Jean Stefancic; and *Before the Beginning: Our Universe and Others* by Martin Ress.

Westview Press does not accept unsolicited manuscripts or book proposals. Direct queries with SASEs to:

Cathleen Tetro, Associate Publisher

Karl Yambert, Senior Editor—Anthropology, archaeology, area studies

Steve Catalano, Senior Editor—History, politics

PETERSON'S

A Division of the Thomson Corporation

Princeton Pike Corporate Center

2000 Lenox Drive, P.O. Box 67005, Lawrenceville, NJ 08648

609-896-1800

www.petersons.com

Peterson's is one of the nation's most comprehensive education resources. Since 1966 Peterson's has helped to connect individuals, educational institutions, and corporations through critically acclaimed books. The house reaches an estimated 105 million consumers annually with information about colleges and universities, career schools, graduate programs, distance learning, executive training, private secondary schools, summer opportunities, study abroad, financial aid, test preparation, and career exploration.

Peterson's is part of the Thomson Corporation, a global leader in providing integrated information solutions to business and professional customers.

Titles from Peterson's include *Master the GRE 2010* by Mark Allen Stewart; *Nursing Programs 2010*; *The Russia Balance Sheet* by Anders Aslund and Andrew Kuchins; *Global Warming and the World Trading System* by Steve Charnovitz et al; and *US Pension Reform: Lessons from Other Countries* by Martin Neil Baily and Jacob Kirkegaard.

Query letters and SASEs should be directed to the Editorial Department.

Therese D'Angelis, Senior Editor

THE PILGRIM PRESS

UNITED CHURCH PRESS

700 Prospect Avenue, East Cleveland, OH 44115-1100

216-736-3764   fax: 216-736- 2207

www.pilgrimpress.com   email: pilgrim@ucc.org

The Pilgrim Press (founded in 1645 and established in the U.S. in 1895) is the book publishing banner of the publishing wing of the United Church of Christ. The house has a tradition of publishing books and other resources that challenge, encourage, and inspire, and are crafted in accordance with fine standards of content, design, and production.

Comprised of two imprints—Pilgrim Press and United Church—Pilgrim's trade motto is: Books at the Nexus of Religion and Culture. The Pilgrim Press is a Christian-related imprint that focuses on three areas: theological ethics (including science, technology, and medicine); human identity, relationships, and sexuality (including feminist and gay/lesbian issues); and activist spirituality (having a social dimension).

Titles indicative of the Pilgrim list include *Equipping the Saint: Best Practices in Contextual Theological Education* edited by David Jenkins and P. Alice Rogers; *Forgiving Yourself: Why You Must, How You Can* by Robert and Jeanette Lauer; *Our Money, Our Values: Building a Just and Sustainable World* by Holley Hewitt Ulbrich and Catherine Mobley; and *Water Bugs and Dragonflies: Explaining Death to Young Children* by Doris Stickney.

UNITED CHURCH PRESS

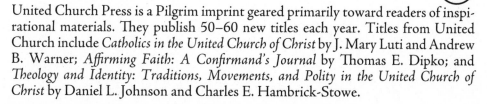

United Church Press is a Pilgrim imprint geared primarily toward readers of inspirational materials. They publish 50–60 new titles each year. Titles from United Church include *Catholics in the United Church of Christ* by J. Mary Luti and Andrew B. Warner; *Affirming Faith: A Confirmand's Journal* by Thomas E. Dipko; and *Theology and Identity: Traditions, Movements, and Polity in the United Church of Christ* by Daniel L. Johnson and Charles E. Hambrick-Stowe.

The Pilgrim Press oversees its own distribution.

See the website for an email submission form. As well, queries may be sent via regular mail with SASE to:

Kim Sadler; Editorial Director; sadlerk@ucc.org

PINNACLE BOOKS [SEE KENSINGTON PUBLISHING]

PLATINUM PRESS [SEE ADAMS MEDIA]

POLKA DOT PRESS [SEE ADAMS MEDIA]

POMEGRANATE COMMUNICATIONS, INC.

775A Southpoint Boulevard, Petaluma, CA 94954-1495

Mailing address:

P.O. Box 808022, Petaluma, CA 94975-8022

707-782-9000/800-227-1428   fax: 707-782-9810

www.pomegranatecommunications.com   email: info@pomegranate.com

Pomegranate publishes an attractive array of lavish graphic titles and specialty items around subjects such as fine art, architecture, travel, ethnic culture, and crafts. Pomegranate is also among the premier publishers of calendars, posters and poster art, note cards, games, puzzles, specialty sets, and popular topical card decks. The house is located in Northern California.

Pomegranate has its roots in San Francisco's 1960s psychedelic art explosion, when founder Thomas F. Burke distributed posters from the Avalon Ballroom and the Fillmore Auditorium. He worked with seminal poster companies such as East

Totem West—two of whose iconic posters, White Rabbit and Cheshire Cat, are still in Pomegranate's line.

Recent titles include *Monet's Passion: The Gardens at Giverny Deluxe Address Book* by Elizabeth Murray; *Constructive Spirit: Abstract Art in South and North America, 1920s–50s* edited by Mary Kate O'Hare; *The Jumblies* by Edward Lear; *The Dong with a Luminous Nose* by Edward Lear; and *Hughie Lee-Smith* by Leslie King-Hammond.

Email queries are not accepted. Query letters and SASEs should be directed to the Submissions Editor.

Thomas F. Burke, President

Zoe Katherine (Katie) Burke, Publisher

POTOMAC BOOKS, INC.

22841 Quicksilver Drive, Dulles, VA 20166

703-661-1548   fax: 703-661-1547

www.potomacbooksinc.com   email: pbimail@presswarehouse.com

Founded in 1983 as part of Brassey's Ltd., a distinguished British publishing house dating back to the 19th century, Potomac Books was acquired by American book distributor Books International in 1999. With strong roots in military history, Potomac Books has expanded its editorial focus to include general history, world and national affairs, foreign policy, defense and national security, intelligence, memoirs, biographies, and sports. The house publishes 85 new titles per year.

Recent titles include *The World Factbook: 2010 Edition; Celebrities Most Wanted* by Marjorie Hallenbeck-Huber; *Long-Range Goals: The Success Story of Major League Soccer* by Beau Dure; *The Secrets of Abu Ghraib Revealed: American Soldiers on Trial* by Christopher Graveline and Michael Clemens; and *How the Cold War Ended: Debating and Doing History* by John Prados.

Email submissions can be sent to either Elizabeth or Hilary. See website for further details. Query letters and proposals with SASEs may be directed to the Editorial Department.

Elizabeth Demers, Editor—History: military and naval, diplomatic, political, and other, current events, international relations, intelligence, security studies, terrorism, and military life; Elizabeth.Demers@booksintl.com

Hilary Claggett, Editor—Politics, public policy, current events, environment energy, media, democracy, and social movements; Hilary.Claggett@booksintl.com

Kathryn Owens, Editor—Most Wanted™ Series; Kathryn@booksintl.com

PRAEGER [SEE GREENWOOD PUBLISHING GROUP]

PRESBYTERIAN PUBLISHING CORPORATION

GENEVA PRESS

WESTMINSTER/JOHN KNOX

100 Witherspoon Street, Room 2047, Louisville, KY 40202-1396

502-569-5052/800-227-2872   fax: 502-569-5113/800-541-5113

www.ppcbooks.com   email: customer_service@presbypub.com

The Presbyterian Publishing Corporation (PPC) is the denominational publisher for the Presbyterian Church (USA), but the materials it issues under its Westminster John Knox Press imprint cover the spectrum of modern religious thought and represent the work of scholarly and popular authors of many different religious affiliations. PPC's Geneva Press imprint is for a specifically Presbyterian audience. The house publishes 95 new books each year and manages a backlist of over 1,600 titles.

For 160 years, PPC and its predecessors have served clergy, scholars, students, and lay people. Most of its publications are used in the spiritual formation of clergy and laity, the training of seminarians, the dissemination of religious scholars' work, and the preparation for ministry of lay church leaders. One of PPC's principal aims is to help readers of its publications achieve biblical and theological literacy. It is a nonprofit corporation, sustained by its sales.

Geneva Press titles include *A Children's Guide to Worship* by Ruth Boling et al; *Making Worship Real* by Aimee Wallis Buchanan et al; *Following Jesus* by Sonja Stewart; and *Come Worship Me* by Ruth Boling and Tracy Carrier.

WESTMINSTER/JOHN KNOX

Westminster/John Knox (WJK) represents the publications unit of the Presbyterian Church (USA). The house unites the former independents Westminster Press and John Knox Press, which were originally founded as one entity in 1838, then separated into distinct enterprises, and again merged as WJK following the reunion of the Northern and Southern Presbyterian Churches in 1983.

WJK publishes general-interest religious trade books, as well as academic and professional works in biblical studies, theology, philosophy, ethics, history, archaeology, personal growth, and pastoral counseling. Among its series are Literary

Currents in Biblical Interpretation, Family Living in Pastoral Perspective, Gender and the Biblical Tradition, and the Presbyterian Presence: The Twentieth-Century Experience. It has also gained popularity for its unofficial series of "Gospel According to…" books that explore religion and pop culture.

WJK's recent titles include *Journey to the Common Good* by Walter Brueggemann; *Making Sense of Evolution: Darwin, God, and the Drama of Life* by John F. Haught; *Halos and Avatars: Playing Games with God* edited by Craig Detweiler; *Mark's Gospel from Scratch: The New Testament for Beginners* by Donald Griggs and Charles Myers, Jr.; and *Making Space for the Spirit: 100 Simple Ways to Nurture Your Soul* by Kathleen Long Bostrom.

WJK distributes its list through Spring Arbor. The house also represents titles from other publishers, including Orbis Books, Pilgrim Press, Saint Andrew Press of Scotland, and Presbyterian Publishing Corporation.

Email queries are fine. Query letters and SASEs should be directed to:

Jana Riess, Acquisitions Editor; jreiss@wjkbooks.com

Don McKim, Theology and Reference Editor; dmckim@wjkbooks.com

Jon Berquist, Editor; jberquist@wjkbooks.com

David Maxwell, Executive Editor (Geneva Press); dmaxwell@wjkbooks.com

David Dobson, Executive Director of Publishing and Editorial

PROFESSIONAL PUBLICATIONS

1250 Fifth Avenue, Belmont, CA 94002

650-593-9119/800-426-1178   fax: 650-592-4519

www.ppi2pass.com   email: acquisitions@ppi2pass.com

Professional Publications, located in Belmont, California, was established as an independent publisher of professional licensing exam review materials since 1975. The house maintains a reputation as a leader in engineering, architecture, and interior design exam review. More than 800,000 exam candidates have used these publications. The mission is simple: to help readers pass their exams.

PPI is currently looking for Civil and Structural PEs with code, timber, and bridges expertise.

PPI titles include *Mechanical PE Sample Examination* by Michael R. Lindeburg; *Electrical Engineering Practice Problems for the Power, Electrical/Electronics, and Computer PE Exams* by John A. Camara; and *Seismic Principles Practice Exams for the California Special Civil Engineer Exam* by Majid Baradar.

Queries may be directed to acquisitions@ppi2pass.com or to the Acquisitions Editor at the mailing address above.

PROMETHEUS BOOKS

HUMANITY BOOKS

PYR

59 John Glenn Drive, Amherst, NY 14228-2197

716-691-0133/800-421-0351   fax: 716-564-2711

www.prometheusbooks.com   email: editorial@prometheusbooks.com

www.pyrsf.com   Pyr blog: pyrsf.blogspot.com

One of the leading publishers in philosophy, popular science, and critical thinking, Prometheus Books has more than 1,500 books in print and produces an average of 100 new titles each year. Founded in 1969, this house took its name from the courageous Greek god who gave fire to humans, lighting the way to reason, intelligence, and independence, among other things. The house is located near Buffalo, New York.

Among the categories of books published are popular science, science and the paranormal, contemporary issues, social science and current events, children's fiction and nonfiction, history, religion and politics, philosophy, humanism, Islamic studies, Jewish studies, biblical criticism, psychology, women's issues, health, self-help, sexuality, reference, and more. Prometheus also maintains a strong backlist that includes hundreds of established classics in literature, philosophy, and the sciences.

Recent titles from Prometheus include *Deep Postmodernism: Whitehead, Wittgenstein, Merleau-Ponty, and Polanyi* by Jerry Gill; *Hemingway: So Far from Simple* by Donald Bouchard; *I, Monster: Serial Killers in Their Own Chillling Words* by Tom Philbin; and *My Brother, My Enemy: America and the Battle of Ideas Across the Islamic World* by Philip Smucker.

HUMANITY BOOKS

Humanity Books publishes academic works across the humanities. Recent Humanity Books titles include *Citizen's of the World: Cosmopolitan Ideals for the 21st Century* edited by Hugh Silverman et al; *Beyond God: Evolution and the Future of Religion* by Kenneth Kardong; *Democracy's Debt: The Historical Tensions Between Political and Economic Liberty* by M. Lane Bruner; and *Culture and Conflict in the Middle East* by Philip Carl Salzman.

PYR

Pyr (the Greek word for fire) publishes science fiction and speculative fiction. Recent titles from Pyr include *Ares Express* by Ian McDonald; *The Dervish House* by Ian McDonald; *The Hounds of Avalon: Dark Age Book 3* by Mark Chadbourn; *The Office of Shadow* by Matthew Sturges; *The Queen of Sinister: Dark Age Book*

2 by Mark Chadbourn; and *The Ragged Man: Book Four of the Twilight Reign* by Tom Lloyd.

Query via regular mail or email (do not send attachments with emails).

Steven L. Mitchell, Editor-in-Chief; editorial@prometheusbooks.com

PROVENANCE PRESS [SEE ADAMS MEDIA]

PYR [SEE PROMETHEUS BOOKS]

QUARRY BOOKS [SEE QUAYSIDE PUBLISHING GROUP]

QUAYSIDE PUBLISHING GROUP

FAIR WINDS PRESS

QUARRY BOOKS

QUIVER

ROCKPORT

100 Cummings Center. Suite 406-L., Beverly, MA 01915

978-282-9590   fax: 978-283-2742

www.quaysidepublishinggroup.com

CREATIVE PUBLISHING INTERNATIONAL

MOTORBOOKS

MVP BOOKS

VOYAGEUR PRESS

400 First Avenue North, Suite 300, Minneapolis, MN 55401

612-344-8100/800-328-0590 fax: 612-344-8691

The Quayside Publishing Group was formed in 2004 upon Rockport Publishers' acquisition of Creative Publishing International. In 2007, Quayside acquired the MBI Publishing Company and its three imprints: Motorbooks, Voyageur Press, and Zenith Press. In 2009, it launched sports and fitness imprint MVP Books.

In 2001, Rockport Publishers launched Fair Winds Press to focus on a wide range of mind, body, and spirit topics that excite readers and help them answer life's fundamental questions. The Quarry Books imprint, launched in 2003, provides practical general reference in categories such as crafts, home style, pet care, and personal improvement. Quiver, launched in 2006, offers titles about sex.

CREATIVE PUBLISHING INTERNATIONAL

Founded in 1969, Creative Publishing International is a worldwide publisher of how-to books. They offer books on home improvement, home decorating, sewing, crafting, hunting, fishing, and photography. Over the past 15 years CPI has developed high-quality photography step-by-step books with nationally recognized brands like Black and Decker and Singer.

Some titles include *The Complete Guide to Garages: Ideas and Projects for Creating the Perfect Garage* by Chris Marshall; *Amigurumi Knits: Patterns for 20 Cute Mini Knits* by Hansi Singh; and *Fabric Art Projects: Fashion and Home Decor Items Made from Artfully Altered Fabric* by Susan Stein.

FAIR WINDS PRESS

Fair Winds offers nonfiction books in a range of practical categories, including cooking, health, household hints, fitness, and self-improvement. Fair Winds books are distinguished by their unique approaches to popular subjects, innovative packaging, and dynamic authors.

Recent Fair Winds titles include *Whole Body Healing Pack: Simple Techniques That Relieve Pain, Restore Health, and Soothe Body, Mind, and Spirit* by Skye Alexander and *Boost Your Fertility: New Solutions for Conceiving Quickly and Having a Healthy Pregnancy as Soon as Possible* by Marilyn Glenville, PhD.

MOTORBOOKS

Motorbooks began in the garage of founder Thomas Warth in 1965, when the automobile aficionado was unable to find quality car, motorcycle, and racing books. It continued to grow and was acquired by the Quayside Publishing Group in 2007.

Some titles include *How to Keep Your Muscle Car Alive* by Harvey White, Jr.; *Chevy Small-Block V-8 Interchange Manual* by David Lewis; *How to Paint Your Tractor* by Tharran E. Gaines; and *The Lamborghini Miura Bible* by Joe Sackey.

MVP BOOKS

Established in 2009, MVP Books is an expansion of the sports category begun under Voyageur Press. Built on a decade of sports publishing experience, their versatile list of books is highlighted by four-color photography and informative, entertaining text, providing high-quality publishing for the sports and fitness enthusiast.

Some recent releases by MVP Books include *Dodgers: Past and Present* by Steven Travers; *New York Yankees and the Meaning of Life* by Derek Gentile; and *Titans: Muhammad Ali and Arnold Schwarzenegger* by Al Satterwhite.

QUARRY BOOKS

Quarry Books provides practical reference in categories such as artisan crafts, home style, pet care, and hobbies. Their books are defined by their full-color photography and illustration, and their informative text.

Recent Quarry titles include *Re-Bound: Creating Handmade Books from Recycled and Repurposed Materials* by Jeannine Stein; *Vintage Spirits and Forgotten Cocktails* by Ted Haigh; and *Cloth Doll Artistry: Design and Costuming Techniques for Flat and Fully Sculpted Figures* by Barbara Willis.

QUIVER

Quiver books are for couples who want to take their sex lives to the next level. Their books feature sex positions, techniques, erotic stories, color photography, kama sutra, and tantra. Their books celebrate erotic pleasure and intimacy through beautiful, sophisticated photography and inspiring text.

Recent Quiver titles include *The Orgasm Loop: The No-Fail Technique for Reaching Orgasm During Sex* by Susan Crain Bakos; *8 Erotic Nights: Passionate Encounters that Inspire Great Sex for a Lifetime* by Charla Hathaway; and *The Sex Bible for Women: The Complete Guide to Understanding Your Body, Being a Great Lover, and Getting the Pleasure You Want* by Susan Crain Bakos.

ROCKPORT

Rockport Publishers creates beautiful illustrated source books for professional designers and artisans of all types. Their books present the best design work from around the world, showing how work gets done, and the inspiration behind the art. Rockport's editors are constantly looking for the newest and most noteworthy trends in the design industry as well as keeping abreast of the best work being done in the traditional areas of commercial design and art.

Recent Rockport titles include *What Is Interior Design?* by Graeme Brooker and Sally Stone; *Remodeled Homes* by Ethel Baraona; *Good Design: Deconstructing Form, Function, and What Makes Design Work* by Terry Marks; *LogoLounge 5: 2000 International Identities by Leading Designers* by Bill Gardner and Catherine Fishel; and *Typography Essentials: 100 Design Principles for Working with Type* by Ina Saltz.

VOYAGEUR PRESS

Since 1972, Voyageur Press has published books and calendars on subjects like nature, science, regional interest, travel, American heritage, country life, crafts, sports, wild animals, pets, and more.

Some titles from Voyageur Press include *Backroads of Florida: Your Guide to Great Day Trips and Weekend Getaways* by Paul M. Franklin and Nancy Mikula; *For the Love of Knitting: A Celebration of the Knitters Art* by Kari Cornell; and *How to Raise Goats* by Carol Amundson.

Direct queries and SASEs to:

Emily Potts, Acquisitions Editor

Winnie Prentiss, Publisher (Rockport, Quarry, CPI Lifestyles)

Bryan Trandem, Publisher (CPI Home Improvement and Outdoor Recreation)

William Kiester, Publisher (Fair Winds, Quiver)

Zack Miller, Publisher (Motorbooks)

Michael Dregni, Publisher (Voyageur Press)

Richard Kane, Publisher (Zenith Press)

QUIRK BOOKS

215 Church Street, Philadelphia, PA 19106

215-627-3581   fax: 215-627-5220

www.irreference.com   email: general@quirkbooks.com

Founded by the folks who authored the Worst-Case Scenario franchise, Quirk Books editors seek to be publishers of high-quality irreverence. The mission of this house is to originate, develop, and publish nontraditional and innovative nonfiction books that are objects of desire editorially, graphically, and physically. Quirk also functions as a book packager, developing and selling recent titles to St. Martin's and Potter, among others.

Quirk's recent titles include *The Geometry of Pasta* by Caz Hildebrand and Jacob Kenedy; *Disneystrology* by Lisa Finander; *Night of the Living Trekkies* by Kevin Anderson and Sam Strall; *Soil Mates* by Sara Alway; and *Android Karenina* by Leo Tolstoy and Ben Winters.

Direct brief queries to Editorial Submissions via fax, email (submissions@quirkbooks.com), or regular mail with SASE.

Jason Rekulak, Editorial, Submissions, and Design; jason@quirkbooks.com

Margaret McGuire, Editor

Stephen H. Segal, Editor

QUIVER [SEE QUAYSIDE PUBLISHING GROUP]

RAGGED MOUNTAIN PRESS [SEE MCGRAW-HILL]

RED DRESS INK [SEE HARLEQUIN ENTERPRISES, LTD.]

RED WHEEL/WEISER

CONARI PRESS

WEISER BOOKS

500 Third Street, Suite 230, San Francisco, CA 94107

www.redwheelweiser.com

www.conari.com

Red Wheel/Weiser, LLC, is the publisher of Weiser and Conari Press. The house primarily publishes in the category of body/mind/spirit, about 60 books per year among the three imprints.

In 2006, the entire Red Wheel/Weiser Conari editorial department relocated from Boston to San Francisco. At the same time, Red Wheel/Weiser Conari consolidated its Maine operations department and the Boston sales and marketing department moved to a new office in Newburyport, Massachusetts.

CONARI PRESS

Conari Press, founded in 1989 in Berkeley, California, was acquired by Red Wheel/ Weiser in 2002. Conari topics include spirituality, personal growth, parenting, and social issues. Some titles include *Get Up: A 12-Step Recovery Guide for Misfits, Freaks, and Weirdos* by Bucky Sinister; *Change Your Mind and Your Life Will Follow: 12 Simple Principles* by Karen Casey; and *100 Sweet Nothings for Baby* by Mina Parker.

WEISER BOOKS

Weiser Books has a long history as one of America's preeminent publishers of esoteric and occult teachings from traditions around the world and throughout time. Areas of Weiser publishing interest include self-transformation, alternative healing methods, meditation, metaphysics, consciousness, magic, astrology, tarot, astral projection, Kabbalah, earth religions, Eastern philosophy and religions, Buddhism, t'ai chi, healing, and Tibetan studies. The publisher specializes in books relating to all facets of the secret and hidden teachings worldwide.

Recent titles from Weiser include *The Essential Laws of Fearless Living: Find the Power and Never Feel Powerless Again* by Guy Finley; *Asthma-Free Naturally: Everything You Need to Know to Take Control of Your Asthma* by Patrick McKeown; and *Magic When You Need It: 150 Spells You Can't Live Without* by Judika Illes.

Submissions are accepted via regular mail only. For both imprints, query letters, proposals, or manuscripts with SASEs should be directed to:

Caroline Pincus, Editor

Jan Johnson, Publisher

REGAL BOOKS [SEE GOSPEL LIGHT PUBLICATIONS]

REGNERY

A Division of Eagle Publishing

One Massachusetts Avenue, North West, Washington, DC 20001

202-216-0600/888-219-4747   fax: 202-216-0612

www.regnery.com   email: submissions@regnery.com

Founded in 1947, Regnery has become the country's most popular publisher of books for conservatives. Regnery publishes books in the fields of current affairs, politics, history, culture, and biography.

In 1993 Regnery became part of the newly founded Eagle Publishing, which also includes Human Events, the national conservative weekly; the Conservative Book Club; and the Evans & Novak Political Report.

Recent titles include *To Save America* by Newt Gingrich; *Ted, White, and Blue* by Ted Nugent; *Power Grab* by Christopher C. Horner; *That's No Angry Mob,*

That's My Mom by Michael Graham; and *The Truth About the Shroud of Turin* by Robert K. Wilcox.

Regnery only accepts manuscripts and proposals submitted by agents.

Marji Ross, Publisher

FLEMING H. REVELL [SEE BAKER PUBLISHING GROUP]

RIZZOLI, USA

UNIVERSE INTERNATIONAL PUBLICATIONS

A Division of RCS Media Group, Italy

300 Park Avenue South, 3rd Floor, New York, NY 10010

212-387-3400   fax: 212-387-3535

www.rizzoliusa.com   email: submissions@rizzoliusa.com

Rizzoli began its New York operations in 1974 as an integral part of its parent company, the Italian communications giant, RCS Media Group. The house is a leader in illustrated books in the fields of art, architecture, interior design, photography, haute couture, and gastronomy. In 1990, Rizzoli added the Universe imprint, marking Rizzoli's entrée into the pop-culture worlds of humor, fashion, beauty, sports, performing arts, and gay and alternative lifestyles. It also contributed a successful calendar program and published economical versions of Rizzoli books.

Under the direction of Senior Editor Robb Pearlman, who joined the company in 2006, the company plans to expand its children's book and calendar lines.

Recent Rizzoli titles include *1001 Albums You Must Hear Before You Die* edited by Robert Dimery; *1001 Beers You Must Taste Before You Die* edited by Adrian Tierney-Jones; *The Allure of the Automobile* by Ronald Labaco and Ken Gross; *The Architecture of Atelier Bow-Wow* by Atelier Bow-Wow et al; *Buildings without Architects* by John May; and *Christian Boltanski* by Catherine Grenier and Daniel Mendelsohn.

Rizzoli titles are distributed through St. Martin's Press.

Rizzoli does accept unsolicited proposals. Email proposals can be sent to submissions@rizzoliusa.com. All queries with SASEs should be directed to Editorial Submissions.

Charles Miers, Publisher

Robb Pearlman, Senior Editor—Children's books, calendars, licensing

RODALE, INC.

33 East Minor Street, Emmaus, PA 18098-0099

610-967-5171   fax: 610-967-8963

New York address:

733 Third Avenue, 15th Floor, New York, NY 10017-3204

212-697-2040   fax: 212-682-2237

www.rodale.com   email: reader_service@rodale.com

Rodale publishes acclaimed nonfiction books on health, fitness, cooking, gardening, spirituality, self-help, nature, and more. Recent *New York Times* bestsellers include Al Gore's *An Inconvenient Truth*; *The Abs Diet for Women* by David Zinczenko; *LL Cool J's Platinum Workout* by LL Cool J; *The South Beach Heart Program* by Arthur Agaston; and *Joy Bauer's Food Cures* by Joy Bauer.

Rodale Books has also been developing titles in new genres including memoirs, biographies, narrative nonfiction, self-help, science and nature, psychology, current events, and personal finance.

Recent titles include *Organic Manifesto* by Maria Rodale; *The Kind Diet* by Alicia Silverstone; *Walk Off Weight* by Michael Stanten; *400 Calorie Fix* by Liz Vaccariello; *2-Week Turnaround Diet Cookbook* by Heather K. Jones; and *Cook This, Not That! Kitchen Survival Guide* by David Zinczenko and Matt Goulding.

Please send proposals and SASEs to the editors via regular mail or email at bookproposals@rodale.com.

Pam Krauss, Vice President, Publishing Director

Colin Dickerman, Vice President, Publishing Director

Julie Will, Senior Editor

Courtney Conroy, Editor

ROUTLEDGE

An Imprint of Taylor and Francis Books

270 Madison Avenue, New York, NY 10016

212-216-7800   fax: 212-563-2269

www.routledge-ny.com

Routledge produces adult nonfiction for the trade and academic markets. The house produces titles in the humanities and social sciences with more specific focus on current events, communications, media, cultural studies, education, self-improvement, world political studies, philosophy, economics, feminist theory, gender studies, history, and literary criticism. Routledge is an imprint of the Taylor and Francis Group.

Recent titles include *400 Rabbits: Thet Pleasure and Pain of Drunkenness* edited by Anne Fox; *Mental Health Services for Adults with Intellectual Disability* edited by Nick Bouras; *Teaching World History as Mystery* by David Gerwin and Jack Zevin; and *Teaching Online: A Practical Guide* by Susan Ko and Steve Rossen.

See the website for submission guidelines. Send your proposal with SASE via regular mail to the Editorial Department; your proposal will be forwarded to the appropriate editor.

Michael Kerns, Politics

Catherine Bernard, Education

Matthew Byrnie, Media studies, communications, literature, cultural studies

Kimberly Guinta, History

Constance Ditzel, Music

INDEPENDENT U.S. PRESSES

ROWMAN & LITTLEFIELD PUBLISHING GROUP

ALTAMIRA

HAMILTON BOOKS

JASON ARONSON, INC., PUBLISHERS

LEXINGTON BOOKS

SCARECROW PRESS

SHEED & WARD

UNIVERSITY PRESS OF AMERICA

4501 Forbes Boulevard, Suite 200, Lanham, MD 20706

301-459-3366 fax: 301-429-5748

www.rowmanlittlefield.com

www.hamiltonbooks.com

www.lexingtonbooks.com

www.aronson.com

www.univpress.com

New York office:

200 Park Avenue South, Suite 1109, New York, NY 10003

212-529-3888   fax: 212-529-4223

TAYLOR TRADE

M. EVANS

5360 Manhattan Circle #100, Boulder, CO 80303

www.rlpgtrade.com   email: tradeeditorial@rowman.com

IVAN R. DEE, PUBLISHER

NEW AMSTERDAM BOOKS

J. S. SANDERS

1332 North Halsted Street, Chicago, IL, 60622-2694

312-787-6262   fax: 312-787-6269

www.ivanrdee.com   email: elephant@ivanrdee.com

The Rowman & Littlefield Publishing Group is one of the largest and fastest-growing independent publishers and distributors in North America. The company publishes more than 20 imprints in virtually all fields in the humanities and social sciences for the academic and trade markets. Rowman & Littlefield also owns National Book Network, which is North America's second-largest distributor of independent trade book publishers. NBN recently created two new divisions: Biblio Distribution for small trade publishers and FaithWorks for CBA publishers.

RLPG built its list quickly by acquiring small companies and niche publishers, especially over the past five years. These have been either merged into existing imprints or have continued to exist as stand-alone RLPG imprints.

Rowman & Littlefield is an independent press devoted to publishing scholarly books in the best tradition of university presses; innovative, thought-provoking texts for college courses; and crossover trade books intended to convey scholarly trends to an educated readership.

Recent titles include *Coming Climate Crisis?: Consider the Past, Beware the Big Fix* by Claire L. Parkinson; *United States Protocol: The Guide to Official Diplomatic*

Etiquette by Ambassador Mark Mel French; *Why We're All Romans: The Roman Contribution to the Western World* by Carl Richard; *The African American Experience During World War II* by Neil A. Wynn; and *Polyamory in the 21st Century: Love and Intimacy with Multiple Partners* by Deborah Anapol.

An academic or scholarly author would do well to explore online the various RLPG imprints, or to query this publisher for guidelines. To submit to Rowman & Littlefield, direct your query to the appropriate editor:

Jonathan Sisk, Senior Editor (MD)—American government, philosophy, political theory, public policy; jsisk@rowmanlittlefield.com

Jack Meinhardt, Acquisitions Editor (MD)—Anthropology, archaeology, Smithsonian Institution Scholarly Press; jmeinhardt@rowman.com

Sarah Stanton, Associate Editor (MD)—Sociology, religion, Cowley Publications; sstanton@rowman.com

Suzanne Staszak-Silva, Senior Editor (MD)—Crime/criminal justice, health, psychology; sstaszak-silva@rowman.com

Patti Belcher, Acquisitions Editor for Education, ACE and AERA

ALTAMIRA

AltaMira Press exists to disseminate high quality information to those who research, study, practice, and read the humanities and social sciences, with a particular focus on helping in the professional development of those who work in the cultural life of a community—the museum, historical society, arts center, and church. They are a preeminent publisher in the field of archaeology, and also publish in anthropology, Asian American studies, Native American studies, and comparative religion. AltaMira welcomes submissions from prospective authors.

Some titles include *The Gift of a Bride: A Tale of Anthropology, Matrimony, and Murder* by Serena Nanda and Joan Gregg; *Ancestors and Elites: Emergent Complexity and Ritual Practices in the Casas Grandes Polity* by Gordon F. M. Rakita; and *Planning Successful Museum Building Projects* by Walter L. Crimm et al.

HAMILTON BOOKS

Hamilton Books was launched as a new imprint of the Rowman and Littlefield Publishing Group in 2003. Potential authors include corporate leaders, politicians, scholars, war veterans, and family historians. Their publishing program is based on an alternative model, where the author is offered a contract that specifies a quantity for pre-publication purchase by the author to share a portion of up-front production expenses. Hamilton covers the costs of all copies beyond the initial order, no matter what the quantity.

Some titles include *Lurps: A Ranger's Diary of Tet, Khe Sanh, A Shau, and Quang Tri, Revised Edition* by Robert C. Ankony; *Objectivism in One Lesson: An Introduction to the Philosophy of Ayn Rand* by Andrew Bernstein; and *What's The*

Beef? Sixty Years of Hard-Won Lessons for Today's Leaders in Labor, Management, and Government by Wayne L. Horvitz.

JASON ARONSON, INC., PUBLISHERS

Jason Aronson is the publisher of highly regarded psychotherapy and Judaica books. Dedicated to publishing professional, scholarly works, their list of Judaica authors spans the entire spectrum of approaches to Jewish tradition: Orthodox, Hasidic, Reconstructionist, Reform, Conservative, Renewal, unaffiliated, and secular. Topics include anti-Semitism, Baal Shem Tov, classics in translation, family, folklore and storytelling, Gematria, Hasidism, history, holidays, Holocaust, Israel, Jewish law, kabbalah, Maimonides, marriage, meditation, prayer, Talmud, theology, Torah, travel, women's studies, and more.

In the subject of psychotherapy, Jason Aronson, Inc., offers more titles from a broader range of psychotherapists than any other publisher. Topics include child therapy, family therapy, eating disorders, substance abuse, short-term therapy, bereavement, stress, trauma, object relations therapy, personality disorder, depression, couple therapy, sexual abuse, play therapy, psychoanalysis, psychology, transference, and more.

Some titles include *The Damaged Core: Origins, Dynamics, Manifestations, and Treatment* by Salman Akhtar; *Psychoanalysis and Male Homosexuality* by Kenneth Lewes; *The Problem Is the Solution: A Jungian Approach to a Meaningful Life* by Marcella Bakur Weiner and Mark B. Simmons; and *Unfree Association: Inside Psychoanalytic Institutes* by Douglas Kirsner.

Send proposal with CV and SASE to:

Arthur T. Pomponio, Editorial Director for Jason Aronson (NY); apomponio@rowman.com

Mary Catherine La Mar, Acquisitions Editor for Jason Aronson (NY); mlamae@rowman.com

LEXINGTON BOOKS

Lexington Books is Rowman & Littlefield's division for publishing specialized new work by established and emerging scholars. Lexington publishes high-quality scholarly work that may not have a wide audience but makes a substantial contribution to scholarship in particular and related fields.

Lexington welcomes proposals in the fields of Africana studies, American history, American studies, anthropology, archaeology, Asian studies, cultural studies, geography, history, international relations, literary criticism, Middle East studies, philosophy, political science, political theory, public policy, religion, and sociology.

Some titles include *Language and Collective Mobilization* by Nadrea Hashim; *A Matter of Honour: Being Chinese in South Africa* by Yoon Park; *Ourselves and*

Our Posterity: Essays in Constitutional Originalism by Bradley C. S. Watson; and *Thinking History, Fighting Evil* by David MacDonald.

SCARECROW PRESS

Scarecrow Press was purchased by R&L in 1995 and is known for their scholarly bibliographies, historical dictionaries, library science, and reference working in the humanities, particularly music and film. They are broadening their list to include textbooks in library and information science, new series that address the technological frontiers of the profession, handbooks for librarians serving children, and a greater scope of materials in music.

Some titles include *In the Heart of the Beat: The Poetry of Rap* by Alexs Pate; *The Postmodern Humanism of Philip K. Dick* by Jason P. Vest; *Channeling the Future: Essays on Science Fiction and Fantasy Television* by Lincoln Geraghty; and *The Biology of Musical Performance* by Alan H. D. Watson.

SHEED & WARD

Founded in 1926 by Australian lawyer Francis Joseph Sheed and his British wife Maisie Ward, Sheed & Ward is one of the most eminent Catholic publishing houses in the world today. Some of their titles include *The Gospel of Cesar Chavez: My Faith in Action* by Mario T. Garcia; *Before I Go: Letters to Our Children about What Really Matters* by Peter Kreeft; and *The Genius of Pope John Paul II: The Great Pope's Moral Wisdom* by Richard A. Spinello.

UNIVERSITY PRESS OF AMERICA

The University Press of America is an academic publisher committed to the belief that the most important question relevant to the publication decision is: Does this work provide a significant contribution to scholarship?

The UPA publishes works across disciplines as various as African American studies, African studies, American history, American literature, anthropology, art history, Asian studies, biblical studies, Catholicism, classics, communications, criminology, Eastern European studies, economics, education, ethics, GLBT studies, gender studies, geography, history, international studies, Jewish studies, language studies, Latin American studies, legal studies, literary studies, marketing, minority studies, organization, peace and conflict studies, philosophy, political science, psychology, public health, religious studies, sociology, U.S. public policy, and world history.

Some titles include *A Roadmap to Education: The CRE-ACT Way* by Dorothy Prokes; *This Is My Body: An Existential Analysis of the Living Body* by William C. Springer; *Maybe I Should…Case Studies on Ethics for Student Affairs Professionals* by Florence A. Hamrick and Mimi Benjamin; and *Ox Cart to Automobile: Social Change in Western New York* by Thomas Rasmussen.

Prospective authors can visit their website to view the proposal questionnaire.

TAYLOR TRADE

The Taylor Trade Publishing program consists of an award-winning list of books on gardening, health, history, family issues, sports, entertainment, nature, field guides, house and home, cooking, Texana/Western history, and children's titles. Taylor Trade operates out of Boulder, Colorado.

Recent Taylor titles include *Recipes from Historic New England: A Restaurant Guide and Cookbook* by Lind Bauer; *Someone's Daughter: In Search of Justice for Jane Doe* by Silvia Pettem; *This Day in Football: A Day-by-Day Record of the Events that Shaped the Game* by Terence Troup; *Paul Newman: A Life* by Lawrence J. Quirk; and *Old Ironsides: Eagle of the Sea* by David Fitz-Enz.

M. EVANS

Recently acquired by Rowman & Littlefield, M. Evans and Company, Inc., has been publishing thought-provoking titles with a clear, constantly honed commercial focus in its favored market niches for over 40 years. M. Evans has become an imprint of Taylor Trade, with editorial operations in Colorado, as well.

The M. Evans front list features high-profile offerings in topical issues, investigative stories in politics, business, and entertainment, and popular biography. The core Evans program accents popular nonfiction books, primarily self-help related, in the areas of health and fitness, human relationships, business and finance, and lifestyle and cuisine.

Recent M. Evans titles include *Beyond Alzheimer's: Avoiding the Dementia Epidemic* by Scott D. Mendelson; *Born in Blood: The Lost Secrets of Freemasonry* by John J. Robinson; *Breaking Into the Boys' Club: 8 Ways for Women to Get Ahead in Business* by Molly D. Shepard et al; and *The Good Girl's Guide to Bad Girl Sex: An Indispensable Resource for Pleasure and Seduction* by Barbara Keesling.

Query letters and SASEs should be directed to the Editorial Department; email generates the quickest response. If querying by email, note "Book Proposal" in the subject line.

Rick Rinehart, Editorial Director; rrinehart@rowman.com

Dulcie Wilcox, Acquisitions Editor; dwilcox@rowman.com

IVAN R. DEE, PUBLISHER

Ivan R. Dee publishes serious nonfiction trade books in history, politics, biography, literature, philosophy, and theater. Similar to Basic Books and the Free Press in their heyday, Ivan R. Dee produces books that are provocative, controversial, and aimed at the intelligent layperson. They are routinely reviewed in the *New York Times*, the *Washington Post*, the *New York Review of Books*, and other influential publications. Ivan R. Dee paperbacks are also used extensively in college courses as supplementary reading.

Founded in 1988 by Ivan Dee, the house was acquired in 1998 by the Rowman

& Littlefield Publishing Group. Ivan Dee continues as publisher in the company's Chicago headquarters.

Some titles include *Rethinking Kennedy: An Interpretive Biography* by Michael O'Brien; *Pay to Play: How Rod Blagojevich Turned Political Corruption into a National Sideshow* by Elizabeth Brackett; and *No Sense of Decency: The Army-McCarthy Hearings* by Robert Shogan.

NEW AMSTERDAM BOOKS

New Amsterdam Books, an imprint of Ivan R. Dee, Publisher, publishes distinguished books for the serious general reader. Highlights include art and art history, fiction in translation, theater, Scottish studies, Victorian studies, religion, and history. New Amsterdam Books is not currently accepting submissions.

Some titles are *Broken April* by Ismail Kadare; *Understanding Design* by Kees Dorst; and *The Immortal Dinner: A Famous Evening of Genius and Laughter in Literature* by Penelope Hughes-Hallett.

J. S. SANDERS

J.S. Sanders & Company, an imprint of Ivan R. Dee, Publisher, was founded by John Sanders of Nashville, Tennessee, to publish and republish general trade books on Southern culture, history, and literature, including the Southern Classics series, which "restores to our awareness some of the South's most important writers of the nineteenth and twentieth centuries" (Hudson Review). Many classic novels about the South, as well as histories and biographies of the region and its leaders, are still in print today thanks to J.S. Sanders. J.S. Sanders is not currently accepting submissions.

Some titles include *Nashville 1864* by Madison Jones; *The War the Women Lived* by Walter Sullivan; *Bedford Forrest and His Critter Company* by Andrew Nelson Lyte; and *John Brown: The Making of a Martyr* by Robert Penn Warren.

J. S. SANDERS [SEE ROWMAN & LITTLEFIELD]

SASQUATCH BOOKS

119 South Main Street, Suite 400, Seattle, WA 98104
206-467-4300/800-775-0817   fax: 206-467-4301
www.sasquatchbooks.com

Sasquatch Books is one of the nation's premier regional presses, with titles for and about the Pacific Northwest, Alaska, and California. Founded in 1986, Sasquatch's publishing program celebrates regionally written works. Their top-selling Best Places travel guides serve the most popular destinations and locations of the West. Sasquatch also publishes widely in the subjects of food, wine, gardening, nature, photography, children's books, and regional history. With more than 200 books on the West, this house offers an exploration of the lifestyle, landscape, and worldview of its region.

Some titles include *The Creaky Knees Guide Oregon* by Seabury Blair, Jr.; *Larry Gets Lost in San Francisco* by John Skewes; *Swirl, Sip & Savor: Northwest Wine and Small Plate Pairings* by Carol Frieberg; *Pugetopolis: A Mossback Takes on Growth Addicts, Weather Wimps, and the Myth of Seattle Nice* by Knute Berger; and *The Collector: David Douglas and the Natural History of the Northwest* by Jack Nisbet.

Email queries are not accepted at this time. Submit a query, proposal, or complete manuscript to the Acquisitions Department.

Gary Luke, President and Publisher

Terence Maikels, Acquisitions Editor

SCHAUM'S MCGRAW-HILL [SEE MCGRAW-HILL]

SCHOLASTIC, INC.

ARTHUR A. LEVINE BOOKS

THE BLUE SKY PRESS

CARTWHEEL BOOKS

557 Broadway, New York, NY 10012

212-343-6100

www.scholastic.com

KLUTZ

KLUTZ LATINO

CHICKEN SOCKS

450 Lambert Avenue, Palo Alto, CA 94306

650-857-0888/800-737-4123

www.klutz.com   email: thefolks@klutz.com

Scholastic is a global children's publishing and media company and is the USA's largest publisher and distributor of children's books. Recognizing that literacy is the cornerstone of a child's intellectual, personal, and cultural growth, Scholastic creates quality products and services that educate, entertain, and motivate children, and are designed to help enlarge their understanding of the world around them.

Scholastic publishes over 750 new books each year. The list includes *Harry Potter, Captain Underpants, Clifford the Big Red Dog, I Spy*, and *The Magic Schoolbus*. Best-selling titles include *How Do Dinosaurs Say Goodnight?, No, David!, Inkheart, Charlie Bone, Chasing Vermeer*, and *The Day My Butt Went Psycho*.

Scholastic imprints include Scholastic Press, Arthur A. Levine Books, Cartwheel Books, and The Blue Sky Press. Scholastic acquired Klutz (see below) five years ago.

Scholastic Library Publishing is a leading provider of print and online reference products for school and public libraries, with a broad array of products through its well-known Grolier, Children's Press, Franklin Watts, and Grolier Online imprints.

Recent titles include *Fever Crumb* by Philip Reeve; *Farm* by Elisha Cooper; *The Dreamer* by Pam Munoz Ryan; and *Glitter Girls and the Great Fake Out (Allie Finkle #5)* by Meg Cabot.

ARTHUR A. LEVINE BOOKS

Arthur A. Levine Books was founded at Scholastic, Inc., in 1996, publishing their first book, *When She Was Good* by Norma Fox Mazer, in the fall of 1997. Since then, they publish a small high-quality list of hardcover literary fiction, picture books, and nonfiction for children and teenagers.

Some of their titles include *Absolutely Maybe* by Lisa Yee; *Marcelo in the Real World* by Francisco X. Stork; and *Tales from Outer Suburbia* by Shaun Tan.

THE BLUE SKY PRESS

The Blue Sky Press publishes picture books and chapter books for grade schoolers. Some titles from The Blue Sky Press include *Our Abe Lincoln* by Jim Aylesworth; *Living Sunlight: How Plants Bring the Earth to Life* by Molly Bang and Penny Chisholm; *Dumb Bunnies' Easter* by Dav Piley; and *Book of Love for Mothers and Sons* by Rob D. Walker.

CARTWHEEL BOOKS

Cartwheel Books publishes picture books for toddlers. Some titles from Cartwheel Books include *Bedtime Kiss for Little Fish* by Lorie Ann Grover; *Don't Lose Your Shoes!* by Elizabeth Mills; *Lily's Twinkly Bedtime* by Katie Peters; and *What Do You See?* by Reyna Lindert.

Scholastic considers submissions from agents or previously published authors.

Arthur A. Levine considers queries from everyone. Submissions and SASEs should be directed to David Saylor.

David Saylor, Editor

Andrea Davis Pinkney, Vice President—Hardcover and Early Childhood

David Levithan, Executive Editor—Trade

Arthur A. Levine, Vice President and Editorial Director (Arthur A. Levine Books)

KLUTZ

Based in Palo Alto, California, Klutz is the creator of kids' activity products including books, kits, toys, and other kids' stuff that stimulate their growth through creativity. Klutz products combine clear instructions with everything you need to give kids a hands-on learning experience that ranges from the artistic to the scientific, and beyond. Founded in 1977 by three Stanford students, Klutz was purchased by Scholastic in 2002, but maintains editorial offices in California's Silicon Valley. Klutz makes cool stuff; their credo is: create wonderful things, be good, have fun.

Imprints include Klutz Latino (Spanish language) and Chicken Socks (for readers ages 4–8).

Recent titles include *Klutz Build-a-Book*: *My Really Good Friends* by the Editors of Klutz; *Paper Beads* by Anne Aker Johnson; *Nail Art* by Sherri Haab; and *Fuzzimal Puppies* by Theresa Hutnik and Megan Smith.

Query with SASE to:

John Cassidy, Founder and Chief Creative Officer

SEAL PRESS [SEE PERSEUS BOOKS GROUP]

SECOND CHANCE PRESS [SEE PERMANENT PRESS]

SELF-COUNSEL PRESS

1704 North State Street, Bellingham, WA 98225

360-676-4530/877-877-6490   fax: 360-676-4549

www.self-counsel.com   email: orderdesk@self-counsel.com

Vancouver editorial office:

1481 Charlotte Road, North Vancouver, BC V7J 1H1 Canada

604-986-3366

A pioneer in the self-help law titles in North America, Self-Counsel Press published its first Divorce Guide in 1971. Self-Counsel produces business how-to, legal reference, self-help, and practical psychology books. Topical areas include entrepreneurship, the legal system, business training, the family, and human resources development and management. The house also produces titles geared to lifestyles and business and legal issues in Florida, Oregon, and Washington.

The house tries to anticipate a need for basic, understandable information and fill that need by publishing an informative, clearly written, and reasonably priced how-to book for the layperson. They publish as many as 30 new titles each year, as well as revising more than 50 of their backlist titles to ensure that their books are always up to date regarding changes in legislation or current procedures and practices. All legal titles are authored by lawyers.

Some titles include *19 Ways to Survive: Small-Business Strategies for a Tough Economy* by Lynn Spry and Philip Spry; *Employee Management for Small Business* by Lin Grensing-Pophal, SPHR; *Estate Planning Through Family Meetings* by Lynne Butler; *Managing Off-Site Staff* by Lin Grensing-Pophal, SPHR; and *Marketing Your Product* by Donald Cyr and Douglas Gray.

Email queries can be sent to orders@self-counsel.com. Direct physical proposals and SASEs to the Acquisitions Editor in either Canada or the U.S., depending on the market for which you are writing.

Diana Douglas, President, ddouglas@self-counsel.com

INDEPENDENT U.S. PRESSES

SEVEN STORIES

SIETE CUENTOS

140 Watts Street, New York, NY 10013

212-226-8760   fax: 212-226-1411

www.sevenstories.com   email: info@sevenstories.com

Seven Stories Press is an independent book publisher based in New York City, with distribution throughout the U.S., Canada, England, Australia, and New Zealand. Under the direction of publisher Dan Simon, perhaps no other small independent house in America has consistently attracted so many important voices away from the corporate publishing sector.

Authors include Nelson Algren, Kate Braverman, Octavia Butler, Harriet Scott Chessman, Assia Djebar, Ariel Dorfman, Martin Duberman, Alan Dugan, Annie Ernaux, Barry Gifford, Stanley Moss, Peter Plate, Charley Rosen, Ted Solotaroff, Lee Stringer, Alice Walker, Martin Winckler, and Kurt Vonnegut, together with political titles by voices of conscience, including Daw Aung San Suu Kyi, Tom Athanasiou, the Boston Women's Health Book Collective, the Center for Constitutional Rights, Fairness & Accuracy in Reporting, Noam Chomsky, Angela Davis, Shere Hite, Robert McChesney, Phil Jackson, Ralph Nader, Gary Null, Benjamin Pogrund, Project Censored, Luis J. Rodriguez, Barbara Seaman, Vandana Shiva, Leora Tanenbaum, Koigi wa Wamwere, Gary Webb, and Howard Zinn.

On several notable occasions, Seven Stories has stepped in to publish—on First Amendment grounds—important books that were being refused the right to publish for political reasons, including Pulitzer Prize-winning journalist Gary Webb's *Dark Alliance*, about the CIA-Contra-crack cocaine connection; Carol Felsenthal's biography of the Newhouse family, *Citizen Newhouse*; and distinguished journalist and death row inmate Mumia Abu-Jamal's censored essays in *All Things Censored*.

Recent Seven Stories titles include *Racing While Black* by Leonard Miller and Andrew Simon; *Jesus of Nazareth* by Paul Verhoeven; *Talk Softly* by Cynthia O'Neal; *Bad Shoes and the Women Who Love Them* by Leora Tanenbaum; and *Propaganda Inc.: Selling America's Culture to the World* by Nancy Snow.

SIETE CUENTOS

Siete Cuentos, Seven Stories' Spanish-language imprint, launched in 2000 and now edited by Sara Villa, represents a major ongoing effort on the part of Seven Stories to introduce important English-language texts to Spanish-language readers on the one hand, for example the Spanish-language editions of *Our Bodies, Ourselves, Nuestros cuerpos, nuestras vidas*, a project of the Boston Women's Health Book Collective; and Howard Zinn's *A People's History of the United States, La otra historia de los Estados Unidos*; and on the other hand to provide Spanish-language readers in the U.S.

with the best in fiction and literature written in Spanish. The literary side of Siete Cuentos has published new and classic texts by Ariel Dorfman, including *Death and the Maiden, La muerte y la doncella* and *Heading South, Looking North, Rumbo al sur, deseando el norte,* and new fiction by Ángela Vallvey and Sonia Rivera-Valdés.

Titles from Siete Cuentos include *11 de Septiembre* by Noam Chomsky; *A la caza del ultimo hombre salvaje* by Angela Vallvey; *La muerte y la doncella* by Ariel Dorfman; and *Nuestros cuerpos, nuestras vidas* by the Boston Women's Health Book Collective.

Seven Stories is accepting submissions of query letters with one or two sample chapters only. Direct your submission to Acquisitions.

Dan Simon, Publisher

SHAMBHALA

NEW SEEDS

TRUMPETER BOOKS

WEATHERHILL BOOKS

P.O. Box 308, Boston, MA 02115

617-424-0030   fax: 617-236-1563

www.shambhala.com   email: editors@shambhala.com

With classic titles like *Meditation in Action* by Chögyam Trungpa, *Writing Down the Bones* by Natalie Goldberg, and *The Tao of Physics* by Fritjof Capra, Shambhala is a foremost representative of the wave of publishers specializing in the arena of contemporary globalized spiritual and cultural interest. Since Shambhala's inception (the house was founded in 1969), the field has blossomed into a still-burgeoning readership, as underscored by the many smaller independent presses and large corporate houses that tend this market. Yet Shambhala quietly continues to publish "what's real and not the glitz."

Shambhala publishes hardcover and paperback titles on creativity, philosophy, psychology, medical arts and healing, mythology, folklore, religion, art, literature, cooking, martial arts, and cultural studies. Shambhala generally issues a modest list of new titles each year and tends a flourishing backlist; the house periodically updates some of its perennial sellers in revised editions.

Shambhala produces a number of distinct lines, including gift editions and special interest imprints. Shambhala Dragon Editions accents the sacred teachings of Asian masters. Shambhala Centaur Editions offers classics of world literature in small-sized gift editions. The New Science Library concentrates on titles relating to science, technology, and the environment. Shambhala co-publishes C.G. Jung

Foundation Books with the C.G. Jung Foundation for Analytical Psychology. Shambhala Redstone Editions are fine-boxed sets composed of books, postcards, games, art objects, and foldouts. Shambhala Lion Editions are spoken-word audiotape cassette presentations. New Seeds publishes such Christian mystics as Thomas Merton; Trumpeter Books publishes humanistic titles with mainstream marketability. Integral Books, an imprint with author Ken Wilber as editorial director, was launched in 2007. Shambhala purchased Weatherhill in 2004, giving it the classic *Zen Mind, Beginner's Mind* by Japanese Zen master Shunryu Suzuki.

Recent titles from Shambhala include *The Fearless Heart: The Practice of Living with Courage and Compassion* by Pema Chödrön; *Turning the Wheel of Truth: Commentary on the Buddha's First Teaching* by Ajahn Sucitto; *Genius of the Transcendent: Mystical Writings of Jakob Boehme* translated by Michael Birkel and Jeff Bach; and *Things Pertaining to Bodhi: The Thirty-Seven Aids to Enlightenment* by Chan Master Sheng Yen.

NEW SEEDS

New Seeds is a new imprint dedicated to publishing books that present the wisdom of the Christian faith for everyone—with a special emphasis on prayer and contemplation. Some new titles include *Where God Happens: Discovering Christ in One Another* by Rowan Williams; *The Practice of the Presence of God* by Brother Lawrence; and *No Man Is an Island* by Thomas Merton.

TRUMPETER BOOKS

Trumpeter Books is a new imprint from Shambhala covering a broad range of topics and genres—including psychology, health, literature, and personal growth—all aimed at nourishing and celebrating our positive human potential. Some titles include *The Autism Mom's Survival Guide (for dads, too!)* by Susan Senator; *Beyond the Abbey Gates* by Catherine MacCoun; *Black Elk in Paris* by Kate Horsley; *Climbing Jacob's Ladder: One Man's Journey to Rediscover a Jewish Spiritual Tradition* by Alan Morinis; and *The Creative Family: How to Encourage Imagination and Nurture Family Connections* by Amanda Blake Soule.

WEATHERHILL BOOKS

Weatherhill specializes in books on art, martial arts, and Eastern culture. Shambhala purchased Weatherhill and its backlist of 150 titles in 2004. Some Weatherhill titles are *77 Dances: Japanese Calligraphy by Poets, Monks, and Scholars 1568–1868* by Stephen Addiss; *The Art of Ancient India* by John Huntington et al; and *The Art of Ground Fighting: Principles and Techniques* by Marc Tedeschi.

Shambhala distributes to the trade via Random House and also services individual and special orders through its own house fulfillment department.

Proposals and SASEs should be directed to the Editorial Assistant, James Rudnickas. Email submissions can go to customerservice@shambhala.com.

James Rudnickas, Editorial Assistant

Jonathan Green, Associate Publisher

David O'Neal, Senior Editor

Emily Bower, Editor

Eden Steinberg, Editor (Trumpeter Books)

M. E. SHARPE

EAST GATE BOOKS

SHARPE REFERENCE

80 Business Park Drive, Armonk, NY 10504

914-273-1800/800-541-6563   fax: 914-273-2106

www.mesharpe.com

Founded in 1958, M.E. Sharpe is a privately held publisher of books and journals in the social sciences and humanities, including economics, political science, management, public administration, and history. They also publish both original works and translations in Asian and East European studies. Several Nobel Prize winners, including Ōe Kenzaburo and Wasily Leontief, are among the M.E. Sharpe authors.

The East Gate imprint publishes in Asian studies. M.E. Sharpe also publishes single- and multivolume reference works designed to meet the needs of students and researchers from high school through college under the Sharpe Reference imprint.

Recent titles include *The Foreign Policy of Russia: Changing Systems, Enduring Interests* by Robert Donaldson and Joseph Nogee; *Handbook of Urban Services: A Basic Guide for Local Governments* by Charles K. Coe; *Dagestan: Russian Hegemony and Islamic Resistance in the North Caucasus* by Robert Ware and Enver Kisriev; and *Entrepreneurial Financial Management: An Applied Approach* by Jeffery Cornwall et al.

EAST GATE BOOKS

The East Gate Books imprint is dedicated to the publication of works that lead to a greater understanding of Asia and its peoples. It represents the best in Asian Studies publishing by scholars, students, and general interest audiences. Recent titles include *Christianity in China: A Scholars' Guide to Resources in the Libraries* by Xiaoxin Wu; *End of the Maoist Era: Chinese Politics During the Twilight of Cultural Revolution 1972–1976* by Frederick Teiwes and Warren Sun; and *Modern East Asia: An Introductory History* by John H. Miller.

SHARPE REFERENCE

Sharpe Reference was created to meet the needs of students and researchers in the high school, public, and college library. Their books provide easy access to a broad array of curriculum related information in the social sciences and humanities; music, art, history, politics, and civil rights are among the fields covered.

Some titles include *Booms and Busts: An Encyclopedia of Economic History from Tulipmania of the 1630s to the Global Financial Crisis of the 21st Century* by James Ciment; and *The Early Republic and Antebellum America: An Encyclopedia of Social, Political, Cultural, and Economic History* by Christopher G. Bates.

All queries with SASEs may be directed to Patricia Kolb. Please, no email queries.

Patricia Kolb, Editorial Director—All areas, all disciplines; pkolb@mesharpe.com

Lynn Taylor, Executive Editor—Economics, business, media studies; ltaylor@mesharpe.com

Harry Briggs, Executive Editor—Management, marketing, public administration; hbriggs@mesharpe.com

---

SIERRA CLUB BOOKS

85 Second Street, 2nd Floor, San Francisco, CA 94105

415-977-5500   fax: 415-977-5799

www.sierraclub.org/books   email: books.publishing@sierraclub.org

The Sierra Club, founded in 1892 by John Muir, has for more than a century stood in the forefront of the study and protection of the earth's scenic, environmental, and ecological resources; Sierra Club Books is part of the nonprofit effort the club carries on as a public trust.

Sierra Club publishes works in the categories of nature, technology, outdoor activities, mountaineering, health, gardening, natural history, travel, and environmental issues. Sierra Club series include the Adventure Travel Guides, Sierra Club Tote books, Naturalists Guides, Natural Traveler, the John Muir Library, and Guides to the Natural Area of the United States. Sierra Club Books has a strong division that publishes works dedicated to children and young adults.

The books represent the following areas: the finest in outdoor photographic artistry; thought-provoking discussions of ecological issues; literary masterworks by naturalist authors; and authoritative handbooks to the best recreational activities the natural world offers. Today, the need to protect and expand John Muir's legacy is greater than ever—to help stop the relentless abuse of irreplaceable wilderness land, save endangered species, and protect the global environment.

Recent titles include *Gloryland* by Shelton Johnson; *Coal Country: Rising Up Against Mountaintop Removal Mining* edited by Shirley Stewart Burns et al; *Ancient Futures: Lessons from Ladakh for a Globalizing World* by Helena Norberg-Hodge; *Bike Touring: The Sierra Club Guide to Travel on Two Wheels* by Raymond Bridge; and *Coming Clean: Breaking America's Addiction to Oil and Coal* by Michael Brune.

Sierra Club Books are distributed by the University of California Press.

Email submissions will not be accepted. Sierra Club Books for Children is not currently accepting any unsolicited manuscripts. Direct queries and SASEs to the Editorial Department.

Helen Sweetland, Publisher

Ellen Landau, Acting Editorial Director

SIETE CUENTOS [SEE SEVEN STORIES]

SIGNATURE BOOKS

564 West 400 North Street, Salt Lake City, UT 84116-3411

801-531-1483   fax: 801-531-1488

www.signaturebooks.com   email: people@signaturebooks.com

Signature Books was founded in 1980 to promote the study of Mormonism and related issues pertaining to the Rocky Mountain area. The Signature list emphasizes contemporary literature, as well as scholarly works relevant to the Intermountain West. Signature Books publishes subjects that range from outlaw biographies and Mormonism to speculative theology, from demographics to humor. In addition, Signature publishes novels and collections of poetry of local interest. They publish 12 new titles per year.

Recent titles include *A Sense of Order and Other Stories* by Jack Harrell; *Candid Insights of a Mormon Apostle: The Diaries of Abraham H. Cannon, 1889–1895* by Edward Lyman; *Dimensions of Faith: A Mormon Studies Reader* by Stephen C. Taysom; *Her Side of It* by Marilyn Bushman-Carlton; and *The Amazing Colossal Apostle: The Search for the Historical Paul* by Robert M. Price.

Signature Publications oversees distribution of its titles via in-house ordering services and a national network of wholesalers. Their acquisitions editors prefer submissions from authors who have been previously published in peer-reviewed forums. Query letters and SASEs should be directed to the Acquisitions Editor.

Gary James Bergera, Acquisitions Editor

Ron Priddis, Managing Director

Jani Fleet, Editor

SILHOUETTE [SEE HARLEQUIN ENTERPRISES, LTD.]

SIMCHA PRESS [SEE HEALTH COMMUNICATIONS, INC.]

GIBBS SMITH, PUBLISHER

P.O. Box 667, Layton, UT 84041

801-544-9800   fax: 801-546-8852

www.gibbs-smith.com

Founded in 1969, Gibbs Smith, Publisher, specializes in beautifully illustrated lifestyle books, with topics including design and architecture, cooking, business, holiday, sports, and children's books. From their farm in Utah, the editors produce books with a mission to enrich and inspire humankind the world over.

Recent titles include *Pink Princess Cupcakes* by Barbara Beery; *Pocketdoodles for Boys* by Chris Sabatino; *Pocketdoodles for Girls* by Gibbs M. Smith; *The Big Book of Gross Stuff* by Bart King; *Origami Toys* by Paul Jackson; *Chinese Slanguage* by Michael Ellis; and *Southern Bouquets* by Melissa Binger.

Gibbs Smith no longer accepts physical manuscripts. Email duribe@gibbs-smith.com for manuscript submission guidelines.

Suzanne Taylor, Vice President and Editorial Director

Linda Nimori, Editor

Melissa Barlow, Editor

Jennifer Grillone, Senior Editor

SOHO PRESS, INC.

SOHO CONSTABLE

SOHO CRIME

853 Broadway, New York, NY 10003

212-260-1900   fax: 212-260-1902

www.sohopress.com   email: soho@sohopress.com

Soho Press, Inc., an independent press established in 1986, publishes literary fiction and nonfiction.

Soho Press primarily publishes fiction, with the occasional autobiography or cultural historical account. They are eager to find work from new writers and place a high priority on publishing quality unsolicited materials.

Recent titles include *Stettin Station* by David Downing; *Gunshot Road* by Adrian Hyland; and *The Broken Circle* by Shirley Wells.

SOHO CONSTABLE

Soho Constable is a new imprint launched in 2008. The press will be releasing mysteries published across the pond by British house Constable & Robinson. The books are both historical and modern-day mysteries set mostly in England and Scotland. Some recent titles include *Strange Images of Death* by Barbara Cleverly; *The Curious Incident at Claridge's* by R.T. Raichev; and *The Pull of the Moon* by Diane Jane.

SOHO CRIME

The Soho Crime imprint focuses on procedurals set in exotic locales. Some recent titles include *Blood Moon* by Garry Disher; *A Deadly Paradise* by Grace Brophy; *The Lord of Death* by Eliot Pattison; and *Random Violence* by Jassy Mackenzie.

No submissions via email. The editors prefer a query letter with three chapters of a completed work (preferably the first three chapters), with a brief outline and CV. Direct submissions with SASEs to:

Laura Hruska, Publisher and Editor-in-Chief

Katie Herman, Editor

Ron Ben Hruska, Editor

INDEPENDENT U.S. PRESSES

SOURCEBOOKS, INC.

CUMBERLAND HOUSE

LANDMARK

MEDIAFUSION

SPHINX PUBLISHING

1935 Brookdale Road, Suite 139, Naperville, IL 60563

630-961-3900/800-43-BRIGHT   fax: 630-961-2168

www.sourcebooks.com   email: info@sourcebooks.com

CASABLANCA

995 Connecticut Ave, Suite 5310, Bridgeport, CT 06607

203-333-9399

FIRE

JABBERWOCKY

390 Fifth Ave, Suite 907, New York, NY 10018

212-414-1701

Chicago's leading independent book publisher, Sourcebooks is exceptionally strong in reference, romance, parenting, self-help, children's, and fiction titles. Under the MediaFusion imprint, Sourcebooks also publishes mixed media titles including *Poetry Speaks to Children* and the Sourcebooks Shakespeare series. The house was founded in 1987 by Dominique Raccah, and it has been one of the fastest-growing companies in America, with many bestsellers.

Sourcebooks is the new publisher for *Jeff Herman's Guide to Book Publishers, Editors, and Literary Agents*.

In 2007, Sourcebooks launched the Jabberwocky imprint for children's and young-adult titles, including *The Fairy Chronicles* by J. H. Sweet and *New York Times* bestseller *I Love You More* by Laura Duksta, illustrated by Karen Keesler. In the Landmark fiction imprint, the house has done very well with books that continue famous stories from Jane Austen including *Mr. Darcy's Diary* and *More Letters from Pemberley: Mrs. Darcy's Story Unfolds* by Jane Dawkins.

Other Sourcebooks imprints include Casablanca Press, with romance genre fiction and nonfiction titles and Sphinx Publishing, which focuses on self-help law titles. In 2008, Sourcebooks acquired Cumberland House, publishers of Gregory Lang's *Why a Daughter Needs a Dad* and other various titles.

Recent Sourcebooks titles include *2011 The Naked Roommate Boxed Calender* by Harlan Cohen; *Cottage by the Sea* by Ciji Ware; *Give Us This Day* by R. F. Delderfield; and *I Love This Bar* by Carolyn Brown.

Sourcebooks is actively seeking romance fiction, and authors of romance may submit a Word document including their first four chapters via email to deb.werksman@sourcebooks.com. For all genres other than romance, the house is only accepting fiction from agents. Nonfiction authors should direct book proposals by mail to Editorial Submissions. No email submissions or phone calls (with the exception of romance or children's titles). Please see the Sourcebooks website for additional information.

Agents may direct submissions to:

Todd Stocke, Editorial Director—General nonfiction, reference, multimedia formats; todd.stocke@sourcebooks.com

Peter Lynch, Editorial Manager, Trade—Business, general nonfiction, fiction; peter.lynch@sourcebooks.com

Shana Drehs, Senior Editor—Adult trade, gift books; shana.drehs@sourcebooks.com

Deborah Werksman, Editorial Manager, Romance—deb.werksman@sourcebooks.com

Rebecca Frazer, Editor, Children's—Picture books, beginning chapter books, and middle-grade fiction, both series and stand-alone titles; genres include friendship, mystery, humor, fantasy, and historical fiction; rebecca.frazer@sourcebooks.com

SPIRE BOOKS [SEE BAKER PUBLISHING GROUP]

SPRINGER

233 Spring Street, New York, NY 10013

212-460-1500/800-SPRINGER   fax: 212-460-1575

www.springer.com   email: service-ny@springer.com

Springer is one of the world's most renowned scientific publishing companies. Its publications cover subjects ranging from the natural sciences, mathematics, engineering, and computer science to medicine and psychology. In the fields of economics and law, Springer offers an increasing number of books in management science. Since the 2004 merger with Dutch scientific house Kluwer Academic Publishing, the range of products has increased; it now includes publications on the arts and social science.

Springer's authors are highly qualified experts. More than 150 Nobel Prize winners, plus scientists, doctors, and engineers such as Robert Koch, Fredinand Sauerbruch, Albert Einstein, Werner von Siemens, and Otto Hahn have published their works at Springer.

Recent titles include *Deconvolution Problems in Nonparametric Statistics* by A. Meister; *Non-Life Insurance Mathematics: An Introduction with the Poisson Process* by Thomas Mikosch; and *Large Random Matrices: Lectures on Macroscopic Asymptotics* by Alice Guionner.

Submit proposals and SASEs to:

William Curtis, Editorial Director—Life sciences and medicine; william.curtis@springer.com

Hans Koelsch, Directorial Editor—Mathematics, physics, engineering; hans.koelsch@springer.com

John Kimmel, Executive Editor—Statistics, computer science; john.kimmel@springer.com

SQUARE ONE PUBLISHERS

115 Herricks Road, Garden City Park, NY 11040

516-535-2010/877-900-BOOK   fax: 516-535-2014

www.squareonepublishers.com

Square One publishing sees itself as recapturing the spirit of the 1920s, '30s, and '40s: the Golden Age of independent publishing. They feel that advances in print technology have given birth to a revival of the original sense of entrepreneurial spirit and excitement that characterized the early pioneers. Supporting this conviction, *Publishers Weekly* has named Square One Publishers one of the fastest-growing indie publishers in the U.S. for the third year in a row. Square One is interested in manuscripts on alternative health, collectibles, cooking, gambling, health, how-to, parenting, personal finance, postcards, self-help, and writing.

Recent titles from Square One include *Acid-Alkaline Cookbook* by Bonnie Ross; *Creative Therapy* by Janet Tubbs; *Fifty Money-Saving Tips for Every Landlord* by Mike McLean; *Health from the Hive: Your Beeline to Health, Beauty, and Longevity* by Julie and Richie Gerber; and *Introducing Macrobiotic Cooking* by Wendy Esko and Aveline Kushi.

Address queries and SASEs to the Acquisitions Editor.

ST. ANTHONY MESSENGER PRESS

Franciscan Communications

28 West Liberty Street, Cincinnati, OH 45202

513-241-5615 /800-488-0488   fax: 513-241-0399

www.sampbooks.org   email: samadmin@americancatholic.org

St. Anthony Messenger Press (founded in 1970) and Franciscan Communications publishes Catholic religious works and resources for parishes, schools, and individuals. The house also owns the video/print imprints Ikonographics and Fischer Productions.

Areas of St. Anthony Messenger's publishing interest include Franciscan topics, Catholic identity, family life, morality and ethics, parish ministry, pastoral ministry, prayer helps, sacraments, saints and Christian heroes, Scripture, seasonal favorites, small-group resources, spirituality for every day, children's books, and youth ministry. The house produces books (hardcover and paperback, many in economically priced editions), magazines, DVDs and CDs, as well as educational programs and an award-winning Website.

Recent titles include *The Simple Way: Meditations on the Words of Saint Francis* by Murray Bodo; *Awakening to Prayer: A Woman's Perspective* by Claire Wagner; *Embracing Latina Spirituality* by Michelle A. Gonzales; and *John Dear on Peace: An Introduction to His Life and Work* by Patricia P. Normile, SFO.

St. Anthony Messenger Press also offers music CDs, computer software, and DVDs.

St. Anthony Messenger Press distributes books through Ingram, Spring Arbor, Riverside Distributors, Appalachian, Inc., Baker & Taylor, and ABS/Guardian.

Query letters and SASEs should be directed to:

Lisa Biedenbach, Editorial Director, Books, LisaB@AmericanCatholic.org

STEEPLE HILL [SEE HARLEQUIN ENTERPRISES, LTD.]

STERLING PUBLISHING CO., INC.

A division of Barnes and Noble

387 Park Avenue South, 10th Floor, New York, NY 10016-8810

212-532-7160

www.sterlingpublishing.com   email: specialsales@sterlingpublishing.com

Sterling Publishing (founded 1949 and acquired by Barnes and Noble in 2003) is one of the world's leading publishers of nonfiction titles with more than 5,000 books in print. Among its bestselling titles are *The Big Book of Knitting*, *The Good Housekeeping Cookbook*, and *Windows on the World Complete Wine Course*. Subject categories in which the company excels include puzzles and games, crafts, gardening, woodworking, health, and children's books.

With an unusual title and packaging, *Yoga for Wimps* became a bestseller in 2001 and marked the launch of an ongoing series that includes *Orchids for Wimps* and *Meditation for Wimps*. Another success is the novelty-packaged Sit and Solve series. Many of Sterling's children's books, such as *Sometimes I Like to Curl Up in a Ball* and *I Know a Rhino*, are critically acclaimed bestsellers.

Recent titles include *The New Sonoma Diet* by Connie Gutterson Rd, PhD; *Clean Start* by Terry Walters; *I Can Make You Confident* by Paul McKenna; and *Rose Elliot's New Complete Vegetarian* by Rose Elliot.

To submit to Sterling, send a proposal with CV and SASE via regular mail. Submissions should be sent to the attention of the category editor, e.g., the material on a woodworking book should be addressed to the Woodworking Editor; a craft book proposal should be addressed to the Craft Editor; and so on. All children's book submissions should be sent to the attention of the Children's Book Editor.

Michael Fragnito, Vice President, Editorial Director

Barbara Berger, Executive Editor

Jennifer Williams, Senior Editor

Laura Swerdloff, Editor

Kate Zimmermann, Associate Editor

Melanie Madden, Assistant Editor

STEWART, TABORI & CHANG [SEE HARRY N. ABRAMS, INC.]

SYBEX, INC. [SEE JOHN WILEY & SONS]

TAYLOR TRADE [SEE ROWMAN & LITTLEFIELD]

THAMES & HUDSON, INC.

500 Fifth Avenue, New York, NY 10110

212-354-3763   fax: 212-398-1252

www.thamesandhudsonusa.com   email: BookInfo@thames.wwnorton.com

Thames & Hudson is one of the world's most eminent publishers of illustrated books. The house releases high-quality, well-printed books on art, architecture, design, photography, decorative arts, archaeology, history, religion, and spirituality, as well as a number of titles for children.

Recent titles include *The Andy Goldsworthy Project* by Molly Donovan et al; *Paris Vogue Covers 1920–2009* by Sonia Rachline; *The Hermes Scarf* by Nadine Coleno; *The Jewelry of Southeast Asia* by Anne Richter; *In the Darkroom: An Illustrated Guide to Photographic Processes Before the Digital Age* by Sarah Kennel et al; *The World of the Ancient Greeks* by John Camp and Elizabeth Fisher; and *The Highland Clans* by Alistair Moffat.

Thames & Hudson is distributed in the U.S. by W.W. Norton & Company, Inc., and in Canada by Penguin.

Authors send queries with SASE to Submissions or email BookInfo@thames .wwnorton.com.

Peter Warner, President

Susan Dwyer, Vice President

THEATRE COMMUNICATIONS GROUP

520 Eighth Avenue, 24th Floor, New York, NY 10018-4156

212-609-5900   fax: 212-609-5901

www.tcg.org   email: tcg@tcg.org

The mission of the Theatre Communications Group is to strengthen, nurture, and promote the not-for-profit professional American theater by celebrating differences in aesthetics, culture, organizational structure and geography. The house produces *American Theatre* magazine and the ArtSEARCH employment bulletin. They also publish plays, translations, and theater reference books. TCG awards grants to individuals and institutions; interested authors should peruse the house website for a myriad of opportunities to connect to the professional theater world.

Recent titles include *Road Show* by Stephen Sondheim; *Plays from the Boom Box Galaxy* edited by Kim Euell & Robert Alexander; *Birth and After Birth and Other Plays* by Tina Howe; and *Salaam.Peace* by Holly Hill and Dina Amin.

Direct queries with SASEs to either Kathy or Molly. Email submissions can be sent to tcg@tcg.org.

Terence Nemeth, Publisher

Kathy Sova, Editorial Director

Molly Metzler, Associate Editor

Alexander Barreto, Associate Editor

TIN HOUSE BOOKS

2601 N.W. Thurman Street, Portland, OR 97210

503-473-8663

www.tinhouse.com/books

After three years working with Bloomsbury USA on a joint publishing venture known as Tin House Books/Bloomsbury, Tin House Books is now an independent company with offices in Portland, Oregon. Tin House continues to publish new literary voices as well as reprints of contemporary and classic works of fiction and nonfiction. The mission of Tin House Books remains constant: to publish compelling and authentic narratives of our time. Tin House salutes the artistic edge but remains rooted in the tenets of the classic storytelling tradition.

Tin House Books' first focus is the launch of the New Voice Series: story cycles, collections, novels, and memoir by first-time authors. The house also publishes the *Tin House* literary journal.

Recent titles include *The Hour: A Cocktail Manifesto* by Bernard DeVoto; *Mentor: A Memoir* by Tom Grimes; *River House* by Sarahlee Lawrence; and *A Householder's Guide to the Universe* by Harriet Fasenfest.

Tin House Books no longer reads unsolicited submissions by authors without representation, but this may change. Check the Tin House Books website for more information.

Lee Montgomery, Editorial Director

Meg Storey, Associate Editor

Tony Perez, Associate Editor

TRAFALGAR SQUARE BOOKS

PO Box 257, 388 Howe Hill Road, North Pomfret, VT 05053

802-457-1911/800-423-4525

www.horseandriderbooks.com   email: info@horseandriderbooks.com

Trafalgar Square published its first horse book, *Centered Riding* by Sally Swift, in 1985 and the book remains one of the bestselling horse books of all time. This book was the spark that led Ted and Caroline Robbins, Trafalgar Square's owners, to start up a horse book publishing business. Previously, Trafalgar Square was a book distribution outlet for British publishers. Since its beginnings in 1985, Trafalgar Square has published over 85 horse books, and has a growing list of titles on dressage, jumping, training, western riding, horse care, driving, and more. Trafalgar Square has also ventured into video, DVD, and audio publishing.

Trafalgar Square has published such authors as Jane Savoi, Linda Tellington-Jones, William Steinkraus, Mary Wanless, Clinton Anderson, Charles de Kunffy, Sylvia Loch, Richard Shrake, Betsy Steiner, Kyra Kyrklund, Alois Podhajsky, Paul Belasik, Jessica Jahiel, and more.

Recent titles from Trafalgar Square include *Better than Bombproof* by Sergeant Rick Pelicano; *Beyond a Whisper* by Ryan Gingerich; *Clinton Anderson's Lessons Well Learned*; *Donkeys: Miniature, Standard, and Mammoth* by Stephen R. Purdy, DVM; and *Dressage Training—Customized* by Britta Schöffmann.

Send queries and SASEs by email to info@horseandriderbooks.com.

TUTTLE PUBLISHING

A Member of the Periplus Publishing Group

364 Innovation Drive, North Clarendon, VT 05759

802-773-8930/800-526-2778   fax: 802-773-6993/800-329-8885

www.tuttlepublishing.com   email: info@tuttlepublishing.com

Tuttle Publishing was founded by Charles Tuttle in Tokyo in 1948. The publisher's mission was to publish "books to span the East and West." In the early 1950s the company began publishing a large number of titles on Japanese language, arts, and culture. In 1983, Charles Tuttle was awarded the Order of the Sacred Treasure by the Emperor of Japan for his services to Japanese-American understanding. Tuttle is now the USA arm of the Periplus Publishing Group, the world's leading publisher of books on Asia.

Eric Oey, a cousin of Charles E. Tuttle, founded Periplus Editions in 1988 in Berkeley, California, and merged the two companies in 1996. With offices in Vermont, Singapore, Tokyo, Hong Kong, and Jakarta, Tuttle Publishing has become the largest English-language book publishing and distribution company in Asia.

Recent titles include *At Home & In the Mood* by Luke Mangan; *Sri Lankan Cooking* by Douglas Bullis; *A Cook's Journey to Japan* by Sarah Marx Feldner; *Rosalind Creasy's Recipes from The Garden*; and *Malaysian Cooking* by Carol Selva Rajah.

No email submissions, please. To submit, send a complete book proposal and SASE to Editorial Acquisitions.

William Notte, Associate Editor, Acquisitions

TYNDALE HOUSE PUBLISHERS

351 Executive Drive, Carol Stream, IL 60188

800-323-9400   fax: 800-684-0247

www.tyndale.com   email: customer@tyndale.com

Tyndale House Publishers (founded in 1962) offers a comprehensive program in Christian living: devotional, inspirational, and general nonfiction, from a nondenominational evangelical perspective. Tyndale's publishing interest also encompasses religious fiction and children's books. The house publishes the bestselling Living Bible and the Left Behind series. Tyndale produces hardcover, trade paperback, and mass-market paperback originals, as well as reprints.

Tyndale Children's books target all ages from birth through high school. Most are on topics of specific interest to children in Christian families (*i.e.*, the Bible or prayer). The others are on themes that interest all children (*i.e.*, friends or fears), but these themes are presented from a clearly Christian perspective.

Tyndale fiction includes mainstream novels, as well as a number of inspirational romance series, including works set in Revolutionary War and Civil War milieus. The house is interested in evangelical Christian-theme romance in other historical periods (including Regency), as well as those with a humorous twist.

Recent Tyndale titles include *Crossing Oceans* by Gina Holmes; *Why I Stayed* by Gayle Haggard; *The One Year Mother-Daughter Devo* by Dannah Gresh; *The Daily God Book—Through the Bible* by Skip Heitzig; and *An Army of Ordinary People* by Felicity Dale.

Tyndale House oversees its own distribution. Tyndale also distributes books from Focus on the Family.

Tyndale is not accepting manuscript proposals from anyone except literary agents or writers whose work has already been published.

Jonathan Farrar, Acquisitions Director
Carol Traver, Acquisitions Editor

UNIVERSE INTERNATIONAL PUBLICATIONS [SEE RIZZOLI, USA]

UNITED CHURCH PRESS [SEE THE PILGRIM PRESS]

UPPER ROOM PUBLISHING

DISCIPLESHIP RESOURCES

Delivery address:

1908 Grand Avenue, Nashville TN 37212

Mailing address:

P.O. Box 840, Nashville, TN 37202-0840

615-340-7200

www.upperroom.org

A program of the General Board of Discipleship, Upper Room is an ecumenical nonprofit religious publisher focused on books that help readers discover, develop, and enrich a life of devotion and attention to God. Books published by Upper Room present to individuals and groups the possibility and promise of an intimate, life-giving relationship with God. These books further assist readers along their spiritual path by offering guidance toward a disciplined life that includes prayer and action. The Upper Room publishes between 25 and 30 books each year.

Recent titles from Upper Room Books include *52 Ways to Create an AIDS-Free World* by Donald E. Messer; *Aging and Ministry in the 21st Century* by Richard H. Gentzler, Jr.; *Being the Presence of Christ* by Daniel Vestal; *Compassion: Cultivating a Good Heart* by Amy Lyles Wilson; and *Do Not Live Afraid: Faith in a Fearful World* by John Indermark.

DISCIPLESHIP RESOURCES

Discipleship Resources is now an imprint of Upper Room Publishing. Areas of publishing interest encompass United Methodist history, doctrine, and theology, as well as Bible study, Christian education, ethnic church concerns, evangelism, ministry of the laity, stewardship, United Methodist men, and worship.

The mission of Discipleship Resources is "to provide quality resources that respond to the needs of United Methodist leaders and congregation members, as they seek to become and encourage others to become disciples of Jesus Christ."

Recent titles from Discipleship Resources include *Does Your Church Have a Prayer? In Mission Toward the Promised Land* by Marc Brown et al; *What Kind of Man Is Joseph, and What Kind of Man Are You?* by Eugene Blair; *A Blueprint for Discipleship: Wesley's General Rules as a Guide for Christian Living* by Kevin Watson; and *Not Just a One-Night Stand: Ministry with the Homeless* by John Flowers and Karen Vannoy.

Query letters with one sample chapter and SASEs should be directed to the Editor; email submissions may be sent to kduncan@gbod.org.

URJ PRESS

633 Third Avenue, New York, NY 10017

888-489-8242/212-650-4120   fax: 212-650-4119

www.urjpress.com   email: press@urj.org

Formerly UAHC Press, URJ Press publishes in the areas of religion (Jewish), Reform Judaism, textbooks, audiovisual materials, social action, biography, and life cycles and holidays. In its trade categories, URJ Press accents juvenile fiction and adult nonfiction books, as well as titles in basic Judaism and inspirational works. The house catalogs books, CDs, DVDs, and multimedia products, suitable for use in both the classroom and the home.

URJ Press provides the highest quality in religious educational materials and has done so for well over 100 years. The publishers are committed to providing their readers with the foremost in materials and service, to be a continuing resource for books, publications, CDs, DVDs, and multimedia.

Indicative of URJ Press interests are *Anthology of Jewish Art Song, Vol. III: A Sametenem Ponim* by Richard Hereld; *Did Moses Really Have Horns? And Other Myths About Jews and Judaism* by Rifat Sonsino; *Entrée to Judaism: A Culinary Exploration of the Jewish Diaspora* by Tina Wasserman; and *Galilee Diary: Reflections on Daily Life in Israel* by Marc Rosenstein.

Query letters, proposals, and SASEs should be directed to:

Michael H. Goldberg, Editor-in-Chief

VEDANTA PRESS

Vedanta Society of Southern California

1946 Vedanta Place, Hollywood, CA 90068

800-816-2242   323-960-1736

www.vedanta.com   email: info@vedanta.com

Vedanta's publishing interests include meditation, religions and philosophies, and women's studies. In addition to its list of titles imported from the East (primarily from Indian publishers), Vedanta's program embraces works of Western origin. The publisher catalogs titles from other publishers and also sells CDs and DVDs.

The house publishes books on the philosophy of Vedanta, with an aim to engage a wide variety of temperaments, using a broad spectrum of methods, in order to attain the realization of each individual personality's divinity within. Vedanta Press (founded in 1947) is a subsidiary of the Vedanta Society of Southern California.

Recent titles include *Eminent Indian Women: From the Vedic Age to the Present*; *Inner Peace in a Busy World* by Cliff Johnson; *Swami Vivekananda on Himself* by Swami Vivekananda; and *Self Mastery* by Swami Paramananda.

Vedanta publishes many classic Vedic works in a variety of editions and translations. Among them is *Bhagavad Gita: The Song of God* (translated by Swami Prabhavananda and Christopher Isherwood; introduction by Aldous Huxley).

Vedanta Press handles its own distribution, with many titles available from Baker and Taylor, DeVross and Company, and New Leaf Distributors.

Vedanta's books originate in-house, though the publisher is open to considering additional projects that may fall within its program. Vedanta does not wish to receive unsolicited manuscripts.

Query letters and SASEs should be directed to:

Bob Adjemian, General Manager

VERSO

20 Jay Street, 10th Floor, Brooklyn, NY 11201-8346

718-246-8160   fax: 781-246-8165

www.versobooks.com   email: versony@versobooks.com

With global sales approaching $3 million per year and over 350 titles in print, Verso can justifiably claim to be the largest radical publisher in the English-language world. The house publishes critical nonfiction in social science, humanities, history, and current affairs, such as Tariq Ali's *The Clash of Fundamentalism* and Laura Flanders' *Bushwomen: How They Won the White House for Their Man*; and trade titles such as Karen Finley's *George and Martha*.

Verso (meaning in printers' parlance "the lefthand page") was founded in 1970 by the London-based New Left Review, a journal of left-wing theory with a worldwide readership of 40,000. The company remains independent to this day. The company's head office is located in London, where a staff of 12 produces a program of 60 new titles each year.

Originally trading as New Left Books, the company developed an early reputation as a translator of classic works of European literature and politics by authors such as Jean-Paul Sartre, Walter Benjamin, Louis Althusser, Theodor Adorno, Herbert Marcuse, Ernest Mandel and Max Weber. More recent translations include the work of Giovanni Arrighi, Norberto Bobbio, Guy Debord, Giles Deleuze, Che Guevara, Carlo Ginzburg, André Gorz, Jürgen Habermas, Gabriel García Marquez, and Paul Virilio.

Commissioning intelligent, critical works located at the intersection of the academic and trade markets, Verso has many key authors in English in the social sciences and humanities, with particular strength in politics, cultural studies, history, philosophy, sociology, and literary criticism. Such writers include Tariq Ali, Benedict Anderson, Perry Anderson, Michèle Barrett, Robin Blackburn, Terry Eagleton, Paul Gilroy, Stuart Hall, Eric Hobsbawm, Victor Kiernan, Steven Lukes, E.P. Thompson, and Raymond Williams.

From early on in its life, the company retained U.S. rights and has added to its imports a range of distinguished North American-based writers. Editors located on both East and West coasts have signed authors including Noam Chomsky, Alexander Cockburn, Marc Cooper, Mike Davis, Juan Gonzalez, Christopher Hitchens, Frederic Jameson, Andrew Kopkind, Lewis Lapham, Manning Marable, David Roediger, Andrew Ross, Edward Said, and Michele Wallace.

North America today comprises 65 percent of the company's worldwide sales. In the spring of 1995 Verso opened an office in New York. Primarily handling marketing and publicity work, the American office now has a staff of four.

Verso stands today as a publisher combining editorial intelligence, elegant production, and marketing flair. Having quadrupled in size over the past decade, the company will continue its progress towards the mainstream of the industry without compromising its radical commitment.

Recent titles include *Night of the Golden Butterfly* by Tariq Ali; *The Communist Hypothesis* by Alain Badiou; *A Painter of Our Time* by John Berger; *The Necessity of Art* by Ernst Fischer; and *In Search of a Past* by Ronald Fraser.

Email queries are preferred; send them to verso@versobooks.com. Send proposals (lengths of ten pages or fewer) and SASEs to the Editorial Department.

VISIBLE INK PRESS

43311 Joy Road, #414, Canton, MI 48187-2075

734-667-3211   fax: 734-667-4311

www.visibleink.com

A Detroit phenomena since 1990 and a continuing surprise to everyone involved, Visible Ink Press publishes mega-works of popular reference that inform and entertain in the areas of culture, science, history, religion, and government. All of their titles could be classified as popular reference.

Recent titles include *The Handy Dinosaur Answer Book* by Patricia Barnes-Svarney and Thomas E Svarney; *Hidden Realms, Lost Civilizations, and Beings from Other Worlds* by Jerome Clark; *The Handy Law Answer Book* by David L. Hudson, Jr.; *Real Vampires, Night Stalkers, and Creatures from the Darkside* by Brad Steiger.

Visible Ink is not currently accepting unsolicited manuscripts, but the editors encourage authors to check the website as this policy may soon change. Direct queries and SASEs to:

Roger Janecke, President

Megan Hiller, Editorial Director

WALKER PUBLISHING [SEE BLOOMSBURY USA]

WATERBROOK MULTNOMAH [SEE RANDOM HOUSE]

WEISER [SEE RED WHEEL/WEISER]

WESTVIEW [SEE PERSEUS]

JOHN WILEY & SONS

WILEY HIGHER EDUCATION

WILEY PROFESSIONAL/TRADE

FISHER INVESTMENTS PRESS

JOSSEY-BASS

SYBEX

WILEY-BLACKWELL

WILEY CHILDREN'S BOOKS

111 River Street, Hoboken, NJ 07030-5774
201-748-6000   fax: 201-748-6088
www.wiley.com   email: info@wiley.com
Indianapolis address:
10475 Crosspoint Boulevard, Indianapolis, IN 46256
317-572-3000
www.dummies.com
Jossey-Bass and Sybex address:
989 Market Street, San Francisco, CA 94103-1741
415-433-1740   fax: 415-433-0499
www.josseybass.com
www.sybex.com   email: sybexproposals@wiley.com

Wiley-Blackwell address:

Commerce Place, 350 Main Street, Malden, MA 02148

781-388-8200   fax: 781-388-8210

www.blackwellpublishing.com

Wiley-Blackwell Publishing Professional address:

2121 State Avenue, Ames, IA 50014-8300

www.blackwellprofessional.com

Wiley was founded in 1807, during the Jefferson presidency. In the early years, Wiley was best known for the works of Washington Irving, Edgar Allan Poe, Herman Melville, and other 19th-century American literary giants. By the turn of the century, Wiley was established as a leading publisher of scientific and technical information. The company went public in 1962 and was listed on the NYSE in 1995.

In 2007, Wiley acquired academic and professional publisher Blackwell Publishing for over $1 billion. Blackwell was merged into Wiley's global scientific, technical, and medical business. Also in 2007, its bicentennial year, Wiley announced record revenue.

Wiley is a global publisher of print and electronic products, specializing in scientific, technical, and medical books and journals under the Wiley-Blackwell Division; professional and consumer books under the Wiley Professional and Trade Division; and textbooks and other educational materials for undergraduate and graduate students as well as lifelong learners under the Wiley Higher Education Division. Wiley publishes in a variety of formats.

Wiley's proposal submission guidelines are rather specific. Please see the page "Submission Guidelines" on the website. It is Wiley's policy not to accept unsolicited proposals for books in the *For Dummies* series. For everything else, send a proposal with SASE to the attention of the appropriate division (Professional and Trade Division or Scientific, Technical, and Medical Division).

WILEY HIGHER EDUCATION

Wiley Higher Education publishes textbooks and other educational materials in English, German, and Chinese (and translated into many other languages) in a variety of formats, both print and online, in the United States, Canada, Europe, Asia, and Australia. Their products are used globally by undergraduate and graduate students, educators, and lifelong learners. Wiley's higher education programs are targeted toward two- and four-year colleges and universities, for-profit career colleges, and advanced placement classes. They are a leader in courses in the sciences, engineering, computer science, mathematics, business and accounting, statistics, geography, hospitality, and the culinary arts, with a growing presence in education, psychology, and modern languages.

WILEY PROFESSIONAL/TRADE

The Professional and Trade Division produces nonfiction books and electronic products for the professional, business, and general interest consumer markets. Its primary fields of interest are accounting, architecture, engineering, business, finance and investment, children, computers, society (including current affairs, health, parenting, self-help, reference, history, biography, science, and nature), hospitality, law, psychology, and real estate. Also included are the following Wiley brands: Betty Crocker, Bible, CliffsNotes, Cracking the Code, Dummies, Frommer's, Howell, Novell Press, Secrets, 3D Visual, Webster's New World Dictionary, Weekend Crash Course, and Weight Watchers. Wiley content travels well. Approximately 40 percent of the company's revenue is generated outside the United States.

The company provides "must-have" content to targeted communities of interest. Wiley's deep reservoir of quality content, constantly replenished, offers a tremendous source of competitive advantage. Technology is making this content more accessible to customers worldwide and is adding value for them by delivering it in interactive and/or fully searchable formats. Approximately 25 percent of global revenue is currently Web-enabled.

With about 3,500 employees worldwide, Wiley has operations in the United States, Europe (England, Germany, and Russia), Canada, Asia, and Australia. The Company has U.S. publishing, marketing, and distribution centers in New Jersey, California, Virginia, Illinois, Indiana, and Ohio. Wiley's worldwide headquarters are located in Hoboken, New Jersey, just across the river from Manhattan.

Recent titles from the Wiley Professional/Trade division include *Cooking Know-How: Be a Better Cook with Hundreds of Easy Techniques, Step-by-Step Photos, and Ideas for Over 500 Great Meals* by Bruce Weinstein et al; *Corporate Finance: Theory and Practice* by Pierre Vernimmen and Pascal Quiry; *Creativity Unlimited* by Micael Dahlén; and *Digital Wedding Photography Secrets* by Rick Sammon.

Steven Smith, CEO

David Pugh, Senior Editor—Finance, investing, e-commerce, corporate tie-ins (NJ)

John Czarnecki, Senior Editor—Architecture and design

Shannon Vargo, Associate Editor—Business Subjects (NJ)

Stephen Power, Senior Editor—Popular science, current events (NJ)

Tom Miller, Executive Editor—General interest (NJ)

Debra Englander, Executive Editor—Investing, finance, money (NJ)

Hana Lane, Executive Editor—History/biography (NJ)

Sheck Cho, Executive Editor—Technology, business, politics (NJ)

Richard Narramore, Senior Editor—General business (NJ)

Matthew Holt, Senior Editor—General business, marketing, careers (NJ)

Kathleen Cox, Acquisitions Editor—For Dummies series (IN)

Mike Lewis, Editor—Dummies series (NJ)

Linda Ingroia, Editor—Cooking and restaurant management (NJ)

Crystel Winkler, Editor—Health, popular psychology, relationships

FISHER INVESTMENTS PRESS

Fisher Investments Press draws upon the expertise of bestselling author Ken Fisher to offer investing advice and education for a wide audience. Says Ken Fisher: "Our goal in partnering with Wiley to create Fisher Investments Press was to reach a wide and diverse investment audience. Working together, we've developed an investment series that can offer insight to the full spectrum of investors, from novices to professionals." The first Fisher Investments title, *10 Roads to Riches* by Ken Fisher, focuses on various methods of wealth accumulation, from old-fashioned saving to inheritance and business enterprise.

More titles from Fisher Investments Press include *Fisher Investments on Industrials* by Matt Schraeder; *Fisher Investments on Emerging Markets* by Austin Fraser; *Fisher Investments on Technology* by Brendan Erne; and *The Global Energy Investment Guide* by Aaron Azelton.

David Pugh, Senior Editor

JOSSEY-BASS

Jossey-Bass publishes books, periodicals, and other media to inform and inspire those interested in developing themselves, their organizations, and their communities. Jossey-Bass publications feature the work of some of the world's best-known authors in leadership, business, education, religion and spirituality, parenting, nonprofit, public health and health administration, conflict resolution, and relationships. Publishing nearly 250 new titles each year, Jossey-Bass was acquired by Wiley in 1999, but maintains largely independent operations in San Francisco.

In religion and spirituality, Jossey-Bass publishes a broad range of trade books that support readers in their spiritual journeys, including some that combine general spirituality and self-improvement. Most of their books have been drawn from Christian and Jewish traditions, but they are looking to expand in a thoughtful way into other traditions. They are also looking for books on the intersection of faith/spirituality, culture, and history.

Recent titles include *Dr. Ruth's Top Ten Secrets for Great Sex: How to Enjoy It, Share It, and Love It Each and Every Time* by Dr. Ruth K. Westheimer; *Hands-On Math Projects with Real-Life Applications: Grades 3–5* by Gary Robert Muschla; and *The Deciding Factor: The Power of Analytics to Make Every Decision a Winner* by John Nash and Larry E. Rosenberger.

Submit proposals, queries, and SASEs to the Editorial Assistant for the relevant series (Business, Education, Health, Higher Education, Nonprofit and Social Leadership, General Interest, Psychology, or Religion).

Cedric Crocker, Vice President and Publisher

Susan Williams, Executive Editor—Business and management; swilliams@wiley.com

Karen Murphy, Senior Editor, kmurphy@wiley.com

Genovesa Llosa, Editor, gllosa@wiley.com

SYBEX

Sybex pioneered computer book publishing in 1976 and has as its mission to bring practical skills to computer users through comprehensive, high-quality education and reference materials. Their series range from the reputable Mastering best-sellers, used by millions to gain in-depth understanding of the latest computer topics, to certification Study Guides that help students prepare for challenging exams, to Maya Press books that service the needs of highly specialized 3D imaging and design markets. Sybex was acquired by John Wiley & Sons in 2005 and publishes about 100 new books per year.

Recent titles include *Action! Acting Lessons for CG Animators* by John Kundert-Gibbs; *Configuring SAP ERP Financials and Controlling* by Peter Jones and John Burger; *Project Manager's Guide to Microsoft Office Project 2007* by Dennis C. Brewer; and *Photoshop for Right-Brainers: The Art of Photomanipulation* by Al Ward.

Direct queries and proposals to sybexproposals@wiley.com and include the word Proposal at the beginning of the subject line.

WILEY-BLACKWELL

Wiley-Blackwell was formed in February 2007 as a result of the merger between Blackwell Publishing Ltd. and John Wiley & Sons, Inc.'s Scientific, Technical, and Medical business. Wiley-Blackwell is organized into five broad divisions: Life Science, Physical Sciences, Professional, Medical, Social Sciences, and Humanities. Blackwell-Wiley is run by Senior Vice President for Scientific, Technical, and Medical Publishing, Eric Swanson. By June 2008, Wiley-Blackwell integrated the two businesses by combining many infrastructure and distribution processes as well as launching a single Web platform.

Recent titles from Wiley-Blackwell include *Designing and Implementing Global Selection Systems* by Ann Marie Ryan; *The Epigenics of Autoimmune Diseases* by Moncef Zouali; *Essential Mathematics and Statistics for Science* by Graham Currell; *The European Reformations* by Carter Lindberg; and *Planets and Planetary Systems* by Stephen Eales.

Recent titles from Wiley-Blackwell Professional include *Carbon Capture and Sequestration: Integrating Technology, Monitoring, Regulation* by Elizabeth Wilson and David Gerard; *Physics at a Glance* by Tim Mills; *Structure and Reactivity in Organic Chemistry* by Mark Moloney; *Trans Fatty Acids* by Alberst Dijkstra, Richard J. Hamilton, and Wolf Hamm.

If you have an idea for a new book, journal, or electronic product that falls into the chemistry, life sciences, medicine, mathematical and physical sciences, humanities, and social sciences, and would like to be contacted by an editor, please send your proposal to John Wiley & Sons, Wiley Blackwell Division.

WENNER BOOKS [SEE HYPERION]

WESTMINSTER JOHN KNOX PRESS [SEE PRESBYTERIAN PUBLISHING CORPORATION]

WILLOW CREEK PRESS, INC.

P.O. Box 147, Minocqua, WI 54548

715-358-7010/800-850-9453

www.willowcreekpress.com   email: info@willowcreekpress.com

Willow Creek Press is a publisher whose primary commitment is to publish books specializing in nature, outdoor and sporting topics, gardening, wildlife and animal books, and cookbooks. They also publish nature, wildlife, fishing, and sporting calendars.

Its location in the Wisconsin Northwoods helps keep Willow Creek Press off the publishing world's radar. But, a few years ago, the house did get noticed with the release of *Just Labs*, a unique and colorful tribute to Labrador retrievers. The book quickly became a bestseller (with over 250,000 copies in print). Now an entire line of popular Willow Creek Press titles evokes the myriad joys of dog and cat ownership. Today they are known for these high-quality, light-hearted books and feature over 40 such titles in a continually expanding line.

Recent titles include *Laugh It Up in Deer Camp: The Very Best American Deer Hunting Humor* by Brian R. Peterson; *Bulldog Bad Boys: And Some Pretty Uncontrollabull Girls Too!*; *Retirement Is a Full Time Job: And You're the Boss!* by Bonnie Louise Kuchler; and the *Horse Country 2010 Wall Calendar*.

Please provide SASE with all correspondence if you want your materials returned. Address all inquiries or proposals to:

Donnie Rubo, Acquisitions, Donnie@willowcreekpress.com

WISDOM PUBLICATIONS

199 Elm Street, Somerville, MA 02144

617-776-7416   fax: 617-776-7841

www.wisdompubs.org   email: editors@wisdompubs.org

Wisdom Publications, a not-for-profit publisher, is dedicated to making available authentic Buddhist works for the benefit of all. The house publishes translations of the sutras and tantras, commentaries and teachings of past and contemporary Buddhist masters, and original works by the world's leading Buddhist scholars. Wisdom Publications was named one of the top 10 fastest-growing small publishers in the country (the company has been in the United States since 1989) by *Publishers Weekly* in 1996.

Wisdom titles are published in appreciation of Buddhism as a living philosophy and with the commitment to preserve and transmit important works from all the major Buddhist traditions. Wisdom products are distributed worldwide and have been translated into a dozen foreign languages.

Wisdom publishes the celebrated Tibetan Art Calendar, containing 13 full-color reproductions of the world's finest Indo-Tibetan thangka paintings, accompanied by detailed iconographical descriptions.

Wisdom Publications has made a commitment to producing books with environmental mindfulness.

Recent Wisdom titles include *Dignity & Discipline: Reviving Full Ordination for Buddhist Nuns* by Thea Mohr and Ven. Jampa Tsedroen; *Awakening the Kind Heart: How to Meditate on Compassion* by Kathleen McDonald; *How Much Is Enough?: Buddhism, Consumerism, and the Human Enviroment* by Richard Payne; *Natural Perfection: Lonchenpa's Radical Dzogchen* by Keith Dowman; and *Unlimiting Mind: The Radically Experiential Psychology of Buddhism* by Andrew Olendzki.

Wisdom Publications is distributed to the trade in the United States and Canada by National Book Network (NBN). Query letters and SASEs should be directed to Acquisitions Editor via regular mail or email. Complete proposal specifications are available on the website.

Tim McNeill, Publisher

WORKMAN PUBLISHING GROUP

ALGONQUIN BOOKS OF CHAPEL HILL

SHANNON RAVENEL BOOKS

P.O. Box 2225, Chapel Hill, NC 27515

919-967-0108   fax: 919-933-0272

www.algonquin.com   email: inquiry@algonquin.com

ARTISAN BOOKS

WORKMAN PUBLISHING COMPANY

225 Varick St., New York, NY 10014-4381

212-254-5900   fax: 212-677-6692

www.workman.com

www.artisanbooks.com   email: artisaninfo@workman.com

BLACK DOG AND LEVENTHAL

151 West 19th Street, New York, NY 10011

212-647-9336   fax: 212-871-9530

www.blackdogandleventhal.com   email: information@blackdogandleventhal.com

STOREY PUBLISHING

210 MASS MoCA Way, North Adams, MA 01247

413-346-2100   fax: 413-346-2199

www.storey.workman.com

TIMBER PRESS

113 SW 2nd Avenue, Suite 450, Portland, OR 97204

503-227-2878   fax: 503-227-3070

www.timberpress.workman.com   email: info@timberpress.com

Workman Publishing Company, a medium-sized independent publisher, is the creator of calendars; cookbooks; parenting/pregnancy guides; fun, educational children's titles; gardening; humor; self-help; and business books. They also include several imprints, including Algonquin Books of Chapel Hill, Artisan, HighBridge Audio, Storey Publishing, and Timber Press, as well as acting as distributor for Black Dog and Leventhal, Greenwich Workshop Press, and Fearless Critic Media.

INDEPENDENT U.S. PRESSES

ALGONQUIN BOOKS OF CHAPEL HILL

Algonquin Books was founded in 1982 with the mission statement, "Though we hope and expect that our books will gain their share of book club adoptions, mass paperback sales, and movie and television adaptations, it is their quality that will be our foremost consideration, for we believe that it is still possible to publish worthy fiction and nonfiction that will also be financially profitable for author, publisher, and bookseller."

This division of Workman Publishing Company maintains a literary orientation in commercial fiction and nonfiction. The house list represents the American tradition, ranging from the homespun to the progressive. Algonquin Books of Chapel Hill presents its titles in hardcover and trade paper editions with a look and feel befitting the publisher's emphasis on both the classical and contemporary—books designed to be comfortably handled when read. The Algonquin editorial organization operates from both the Chapel Hill and New York Workman offices. They publish 20–25 new books per year, of fiction, nonfiction, cookbooks, and lifestyle books.

Recent Algonquin titles include *Mudbound* by Hillary Jordan; *Lincoln As I Knew Him: Gossip, Tributes, and Revelations from His Best Friends and Worst Enemies* by Harold Holzer; *The Music Teacher* by Barbara Hall; and *A Rose By Any Name: The Little-Known Lore and Deep-Rooted History of Rose Names* by Douglas Brenner and Stephen Scannniello.

Ina Stern, Associate Publisher (Algonquin)

Chuck Adams, Executive Editor—Fiction

Amy Gash, Editor—Nonfiction

Jay Shaefer, Editor-at-Large

Jane Roseman, Editor

SHANNON RAVENEL BOOKS

Algonquin founder Shannon Ravenel's imprint at Algonquin publishes both nonfiction and fiction with titles such as *Brave Enemies: A Novel of the American Revolution* by Robert Morgan; *The Ghost at the Table: A Novel* by Suzanne Berne; *On Agate Hill: A Novel* by Lee Smith; and *Saving the World* by Julia Alvarez.

Shannon Ravenel, Director

ARTISAN BOOKS

Artisan Books, another division of Workman, is known for excellence of content, quality of illustration, and innovative printing. Their authors seek to contribute to the cultural life of a diverse and visually sophisticated readership. Recent tiles include *How to Build an A* by Sara Midda; *Tavern on the Green* by Kay LeRoy and Jennifer Oz LeRoy; *Frank Stitt's Bottega Favorita: A Southern Chef's Love Affair with*

Italian Food by Frank Sitt; *Under Pressure: Cooking Sous Vide* by Thomas Keller; and *Medal of Honor: Portraits of Valor Beyond the Call of Duty* by Nick Del Calzo and Peter Collier.

Ann Bramson, Publisher

Ingrid Bramozitch, Editor—Home and style, general

WORKMAN PUBLISHING COMPANY

Books, calendars, trends. Workman is a publisher that's always around big ideas. *B. Kliban's Cat, 1,000 Places to See Before You Die, The Silver Palate Cookbook, Bad Cat* the original *Page-A-Day Calendars*, the *What to Expect* books, *BRAIN QUEST*— landmark bestsellers such as these reflect a knack for publishing books and calendars that lead.

Workman's first book, 1968's *Yoga 28-Day Exercise Plan* is currently in its 28th printing. Their books are known for having an appealing trade-paperback format with high standards of design and production. Authors who are authorities, who tour extensively and are spokespeople for their subjects, work with Workman. Workman also sometimes goes with unexpected formats such as the packaging of books with objects. And above all, the house prides itself on value through conscientious, aggressive pricing.

Once a book is published, Workman stays after it through promotion and publicity. Take, for example, the case of *The Official Preppy Handbook*, and how an idiosyncratic bestseller was transformed into a phenomenon, complete with posters and stationery—even pins and nightshirts. Or *What to Expect When You're Expecting*, which started with a modest 6,700-copy advance in 1984 and has grown into America's pregnancy bible, currently with 10 million copies in print.

Perhaps more telling is the fact that over two-thirds of all the books the house has published in the last 28 years are still in print, with a fair share of titles that have over one million copies in print, including *BRAIN QUEST, The Silver Palate Cookbook, The New Basics Cookbook, All I Need to Know I Learned from My Cat, The Magic Locket,* and *The Bones Book & Skeleton*.

Some recent titles from Workman include *I Will Teach You to Be Rich* by Ramit Sethi; *Sell Your Business for the Max!* by Steve Kaplan; *Good Egg* by Barney Saltzberg; and *How to Make Someone Fall in Love with You in 90 Minutes or Less* by Nicholas Boothman.

Peter Workman, Publisher

Susan Bolotin, Editor-in-Chief

Suzanne Rafer, Executive Editor

Janet Harris, Editor—Non-book products (calendars)

Raquel Jaramillo, Director of Children's Publishing

BLACK DOG AND LEVENTHAL

Black Dog and Leventhal seeks to publish strikingly original books of light reference, humor, cooking, sports, music, film, mysteries, entertainment, history, biography, and more. Many are unusual in format and rich with color and imagery. Titles include *The Manhattan Project: The Birth of the Atomic Bomb in the Words of Its Creators, Eyewitnesses, and Historians* by Cynthia Kelly; *Blue Ribbon Recipes* by Barbara Greenman; *The Cube: The Ultimate Guide to the World's Best-Selling Puzzle: Secrets, Stories, Solutions* by Jerry Slocum et al; *Splitters, Squeezes, and Steals: The Inside Story of Baseball's Greatest Techniques, Strategies, and Plays* by Derek Gentile; and *Hopes and Dreams: The Story of Barack Obama: The Inaugural Edition* by Steve Dougherty.

Liz Van Doren, Editor-in-Chief

STOREY PUBLISHING

Storey Publishing began on July 1, 1983, with about 65 books and 100 bulletins on topics as varied as building your own log cabin, tanning leather yourself, and canning your garden's bumper crop of fruits and vegetables. Since then, Storey has maintained its independent streak while keeping a backlist of more than 450 titles. Storey wants books that offer fresh ideas, lend encouragement, and help the reader succeed at something specific.

Recent titles from Storey press include *Sew What! Bags: 18 Pattern-Free Projects You Can Customize to Fit Your Needs* by Lexi Barnes; *The Gardener's A-Z Guide to Growing Organic Food* by Tanya Denckla; *Growing Chinese Vegetables in Your Own Backyard* by Geri Harrington; *Happy Baby, Happy You: Quick Tips for Nurturing, Pampering, and Bonding with Your Baby* by Karyn Siegel-Maier; *The Cattle Health Handbook* by Heather Smith Thomas; and *The Ever-Blooming Flower Garden: A Blueprint for Continuous Bloom* by Lee Schneller.

Deborah Balmuth, Editorial Director—Building and mind/body/spirit

Deborah Burns, Acquiring Editor—Equine, animals, nature

Gwen Steege, Acquiring Editor—Gardening and crafts

Margaret Sutherland, Acquiring Editor—Cooking, wine, and beer

Carline Perkins, Acquiring Editor

TIMBER PRESS

Timber Press, located in Portland, Oregon, has over 400 titles in print and is considered the preeminent publisher of horticulture books. Timber Press began in 1980, publishing J.D. Vertee's *Japanese Maples*, which is still in print. Besides horticulture, Timber Press also seeks to publish books about landscape design, food-related topics, fruit-growing titles, natural history, and the Pacific Northwest.

Timber Press titles include *Huntleyas and Related Orchids* by Patricia A.

Harding; *The Pruning of Trees, Shrubs, and Conifers* by George Brown and Tony Kirkham; *The Oregon Companion: A Historical Gazetter of the Useful, the Curious, and the Arcane* by Richard H. Engeman; *Green Flowers: Unexpected Beauty for the Garden, Container, or Vase* by Alison Hoblyn; *Perennial Companions: 100 Dazzling Plants for Every Season* by Tom Fischer and Richard Bloom; and *The Art of Botanical Drawing* by Agathe Ravet-Haevermans.

To submit your manuscript, send a 20-page sample of your work, a cover letter, a self-addressed envelope, and a check to cover return postage to the attention of the Editorial Department.

Tom Fischer, Editor-in-Chief

Eve Goodman, Editorial Director

Juree Sondker, Acquisitions Editor

WRIGHT GROUP/MCGRAW-HILL [SEE MCGRAW-HILL]

WRITER'S DIGEST

4700 E. Galbraith Road, Cincinnati, OH 45236

513-531-2690

www.writersdigest.com   email: writersdig@fwpubs.com

Writer's Digest is the world's leading magazine for writers, founded in 1920. Today this house provides a variety of books, magazines, special interest publications, educational courses, conferences, websites, and more.

Publications include: *Writer's Yearbook,* published annually, *Scriptwriting Secrets, Getting Started in Writing, Start Writing Now,* and a variety of other special interest publications for writers.

All are part of F&W Publications, a leading publisher of books and magazines for creative people. F&W Publications is headquartered in Cincinnati, Ohio, with additional offices in New York, Denver, and Devon, England.

Recent titles include *Write That Book Already! The Tough Love You Need to Get Published Now* by Sam Barry and Kathi Kamen Goldmark; *Get an Agent 2010; The 3 A.M. Epiphany* by Brian Kiteley; and *A Civilian's Guide to the U.S. Military* by Barbara Shading.

Send a query and SASE to:

Jane Friedman, Editorial Director; jane.friedman@fwpubs.com

ZEBRA BOOKS [SEE KENSINGTON PUBLISHING]

SECTION THREE

UNIVERSITY PRESSES

THE UNIVERSITY AS PUBLISHER

FROM ACADEMIC PRESS TO COMMERCIAL PRESENCE

WILLIAM HAMILTON
Director, University of Hawaii Press
2840 Kolowalu Street, Honolulu, HI 96822

You nod as you glance at the ads in the book reviews, you are aware of the spots you heard or saw on radio and late-night television, and you recognize the authors from television interviews and radio call-in shows. So you know that today's university presses publish much more than scholarly monographs and academic tomes.

Although the monograph is—and will always be—the bread and butter of the university press, several factors over the past quarter century have compelled university presses to look beyond their primary publishing mission of disseminating scholarship. The reductions in financial support from parent institutions, library-budget cutbacks by federal and local governments, and the increasing scarcity of grants to underwrite the costs of publishing monographs have put these presses under severe financial pressure. The watchword for university presses, even in the 1970s, was survival.

While university presses were fighting for their lives, their commercial counterparts also experienced difficult changes. The commercial sector responded by selling off unprofitable and incompatible lists or merging with other publishers; many houses were bought out by larger concerns. Publishers began to concentrate their editorial and marketing resources on a few new titles that would generate larger revenues. Books that commercial publishers now categorized as financial risks, the university presses saw as means of entry into new markets and opportunities to revive sagging publishing programs.

Take a look through one of the really good bookstores in your area. You'll find university press imprints on regional cookbooks, popular fiction, serious nonfiction, calendars, literature in translation, reference works, finely produced art books, and a considerable number of upper-division textbooks. Books and other items normally associated with commercial publishers are now a regular and important part of university press publishing.

There are approximately 100 university presses in North America, including U.S. branches of the venerable Oxford University Press and Cambridge University Press. Of the largest American university presses—California, Chicago, Columbia, Harvard, MIT, Princeton, Texas, and Yale—each publishes well over 100 books per year. Many of these titles are trade books that are sold in retail outlets throughout the world.

The medium-sized university presses—approximately 20 fit this category—publish between 50 and 100 books a year. Presses such as Washington, Indiana, Cornell, North Carolina, Johns Hopkins, and Stanford are well established as publishers of important works worthy of broad circulation.

All but the smallest university presses have developed extensive channels of distribution, which ensure that their books will be widely available in bookstores and wherever serious books are sold. Small university presses usually retain larger university presses or commissioned sales firms to represent them.

University Press Trade Publishing

The two most common trade areas in which university presses publish are (1) regional titles and (2) nonfiction titles that reflect the research interests of their parent universities.

For example, University of Hawaii Press publishes approximately 30 new books a year with Asian or Pacific Rim themes. Typically, 8 to 10 of these books are trade titles. Recent titles have included Japanese literature in translation, a lavishly illustrated book on Thai textiles, books on forms of Chinese architecture, and a historical guide to ancient Burmese temples. This is a typical university press trade list—a diverse, intellectually stimulating selection of books that will be read by a variety of well-informed, responsive general readers.

For projects with special trade potential, some of the major university presses enter into copublishing arrangements with commercial publishers—notably in the fields of art books and serious nonfiction with a current-issues slant—and there seems to be more of these high-profile projects lately.

Certain of the larger and medium-sized university presses have in the past few years hired editors with experience in commercial publishing to add extra dimensions and impact to the portion of their program with a trade orientation.

It's too early to know whether these observations represent trends. Even if so, the repercussions remain to be seen. Obviously, with the publishing community as a whole going through a period of change, it pays to stay tuned to events.

University Press Authors

Where do university press authors come from? The majority of them are involved in one way or another with a university, research center, or public agency, or are experts in a particular academic field. Very few would list their primary occupation as author. Most of the books they write are the result of years of research or reflect years of experience in their fields.

The university press is not overly concerned about the number of academic degrees following its trade book authors' names. What matters is the author's thoroughness in addressing the topic, regardless of his or her residence, age, or amount of formal education. A rigorous evaluation of content and style determines whether the manuscript meets the university press's standards.

University Press Acquisition Process

Several of the other essays in this volume provide specific strategies for you to follow to ensure that your book idea receives consideration from your publisher of choice—but let me interject a cautionary note: The major commercial publishers are extremely difficult to approach unless you have an agent, and obtaining an agent can be more difficult than finding a publisher!

The commercial publishers are so overwhelmed by unsolicited manuscripts that you would be among the fortunate few if your proposal or manuscript even received a thorough reading. Your unagented proposal or manuscript will most likely be read by an editorial assistant, returned unread, or thrown on the slush pile unread and unreturned.

An alternative to the commercial publisher is the university press. Not only will the university press respond; but the response will also generally come from the decision maker—the acquisitions editor.

Before approaching any publisher, however, you must perform a personal assessment of your expectations for your book. If you are writing because you want your book to be on the bestseller list, go to a medium to large commercial press. If you are writing to make a financial killing, go to a large commercial publisher. If you are writing in the hope that your book will be a literary success, contribute to knowledge, be widely distributed, provide a modest royalty, and be in print for several years, you should consider a university press.

Should a University Press Be Your First Choice?

That depends on the subject matter. It is very difficult to sell a commercial publisher on what appears on the surface to be a book with a limited market. For example, Tom Clancy was unable to sell *The Hunt for Red October* to a commercial publisher because the content was considered too technical for the average reader of action-adventure books. Clancy sent the manuscript to a university press that specialized in military-related topics. Naval Institute Press had the foresight to see the literary and commercial value of Clancy's work. As they say, the rest is history. Tom Clancy created the present-day technothriller genre and has accumulated royalties well into the millions of dollars. Once Clancy became a known commodity, the commercial publishers began courting him. All of his subsequent books have been published by commercial houses.

How do you find the university press that is suitable for you? You must research the university press industry. Start by finding out something about university presses. In addition to the listings in the directory of publishers and editors appearing in this book, most university presses are listed in *Literary Market Place*.

A far better and more complete source is *The Association of American University Presses Directory*. The AAUP directory offers a detailed description of each AAUP member press, with a summary of its publishing program. The directory lists the names and responsibilities of each press's key staff, including the acquisitions editors. Each press states its editorial program—what it will consider for publication. A section on submitting manuscripts provides a detailed description of what the university press expects a proposal to contain. Another useful feature is the comprehensive subject grid, which identifies more than 125 subject areas and lists the university presses that publish in each of them.

An updated edition of *The Association of American University Presses Directory* is published every fall and is available for a nominal charge from the AAUP central offices in New York City or through its distributor, University of Chicago Press.

Most university presses are also regional publishers. They publish titles that reflect local interests and tastes and are intended for sale primarily in the university press's local region. For example, University of Hawaii Press has more than 250 titles on Hawaii. The books—both trade and scholarly—cover practically every topic one can think of. Books on native birds, trees, marine life, local history, native culture, and an endless variety of other topics can be found in local stores, including chain bookstores.

This regional pattern is repeated by university presses throughout the country. University of Washington Press publishes several titles each year on the Pacific Northwest and Alaska. Rutgers University Press publishes regional fiction. University of New Mexico Press publishes books on art and photography, most dealing with the desert Southwest. Louisiana State University Press publishes Southern history and literature. Nebraska publishes on the American West.

Almost all university presses publish important regional nonfiction. If your book naturally fits a particular region, you should do everything possible to get a university press located in that region to evaluate your manuscript.

Do not mistake the regional nature of the university press for an inability to sell books nationally—or globally. As mentioned earlier, most university presses have established channels of distribution and use the same resources that commercial publishers use for book distribution. The major difference is that the primary retail outlets for university press books tend to be bookstores associated with universities, smaller academic bookstores, specialized literary bookstores, and independent bookstores that carry a large number of titles.

Matching books to buyers is not as difficult as you might think. Most patrons of university press bookstores know these stores are likely to carry the books they want.

Traditionally, very few university press titles are sold through major chain bookstores outside their local region. Even so, this truism is subject to change. Some of the biggest bookstore chains are experimenting with university press sections in their large superstores.

What to Expect at a University Press

You should expect a personal reply from the acquisitions editor. If the acquisitions editor expresses interest, you can expect the evaluation process to take as long as six to eight months. For reasons known only to editorial staffs—commercial, as well as those of university presses—manuscripts sit and sit and sit. Then they go out for review, come back, and go out for review again!

Once a favorable evaluation is received, the editor must submit the book to the press's editorial board. It is not until the editorial board approves the manuscript for publication that a university press is authorized to publish the book under its imprint.

A word about editorial boards: The imprint of a university press is typically controlled by an editorial board appointed from the faculty. Each project presented to the editorial board is accompanied by a set of peer reviews, the acquisitions editor's summary of the reviews, and the author's replies to the reviews. The project is discussed with the press's management and voted upon.

Decisions from the editorial board range from approval, through conditional approval, to flat rejection. Most university presses present to the editorial board only those projects they feel stand a strong chance of acceptance—approximately 10 to 15 percent of the projects submitted annually. So if you have been told that your book is being submitted to the editorial board, there's a good chance that the book will be accepted.

Once a book has been accepted by the editorial board, the acquisitions editor is authorized to offer the author a publishing contract. The publishing contract of a university press is quite similar to a commercial publisher's contract. The majority of the paragraphs read the same. The difference is most apparent in two areas— submission of the manuscript and financial terms.

University presses view publishing schedules as very flexible. If the author needs an extra six to twelve months to polish the manuscript, the market is not going to be affected too much. If the author needs additional time to proofread the galleys or page proofs, the press is willing to go along. Why? Because a university press is publishing for the long term. The book is going to be in print for several years. It is not unusual for a first printing of a university press title to be available for ten or more years. Under normal circumstances the topic will be timeless, enduring, and therefore of lasting interest.

University presses go to great lengths to ensure that a book is as close to error-free as possible. The academic and stylistic integrity of the work is foremost in the editor's mind. Not only the content, but the notes, references, bibliography, and index should be flawless—and all charts, graphs, maps, and other illustrations perfectly keyed.

It does not matter whether the book is a limited-market monograph or serious nonfiction for a popular trade. The university press devotes the same amount of care to the editorial and production processes to ensure that the book is as accurate and complete as possible. Which leads us to the second difference—the financial terms.

Commercial publishers follow the maxim that time is money. The goal of the organization is to maximize shareholder wealth. Often the decision to publish a book is based solely on financial considerations. If a book must be available for a specific season in order to meet its financial goals, pressure may be applied to editorial by marketing, and editorial in turn puts pressure on the author to meet the agreed-upon schedule. This pressure may result in mistakes, typos, and inaccuracies—but will also assure timely publication and provide the publisher with the opportunity to earn its expected profit. At the commercial publishing house, senior management is measured by its ability to meet annual financial goals.

University presses are not-for-profit organizations. Their basic mission is to publish books of high merit that contribute to universal knowledge. Financial considerations are secondary to what the author has to say. A thoroughly researched, meticulously documented, and clearly written book is more important than meeting a specific publication date. The university press market will accept the book when it appears.

Do not get the impression that university presses are entirely insensitive to schedules or market conditions. University presses are aware that certain books—primarily textbooks and topical trade titles—must be published at specific times of the year if sales are to be maximized. But less than 20 percent of any year's list would fall into such a category.

University Presses and Author Remuneration

What about advances? Royalties? Surely, university presses offer these amenities—which is not to suggest they must be commensurate with the rates paid by commercial houses.

No and yes. No royalties are paid on a predetermined number of copies of scholarly monographs—usually 1,000 to 2,000.

A royalty is usually paid on textbooks and trade books. The royalty will be based on the title's sales revenue (net sales) and will usually be a sliding-scale royalty, ranging from as low as 5 percent to as high as 15 percent.

As with commercial publishers, royalties are entirely negotiable. Do not be afraid or embarrassed to discuss them with your publisher. Just remember that university presses rarely have surplus funds to apply to generous advances or high royalty rates. However, the larger the university press, the more likely you are to get an advance for a trade book.

Never expect an advance for a monograph or supplemental textbook.

When Considering a University Press

When you're deciding where to submit your manuscript, keep the following in mind. University presses produce approximately 10 percent of the books published in the United States each year. University presses win approximately 20 percent of the annual major book awards. Yet university presses generate just 2 percent of the annual sales revenue.

So if you want to write a book that is taken seriously and will be carefully reviewed and edited; if you want to be treated as an important part of the publishing process and want your book to have a good chance to win an award; and if you are not too concerned about the financial rewards—then a university press may very well be the publisher for you.

CAMBRIDGE UNIVERSITY PRESS

32 Avenue of the Americas, New York, NY 10013-2473

212-924-3900 fax: 212-691-3239

www.cambridge.org/us

Cambridge University Press is the world's oldest printing and publishing house, and is dedicated to the advancement and dissemination of knowledge. Internationally, Cambridge publishes over 2,500 titles and 200 journals every year.

The Manhattan office acquires and publishes books in many areas of the humanities and social sciences, with particular focus on subjects including law, history, political science, and economics; it is also active across a broad spectrum of science and medicine publishing. It administers some of the prestigious journals issued by the press and it also publishes an extremely successful list of books aimed at those learning American English as a foreign or second language.

The press is now in a real sense a "world publisher." English is the dominant world language of scholarship and science, and the press seeks to attract the best authors and publish the best work in the English language worldwide; it currently has over 36,000 authors in 120 countries, including well over 8,000 in the USA, over 1,300 in Australia, and over 100 each (and rising fast) in countries as various as Japan, Russia, South Africa, Spain, and Israel. The press publishes and distributes the whole of this varied output through its own network around the world: There are branches in North America, Australia, Africa, Brazil, and Spain, all representing the whole list, supported by sales offices in every major center; there are editorial offices in New York, Melbourne, Cape Town, Madrid, Singapore, and Tokyo, each contributing to it their own related publishing programs; and the press's websites are visited by over 2.5 million people worldwide.

Recent Cambridge University titles include *Yalta 1945* by Fraser J. Harbutt; *Friedrich Nietzsche* by Julian Young; *An Introduction to Kant's Moral Philosophy* by Jennifer K. Uleman; *Jihad in Saudi Arabia* by Thomas Hegghammer; and *The American Public Mind* by William J.M. Claggett and Byron E. Shafer.

Submit queries (with SASEs if by regular mail) to the appropriate editor:

Andrew Beck—Anthropology, Jewish studies, religion; abeck@cambridge.org

Frank Smith—American history, business history, economic history, history of science, Latin American studies, African studies; fsmith@cambridge.org

Beatrice Rehl—Philosophy, classical art and archaeology; brehl@cambridge.org

Eric Crahan—History and political science; ecrahan@cambridge.org

Scott Parris—Economics and finance; sparris@cambridge.org

John Berger—Law; jberger@cambridge.org

Andrew Winnard—Language and linguistics; awinnard@cambridge.org

Marigold Acland—The Middle East, Asia Islamic studies; macland@cambridge.org

Ed Parsons—Textbooks in political science, sociology, and criminology; eparsons@cambridge.org

Lewis Bateman—Political science, history; lbateman@cambridge.org

Simina Calin—Psychology; scalin@cambridge.org

Lauren Cowles—Academic computer science, statistics; lcowles@cambridge.org

Mark Strauss—Anesthesia, emergency medicine, psychiatry, pathology, OB/GYN/repro medicine, dermatology, gastroenterology, hematology/oncology, neurology; mstrauss@cambridge.org

Allan Ross—Biotechnology, pharmacology, molecular biology, genetics, and neuroscience; aross@cambridge.org

Heather Bergman—Computer science; hbergman@cambridge.org

Chris Curcio—Ecology, conservation biology, evolution, and neuroscience; ccurcio@cambridge.org

Peter Gordon—Mechanical, chemical and aerospace engineering; pgordon@cambridge.org

Richard Westood—Education: literacy/English, mathematics/numeracy, cross-curricular; rwestwood@cambridge.org

Peter Canning—Education: secondary assessment, history, music, languages, geography, environment, information/communications technology, mathematics and all areas not otherwise listed; pcanning@cambridge.org

Matthew Winson—Education: secondary English and classics; mwinson@cambridge.org

Kat Booth—Education: sciences, design technology; kbooth@cambridge.org

Noel Kavanagh—International: Caribbean; nkavanagh@cambridge.org

Simon Read—International: IGCSE, IB and other; sread@cambridge.org

Claudia Bickford-Smith—International, IB and other; cbickford-smith@camridge.org

Debbie Goldblatt—English for language teaching: adult courses; dgoldblatt@cambridge.org

Bruce Myint—English for language teaching: adult education; bamyint@cambridge.org

Kathleen Corley—English for language teaching: applied linguistics and professional books for teachers; kcorley@cambridge.org

Bernard Seal—English for academic purposes and pre-academic ESL reading and writing; bseal@cambridge.org

Jane Mairs—Grammar, pronunciation and exams; jmairs@cambridge.org

Lesley Koustaff—Primary and secondary courses; lkoustaff@cambridge.org

Paul Heacock—Reference and vocabulary; pheacock@cambridge.org

Karen Brock—Short courses and general EFL listening, speaking, reading, and writing; kbrock@cambridge.org

COLUMBIA UNIVERSITY PRESS

61 W. 62nd Street, New York, NY 10023

212-459-0600 fax: 212-459-3678

www.columbia.edu/cu/cup

Columbia University Press was founded in 1893 as a nonprofit corporation, separate from Columbia University although bearing its name and associated closely with it. The purpose of the press expressed in the Certificate of Incorporation was to "promote the study of economic, historical, literary, scientific and other subjects; and to promote and encourage the publication of literary works embodying original research in such subjects."

In its first quarter century, the list focused on politics with books by two U.S. presidents, Woodrow Wilson and William Howard Taft. In 1927, the press began publishing major multivolume works. By 1931 the press had grown to such an extent that it published an annual list of 83 new titles—more than any other American university press and 25th among all U.S. publishers.

With the publication of *The Columbia Encyclopedia* in 1935, the press began to develop a list of general reference works in print (several are now in electronic form) that has set it apart from all other American university presses. King's Crown Press was established in 1940 as an imprint for Columbia dissertations: publication was a requirement for a Columbia PhD until the 1950s. In addition, Columbia University's professional program in social work stimulated a strong list of books in that field.

In the 1960s the press became the first—and it is still the only—American university press to publish music. The imprints Columbia University Music Press (for BMI composers) and King's Crown Music Press (for ASCAP composers) were created to publish new music written by Americans. Twentieth-Century Continental Fiction, the press's first fiction series, was launched in the 1980s with novels by Juan Benet (*Return to Region*, translated by Gregory Rabassa) and other leading Iberian Spanish writers not before published in English. In 2007 the Press launched Columbia Business School Publishing, an imprint that publishes practical works of importance by academic and financial professionals.

Columbia now publishes around 160 titles a year in the areas of Asian studies, literature, biology, business, culinary history, current affairs, economics, environmental sciences, film and media studies, finance, history, international affairs, literary studies, Middle Eastern studies, New York City history, philosophy neuroscience, paleontology, political theory, religion, and social work.

Recent titles include *My Life with the Taliban* by Abdul Salam Zaeef; *Smart Growth: Building an Enduring Business by Managing the Risks of Growth* by Edward D. Hess; *India, Pakistan, and the Bomb: Debating Nuclear Stability in South Asia* by Šumit Ganguly and S. Paul Kapur; and *The Matthew Effect: How Advantage Begets Further Advantage* by Daniel Rigney.

Columbia University Press accepts proposals by email or regular mail. However, do not send large files by email. Direct proposals (with SASEs if by regular mail) to the appropriate editor:

Jennifer Crewe, Associate Director and Editorial Director—Asian humanities, film, food history, New York City; jc373@columbia.edu

Lauren Dockett, Executive Editor—Gerontology, psychology, social work; ld2237@columbia.edu

Patrick Fitzgerald, Publisher for the Life Sciences—Conservation biology, environmental sciences, ecology, neuroscience, paleobiology, public health, biomedical sciences; pf2134@columbia.edu

Philip Leventhal, Associate Editor—Literary studies, cultural studies, journalism, media; pl2164@columbia.edu

Wendy Lochner, Senior Executive Editor—Animal studies, religion, philosophy; wl2003@columbia.edu

Anne Routon, Associate Editor—Asian history, international relations, anthropology; akr36@columbia.edu

Myles Thompson, Publisher, Finance and Economics—Finance, economics; mt2312@columbia.edu

CORNELL UNIVERSITY PRESS

Sage House, 512 East State Street, Ithaca, NY 14850

607-277-2338   fax: 607-277-2374

www.cornellpress.cornell.edu

Cornell University Press was established in 1869, giving it the distinction of being the first university press to be established in the United States, although it was inactive for several decades between 1890 and 1930. The house offers 150 new titles a year in many disciplines, including anthropology, Asian studies, biological sciences, classics, cultural studies, history, industrial relations, literary criticism and theory, medieval studies, philosophy, politics and international relations, psychology and psychiatry, veterinary subjects, and women's studies. Submissions are not invited in poetry or fiction. Their many books in the life sciences and natural history are published under the Comstock Publishing Associates imprint, and a list of books in industrial and labor relations is offered under the ILR Press imprint.

Recent titles include *Wild Urban Plants of the Northeast: A Field Guide* by Peter Del Tredici; *Protection for Exporters: Power and Discrimination in Transatlantic Trade Relations, 1930–2010* by Andreas Dür; *Red to Green: Environmental Activism in Post-Soviet Russia* by Laura A. Henry; *Royal Poetrie: Monarchic Verse and the Political Imaginary of Early Modern England* by Peter C. Herman; and *Why Intelligence Fails: Lessons from the Iranian Revolution and the Iraq War* by Robert Jervis.

The house distributes its own titles. Queries and SASEs may be directed to:

Peter J. Potter, Editor in Chief—Literature, medieval studies, classics, and ancient history; pjp33@cornell.edu

John G. Ackerman, Director—European history, intellectual history, Russian/East European studies, music; jga4@cornell.edu

Frances Benson, Editorial Director—Business, labor, workplace issues, health care; fgb2@cornell.edu

Roger Haydon, Executive Editor—Political science, international relations, Asian studies, philosophy; rmh11@cornell.edu

Michael J. McGandy, Acquisitions Editor—American history, American politics, law, New York State, regional books; mjm475@cornell.edu

Heidi Steinmetz Lovette, Science Acquisitions Editor, Comstock Publishing Associates—Biology and natural history, ornithology, herpetology, ichthyology, mammology, entomology, botany, plant sciences; hsl22@cornell.edu

Sara R. Ferguson, Editorial Assistant—srf3@cornell.edu

Rachel E. Post, Editorial Assistant—rep94@cornell.edu

Emily A. Zoss, Editorial Assistant—eaz27@cornell.edu

DUKE UNIVERSITY PRESS

905 West Main Street, Suite 18B, Durham, NC 27701

919-687-3600 fax: 919-688-4574

www.dukeupress.edu email: dukepress@duke.edu

Duke University Press publishes approximately 120 books annually and more than 30 journals. This places the press's books publishing program among the 20 largest at American university presses, and the journals publishing program among the five largest. The relative magnitude of the journals program within the press is unique among American university presses: There is no other publisher of more than 15 journals that also publishes fewer than 175 books per year.

The press publishes primarily in the humanities and social sciences and issues a few publications for primarily professional audiences (e.g., in law or medicine). It is best known for its publications in the broad and interdisciplinary area of theory and history of cultural production, and it is known in general as a publisher willing to take chances with nontraditional and interdisciplinary publications, both books and journals.

Like many other university presses, in addition to scholarly titles, Duke looks for books with crossover appeal for general audiences. For example, *Good Bread Is Back: A Contemporary History of French Bread, the Way It Is Made, and the People Who Make It* by Steven Kaplan appeals to "foodies" as well as scholars.

Other recent titles include *Tropical Zion: General Trujillo, FDR and the Jews of Sousa* by Allen Wells; *Untimely Bollywood: Globalization and India's New Media Assemblage* by Amit Rai; *The Woman in the Zoot Suit: Gender, Nationalism, and the Cultural Politics of Memory* by Catherine Ramiacute; *Fixing Sex: Intersex, Medical Authority, and Lived Experience* by Katrina Karkazis; and *Surviving Against the Odds: Village Industry in Indonesia* by S. Ann Dunham.

Duke University Press requests that you submit a printed copy of your proposal by mail. If you'd like to inquire about potential interest in your project, you may submit a short query by email. Do not submit full proposals electronically unless specifically asked to do so. Direct queries and submissions to:

Ken Wissoker, Editorial Director—Anthropology, cultural studies, postcolonial theory, lesbian and gay studies, construction of race, gender, and national identity, social studies of science, new media, literary criticism, film and television, popular music, visual studies; kwiss@duke.edu

Valerie Millholland, Senior Editor—Latin American history and politics, European history and politics, American history, women's history, environmental studies, labor history, political science; vmill@duke.edu

Miriam Angress, Associate Editor— Religion, women's studies, world history, humanities, cultural studies; mangress@dukeupress.edu

Courtney Berger, Assistant Editor—Political theory, social theory, film and television, geography, gender studies, American studies, Asian American studies, cultural studies of food; cberger@dukeupress.edu

THE FEMINIST PRESS AT THE CITY UNIVERSITY OF NEW YORK

The Graduate Center, 365 Fifth Avenue, Suite 5406, New York, NY 10016

212-817-7925   fax: 212-817-1593

www.feministpress.org

The mission of the Feminist Press is to publish and promote the most potent voices of women from all eras and all regions of the globe. Now in its 39th year, the press has brought more than 300 critically acclaimed works by and about women into print, enriching the literary canon, expanding the historical record, and influencing public discourse about issues fundamental to women.

In addition to publishing new works, this renowned house recovers precious out-of-print and never-in-print documents, establishing the history of women around the globe. The press develops core curriculum materials for all classroom levels, providing young women with strong role models. In recognition of its special role in bringing awareness to international women's issues, the Feminist Press was granted NGO status with the Economic and Social Council of the United Nations in 2000.

The Feminist Press is interested in acquiring primary texts that will have broad, long-term sales in bookstores, as well as the possibility of consistent adoption for college classrooms or use in secondary school classrooms. Through publications and projects, The Feminist Press attempts to contribute to the rediscovery of the history of women in the United States and internationally and to the emergence of a more humane society.

Please note that this house does not publish original fiction, original poetry, drama, doctoral dissertations, or original literary criticism. For the time being, the house has also ceased publishing books for children.

Recent titles from the Feminist Press include *Women in Science: Then and Now* by Vivan Gornick; *Base Ten* by Maryann Lesert; *Walking the Precipice: Witness to the Rise of the Taliban in Afghanistan* by Barbara Bick; *From Eve to Dawn: A History of Women in the World, Vol. III* by Mailyn French; *Dream Homes: From Cairo to Katrina, An Exile's Journey* by Joyce Zonana; and *Inventing the Real: 2008 Edition* by Henry James and Edith Wharton.

To submit, send an email of no more than 200 words describing your book project with the word "submission" in the subject line. Your email should very briefly explain the type of book you are proposing and who you are. Do not send a proposal unless the editors request it, as they will discard all submission materials that arrive without an invitation. Send email query to:

Jeanann Pannasch, Managing Editor; jpannasch@gc.cuny.edu

FORDHAM UNIVERSITY PRESS

University Box L, 2546 Belmont Avenue, Bronx, NY 10458

718-817-4795   fax 718-817-4785

www.fordhampress.com

Fordham University Press was established in 1907 not only to represent and uphold the values and traditions of the University itself, but also to further those values and traditions through the dissemination of scholarly research and ideas.

The press publishes primarily in the humanities and the social sciences, with an emphasis on the fields of philosophy, theology, history, classics, communications, economics, sociology, business, political science, and law, as well as literature and the fine arts. Additionally, the press publishes books focusing on the metropolitan New York region and books of interest to the general public.

Recent titles include *Dutch New York: The Roots of Hudson Valley Culture* by Roger Panetta; *The Hudson-Fulton Celebration: New York's River Festival of 1909 and the Making of a Metropolis* by Kathleen Johnson; *Multiversal* by Amy Catanzano; *Clint Eastwood and Issues of American Masculinity* by Drucilla Cornell; and *On the Commerce of Thinking: On Books and Bookstores* by Jean-Luc Nancy.

Submissions are not accepted via email. Direct proposals and SASEs to:

Helen Tartar, Editorial Director—Philosophy, religion, theology, literary studies, anthropology, law, or any other fields in the humanities or social sciences

Mary-Lou Elias Pena, Assistant to the Director—History, especially World War II, the Civil War and Reconstruction, politics, urban and ethnic studies, media, and New York and the region

GEORGETOWN UNIVERSITY PRESS

3240 Prospect Street, NW, Washington, DC 20007

202-687-5889   fax: 202-687-6340

press.georgetown.edu   email: gupress@georgetown.edu

Georgetown University Press supports the academic mission of Georgetown University by publishing scholarly books and journals for a diverse, worldwide readership. These publications, written by an international group of authors representing a broad range of intellectual perspectives, reflect the academic and institutional strengths of the university. They publish peer-reviewed works in five subjects: bioethics; international affairs and human rights; languages and linguistics; political science, public policy, and public management; and religion and ethics.

The beginnings of Georgetown University Press can be traced to 1964; they currently publish approximately 40 new books a year, as well as two journals, with an active list of close to 500 titles. These publications primarily service the scholarly community, and many also reach into the general reading public. Many help to unite people speaking different languages, literally and figuratively, and all attempt to illuminate, clarify, and respond to the world's most difficult questions.

Recent titles include *A Handbook of Bioethics Terms* by James B. Tubbs, Jr.; *Little Words: Their History, Phonology, Syntax, Semantics, Pragmatics, and Acquisition* by Ronald P. Leow et al; *Ethics and International Affairs: A Reader* by Joel H. Rosenthal and Christian Barry; *Thwarting Enemies at Home and Abroad: How to Be a Counterintelligence Officer* by William R. Johnson; and *Islamic Radicalism and Global Jihad* by Devin R. Springer, James L. Regens, and David N. Edger.

Georgetown University Press does not publish poetry, fiction, memoirs, children's books, *Festschriften*, symposium proceedings, or unrevised dissertations. Send cover letter, prospectus, and SASE via regular mail:

Richard Brown, PhD, Director—Bioethics, international affairs and human rights, religion and politics, and religion and ethics; reb7@georgetown.edu

Gail Grella, Associate Director and Acquisitions Editor—Languages, linguistics; grellag1@georgetown.edu

Donald Jacobs, Acquisitions Editor—International affairs, human rights, public policy, public management; dpj5@georgetown.edu

HARVARD BUSINESS SCHOOL PRESS

60 Harvard Way, Boston, MA 02163

617-783-7400   fax: 617-783-7555

New York office:

75 Rockefeller Plaza, 15th Floor, New York, NY 10019-6926

www.hbsp.harvard.edu   email: asandoval@hbsp.harvard.edu

Harvard Business School Press seeks to influence real-world change by maximizing the reach and impact of its essential offering—ideas. The editors accept proposals for books that take a harder, broader look at the questions that business people face every day. The press is a business unit of Harvard Business School Publishing (HBSP).

HBSP was founded in 1994 as a not-for-profit, wholly-owned subsidiary of Harvard University. Its mission is to improve the practice of management in a changing world. HBSP does this by serving as a bridge between academia and enterprises around the globe through its publications and reach into three markets: academic, enterprise, and individual managers.

HBSP has about 250 employees, primarily based in Boston, with an office in New York City. Its business units are Harvard Business Review magazine and article reprints, Harvard Business School Press, Harvard Business School Publishing Newsletters, Harvard Business School Publishing Conferences, Harvard Business School Publishing Higher Education, and Harvard Business School Publishing eLearning.

Recent titles include *The Lords of Strategy: The Secret Intellectual History of the New Corporate World* by Walter Kiechel; *Seizing the White Space: Business Model Innovation for Growth and Renewal* by Mark W. Johnson; *Winning in Emerging Markets: A Road Map for Strategy and Execution* by Tarun Khanna and Krishna Palepu; *The India Way: How India's Top Business Leaders are Revolutionizing Management* by Peter Cappelli, Harbir Singh, Jittendra Singh, and Michael Useem; and *Earth, Inc.: Using Nature's Rules to Build Sustainable Profits* by Gregory Unruh.

Harvard Business School Press distributes through Perseus.

Send proposals and SASEs via regular mail or email to Courtney E. Schinke, Editorial Coordinator (Boston); cschinke@hbsp.harvard.edu.

Jacqueline Murphy, Senior Editor (Boston)

Jeff Kehoe, Senior Editor (Boston)

Melinda Adams Merino, Editor (Boston)

Kirsten D. Sandberg, Executive Editor (NY)

HARVARD UNIVERSITY PRESS

BELKNAP PRESS

79 Garden Street, Cambridge, MA 02138

800-405-1619/401-531-2800   fax: 401-531-2801

www.hup.harvard.edu   email: contact_HUP@harvard.edu

blog: harvardpress.typepad.com

podcast: www.hup.harvard.edu/audio/index.html

Publisher of enduring tomes such as Lovejoy's *Great Chain of Being*; Giedion's *Space, Time, and Architecture*; Langer's *Philosophy in a New Key*; and Kelly's *Eleanor of Aquitaine and the Four Kings*; Harvard University Press (HUP) holds an exalted position within the university press world. Still, its editors look to attract an audience of general readers as well as scholars, and the press welcomes considered nonfiction proposals.

HUP publishes scholarly books and thoughtful books for the educated general reader in history, philosophy, American literature, law, economics, public policy, natural science, history of science, psychology, and education, and reference books in all the above fields. The Belknap Press imprint, established in 1949, strives to publish books of long-lasting importance, superior scholarship and production, chosen whether or not they might be profitable, thanks to the bequest of Waldron Phoenix Belknap, Jr.

Recent HUP titles include *Lake Views: This World and the Universe* by Steven Weinberg; *Avengers of the New World: The Story of the Haitian Revolution* by Laurent DuBois; *We Ain't What We Ought to Be: The Black Struggle from Emancipation to Obama* by Stephen Tuck; *Natural Experiments in History* by Jared Diamond; and *Coyote at the Kitchen Door: Living with Wildlife in Suburbia* by Stephen DeStephano.

All HUP books are published in English, with translation rights bought by publishers in other countries. The house does not publish original fiction, original poetry, religious inspiration or revelation, cookbooks, guidebooks, children's books, art and photography books, *Festschriften*, conference volumes, unrevised dissertations, or autobiographies.

The HUP website offers photographs of the editors that you may or may not wish to peruse prior to submitting, as well as detailed submission guidelines that you will not want to miss. No electronic submissions. Submit proposals and SASEs to:

Susan Wallace Boehmer, Editor-in-Chief

Michael Fisher, Editor-in-Chief—Evolutionary theory, evolutionary developmental biology, biological and evolutionary anthropology, neuroscience, systems biology and bioinformatives, human genetics, science and society, animal cognition and behavior, history of technology; also books for general readers in physics, astronomy, earth science, chemistry, engineering, and mathematics

Joyce Seltzer, Senior Executive Editor for History and Contemporary Affairs—Serious and scholarly nonfiction that appeals to a general intellectual audience as well as to students and scholars in a variety of disciplines, especially history across a broad spectrum, American studies, contemporary politics, social problems, and biography

Lindsay Waters, Executive Editor for the Humanities—Philosophy, literary studies, cultural studies, film, Asian cultural studies, pop culture, conflicting relations among the races in the United States and around the world

Michael Aronson, Senior Editor for Social Sciences—Economics, business, law, political science, sociology, especially the problems of capitalism such as distribution and inequality

Ann Downer-Hazell, Editor for Life Sciences and Health—Life sciences including natural history, non-primate animal behavior, and evolutionary and organismic biology; consumer and public health medicine, history of medicine, history of life sciences; marine biology, botany/ethnobotany, paleontology, microbiology

Elizabeth Knoll, Senior Editor for Behavioral Sciences and Law—Education, psychology, law, especially political and social aspects of education, universities, and developmental psychology

Shamila Sen, Editor for the Humanities—World religions, classics, ancient history, religion

Kathleen McDermott, Editor for History and Social Sciences—American history, Atlantic history, European history from late medieval to modern, Russian and Central European history, Asian history, international relations, global history, military history, U. S. Western history, Native American history, legal history

Jennifer Snodgrass, Editor for Reference and Special Projects—Reference books and related projects, electronic or multimedia proposals, Loeb Classical Library, The I Tatti Renaissance Library

John Kulka, Executive Editor-At-Large—American, English, and world literature, modernism, history of criticism, theory, the American publishing industry, political journalism, globalization, democracy, and human dignity

---

HOWARD UNIVERSITY PRESS

2225 Georgia Avenue, NW, Suite 718, Washington, DC 20059

202-238-2570   fax: 202-588-9849

www.hupress.howard.edu   email: howardupress@howard.edu

Howard University Press is dedicated to publishing noteworthy new scholarship that addresses the contributions, conditions, and concerns of African Americans, other people of African descent, and people of color around the globe.

Recent titles include *No Boundaries: A Cancer Surgeon's Odyssey* by LaSalle D. Leffall, Jr. MD; *Horace T. Ward: Desegregation of the University of Georgia, Civil Rights Advocacy* by Maurice C. Daniels; *And Then We Heard the Thunder* by John Oliver Killens; *First Freed: Washington D.C. in the Emancipation Era* edited by Elizabeth Clark-Lewis; *One-Third of a Nation: African American Perspectives* edited by Lorenzo Morris and Ura Jean Oyemade Bailey; *The American Paradox: Politics and Justice* by Patrick J. Gallo; *The Black Seminole Legacy and North American Politics, 1693–1845* by Bruce Edward Tyman; *Genocide in Rwanda: A Collective Memory* edited by John A. Berry and Carol Pott Berry; and *Manichean Psychology: Racism and the Minds of People of African Descent* by Camera Jules P. Harrell.

Please submit proposals, résumés, and SASEs by regular mail to the attention of the Editorial Department.

D. Kamali Anderson, Director; danderson@howard.edu

INDIANA UNIVERSITY PRESS

QUARRY BOOKS

601 N. Morton Street, Bloomington, IN 47404

(812) 855-8817/800-842-6796

www.iupress.indiana.edu   email: iupress@indiana.edu

Currently the second-largest public university press, Indiana University Press (IU Press) wants to publish books that will matter 20 or even a 100 years from now—books that make a difference today and will live on into the future through their reverberations in the minds of teachers and writers. IU Press also publishes books with Midwest regional interest through their Quarry Books imprint.

As an academic press, their mandate is to serve the world of scholarship and culture as a professional, not-for-profit publisher. Founded in 1950, IU Press is recognized internationally as a leading academic publisher specializing in the humanities and social sciences. They produce more than 140 new books annually, in addition to 30 journals, and maintain a backlist of some 2,000 titles. The press emphasizes scholarship but also publishes text, trade, and reference titles. Their program is financed primarily by income from sales, supplemented, to a minor extent, by gifts and grants from a variety of outside sources.

IU Press books have won many awards for scholarly merit and design, including two National Book Awards, three Herskovits Awards in African studies, and several National Jewish Book Awards. Numerous IU Press titles are selected every year by Choice as outstanding academic books.

Major subject areas include African, African American, Asian, cultural, Jewish and Holocaust, Middle East, Russian and East European, gender studies, anthropology, film, history, bioethics, music, paleontology, philanthropy, philosophy, and religion.

Recent titles include *Prince Twins Seven-Seven: His Art, His Life in Nigeria, His Exile in America* by Henry Glassie; *A Personal Memoir: Fragments for an Autobiography* by Antoni Tàpies; *Rediscovering Traces of Memory: The Jewish Heritage of Polish Galicia* by Jonathan Webber; *Albee in Performance* by Rakesh H. Solomon; and *Cinema as History: Michel Brault and Modern Quebec* by André Loiselle.

Quarry books focuses on everything about Indiana and the Midwest, exploring subjects such as photography, history, gardening, cooking, sports, leisure, people, and places. Some books from Quarry include *An American Hometown: Terre Haute, Indiana 1927* by Tom Roznowski; *An Amish Patchwork: Indiana's Old Orders in the Modern World* by Thomas J. Meyers and Steven M. Nolt; *The Artists of Brown County* by Lyn Letsinger-Miller; and *Bean Blossom Dreams: A City Family's Search for a Simple Country Life* by Sallyann J. Murphy.

Please submit your inquiry to one editor only. Preliminary inquiries without attachments may be posted by email, but it is recommended that submissions be sent by mail. Direct submissions to:

Janet Rabinowitch, Director—Russian and East European studies, art, Jewish and Holocaust studies, international studies; jrabinow@indiana.edu

Robert Sloan, Editorial Director—U.S. history, African-American studies, bioethics, philanthropy, military history, paleontology, natural history; rjsloan@indiana.edu

Dee Mortensen, Senior Sponsoring Editor—African studies, religion, philosophy; mortense@indiana.edu

Jane Behnken, Sponsoring Editor—Music, cinema, media studies; jbehnken@indiana.edu

Rebecca Tolen, Sponsoring Editor—Anthropology, Asian studies, political science/international relations, folklore; retolen@indiana.edu

Linda Oblack, Assistant Sponsoring Editor—Regional trade, regional natural history, railroads past and present; loblack@indiana.edu

JOHNS HOPKINS UNIVERSITY PRESS

2715 North Charles Street, Baltimore, MD 21218-4363

410-516-6900   fax: 410-516-6968

www.press.jhu.edu

Daniel Coit Gilman, the first president of the Johns Hopkins University, inaugurated the press in 1878. For Gilman, publishing, along with teaching and research, was a primary obligation of a great university. Since that time, the Johns Hopkins University Press has carried the name and mission of the university to every corner of the world. The press has published more than 6,000 titles, of which almost half remain in print today.

The press began as the University's Publication Agency, publishing the *American Journal of Mathematics* in its first year and the *American Chemical Journal* in its second. The agency published its first book, *Sidney Lanier: A Memorial Tribute*, in 1881 to honor the poet who was one of the university's first writers in residence. In 1891, the Publication Agency became the Johns Hopkins Press; since 1972, it has been known as the Johns Hopkins University Press (JHU Press). Today JHU Press is one of the world's largest university presses, publishing 60 scholarly periodicals and more than 200 new books each year.

Recent JHU Press titles include *Moses of South Carolina* by Benjamin Ginsberg; *For Business and Pleasure* by Mara L. Keire; *Managing the President's Message* by

Martha Joyce Kumar; *Pursuing Power and Light* by Bruce J. Hunt; and *An Amish Paradox* by Charles E. Hurst and David L. McConnell.

Direct queries with SASEs to the appropriate acquiring editor:

Trevor C. Lipscombe, Editor-in-Chief—Mathematics, physics, astronomy; tcl@press.jhu.edu

Jacqueline C. Wehmueller, Executive Editor—Consumer health, history of medicine, education; jcw@press.jhu.edu

Henry Y.K. Tom, Executive Editor —Social sciences; hyt@press.jhu.edu

Wendy Harris, Senior Acquisitions Editor—Clinical medicine, public health, health policy; wah@press.jhu.edu

Robert J. Brugger, Senior Acquisitions Editor—American history, history of science and technology, regional books; rjb@press.jhu.edu

Vincent J. Burke, Senior Acquisitions Editor—Biology and life sciences; vjb@press.jhu.edu

Ashleigh Elliot McKown, Assistant Editor—Higher education; aem@press.jhu.edu

KENT STATE UNIVERSITY PRESS

1118 University Library, 1125 Risman Drive, PO Box 5190, Kent, OH 44242-0001

330-672-7913 fax: 330-672-3104

upress.kent.edu email: ksupress@kent.edu

The Kent State University Press began in 1965 under the direction of Howard Allen and published in the university faculty strengths in literary criticism. In 1972 Paul Rohmann became the press's second director and expanded the press's publishing program to include regional studies and ethnomusicology. In 1985 historian John Hubbell assumed the directorship and for 15 years saw the staff and publishing program grow to include widely regarded lists in Civil War history and Ohio history. Today, under director Will Underwood, the press publishes 30–35 titles a year and reaches a large and appreciative audience.

The Kent State University Press is especially interested in acquiring scholarly works in history, including military, Civil War, U.S. diplomatic, American cultural, women's and art history; literary studies; titles of regional interest for Ohio; scholarly biographies; archaeological research; the arts; and general nonfiction.

Recent titles include *A Passion for the Land: John F. Seiberling and the Enviromental Movement* by Daniel Nelson; *All Man: Hemingway, 1950s Men's Magazines, and the Masculine Persona* by David M. Earle; *Scars to Prove It: The Civil War Soldier and*

American Fiction by Craig A. Warren; *The Indian Hater and Other Stories* by James Hall; and *Circus Parade* by Jim Tully.

Direct query letters with SASEs to:

Joyce Harrison, Acquiring Editor

Will Underwood, Director

Mary D. Young, Managing Editor

LOUISIANA STATE UNIVERSITY PRESS

P.O. Box 25053, Baton Rouge, LA 70894-5053

800-848-6224 fax: 225-576-6461

www.lsu.edu/lsupress

Founded in 1935, the Louisiana State University Press is a nonprofit book publisher dedicated to the publication of scholarly, general interest, and regional books. As an integral part of LSU, the press shares the university's goal of the dissemination of knowledge and culture. LSU Press is one of the oldest and largest university presses in the South and only university press to have won a Pulitzer Prize in both fiction and poetry.

The press is perhaps most widely recognized as the original publisher of John Kennedy Toole's Pulitzer Prize-winning novel *A Confederacy of Dunces*. The winner of the 2006 Pulitzer Prize for poetry, *Late Wife* by Claudia Emerson, was also published by the press. Through the years, its books have earned many prestigious honors, including a total of three Pulitzer Prizes, the National Book Award, the National Book Critics Circle Award, the Booker Prize, the American Book Award, the Los Angeles Times Book Prize, the Bancroft Prize, the Lincoln Prize, the Lamont Poetry Selection by the Academy of American Poets, and numerous others.

LSU Press publishes approximately 80 new books each year as well as a backlist of some 1,000 titles. Their primary areas of focus include Southern history, biography, and literature; the Civil War and World War II; poetry; political philosophy and political communications; music studies, particularly jazz; geography and environmental studies; and illustrated books about the Gulf South region. In the mid-1990s the press launched the acclaimed paperback fiction reprint series Voices of the South and in 2005, after a hiatus of about a decade, resumed publishing original fiction under the new series Yellow Shoe Fiction, edited by Michael Griffith.

This is a press that cares whether people outside a narrow theory specialty will understand a text. "We want work that is as accessible as possible," said executive editor John Easterly.

Recent titles include *On the Front Lines of the Cold War: An American Correspondent's Journal from the Chinese Civil War to the Cuban Missile Crisis and Veitnam* by Seymour Topping; *Stations West: A Novel* by Allison Amend; *Lincoln, the Cabinet, and the Generals* by Chester G. Hearn; *Murder in the Metro: Laetitia Toureaux and the Cagoule in 1930s France* by Gayle K. Brunelle and Annette Finley-Croswhite; and *Mosquito Soldiers: Malaria, Yellow Fever, and the Course of the American Civil War* by Andrew McIlwaine Bell.

Proposals for everything except fiction should include a cover letter, table of contents, sample chapters, information about competitive titles, and a résumé or curriculum vitae. Fiction proposals should include a cover letter, a one-page summary of the work, a brief sample from the work, and a résumé. The press is not currently accepting poetry manuscripts. Submit to the appropriate acquisitions editor by regular mail:

John Easterly, Executive Editor—Poetry, fiction, literary studies, regional interest

Rand Dotson, Senior Editor—Slavery, Civil War, Reconstruction, 19th- and 20th-century South, Louisiana roots music

Margaret Hart, Trade Editor—General interest

Alisa Plant, European/Atlantic World History, and Media Studies Editor

MASSACHUSETTS INSTITUTE OF TECHNOLOGY/ THE MIT PRESS

55 Hayward Street, Cambridge, MA 02142-1493

617-253-5646 fax: 617-258-6779

mitpress.mit.edu blog: mitpress.typepad.com

The MIT Press is the only university press in the United States whose list is based in science and technology. This does not mean that science and engineering are all they publish; rather, they are committed to the edges and frontiers of the world—to exploring new fields and new modes of inquiry.

The press publishes about 200 new books a year and are a major publishing presence in fields as diverse as architecture, social theory, economics, cognitive science, and computational science. The MIT Press has a long-term commitment to both design excellence and the efficient and creative use of new technologies. Their goal is to create books that are challenging, creative, attractive, and yet affordable to individual readers.

The MIT Press history starts in 1926 when the physicist Max Born visited MIT to deliver a set of lectures on Problems of Atomic Dynamics. The institute published the lectures under its own imprint, and that book is numbered 1 in the archives of

The MIT Press. In 1932, James R. Killian, Jr.—editor of MIT's alumni magazine and future scientific advisor to President Kennedy and tenth president of MIT—engineered the creation of an institute-sponsored imprint called Technology Press, which published eight titles over the next five years. In 1937, John Wiley & Sons took on editorial and marketing functions for the young imprint, which during the next 25 years published 125 titles. In 1962, MIT amicably severed the Wiley connection and upgraded its imprint to an independent publishing house, naming it The MIT Press.

The creative burst and explosive growth of the 1960s slackened with the library cutbacks of the early 1970s, and by the end of that decade the press knew that it had to rethink what it was doing. They developed a strategy of focusing the list on a few key areas and publishing in depth in those areas. The initial core consisted of architecture, computer science and artificial intelligence, economics, and the emerging interdiscipline of cognitive science. The plan worked wonderfully, and by the mid-1980s the press was again thriving. As the list developed, occasional offshoots sprouted (neuroscience, for example, was spun off from cognitive science in 1987), while a few smaller areas in which they continued to publish—technology studies, aesthetic theory, design, and social theory—have remained viable and interesting components of what has become a unique mix. Their latest addition was an environmental science list, started in the early 1990s.

Recent titles include *ThermoPoetics: Energy in Victorian Literature and Science* by Barri J. Gold; *Living Through the End of Nature: The Future of American Environmentalism* by Paul Wapner; *Art School (Propositions for the 21st Century)* by Steven Henry Madoff; and *The Inner Touch: Archaeology of a Sensation* by Daniel Heller-Roazen.

The MIT Press accepts proposals via email or regular mail with SASE. Submit your proposal to the appropriate editor:

Gita Manaktala, Editorial Director; manak@mit.edu

Phillip Laughlin, Senior Acquisitions Editor—Cognitive science, philosophy; laughlin@mit.edu

Roger Conover, Executive Editor—Art, architecture: visual and cultural studies; conover@mit.edu

Tom Stone, Senior Acquisitions Editor—Cognitive science, linguistics, philosophy, Bradford Books, Zone Books; tstone@mit.ecu

Ada Brunstein, Acquisitions Editor—Computer science, linguistics; adab@mit.edu

John S. Covell, Senior Acquisitions Editor—Economics, finance, business; jcovell@mit.edu

Jane Macdonald, Acquisitions Editor—Economics, finance, business; janem@mit.edu

Clay Morgan, Senior Acquisitions Editor—Environmental and political science, bioethics; claym@mit.edu

Robert Prior, Executive Editor—Life Sciences, neuroscience, biology; prior@mit.edu

Doug Sery, Senior Acquisitions Editor—Design, new media, game studies; dsery@mit.edu

Marguerite Avery, Acquisitions Editor—Science, technology and society, information science; mavery@mit.edu

NEW YORK UNIVERSITY PRESS

838 Broadway, 3rd Floor, New York, NY 10003-4812

212-998-2575   fax: 212-995-3833

www.nyupress.org   email: information@nyupress.org

The NYU Press believes in the idea that academic research and opinion can and should have a prominent place at the table of public debate. At a time of continued upheaval in publishing, some presses, NYU Press among them, detect profound opportunities in this unstable landscape. Rather than bemoaning a lost age, when libraries more or less financed university press operations, these presses are emphasizing their strengths. Convinced that intellectual heft and a user-friendly efficiency need not be mutually exclusive, the staff at NYU Press has sought, in recent years, to redefine what it means to be a university press.

Most importantly, they do not believe that the sole purpose of a university press is to publish works of objective social science, though to be sure this remains an important role of the house mandate. Rather, NYU Press also eagerly embraces the role of a gadfly. They oftentimes publish books on the same issue from different poles of the political spectrum in the same catalog, to generate dialogue, engender debate, and resist pat categorization of the publishing program. Rather than praise diversity as an abstract goal, they embrace ideological diversity as a crucial, defining ingredient for a healthy program. They do so with a list of around 100 new books a year and a backlist of over 1,500 titles.

On a logistical level, NYU Press believes that, in the world of nonfiction publishing, the scales have far too long been tipped in favor of the publishers. The house therefore rejects exclusive review, encouraging authors to submit their manuscripts widely, should they wish to do so, to ensure their decision, if they publish with this house, is an educated one, not the result of artificial restrictions. NYU Press believes that any long-term relationship between an author and publisher must be predicated on mutual respect. Thus, they place enormous emphasis on a close working relationship with authors. Further, they provide high-quality production and decades of craft experience. Importantly, they can provide all these advantages alongside one crucial guarantee: No one will ever take this house over.

NYU Press is interested in titles that explore issues of race and ethnicity. They are also highly interested in media studies and American studies.

Recent titles include *Dangerous Curves* by Isabel Molina-Guzman; *Empire of Sacrifice* by Jon Pahl; *Musical ImagiNation* by Maria Elena Cepeda; *The Politics of Protest* by Jerome H. Skolnick; *Who You Claim* by Lola Williamson; *Inside Insurgency* by Claire Metelits; and *On the Make* by Brian P. Luskey.

No submissions through email. Query letters and SASEs should be directed to:

Eric Zinner, Editor-in-Chief—Literary criticism and cultural studies, media studies, American history; eric.zinner@nyu.edu

Ilene Kalish, Executive Editor—Sociology, criminology, politics; ilene.kalish@nyu.edu

Jennifer Hammer, Editor—Religion, psychology, anthropology; jennifer.hammer@nyu.edu

Deborah Gershenowitz, Senior Editor—American history to 1900, American military history, law; deborah.gershenowitz@nyu.edu

NORTHWESTERN UNIVERSITY PRESS

629 Noyes Street, Evanston, IL 60208-4210

847-491-2046 fax: 847-491-8150

nupress.northwestern.edu email: nupress@northwestern.edu

From its inception Northwestern University Press has striven to be at the forefront in publishing not only scholarly works in different disciplines, but also quality works of fiction, nonfiction, and literary criticism.

Founded in 1893, the early years of the press were dedicated to the publication of legal periodicals and scholarly books dealing with the law. In 1957 the press was established as a separate university publishing company and began expanding its offerings with new series in various fields, including African studies, phenomenology and existential philosophy, literature, and literary criticism.

In the late 1960s, the press published Viola Spolin's landmark volume, *Improvisation for the Theater: A Handbook of Teaching and Directing Techniques*. This "bible" of improvisational theater has sold more than 100,000 copies since its publication and, with several other Spolin titles, forms a cornerstone of the press's publishing program. The press continues its commitment to theater and performance studies, most recently with the publication of Mary Zimmerman's *Metamorphoses*, the script of her Broadway show that was nominated for the 2002 Tony award for Best Play and Best Scenic Design, and won the 2002 Tony award for Best Director.

Since 1992 Northwestern University Press has doubled its publishing output.

In addition to the works of contemporary European writers, the press has also begun to reissue lost or previously untranslated works of important European authors, including Nobel Prize winners Heinrich Böll and Grazia Deledda. Scholarly series include Rethinking Theory, Studies in Russian Literature and Theory, Writings from an Unbound Europe, Avant-Garde and Modernism Studies, and Studies in Phenomenology and Existential Philosophy. In 1992 the press joined forces with *TriQuarterly* magazine—Northwestern University's innovative literary journal aimed at a sophisticated and diverse readership—to establish the TriQuarterly Books imprint, which is devoted primarily to contemporary American fiction and poetry. In addition, the press has a second trade imprint, Hydra Books, which features contemporary fiction, poetry, and nonfiction in translation. In 1997 *TriQuarterly* magazine itself became a publication of the press. In 2002 the press began publishing Chicago regional titles, such as *A Court That Shaped America: Chicago's Federal Court from Abe Lincoln to Abbie Hoffman* by Richard Cahan.

Recent titles include *The Conservative Resurgence and the Press: The Media's Role in the Rise of the Right* by James McPherson; *Harvest of Blossoms: Poems of a Life Cut Short* by Selma Meerbaum-Eisinger; *Hegel of Hamann* by G.W.F. Hegel; *Isaac B. Singer: A Life* by Florence Noiville; and *The Moral Obligation to Be Intelligent* by Lionel Trilling.

To submit fiction, poetry, or general nonfiction, please send the complete manuscript or several sample chapters along with biographical information on the author, including a list of previously published books. Because of the high volume of submissions, allow at least 16 weeks for the review of your manuscript.

To submit a scholarly manuscript, please send a proposal, cover letter, and CV. Allow approximately 12 weeks for the review of your manuscript.

Please do not call. Send queries and SASEs to: Acquisitions Department.

Henry L. Carrigan Jr., Senior Editor; h-carrigan@northwestern.edu

Mike Levine, Acquisitions Editor; mike-levine@northwestern.edu

Jenny Gavacs, Assistant Acquisitions Editor; j-gavacs@northwestern.edu

Anne Gendler, Managing Editor; a-gendler@northwestern.edu

Serena Brommel, Senior Project Editor; s-brommel@northwestern.edu

Heather Antti, Senior Project Editor; h-antti@northwestern.edu

OHIO STATE UNIVERSITY PRESS

180 Pressey Hall, 1070 Carmack Road, Columbus, OH 43210-1002
614-292-6930   fax: 614-292-2065
www.ohiostatepress.org

The Ohio State University Press was established in 1957 and currently publishes 30 new books a year. Areas of specialization include literary studies, including narrative theory; history, including business history, medieval history, and history of crime; political science, including legislative studies; and Victorian studies, urban studies, and women's health. They also publish annual winners of short fiction and poetry prizes, the details of which are available at www.ohiostatepress.org.

Recent titles include *Basics of Language for Language Learners* by Peter W. Culicover and Elizabeth V. Hume; *The Affective Life of the Average Man: The Victorian Novel and the Stock-Market Graph* by Audrey Jaffe; *Educating Seeta: The Anglo-Indian Family Romance and the Poetics of Indirect Rule* by Shuchi Kapila; *Tabloid, Inc.: Crimes, Newspapers, Narratives* by V. Penelope Pelizzon and Nancy M. West; *Darkly Perfect World: Colonial Adventure, Postmodernism, and American Noir* by Stanley Orr; and *Uncanny Subjects: Aging in Contemporary Narrative* by Amerlia DeFalco.

Ohio State University Press oversees its own sales and distribution.

Scholars proposing manuscripts for publication should submit whatever materials they feel are necessary for the acquisitions department at Ohio State University Press to make informed decisions about the project. Query letters and SASEs should be directed to:

Sandy Crooms, Senior Editor—Literary studies, Victorian studies, narrative, American studies, women's studies, women and health; sandy.crooms@osupress.org

Malcolm Litchfield, Acquisitions Editor—Medieval studies, literary theory other than narrative; ml@osupress.org

Eugene O'Connor, PhD, Acquisitions Editor—Classics; Eugene@osupress.org

OXFORD UNIVERSITY PRESS

198 Madison Avenue, New York, NY 10016

212-726-6003

www.oup-usa.org blog: blog.oup.com

Oxford University Press, Inc. (OUP USA), is by far the largest American university press and perhaps the most diverse publisher of its type. It publishes works that further Oxford University's objective of excellence in research, scholarship, and education.

The press had its origins in the information technology revolution of the late 15th century, which began with the invention of printing from movable type. The first book was printed in Oxford in 1478. In 1586, the university itself obtained a decree confirming its privilege to print books. This was further enhanced in the

Great Charter secured by Archbishop Laud from King Charles I, which entitled the university to print "all manner of books." The university first appointed delegates to oversee this privilege in 1633. Minutes recording their deliberations date back to 1668, and OUP as it exists today began to develop in a recognizable way from that time.

OUP's international expansion began with the opening of a U.S. office in 1896. The office was established initially simply to sell bibles published in Oxford, but by the 1920s, the office began to produce books on its own. The first nonfiction work published by OUP USA, *The Life of Sir William Osler*, won the Pulitzer Prize in 1926. Six more Pulitzers, several National Book Awards, and over a dozen Bancroft Prizes in American history have followed since.

Oxford's New York office is editorially independent of the British home office and handles distribution of its own list, as well as titles originating from Oxford's branches worldwide. OUP USA publishes at a variety of levels, for a wide range of audiences in almost every academic discipline. The main criteria in evaluating new titles are quality and contribution to the furtherance of scholarship and education. OUP USA produces approximately 500 titles each year, of which 250 are scholarly research monographs, and imports close to 800 such works from their UK and branch offices. OUP USA has 3,300 scholarly books in print and stocks another 8,700 imports from other OUP offices around the world. All publications are first vetted by OUP's delegates, who are leading scholars at Oxford University and from other top U.S. institutions.

OUP editor Shannon McMahan said recently that the press is especially interested in acquiring titles that explore "material based studies," and such topics as print culture, environmentalism, and literature and the law.

Recent titles include *Naked City: The Death and Life of Authentic Urban Places* by Sharon Zukin; *The Oxford Companion to the Book* by Michael Suarez SJ; *A Genius for Deception: How Cunning Helped the British Win Two World Wars* by Nicholas Rankin; *Red Families v. Blue Families: Legal Polarization and the Creation of Culture* by Naomi Cahn; and *Always On: Language in an Online and Mobile World* by Naomi Baron.

OUP USA welcomes submissions. Potential authors should include a cover letter, a copy of their CV, a prospectus, and sample chapters from the work (if available). In general all material should be unbound and double-spaced on single-sided paper. Material may be sent in care of the appropriate editor:

Niko Pfund, Academic Publisher

Stefan Vranka, Editor—Classical studies; stefan.vranka@oup.com

James Cook, Editor—Criminology; james.cook@oup.com

David McBride, Editor—Current affairs, political science, law, (Trade), sociology (Trade); david.mcbride@oup.com

Sarah Harrington, Editor—Developmental psychology; sarah.harrington@oup.com

Joan Bossert, Associate Publisher—Neuroscience, consumer health, psychological and behavioral sciences; joan.bossert@oup.com

Catharine Carlin, Associate Publisher—Cognitive neuroscience, ophthalmology, cognitive psychology; catharine.carlin@oup.com

Susan Ferber, Editor—American and world history, art history, academic art and architecture; susan.ferber@oup.com

Larry Selby, Editor—Law (Practitioner); larry.selby@oup.com

Chris Collins, Editor—Law (Academic); chris.collins@oup.com

Tisse Takagi, Editor—Life Sciences; tisse.takagi@oup.com

Jeremy Lewis, Editor—Chemistry; jeremy.lewis@oup.com

Peter Ohlin, Editor—Bioethics, linguistics, philosophy; peter.ohlin@oup.com

Phyllis Cohen, Editor—Mathematics and statistics; phyllis.cohen@oup.com

Cynthia Read, Senior Editor—Religion (trade); cynthia.read@oup.com

Donald Kraus, Executive Editor—Bibles; donald.kraus@oup.com

Andrea Seils, Anesthesiology; andrea.seils@oup.com

Shannon McLachlan, Editor—American studies, classical studies, English language and literature, literary studies, film; shannon.mclachlan@oup.com

Terry Vaughn, Editor—Business management, economics, finance and financial economics; terry.vaughn@oup.com

Mariclaire Cloutier, Editor—Forensic psychology, clinical psychology; mariclaire.cloutier@oup.com

Craig Panner, Editor—Neurology; craig.panner@oup.com

Shelley Reinhardt, Editor—Neuropsychology; shelley.reinhardt@oup.com

Lori Handelman, Editor—Social psychology; lori.handelman@oup.com

Maura Roessner, Editor—Social work; maura.roessner@oup.com

Theo Calderera, Editor—Religion (academic); theo.calderera@oup.com

William Lamsback, Editor—Medicine, neurology, public health; william.lamsback@oup.com

Suzanne Ryan, Editor—Music (books); suzanne.ryan@oup.com

Todd Waldman, Editor—Music (sheet music); todd.waldman@oup.com

Sonke Adlung, Editor—Physics; sonke.adlung@oup.com

PENN STATE UNIVERSITY PRESS

820 North University Drive, University Support Building 1, Suite C, University Park, PA 16802-1003

814-865-1327 fax: 814-863-1408

www.psupress.psu.edu email: info@psupress.org

The Penn State University Press is dedicated to serving the university community, the citizens of Pennsylvania, and the worldwide network of scholars by publishing books and journals of the highest quality. In fulfilling its role as part of the University's division of research and graduate education, the press promotes the advance of scholarship by disseminating knowledge—new information, interpretations, methods of analysis—and strives to reflect academic strengths of the university. As an integral part of the university community, the press collaborates with alumni, friends, faculty, and staff in producing books about aspects of university life and history. As the publishing arm of a land-grant and state-supported institution, the press recognizes its special responsibility to develop books about Pennsylvania, both scholarly and popular, that enhance interest in the region and spread awareness of the state's history, culture, and environment.

The origins of the press go back to 1945, when a committee at the university was appointed "to study the advisability and practicability of establishing a Pennsylvania State College Press." No immediate action was taken, but in 1953, as a first experiment in university press publishing, the Department of Public Information (then directed by Louis H. Bell) issued a book entitled *Penn State Yankee: The Autobiography of Fred Lewis Pattee*, which Mr. Bell himself edited and designed. The experiment evidently proved successful enough to persuade the trustees board in 1956 to establish the Pennsylvania State University Press "on an experimental basis."

The press's strengths include core areas such as art history and literary criticism as well as fields such as philosophy, religion, history (mainly U.S. and European), and some of the social sciences (especially political science and sociology).

Recent titles include *Dapper Dan Flood: The Controversial Life of a Congressional Power Broker* by William C. Kashatus; *The First White House Library: A History and Annotated Catalogue* edited by Catherine M. Parisian; *David Franks: Colonial Merchant* by Mark Abbott Stern; *Rural Education for the Twenty-First Century: Identity, Place, and Community in a Globalizing World* edited by Kai A. Schafft and Alecia Youngblood Jackson; and *Gender and Populism in Latin America: Passionate Politics* edited by Karen Kampwirth.

If you have questions about submissions, Penn State Press invites you to call or email with Manuscript Submissions in the subject line. Direct queries and SASEs to:

Patrick H. Alexander, Editor-in-Chief—American studies, European history and culture, history, medieval and early modern studies, philosophy, regional studies, religion, religious studies, romance studies, and Slavic studies; pha3@psu.edu

Eleanor Goodman PhD, Executive Editor for the Arts & Humanities—Art and art history, architectural history, European history and culture (Spanish, French), literature, medieval and early modern studies, visual culture; ehg11@psu.edu

Sanford G. Thatcher, Director—Latin American studies, law, philosophy (feminist, legal, political), political science, and sociology; sgt3@psu.edu

PRINCETON UNIVERSITY PRESS

41 William Street, Princeton, NJ 08540-5237

609-258-4900   fax: 609-258-6305

www.pup.princeton.edu

UK office:

3 Market Place, Woodstock, Oxfordshire OX20 1SY, UK

011-44-1993-814500

Princeton University Press, which celebrated its 100th anniversary in 2005, is one of the country's largest and oldest university presses. The press publishes some 200 new books in hardcover each year and another 90 paperback reprints. With a goal to disseminate scholarship both within academia and to society at large, the press produces publications that range across more than 40 disciplines, from art history to ornithology and political science to philosophy.

The press is an independent publisher with close connections, both formal and informal, to Princeton University. Its five-member editorial board, which makes controlling decisions about which books will bear the press's imprint, is appointed from the faculty by the president of the university, and 9 of the 15 members of the press's board must have a Princeton University connection.

Recent titles include *The Best of All Possible Worlds: A Story of Philosophers, God, and Evil in the Age of Reason* by Steven Nadler; *The Church in the Shadow of the Mosque: Christians and Muslims in the World of Islam* by Sidney H. Griffith; *Democracy and Knowledge: Innovation and Learning in Classical Athens* by Josiah Ober; *God and Race in American Politics: A Short History* by Mark A. Noll; *Greece—A Jewish History* by K.E. Fleming; and *Luxury Fever: Money and Happiness in an Era of Excess* by Robert H. Frank.

The Bollingen Series, established in 1941, is sponsored by the Bollingen Foundation and has been published by Princeton since 1967. Bollingen titles are works of original scholarship, translations, or new editions of classics. An ongoing

Bollingen project is Mythos: The Princeton/Bollingen series in world mythology. Titles representative of the list include *The Collected Works of Samuel Taylor Coleridge, Volume 15: Opus Maximum*, edited by Thomas McFarland; *The I Ching or Book of Changes* edited by Hellmut Wilhelm, translated by Cary F. Baynes; and *Essays on a Science of Mythology: The Myth of the Divine Child and the Mysteries of Eleusis* by C.G. Jung and C. Kerényi.

Books from the Princeton Science Library include *Fearful Symmetry: The Search for Beauty in Modern Physics* by A. Zee; *Eye and Brain: The Psychology of Seeing* by Richard L. Gregory; *Flatland: A Romance of Many Dimensions* by Edwin Abbott; and *Why Big Fierce Animals Are Rare: An Ecologist's Perspective* by Paul A. Colinvaux.

Princeton University Press handles distribution through the offices of California/Princeton Fulfillment Services, as well as regional sales representation worldwide. Princeton University Press does not accept unsolicited proposals or manuscripts via email. Queries or brief proposals along with a copy of your CV and SASEs should be mailed via regular mail addressed to the Editorial Administrator.

Peter Dougherty, Director

Brigitta van Rheinberg, Editor-in-Chief—History (American, European, Middle Eastern, Jewish, Asian, Medieval, Ancient, and World)

Fred Appel, Associate Editor—Music, anthropology, literature

Seth Ditchik, Senior Editor—Economics, finance, behavioral and cognitive sciences

Ingrid Gnerlich, Senior Editor—Physical sciences, earth sciences

Alison Kalett, Editor—Biology, earth sciences

Vickie Kearn, Executive Editor—Mathematics

Robert Kirk, Executive Editor—Natural history, biology, ornithology, field guides

Chuck Myers, Executive Editor—Political science, law

Clara Platter, Assistant Editor—American history

Anna Savarese, Senior Editor—Reference

Eric Schwartz, Editor—Sociology, cognitive sciences

Robert Tempio, Editor—Philosophy, classics, ancient world

Hanne Winarsky, Editor—Literature, art

RUTGERS UNIVERSITY PRESS

RIVERGATE BOOKS

100 Joyce Kilmer Avenue, Piscataway, NJ 08854-8099

732-445-7762 ext. 605   fax: 732-445-7039

rutgerspress.rutgers.edu

Since its founding in 1936 as a nonprofit publisher, Rutgers University Press has been dedicated to the advancement and dissemination of knowledge to scholars, students, and the general reading public. An integral part of one of the leading public research and teaching universities in the U.S., the press reflects and is essential to the university's missions of research, instruction, and service. To carry out these goals, the house publishes books in print and electronic format in a broad array of disciplines across the humanities, social sciences, and sciences. Fulfilling a mandate to serve the people of New Jersey, it also publishes books of scholarly and popular interest on the state and surrounding region.

Working with authors throughout the world, the house seeks books that meet high editorial standards, facilitate the exchange of ideas, enhance teaching, and make scholarship accessible to a wide range of readers. The press's overriding ambition is nothing less than to help make the world better, one book at a time, through a publication program of superior scholarship and popular appeal. The press celebrates and affirms its role as a major cultural institution that contributes significantly to the ideas that shape the critical issues of our time.

The press's strengths include history, sociology, anthropology, religion, media, film studies, women's studies, African American studies, Asian American studies, public health, history of medicine, evolutionary biology, the environment, and books about the Mid-Atlantic region.

Recent titles published by Rutgers University Press include *Girlhood: A Global History* edited by Colleen A. Vasconcellos; *New Blood: Third-Wave Feminism and the Politics of Menstruation* by Chris Bobel; *Through Our Eyes: African American Men's Experiences of Race, Gender, and Violence* by Gail Garfield; *Surveillance in the Time of Insecurity* by Torin Monahan; and *Managing Ethnic Diversity After 9/11: Intergration, Security, and Civil Liberties in Transatlantic Perspective* edited by Ariance Chebel d'Appollonia and Simon Reich.

Rutgers is proud to announce Rivergate Books, an imprint devoted to New Jersey and surrounding states. New titles from Rivergate include *Knickerbocker: The Myth Behind New York* by Elizabeth L. Bradley; *No Minor Accomplishment: The Revival of New Jersey Professional Baseball* by Bob Golon; *How Newark Became Newark: The Rise, Fall, and Rebirth of an American City* by Brad R. Tuttle; *Local Heroes: The Asbury Park Music Scene* by Anders Martensson; and *The George Washington Bridge: Poetry in Steel* by Michael Aaron Rockland.

Rutgers University Press handles its own distribution.
Query letters and SASEs should be directed to:

Leslie Mitchner, Associate Director and Editor-in-Chief—Humanities, literature, film, communications; lmitch@rutgers.edu

Peter Mickulas, Editor; mickulas@rutgers.edu

Katie Keeran, Editorial Assistant; ckeeran@rutgers.edu

STANFORD UNIVERSITY PRESS

1450 Page Mill Road, Palo Alto, CA 94304-1124

650-723-9434 fax: 650-725-3457

www.sup.org email: info@www.sup.org

Stanford University Press maintains specific publishing strategies that mirror not only Stanford's commitment to the unfettered creation and communication of new knowledge, but also its commitment to offering an undergraduate education that is unrivaled among research universities, and its commitment to training tomorrow's leaders in a range of graduate professional disciplines.

They do this by making available a range of highly specialized and peer-reviewed research that otherwise might not be published; making major foreign-language works available in translation here, and making books available in foreign-language editions abroad; keeping books in print and debate alive, often for decades; publishing the work of new scholars, thereby adding their voices and views to ongoing debates—and often precipitating new ones; publishing textbooks for upper-level undergraduate courses and graduate courses; publishing reference works for professional practitioners; making all works for which the house has electronic rights available through the main electronic aggregators, including ebrary, netLibrary, Questia, Google, and Books 24x7.

In pursuit of these strategies, the press publishes about 130 books per year. About two-thirds of these books are scholarly monographs and textbooks in the humanities and the social sciences, with a strong concentration in history, literature, philosophy, and Asian studies, and growing lists in politics, sociology, anthropology, and religion. The remaining one-third are textbooks, professional reference works, and monographs in law, business, economics, public policy, and education. Tenure monographs account for about 20 percent of their scholarly output, and translations account for about 12 percent.

In keeping with the high intellectual quality of the works the house publishes, the press ensures that every title it releases benefits from exacting professional standards for editing, design, and manufacturing. It also ensures that each book is carefully positioned in the market channel most appropriate for reaching its primary audience—that is, libraries, bookstores, online vendors, electronic collections, and searchable databases.

Working hard to maintain this commitment to intellectual quality and high production values is a creative, energetic, and enthusiastic staff who work closely together to make the whole process from manuscript creation to publication both seamless for the author and timely for the buyer. Their efforts are augmented by a global sales, marketing, and distribution network that gives access to wholesale and retail buyers in all the key markets of the Americas, Europe, Asia, and Australia.

Recent titles include *The Politics of Trafficking: The First International Movement to Combat the Sexual Exploitation of Women* by Stephanie A. Limoncelli; *Corporate Community Involvement: The Definitive Guide to Maximizing Your Business' Societal Engagement* by Nick Lakin and Veronica Scheubel; *Henry Kaplan and the Story of Hodgkin's Disease* by Charlotte DeCroes Jacobs; *Your Career Game: How Game Theory Can Help You Achieve Your Professional Goals* by Nathan Bennett and Stephen A. Miles; and *The Power of Song: Music and Dance in the Mission Communities of Northern New Spain, 1590–1810* by Kristin Dutcher Mann.

Stanford University Press books are distributed by Cambridge University Press Distribution Center.

Initial inquiries about publication should be made directly to the appropriate sponsoring editor at the press. Do not send complete manuscripts until invited to do so by the editor. Query letters and SASEs should be directed to:

Geoffrey Burn, Director and Acquisitions Editor—Business strategy and security studies; grhburn@stanford.edu

Alan Harvey, Deputy Director and Editor-in-Chief; aharvey@stanford.edu

Norris Pope, Director of Scholarly Publishing—History, Latin American studies, Jewish studies; npope@stanford.edu

Kate Wahl, Executive Editor—Sociology, law, Middle East studies; kwahl@stanford.edu

Margo Beth Crouppen, Acquisitions Editor—Economics and organizational studies; mbcrouppen@stanford.edu

Stacy Wagner, Acquisitions Editor—Asian studies, Asian American studies, political science; swagner@stanford.edu

Emily-Jane Cohen, Acquisitions Editor—Literature, philosophy, religion; beatrice@stanford.edu

Jennifer Hele, Acquisitions Editor—Anthropology, education; jhele@stanford.edu

STATE UNIVERSITY OF NEW YORK PRESS

EXCELSIOR EDITIONS

194 Washington Avenue, Suite 305, Albany, NY 12210-2384

518-472-5000 fax: 518-472-5038

www.sunypress.edu email: info@sunypress.edu

State University of New York Press (SUNY Press) publishes scholarly and trade books in support of the university's commitments to teaching, research, and public service. With an editorial board made up of SUNY faculty from throughout the state, SUNY Press has a large catalog, featuring authors from around the world.

From a modest beginning in 1966, SUNY Press has become one of the largest public university presses in the U.S., with an annual output of some 170 books and a backlist of more than 4,000 titles. The press publishes chiefly in the humanities and social sciences, and has attained national recognition in the areas of education, philosophy, religion, Jewish studies, Asian studies, political science, and sociology, with increasing growth in the areas of literature, film studies, communication, women's studies, and environmental studies.

Recent titles include *In the Hamptons Too: Further Encounters with Farmers, Fisherman, Artists, Billionaires, and Celebrities* by Dan Rattinere; *Blows to the Head: How Boxing Changed My Mind* by Binnie Klein; *Truckin' with Sam: A Father and Son, The Mick and the Dyl, Rockin' and Rollin', on the Road* by Lee Gutkind; *The Italian Actress: A Novel* by Frank Lentricchia; and *The Smoking Horse: A Memoir in Pieces* by Stephen Spotte.

Excelsior Editions showcases the history of New York and surrounding states while at the same time making available noteworthy and essential popular books, both classic and contemporary. Some titles from Excelsior Editions include *The Revelation of the Breath: A Tribute to Its Wisdom, Power, and Beauty* by Sharon G. Mijares; *Frank, The Story of Frances Folsom Cleveland, America's Youngest First Lady* by Annette Dunlap; *Once an Engineer: A Song of the Salt City* by Joe Amato; *Letters to a Best Friend* by Richard Seltzer; and *The Firekeeper: A Narrative of the New York Frontier* by Robert Moss.

SUNY Press accepts simultaneous submissions of proposals; however, at the manuscript review stage they prefer an exclusive review. To submit, send a proposal with SASE to:

Jane Bunker, Editor-in-Chief—Philosophy, transpersonal psychology; jane.bunker@sunypress.edu

Larin McLaughlin, Acquisitions Editor—Women's and gender studies, African American studies, queer studies; larin.mclaughlin@sunypress.edu

Amanda Lanne, Editorial Assistant

Andrew Kenyon, Editorial Assistant

Zachary Moning, Editorial Assistant

Nancy Ellegate, Senior Acquisitions Editor—Religious studies, Asian studies; nancy.ellegate@sunypress.edu

James Peltz, Associate Director—Excelsior Editions; james.peltz@sunypress.edu

SYRACUSE UNIVERSITY PRESS

621 Skytop Road, Suite 110, Syracuse, NY 13244-5290

315-443-5534 fax: 315-443-5545

www.syracuseuniversitypress.syr.edu email: supress@syr.edu

Syracuse University Press was founded in 1943 by Chancellor William Pearson Tolley, with the intent to enhance the school's academic standing. With more than 1,200 titles in print today, the press consistently earns international critical acclaim and attracts award-winning authors of note.

Each year Syracuse University Press publishes new books in specialized areas including New York State, Middle East Studies, Judaica, geography, Irish studies, Native American studies, religion, television, and popular culture.

Recent titles include *Feeding Mrs. Moskowitz and The Caregiver: Two Stories* by Barbara Pokras and Fran Pokras Yariv; *Missing a Beat: The Rants and Regrets of Seymour Krim* by Mark Cohen; *The Man Who Guarded the Bomb: Stories* by Gregory Orfalea; *Martyrdom Street* by Firoozeh Kashani-Sabet; *One Family's Response to Terrorism: A Daughter's Memoir* by Susan Kerr van de Ven.

Syracuse University Press distributes its list via its own in-house offices and utilizes a variety of distribution services worldwide.

Please send a proposal, abstract, and CV with SASE to:

Mary Selden Evans, Executive Editor; msevans@syr.edu

Annelise Finegan, Acquisition Editor; amfinega@syr.edu

Marcia Hough, Acquisitions Assistant; mshough@syr.edu

TEXAS A&M UNIVERSITY PRESS CONSORTIUM

John H. Lindsey Building, Lewis Street, 4354 TAMU, College Station, TX, 77843-4354

979-845-1436 fax: 949-847-8752

www.tamu.edu/upress email: dlv@tampress.tamu.edu

TEXAS STATE HISTORICAL ASSOCIATION PRESS

1155 Union Circle #311580, Denton, TX 76203-5017

940-369-5200 fax: 940-369-5248

www.tshaonline.org

TEXAS CHRISTIAN UNIVERSITY PRESS

3000 Sandage, Fort Worth, TX 76109

817-257-7822 fax: 817-257-5075

www.prs.tcu.edu

UNIVESITY OF NORTH TEXAS PRESS

1155 Union Circle #311336, Denton, TX 76203-5017

940-565-2142 fax: 940-565-4590

www.unt.edu/untpress

SOUTHERN METHODIST UNIVERSITY PRESS

PO Box 750415, Dallas, TX 75275-0415

214-768-1432 fax: 214-768-1428

www.smu.edu

STATE HOUSE PRESS/MCWHINEY FOUNDATION PRESS

PO Box 818, Buffalo Gap, TX 79508

325-572-3974 fax: 325-572-3991

www.tshaonline.org

TEXAS REVIEW PRESS

PO Box 2146, SHSU Div. of English and Foreign Languages, Evans Bldg., Rm. #152, Huntsville, TX 77341-2146

936-294-1992 fax: 936-294-3070

www.shsu.edu/~www_trp

Founded in 1974, Texas A&M University Press is the principal publishing arm of one of this nation's leading research institutions. The press's primary mission is to select, produce, market, and disseminate scholarly publications of outstanding quality and originality and thereby help the university achieve its paramount purposes of teaching, research, public service, and dissemination of the results of scholarly inquiry. In conjunction with the long-term development of its editorial program, the press draws on and supports the intellectual activities of the university and reflects the standards and stature of scholarship that are fostered by this institution.

The press falls under the administrative aegis of the provost, the chief academic officer of the University, and is an integral part of its parent institution. The press imprint is controlled by an advisory committee composed of senior members of the university's faculty, who are chosen for their own scholarly acumen and publishing experience. Manuscripts, whether by outside authors or by members of the Texas A&M faculty (currently around 15 percent of the total author list), must have been reviewed favorably by both the press's director and editorial staff and at least two experts in that field before being submitted to the faculty advisory committee for approval. Of the hundreds of manuscripts and proposals that come to the press each year, most do not survive this rigorous selection process.

The press's editorial interests span a range of significant fields, including agriculture, anthropology, nautical archaeology, architecture, borderland studies, Eastern Europe, economics, military history, natural history, presidential studies, veterinary medicine, and works on the history and culture of Texas and the surrounding region. Many of these fields of interest reflect outstanding departmental and programmatic strengths at Texas A&M University. Overall, the press seeks to maintain high standards in traditional areas of academic inquiry while also exploring innovative fields of research and new forms of scholarly communication.

The press currently publishes more than 70 new titles a year in these fields. Of the total of nearly 930 books published by the press in its 34-year history, the great majority remains in print or are available in on-demand and electronic editions.

Recent titles include *Waiting* by Linda Moore-Lanning; *Lovin' that Lone Star Flag* by E. Joe Deering; *Spanish Water, Anglo Water: Early Development in San Antonio* by Charles R. Porter Jr.; *To the Line of Fire!: Mexican Texans and World War I* by Jose A. Ramirez; *War and the Environment: Military Destruction in the Modern Age* edited by Chalres E. Closmann; and *13 Days to Glory: The Siege of the Alamo* by Lon Tinkle.

The Texas State Historical Association was the first member of the Texas A&M University Press Consortium. Founded in 1897, the TSHA Press specializes in books of Texas History and Texana, both new titles and reprints of classics. Some new titles include *Road, River, and Ol' Boy Politics: A Texas County's Path from Farm to Supersuburb* by Linda Scarbrough; *Giant under the Hill: A History of the Spindletop Oil Discovery at Beaumont, Texas, in 1901* by Jo Ann Stiles et al; *General Vicente Filisola's Analysis of Jose Urrea's Military Diary* by Gregg J. Dimmick; and *Biracial Unions on Galveston's Waterfront, 1865–1925* by Clifford Farrington.

Texas Christian University Press is among the smallest university publishers in the nation, deciding that it was more important to do a few books well than increase the list. TCU Press focuses on the history and literature of the American Southwest. Some recent titles include *Walk Across Texas* by Jon McConal; *Purple Hearts* by C. W. Smith; and *Manhunters* by Elmer Kelton.

Southern Methodist University Press publishes 10 to 12 titles a year in the areas of ethics and human values, literary fiction, medical humanities, performing arts, Southwestern studies, and sport. Some titles include *The End of the Straight and Narrow* by David McGlynn; *The Trespasser* by Edra Ziesk; *Desert Days: My Life as a Field Archaeologist* by Fred Wendorf; and *Silence Kills: Speaking Out and Saving Lives* by Lee Gutkind.

State House Press and the McWhiney Foundation Press are located in Buffalo Gap, Texas. They see their missions as making history approachable, accessible, and interesting with special emphasis on Texas, West Texas, the Civil War, military, and southern history. New titles include *The Illustrated Alamo 1836: A Photographic Journey* by Mark Lemon; *The States Were Big and Bright, Vol. 1: The United States Army Air Forces and Texas During World War II* by Thomas E. Alexander; and *Texian Macabre: A Melancholy Tale of a Hanging in Early Houston* by Stephen L. Hardin.

Texas Review Press was established in 1979 but published only chapbooks and an occasional anthology until 1992 when it introduced the Southern and Southwestern Writers Breakthrough Series. It now publishes six to eight books a year and has over 40 titles in print in fiction, poetry, and prose nonfiction. Some books include *The Southern Poetry Anthology: South Carolina* by Stephen Gardner and William Wright; *Splinterville* by Cliff Hudder; and *Far-From-Equilibrium Conditions* by Michael Lieberman.

Query letters and SASEs for TAMU Press should be directed to Diana L. Vance:

Diana L. Vance, Editorial Assistant, Acquisitions (TAMU Press); dvance@tamu.edu

Mary Lenn Dixon, Editor-in-Chief (TAMU Press); mary-dixon@tamu.edu

Shannon Davies, Senior Editor, Natural Sciences (TAMU Press); sdavies@tamu.edu

Thom Lemmons, Managing Editor (TAMU Press); thom.lemmons@tamu.edu

Kent Calder, Director (TSHA Press); kent.calder@tshaonline.org

Judy Alter, Director (TCU Press); j.alter@tcu.edu

Susan Petty, Editor (TCU Press); s.petty@tcu.edu

Ron Chrisman, Director (UNT Press); ronald.chrisman@unt.edu

Karen DeVinney, Managing Editor (UNT Press); karen.devinney@unt.edu

Amy E. Smith, Executive Director (SHP/McWhiney Foundation Press); asmith@mcm.edu

Paul Ruffin, Executive Director (Texas Review Press); eng_pdr@shsu.edu

UNIVERSITY OF ALABAMA PRESS

USPS Address: Box 870380, Tuscaloosa, AL 35487-0380

Physical/Shipping Address: 200 Hackberry Lane, 2nd Floor McMillan Bldg., Tuscaloosa, AL 35401

205-348-5180 fax: 205-348-9201

www.uapress.ua.edu

As the university's primary scholarly publishing arm, the University of Alabama Press seeks to be an agent in the advancement of learning and the dissemination of scholarship. The press applies the highest standards to all phases of publishing, including acquisitions, editorial, production, and marketing. An editorial board comprised of representatives from all doctoral degree-granting state universities within Alabama oversees the publishing program. Projects are selected that support, extend, and preserve academic research. The press also publishes books that foster an understanding of history of cultures of this state and region.

The University of Alabama Press publishes in the following areas: American history; Southern history and culture; American religious history; Latin American history; American archaeology; Southeastern archaeology; Caribbean archaeology; historical archaeology; ethnohistory; anthropology; American literature and criticism; rhetoric and communication; creative nonfiction; linguistics, esp. dialectology; African American studies; Native American studies; Judaic studies; public administration; theater; natural history and environmental studies; American social and cultural history; sports history; military history; regional studies of Alabama and the southern U.S., including trade titles. Submissions are not invited in poetry, fiction, or drama.

Special series from Alabama include Classics in Southeastern Archaeology; Contemporary American Indian Studies; Deep South Books; Alabama: The Forge of History; Judaic Studies; Library of Alabama Classics; Modern and Contemporary Poetics; The Modern South; Religion and American Culture; Rhetoric, Culture, and Social Critique; and Studies in American Literary Realism and Naturalism.

Recent Alabama titles include *The Song Is Over: Survival of a Jewish Girl in Dresden* by Henny Brenner; *A Morning in June: Defending Outpost Harry* by James W. Evans; *The Victory Album: Reflections on the Good Life After the Good War* by Phillip D. Beidler; *Dixie Walker of the Dodgers: The People's Choice* by Maury Allen with Susan Walker; *Going for Gold: The History of Newmont Mining Corporation* by Jack H. Morris; and *Spirit Wind* by Jon L. Gibson.

Submit your proposal with cover letter and CV by regular mail to the appropriate acquisitions editor (for questions, feel free to contact the appropriate editor by email):

Daniel J.J. Ross, Director—American history, Southern history and culture, American military history, American religious history, Latin American history, Jewish studies, regional studies of Alabama and the southern U.S., including regional trade titles; danross@uapress.ua.edu

Judith Knight, Senior Acquisitions Editor—American archaeology, Southeastern archaeology, Caribbean archaeology, historical archaeology, Native American studies, ethnohistory, anthropology; jknight@uapress.ua.edu

Daniel Waterman, Acquisitions Editor for Humanities—American literature and criticism, rhetoric and communication, creative nonfiction, linguistics,

African American studies, public administration, theater, natural history and environmental studies; waterman@uapress.ua.edu

Elizabeth Motherwell, Acquisitions Editor for Natural History and the Environment—Natural history and environmental trade titles; emother@uapress.ua.edu

Claire Lewis Evans, Associate Editor for Digital and Electronic Publishing—Digital projects; cevans@uapress.ua.edu

UNIVERSITY OF ARIZONA PRESS

355 S. Euclid Avenue, Suite 103, Tucson, AZ 85719

520-621-1441 fax: 520-621-8899

www.uapress.arizona.edu   email: uapress@uapress.arizona.edu

The University of Arizona Press, founded in 1959 as a department of the University of Arizona, is a nonprofit publisher of scholarly and regional books. As a delegate of the University of Arizona to the larger world, the press publishes the work of scholars wherever they may be, concentrating on scholarship that reflects the special strengths of the University of Arizona, Arizona State University, and Northern Arizona University.

The University of Arizona Press publishes about 55 books annually and has some 783 books in print. These include scholarly titles in American Indian studies, anthropology, archaeology, environmental studies, geography, Chicano studies, history, Latin American studies, and the space sciences.

The UA Press also publishes general interest books on Arizona and the Southwest borderlands. In addition, the press publishes books of personal essays, such as Nancy Mairs's *Plaintext* and two series in literature: Sun Tracks: An American Indian Literary Series and Camino del Sol: A Chicana/o Literary Series.

Recent titles include *Life in the Hothouse: How a Living Planet Survives Climate Change* by Melanie Lenart; *The Permit that Never Expires: Migrant Tales from the Ozark Hills and the Mexican Highlands* by Philip Garrison; *Crossing with the Virgin: Stories from the Migrant Trail* by Kathryn Ferguson, Norma A. Price, and Ted Parks; *Camino del Sol: Fifteen Years of Latina and Latino Writing* edited by Riboberto Gonzalez; and *Flamenco Hips and Red Mud Feet* by Dixie Salazar.

University of Arizona Press handles its own distribution and also distributes titles originating from the publishing programs of such enterprises and institutions as Oregon State University Press, the Arizona State Museum, and archaeological and environmental consulting firms.

Query letters and SASEs should be directed to:

Allyson Carter, Editor-in-Chief, Social Sciences and Sciences—Anthropology, archaeology, ecology, geography, natural history, environmental science, astronomy and space sciences, and related regional titles; acarter@uapress@arizona.edu

Patti Hartmann, Senior Acquiring Editor, Humanities—Native American literature and studies, Latina/o literature and studies, border studies, and related regional titles; hartmann@uapress.arizona.edu

Kristen Buckles, Acquiring Editor—Chicana and Latino studies and literature, environmental and western history, related regional titles; kbuckles@uapress.arizona.edu

UNIVERSITY OF ARKANSAS PRESS

McIlroy House, 105 N. McIlroy Ave, Fayetteville, AR 72701

479-575-3246/800-626-0090 fax: 479-575-6044

www.uapress.com email: uapress@uark.edu

The University of Arkansas Press was founded in 1980 as the book publishing division of the University of Arkansas. A member of the Association of American University Presses, it publishes approximately 20 titles a year in the following subjects: history, Southern history, African American history, Civil War studies, poetics and literary criticism, Middle East studies, Arkansas and regional studies, music, and cultural studies. About a third of its titles fall under the general heading of Arkansas and Regional Studies. The press also publishes books of poetry and the winners of the Arabic Translation Award.

The press is charged by the university's trustees with the publication of books in service to the academic community and for the enrichment of the broader culture, especially works of value that are likely to be turned aside by commercial houses. This press, like all university presses, has as its central and continuing mission the dissemination of the fruits of research and creative activity.

Recent titles include *The Dirt Riddles* by Michael Walsh; *Sacred Spaces: The Architecture of Fay Jones* by Larry Foley and Dale Carpenter; *Looking Back to See: A Country Music Memoir* by Maxine Brown; *Harm's Way* by Eric Leigh; and *Another Creature* by Pamela Gemin.

Query letters and SASEs should be directed to:

Lawrence J. Malley, Director and Acquisitions Editor—U.S. history, African American history, civil rights studies, Middle East studies, sport history; lmalley@uark.edu

Julie Watkins, Editor—Southern history, Civil War, Arkansas, regional studies; jewatki@uark.edu

Enid Shomer, Series Editor—Poetry

UNIVERSITY OF CALIFORNIA PRESS

2120 Berkeley Way, Berkeley, CA 94720-1012

510-642-4247 fax: 510-643-7127

www.ucpress.edu   email: askucp@ucpress.edu

Founded in 1893, University of California Press is one of the nation's largest and most adventurous scholarly publishers. Each year they publish approximately 200 new books and 50 multi-issue journals in the humanities, social sciences, and natural sciences and keep about 4,000 book titles in print.

The nonprofit publishing arm of the University of California system, UC Press attracts manuscripts from the world's foremost scholars, writers, artists, and public intellectuals. About one-fourth of its authors are affiliated with the University of California.

UC Press publishes in the areas of art, music, cinema and media studies, classics, literature, anthropology, sociology, archaeology, history, religious studies, Asian studies, biological sciences, food studies, natural history, and public health.

Recent titles include *The Gastronomica Reader* edited by Darra Goldstein; *Life: Extraordinary Animals, Extreme Behavior* by Martha Holmes and Michael Gunton; *Arctic Labyrinth: The Quest for the Northwest Passage* by Glyn Williams; *Europe's Promise: Why the European Way Is the Best Hope in an Insecure Age* by Steven Hill; and *Death in a Church of Life: Moral Passion During Botswana's Time of AIDS* by Frederick Klaits.

University of California Press distributes its own list.

Query letters and SASEs should be directed to:

Rachel Berchten, Editor—Poetry, poetics

Laura Cerruti, Editor—Online references

Chuck Crumly, Editor—Organismal biology, ecology, evolution, environment

Blake Edgar, Editor—Enology, biology, archaeology, viticulture

Stephanie Fay, Editor—Art history, classical studies

Mary Francis, Editor—Music, cinema

Niels Hooper, Editor—History (except Asia), American studies

Deborah Kirshman, Editor—Museum co-publications

Sheila Levine, Editorial Director—Food studies, regional studies

Reed Malcolm, Editor—Religion (sociology/history/anthropology), politics, Asian studies

Naomi Schneider, Executive Editor—Sociology, politics, anthropology, Latin American studies

Jenny Wapner, Editor—Natural history, organismal biology

Lynne Withey, Editor—Public health

UNIVERSITY OF CHICAGO PRESS

1427 East 60th Street, Chicago, IL 60637

773-702-7700   fax: 773-702-9756

www.press.uchicago.edu   blog: http://pressblog.uchicago.edu

Since its founding in 1891 as one of the three original divisions of the University of Chicago, the press has embraced as its mission the obligation to disseminate scholarship of the highest standard and to publish serious works that promote education, foster public understanding, and enrich cultural life. Through their books and journals programs, they seek not only to advance scholarly conversation within and across traditional disciplines but, in keeping with the University of Chicago's experimental tradition, to help define new areas of knowledge and intellectual endeavor.

In addition to publishing the results of research for communities of scholars, the press presents innovative scholarship in ways that inform and engage general readers. The editors develop reference works and educational texts that draw upon and support the emphases of the university's scholarly programs and that extend the intellectual reach of the press. The house publishes significant nonscholarly work by writers, artists, and intellectuals from within and beyond the academy; translations of important foreign-language texts, both historical and contemporary; and books that contribute to the public's understanding of Chicago and its region. In all of this, the press is guided by the judgment of individual editors who work to build a broad but coherent publishing program engaged with authors and readers worldwide.

Recent titles include *Nature's Ghosts: Confronting Extinction from the Age of Jefferson to the Age of Ecology* by Mark V. Barrow, Jr.; *Uncommon Sense: Economic Insight, from Marriage to Terrorism* by Gary S. Becker and Richard A. Posner; *Is It Good for the Jews?: Many Stories from the Old Country and the New* by Adam Biro; *In the Forest of Faded Wisdom: 104 Poems* by Gendun Chopel; *A Bilingual Edition* by Gendun Chopel; and *Sexy Orchids Make Lousy Lovers & Other Unusual Relationships* by Marty Crump.

University of Chicago Press distributes its own list.

Query letters and SASEs should be directed to:

Paul Schellinger, Editorial Director, Reference—Dictionaries, encyclopedias, guides, atlases, and other general reference; pschellinger@press.uchicago.edu

Alan G. Thomas, Editorial Director, Humanities and Sciences—Literary criticism and theory, religious studies; athomas@press.uchicago.edu

John Tryneski, Editorial Director, Social Sciences and Paperback Publishing—Political science, law and society; jtryneski@press.uchicago.edu

Susan Bielstein, Executive Editor—Art, architecture, ancient archeology, classics, film studies; sbielstein@press.uchicago.edu

T. David Brent, Executive Editor—Anthropology, paleoanthropology, philosophy, psychology; dbrent@press.uchicago.edu

Karen Merikangas Darling, Editor—Science studies (history, philosophy, social studies of science, medicine, technology); kdarling@press.uchicago.edu

Robert P. Devens, Editor—American history, Chicago, other regional publishing; redevens@press.uchicago.edu

Elizabeth Branch Dyson, Associate Editor—Ethnomusicology, interdisciplinary philosophy, education; ebranchdyson@press.uchicago.edu

Kathleen K. Hansell, Editor—Music; khansell@press.uchicago.edu

Christie Henry, Executive Editor—Biological science, behavior, conservation, ecology, environment, evolution, natural history, paleobiology, geography, earth sciences; chenry@press.uchicago.edu

Margaret Hivnor, Paperback Editor; mhivnor@press.uchicago.edu

Jennifer S. Howard, Associate Editor—Physical sciences (astrophysics, general physics, mathematics); jhoward@press.uchicago.edu

Douglas Mitchell, Executive Editor—Sociology, history, sexuality studies, rhetoric; dmitchell@press.uchicago.edu

David Morrow, Senior Editor—Reference works, including regional reference; dmorrow@press.uchicago.edu

David Pervin, Senior Editor—Economics, economic history, business, law; dpervin@press.uchicago.edu

Randolph Petilos, Assistant Editor—Medieval studies, poetry in translation; rpetilos@press.uchicago.edu

UNIVERSITY OF GEORGIA PRESS

330 Research Drive, Athens, GA 30602-4901

706-369-6130   fax: 706-369-6131

www.ugapress.uga.edu   email: books@ugapress.uga.edu

The University of Georgia Press is the oldest and largest publishing house in the state and one of the largest publishing houses in the South. The press publishes 70–80 titles each year, in a range of academic disciplines as well as books of interest to the general reader, and has nearly a thousand titles in print.

Since its founding in 1938, the University of Georgia Press has as its primary mission to support and enhance the university's place as a major research institution by publishing outstanding works of scholarship and literature by scholars and writers throughout the world as well as the university's own faculty.

As the publishing program of the press has evolved, this mission has taken on three distinct dimensions:

Works of scholarship. The press is committed to publishing important new scholarship in the following subject areas: American and Southern history and literature, African American studies, civil rights history, legal history, Civil War studies, Native American studies, folklore and material culture, women's studies, and environmental studies.

Regional books. The press has a long history of publishing books about the state and region for general readers. Their regional publishing program includes architectural guides, state histories, field guides to the region's flora and fauna, biographies, editions of diaries and letters, outdoor guides, and the work of some of the state's most accomplished artists, photographers, poets, and fiction writers.

Creative and literary works. This area of the list includes books published in conjunction with the Flannery O'Connor Award for Short Fiction, the Associated Writing Programs Award for Creative Nonfiction, and the Cave Canem Poetry Prize. Please write to the press for entry requirements and submission guidelines for these awards.

Recent titles include *A Wreath of Down and Drops of Blood* by Allen Braden; *In the World He Created According to His Will* by David Caplan; *Ice Age: Stories* by Robert Anderson; and *Johnny Mercer: Southern Songwriter for the World* by Glenn T. Eskew.

The University of Georgia Press oversees its own distribution.

Query letters and SASEs should be directed to:

Nancy Grayson, Associate Director and Editor-in-Chief—American and Southern history, American literature, Southern studies, African American studies, legal history, women's studies, international affairs; ngrayson@ugapress.uga.edu

Derek Krissoff, Senior Acquisitions Editor—American and Southern history, urban studies, African American studies, civil rights, popular music; dkrissoff@ugapress.uga.edu

Judy Purdy, Acquisitions Editor—Natural history, environmental studies, nature writing, nature photography, horticulture, botany; jpurdy@ugapress.uga.edu

Erika Stevens, Acquisitions Editor—American studies, environmental history, popular culture and cultural studies, cinema/media studies, current events, Appalachian studies; estevens@ugapress.uga.edu

Nicole Mitchell, Director—General interest books about Georgia and the South; mitchell@ugapress.uga.edu

UNIVERSITY OF HAWAI`I PRESS

2840 Kolowalu Street, Honolulu, HI 96822-1888

1-808-956-8255 fax: 808-988-6052

www.uhpress.hawaii.edu email: uhpbooks@hawaii.edu

Areas of University of Hawai`i Press (UHP) publishing interest include cultural history, economics, social history, travel, arts and crafts, costume, marine biology, natural history, botany, ecology, religion, law, political science, anthropology, and general reference; particular UHP emphasis is on regional topics relating to Hawaii, and scholarly and academic books on East Asia, South and Southeast Asia, and Hawai`i and the Pacific.

University of Hawai`i Press (started in 1947) publishes books for the general trade, as well as titles keyed to the academic market. UHP also issues a series of special-interest journals. The house maintains an established backlist.

Recent titles include *Gender, Ritual and Social Formation in West Papua: A Configurational Analysis Comparing Kamoro and Asmat* by Jan Power; *Experimental Essays on Zhuangzi* edited by Victor Mair; *Population, Family and Society in Pre-Modern Japan* by Akira Hayami; *Peking: A Social Survey* by Sidney D. Gamble; and *Polynesia: The Mark and Carolyn Blackburn Collection of Polynesian Art* by Adrienne Kaeppler.

The University of Hawai`i Press handles its own distribution via a network that includes in-house fulfillment services, as well as independent sales representatives.

Query letters and SASEs should be directed to:

Patricia Crosby, Executive Editor—East Asian studies (all disciplines except literature), anthropology, Buddhist studies; pcrosby@hawaii.edu

Masako Ikeda, Acquisitions Editor— Hawai`ian and Pacific studies (all disciplines), Asian American studies (all disciplines), general interest books on Hawai`i and the Pacific; masakoi@hawaii.edu

Pamela Kelley, Acquisitions Editor—Southeast Asian studies (all disciplines), East Asian literature; pkelley@hawaii.edu

Keith Leber, Acquisitions Editor—Natural history and science, scholarly and popular guide books, reference books; kleber@hawaii.edu

Cheri Dunn, Managing Editor; cheri@hawaii.edu

Ann Ludeman, Managing Editor; aludeman@hawaii.edu

UNIVERSITY OF ILLINOIS PRESS

1325 South Oak Street, Champaign, IL 61820-6903

217-333-0950 fax: 217-244-8082

www.press.uillinois.edu email: uipress@uillinois.edu

The University of Illinois Press was established in 1918 as a not-for-profit scholarly publisher at the university. It became one of the founding members of the Association of American University Presses in 1937 and now ranks as one of the country's larger and most distinguished university presses. The house publishes works of high quality for scholars, students, and the citizens of the state and beyond. Its local staff of 46 brings out about 120 books each year, as well as 26 journals.

The University of Illinois Press publishes scholarly books and serious nonfiction, with special interests in Abraham Lincoln studies; African American studies; American history; anthropology; Appalachian studies; archaeology; architecture; Asian American studies; communications; folklore; food studies; immigration and ethnic history; Judaic studies; labor history; literature; military history; Mormon history; music; Native American studies; philosophy; poetry; political science; religious studies; sociology; southern history; sport history; translations; transnational cultural studies; western history; and women's studies. Note that this press does not publish original fiction, and only considers poetry submissions in February.

Recent titles include *The Genius and the Goddess: Arthur Miller and Marilyn Monroe* by Jeffrey Meyers; *Freeing Charles: The Struggle to Free a Slave on the Eve of the Civil War* by Scott Christianson; *Blues Before Sunrise: The Radio Interviews* by Steve Cushing; *Serving Genius: Carlo Maria Giulini* by Thomas D. Saler; and *Talking with the Children of God: Prophecy and Transformation in a Radical Religious Group* by Gordon and Gary Shepard.

The University of Illinois Press distributes its own list, as well as books from other university publishers, including Vanderbilt University Press.

Proposals and SASEs should be directed to the appropriate editor:

Willis G. Regier, Director—Lincoln studies, Nietzsche studies, classics, translations, sports history, military history, ancient religion, literature; wregier@uillinois.edu

Joan Catapano, Associate Director and Editor-in-Chief—Feminist studies, African American studies, film, dance, anthropology, cultural studies, history, philosophy; jcatapan@uillinois.edu

Laurie Matheson, Senior Acquisitions Editor—American history, Appalachian studies, labor history, music, sociology; lmatheso@uillinois.edu

Kendra Boileau, Senior Acquisitions Editor—Asian American studies, communications studies, food studies, history, Mormon studies, religion; kboileau@uillinois.edu

David Nasset, Assistant Acquisition Editor; dnasset@uillinois.edu
Vijay Shah, Assistant Acquisition Editor; vshah@uillinois.edu

UNIVERSITY OF IOWA PRESS

119 West Park Road, 100 Kuhl House, Iowa City, IA 52242-1000

319-335-2000   fax: 319-335-2055

www.uiowapress.org   email: uipress@uiowa.edu

Established in 1938, the University of Iowa Press operated for many years as an irregular imprint of the university. In 1969, John Simmons was named the first director of the press and the imprint was officially organized under a board of faculty advisors. Since 1985, the press has published 30–35 new titles a year. As always, it seeks good manuscripts from campus authors, but its efforts have expanded significantly, and press authors and customers now come from countries around the world. As Daniel Coit Gilman, founder of the first university press at Johns Hopkins University, said, it is a university's task to "advance knowledge, and to diffuse it not merely among those who can attend the daily lectures—but far and wide." The University of Iowa Press considers this to be its main trust.

As one of the few book publishers in the state of Iowa, the press considers it a mission to publish excellent books on Iowa and the Midwest. But since the press's role is much broader than that of a regional press, the bulk of its list appeals to a wider audience. The University of Iowa Press books receive national attention in a great variety of scholarly journals, newspapers, magazines, and other major book-reviewing media.

The University of Iowa Press seeks proposals to add to its list in the following areas: literary studies, including Whitman studies and poetics; letters and diaries; American studies, literary nonfiction and thematic edited anthologies, particularly poetry anthologies; the craft of writing; literature and medicine; theater studies; archaeology; the natural history of the Upper Midwest; and regional history and culture. Single Author short fiction and poetry are published through series only.

Moreover, the press is actively looking for literary works dealing with the intersection of the humanities and medicine, works of narrative medicine, fiction, poetry, and memoir by health care professionals and patients, and conceptual works that illuminate health and illness from the perspective of the humanities. They have recently published titles on Midwestern archeology and the Andean region.

Recent titles include *Starting Today: 100 Poems for Obama's First 100 Days* edited by Rachel Zucker and Arielle Greenburg; *Brave New Words: How Literature Will Save the Planet* by Elizabeth Ammons; *Democratic Vistas: The Original Edition in Facsimile* by Walt Whitman; *Poetry of the Law: From Chaucer to the Present* edited by David Kader and Michael Stanford; and *Like a Sea* by Samuel Amadon.

University of Iowa Press books are distributed by the University of Chicago Distribution Center.

Query letters and SASEs should be directed to:

Holly Carver, Director and Editor; holly-carver@uiowa.edu

Joseph Parsons, Acquiring Editor; joseph-parsons@uiowa.edu

Charlotte Wright, Managing Editor; charlotte-wright@uiowa.edu

Faye Schillig, Assistant to the Director; faye-schillig@uiowa.edu

UNIVERSITY OF MASSACHUSETTS PRESS

P.O. Box 429, Amherst, MA 01004

413-545-2217 fax: 413-545-1226

www.umass.edu/umpress   email: info@umpress.umass.edu

Founded in 1963, the University of Massachusetts Press is the book publishing arm of the University of Massachusetts. Its mission is to publish first-rate books, edit them carefully, design them well, and market them vigorously. In so doing, it supports and enhances the university's role as a major research institution.

The editors at UMass Press think of book publishing as a collaborative venture—a partnership between author and press staff—and they work hard to see that their authors are happy with every phase of the process.

Since its inception, the press has sold more than 2,000,000 volumes. Today it has over 900 titles in print. Seven employees, along with student assistants and outside sales representatives, produce and distribute some 30–40 new titles annually.

The press imprint is overseen by a faculty committee, whose members represent a broad spectrum of university departments. In addition to publishing works of scholarship, the press produces books of more general interest for a wider readership. With the annual Juniper Prizes, the press also publishes fiction and poetry. For the rules of the contests, please refer to the website or request guidelines via regular mail.

Recent titles include *Shadows in the Valley: A Cultural History of Illness, Death and Loss in New England, 1840–1916* by Alan Swedlund; *The Dragon's Tail: Americans Face the Atomic Age* by Robert A. Jacobs; *Upstaging the Cold War: American Dissent and Cultural Diplomacy, 1940–1960* by Andrew J. Falk; *Framing the Sixties: The Use and Abuse of a Decade from Ronald Reagan to George W. Bush* by Bernard von Bothmer; and *Practicing Medicine in a Black Regiment: The Civil War Diary of Burt G. Wilder, 55th Massachusetts* edited by Richard M. Reid.

The University of Massachusetts Press publishes scholarly books and serious nonfiction. Please note that they consider fiction and poetry only through their annual Juniper Prize contests. Also, they do not normally publish *Festschriften*, conference proceedings, or unrevised doctoral dissertations.

Submit proposals with SASEs or email queries to:

Clark Dougan, Acquisitions Editor; cdougan@umpress.umass.edu

Bruce Wilcox, Acquisitions Editor; wilcox@umpress.umass.edu

UNIVERSITY OF MICHIGAN PRESS

ANN ARBOR PAPERBACKS

839 Greene Street, Ann Arbor, MI 48104-3209

734-764-4388 fax: 734-615-1540

www.press.umich.edu

University of Michigan Press publishes trade nonfiction and works of scholarly and academic interest. Topic areas and categories include African American studies, anthropology, archaeology, Asian studies, classical studies, literary criticism and theory, economics, education, German studies, history, linguistics, law, literary biography, literature, Michigan and the Great Lakes region, music, physical sciences, philosophy and religion, poetry, political science, psychology, sociology, theater and drama, women's studies, disability studies, and gay and lesbian studies.

Recent titles include *Understanding Torture: Law, Violence and Political Identity* by John T. Parry; *Sacred Violence: Torture, Terror, and Sovereignty* by Paul W. Kahn; *Bath Massacre: America's First School Bombing* by Arnie Bernstein; *The Invention of Coinage and the Monetization of Ancient Greece* by David M. Schaps; and *Racial Union: Law Intimacy, and the White State in Alabama, 1865–1954* by Julie Novkov.

Query letters and SASEs should be directed to:

Ellen Bauerle, Manager, Acquisitions Department—Classics, archaeology, German studies, music, fiction, early modern history; bauerle@umich.edu

Tom Dwyer, Acquiring Editor—Communications studies, new media, literary studies, cultural studies; thdwyer@umich.edu

LeAnn Fields, Senior Executive Editor—Class studies, disability studies, theater, performance studies; lfields@umich.edu

Christopher J. Hebert, Editor at Large—Popular music, jazz; hebertc@umich.edu

Melody Herr, Acquiring Editor—Politics, law, American history; mrherr@umich.edu

Ellen McCarthy, Senior Acquiring Editor—Michigan and Great Lakes titles; emcc@umich.edu

Phil Pochoda, Acquiring Editor—Contemporary political and social issues; pochoda@umich.edu

Kelly Sippell, Executive Editor—ESL, applied linguistics; ksippell@umich.edu

---

UNIVERSITY OF MINNESOTA PRESS

111 Third Avenue South, Suite 290, Minneapolis, MN 55401

612-627-1970 fax: 612-627-1980

www.upress.umn.edu email: ump@umn.edu

The University of Minnesota Press (founded in 1925) is a not-for-profit publisher of academic books for scholars and selected general interest titles. Areas of emphasis include American studies, anthropology, art and aesthetics, cultural theory, film and media studies, gay and lesbian studies, geography, literary theory, political and social theory, race and ethnic studies, sociology, and urban studies. The Press is among the most active publishers of translations of significant works of European and Latin American thought and scholarship. The press also maintains a long-standing commitment to publish books that focus on Minnesota and the Upper Midwest, including regional nonfiction, history, and natural science. They do not publish original fiction or poetry.

Recent titles include *Bad for Democracy: How the Presidency Undermines the Power of the People* by Dana Nelson; *Victorian Vogue* by Dianne Sadoff; *Midnight at the Barrelhouse: The Johnny Otis Story* by George Lipsitz; and *Screens: Viewing Media Installation Art* by Kate Mondloch.

University of Minnesota Press order fulfillment is handled by the Chicago Distribution Center and in the UK and Europe through Plymbridge Distributors, Ltd.

Proposals in areas not listed below should be addressed to the Executive Editor. Query letters, proposals, and SASEs should be directed to:

Richard Morrison, Executive Editor—American studies, art and visual culture, literary and cultural studies; morri094@umn.edu

Todd Orjala, Senior Editor for Regional Studies and Contemporary Affairs—Regional history and culture, regional natural history; t-orja@umn.edu

Pieter Martin, Editor—Architecture, legal studies, politics and international studies, Scandinavian studies, urban studies; marti190@umn.edu

Jason Weidemann, Editor—Anthropology, Asian culture, cinema and media studies, geography, native studies, sociology; weide007umn.edu

UNIVERSITY OF MISSOURI PRESS

2910 LeMone Boulevard, Columbia, MO 65201

573-882-7641 fax: 573-884-4498

www.umsystem.edu/upress email: upress@umsystem.edu

The University of Missouri Press was founded in 1958 by William Peden, writer and dedicated member of Missouri's English Department faculty. The press has now grown to publish more than 70 titles per year in the areas of American and world history, including intellectual history and biography; African American studies; women's studies; American, British, and Latin American literary criticism; journalism; political science, particularly philosophy and ethics; regional studies of the American heartland; short fiction; and creative nonfiction.

The University of Missouri Press's chief areas of publishing emphasis are American history, political philosophy, journalism, and literary criticism with a primary focus on American and British literature. However, they are glad to receive inquiries from almost any area of work in the humanities. They do publish creative nonfiction and an occasional short-story collection, but no poetry or original novels.

Recent titles include *Chewing Gum, Candy Bars, and Beer: The Army PX in World War II* by James J. Cooke; *Gilbert and Gubar's the Madwoman in the Attic after Thirty Years* edited by Annette R. Federico; *In the Company of Generals: The World War I Diary of Pierpont L. Stackpole* edited by Robert H. Ferrell; *Lincoln and the Politics of Christian Love* by Grant N. Havers; and *Animals Always: 100 Years at the Saint Louis Zoo* by Mary Delach Leonard.

Query letters and SASEs should be directed to Mr. Clair Willcox.

Clair Willcox, Acquisitions Editor

Beverly Jarrett, Director and Editor-in-Chief

Gary Kass, Acquisitions Editor

UNIVERSITY OF NEBRASKA PRESS

BISON PRESS

1111 Lincoln Mall, Lincoln, NE 68588-0630

402-472-3581 fax: 402-472-6214

www.nebraskapress.unl.edu email: pressmail@unl.edu

As a publisher of scholarly and popular books for more than 60 years, the University of Nebraska Press is a distinctive member of the University of

Nebraska-Lincoln community. Through the work of its staff and resulting publications, the press fulfills the three primary missions of its host university: research, teaching, and service. Reporting to the vice chancellor for research and in cooperation with a faculty advisory board, the press actively encourages, develops, publishes, and disseminates first-rate, creative literary work, memoirs, and the results of national and international scholarly research in several fields. The press facilitates teaching through its publications and develops projects particularly suited for undergraduate and graduate university classrooms. The press serves the university community directly by publishing the work of many UNL faculty authors, maintaining long-term publishing associations with prominent university organizations, sponsoring campuswide events, hosting publishing workshops, and enhancing the international visibility of the university through its publicity efforts and reviews of its books. The press's sustained commitment to publications on the peoples, culture, and heritage of Nebraska reflect decades of service to its home state.

Recent University of Nebraska Press titles include *Goodbye Wives and Daughters* by Susan Kusner Resnick; *Journeys West* by Virginia Kerns; *Kansas Politics and Government: The Clash of Political Cultures* by H. Edward Flentje; *Driving with Dvorak: Essays of Memory and Identity* by Fleda Brown; and *Never Land: Adventures, Wonder, and One World Record in a Very Small Plane* by W. Scott Olsen.

Bison Books is the quality trade paperback imprint of the University of Nebraska Press. Launched in 1960, priced inexpensively, and sold in drugstores and highway tourist gift shops as well as bookstores, the Bison Books line appeared as an affordable means of publishing "original works and reissues of books of permanent value in all fields of knowledge." The idea of the Bison Books imprint was a particularly bold and far-sighted move for a smallish university press in 1960—publishing scholarship in paperback, rather than the more "dignified" cloth, was a rather radical notion, as was selling books in drugstores and gift shops. Today Bison Books publishes in a wide variety of subject areas, including Western Americana; Native American history and culture; military history; sports; Bison Frontiers of Imagination, a science fiction line; classic Nebraska authors, including Willa Cather, Mari Sandoz, John G. Neihardt, Wright Morris, Weldon Kees, and Loren Eiseley; and philosophy and religion.

Recent titles from Bison Books include *Ed Barrow: The Bulldog Who Built the Yankees' First Dynasty* by Daniel R. Levitt; and *The Recipe Reader: Narratives, Contexts, Traditions* edited by Janet Floyd and Laurel Forster.

Queries and SASEs should be directed to:

Matt Bokovoy, Acquiring Editor—Native studies; mbokovoy2@unl.edu

Kristen Elias Rowley, Humanities Editor; keliasrowley2@unl.edu

Rob Taylor, Acquiring Editor—Sports; rtaylor6@unl.edu

Heather Lundine, Editor-in-Chief—History; hlundine2@unl.edu

Tom Swanson, Manager (Bison Books); tswanson3@unl.edu

Alicia Christensen, Bison Books Editor; achristensen6@unl.edu

Bridget Barry, Associate Acquisitions Editor; bbarry2@unl.edu

Elisabeth Chretien, Associate Acquisitions Editor; echretien2@unl.edu

UNIVERSITY OF NEW MEXICO PRESS

1312 Basehart Road SE, Albuquerque, NM 87106-4363

800-249-7737   fax: 505-272-7778

www.unmpress.com   email: unmpress@unm.edu

University of New Mexico Press (UNM Press) is a publisher of general, scholarly, and regional trade books in hardcover and paperback editions. Among areas of strong New Mexico interest are anthropology, archaeology, cultures of the American West, folkways, Latin American studies, literature, art and architecture, photography, crafts, biography, women's studies, travel, and the outdoors. UNM Press offers a robust list of books in subject areas pertinent to the American Southwest, including native Anasazi, Navajo, Hopi, Zuni, and Apache cultures; Nuevomexicano (New Mexican) culture; the pre-Columbian Americas; and Latin American affairs. UNM Press also publishes works of regional fiction and belles lettres, both contemporary and classical.

Recent titles include *Constructing Lives at Mission San Francisco: Native Californians and Hispanic Colonists, 1776–1821* by Quincy Newell; *The American Military Frontiers: The United States Army in the West, 1783–1900* by Robert Wooster; *Country of Bullets: Chronicles of War* by Juanita Leon; *A Field Guide to the Plants and Animals of the Middle Rio Grande Bosque* by Jean-Luc Caron et al; *Dark Spaces: Montana's Historic Penitentiary and Deer Lodge* by Ellen Baumler; and *Creek Indian Medicine Ways: The Enduring Power of the Mvskoke Religion* by David Lewis Jr. and Ann T. Jordan.

Query letters and SASEs should be directed to:

W. Clark Whitehorn, Editor-in-Chief; wcwhiteh@unm.edu

Elise M. McHugh, Production Editor

Elizabeth Albright, Professional Intern

UNIVERSITY PRESSES

UNIVERSITY OF NORTH CAROLINA PRESS

116 South Boundary Street, Chapel Hill, NC 27514-3808

919-966-3561 fax: 919-966-3829

www.uncpress.unc.edu email: uncpress@unc.edu

For more than 80 years, the University of North Carolina Press (UNC Press) has earned national and international recognition for quality books and the thoughtful way they are published. A fundamental commitment to publishing excellence defines UNC Press, made possible by the generous support of individual and institutional donors who created its endowment.

Reflecting the mission of its parent institution, the 16-campus UNC system, the press exists both to advance scholarship by supporting teaching and research and to serve the people of the state and beyond. Since 1922, the first university press in the South and one of the first in the nation, UNC Press has published outstanding work in pursuit of its dual aims.

UNC Press books explore important questions, spark lively debates, generate ideas, and move fields of inquiry forward. They illuminate the life of the mind. With more than 4,000 titles published and almost 1,500 titles still in print, UNC Press produces books that endure.

When the press was founded in 1922, university presses published work strictly for scholars and by scholars, primarily those from the home faculty. Today, press authors come from all across the nation and around the world. UNC Press's readers come from inside and outside academia, as the press reaches a crossover audience of general readers with titles like *Pets in America: A History* by Kathleen C. Grier and *Gardening with Heirloom Seeds* by Lynn Coulter.

Areas of interest include American studies, African American studies, American history, literature, anthropology, business/economic history, Civil War history, classics, ancient history, European history, folklore, gender studies, Latin American and Caribbean studies, legal history, media studies, Native American studies, North Caroliniana, political science, public policy, regional books, religious studies, rural studies, social medicine, southern studies, and urban studies.

Other recent titles include *Give My Poor Heart Ease: Voices of the Mississippi Blues* by William Ferris; *Sweet Carolina: Favorite Desserts and Candies from the Old North State* by Foy Allen Edelman; *Carolina Basketball: A Century of Excellence* by Adam Lucas; and *Disunion! The Coming of the American Civil War, 1789–1859* by Elizabeth R. Varon.

University of North Carolina Press handles its own distribution with the assistance of regional sales representatives.

Query letters and SASEs should be directed to:

David Perry, Assistant Director and Editor-in-Chief—History, regional trade, Civil War; david_perry@unc.edu

Charles Grench, Assistant Director and Senior Editor—American history, European history, law and legal studies, classics and ancient history, business and economic history, political science, social science; charles_grench@unc.edu

Elaine Maisner, Senior Editor—Religious studies, Latin American studies, Caribbean studies, regional trade; elaine_maisner@unc.edu

Sian Hunter, Senior Editor—African American studies, American studies, gender studies, cultural studies, social medicine, Appalachian studies; sian_hunter@unc.edu

Mark Simpson-Vos, Editor—Native American studies, ethnohistory, electronic publishing; mark_simpson-vos@unc.edu

Katy O'Brien, Assistant Editor—Assists Mr. Grench

Zachary Read, Assistant Editor—Assists David Perry

UNIVERSITY OF OKLAHOMA PRESS

1005 Asp Avenue, Norman, OK 73019-6051

405-325- 2000

www.oupress.com   email: acquisitions@ou.edu

During its more than 75 years of continuous operation, the University of Oklahoma Press (OU Press) has gained international recognition as an outstanding publisher of scholarly literature. It was the first university press established in the Southwest, and the fourth in the western half of the country.

The press began as the idea of William Bennett Bizzell, fifth president of the University of Oklahoma and a wide-ranging humanist and book collector. Over the years, the press has grown from a staff of one—the first director, Joseph A. Brandt—to an active and capable team of some 50 members.

Building on the foundation laid by their four previous directors, OU Press continues its dedication to the publication of outstanding scholarly works. Under the guidance of the present director, John Drayton, the major goal of the press is to strengthen its position as a preeminent publisher of books about the American West and American Indians, while expanding its program in other scholarly disciplines, including classical studies, military history, political science, and natural science.

Recent titles include *A Rough Ride to Redemption: The Ben Daniels Story* by Robert K. DeArment; *After My Lai: My Year Commanding First Platoon, Charlie Company* by Gary W Bray; *All for the King's Shilling: The British Soldier under Wellington, 1808–1814* by Edward J Coss; *American Indians and the Fight for Equal Voting Rights* by Laughlin McDonald; *Art as Performance, Story as Criticism:*

Reflections on Native Literary Aesthetics by Craig S. Womack; and *Art of the Oklahoma State Capitol: The Senate Collection* by Bob Burke.

For additional information, email acquisitions@ou.edu. Query letters with SASEs should be directed to:

Charles E. Rankin, Associate Director, Editor-in-Chief—American West, military history; cerankin@ou.edu

Allessandra Tamulevich, Editor—American Indian, Mesoamerican, Latin American studies; jacobi@ou.edu

John Drayton, Senior Associate Director and Publisher—Classical studies; jdrayton@ou.edu

Connie Arnold, Administrative Assistant; carnold@ou.edu

Jay Dew, Editor—Twentieth-century American West, Texas history, politics and political history, environmental history; jaydew@ou.edu

UNIVERSITY OF SOUTH CAROLINA PRESS

1600 Hampton Street, 5th Floor, Columbia, SC 29208

803-777-5245 fax: 803-777-0160

www.sc.edu/uscpress

The University of South Carolina Press shares the central mission of its university: to advance knowledge and enrich the state's cultural heritage. Established in 1944, it is one of the oldest publishing houses in the South and among the largest in the Southeast. With more than 1,500 published books to its credit, 800 in print, and 50 new books published each year, the press is important in enhancing the scholarly reputation and worldwide visibility of the University of South Carolina.

The University of South Carolina Press publishes works of original scholarship in the fields of history (American, African American, Southern, Civil War, culinary, maritime, and women's), regional studies, literature, religious studies, rhetoric, and social work.

Recent titles include *Authors Out Here: Fitzgerald, West, Parker, and Schulberg in Hollywood* by Tom Cerasulo; *Bill Arp's Peace Papers: Columns on War and Reconstruction, 1861–1873* by Charles Henry Smith; *The Boykin Spaniel: South Carolina's Dog Revised Edition* by Mike Creel and Lynn Kelley; *City of the Silent: The Charlestonians of Magnolia Cemetery* by Ted Ashton Phillips, Jr.; *The Day the Johnboat Went Up the Mountain: Stories from My Twenty Years in South Carolina Maritime Archaeology* by Carl Naylor; and *Democracy and Rhetoric: John Dewey on the Arts of Becoming* by Nathan Crick.

Queries with SASEs should be directed to:

Linda Haines Fogle, Assistant Director for Operations—Trade titles, literature, religious studies, rhetoric, social work, general inquiries; lfogle@gwm.sc.ude

Alexander Moore, Acquisitions Editor—History, regional studies; alexm@gwm.sc.edu

Jim Denton, Acquisitions Editor—Literature, religious studies, rhetoric, social work; dentoja@mailbox.sc.edu

UNIVERSITY OF TENNESSEE PRESS

110 Conference Center, 600 Henley Street, Knoxville, TN 37996-4108

865-974-3321 fax: 865-974-3724

www.utpress.org

The University of Tennessee Press is dedicated to playing a significant role in the intellectual life of the University of Tennessee system, the academic community in general, and the citizens of the state of Tennessee by publishing high-quality works of original scholarship in selected fields as well as highly accurate and informative regional studies and literary fiction. By utilizing current technology to provide the best possible vehicles for the publication of scholarly and regional works, the press preserves and disseminates information for scholars, students, and general readers.

The University of Tennessee Press was established as a scholarly publisher in 1940 by the university trustees. Its mandate was threefold: to stimulate scholarly research in many fields; to channel such studies to a large readership; and to extend the university's regional leadership by publishing worthy projects about the South, including those by non-university authors.

Recent titles include *Appalachians All: East Tennesseans and the Elusive History of an American Region* by Mark T. Banker; *The Battles of Chickamauga and Chattanooga and the Organizations Engaged* by Henry V. Boynton; *A Nation Forged in War: How World War II Taught Americans to Get Along* by Thomas Bruscino; *Virginia Broughton: The Life and Writings of a National Baptist Missionary* by Tomeiko Ashford Carter, ed.; *Murphy Station: A Memoir from the American South* by David Donovan; and *Napoleon and Egyptomania in Tennessee* by Elaine Altman Evans.

Query letters and SASEs should be directed to:

Scot Danforth, Acquisitions Editor—African American studies, American religion, Appalachian studies, folklore, history, literature, material culture, sport and popular culture, vernacular architecture; danforth@utk.edu

Carrie Webb, Editorial Assistant; cwebb@utk.edu

UNIVERSITY OF TEXAS PRESS

P.O. Box 7819, Austin, TX 78713-7819

512-471-7233 fax: 512-232-7178

www.utexas.edu/utpress email: utpress@uts.cc.utexas.edu

By launching a scholarly press in 1950, the University of Texas made several important statements: books matter; books educate; and publishing good books is a public responsibility and a valuable component of the state's system of higher education.

As part of its mission to serve the people of Texas, the press also produces books of general interest for a wider audience, covering, in particular, the history, culture, arts, and natural history of the state. To these, the press has recently added accounts of the contributions of African and Native Americans, Latinos, and women. Major areas of concentration are anthropology, Old and New World archaeology, architecture, art history, botany, classics and the Ancient World, conservation and the environment, Egyptology, film and media studies, geography, landscape, Latin American and Latino studies, literary modernism, Mexican American studies, marine science, Middle Eastern studies, ornithology, pre-Columbian studies, Texas and Western studies, and women's studies.

The University of Texas Press has published more than 2,000 books over five decades. Currently a staff of 50, under the direction of Joanna Hitchcock, brings out some 90 books and 11 journals annually.

Recent titles include *Revolution on Paper: Mexican Prints 1910–1960* by Dawn Ades and Alison McClean; *Toward a Cognitive Theory of Narrative Acts* edited by Frederick Luis Aldama; *Terry Allen* by Terry Allen; *Dreamland: The Way of Juarez* by Charles Bowden and Alice Leora Briggs; and *House of Hits: The Story of Houston's GoldStar/SugarHill Recording Studios* by Andy Bradley and Roger Wood.

University of Texas Press handles its own distribution.

Query letters and SASEs should be directed to:

Theresa May, Editor-in-Chief—Latin American studies, Latino/a studies, Native American studies, anthropology, New World archaeology, photography

William Bishel, Sponsoring Editor—Texana, ornithology, botany, natural history, environmental studies

Jim Burr, Sponsoring Editor—Classics and ancient world, film and media studies, Middle East studies, Jewish studies, Old World archaeology, architecture, applied languages

Allison Faust, Sponsoring Editor—Music, geography, art, Texas art, culture; Alison@utpress.ppb.utexas.edu

Casey Kittrell, Assistant Editor—Fiction in translation; casey@utpress.ppb.utexas.edu

UNIVERSITY OF VIRGINIA PRESS

Box 400318, Charlottesville, VA 22904

Phone: 434-924-3468

www.upress.virginia.edu   email: upressva@virginia.edu

The University of Virginia Press (UVaP) was founded in 1963 to advance the intellectual interests not only of the University of Virginia, but of institutions of higher learning throughout the state. UVaP currently publishes 50–60 new titles annually.

The UVaP editorial program focuses primarily on the humanities and social sciences with special concentrations in American history, African American studies, Southern studies, literature, ecocriticism, and regional books. While it continuously pursues new titles, UVaP also maintains a backlist of over 1,000 titles in print.

Active series include the Papers of George Washington; the Papers of James Madison; the Victorian Literature and Culture Series; CARAF Books (translations of Francophone literature); New World Studies; the Carter G. Woodson Institute Series in Black Studies; Under the Sign of Nature: Explorations in Ecocriticism; The American South Series; A Nation Divided: New Studies in the Civil War; Constitutionalism and Democracy; Race, Ethnicity, and Politics; Reconsiderations in Southern African History; Studies in Early Modern German History; Studies in Religion and Culture; Southern Texts Society; and the Virginia Bookshelf series of regional reprints.

Other recent titles include *Parallel Worlds: The Remarkable Gibbs-Hunts and the Enduring (In)significance of Melanin* by Adele Logan Alexander; *Mongrel Nation: The America Begotten by Thomas Jefferson and Sally Hemings* by Clarence E. Walker; *The Great Virginia Triumvirate: George Washington, Thomas Jefferson, and James Madison in the Eyes of Their Contemporaries* by John P. Kaminski; *On the Trail of the D.C. Sniper: Fear and the Media* by Jack R. Censer; and *The Virtues of Mendacity: On Lying in Politics* by Martin Jay.

The Electronic Imprint of the UVaP publishes digital scholarship in the humanities and social sciences issued under the Rotunda imprint (rotunda.upress.virginia.edu). Rotunda was created for the publication of original digital scholarship along with newly digitized critical and documentary editions in the humanities and social sciences. For further information, contact Rotunda via email at rotunda-upress@virginia.edu.

Submit UVaP queries and SASEs to:

Cathie Brettschneider, Humanities Editor; cib8b@virginia.edu

Richard K. Holway, History and Social Sciences Editor; rkh2a@virginia.edu

Boyd Zenner, Architecture and Environmental Editor; bz2v@virginia.edu

UNIVERSITY OF WASHINGTON PRESS

P.O. Box 50096, Seattle, WA 98145-5096

206-543-4050   fax: 206-543-3932

www.washington.edu/uwpress   email: uwpress@u.washington.edu

The University of Washington Press (UW Press) publishes titles that cover a wide variety of academic fields, with especially distinguished lists in Asian studies, Middle Eastern studies, environmental history, biography, anthropology, Western history, natural history, marine studies, architectural history, and art. The Press has published approximately 3,800 books, of which about 1,400 are still in print. UW Press publishes about 60 new titles a year.

The press is recognized as the world's foremost publisher on the art and culture of the Northwest Coast Indians and Alaskan Eskimos, and as the leader in the publication of materials dealing with the Asian American experience. Such series as A History of East Central Europe, Studies in Modernity and National Identity, American Ethnic and Cultural Studies, Asian Law Series, Korean Studies of the Henry M. Jackson School of International Studies, Studies on Ethnic Groups in China, Literary Conjugations, In Vivo, and the Pacific Northwest Poetry Series, have brought distinction to the press and the university.

The imprint of the University of Washington Press is under the control of a faculty committee appointed by the university's president. The approval of the University Press Committee is required before any book may be published. The press's editors work closely with the faculty committee to select those books that will carry the University of Washington imprint. About one-third of the books published by the press originate within the University of Washington. Of the manuscripts and proposals that are submitted annually from all over the world, less than 5 percent are accepted for publication.

Recent titles include *China Watcher: Confessions of a Peking Tom* by Richard Baum; *The Dawn of Conservation Diplomacy: U.S.-Canadian Wildlife Protection Treaties in the Progressive Era* by Kurkpatrick Dorsey; *Ichishkiin Sinwit Yakama/Yakima Sahaptin Dictionary* by Virginia Beavery and Sharon Hargus; *Landscapes of Conflict: The Oregon Story, 1940–2000* by William Robbins; *Making Mountains: New York City and the Catskills* by David Stradling; and *The Nature of Gold: An Enviromental History of the Klondike Gold Rush* by Kathryn Morse.

Query letters and SASEs should be directed to:

Lorri Hagman, Executive Editor—Asian studies, cultural and environmental anthropology; lhagman@u.washingon.edu

Marianne Keddington-Lang, Acquisitions Editor—Western history, environmental studies, Native American studies; mkedlang@u.washington.edu

Beth Fuget, Acquisitions Editor—International studies, American ethnic studies, architecture, natural history; uwpacq@u.washington.edu

UNIVERSITY OF WISCONSIN PRESS

1930 Monroe Street, 3rd Floor, Madison, WI 53711-2059

608-263-1110   fax: 608-263-1120

www.wisc.edu/wisconsinpress   email: uwiscpress@uwpress.wisc.edu

Located in Madison, Wisconsin, the University of Wisconsin Press was founded in 1936, and publishes both books and journals. Since its first book appeared in 1937, the press has published and distributed more than 3,000 titles. They have more than 1,400 titles currently in print, including books of general interest (biography, fiction, natural history, poetry, photography, fishing, food, travel, etc.), scholarly books (American studies, anthropology, art, classics, environmental studies, ethnic studies, film, gay and lesbian studies, history, Jewish studies, literary criticism, Slavic studies, etc.), and regional books about Wisconsin and the Upper Midwest. They publish and distribute new books each year in these fields.

Among their book series are the Brittingham Prize in Poetry, the Felix Pollak Prize in Poetry, Wisconsin Studies in Autobiography, Wisconsin Studies in Classics, Living Out: Gay and Lesbian Autobiography, Studies in Dance History, George L. Mosse Series in Modern European Cultural and Intellectual History, The History of American Thought and Culture, and Publications of the Wisconsin Center for Pushkin Studies.

The press is a division of the Graduate School of the University of Wisconsin–Madison. Residing within the university's graduate school, UW Press draws on and supports the intellectual activities of the graduate school and its faculty and enhances the university's overall missions of research and instruction. Although they publish many books and journals produced by faculty from the University of Wisconsin campuses, they also publish books and journals from scholars around the U.S. and the world. The house has authors residing in many different countries, from Australia to Zimbabwe. They have co-published English-language books with publishers in England, Ireland, Turkey, Italy, and Japan. The University of Wisconsin Press books have been translated into dozens of foreign languages.

Recent titles include *A Nation of Politicians: Gender, Patriotism, and Political Culture in Late Eighteenth-Century Ireland* by Padhraig Higgins; *Captain Rock: The Irish Agrarian Rebellion of 1821–1824* by James S. Donnelly, Jr.; *Spirits of Earth: The Effigy Mound Landscape of Madison and the Four Lakes* by Robert A. Birmingham; and *The Prints of Warrington Colescott: A Catalogue Raisonne, 1948–2008* by Mary Weaver Chapin.

Query letters and SASEs should be directed to:

Raphael Kadushin, Senior Acquisitions Editor—autobiography/memoir, biography, classical studies, dance, performance, film, food, gender studies, GLBT studies, Jewish studies, Latino/a memoirs, travel; kadushin@wisc.edu

Gwen Walker, PhD, Acquisitions Editor—African studies, anthropology, environmental studies, Irish studies, Latin American studies, Slavic studies, Southeast Asian studies, U.S. history; gcwalker@wisc.edu

---

UNIVERSITY PRESS OF COLORADO

5589 Arapahoe Avenue, Suite 206C, Boulder, CO 80303

720-406-8849   fax: 720-406-3443

www.upcolorado.com

Founded in 1965, the University Press of Colorado is a nonprofit cooperative publishing enterprise supported, in part, by Adams State College, Colorado State University, Fort Lewis College, Mesa State College, Metropolitan State College of Denver, University of Colorado, University of Northern Colorado, and Western State College of Colorado. The press publishes 30–35 new titles each year, with the goal of facilitating communication among scholars and providing the peoples of the state and region with a fair assessment of their histories, cultures, and resources. The press has extended the reach and reputation of supporting institutions and has made scholarship of the highest level in many diverse fields widely available.

The University Press of Colorado is currently accepting manuscript proposals in anthropology, archaeology, environmental studies, history, law, Native American studies, and the natural sciences as well as projects about the state of Colorado and the Rocky Mountain region. They are also accepting submissions for the following series: Atomic History & Culture, Mesoamerican Worlds, Mining the American West, Timberline Books, and The Women's West (nonfiction only). The University Press of Colorado is not currently accepting proposals in fiction or poetry.

Recent titles include *Adventures in Eating: Anthropological Experiences in Dining from Around the World* edited by Helen R. Haines and Clare A. Sammells; *Anthropology without Informants: Collected Works in Paleoanthropology* by L.G. Freeman; *The Beast* by Benjamin B. Lindsey; *Colorado Water Law for Non-Lawyers* by P. Andrew Jones and Tom Cech; and *Dr. Charles David Spivak: A Jewish Immigrant and the American Tuberculosis Movement* by Jeanne Abrams.

Scholars proposing manuscripts for publication should submit a prospectus to the acquisitions department before submitting a complete manuscript. Submissions are accepted via mail and email. No phone calls. Address manuscript submission inquiries to:

Darrin Pratt, Director and Acquiring Editor; darrin@upcolorado.com

UNIVERSITY PRESS OF FLORIDA

15 NW 15th Street, Gainesville, FL 32611

352-392-1351/800-226-3822   fax: (352) 392-0590

www.upf.com   email: press@upf.com

The University Press of Florida, the scholarly publishing arm of the State University System, representing all ten universities, is charged by the Board of Regents with publishing books of intellectual distinction and significance, books that will contribute to improving the quality of higher education in the state, and books of general and regional interest and usefulness to the people of Florida, reflecting its rich historical, cultural, and intellectual heritage and resources. The press may publish original works by State University System faculty members, meritorious works originating elsewhere, important out-of-print books, and other projects related to its backlist that will contribute to a coherent and effective publishing program—one that will supplement and extend programs of instruction and research offered by the universities.

UPF has published over 2,500 volumes since its inception and currently releases nearly 100 new titles each year.

Subjects include African studies, anthropology and archaeology, art, dance, music, law, literature, Middle East studies, natural history, Russian studies, history, Florida, Latin America studies, political science, science and technology, and sociology.

Recent titles include *Tales from the 5th Street Gym: Ali, the Dundees, and Miami's Golden Age of Boxing* by Ferdie Pacheco; *Guy LaBree: Barefoot Artist of the Florida Seminoles* by Carol Mahler; *Thunder on the River: The Civil War in Northeast Florida* by Daniel L. Schafer; *Cruise of the Dashing Wave: Rounding Cape Horn in 1860* by Philip Hichborn; and *Lucky 73: USS Pampanito's Unlikely Rescue of Allied POWs in WWII* by Aldona Sendzikas.

To submit a manuscript, send a one-page letter of inquiry to Editor-in-Chief John Byram, to determine the University Press of Florida's interest in your project. Please include your full postal address.

John Byram, Associate Director and Editor-in-Chief

Amy Gorelick, Assistant Director and Assistant Editor-in-Chief

Heather Romans-Turci, Acquisitions Assistant

Kara Schwartz, Acquisitions Assistant

UNIVERSITY PRESS OF KANSAS

2502 Westbrooke Circle, Lawrence, KS 66045-4444

785-864-4155   fax 785-864-4586

www.kansaspress.ku.edu   email upress@ku.edu

The University Press of Kansas publishes scholarly books that advance knowledge and regional books that contribute to the understanding of Kansas, the Great Plains, and the Midwest. Founded in 1946, it represents the six state universities: Emporia State University, Fort Hays State University, Kansas State University, Pittsburg State University, the University of Kansas, and Wichita State University.

Profiled by *The Chronicle of Higher Education* (3 July 1998) as "a distinctive model of success in turbulent times," the press focuses generally on history, political science, and philosophy. More specifically, it concentrates on presidential studies, military studies, American history (especially political, cultural, intellectual, and western), U.S. government and public policy, legal studies, and social and political philosophy.

Direct queries, proposals, and SASEs to:

Fred M. Woodward, Director—American government and public policy, presidential studies, American political thought, urban politics, Kansas and regional studies; fwoodward@ku.edu

Michael Briggs, Editor-in-Chief—Military history and intelligence studies, law and legal history, political science; mbrigss@ku.edu

Ranjit Arab, Acquisitions Editor—Western history and Native American studies, environmental studies, American studies, women's studies; rarab@ku.edu

Amy Sherman, Editorial Assistant; edassist.ku.edu

UNIVERSITY PRESS OF MISSISSIPPI

3825 Ridgewood Road, Jackson, MS 39211-6492

601-432-6205/800-737-7788   fax: 601-432-6217

www.upress.state.ms.us   email: press@ihl.state.ms.us

The University Press of Mississippi was founded in 1970 and is supported by Mississippi's eight state universities. UPM publishes scholarly books and books that interpret the South and its culture to the nation and the world. From its offices in Jackson, the University Press of Mississippi acquires, edits, distributes, and promotes more than 60 new books every year. Over the years, the press has published more than 900 titles and distributed more than 2,500,000 copies worldwide, each with the Mississippi imprint. Out of the approximately 600 submissions they receive, the UPM publishes an average of 60 manuscripts a year.

The University Press of Mississippi is a nonprofit publisher that serves an academic and general audience. The editorial program focuses on the following areas: scholarly and trade titles in African American studies; American studies, literature, history, and culture; art and architecture; biography and memoir; ethnic studies; film studies; folklore and folk art; health; memoir and biography; military history; music; natural sciences; performance; photography; popular culture; reference; Southern studies; sports; women's studies; other liberal arts. Special series include American Made Music, Chancellor Porter L. Fortune Symposium in Southern History, Conversations with Comic Artists, Conversations with Filmmakers, Faulkner and Yoknapatawpha, Hollywood Legends, Literary Conversations, Margaret Walker Alexander Series in African American Studies, Southern Icons, Studies in Popular Culture, Understanding Health and Sickness, Willie Morris Books in Memoir and Biography, and Writers and Their Works.

Recent titles include *My Life with Charlie Brown* by Charles M. Schultz; *The Comics of Chris Ware: Drawing Is a Way of Thinking* edited by David M. Ball and Martha B. Kuhlman; *Drawing France: French Comics and the Republic* by Joe E. Vessels; *Inside the Hollywood Fan Magazine: A History of Star Makers, Fabricators, and Gossip Mongers* by Anthony Slide; *American Horror Film: The Genre at the Turn of the Millennium* edited by Steffen Hantke; and *Banjo on the Mountain: Wade Mainer's First Hundred Years* by Dick Spottswood.

Submit proposal, CV, and SASE to the appropriate editor:

Leila W. Salisbury, Director—American studies, film studies, popular culture; lsalisbury@ihl.state.ms.us

Craig Gill, Assistant Director and Editor-in-Chief—Art, architecture, folklore and folk art, history, music, natural sciences, photography, Southern studies; cgill@ihl.state.ms.us

Anne Stascavage, Managing Editor—Performance studies; astascavage@ihl.state.ms.us

Walter Biggins, Acquiring Editor—American literature, comics studies, American studies, Caribbean studies; wbiggins@ihl.state.ms.us

Valerie Jones, Editorial Assistant; vjones@mississippi.edu

UNIVERSITY PRESS OF NEW ENGLAND (TUFTS, NORTHEASTERN, DARTMOUTH, BRANDEIS, VERMONT, NEW HAMPSHIRE)

1 Court Street, Suite 250, Lebanon, NH 03766

603-448-1533 fax: 603-448-7006

www.upne.com

University Press of New England (UPNE) is an award-winning university press supported by a consortium of schools—Brandeis University, Dartmouth College, the University of New Hampshire, Northeastern University, Tufts University, and University of Vermont—and based at Dartmouth College since 1970. UPNE has earned a reputation for excellence in scholarly, instructional, reference, literary and artistic, and general-interest books. Many of these are published cooperatively with one of the member institutions and carry a joint imprint. Others are published under the University Press of New England imprint.

The publishing program reflects strengths in the humanities; liberal arts; fine, decorative, and performing arts; literature; New England culture; and interdisciplinary studies. The press publishes and distributes more than 80 titles annually, with sales of more than $2.5 million. A professional staff of 24 maintains high standards in editorial, design and production, marketing, order fulfillment, and business operations.

University Press of New England publishes books for scholars, teachers, students, and the general public. The press concentrates in American studies; literature; history; cultural studies; art, architecture, and material culture; ethnic studies (including African American, Jewish, Native American, and Shaker studies); international studies; nature and the environment; and New England history and culture. The Hardscrabble Books imprint publishes fiction of New England.

Recent titles include *Inspired Innovations: A Celebration of Shaker Ingenuity* by M. Stephen Miller; *Excavating the Sutlers' House: Artifacts of the British Armies in Fort Edward and Lake George* by David R. Starbuck; *Sviatoslav Richter: Pianist* by Karl Aage Rasmussen; *Hard Lives, Mean Streets: Violence in the Lives of Homeless Women* by Jana L. Jasinski; and *The Women Who Recontructed American Jewish Education, 1910–1965* by Caroll K. Ingall.

It is best to contact this press early in one's development process, even at the proposal stage. Send a proposal with SASE to:

Michael P. Burton, Director—Art, photography, decorative arts, material culture, historic preservation, distribution titles; michael.p.burton@dartmouth.edu

Phyllis Deutsch, Editor-in-Chief—Jewish studies, nature and environment, environment and health, sustainability studies, nineteenth century studies,

American studies, criminology with a gendered component; phyllis.d.deutsch@
dartmouth.edu

Stephen Hull, Acquisitions Editor —New England regional, African American
studies, New England sports, sports and society, music and technology, international studies with a civil society component; stephen.p.hull@dartmouth.edu

Richard Pult, Acquisitions Editor—New England regional/Boston, New
England sports, marine biology/ecology, criminology, music/opera, Native
American studies, American studies, visual culture, institutional histories;
richard.pult@dartmouth.edu

Lorri Miller, Editorial Assistant—New England regional, African American
studies, women's studies, American studies, ethnic studies, arctic studies,
Canadian-American border studies, political science, historic preservation,
material culture, decorative arts; lori.miller@dartmouth.edu

UTAH STATE UNIVERSITY PRESS

7800 Old Main Hill, Logan, UT 84322

435-797-1362   fax: 435-797-0313

www.usu.edu/usupress

Utah State University Press is a refereed scholarly publisher and division of Utah
State University. Established in 1972, the press's mandate is to acquire and publish books of superior quality that win the esteem of readers and that appropriately represent the university to the community of scholars. Vital also to their
mission is publication for a broader community, including students, who use the
books in their studies, and general readers, who find in them enjoyment as well
as enlightenment.

Utah State University Press is an established publisher in the fields of composition studies, creative writing, folklore, Native American studies, nature and environment, and Western history, including Mormon history and Western women's
history. They also sponsor the annual May Swenson Poetry Award.

Recent titles include *Peculiar Portrayals: Mormons on the Page, Stage, and Screen*
edited by Mark T. Decker and Michael Austin; *Folklore and the Internet: Vernacular
Expression in a Digital World* edited by Trevor J. Blank; *The Fierce Tribe: Masculine
Identity and Performance in the Circuit* by Mickey Weems; *Jesus in America and Other
Stories from the Field* by Claudia Gould; and *The River Knows Everything: Desolation
Canyon and the Green* by James M. Aton.

Direct proposals with SASEs to:

Michael Spooner, Director; michael.spooner@usu.edu

John Alley, Executive Editor; john.alley@usu.edu

VANDERBILT UNIVERSITY PRESS

VU Station B, Box 351813, Nashville, TN 37235-1813

615-322-3585 fax: 615-343-8823

www.vanderbilt.edu/vupress email: vupress@vanderbilt.edu

Established in 1940, Vanderbilt University Press is the principal publishing arm of one of the nation's leading research universities. The press's primary mission is to select, produce, market, and disseminate scholarly publications of outstanding quality and originality. In conjunction with the long-term development of its editorial program, the press draws on and supports the intellectual activities of the university and its faculty. Although its main emphasis falls in the area of scholarly publishing, the press also publishes books of substance and significance that are of interest to the general public, including regional books. In this regard, the press also supports Vanderbilt's service and outreach to the larger local and national community.

The editorial interests of Vanderbilt University Press include most areas of the humanities and social sciences, as well as health care and education. The press seeks intellectually provocative and socially significant works in these areas, as well as works that are interdisciplinary or that blend scholarly and practical concerns. In addition the press maintains an active co-publishing program with Nashville-based Country Music Foundation Press. At present, Vanderbilt publishes some 20 new titles each year. Of the total of some 300 works published by the press in its five-decade history, more than 125 remain in print.

Recent titles include *The DeMarco Factor* by Michael Pertschuk; *Chasing Polio in Pakistan: Why the World's Largest Public Health Initiative May Fail* by Svea Closser; *Living on the Edge in Suburbia: From Welfare to Workforce* by Terese Lawinski; *The American Impressionists in the Garden* by May Brawley Hill; and *Locked Up, Locked Out: Young Men in the Juvenile Justice System* by Anne M. Nurse.

Direct query letters and SASEs to:

Michael Ames, Director; vupress@vanderbilt.edu

Eli Bortz, Acquisitions Editor; eli.bortz@vanderbilt.edu

Jessie Hunnicutt, Managing Editor; jessie.hunnicutt@vanderbilt.edu

WAYNE STATE UNIVERSITY PRESS

The Leonard N. Simons Building, 4809 Woodward Avenue, Detroit, MI 48201-1309

313-577-6120 fax: 313-577-6131

wsupress.wayne.edu

Wayne State University Press is a distinctive urban publisher committed to supporting its parent institution's core research, teaching, and service mission by generating high quality scholarly and general interest works of global importance. Through its publishing program, the press disseminates research, advances education, and serves the local community while expanding the international reputation of the press and the university.

Wayne State University Press is an established midsize university press that publishes approximately 40 new books and 6 journals per year. Subject areas featured in the current publishing program include Africana studies, Armenian studies, children's studies, classical studies, fairy-tale and folklore studies, film and television studies, German studies, Great Lakes and Michigan, humor studies, Jewish studies, labor and urban studies, literature, and speech and language pathology.

Recent titles include *Byron and the Jews* by Sheila A. Spector; *Yannai on Genesis: An Invitation to Piyyut* by Laura S. Lieber; *Let's Read: A Linguistic Approach* by Cynthia A. Barnhart and Robert K. Barnhart; *Picturing Hemingway's Michigan* by Michael R. Federspiel; and *Leave Me Hidden* by Franz Wright.

To submit, send a letter of inquiry or proposal with SASE to:

Kathryn Wildfong, Acquisitions Manager—Africana studies, Jewish studies, Great Lakes and Michigan; k.wildfong@wayne.edu

Annie Martin, Acquisitions Editor—Film and TV studies, fairy-tale studies, children's studies, Made in Michigan Writers Series, speech and language pathology; annie.martin@wayne.edu

WESLEYAN UNIVERSITY PRESS

215 Long Lane, Middletown, CT 06459

860.685.7711 fax: 860.685.7712

www.wesleyan.edu/wespress

The mission of Wesleyan University Press is to develop and maintain a sound and vigorous publishing program that serves the academic ends and intellectual life of the university. In addition, the press formulated three broad goals meant to ensure that the press would fulfill its mission:

"To acquire and publish scholarly and broadly intellectual works that make significant contributions to knowledge in traditional fields of inquiry or expression, and to new and cross-disciplinary fields of inquiry or expression; to enhance the intellectual life of the Wesleyan community through the involvement of faculty and students in the publishing programs and activities of the press; and to project the name and image of the university and to enhance its reputation as an academic institution of the highest quality."

Publishing in its current form since 1959, Wesleyan University Press has lived through many transitions while continuing to thrive. It has published an internationally renowned poetry series since its inception, releasing more than 250 titles and collecting four Pulitzer Prizes, a Bollingen, and two National Book Awards in that one series alone.

Recent titles include *Mirrors and Scrims: The Life and Afterlife of Ballet* by Marcia B. Siegel; *Movable Pillars: Organizing Dance, 1956–1978* by Katja Kolcio; *Balasaraswati: Her Art and Life* by Douglas M. Knight, Jr.; *The South Korean Film Renaissance: Local Hitmakers, Global Provocateurs* by Jinhee Choi; and *Grace, Fallen from* by Marianne Boruch.

The Wesleyan Poetry Program accepts manuscripts by invitation only until further notice. Their publications in nonfiction concentrate in the areas of dance, music/culture, film/TV and media studies, and science-fiction studies. They will accept proposals for books in these areas only. The equivalent of a cover letter may be submitted by email/attachment, but do not submit full proposals electronically unless asked to do so.

Direct queries with CVs and SASEs to:

Suzanna Tamminen, Director and Editor-in-Chief—Dance; stamminen@wesleyan.edu

Parker Smathers, Editor—Music/culture, film/TV and media studies, science-fiction studies, Connecticut history; psmathers@wesleyan.edu

YALE UNIVERSITY PRESS

302 Temple Street, New Haven, CT 06511

P.O. Box 209040, New Haven, CT 06520-9040

203-432-0960 fax: 203-432-0948

www.yale.edu/yup email: yupmkt@yalevm.cis.yale.edu

London office:

47 Bedford Square, London WC1B3DP

020 7079 4900 fax: 020 7029 4901

www.yalebooks.co.uk

blog: yalepress.typepad.com/yalepresslog

By publishing serious works that contribute to a global understanding of human affairs, Yale University Press aids in the discovery and dissemination of light and truth, *lux et veritas*, which is a central purpose of Yale University. The press's publications are books and other materials that further scholarly investigation, advance interdisciplinary inquiry, stimulate public debate, educate both within and outside the classroom, and enhance cultural life. Through the distribution of works that combine excellence in scholarship with skillful editing, design, production, and marketing, the press demonstrates its commitment to increasing the range and vigor of intellectual pursuits within the university and elsewhere. With an innovative and entrepreneurial spirit, Yale University Press continually extends its horizons to embody university press publishing at its best.

One hundred years and over 7,000 titles ago Yale University Press was founded by a young graduate and his wife. In its first few years, owned entirely by the founders and guided by a committee of the Yale Corporation, whimsy played a part in the publishing of dozens of books of poetry, many from the literary renaissance then at Yale—MacLeish, Farrar, Luce, and the Benéts, for example—and soon the Yale Shakespeare, and the Yale Series of Younger Poets, which are going strong today. Then there were the many books for children, another surprise from a university press. These were in addition to such works of solid scholarship as Farrand's 1911 Records of the 1787 Constitutional Convention, also still in print, and the Chronicles of America, the Yale Review from time to time, and the many long Yale series of studies in history and literature and economics and language. Beyond their content, these books were distinguished by their looks, for Carl Purington Rollins designed them over three decades, gathering praise all the while. Among its series then and now are the many shelves of volumes of the papers of Walpole and Franklin and Edwards, and today's new and ambitious series on the Culture & Civilization of China and the Annals of Communism. The Yale Pelican History of Art recently joined a long list of art books that was already perhaps the best in the world.

The London office of the Yale Press was first established in 1961 as a marketing base, and in 1973 commenced publishing its own list. It now has a unique position as the only American university press with a full-scale publishing operation and publishing program in Europe. Working closely with the Paul Mellon Centre for Studies in British Art, it swiftly built a preeminent reputation for its art history and architecture titles. Its range now extends to trade history and biography, politics, music, religion, literature, and contemporary affairs, and its books have won many of the leading British literary prizes and awards, as well as receiving notable attention in reviews, journals, and broadcasting.

Recent titles include *Alice Neel: Painted Truths* by Barry Walker, Jeremy Lewison, Robert Storr, and Tamar Garb; *Architecture as Icon: Perceptions and Representations of Architecture in Byzantine Art* edited by Slobodan Curcic and

Evangelia Hadjitryphonos; *The Crisis of Islamic Civilization* by Ali A. Allawi; *Yemen: Dancing on the Heads of Snakes* by Victoria Clark; *Churchill's Bunker: The Cabinet War Rooms and the Culture of Secrecy in Wartime London* by Richard Holmes; and *Russian Orientalism: Asia in the Russian Mind from Peter the Great to the Emigration* by David Schimmelpenninch van der Oye.

Query letters, proposals, and SASEs should be directed to:

New Haven Office:

Jean E. Thomson Black, Executive Editor—Life sciences, physical sciences, environmental sciences, medicine

Jennifer Banks, Editor—Literature in translation, religion

Jonathan Brent, Editor-at-Large—Literature, literary studies, theater, Slavic studies

Laura Davulis, Assistant Editor, Coordinator of Editorial Internships—history, current events

Patricia Fidler, Publisher—Art and architecture

William Frucht, Executive Editor—Political science, international relations

Michelle Komie, Senior Editor—Art and architecture

Sarah Miller, Assistant Editor

Michael O'Malley, PhD, Executive Editor—Business, economics, law

Mary Jane Peluso, Publisher—Foreign languages and ESL

Christopher Rogers, Executive Editor—History, current events

Tim Shea, Development Editor—Foreign languages and ESL

Vadim Staklo, Associate Editor—Reference

Alison MacKeen, Editor—Media and technology, literary studies, education

Ileene Smith, Editor-at-Large—Trade list

Lindsay Toland, Publishing Coordinator—Art and architecture

London Office:

Robert Baldock, Managing Director, London, and Editorial Director (Humanities)—History, biography, politics, music, history of religion, contemporary affairs

Gillian Malpass, Publisher (Art & Architecture)—History of art, history of architecture, history of fashion

Heather McCallum, Publisher, Trade Books, London—History, politics, current affairs, international affairs, biography, history of science

Sally Salvesen, Publisher (Pevsner Architectural Guides)—Politics, economics, current affairs

SECTION FOUR

CANADIAN BOOK PUBLISHERS

CANADIAN BOOK PUBLISHING

AND THE CANADIAN MARKET

GREG IOANNOU
President
Colborne Communications, Toronto
www.colcomm.ca   email: greg@colcomm.ca
tel: 416-214-0183

Colborne Communications provides a full range of services to the book publishing industry, taking books from initial conception through writing, editing, design, layout, and print production.

There's good and bad news about the Canadian publishing industry for writers. First, the bad: Breaking in isn't easy. The good news: Most Canadian publishers are interested in new writers. They have to be, because small- to mid-sized Canadian houses operate mainly on government grant money. In order to get that grant money, houses must publish Canadian authors. They also can't afford bidding wars. Instead, they often find new authors, develop them, and hope they stay—or that their fame will add value to the house's backlist.

The key to getting published is to make sure that you're sending the right manuscript to the right publisher, using an appropriate style for submissions. Publishers are less frustrated by poor writing than they are by poorly executed submissions.

If you've written a nonfiction book about rural Nova Scotia, don't send your manuscript to a children's publisher in Vancouver. Research the publishers first instead of spamming busy editors with manuscripts that don't fit their house's list.

The Internet is a fantastic tool for writers. It's easier to research potential publishers online than it is to sit at the library and search through Quill & Quire's Canadian Publishers Directory—though that is still a valuable resource.

Do an online search for Canadian publishers. A few places to start are the Association of Canadian Publishers—who provide a search form by genre and province—and the Canadian Publishers' Council. The Canadian Children's Book Centre is particularly focused and has an annual publication that lists publishers who accept unsolicited manuscripts and artwork. If you see a publisher whose mandate seems to match your book idea, visit their website and locate their submission requirements, or contact a Canadian agent.

Rather than sending your manuscript everywhere, write custom proposals that show the publisher that you know what they publish, you've read their submission guidelines thoroughly, and your manuscript adheres to those requirements. It is okay to show enthusiasm for the press, or to suggest where you think your manuscript fits on their list. But don't act as though the publisher would be lucky to get your book. Do not threaten publishers with deadlines; you may bully yourself into an automatic rejection. Take the time to write a brief but informative proposal, including a chapter-by-chapter outline if appropriate, and *send a sample* of your work. Include the approximate word count, genre, and reading level in the cover letter. Consider contacting the Canadian Authors Association or The Writers' Union of Canada for more information on writing for the Canadian market.

If you're a foreign writer hoping to be published in Canada, offer some form of subject-matter expertise. It's like immigrating to another country: You need to have a skill that a Canadian doesn't have.

American writers should remember that Canada is not part of the United States; Canadian publishers cannot use U.S. stamps to return manuscripts. Use International Reply Coupons (available at any post office) instead.

ANNICK PRESS LIMITED

15 Patricia Avenue, Toronto, ON M2M 1H9, Canada

416-221-4802   fax: 416-221-8400

www.annickpress.com

Annick Press publishes children's literature, specifically picture books, nonfiction, and juvenile and young-adult novels. The company has won many prestigious design and publishing awards. Annick Press was the first children's publisher to receive the Canadian Booksellers Association's Publisher of the Year award. Annick publishes books for children ages six months to 12 years and for young adults, approximately 30 titles annually. A select number of books are published in French and Spanish editions.

While continuing to publish picture books, Annick has added contemporary fiction and nonfiction to its list. It seeks titles that speak to issues young people deal with every day, such as bullying, teen sexuality, advertising, and alienation. It also publishes books on science, fantasy, pop culture, and world conflict.

Recent titles include *Dear Diary, I'm Pregnant* by Anrenée Enlander; *I.D.: Stuff That Happens to Define Us* by Kate Scowen and Peter Mitchell; *Just Julie/ I Am Not Emmanuelle* by Nadia Xerri-L and Carine Tardieu; and *Munsch at Play: Eight Stage Adaptations for Young Performers* by Irene N. Watts and Robert Munsch.

Annick Press is committed to publishing only Canadian authors. Further, they are not currently accepting manuscripts for picture books. However, they are interested in receiving manuscripts featuring teen fiction, middle-reader (ages 8–11) fiction, and middle-reader and teen nonfiction. Address all submissions to The Editors, so that they may properly register your manuscript. Do not send manuscripts by email or fax.

Rick Wilks, Director

Colleen MacMillan, Associate Publisher

ANVIL PRESS

278 East First Avenue, Vancouver, BC V5T 1A6, Canada

604-876-8710   fax: 604-879-2667

www.anvilpress.com

Anvil Press is a literary publisher interested in contemporary, progressive literature in all genres. It was created in 1988 to publish *sub-TERRAIN* magazine, which explores alternative literature and art; three years later the press moved into publishing books as well. The Anvil Press mission is to discover, nurture, and promote new and established Canadian literary talent. They publish 8–10 titles per year and sponsor the International 3-Day Novel Contest, which involves writing an entire novel over the Labour Day Weekend and is explained in detail at www.3daynovel.com. They are not interested in publishing genre novels (sci-fi, horror, romance, etc).

Recent Anvil titles include *Frenzy* by Catherine Owen; *The Skeleton Dance* by Philip Wuinn; *Wild at Heart: The Films of Nettle Wild* by Mark Harris and Claudia Medina; *Kaspoit!* by Dennis E. Bolen; and *Private Grief, Public Mourning: The Rise of the Roadshire Shrine in British Columbia* by John Belshaw and Diane Purvey.

Direct query letters and SASEs to:

Brian Kaufman, Publisher

Jenn Farrell, Assistant Editor

ARSENAL PULP PRESS

341 Water Street, Suite 200, Vancouver, BC V6B 1B8, Canada

604-687-4233/888-600-PULP   fax: 604-687-4283

www.arsenalpulp.com

Arsenal Pulp Press is a publisher of over 200 provocative and stimulating books in print that challenge the status quo in the following genres: cultural studies, political/sociological studies, regional studies and guides (particularly for British Columbia), cookbooks, gay and lesbian literature, visual art, multicultural literature, literary fiction, youth culture, and health. No genre fiction, such as sci-fi, thrillers, or romance. They have had particular success with cookbooks and publish around 12 to 18 new titles a year.

Recent Arsenal titles include *American Hunks: The Muscular Male Body in Popular Culture: 1860–1970* by David L. Chapman and Brett Josef Grubisic; *Automaton Biographies* by Larissa Lai; *Gods and Monsters: A Queer Film Classic* by Noah Tsika; *Hard Core Logo* by Michael Turner; and *How It All Vegan! 10th Anniversary: Irresistible Recipes for an Animal-Free Diet* by Sarah Kramer and Tanya Barnard.

Submissions should include a marketing analysis, synopsis, and a 50- to 60-page sample. Direct your query and SASE to the Editorial Board.

Brian Lam, Publisher

Robert Ballantyne, Associate Publisher

Susan Safyan, Associate Editor

BEACH HOLME PUBLISHING

409 Granville Street, Suite 1010, Vancouver, BC V6C 1T2, Canada

604-733-4868   fax: 604-733-4860

Beach Holme Publishing specializes in Canadian literary fiction, plays, poetry, literary nonfiction, and young-adult fiction. They bring indigenous creative writing to a wider Canadian audience and have published award-winning authors including Evelyn Lau, Joe Rosenblatt, and Dorothy Park.

Beach Holme's line of young-adult fiction is geared to children ages 8–13, and often features historical Canadian settings and situations.

Recent titles include *White Jade Tiger* by Julie Lawson; *False Shuffles* by Jane Urquhart; *Last Days in Africaville* by Dorothy Perk; *Little Emperors: A Year with the Future of China* by JoAnn Dionne; *Natural Disasters* by Andrea MacPherson; and *Hesitation Before Birth* by Bert Almon.

Direct queries and SASEs to:

Michael Carroll, Publisher; bhp@beachholme.bc.ca

BRICK BOOKS

431 Boler Road, Box 20081, London, ON N6K 4G6, Canada

519-657-8579

www.brickbooks.ca   email: brick.books@sympatico.ca

Brick Books is a small literary press based in London, Ontario, which seeks to foster interesting, ambitious, and compelling work by Canadian poets. Brick Books was nominated for the prestigious Canadian Booksellers Association Libris Award for Best Small Press Publisher of the Year 2006. They publish 7 new books and 3–14 reprints every year.

Recent titles include *Lost Gospels* by Lorri Neilsen Glenn; *The Secret Signature of Things* by Eve Joseph; *Alien, Correspondent* by Anthony Di Nardo; and *The Good News About Armageddon* by Steve McOrmond.

Brick Books can publish only authors who are Canadian citizens or landed immigrants. To submit, you may send the fully completed manuscript or a sample of eight to ten poems. Please note that they will only accept submissions between January 1 and April 30. Submissions received outside of the reading period will be returned. Email submissions are not accepted. Please address submissions to Brick Books and allow three to four months for a response.

Don McKay, Co-Publisher

Stan Dragland, Co-Publisher

Barry Dempster

John Donlan

Alayna Munce

Marnie Parsons

Elizabeth Philips

Jan Zwicky

CORMORANT BOOKS

215 Spadina Avenue, Studio 230, Toronto, ON M5T 2C7, Canada

416-929-4957   fax: 416-929-3596

www.cormorantbooks.com

Cormorant Books seeks to publish the best new work in the area of literary fiction and creative nonfiction for the adult market. This award-winning house publishes a select list of literary fiction, trade nonfiction, and works of fiction in translation.

Recent titles from Cormorant include *Underground* by Jane Hutton; *From This Distance* by Karen McLaughlin; *The Queen of Unforgetting* by Sylvia Maultash Warsh; *Witness to a City* by David Miller and Douglas Arrowsmith; *The Goodtime Girl* by Tess Fragoulis; *It's All About Kindness* by Margaret McBurney; *Curtains for Roy* by Aaron Bushkowsky; *Moon Over Marrakech* by Nazneen Sheikh; and *Waiting for the Revolution* by Sally Clark.

Cormorant Books is not currently accepting unsolicited manuscripts, and unsolicited manuscripts will be recycled. Check their website to see if this policy is changed.

Query letters and SASEs should be directed to:

J. Marc Côté, President and Publisher

Robyn Sarah, Poetry Editor

COTEAU BOOKS

2517 Victoria Avenue, Regina, SK S4P 0T2, Canada

306-777-0170   fax: 306-522-5152

www.coteaubooks.com   coteau@coteaubooks.com

Based in Regina, Coteau publishes novels, juvenile fiction, regional and creative nonfiction, drama, and authors from all parts of Canada. The press seeks to give literary voice to its community, and places a special emphasis on Saskatchewan and prairie writers. It also has an active program of presenting and developing new writers. Coteau releases more than a dozen new titles each year. They publish novels for young readers aged 9–12, ages 13–15, and 16 and up. They do not publish kids' picture books.

Recent Coteau titles include *Crow Boy* by Maureen Bush; *Euphoria* by Cora Taylor; *Katie Be Quiet* by Connie Gault; *The Factory Voice* by Jeanette Lynes; *Fishtailing* by Wendy Phillips; *For the Love of Strangers* by Brenda Niskala; *Interruptions in Glass* by Tracy Hamon; *The Knife Sharpener's Bell* by Rhea Tregebov; and *Molly's Cue* by Alison Acheson

Coteau publishes only authors who are Canadian citizens. No simultaneous submissions, and only hard copy submissions are considered. You may send the full manuscript or a sample (3–4 stories or chapters; 20–25 poems) accompanied by a self-addressed envelope of appropriate size to:

Nik Burton, Managing Editor

D&M PUBLISHERS, INC.

GREYSTONE BOOKS

NEW SOCIETY PUBLISHERS

NEW CATALYST BOOKS

Suite 201, 2323 Quebec Street, Vancouver, BC V5T 4S7, Canada

604-254-7191/1-800-667-6902 fax: 604-254-9099

Toronto office:

Suite 500 720, Bathurst Street, Toronto, ON M5S 2R4, Canada

416-537-2501 fax: 416-537-4647

www.dmpibooks.com

New Society Publishers:

P.O. Box 189, Gabirola Island, BC, V0R 1X0, Canada

250-247-9737 fax: 250-247-7471

www.newsociety.com email: info@newsociety.com

D&M Publishers, Inc., recently changed its name from Douglas & McIntyre Publishing Group after the acquisition of New Society Publishers. D&M is an independent publishing house with three unique imprints: Douglas & McIntyre,

Greystone Books, and New Society Publishers. The group publishes popular Canadian trade books for a global market, with many international successes, particularly in the areas of natural science and the environment.

Douglas & McIntyre publishes a broad general program of adult fiction and nonfiction, with an emphasis on art and architecture, Native studies, Canadian history, biography and social issues, aviation, popular memoir, and food and wine. It publishes around 35 nonfiction books a year while maintaining a distinguished literary fiction list.

Greystone Books titles focus on natural history and science, the environment, popular culture, travel books, guidebooks, and health and sports. It publishes around 30 new books a year.

New Society Publishers is an activist press focused on solutions and social change. Their mission is to publish books that contribute in fundamental ways to building an ecologically sustainable and just society, and all their books are printed on 100 percent post-consumer recycled paper with vegetable based inks.

New Society Publishers has an imprint of its own, New Catalyst Books, that takes advantage of recent technological advances that allow books to be printed rapidly and cost-effectively on an as-needed basis. Its Sustainability Classics series is designed to keep books in print that have enduring value in the field of sustainability.

Recent titles from Douglas & McIntyre include *Darwin's Bastards* by Zsuzsi Gartner; *Who We Are* by Ruyard Griffiths; *Operation Husky* by Mark Zuehlke; and *Brian Jungen* by Daina Augaitis.

Some titles indicative of the Greystone list include *Ten Technologies to Save the World* by Chris Goodall; *Tar Sands: Revisited and Updated* by Andrew Nikiforuk; *Abundant Beauty* by Marianne North; and *A Woman in the Polar Night* by Christiane Ritter.

Recent titles from New Society Publishers include *Transport Revolutions: Moving People and Freight without Oil* by Richard Gilbert and Anthony Perl; and *From Container to Kitchen: Growing Fruits and Vegetables in Pots* by D.J. Herda.

Query letters and SASEs should be directed to the Editorial Panel.

Scott McIntyre, Publisher (Douglas & McIntyre)

Chris Labonté, Editor—Fiction (Douglas & McIntyre)

Rob Sanders, Publisher (Greystone Books)

Judith Plant, Publisher (New Society Publishers)

Chris Plant, Acquisitions Editor, Editorial Director (New Society Publishers)

DRAWN AND QUARTERLY

P.O. BOX 48056, Montréal, QB H2V 4S8, Canada

514-279-2221

www.drawnandquarterly.com

Drawn and Quarterly is an award-winning publisher of graphic novels, comic books, and comic book series with over 20 new titles per year. The publisher acquires new comic books, art books, and graphic novels by renowned cartoonists and newcomers from around the globe.

Drawn & Quarterly welcomes submissions for consideration in a number of their publishing venues, including a new talent forum (Drawn & Quarterly Showcase), a regular anthology (Drawn & Quarterly), and a seasonal selection of general graphic novels, comic books, and comic book series.

Drawn & Quarterly prefers to receive electronic submissions. Email website URLs or JPEG samples of your work to: chris@drawnandquarterly.com.

If you are unable to submit via email, mail b&w photocopies of your work, no more than 8 pages. Do not include SASE as Drawn and Quarterly will not return work and will contact you only if they're interested in publishing your art.

Chris Oliveros, Publisher, chris@drawnandquarterly.com

THE DUNDURN GROUP

NATURAL HERITAGE BOOKS

3 Church Street, Suite 500, Toronto, ON M5E 1M2, Canada

416-214-5544   fax: 416-214-5556

www.dundurn.com   email: info@dundurn.com

The Dundurn Group began as Dundurn Press Limited, established in 1972 to bring Canadian history and biography to a general readership. Politics, history, and biography were the original mandate, which quickly expanded to include literary and art criticism, and large illustrated art books.

In the 1990s, Dundurn acquired three other Canadian publishing houses: Hounslow Press, Simon & Pierre, and Boardwalk Books. These companies further broadened Dundurn's editorial mandate to include popular nonfiction, literary fiction, young-adult books, and mysteries. It publishes about 75–80 new titles a year and is now one of the largest publishers of adult and children's fiction and nonfiction in Canada.

In 2007, Dundurn acquired the assets of Natural Heritage Books, which concentrates on publishing titles that focus on Canadian heritage, natural history, and biography. Natural Heritage releases 7–12 new books a year.

Recent titles include *Blood and Groom: A Sasha Jackson Mystery* by Jill Edmondson; *Grave Doubts: A Quin and Morgan Mystery* by John Moss; *Reading Rock Art: Interpreting the Indian Rock Paintings of the Canadian Shield* by Grace Rajnovich; and *Something Remains* by Hassan Ghedi Santur.

To submit, please send the complete proposal or manuscript or three sample chapters to the attention of the Acquisitions Editor. Fiction submissions will be reviewed twice annually, in the spring and in the fall. Email submissions are not considered. While authors outside Canada are considered, be sure to include an international reply coupon with the SASE.

Kirk Howard, President and Publisher

Michael R. Carroll, Editorial Director

Shannon Whibbs, Senior Editor

Allison Hirst, Assistant Editor

ECW PRESS

2120 Queen Street East, Suite 200, Toronto, ON M4E 1E2, Canada

416-694-3348   fax: 416-698-9906

www.ecwpress.com   email: info@ecwpress.com

ECW Press publishes nonfiction and fiction for the adult market. ECW has published close to 1,000 books that are distributed throughout the English-speaking world and translated into dozens of languages. Their list includes poetry and fiction, pop culture and political analysis, sports books, biography, and travel guides. ECW releases around 50 new titles per year.

Recent titles include *Adventures in Larryland!: Life in Professional Wrestling* by Larry Zbyszko; *Beyond Ego: Influential Leadership Starts Within* by Art Horn; *Darwin's Nightmare* by Mike Knowles; *Give Smart: How to Make a Dramatic Difference with Your Donation Dollar* by Elaine R. Kelly; *Punk Rock Fun Time Activity Book* by Aye Jay Morano; and *The Show That Smells* by Derek McCormack.

ECW publishes only Canadian-authored poetry and fiction. For nonfiction (literary and commercial) they consider proposals from anywhere. Instead of an SASE, you may include an email address in your cover letter where they could email a reply to your query. Please send a proposal and SASE to the appropriate editor:

Jack David, Co-Publisher—Business, sports, mystery fiction, true crime, biographies

David Caron, Co-Publisher—Sci-fi, graphic novels, history

Jennifer Hale, Senior Editor—Pop culture, music, celebrity biographies, television, film, fiction, creative nonfiction

Michael Holmes, Senior Editor—Literary fiction, poetry, wrestling

Erin Creasey, Publishing Manager

FIREFLY BOOKS LTD

66 Leek Crescent, Richmond Hill, ON L4B 1H1, Canada

416-499-8412   fax: 416-499-8313

www.fireflybooks.com   email: service@fireflybooks.com

Firefly Books, established in 1977, is a North American publisher and distributor of nonfiction and children's books. Firefly's admirable goal is to bring readers beautifully produced books written by experts at reasonable prices.

Firefly Books has particular strengths in cookbooks, gardening, astronomy, health, natural history, pictorial books, reference books (especially for children), and sports. Firefly has published books as diverse as Robert Munsch and Sheila McGraw's *Love You Forever* (over 17 million copies in print) and Terence Dickinson's *Nightwatch: A Practical Guide to Viewing the Universe (Third Edition: Revised and Expanded for Use Through 2010).*

Recent titles include *The Backyard Astronomer's Guide* by Terence Dickinson and Alan Dyer; *An American History Album: The Story of the United States Told Through Stamps* by Michael Worek and Jordan Worek; *Amazing Baby* by Desmond Morris; and *The Pregnancy Bible: Your Complete Guide to Pregnancy and Early Parenthood* by Joanne Stone MD and Keith Eddelman MD.

Firefly Books does not accept unsolicited manuscripts. However, it does accept proposals for illustrated nonfiction. Firefly does not publish children's books. Direct queries and SASEs to:

Lionel Koffler, President and Publisher

Michael Warrick, Associate Publisher

FITZHENRY & WHITESIDE LTD.

195 Allstate Parkway, Markham, ON L3R 4T8, Canada

905-477-9700/800-387-9776   fax: 800-260-9777

www.fitzhenry.ca

FIFTH HOUSE PUBLISHERS

1511-1800 4 Street SW, Calgary, AB T2S 2S5, Canada

403-571-5230

Fitzhenry & Whiteside Ltd. specializes in trade nonfiction and children's books. The firm also offers a textbook list and a small list of literary fiction. They publish or reprint 60–80 titles per year. The house specializes in history, natural sciences, forestry, ecology, biography, psychology, reference, Canadiana, antiques, art, photography, children's and young-adult fiction and nonfiction.

Fitzhenry & Whiteside nonfiction titles range throughout Canadian history, biography, Native studies, nature, and antiques and collectibles. The children's book list includes early readers, picture books, and middle-grade and young-adult novels. Markets include trade, school, library, professional and reference, college, mail order, and specialty.

In 1998 Fitzhenry & Whiteside purchased the Calgary-based publisher Fifth House Publishers. It selects books that contribute to the understanding of western-Canadian history, culture, and environment, publishing around 15 titles a year.

Recent Fitzhenry & Whiteside titles include *Beginner's Guide to Minerals and Rocks* by Joel Grice; *Five Days of the Ghost* by William Bell; *Hockey Talk* by John Goldner; *Sila's Revenge* by Jamie Bastedo; and *The Nine Lives of Travis Keating* by Jill MacLean.

Titles from Fifth House include *A Bend in the Willows* by Paul Dolphin; *Against the Flow: Rafferty-Alameda and the Politics of the Environment* by George N. Hood; and *Mustang Wranglers* by Curly R.V. Guenter.

Query letters and SASEs should be directed to:

Sharon Fitzhenry, President

Gail Winskill, Publisher—Children's Books

Stephanie Stewart, Publisher; stewart@fifthhousepublishers.ca

GASPEREAU PRESS

47 Church Avenue, Kentville, NS B4N 2M7, Canada

1-902-678-6002/877-230-8232   fax: 902-678-7845

www.gaspereau.com   email: info@gaspereau.com

Gaspereau Press is a Nova Scotia-owned and operated trade publisher specializing in short-run editions of both literary and regional interest for the Canadian market. Their list includes poetry, local history books, literary essays, novels, and short story collections. Gaspereau was nominated for the prestigious Canadian Booksellers Association's Libris Award for Best Small Press Publisher of the Year 2006.

Gaspereau is one of a handful of Canadian trade publishers that prints and binds books in-house. With only 16 paces between the editor's desk and the printing press, Gaspereau Press practices a form of "craft" publishing that is influenced more by William Morris and the private press movement of the 19th century than by the contemporary publishing culture.

Recent titles include *A Short History of Forgetting* by Paul Tyler; *I Do Not Think That I Could Love a Human Being* by Johanna Skibsrud; *The Annotated Bee and Me* by Tim Bowling; *The Geography of Arrival: A Memoir* by George Sipos; and *Through Darkling Air: The Poetry of Richard Outram* by Peter Sanger.

When submitting, please include a cover letter, a list of previous publications, and an SASE. Email submissions are not considered. It typically takes four to eight months to hear back from this publisher.

Gary Dunfield, Publisher

Andrew Steeves, Publisher

GOOSE LANE EDITIONS

500 Beaverbrook Court, Suite 330, Fredericton, NB E3B 5X4, Canada

888-926-8377 fax: 506-459-4991

www.gooselane.com email: info@gooselane.com

Canada's oldest independent publisher, Goose Lane Editions is a small publishing house that specializes in literary fiction, poetry, and a select list of nonfiction titles including history, biography, Canadiana, and fine art books. It does not publish commercial fiction, genre fiction, or confessional works of any kind. Nor does it publish for the children's market.

Recent titles include *Therefore Choose* by Keith Oatley; *Birding in New Brunswick* by Roger Burros; *For and Against* by Sharon McCartney; and *Trails of Halifax Regional Municipality* by Michael Haynes.

Goose Lane considers submissions from outside Canada only rarely, and only when both the author and the material have significant Canadian connections and the material is of extraordinarily high interest and literary merit. Writers should submit a synopsis, outline, and sample (30–50 pages) with an SASE if in Canada; international authors should include SASEs and international reply coupons with submissions. No electronic submissions.

Please query by mail or phone before submitting; direct queries and SASEs to:

Susanne Alexander, Publisher

Angela Williams, Publishing Assistant

Akoulina Connell, Managing Editor

Ross Leckie, Editor—Poetry

Bethany Gibson, Editor—Fiction

GREAT PLAINS PUBLICATIONS

GREAT PLAINS TEEN FICTION

ENFIELD & WIZENTY

955 Arthur Street, Suite 345, Winnipeg, MB R3B 1G7, Canada

204-475-6799   fax: 204-475-0138

www.greatplains.mb.ca   email: info@greatplains.mb.ca

Great Plains Publications is an award-winning prairie-based, general trade publisher specializing in regional history and biography. It has recently established two new imprints, Enfield & Wizenty and Great Plains Teen Fiction.

Great Plains Publications' mandate is to publish books that are written by Canadian prairie authors. They also publish books by Canadian authors not living on the prairies, but of specific interest to people living in this region (content, setting). Great Plains Teen Fiction and Enfield & Wizenty publish fiction from across the country.

Recent titles from Great Plains Publications include *A Memory of Sky: A Pilot's View of Canada's Century of Flight* by Jim Shilliday; *Every Stone a Story II: Manitoba's Buried History* by Dale Brawn; *Impact: A History of Disasters in Manitoba* by Brock Holowachuk; *Devil Among Us* by Mike McIntyre; and *Noah's Last Canoe* by Doug Evans.

Recent titles from Great Plains Teen Fiction include *Black Bottle Man* by Craig Russell; *Illegally Blonde* by Nelsa Roberto; *Spirit Quest* by Susan Rocan; and *Dreamfire* by Nicole Luiken.

Recent titles from Enfield and Wizenty include *Rats of Las Vegas* by Lisa Pasold; *The Moon of Letting Go and Other Stories* by Richard Van Camp; and *10 Things to Ask Yourself in Warsaw and Other Stories* by Barbara Romanik.

Currently, Great Plains is not accepting proposals or manuscripts for poetry or children's picture books, how-to books, cookbooks, or self-help books. Address queries with sample chapters and SASEs to the attention of the Fiction Editor, Nonfiction Editor, or Young Adult Editor, depending on the genre of your work.

Gregg Shilliday, Publisher

Ingeborg Boyens, Executive Editor

Maurice Mierau, Associate Editor (Enfield & Wizenty)

Anita Daher, Associate Editor (Great Plains Teen Fiction)

HARLEQUIN ENTERPRISES LIMITED

HARLEQUIN BOOKS (CANADA)

MILLS & BOON/HARLEQUIN ENTERPRISES LTD.

WORLDWIDE LIBRARY

225 Duncan Mill Road, Don Mills, ON M3B 3K9, Canada

416-445-5860

press.eharlequin.com

www.millsandboon.co.uk

Harlequin Enterprises Limited is the world's leading publisher of romance fiction and women's fiction. The Toronto-based company publishes over 120 titles a month in 29 languages in 107 international markets on six continents. These books are written by more than 1,200 authors. With 130 million books sold in 2007— 50 percent overseas and 96 percent outside Canada—it is both the country's most successful publisher and one of its most international businesses.

The Harlequin Enterprises home base in Ontario, Canada, issues the greater portion of the Harlequin Books series, while the New York office issues several Harlequin series, as well as the HQN, Kimani, Red Dress, Steeple Hill, and Silhouette lists (please see listing for Harlequin Books in the directory of Independent United States Presses). The editorial acquisitions departments for Mills & Boon, Harlequin Romance, and Harlequin Presents are located at the operation's United Kingdom offices (listed below). Harlequin Enterprises Limited in Canada also publishes the Worldwide Library, which features titles in the mystery, suspense, and thriller genres.

Each of the various lines within the Harlequin series of romance novels published in Canada, like their American counterparts, stakes out particular market-niche segments of reader interest within the overall categories of romance fiction and women's fiction. There are 33 lines altogether, and each has its own submission and editorial guidelines. These guidelines are explored in great detail on the Harlequin website.

HARLEQUIN BOOKS (CANADA)

Harlequin Books (Canada) is home to Harlequin Everlasting, American Romance, Blaze, Superromance, MIRA, and Spice. The best way to learn which imprint is appropriate for your manuscript is to read books already in print. Harlequin offers detailed tip sheets on their website, eHarlequin.com, or by written request. Following are general guidelines to the imprints handled in Canada:

Harlequin Everlasting, brand-new in 2007, is a contemporary romance series. The novels in this series follow the life and relationship/s of one couple. These emotionally intense stories span considerably more time than the typical series romance—years or even an entire lifetime—and at 75,000 words, the books are longer than usual as well. Recent titles include *Pictures of Us* by Amy Garvey; *Meant for Each Other* by Lee Duran; *A Christmas Wedding* by Tracy Wolff; and *Always a Mother* by Linda Warren.

American Romance features fast-paced, heartwarming stories about the pursuit of love, marriage, and family in America today. They're set in small towns and big cities, on ranches and in the wilderness, from Texas to Alaska—everywhere people live and love. For this series, Harlequin is looking for energetic writing and well-constructed plots based on contemporary characters. Titles indicative of the list include *His Baby Surprise* by Lisa Childs; *A Mother's Wedding Day* by Rebecca Winters and Dominique Burton; and *An Unexpected Father* by Lisa Ruff.

The Harlequin Blaze series features sensuous, highly romantic, innovative stories that are sexy in premise and execution. The tone of the books can run from fun and flirtatious to dark and sensual. Writers can push the boundaries in terms of characterization, plot, and sexual explicitness. Recent titles include *Just Fooling Around* by Julie Kenner and Kathleen O'Reilly; *The Drifter* by Kate Hoffmann; and *While She Was Sleeping...* by Lisabel Sharpe.

The aim of a Harlequin Superromance novel is to produce a contemporary, involving read with a mainstream tone in its situations and characters, using romance as the major theme. To achieve this, emphasis should be placed on individual writing styles and unique and topical ideas. Titles include *Her Best Friend* by Sarah Mayberry; *Trusting the Bodyguard* by Kimberly Can Meter; and *Always a Temp* by Jeannie Watt.

MIRA Books is dedicated to mainstream single-title women's fiction in hardcover and paperback editions. Of interest to a primarily women's readership, MIRA titles span all genres, including thrillers, historical romances, relationship novels, and suspense. Recent titles include *The Memorist* by M.J. Rose; *Home in Carolina* by Sherryl Woods; and *Out of Mind* by Stella Cameron.

New in 2006, SPICE is Harlequin's single-title imprint for erotic fiction for the modern woman who also wants a great read. Titles include *Rampant* by Saskia Walker; *Naughty Bits* by Lacy Danes et al; *Addicted* by Charlotte Featherstone; *Stranger* by Megan Hart; *The Duchess, the Maid, the Groom & Their Lover* by Victoria Janssen; *Enchanted Again* by Nancy Madore; *The Diary of Cozette* by Amanda McIntrye; and *Obsession* by Kayla Perrin.

Harlequin will send prospective authors full editorial guidelines with suggested heroine and hero profiles, as well as information pertaining to manuscript length, setting, and sexual approach and content. This information is available upon written request from the publisher and online at eHarlequin.com.

Harlequin invites submissions from both published and unpublished writers. They prefer a query with synopsis and 1–3 chapters. Make sure your query is clear as to which line it is intended for: Harlequin Everlasting, American Romance, Blaze, Harlequin Superromance, MIRA, or Spice. Direct your submission to:

Valerie Grey, Executive Editor—MIRA Books, Spice

Wanda Ottewell, Senior Editor—Harlequin Superromance

Paula Eykelhof, Executive Editor—Single titles

Kathleen Scheibling, Senior Editor—American Romance

Susan Swinwood, Editor—MIRA Books

Brenda Chin, Senior Editor—Blaze

Victoria Curran, Editor—Superromance

Kathyrn Lye, Editor—Blaze, RDI

Johanna Raisanen, Associate Editor—American Romance

MILLS & BOON/HARLEQUIN ENTERPRISES LTD.

HARLEQUIN PRESENTS

HARLEQUIN ROMANCE

Eton House, 18-24 Paradise Road, Richmond, Surrey TW9 1SR, United Kingdom

Acquisitions for Mills & Boon, Harlequin Romance, and Harlequin Presents are through the United Kingdom offices. You may query the offices to request a set of editorial guidelines supplied to prospective authors or read them online at eHarlequin.com.

A new line, Mills & Boon Modern books explore cosmopolitan, city romances between upscale men and women. Young characters in affluent urban settings—either North American or international—meet, flirt, share experiences, have great, passionate sex and fall in love, finally making a commitment that will bind them together, forever. Titles include *Greek Tycoon, Wayward Wife* by Sabrina Philips; *The Italian's Passionate Revenge* by Lucy Gordon; *The Greek Tycoon's Baby Bargain* by Sharon Kendrick; *Di Cesare's Pregnant Mistress* by Chantelle Shaw; *The Billionaire's Virgin Mistress* by Sandra Field; *At the Sicilian Count's Command* by Carole Mortimer; and *Blackmailed for Her Baby* by Elizabeth Power.

The Mills & Boon Medical Romance line involves intense emotional romances and medical drama set in a modern medical community. Recent titles include *Her Long-Lost Husband* by Josie Metcalfe; *English Doctor, Italian Bride* by Carol Marinelli; *The Heart Surgeon's Baby Surprise* by Meredith Webber; *A Wife for the Baby Doctor* by Josie Metcalfe; and *Surgeon Boss, Surprise Dad* by Janice Lynn.

Mills & Boon Historical Romance novels cover a wide range of British and European historical civilizations up to and including the Second World War. Titles include *Untamed Rogue, Scandalous Mistress* by Bronwyn Scott; *Kidnapped: His Innocent Mistress* by Nicola Cornick; *His Cavalry Lady* by Joanna Maitland; *Questions of Honor* by Kate Welsh; and *Conquering Knight, Captive Lady* by Anne O'Brien.

Harlequin Romance is the original line of romance fiction, the series that started it all—more than 35 years ago. These are warm, contemporary novels, filled with compassion and sensitivity, written by world-famous authors and by newcomers. Titles include *Brady: The Rebel Rancher* by Patricia Thayer; *Italian Groom, Princess Bride* by Rebecca Winters; *Falling for Her Convenient Husband* by Jessica Steele; and *Cinderella's Wedding Wish* by Jessica Hart.

Harlequin Presents is overall the bestselling Harlequin line, published in 16 different languages and sold in almost every country of the world. This line features heartwarming romance novels about spirited, independent women and strong, wealthy men. Although grounded in reality and reflective of contemporary, relevant trends, these fast-paced stories are essentially escapist romantic fantasies that take the reader on an emotional roller-coaster ride. Written in the third person, they can be from the male or female point of view, or seen through the eyes of both protagonists. Titles include *The Italian's Ruthless Marriage Command* by Helen Bianchin; *The Spaniard's Virgin Housekeeper* by Diana Hamilton; *The Greek's Million-Dollar Baby Bargain* by Julia James; and *At the Argentinean Billionaire's Bidding* by India Grey.

Please submit the first three chapters along with a one to two page synopsis of your novel, with appropriate SASE to:

Tessa Shapcott, Senior Editor—Harlequin Presents (Mills & Boon Modern Romance), Modern Xtra Sensual

Bryony Green, Senior Editor—Harlequin Romance (Mills & Boon Tender Romance)

Linda Fildew, Senior Editor—Historical Romance

Sheila Hodgson, Senior Editor—Medical

WORLDWIDE LIBRARY

WORLDWIDE MYSTERY

GOLD EAGLE BOOKS

The Worldwide Library division of Harlequin Enterprises hosts two major imprints, Worldwide Mystery and Gold Eagle Books. Worldwide Library emphasizes genre fiction in the categories of mystery and suspense, action-adventure, futuristic fiction, war drama, and post-Holocaust thrillers. The house gives its titles (primarily mass-market paperbacks) solid marketing and promotional support.

The Worldwide Mystery imprint specializes in mainstream commercial mystery and detective fiction in reprint. This imprint has not been issuing previously unpublished, original fiction; however, Worldwide is not to be overlooked as a resource regarding potential reprint-rights sales in this field. The house generally keeps lines of popular writers' ongoing series in print for a number of seasons, sometimes indefinitely. Titles at Worldwide include *Of All Sad Words* by Bill Crider; *Flawed* by Jo Bannister; and *Murder at Wrightsville Beach* by Ellen Elizabeth Hunter.

Gold Eagle Books is known for a fast-and-furious slate of men's action and adventure series with paramilitary and future-world themes. Series include Deathlands, the Destroyer, the Executioner, and Stony Man. Gold Eagle also publishes Super Books keyed to the various series—longer novels with more fully developed plots. Prospective authors should be familiar with the guidelines and regular characters associated with each series.

Query letters and SASEs should be directed to:

Feroze Mohammed, Senior Editor

Nicole Brebner, Editor

HOUSE OF ANANSI PRESS

GROUNDWOOD BOOKS

LIBRO TIGRILLO

110 Spadina Avenue, Suite 801, Toronto, ON M5V 2K4, Canada

416-363-4343   fax: 416-363-1017

www.anansi.ca

www.groundwoodbooks.com

House of Anansi Press specializes in finding and developing Canada's new writers of literary fiction, poetry, and nonfiction and in maintaining a culturally significant backlist that has accumulated since the house was founded 42 years ago.

Anansi started as a small press with a mandate to publish only Canadian writers, and quickly gained attention for publishing significant authors such as Margaret Atwood, Matt Cohen, Michael Ondaatje, and Erin Mouré, as well as George Grant and Northrop Frye. French-Canadian works in translation have also been an important part of the list, and prominent Anansi authors in translation include Roch Carrier, Anne Hébert, Lise Bissonnette, and Marie-Claire Blais.

Today, Anansi publishes Canadian and international writers of literary fiction, poetry, and serious nonfiction. They do not publish genre fiction (mysteries, thrillers, science fiction, or romance novels), nor do they publish self-help nonfiction.

New titles include *Guilt About the Past* by Bernhard Schlink; *Ways of Staying* by Kevin Bloom; *The Irrationalist* by Suzanne Buffam; *Patient Frame* by Steven Heighton; *Bloom* by Michael Lista; and *Holding Still as Long as Possible* by Zoe Whittall.

GROUNDWOOD BOOKS

Groundwood Books, an independent imprint of House of Anansi Press, is based in Toronto and publishes children's books for all ages, including fiction, picture books, and nonfiction.

Their primary focus has been on works by Canadians, though they sometimes also buy manuscripts from authors in other countries. Many of their books tell the stories of people whose voices are not always heard. Books by the First Peoples of this hemisphere have always been a special interest, as well as French-Canadian works in translation. Since 1998, Groundwood has been publishing works by people of Latin American origin living in the Americas both in English and in Spanish under their Libros Tigrillo imprint.

In lieu of sending complete unsolicited manuscripts, House of Anansi prefers to receive proposals in hard copy along with a detailed literary curriculum vitae and a 10- to 15-page sample from the manuscript. These materials should be sent to Manuscript Submissions.

Groundwood Books is always looking for new authors of novel-length fiction for children in all age areas, but does not accept unsolicited manuscripts for picture books. They like character-driven literary fiction and note that they do not publish high-interest/low-vocabulary fiction or stories with anthropomorphic animals or elves/fairies as their main characters.

Lynn Henry, Publisher (Anansi)

Janey Yoon, Managing Editor (Anansi)

Patsy Aldana, Vice President and Publisher (Groundwood)

Nan Froman, Managing Editor (Groundwood)

INSOMNIAC PRESS

520 Princess Avenue, London, ON N6B 2B8, Canada

416-504-6270   fax: 416-504-9313

www.insomniacpress.com

Insomniac Press is a midsize independent press that publishes nonfiction, fiction, and poetry for the adult markets. Insomniac always strives to publish the most exciting new writers it can find. Celebrated authors like Natalee Caple, Lynn Crosbie, Stephen Finucan, and A.F. Moritz either got their start at Insomniac, or have published important books with the house.

While it publishes a broad range of titles, Insomniac has also developed special niche areas, including black studies books, gay and lesbian books, celebrity musician-authored books (including titles by Matthew Good, Jann Arden, and Terri Clark), and gay mysteries. Insomniac is actively seeking commercial and creative nonfiction on a wide range of subjects, including business, personal finance, gay and lesbian studies, and black Canadian studies.

Recent titles include *Bird Eat Bird* by Katrina Best; *Date With a Sheesha: A Russell Quant Mystery* by Anthony Bidulka; *Inspire Your Career: Strategies for Success in Your First Years at Work* by Patricia Barbato; *Tiny, Frantic, Stronger* by Jeff Latosik; and *Why Are You So Long and Sweet?* by David McFadden.

The house does not publish science fiction, cookbooks, romance, or children's books. The poetry list is also full for the foreseeable future. Insomniac does accept unsolicited manuscripts, but suggests that you query first with a short letter or email describing the project. Email mike@insomniacpress.com.

Queries and SASEs can be directed to:

Mike O'Connor, Publisher, mike@insomniacpress.com

Dan Varrette, Managing Editor, dan@insomniacpress.com

JAMES LORIMER & COMPANY LIMITED

317 Adelaide Street West, Suite 1002, Toronto, ON M5V 1P9, Canada

416-362-4762   fax: 416-362-3939

www.lorimer.ca

James Lorimer is a publisher of nonfiction, children's young-adult novels, and illustrated guide books. They publish Canadian authors for a Canadian audience and are currently seeking manuscripts in the following genres: cultural or social history, natural history, cookbooks with a Canadian or regional focus, education, public issues, travel and recreation, and biography. They are especially interested in projects for the southwestern Ontario marketplace.

Recent titles include *Ghost Town Stories of Ontario* by Maria Da Silva and Andrew Hind; *Great Canadian Imposters* by Cheryl MacDonald; *Immodest and Sensational: 150 Years of Canadian Women in Sport* by M. Ann Hall; *How We Almost Gave the Tories the Boot: The Inside Story Behind the Coalition* by Brian Topp; and *Journey to the Tar Sands* edited by Tim Murphy.

Do not send entire manuscripts, just a proposal. Email queries are not acceptable. Queries and SASEs should be mailed to the attention of the Acquisition Editor.

Diane Young, Managing Editor; diane.young@lorimer.ca

Carrie Gleason, Children's Book Editor; childrenseditor@lorimer.ca

KEY PORTER BOOKS LTD.

6 Adelaide Street East, 10th Floor, Toronto, ON M5C 1H6, Canada
416-862-7777   fax: 416-862-2304

www.keyporter.com

Key Porter Books Limited is one of Canada's most prominent independent publishers, launching more than 100 new books per year with over 500 titles in print. The company is known internationally for its high-quality illustrated books and in Canada for its mainstream books of national interest. Key Porter publishes trade nonfiction, fiction, and children's books. Their areas of specialization include Canadian politics, fiction, history biography, environmental and social issues, children's literature, health, wildlife, conservation, sports, business, cookbooks, and photography.

Recent titles include *Smart Tax Tips: Winning Strategies to Reduce Your Taxes* by Grant Thornton and Karen Yull; *Always Change a Losing Game: Winning Strategies for Work, for Home and for Your Health* by David Posen; and *Max and Ruby: The Big Picture; and Supereating: A Revolutionary Way to Get More from the Foods You Eat* by Ian Marber.

Key Porter Books does not accept unsolicited manuscript submissions, but will review queries and proposals. Send queries and SASEs Attention: Submissions.

Jordan Fenn, Vice President and Publisher

LOBSTER PRESS LTD.

1620 Sherbrooke Street West, Suites C & D, Montreal, QC H3H 1C9, Canada
514-904-1100   fax: 514-904-1101

www.lobsterpress.com

Lobster Press publishes fiction and nonfiction books for children, tweens, teens, and their families. Lobster Press is seeking fresh, edgy fiction for young adults, high interest fiction for reluctant readers, and nonfiction for preteens and teens. They particularly seek titles that appeal to boys. Lobster Press also publishes a bestselling series of family guidebooks, *The Lobster Kids' Guides to Cities in the USA and Canada*.

Recent titles include *Green Careers: You Can Make Money AND Save the Planet* by Jennifer Power Scott; and *Grim Hill* by Linda DeMeulemeester.

They are actively seeking new authors and manuscripts. Please send a complete manuscript, accompanied by a cover letter, résumé, and synopsis of the story.

Specify the genre of your work clearly on the envelope. Do not include a SASE as Lobster Press will recycle unwanted manuscripts and contact only those authors they wish to publish.

Alison Fripp, President and Publisher

Mahak Jain, Acting Managing Editor

MAPLE TREE PRESS

10 Lower Spadina Avenue, Suite 400, Toronto, Ontario M5V 2Z2, Canada

416-340-2700   fax: 416-340-9767

www.mapletreepress.com   email: owlkids@owlkids.com

Based in Toronto, Maple Tree Press has been publishing children's books for more than 30 years. They specialize in science and nature titles, but also look for nonfiction in a wide range of subjects, including Canadian culture, sports, crafts, activities, history, humor, and picture books.

Recent titles from Maple Tree Press include *Magic Up Your Sleeve: Amazing Illusions, Tricks, and Science Facts You'll Never Believe* by Helaine Becker; *SOS! Titanic!: Canadian Flyer Adventures #14* by Frieda Wishinsky; and *Wow Canada!: Exploring this Land from Coast to Coast to Coast* by Vivien Bowers.

Maple Tree Press publishes Canadian authors almost exclusively. They especially welcome submissions for children's books targeted to ages 3–12. Please send to the attention of the Submissions Editor.

Sheba Meland, Publisher

MCCLELLAND & STEWART

DOUGLAS GIBSON BOOKS

TUNDRA BOOKS

75 Sherbourne Street, 5th Floor, Toronto, ON M5A 2P9, Canada

416-598-1114   fax: 416-598-7764

www.mcclelland.com   email: mail@mcclelland.com

www.tundrabooks.com

Celebrating its 103rd anniversary this year, McClelland & Stewart (M&S) is something of a Canadian institution and was an early publisher of Lucy Maud

Montgomery's *Anne of Green Gables* and Winston Churchill's *History of the English Speaking Peoples*. Today, they publish a wide range of poetry, fiction, and nonfiction.

M&S authors include Margaret Atwood, Sandra Birdsell, Mavis Gallant, Jack Hodgins, Alistair MacLeod, Rohinton Mistry, Alice Munro, Michael Ondaatje, and Jane Urquhart, but they also publish debut authors like Madeleine Thien.

Recent titles include *Map of the Invisible World* by Tash Aw; *Piece of My Heart* by Peter Robinson; *The Rehearsal* by Eleanor Catton; *Cities of Refuge* by Michael Helm; and *Brooklyn* by Colm Toibin.

TUNDRA BOOKS

In 1995, M&S bought Tundra, a children's book publisher known for combining art and story in innovative ways. The previous publisher of Tundra, Douglas Gibson, is now the publisher of his own imprint within Tundra Books.

Tundra's newest venture is the re-introduction of a storybook format, which had been popular before World War II, to combine the beauty of picture books with more complex and longer stories.

Recent titles from Tundra include *Alison Dare, Little Miss Adventure* by J. Torres; *Cyclist BikeList: The Book for Every Rider* by Laura Robinson; *Folly* by Marthe Jocelyn; *Grand* by Marla Stewart Konrad; and *Grease Town* by Ann Towell.

Douglas Gibson was the first editorial imprint in Canada when it was established in 1986. The list is kept small at five to ten titles a year, and represents Gibson's eclectic tastes in politics, history, biography, high adventure, and fine fiction.

Recent titles from Douglas Gibson include *Memoirs: 1939–1993* by Brian Mulroney; *My Mother's Daughter* by Rona Maynard; *Hot Air: Meeting Canada's Climate Change Challenge* by Jeffrey Simpson, Mark Jaccard, and Nic Rivers; *Raisin Wine: A Boyhood in a Different Muskoka* by James Bartleman; and *King John of Canada* by Scott Gardinier.

Please do not send manuscript submissions by email. Tundra does not accept unsolicited manuscripts for picture books. Direct queries and SASEs to:

Douglas Pepper, President and Publisher (McClelland & Stewart)

Ellen Seligman, Vice President and Publisher (McClelland & Stewart)

Susan Renouf, COO—Nonfiction (McClelland & Stewart)
Kathy Lowinger, Publisher (Tundra Books)
Douglas Gibson, Publisher (Douglas Gibson Books)

MCGILL-QUEEN'S UNIVERSITY PRESS

Montreal office:

McGill University, 3430 McTavish Street, Montreal, QC H3A 1X9, Canada

514-398-3750   fax: 514-398-4333

Kingston office:

Queen's University, Kingston, ON K7L 3N6, Canada

613-533-2155   fax: 613-533-6822

www.mqup.mcgill.ca   email: mqup@mcgill.ca

McGill-Queen's University Press (MQUP) publishes original scholarly books and well-researched general interest books in all areas of the social sciences and humanities. While their emphasis is on providing an outlet for Canadian authors and scholarship, some of their authors are from outside Canada. More than half of their sales are international.

A joint venture of McGill University in Montreal, Quebec, and Queen's University in Kingston, Ontario, MQUP is both a specialist in the Canadian perspective and a publisher of international themes. A Canadian press with a global reach, the house aims to advance scholarship and contribute to culture by selling books.

Recent titles include *The New Pragmatism* by Alan Malachowski; *Delayed Impact* by Franklin Bialystok; *Virgil the Blind Guide* by Lloyd H. Howard; *Into Deep Waters* by Daniel C. Goodwin; and *Cast from Bells* by Suzanne Hancock.

Extensive submitting details are on their website. In general, they welcome proposals quite early in the development process. Query letters and SASEs should be directed to:

Donald H. Akenson, Senior Editor (Kingston)

Joan Harcourt, Editor (Kingston)

Jeffrey Brison, Deputy Senior Editor; bjh@queensu.ca

Mary-Lynne Ascough, mqup@queensu.ca

Philip J. Cercone, Executive Director and Senior Editor (Montreal)

Joan McGilvray, Coordinating Editor (Montreal)

John Zucchi, Senior Editor

Kyla Madden, Editor; kyla.madden@mcgill.ca

Mark Abley, Editor; mark.abley@mcgill.ca

Jonathon Crago, Editor (Montreal)

CANADIAN BOOK PUBLISHERS

MCGRAW-HILL RYERSON LTD.

300 Water Street, Whitby, ON L1N 9B6, Canada

1-800-565-5758

www.mcgrawhill.ca

One of the 111 McGraw-Hill Companies around the globe, McGraw-Hill Ryerson is staffed and managed by Canadians but reports to its parent company in New York. Though primarily an educational division, McGraw-Hill Ryerson also has a thriving trade arm.

McGraw-Hill Ryerson's trade division publishes and distributes reference books on a wide array of subjects, including business, computing, engineering, science, reference, travel, and self-study foreign language programs. Other areas include outdoor recreation, child care, parenting, health, fine arts, music, sports, fitness, cooking, and crafts.

Recent titles include *Wake Up Now: A Guide to the Journey of Spiritual Awakening* by Stephan Bodian; *Awaken Your Strongest Self: Break Free of Stress, Inner Conflict, and Self-Sabotage* by Neil Fiore; and *Fetology: Diagnosis and Management of the Fetal Patient* by Diana W. Bianchi.

Query letters and SASEs should be directed to:

Claudio Pascucci, President of Professional Division

Lynda Walthert, Assistant to the President of Professional Division

THE MERCURY PRESS

P.O. Box 672, Station P, Toronto, ON M5S 2Y4, Canada

416-531-4338   fax: 416-531-0765

www.themercurypress.ca   email: contact@themercurypress.ca

The Mercury Press, shortlisted for 1997 Publisher of the Year by the Canadian Booksellers Association, specializes in cutting-edge fiction and poetry, as well as nonfiction and murder mysteries. All titles are Canadian-authored.

The Mercury Press also publishes *Word: Canada's Magazine for Readers + Writers. Word* features literary event listings, columns, and reviews, and is a good starting place for learning about this publisher.

Recent Mercury Press titles include *Bouncin' with Bartok* by Jack Chambers; *A Debt of Death* by John Worsley Simpson; *The Hostage Taker* by D.O. Dodd; *Zong!* by M. Nourbese Philip; *A Painter's Journey: Volume II, 1974–1979* by Barbara Caruso; and *Between You and Me* by Lesley McAllister.

Mercury Press does not consider electronic submissions. Direct queries via regular mail with SASEs to:

Beverley A. Daurio, Editor

NOVALIS

Novalis—Toronto:

10 Lower Spadina Ave, Suite 400, Toronto, Ontario M5V 2Z2, Canada

416-363-3303   fax: 416-363-9409

Novalis—Montreal:

4475 Frontenac Street, Montreal, Quebec H2H 2S2, Canada

514-278-3020   fax: 514-278-0072

Novalis—Ottawa:

223 Main Street, Ottawa, Ontario K1S 1C4, Canada

613-236-1393   fax: 613-782-3004

www.novalis.ca

Novalis is a religious publishing house in the Catholic tradition and is a part of Saint Paul University. Novalis publishes and distributes periodicals, books, brochures, and audio-visual resources touching on all aspects of spiritual life, especially from the Christian and Jewish traditions. While the greater part of its production is for the general public, Novalis also publishes more specialized works in the area of theology and religious studies.

Subjects include personal growth, self-help, spirituality and prayer, children's books, gardening, meditation, Church history, and Celtic spirituality, among others. Novalis has equally strong publishing programs in both of Canada's official languages.

Recent titles include *2009 Sunday Missal for Young Catholics*; *Seraphic Singles* by Dorothy Cummings; *Forgiveness: One Step at a Time* by Joseph F. Sica; *On Earth as It Is in Heaven* by Josephine Lombardi; *A View from the Trenches* by Dennis Murphy; and *Drumming from Within* by Sylvain Lavoie.

Direct queries and SASEs to:

Joseph Sinasac, Publishing Director; joseph.sinasac@novalis.ca

Grace Deutsch, Editorial Director; grace.deutsch@novalis.ca

Anne-Loiuse Mahoney, Managing Editor; anne-louise.mahoney@novalis.ca

OOLICHAN BOOKS

P.O. Box 2278, Fernie, BC V0B 1M0, Canada

250-423-7461   fax: 866-299-0026

www.oolichan.com   email: oolichanbooks@telus.net

Oolichan Books is a literary press, publishing poetry, fiction, and creative nonfiction titles including literary criticism, memoirs, and books on regional history, First Nations, and policy issues. Their name is taken from the small fish, once plentiful in West Coast waters and a staple in the diet of First Nations people to whom it was sacred. The oolichan, often referred to as the candlefish, is believed to possess healing powers and guarantee longevity.

Recent Oolichan titles include *Words* by Mark Ellis and Ruth Campbell; *The Blue Sky* by Galsan Tschinag, translated by Katharina Rout; *The Aviary* by Miranda Pearson; *Writing on Stone* by Michael Elcock; *Elliot & Me* by Keith Harrison; *Touching Ecuador* by W.H. New; and *Time Out Of Mind* by Laurie Block.

Oolichan Books publishes only Canadian authors. Please send up to ten poems and three chapters of a manuscript along with a cover letter and CV. Note that they will not read a submission that arrives without a proper SASE for its return. You may direct submissions to:

Randal Macnair, Publisher

Ron Smith, Publisher

Pat Smith, Consulting Editor

ORCA BOOK PUBLISHERS

P.O. Box 5626, Station B, Victoria, BC V8R 6S4, Canada

800-210-5277   fax: 877-408-1551

www.orcabook.com   email: orca@orcabook.com

Orca Book Publishers focuses on children's books: picture books, and juvenile and young-adult fiction. Their limited adult list focuses on general trade nonfiction, including travel and recreational guides, regional history, and biography. They release books in their Orca Soundings, Orca Currents, Orca Sports, Orca Echoes, and Orca Young Readers lines.

Orca is presently seeking manuscripts written by Canadian authors in the following genres: children's picture books, early chapter books, juvenile fiction, young-adult fiction, and graphic novels. They are not seeking seasonal stories, board books, or "I Can Read" books.

Recent titles include *Craigdarroch* by Terry Reksten; *In the Company of Whales* by Alexander Morton; and *Once Upon a Time: My Life with Children's Books* by Sheila Egoff and Wendy Sutton.

The Orca Soundings line features short, high-interest novels with contemporary themes written expressly for teens reading below grade level. New releases include *Back* by Norah McClintock; *Comeback* by Vicki Grant; *Hannah's Touch* by Laura Langston; and *Impact* by James C. Dekker.

The Orca Currents line seeks short, high-interest novels with contemporary themes written expressly for middle-school students reading below grade level. Titles include *Bear Market* by Michele Martin Bossley; *Blob* by Frieda Wishinsky; and *Branded* by Eric Walters.

Their Orca Sports line features sports action combined with mystery/suspense. For ages 10+, Orca Sports seeks strong plots, credible characters, simple language, and high-interest chapters. Some Orca Sports books include *Absolute Pressure* by Sigmund Brouwer; *Paralyzed* by Jeff Rud; *Slam Dunk* by Kate Jaimet; and *Venom* by Nikki Tate.

The Orca Echoes line features early chapter books for readers ages seven to nine with a Grade 2 reading level with engaging characters, easy-to-follow plots with exciting stories, and generous illustrations. Some titles include *Marsh Island* by Sonya Spreen Bates; *Sam's Ride* by Becky Citra; *The Fossil Hunters* by Marilyn Helmer; and *Timberwolf Rivals* by Sigmund Brouwer.

The Orca Young Readers line has historical and contemporary stories for ages 8–11, with age appropriate plots and story lines. Orca Young Readers has had many bestsellers and award-winning titles. Some recent titles include *Addison Addley and the Trick of the Eye* by Melody DeFields McMillan and *After Peaches* by Michelle Mulder.

While picture books submissions may be sent in their entirety, all other authors should query with sample chapters prior to sending the complete manuscript. Please send to the appropriate editor, or check the website for further information.

Andrew Woolridge, Publisher—Teen novels aimed at reluctant readers

Bob Tyrrell, Editorial Director

Christi Howes, Editor—Children's and picture books (Orca Echoes)

Sarah Harvey, Editor—Young readers, juvenile novels, teen fiction

Melanie Jeffs, Editor—Intermediate novels aimed at reluctant readers

PENGUIN GROUP (CANADA)

HAMISH HAMILTON CANADA

PUFFIN CANADA

VIKING CANADA

90 Eglinton Avenue East, Suite 700, Toronto, ON M4P 2Y3, Canada

416-925-2249   fax: 416-925-0068

www.penguin.ca   email: info@ca.penguingroup.com

Penguin Group (Canada)—once called Penguin Books—was founded in 1974. Initially a distribution arm for Penguin International, Penguin Books began publishing indigenous Canadian work in 1982 with such notable titles as Peter C. Newman's landmark history of the Hudson's Bay Company, *Company of Adventurers*, and fiction by Robertson Davies, Timothy Findley, Alice Munro, and Mordecai Richler. It also publishes books under three imprints, Hamish Hamilton Canada, Puffin Canada, and Viking Canada.

Penguin Group (Canada) is determined to publish books that speak to the broadest reading public and address leading issues of social importance. Penguin's books cover subjects as diverse as Canadian nationalism, homelessness and mental illness, and health care and education.

Recent titles include *Gods and Human Beings* by François Voltaire and Michael Shreve; *The Girl Next Door* by Elizabeth Noble; *The Selected Works of T.S. Spivet* by Reif Larsen; *Dog House: A Love Story* by Carol Prisant; and *The Marks of Cain: A Novel* by Tom Knox.

Hamish Hamilton Canada is the Canadian counterpart of one of Britain's most distinguished literary lists. Hamish Hamilton has provided a home for an exciting and eclectic group of authors united by the distinctiveness and excellence of their writing. Hamish Hamilton Canada will maintain a deep commitment to literary value, embracing both young and old, the experimental and the new, and continuing to be selective with a list of five to ten titles a year.

Puffin Canada publishes juvenile fiction and nonfiction in hardcover and paperback. Titles from Puffin Canada include *Mine for Keeps* by Jean Little; *Daring Game* by Kit Pearson; *Royal Ransom* by Eric Walters; and *Hamish X and the Hollow Mountain* by Sean Cullen.

Viking Canada, Penguin Canada's counterpart to the Viking Press, publishes adult and juvenile material. Titles include *Promises to Keep* by Jane Green; *Songs of Blood and Sword: A Daughter's Memoir* by Fatima Bhutto; *Under Heaven* by Guy Gavriel Kay; and *Nice Recovery* by Susan Juby.

Penguin Group (Canada) no longer accepts unsolicited manuscripts, and will not enter into correspondence about unpublished work, except with literary agents.

David Davidar, Publisher/President

Diane Turbide, Editorial Director

Laura Shin, Editor—Crimes, thrillers, romance

Helen Rees, Senior Editor—General nonfiction

Nicole Winstanley, Executive Editor—Children's literature

PLAYWRIGHTS CANADA PRESS

215 Spadina Avenue, Suite 230, Toronto, ON M5T 2C7, Canada

416-703-0013   fax: 416-408-3402

www.playwrightscanada.com

Playwrights Canada Press publishes Canadian plays, theater criticism, history, biographies, and memoirs, and is the largest exclusive publisher of Canadian drama. It publishes roughly thirty books of plays, theater history, and criticism every year. This publisher exists to raise the profile of Canadian playwrights and Canadian theater and theater practitioners. French plays by Canadian authors are published in translation, and the Press's mandate includes printing plays for young audiences.

Recent titles include *Toronto the Good* by Andrew Moodie; *Scratch* by Charlotte Corbeil-Coleman; *Forests* by Wajdi Mouowad; *While We're Young* by Don Hannah; and *Billy Twinkle: Requiem for a Golden Boy* by Ronnie Burkett.

Query letters and SASEs should be directed to:

Annie Gibson, Publisher; publisher@playwrightscanada.com

Blake Sproule, Editorial and Production Manager; editor@playwrightscanada .com

THE PORCUPINE'S QUILL

68 Main Street, Erin, ON N0B 1T0, Canada

519-833-9158   fax: 519-833-9845

http://porcupinesquill.ca   email: pql@sentex.net

Since 1974, The Porcupine's Quill has been publishing literary titles, especially novels, short stories, and poetry. The Porcupine's Quill is a small publisher with a tradition of publishing first books of poetry; they are proud that many of their writers graduated to large trade houses to publish bestsellers. Today they publish some 12 books per year.

Recent titles include *A Suit of Nettles* by James Reaney; *My Other Women* by Pauline Carey; *Wanderlust* by Megan Speers; and *A Kind of Perseverance* by Margaret Avison.

The Porcupine's Quill does not accept unsolicited work. Instead, they seek out writers whose work has appeared in literary magazines such as *The New Quarterly*. Direct your query and SASE to:

Tim Inkster, Publisher

Doris Cowan, Fiction Editor

George A. Walker, Graphic Novels Editor

Carmine Starnino, Nonfiction Editor

Wayne Clifford, Poetry Editor

RANDOM HOUSE CANADA

ANCHOR CANADA

BOND STREET BOOKS

DOUBLEDAY CANADA

KNOPF CANADA

RANDOM HOUSE CANADA

SEAL BOOKS

VINTAGE CANADA

One Toronto Street, Suite 300, Toronto, ON M5C 2V6, Canada

416-364-4449   fax: 416-364-6863

www.randomhouse.ca

Random House of Canada was established in 1944 and in 1986 established its own indigenous Canadian publishing program. As a separate company, Doubleday Canada has been one of Canada's most prominent publishers for more than 40 years. Following the international merger of Random House and Bantam Doubleday in 1998, the two companies officially became one in Canada in 1999, representing sister companies' titles in this country and maintaining thriving Canadian publishing programs.

The Random House Canada imprint features a diverse list of literary and commercial fiction, Canadian and international cookbooks, and bold nonfiction. Some titles include *Making an Elephant* by Graham Swift; *Border Songs* by Jim Lynch; *Why Your World Is About to Get a Whole Lot Smaller* by Jeff Rubin; *The G.I. Diet Menopause Clinic* by Rick Gallop; and *Murder Without Borders: Dying for the Story in the World's Most Dangerous Places* by Terry Gould.

Anchor Canada is a publisher of quality trade paperback books, fiction and non-fiction. Launched in 2001, it began by publishing affordable editions of Doubleday Canada's hardcover titles and other titles published elsewhere. In 2002 Anchor Canada published its first Anchor Trade Paperback Original and continues to produce original fiction and nonfiction works. Some titles include *Devil May Care* by Sebastian Faulks; *Loyalists and Layabouts: The Rapid Rise and Faster Fall of Shelburne, Nova Scotia* by Stephen Kimber; *One to Nine: The Inner Life of Numbers* by Andrew Hodges; *Trauma* by Patrick McGrath; and *The Fruit Hunters: A Story of Nature, Adventure, Commerce, and Obsession* by Adam Gollner.

The Bond Street Books imprint was launched in 2005, taking its name from the small historic street from which Doubleday Canada began publishing more than 50 years ago. It is dedicated to publishing fiction and nonfiction titles from around the world. Bond Street Books are supported by an encompassing, dynamic marketing campaign to ensure they reach a wide readership in Canada. Some titles include *The Invisible Mountain* by Carolina De Robertis; *Burnt Shadows* by Kamila Shamsie; *Direct Red: A Surgeon's View of Her Life-or-Death Profession* by Gabriel Weston; *Bits of Me Are Falling Apart: How We Get Older and Why* by William Leith; and *The Siege* by Ismail Kadare.

Doubleday Canada has been one of Canada's most prominent publishers for over 50 years and is committed to producing fine fiction from both established and new voices and developing challenging and entertaining nonfiction. It also maintains a Young Adult publishing program. Some titles include *Tell Me Why: How Young People Can Change the World* by Eric Walters; *Not Yet: A Memoir of Living and Almost Dying* by Wayson Choy; *Automatic World* by Struan Sinclair; *A Walk Through a Window* by KC Dyer; and *The Sweetness at the Bottom of the Pie* by Alan Bradley.

Knopf Canada was launched in 1991 when Sonny Mehta, president of Alfred A. Knopf, approached prominent editor Louise Denny to create and run a Canadian arm of Knopf in the offices of Random House Canada. It is interested in thoughtful nonfiction and fiction with literary merit and strong commercial potential. Some titles include *The Dead Republic* by Roddy Doyle; *Every Lost Country* by Steven Heighton; *Girl from the South* by Joanna Trollope; and *The Shadows in the Street* by Susan Hill.

Seal Books is a mass-market publishing house, publishing original books and specializing in reprints of major hardcover fiction titles, such as books by Margaret Atwood and Lucy Maud Montgomery. Some of their titles include *The Purity Myth: How America's Obsession with Virginity Is Hurting Young Women* by Jessica Valenti; *Travel Therapy: Where Do You Need to Go?* by Karen Schaler; *When the Piano Stops: A Memoir of Healing from Sexual Abuse* by Catherine McCall; *Charley's Web* by Joy Fielding; and *Open: Love, Sex, and Life in an Open Marriage* by Jenny Block.

Vintage Canada publishes quality trade paperback editions, selecting its books primarily from titles originally published by Knopf Canada and Random House Canada.

Random House Canada does not accept unsolicited manuscripts. Query letters and SASEs should be directed to:

Louise Dennys, Publisher

Bhavna Chauhan, Assistant to the Publisher (Anchor, Doubleday, Bond Street)

Nita Pronovost, Senior Editor (Anchor, Doubleday, Bond Street)

Diane Martin, Acquisitions Editor (Knopf, Seal, Vintage Canada)

Michael Schellenberg, Acquisitions Editor (Knopf, Seal, Vintage Canada)

Angelika Glover, Acquisitions Editor (Knopf, Seal, Vintage Canada)

Marion Garner, Acquisitions Editor (Knopf, Seal, Vintage Canada)

RED DEER PRESS

ROBERT J. SAWYER BOOKS

195 Allstate Parkway, Markham, Ontario L3R 4T8 Canada

1-800-387-9776

www.reddeerpress.com

Red Deer Press is an award-winning publisher of literary fiction, nonfiction, children's illustrated books, juvenile fiction, teen fiction, drama, and poetry. Red Deer Press's mandate is to publish books by, about, or of interest to Canadians, with special emphasis on the Prairie West. Red Deer Press publishes 18–20 new books per year, all written or illustrated by Canadians. Approximately 20 percent of their program is comprised of first-time authors and illustrators.

Recent titles indicative of the list include *Acting Up* by Ted Stauton; *The McGuillicuddy Book of Personal Records* by Colleen Sydor; and *How to Ruin Your Life: And Other Lessons You Don't Learn in School* by Carolyn McTighe.

In 2004, Red Deer Press launched the Robert J. Sawyer Books imprint, a line of literate, philosophically rich science-fiction titles personally selected by "the dean of Canadian Science Fiction." The books in this imprint appeal to both SF fans and general readers who enjoy a mingling of the intimately human with the grandly cosmic.

Some titles from this imprint include *Valley of the Day-Glo* by Nick DiChario; *Identity Theft: And Other Stories* by Robert J. Sawyer; *Birthstones* by Phyllis Gotlied; *The Commons* by Matthew Hughes; *Sailing Time's Ocean* by Terence M. Green; and *Rogue Harvest* by Danita Maslan.

Send queries and SASEs to:

Richard Dionne, Publisher
Val Burke-Harland, Associate Publisher
Peter Carver, Children's Editor
Robert J. Sawyer, Publisher (Robert J. Sawyer Books)

RONSDALE PRESS

3350 West 21st Avenue, Vancouver, BC V6S 1G7, Canada
604-738-4688   fax: 604-731-4548
www.ronsdalepress.com   email: ronsdale@shaw.ca

A literary publishing house, Ronsdale Press is dedicated to publishing books from across Canada and books that give Canadians new insights into themselves and their country. Ronsdale publishes fiction, poetry, regional history, biography and autobiography, plays, books of ideas about Canada, and children's books. The press looks for thoughtful works that reveal the author has read deeply in contemporary and earlier literature and is working to create a text with innovative combinations of form and content that can bring genuinely new insights. Ronsdale accepts submissions only from Canadian authors.

Recent titles include *Chasing a Star* by Norma Charles; *The Dead Can't Dance* by Pam Calabrese MacLean; *From a Speaking Place: Writings from the First Fifty Years of Canadian Literature* edited by W.H. New; *In the Wake of Loss* by Sheila James; and *Journey to Atlantis* by Philip Roy.

Authors are welcome to send finished manuscripts or queries with samples, along with SASEs.

Ronald B. Hatch, General Acquisitions Editor
Veronica Hatch, Children's Acquisition Editor

SECOND STORY PRESS

20 Maud Street, Suite 401, Toronto, ON M5V 2M5, Canada
416-537-7850   fax: 416-537-0588
www.secondstorypress.ca   email: info@secondstorypress.ca

The Second Story Press list spans adult fiction and nonfiction, children's fiction, nonfiction and picture books, and young-adult fiction and nonfiction. As a feminist press, they look for manuscripts dealing with the many diverse and varied aspects of the lives of girls and women. Some of their special interest areas include Judaica, ability issues, coping with cancer, and queer rights. They publish about 16 new books per year, primarily from Canadian authors.

Recent titles include *Madwoman of Bethlehem* by Rosine Nimeh-Mailloux; *Tell Me a Story, Tell Me the Truth* by Gina Roitman; *White Space Between* by Ami Sands Brodoff; *Woman's Agenda 2009* by Kathy White and Kerry Cathers; *Fantastic Female Filmmakers* by Suzanne Simoni; *Headline Murder* by April Lindgren; and *Maggie and the Chocolate War* by Michelle Mulder.

Second Story accepts unsolicited manuscripts with SASEs. Email manuscripts are not considered. Direct submissions to:

Margie Wolfe, Publisher

Carolyn Jackson, Managing Editor

TALON BOOKS LTD.

P.O. Box 2076, Vancouver BC V6B 3S3, Canada

604-444-4889; Outside Vancouver: 1-888-445-4176   fax: 604-444-4119

www.talonbooks.com   email: info@talonbooks.com

Talon Books publishes drama, fiction, and nonfiction of the political, social, critical, and ethnographic variety.

Recent titles include *After Jack* by Garry Thomas Morse; *Asian Skies* by Ken Norris; *Bardy Google* by Frank Davey; *Decompositions* by Ken Belford; and *How to Write* by Derek Beaulieu.

Submissions of drama, fiction, criticism, history, and cultural studies are welcomed. Poetry, self-help, how-to, children's books, and genre books are not considered. Send submission and SASE to:

Kevin Williams, President

Karl Siegler, Publisher

TRANSIT PUBLISHING

1996 Saint-Joseph Boulevard East, Montréal, QC H2H 1E3
514-273-0123   fax: 1-866-258-7772
www.transitpublishing.com   email: direction@transitmedias.com

Transit Publishing, founded in March 2009, primarily publishes celebrity-oriented investigative journalism. Additionally, Transit is looking to expand into differing genres of fiction, including mystery, as well as health and lifestyle books.

Recent titles include *David Carradine: The Eye of My Tornado* by Marina Anderson; *Behind the Bell: Dustin Diamond* by Dustin Diamond; *Britney Spears: Little Girl Lost* by Christopher Heard; *Blood for Blood* by Gipsy Paladini; and *Mickey Rourke: Wrestling with Demons* by Sandro Monetti.

Send submission and SASE to:

Pierre Turgeon, President and Publisher; direction@transitmedias.com

UNIVERSITY OF ALBERTA PRESS

Ring House 2, University of Alberta, Edmonton, AB T6G 2E1, Canada
780-492-3662   fax: 780-492-0719
www.uap.ualberta.ca

A scholarly house, the University of Alberta Press publishes in the areas of biography, history, language, literature, natural history, regional interest, travel narratives, and reference books. The press seeks to contribute to the intellectual and cultural life of Alberta and Canada by publishing well-edited, research-based knowledge and creative thought that has undergone rigorous peer-review, is of real value to natural constituencies, adheres to quality publication standards, and is supported by diligent marketing efforts.

The University of Alberta Press is looking for original works of significant scholarship that are written for a reasonably wide readership. Canadian works that are analytical in nature are especially welcome, as are works by scholars who wish to interpret Canada, both past and present.

Recent titles include *Bosnia: In the Footsteps of Gavrilo Princip* by Tony Fabijancic; *Wild Horses* by Rob McLennan; *Too Bad: Sketches Toward a Self-Portrait* by Robert Kroetsch; and *Memory's Daughter* by Alice Major.

Submit queries and SASEs to:

Linda Cameron, Director; linda.cameron@ualberta.ca

Peter Midgley, Senior Acquisitions Editor; petem@ualberta.ca

UNIVERSITY OF BRITISH COLUMBIA PRESS

2029 West Mall, Vancouver, BC V6T 1Z2, Canada

604-822-5959   fax: 604-822-6083

www.ubcpress.ubc.ca   email: frontdesk@ubcpress.ca

University of British Columbia Press (UBC Press) is the publishing branch of the University of British Columbia. Established in 1971, it is among the largest university presses in Canada. It publishes 50 to 60 new books annually and has an active backlist of more than 800 titles.

UBC Press is widely acknowledged as one of the foremost publishers of political science, Native studies, and forestry books. Other areas of particular strength are Asian studies, Canadian history, environmental studies, planning, and urban studies. The Press publishes several series: Legal Dimensions, Law and Society, Canada and International Relations, Studies in Canadian Military History, Sexuality Studies, Sustainability and the Environment, Urbanization in Asia, First Nations Languages, Contemporary Chinese Studies, Pioneers of British Columbia, Pacific Rim Archaeology, and the Brenda and David McLean Canadian Studies series.

Recent titles include *Art in Turmoil: The Chinese Cultural Revolution 1966–76* edited by Richard King; *One of the Family: Metis Culture in Nineteenth-Century Northwestern Saskatchewan* by Brenda Macdougall; and *The Hero and the Historians: Historiography and the Uses of Jacques Cartier* by Alan Gordon.

Query letters and SASEs should be directed to:

Peter Milroy, Director—Special projects, international rights

Emily Andrew, Senior Editor—Asian studies, political science and political philosophy, military history, transnational and multicultural studies, communications

Randy Schmidt, Senior Editor—Forestry, environmental studies, urban studies and planning, sustainable development, geography, law and society

Melissa Pitts, Acquisitions Editor—Canadian history, sociology, urban studies and planning

David Cullen, Acquisitions Editor—Canadian history, regional, native studies, sexuality studies, northern and arctic studies, health studies, education

UNIVERSITY OF MANITOBA PRESS

301 St. John's College, University of Manitoba, Winnipeg, MB R3T 2M5
Canada

204-474-9495   fax: 204-474-7566

www.umanitoba.ca/uofmpress

Founded in 1967, the University of Manitoba Press publishes innovative and exceptional books of scholarship and serious Canadian nonfiction. Their list includes books on Native studies, Canadian history, women's studies, Icelandic studies, aboriginal languages, film studies, biography, geography, nature, and Canadian literature and culture. They publish five to eight books a year, meaning each book receives the concentrated focus and attention that is often not possible in a larger press.

Recent titles include *The Clay We are Made Of: Haudenosaunee Land Tenure on the Grand River* by Susan M. Hill; *Families, Lovers, and Their Letters: Italian Postwar Migration to Canada* by Sonia Cancian; *Sounds of Ethnicity: Listening to German North America, 1850–1914* by Barbara Lorenzkowski; and *All Our Changes: Images from the Sixties Generation* by Gerry Kopelow.

Queries and SASEs may be submitted to:

David Carr, Director and Editor; carr@cc.umanitoba.ca

Jean Wilson, Senior Acquisitions Editor; jeanwilson@shaw.ca

Glenn Bergen, Managing Editor

UNIVERSITY OF OTTAWA PRESS/LES PRESSES DE L'UNIVERSITÉ D'OTTAWA

542 King Edward, Ottawa, ON K1N 6N5, Canada

613-562-5246   fax: 613-562-5247

www.press.uottawa.ca   email: puo-uop@uottawa.ca

As Canada's only officially bilingual press, the University of Ottawa Press (UOP) is both uniquely Canadian and unique in Canada. Since 1936, UOP has supported cultural development through the publication of books in both French and English aimed at a general public interested in serious nonfiction.

UOP's editorial team works closely with its authors. Writers are supported in the preparation of their manuscript through peer reviews that help tighten the focus of the work before its final submission. By the time a manuscript is submitted to the Editorial Board to decide if it will be published, it has received a good deal of editorial development and revision.

Recent titles include *My Life: The Memoirs of Sofia Andreevna Tolstaya* edited by Andrew Donskov; *RE: Reading the Postmodern: Canadian Literature and Criticism After Modernism* edited by Robert David Stacey; and *DanceHall: From Slave Ship to Ghetto* by Sonjah Stanley Niaah.

Please direct query and SASE to:

Michael O'Hearn, Director; michael.ohearn@uottawa.ca

Marie Clausén, Managing Editor; msec@uottawa.ca

Eric Nelson, Acquisitions Editor; enelson@uottawa.ca

Mariam Faye, Editor; mariam.faye@uottawa.ca

UNIVERSITY OF TORONTO PRESS

10 Saint Mary Street, Suite 700, Toronto, ON M4Y 2W8, Canada
416-978-2239   fax: 416-978-4738
www.utpress.utoronto.ca

University of Toronto Press is Canada's oldest and largest scholarly publisher, and is among the top 15 university presses in North America in size. It is always on the lookout for strong, innovative, and interesting works of scholarship.

Established in 1901, University of Toronto Press publishes scholarly, reference, and general interest books on Canadian history and literature, medieval studies, and social sciences among other subjects, as well as scholarly journals. Approximately 150 new titles are released each year, and a backlist of more than 1,000 titles is maintained in print.

The house publishes in a range of fields, including history and politics; women's studies; health, family, and society; law and crime; economics; workplace communication; theory/culture; language, literature, semiotics, and drama; medieval studies; Renaissance studies; Erasmus; Italian-language studies; East European studies; classics; and nature. The list includes topical titles in Canadian studies, Native studies, sociology, anthropology, urban studies, modern languages, and music. A complete list of subjects as well as details on creating and submitting a manuscript are available on the University of Toronto Press website.

Recent titles include *Parliamentary Democracy in Crisis* edited by Peter H. Russell and Lorne Sossin; *Civility: A Cultural History* by Benet Devetian; *Newfoundland and Labrador: A History* by Sean T. Cadigan; and *1 Way 2 C the World* by Marilyn Waring.

Query letters and SASEs should be directed to:

Virgil Duff, Executive Editor—Social sciences, scholarly medical books, law and criminology, women's studies

Len Husband, Editor—Canadian history, natural science, philosophy

Stephen Kotowych, Editor—Social sciences

Richard Ratzoff, Editor—Book history, English literature, modern languages, Victorian studies

Siobhan McMenemy, Editor—Cultural studies, digital futures, film studies

Suzanne Rancourt, Editor—Humanities, rights and translations, classics, medieval and renaissance studies, music, religion and theology

Ron Schoeffel, Editor—Erasmus studies, Italian studies, literary criticism, religion and theology

VÉHICULE PRESS

SIGNAL EDITIONS

ESPLANADE BOOKS

P.O.B. 125, Place du Parc Station, Montreal, QC H2X 4A3, Canada

514-844-6073   fax: 514-844-7543

www.vehiculepress.com   email: vp@vehiculepress.com

For more than 30 years, Véhicule Press has been publishing prize-winning poetry, fiction, social history, Quebec studies, Jewish studies, jazz history, and restaurant guides.

Signal Editions is the poetry imprint of Véhicule Press. Since 1981, 65 poetry titles have been published, one-third of those by first-time authors. Esplanade Books is the fiction imprint of Véhicule Press. Esplanade publishes novels, novellas, and short story collections—books that fall between the cracks, works of unusual structure and form, and short sharp monologues.

Recent Véhicule Press titles include *Circus* by Michael Harris; *Paul Bley: The Logic of Chance* by Arrigo Cappelletti; *The Third Seder: A Haggadah for Yom Hashoah* by Irene Lilienheim Angelico and Yehudi Lindeman; *The Crime on Cotes de Neiges* by David Montrose; and *A Place in Mind: The Search for Authenticity* by Avi Friedman.

For poetry and nonfiction submissions, please query first. For fiction submissions, please include a 25- to 30-page excerpt. Véhicule mostly publishes Canadian authors.

Simon Dardick, Publisher

Nancy Marrelli, Publisher

Andrew Steinmetz, Editor—Esplanade Books

Carmine Starnino, Editor—Signal Editions

WHITECAP BOOKS

WALRUS BOOKS

351 Lynn Avenue, North Vancouver, BC V7J 2C4, Canada

604-980-9852   fax: 604-980-8197

www.whitecap.ca

Whitecap Books is one of Canada's largest independent publishers. In addition to the cookbooks, gift books, and coffee table books that it is primarily known for, Whitecap publishes gardening and crafts, photo-scenic, history, arts and entertainment, children's fiction and nonfiction, travel, sports, and transportation books. Walrus Books is their imprint for children's books, publishing series fiction for teenagers and science nonfiction.

With a head office in Vancouver, British Columbia, and warehouse operations in Markham, Ontario, the house generates sales across Canada, from coast to coast to coast. In addition to traditional bookstores, Whitecap books can be found in many retail outlets, ranging from museums and clothing stores to gardening centers and cookware suppliers, thus special sales manuscripts might be successfully placed here.

Recent titles include *The Best Chef at Home* by Michael Smith; *Children of the Klondike* by Frances Backhouse; and *Day Trips from Calgary: Revised and Updated* by Bill Corbett.

Whitecap is delighted to receive submissions of queries with proposals and sample chapters. Be sure to include SASEs (and international reply coupons) and direct to Rights and Acquisitions.

Robert McCullough, Publisher

Taryn Boyd, Managing Editor

Grace Yaginuma, Editor

SECTION FIVE

LITERARY AGENTS

WHAT MAKES THIS AGENT DIRECTORY SPECIAL?

JEFF HERMAN

There are many books and websites that include lists of literary agents, but this directory is truly extraordinary because we go way beyond providing names, addresses and basic statistics. We have offered the agents included here the chance to "talk" about themselves, both professionally and personally, and to share their insights about all aspects of the publishing business. You will not only know who represents what and how to solicit them, but you will also get a sense about many of them as human beings and as potential business partners.

I am frequently asked why certain agents are not listed. I wish to be clear that literally dozens of excellent agents are not listed here, though I would like them to be. Each year I invite the 200-plus members of the Association of Author Representatives (AAR), as well as many excellent nonmember agents, to be in this book. However, just because an agent is not here does not mean that that agent is not qualified to be. The truth is that many agents are already saturated with as many clients as they can handle, or want to handle. They are not eager to invite unsolicited submissions from the general public, because their existing rosters and a few trusted referrals are more than they want to handle. Most agencies are small "mom and pop" businesses that are not inclined to take on a lot of staff and overhead. Their business model is to maximize revenues by limiting expenses and administrative tasks. Yet many qualified agents happily accept my invitation to be listed because they want to hear from as many fresh prospects as possible. If an agent does not explicitly confirm that he or she wants to be in this book, then that agent is not included here.

Each year many "false agents" endeavor to be included, and we do our best to keep them out. A false agent is anyone who masquerades as an agent for the sole purpose of stealing money from writers through various acts of clever deception. Letting such people into this book would be tantamount to inviting Col. Sanders into a hen house. With regret, I must concede instances in the past where I have been deceived by some of these deceivers. The consequences for these errors were predictable: I would receive numerous complaints from writers who came close to getting snagged by these hoodlums. Fortunately, most of the writers smelled the odor before it was too late; but sometimes I would hear from writers who didn't know what hit them until they were already pinched for a few bucks.

The bottom line is that my staff and I exercise due diligence about who gets listed. Nevertheless, some charlatans may manage to slip through our filters. Like hybrid software viruses, some of these serial grifters have the chutzpah to simply change their names and addresses as soon as word gets out about their scams. I am largely dependent upon you, the writers, to immediately let me know about any wrongful experiences you might have with any of the agencies in this book. That is how I can keep them out of future editions and help sound the alarm elsewhere, as can you. Please see the essay section for more information about this issue. Of course, do not shoot venom only because someone has rejected or disrespected you.

I am not trying to spread fear and paranoia. These unfortunate situations are very much the exception, not the rule. Any agent who has a bona fide list of sales to recognized publishers is legitimate.

AEI/ATCHITY ENTERTAINMENT INTERNATIONAL, INC (BOOK/FILM)

518 S. Fairfax Ave., Los Angeles CA 90036

Agent's name: Dr. Kenneth Atchity

Born: Eunice, Louisiana.

Education: BA, Georgetown; M.Phil., theater history—PhD, comparative literature, Yale.

Career history: Professor of comparative literature (classics, medieval, Renaissance creative writing), Occidental College (1970–1987); Instructor, UCLA Writer's Program (1970–1987). Author of 14 books, including *How to Escape Lifetime Security to Pursue Your Impossible Dream: A Guide to Transforming Your Career* (Helios); *How to Publish Your Novel* (SquareOne Books); *A Writer's Time: A Guide to the Creative Process, from Vision Through Revision* (Norton); and *Writing Treatments That Sell* (with Chi-Li Wong; Owl Books). Producer of 22 films, including *The Madam's Family: The Truth about Canal Street Brothel* (Ellen Burstyn, Annabella Sciorra, Dominique Swain) for CBS; *Life or Something Like It* (Angelina Jolie, Ed Burns) for 20th Century Fox, *Joe Somebody* (Tim Allen, Jim Belushi, Julie Bowen) for 20th Century Fox, *Champagne for Two* (Cinemax-HBO), *Amityville: The Evil Escapes* (NBC) *Shadow of Obsession* (NBC), and *Falling Over Backwards*. Sold *Ripley's Believe-It-Or-Not!* franchise to Paramount Pictures, AEI to produce with Alphaville (*The Mummy*) and Richard Zanuck (*Jaws*), script by Scott Alexander and Larry Karazewski (*The People vs. Larry Flynt*), Tim Burton directing, Jim Carrey starring; Steve Alten's *Meg* to New Line, script by Shane Salerno (*Shaft, Armageddon*), directing Jan de Bont, AEI producing with Larry Gordon Productions (*Lara Croft*), Guillermo del Toro (*Hellboy*) and Nick Nunziata; John Scott Shepherd's *Henry's List of Wrongs* to New Line, script by Harley Peyton (*Less Than Zero, Moon Over Miami*), Marc Waters to direct, AEI producing with Zide-Perry Films (*American Pie, Final Destination*); Royce Buckingham's *Demon Keeper* to Fox 2000, etc.

Hobbies/personal interests: Collecting autographed editions, pitchers; tennis; travel.

Categories/subjects that you are most enthusiastic about agenting: We are focused on storytellers with bestselling potential in both New York publishing and Hollywood films. Basically don't send us material that doesn't have potential both as a book and as a television or film project. We love comedy; male action; young adult—with strong narrative line, and not Harry Potter look alike; celebrity or "branded" books, biography or otherwise; comic books, and films that can be franchises; personal achievement by nationally known names; nonfiction with national impact and national platform; business nonfiction by distinguished business leaders with built-in corporate tie-in potential; female novel authors with fresh

LITERARY AGENTS

contemporary voice and/or film potential; visionary, heroic, and true stories of every kind, including true crime; general interest and/or narrative nonfiction, especially true stories with TV or film potential; celebrity biographies. Aside from that, we're dying to discover (a) the next Michael Chabon and/or (b) the next mainstream Hispanic American, Asian American, or African American novelist. The key is combining a major platform with a major message for the general public. Screenplays: All motion picture, as well as specific television movie, categories. Especially comedy (both broad comedy and romantic comedy); action franchise; adaptations of classics to modern times; new-angle horror; heroic true stories (past or present); families in crisis; serious drama for top stars; female-driven heroic stories.

What you don't want to agent: Drug-related, religious, category romance, small niche subjects, category mystery or Western, poetry, "interior" confessional fiction; novelty books.

If you were not an agent, what might you be doing instead: If I weren't a literary manager, writer, and producer, I'd be doing the same thing and calling it something else. A story merchant: finding, perfecting, selling and producing stories by serious storytellers determined to become globally known for their art and craft.

What's the best way for writers to solicit your interest: Query letter, including synopsis (with SASE). Please note: All submissions to Jennifer Pope.

Do you charge reading or management fees: NO.

Can you provide an approximation by percent of what you tend to represent by category: Fiction 30 percent, nonfiction 40 percent, screenplays 30 percent.

How would you describe the client from hell: He or she is so self-impressed it's impossible to provide constructive criticism; makes his package impossible to open, provides return envelope too small to be used, and tells us how to run our business.

How would you describe the perfect client: He or she comes in with an outstanding action or high-concept fiction or nonfiction book, plus an outline for two more, is delighted to take commercial direction on the writing and the career, markets his or her book relentlessly. The higher the concept the better.

How and why did you ever become an agent: Nearly two decades of teaching comparative literature and creative writing at Occidental College and the UCLA Writers Program, reviewing for the *Los Angeles Times Book Review*, and working with the dreams of creative people through DreamWorks (which I co-founded with Marsha Kinder) provided a natural foundation for this career. I made the transition from academic life through producing, but continued my publishing-consulting business by connecting my authors with agents. As I spent more and more time developing individuals' writing careers, as well as working directly with publishers in my search for film properties, it became obvious that literary management was the next step. True or fiction, what has always turned me on is a good story.

What do you think the future holds for writers, publishers, and agents: Nothing but continued growth and excitement as the distribution channels continue to evolve rapidly: all that remains the same is the insatiable need for stories and information.

MIRIAM ALTSHULER LITERARY AGENCY

53 Old Post Road North, Red Hook, NY 12571

845-758-9408   fax: 845-758-3118

www.miriamaltshulerliteraryagency.com   email: miriam@maliterary.com

Agent's name: Miriam Altshuler

Born: New York, New York.

Education: Middlebury College.

Career history: Agent for 12 years at Russell and Volkening, Inc. Started my own agency in 1994.

Hobbies/personal interests: Reading, skiing, horseback riding, the outdoors, my children.

Categories/subjects that you are most enthusiastic about agenting: Literary/commercial fiction and nonfiction, narrative nonfiction, memoirs, young-adult novels. See my website: www.miriamaltshulerliteraryagency.com for further guidelines.

What you don't want to agent: Genre fiction, how-to, romance. See my website: www.miriamaltshulerliteraryagency.com, for further guidelines.

Do you charge reading or management fees: No reading fees.

How and why did you ever become an agent: I love reading books and love working with people.

ARCADIA

31 Lake Place North, Danbury, CT 06810

203-797-0993

Website under construction

Agent's name: Victoria Gould Pryor, arcadialit@sbcglobal.net

Born: New York City

Education: BA Pembroke College/Brown University (modern literature/history); MA NYU (modern literature).

Career Story: My first job after college was at the John Cushman Agency. Moved to the Sterling Lord Agency and became hooked on agenting. At the Harold Matson Agency I began representing authors and then helped found Literistic, Ltd. Arcadia was begun in 1986.

Hobbies and special personal interests: Science, medicine, classical music and choral singing, gardening, current/foreign affairs, reading, art, woodworking.

Subjects and categories you like to agent: Nonfiction: science/medicine, current affairs/popular culture, history, psychology, true crime, true business, investigative journalism, women's issues, biography, classical music, memoir, literary fiction.

Subjects and categories writers shouldn't bother pitching to you: Children's/YA, science fiction/fantasy, horror, humor, chick lit, technothrillers, picture books, memoirs about overcoming addiction or abuse.

What might you be doing if you weren't agenting: I'd be an unhappy and reasonably solvent doctor or lawyer, a content and struggling woodworker or landscape architect, or if I had a much better voice, an ecstatic and prosperous Wagnerian opera singer.

What's the most effective ways for writers to grab your attention: For fiction: a concise query letter with brief sample material (the novel's opening paragraphs, pages or chapters) and an SASE. In a query letter, I'm more drawn to a novel's description and themes, as opposed to a detailed plot synopsis.

For nonfiction: a detailed query letter and SASE. It's fine to send a proposal with the letter, but please take the time to analyze what comparable books are already on the market and how your proposed book fills a niche.

Email queries without attachments are fine. If your subject and query letter are enticing, I'll ask you to send the file—either proposal or manuscript—as an attachment.

Do you charge fees separate from your commission, or offer non-agenting fee-based services: No fees or fee-based services.

Representative titles: Anjana Appachana: *Listening Now* (Random House); Philip Dine: *State of the Unions: How Labor Can Revitalize Itself, Seize the National Debate on Values and Help Win Elections* (McGraw-Hill); Rob Dunn, PhD: *Every Living Thing: Man's Obsessive Quest To Catalog Life, From Nanobacteria to New Monkeys* (Smithsonian Books); *Haunted by Nature: How Clean Living Has Left Us Sick, Xenophobic and Discontented* (Smithsonian Books); Kristin Luker, PhD: *When Sex Goes to School: Warring Views on Sex Since the Sixties* (Norton), *Salsa Dancing into the Social Sciences* (Harvard University Press); Avner Mandelman: *Talking to the Enemy* (Seven Stories Press), *Sleuth Investor* (McGraw-Hill), *The Debba* (Other Press); Diane Powell, MD: *The ESP Enigma: The Scientific Case for Psychic Phenomena* (Walker); Dr. Bernie Siegel: *Love, Medicine and Miracles, Peace, Love and Healing, How to Live Between Office Visits*, and *Prescriptions for Living* (HarperCollins), *Help Me to Heal* (Hay House); Jane Anne Staw: *Unstuck: A Supportive and Practical Guide to Working Through Writer's Block* (St. Martin's); Frank T. Vertosick, Jr., MD: *When the Air Hits Your Brain: Tales of Neurosurgery* (Norton); *Why We Hurt: The Natural History of Pain* and *The Genius Within: Discovering the Intelligence of Every Living Thing* (Harcourt); Jonathan Weiner: *Planet Earth* and *The Next One Hundred Years* (Bantam), *The Beak of the Finch* and *Time, Love, Memory* (Knopf).

Why did you become an agent, and how did you become one: The luck of the draw; I stumbled into the perfect (for me) field, combining a love of reading, people and business with a smattering of law and social work thrown in on the side.

How do you feel about writers: They're the most fascinating, delightful, talented, hard-working people I know, and life would be very dull without them. Most editors are talented, dedicated, professional, valiant and extremely overworked. They're often caught in a squeeze between trying to do right by an author and obligations to their employer's bottom line.

What do you tell entities from other planets and dimensions about your job: An agent is a combination industrial-strength reader, talent scout, business manager/career planner/matchmaker, developmental editor, midwife to creativity and supporter of professional dreams.

What are your favorite books, movies, TV shows, and why: Not including my own clients' work, I admire nonfiction that helps us understand and/or changes the way we look at the world past and present (*History of the Jews, Embracing Defeat, And the Band Played On, What's the Matter with Kansas, Temperament*), illuminates areas of science (*Our Kind, How We Die, Love's Executioner, The Man Who Mistook His Wife for a Hat, Anatomy of Love*), introduces us to people who lived fascinating lives (*Nora*), quirky and compelling narratives (*Year of Reading Proust, A Heartbreaking Work of Staggering Genius*).

Novels by Melville, Faulkner, Greene, Roth, Le Carré, and Turow. *The Tin Drum, Love in the Time of Cholera, Ragtime, Life of Pi, Atonement*, etc., and I'm a sucker for literate, character-driven thrillers.

TV: Not a lot of time to watch, but I'm a fan of *In Treatment* and any series moderated by Simon Schama.

Movies: Another year…

How would you describe the writer from hell: The writer from hell is not respectful of an agent's or editor's time. He/she is unable to hear or apply whatever information or advice is offered, and assumes that business ground rules be set aside for his/her work. Fortunately I don't represent anyone who resembles this.

How would you describe the publisher and/or editor from hell: Nonresponsive (or very slow to respond); less than flexible and supportive.

What do you like best about your clients, and the editors and publishers you work with: At its best, my job is about being part of a team of talented, dedicated professionals. It's thrilling to see a book grow from the germ of an idea to a manuscript and then to see the magic that can result when the publisher's expertise and support are added. And it's even more thrilling to help guide an author's career.

Will our business exist as we know it in ten years or so: The book business will keep chugging along. The trappings will be different but the core will still be the development and spreading of ideas. Creativity and the imagination will not have changed, and will still need nurturing.

ARTISTS AND ARTISANS, INC.

244 Madison Avenue, Suite 334, New York, NY 10016

212-924-9619 fax: 212-931-8377

www.artistsandartisans.com

Agents' names: Adam Chromy; Michelle Wolfson; Jamie Brenner, Jamie@ artistsandartisans.com.

The following information pertains to Jamie Brenner.

Born: Philadelphia, Pennsylvania, 1974.

Education: The George Washington University, BA English.

Career story: Started in publishing as a publicity assistant at HarperCollins. I worked on books by super-talented writers like Barbara Kingsolver, Louise Erdrich, and Erica Jong. Then a former colleague lured me over to Barnes & Noble—the company was just launching their online store to compete with Amazon. I worked there as an editor/buyer for a few years. During this time, a film industry connection got me a freelance job reading manuscripts for Miramax films, and I eventually became a book scout for a film production company. In 2007 I started at Artists and Artisans as a literary agent.

Hobbies and special personal interests: I'm very into pop culture, music, film. I'm fascinated by ballet. I'm interested in politics though I try not to be because there's so much disappointment.

Subjects and categories you like to agent: Women's fiction, especially novels straddling the line between commercial and literary fiction. I like horror novels that have a strong psychological element. I am always looking for memoir. I like political thrillers and literary mysteries.

Subjects and categories writers shouldn't bother pitching to you: Children's books, fantasy, science fiction, sports, spirituality.

What might you be doing if you weren't agenting: I don't know—but it would be something with books.

What's the most effective ways for writers to grab your attention: A simple email query that gives me a clear pitch for the book and an idea who the writer is.

Do you charge fees separate from your commission, or offer non-agenting fee-based services: I never charge separate fees, nor do I offer fee-based services.

What are representative titles you have sold to publishers: *Insatiable, A Memoir* by Erica Rivera (Berkeley); *Liver Let Die* by Annelise Ryan (Kensington).

Why did you become an agent, and how did you become one: When I was scouting books for a film company, I routinely met with agents to hear about the books they had coming down the pike. One of these was my current colleague,

Adam Chromy. It was his idea that I try agenting. Needless to say, he was very persuasive. And it was one of the best decisions I ever made.

How do you feel about writers: Writers are the people who helped shaped me. It is their words, stories, pain, insight, that have influenced the way I see the world and even brought the world to me when I was just a suburban girl. To me, they are the most important artists.

What do you tell entities from other planets and dimensions about your job: I never talk to entities from other planets about my job. Like Europeans, they think we discuss work too much.

What are your favorite books, movies, TV shows, and why: Favorite books— I could go on forever. I've read almost every Nelson DeMille book. I loved Cathi Hanauer's *Sweet Ruin*. I'm a big fan of Dani Shapiro's *Black and White* and *Slow Motion*. For family sagas, I love Susan Howatch's *The Wheel of Fortune*. Favorite in horror is Bentley Little's *The Mailman*. I have to stop now! Favorite films: *25th Hour, Pulp Fiction, Roger Dodger, A Walk on the Moon, About Last Night, High Art.*

How would you describe the writer from hell: One who doesn't take the time to understand that this is a business.

How would you describe the publisher and/or editor from hell: One who could just as easily be buying/selling widgets.

What do you like best about your clients, and the editors and publishers you work with: At the end of the day, we share a passion.

The following information pertains to Adam Chomry.

Education: New York University Stern School of Business, BS, 1992.

Career history: After a brief stint at a renowned literary agency, Adam Chomry went out on his own to represent a novel written by a close friend. The gamble paid off and the book was sold on a preemptive offer. Since that auspicious start in 2002, Adam's fresh, rule-breaking approach has led to dozens of book deals at major publishing houses, a national and *New York Times* bestseller, and a number of film deals for his clients' projects.

Categories/subjects that you are most enthusiastic about agenting: I am still signing authors of fiction and narrative nonfiction as long as the writing is exceptional and the authors have something truly unique to say. He is also interested in practical nonfiction from authors with strong platforms and/or a point of view that challenges the status quo.

What you don't want to agent: Screenplays, photo or children's books.

What's the best way for writers to solicit your interest: Read and follow the submission guidelines on my website—www.artistsandartisans.com.

What are the most common mistakes writers make when pitching you: Pitching halfbaked ideas or projects is a turn-off.

Do you charge reading or management fees: No.

Can you provide an approximation by percent of what you tend to represent

by category: I spend half my time on fiction and [half on] nonfiction but because fiction is a tougher sell we end up with a list comprised of slightly more nonfiction.

How would you describe the client from hell: I do not have any (at least not for long).

How would you describe the perfect client: They understand that being a professional author is 50 percent writing and 50 percent marketing and they energetically and enthusiastically pursue both.

What, if anything, can a writer do to increase the odds that you will become his or her agent: The author should do everything possible to make sure their book is of the highest quality AND make sure they understand their book's market and how to reach it. If they make this clear in a query, then it is hard to pass up.

How would you describe to someone (or something) from another planet what it is that you do as an agent: I wouldn't waste time telling someone from another planet what I do, I would be trying to sign them for their memoir.

What do you think the future holds for writers, publishers, and agents: I like to remind my authors about the railroad companies of the last century and how they went out of business because they thought of themselves as "railroad companies" and not "transportation companies." So we don't just focus on author's books, we focus on the value of their stories and messages as intellectual property and plan ahead for delivering that IP through books, websites, TV, film or anything else that comes along.

On a personal level, what do you think people like about you and dislike about you: I think I get both reactions because I am a straight shooter.

Please list representative titles you have sold: *The Hookup Handbook,* (Simon Spotlight; film setup at Weinstein Bros.); *Pomegranate Soup* (Random House, international bestseller); *Jewtopia* (Warner, based on the hit off-Broadway play); *World Made by Hand* and the sequel to the bestseller *The Long Emergency,* (Grove/Atlantic); additional titles on my website.

This information pertains to Michelle Wolfson.

Education: Dartmouth College, BA 1995; NYU Stern School of Business MBA 2001.

Career history: After working outside of publishing for several years, first in nonprofit and then finance, I made a switch to agenting. I worked for two years at Ralph M. Vicinanza, Ltd. and then joined Artists and Artisans Inc. in March 2006.

Categories/subjects that you are most enthusiastic about agenting: Mainstream and women's fiction, mysteries and thrillers; practical and narrative nonfiction, particularly of interest to women; humorous nonfiction.

What you don't want to agent: Screenplays, children's, science fiction, or horror.

What's the best way for writers to solicit your interest: email query.

Do you charge reading or management fees: No.

What are the most common mistakes writers make when pitching you: Apologizing for their ideas/presentation. If you don't love it, why would I?

How would you describe the perfect client: They understand that I want the same things for them that they want for themselves and we work together as a team to achieve success.

How and why did you ever become an agent: It's never the same on any two days but it's all directed towards books and reading, which I love.

What, if anything, can a writer do to increase the odds of your becoming his or her agent: Make your project as good as you possibly can without me, then work hard on your query letter so that it grabs my attention.

On a personal level, what do you think people like about you and dislike about you: I'm straightforward and honest, yet tactful.

Please list representative titles you have sold: *Embracing Your Big Fat Ass* by Laura Banks and Janette Barber, the bestselling authors of *Breaking the Rules,* (Atria); *Who's Your Birth Order Love Match* (Marlowe And Company); *A Guide to Compatibility in Relationships from a Birth Order Perspective* by William Cane (the bestselling author of *The Art of Kissing*); *Love Lessons from Arranged Marriages: Seven Surprising Secrets that Will Improve Your Relationship* by Reva Seth (Touchstone Fireside).

THE AUGUST AGENCY, LLC

www.augustagency.com

Agents' names: Cricket Freeman, Jeffery McGraw

Career story: Cricket Freeman, co-founder and agent: After years as a business owner engaged in sales and marketing, Cricket redirected her creativity toward the writing business, freelancing for magazines (more adventure than money) and business clients (more money than adventure). For a time she even slaved daily as the editor-in-chief of a national full-color glossy. In 1991, Cricket intertwined her art education, business experience, and writing skills to establish Possibilities Press to support small book publishers with writing, editing, design, and production services. Ever the entrepreneur, a decade later she shifted her focus exclusively to literary representation and founded The Christina Pechstein Agency. In 2004 she saw another fine opportunity to expand her business and her horizons and joined forces with Jeffery McGraw to launch The August Agency, where she operates from its headquarters in Florida.

Jeffery McGraw, co-founder and agent: Jeffery directs the New York operations of The August Agency LLC. He brings to the company a wide range of experience in publishing and television, with a concentrated background in editorial, legal, publicity, and content sales. He has worked for magazine and book publishers large and small, including *Soap Opera Weekly* as contributing reporter, HarperCollins as editor, Harry N. Abrams as publicity manager, and Leisure Publishing as magazine columnist. Throughout his career he has had the privilege to work with many different types of books—from exquisite art and illustrated coffee table tomes to *New York Times* bestselling fiction and nonfiction—and an equally diverse roster of remarkable authors and artists—among them Nancy Bartholomew,

Elizabeth Berg, Cathy East Dubowski, Patricia Gaffney, Olivia Goldsmith, Andy Goldsworthy, Al Hirschfeld, Mary-Kate and Ashley Olsen, Bill O'Reilly, Joanne Pence, Betty Rollin, Ben Schonzeit, and Hunt Slonem.

Our company mind-set: Of any national literature, "the Augustan age" is considered the period of its highest state of excellence and refinement. The expression originated with the reign of the emperor Augustus, who fostered the golden age of Roman literature. Since then, the name has been ascribed to subsequent eras of great prosperity in artistic writing. The August Agency is founded on many of the same principles Augustus set in place to facilitate a stimulating venue where distinguished writers could flourish. More than just another literary and media management company in the business of selling creative projects, we approach the industry with a fresh point of view and innovative strategies that set us apart from other agencies. We firmly believe an agent is, among other things, an author's ultimate advocate, anchor, arbitrator, and advisor. At the August Agency, we not only embrace our authors' works but also the writers themselves and their careers.

What writers can expect from the August Agency: With our rich background of experience, we have developed a unique approach to the publishing industry that seems to work well for us and for our authors. Our fundamental belief is that we are all in this together. Neither of us is the employer, nor the employee, and we don't treat each other that way. Instead, we prefer to think of both parties as business partners in a mutually thrilling venture. The August Agency is a nurturing place where we all learn from each other, sell a lot of books, and have fun along the way. Our primary commitment as agents is taking care of our authors, helping to get their proposals in the best shape possible, and effectively marketing their work to publishing houses and beyond. We encourage our authors to follow our lead: Be a team player, meet deadlines, honor contracts, and, no matter how anxious they are about their work, try to have reasonable expectations. While we cannot promise publication for every writer's project, we can guarantee that their work will be put in front of the right people at the right time with the right degree of passion and enthusiasm behind it.

Subjects and categories you like to agent: The August Agency accepts electronic queries exclusively. We actively pursue a diverse array of writers to represent, with an emphasis in the following areas: Media/current events (seasoned journalists receive special favor here), popular culture, arts, and entertainment, political science, self-help, health, and spirituality, lifestyle, family, and home (including cookbooks, diet, and fitness), science, social sciences, criminology and investigation, history, economics, business and technology, biographies and memoirs, creative narrative nonfiction. In particular, we favor persuasive and prescriptive works, each with a full-bodied narrative command and an undeniable contemporary relevance.

Subjects and categories writers shouldn't bother pitching to you: At this time, we are not accepting submissions in the following areas: Self-published works, screenplays, children's books, cozy mysteries, genre romance, horror, poetry, science fiction, fantasy, short story collections, Westerns, projects by blowhards, bigots, braggarts, bitches, and bastards!

What's the most effective ways for writers to grab your attention: To submit, please visit www.augustagency.com for complete details of and any updates to our submission guidelines, which currently include sending an email to submissions@augustagency.com containing the following: 1) The word "query" in the subject line, 2) A detailed summary of your book (one to two paragraphs only), 3) A chapter outline (for nonfiction only), 4) A brief paragraph explaining who you are and why you have chosen to write this particular book, 5) MOST IMPORTANT: The first 1,000 words or first chapter (note: this must be pasted within the body of your email; all emails with unsolicited attachments or lack of this writing sample within the body of the email may be deleted without being read), 6) The total page or word count of your completed manuscript, 7) Your full contact information (including telephone and email address).

If you want to be an ordinary writer, write an ordinary book. But if you want to be an extraordinary author, be prepared to go the extra mile. Our staff is made up of highly selective, seasoned publishing professionals who will give serious consideration to original, creative, and quality manuscripts from extraordinary authors.

Due to the volume of submissions we receive, we are unable to respond to all incoming email. However, please note that every query is read and thoroughly reviewed by our staff. If we are interested in your project, you should receive a response to your email within two to three weeks. At that time you will receive further instructions on how to submit a full-length copy of your proposal. We appreciate the opportunity to review your work and look forward to hearing from you.

Do you charge fees separate from your commission, or offer non-agenting fee-based services: We do not charge a reading fee. The August Agency retains a commission of fifteen percent (15 percent) of all domestic sales and twenty percent (20 percent) of all foreign, film, dramatic, merchandising, and other sales.

BARER LITERARY, LLC

270 Lafayette Street, Suite 1504, New York, NY 10023
212-6913513   fax: 212-691-3540

Agent's name: Julie Barer
Born: New York, New York.
Education: Vassar College.
Career story: After working for six years at the prestigious New York literary agency Sanford J. Greenburger Associates, I left to start my own agency, Barer Literary, in December 2004. I represent a wide range of fiction writers who publish across the literary spectrum, and I am especially attracted to voice-driven projects that feel original and fresh. My list is extremely selective and I

am interested in developing long-term relationships with my clients. I attended the Jerusalem Book Fair as an Agent Fellow in 2003 and I am a member of the Association of Authors' Representatives. Before becoming an agent, I worked at Shakespeare & Co. Booksellers in New York City.

Subjects and categories you like to agent: Literary fiction, historical fiction, women's fiction, international fiction and nonfiction, narrative nonfiction, history, biography, memoir, travel.

Subjects and categories writers shouldn't bother pitching to you: Barer Literary does NOT handle the following: Health and fitness; business, investing, or finance; sports; mind, body, and spirit; reference; thrillers or suspense; military; romance; children's books, picture books, or young-adult books; screenplays.

What might you be doing if you weren't agenting: As old-fashioned as it sounds, if I wasn't an agent, I'd love to own a bookstore.

What's the most effective ways for writers to grab your attention: Do your research and make sure that our agency represents the kind of book you've written. Then send a well-written and professional query letter with a self-addressed stamped envelope.

Do you charge fees separate from your commission, or offer non-agenting fee-based services: No.

What are representative titles you have sold to publishers: *Then We Came to the End* by Joshua Ferris (Little, Brown & Co.); *Still Life with Husband* by Lauren Fox (Alfred A. Knopf); *What You Have Left* by Will Allison (Free Press); *Finding Nouf* by Zoe Ferraris (Houghton Mifflin); *People I Wanted to Be: Stories* by Gina Ochsner (Houghton Mifflin).

Why did you become an agent, and how did you become one: I became an agent first and foremost because I love to read, and I love the moment of discovering a wonderful novel or story that no one else has read yet, and being the person who helps bring that book out into the world. I also love being able to work closely with writers, and help shape their work, as well as their careers. Being an agent allows me to be involved with so many aspects of a book's life—from editing and placing a book with the right publisher to helping conceptualize cover art and promotion and beyond.

MEREDITH BERNSTEIN LITERARY AGENCY

2095 Broadway, Suite 505, New York, NY 10023
212-799-1007   fax: 212-799-1145

Agent's name: Meredith Bernstein

Born: Hartford, Connecticut.

Education: BA, University of Rochester.

Career history: Story editor to film producers; literary agent.

Hobbies/personal interests: Reading, of course; travel; film; art; theater; ballet; fashion; contemporary art/craft; jewelry; meeting new people.

Categories/subjects that you are most enthusiastic about agenting: Young adult. Almost anything wherein I can learn something new.

What you don't want to agent: Military history.

If you were not an agent, what might you be doing instead: Curating a craft museum; owning a store like Julie on Madison Avenue.

DANIEL BIAL AGENCY

41 W. 83rd St., Suite 5C, New York, NY 10024

212-721-1786

email: dbialagency@msn.com

Agent's name: Daniel Bial

Education: BA, Trinity College, English.

Career history: Editor for 15 years, including 10 years at HarperCollins. Founded agency in 1992.

Hobbies/personal interests: Travel, cooking, music, parenting.

Categories/subjects that you are most enthusiastic about agenting: Nonfiction: Biography, business, cooking, current events, history, how-to, humor, Judaica, language, narrative nonfiction, popular culture, popular reference, popular science, psychology, sports, travel. Fiction: Quality fiction.

What you don't want to agent: Nonfiction: Academic treatises, crafts, gift books. Fiction: Children's books, genre fiction, poetry, novels by first-time authors with no publishing credits.

If you were not an agent, what might you be doing instead: Writer, book doctor, or maybe a freelance celebrity advisor.

What's the best way for writers to solicit your interest: Email (about one page long with no attachments) or query letter with SASE.

What are the most common mistakes writers make when pitching you: A surprising number of writers devote time in their query letter to telling me about their shortcomings or previous failures. They essentially reject themselves.

Do you charge reading or management fees: No.

Can you provide an approximation by percent of what you tend to represent by category: Nonfiction: 95 percent, fiction: 5 percent.

How would you describe the perfect client: Perfect clients produce trim, tight, ready-to-sell material. They know the business and how to get ahead. They recognize the importance of marketing and know that good intentions don't sell books, hard work does. They take pride in their work and their relationships.

How and why did you ever become an agent: I love books, good writing, interesting ideas, and love being part of the fascinating industry that makes it all happen.

What do you think the future holds for writers, publishers, and agents: Ever since the advent of the computer age, publishers have gotten smarter, and so have most agents and many writers. The old belief that quality sells itself has been proved wrong, and replaced with a more practical knowledge of what sells. As a result, publishers are selling more copies, and there are more blockbuster authors than ever before. Publishing has long been threatened by many other entertainment options (movies, games, etc.), and illiteracy remains a problem for the nation as a whole. But despite the occasional doom-and-gloom prediction, the overall business is chugging along quite well.

BLEECKER STREET ASSOCIATES, INC.

217 Thompson St., #519, New York, NY 10012

212-677-4492   fax: 212-388-0001

Agent's name: Agnes Birnbaum

Born: Budapest, Hungary.

Career history: 16 years as editor before starting agency in 1984; senior editor at Pocket, NAL; editor-in-chief of Award Books, later a division of Berkley.

Categories/subjects that you are most enthusiastic about agenting: History, biography, science, investigative reporting, true crime, health, psychology, true adventure, women's issues, also mystery/suspense, women's fiction.

What you don't want to agent: Poetry, science fiction, western, children's, film/TV scripts, plays, professional/academic books.

What's the best way for writers to solicit your interest: Short letter with SASE. No fax or email.

Do you charge reading or management fees: No.

Can you provide an approximation by percent of what you tend to represent by category : Fiction: 10 percent, Nonfiction: 90 percent.

How and why did you ever become an agent: Love to read.

What, if anything, can a writer do to increase the odds of your becoming his or her agent: Send a great short letter about the book and themselves. We don't respond without an SASE.

Do you have any particular opinions or impressions of editors and publishers in general: I like them; having been an editor I can understand their problems.

What are your favorite books, movies, TV shows, and why: The movie *The Big Lebowski*—wonderfully funny.

Please list representative titles you have sold: *The Indifferent Stars Above* by Daniel James Brown (Morrow); *Surviving the College Search* (St. Martin's); *Inside the Nazi War Machine* (NAL); *Fossil Hunter* (Palgrave Macmillan); *Everyday Ethics* (Viking); *Ophelia Speaks* (HarperCollins); *How the South Could Have Won the Civil War* (Crown); *Sex, Lies, and Handwriting* (Simon & Schuster); *Puppy Miracles* (Adams); *Big, Beautiful, and Pregnant* (Marlowe & Co.); *Buddha Baby* (Avon); *Phantom Warrior* (Berkley); *The Flag, the Poet, and the Song* (Dutton).

THE BLUMER LITERARY AGENCY, INC.

809 W. 181 Street, Suite 201, New York, NY 10033

212-947-3040   fax: 212-947-0460

Agent's name: Olivia B. Blumer; blumerliterary@earthlink.net
Born: Long Island, New York.
Education: BA, English from Goucher College.
Career history: Worked for three publishers (Doubleday, Atheneum, and Warner Books) before becoming an agent fifteen years ago.
Hobbies/personal interests: Gardening, food and cooking, travel, tennis, reading (believe it or not).
Categories/subjects that you are most enthusiastic about agenting: Memoirs with a larger purpose, expository books on social and cultural phenomena, books that spark interest in both ordinary and extraordinary things, groundbreaking guides/how-to books, novels that explore the unexplored (in literature and in life).
What you don't want to agent: Victim lit, PhD theses turned "intellectual" exposés, opportunistic books with no larger picture, science fiction, category romance.
If you were not an agent, what might you be doing instead: Animal rescue.
What's the best way for writers to solicit your interest: A well-crafted, short, unambiguous letter with neither hype nor typos. Just the facts, please.
Do you charge reading or management fees: No.
Can you provide an approximation by percent of what you tend to represent by category: Nonfiction: 60 percent, fiction: 40 percent.
What are the most common mistakes writers make when pitching you: Too much author bio and not enough information about the actual book (or vice versa); self-congratulatory author bio; don't tell me that all your friends love your book; non-standardized, small (less than 12-point) type that is not double-spaced drives us crazy!
How would you describe the client from hell: Those deaf to suggestions and those eager to please; whiners.
How would you describe the perfect client: Thick-skinned, talented, patient, hard working, long-term vs. short-term thinker who is not looking to get rich quick, attentive to suggestions and thorough in their execution.

How and why did you ever become an agent: A chance to invest in my own taste.

What, if anything, can a writer do to increase the odds of your becoming his or her agent: Don't nag, let your writing speak for itself.

How would you describe to someone (or something) from another planet what it is that you do as an agent: Matchmaker, manager of expectations, career counselor.

Do you have any particular opinions or impressions of editors and publishers in general: Majority is overworked and risk-averse.

On a personal level, what do you think people like about you and dislike about you: Dislike: Direct, impatient; Like: Passionate, organized, eclectic taste, lots of varied experience in the book biz from retail to rights to publicity to editorial.

BOOKS & SUCH LITERARY AGENCY

52 Mission Circle, Suite 122, PMB 170, Santa Rosa, CA 94509

www.booksandsuch.biz

email: representation@booksandsuch.biz

Agents' names: Janet Kobobel Grant, Wendy Lawton, Etta Wilson, Rachel Zurakowski

Subjects and categories you are interested in agenting, including fiction and nonfiction: Adult fiction and nonfiction, teen, middle readers.

Subjects and categories writers shouldn't even bother pitching to you: Fantasy, sci-fi, paranormal, gift books, poetry, plays.

What would you do if you weren't agenting: Edit fiction.

What's the best way for fiction writers to solicit your interest: Have a short, snappy hook that piques my interest. A great title also helps.

What's the best way for nonfiction writers to solicit your interest: Focus the idea on a specific but significantly populated group of potential readers, and a unique approach to a perennially popular topic.

Do you charge reading or any upfront fees: No.

In your experience, what are the most common pitching mistakes writers make: Not being able to talk about an idea succinctly. I don't want to hear an entire plotline nor an entire history of why someone wrote a manuscript.

Describe the client from hell, even if you don't have any: Emails several times a day; suffers from huge insecurity and needs to be assured several times a week that, yes, publishing is insane but he/she is not; unrealistic expectations in terms of the financial reward of writing; unwilling to take criticism of work; doesn't meet deadlines; isn't willing to do the hard work of actually writing a great book—and a great proposal.

What's your definition of a great client: An innate sense of where the market is and how to write accordingly; capable of putting together a dazzling title and concept; works hard at improving the craft; has strong ideas on how to publicize him/

herself as well as his/her writing; has the smarts to know when we need to talk and when we don't; relates well with everyone.

How can writers increase the odds that you will offer representation: Study our website to learn what type of writing really interests us and query us in the way we ask to be queried. An author who think his/her work is worthy of making an exception to the query process is just asking to be turned down.

Why did you become an agent, and how did you become one: As an editor, I found what I loved most about the publishing process was discovering authors and introducing them to the reading world. Eventually it occurred to me that agents do that a much higher percentage of the time than editors.

In your opinion, what do editors think of you: I've often been told that I'm tough but fair, that I have good instincts about what each publishing house is looking for.

What are some representative titles that you have sold: *Hideaway Series* by Robin Jones Gunn (Simon & Schuster); *One Simple Act* by Debbie Macomber (Simon & Schuster); *A Woman Named Sage* by DiAnn Mills (Zondervan); *Breach of Trust* by DiAnn Mills (Tyndale); *Smotherly Love* by Debi Stack (Thomas Nelson); *Unleashing the Courageous Faith* by Paul Coughlin (Bethany House); *Murder by Family* by Kent Whitaker (Simon & Schuster); *Getting Old Ain't for Wimps* by Karen O'Connor (Harvest House); *Having a Mary Heart in a Martha World* by Joanna Weaver (WaterBrook); *Summer of Light* by Dale Cramer (Bethany House).

RICK BROADHEAD & ASSOCIATES

47 St. Clair Avenue West, Suite #501, Toronto, Ontario, Canada M4V 3A5
416-929-0516
www.rbaliterary.com   email: rba@rbaliterary.com

Don't be scared off by my address! I represent many American authors and I have made dozens of sales to major American publishers (see below). I welcome queries by email.

Agent's name: Rick Broadhead

Education: BBA, York University; MBA, Schulich School of Business, York University.

Career history or story: I opened my literary agency in 2002 and quickly established myself as one of the leading agencies in the business. In addition to being one of the few literary agents who has a business background and MBA, I have the rare distinction of being a bestselling author. I wrote and co-wrote over 30 books prior to establishing my literary agency and this affords me a unique perspective on the industry that few agents possess. I have secured dozens and dozens of deals for my authors with large publishing houses across the United States, including Random House, HarperCollins, Hyperion, Penguin, St. Martin's Press, Running Press, Ten Speed Press, Wiley, Simon & Schuster, Harlequin, Jossey-Bass, Da Capo Press, Rodale, Thomas Nelson, Chronicle Books, Adams Media, Abrams, Warner Books/Hachette Book Group, and more.

Books represented by my agency have appeared on bestseller lists, been shortlisted for literary awards, translated into multiple languages, and through my agency's partnerships in Hollywood, been optioned for film and television development.

One of my first book sales was quickly optioned by Paramount/CBS for development as a television sitcom.

My marketing and business expertise were acknowledged by my alma mater, York University, which awarded me their prestigious marketing medal for demonstrated excellence in marketing.

My vast knowledge of the publishing industry, both as an author and an agent, and my strong relationships with editors have allowed me to consistently negotiate excellent deals for my clients. I'm a meticulous negotiator and I have secured many six-figure deals for my clients.

Subjects and categories you are interested in agenting, including fiction and nonfiction: The agency's clients include accomplished journalists, historians, physicians, television personalities, bloggers and creators of popular websites, successful business executives, and experts in their respective fields. They include Yale University physician and *Oprah Magazine* columnist Dr. David Katz; survival skills expert and Discovery Channel host Les Stroud (*Survivorman*); Alex Debogorski, co-star of The History Channel's hit show, *Ice Road Truckers*; intelligence historian and National Security Archive fellow Matthew Aid; *Wall Street Journal* bestselling author and marketing guru Ryan Allis; award-winning military historian Tim Cook; ornithologist/biologist Dr. Glen Chilton; musician Steven Page, former lead singer of the Barenaked Ladies; comic book blogger Brian Cronin; and science journalist Sam Kean. I love history, politics, natural history (birding/nature/environment); current affairs, biography, science, pop culture, relationships, self-help, health, medicine, military history, national security/intelligence, business, pop culture, and humor. I especially love working with journalists and I have found many of my best clients after seeing their work in magazines or newspapers. I've also sold many books based on popular websites.

Subjects and categories writers shouldn't even bother pitching to you: Fiction, children's books, poetry, screenplays.

What's the best way for nonfiction writers to solicit your interest: A short query letter is best. Describe the book project and your credentials/platform.

Do you charge reading or any upfront fees: There are no reading or upfront fees.

In your experience, what are the most common pitching mistakes writers make: Overly long query letters; sending me a proposal that has clearly not been vetted for grammar and spelling mistakes; not having confidence in your work; pasting chapters into the body of an email; sending attachments without asking first; cc-ing the same query letter to multiple literary agents simultaneously; not personalizing a query letter; sending a manuscript (electronically or in hard copy) before an agent has requested it; pitching multiple book projects simultaneously. It can be overwhelming when an author pitches four to five ideas or projects at once. It implies that you're scattered and unfocused. Make sure you have a solid proposal ready before you contact a literary agent. It's quite demotivating when an author pitches an idea, gets me excited, then tells me the proposal is still in progress and weeks away from completion.

What's your definition of a great client: The best clients, not surprisingly, are those who make my job easier. They're professional, patient, prepared, flexible, open to my input, prompt to respond to my questions and needs, and their proposals are outstanding. Incessant phone calls and emails make my job very difficult since they take time away from selling. I really enjoy working with journalists and historians.

How can writers increase the odds that you will offer representation: First of all, you should know what types of books I'm most interested in, as I'm most likely to be receptive to a pitch if the book fits my interests and the subject categories I'm looking for. There are three major criteria I look for when evaluating book proposals (and query letters): 1) a talented writer; 2) a great concept (ideally, a book that is different from other books currently on the market); 3) an author with a platform, credentials, and the relevant expertise.

Books rarely sell themselves these days, so I look for authors who have a "platform." If you're a leading expert in your field or you have experience writing for major newspapers or magazines, I'm more likely to have success selling you to a major publisher. Similarly, if you have a popular blog or website or you're affiliated with a major organization or university/college, publishers are more likely to be interested in you.

Remember that I have to sell your project to an editor, and then the editor has to sell your project internally to his/her colleagues (including the marketing and sales staff), and then the publisher has to sell your book to the book buyers at the chains and bookstores. You're most likely to get my attention if you write a succinct query letter that demonstrates your platform, the market potential of your book, and why your book is different. In short—get me excited!

I'm particularly interested in experts and journalists who have had their work published in major newspapers and magazines. In the marketing section of your proposal, do not put together a full-blown marketing plan that includes a laundry list of ideas for book signings, press releases, a website, etc. This is one of the biggest mistakes authors make when crafting a book proposal. Publishers are most interested in the existing connections and relationships you have (with newspapers, television shows, websites, etc.) that will help the publisher sell your book when it's published.

Why did you become an agent, and how did you become one: I'm an entrepreneur at heart and I love the business side of publishing—finding great authors, pitching book ideas, negotiating deals, and being a part of an exciting and dynamic industry. I became a bestselling author early in my career, and eight years later, after several successive bestsellers, I decided to put my business savvy and passion for publishing to work for other authors. I love what I do, and I love getting excited about a new book project that I can pitch to the editors I work with. There's something special about holding a book in your hand and realizing you played a part in its creation.

Describe to someone from another planet what you do as an agent: I help make dreams come true! A lot of writers question the value of an agent but my involvement will always result in a better deal for the author, whether it's in the advance/royalties, the selection of the publisher/editor, or better contract terms.

What are some representative titles that you have sold: *The Curse of the Labrador Duck: My Obsessive Quest to the Edge of Extinction* by ornithologist Dr. Glen Chilton (Simon & Schuster); *Northern Armageddon: The Battle of the Plains of Abraham* by military historian Peter MacLeod (Knopf/Random House USA); *Survive: Essential Skills and Tactics to Get You Out of Anywhere—Alive* by survival skills expert Les Stroud, host of *Survivorman* on the Discovery Channel (Collins/HarperCollins); *The Secret Sentry: The Top-Secret History of the National Security Agency* by intelligence historian Matthew Aid (Bloomsbury Press/Bloomsbury USA); *The Flavor Point Diet* by Yale University Associate Professor and ABC News medical contributor David Katz MD (Rodale); *Do Gentlemen Really Prefer Blondes?* by former Random House editor Jena Pincott (Bantam Dell/Random House USA); *Insultingly Stupid Movie Physics* by engineer and science teacher Tom Rogers (Sourcebooks); *The Quantum Ten: A Story of Passion, Tragedy, Ambition and Science* by science journalist Sheilla Jones (Oxford University Press USA); *101 Foods That Could Save Your Life* by Registered Dietician David Grotto (Bantam Dell/Random House USA); *Bad Bridesmaid: Bachelorette Brawls and Taffeta Tantrums—What We Go Through for Her Big Day* by journalist Siri Agrell (Henry Holt); *Ten Years Thinner: The Ultimate Lifestyle Program for Winding Back Your Physiological Clock—and Your Bathroom Scale* by Christine Lydon MD (Da Capo Press/Perseus Books Group); *The Menopause Makeover* by Staness Jonekos (Harlequin); *It's a Dog's Life…and It's a Cat's World* by veterinarian Justine Lee (Three Rivers Press/Random House USA); *Zero to a Million: How I Built a Company to $1 Million in Sales and How You Can, Too* by CEO and entrepreneur Ryan Allis (McGraw-Hill USA); *The Trouble with Africa: Why Foreign Aid Isn't Working* by former World Bank executive Robert Calderisi (Palgrave USA/St. Martin's Press); *Connected Parenting: Transform Your Challenging Child and Build Loving Bonds for Life* by parenting expert Jennifer Kolari (Avery/Penguin Group USA); *Was Superman a Spy? and Other Comic Book Urban Legends Revealed* by comic book expert and blogger Brian Cronin (Plume/Penguin Group USA); *Twisted Triangle* by Pulitzer Prize–nominated investigative journalist Caitlin Rother (Jossey Bass); *The Love Pirate: Murder, Sin, and Scandal in the Shadow of Jesse James* by true crime historian Laura James (Sterling).

ANDREA BROWN LITERARY AGENCY

650-853-1976

www.andreabrownlit.com   email: laura@andreabrownlit.com

We accept email queries only. Please see our agency website for submission guidelines.

Agents' names: Andrea Brown, President. Laura Rennert, Senior Agent. Other agents also at the agency are Caryn Wiseman, Jennifer Jaeger, and Michelle Andelman.

The following information pertains to Andrea Brown.

What are representative titles you have sold to publishers: *Unwind* by Neal Shusterman (Simon & Schuster); *Circle Unbroken* by Margot Theis Raven (Farrar, Straus & Giroux).

How do you feel about writers: I got into publishing because I loved books, but I realized after becoming an agent, that I really loved writers even more than books. I am still, after 26 years as an agent, in awe of writers who can finish a book and keep a reader hooked.

What do you tell entities from other planets and dimensions about your job: I tell everyone who will listen that I have the best career: I get to work with intelligent, creative, wonderful people every day (that includes all my associates at the agency, not just our fabulous clients).

You're welcome to share your thoughts and sentiments about the business of writing and publishing: It is a wonderful time for children's book authors—the best in the 30 years I [have been] in the business. It is also imperative that writers think about their audience more than ever. They must write the best book possible and also make certain that it is commercial. Ask, "Would you pay $25 for this book?"

Will our business exist as we know it in ten years or so: I think book publishing will always exist, but I think big changes are on the horizon, and the authors that can adapt will continue to be published. I don't think it will exist as it is.

The following information pertains to Laura Rennert.

Education: PhD in English Literature, University of Virginia, BA, *magna cum laude*, Cornell University.

Career history: Literary agent, ten years. Professor, eight years of teaching English literature at Santa Clara University, the University of Virginia, and visiting professor at Osaka University of Foreign Studies in Japan.

Hobbies/personal interests: Travel, movies, theater, good food and wine, reading and writing, of course.

Categories/subjects that you are most enthusiastic about agenting: Ambitious voice-driven fiction, whether children's books or adult; literary mysteries and thrillers, compelling story-based narrative nonfiction; literary-commercial middle-grade and young-adult fiction; crossover fiction; fiction. Regardless of genre, I look for works that are emotionally powerful and resonant.

What you don't want to agent: Westerns, adult fantasy, adult science fiction, prescriptive nonfiction, screenplays, New Age fiction, and nonfiction.

What's the best way for fiction writers to solicit your interest: Follow the guidelines on our website (www.andreabrownlit.com), and choose one agent to e-query. Target the agent for whom you feel your work is the best fit and take the time to do a little research. A strong query that demonstrates you've done your homework makes a good first impression. When someone tells me why they're approaching me, particularly, and demonstrates some knowledge of the market, I look closely at their work. Professionalism, passion, and confidence (not hubris) are attractive. A strong voice is one of my main criteria in work I choose to take on, and I'm already on the look out for it as I read query letters.

What's the best way for nonfiction writers to solicit your interest: I'm looking for a strong proposal and sample chapters—and pretty much look for the same criteria I mention above for fiction.

If you were not an agent, what might you be doing instead: If I weren't agenting, I'd probably be an editor, a professor of English literature, or a writer...pretty predictable, I'm afraid, although I do also have a secret fascination with dinosaurs—so maybe also paleontologist.

Do you charge reading or management fees: No.

Can you provide an approximation by percent of what you tend to represent by category: Children's books: 70 percent, adult fiction and Nonfiction: 30 percent.

How would you describe the client from hell: The client from hell wants constant updates, handholding, and attention all the time.

What are your favorite books, movies, TV shows, and why: Some of my favorite books are Jonathan Lethem's *Motherless Brooklyn*, A. S. Byatt's *Possession*, Barry Eisler's *The Last Assassin*, J. K. Rowling's *Harry Potter* novels, Terry Pratchett's *Wee Free Men* trilogy, all of Jane Austen's novels, and Madeleine L'Engle's *A Wrinkle in Time*. Although they are very different, what all of these works have in common is a marvelous, individualistic voice; characters that get under your skin; emotional power and resonance, masterful storytelling; a unique perspective; and vivid, evocative, visceral writing.

Please list representative titles you have sold: *The Five Ancestors Series* (Random House); *Becoming Chloe* (Knopf); *Storky: How I Won the Girl and Lost My Nickname* (Putnam); *Monsoon Summer* (Random House); *The Squishiness of Things* (Knopf); *The Strongbow Saga: Viking Warrior Book 1* (HarperCollins); *First Daughter: Extreme American Make-Over* (Dutton); *Revolution Is Not a Dinner Party* (Holt); *Evolution, Me, and Other Freaks of Nature* (Knopf); *Glass* (Margaret Mcelderry/Simon & Schuster); *Love in the Present Tense* (Doubleday); *Thirteen Reasons Why* (Razorbill/Penguin Group); *The Day I Killed James* (Knopf); *Chasing Windmills* (Doubleday) and *Madapple* (Knopf).

The following information pertains to **Jennifer Jaeger.**

Born: Los Angeles, California

Education: BA in English from UC Davis; minor in social and ethnic relations with a focus on multicultural literature. Spent one year at the University of East Anglia in England. Studied education at Dominican University.

Career history or story: I worked in journalism and education before becoming a literary agent.

Hobbies, interests: Reading (of course), cooking, martial arts, stock market, travel, spa days, theater, early U.S. history.

Subjects and categories you are interested in agenting, including fiction and nonfiction: Picture books through YA, with a special interest in middle-grade. I like humorous, literary, multicultural, edgy and offbeat material. I enjoy some paranormal, fantasy and historical manuscripts. Though I do not represent adult fiction, I am interested in crossover fiction.

Subjects and categories writers shouldn't even bother pitching to you: Please, no adult works.

What would you do if you weren't agenting: I would be teaching, learning languages in foreign countries, or working the counter at a bakery.

What's the best way for fiction writers to solicit your interest: Please email your query along with the first ten pages of your manuscript in the body of an email. For picture books, include the entire manuscript. No attachments, please.

Do you charge reading or any upfront fees: No.

In your experience, what are the most common pitching mistakes writers make: No personalized greeting, no knowledge about my interests or the Andrea Brown Literary Agency, and unprofessional and unpolished query letters.

Describe the client from hell, even if you don't have any: Such a client would be inflexible, greedy, and unnecessarily dramatic.

What's your definition of a great client: Great clients know their market and the business, they work tirelessly on their craft, they're open to revising and are willing to promote their work. They're also very patient.

Why did you become an agent, and how did you become one: Agenting is the perfect combination of my skills and interests: writing and editing, communication, and business. It is thrilling to know that I play a role in helping great and important books get published.

How do you feel about writers: I think authors are brave souls and the true celebrities.

What are your favorite books, TV shows, movies, and why: Books: *Even Cowgirls Get the Blues*; *Catherine Called Birdy*; *The Schwa Was Here*; *A Passage to India*; and books by Jonathan Safran Foer and Toni Morrison. TV shows: *The Office*. Movies: *Dirty Dancing*, *Rushmore*, *Sweet Home Alabama*, and *Little Miss Sunshine*.

What are some representative titles that you have sold: (Please note that titles are subject to change.) *The Down-to-Earth Guide to Global Warming* (Orchard/Scholastic); *Las Mantas de Milagros* (Holt); *Farwalker* (Bloomsbury); *Before You Were Here* and *The Cazuela that the Farm Maiden Stirred* (Viking and Charlesbridge, respectively); *Paris Pan Takes the Dare* (Puffin and Putnam/Penguin).

The following information pertains to Caryn Wiseman.

Education: MBA, Anderson School, UCLA; BS, University of Virginia.

Career history or story: Caryn's fifteen years of business experience prior to joining the agency emphasized editing and writing as well as sales, negotiation and client management.

Subjects and categories you are interested in agenting, including fiction and nonfiction: I handle children's books only: young-adult and middle-grade fiction and nonfiction, chapter books, and picture books. I am particularly interested in sports; humorous chapter books and middle-grade fiction; "boy" books; YA that falls at the intersection of commercial and literary; YA that is edgy without being gratuitous; magical realism and reality-based fantasy; biography for kids of all ages; unique nonfiction; and African American and Latino-themed literature in all age groups. I am always open to terrific children's work that doesn't fit these categories, however. For fiction, a fresh, unique voice is paramount, but the story must have great characterization and plot as well. I loves nonfiction that reads like fiction; that has a great "story behind the story." I do not represent adult projects. Please do not query her regarding adult work.

Subjects and categories writers shouldn't even bother pitching to you: Any adult projects.

What are some representative titles that you have sold: Some recent and forthcoming titles include: *The Qwikpick Adventure Society* by Sam Riddleburger (Dial); *Beneath My Mother's Feet* by Amjed Qamar (Mcelderry); *Flying Beneath the Radar* by Lisa Kline (Delacorte); *Beanball* by Gene Fehler (Clarion); *The Great Walloper Series* by Kevin Markey (HarperCollins); *Life in the Wild: The George Schaller Story* by Pamela S. Turner (FSG); *The Man Who Flies with Birds* by Carole G. Vogel (Millbrook).

CURTIS BROWN LTD.

10 Astor Place, New York, NY 10003

212-473-5400

Agents' names: Elizabeth Harding, Ginger Knowlton, Laura Blake Peterson.

The following information pertains to Elizabeth Harding.

Education: BA in English, University of Michigan (Ann Arbor).

Categories/subjects that you are most enthusiastic about agenting: Children's literature.

What's the best way for writers to solicit your interest: Query letter or sample chapters.

Can you provide an approximation by percent of what you tend to represent by category: Children's: 100 percent.

The following information pertains to Ginger Knowlton.

Born: Before the 1960s in Princeton, New Jersey.

Education: Questionable, Navy brat–quality.

Career history: I worked in a factory assembling display cases in Mystic, Connecticut, for a time. Gained numerous pounds one summer working in a bakery in Mendocino, California. I've taught preschool and I directed an infant and toddler child-care center. That means I organized a lot of fundraisers. I started working at Curtis Brown in 1986.

Categories/subjects that you are most enthusiastic about agenting: Middle-grade and teenage novels.

What you don't want to agent: I prefer to remain open to all ideas.

What's the best way for writers to solicit your interest: A simple, straightforward letter with a return envelope works well.

If you were not an agent, what might you be doing instead: I love my job, but if I had the luxury of not having to work, I would play tennis even more than I already do; I would tend my gardens more fastidiously; and I would spend more time playing with others.

Can you provide an approximation by percent of what you tend to represent by category: Nonfiction, 5 percent; fiction, 5 percent; children's, 90 percent.

What are the most common mistakes writers make when pitching you: Expecting an answer within a week, but mostly poor-quality writing.

How would you describe the client from hell: Happy to report that I still don't have firsthand experience with a "client from hell," so once again I will refrain from describing one (for fear of a self-fulfilling prophecy).

How would you describe the perfect client: Professional authors who respect my job as I respect theirs, who will maintain an open dialogue so we may learn from each other and continue to grow, who are optimistic and enthusiastic, and who continue to write books worthy of publication.

How and why did you ever become an agent: I asked Dad for money for graduate school. He offered me a job at Curtis Brown instead.

Do you have any particular opinions or impressions of editors or publishers in general: I have a lot of respect for editors and I think they have an incredibly difficult job. As in all professions, some are more gifted than others.

The following information pertains to Laura Blake Peterson.

Education: BA, Vassar College.

Career history: 1986–present, Curtis Brown, Ltd.

Hobbies/personal interests: Gardening, pets, regional equestrian competitions.

Areas most interested in agenting: Exceptional fiction, narrative nonfiction, young-adult fiction, anything outstanding.

What you don't want to agent: Fantasy, science fiction, poetry.

If you were not an agent, what might you be doing instead: Teaching, gardening, who knows?

What's the best way for writers to solicit your interest: The best way is through a referral from either a client of mine or an editor with whom I work.

Can you provide an approximation by percent of what you tend to represent by category: Fiction: 40 percent; nonfiction: 40 percent; children's: 20 percent.

What are the most common mistakes writers make when pitching you: Calling, rather than sending a query letter.

How would you describe the client from hell: Authors who call incessantly, preventing me from accomplishing anything on their behalf.

How would you describe the perfect client: A talented writer who knows the idiosyncrasies of the publishing business yet nonetheless remains determined to be a part of it; a writer with the skills and patience to participate in an often frustrating and quirky industry.

How and why did you ever become an agent: I love language. I can't imagine a better job than helping to bring a skilled writer to the attention of the book-buying public.

What, if anything, can a writer do to increase the odds that you will become his or her agent: Do their homework. Find out what I (or whoever they're contacting) like to read and represent, what books I've sold in the past, etc. Read this survey!

TRACY BROWN LITERARY AGENCY

P.O. Box 88, Scarsdale, NY 10583

914-400-4147   email: tracy@brownlit.com

Agent's name: Tracy Brown

Born: Omaha, Nebraska.

Education: Williams College; Columbia University.

Career story: I worked my way up (and down) the book publishing editorial ladder for 25 years before becoming an agent in 2004. I came into the business at the age of 28 as an assistant in the publicity department at E. P. Dutton and then moved to junior editorial positions at Holt and Penguin. In 1988 I was offered the job of editorial director of Quality Paperback Book Club. Returning briefly to trade publishing in 1992, I initiated a new trade paperback list at Little, Brown called Back Bay and served as its first editorial director. In 1993 I returned to the book clubs when I was offered the position of editor-in-chief of Book-of-the-Month Club, a position I held until 1996 when I returned to the trade as an acquiring editor at Holt and then at Ballantine. In 2004 I decided to become an agent. My first three years were spent in association with Wendy Sherman Associates. I opened my own agency in 2007.

Hobbies and special personal interests: Travel, cooking, farmer's markets, Bob Dylan's music.

Subjects and categories you like to agent: 80 percent nonfiction: Current affairs, memoir, psychology, travel, nature, health; 20 percent literary fiction.

Subjects and categories writers shouldn't bother pitching to you: Science fiction, romance, YA.

What might you be doing if you weren't agenting: That's a scary thought.

What's the most effective ways for writers to grab your attention: Write a succinct and informative query letter that clearly states who you are and what you want to write about.

Do you charge fees separate from your commission, or offer non-agenting fee-based services: No fees.

What are representative titles you have sold to publishers: *Mating in Captivity: Unlocking Erotic Intelligence* by Esther Perel (HarperCollins); *Perfect Girls, Starving Daughters* by Courtney E. Martin (Free Press); *The Man in the White Sharkskin Suit* by Lucette Lagnado (Ecco); *Why We're Losing the War on Cancer* by Clifton Leaf (Knopf); *Full Frontal Feminism* by Jessica Valenti (Seal Press); *Super in the City: A Novel* by Daphne Uviller (Bantam).

Why did you become an agent, and how did you become one: I'm amazed that I survived in corporate publishing for 25 consecutive years. Then there came a time when I wanted more freedom to select the authors I want to work with. The transition from editor to agent was relatively easy for me; acquiring books and selling them involve essentially the same skills.

How do you feel about writers: Their words have impacted my life more than any other art form.

What do you tell entities from other planets and dimensions about your job: Don't even try to make sense of the book business. Nobody knows why some books sell and others don't. This irrationality can be frustrating at times but is also a large part of why so many of us are attracted to the challenge of bringing worthy books to the public's attention.

How would you describe the writer from hell: A client needs to trust that an agent knows how to do his/her job. Trying to micro-manage the process is going to make everyone miserable.

How would you describe the publisher and/or editor from hell: I've known a few (luckily very few) editors and publishers who seem to feel that the agent is nothing but a troublemaker who must be thwarted at every turn.

What do you like best about your clients, and the editors and publishers you work with: I enjoy these relationships most when the topic of conversation is not always about work.

Do you wish to describe who you are: I receive a lot of queries addressed to "Ms" Tracy Brown. I'm used to this and don't mind, but it's probably best for potential clients to know that I'm one of the rare males with the name Tracy.

Will our business exist as we know it in ten years or so: Definitely not as we know it today. But there will always be people who want to tell stories and other people will want to hear them. So most likely there will be a need for somebody to facilitate the process. I'm not worried—yet.

PEMA BROWNE, LTD.

11 Tena Place, Valley Cottage, NY 10989

845-268-0026

www.pemabrowneltd.com

Agent's name: Pema Browne

What are some representative titles that you have sold: *Taming the Beast* by Heather Grothaus (Kensington/Zebra Historical); *Highlander's Honor* by Michele Sinclar (Kensington/Zebra Historical); *Kisses Don't Lie* by Alexis Darin (Zebra Contemporary Romance); *The Daring Ms. Quimby* by Suzanne Whitaker (Holiday House).

SHEREE BYKOFSKY ASSOCIATES, INC.

P.O. Box 706, Brigantine, NJ 08203

Agent's name: Sheree Bykofsky

Born: September 1956, Queens, New York.

Education: BA, State University of New York, Binghamton; MA, in English and comparative literature, Columbia University.

Career history or story: Executive editor/book producer, the Stonesong Press (1984–1996); freelance editor/writer (1984); general manager/managing editor, Chiron Press (1979–1984); author and co-author of a dozen books, including three poker books with co-author Lou Krieger.

Hobbies, interests: Poker, Scrabble.

Subjects and categories that you are interested in agenting, including fiction and nonfiction: Popular reference, adult nonfiction (hardcovers and trade paperbacks), quality literary and commercial fiction (highly selective).

Subjects and categories writers shouldn't even bother pitching to you: Children's, young adult, genre romance, science fiction, horror, Westerns, occult and supernatural, fantasy.

What's the best way for fiction writers to solicit your interest: Send an e-query letter, pasted into the body of your email, to submitbee@aol.com. No attachments will be opened.

What's the best way for nonfiction writers to solicit your interest: See above.

Do you charge reading or any upfront fees: No.

In your experience, what are the most common pitching mistakes writers make: Excessive hubris; not explaining what the book is about; comparing book to bestsellers rather than showing how it is unique; paranoia (we're not going to steal your idea); sloppy grammar, punctuation, and spelling.

What's your definition of a great client: One who is not only a talented writer but also who is professional in every sense.

How can writers increase the odds that you will offer representation: I love a query letter that is as well written as the proposed book, or a polished, perfect, professional proposal.

Please list representative titles you have sold: *Boyfriend University* (Wiley); *1001 Ways to Live Green* (Berkley); *Conspiracy Nation* (Chicago Review); *Junk Jewelry* (Clarkson Potter); *The Thrill of the Chaste* (Thomas Nelson); *When the Ghost Screams* (Andrews McMeel); *Death Waits for You* (Pocket).

CASTIGLIA LITERARY AGENCY

1155 Camino del Mar, Del Mar, CA 92014

Agents' names: Julie Castiglia, Winifred Golden, Sally Van Haitsma, Deborah Ritchken

Subjects and categories writers shouldn't even bother pitching to you: Horror, fantasy, poetry.

What would you do if you weren't agenting: Making movies, gardening, reading, traveling, cooking and lying on the beach.

What's the best way for fiction writers to solicit your interest: Query letter, two pages of sample writing plus a synopsis, publishing credits.

What's the best way for nonfiction writers to solicit your interest: Query letter listing credentials, education and experience plus any marketing ability, connections, etc.

Do you charge reading or any upfront fees: No.

In your experience, what are the most common pitching mistakes writers make: Unprofessional presentation, spelling errors, lack of knowledge about the publishing industry. Lack of information about themselves. Calling instead of writing. Lack of brevity. Submitting more than one project at a time to more than one agent in our office.

Describe the client from hell, even if you don't have any: Not listening to our advice, not trusting our judgment. Telling us what to do and how to do it.

What's your definition of a great client: Appreciative, loyal, trusting, trustworthy, knowing that we care deeply about their work. Sense of humor, sends chocolates.

How can writers increase the odds that you will offer representation: Write a query that will knock our socks off. Be referred by editors, clients, other professionals or simply be a brilliant writer.

Why did you become an agent, and how did you become one: It was my destiny (Castiglia); I thought it was the CIA (Golden); I was seduced by the ghost of Thomas Hardy (Van Haitsma); The Devil made me do it. (Ritchken).

Describe to someone from another planet what you do as an agent: We sell manuscripts from writers unknown and known to publishers who magically turn them into books.

How do you feel about editors and publishers: Thank God for all of them.

How do you feel about writers: It depends if they can write.

What do you see in the near future for book publishing: I don't want to think about it.

What are your favorite books, TV shows, movies, and why: *Child 44*; *The Perfect Storm*; *Atonement*; *The Glass Castle*; *The Nature of Air and Water*; *Motherless Brooklyn*, *The Devil in the White City*. TV Shows: *House*; *24*; design and architecture shows; *Chopping Block Movies*; *Slumdog Millionaire*; *Empire of the Sun*; *La Strada*; *Notes on a Scandal*; *The Reader*.

In your opinion, what do editors think of you: They respect and like us. We are consummate professionals, aggressive when we need to be but always polite and pleasant. They recognize integrity and they are aware of our good reputation.

On a personal non-professional level, what do you think people think of you: Everyone loves us, why wouldn't they? Our friends think we have a very glamorous job. We don't tell them the truth.

What are some representative titles that you have sold: *The Islanders* (HarperCollins) by Sandra Rodriguez Barron; *Freefall* by Reese Hirsch (Berkley); *America Libre* by Raul Ramos y Sanchez (Grand Central); *Why Did He Cheat on Me?* (Adams Media) by Rona Subotnik; *The Leisure Seeker* by Michael Zadoorian (Morrow/Harper); *Waiting for the Apocalypse* by Veronica Chater (Norton); *From Splendor to Revolution* by Julia Gelardi (St. Martin's); *Beautiful: The Life of Hedy Lamar* by Stephen Shearer (St. Martin's); *Forever L.A.* by Doug Keister (Gibbs Smith); *Barry Dixon Interiors* by Brian Coleman (Gibbs Smith); *Wesley the Owl* by Stacey O'Brien (Free Press/Simon & Schuster).

FRANCES COLLIN, LITERARY AGENT

P.O. Box 33, Wayne, PA 19087 0033

Tel 610 254 0555 • Fax 610 254 5029

www.francescollin.com

Agents' names: Frances Collin, Sarah Yake; queries@francescollin.com (Both agents see all queries sent to this address.)

The following information pertains to Sarah Yake.

Education: MA, English literature, West Chester University

Career Story: Bookstore manager for five years, worked in sales for a major publisher for three years, have been with Fran Collin for five years and building my own client list for two years.

Subjects and categories you like to agent: YA, literary fiction, memoir, narrative nonfiction, travel narrative.

I love the West, wilderness, nature and the great outdoors on a grand scale and am always open to both fiction and nonfiction that can transport me there, especially if it features a strong woman character.

Subjects and categories writers shouldn't bother pitching to you: Children's picture books, cooking, poetry, crafts, photography.

What might you be doing if you weren't agenting: Librarian, bookseller, English teacher; definitely something bookish.

What's the most effective ways for writers to grab your attention: Personally, I would rather be wooed than grabbed right off the bat. Often the writers who grab my attention do so for all the wrong reasons and their queries stick out like sore thumbs, so to speak. A writer woos me by following the generally accepted guidelines for a good, solid, well-written query. Once the query woos me, the writing itself should grab me.

Do you charge fees separate from your commission, or offer non-agenting fee-based services: No.

Why did you become an agent, and how did you become one: After years spent in other areas of the book business a series of tiny quirks of fate led me to Fran at just the right time.

How do you feel about writers: I love them!

What do you tell entities from other planets and dimensions about your job: I try to explain it in the simplest terms and from the ground up. I remember what it's like to know nothing of the strange world of publishing.

What are your favorite books, movies, TV shows, and why: *Fugitive Pieces* by Anne Michaels, anything by Virginia Woolf, *Zero, Three, Bravo* by Mariana Gosnell, *Cowboys Are My Weakness* by Pam Houston, any of the books by Emily Carr, who was just as good a writer as she was a painter, Philip Pullman's *His Dark Materials* trilogy.

TV: *The Vicar of Dibley*, the new *Doctor Who*, *Ace of Cakes*.

What do they all, fiction and nonfiction alike, have in common? GREAT characters!

What do you like best about your clients, and the editors and publishers you work with: I'm lucky to be in contact, every day, with people who love books and are dedicated to the art and craft of writing.

You're welcome to share your thoughts and sentiments about the business of writing and publishing: It's a tough business, and there's no mistaking the fact that it is a business, but there's always room for enthusiasm and passion. It's an honor to be a part of the industry; sounds hokey, but it's true.

CREATIVE CONVERGENCE

11040 Santa Monica Blvd., Suite 200, Los Angeles, CA 90025

310-954-8480   fax: 310-954-8481

www.creativecvg.com

Agent's name: Philippa Burgess

Born: October 1974 in Trenton, New Jersey.

Education: Grew up in Upper Montclair, New Jersey and New York City. Graduated from USC: studied international relations and cinema-television.

Career history or story: Started at ICM and went on to found boutique literary management company that evolved into Creative Convergence.

Subjects and categories you are interested in agenting, including fiction and nonfiction: We represent and co-represent published literary properties to bring to film and television, as well as work with branded clients to develop literary properties that are part of a larger media brand.

What would you do if you weren't agenting: We love entertainment, media and entrepreneurship. When we are not representing clients or packaging projects, we are writing, teaching, and speaking to writers and content creators.

What's the best way for fiction writers to solicit your interest: Referrals, published, credited, or branded.

What's the best way for nonfiction writers to solicit your interest: Referrals, published, credited, or branded.

Do you charge reading or any upfront fees: Our literary management department represents screenwriters and directors on commission only. Our production department is paid fee for services and is paid by the studio. Our entertainment consulting services provides brand development and brand management for business endeavors that can be a combination of fees, commissions, or profit participation depending on the nature of the services rendered, that often include PR, media and business development. We also offer a brand development course entitled "Your Signature Story: From Content Creator to Media Brand" for a nominal fee.

In your experience, what are the most common pitching mistakes writers make: Lack clarity about what the author brings to the story from their own experience; what they bring to the table in terms of knowledge about the industry; who their audience is and how this story is relevant to them; what type of platform they are building to reach and remain engaged with their audience.

Describe the client from hell, even if you don't have any: A general lack of respect for our time and the realities of the business is a turn-off. Not to mention a gross sense of entitlement that [is] often tied to a lack of ability or interest in doing their work to deliver a quality product.

What's your definition of a great client: Someone who takes responsibility for doing their work well, and continues to grow in their craft, relationships, and understanding of the business. We want a client to see our relationship as a team effort.

How can writers increase the odds that you will offer representation: Give us something amazing. Get it to us through a referral. Otherwise keep growing and learning, and it will come back around if it really is the right match.

Why did you become an agent, and how did you become one: Started at ICM and really liked it but saw there was a knowledge gap so I moved into management. The business kept changing and I found the knowledge gap was widening and a lot more people needed the information and coaching, specifically media brands. We retained our literary management while expanding into film and television production and entertainment consulting.

Describe to someone from another planet what you do as an agent: We take books and package them for film and television. Specifically in television we are looking for properties that we can package for network and cable series. We also look to work with content creators that are media brands that we can work to move their content across media platforms.

How do you feel about editors and publishers: We can only manage so many relationships, so we don't actually deal very often with editors and publishers. Rather we work through literary agents when it comes to the publishing side of things. Being an entertainment company in Los Angeles we work closely with the equivalent in film and television.

How do you feel about writers: We love the smart ones! No really, we are passionate about writers and content creators. Beyond representing clients, packaging literary properties, or managing media brands, we look to be a resource to writers are frequently found at writers conferences or teaching classes about the business.

What do you see in the near future for book publishing: Film, television, media, and publishing all need each other more than ever before. There is going to be a lot more cooperation between these different arenas of entertainment and media. However, the author needs to recognize that these professionals don't all speak the same language and thus needs to take a greater responsibility for moving their message across media platforms (and in doing so well, will stand to gain a lot more attention and regard from all parties).

In your opinion, what do editors think of you: We'd like to think that industry professionals see us as professional, resourceful, and forthright.

On a personal non-professional level, what do you think people think of you: We'd like to think that people see us as professional, resourceful, and forthright.

What are some representative titles that you have sold: *52 Fights* by Jennifer Jeanne Patterson (Penguin/Putnam), sold and produced as a TV pilot for ABC/Touchstone; *Men's Guide to the Women's Bathroom* (HarperCollins), sold as a TV pilot to CBS/Paramount (slated for production); *Thieves of Baghdad* (Bloomsbury) sold as a feature film to Warner Brothers with our client Jonathan Hunt co-producing; *They Come Back*, an original script written by Gary Boulton-Brown sold and produced for Lifetime; *Queensize*, an original script written by Rod Johnson sold to Lifetime (slated for production).

CROSSMAN LITERARY AGENCY

65 East Scott Street, Suite 12E, Chicago, IL 60610

312-664-6470   fax: 312-664-7137

email: crossmanla@aol.com

Agent's name: Nancy Crossman
Born: Chicago, Illinois.
Education: BA with honors, English literature, DePaul University, Northwestern University School of Education.
Career history: Vice president, editorial director, associate publisher: Contemporary Books, Inc. 1979–1997.
Hobbies/personal interests: Golf, travel, classical music.
Categories/subjects that you are most enthusiastic about agenting: General nonfiction, self-improvement, health, medicine, nutrition, fitness, cooking, sports, women's issues, pop culture, travel, business, parenting.
What you don't want to agent: Children's, young adult titles, poetry.
If you were not an agent, what might you be doing instead: Teaching, coaching girls' sports.
What's the best way for writers to solicit your interest: Query with synopsis and SASE.
Do you charge reading or management fees: No reading fees.
How would you describe the perfect client: Dream clients are professional and talented, work as team players and are passionate about their work.
How and why did you ever become an agent: After 18 years as the director of a publishing house, I left so that I could work on a variety of projects that personally interested me, as well as have more time to spend with my children.
What, if anything, can a writer do to increase the odds of your becoming his or her agent: Generate solid, convincing proposals. Be patient and have a good sense of humor.

Please list representative titles you have sold: *The Cake Mix Doctor* Cookbook Series (Workman); *Rules Brittania* (St. Martin's); *The Pocket Parent* (Workman); *The Petit Appetit* (Perigee Penguin); *What Your Doctor May Not Tell You About Fibrosis* (Warner).

CS INTERNATIONAL LITERARY AGENCY

43 West 39th St., New York, NY 10018

212-921-1610

www.csliterary.com   email: csliterary@aol.com

Agent's name: Cynthia Neeseman

Education: Columbia University.

Subjects and categories you are interested in agenting, including fiction and nonfiction: Fiction, nonfiction, screenplays.

Subjects and categories writers shouldn't even bother pitching to you: Pornography.

What would you do if you weren't agenting: Real estate and writing.

What's the best way for fiction writers to solicit your interest: Send short query letters that grab one's attention. Include telephone numbers, if available, as well as email and snail mail addresses. I like to talk to potential clients over the phone as a fast and efficient way to determine whether we will connect and be able to work together.

What's the best way for nonfiction writers to solicit your interest: See above.

Do you charge reading or any upfront fees: I charge reading fees if I believe a writer might need revision and/or I have doubts about marketability of subject matter and/or interest in submitted subject. I expect a writer to pay for expenses as they occur. My fees are very fair and moderate. I analyze manuscripts and screenplays as well as agenting because many writers benefit from revision. I like to help writers produce material that will sell and therefore I discuss all aspects of their efforts including marketability up front. It saves time and effort. I also read partial manuscripts. Sometimes a smaller first submission can be beneficial.

In your experience, what are the most common pitching mistakes writers make: They have not mastered the art of being succinct but pithy. In short, they ramble.

Why did you become an agent, and how did you become one: I have always been interested in writing and obtaining interesting information. I was a foreign correspondent and worked for a literary agent.

How do you feel about writers: Writers are wonderful.

What do you see in the near future for book publishing: More and more self-publishing. Marketing is often the secret to becoming a successful writer.

D4EO LITERARY AGENCY

7 Indian Valley Road, Weston, CT 06883

203-544-7180   fax: 203-544-7160

email: d4eo@optonline.net

Agents' names: Robert G. (Bob) Diforio, Mandy Hubbard, mandy@d4eo .com, www.mandyhubbard.com

The following information pertains to Robert Diforio.

Born: March 19, 1940; Mamaroneck, New York.

Education: Williams College 1964, Advanced Management Program (AMP) at Harvard Business School 1978.

Career history: Kable News Company 1964–1972; book and magazine sales rep 1964–1966, manager, paperback Books Division 1966, VP book sales 1969; New American Library 1972–1989, VP general sales manager 1972–1974, senior VP marketing director 1975–1978, executive VP 1979, president, publisher 1980, chairman and CEO 1981–1989; founded D4EO Literary Agency 1989.

Hobbies/personal interests: Golf.

Categories/subjects that you are most enthusiastic about agenting: Commercial fiction and nonfiction.

What you don't want to agent: Anything I don't like.

If you were not an agent, what might you be doing instead: Publisher.

What's the best way for writers to solicit your interest: Recommendation from a publisher or client.

Do you charge reading or management fees: No.

How and why did you ever become an agent: As a publisher I loved launching new writers, now I do it as an agent.

What, if anything, can a writer do to increase the odds that you will become his or her agent: Send me a MS that I absolutely love.

How would you describe to someone (or something) from another planet what it is that you do as an agent: I find the right editor/publisher for my client's work.

Please list representative titles you have sold: *To Sin With a Scoundrel, To Surrender to a Rogue +1* (Mira); *The Hunt Chronicles trilogy* (Tor and Droemer Knaur); *Game Over trilogy* (Tor); *Libertine's Kiss* (Harlequin); *Boca Knights and Boca Mournings* (Tor), *Reindeer Christmas* and *The Very Best Pumpkin* (Paula Wiseman/S&S); *Betrayed, Captured, Escape, Malice, Counterplay, Hoax, Fury* (all of the Butch Karp legal thrillers by Roberth Tanenbaum; Vanguard/Atria Books/ Pocket Books); *Havoc, Deep Fire Rising, River of Ruin, Medusa Stone, Pandora's Curse, Charon's Landing, Vulcan's Forge* (Dutton/NAL); *Felony Murder, Shoot the Moon, Flat Lake in Winter, Irreparable Damage, Fog* (St. Martin's Press); *My*

Name Is Jillian Gray (Albin Michel); *The Mermaid's Song* (Delacort); *The 10th Case*, *Bronx Justice* and *Depraved Indifference* (Mira); *Anxiety Free* and *Here Comes the Sun* (Hay House); *Putting My Way* [Jack Nicklaus, Ken Bowden] (John Wiley & Sons); *Debates on Science*, seven-book series (Facts on File); *The Words You Should Know to Sound Smart* (Adams Media); *Don't Be That Boss* (John Wiley); *Age of Fire* (St. Martin's); Michael Phelps biography (St. Martin's); *S.K.I.R.T.S. in the Boardroom* (John Wiley); *Undress for Success* (John Wiley); *Murder for Hire* (St. Martin's); *The CIG to Biology* (Alpha); *Roux Memories Cookbook* and *Knack Chinese Cooking* (Globe Pequot); *Everything Soup, Stew & Chili* (Adams Media), *Knack Drums* (Globe Pequot); *Starting a Web Based Business* (Adams Media); *The Wealthy Freelancer* (Adams Media); *Bear Trap* (foreign sales China, Taiwan; Korea & Poland); *Hyper-performance* (Jossey Bass); *New Résumé New Career* (Alpha Books); *The Little Book of Bullet-Proof Investing* (John Wiley); *Betrayal* (Union Square Press); *Reel Terror* (St. Martin's Press); *Teeing Off* (Triumph Books); *Everything I Needed to Know I Learned at McDonald's* (McGraw-Hill); *Accidental Landlord* and *Accidental Tycoon* (Alpha Books); *The Faraway Fairies* (Hatchette Australia); *Reindeer Christmas* (Paula Wiseman/Simon & Schuster); *The History of Medicine* and *Controversies in Science* and *Ocean Sciences*, multi-book series (Facts on File); *Crazy Love, Cruising* (Pocket Books); *Expired, Criss Cross, Out a Order* (Kensington); *The Tiger's Mistress, Kiss of Spice* (Pocket Books); *Hellions* (Warner); *Take Me Out of the Bathtub, I'm Still Here in the Bathtub* (Margaret McElderry); *McKeag's Mountain, Wolf Mountain, Stranahan, Gavagan, O'Rourke's Revenge* (Kensington); *House of Pain, Behold a Pale Horse* (Tor); *The Last Pope* (Sourcebooks); *Via Magna*—Spain, *DiFel*—Portugal, *Eddie's World, Jimmy Bench Press, Charlie Opera, Cheapskates* (Carroll & Graf + UK and Russia sales); *Shakedown* (Pegasus); *Rift Zone* (Tor); *4th & Fixed* (Sourcebooks); *Dangerous Deceptions* (NAL); *Red Meat Cures Cancer* (Vintage); *Heretic, The Templar Chronicles* (Pocket Books); *Droemer-Knaur*—Germany, *Alfaret*—Russia, *Pleasure Control* Trilogy (Avon Red); *Allure Author's Anthology* (Avon Red); *Sexy Beast, Hell Kat, Inferno* (Aphrodisia); *Wild Wild Women of the West* (Aphrodisia); *Vampire Erotica 1* and *2* (Avon Red); *Solomon's Code, The Voynich Code* (sales in Russia, Bulgaria, Brazil); *The Worry Cure* (Harmony Books); *Application Suicide* (Gotham); *Madscam* (Entrepreneur Press); *Commissions at Risk*—Dearborn (Kaplan); *How to Earn a Living Teaching On Line* (John Wiley); *The Secret of Hogan's Swing* (John Wiley); *The Blog Book* (Nelson Business); *The Expert's Guide to Poker Tells* (Triumph); *Collaborative Divorce* (Nolo); *The Trans Fat Free Kitchen* (HCI); *Feeding Your Kids Right* (Career Press); *Harriet Roth's Fat Counter* (NAL); *You Lost Them at Hello* (AMACOM); *Interactive Selling* (Career Press); *American*

Geisha (Hunter House); *Presentation SOS* (Warner Books); *Their Last Words—A Tribute to Soldiers Who Lost Their Lives in Iraq* (Berkley Books); *Bringing the Thunder* (Stackpole); *Thunderhorse Six* (Citadel); *Cashing In on the Coming Real Estate Crash* (John Wiley); *Operation Black Biscuit* (Lyons Press); *Living Longer, Learning Later* (Sentient); *The S Factor: Sheila Kelley's Strip Workouts for Every Woman* (Workman Publishing); *Heart of the Storm* (John Wiley); *Leadership Secrets of the World's Best CEOs* (Dearborn); *That's Not in My Science Book* (Taylor Trade Publishing); *Divorce Guide for Fathers: Nurturing the Extended Family* (Nolo); *Stop the Show!* (Thunder Mouth); *My Year in the Blogosphere* (Nelson Business Books); *The Cosmic Laws of Golf* (Berkley); *Seeing Lessons* (John Wiley); *The Gal's Got Bite* (St. Martin's Press); *Start Small Finish Big* (Warner); Morgan Freeman Bio (Barricade Books); *Living Well with Endometriosis* (Collins Reference); *Sex Secrets of Escorts* (Alpha Books); Ellen Degeneres updated edition (Citadel/Kensington); *Living Well with Anxiety* (HarperResource); *Living Well with Menopause* (Collins Reference); *Business Lunchatations* (Chamberlain Bros.); *Sell Your Own Home* (Career Press); *The Science Teacher's Almanac* (John Wiley & Sons); *Fire Someone Today* (Nelson Books); *Out of the Pens of Kids* (Sasquatch Books); *The Golden State of Golf* (Sports Media); *Odyssey of an Eavesdropper* (Carroll & Graf); *The Future of Golf* (Sasquatch); *Major Memories Minor Moments* (Lyons Press); *ABLE!: One Company's Loyal, Disabled Workers Show That Love and Compassion Makes Good Business Sense* (BenBella Books); *Don't Chew Jesus* (BenBella Books); *Magnetic Selling* (AMACOM); *Winning the Interview Game—Everything You Need to Know to Land the Job* (AMACOM); *Rosie O'Donnell* (Carroll & Graf); *Eating with Your Anorexic* (McGraw-Hill/Contemporary); *The Mojo Triangle: A Cultural History of American Music* (Schirmer); *Life Isn't Fair* (Sourcebooks); *Profitable Candlestick Trading* (John Wiley); *Getting Started as a Freelance Writer* (Filbert); *From Science Fiction to Science Fantasy* (Ben Bella); *Real World Software Testing* (Charles River Media); *Howard Dean: In His Own Words* (Rogak St. Martin's Press instant book); *Getting Entrepreneurial* (John Wiley); *I'm Right, You're Wrong, Now What?* (Sourcebooks); Diana Riggs Biography (BenBella Books); *People, Performance and Pay, The Hay Compensation Guide* (The Free Press); *Google Earth for Dummies, The PIG to Texas Hold'em, The PIG to Interviews, The PIG to Potty Training the Reluctant Child; The Pig to Stock Picking; The CIG to Real Estate Basics, The CIG to Designing Your Own Home, The CIG to Faith, The CIG to Party Plan Selling, The CIG to Success as a Mortgage Broker, The CIG to Successful Interviews, The CIG to Successful Business Plans, The CIG to Portrait Photography.*

The following information pertains to Mandy Hubbard.

When and where you were born: Enumclaw, Washington.

Your formal education: Associate of Arts Degree, Green River Community College.

Your professional story: Mandy Hubbard began her career in publishing on the other side of the desk: as an author. Her titles include *Prada & Prejudice* (Razorbill/Penguin, 2009); *Driven* (Harlequin, 2010); *You Wish* (Razorbill/Penguin, 2010); and *Shattered* (Flux, 2011). She interned with The Bent Agency before joining D4EO Literary, where she is now building a list of middle-grade and young-adult fiction.

Your personal interests/hobbies: Hiking, reading, horseback riding, ATVs, camping.

The subjects and categories you tend to agent: middle-grade and young-adult fiction.

What writers shouldn't even try pitching to you: Nonfiction, books for the adult market, poetry, screenplays, picture books.

What would you have been, or be, if not an agent: I am currently—and always will be—an author.

Do you charge fees or offer fee-based services: No.

Approximately ten titles you recently sold: As a new agent, I am currently building my list.

Why did you choose to become an agent and how did it happen: As an author, I've had many, many writers come to me for advice. This industry is crazy and maddening and so dang hard to break into. I really love trying to play tour guide and help writers as much as I can. Prior to becoming an agent, I worked heavily on revising manuscripts with authors I truly believed in. A few of my friends nearly rewrote their novel with my advice, and ended up signing an agent quite quickly afterward. At some point, I realized that if I was an agent, I wouldn't have to "give up" playing tour guide—I could continue guiding them throughout their career. Interning with The Bent Agency confirmed that desire for me.

How do you really feel about writers: I love them, of course! My closest friends are writers or published authors.

How do you really feel about editors and publishers: Editors are so much like me—they share the same passion for books. They may seem like the bad guys when they are rejecting a project, but they very much want to find the next amazing project.

Describe your job to a visitor from another planet, or a moron you just met at a bar: I get to spend all day with the written word—whether that means screening new queries or working with clients on revisions or pitching exciting projects to editors. Plus, I spend copious amounts of time reading published works in order to say up on market trends.

What are your favorite books, TV shows, movies, and why: Books: *The Season* by Sarah Maclean, *A Match Made in High School* by Kristin Walker, *Hate List* by Jennifer Brown, *Amaranth Enchantment* by Julie Berry, *Wintergirls* by Laurie Halse Anderson, *Hunger Games* by Suzanne Collins...I could go on forever. Movies: I am forever quoting *Empire Records*. There's just something addictive about it. Television: *Veronica Mars* (love her snarky quips!); *House* (I'm sensing a snarky quip trend…); and *The OC* (love the romance and drama!).

Describe the writer/client from hell: Someone who is inflexible with their craft. You simply must be open to revision if you expect to find success in this industry. Work with me (and later, your editor) on polishing your manuscript and meet your deadlines and we'll be in good shape.

Describe yourself: Driven, enthusiastic, hard-working. My debut novel, *Prada & Prejudice*, was rejected 26 times. I started over from scratch and totally rewrote it, and then we received two offers. If I believe in your project, I'll work just as hard on selling your manuscript as I did on breaking into this industry.

Describe the publisher and/or editor from hell: There are two sorts of editors who can be difficult to work with: the one who is adamant that things be done a certain way—and demands that the revisions be done exactly as they've described—and an editor who waffles, putting the writer through round after round of revisions, sometimes undoing the very things they asked for the first time.

Describe hell: An eternal waiting room with no books to read. Seriously, I can sit around all day every day if I can read. But remove the books from the equation and I'm the most fidgety, irritable person ever.

What are your preferred ways for writers to pitch you: E-queries! I do not accept snail mail queries at all.

Do you think the e-readers and similar devices will significantly change the publishing business: I do think e-readers are going to have a major impact on the industry, but I, personally, believe it'll be decades before we really know what to make of them. At the risk of having rocks thrown at me, I own a Kindle and I love it. I could not live without it. But I don't use it for published books (I still like the paper ones. I collect them like trophies), I use it for manuscripts. I can have dozens of them loaded onto the Kindle and read them anywhere, rather than be tied to a computer.

Are you optimistic, pessimistic, neutral, or catatonic about the book business into the knowable future: Optimistic. I'm a pretty glass-half-full sort of person. This industry will always exist in some form or another. As long as we're flexible and adjust to the changing times, we can find success. It's not like it was ever an easy business to begin with!

Explain what you like and don't like about your job: My favorite part is falling in love with a new manuscript. There are times I have butterflies and am nearly holding my breath for the hours it takes to read it. It's a total adrenaline rush to find something great. My least favorite parts: rejecting authors; being one of a half-dozen agents to love a manuscript and not being the one the writer picks for representation; sharing rejections with authors.

Describe a book you might like writing: Since I'm also an author, I already write the books I want to write.

DANIEL LITERARY GROUP

1701 Kingsbury Dr., Ste 100, Nashville, TN 37215
615-730-8207
www.danielliterarygroup.com   email: submissions@danielliterarygroup.com

Agent's name: Greg Daniel

Born: Lubbock, Texas.

Education: BA, Wheaton College (Communications); MA, *summa cum laude,* Trinity Divinity School (Theology).

Career story: I founded Daniel Literary Group in April 2007 after more than ten years in publishing, six of which were at the executive level at Thomas Nelson Publishers, the largest Christian publisher in the world. Most recently I was vice president and associate publisher for W Publishing Group (formerly Word Publishing), a trade-book division of Thomas Nelson.

Hobbies and special personal interests: Ultra endurance cycling, golf, motorcycling, crosswords, taxi driver for my kids.

Subjects and categories you like to agent: Nonfiction areas: Biography/autobiography; business/economics; child guidance/parenting; current affairs; health/medicine; history; how-to; humor/satire; memoirs; nature/environment; popular culture; religious/inspirational; self-help/personal improvement; sports; theater/film; women's issues. Fiction areas: Action/adventure; contemporary issues; detective/police/crime; family saga; historical; humor/satire; literary; mainstream/contemporary; mystery/suspense; religious/inspirational; thriller; young adult.

Subjects and categories writers shouldn't bother pitching to you: Poetry, romance, science fiction, children's, screenplays, short stories, erotica.

What might you be doing if you weren't agenting: Nuclear physicist or gangster rapper.

What's the most effective ways for writers to grab your attention: Do your homework on what I represent and don't represent, and follow my submission guidelines. Sounds basic, but amazingly, 90 percent of the queries I receive ignore this advice. And please don't tell me that your Aunt Ethel or your pet cat read your manuscript and told you it was the most brilliant thing they'd ever read.

Do you charge fees separate from your commission, or offer non-agenting fee-based services: No.

What are representative titles you have sold to publishers: *Green Gospel* (HarperOne); *Peaches and Daddy* (Overlook Press); *The Collapse of Distinction* (Thomas Nelson); *My Life as a Holy Roller* (WaterBrook/Multnomah Press); *Finding God in the Other* (Jossey-Bass/Wiley); *Wild Things* (Tyndale House); *The Sacredness of Questioning Everything* (Zondervan); *Reimagining Church* (Cook); *Holy*

Stability (Paraclete); *Saints in Limbo* (WaterBrook/Multnomah Press); *Making the World Human Again* (Zondervan).

Why did you become an agent, and how did you become one: I loved being an editor and publisher, but I always envied the diversity of writers that an agent could choose to work with and the ability to concentrate on a smaller group of authors, building their careers and brands. So I finally took the plunge and left life as an editor/publisher to launch my own agency. It's been everything I hoped it would be.

What are your favorite books, movies, TV shows, and why: I love books, TV shows, and movies that are entertaining on one level but with a deeper level of meaning that keep me pondering them for days afterward. Movies such as *Seven Samurai, Babette's Feast, The Godfather,* and *Lars and the Real Girl.* And books such as *Peace Like a River, The Road, Brother to a Dragonfly,* and anything by Frederick Buechner.

How would you describe the writer from hell: One with horns, a tail, and a pitchfork.

What do you like best about your clients, and the editors and publishers you work with: Book people, whether they're authors or editors, are absolutely the greatest group of people in the world to hang out with. Smart, witty, interesting, and fresh minty breath.

LIZA DAWSON ASSOCIATES

350 7th Avenue, Suite 2003, New York, NY 10001

212-465-9071   fax: 212-947-0460

www.lizadawsonassociates.com

Agents' names: Liza Dawson, queryLiza@lizadawsonassociates.com; Caitlin Blasdell, queryCaitlin@lizadawsonassociates.com; Anna Olswanger, queryAnna@lizadawsonassociates.com; Karen E. Quinones Miller, queryKaren@lizadawsonassociates.com; Havis Dawson, queryHavis@lizadawsonassociates.com; Victoria Horn, queryVictoria@lizadawsonassociates.com

The following information pertains to Liza Dawson.

Education: BA in history, Duke University; graduate of Radcliffe's Publishing Procedure Course.

Career history or story: Founded Liza Dawson Associates in 1998 after twenty years as executive editor and vice president at William Morrow and Putnam.

Hobbies, interests: Local and national politics, archaeology, gardening, nagging spacey teenagers.

Subjects and categories you are interested in agenting, including fiction and nonfiction: Plot-driven literary fiction; upscale historicals and mysteries; pacey, well-textured thrillers; multicultural fiction written in a distinctive, memorable voice; parenting books by authors with platforms; history (especially ancient) written by excellent writers; psychology that says something fresh; politics with a point of view; narrative nonfiction, travel, and memoirs written in a lively, moving tone which take you someplace unexpected.

Subjects and categories writers shouldn't even bother pitching to you: Poetry, Westerns, science fiction.

What would you do if you weren't agenting: Digging for ancient treasure in Italy.

What's the best way for writers to solicit your interest: Query via snail mail or email.

Do you charge reading or any upfront fees: No reading fee.

What's your definition of a great client: A brilliant, funny, focused, fearless workaholic with lots of friends in the media.

What are some representative titles that you have sold: *Sister Mine* by Tawni O'Dell (Crown); *The Genius* by Jesse Kellerman (Putnam); *Mozart and the Whale: An Asperger's Love Story* by Jerry and Mary Newport; *Zeus: Traveling through Greece with the God of Gods* by Tom Stone (Bloomsbury); *The Darker Side* by Cody McFadyen (Bantam); *The Guernsey Literary and Potato Peel Pie Society* by Mary Ann Shaffer (Dial); *Passin'* by Karen E. Quinones Miller (Grand Central).

The following information pertains to Caitlin Blasdell.

Education: BA, Williams College.

Career history or story: Senior editor at Harper and Avon. With the agency since 2002.

Hobbies, interests: In the dim past, before being the mother of three small boys, I remember liking cross-country skiing, perennial gardening, baking, and art history.

Subjects and categories you are interested in agenting, including fiction and nonfiction: Science fiction, fantasy (for both adults and young adults), parenting, business, thrillers, and women's fiction.

Subjects and categories writers shouldn't even bother pitching to you: Horror, especially any books where small children die brutally; Westerns, poetry, cookbooks, business.

What would you do if you weren't agenting: Organizing quality flexible child care for working mothers.

What's the best way for writers to solicit your interest: Query via snail mail or email.

Do you charge reading or any upfront fees: No reading fee.

What are some representative titles that you have sold: *Saturn's Children* by Charles Stross (Berkeley); *A Writer's Coach: An Editor's Guide to Words that Work* by Jack Hart (Pantheon).

The following information pertains to Anna Olswanger.

Education: BA, Phi Beta Kappa, Rhodes College; MA, University of Memphis; Certificate in Book Publishing, NYU.

Career history or story: With the agency since 2005. Coordinates the Jewish

Children's Book Writers' Conference every fall at the 92nd Street Y. Teaches business writing at the Center for Training and Education at Johns Hopkins University and writing for physicians at Stony Brook University Hospital. Author of a children's book. She recently launched www.Host-a-Jewish-Book-Author.com.

Hobbies, interests: Birds, fine art, Israel.

Subjects and categories you are interested in agenting, including fiction and nonfiction: Gift books for adults, young-adult fiction and nonfiction, children's illustrated books, and Judaica.

Subjects and categories writers shouldn't even bother pitching to you: Horror, occult, military/war, poetry, short story collections, government/politics, technical, textbooks.

What would you do if you weren't agenting: Building tree houses, traveling, photographing and painting, writing.

What's the best way for writers to solicit your interest: Query via snail mail or email.

Do you charge reading or any upfront fees: No reading fee.

What are some representative titles that you have sold: *The Jewish Woman's Weekly Planner 2010* (Pomegranate); *Ant & Grasshopper* (McElderry/Simon & Schuster), *Sylvie* (Random House Children's Books).

The following information pertains to **Karen E. Quinones Miller.**

Education: BA in journalism, Temple University.

Career history or story: With the agency since 2006; author of five Essence bestselling novels; a client since 2002.

Hobbies, interests: National politics, Harlem Renaissance.

Subjects and categories you are interested in agenting, including fiction and nonfiction: Science fiction, fantasy (for both adults and young adults), parenting, business, thrillers, and women's fiction.

Subjects and categories writers shouldn't even bother pitching to you: Poetry.

What would you do if you weren't agenting: Running a luxury bed and breakfast in Harlem.

What's the best way for writers to solicit your interest: Query via snail mail or email.

Do you charge reading or any upfront fees: No reading fee.

What are some representative titles that you have sold: *A Rich Man's Baby* by Daaimah Poole; *All I Want Is Everything* (Kensington); *Hiding in Hip-Hop* (Atria); *We Take This Man* (Grand Central) co-agented with Audra Barrett of Audra Barrett Books; *Diamond Playgirls* (Kensington).

The following information pertains to **Havis Dawson.**

Education: BA, Duke University.

Career history or story: Joined Liza Dawson Associates after twenty years of editing business-trade magazines.

Hobbies, interests: Smoking cigars and driving cheap, clapped-out sports cars (preferably doing both simultaneously).

Subjects and categories you are interested in agenting, including fiction and

nonfiction: Military memoirs, southern fiction, fantasy, science fiction, thrillers, business and practical books as wells as spiritual books.

Subjects and categories writers shouldn't even bother pitching to you: Photo books, poetry, sports.

What would you do if you weren't agenting: The pleasantly sinew-taxing chores of gardening: digging holes, chopping tree roots, rolling big stones...

What's the best way for writers to solicit your interest: Query via snail mail or email.

Do you charge reading or any upfront fees: No reading fee.

What are some representative titles that you have sold: *Flying Through Midnight: A Pilot's Dramatic Story of His Secret Missions Over Laos During the Vietnam War* by John T. Halliday (Scribner); *Law of Attraction: The Science of Attracting More of What You Want and Less of What You Don't* by Michael J. Losier (Grand Central)—co-agented with L. Dawson.

The following information pertains to Victoria Horn.

Education: BA in English, Grinnell College.

Career history or story: Victoria came to Liza Dawson Associates in April, 2008 after two years with Trident Media Group as an assistant.

Subjects and categories you are interested in agenting, including fiction and nonfiction: YA fiction, adult women's fiction, romance and literary fiction. She can't get enough truly well done magical realism and is a sucker for great historical novels. Victoria is open to narrative nonfiction, travel, memoir, pop culture or social science takes on current debates. She looks for sharp humor in unexpected places, a story that places her firmly in another world, and characters she can't leave behind. She loves strong voices and high concept hooks, or really well written stories about timeless subjects.

What's the best way for writers to solicit your interest: Query via snail mail or email.

Do you charge reading or any upfront fees: No reading fee.

THE JENNIFER DECHIARA LITERARY AGENCY

31 East 32nd Street, Suite 300, New York, NY 10016

212-481-8484 ext. 362 fax: 212-481-9582

www.jdlit.com   email: jenndec@aol.com

Agents' names: Jennifer DeChiara, Stephen Fraser

Born: New York, New York.

Career history: Freelance book editor for Simon & Schuster, and Random House; writing consultant for several major New York City corporations; literary agent with Perkins, Rubie Literary Agency and the Peter Rubie Literary Agency; founded the Jennifer DeChiara Literary Agency in 2001.

Hobbies/personal interests: Reading, movies, music, ballet, photography, sports, travel.

Categories/subjects that you are most enthusiastic about agenting: Children's books (picture books, middle grade, young adult), literary fiction, commercial fiction, chick lit, celebrity bios, mysteries/thrillers, self-help, parenting, humor, pop-culture; in general almost any well-written book, either fiction or nonfiction.

What you don't want to agent: Romance, erotica/porn, horror, science fiction, poetry.

What's the best way for writers to solicit your interest: Email queries only, with "Query" in the subject line of the email. No attachments. Go to our website for details: www.jdlit.com

Do you charge reading or management fees: No.

Can you provide an approximation by percent of what you tend to represent by category: Children's books: 50 percent, adult fiction: 25 percent, adult non-fiction: 25 percent.

What are the most common mistakes writers make when pitching you: Phoning or faxing queries; calling to check that we received query letter or manuscript; expecting to meet me or showing up uninvited before I've agreed to represent them; interviewing me instead of the other way around; someone who raves about their material when the work has to speak for itself; someone who is more concerned about possible movie deals and marketing angles and the prestige of being an author rather than the actual writing; queries and manuscripts that are poorly written or that have typos; not sending an SASE.

How would you describe the client from hell: Someone who calls or emails constantly for news; expects a phone call when there's nothing to discuss; expects me to perform according to their timetable; has no knowledge of the publishing business and doesn't think it's their job to learn; doesn't want to work on next book until the first one is sold; can't accept rejection or criticism; needs a lot of hand-holding; has a negative attitude; fails to work as part of a team. Every once in a while a Client from hell slips into the agency, but once they show us their horns, we send them back to the inferno.

How would you describe the perfect client: Someone who is passionate about writing; thoroughly professional; appreciative and understanding of my efforts; and who works as part of a team.

How would you describe to someone (or something) from another planet what it is that you do as an agent: I help make dreams come true.

Please list representative titles you have sold: *Naptime for Barney* by Danny Sit (Sterling Publishing); *Heart of a Shepherd* by Rosanne Parry (Random House); *The Chosen One* by Carol Lynch Williams (St. Martin's Press); *A Glimpse Is All I Can Stand* by Carol Lynch Williams (Simon & Schuster); *The Clockmaker's Grimoire* by Matthew Kirby (Scholastic); *The Screwed-Up Life of Charlie the Second* by Drew Ferguson (Kensington Publishing); *Geography Club* by Brent Hartinger (HarperCollins); *The 30-Day Heartbreak Cure* by Catherine Hickland (Simon & Schuster); *His Cold Feet* by Andrea Passman Candell (St. Martin's Press); *The*

Ten-Minute Sexual Solution by Dr. Darcy Luadzers, PhD (Hatherleigh Press); *The Write-Brain Workbook* by Bonnie Neubauer (Writer's Digest).

DEFIORE AND COMPANY

97 E. 19th Street, 3rd Floor, New York, NY 10003

Agent's name: Brian DeFiore

Born: August 1956, Brooklyn, New York.

Education: BA, S.U.N.Y. at New Paltz and Queens College.

Career history: 1999–Present: president, DeFiore and Co.; 1997–1998: SVP and publisher, Villard Books, Random House; 1992–1997: VP and editor-in-chief, Hyperion; 1988–1992: senior editor/VP and editorial director, Dell/Delacorte Press; 1983–1988: editor, St. Martin's Press.

Hobbies/personal interests: Movies, theater, cycling, cooking, being a good dad to my daughters.

Categories/subjects that you are most enthusiastic about agenting: Intelligent commercial fiction, suspense fiction, narrative nonfiction, psychology/self-help, business, humor, virtually anything that is written beautifully.

What you don't want to agent: Category romance, poetry, computer books, anything written pedantically.

If you were not an agent, what might you be doing instead: Psychotherapy.

What's the best way for writers to solicit your interest: A drop-dead brilliant letter (sent by mail or email). Publishing is a medium about the written word; a persuasively written letter indicates the right sort of talent. A sloppy or trite letter indicates the opposite.

Do you charge reading or management fees: No.

Can you provide an approximation by percent of what you tend to represent by category: Fiction: 35 percent, children's: 10 percent, nonfiction: 55 percent.

What are the most common mistakes writers make when pitching you: Pitching several books at once. Telling me how many other agents and/or publishers loved their work, but simply aren't taking new clients (yes, people really do this!).

How would you describe the client from hell: Someone who hears but doesn't listen. Someone who thinks an agent's job is solely to bully publishers. Someone who has a cynical "I'll write whatever sells" attitude about their work.

How would you describe the perfect client: Someone whose work inspires me, and who respects and appreciates my role in the process.

How and why did you ever become an agent: After 18 years on the publishing and editorial side of the business, I was ready for a more entrepreneurial challenge. I love the publishing process, but I felt that too much of my time was spent on corporate posturing and not enough on books and authors. Now I can have it both ways.

What, if anything, can a writer do to increase the odds of your becoming his or her agent: Write brilliantly. There's not much else. Don't send me something until it's absolutely as good as it possibly can be.

How would you describe to someone (or something) from another planet what it is that you do as an agent: I search for talented authors. Using my experience as a publisher, I work with my clients to get their submission material (manuscript or proposal) into the best possible shape to elicit a positive response from publishers. I orchestrate the sale to get the best combination of deal points and publishing house for the project. I negotiate the contract. I sell the subsidiary rights to those projects, often in concert with co-agents in Los Angeles and cities around the world. I oversee the publication effort and make sure the publisher is doing what needs to be done. I interpret the publisher's business needs for the author and vice versa. I strategize with my clients to develop their careers.

Do you have any particular opinions or impressions of editors and publishers: I admire the work they do; indeed I did it myself for several years. I think most editors and publishers have their hearts firmly planted in the right place. I wish that their corporate masters gave them more time and support to do their jobs well. They are under such pressure these last few years that editorial nurturing of authors has evolved into an obsessive quest for "the next big thing." It's always lovely to have "the next big thing," but I've yet to meet the publishing team who always knew what that was eighteen months in advance. I firmly believe that those publishers who focus on editorial quality and integrity over high concept and "platform" are the ones who will win in the end.

What are your favorite books, movies, TV shows, and why: TV: *The Sopranos, The Daily Show, 30 Rock*. Movies: *The Philadelphia Story, Network, Star Wars*.

Please list representative titles that you have sold: *Lighten Up!* (Hay House); *Other People's Love Letters* (Clarkson Potter); *The Monstrumologist* (Simon & Schuster); *Panic Attack* (St. Martin's); *The Extraordinary Adventures of Alfred Kropp* (Bloomsbury); *Post Secret: Extraordinary Confessions from Ordinary Lives* (Morrow); *Target Underwear and a Vera Wang Gown* (Gotham); *All for a Few Perfect Waves* (William Morrow).

JOELLE DELBOURGO ASSOCIATES, INC.

516 Bloomfield Ave., Suite 5, Montclair, NJ 07042
fax: 973-783-6802
www.delbourgo.com   email: info@delbourgo.com

Agents' names: Joelle Delbourgo, Molly Lyons
The following information pertains to Joelle Delbourgo.
Education: BA, *magna cum laude*, Phi Beta Kappa, Williams College

(double-major in history and English literature); MA with honors in English literature from Columbia University.

Career history or story: Fall 1999 to present, president and founder of Joelle Delbourgo Associates, Inc. 1996–1999, HarperCollins (1996–1997, vice president, editorial director; 1997–1999, senior vice president, editor-in-chief and associate publisher); 1980–1996 held various positions from Senior Editor to Vice President, Editor-in-Chief of Hardcover and Trade Paperback; 1976–1980, various editorial positions at Bantam Books.

Hobbies, interests: Cooking, travel.

Subjects and categories you are interested in agenting, including fiction and nonfiction: Serious nonfiction, including narrative nonfiction, history, psychology, women's issues, medicine and health, business, science, biography, memoir, sports, popular culture, lifestyle, thesis-based books and interdisciplinary approaches to nonfiction subjects, literary fiction, some commercial fiction, some historical fiction, and young-adult books both fiction and nonfiction. I'm interested in serious thinkers, original ideas, and in a story well told.

Subjects and categories writers shouldn't even bother pitching to you: No category fiction (including romance, Westerns, science fiction, and fantasy). No children's books or technical books.

What would you do if you weren't agenting: I would be a college professor or dean, perhaps, or a writer myself. Anything that involved life as learning. Publishing has been a continuous graduate school for me and has allowed me to hone my skills and knowledge, while pushing the envelope in those areas I'm curious about. My authors are often pioneers in their fields, and I get a firsthand education working with them. It really works both ways.

Do you charge reading or any upfront fees: We do not charge to read submissions, but by the same token, we are not obligated to analyze your work for you unless you become a client.

Can you provide an approximation by percent of what you tend to represent by category: Fiction: 20 percent, nonfiction: 80 percent.

In your experience, what are the most common pitching mistakes writers make: Pretending they know me when they don't; not sending an SASE; writing letters telling me how many other agents have rejected them already, or how little they know about the process. Good-bye!

Describe the client from hell, even if you don't have any: Someone who approaches me by phone, sends materials in minuscule type without an SASE, calls to find out if the package has arrived, won't take no for an answer; clients with a smattering of publishing knowledge that makes them second-guess the agent's every step.

What's your definition of a great client: A naturally gifted writer and thinker. The client who has been thinking about the idea or book for a long time and perhaps has tested the idea through research, or presentations such as lectures and workshops; who is passionate, committed, serious, respectful, and works hard over the long term to do right by the book. The client who understand that this is a partnership, between agent and client at first, and then with the editor and publisher.

LITERARY AGENTS

The client who is willing to market a book and is open to being guided in the process. My role is to guide, advise, cheer, facilitate, boost egos, solve problems, and be there when the going gets rough.

How can writers increase the odds that you will offer representation: Write me a fabulous and respectful query and follow the guidelines on my website.

Why did you become an agent, and how did you become one: I had put in 25 years on the corporate side, climbing the ladder from editorial assistant to many years as a top executive. I loved the publishing process, but it also grinds you down. I wanted to get back to what got me into publishing in the first place: working with writers and editors again. I also wanted to work for a company in which I could set the tone, one that is professional and generous and respectful, and the best way to do it seemed to be to create it myself!

Describe to someone from another planet what you do as an agent: I see myself as helping to shape the culture, by choosing to support and develop ideas I find exciting, bodies of information that need to be shared, and literary experiences that will touch readers' hearts and minds. I like being a catalyst in people's lives, occasionally helping them to live their dreams. I am a muse, mother, therapist, advocate, CEO, and friend. Sometimes I wish I had someone like that in my life!

How do you feel about editors and publishers: I'm nuts about them. Occasionally you meet those who aren't smart or good at their job, but most are exceptional. They love what they do and live every day in the hope that they'll discover something that can sell. I love the older, wiser, experienced ones who have perfected their craft, but I'm also very impressed with the taste and talents of the many young editors in the business who have the ear of their management and take their responsibilities very seriously.

How do you feel about writers: I have a great deal of respect for good writers. It is really challenging for any talented person to envision a work and bring it into being. It involves vision, dedication, hard work and the ability to sustain these qualities on a solitary basis.

What do you see in the near future for book publishing: I get really irritated by all of the gloom and doom about publishing. It's true that the traditional world of book publishing is shrinking, but it's equally true that there are marvelous new opportunities if you keep your eyes open. I'm fascinated with the opportunity that university presses have, for example, to develop what the "big" firms call "mid-list," or by the new trade lists being developed by McGraw-Hill, which was formally thought of primarily as a business publisher, and Rodale Books, which is rapidly expanding beyond direct mail. More and more, we need to think about new formats, novel ways to market content and creative new business models. While I am a realist, my philosophy is to think positively and go where the opportunity is. I hate it when people don't agree with me, but, hopefully, I'm right about books more often than I'm wrong; no one "owes" you anything. You want to sell books because they are good and because someone at the publishing house has a vision for how to bring them to market. When it works correctly, it's a beautiful thing.

What are your favorite books, TV shows, movies, and why: I am a fierce admirer of *Friday Night Lights*, which is one of the smartest series on TV, and AMC's stylish *Mad Men*. I devour anything by Philip Roth, who is probably my favorite American writer, but also read lighter fare such as Elinor Lipman's novels. This year's great reads included Anita Shreve's *Testament*, Richard Russo's *Bridge of Sighs*, David Scharch's *Passionate Marriage*, and Daniel Mendelsohn's extraordinary *The Host: A Search for Six of Six Million*. I also read a lot of history, current affairs, and narrative nonfiction.

In your opinion, what do editors think of you: You should ask them! Once an editor, always an editor. Given my editorial background, they recognize me as a member of the tribe, as opposed to an adversary. I believe most respect my judgment, my sense of fairness and my professional integrity.

One a personal non-professional level, what do you think people think of you: Warm, intense, focused, occasionally intimidating but most people who are drawn to me like my ability to listen and connect with them.

What are some representative titles that you have sold: *BustedHalo's Freshman Survival Guide* by Nora Bradbury-Haehl with Bill McGarvey (Grand Central), *Talk to Me Like I'm Someone You Love* by Nancy Dreyfus, PhD (Jeremy Tarcher/Penguin), *Summer Shift* by Lynn Bonasia (Touchstone/Simon & Schuster), *Lessons from the Fat-O-Sphere* by Kate Harding and Marianne Kirby (Perigee/Penguin), *To Kill a Tiger: A Memoir of Korea* by Jid Lee (Overlook Press), *Amen, Amen, Amen* by Abby Sher (Simon & Schuster), *The Sneaky Chef to the Rescue* by Missy Chase Lapine (Running Press/Perseus Publishing), *You Can't Predict a Hero: Leadership in Times of Crisis from Vietnam to Wall Street* by Joseph J. Grano (Jossey-Bass/John Wiley), *The Resilient Stepmother* by Rachelle Katz, EdD (Harlequin Nonfiction), *The Napkin, The Melon, and the Monkey: How to be Happy at Work and In Life* by Barbara Burke (Hay House), *The Good Girl's Guide to Getting it On* by Joselin Linder and Elena Donavan Mauer (Adam's Media), *Greening Your Small Business* by Jennifer Kaplan (Perigee/Penguin), and *The Gift of Neurodiversity: The Hidden Strengths of Autism, ADHD, Dyslexia, and Other Brain Differences* by Thomas Armstrong (Da Capo/Perseus Publishing).

SANDRA DIJKSTRA LITERARY AGENCY

1155 Camino del Mar, PMB 515, Del Mar, CA 92014

Agent's name: Sandra Dijkstra

Born: New York, New York.

Education: BA in English, Adelphi; MA in comparative literature, UC Berkeley; PhD in French literature, UC San Diego.

Career history or story: University professor, literary agent.

Hobbies, interests: Reading, films.

Subjects and categories you are interested in agenting, including fiction and nonfiction: Specialize in literary and commercial fiction and nonfiction, especially biography, business, current affairs, health, history, psychology, popular culture, science, self-help, narrative nonfiction.

Subjects and categories writers shouldn't even bother pitching to you: Westerns, science fiction, romance, poetry collections, screenplays.

What would you do if you weren't agenting: I would be an editor and/or college professor.

What's the best way for fiction writers to solicit your interest: Please send a query letter by regular mail (email submissions are NOT accepted) with 50 sample pages of your manuscript (double-spaced, single-sided), and a one- to two-page synopsis. Please refer to our website, www.dijkstraagency.com, for our most updated submission guidelines.

What's the best way for nonfiction writers to solicit your interest: Send one to two sample chapters, profile of competition, intended audience and market, author bio, and brief chapter outline.

Do you charge reading or any upfront fees: No.

In your experience, what are the most common pitching mistakes writers make: Incessant phone calls to check on the status of their submissions, or demanding reading notes on an unsolicited submission. Writers should also be careful not to over-hype their projects, and to remember to let us know about your platform or previous writing credentials.

Describe the client from hell, even if you don't have any: The client from hell is never satisfied and has expectations that exceed all possibilities of realization.

What's your definition of a great client: Dream clients ask the right questions, offer useful support material, and trust their agents. They do not email and/or call daily. These clients keep us apprised of progress and are professionals who understand that we are their partners and advocates. They help us to represent their best interests, trust us, and work like hell to make [their] book happen after writing the best book possible.

How can writers increase the odds that you will offer representation: They should try to find a publisher, bookseller, librarian, or established author to recommend them to us. They should also try to publish their work in magazines, newspapers, or online—leading us to chase them!

Why did you become an agent, and how did you become one: I became an agent to publish books that help writers realize their dreams and make a difference in the world.

Describe to someone from another planet what you do as an agent: I read manuscripts and hope to fall in love. Then, when I do, I talk on the phone with editors and prepare them to fall in love. When I discover talent, I support it with all my heart, brain, and soul.

How do you feel about editors and publishers: Editors are overworked and underpaid. They are (most of them) dedicated and passionate about authors and books. In a perfect world, publishers would have more support, more money, and more time! Publishers would be "making public the book," in the fullest sense, which they try to do, often.

How do you feel about writers: Writers are our inspiration! Their work drives our work. There's nothing better than nurturing and campaigning for their books in the world.

What do you see in the near future for book publishing: Lots of joy when the publishing process works as it should. Lots of sorrow when it doesn't.

What are your favorite books, TV shows, movies, and why: Bill Maher, Jon Stewart, Keith Olbermann.

In your opinion, what do editors think of you: That I'm pushy—on the front and back end of the publishing process, which is my job.

What are some representative titles that you have sold: Nonfiction: *Devil's Highway* by Luis Urrea (Back Bay Books); *Religious Literacy* by Stephen Prothero (Harper San Francisco); *Winter World* by Bernd Heinrich (Harper Perennial); *God on Trial* by Peter Irons (Viking); *The Little Book that Beat the Market* by Joel Greenblatt (Wiley). Fiction: *Saving Fish from Drowning* by Amy Tan (Ballantine Books); *Snow Flower and the Secret Fan* by Lisa See (Random House); *Empress Orchid* by Anchee Min (Houghton Mifflin); *Lethally Blond* by Kate White (Warner); *Sweet Revenge* by Diane Mott Davidson (William Morrow).

JIM DONOVAN LITERARY

4515 Prentice, Suite 109, Dallas, TX 75206

email queries: jdliterary@sbc.global.net

Agents' names: Jim Donovan, Melissa Shultz
Born: Brooklyn, New York.
Education: BS, University of Texas.
Career history: In books since 1981 as a bookstore manager, chain-store buyer, published writer (*The Dallas Cowboys Encyclopedia*, 1996, Carol Publishing; *Custer and the Little Bighorn*, 2001, Voyager Press; *A Terrible Glory*, 2008, Little, Brown), freelance editor, senior editor: Taylor Publishing, five years. Literary agent since 1993.

Categories/subjects that you are most enthusiastic about agenting: American history, biography, sports, popular culture, health, business, fiction, popular reference. Also, chick lit and parenting (address to Melissa Shultz).

What you don't want to agent: Children's, poetry, short stories, romance, religious/spiritual, technical, computer, fantasy/science fiction.

What's the best way for writers to solicit your interest: Nonfiction: An intelligent query letter that gets to the point and demonstrates that the writer knows the subject and has something to contribute—and it's not just a magazine article stretched to book length. Fiction: Solid writing and some publishing credentials at shorter length. Snail mail with query and SASE or email: jdlqueries@sbcglobal.net. No attachments please. We will respond to email queries only if we are interested.

Do you charge reading or management fees: No.

What are the most common mistakes writers make when pitching you: The top ten query letter turn-offs: 1) Don't use a form letter that begins with "To Whom It May Concern" or "Dear Editor." 2) Don't say your writing is better than bestselling writers'. 3) Don't mention your self-published books unless they've sold several thousand copies. 4) Don't refer to your "fiction novel." 5) Don't brag about how great or how funny your book is. 6) Don't quote rave reviews from your relatives, friends, or editors whom you've paid. 7) Don't tell the agent how you're positive your book will make both of you rich. 8) Don't say it's one of five novels you've finished. 9) Don't tell the editor that he'll be interested because it will make a great movie. 10) Don't ask for advice or suggestions (if you don't think it's ready, why should they?).

What, if anything, can a writer do to increase the odds of your becoming his or her agent: Become published in reputable magazines, reviews, etc. before attempting a book. Most writers simply have no idea how hard it is to garner a contract for an unpublished writer.

Do you have any particular opinions or impressions of editors and publishers: Editors are the miners of the publishing world—they spend days and nights digging through endless layers of worthless material for the occasional golden nugget. Anything the agent or the writer can do to make their job easier is greatly appreciate, so I stress that to potential writers.

What do you think the future holds for writers, publishers, and agents: Most people—and that means most unpublished writers—do not appreciate the importance of good editing and publishing, which is why there will always be a need for editors and publishers—and agents.

Please list representative titles that you have sold: *The Bomber Boys* by Travis Ayres (NAL); *Honor in the Dust* by Gregg Jones (NAL); *Born to Be Hurt* by Sam Staggs (St. Martin's Press); *The Last Real Season* by Mike Shropshire (Grand Central); *To Hell on a Fast Horse* by Mark Gardner (Morrow); *Resurrection* by Jim Dent (St. Martin's Press).

DOYEN LITERARY SERVICES, INC.

1931 660th St., Newell, IA 50568

712-272-3300

www.barbaradoyen.com

    Agent's name: Barbara Doyen, Pres.

    Career story: We own perhaps the only literary agency in the world located on a rural acreage. The editor-in-chief of a national magazine once called from her NYC headquarters to ask us to look out the office windows and describe what we saw. She intended to send a photographer out to take some pictures for an article about virtual businesses, but couldn't fathom our answer: vast fields of corn and soybeans. Even stranger to her was that our office commute had nothing to do with subways, buses or trains. But this was years ago before the world had caught up to us; now many people dream of having successful businesses while living a country lifestyle and modern technology makes it doable from any location. Over 20 years ago, our agency began representing books of all kinds: children's board and picture books, teen and young-adult fiction and nonfiction, and most adult categories. But as the business has grown, we've narrowed our focus to adult nonfiction—the kind of books you find in bookstores for the ordinary reader, plus a few that cross over into the textbook and library markets.

Subjects and categories you like to agent: We offer exceptional service that starts with extensive advice about preparing a winning book proposal and continues beyond the publisher's contract—we're there to assist through the whole process to ensure a positive outcome: successful books. We are known for our outstanding nonfiction authors who write knowledgeably and well and who deliver to deadline. We are primarily interested in acquiring excellent writers for all kinds of adult nonfiction books and a few textbooks. Can't write? If you are an expert with a book idea but writing is not your strength, we may be able to help. We frequently pair authors and experts for successful book projects. Nonfiction topics: Advice/relationships, business/investing/finance, science, health/diet/fitness, history/politics/current affairs, how-to/DIY, lifestyle, psychology, self-improvement, cookbooks, pop culture, reference, narrative nonfiction, inspirational, biography, memoir and more.

Subjects and categories writers shouldn't bother pitching to you: We are not accepting fiction, poetry, or children's projects; however, we cover most adult nonfiction categories. (See the Third Simple Rule, below.)

What's the most effective way for writers to grab your attention: While we have an existing full stable of wonderful authors, we are open to new talent—after all, we started the agency due to our passion for authors and publishing and we love fresh nonfiction voices and ideas. In order to consider new clients, however, we must have a Few Simple Rules: 1) Please make your first contact to us be a query letter only—do not send your material until we request it. 2) You may send your query letter via snail mail or email—the latter can be done through our website, above. 3) Query us about adult nonfiction only. There now, that wasn't so bad, was it? Tip: Include your background and interests when querying us—you just never know what could come of it. We might have a book idea for you.

Do you charge fees separate from your commission, or offer non-agenting fee-based services: Doyen Literary Services, Inc., operates on a commission basis only; we do not charge fees of any kind.

What are representative titles you have sold to publishers: *Healthy Aging for Dummies* by Brent Agin, MD and Sharon Perkins, RN; *The Complete Idiot's Guide to Playing the Fiddle* by Ellery Klein ; *Presidents' Most Wanted* by Nick Ragone.

DUNHAM LITERARY, INC.

156 Fifth Avenue, Suite 625, New York, NY 10010

212-929-0994

www.dunhamlit@yahoo.com

Agents' names: Jennie Dunham, Owner; Chris Morehouse
The following information pertains to Chris Morehouse.
Career story: Attorney admitted to New York State Bar for 25 years. Member of the Entertainment, Arts and Sports Law Section of the NYSBA. Member of AAR.

Subjects and categories you like to agent: I like to represent writers of adult nonfiction books in the categories of memoir, health, parenting, relationships and current affairs. I also represent authors of middle grade and young-adult fiction and nonfiction. Topics of particular interest to me are sports (especially baseball), psychology, and women's issues (motherhood, work, self-help). I am not interested in the paranormal or religious topics.

What's the most effective ways for writers to grab your attention: No email queries please! Send Chris Morehouse query letters to 9 Normandy Lane, Manhasset, NY 11030.

How do you feel about writers: Like motherhood, writing is the hardest and loneliest profession, but the rewards are great when you do it well. I love my writers because they handle criticism and rejection with a sense of humor and as a learning experience.

EBELING & ASSOCIATES

www.ebelingagency.com

Agents' names: Michael Ebeling, ebothat@yahoo.com; Kristina Holmes, kristina@ ebelingagency.com
The following information pertains to Michael Ebeling.
Born: June 13, 1963; Escondido, California.
Education: BS business, Colorado University; MA holistic health and wellness, Naropa University.
Career story: Michael Ebeling brings more than 15 years of publications, consulting, sales and applied management experience to Ebeling & Associates. Michael's experience with leading authors and publishing companies enables him to effectively advise and support clients in the execution of their goals. Michael spent seven years as the CEO of Alan Cohen Publications (ACP), managing

the business and developing Alan's platform and branding from the ground up. During his tenure at ACP, Michael sold several Cohen titles to U.S. publishers and a number of foreign rights to more than ten countries. In addition to increasing overall sales by 30 percent, Michael managed worldwide book tours and retreats, and branded the company message through mediums such as corporate DVDs, websites, promotional materials and press kits. Michael also booked shows for the author on CNN, Fox News with Neil Cavuto, CNBC, and WGN, and had article placements on MSN, CNET and in *Psychology Today's* Blues Buster, *First for Women*, and *Body and Soul*. Previously, Michael was the marketing director for Art After Five, a publishing house and gift line based in Colorado. During this time, he more than doubled sales and increased the client base by 50 percent. Combining a business degree from the University of Colorado and an MA in health and wellness from the Naropa Institute in Boulder, Colorado, along with his travels to India experiencing and studying the teachings of Indian masters, Michael has a unique background that enables him to merge the worlds of business and spirituality. He enjoys developing long-term relationships built with a deep sense of caring and integrity, and enjoys consulting with authors to create platforms and marketing strategies that drive and sell their books.

Hobbies and special personal interests: Surfing, yoga, Ultimate Frisbee, travel and reading.

Subjects and categories you like to agent: Prescriptive nonfiction including health, diet, nutrition, sports, self-help/personal growth, mind/body/spirit, humor, business, finance, and career books.

Subjects and categories writers shouldn't bother pitching to you: Fiction.

What might you be doing if you weren't agenting: I would be a professional traveler.

What's the most effective ways for writers to grab your attention: By adhering to the submission guidelines outlined on our website. We are looking for professional authors with strong platforms that want to get their message out to the world.

Do you charge fees separate from your commission, or offer non-agenting fee-based services: Our agency offers consulting services for non-agented clients— usually involves sales/marketing/platform development coaching.

What are representative titles you have sold to publishers: *Counterintuitive: How Neuroscience Is Revolutionizing Management* by Charles Jacobs, PhD (Portfolio/Penguin); *The Loyalty Cure* by Timothy Keiningham and Lerzan Askoy (Benbella Books); *The Soul Truth: A Guide to Inner Peace* by Sheila and Marcus Gillette with Theo (Tarcher/Penguin); *Defenders of the Heart: 12 Strategies to a Richer, Fuller and More Satisfying Life* by Dr. Marilyn Kagan and Neil Einbund (Hay House); *Connecting to the Infinite: A 10-Step Approach to the Psychology of Yoga Poses* by Robert Butera (Llewellyn).

Why did you become an agent, and how did you become one: Because I love the book business and I love to sell. Put those two together and there you are— an agent.

What are your favorite books, movies, TV shows, and why: TV: *The Daily Show, Boston Legal, Grey's Anatomy, The Sopranos.* Movies: *Ray* and *What The Bleep! Do We Know.*

How would you describe the writer from hell: 1) They call all the time. 2) They don't listen to what you tell them. 3) They think they should be on *Oprah.*

You're welcome to share your thoughts and sentiments about the business of writing and publishing: The publishing industry is going to become more and more competitive. It seems that everyone wants to write a book these days and there is only so much shelf space in the bookstores. Writers are going to have a more challenging time finding agents; agents will find it harder to place their clients; and the publishers' margins are shrinking because of this competition.

The following information pertains to Kristina Holmes.

Education: BA anthropology, University of Hawaii, Manoa 2002.

Career story: After working in a number of editorial and freelance writing capacities, I began my career as a literary agent in 2005 at Ebeling & Associates. With over 15 years in the industry, Michael Ebeling provides much of the sales and marketing expertise with a big eye towards platform, while I have more of the literary eye. I have personally acquired and placed a variety of authors including investigative journalists, professional writers, bloggers, speakers, consultants, celebrities, entrepreneurs, memoirists, mediums, self-help leaders, psychologists and more. I'm very passionate about the type of books we represent—books that makes a positive impact on the world.

Hobbies and special personal interests: Do I dare say reading?! Beyond my love affair with books, I enjoy physical activities like hiking, biking, surfing, swimming, and going to the gym; nutrition, continuing education, astrology, metaphysics, photography, art, yoga, meditation, friends and nature.

Subjects and categories you like to agent: I love prescriptive, narrative, and literary projects (including memoir) in a variety of subjects. Genres I'm actively looking for in the prescriptive realm are health and wellness, mind/body/spirit, spirituality, women's issues, psychology, business, environment/green books, parenting, and pop culture. Prescriptive books must have an established platform and a truly unique premise. Narrative/literary projects vary greatly—the ones that interest me the most have a very strong and polished voice with a great story behind it. In general, our agency is looking for a wide range of intelligent authors, whether they are serious, comic, edgy or eloquent.

Subjects and categories writers shouldn't bother pitching to you: Books that are negatively bent or overly dry; fiction.

What might you be doing if you weren't agenting: Traveling…

What's the most effective ways for writers to grab your attention: Write a succinct and savvy query including a brief statement about your book, why readers will love it and why you're the person to write it. Have solid credentials to write your book and demonstrate that you're a great writer by creating a clever query, proposal and sample material.

What are representative titles you have sold to publishers: See Michael's listing above.

How do you feel about writers: I LOVE WRITERS!! Writers are amazing individuals. True writers are artists, activists, mediators, educators, therapists, and much more. They may bring to light things we all know but in a way most of us can't express. Or perhaps they illuminate aspects of life that we've never considered and need to. I particularly love writers because they can make magic happen. How? By literally changing the way that we think, and as a result, who we are in the world. This is why I'm so passionate about positive change authors, those individuals that promote widespread and immeasurable compassion and integrity among readers through the written word.

How would you describe the writer from hell: Unappreciative with an lack of willingness to do their part (write a great manuscript and book proposal, create and implement a successful promotion plan for the book), unable to accept constructive feedback, overly demanding, doesn't follow through with deadliness.

How would you describe the publisher and/or editor from hell: I haven't yet encountered a truly hellish editor, thankfully! Editors work hard and long hours, and tend to be very appreciative of the authors we bring their way. A few editors are unprofessional or nonresponsive, but the great majority are amazing people. Thank you, gracious colleagues...

What do you like best about your clients, and the editors and publishers you work with: Michael and I meet incredible people through our work and have the honor of guiding authors in their careers. It is a phenomenal business to be in for a variety of reasons. Through our authors and their networks, we are in the middle of a matrix of cutting-edge leaders and thinkers—we become an integral part of exposing their ideas and knowledge to many readers around the world. It is a way for us to advocate certain issues, educate people or just make them laugh! And on a personal level, we love our clients. They are all very cool, fun and savvy individuals!

Do you wish to describe who you are: On a professional level, I'm encouraging, enthusiastic, savvy, determined, focused, motivated and relevant. I represent the younger sector of Americans who have had a lot of freedom to decide what they want in life and less of the societal constrictions that influenced older generations to follow a formulaic approach to life (education, marriage, kids, retirement). This environment has allowed us to consider alternative ways of being and living, which is very necessary for the health of our relationships, environment, economy and personal satisfaction in life. So, a big thanks to the older generations for helping to shape our history here in the U.S., while still so obviously fraught with political and social challenges, we have the opportunity to create our own reality, a freedom that so many others around the world lack. I get a lot of enjoyment out of being a literary agent, but I also look way beyond this to what I'm getting out of and giving to the world. I'm looking forward to being part of the positive growth and evolution occurring globally. Life is a deep mystery and something that I am profoundly grateful to be part of.

THE LISA EKUS GROUP, LLC

57 North Street, Hatfield, MA 01038

413-247-9325   fax: 413-247-9873

www.LisaEkus.com   email: sia@LisaEkus.com

Agent's name: Lisa Ekus-Saffer

Categories/subjects that you are most enthusiastic about agenting: Our primary interest is culinary titles, although we do consider some other nonfiction topics that are complementary, such as books on nutrition, health and wellness, and wine and beverages.

What you don't want to agent: Fiction or poetry.

What's the best way for writers to solicit your interest: We have proposal guidelines and other information about our agency on our website.

What, if anything, can a writer do to increase the odds of your becoming his or her agent: The best way for authors to approach us is with a formal query and/or proposal, and we appreciate if people do not call us. We follow up on all formal queries and submissions. We are a full member of the Association of Authors Representatives.

What do you think the future holds for book publishing: Despite an increasingly competitive marketplace, we continue to believe in a vibrant cookbook industry full of opportunity.

Please list representative titles that you have sold: Our website offers a comprehensive listing of our authors, book projects, and the many publishers with whom we have worked over the years. The agency celebrated its 28th anniversary this year. We began literary agenting services in 2000 and have negotiated book deals for more than 200 books since then. The business has four primary service areas: public relations, literary agenting, media training, and spokesperson opportunities.

THE ETHAN ELLENBERG LITERARY AGENCY

548 Broadway, New York, NY 10012

Agent's name: Ethan Ellenberg

Career history: Contracts Manager at Berkley, associates Contracts Manager at Bantam 1979–1984.

Categories/subjects that you are most enthusiastic about agenting: All commercial fiction: romance, SF, fantasy, thriller, mystery. All children's fiction: picture books, middle-grade, YA. History, health, science, etc.

What you don't want to agent: Poetry

What's the best way for fiction writers to solicit your interest: By mail—see website. Synopsis/first three chapters/SASE.

What's the best way for nonfiction writers to solicit your interest: By mail—see website. Proposal/SASE.

Do you charge reading or management fees: No.

What are the most common mistakes writers make when pitching you: Confusing letters. Too much personal information.

What, if anything, can a writer do to increase the odds of your becoming his or her agent: Write a great book.

Why did you become an agent, and how did you become one: Love books, felt it was the best job.

Describe to someone from another planet what you do as an agent: Represent authors, support them, handle their business.

What do you think the future holds for book publishing: The continued impact of internet will affect us a lot.

Please list representative titles that you have sold: Translation rights to three-time 2009 Hugo Award nominee John Scalzi's *Zoe's Tale* to Heyne in Germany and Eskimo in Russia. Two new UNDEAD titles and one new paranormal romance anthology to Berkley for Mary Janice Davidson. Three new historical romances to NAL for Beatrice Small. Five new military science-fiction titles to Avon for Stephen Coonts' co-author and bestseller William Keith. *The Rogue Agent* series of young-adult fantasy to Harper Australia and Orbit US/UK for Karen Miller (w.a. K.E. Mills). Two new paranormal romance titles for up-and-coming author Jory Strong to Berkley. Six-book deal for bestselling paranormal romance author Christine Warren to St. Martin's. *Last Song*, a new illustrated book by Eric Rohmann to Roaring Brook Press. *Hellcats* by Peter Sasgen to Putnam. *None Left Behind* by Charles Sasser to St. Martin's.

ELAINE P. ENGLISH, PLLC

4710 41st Street, NW Suite D, Washington, DC 20016

202-362-5190   fax: 202-362-5192

www.elaineenglish.com   email: Elaine@elaineenglish.com

Agent's name: Elaine P. English

Born: October 8, 1949; Asheville, North Carolina.

Education: Undergraduate in Latin (*magna cum laude*) at Randolph Macon Woman's College; MEd (counseling and personnel services) University of Maryland; JD National Law Center at George Washington University.

Career history or story: After pursuing careers in teaching, social services, and personnel management, I completed law school and began working as an attorney for a public interest organization representing reporters and journalists on open government and media issues. I then joined a small firm with a publishing law/agenting practice. After that I had my own firm and managed a small literary agency. For more than twenty years in private practice, I have concentrated on media and publishing issues. About six years ago, I decided to expand my practice to include agenting of commercial fiction. Now, on my own, I continue to pursue a practice of both legal and agenting services.

Hobbies, interests: Reading, hiking, nature photography.

Subjects and categories you are interested in agenting, including fiction and nonfiction: Women's fiction, romance of all subgenres (both contemporary, historical, and paranormal but primarily single titles), mysteries, and thrillers.

Subjects and categories writers shouldn't even bother pitching to you: All Nonfiction (including memoirs), children's books, inspirational projects, and science fiction.

What would you do if you weren't agenting: Simply practicing law.

What's the best way for fiction writers to solicit your interest: I accept (prefer) email queries sent to queries@elaineenglish.com. I do not accept attachments to emails. Generally I will not make [a] final decision without reading the entire manuscript.

What's the best way for nonfiction writers to solicit your interest: N/A.

Do you charge reading or any upfront fees: I charge no reading fees or any upfront costs. I may ask for reimbursement for copying and postage expenses only.

In your experience, what are the most common pitching mistakes writers make: I hate to see pitches that get bogged down in too much detail, while not giving a complete overview of the project. Also, I find that too many authors rush into submitting their manuscripts before they have actually completed editing, critiquing, and proofreading [them].

Describe the client from hell, even if you don't have any: The client who is not open to comments and criticism, and who refuses to learn anything about the realities of the publishing business.

What's your definition of a great client: A great client is one who sees his/her relationship with [the] agent as a partnership and is willing to work hard as a professional in this business. Of course, [he/she is] first and foremost an exceptionally talented writer.

How can writers increase the odds that you will offer representation: Know their target market and have a well-written, solid manuscript with an inventive plot, strong commercial hook, good pacing, strong dialogue and realistic, strong characters.

Why did you become an agent, and how did you become one: Because I love books, enjoy working with authors, and wanted to contribute, even in a small way, to the creative process by which the reading public is entertained.

What do you see in the near future for book publishing: The book publishing industry is clearly in a period of transition at the moment, and the precise parameters of the future are not clear. I'm confident, though, that books, in some form, will be with us forever.

What are your favorite books, TV shows, movies, and why: *Jane Eyre* is my all-time favorite book, in part, because it was my introduction into the wonderful world of women's fiction and romance. My taste in TV shows and movies is varied, but I tend to like character driven series. Frankly, with all the reading I do, there's not much TV time.

In your opinion, what do editors think of you: I hope that they think of me as a fair and reasonable professional who brings them quality projects.

What are some representative titles that you have sold: *Bond of Fire* and *Kisses Like a Devil* by Diane Whiteside (Berkley; Kensington); *Fast Forward* by Celeste Norfleet (Kimani TRU); *The Wind Comes Sweeping* by Marcia Preston (Mira), and *Cowtown Confidential* by Joanne Kennedy (Sourcebooks).

THE EPSTEIN LITERARY AGENCY

P.O. Box 356, Avon, MA 02322

www.epsteinliterary.com

Agent's name: Kate Epstein, kate@epsteinliterary.com

Born: New York City.

Education: BA University of Michigan.

Career story: I was an editor at a trade publisher and I loved it. And then one day I kind of stopped loving it. I still loved books, and I still loved working with authors, but a job that had seemed so varied and interesting was beginning to seem boring. The passion was starting to drip away. Since the money isn't that good, I needed to get that back.

One of the best things about making the change to being an agent is that I could follow my heart to be 100 percent the author's advocate. As an editor my sympathies generally lay with the authors, but my paycheck came from elsewhere, so I felt divided ethically. But being your advocate means sometimes telling you that you're wrong.

Hobbies and special personal interests: Raising my two kids. Reading—I've always resisted calling it a "hobby" because I don't consider eating or breathing to be hobbies, and I'm almost that dependent on it. Being very busy I squeeze it in at the oddest times—while doing housework, or brushing my teeth. I actually don't know how to go to sleep without reading. Feminism. I also have a vegetable garden and work out every day, but I'm not necessarily proficient at either.

Subjects or categories you like to agent: 100 percent nonfiction for adults. Particularly interested in (in alpha order):business, crafts, fashion, humor, inspiration, journalism, lifestyles, memoir, nonfiction narrative, parenting, pets, popular culture, reference, relationships, self-help, travel/adventure, women's interest.

Subjects and categories writers shouldn't bother pitching to you: Fiction, children's, poetry, screenplays.

What might you be doing if you weren't agenting: The longer I do it, the harder it is to contemplate not agenting, but I loved being an acquisitions editor and could probably love it again. If I didn't work in publishing, I could imagine being a doula.

What's the most effective ways for writers to grab your attention: Make it clear you've read my website. I'm a sucker for compliments, like anyone else—especially if you've read something I agented. I'll also give special consideration if we share an alma mater.

Do you charge fees separate from your commission, or offer non-agenting fee-based services: Nope.

What are representative titles you have sold to publishers: *A TV Guide to Life* by Jeff Alexander of *Television Without Pity*, Berkley Books; *Whatever You Do, Don't Run* by Peter Allison, Globe Pequot (North America), Nicholas Brealey (UK, South Africa), Allen & Unwin (Australia), Mouria (Dutch); *Don't Look Behind You* by Peter Allison, Globe Pequot (North America), Allen & Unwin (Australia); *Your 401(canine) Plan* by Mary Jane Checchi, T.F.H. Publications, *The Crochet Dude's Designs for Guys* by Drew Emborsky, The Crochet Dude, Lark Books, of Sterling; *Pets and the Planet* by Carol Frischmann, Howell Book House, a division of John Wiley & Sons, Inc.; *Eagle Walker* by Jeffery Guidry, William Morrow; *The Green Bride Guide* by Kate Harrison, Sourcebooks; *Crossing the Gates of Alaska: One Man and Two Dogs 600 Miles Off the Map* by Dave Metz, Citadel, *Knitting the Threads of Time* by Nora Murphy, New World Library; *Stage Right: Professional Advice to Sell Your Home* by Starr C. Osborne, AMACOM Books; *Nail Your Law Job Interview* by Natalie Prescott and Oleg Cross, Career Press.

My website has a complete list.

Why did you become an agent, and how did you become one: I basically became an agent by putting out my shingle. I also took a number of more experienced agents to lunch and picked their brains—a number continue to provide support and advice, and I likewise share my knowledge when it's helpful. Two years in I qualified for membership in the AAR.

How do you feel about writers: Being a solo agent means that writers are my closest colleagues in many ways. I've always loved working with them and have enjoyed nurturing their varied processes—it keeps things interesting.

I'm not hugely hip to fame and I think that's why I like being outside the spotlight, and helping my authors to be in the spotlight. I wasn't cool in high school and I didn't want to be. (I wasn't picked on either. I was ignored by most. Good enough.)

What are your favorite books, movies, TV shows, and why: I'm bad at picking favorite books, and I've become someone that rarely re-reads, so in a way my relationship with a book is always temporary. Though when it changes me that may be permanent.

I read *Chains* by Laurie Halse Anderson recently and found it a throwback to my teen years, so absorbing that nothing else seems real. It's very upsetting though, in a way I think far more upsetting to an adult than to a kid. That's the only book I read recently that I'd recommend really widely, though I just enjoyed *Identical Strangers*, by Elyse Schein and Paula Bernstein, which deftly wove together two personal narratives and all kinds of interesting information about twins and adoption. Dewey was really quite cute.

Favorite TV shows is easy; I like *Battlestar Galactica*, *The Daily Show with Jon Stewart*, and *Saving Grace*. BSG inspires in me a deep love that comes from intriguing plot lines, great characters, and cute boys. As to Jon, he makes the news interesting, which is a feat. I watch while lifting weights the next morning after he broadcasts.

How would you describe the writer from hell: Someone who is abusive to me or to editors. Life is too short to work with some people.

What do you like best about your clients, and the editors and publishers you work with: I love it when we all believe in a book and its capacity to make people's lives better in some way.

You're welcome to share your thoughts and sentiments about the business of writing and publishing: I think what inspires me most is how intimate the act of reading is, how books enter people's homes and lives. Whatever their subject.

Do you wish to describe who you are: In some ways I identify with The Little Engine that Could. I carry fun and nourishment over the mountain, and I'm very determined.

Will our business exist as we know it in ten years or so: Yes, I believe it will, though certainly it will change. I'm hopeful about the electronic future. I haven't got a reader yet—I don't commute so it doesn't seem worth it—but I'm hopeful that it will focus readers' attention on the book's text, which after all is its essence. I used to feel books were great decoration—and I still find it odd when I go into a home and see none of them—but I'm finding I have less interest in keeping large numbers of books around than I used to. I think books are to be read and loved, but their physical presence means little to me. And I wouldn't mind getting out of the tree-killing business.

DIANA FINCH LITERARY AGENCY

116 West 23rd St, Suite 500, New York, NY 10011
646-375-2081

For queries: No phone calls please. Query by mail with SASE or email address for reply, or by email. Please do not include attachments with email queries. The query should be the text of the email, not a separate attachment. Include the word *query* in the subject heading. Email address for queries: queryfinchagency@verizon.net

Agent's name and email address: Diana Finch; diana.finch@verizon.net

Date of birth: September 1954.

Education: Hanover High School, Hanover, NH. 1972, Harvard, BA *cum laude* 1976, University of Leeds, Leeds, England, MA 1977.

Career Story: I opened my own agency in March 2003, following 18 years at the Ellen Levine Literary Agency, where I handled translation rights for Ellen Levine's clients including Russell Banks, Garrison Keillor and Michael Ondaatje, while developing my own client list. My first job in publishing was on the other side of the fence, as an editorial assistant and then assistant editor at St. Martin's Press. On the advice of older editors, I decided to try agenting and joined the literary agency of Sanford J. Greenburger Associates, where I agented my first deals.

I handle translation rights for a select few literary agents. Among their clients whose work I have sold abroad are Stanford mathematics professor Keith Devlin (*The Millennium Problems, The Math Gene* and *Math Instinct*) and the adventurer and philanthropist Greg Mortenson, author with David Oliver Relin of the bestseller *Three Cups of Tea.*

My own client list includes other novelists, journalists and foreign correspondents, freelancers and staff writers at *Newsweek*, the *Wall Street Journal*, CNN, and the BBC, authors of popular self-help and reference books, and award-winning children's book authors.

I have negotiated assignments for my clients with online and print magazines including *Harper's, Salon, GQ, Outside*, the *New York Times*, and *Vanity Fair.*

I am the Chair of the International Committee of the Association of Authors Representatives, the membership trade organization for literary agents. The committee meets monthly to focus on issues involved in selling clients' work to foreign publishers. I attend the Frankfurt Book Fair every year, and London Book Fair every few years

Hobbies and special personal interests: Sports: running, field hockey, soccer. Giants football, RedSox/Yankees baseball, World Cup soccer. Introducing my teenaged daughter to the opera.

Subjects and categories you like to agent: Memoir, progressive politics, popular science, economics, literary fiction.

Subjects and categories writers shouldn't bother pitching to you: Romance fiction.

What might you be doing if you weren't agenting: Certainly a career that involved writing and reading—beyond that it is hard to say: health, social work, education, environmental issues.

What's the most effective ways for writers to grab your attention: Approach me with a polished proposal and sample chapter, have both a developed platform and a website, be original and don't use a query service.

Do you charge fees separate from your commission, or offer non-agenting fee-based services: No.

What are representative titles you have sold to publishers (book title, author,

publisher): Azadeh Moaveni, *Time* correspondent, *Honeymoon in Tehran* (Random House) and *Lipstick Jihad* (Public Affairs); Owen Matthews, *Newsweek* Moscow bureau chief, *Stalin's Children* (Bloomsbury); author and activist Antonia Juhasz, *The Tyranny of Oil* and *The Bush Agenda* (HarperCollins); Robert Marion, MD, *Genetics Rounds* (Kaplan) and the classic *Intern Blues* (HarperCollins); environmental journalist Eric Simons, *Darwin Slept Here* (Overlook); economist Loretta Napoleoni, *Rogue Economics* (Seven Stories Press); novelist and essayist Chris Bauman, *The Ice Beneath You*, *Voodoo Lounge* and most recently *In Hoboken* (Melville House); first novelist Michael FitzGerald, *Radiant Days* (Shoemaker & Hoard); Greg Palast's *Armed Madhouse* and *The Best Democracy Money Can Buy* (Dutton/Plume).

How do you feel about writers: What writers do is very difficult and it usually does not get easier with practice. Figuring out what to write about and planning a book can be as big an undertaking as actually writing the text of the book.

How would you describe the writer from hell: None of my clients fit this description, I'm glad to say.

How would you describe the publisher and/or editor from hell: I consider it part of my job to keep the publishers and editors with whom I work from descending into this realm.

What do you like best about your clients, and the editors and publishers you work with: Their energy and creativity are both inspiring and a pleasure to work with.

You're welcome to share your thoughts and sentiments about the business of writing and publishing: It is not easy and it never gets easier—and it is not always possible to tell what will be the most difficult aspect of writing and publishing a book.

Finally, will our business exist as we know it in ten years or so: No, of course it will be different and probably more different ten years from now than it was ten years ago. The difficult economy will have an impact, and the truly creative will use the Internet and new communication technologies in ways we can't quite predict, and the current edge that celebrities have will I think be diminished as true artists level the playing field.

FINEPRINT LITERARY MANAGEMENT

240 W. 35th Street, Ste. 500, New York, NY 10001

212-279-1282

www.fineprintlit.com

Agents' names: Amy Tipton; amy@fineprintlit.com; Colleen Lindsay, colleen@fineprintlit.com; Diane Freed, diane@fineprintlit.com; Janet Reid, janet@fineprintlit.com, June Clark, june@fineprintlit.com, Meredith Hays, Peter Rubie, peter@fineprintlit.com; Stephany Evans; stephany@fineprintlit.com, Brenden Deenen; brenden@fineprintlit.com

The following information pertains to Amy Tipton.

Born: Jan. 27, Arlington, Texas.

Education: BA from Naropa University, MA and MFA from New College of California.

Career story: I became an agent after working as a literary assistant and office manager at several literary agencies including JCA Literary Agency, Diana Finch Literary Agency, Gina Maccoby Literary Agency, and Liza Dawson Associates. I also worked as a book scout for Aram Fox, Inc. dealing with foreign rights and also worked as a freelance editor to Lauren Weisberger, author of *The Devil Wears Prada*.

Subjects and categories you like to agent: YA, commercial women's fiction.

Subjects and categories writers shouldn't bother pitching to you: Science fiction/fantasy.

What might you be doing if you weren't agenting: Writing or teaching.

Do you charge fees separate from your commission, or offer non-agenting fee-based services: No.

What are representative titles you have sold to publishers: *Cracked Up to Be* by Courtney Summers (St. Martin's Press); *Untitled* by Amy Reed (Simon Pulse).

Why did you become an agent, and how did you become one: I just fell into it. I was Peter Rubie's assistant and he encouraged me to start taking on projects, to see if I could do it.

How do you feel about writers: I love writers. Of course.

What are your favorite books, movies, TV shows, and why: I probably have too many favorites to name…Books, recently? A lot of YA: *13 Reasons Why, Such a Pretty Girl, Looking for Alaska, The Fat Girl, Speak, Cracked Up To Be,* etc. All time? *The Abortion: An Historical Romance 1966, Breakfast at Tiffany's, To Kill a Mockingbird, Catcher in the Rye, The Stranger.* Authors I love: Richard Brautigan, Michelle Tea, Eileen Myles, Dorothy Allison, Tawni O'Dell, E. Lockheart, Patrick Carman, Courtney Summers, Daisy Whitney, Lauren Weisberger…As for movies, I love *Breakfast at Tiffany's, Surviving Desire, Secretary, Eternal Sunshine of the Spotless Mind, Down By Law, Ghost World, Serial Mom, Hedwig and the Angry Inch, Muriel's Wedding, Heathers*…I love these books/authors and movies because each one tells a great story.

How would you describe the writer from hell: A writer who is (emotionally) high-maintenance is hard to work with; someone who has ego and/or is constantly demanding attention—in the form of email or phone conversations—and second-guessing you as an agent is difficult to work with.

The following information pertains to Colleen Lindsay.

Born: Burlingame, California; April 13.

Education: Life!

Career story: I spent most of my formative years hiding beneath the blankets with a flashlight and a book. My first job in publishing was in Northern California as a mass merchandise sales rep for Ballantine Books. For five years I served as director of publicity for Del Rey Books, a division of the Random House Publishing Group, where I specialized in the creative publicity and marketing of science fiction, fantasy, pop culture, YA fantasy, graphic novels and third-party licensed media. I've also worked as a freelance publicist and copywriter for several major trade publishers and as a book reviewer for the *San Francisco Chronicle* under the inimitable Pat Holt. My background in independent book publishing goes even further back to my first job as a bookstore manager in 1984 at the now-defunct San Francisco Bay Area bookstore Central Park Books. I also worked at Printers, Inc. Books in Palo Alto and spent six years as the marketing and events manager at Stacey's Bookstore in San Francisco.

Hobbies and special personal interests: Being faster than a speeding bullet. Gratuitous lifting of heavy objects in front of a mirror. Nerd-herding. Extracting cat claws from sofa. Occasionally getting Monopoly and Risk confused, thus resulting in the occasional unfortunate placement of hotels in the Ural Mountains while my army unwittingly invades Park Place. (Tragic!) Photography. Writing. Blogging. Sleeping whenever possible. And, of course, reading.

Subjects and categories you like to agent: Fiction of all types, both literary and commercial. I love writers who can engage me with amazing characters and a strong voice. Above all, I'm looking for writers who understand the importance of storytelling. I have a particular soft spot for and specialize in genre fiction: science fiction, fantasy, urban fantasy, paranormal romance, slipstream, new weird, horror, steampunk, space opera, military SF, cyberpunk and surrealism. I love YA and YA fantasy, too. In nonfiction, I'm looking for eloquent narrative nonfiction, works of LGBT interest and pop culture. I'd also like to see business or career books geared toward young women. And I'm very interested in graphic novels!

Subjects and categories writers shouldn't bother pitching to you: I don't represent any Christian fiction or nonfiction, inspirational, category romance, children's books, poetry or short stories.

What might you be doing if you weren't agenting: When I was a kid, I wanted to be (in the following order): A small Mexican boy named Pedro (in my head I had a sombrero and a burro), an astronaut, a veterinarian, a writer and an archaeologist. When I grown up, I still hope to become Indiana Jones. But for now, agenting fits nicely.

What's the most effective ways for writers to grab your attention: Shout? Wave? Throw an angry Pomeranian at me? Oh, wait, you mean as a writer? The most effective way to make me sit up and take notice is to write a damned good query letter with a strong hook. Let me know that you've actually read my submissions guidelines. This shows me that you're a professional, that you take your own career as seriously as I do.

Do you charge fees separate from your commission, or offer non-agenting fee-based services: I'm a freelance copywriter for several large publishers. I specialize in press materials and author Q&As.

What are representative titles you have sold to publishers: *Better Part of Darkness* by Kelly Gay (Pocket Books), *Total Oblivion, More or Less* by Alan Deniro (Bantam).

Why did you become an agent, and how did you become one: I'd been working in publishing for a number of years in marketing and publicity. While I really enjoyed the work, I also longed to be able to only work on those titles I really felt passionate about. After a layoff in 2007, several of my author and editor friends encouraged me to try to become an agent. The idea appealed to me but I didn't want to simply hang up my shingle and call myself an agent; too many people try this and they do a terrible disservice to their clients. I decided the best way to go about it was to do set up some informational interviews with agents to learn more about it. I'd done close to twenty informational interviews by the time I met with Peter Rubie and Stephany Evans at FinePrint. We had a great conversation, talked for a couple of hours and by the time I got home later than evening, there was a job offer on my voicemail. It was kismet, I guess.

How do you feel about writers: I love writers. They make what I do possible.

What do you tell entities from other planets and dimensions about your job: If I met an entity from another planet, I'd be too busy buying him/her a beer and listening to his/her story so I could sell it!

What are your favorite books, movies, TV shows, and why: TV Shows: The new *Battlestar Galactica*: hands-down the strongest writing, ensemble cast and cinematography on television. Why this show hasn't won any Emmys for writing is seriously beyond me. Books: Oh, don't ask me that! I've worked in publishing or bookselling for more than twenty-three years. It would take all day to list all of my favorite books. Here's a random sampling: *Les Miserables* by Victor Hugo, *Always* by Nicola Griffith, *Dark Water's Embrace* by Stephen Leigh, *Perdido Street Station* by China Mieville, *Fall on Your Knees* by Anne Marie McDonald and *Operation Wandering Soul* by Richard Powers. I love good science fiction, fantasy, mystery, literary fiction, and queer stuff, with the occasional baffling foray into history. (Go figure.) Movies: Movies where things explode and pretty people disrobe. *The Lord of the Rings, Serenity, Wings of Desire, Children of Paradise*, Myazaki things.

How would you describe the writer from hell: High-maintenance. Life is too short for divas, and there are plenty of other writers out there who won't make an agents or editor's life miserable.

How would you describe the publisher and/or editor from hell: Editors who are non-responsive: they sit on manuscripts for months, sometimes years! They don't answer emails or return phone calls.

What do you like best about your clients, and the editors and publishers you work with: I love pretty much everything about what I do, honestly. I just wish I had more hours in the day to do it.

Do you wish to describe who you are: Professional nerd. Also, an amateur nerd of epic proportions. It's all good. I've recently overcome my terror of dancing in public. This mustn't be confused with an actual ability to dance, however.

Will our business exist as we know it in ten years or so: Absolutely! And with the growing acceptance of e-book readers, books will become more accessible than ever before.

The following information pertains to Diane Freed.

Born: Sandwich, Illinois.

Education: BS in journalism, University of Illinois.

Career story: I've worked in the field of book publishing my entire career. I began at Prentice Hall as an editor/production coordinator, then on to *U.S. News & World Report* as a book editor and production supervisor. At Time-Life Books I produced direct mail promotional materials, and at Addison-Wesley/Pearson I was a book production supervisor. As owner and manager of my own publishing services company I worked as a book packager, producing titles for publishers from raw manuscript through electronic files to the printer. I became an agent when I joined the Peter Rubie Literary Agency, which later became FinePrint Literary Management in September 2007. Initially I focused on selling nonfiction, but now I'm representing fiction writers as well and enjoying it tremendously.

In each capacity, I've worked closely with authors in one way or another, so one of my strengths is the ability to collaborate well with them when producing proposals and working on manuscripts. I consider myself a sculptor of sorts: I like putting all the book parts together to make a product that readers can sit with and enjoy, and that they can learn from as well.

Hobbies and special personal interests: Swimming, boating, cooking, travel, movies, theater.

Subjects and categories you like to agent: Nonfiction: Primarily relationship/advice, self-help, spirituality, health/fitness, memoir, current affairs, popular culture, women's issues, environment, humor. Fiction: commercial and literary fiction, partial to women's fiction. Generally, I can't resist a theme, fiction or nonfiction, in which the characters demonstrate real compassion for others in the lives they lead.

Subjects and categories writers shouldn't bother pitching to you: Poetry, science fiction.

What might you be doing if you weren't agenting: I'd be a book editor full time or seriously take up a favorite sport.

What's the most effective ways for writers to grab your attention: Write an honest, well-written query letter that tells me why your book is important, why it should be published now, and why you are the person to write it.

Do you charge fees separate from your commission, or offer non-agenting fee-based services: As an agent, I do not charge fees separate from my commission. However, I do take on occasional, completely separate, editing and proofreading projects.

What are representative titles you have sold to publishers: *Natural Flexibility* by Charles Kenny (Hatherleigh); *Bufflehead Sisters* by Patricia DeLois (Berkley/Penguin); *Penguins in Amsterdam* by Patricia DeLois (Berkley/Penguin); *The*

Language of Comforting by Val Walker (Jeremy Tarcher/Penguin); *Getting Past Your Breakup* by Susan Elliot (Da Capo/Perseus).

Why did you become an agent, and how did you become one: I became an agent because I like discovering new writers and being tuned in to what's on everyone's minds. I took Peter Rubie's course on the role of the literary agent, through New York University, which launched my agenting career.

How do you feel about writers: I can't help but like them a lot, given what I do for a living! Most of all, I admire and respect them incredibly for their patience and perseverance.

What do you tell entities from other planets and dimensions about your job: I match up aspiring writers with editors at publishing houses that sell the type of books they have written.

What are your favorite books, movies, TV shows, and why: Tops on my book list would be any and all that had an impact on me when I was growing up, enabled me to see the bigger world, to walk in someone else's shoes: *Black Like Me, All Quiet on the Western Front, To Kill a Mockingbird,* Pearl Buck's stories. Favorite authors today include Lara Vapnyar, Geraldine Brooks, Larry McMurtry, Colm Toibin, Frank McCourt, John Irving, Anne Tyler, Alice Hoffman, Sedaris, Burroughs, and Keillor. Memoir: *Reading Lolita in Tehran* by Azar Nafisi, *The Glass Castle* by Jeannette Walls. Movies: *Thelma and Louise, Send Me No Flowers, Matchstick Men, The Sound of Music, Pulp Fiction, West Side Story.* TV: *Boston Legal, Sopranos, The Office, Charlie Rose Show.* Why? Not sure, but common threads might be that they feature inspirational characters that somehow touch me emotionally, or they just make me laugh. Or best of all, do both.

How would you describe the writer from hell: Someone looking for an agent who calls out of the blue or emails me a chapter asking if I'll give it a quick critique. Then there is the client who calls at least once a day just to check up on how things are going.

How would you describe the publisher and/or editor from hell: Someone with poor communication skills and/or who doesn't follow up on things, but fortunately most editors aren't like this.

What do you like best about your clients, and the editors and publishers you work with: With clients, I like the collaboration process, discussing how to present the material—both the proposal and the text—in the best way possible so that it will catch an editor's eye. With editors, what I like best is the good feeling we each have upon discovering a new author/book, knowing that we both can appreciate and are excited about promoting what this person has written.

You're welcome to share your thoughts and sentiments about the business of writing and publishing: As an author, you should write from your heart, but be real about what's ahead if you want to be published. It's all about matchmaking from the moment you begin your search for a publisher: finding the right agent who believes in you and what you've written, who'll then find an editor/publisher who feels the same way, who'll in turn find—match you up with—that bigger audience who'll want to read and buy your book. And, as if you haven't heard this before: The best strategy you can have is to build your platform, especially for nonfiction, as editors always want a strong platform to show that you're getting yourself out there and have real credibility. Blogging regularly shows you have an audience; it's instant, free publicity for the publisher, so consider having your own blog if you don't already.

Do you wish to describe who you are: (See above.)

Will our business exist as we know it in ten years or so: I hope so, but I think there will be much more niche stuff given how we can personalize our tastes more now with websites, blogging, and so forth. Perhaps agents will focus on fewer types of books. And I do think that e-books will survive, although I'd predict that they will be more popular as reference books, texts, and the like rather than as mainstream fiction and nonfiction.

The following information pertains to Janet Reid.

Born: Seattle, Washington.

Hobbies and special personal interests: Contemporary art, contemporary music, justice and death penalty issues.

Subjects and categories you like to agent: Crime fiction, literary fiction tied to the West, cowgirl noir, how-to books, interesting and provocative books that everyone else sneers at.

Subjects and categories writers shouldn't bother pitching to you: Domestic, sexual, pastoral abuse. Poetry (although I represent poets for their narrative work), screenplays.

What might you be doing if you weren't agenting: Stalking Jack Reacher.

What's the most effective ways for writers to grab your attention: Write a compelling query letter on a twenty-dollar bill.

Do you charge fees separate from your commission, or offer non-agenting fee-based services: No.

What are representative titles you have sold to publishers: *Where Hope Begins* by Alysia Sofios (Pocket); *First Contact* by Evan Mandery (Harper); *Even* by Andrew Grant (Thomas Dunne Books); *The Breach* by Patrick Lee (Harper); *All Roads Lead Me Back to You* by Kennedy Foster (Pocket); *The Little Book of Curses and Maledictions for Everyday Use* by Dawn Rae Downton (Skyhorse); *Chasing Smoke* by Bill Cameron (Bleak House Books); *Eternal Prison* by Jeff Somers (Orbit).

How do you feel about writers: Their work and their confidence in me allows me to earn a living doing what I love.

What do you tell entities from other planets and dimensions about your job: I try not to discuss my work when on vacation.

What are your favorite books, movies, TV shows, and why: *The Wire*. No further explanation needed.

How would you describe the writer from hell: Well, I am Satan's literary agent, so I describe him as "mine."

How would you describe the publisher and/or editor from hell: There are no publishers or editors in hell. They rejected it as "not quite right for them."

What do you like best about your clients, and the editors and publishers you work with: Their brilliant writing and creativity. And they are hilarious. I'm so, so fortunate to have them on my list. As for editors: They work magic.

Do you wish to describe who you are: No. I don't want to scare anyone...yet.

Will our business exist as we know it in ten years or so: Yes.

The following information pertains to June Clark.

Education: BA in creative writing/mass media, Queens College, NY; MA in writing and publishing, Emerson College, Boston, MA.

Career story: Marketing and promotion in cable TV, professional copywriter, published author, and playwright.

Hobbies and special personal interests: Writing, reading, traveling, music, food and wine, pets.

Subjects and categories you like to agent: Accepting limited submissions exclusively in commercial nonfiction areas of film/TV/theater; entertainment biographies; health and beauty; reference and how-to; women's issues; relationships; self-help and pop psychology; food, cocktails and wine.

Subjects and categories writers shouldn't bother pitching to you: Sci-fi, horror, fantasy; military history; politics; Westerns; poetry; children's books; memoirs; short stories/novellas.

What might you be doing if you weren't agenting: Writing full time or working in theater.

What's the most effective ways for writers to grab your attention: Learn about the types of books I represent and tell me why you think I'm the right agent for your work. Then, show a strong platform or experience in the topic being written about and presenting a compelling query about your book.

Do you charge fees separate from your commission, or offer non-agenting fee-based services: I have provided freelance writing/editing services, but this work is always separate from our agency.

What are representative titles you have sold to publishers: *Black Comedians on Black Comedy: How African Americans Taught Us How to Laugh* by Darryl Littleton (Applause); *Eve's Bible: A Woman's Guide to the Old Testament* by Sarah Forth (St. Martin's Press); *The Vampress Girls* series by Jacy and Nik Nova (Kensington); *Beatleology: Embracing Your Inner Beatle* by Adam Jaquette and Roger Jaquette (Adams Media); *Simply Elegant Flowers* by Michael George (North Light); *Friends on a Rotten Day* by Hazel Dixon-Cooper (Weiser Books); *Bad Bosses, Crazy Coworkers & Other Office Idiots: 201 Smart Solutions to Every Problem at Work* by Vicky Oliver (Sourcebooks); *Obscene, Indecent, Immoral and Offensive: 100+ Years of Censored, Banned, and Controversial Films* by Stephen Tropiano (Limelight).

Why did you become an agent, and how did you become one: Was helping my agent, Peter Rubie, read query letters and found several projects I liked and was encouraged to pursue them. I continued agenting because it's a sociable job with exposure to interesting ideas and people. And as a writer myself, I can offer a well-rounded perspective to my clients.

How do you feel about writers: Sadly, I feel that being a talented writer is not enough in today's market. It is now necessary to have a great outreach and a reputation in your field or genre in order to get noticed by publishers. That means writers always need to be cultivating an audience for themselves and that's a tall order for many.

What do you tell entities from other planets and dimensions about your job: Not much, since they've never asked!

What are your favorite books, movies, TV shows, and why: In books, I enjoy edgy or witty writers that entertain like Dave Barry, David Sedaris, and Nora Ephron. On TV, I enjoy *In Treatment, Dexter, Real Time with Bill Maher, 30 Rock*, and a few guilty pleasures like *Top Chef* and *American Idol*. Movies…I rarely, if ever, go to the movies; I prefer live theater.

How would you describe the writer from hell: Writers from hell are close-minded and resistant to suggestions on how to improve their work. They have difficulty meeting deadlines or effectively communicating with their editors and treat their agent like a secretary.

How would you describe the publisher and/or editor from hell: Publishers/editors from hell are those who don't return emails or phone calls from agents (and their authors), ask to see material but never respond to it, and expect the author to jump through unreasonable hoops or unrealistic delivery of material and then sit on the author's final manuscript for months without reading or honoring their end of the deal.

What do you like best about your clients, and the editors and publishers you work with: Open communication, positive attitude, respect for an author's work and editor's time, taking initiative, being proactive in their job or career, and acting professionally.

You're welcome to share your thoughts and sentiments about the business of writing and publishing: Publishing is going to have to reinvent itself, especially in our rapidly changing technology age. I think there will be a rise in e-books and print on demand, both of which will make more sense, economically, in the long term. The challenge for all of us, particularly agents, will be in making sure that authors' rights and royalties will be protected. Publishers also need to put more efforts into promotion and place some focus on great concepts and great writing in balance with the whole "platform" issue.

Will our business exist as we know it in ten years or so: I think publishing may go the way of the music business. Writers will become more creative in getting their work seen by the masses and possibly bypass publishers, due to the Internet. I also think the readers of tomorrow will become more comfortable with e-books and there may be [fewer] printed books (saves paper and trees!).

The following information pertains to Meredith Hays.

Born: July 28, 1969 in Lynn, Massachusetts.

Education: BA from Skidmore College.

Career story: After attending the Radcliffe Publishing Program, I worked at Houghton Mifflin Co. in Boston in the now defunct Trade/Reference division, specializing in dictionaries. Moved to NYC and switched gears and worked at agencies, first Writers House, then Linda Chester & Associates, then Judith Ehrlich Literary Management and now FinePrint.

Hobbies and special personal interests: My family (husband, Reed, and son, Henry); animals (especially my cats).

Subjects and categories you like to agent: Fiction: Exceptionally crafted novels only; must be surprising, refreshing, and deeply satisfying no matter the subject. Nonfiction: Lifestyle; pop culture; animals/nature; memoir (but no depressing or tragic stories!); crafts.

Subjects and categories writers shouldn't bother pitching to you: Fiction: No romance, Westerns, sci-fi, fantasy, historical fiction, young adult, children's. Nonfiction: Cookbooks, diet, fitness, politics, finance.

What might you be doing if you weren't agenting: Dog trainer.

What's the most effective ways for writers to grab your attention: A short, well crafted, spell-checked query letter.

Do you charge fees separate from your commission, or offer non-agenting fee-based services: No.

What are representative titles you have sold to publishers: *Rollergirl: Totally True Tales from the Track* by Melissa "Melicious" Joulwan (Touchstone); *Lonesome For Bears: A Woman's Journey in the Tracks of the Wilderness* by Linda Jo Hunter (The Lyons Press); *Feltique* by Nikola Davidson (PotterCraft); *The Good Cat Spell Book* by Gillian Kemp (Celestial Arts/Ten Speed Press).

Why did you become an agent, and how did you become one: I went into publishing when I was right out of college and convinced that books were better company than people. When I moved to NYC the first job I was offered was at an agency and I liked how hands-on agenting is—how satisfying it is to follow a book from an idea to a manuscript to a finished published book.

How do you feel about writers: I admire their ability to stick with a subject long enough to create a book-length work.

What do you tell entities from other planets and dimensions about your job: Lots of work, little money.

What are your favorite books, movies, TV shows, and why: Books: *The Giant's House* by Elizabeth McCracken (because it's a lovely twisted love story); *The Time Traveler's Wife* by Audrey Niffenegger (because it's one of the only truly brave, unique, and memorable stories I've come across); all of Jane Austen (because it's Jane Austen); all of Hemingway (because his dialogue cracks me up); *The End of the Affair* (because it's heart-wrenching). Movies: *Rebecca* (because it's pure gothic charm); BBC's *Pride & Prejudice* (because Colin Firth); *Bridget Jones' Diary* (because it's a guilty pleasure); *The Wedding Singer* (because of the music). TV:

Buffy the Vampire Slayer (because it's brilliant); original *Mission Impossible* (because it's so stylized).

How would you describe the writer from hell: One who is clueless about the industry. Oh, and impatient and unkind and contacts me all the time.

How would you describe the publisher and/or editor from hell: One who is mean and not willing to take risks or collaborate.

What do you like best about your clients, and the editors and publishers you work with: I like to work in tandem with clients and editors to create the best project possible. I'm open to new ideas and suggestions and am all for tweaking a manuscript if it will make it better.

Will our business exist as we know it in ten years or so: Can't say because as a new mom I don't even know what's on my schedule for tomorrow!

The following information pertains to Peter Rubie.

Date and location of birth: Taplow, England, 1950.

Education: UK education system, NTCJ (journalism degree equivalent).

Career story: After college I worked in local and regional newspapers before moving to London to work in Fleet Street and then BBC Radio News. In 1981 I moved to the U.S. and worked a variety of jobs including editor-in-chief of a local Manhattan, NY newspaper and freelance editor in publishing before becoming the fiction editor at Walker & Co., for six years or so. I left to become a partner in a small two-person literary agency, and started my own agency in 2000. In 2007 I merged my company with Imprint to form FinePrint (a company with nine agents as of this writing), of which I am the CEO.

Hobbies and special personal interests: Music, movies, Go, chess, reading, woodworking, computing, parenting, writing.

Subjects and categories you like to agent: Narrative nonfiction, parenting, pop science, history, current events, business; crime fiction, thrillers, offbeat literary, history, young-adult and middle-grade, literate SF and fantasy, things that excite and interest me.

Subjects and categories writers shouldn't bother pitching to you: Romance, women's fiction, scripts, poetry, poorly written material of any genre.

What might you be doing if you weren't agenting: Being a professional writer and jazz musician and earning a living as a carpenter (I'd have to be to do the other two things).

What's the most effective ways for writers to grab your attention: Write really well. Not gimmicky but just with a love of, and grasp of, graceful English. Writing is about THINKING, so I'm looking for that VOICE that will engage me from word one.

Do you charge fees separate from your commission, or offer non-agenting fee-based services: No.

What are representative titles you have sold to publishers: Atherton series (Little Brown), Land of Elyon series (Scholastic), and *Skeleton Creek* (Scholastic)—a cutting-edge multimedia book Internet project—by Patrick Carman; *First Copernican* by Dennis Danielson (Walker); *Enemy of the State* by Michael Scharf and Michael Newton (St. Martin's Press); *On Night's Shore* by Randall Silvis (St. Martin's); *Coyote's Wife* by Aimee and David Thurlo (Tor); *Soul Patch* by Reed Farrell Coleman (Bleak House).

Why did you become an agent, and how did you become one: I decided I spent so much time as an editor arguing on behalf of an author in-house it made sense to actually cross over and become an author's representative. I was one of several people let go by the house I was working for after my boss had the bad taste to accidentally drown, and so it made sense to make the move at that point.

How do you feel about writers: I spend every day talking with writers. The best are smart, funny, imaginative just who you would want to spend time with at work or at leisure. I have many friends who are writers, artists, and musicians. The worst are whiny, feel entitled for no good reason, feel aggrieved they're not getting their "due" and are unprofessional in their behavior, acting worse than my six-year-old. Guess who I prefer to be around.

What do you tell entities from other planets and dimensions about your job: Me, human. Do you know what a book is? It's where human beings do their best thinking and express their best ideas, sometimes in the most beautiful language you can imagine.

What are your favorite books, movies, TV shows, and why: Too many to mention. All are what I would consider imaginative and well crafted pieces that throw a light on our world and how we deal with the people in it and our relationships to them.

How would you describe the writer from hell: Unprofessional, demanding, doesn't get the industry and is only concerned with their ill-informed opinion of what life should be, not dealing with what life actually is and making the most of that.

How would you describe the publisher and/or editor from hell: Don't communicate, lie to you, fail to keep promises, fail to follow up and look after your author in-house, are rude and dismissive, too lazy and too ignorant to edit properly.

What do you like best about your clients, and the editors and publishers you work with: They are smart, funny, imaginative, stimulating people who are a blast to hang out with and work with.

You're welcome to share your thoughts and sentiments about the business of writing and publishing: Publishing at present is struggling to come to terms with the speed that technology is changing the way we do things. The issue is not technology though, but how technology is changing how things have always been done and what model or models are going to replace the old ways. It's one reason senior publishing executives are leaving their institutions and starting up their own businesses based on their perception of how the industry is moving forward. Writers need to be writing about and coming to terms with these profound changes in the way we view and live our lives for better or worse, but too few are. Save me from another book about a dysfunctional childhood or relationship that is totally engrossed in its own misery and can't or won't relate to the lives of others.

Do you wish to describe who you are: Still figuring this one out.

Will our business exist as we know it in ten years or so: Yes, but in 25 years—ah, that's a completely different question. People always want to read, and always want stories so publishing and books will still be around and valid. But in what form? Your guess is as good as mine.

The following information pertains to Stephany Evans.

Born: October 11, 1957; West Chester, Pennsylvania.

Education: Elizabethtown College, Elizabethtown, PA.

Hobbies and special personal interests: Running, mosaics, gallery-hopping, movies, reading, travel.

Subjects and categories you like to agent: Health, wellness, spirituality, food and wine, green/sustainability; narrative nonfiction; literary fiction, mysteries, women's fiction—both literary and commercial (romance, light suspense, paranormal, historical).

Subjects and categories writers shouldn't bother pitching to you: Poetry, screenplays, children's books, parenting, true crime, fantasy, sci-fi, overtly moralistic tales; no abused women, no abused children.

What might you be doing if you weren't agenting: Reading, painting, home renovation, operate an art gallery.

What's the most effective ways for writers to grab your attention: Fine wine, flowers…but seriously: write well!

Do you charge fees separate from your commission, or offer non-agenting fee-based services: No.

What are representative titles you have sold to publishers: *Solar Power Your Home and Alternative Energy* by Rik DeGunther (Wiley/For Dummies); *A Geography of Oysters, Fruitless Fall,* and *American Terroir* by Rowan Jacobsen (Bloomsbury USA); *Do Dead People Watch You Shower?* by Concetta Bertoldi (HarperCollins); *Ina May's Guide to Childbirth* by Ina May Gaskin (BantamDell); *Fully Present: The Art & Science of Mindfulness* by Susan Smalley, PhD and Diana Winston (Da Capo); *Soul Currency* by Ernest Chu (New World Library); *The Wisdom to Know the Difference* by Eileen Flanagan (Tarcher); *The Extra Mile* by Pam Reed (Rodale); *Something Borrowed* and *Love the One You're With* by Emily Giffin (St. Martin's Press); *The Rose Variations* by Marisha Chamberlain (Soho Press); *Lee* and *Fields of Asphodel* by Tito Perdue (Overlook Press); *SEALed with a Kiss* by Mary Margret Daughtridge (Sourcebooks/Casablanca); *Nice Girls Don't Have Fangs* by Molly Harper (Pocket Books).

Why did you become an agent, and how did you become one: I never had any idea of being an agent. I feel extremely lucky to have met someone who offered me the opportunity, I loved it, and couldn't think of anything I'd like to do more.

How do you feel about writers: Lovely creatures! Many are my best friends.

What do you tell entities from other planets and dimensions about your job: I so rarely get to talk to such folk at all. We're usually catching up on other subjects.

What are your favorite books, movies, TV shows, and why: Too many too many too many too many! In books and movies, I tend to gravitate in two directions, either toward something light and funny, or something dark and beautiful. In either case, the heart is most important, not the spectacle. TV is where I slum. Aside from PBS' News Hour and Washington Week, I most often will watch all the reality shows (except the ones where contestants eat gross things). In the little box, spectacle rules.

What do you like best about your clients, and the editors and publishers you work with: Their creativity, intelligence, heart, responsiveness, and their willingness to extend themselves, both to further their own careers and to make the world a better, more interesting place.

The following information pertains to Brendan Deneen.

Born: Hartford, CT

Education: University of Scranton, University of Glasgow (Scotland).

Career Story: Assistant agent at William Morris Agency, story editor at Scott Rudin Productions, director of development at Miramax/Dimension Films, director of production and development at The Weinstein Company, senior vice president at Objective Entertainment. Now with FinePrint Literary.

Hobbies and special personal interests: Comic book nerd. Film buff.

Subject and categories you like to agent: All, but particularly interested in thrillers and YA right now.

Subjects and categories writers shouldn't bother pitching to you: None. If it's a great idea, I'm interested.

What might you be doing if you weren't agenting: Professional breakdancing.

What's the most effective way for writers to grab your attention: A smart, funny, concise cover letter.

Do you charge fees separate from your commission, or offer non-agenting fee-based services: I help my clients develop their ideas for the low, low cost of "free."

What are representative titles you have sold to publishers: *Death's Daughter* by Amber Benson, *Killer's Diary* by Brian Pinkerton, *Drama High* by L. Divine, *The Wildman* by Rick Hautala, *The Hydes* by James A. Moore.

Why did you become an agent, and how: I became an agent because I love the idea of discovering and fostering new talent. I became an agent pretty much by accident.

How do you feel about writers: I love writers, especially ones who understand that this business is all about patience, mixed with a healthy dose of workaholism.

What are your favorite books movies, TV shows, and why: My favorite books include *Grendel* by John Gardner and *Geek Love* by Katherine Dunn. My favorite movies include *Ed Wood* and *Blade Runner*. My favorite TV shows include *Lost* and *The Office*.

How would you describe the writer from hell: Someone who thinks constantly badgering me makes me more likely to work hard for them.

How would you describe the publisher and/or editor from hell: Someone who doesn't return calls or emails.

What do you like best about your clients, and the editors and publishers you work with: Patience in my clients and responsiveness from editors/publishers.

Will our business exist as we know it in ten years or so: It may be altered somewhat but people will always read and watch movies, so I'll still have a job.

FIREBRAND LITERARY

285 West Broadway, Suite 520, New York, NY 10013

212-334-0025

www.firebrandliterary.com

Individual agent(s) name and email address: Danielle Chiotti; Danielle@firebrandliterary.com

Date and location of birth: September 3, Pittsburgh, PA.

Education: University of Pittsburgh, BA, creative writing and communications.

Career Story: Danielle Chiotti has nearly ten years' experience with trade fiction and nonfiction publishing. Formerly a senior editor at both Kensington Publishing and Adams Media, she has worked on a wide variety of books ranging from contemporary women's fiction to narrative nonfiction, romance, relationships, humor, and young adult.

Subjects and categories you like to agent: For fiction: Commercial fiction, multicultural fiction (with a slightly literary edge), romance, paranormal romance, and young-adult fiction for girls. I tend to favor fish-out-of-water stories and stories in which characters get themselves in very sticky situations and must find a way out. I am drawn to gorgeous writing and strong, flawed characters who aren't afraid to take big chances or show a little bit of a dark side.

For nonfiction: Narrative nonfiction, memoir, self-help, dating/relationships, humor, current events, women's issues, and cooking (including cookbooks and food narrative). I am looking for compelling projects that present an author's unique voice and point of view, or that sheds light on a previously unexplored topic.

Subjects and categories writers shouldn't bother pitching to you: Abuse memoirs, sports, New Age nonfiction, children's books, sci-fi/fantasy, romantic suspense, thrillers, poetry, anything that is described as the "new *Bridget Jones's Diary.*"

What might you be doing if you weren't agenting: Writing.

What's the most effective ways for writers to grab your attention: For fiction: Have a great first line that provides an immediate insight into your protagonist.

For nonfiction: Have a unique/original idea and strong, clear writing. Know your subject area and the audience you're trying to reach, and how you can reach them. Be able to describe your project in one sentence: "It's *The Secret* meets *He's Just Not That Into You.*" Know your competition!

Do you charge fees separate from your commission, or offer non-agenting fee-based services: No.

What are representative titles you have sold to publishers: As I fill out this questionnaire, I am brand-new to agenting, so no sales yet!

Why did you become an agent, and how did you become one: How: I became an agent through serendipitous circumstances, which is the way I got into publishing, and the way I've gotten all of my jobs in publishing.

Why: I became an agent so I could deal more creatively with a wider variety of authors and genres.

What are your favorite books, movies, TV shows, and why: Books I come to again and again for inspiration and comfort: *The Mysteries of Pittsburgh* by Michael Chabon, *The American Woman in the Chinese Hat* by Carole Maso, *Great With Child* by Beth Ann Fennelly, *Charlotte's Web* by E. B. White, *No One Belongs Here More Than You* by Miranda July.

Books that are plain old fun: *Valley of the Dolls* by Jacqueline Susann, *Bittersweet* by LaVyrle Spencer, anything by Emily Giffin.

How would you describe the writer from hell: A writer who balks at constructive criticism, who refuses to look outside of themselves and get a sense of the "bigger picture," and who lacks patience with the submission and publishing process.

How would you describe the publisher and/or editor from hell: Lack of communication between editor and author/agent. Lack of transparency on the part of the publisher in terms of in-house process, sales figures, publicity/marketing plans for the author.

What do you like best about your clients, and the editors and publishers you work with: The buzz of excitement when we fall in love with an amazing writer/project, the constant exchange of ideas.

THE FIRM

9465 Wilshire Blvd., 6th floor, Beverly Hills, CA 90212

310-860-8000   fax: 310-860-8132

Agent's name: Alan Nevins

Education: Dual Major: BS, economics, UCLA; BA, motion picture/television studies, UCLA.

Career history: Created in August 2002, and comprising department head Alan Nevins and a team of literary associates, The Firm's book division rose from the ashes of Renaissance, a successful literary agency of nine years' standing, founded by Alan Nevins and two partners in 1993. Renaissance acquired the Irving Paul Lazar agency in 1993 after the death of famed super agent Irving "Swifty" Lazar. Alan Nevins had been Lazar's final and sole associate prior to forming Renaissance and the estate approached Nevins about acquiring the Lazar enterprise. This acquisition, and that of the H. N. Swanson Agency, gave the infant Renaissance the enviable legacy of two of Hollywood's most colorful literary agents and solidified its place as a powerhouse literary firm supplying material to the New York publishers as well as the film/television community.

When Renaissance dissolved in 2002, Nevins joined music and film mogul The Firm as head of the book division. With longstanding and impressive relationships in Hollywood, London and New York, the agency currently represents more than 125 writers, boasts an extensive estate list and partners with more than thirty agencies worldwide for their film and ancillary rights. The Firm book division has major properties in development at the Hollywood studios and with the leading networks, a substantial backlist, and continues to attract some of the world's most sought-after writers for both publishing and film representation.

Awards: Emmy nomination, Executive Producer, *Homeless to Harvard: The Liz Murray Story*; Christopher Award, Executive Producer, *Homeless to Harvard: The Liz Murray Story*.

Categories/subjects that you are most enthusiastic about agenting: commercial fiction, literary fiction, historical fiction, narrative nonfiction, current affairs, lifestyle, women's fiction/chick lit (original voices and storylines), business; children's: unique illustrations and creative storylines that truly stand out; YA fiction: focus on strong storytelling, prose and characters.

What you don't want to agent: Poetry, short stories.

What's the best way for writers to solicit your interest: Email query letter and synopsis to query@thefirmbooks.com.

What are the most common mistakes writers make when pitching you: Sending a proposal or manuscript without first contacting us. Sending single-spaced or otherwise improperly formatted manuscripts.

Please list representative titles you have sold: *What to Expect When You're Expecting* Series (Workman); *A Lotus Grows in the Mud* (Putnam); *Memories are Made of This* (Harmony); *By Myself and Then Some* by Lauren Bacall (HarperCollins); *Learning to Sing* (Random House); *Lost Laysen* (Scribner); *Tickled Pink* (Time Warner); *Deaf Child Crossing* (Simon & Schuster); *Less Is More* (Portfolio); *The Doors* (Hyperion); Larry Collins and Dominique Lapierre (All Titles); *The Black Dahlia Files* (HarperCollins); *Real Life Entertaining* (William Morrow); *Warren Beatty: A Private Man* (Harmony); *Audrey Hepburn: An Elegant Spirit* (Atria); Hank Zipzer YA Series (Penguin); *Baggage Claim* (Simon & Schuster); *Love on the Dotted Line* by David E. Talbert (Simon & Schuster); *Emily's Reasons Why Not* (HarperCollins); *Tonight, Somewhere in New York* (Carroll & Graf); *Sins of the Seventh Sister* (Harmony); Roman Sub Rosa Series (St. Martin's); *The Sword of Attila* (St. Martin's); *Tomorrow to Be Brave* (Free Press).

FOLIO LITERARY MANAGEMENT, LLC

New York: 505 8th Avenue, Suite 603, New York, NY 10018

Washington, DC: 627 K St. NW, Suite 1200, Washington, DC 20006

212-400-1494   fax: 212-967-0977

www.foliolit.com   email: See individual agent listings on website

Agents' names: Jeff Kleinman, Paige Wheeler, Scott Hoffman, Erin Cartwright Niumata, Rachel Vater, Laney Katz Becker

The following information pertains to Jeff Kleinman.

Born: Cleveland, Ohio.

Education: BA with High Distinction, University of Virginia (English/modern studies) MA, University of Chicago (Italian language/literature) JD, Case Western Reserve University.

Career history or story: After graduating from the University of Virginia, I studied Renaissance history in Italy for several years, went to law school, and then joined an art and literary law firm. A few years later, I joined the Graybill & English Literary Agency before becoming one of the founders of Folio in 2006.

Hobbies, interests: Art, history, animals, especially horses (train dressage and event horses).

Subjects and categories you are interested in agenting, including fiction and nonfiction: Very well-written, character-driven novels; some suspense, thrillers, historicals; otherwise mainstream commercial and literary fiction. Prescriptive nonfiction: Health, parenting, aging, nature, pets, how-to, etc. Narrative nonfiction: Especially books with a historical bent, but also art, nature, ecology, politics, military, espionage, cooking, equestrian, pets, memoir, biography.

Subjects and categories writers shouldn't even bother pitching to you: No mysteries, romance, Westerns, SF&F, children's or young adult, poetry, plays, screenplays.

What would you do if you weren't agenting: Practicing intellectual property law or training horses, or both.

What's the best way for fiction writers to solicit your interest: Email preferred (no attachments, please); include a cover letter and the first few pages of the novel.

What's the best way for nonfiction writers to solicit your interest: Email preferred (no attachments, please); otherwise snail mail. Include a cover letter and perhaps a few pages of a sample chapter, and/or an outline.

Do you charge reading or any upfront fees: No charges. AAR members.

In your experience, what are the most common pitching mistakes writers make: Groveling—just pretend this is a job application, and act like a professional; providing too much information—telling too much about the project, rather than being able to succinctly summarize it; sending a poorly formatted, difficult-to-read manuscript.

Describe the client from hell, even if you don't have any: Someone who doesn't listen, doesn't incorporate suggestions, and believes that the world "owes" him (or her) a bestseller.

What's your definition of a great client: Someone who writes beautifully, who has marketing savvy and ability, who is friendly, accessible, easy to work with, fun to talk to, can follow directions and guidance without taking offense.

How can writers increase the odds that you will offer representation: For fiction, write a fabulous book with a fresh voice and compelling, unique perspective, and be able to sum up that book in a single, smart, intriguing sentence or two. For nonfiction, ENHANCE YOUR CREDENTIALS. Get published, or have some kind of platform or fresh perspective that really stands out above the crowd. Show me (so I can show a publisher) that you're a good risk for publication.

Why did you become an agent, and how did you become one: My law firm shared offices with an agency, and I did several book contracts. Gradually, I started reading manuscripts, talking to writers, and before long, there I was—a literary agent.

How do you feel about editors and publishers: I think that too often they're overworked and underpaid, and often don't have the time to really "connect the dots" in a manuscript or a proposal—so it's crucial that we (the writer and I) connect the dots for them.

How do you feel about writers: It depends on the writer.

What do you see in the near future for book publishing: Something utterly new, that we haven't seen before. Maybe Microsoft will design it; maybe Pixar; but it's coming, and it'll revolutionize the industry.

In your opinion, what do editors think of you: That I'm honest, ethical, and have a solid list of clients.

What are some representative titles that you have sold: *The Widow of the South* by Robert Hicks (Warner); *Mockingbird* and *So It Goes* by Charles Shields' (both to Holt); *Freezing Point* by Karen Dionne (Berkley); *I Was Only Trying to Help* by Quinn Cummings (Hyperion); *Finn* by Jon Clinch (Random House).

The following information pertains to Scott Hoffman.

Born: Holmdel, New Jersey.

Education: BA in government from the College of William and Mary; MBA in finance from New York University's Leonard N. Stern School of Business.

Career history or story: Publishing is a second career for me; before becoming a literary agent I ran a lobbying firm in Washington, DC. After a brief flirtation with finance, I realized my two favorite things in life were books and deals—so I figure out a way to do book deals for a living. In 2006, I was fortunate enough to find Jeff and Paige and start Folio with them.

Hobbies, interests: Chess, poker, opera, Bridge, golf, wine.

Subjects and categories you are interested in agenting, including fiction and nonfiction: Novels that fit perfectly in that sweet spot between really well-written commercial fiction and accessible literary fiction (book-club type books); literary science fiction and fantasy; thrillers of all types; all kinds of narrative nonfiction, journalistic or academic nonfiction; edgy, cool pop-culture nonfiction.

Subjects and categories writers shouldn't even bother pitching to you: No kids' books, category romance, Westerns, cozy mysteries, poetry, short stories, stage plays or screenplays.

What would you do if you weren't agenting: In venture capital or running for office.

What's the best way for fiction writers to solicit your interest: Check out our guidelines at www.foliolit.com

What's the best way for nonfiction writers to solicit your interest: Check out our guidelines at www.foliolit.com

Do you charge reading or any upfront fees: No charges. AAR members.

How do you feel about editors and publishers: I think there are many, many things traditional publishers do very well, and some other things they don't. One of the reasons we started Folio was to help authors market their own works—figure out ways to get individuals into bookstores to pick up their specific title.

How do you feel about writers: It takes a special kind of personality to be able to spend a year in a closet writing a book. I like special personalities.

What do you see in the near future for book publishing: Authors and their agents will begin to take a much more active approach in marketing their titles.

In your opinion, what do editors think of you: That I'm a fair and kind agent with a great eye for talent who's tough enough to always look out for his clients' best interests.

What are some representative titles that you have sold: *Lessons from the CEO's Boss* by Anne Marie Fink (Crown Business); *The Fug Awards* by Heather Cocks and Jessica Morgan (Simon Spotlight Entertainment); *Volk's Game* by Brent Ghelfi (Holt); *The Kommandant's Girl* by Pam Jenoff (Mira); *The Preservationist* by David Maine (St. Martin's Press); *The Superman Wish* by John Hideyo Hamamura (Doubleday).

The following information pertains to Erin Cartwright Niumata.

Born: Scranton, Pennsylvania.

Education: BA University of Delaware.

Career history or story: Erin has been in publishing for over fifteen years. She started as an editorial assistant at Simon & Schuster in the Touchstone/Fireside paperback division for several years; then moved over to HarperCollins as an editor, and then she went to Avalon Books as the editorial director, working on romance, mysteries, and Westerns. Erin has edited many authors including Leon Uris, Stuart Woods, Phyllis Richman, Senator Fred Harris, Dean Ornish, Michael Lee West, Debbie Fields, Erica Jong, Brenda Maddox, Lawrence Otis Graham, and Joan Rivers.

Hobbies, interests: Dogs, reading, cycling, running, knitting, sewing.

Subjects and categories you are interested in agenting, including fiction and nonfiction: Fiction: Commercial women's fiction, historical fiction, psychological thrillers, suspense, humor. I love sassy Southern and/or British heroines. Nonfiction: Cookbooks, biographies, petcare/pets, parenting, self-help, pop-culture, humor, women's issues, fashion, decorating.

Subjects and categories writers shouldn't even bother pitching to you: Absolutely no romance, Westerns, cozy mysteries, poetry, short story collections, business, travel memoirs, young adult, or picture books.

What would you do if you weren't agenting: I would be an editor or a teacher.

What's the best way for fiction writers to solicit your interest: I prefer a proposal (nonfiction) or a brief synopsis with the first 50 pages (fiction) with SASE. I receive too many emails to handle.

What's the best way for nonfiction writers to solicit your interest: Cover letter pitch explaining the book and the author's platform along with sample chapters and an outline.

Do you charge reading or any upfront fees: No charges. AAR members.

In your experience, what are the most common pitching mistakes writers make: Not following the submission guidelines and sending me something I don't represent. Or telling me that random people have read the book and think it's fantastic.

Describe the client from hell, even if you don't have any: Someone who fights every piece of advice and calls/emails incessantly wanting updates or just to "chat."

What's your definition of a great client: Someone who is talented, has a great project, an open-minded attitude, eager to learn, ready to promote the book, and is happy to hear suggestions.

Why did you become an agent, and how did you become one: I was an editor for 16 years and decided to try my hand at agenting. So far, so good.

How do you feel about editors and publishers: Editors are overworked, attend entirely too many meetings, have piles of manuscripts that are all urgent, have very little time for anything—which is why agents are crucial for authors.

How do you feel about writers: Most are fantastic.

What are some representative titles that you have sold: *The House on Briar Hill* by Holly Jacobs (Harlequin); *Things That Make Us (Sic)* by Martha Brockenbrough (St. Martin's); *Fabulous Felines* by Sandie Robins (TFH); *Sleeping with Ward Cleaver* by Jenny Gardiner (Dorchester).

The following information pertains to Rachel Vater.

Born: Covington, Kentucky.

Education: BA Northern Kentucky University.

Career history or story: Worked as an editor at Writer's Digest Books before moving to New York City to be an assistant agent at the Donald Maass Literary Agency and then a literary agent with Lowenstein-Yost Associates. She joined Folio in 2007.

Hobbies, interests: Art, piano, theater.

Subjects and categories you are interested in agenting, including fiction and nonfiction: Fiction: Fantasy, urban fantasy or anything with a paranormal element, YA novels (especially fantasy but also historical or anything dealing with contemporary teen issues), MG novels with a fun hip voice young teens can relate to. Nonfiction: Pop culture, business, self-help or humor appealing to professional women.

Subjects and categories writers shouldn't even bother pitching to you: No category romance, Westerns, poetry, short stories, screenplays, nor anything graphically violent.

What would you do if you weren't agenting: I would be an editor, designer, or musician.

What's the best way for fiction writers to solicit your interest: Email or postal mail. Query letter with first few pages. No attachments.

What's the best way for nonfiction writers to solicit your interest: Query via email or postal mail, including credentials, platform, and outline.

Do you charge reading or any upfront fees: No charges. AAR members.

In your experience, what are the most common pitching mistakes writers make: Not knowing what their hook is—what makes the book stand out from the rest out there like it, and failing to emphasize that in the query.

Describe the client from hell, even if you don't have any: A writer who won't gracefully accept editorial notes, and if he/she disagrees with any points, argues angrily instead of working with me/the editor to make the manuscript stronger or more clear.

What's your definition of a great client: A writer who mulls over edit notes carefully and implements them well and quickly, keeps a positive attitude, expresses gratitude to his/her agent and editor, is willing to promote his/her books with tireless enthusiasm.

How can writers increase the odds that you will offer representation: Know the market. Read a lot in your chosen genre and know what makes your book/series different and special.

Why did you become an agent, and how did you become one: I was an editor with Writer's Digest Books, where I edited *The Guide to Literary Agents*. I had a chance to meet and interview a lot of agents. It sounded like a dream job to me, and it is.

How do you feel about editors and publishers: It's crucial for agents to know the preferences and quirks of each publishing house and the editors there. Several editors at the same imprint may all have different tastes, so it's important to keep up on who's looking for exactly what.

How do you feel about writers: Without them, I wouldn't have a job.

What do you see in the near future for book publishing: The ways in which an author can promote his/her book will keep expanding. New technology makes it easier, faster and cheaper to find and reach your target readership.

In your opinion, what do editors think of you: I'm a young ambitious agent building a great list.

What are some representative titles that you have sold: *Wicked Lovely* by Melissa Marr (HarperCollins Children's Books); *Halfway to the Grave* by Jeaniene Frost (Avon/HarperCollins); *Night Life* by Caitlin Kittredge (St. Martin's Press); *I So Don't Do Mysteries* by Barrie Summy (Delacorte Press); *Unpredictable* by Eileen Cook (Berkley).

The following information pertains to Laney Katz Becker.

Born: Toledo, Ohio.

Education: BS, School of Communication, Northwestern University.

Career history or story: My background is as a writer. I started as a copywriter at the ad agency J. Walter Thompson. Over the next two decades I also worked as a freelance journalist; my articles appeared in more than 50 magazines, including

Self, Health, Seventeen, First for Women. I'm also an author (*Dear Stranger, Dearest Friend; Three Times Chai*). Somewhere along the way, I decided that spending seven hours a day in my basement writing books was too solitary for me. I wanted to use my marketing, writing, and reading skills in a new and different way. The agenting world allows me to do just that—and it's never, ever solitary!

Hobbies, interests: Tennis, sewing, reading, writing, theater, spending time with my family, snuggling with my dog.

Subjects and categories you are interested in agenting, including fiction and nonfiction: Fiction: Anything well-suited to book club discussion; anything with a fresh voice; commercial/women's/mainstream/literary. Smart, psychological thrillers. Nonfiction: Memoir; narratives about fascinating subjects that teach me something new and/or expose me to different ideas, cultures, etc.; stories about people who make a difference in the world. Also: Pets, family, kids, relationships, women's issues, the environment and everything else that relates to my life.

Subjects and categories writers shouldn't even bother pitching to you: No romance, genre mysteries, children's, fantasy, science fiction, horror, Westerns.

What would you do if you weren't agenting: Something where I could continue to use my skills as a writer and voracious reader.

What's the best way for fiction writers to solicit your interest: I only accept email queries. Authors are encouraged to include the first few pages (or chapter) in the body of the email. (No attachments, please.)

What's the best way for nonfiction writers to solicit your interest: Query via email, only. Convince me there's a need for your book and why you're uniquely qualified to write it. Feel free to include your proposal in the body of the email. (No attachments, please.)

Do you charge reading or any upfront fees: No charges. AAR members.

In your experience, what are the most common pitching mistakes writers make: Long, rambling query letters that leave me bored or confused. Being addressed as "Dear Agent," or "Dear Sir/Madam," or anything else that shows the author didn't bother to do his/her homework about me.

Describe the client from hell, even if you don't have any: Defensive writers who don't want to revise, don't want to listen and view agents simply as gatekeepers to editors. I'm also not a fan of writers who fail to say thank you. Writers who, because of my writing background, expect me to do their work for them because, "You know how to do this," are also writers I try to avoid. And finally, writers who immediately send back revisions, rather than taking time to let things sit, reread what they've written and then—only then—once they're certain their work can't be any better, send it back to me for my review.

What's your definition of a great client: A talented writer who is also a wonderful, thoughtful person. Someone who understands that revision is part of the writing process and is willing to go the distance to make their project the very best it can be.

How can writers increase the odds that you will offer representation: If your work is compelling, thought-provoking and well-written, you'll get my attention. If your work is fresh and I don't feel like I've seen the idea/theme a million times before you'll stand an even better chance of winning me over.

Why did you become an agent, and how did you become one: Being an agent allows me to use all the skills I've developed as a writer/reader. Plus, I get to work with lots of interesting people—on all sides of the business.

Describe to someone from another planet what you do as an agent: Read, edit, find talented writers, help authors improve their projects, spend time with editors getting to know their tastes/preferences, sell wonderful manuscripts, help authors understand the publishing process, negotiate contracts, come up with fresh ideas about how to promote authors' works, pitch ideas, and finally...practice conflict resolution and hold an occasional hand or two.

How do you feel about editors and publishers: I think that agents and editors are more alike than different. We've all got piles of manuscripts on our desks and we're all trying to make the right connections. We love to read and are busy trying to shepherd projects we're passionate about through the process. We're all overworked/underpaid but we're doing what we do because we love it.

What are your favorite books, TV shows, movies, and why: Although it's no longer on the air, my favorite TV show of all time is *The West Wing*. My favorite movie is *Apollo 13*. My favorite book? I can't decide on just one.

In your opinion, what do editors think of you: They like the fact that I work so closely with my authors on revisions before I submit anything to them, the publishers. They also like that I've already done the writing thing and bring those experiences and sensibilities to the table. They tell me they think I've got a good eye and great taste in the projects/authors I represent—and of course, I agree!

On a personal non-professional level, what do you think people think of you: I'm strong and I don't give up. I've faced many challenges—and keep battling back; I'm a good juggler (of family/friends/work) and a "good picker," as my grandma said, when I introduced her to my future husband.

What are some representative titles that you have sold: *Obedience* by Will Lavender (Crown Books/Shaye Areheart); *First Comes Love, Then Comes Malaria* by Eve Brown-Waite (Broadway Books); *Life's That Way* by Jim Beaver (Putnam/Amy Einhorn Books); *The Crying Tree* by Naseem Rakha (Broadway Books); *The Six Men All Women Should Marry* by Dr. Steven Craig (Simon & Schuster); *The Business of Happiness* by Ted Leonsis (Eagle/Regnery).

The following information pertains to Paige Wheeler.

Born: Richmond, Virginia.

Education: BA, *magna cum laude*, Boston University.

Career history or story: After working in bookstores in college, I moved to London and worked for a financial publisher. My first publishing job in the U.S. was working in editorial for Harlequin/Silhouette. I then worked as an editor for an investment bank before switching over to agenting. My first agenting job was at Artists Agency, where I repped writers for TV, producers, celebrities as well as book authors. I started my own agency, Creative Media Agency Inc, and ran that for nine years before I met Jeff and Scott. Together we decided to form Folio in 2006 to meet the changing needs of authors.

Hobbies, interests: My puppy, reading (!), wine, antiques, interior design/reno.

Subjects and categories you are interested in agenting, including fiction and nonfiction: Fiction: I'm looking for very well-written commercial and upscale fiction—it should have a fresh and fabulous voice; women's fiction, mysteries and thrillers (the smarter the better). Nonfiction: Narrative and prescriptive—self-help, how-to, women's issues, business books (all types), pop culture, soft science, politics, travel, design.

Subjects and categories writers shouldn't even bother pitching to you: No Westerns, SF&F, children's, poetry, plays, screenplays.

What would you do if you weren't agenting: There's another option???

What's the best way for fiction writers to solicit your interest: I prefer an email query with a synopsis, the first few pages embedded (no attachments). I also accept submissions by snail mail.

What's the best way for nonfiction writers to solicit your interest: Email query preferred but snail mail is fine, with a lot of information about the author and his/her platform. What is unique about this project and why is the author the perfect person to write it?

Do you charge reading or any upfront fees: No charges. AAR members.

In your experience, what are the most common pitching mistakes writers make: Oooh, I love groveling! Seriously, forgetting to include specifics (what the project is about), and not understanding the market for the book.

Describe the client from hell, even if you don't have any: Writers who fail to realize that they are not my only client and aren't appreciative of all the things that I do behind the scenes.

What's your definition of a great client: A fabulous writer who understands the process of publishing, is a go-getter but is also patient and understanding of time constraints, and is appreciative of my hard work.

How can writers increase the odds that you will offer representation: If you're an outstanding writer with fresh ideas and an engaging voice, you'll get my attention. For nonfiction, it's about platform, platform, platform—and a unique slant on a concept or idea.

Why did you become an agent, and how did you become one: Again, there's another option????

Describe to someone from another planet what you do as an agent: Um, I don't handle SF& F so I wouldn't be able to communicate with them.

How do you feel about editors and publishers: I think pairing an author with the perfect editor for a project is the difference between merely getting published and building a very successful career. It's our job to find the perfect editor for a particular project.

How do you feel about writers: One of the things I love about this business is that I work with smart and talented people. In general, most writers are super-informed and passionate people who are eager to share their ideas with a larger audience. I like people who possess a viewpoint or don't shy away from an idea and have the information to back it up.

What do you see in the near future for book publishing: Faster adaptation to emerging technologies—as long as it's financially beneficial to the publisher.

In your opinion, what do editors think of you: I'm both intrigued and horrified to find out, but I do hope it's that I'm tenacious, ambitious, and have the drive to succeed.

On a personal non-professional level, what do you think people think of you: Friends and family think that I should probably work less and enjoy life more.

What are some representative titles that you have sold: *On the Edge of the Woods* by Diane Tyrrel (Berkley Sensation); *Targeting the Job You Want* by Kate Wendleton (Career); *Once Upon a Time in Great Britain* by Melanie Wentz (Travel) (St. Martin's); *On Strike for Christmas* by Sheila Roberts (St. Martin's); *An Affair Most Wicked* by Julianne Maclean (Avon); *Don of the Dead* by Casey Daniels (Avon); *Sit Stay Slay* by Linda O. Johnston (Berkley Prime Crime).

The following information pertains to Celeste Fine.

Born: Redlands, California.

Education: BA in government, *magna cum laude*, Harvard University.

Career history or story: After working as an assistant, foreign rights agent, foreign rights manager, and literary agent at Vigliano Associates and Trident Media Group, I joined Folio Literary Management in 2006.

Hobbies, interests: Pool, music, games, tequila.

Subjects and categories you are interested in agenting, including fiction and non-fiction: Nonfiction: 90 percent of my list is nonfiction—mostly platform-driven projects. Fiction: I do a select list of fiction—mostly projects with memorable characters.

Subjects and categories writers shouldn't even bother pitching to you: Women's fiction, romance, graphic novels.

What would you do if you weren't agenting: Rockstar.

What's the best way for fiction writers to solicit your interest: Email.

What's the best way for nonfiction writers to solicit your interest: Email.

Do you charge reading or any upfront fees: No charges. AAR members.

In your experience, what are the most common pitching mistakes writers make: Not being able to provide a compelling sound bite of the project and not knowing their competition.

What's your definition of a great client: A client who is talented, expects to work as hard as I [do] on their project, and understands the business of publishing.

How can writers increase the odds that you will offer representation: Be an expert on your subject.

Why did you become an agent, and how did you become one: I fell in love with partnering with authors to make the most of their careers.

How do you feel about writers: A talented writer can change you. That is extraordinary.

What do you see in the near future for book publishing: I imagine there will be a lot of differences. Very exciting.

What are your favorite books, TV shows, movies, and why: *Tale of Two Cities* and *The Apologist*; *Arrested Development* and *The Closer*; *Confessions of a Dangerous Mind* and *The Departed*.

What are some representative titles that you have sold: *The Alchemy of Aging Well* by Randy Raugh (Rodale); *The LCA's The 30-Day Diabetes Miracle And Cookbook* (Perigee); *The 99¢ Only Store Cookbook* by Christiane Jory (Adams Media); *Eat, Drink, and Be Gorgeous* by Esther Blum (Chronicle); *Unusually Stupid Celebrities* and *Unusually Stupid Politicians* by Kathy and Ross Petras (Villard); *It's Not News, It's Fark* by Drew Curtis (Gotham); *Good Granny, Bad Granny* by Mary Mchugh (Chronicle); *Confessions of a Gambler* by Rayda Jacobs (Overlook); *Rightsizing* by Ciji Ware (Springboard Press).

FOUNDRY LITERARY MEDIA

33 West 17th Street, PH, New York, New York 10011

212.929.5064   fax: 212.929.5471

http://www.foundrymedia.com/

Agent names: Peter H. McGuigan, Yfat Reiss Gendell, Stéphanie Abou, Hannah Brown Gordon, Chris Park, Lisa Grubka, Mollie Glick; mglick@foundry media.com, Stephen Barbara; sbarbara@foundrymedia.com

The following applies to Lisa Grubka.

Born: April 19, 1950, Mineola, New York.

Education: University of Michigan.

Career Story: Began career at the publishing house of Farrar, Straus & Giroux, then spent six years at the William Morris Agency before joining Foundry.

Subjects and categories you like to agent: Fiction: Literary, young adult, and upmarket women's fiction. Nonfiction: Food and wine, memoir, pop-science, narrative.

Subjects and categories writers shouldn't bother pitching to you: Sci-fi, fantasy, romance, crime, mystery, suspense, thrillers.

What's the most effective ways for writers to grab your attention: An engaging and well-written query letter that gives me a sense of the writer's voice, provides me with a thoughtful synopsis, and tells me a bit about the writer.

Do you charge fees separate from your commission, or offer non-agenting fee-based services: No.

What do you like best about your clients, and the editors and publishers you work with: I adore my authors—they work hard, are fantastic human beings, and most importantly they love what they do and it shows in their writing.

The following applies to Mollie Glick.

Career Story: After graduating from Brown University, Mollie began her publishing career as a literary scout, advising foreign publishers regarding the acquisition of rights to American books. She then worked as an editor at the Crown imprint of Random House, before switching over to "the other side" and becoming an agent at

JVNLA (The Jean V. Naggar Literary Agency) in 2003. She joined the Foundry Media team in September, 2008. Mollie's list includes literary fiction, narrative nonfiction, and a bit of practical nonfiction. She's particularly interested in fiction that bridges the literary/commercial divide, combining strong writing with a great plot, and nonfiction dealing with popular science, medicine, psychology, cultural history, memoir and current events. She's very hands-on, working collaboratively with her authors to refine their projects, then focusing on identifying just the right editors for the submissions.

In addition to her work as a literary agent, Mollie also teaches classes on nonfiction proposal writing at MediaBistro, and a copy of her instructional article on nonfiction proposal writing will be featured in this year's edition of the *Writer's Digest* guide to literary agents.

Hobbies and special personal interests: I'm a bit of a foodie, an amateur film critic, and I love to travel.

Subjects and categories you like to agent: Literary fiction, narrative nonfiction, memoir, YA.

Subjects and categories writers shouldn't bother pitching to you: Genre that doesn't cross over. Picture books. Romance

What might you be doing if you weren't agenting: I'd be a food writer, costume designer or film producer.

What's the most effective ways for writers to grab your attention: With a killer query letter and great sample chapters.

Do you charge fees separate from your commission, or offer non-agenting fee-based services: No.

What are representative titles you have sold to publishers: *Drawing in the Dust* by Zoe Klein (Pocket Books); *All About Lulu* by Jonathan Evison (Soft Skull); *Pop Tart* by Kira Coplin and Julianne Kaye (Avon); *Shut Up, I'm Talking: And Other Diplomacy Lessons I Learned in the Israeli Government* by Greg Levey (The Free Press); *Shiny Objects: How We Lost Our Way on the Path to the American Dream and How We Can Find Our Way Back* by Dr. Jim Roberts (HarperOne); *Wounded Warriors* by Mike Sager (Da Capo); *Queen of the Road* by Doreen Orion (Broadway).

Why did you become an agent, and how: I love the thrill of being the first one to discover a great new writer, and I really enjoy collaborating with my writers.

What are your favorite books, movies, TV shows, and why: *Lost, Mad Men, Eastbound and Down*. All three shows have strong aesthetic viewpoints, waver between humor and drama, and [have] great character development.

How would you describe the writer from hell: A writer who is too insecure or untrusting to collaborate on his/her work.

What do you like best about your clients, and the editors and publishers you work with: I love clients who take editorial notes and run with them, who strive to understand the business of writing, and who have got original, fresh voices.

Finally, will our business exist as we know it in ten years or so: Right now, my eyes are on Amazon. Between their Amazon Shorts program, their look-inside-the-book features, and the Kindle, they're reeling out the innovations, and I hope publishers will soon follow their lead.

The following information pertains to **Stephen Barbara.**

Date and location of birth: Born August 1980 in New Haven, Connecticut to Italian-American family.

Education: BA '02 in English literature (with a focus on literary criticism), University of Chicago.

Career Story: After working briefly on the editorial side at HarperCollins, I spent a year as an assistant at the Fifi Oscard Agency. Then in January of 2006 I became agent and contracts director at the Donald Maass Literary Agency. In early 2009 I brought all of my clients to Foundry, where I'm now a full-time agent.

Hobbies and special personal interests: I follow Italian soccer, enjoy traveling, and am an avid reader of business and narrative nonfiction books.

Subjects and categories you like to agent: Literary fiction, commercial fiction, young adult, children's, memoirs, business, narrative nonfiction, health and fitness, humor.

Subjects and categories writers shouldn't bother pitching to you: Romance novels and screenplays.

What might you be doing if you weren't agenting: Cry, gnash my teeth, pull my hair out. I love my job!

What's the most effective ways for writers to grab your attention: Send me a one-page query letter via email with the first five pages pasted into the body of the email. Please mention any writing credits you have and/or endorsements you've received from other writers.

Do you charge fees separate from your commission, or offer non-agenting fee-based services: No.

What are representative titles you have sold to publishers: *The Thing about Georgie* by Lisa Graff (HarperCollins Children's); *The Big Splash* by Jack D. Ferraiolo (Amulet Books); *Dead Is the New Black* by Marlene Perez (Houghton Mifflin Harcourt); *The Little Sleep* by Paul Tremblay (Henry Holt); *The Secret of Zoom* by Lynne Jonell (Holt Books for Young Readers); *If I Should Fall* by Lauren Oliver (Harper Teen); *The November Criminals* by Sam Munson (Knopf Doubleday); *Wish You Were Dead* by Todd Strasser (Egmont USA); *The Body Fat Solution* by Tom Venuto (Avery). Other clients include Newbery Medal winner Laura Amy Schlitz and fitness expert Hugo Rivera.

Why did you become an agent, and how did you become one: Edmund Wilson was probably the writer who most filled me with awe of the New York publishing world when I was growing up, and I knew even in college I wanted to enter into that world and become an editor or agent. But agenting best suited my independent, entrepreneurial instincts.

What are your favorite books, movies, TV shows, and why: Some of my favorite books include *Feed* by M.T. Anderson, *Liar's Poker* by Michael Lewis, *The Russian Debutante's Handbook* by Gary Shteyngart, *Small Is the New Big* by Seth Godin, and the *Artemis Fowl* series. I'm a big fan of *Burn Notice* and *House*, in terms of TV series. (Hint: I like brash and offbeat heroes and protagonists.)

How would you describe the writer from hell: I am happy to report that all my clients are nice, pleasant people in addition to being brilliant writers.

How would you describe the publisher and/or editor from hell: Many of your problems as an agent go away by signing great writers and pairing them with the most committed and caring editors. By and large I've managed to avoid the nightmares many agents report—editors who disappear, editors who package and publish badly, or even simply fail to create enthusiasm for their authors' books in-house.

What do you like best about your clients, and the editors and publishers you work with: What I like is waking up each day and not knowing what I'll discover next: perhaps a wonderful new writer, perhaps an incredible new work by an existing client. There is the joy of always falling in love with a great new project. Then too I like to obsess over the roll-out of a client's book; it's satisfying to see a book released to good reviews and a positive reception with readers.

Finally, will our business exist as we know it in ten years or so: Certainly not. The current economic recession has highlighted a number of issues the industry must address and respond to: the problem of over-publishing; the coming e-book revolution; the struggles of the chains to maintain profitability; redundant imprints, among others. But at Foundry we're very optimistic about the future. There will always be readers for a great book.

The following information pertains to Chris Park.

Education: BA, English, Harvard University.

Career Story: I spent most of my publishing career on the editorial side—working at Random House and Hachette among other companies—before joining Foundry as an agent in 2007.

Subjects and categories you like to agent: Memoirs, narrative nonfiction, sports, Christian nonfiction and women's fiction.

Subjects and categories writers shouldn't bother pitching to you: Genre fiction, New Age.

What's the most effective way for writers to grab your attention: Email query.

Do you charge fees separate from your commission, or offer non-agenting fee-based services: No!

What are representative titles you have sold to publishers: *Bible Babel: Making Sense of the Most Talked-about Book of All Time* by Kristin M. Swenson (HarperCollins); *Love, Daddy: A Memoir* by Kambri Crews (Villard/Random House); *High Heat: The Search for the Fastest Pitcher of All Time* by Tim Wendel (DaCapo Press); *How to Be Like God: One Church's Experiment with Living the Old Testament Book of Leviticus* by Daniel M. Harrell (FaithWords).

Why did you become an agent, and how did you become one: I loved my time as an editor, but felt that it was increasingly difficult to be the kind of advocate that I wanted to be for my authors. Agenting seemed to feature the perks of being an editor (working closely with authors, editing, advocating) without the unpleasant aspects of working within corporate publishing (having to pledge my firstborn child to get attention for a book).

What do you tell entities from other planets and dimensions about your job: It's like the movie *Jerry Maguire*, but with less running and more emailing.

JEANNE FREDERICKS LITERARY AGENCY, INC.

221 Benedict Hill Road, New Canaan, CT 06840

203-972-3011

www.jeannefredericks.com   email: jeanne.fredericks@gmail.com

Agent's name: Jeanne Fredericks

Born: April 19, 1950, Mineola, New York.

Education: BA Mount Holyoke College, 1972, major in English; Radcliffe Publishing Procedures Course, 1972. MBA, New York University Graduate School of Business (now called Stern), major in marketing, 1972.

Career history: Established own agency in 1977 after being an agent and acting director of Susan P. Urstadt (1990–1996). Prior to that, I was an editorial director of Ziff-Davis Books (1980–1981), acquiring editor and the first female managing editor of Macmillan's Trade Division (1974–1980), and assistant to the editorial director and foreign/subsidiary rights director of Basic Books (1972–1974). Member of AAR and Authors Guild.

Hobbies/personal interests: Crew, swimming, yoga, reading, traveling, casual entertaining, gardening, photography, family activities, volunteering at church.

Categories/subjects that you are most enthusiastic about agenting: Practical, popular reference by authorities, especially in health, science, fitness, gardening, and women's issues. Also interested in business, cooking, elite sports, parenting, travel, and antiques/decorative arts.

What you don't want to agent: Horror, occult fiction, true crime, juvenile, textbooks, poetry, essays, plays, short stories, science fiction, pop culture, guides to computers and software, politics, pornography, overly depressing or violent topics, memoirs that are more suitable for one's family or that are not compelling enough for the trade market, romance, manuals for teachers.

If you were not an agent, what might you be doing instead: Reading and traveling more for pleasure, volunteering more, learning to play piano, writing or perhaps running a publishing company.

What's the best way for writers to solicit your interest: Please query with an SASE (or by email without attachments to jeanne.fredericks@gmail.com). No phone calls, faxes, or deliveries that require signatures.

Do you charge reading or management fees: No.

Can you provide an approximation by percent of what you tend to represent by category: 1 percent fiction (just from existing nonfiction clients); 0 percent children's; 99 percent nonfiction.

What are the most common mistakes writers make when pitching you: Calling me to describe their proposed books and giving me far too much detail. I'd much rather see that potential clients can write well before I spend valuable phone time with them. Also, claiming to have the only book on a subject when a quick check on the Internet reveals that there are competitive titles.

How would you describe the client from hell: An arrogant, pushy, self-centered, unreliable writer who doesn't understand publishing or respect my time, and who vents anger in an unprofessional way.

How would you describe the perfect client: A creative, cooperative, media-savvy professional who is an expert in his or her field and who can offer information and guidance that is new and needed by a sizeable audience.

How and why did you ever become an agent: I reentered publishing as an agent because the flexible hours and home-based office were compatible with raising children. I enjoy working with creative authors who need my talents to find the right publishers for their worthy manuscripts and to negotiate fair contracts on their behalf. I'm still thrilled when I open a box of newly published books by one of my authors, knowing that I had a small role in making it happen. I'm also ever hopeful that the books I represent will make a positive difference in the lives of many people.

What, if anything, can a writer do to increase the odds that you will become his or her agent: Show me that they have thoroughly researched the competition and can convincingly explain why their proposed books are different, better, and needed by large, defined audiences. Be polite, patient, and willing to work hard to make their proposals ready for submission. Build their media experience and become in demand for regular workshops/presentations.

How would you describe to someone (or something) from another planet what it is that you do as an agent: I select authors, find them the right publishers, negotiate the best deal for them, act as their advocate and diplomat through the publishing process, and handle the money side of the business for them so that they can concentrate on what they do best.

Do you have any particular opinions or impressions of editors and publishers in general: Having been on the editorial side of publishing for about ten years, I have great respect for the demands on the time of a busy editor. I therefore try to be targeted and to the point when I telephone or email them and provide them with a one-page pitch letter that gives them the essence of what they need to make a proposal to management. I also make sure that the proposals I represent are focused, complete, and professional to make it easy for an editor to grasp the concept quickly and have a good sense of what the book will be like and why it will sell well. With few exceptions, editors value the creativity and hard work of authors and are intelligent and well meaning. Since they are often overwhelmed with manuscripts, paperwork, and meetings, though, they sometimes neglect some of their authors and need an agent's nudging and reminders. I think that some editors are frustrated by the emphasis on celebrity and platform in the selection process and wish there were more publishers willing to build the careers of authors who have writing talent and authority in their fields of expertise. I share that frustration with them.

Please list representative titles you have sold: *Your New Green Home* and

Beautiful Solar Homes by Stephen Snyder and Dave Bonte (Gibbs Smith); Lilias! Yoga Gets Better with Age by Lilias Folan (Rodale); Waking the Warrior Goddess: Dr. Christine Horner's Program to Protect Against and Fight Breast Cancer by Christine Horner, MD (Basic Health); The Generosity Plan by Kathy LeMay (Beyond Words/Atria); Canadian Vegetable Gardening by Doug Green (Cool Springs); Food Fray: Inside the Controversy Over Genetically Modified Food by Lisa Wessel, PhD (AMACOM); Stealing with Style and The Big Steal (novels) by Emyl Jenkins (Algonquin); Raising an Optimistic Child by Bob Murray, PhD and Alicia Fortinberry (McGraw-Hill); Palm Springs Gardening by Maureen Gilmer (Contemporary/McGraw-Hill); Sentinel of the Seas: Life and Death at the Most Dangerous Lighthouse Ever Built by Dennis Powers (Kensington); Melanoma by Catherine M. Poole and Dupont Guerry, MD (Yale University Press); Heal Your Heart with EECP by Debra Braveman, MD (Celestial Arts); Homescaping by Anne Halpin (Rodale); The Monopoly Guide to the Real Estate Marketplace by Carolyn Janik (Sterling); Cowboys and Dragons: Shattering Cultural Myths to Advance Chinese-American Business by Charles Lee, PhD (Dearborn); The American Quilt by Robert Shaw (Sterling); No Limit: From the Cardroom to the Boardroom by Donald Krause and Jeff Carter (AMACOM); Rough Weather Seamanship for Sail and Power by Roger Marshall (International Marine/McGraw-Hill); Building Within Nature by Andy and Sally Wasowski (University of Minnesota Press); The Green Market Baking Book by Laura Martin (Sterling); I Ching for Executives by Donald Krause (AMACOM); Taking the Sea: Perilous Waters, Sunken Ships, and the True Story of the Wrecker Captains, Tales of the Seven Seas by Dennis Powers (Taylor); The Budget Gardener by Maureen Gilmer (Cool Springs); Techniques of Graphite Pencil Drawing by Katie Lee (Sterling); Artful Watercolor by Carolyn Janik and Lou Bonamarte (Sterling).

HALSTON FREEMAN LITERARY AGENCY, INC.

140 Broadway, 46th Floor New York, NY 10005

Contact: Molly Freeman, Betty Halston. Snail mail or email only; queryhalston freemanliterary@hotmail.com

Career Story: Prior to becoming an agent, Ms. Halston was a marketing and promotion director for a local cable affiliate.

Hobbies and Special Interests: Travel, yoga, tennis, and a nice glass of wine with dinner.

Subjects and categories we like to agent: Betty Halston—80 percent nonfiction—20 percent fiction. Does not want to see children's books, poetry, text books, erotica, young adult.

Molly Freeman—75 percent nonfiction—25 percent fiction. Does not want to see children's books, poetry, textbooks, New Age, erotica, horror.

Most effective ways for writers to grab our attention: Write a compelling query letter.

For nonfiction include sample chapters, overview, why you are qualified to write on your subject, biography, and details about any marketing platform you might have.

For fiction include synopsis and first three chapters.

Email or snail mail only. No faxes, phone calls, or attachments. If you email your query, include sample chapters and other requested material in text of the email. Include SASE if you query by snail mail.

Fees: We do not charge reading or editorial fees. We charge for photocopying, if we accept someone as a client.

Representative titles: Presently, we have a half-dozen deals pending that should be closing in May or June.

What we like about our clients: We are a hands-on agency specializing in quality nonfiction and fiction. As a new agency, it is imperative that we develop relationships with good writers who are smart, hardworking, and understand what's required of them to promote their work.

Writer from hell is a person who won't listen and is, more often than not, late getting requested material submitted.

It is our belief that the publishing industry will be predominantly e-books in ten years. Technology will improve and become less expensive, making it attractive, especially to younger people, to download books. Brick-and-mortar stores will begin to disappear unless independents and chains can service the e-book market as competitively as online sellers.

SARAH JANE FREYMANN LITERARY AGENCY

59 West 71st Street, #9b, New York, NY 10023

212-362-9277   Steve Schwartz: 212-362-1998

www.sarahjanefreymann.com

email: sarah@sarahjanefreymann.com, steve@sarahjanefreymann.com

Please send submissions to submissions@sarahjanefreymann.com

Agents' names: Sarah Jane Freymann; Steve Schwartz (Associate); Jessica Sinsheimer, jessica@sarahjanefreymann.com; Katharine Sands, katharinesands@nyc.rr.com

The following information pertains to Sarah Jane Freymann.

Born: London.

Education: Although I spent most of my childhood in New York City, I went to a French school—the Lycée Français de New York. I also studied ballet with

Balanchine and grew up in a home where the environment was intensely 19th-century European.

Career history or story: My first job was with the United Nations. I also worked as a model...in real estate...and as an editor in a publishing company.

Hobbies, interests: I am interested in journeys and adventures of every kind—both inner and outer. My personal interests and hobbies keep changing. Right now, I am into teaching...yoga...and, as soon as my shoulder heals, kayaking.

Subjects and categories you are interested in agenting, including fiction and nonfiction: Sarah Jane: Nonfiction: Spirituality, psychology, self-help; women's issues, health/medicine (conventional and alternative); cookbooks; narrative nonfiction; natural science, nature; memoirs; cutting-edge journalism; multi-cultural issues; parenting; lifestyle; history. Fiction: Sophisticated mainstream and literary fiction with a distinctive voice: historical and biblical fiction; edgy young-adult fiction.

Steve Schwartz: Nonfiction: Business; sports; humor; men's issues; politics; new technology. Fiction: Mystery/crime; thrillers, fantasy; historical sagas; adventure; sports—popular fiction in almost any genre as long as it grabs me from the first paragraph and doesn't let go.

Jessica Sinsheimer: Nonfiction or fiction: Works that speak to life in the 21st century.

Subjects and categories writers shouldn't even bother pitching to you: Westerns, screenplays, and almost anything channeled.

What would you do if you weren't agenting: Working with Doctors Without Borders; with children and adolescents; competitive ballroom dancing; singing opera (if I could); cultivating a quiet haven by the sea.

What's the best way for fiction writers to solicit your interest: Via a well-written and interesting query letter (include email address), or via an email query (with no attachments). Please send queries to submissions@sarahjanefreymann.com.

What's the best way for nonfiction writers to solicit your interest: Via a well-written and interesting query letter (include email address), or via an email query (with no attachments). Please send queries to submissions@sarahjanefreymann.com.

Do you charge reading or any upfront fees: There are no reading or upfront fees.

In your experience, what are the most common pitching mistakes writers make: Calling and attempting to describe projects over the phone; characterizing a project as "The best...Startling...Never before in publishing history..." and so on...

Describe the client from hell, even if you don't have any: I honestly wouldn't know because I've always made sure never to take on such a client, but it would be someone who isn't honest with us about themselves, the work, or who has seen it in the past or is reviewing it now. Or someone who is a generally difficult, mean-spirited human being.

What's your definition of a great client: Someone who is not only a natural storyteller and writes beautifully, with passion and intelligence, but who is also a nice human—in other words, a "mensch." Someone with a sense of humor, who has the patience, the willingness, and the humility to rewrite their material when necessary. And someone who appreciates the hard work and the passion that their agent brings to the job. I am fortunate to have several such clients.

How can writers increase the odds that you will offer representation: Submit a strong, clear, well-written query that sells both the book and its author, with the promise of substance rather than hype.

Why did you become an agent, and how did you become one: I became an agent by rushing in where angels feared to tread, and if I knew then what I know now…I'd do the same thing all over again.

Describe to someone from another planet what you do as an agent: That I am a treasure hunter in search of new universes and galaxies, and of new ways of looking at our old, familiar universe. That I assist writers in getting published by helping them edit and shape their proposals, and then by being a deal-maker, a matchmaker, and a negotiator once the work is ready to be launched.

How do you feel about editors and publishers: I love editors. They are intelligent, idealistic, well-informed, incredibly hardworking, and absolutely devoted to their books and to their authors.

How do you feel about writers: I have great respect for writers. They have the capacity to reveal the truth and create new visions for the world.

What do you see in the near future for book publishing: Like all arts and industries, publishing is going through a sometimes painful transition. In large measure, due to the Internet, the publishing universe (like the rest of the world) is becoming increasingly global. This is a challenge—but a challenge we should accept and even welcome.

In your opinion, what do editors think of you: I would imagine editors think I'm a straight shooter and a tough negotiator—but someone who is always fair, invariably gracious, and has terrific projects.

On a personal, nonprofessional level, what do you think people think of you: People say that I am charming, generous, elegant, warm, intuitive, kind and passionate about life. By the same token, I have strong opinions and at times, according to my daughter, I can be self-righteous.

What are some representative titles that you have sold: *Souls of the Air: Invoking the Essence of Birds* by Sy Montgomery (Simon & Schuster); *The Perfect One-Dish: Simple Meals for Family and Friends* by Pam Anderson (Houghton Mifflin); *Mediterranean Hot & Spicy* by Aglaia Kremezi (Random House/Broadway); *Birth Day: A Pediatrician Explores the Science, the History, and the Wonder of Childbirth* by Dr. Mark Sloan (Random House/Ballantine); *100 Places Every Woman Should Go* by Stephanie Elizando Griest (Traveler's Tales) and *Mexican Enough* (Simon & Schuster/Atria); *Stylish Sheds and Elegant Hideaways* by Debra Prinzing and William Wright (Clarkson Potter); *Tossed & Found: Customization, Reclamation, & Personification for Your Home* by John and Linda Meyers (Stewart, Tabori & Chang); *I Want to be Left Behind: Rapture Here on Earth* Brenda Peterson (a Merloyd Lawrence book); *That Bird Has My Wings: The Autobiography of an Innocent Man on Death Row* with an Introduction by Pema Chodrun (Harper One); *Taxpertise* by Bonnie Lee (agent Katharine Sands) (Entrepreneur Press); *How to Make Love to a Plastic Cup: and Other Things I Learned While Trying to Knock Up My Wife* by Greg Wolfe (HarperCollins); *The Fatigue Prescription* by Linda Hawes Clever MD (Viva/

Cleis Press); *Wisdom 2.0: Ancient Secrets for the Creative & Constantly Connected* by Soren Gordhamer (HarperOne); *Emptying the Nest: Launching Your Reluctant Young Adult* by Dr. Brad Sachs (Palgrave Macmillan).

FULL CIRCLE LITERARY, LLC.

7676 Hazard Center Drive, Suite 500, San Diego, CA 92180

858-824-9269 (No phone queries, please!)

www.fullcircleliterary.com   www.fullcirclelit.blogspot.com

Agents' names: Lilly Ghahremani, Stefani Von Borstel. For adult fiction and nonfiction, please email query to submissions@fullcircleliterary.com.

Born: Lilly: November 8, Chicago. Stefanie: Libra born in San Antonio, Texas.

Education: Lilly: JD from UCLA School of Law; BA in English from University of Michigan; MBA from San Diego State University (expected 2009). Stefanie: BA in English and Professional Marketing Program, University of California, San Diego.

Career history: Lilly: Following law school, I decided to "use my powers for good." With some editing experience under my belt, I formally began my publishing career with a small firm that specialized in authors' affairs. Although I loved helping authors finalize the paperwork, addressing copyright affairs and doing some pitching to publishers, I wanted to really dig in and be involved in the creative process more, finding and growing talent and carrying it through to completion, so we launched Full Circle in 2004 to allow us to do just that. Stefanie: As an undergrad English Lit student, I started my first internship in the editorial department of Penguin/PSS, where my first duties included reading submissions and testing copy for *Mad Libs!* I thought, wow, what a fun industry, this is for me! I moved on to working in the marketing department at Harcourt, where I worked over the course of seven years in various publicity, advertising, and promotions positions. After experiencing both the editorial and marketing/sales side of trade publishing, I decided to combine my experience to help writers navigate the publishing world as an agent.

Hobbies and special personal interests: Lilly: Traveling, reading (of course!), dancing, collecting random pop trivia, yoga. Stefanie: Cooking and entertaining, flamenco and salsa dancing, tennis, travel, and foreign films.

Categories/subjects that you are most enthusiastic about agenting: Lilly: Green living, crafting books/do-it-yourself, pop culture, nonfiction how-to books written by an expert with a funny writing voice, and young adult. Stefanie: Multicultural fiction for adults, teens, and children (especially Latino), nonfiction how-to including parenting, green living, women's interest, and crafts.

What might you be doing if you weren't agenting: Lilly: Realistically I'd be doing the lawyer grind. Blech. Stefanie: I think I'd like to own a chocolate shop–children's boutique–bookstore—a combination of a few of my favorite things!

What's the most effective ways for writers to grab your attention: Lilly: Professionalism is underrated! Authors who do their research and are clear about why they're pitching to me (correctly!) will have my attention. Stefanie: I am always impressed when a writer is familiar with books and authors we've represented.

Do you charge fees separate from your commission, or offer non-agenting fee-based services: Absolutely not. Full Circle does not charge any additional fees for its services, nor do we charge a reading fee.

Why did you become an agent, and how did you become one: Stefanie: After working in both the editorial and marketing/sales side of trade publishing, I found that agenting is a great way to be involved in a book from the beginning. So I put my publishing experience to work and I became an agent to connect books with readers!

How do you feel about writers: Lilly: Writers are often the most unappreciated artists out there. Writing a book is no small feat, and writers are some of the most articulate clients you could possibly dream to work with. Plus they are fellow readers, which automatically brings them close to my heart! Stefanie: I am always amazed at the creative ideas and imagination that seem to fill writers from head to toe. Writing is a true craft!

What do you tell entities from other planets and dimensions about your job: Lilly: I tell them no, I didn't agent *The Da Vinci Code*! Stefanie: Many times people think that since I work with books that I must be a writer OR that I can print their book. I have to explain that I am fortunate to work with both writers and publishers, but I don't write or publish!

How would you describe the writer from hell: The problem writer wouldn't take the time to learn about the industry and what are (or aren't) realistic expectations of an agent or, more importantly, a publisher! On the flipside, a dream author is a self-starter, a self-promoter who realizes they are the foundation of a successful book, and that never changes, even with the biggest publisher or marketing budget.

How would you describe the publisher and/or editor from hell: Lack of communication. Sending a manuscript and not hearing back is purgatory for agents, whether it's in the submission stage or delivery of a final manuscript.

What do you like best about your clients, and the editors and publishers you work with: Lilly: In general, I try to work with editors I feel a personal connection with—it's important to me that I leave my books in capable, caring hands. I am proud to work with publishers who bring enthusiasm and incredible insight into the projects we share. Stefanie: I have a passion for the books I represent that I truly share with my authors and the editors I work with. I love the spark of a new idea and seeing it transformed (after lots of work, of course) into a beautiful, printed page!

You're welcome to share your thoughts and sentiments about the business of writing and publishing: Stefanie: Everyone in our industry is in it because they love what they do. I think we're at a time when it's important to support each other and produce the best books that we all can so that readers will continue to read! And more often and at even the earliest age—we all win when there are more lifelong readers!

What are representative titles you have sold to publishers: Lilly's recent titles: *The Work-at-Home Success Bible* (Leslie Truex); *Sewing Green* by Betz White (Stewart, Tabori, & Chang); *Hit Me with Your Best Shot* by Raina Lee (Chronicle Books); *Rockabye Baby* by Penny Warner (Chronicle Books). Stefanie's recent titles: *Preggatinis* by Natalie Boris Nelson; *The Bilingual Edge: Why, When and How to Teach Your Child a Second Language* by Kendall King and Alison Mackey (HarperCollins); *I Love Dirt!: 52 Activities to Help You and Your Kids Discover the Wonders of Nature* by Jennifer Ward (Shambhala); *Confetti Girl* by Diana Lopez (Little, Brown); *Pele: King of Soccer (Pelé: El Rey del Fútbol)* by Monica Brown and illustrated by Rudy Guiterrez (Rayo/HarperCollins); *What Can You Do with a Paleta?* by Carmen Tafolla and illustrated by Magaly Morales (Tricycle Press). Jointly agented: *Exclusively Chloe* by Jon Yang.

MAX GARTENBERG LITERARY AGENCY, LLC.

912 N. Pennsylvania Ave., Yardley, PA 19067

215-295-9230   fax: 215-295-9240

www.maxgartenberg.com   email: agdevlin@aol.com

Agent name: Anne G. Devlin

Career history: The Max Gartenberg Literary Agency has long been recognized as a source for fine fiction and nonfiction. Established in 1954 in New York City, the agency has migrated to the Philadelphia area, growing by two agents in the latest move.

Categories/subjects that you are most enthusiastic about agenting: Special interests: Nonfiction, current events, women's issues, celebrity, health, literary fiction, true crime, commercial fiction, sports, politics, popular culture, biography, environment, narrative nonfiction, and multicultural nonfiction.

What you don't want to agent: Poetry, New Age, fantasy.

What's the best way for writers to solicit your interest: Writers desirous of having their work handled by this agency should first send a one- or two-page query letter. Simply put, the letter should describe the material being offered as well as relevant background information about the writer, and include an SASE for a reply. If the material is of interest, an agent may request a sample or the entire manuscript. Unsolicited material will be returned unread if accompanied by sufficient postage for its return.

Do you charge reading or management fees: No.

Can you provide an approximation by percent of what you tend to represent by category: Fiction: 15 percent, nonfiction: 85 percent.

What are the most common mistakes writers make when pitching you: Rather than describing his material and summarizing his qualifications, the writer's query letter asks for information about the agency, information readily available in such directories as *Jeff Herman's Guide and Literary Market Place* or on the Web. This tells that the writer is too lazy to do his homework and is probably a poor researcher, to boot.

How would you describe the client from hell: Client who demands unceasing attention and is never satisfied with the deal the agent brings him (he always has friends whose agent got twice as much), who delivers his manuscript late and in such disrepair that it is unacceptable at first glance. And blames the agent for his mess. This is not an imaginary character.

How would you describe the perfect client: A writing professional who can be counted on to produce a well-made, literate, enlightening, and enjoyable book with a minimum of Sturm and Drang. Fortunately, this is not an imaginary character, either.

What, if anything, can a writer do to increase the odds that you will become his or her agent: Write a brilliant query letter and, when asked, follow it up with a manuscript or proposal that is even better. Remember that the waiting is the hardest part.

Please list representative titles that you have sold: *Charles Addams: A Cartoonist's Life* (Random House); *Ogallala Blue* (W.W. Norton); *Encyclopedia of Pollution* and *Encyclopedia of Earthquakes and Volcanoes* (Facts On File); *Jack and Lem* (DaCapo Press); *Passing Gas and Other Towns Along the American Highway* (Ten Speed Press); *What Patients Taught Me and Country Hospital* (Sasquatch Books); *Winning the Disability Challenge* (New Horizon Press); *How to Talk to Your Child's Doctor* (Prometheus Press).

FRANCES GOLDIN LITERARY AGENCY, INC.

57 E. 11th St. Suite 5B, New York, NY 10003

212-777-0047   fax: 212-228-1660

www.goldinlit.com

Agents' names: Ellen Geiger, eg@goldinlit.com; Sam Stoloff, ss@goldinlit.com; Matt McGowan

The following information pertains to Ellen Geiger.

Born: New York, New York.

Education: BA, Barnard; MA, University of California.

Career history or story: I started agenting while working as an executive at a PBS station almost 20 years ago and have been at it ever since.

Hobbies, interests: Shockingly enough, I still love to read. I'm also a politics and history fan, and play a mean game of Scrabble.

Subjects and categories you are interested in agenting, including fiction and nonfiction: Serious nonfiction of all sorts, history, science, current affairs, business, progressive politics, arts and culture, film, interesting memoirs, cutting-edge issues. In fiction, literary fiction, women's fiction, thrillers, mysteries, historical.

Subjects and categories writers shouldn't even bother pitching to you: No New Age or flaky science, romance novels or science fiction.

What would you do if you weren't agenting: Travel and do more volunteer work; although these days I could work from anywhere if I had my Blackberry along.

What's the best way for fiction writers to solicit your interest: Be able to write well and have an original idea, which is surprisingly hard to find. Understand the genre you're writing in. Have a track record, ideally, or some writing classes under your belt so you have a good sense of the form. Have done several drafts of your novel: there's nothing that makes my heart sink faster than to read that I'm the first one to read your first draft.

What's the best way for nonfiction writers to solicit your interest: Have a good grasp of your idea and some credentials to back it up. Have researched the market and the competition. Have good writing skills or be willing to team up with a writer to make the book the best it can be.

Do you charge reading or any upfront fees: Absolutely not. No real agent who is a member of the AAR (Association of Author's Representatives) does.

In your experience, what are the most common pitching mistakes writers make: To tell me what a great FILM their book will make. To not be able to summarize the plot briefly or create an interesting hook to get me eager to read more. To submit a query letter filled with typos and grammatical errors.

Describe the client from hell, even if you don't have any: Worst is the writer who doesn't trust the agent and second-guesses your decisions, typically someone who solicits advice from everyone in their family including the dog. Another no-no is a bitter, pessimistic person who can't be pleased no matter what happens: If the review of their book is on page 3 of the *NY Times*, they're angry it's not on page 1. Usually I can screen these people out early on, but occasionally I am surprised, as they often masquerade as nice people until publication time.

What's your definition of a great client: Easy. Someone who can write well, and deliver on time! And it's great if that person is also someone who is emotionally mature enough to withstand the natural ups and downs of the publishing process.

How can writers increase the odds that you will offer representation: A referral is guaranteed to get immediate attention. Having a track record and/or good credentials. Having a promotional platform for your book or a good plan for one. Having studied the craft of writing at reputable schools and workshops. Being educated and realistic about the realities of the publishing world.

Why did you become an agent, and how did you become one: It's my calling; I've always worked in arts representation. When I was 25 I owned part of a nightclub, and in a sense, I've been doing that kind of work ever since. I was mentored into the business by a top agent.

Describe to someone from another planet what you do as an agent: In the most general way, do everything possible to get the writer a great deal and help them achieve the best possible publication and promotion of their work. Then make sure they get paid.

How do you feel about editors and publishers: I realize they are under enormous pressure to perform to today's bottom-line oriented standards. Still, I wish they would take more chances and back up their books with real promotion.

How do you feel about writers: By nature, I am predisposed to like creative people and admire those who have the courage of their convictions and believe in their talent.

What do you see in the near future for book publishing: I hope publishers will understand that they must promote the books they buy better. Promotion is the weak link in the chain. We're now in a period of wild experimentation with web-based content, and I think that will shake out in the next few years. And, no matter how sexy they make those e-book readers, people will always prefer holding a real book in their hands.

What are your favorite books, TV shows, movies, and why: Among our clients, our author Barbara Kingsolver's *Poisonwood Bible* for its sweep, narrative brilliance and social relevance, our author Ann Jones's *Kabul in Winter: Life Without Peace in Afghanistan,* for its brilliant depiction of the forgotten lives of women and men in wartime, our author Dorothy Allison's *Bastard out of Carolina* because it's just one of the best memoirs ever written. *Suite Francaise* for its historical impact and moving origins, *Fieldwork* by Mischa Berlinski for its scope and ideas, Jeffrey Eugenides's *Middlesex* because it's a *tour de force* of writing and history, *Then We Came to the End* for its shrewd, ironic and ultimately moving insights into contemporary culture. In TV: *Mad Men* for its genius depicting the 1960s era, *The Closer* for Kyra Sedgwick's fab character, *Six Feet Under* and *The Sopranos* for their high-water marks in narrative storytelling. In theater: I love all kinds of theater but recently saw the superb revival of *Sunday in the Park with George* and love it for its tribute to the glory, persistence and purity of art—surely a theme anyone in our profession can embrace.

In your opinion, what do editors think of you: Smart, fair, dedicated, experienced, a good negotiator, tough on contracts.

On a personal non-professional level, what do you think people think of you: Together, organized, friendly, a bit of an egghead, good sense of humor.

What are some representative titles that you have sold: Fiction: *Monkeewrench* by PJ Tracy (Putnam); *The Sunday List of Dreams* by Kris Radish (Bantam); *The Penguin Who Knew Too Much* by Donna Andrews (St. Martin's); *The Saddlemaker's Wife* by Earlene Fowler (Berkley). Nonfiction: *Kabul in Winter: Life Without Peace in Afghanistan* by Ann Jones (Holt/Metropolitan); *The American Plague: The Untold Story of Yellow Fever, the Epidemic that Shaped Our History* by Molly Crosby (Berkley); *If the Creek Don't Rise: My Life Out West with the Last Black Widow of the Civil War* by Rita Williams (Harcourt); *How to Read the Bible* by James L. Kugel (Free Press); *Gringos in Paradise* by Barry Golson (Scribner); *Free Exercise, Expensive Gas: A Church-State Road Trip* by Jay Wexler (Beacon).

The following information pertains to Sam Stoloff.

Born: Nov. 14, 1960, New York City.

Education: BA, Columbia University, 1984; MFA, Cornell University, 1988; MA, Cornell University, 1991; PhD, Cornell University (defended dissertation but have not yet received degree, and I may never, just out of laziness).

Career history or story: I taught college courses in English literature, creative writing, American history, and film studies for a number of years, at Cornell, Ithaca College, and the State University of New York. I've been with the Frances Goldin Agency since 1997. Being an agent is better.

Hobbies, interests: I spend most of my non-working time these days with my kids, so you could call that my main hobby. I love to cook and I'm a bit of a foodie and small-time gardener, I sort-of-collect wine, I'm a big fan of the New York Mets, I play tennis, I'm a bit of a political junkie and obsess to an unhealthy degree about the outrages of the Bush administration, and I read books (novels, journalism, history) for pleasure when I can. I like a good game of Scrabble or poker. I love movies, but haven't seen many since my first kid was born.

Subjects and categories you are interested in agenting, including fiction and nonfiction: Smart journalism, history, books on current events and public affairs, books about food, sports, popular culture, economics, psychology, original graphic works, wonderfully written novels, stories and memoirs.

Subjects and categories writers shouldn't even bother pitching to you: Most genre fiction (unless literary), self-help, diet books, practical nonfiction, pet books, celebrity bios, screenplays.

What would you do if you weren't agenting: I'd probably either be a professor of American studies (literature, history, film), or a writer. Possibly a Washington think-tank type.

What's the best way for fiction writers to solicit your interest: Write a smart, succinct query letter describing the book (only one book, not every available manuscript), and previous publications, if any. I still prefer paper to email, although I can see the writing on the wall.

What's the best way for nonfiction writers to solicit your interest: Write a smart, succinct query letter describing a fabulous project, and previous publications or other credentials, if any.

Do you charge reading or any upfront fees: No.

In your experience, what are the most common pitching mistakes writers make: Failure to actually describe the project. Pitching more than one thing at a time. Telling me my business (e.g. "Knopf would be the ideal publisher for this book"). Assuming an unearned familiarity.

Describe the client from hell, even if you don't have any: Thin-skinned, with an aversion to editorial feedback, and an inflated sense of literary importance and wildly unrealistic expectations about what publishing a book means; unable to acknowledge the work of others on their behalf.

What's your definition of a great client: Thick-skinned, welcoming of editorial feedback, and with a becoming sense of modesty about themselves; freely expressive of gratitude for the work others do on their behalf. And wonderfully talented, of course.

How can writers increase the odds that you will offer representation: Be professional and courteous.

Why did you become an agent, and how did you become one: Frances Goldin is an old family friend, and I have long admired her integrity, her dedication, her loyalty to her clients, and the quality of the writers she has worked with. It looked pretty good to me!

What do you see in the near future for book publishing: The transition to electronic books will be a gradual one. Reading on paper and on screen will co-exist for some time, although I think that when there's a knockout e-book reader with a great screen and a decent price, the migration to e-books will begin in earnest. Book publishers will struggle to adapt, as the means for distributing and consuming words continue to change. Writers will still write, agents will still represent them, but publishers and booksellers face big institutional upheavals.

What are your favorite books, TV shows, movies, and why: My favorite movie is *Vertigo*. My favorite book is probably *The Great Gatsby*, or maybe *House of Mirth*. My favorite TV show is *The Wire*.

What are some representative titles that you have sold: *A Brief History of the Flood* by Jean Harfenist (Knopf); *Jesus Land* by Julia Scheeres (Counterpoint); *Too Late to Die Young* by Harriet McBryde Johnson (Holt); *Blocking the Courthouse Door* by Stephanie Mencimer (Free Press); *Lullabies for Little Criminals* by Heather O'Neill (HarperCollins); *A People's History of Science* by Clifford Conner (Nation Books); *The Daring Book for Girls* by Miriam Peskowitz and Andrea Buchanan (HarperCollins); *Dirty Diplomacy* by Craig Murray (Scribner); *New York at War* by Steven Jaffe (Basic Books).

The following information pertains to Matt McGowan.

Born: June 19, 1972; Antwerp, Belgium.

Education: BA, Colby College.

Career history: I started in 1994 as an assistant at St. Martin's Press. After a year I moved on to assist retired Pantheon publisher Fred Jordan revive a small press called Fromm International. Fred was very generous, encouraging me to try just about anything from designing jackets to acquiring books. He was also inspiring in that he had published these icons like Jack Kerouac and Allen Ginsberg during the heyday of Grove Press/Evergreen Review, where he worked for over 30 years, and had these absurd stories about going to a Mets game with Samuel Beckett, drinking in Paris with William Burroughs, and being chased around the Grove offices by Valerie Solanas and her ice pick. I've always looked up to the Grove legacy and Grove founder Barney Rosset and think landing at Frances Goldin, after a short stint at another agency, was really fortunate as Frances has similar convictions about books and writers.

Categories/subjects that you are most enthusiastic about agenting: Narrative nonfiction; literary, unusual, and/or humorous essays; travel; sports narratives (particularly soccer); smart commercial fiction; distinctive literary fiction; pop culture; music; peculiar histories; quirky and accessible food, business, science, or sociology.

What you don't want to agent: Romance, religion, diet, reference; I see a lot of "edgy" first novels that romanticize drug use or depravity, which I quickly pass on.

What's the best way for writers to solicit your interest: Query letter or brief email.

Do you charge reading or management fees: No.

What are the most common mistakes writers make when pitching you: Making letters too "pitchy." I like a straight-forward, informational query letter.

How and why did you ever become an agent: I read a novel in college which I learned had a really difficult time getting published and that bred these idealistic notions about publishing and recognizing talented writers and helping them break through. That led to me doing an internship in New York my senior year and I was actually attracted to the business of it all as much as anything.

What do you think the future holds for writers, publishers, and agents: I doubt books as we think of them today will survive, technology seems to be developing too fast, as well as consumer expectations, but authors and ideas will always be around and there should always be a market for them.

What are your favorite books, movies, TV shows, and why: TV: *Entourage, Scrubs, Flip This House*, Anthony Bourdain's show, *No Reservations*. Books: *I am Not Jackson Pollock* by John Haskell; *Natasha* by David Bezmogzis; *The Miracle of Castel di Sangro* by Joe McGinniss; *Where I Was From* by Joan Didion.

On a personal level, what do you think people like about you and dislike about you: I think my some of my more difficult and literary clients are appreciative that I work hard for them when their work is not clearly commercial. One of them sends me a fruit basket every Christmas, at least. I'm sure there are some things people don't like but let's not go there.

Please list representative titles you have sold: *The Lifespan of a Fact: An Essay* (FSG); *The Open Curtain: A Novel* (Coffee House); *To Air Is Human: One Man's Quest to Become the World's Greatest Air Guitarist* (Riverhead); *Kicking Out, Kicking On: On the Road with the Fans, Freaks, and Fiends at the World's Biggest Sporting Event, World Cup 2006* (Harcourt); *Neck Deep: Odd Essays* (Graywolf); *The Perfect Baby Handbook: A Guide for the Excessively Motivated New Parent* (HarperCollins); *Bank: A Novel* (Little Brown).

IRENE GOODMAN

27 West 24th St. Suite 700B, New York, NY 10010

(212) 604-0330

www.irenegoodman.com

Agents' names: Irene Goodman, Miriam Kriss, Barbara Poelle, and Jon Sternfeld
The following applies to Irene Goodman.

Education: BA and MA from the University of Michigan.

Career history or story: I've been an agent for 29 years and counting. I've had my share of major bestsellers, discoveries in the slush, and wonderful long-term relationships.

Subjects and categories you are interested in agenting, including fiction and nonfiction: Quality fiction, including genre fiction; narrative and prescriptive nonfiction.

What would you do if you weren't agenting: I don't know how to do anything else. Fortunately, I'm very good at this.

What's the best way for fiction writers to solicit your interest: Briefly.

What's the best way for nonfiction writers to solicit your interest: With a solid, clever idea and a strong platform.

Do you charge reading or any upfront fees: No.

In your experience, what are the most common pitching mistakes writers make: They are boring.

Describe the client from hell, even if you don't have any: I'm too polite to say.

What's your definition of a great client: That would be someone who is talented, ambitious, and smart but who has a healthy sense of humor about his or her work and doesn't take it all too seriously.

How can writers increase the odds that you will offer representation: By being that good.

Why did you become an agent, and how did you become one: I started as an editorial assistant to a publisher and then worked for an agent. I quickly saw that I was suited to it.

How do you feel about editors and publishers: I love them.

How do you feel about writers: I love them too.

What are your favorite books, TV shows, movies, and why: *Jane Eyre, The Godfather, Of Human Bondage, Boston Legal, The Sopranos.*

In your opinion, what do editors think of you: They respect me. They like me, but know I will kill for my authors.

ASHLEY GRAYSON LITERARY AGENCY

1342 W. 18th Street, San Pedro, CA 90732

310-514-0267 or 310-548-4672   fax: 310-831-0036

www.graysonagency.com

Agents' names: Ashley Grayson, graysonagent@earthlink.net; Carolyn Grayson, carolyngraysonagent@earthlink.net; Denise Dumars, denise.graysonagent@earth link. net; Lois Winston, lois.graysonagent@earthlink.net

Education: A. Grayson: BS in Physics. C. Grayson: BA, English, Wellesley College; MBA, U.C.L.A. Dumars: BA in English/creative writing, Cal State Univ. Long Beach; MA in English/creative writing, Cal State Univ. Dominguez Hills. Winston: BFA graphic design/illustration, Tyler School of Art/Temple University.

Career story: A. Grayson: computer sales, management consultant, founded Ashley Grayson Literary Agency in 1976. C. Grayson: market research analyst; marketing consultant; agent since 1994. Dumars: library professional, college English instructor, journalist, literary agent, published author of three books, five chapbooks and numerous articles, reviews, poems, and short stories. Winston: art director, designer and editor in consumer crafts industry; published author of two novels, contributor to three fiction and one nonfiction anthologies; author of numerous magazine articles; agent since 2005.

Hobbies and special personal interests: A. Grayson: languages, opera, gardening. C. Grayson: reading, gardening, roses, beach, investing, wine, cooking. Dumars: travel, horror films, metaphysics, attending poetry readings, experimental theater and punk rock concerts. Winston: Broadway theater, reading, travel, wandering around art museums.

Subjects and categories you like to agent: We love to agent books that make us want to run out and tell the world about the book and the author. We love novels that are exceedingly well-written, with characters we want to spend time with; clever, high-concept ideas often with a good dose of humor; wonderful, fresh stories that draw us in, keep us turning the pages, and are just so darn fun to read. In nonfiction, we look for books that are fresh, commercial, high-concept and promotable, from an author with a national platform. We're especially looking for narrative-driven nonfiction books about health and science topics and cultural history. In children's books: we seek authors and books with unique voice and the right sensibilities for the market, whether quirky and fun or more serious. We are extremely selective about children's nonfiction.

A. Grayson: Strong, well-written literary and commercial fiction, historical fiction, dark fantasy, mysteries, thrillers, young adult, humorous or edgy children's fiction. C. Grayson: Women's fiction (including romance and multicultural); historical fiction; mysteries; suspense; women-oriented fantasy; horror; children's books, from chapter books to YA. Nonfiction: contemporary self-help, business, pop culture, science, true crime, and a very few gift or highly illustrated books, narrative nonfiction. Dumars: Horror and dark fantasy fiction, offbeat literary and women's fiction, ethnic fiction; and nonfiction that is related to pop-culture topics, especially Goth and noir, and metaphysical writings, especially related to Wicca, paganism, magick, goddess religion and general New Age topics—as long as it is positive in tone. Winston: women's fiction, romance (all sub-genres except inspiration romance), romantic suspense, thrillers, and traditional mysteries. Humor is always a plus but not slapstick.

Subjects and categories writers shouldn't bother pitching to you: The Agency does not represent screenplays, poetry, short stories, novellas, most novelty books, textbooks, or most memoirs, especially stories of abuse or addiction recovery. In fiction: Dark fiction is fine; gore solely for the sake of shocking the reader is not for us. C. Grayson: I'm not inclined to read and represent women's fiction in which the life of the heroine is full of depression and angst; I do like a happy ending. Winston: I'm not partial to dark paranormals (light and/or humorous paranormals are okay), and I prefer historical novels over historical romances.

What might you be doing if you weren't agenting: Dumars: Writing, teaching, and traveling, which I pretty much do already. Winston: Working on my own novels.

What's the most effective ways for writers to grab your attention: Send us something smart, fresh, captivatingly written, and beautifully crafted.

Dumars: Write a book that is truly new and fills a need, not just a version of something that's currently popular. My interests are very specific, so research them carefully before sending your work to me. List publications you've published in, and organizations you belong to that demonstrate your interest in the field.

For fiction: We are still accepting clients who are previously published by a known publisher. The agency is temporarily closed to queries from writers who are not published at book length, with the following exceptions: 1) Authors recommended by a client, published author, or editor who has read the work in question; 2) Authors we have met at conferences and from whom we have requested submissions; 3) Authors who have been published in quality small presses or magazines. We have had excellent success selling first-time novelists, but at this time we must concentrate on the needs of professional authors who need our intellectual property management skills and financial skills. If you meet these criteria, please query us, listing publishing credits with titles, publishers, and dates published. Query Ashley Grayson, Carolyn Grayson, and Lois Winston by email only. Include the first three pages of the manuscript in the body of your email; do not send attachments unless requested. Denise Dumars prefers queries sent by ordinary post; include first three pages and SASE. Do not send queries by overnight service and never ever by certified mail. Do not query more than one agent in our agency, whether by email or post; we will make sure that your query reaches the right person.

For nonfiction: query with proposal. Note: We cannot review self-published works to evaluate moving them to mainstream publishers. Please send query letter by email, including brief bio or CV, and the Market and Competition sections of your proposal.

Do you charge fees separate from your commission, or offer non-agenting fee-based services: We do not offer non-agenting fee-based services. We do charge for some extraordinary expenses such as bank wires, overnight mail delivery, or posting books to foreign lands.

What are representative titles you have sold to publishers: *Tales of the Madman Underground* by John Barnes (Viking Children's Books); *Move Your Stuff, Change Your Life* by Karen Rauch Carter (Simon & Schuster); *The Middle of Somewhere* by J.B. Cheaney (Knopf Books for Young Readers); *Moongobble and Me* (series) by Bruce Coville (Simon & Schuster Children's Books); *Ball Don't Lie* by Matt de la Peña (Delacorte); *Be Blesséd* by Denise Dumars (New Page); *Grease Monkey* by Tim Eldred (Tor); *Bride of the Fat White Vampire* by Andrew Fox (Ballantine); *Child of a Dead God* by Barb and J. C. Hendee (ROC/Penguin); *Mars Crossing* by Geoffrey A. Landis (Tor); *Tiny Little Troubles* by Marc Lecard (St. Martin's); *Sleeping Freshmen Never Lie* by David Lubar (Dutton); *Théâtre Illuminata: Eyes Like Stars* by Lisa Mantchev (Feiwel and Friends); *The Healing Power of Faery* by Edain McCoy (Provenance/Adams Media); *Sex Starved and Sex Drive* by Jill Myles (Pocket Books); *But I Don't Feel Too Old to Be a Mommy* by Doreen Nagle (Health Communications); *Phoenix Unrisen* by Kathleen Nance (Dorchester); *Alosha* by Christopher Pike (Tor/Forge); *Cave Paintings to Picasso* by Henry Sayre (Chronicle Books); *Wiley and Grampa's Creature Features* (series) by Kirk Scroggs (Little Brown Books for Young Readers); *Cat Yoga* by Rick Tillotson (Clarkson Potter); *The Boy with the Lampshade on His Head* by Bruce Wetter (Atheneum); *Raven* by Allison van Diepen (Simon Pulse); *Kitty and the Silver Bullet* by Carrie Vaughn (Warner); *I Wish I Never Met You* by Denise Wheatley (Simon & Schuster/Touchstone); *Love, Lies and a Double Shot of Deception* by Lois Winston (Dorchester).

Why did you become an agent, and how did you become one: A. Grayson: I love to read books and sell new ideas. The real reason I became an agent is that Judy-Lynn Del Rey (the late founder of the Del Rey imprint at Random House) told me in 1976 that I should. She had great insight—I'm still having a great time. C. Grayson: I love to read, including contracts, and I love to help authors move up in their careers. Dumars: Because I was tired of seeing people signing book contracts without understanding them. I wanted to help authors, especially those I knew in the genre fiction and New Age arenas. On suggestion from Dan Hooker, Ashley Grayson took me on as a manuscript evaluator, reading the slush pile, and gradually I worked my way up to agent. Winston: Ashley thought I'd be an asset to the agency, and like Denise, I've worked my way up to agenting.

How do you feel about writers: Dumars: I think I'm quoting Ben Franklin here when I say we have to hang together or they'll hang us all separately. Winston: Ditto what Denise said.

What do you tell entities from other planets and dimensions about your job:

Many people think we get paid to read for a living, but that's only the beginning of what we do. We use our judgment to select and market wonderful manuscripts to the most appropriate editors at the most appropriate houses; we read contracts with a thoroughgoing understanding of terms and negotiate the best terms we can in every deal; read royalty statements with an eagle eye; work with publishers and authors to promote the books; sell subrights, including negotiating contracts for foreign editions, film and TV; and are the authors' advocates in all publishing matters.

What are your favorite books, movies, TV shows, and why: C. Grayson: My favorite books are my clients' of course; I like movies with clever screenwriting: many of the Coen Brothers movies, especially *Barton Fink* and *The Man Who Wasn't There*; TV Shows: *Law & Order*; *CSI: Las Vegas*; *Mystery!* Winston: Books: Ditto what Carolyn said about my clients' books; TV: *House, Lost, Bones, The Shield, Burn Notice, Law & Order*; Movies: *Chicago, Casablanca, Singing in the Rain, Same Time Next Year, Shakespeare in Love*. Dumars: Favorite TV shows: currently, *Lost* and *Heroes*. Movies: My all-time favorite movies are *Repo Man, Casablanca*, and *Interview with the Vampire*. I also enjoyed *Pan's Labyrinth*.

How would you describe the writer from hell: A. Grayson: Of course, we don't represent any writers from hell, but such a person is more interested in the celebrity of being an author than in actually writing books. Anyone who doesn't work on the next book until the present one sells. Any clients who want to second-guess their agent. Dumars: A person who is unprofessional—doesn't return calls or make deadlines. Someone who is not interested in being a professional writer but instead sees writing only as advancing an agenda or as a charity project; clients who listen to gossip and believe it instead of believing their agent. Not that I've ever heard of such a writer, of course. Winston: An author who believes every word he/she has written is etched in platinum and refuses to even consider revising.

How would you describe the publisher and/or editor from hell: We love our clients—they always have great ideas simmering for the next book or two, their works are continually fresh and exciting, they continue to charm and delight us with their innovative and creative ideas and work, are genuinely enthusiastic about the business, and they understand publishing is a business. They are relentlessly surprising, and never bewildering—their work is stunning. We love editors for their enthusiasm for books and authors. We look forward to continuing to work with editors and publishers to find ways to publish and sell creative works as technology, industry business models, and even the form of the book, change.

Will our business exist as we know it in ten years or so: No, it will not. Readers have changed in their style of reading and reasons to read, as well as in what they read, and where and how they read. The new Generation Y population neither lives like, nor thinks like, nor reads like the Boomers and Gen X readers. New bestsellers must address these changes and authors must adapt to sell big now and continue to win loyal readers in the next fifteen years. Publishers, distributors and retailers have demonstrated repeatedly that they do not want to continue performing the activities associated with their traditional businesses and desire to move to a model in which no book is manufactured or stocked until the customer buys it. This works well for downloadable games and software and it is inevitable that books will be next. As an agency, we are prepared to operate in such a future and to protect and grow our client's intellectual property investments. We are paying attention, but are not worried.

Dumars: Niche marketing, which is what I see already on MySpace and similar areas. When my students started wearing T-shirts of death metal bands from Outer Mongolia that I had never heard of, and they in turn had never heard of the MTV and VH1 rock bands I listen to, I realized that there had been a quantum shift in how people relate to entertainment in general. Maybe it will signal a return to the independent bookstore that caters to a particular clientele. We can only hope.

SANFORD J. GREENBURGER ASSOCIATES

55 Fifth Ave., New York, NY 10003

Agent's name: Matt Bialer

Born: December 20, 1962.

Education: BA, Vassar College.

Career history or story: Spent 14 years in the book department at the William Morris Agency. Have been in the business since 1985.

Hobbies, interests: Painting, photography, outdoors, music (rock, jazz, classical).

Subjects and categories you are interested in agenting, including fiction and non-fiction: Thrillers, urban fantasy, epic fantasy, cross-over science fiction, some romance, pop music books, narrative nonfiction, literary fiction, women's fiction, sports.

Subjects and categories writers shouldn't even bother pitching to you: Self-help, diet books.

What would you do if you weren't agenting: Paint (watercolor) and take black and white street photographs.

What's the best way for fiction writers to solicit your interest: Be aware of what I represent (at least some of it) and see if what you wrote jives with my taste.

What's the best way for nonfiction writers to solicit your interest: Letter.

Do you charge reading or any upfront fees: No.

In your experience, what are the most common pitching mistakes writers make: They just shotgun it out there without any thought as to who the agent is and what they do.

Describe the client from hell, even if you don't have any: That's a tough one. Generally speaking it is a client who does not listen, who does not get how things are properly done in the business.

What's your definition of a great client: Listens. Trusts. And has a good rapport. A great relationship with the client is me not telling the writer what to do by an ongoing dialogue. I like clients who can teach me a thing or two.

How can writers increase the odds that you will offer representation: Do the homework on what is out there and successful that is like your project. And be realistic about it. And find out about the agent you are pitching.

Why did you become an agent, and how did you become one: I love books and publishing. I like creativity. I like to help make a project come to fruition. I became one because I started at an agency and just never looked back.

Describe to someone from another planet what you do as an agent: I manage book careers. I help a writer sell their book to a publisher. I am a matchmaker between project and editor/publisher and then I help manage the publishing of the book in both the U.S. and throughout the world.

How do you feel about editors and publishers: In a perfect world, I love them both but of course I have my preferences. Some editors and publishers are more effective than others or better at a certain kind of book.

How do you feel about writers: Love them.

What do you see in the near future for book publishing: Still trying to find itself in a world full of competing media whether a million TV channels, computers, iPods, etc.

What are your favorite books, TV shows, movies, and why: Books: Cormac McCarthy, Tolkien, Stephen King, Hemingway, Dennis Lehane, Tad Williams, Pynchon, Phil Dick. TV: *Heroes, Without a Trace*. Movies: Too many to name.

In your opinion, what do editors think of you: I think I am well respected and am well known in the industry.

On a personal non-professional level, what do you think people think of you: They love me!

What are some representative titles that you have sold: *Otherland and Shadowmarch* series by Tad Williams; *The Name of the Wind* by Patrick Rothfuss; *The Ice-Man: Confessions of a Mafia Contract Killer* by Philip Carlo; *The People Series* by Michael Gear and Kathleen O'Neal Gear; *Truancy: Some Kids Were Rebellious* by Isamu Fukui; *Zanesville* by Kris Saknussemm; *The Bone Thief* by Thomas O'Callaghan.

THE CHARLOTTE GUSAY LITERARY AGENCY

10532 Blythe Avenue, Los Angeles, CA 90064

310-559-0831   fax: 310-559-2639

www.gusay.com   email: gusay1@ca.rr.com (For Queries Only)

Agent's name: Charlotte Gusay

Education: BA in English literature/theater; General Secondary Life Teaching Credential.

Career history: Taught in secondary schools for several years. Interest in film-making developed. Founded (with partners) a documentary film company in the early 1970s. Soon became interested in the fledgling audio-publishing business. Became the Managing Editor for the Center for Cassette Studies/Scanfax, producing audio programs, interviews, and documentaries. In 1976 founded George Sand, Books, in West Hollywood, one of the most prestigious and popular bookshops in Los Angeles. It specialized in fiction and poetry, sponsored readings and events. Patronized by the Hollywood community's glitterati and literati, George Sand, Books, was the place to go when looking for the "best" literature and quality books. It was here that the marketing of books was preeminent. It closed in 1987. Two years later the Charlotte Gusay Literary Agency was opened.

Hobbies/personal interests: Gardens and gardening, architecture, magazines (a magazine junkie), good fiction (especially juicy novels), reading, anything French, anything Greek.

Categories/subjects that you are most enthusiastic about agenting: I enjoy both fiction and nonfiction. Prefer commercial, mainstream but quality material. Especially like books that can be marketed as film material. Also, like material that is innovative, unusual, eclectic, nonsexist. Will consider literary fiction with crossover potential. TCGLA is a signatory to the Writers' Guild and so represents screenplays and screenwriters selectively. I enjoy unusual children's books and illustrators, but have begun to limit children's projects to young-adult novels, especially if they have film possibilities.

What you don't want to agent: Prefer not [to] consider science fiction or horror, poetry or short stories (with few exceptions), or the romance genres per se.

If you were not an agent, what might you be doing instead: I would travel to Istanbul and become a foreign agent. I would re-read all of Marcel Proust. I would re-read Jane Austen. Work on my French. Study Greek (actually I do now). Play the piano. Tap dance.

What's the best way for writers to solicit your interest: First: Send one-page query letter with SASE. Then: After we've read your query and if we request your material (book, proposal, whatever it is), note the following guidelines: For fiction: Send approximately the first 50 pages and a synopsis, along with your credentials (i.e., list of previous publications, and/or list of magazine articles, and/or any pertinent information, education, and background.) For nonfiction: Send a proposal consisting of an overview, chapter outline, author biography, sample chapters, marketing and audience research, and survey of the competition. Important note: Material will not be returned without an SASE. Second important note: Seduce me with humor and intelligence. Always be polite and professional.

Do you charge reading or management fees: No reading fee. No editorial fees. When a client is signed, the client and I share 50/50 percent out-of-pocket expenses. In certain cases, I charge a nominal processing fee, especially when considering unsolicited submissions decided upon as and when queries arrive in my office. (Note: Charlotte—ever the teacher—sponsors a mentoring internship program for young college graduates interested in entering and training in the publishing/book business. Any such Processing Fees help fund this program.)

Can you provide an approximation by percent of what you tend to represent

by category: Nonfiction, 40 percent; fiction, 15 percent; children's, 10 percent; books to film/screenplays, 35 percent.

What are the most common mistakes writers make when pitching you: Clients must understand the role of agents and that agents represent only the material they feel they can best handle or—more importantly—material they are completely enthusiastic about and feel they can sell. Potential clients must understand that any given agent may or may not be an editor, a sounding board, a proposal writer, or a guidance counselor. Because of the enormous amount of submissions, queries, and proposals, we most often have only time to say yes or no to your project. Above all, when clients don't understand why in the world we can't respond to a multiple submission with regard to their "900-page novel" within a few days, all we can do is shake our heads and wonder if that potential client realizes we are human.

How would you describe the client from hell: The client from hell is the one who does not understand the hard work we do for our clients. Or the one who refuses to build a career in a cumulative manner, but rather goes from one agent to the next and so on. Or clients who circulate their manuscripts without cooperating with their agents. Or those who think it all happens by magic. Or those who have not done their homework and who do not understand the nuts and bolts of the business.

How would you describe the perfect client: The perfect client is the one who cooperates. The one who appreciates how hard we work for our clients. The one who submits everything on time, in lean, edited, proofed, professional copies of manuscripts and professionally prepared proposals. Clients who understand the crucial necessity of promoting their own books until the last one in the publisher's warehouse is gone. Those who work hard on their book selling in tandem with the agent. The author/agent relationship, like a marriage, is a cooperative affair built on mutual trust, and it is cumulative. The dream client will happily do absolutely whatever is necessary to reach the goal.

How and why did you ever become an agent: With a great entrepreneurial spirit, cold calls, seat-of-the-pants daring, 12 years in the retail book business (as founder and owner of a prestigious book shop in Los Angeles called George Sand, Books), and 25 years of business experience, including producing films and editing spoken-word audio programs. Agenting is the most challenging and rewarding experience I've ever had.

What, if anything, can a writer do to increase the odds of your becoming his or her agent: A writer must be professional. Be courteous. Be patient. Understand that we are human. Pay careful attention to the kinds of projects we represent. Query us only if your project fits with our agency profile. Know what we are overworked, always swamped with hundreds of queries. Know that we love and understand writers.

How would you describe to someone (or something) from another planet what it is that you do as an agent: My job is essentially that of a bookseller. I sell books. To publishers, producers, and ultimately to the retail book trade.

Sometimes, I develop a book idea. Sometimes, I develop someone's story, help the writer get a proposal written. I've even written proposals myself because I believed strongly in the book, or the person's story, or the salability of an idea. For fiction writers with potential, I sometimes make cursory suggestions. However, I must be clear—I am not an editor. Most often I help writers find a professional editor to work on their novel before it is submitted to a publishing house. That is key. The manuscript must be pristine. I repeat: A manuscript must be complete, polished, and professional.

Do you have any particular opinions or impressions of editors and publishers in general: Publishers continue to be in great flux and continue to have a difficult time these days. The "conglomeratizing" and "electrifying" aspects of the publishing business are taking over the publishing/book businesses. It's going to be very interesting to see where especially the electronics of the book business ends up. However, still and all, publishers are still and always looking for the next great writer, the next great book, and a way to make both successful. (That means making money.)

Editors are still overworked and underpaid. Therefore, if you wish to have the best chance of having your work accepted, you must do their work for them and don't complain. That is the reality of the editor's milieu. Editors are usually very smart. Most always, if they're any good, they are temperamental, and they know their particular publisher's market. If interested, they know how to make your work fit into their list. Do what your editor (and agent) tells you. No argument.

The publishing business continues to be overpublished. I read somewhere that 240,000 books were published within the last year. Be reminded that only one percent (1 percent) of manuscripts submitted to publishing houses were actually accepted for publication (according to Dee Power, co-author with Brian Hill, in their book *The Making of a Bestseller*.)

What do you think the future holds for writers, publishers, and agents: As long as there is intelligent life on Earth, there will be writers who must express themselves in whatever way or medium they will. As to whether that work will be published—in book form by a major, established publisher paying actual money for it—is doubtful. I repeat my note above, only one percent (1 percent) of manuscripts submitted to publishing houses will actually be accepted for publication. If you have an agent who is enthusiastic about your work, or your book, you will certainly increase your odds of being in that percentage. Remember that most major publishing houses will accept manuscripts only from agents.

What are your favorite books, movies, TV shows, and why: Recent films and not-so-recent films I liked: *Shakespeare in Love, Slam, Chasing Amy*, Bas Luhrman's *Romeo and Juliet*, the Marx Brothers films. A few of my all-time favorite films are *Runaway Train, The English Patient, Dr. Zhivago, Cabaret, Rebel Without a Cause, Woman in the Dunes*. A few favorite television shows: Any *Masterpiece Theatre*; *American Idol, Entourage, Weeds*. And many, many books—a few all-time favorites: Austen's *Pride and Prejudice*; Hemingway's *The Sun Also Rises*; *The English Patient, Dr. Zhivago, Housekeeping*, and many more. The one thing these have in common for me: They held my attention and I was moved in some important way, and the writing is superb.

On a personal level, what do you think people like about you and dislike about you: People like my intelligence and enthusiasm. In my agent mode, people don't like my selectivity or they don't understand it. If I reject a project, often the writer feels bleak and…well…rejected. Hopefully, writers will come to understand that I accept projects, very selectively. That is important for writers to understand.

Please list representative titles you have sold: *Wild West 2.0: Reputation and Privacy on the Digital Frontier—The Battle to Take Back Your Good Name and Regain Your Privacy* (forthcoming from AMACOM Books); *Mother Ash* (forthcoming from Red Hen Press) and *American Fugue* (Etruscan Press) both by National Endowment of the Arts International Award Recipient Alexis Stamatis (from Greece); *Honesty Sells: How to Make More Money and Increase Business Profits* (forthcoming 2009, John Wiley and Sons Inc. Publishers); *Forty-One Seconds: From Terror to Freedom* (Presidio Press/Ballantine); *Richard Landry Estates* (Oro Editions); *Beachglass* (St. Martin's Press); *The Dead Emcee Scrolls: The Lost Teachings of Hip Hop* (MTV/Simon & Schuster); *Said the Shotgun to the Head* (MTV/Simon & Schuster); *Meeting Across the River: Stories Inspired by the Haunting Bruce Springsteen Song,* story contributed by Randy Michael Signor (Bloomsbury Publishing); *Other Sorrows, Other Joys: The Marriage of Catherine Sophia Boucher and William Blake: A Novel* (St. Martin's Press); *Imperial Mongolian Cooking: Recipes from the Kingdoms of Genghis Khan* by Marc Cramer (Hippocrene Publishers); *Somebody's Child: Stories from the Private Files of an Adoption Attorney* by Randi Barrow (Perigee/Penguin Putnam, Inc.); *Retro Chic: A Guide to Fabulous Vintage and Designer Resale Shopping in North America & Online* by Diana Eden and Gloria Lintermans (Really Great Books); *The Spoken Word Revolution:* An essay, poem, and an audio contribution by Saul Williams (Sourcebooks); *Rio L.A.: Tales from the Los Angeles River* by Patt Morrison, with photographs by Mark Lamonica (Angel City Press).

Films: *What Angels Know: The Story of Elizabeth Barrett and Robert Browning,* (screenplay optioned by Producer Marta Anderson); *Somebody's Child: Stories from the Private Files of an Adoption Attorney* by Randi Barrow (Perigee/Penguin Putnam, Inc.), optioned by Green/Epstein/Bacino Productions for a television series; *A Place Called Waco: A Survivor's Story* by David Thibodeau and Leon Whiteson (Public Affairs/Perseus Book Group), optioned to Showtime for a television movie; *Love Groucho: Letters from Groucho Marx to His Daughter Miriam,* edited by Miriam Marx Allen (Faber & Faber, Straus & Giroux U.S., and Faber & Faber U.K.), sold to CBS.

At this writing, we have just signed the film rights to popular Irish novelist Maeve Binchy's novel *Light a Penny Candle* (Viking/NAL/Signet). We have many books in submission and development at this writing and at any given time.

REECE HALSEY NORTH/REECE HALSEY PARIS/REECE HALSEY NEW YORK

Reece Halsey North (Kimberly Cameron, April Eberhardt, Amy Burkhardt): 98 Main Street, #704, Tiburon, CA 94920

415-789-9191

Reece Halsey Paris (Kimberly Cameron)

Reece Halsey New York (Elizabeth Evans):

450 Seventh Avenue, Suite 2307, New York, NY 10123

415 272.4990

www.reecehalseynorth.com

Agents' names: Kimberley Cameron, President, bookgirl2@comcast.net; Elizabeth Evans, elizabeth@reecehalseynorth.com; April Eberhardt, april@reece halseynorth.com; Amy Burkhardt, amy@reecehalseynorth.com

The following information pertains to Elizabeth Evans.

Born: Milwaukee, Wisconsin.

Education: BA Hamilton College, English; MFA in writing, University of San Francisco.

Career story: I interned at *Zyzzyva* magazine before beginning my MFA at the University of San Francisco in 2004. While at USF, I joined Reece Halsey North as a reader and editor. I completed my MFA in 2006 and have been an associate agent since that time. In January of 2009 I relocated to New York City to open Reece Halsey New York.

Hobbies and special personal interests: Hobbies: Hiking in the mountains, anything to do with boats. I like fresh air. When the weather keeps me indoors, I'll cozy up with a good book and a cup of tea. Personal interests: Appetizers, bright colors, travels abroad, flowers, aquariums, angel food cake.

Subjects and categories you like to agent: I represent a wide range of non-fiction and fiction including memoir, pop culture, biography, literary and upmarket commercial fiction, historical fiction, mysteries, YA and middle-grade fiction. I'm especially drawn to voice-driven fiction and narrative nonfiction in unfamiliar or exotic settings. I'm looking for excellent writing that strikes at the heart of the human condition. And I always enjoy a good love story.

Subjects and categories writers shouldn't bother pitching to you: I do not handle picture books or books for young children, poetry, or screenplays.

What might you be doing if you weren't agenting: If not agenting, I would run an organic artisanal cheesery in Wisconsin. Or I'd be a professional organizer.

What's the most effective ways for writers to grab your attention: I prefer a polite, well-written query letter accompanied by the appropriate submission materials (please see our website). Please do not call the office to pitch your project over the phone. Some ideas might stand out, but great writing is what captures my attention.

Do you charge fees separate from your commission, or offer non-agenting fee-based services: No.

What are representative titles you have sold to publishers: *The Dissemblers* (Permanent Press); *The Geography of Love* by Glenda Burgess (Broadway/Doubleday); *Courage to Surrender* by Tommy Hellsten (Ten Speed Press); *A Trace of Smoke* by Rebecca Cantrell (Tor/Forge Books).

Why did you become an agent, and how did you become one: I didn't know about agenting until a writing professor suggested I contact Kimberley Cameron about a reading internship. I knew immediately this was the perfect job for me. Agenting is very business oriented but also appeals to my creative side. I've always enjoyed reading and editing, and I find working with my clients very satisfying. Each day is unique and filled with possibilities.

How do you feel about writers: I have an enormous amount of respect for writers. It takes such determination and discipline to write. And confidence. I admire that. I appreciate the opportunity to read another person's work.

What do you tell entities from other planets and dimensions about your job: Shhh, don't bother me. I'm reading!

What are your favorite books, movies, TV shows, and why: *Don't Let's Go to the Dogs Tonight* by Alexandra Fuller, *Housekeeping* by Marilynn Robinson, *Life and Death in Shanghai* by Nien Cheng, *The Power of One* by Bryce Courtenay, *Reading Lolita in Tehran* by Azar Nafisi, *Child of My Heart* by Alice McDermott, *Woman Hollering Creek* by Sandra Cisneros, *The Virgin Suicides* by Jeffrey Eugenides, *Beloved* and *Jazz* by Toni Morrison, *Prep* by Curtis Sittenfeld, *Howards End* by E.M. Forster, anything by Kazuo Ishiguro. All these books give me shivers when I read them. I tend to like films with a sense of whimsy. Favorite movies are *Big Fish*, *The Neverending Story*, *Moulin Rouge*, *Rushmore*. I don't watch much TV, but I got sucked into *The Tudors* on Showtime. My guilty pleasure is *Gossip Girl*.

How would you describe the writer from hell: The writer from hell shows an unhealthy desperation and forgets his/her manners. I enjoy working with writers who are serious and professional and recognize that publishing is a business.

How would you describe the publisher and/or editor from hell: The publisher/editor from hell? No such thing, they're all angels!

The following information pertains to Kimberley Cameron.

Born: Los Angeles, California.

Education: Marlborough School for Girls, Humboldt State University, Mount St. Mary's College.

Career history: Former publisher, Knightsbridge Publishing Company. She was a partner with Dorris Halsey from 1993 to 2006.

Hobbies/personal interests: France, reading for the sheer pleasure of it.

Categories/subjects that you are most enthusiastic about agenting: Writing that touches the heart.

What you don't want to agent: Children's books, poetry.

If you were not an agent, what might you be doing instead: Reading.

What's the best way for writers to solicit your interest: Please send all query letters by email to Amy Burkhardt at info@reecehalseynorth.com. For nonfiction, please attach a complete proposal with sample chapters. For fiction, please attach the first three chapters and a brief synopsis.

Do you charge reading or management fees: No.

Can you provide an approximation by percent of what you tend to represent by category: Fiction: 50 percent, nonfiction: 50 percent.

What are the most common mistakes writers make when pitching you: We are always impressed by politeness, in a well-written letter or otherwise. Their most common mistake is using too many rhetorical adjectives to describe their own work.

How would you describe the client from hell: One who doesn't know that publishing is a business, and should be conducted in a businesslike manner.

How would you describe the perfect client: A writer who understands the publishing business and is respectful of an agent's time.

How and why did you ever become an agent: We love books and what they have to teach us. We understand how important and powerful the written word is and appreciate what it takes to be a good writer.

What, if anything, can a writer do to increase the odds of your becoming his or her agent: Be polite and do your homework—know what we represent and market your work only when it's ready.

How would you describe to someone (or something) from another planet what it is that you do as an agent: READ. Guide writers through the writing and publishing process...

Do you have any particular opinions or impressions of editors and publishers in general: Editors and publishers are in this business for the love of books—they are all overworked but do the best they can.

What do you think the future holds for writers, publishers, and agents: There will always be readers—what form books will take we cannot imagine. There are searchers for knowledge, spiritual and otherwise that will always be looking for enlightenment.

On a personal level, what do you think people like about you and dislike about you: They like that I'm serious about helping writers—they might dislike that I must be extremely selective about the material I represent...

Please list representative titles you have sold: Please visit my website: www.kimberleycameron.com.

The following information pertains to April Eberhardt.

Date and place of birth: Small-town New Jersey, during a kinder, gentler era.

Education: BA Hamilton College, anthropology and French; CPLF, University of Paris; MBA, finance and marketing, Boston University.

Career history or story: Twenty years as strategist in corporate America; seven years as head of my own women's clothing design company; three years with *Zoetrope: All-Story*; three years as agent.

Hobbies, interests: Hobbies: Designing new ways to do familiar things, introducing people with similar interests, figuring out families. Spending the whole weekend reading and hiking. Personal interests: Smart design. Anything orange or chartreuse. Travel to Paris, Sweden, and Switzerland (or any lush, cool location where I can walk or hike). Rocks, volcanoes and owls. Fifties food, especially offbeat meat loaf recipes, mashed potatoes and butterscotch pudding.

Subjects and categories you are interested in agenting, including fiction and nonfiction: I favor interlinked collections of short stories, as well as contemporary women's fiction featuring smart protagonists. Family fiction always catches my eye, as does the good American novel, albeit nothing too serious, romantic or historical. Extra credit if it's set in a city or New Jersey. I'm a fan of first-time authors, the here and now, a fast pace, irony and bite.

Subjects and categories writers shouldn't even bother pitching to you: I don't represent children's or young-adult works, thrillers, murders or mysteries, Westerns or war themes, history, romance or poetry. No space porn, please. (Yes, it's a genre.)

What would you do if you weren't agenting: If not agenting, I would found a literary magazine dedicated to new writers, or else figure out a way for first-time authors to self-publish and garner worldwide distribution and acclaim quickly, and make money at it too. (I know, I know—that's what the Internet is for.) Or maybe I'd be an inventor, a design and color consultant, or an Alpine hiking guide.

What's the best way for fiction writers to solicit your interest: I prefer a short, concise emailed query accompanied by the first couple of chapters. No snail mail or phone calls. No lengthy synopses. To me the truth is in the writing.

Do you charge reading or any upfront fees: No.

Describe the client from hell, even if you don't have any: The author who calls or emails too often to see what I've done for her today, suggesting she doesn't trust or believe that I'm working really hard to find a good home for her work.

Why did you become an agent, and how did you become one: I became an agent because I take great satisfaction in introducing literary talent to the world, and because it's gratifying to find the right house and editor for an author. You could say I'm a professional cheerleader and matchmaker of sorts.

How do you feel about editors and publishers: The clients and editors I work with are gleamingly five-star. Otherwise why would I keep working with them?

How do you feel about writers: I am in awe of writers and their ability to create stirring, imaginative fiction out of thin air. Nothing thrills or transports me like seeing the world through another person's brain.

What do you see in the near future for book publishing: Back to inventing: I'd love to design a gel-pack type of floppy reader, thin so that it rolls/folds up for travel, but opens out to a big, light, bright screen for day or nighttime reading. You could download your favorite books (and manuscripts) to it wirelessly. Maybe I'd make it microwaveable and freezable, too, so you could put it on your neck when you're tired.

What are your favorite books, TV shows, movies, and why: Best books: *The Girls' Guide to Hunting and Fishing* by Melissa Bank, *Nice Big American Baby* by Judith Budnitz, *The Dive from Clausen's Pier* by Ann Packer. Anything by Laurie Colwin. Favorite films: *Swimming Pool* or *Under the Sand* with Charlotte Rampling; Terrence Malick's *Days of Heaven*; Kathleen Turner in *Body Heat*; *American Gigolo* starring a young Richard Gere and Lauren Hutton.

The following information pertains to Amy Burkhardt.

Location of birth: New Jersey...I spent half of my childhood there and half outside Boston, Massachusetts.

Education: BA in English, Bates College; candidate for MFA in writing, University of San Francisco.

Career Story: I worked for three years in various business positions, then moved to San Francisco to begin my MFA in writing. While working on my graduate degree I began interning as a reader at the Reece Halsey North Literary Agency. Since then, I have added responsibilities as an editor and agent.

Hobbies and special interests: Writing; any kind of dance—I have been a dancer since age five; music; art and art history; travel and foreign languages—I speak German and have studied Spanish; hiking/camping, and generally being outside; cooking (but I'm a novice), baking; trying new restaurants; international news and politics; reading, of course!

Subjects and categories you like to agent: I am open to a wide range of fiction and nonfiction. For fiction, I am drawn to the following categories: literary, upmarket commercial, women's historical, mysteries with a twist. I also enjoy YA or character-driven science fiction, but only manuscripts that create an entirely new world for the reader. For nonfiction, I am interested in voice-driven, narrative nonfiction, memoir, travel, lifestyle, and food books. In any genre, I look for accomplished writing, interesting and quirky characters, fresh voices, timely themes, and a good dose of wit. I enjoy stories that teach the reader something new.

Subjects and categories that writers shouldn't bother pitching to you: Please no children's, poetry, horror, business books, or screenplays.

What might you be doing if you weren't agenting: Writing fiction and reading...oh wait, I already do that. Hmmm...traveling the world, learning languages and local dance forms, and writing about it.

What's the most effective way for writers to grab your attention: A well-written query letter, and a submission that follows or guidelines. For fiction: a one-page synopsis and the first fifty pages of the manuscript. For nonfiction: a proposal and sample chapters. Please no phone pitches...the writing should speak for you.

Do you charge fees separate from your commission, or offer non-agenting services: No.

Why did you become an agent, and how did you become one: I began interning at literary agencies to learn about the industry. I have always loved books and knew I wanted to be involved in creating them. As an agent, I have the opportunity to find new authors, to edit and shape their work, and to help them realize their dream of publication. I also have the freedom to choose projects that I am passionate about.

How do you feel about writers: I have the utmost respect and admiration for them, for their powers of creativity, for their dedication, for their perseverance and the face of rejection.

What are your favorite books, movies, TV shows, and why: I can never pick favorites because it's always changing. Books I like: anything by Edith Wharton and Shakespeare, *To the Lighthouse* by Virginia Woolf, *Atonement* by Ian McEwan, *So Long, See You Tomorrow* by William Maxwell, *The Giver* by Lois Lowry. Movies I like: *Contact*, *The Thomas Crown Affair*, *Chocolat*, and *Little Miss Sunshine*. I don't watch much TV, but I loved *Sex and the City*, *Arrested Development*, and *The Office*.

How would you describe the writer from hell: A writer who is unprofessional or rude, who is unwilling to invest real time and effort in editing their manuscript, and who hasn't done their research/has no understanding of the business.

How would you describe the publisher and/or editor from hell: Are we allowed to say bad things about editors?

What do you like best about your clients and the editors and publishers you work with: Everyone loves books, and they are all in it because they are passionate about them.

Finally, will our business exist as we know it in ten years or so: I wish I knew what it will look like, but I have every confidence it will still exist. People love reading too much for me to imagine a future without books.

HARTLINE LITERARY AGENCY

123 Queenston Dr., Pittsburgh, PA 15235

412-829-2483

www.hartlineliterary.com

Agents' names: Joyce Hart, joyce@hartlineliterary.com; Tamela Hancock Murray, tamela@hartlineliterary.com; Terry Burns, terry@hartlineliterary.com; Diana Flegal, diana@hartlineliterary.com

The following information pertains to Joyce Hart.

Born: August 7, Iowa City, Iowa.

Education: Open Bible College, Des Moines, Iowa (now in Eugene, Oregon).

Career story: Started as a secretary to the vice president and editorial staff at

Whitaker House, Springdale, Pennsylvania in 1978, until 1989. The last three years I was the vice president of marketing. Worked in all aspects of the publishing house.

Hobbies and special personal interests: Reading, traveling, dogs.

Subjects and categories you like to agent: Most adult novels, most genres except fantasy, sci-fi, nonfiction adult books—self-help, spirituality, prayer, family.

Subjects and categories writers shouldn't bother pitching to you: Sci-fi, fantasy, poetry, gay and lesbian, paranormal, memoirs.

What might you be doing if you weren't agenting: Teaching, working in a bookstore, speaking to women's groups.

What's the most effective ways for writers to grab your attention: A well-written, well-researched proposal. Following our guidelines on our website.

Do you charge fees separate from your commission, or offer non-agenting fee-based services: Once in a while we'll charge for postage if it's overnight or very high. Most of the time we don't bother. No fees for non-agenting services. We don't do any editing, etc.

What are representative titles you have sold to publishers: *An Absence So Great* by Jane Kirkpatrick (WaterBrook Multnomah); three-book series *Lancaster County Secrets*, Suzanne Fisher (Revell); *I Don't Want a Divorce*, David Clark (Revell); *Skipping the Narrows*, Kevin Milne (Center Street); *Blood Ransom*, Lisa Harris (Zondervan); *Scattered Petals*, Amanda Cabot (Revell); *Journey to the Well*, Diana Wallis Taylor (Revell); *Through the Eyes of Love*, Dorothy Clark, Harlequin (Steeple Hill); *Love Finds You in Golden New Mexico*, Lena Nelson Dooley, (Summerside Press).

Why did you become an agent, and how did you become one: I became an agent because I quit my corporate job and wanted to stay in this industry. I found my niche. I started Hartline Marketing in 1990 and Hartline Literary in 1992. I was a publisher's rep for 11 or more years and did the literary agency part-time. Eventually, the agency became my full-time job.

How do you feel about writers: I like working with authors for the most part. If they are prima donnas, then it's not so much fun. Most are great and my good friends.

What do you tell entities from other planets and dimensions about your job: I don't know how to answer this one…

What are your favorite books, movies, TV shows, and why: Books: *The Will of Wisteria* by Denise Hildreth, *Shadows of Lancaster County* by Mindy Sterns Clark, *Healing Stones & Healing Waters* by Nancy Rue and Stephen Arterburn, *A Time to Mend* by Sally John and Gary Smalley. Movies: two most favorite are *Sound of Music*, because of the music and the story. *Steel Magnolias*—I love the characters and their relationships with one another. TV Shows: *Murder, She Wrote; Diagnosis Murder, Jane Doe*—all mysteries and I like the characters.

How would you describe the writer from hell: One who rewrites and rewrites, not flexible, calls me all hours of the day and night; hard to work with those.

How would you describe the publisher and/or editor from hell: An editor who never responds to emails or phone calls. Snobbish editors. Most editors and publishers I work with are good friends.

What do you like best about your clients, and the editors and publishers you work with: I like seeing good writing and compelling stories, good nonfiction. I like my clients who are loyal to our agency. Most are willing to work hard and give us a good proposal to present to the editors. Most of the editors are great to work with. I love it when they call me and ask me if I have a client who could write specific book or on a specific subject. I like to help the author and editor develop a good product.

You're welcome to share your thoughts and sentiments about the business of writing and publishing: I love the publishing world. It is not an easy profession, getting harder all the time. Publishers are asking for "household names" more than ever. Sometimes the "market driven" part of the business gets discouraging. Especially when sales turns down a really good book.

Do you wish to describe who you are: A pretty ordinary, hard-working woman. The wife of a minister, a mother and a grandmother. Someone who counts her blessings and is grateful for a job that has brought great satisfaction in her life.

Will our business exist as we know it in ten years or so: I think our business will exist in the next ten years or so. It has changed a lot in the past five years and will continue to change. More and more people are buying online, we're seeing more e-books, but the growth is not huge. However, I think we will always have print books, books that people can hold in their hands.

The following information pertains to **Tamela Hancock Murray**, www.tamelahancockmurray.com, tamelaagents@juno.com.

Born: Petersburg, Virginia; September 6.

Education: Lynchburg College, honors in journalism.

Career story: Tamela has been with Hartline Literary Agency since 2001. She has many happy and successful clients. A professional writer since 1994, she is also an award-winning, bestselling author in her own right.

Hobbies and special personal interests: Reading is Tamela's favorite hobby, a great convenience since her job as an agent requires so much reading! She especially enjoys time spent with her family and friends. Travel fascinates her.

Subjects and categories you like to agent: Tamela's focus is on inspirational titles. She enjoys fiction and nonfiction. Novelists with stories geared to a mainstream audience stand the best chance of gaining her representation. Writers with an outstanding platform have the best chance of success when submitting nonfiction.

Subjects and categories writers shouldn't bother pitching to you: Erotica, science fiction, experimental, stream-of-consciousness, horror. I don't mind seeing Christianity explored in a thoughtful manner, but I will not represent any work that is obviously offensive to Christians.

What might you be doing if you weren't agenting: Writing for newspapers and magazines.

What's the most effective ways for writers to grab your attention: Client referrals are the number-one way to get my attention. Barring a referral, a top-notch proposal showing me how you will partner with your publisher to make your book a success is the best way to gain my attention. I do review each submission so if you don't hear from me in three months, feel free to resubmit and let me know it's your second try. If you are accepted for representation by another agent before hearing back from me, I would greatly appreciate it if you could let me know so I can disregard your submission and wish you the best.

Do you charge fees separate from your commission, or offer non-agenting fee-based services: I charge no fees. No reading fees, no critique fees, nothing but industry standard commission.

What are representative titles you have sold to publishers: *A Promise for Spring* by Kim Vogel Sawyer (Barbour Books); *Jewel of His Heart* by Maggie Brendan (Revell); *Mothers of the Bible Speak to Mothers of Today* by Kathi Macias (New Hope Publishers).

Why did you become an agent, and how did you become one: I believe in the books I present to editors and I love making authors' dreams come true. I became an agent because my agent, Joyce Hart, wanted to expand her business and she was willing to take a chance on me. I'm so glad she did!

How do you feel about writers: I love writers! Since I'm a writer myself, I understand what they go through to get published and to keep their career momentum going. I understand the frustration of the near miss and the pain of multiple rejections. I also celebrate with them when that all-important contract comes through. Gaining new book contracts never gets old for me. The twentieth book is just as exciting as the first.

What do you tell entities from other planets and dimensions about your job: I spend a lot of time reading, advising, answering questions, hand-holding, and making friends.

What are your favorite books, movies, TV shows, and why: My tastes are eclectic. I like to read books on Western mysticism from the Middle Ages. I also enjoy romantic books and suspense. Silent films are a treat. The other night my husband and I stayed up much too late watching *Lorna Doone*. As for TV, *Clean House* is fun to watch. My tastes are often dominated by my mood at the time, whether I want entertainment or wish to be challenged.

How would you describe the writer from hell: This writer would refuse to cooperate with editors, send me lots of chain-letter emails, and be flighty and unpredictable, with a poor work ethic. Thankfully I have wonderful writers who are just super!

How would you describe the publisher and/or editor from hell: I really hate having to act as a bill collector. I like when a publisher pays on time. The hellish editor is one who refuses to answer legitimate calls and/or emails.

What do you like best about your clients, and the editors and publishers you work with: I love how dedicated my clients are to the writing craft, and their wonderful attitudes about complying with editors' requests. I love how my editors don't make irrational, unreasonable requests and how they treat my authors with respect. I love publishers who do a top-notch job of marketing.

You're welcome to share your thoughts and sentiments about the business of writing and publishing: A talented, persistent writer willing to be flexible and sensitive to the market has the best chance of success.

Do you wish to describe who you are: My goal is to be a benefit and a blessing to all who work with me.

Will our business exist as we know it in ten years or so: Yes, and the quality of our books will only get better. Electronic formats may gain in popularity, but I think we'll always have leather-bound, hardback, and paperback books.

The following information pertains to Terry Burns.

Born: August 21, 1942.

Education: BBA West Texas State; advanced studies at Southern Methodist University.

Career story: Chamber of commerce executive for 27 years, professional writer of inspirational fiction 15 years, agent at Hartline for over three years. As a writer I have 24 books in print, and as an agent have a diverse and growing client list.

Hobbies and special personal interests: Camping and RV.

Subjects and categories you like to agent: Historical fiction and romance, mysteries, thriller/suspense, inspirationals, nonfiction, a good well-written book I can see the market for and feel I have the right contacts to address that market.

Subjects and categories writers shouldn't bother pitching to you: Fantasy and sci-fi, erotica, gay or lesbian or anything of that nature. [Writers] should know I don't take hard-copy submissions and should check our submission guidelines.

What might you be doing if you weren't agenting: Writing more.

What's the most effective ways for writers to grab your attention: Read the submission guidelines and send me just exactly what I want to see in the exact manner I ask to see it.

Do you charge fees separate from your commission, or offer non-agenting fee-based services: No; our agency does have a provision to charge for copies and postage if appropriate.

What are representative titles you have sold to publishers: *Rhapsody in Red* (Moody); *The Birth to Five Book* (Revell); *Beyond the Smoke* (BJU Press); *Tribute* (Kregel); Two separate five-book youth series to Capstone Press; *Rekindle Your Dreams* (Bridge Logos); *Love Rescues*: first book in trilogy (Whitaker House); *By Darkness Hid*: first book in three-book series to Marcher Lord Press and Highland Blessings (Abingdon Press).

Why did you become an agent, and how did you become one: The owner of this agency, Joyce Hart, was my agent for a number of years and still is. She recruited me to work with her. I decided I could do more good by helping a number of people get their work out than doing a book or two a year myself, although I do still write.

How do you feel about writers: Most agents come from a publishing background. I came from a writing background. Whether that is an advantage or a disadvantage, it does give me an unusually good rapport with writers.

What do you tell entities from other planets and dimensions about your job: To go home because I don't rep sci-fi.

What are your favorite books, movies, TV shows, and why: I grew up watching *Bonanza* and *Gunsmoke* and Gene and Roy at the movies. I love Westerns. I'd write and rep a bunch of them if there was a market for them right now. As to shows today it takes something pretty interesting to get me away from whatever I'm doing.

How would you describe the writer from hell: Let me put it this way, I don't take orders very well.

How would you describe the publisher and/or editor from hell: The only ones that really bother me are the ones whose idea of a response to a submission is just to never respond. Unfortunately there seems be more doing that.

What do you like best about your clients, and the editors and publishers you work with: The love of the words, the desire to get a good story out there that will entertain, that will impact emotions, that will cause someone to stop and think, possible even bring some change into their lives. I love to work with people on both ends that are trying to make something happen with the written word.

You're welcome to share your thoughts and sentiments about the business of writing and publishing: See above.

Do you wish to describe who you are: Just a good old boy that likes to try and help people get their words out into the marketplace.

Will our business exist as we know it in ten years or so: Yes. There have been changes over the years, but they have tended to be additional sources of publishing, not replacing previous forms. We will see digital and audio and some of the other changes taking place now continue to grow, but we'll still see publishing as we know it continue to exist.

The following information pertains to Diana L. Flegal.

Born: July 24, Johnstown, Pennsylvania.

Education: Certified dental assistant; certified X-ray technologist; 13 credits shy of a degree in anthropology and missions from Maryland Bible College and Seminary.

Career story: Served as a third-world health care giver in Haiti one year. Chairside dental assistant, twenty-three years; apologetics teacher at Grace Bible Academy, Sioux Falls, South Dakota; women's Bible study leader; youth leader; Sunday school leader; pastor's wife; editorial assistant to Joyce Hart, CEO and founder of Hartline Literary Agency; literary agent.

Hobbies and special personal interests: Crafting, decorating my home, reading, gardening, traveling.

Subjects and categories you like to agent: Inspirational nonfiction, inspirational literary fiction, inspirational gift books, animal books (moving stories about animals and the people that love them).

Subjects and categories writers shouldn't bother pitching to you: Gay/lesbian, paranormal, New Age, or anything that is not from a Christian worldview. I'll take a look at most anything else if it is well written.

What might you be doing if you weren't agenting: Life coaching.

What's the most effective ways for writers to grab your attention: Good storyline with a fast pace. Do not bog me down with minute details of your personal life story. Readers do not want to know these things.

Do you charge fees separate from your commission, or offer non-agenting fee-based services: I charge for copies that I must print for submission and the postage for same. That is all. Honest!

What are representative titles you have sold to publishers: *Fat to Skinny Fast & Easy* by Doug Varrieur (Sterling Publishing Co.); *Be Still and Let Your Nail-Polish Dry* by Loree Lough (Summerside Press); *No Strings Attached* by Loree Lough (Whitaker House); *Love Finds You in North Pole Alaska* by Loree Lough (Summerside Press); *Love Finds You in Hershey Pa.* by Cerella Seachrist (Summerside Press).

Why did you become an agent, and how did you become one: A voracious reader from little on, I have always wanted to be paid to read. As Joyce Hart's first reader, I learned what good writing was, what editors were looking for and what did not sell. I began to realize that I could be an agent.

How do you feel about writers: I love writers because before I was an agent, I was a reader. I love the printed word, newspapers, magazines, digests, and novels, how to's etc. so without writers I wouldn't have those precious stolen moments in time when I am swept away to another place and time, country or planet. My life would not be at all as joyful and varied as it is.

What do you tell entities from other planets and dimensions about your job: It is the best reason to relocate to Planet Earth. We have free libraries and they can get their own card. You don't need an extension cord and any battery packs. Just daylight and a comfy chair. It is so worth learning English for!

What are your favorite books, movies, TV shows, and why: The Bible has the top slot to be sure. As to fiction, I love mysteries best, Elizabeth Peters and her pen name Anne Perry is my absolute favorite author. I have read most everything she has written, and that is a lot of books. Google her sometime. Christy Barritt, Ron and Janet Benrey too. Maeve Binchy is my favorite secular author, read everything she has written; then non fiction how-to, John Ortberg, Erwin McManus, T.D. Jakes, Philip Yantzy, Max Lucado, John Maxwell, Donald Miller. Writing Books: Anne Lamott's *Bird by Bird* is one of the best, then Terry Whalin's *How to Write a Nonfiction Book Proposal*, along with Julia Cameron and William Zinsser. Movies: *The Secret Life of Bees*, *Lord of the Rings*, *K-Pax*. TV Shows: *NCIS*, *Bones*, Home & Garden Television.

How would you describe the writer from hell: I try to steer clear of them. But I guess they are the ones that write their life story with every small detail included expecting it to be a bestseller and it is only interesting to them…

How would you describe the publisher and/or editor from hell: Don't know too many, but I would say they are the ones who clear their desk and send out the form rejection letters and never give your proposal a glance. Or at the least fail to tell me what exactly they ARE looking for.

What do you like best about your clients, and the editors and publishers you work with: The creative comments and critiques that editors give help my writers become better writers. You can tell the ones (editors) that truly love what they do and that they care about representing good writing. They take that extra minute to say a nice thing that keeps you trying all the more to make a match for the writer and the editor. As for my clients, they have become my extended family. We support one another with words and deeds. In my case we encourage one another to go beyond our limitations to attempt excellence. I care so much for each one and their stories that I [lie] awake at night trying to strategize a plan to enable their success.

You're welcome to share your thoughts and sentiments about the business of writing and publishing: It is a tough business, getting tougher every year, but I believe this means that the really well-turned phrase and good story will shine forth and find its place. And we will be all the better for having known one another and shared the time it takes to read a book together. My life will be enriched as well as the others that just happen to come across that good read, or received a gift or had nothing better to do so out of boredom picked up a book to fill the time. Their lives will be changed, the world will be a better place to live in and more aliens will desire to visit. They will begin savings accounts and place a poster on the wall of their bedrooms and dream of the day they come to Planet Earth and get their very own library card with their name on it.

Do you wish to describe who you are: I am a lover of books, a dreamer of dreams, an armchair traveler and a visionary and a missionary. I'm also a blond by birth.

Will our business exist as we know it in ten years or so: I plan on being a literary agent until I pass from this life on to the next. It is something that I can do from anyplace in the world. I plan to be so successful that I will travel extensively, representing my authors anywhere I go. I appreciate the technology that allows this and hope I can enjoy the health to follow my dreams of helping dig wells in Africa, build orphanages in third-world countries and help a school in Tanzania where a friend of mine teaches.

JOHN HAWKINS & ASSOCIATES, INC.

71 West 23rd Street, Suite 1600, New York, NY 10019

212-807-7040   fax: 212-807-9555

www.jhalit.com

Agents' names: Anne Hawkins, ahawkins@jhalit.com; Moses Cardona, moses@jhalit.com; William Reiss, reiss@jhalit.com

The following information pertains to Anne Hawkins.

Education: BA, Bryn Mawr College.

Career history: I have been a literary agent for over twelve years. Prior to that, I worked in various businesses and in English education. I also played the bassoon professionally.

Hobbies/personal interests: I love classical music, ballet, opera, and theater. Cooking is one of my favorite forms of weekend relaxation. I also collect African tribal art.

Categories/subjects that you are most enthusiastic about agenting: Adult mainstream literary and commercial fiction, including mystery/suspense/thriller, and historicals. A small number of upper-middle-grade and young-adult projects. Adult nonfiction projects concerning history, public policy, science, medicine, nature/outdoors, and women's issues

What you don't want to agent: Adult fiction: romance, Westerns, horror, science fiction, fantasy. Adult nonfiction: advice/relationships, business, self-help, spirituality, most how-to. Juvenile: picture books or books for very young readers.

If you were not an agent, what might you be doing instead: I might work as a museum curator or in a nursery that specializes in exotic trees and shrubs.

What's the best way for writers to solicit your interest: Write a brief, engaging query letter and include a few sample pages.

Do you charge reading or management fees: No.

Can you provide an approximation by percent of what you tend to represent by category : Adult fiction: 45 percent, adult nonfiction: 45 percent, upper-middle-grade or young-adult fiction: 10 percent.

What are the most common mistakes writers make when pitching you: Pitching multiple, unrelated projects at the same time is a big mistake, since it's hard enough to find the right agent for even one book. Pitching projects of a type that I don't handle is foolish and a waste of everyone's time. (Readers of this book won't have that problem.)

How would you describe the client from hell: Authors can be a quirky bunch, and "quirky" is fine. But arrogant, unreasonably demanding, inflexible, mean-spirited behavior sours an agent-client relationship every time.

How would you describe the perfect client: Glorious talent aside, the perfect client is distinguished by good sense, good humor, and good manners.

How and why did you ever become an agent: My brother-in-law, John Hawkins, encouraged me to join the agency.

What, if anything, can a writer do to increase the odds of your becoming his or her agent: A referral from some I know (author, other publishing professional, or personal friend) will get my immediate attention. Over 50 percent of my clients have come to me through some kind of referral.

How would you describe to someone (or something) from another planet what it is that you do as an agent: I represent the business interests of authors to publishing houses, provide advocacy, act as a sounding board for editorial issues, and help authors make wise career choices.

Do you have any particular opinions or impressions of editors and publishers in general: Most people in this industry are smart, interesting, and fun to work with.

On a personal level, what do you think people like about you and dislike about you: I always try to be forthright and honest. Most people like that, but a few find it daunting.

The following information pertains to Moses Cardona.

Born: October 1966, New York, New York.

Education: BS, New York University.

Career history: All with John Hawkins & Associates: began as bookkeeper, promoted to rights director, and currently general manager/literary agent of the agency.

Hobbies/personal interests: Comics, basketball, jigsaw puzzles.

Categories/subjects that you are most enthusiastic about agenting: Multicultural, gay fiction, literary fiction.

What you don't want to agent: Poetry, children's, military, mafia fiction.

If you were not an agent, what might you be doing instead: Running a bed and breakfast.

What's the best way for writers to solicit your interest: Query letter, with sample chapters, or email query.

Do you charge reading or management fees: No.

Can you provide an approximation by percent of what you tend to represent by category: Multicultural: 50 percent, fiction—mysteries, literary, science fiction/horror: 30 percent, science/business: 10 percent, other: 10 percent.

What are the most common mistakes writers make when pitching you: Pitching more than one project. Misspelling agent's name, information.

How would you describe the client from hell: Having unrealistic ideas about publishing industry.

How would you describe the perfect client: Good manners, patience, a bit of attitude, and a great sense of humor.

How and why did you ever become an agent: I fell into the business through a client of the agency.

What, if anything, can a writer do to increase the odds of your becoming his or her agent: [Have] patience and be a great storyteller.

How would you describe to someone (or something) from another planet what it is that you do as an agent: I help place ideas onto various formats, film, books, magazines for mass distribution around the planet.

What are your favorite books, movies, TV shows, and why: *Mary Tyler Moore Show*, great cast, writing—timeless; *All About Eve*, best movie about art, theater, and people; *The Stand*, probably one of the best epic books about humanity.

On a personal level, what do you think people like about you and dislike about you: I'm brutally honest.

Please list representative titles you have sold: *Tarnished Beauty* (Atria Books); *White Nights* (St Martin's/Minotaur); *Red Bones* (St. Martin's/Minotaur).

The following information pertains to William Reiss.

Born: 1942, New York, New York.

Education: BA, Kenyon College.

Career history: Freelance researcher; editorial assistant to Lombard Jones (a graphic designer and editor), encyclopedia editor, Funk & Wagnalls Standard Reference Library.

Categories/subjects that you are most enthusiastic about agenting: Biographies, nonfiction historical narratives, archaeology, science fiction and fantasy, mysteries and suspense, true-crime narratives, natural history, children's fiction, adult fiction (literary and commercial).

What you don't want to agent: Romance novels, poetry, plays.

What's the best way for writers to solicit your interest: Telephone or send a letter describing the project, with a few sample pages to provide a sense of writing style.

Do you charge reading or management fees: No.

Please list representative titles you have sold: *Shiloh* (S&S/Atheneum Children's Books); *The Madman's Tale* (Ballantine); *White Oleander* (Little, Brown); *Allegiance: Fort Sumter, Charleston, and the Beginning of the Civil War* (Harcourt); *Exit Strategy* (Jove); *Ghosts in the Snow* (Bantam); *Son of a Witch* (Regan Books/HarperCollins).

HEACOCK LITERARY AGENCY, INC.

Catt LeBaigue, AAR; Tom Dark

Author's Representatives

1020 Hollywood Way, #439, Burbank, CA 91505

www.heacockliteraryagency.com

email: catt@heacockliteraryagency.com; tom@heacockliteraryagency.com

Headquarters:

Rosalie Grace Heacock Thompson, AAR

507 Grand Blvd., P.O. Box 226, Cloudcroft, NM 88317-0226

Agent's name: Catt LeBaigue

Born: December 30, California.

Education: BA, music, California State University, San Bernardino; plus a certificate in writing in upper-division and graduate-level courses, CSUSB

Career history: Eighteen years in the television and film industry for Columbia, Lorimar, Sony, Fox, Paramount, and Warner Bros. studios. Catt LeBaigue joined the Heacock Literary Agency, working full time as an agent, in 2005. Tom Dark is our newest agent, joining in 2008.

Hobbies/personal interests: I grew up as an American living abroad in the diplomatic community. A highlight in my life was in 2005, when a full-blooded traditional aboriginal tribe in Australia adopted me, gave me a new name and invited me to dance in their sacred dances. I raise horses and live close to nature. My interests are meditation, dreams, Jung, reading, travel, drawing, sculpting, and animals.

Categories/subjects that you are most enthusiastic about agenting: The Heacock Literary Agency was founded in 1978 with a vision to get significant books into the marketplace, books with the potential to empower and fortify consciousness. Books can change the individual from the inside out and individual consciousness can transform the world. Trade nonfiction: Art, architecture, animal communication, diplomacy, ecology, indigenous cultures, invention, the mind and learning processes, formal science and the connection to inner knowing, social sciences, travel, wilderness awareness, body, mind and spirit. We seek innovative books which present solutions to problems. Trade fiction: Children's, especially middle-grade and YA. Adult fiction: Literary, no short stories.

What you don't want to agent: True crime, abuse accounts and books that do not contribute to the reader's well-being and peace of mind.

If you were not an agent, what might you be doing instead: I see my work as an author's representative, not just as my job, but as the best way that I can contribute to humanity and the health of the planet. If I wasn't agenting, I'd be seeking another way that is just as powerful to make a difference.

What's the most effective ways for writers to grab your attention: Email without attachments, unless requested. Not accepting postal mail queries.

Do you charge reading or any upfront fees: No.

Can you provide an approximation by percent of what you tend to represent by category: 30 percent adult nonfiction, 40 percent children's, 30 percent fiction.

What are the most common mistakes writers make when pitching you: The writer should take care in composing the inquiry since this is the first impression the agent receives of the writer's ability to convey his or her ideas. Any background information will enhance the writer's chance of attracting interest. Nonfiction books should be presented with a book proposal. Including the word count of the final manuscript is helpful.

How would you describe the writer from hell: The client from hell seeks only monetary gain or fame and cannot see beyond themselves.

How would you describe the perfect client: The perfect client delights me with fine writing, is considerate, and expresses appreciation for our efforts.

How and why did you ever become an agent: Since the founding of the agency by my uncle James B. Heacock and my aunt Rosalie Grace Heacock Thompson, in 1978, I knew that one day, after a career in Hollywood, I would turn to agenting books. I focused my education with that in mind and followed the publishing business closely through the years, occasionally working for the agency. After spending eighteen years in the entertainment industry working in film and television, I felt it was time to switch careers. I joined the agency in 2005, as full-time agent, representing trade fiction and nonfiction. We do not handle screenplays at this time.

What, if anything, can a writer do to increase the odds of your becoming his or her agent: Timing is the critical element here. If the author is presenting a simply wonderful book about a very crowded subject which already has wonderful books out, the representative cannot spend his or her time trying to place it. The author should be familiar with what is "out there" and concentrate efforts on what needs to be out there.

How would you describe to someone (or something) from another planet what it is that you do as an agent: The literary agent reads and evaluates book proposals and manuscripts, presents those which are accepted to appropriate publishers, negotiates the very best contract possible and carefully reviews all royalty statements after publication. The literary agent is basically a business manager for the author's writing efforts, serves also as a sounding board when the author wants to test new ideas and distributes the authors' monies promptly.

Do you have any particular opinions or impressions of editors and publishers in general: Editors and publishers impress me as dedicated, book-loving individuals who behave with integrity and honor.

What do you think the future holds for writers, publishers and agents: The future is bright for all three. Books continue to be the thought processes of humanity and to make vast contributions to society.

On a personal level, what do you think people like about you and dislike about you: As Robbie Burns once wrote: "O wad some Power the giftie gie us / To see oursel as ithers see us!"

Please list representative titles you have sold: The Heacock Literary Agency has sold over 1,100 books to over 100 publishers.

DAVID HENDIN

PO Box 805, Nyack, NY 10960

Agent's name: David Hendin

Born: December 16, 1945, St. Louis, Missouri.

Education: BS in biology, education, University of Missouri, Columbia 1967. MA in journalism, University of Missouri, Columbia, 1970.

Career history: Columnist, feature writer, executive (including senior vice president, newspaper syndication, and president, publishing division), United Feature Syndicate, Inc. 1970–1993.

What's the best way for writers to solicit your interest: We are not accepting any new clients.

Do you charge reading or management fees: No.

Can you provide an approximation by percent of what you tend to represent by category: Fiction: 40 percent, nonfiction: 60 percent.

How would you describe to someone (or something) from another planet what it is that you do as an agent: I have fun with writers.

Please list representative titles you have sold: *Miss Manners' Guide to a Surprisingly Dignified Wedding* by Judith and Jacobina Martin (W.W. Norton); *Killer Cuts* by Elaine Viets (NAL/Signet); *The Time Travelers* by David Toomey (W.W. Norton).

THE JEFF HERMAN AGENCY

PO Box 1522 or 3 Elm Street, Stockbridge, MA 01262

413-298-0077   fax: 413-298-8188

www.jeffherman.com   email: jeff@jeffherman.com

Agent's name: Jeff Herman

When and where you were born: December 7, 1958. North Shore Hospital, Manhasset, NY.

Your formal education education: Bachelor's degree in the liberal arts, Syracuse University.

Your professional history: I had a litany of jobs post-college in public relations, marketing, and some journalism. I spent some time in Israel picking apples and catching scared chickens for their ritual demise. They don't kill, pluck and mutilate themselves. I started my literary agency in my latter 20s. I started it in a backwards way. I didn't have clients, hands-on experience or requisite knowledge or connections. But I was much too unaware of reality to know any better, and was gifted with the ability to keep making interesting mistakes at my own expense and the tendency to be pushed forward by raw arrogance. People will often let you do something for them if you show up to do it and seem to be legit, especially if they only have to pay you based upon results. Over the years I have made hundreds of book deals, and am happy to report I still make mistakes and am much less arrogant.

Your personal interests/hobbies: I sing (not well) and speak nonsense to dogs, cats, crows, squirrels, or whatever creatures stand still to listen without trying to have me arrested. I don't know if they say anything in return, but I'm confident that I'm heard, and I don't feel the need to be understood in the conventional sense, since I can rarely be certain I'm saying I might really mean anyway. This is the closest I can come to what might resemble a hobby.

The subjects and categories you tend to agent: I deal with many areas of nonfiction, especially if it regards a practical, Earth-based topic, or something that makes people's eyes go big for a few moments.

What writers shouldn't even try pitching to you: I don't comprehend poetry.

What would you have been, or be, if not an agent: Something else.

Do you charge fees or offer fee-based services: Charging fees would be easy and lucrative, but then I would have to keep performing specific tasks of equal value in return, or else keep changing my name and address. Either way, it seems easier not to charge fees.

Approximately ten titles you recently sold: See www.jeffherman.com.

Why did you choose to become an agent and how did it happen: Well, like I said above, plus I really like ideas and thinking about things, and structuring deals, and being around positive passion.

How do you really feel about writers: I like that they want to express themselves in a way that is perpetual, maybe even eternal. Their words make impressions that bring forth more words, thoughts and deeds by others. Writers help expand the universe.

Describe your job to a visitor from another planet, or a moron you just met at a bar: I help people make statements that benefit other people.

What are your favorite books, TV shows, movies, and why: I like most zombie movies, because the idea of eating another person's living body without remorse, shame, or indigestion is fascinating. I'm intrigued by the raw undefined force that makes them do that. And I like it when serene suburban neighborhoods suddenly erupt into an orgy of zombies eating their still un-zombie neighbors. It seems like it should be something that could actually happen anywhere once in a while. Maybe it does.

Describe the writer/client from hell: People who resent others for not being controlled or manipulated.

Describe yourself: Just watching and waiting while I work and live; like everyone else.

Describe the publisher and/or editor from hell: When someone is deceptive, intentionally destructive, or deliberately unaccountable for the dissonance they sow.

Describe hell: Whatever is seriously unpleasant can qualify, at least for that moment. On the other hand, it's possible that some people are satisfied with a situation that is seemingly hellish. And then there are those who can bring hell to others through the toxins they deliver, but that can be entirely transient and temporal, like a nasty oil spill.

What are your preferred ways for writers to pitch you: Anyway they dare.

Do you think the e-readers and similar devices will significantly change the publishing business: Yes. I'm not sure large traditional publishing infrastructures are able to quickly adapt to new economic models that emerging technologies are imposing on the marketplace, and I don't think they internally understand what's happening. Intellectual products are becoming entirely non-physical, and per-unit pricing is unsettled.

Are you optimistic, pessimistic, neutral, or catatonic about the book business into the knowable future: Optimistic. Especially if some of the large houses and book chains begin to wobble, because good innovations will likely displace them.

Explain what you like and don't like about your job: I don't like that I have to do it almost every day, but I like that it gives me something to do almost every day. I wish I had more time to simply be creative and more attentive to certain tasks.

Describe a book you might like writing: That book would challenge the readers to release everything they believe and replace it with the truth. However, I don't have enough content for even the first sentence, so it obviously wouldn't be nearly long enough.

Do you think some/most of these questions are stupid: I don't think they're stupid for the simple reason that they illicit answers, which creates paths to somewhere.

HIDDEN VALUE GROUP

1240 E. Ontario Ave; STE #102-148, Corona, CA 92881

951-549-8891

www.hiddenvaluegroup.com

Agent's name: Nancy Jernigan, LPF, LPC

Career history or story: *Christianity Today*, Inc.: marketing manager/publishing; Focus on the Family: director of marketing/publishing; Nest Entertainment: director of marketing/publishing and direct mail; BUY.COM: head of customer relationship manager/online and print; Licensed Professional Coach/LPCC; professionally recognized agent.

Hobbies, interests: Rock climbing, reading.

Subjects and categories you are interested in agenting, including fiction and nonfiction: Family, marriage, parenting, fiction, women's issues, inspirational, self-help, etc.

JULIE A. HILL AND ASSOC., LLC

1155 Camino Del Mar #530, Del Mar, CA 92014

www.publishersmarketplace.com/members/hillagent

email: hillagent@aol.com (no e-submissions please)

Agents' names: Julie Hill, hillagent@aol.com

Born: Pasadena, California, May 13.

Education: Education: BA, University of Arizona; UC Berkeley Publishing Course. I am also a guest lecturer at San Diego State University in the graduate level thesis-writing course.

Career story: Writer then agent…see below.

Hobbies and special personal interests: Gardening, cooking, TRAVEL.

Subjects and categories you like to agent: Psychology, memoir, Jewish memoir, especially anything Holocaust-related, self-help, and advice are favorites too and travel, lots of travel. New spins on New Age too.

Subjects and categories writers shouldn't bother pitching to you: Fantasy, horror, children's, business.

What might you be doing if you weren't agenting: Gardening, traveling, eating!

What's the most effective ways for writers to grab your attention: Perfect book proposal! Thorough (please, please) market survey and developed platform, including Internet presence.

Do you charge fees separate from your commission, or offer non-agenting fee-based services: I offer contract consultation at an hourly fee. Often writers sell something themselves and need help with the contract, thus I am here to help! I enjoy contract negotiation.

What are representative titles you have sold to publishers: A few: *Return to Naples: My Italian Bar Mitzvah and Other Discoveries* by Robert Zweig, PhD (Barricade); Frommers and Dummies titles for Walt Disney World and Orlando by Laura Lea Miller (four different titles, revised yearly; Barnes and Noble Travel Bestseller List); *Café Life: Venice*, *Café Life: San Francisco*, and *Café Life: Seattle* by Joe Wolff and Roger Paperno, photographer (Interlink Books)—Their *Café Life: Florence* won a Travel Book of the Year Award for 2006; *A Blessing in Disguise* by Andrea Joy Cohen, MD (Berkely/Penguin)—made the *LA Times* (and others) bestseller list.

Why did you become an agent, and how did you become one: I was writing for periodicals (and online horoscopes) and I watched my friends who were also writers struggling to find good representation, and felt I could help writers get what they deserve. I also wanted to be a career developer and manager, which I do for my authors. Most agents only sell books, which is fine, but there is so much more to making a career out of writing and I want to help my authors prosper.

How do you feel about writers: I love them, of course.

What do you tell entities from other planets and dimensions about your job: That they don't want it. Space travel has many more benefits, including long distance travel without airport hassles.

What are your favorite books, movies, TV shows, and why: *Boston Legal*. So smart, so socially responsible.

How would you describe the writer from hell: Cannot/will not take direction. Calls to chat. May not know the term "platform." Say they are "going to develop a website."

How would you describe the publisher and/or editor from hell: Suggests one of your writers formulate a proposal for something they have conceived, then turns the proposal down. Oh God, I could go on, but mostly I want to go on the record here as appreciating the good ones, and there are far more good ones that bad. Many are even great.

What do you like best about your clients, and the editors and publishers you

work with: Smart, smart, smart. Efficient. Don't need a lot of reminding to get the job done.

You're welcome to share your thoughts and sentiments about the business of writing and publishing: Writers' conferences tend to focus on the theme that unknown writers get huge advances, get discovered by Hollywood, and their lives are forever transformed with one book. You may as well bet on Big Brown to win the Triple Crown. Fun to talk about, but unlikely. Someone, somewhere, said "publishing isn't a business, it's a casino." More true than not, but one can improve one's odds by doing the work, doing it well, and doing it because "it calls you."

Do you wish to describe who you are: A pretty nice but short-tempered woman.

Will our business exist as we know it in ten years or so: A great question... wish I knew...being an astrologer, I forecast more electronic media, but not as much as the electronic people would have you think. I do feel pubs will do more with agents online, in fact, one of my last deals was done totally by email. The book has been released and is very successful, and I've never heard this editor's voice. I know it seems strange, but we are both happy with the efficiency, and happy with having a record of every word that was said and every term every negotiated, and how it went down. Believe me, this can be very useful going forward, both for me, my author and the publisher. Further forecast: Despite hundreds of cable channels to keep us entertained, books will thrive because there is nothing more satisfying than a quiet read provided by a great author...nothing.

HORNFISCHER LITERARY MANAGEMENT, L.P.

P.O. Box 50544, Austin, TX 78703

email: jim@hornfischerlit.com

Agent's name: Jim Hornfischer, President.

Born: 1965, Massachusetts.

Education: BA, Colgate University; JD, University of Texas at Austin.

Career history: President, Hornfischer Literary Management, Austin, 2001–present; agent, Literary Group International, New York, 1993–2001; Editorial positions, McGraw-Hill, HarperCollins, New York, 1987–92.

Categories/subjects that you are most enthusiastic about agenting: All types of high-quality narrative nonfiction, including current events, biography, memoir, U.S. and world history, military history, popular science, medicine/health, business, law and culture.

What you don't want to agent: Fiction and poetry, and most self-help/inspirational.

What's the best way for writers to solicit your interest: A smartly tailored personal letter that suggests professionalism and/or accomplishment, together with thirty to fifty pages of good material that supports your optimism. Please include an overview of the book and its market, author bio (and reviews and other media if available), chapter summaries, and one to three sample chapters.

Do you charge reading or management fees: No reading fees. Commission structure is 15 percent domestic, 25 percent foreign. Sold approximately sixteen titles last year. The approximate percentage of all submissions (from queries through manuscripts) that I rejected?: The same parade-drenching number as the rest of them.

What are the most common mistakes writers make when pitching you: Failing to identify the unique space in the universe (or at least in the bookstore) that their proposed book will occupy. Everything follows from that simple act.

How would you describe the perfect client: Thinks big, drinks from glasses that are half full, writes even grocery lists with narrative momentum, keeps an open ear for useful advice and runs with it in brilliant and surprising ways.

How and why did you ever become an agent: Getting a good book published, especially one that might not otherwise have been, can be rewarding in a life-affirming sort of way.

What, if anything, can a writer do to increase the odds that you will become his or her agent: Grasp the rudiments of the business (even if as an artist you'd prefer not to bother), temper your ambition with patience and a long view, and refine and improve your craft continuously. It's all in the writing.

How would you describe to someone (or something) from another planet what it is that you do as an agent: My wife always tells me that I shatter dreams for a living, because I send back so many rejections. I prefer to think that, for those writers for whom I do useful work, I help make them. I do a little writing, too: www.jameshornfischer.com.

Do you have any particular opinions or impressions of editors and publishers in general: Editors: The good ones are the heart and soul of their companies, and management should listen to them more closely. Publishers: I am in awe of the process by which a talented group of people can rally collectively to insert a new voice into the national conversation. It happens all too rarely, but when it does you look back and marvel at the peculiar alchemy of it all.

Please list representative titles you have sold: *Flags of Our Fathers* by James Bradley with Ron Powers (Bantam); *Traitor to His Class: The Privileged Life and Radical Presidency of Franklin Delano Roosevelt* by H. W. Brands (Doubleday); *The Scent of the Missing: A Handler's Journey Beside a Search-and-Rescue Dog* by Susannah Charleson (Houghton Mifflin); *The Next 100 Years: A Forecast for the 21st Century* by George Friedman (Doubleday); *Ghost: Confessions of a Counterterrorism Agent* by Fred Burton (Random House); *American Pests: The Losing War on Insects, from Colonial Times to DDT* by James E. McWilliams (Columbia); *Rose Bowl Dreams: A*

Memoir of Faith, Family and Football by Adam Jones (Thomas Dunne Books); *How to Break a Terrorist: The U.S. Interrogators Who Used Brains, Not Brutality, to Take Down the Deadliest Man in Iraq* by Matthew Alexander with John Bruning (Free Press); *Mark Twain: A Life* by Ron Powers (Free Press); *Obama: From Promise to Power* by David Mendell (Harper/Amistad); *House to House: A Soldier's Memoir* by David Bellavia with John Bruning (Free Press).

ANDREA HURST LITERARY MANAGEMENT

P.O. Box 19010, Sacramento, CA 95819

5050 Laguna Blvd Ste 112-330, Elk Grove, CA 95758

www.andreahurst.com   email: andrea@andreahurst.com, judy@andreahurst.com

Agents' names: Andrea Hurst, Judy Mikalonis.
The following information pertains to Andrea Hurst.
Born: Los Angeles, California.
Education: Bachelor's degree in expressive arts.
Career history or story: President of Andrea Hurst Literary Management, works with both major and regional publishing houses, and her client list includes emerging new voices and *NY Times* bestselling authors such as Dr. Bernie Siegel. With over 20 years in the publishing industry, Andrea is a published author (*Lazy Dog's Guide to Enlightenment*), skilled acquisition and development editor, speaker, and literary judge. Her areas of expertise include sales, promotion, and production in the publishing and entertainment fields. She is an instructor for the Whidbey Island MA program in creative writing.
Hobbies, interests: Animal welfare, reading fine novels, writing fiction, gourmet natural food.
Subjects and categories you are interested in agenting, including fiction and nonfiction: Prescriptive and narrative nonfiction: Parenting, relationships, women's issues, personal growth, health and wellness, science, business, true crime, animals, pop culture, humor, cookbooks, gift books, spirituality, metaphysical, psychology, and self-help. Fiction: Adult commercial fiction, women's fiction.
Subjects and categories writers shouldn't even bother pitching to you: Science fiction/fantasy, western, horror.
What would you do if you weren't agenting: I would be a bestselling fiction author living on Whidbey Island, although I would still probably keep some of my best clients.
What's the best way for fiction writers to solicit your interest: Take the time to learn the craft of writing and have your work professionally edited before sending it out. Be sure your query letter is compelling and shows off your writing style.
What's the best way for nonfiction writers to solicit your interest: Write a

knockout book proposal with a long and detailed marketing section. Send a query letter first by email.

Do you charge reading or any upfront fees: No.

In your experience, what are the most common pitching mistakes writers make: Not researching to find the appropriate agency match for their work. It is very easy to locate an agent's website and figure out what they are looking for, how they want it submitted, and what their name is! Not following directions and not having a strong query letter.

Describe the client from hell, even if you don't have any: A writer who is not familiar with the publishing business and has unrealistic expectations can turn quickly into a client from hell. Particularly someone who is not willing to edit their work, can't make deadlines, and has an attitude that everyone else should accommodate [them].

What's your definition of a great client: Luckily, I have many of those. A great client follows directions willingly, meets and exceeds deadlines and expectations, and has a can-do attitude. We have a mutual trust and they let me do my job.

How can writers increase the odds that you will offer representation: Write exceptionally well, have a unique, well-researched idea that is pitched through a complete book proposal for nonfiction, or a synopsis and sample chapters for fiction. Have a strong platform that you are building on a daily basis and be committed to a long-term writing career. Be willing to work hard to promote your writing and continue to improve your craft through classes, critique groups, conferences, etc.

Why did you become an agent, and how did you become one: The publishing business has been in my blood from a very early age. As a writer myself, I understand the business from both sides. My first book published was *Everybody's Natural Foods Cookbook* through New World Library. Marc Allen, the publisher, taught me the business from the ground up. After that, I was hooked. I worked as a freelance editor, ghostwriter, and instructor for many years, including a position as an acquisition and development editor for a children's publisher in Seattle. My extensive list of editorial contacts, coupled with my strong marketing background acquired through working at Columbia Records, led me on a natural course to becoming an agent.

Describe to someone from another planet what you do as an agent: Just about everything from editing to selling, and networking to acting as a coach and mentor. The job is never done.

How do you feel about editors and publishers: They are the gatekeepers that provide the opportunity for wonderful books to reach the world.

How do you feel about writers: I am always looking for the exceptional ones that have a great story to tell or wonderful information to share. Every query I receive is another opportunity to discover a great writer.

In your opinion, what do editors think of you: That I am professional, accessible, genuine, and represent talented and reliable clients.

What are some representative titles that you have sold: *Love, Magic & Mudpies* by Dr. Bernie Siegel (Rodale); *Dare to Wear Your Soul on the Outside* by Dr. Gloria Burgess (Jossey-Bass/Wiley); *A Course in Happiness* by Dr. Mardi Horowitz (Tarcher/Penguin); *True Self, True Wealth* by Peter Cole (Daisy Reese); *Beyond Words* (Atria); *Best Recipes from Italy's Food Festivals* by James Fraioli/Leonardo Curti Gibbs (Smith Publishers).

The following information pertains to Judy Mikalonis.

Subjects and categories you are interested in agenting, including fiction and nonfiction: Christian nonfiction, Christian fiction, adult nonfiction, YA fiction.

Subjects and categories writers shouldn't even bother pitching to you: No science fiction, no historical fiction, no supernatural thrillers.

What's the best way for fiction writers to solicit your interest: Write amazingly well and tell a transformative story.

What's the best way for nonfiction writers to solicit your interest: Write a damn good proposal and have an amazing platform.

Do you charge reading or any upfront fees: No.

In your experience, what are the most common pitching mistakes writers make: Not being prepared to sell their story. No immediate relevance to the reader apparent in their pitch. Can't tell me what their protagonist wants (fiction).

How can writers increase the odds that you will offer representation: Write really well. Write a good proposal. Follow directions and email queries only. Do not mail a query.

KELLER MEDIA, INC.

23852 West Pacific Coast Highway, Suite 701, Malibu, CA 90265

310-457-3490

email: Query@KellerMedia.com

Agent's name: Wendy Keller

Born: Chicago, Illinois, 20th century.

Education: Arizona State University, BA, journalism with minors in history and French.

Career history: 1980–1985 Print Journalist; 1988–1989 Agency Aide; 1989–present Literary Agent/Agency Owner.

Hobbies/personal interests: Fighting snails in my garden, managing my teenager's hectic social schedule, part-time taxi service for aforementioned teenager, reading very large stacks of books for fun and profit.

Categories/subjects that you are most enthusiastic about agenting: Any nonfiction book intended for adults, including business (sales, management, marketing and finance); spirituality/inspiration (esp. Divine Feminine/Goddess related); women's issues (any from health to family to relationships to other); self-help (parenting, relationships, mental wellness, health, education, etc.); science/physics (esp. quantum physics); history (any—world, American, esp. European); biography (celebrity or known names only); sports; popular psychology; current affairs; chick lit; how-to (do anything); cookbooks (only by authors with their own show on TV or radio, well-known restaurant or big web presence); consumer reference; gift books (illustrated or not).

What you don't want to agent: NO to juvenile, fiction, Christian, scripts, erotica, poetry, or true crime. No illustrated books. NO to first-person accounts of overcoming some medical, mental, or addiction trauma. NO to first-person accounts of sexual abuse or crime. NO books written from inside penitentiaries. NO books channeled by dead spirits or dead celebrities, e.g., Mother Theresa (she seems to be popular), Princess Di, Kurt Cobain, John Lennon, Einstein, etc. (P.S.—all these names are from queries received in the last six months or so!) NO books written by your dog or cat, goldfish, hamster, etc. That's probably pretty clear. You get the idea, right?

If you were not an agent, what might you be doing instead: Oh, I don't know. I think I'd be running a small, extremely organized, profitable, tidy country somewhere. Or practicing improving my French, Italian or Spanish language skills. Or finally taking that trip to Morocco…

What's the best way for writers to solicit your interest: It's even easier than that! There's only ONE way to really get my interest: SEND AN EMAIL. I prefer it so much to paper queries! Query@KellerMedia.com I promise whoever reads it will really look at it before they decide what to do with it.

Do you charge reading or management fees: Absolutely not! Agents who do should be immediately burned at the stake! Same with agents who ask for exclusive time periods to consider your work. Heck, if it's good, we will be fighting one another for it. Of course, in a genteel way. Send it to all who ask for it, and then if someone actually offers representation, call the slow ones and give them X days to respond. May the best woman win!

Can you provide an approximation by percent of what you tend to represent by category: Nonfiction book rights, English language: 60 percent, speaking fees for clients: 20 percent, foreign rights/audio/ancillary: 20 percent.

What are the most common mistakes writers make when pitching you: They send me stuff that is absolutely NOT what I handle (See "What you don't want to agent" above) OR they have little to no qualifications for their topic. E.g., male authors who want to write a guide to menopause and aren't even doctors, how-to-be-a-millionaire books by paupers, business books by people who know little more than middle management, science books that have so been done a thousand times before.

How would you describe the client from hell: Clients from hell are those who are so convinced they will be on *Oprah*, make the bestseller list, get a major six-figure advance but their book is on something like "start your own home-based fertilizer business" or "The Ten Best Potato Salad Recipes in America Today." Geez! Get real! And, of course, unilaterally I get annoyed with people who won't accept editing well, or who lie about their qualifications.

How would you describe the perfect client: Read my sold list! I have so many wonderful clients. Of course, the perfect ones I do not yet represent are people who have their own TV or radio show (or infomercial) broadcasting nationwide, and/or a national speaking platform in the USA, or who work for a company that is or they themselves are a household name. Pulitzer and Nobel prize winners always welcome!

How and why did you ever become an agent: I was training to be an Olympic typist and I crushed my fingers trying to get spare change out of a public payphone.

What, if anything, can a writer do to increase the odds of your becoming his or her agent: Have a massive, impressive, powerful media or speaking platform already in place, or the finances, drive, team and/or contacts to erect it. Everything else can be arranged.

How would you describe to someone (or something) from another planet what it is that you do as an agent: I make hundreds of phone calls; I fly to New York; I smile at a lot of people, even incoherent cab drivers; I make more phone calls; I cash very, very large checks, skim them for 15 percent (sometimes 20 percent); and I make smart people really, really happy (and sometimes famous).

Do you have any particular opinions or impressions of editors and publishers in general: I worship at the feet of publishers and editors. I am grateful for their wisdom and ability to write very large checks. I honor their ability to motivate their curmudgeonly publicity departments to work hard for my clients' best interests. In summary, they are the blessed souls about to pay for my kid's college education.

What do you think the future holds for writers, publishers, and agents: A lot, lot, lot of books. In many forms and formats, now known or which may be developed at some time in the future.

Do you have any favorite (current) TV shows, films, or books that you especially like and how come: "How come"? Jeff Herman, are you from Texas now?

On a personal level, what do you think people like about you and dislike about you: Authors like two things about me: One, I absolutely get the job done, always. I'm extremely focused, efficient, organized and productive. Two, my mother was a pit bull, my father a Harvard English professor, so I'm a great person to have on your side, unless I skip my distemper shot.

Please list representative titles you have sold: *Our Own Worst Enemy* (Warner Books); *Inner Wisdom* (Simon & Schuster); *Questions from Earth, Answers from Heaven* (St. Martin's Press); *Who's Afraid to be a Millionaire?* (Wiley); *The Ultimate Smoothie Book* (Warner Books); *Raising a Secure Child* (Viking/Penguin); *101 Ways to Promote Yourself* (HarperCollins); *Hiring Smart* (Crown Books); *The Encouraging Parent* (Random House); *Bringing Home the Business* (Penguin/Perigee); *The Power Path* (New World Library); *Secrets of Successful Negotiation for Women* (Career Press); *Ethics and Etiquette* (Entrepreneur Press); *Heart at Work* (McGraw-Hill); *Seven Secrets to Raising a Secure Child* (Penguin); *Never Make Another Cold Call* (Kaplan/Dearborn); *I Closed My Eyes* (Hazelden); *The Acorn Principle* (St. Martin's Press); *Be the Person YOU Want to Be Using NLP* (Random House); *The Jesus Path* (Red Wheel/Weiser).

NATASHA KERN LITERARY AGENCY

P.O. Box 1069, White Salmon, WA 98672

www.natashakern.com   email your queries to: queries@natashakern.com

Education: University of North Carolina, Chapel Hill; Columbia University, New York; New York University.

Career history: Publicist and editor for New York publishers and acquisitions editor for New York agents prior to founding her own agency in 1986, Natasha Kern has personally sold over 700 books and has worked on close to 1,000 during her career in publishing.

Hobbies/personal interests: Gardening, travel, animals and birds, yoga, performing arts, history, geology and, of course, family and reading.

Categories/subjects that you are most enthusiastic about agenting: Fiction: I am actively looking for big historical novels; inspirational fiction; romantic suspense; romantic comedies; mainstream women's fiction; young-adult fiction. Nonfiction: Narrative nonfiction, health, science, women's issues, parenting, spirituality, self-help, social issues—especially topics that inspire positive thought, action or change, and books by authorities in their field.

What you don't want to agent: Fiction: Horror and fantasy, short stories, children's. Nonfiction: True crime, sports, cookbooks, poetry, gift books, coffee-table books, computers, technical, scholarly or reference books, stage plays, scripts or screenplays.

If you were not an agent, what might you be doing instead: I have been an agent for 20 years because I love doing it. This is a calling for me and I can't imagine doing anything else. I love my clients. I love books. I like assisting writers to earn a living at what they do best.

What's the best way for writers to solicit your interest: See submission instructions on the website, www.natashakern.com. Send all queries to: queries@natashakern.com. We do not accept queries by phone or snail mail. We will contact you within three weeks of receipt of your query if we are interested. Please include your phone number and email address.

Do you charge reading fees or management fees: No.

Percentage of representation by category: Fiction: 65 percent, nonfiction: 35 percent.

Approximate number of titles sold during the past year: 43 titles.

Approximately what percentage of all the submissions you receive do you reject: 99 percent of unsolicited; 85 percent solicited partials, proposals and manuscripts; and 30 percent of referrals. From 6,000 queries every year, approximately ten writers are accepted for representation. Write a good query! We are selective, but we do want to find successful writers of the future and have launched the careers of many writers.

What are some of the most common mistakes writers make when pitching

to you: Not researching what we represent! Not describing the material or project adequately. Not knowing the standards and conventions of the genres we represent. Querying by fax, phone, or snail mail. Sending unrequested material. Exaggerated claims or credentials. Comparing themselves favorably to current best-selling authors. Lack of professionalism. Not knowing the craft of writing. Not having an original concept. Omitting the ending from a synopsis. Not following directions. The majority of queries are rejected because the writer has simply not taken the time to learn, study and practice to produce something salable, basically the equivalent of taking a week of music lessons and hoping to play Carnegie Hall.

How would you describe your client from hell: I do not have any clients like this. All of my clients are people I respect and admire as individuals as well as writers. They are committed to their own success and know that I am committed to helping them to achieve it. They understand the complex tasks involved in agenting, including sales, negotiations, editorial, arbitration, foreign and film rights, etc., and we work as a team to ensure the best outcome for their work. Usually problem clients who are difficult to work with are identified before a contract is signed.

How would you describe the perfect client: One who participates in a mutually respectful business relationship, is clear about needs and goals and communicates about career planning. If we know what you need and want, we can help you to achieve it. A dream client has a gift for language and storytelling, a commitment to a writing career, a desire to learn and grow, and a passion for excellence. This client understands that many people have to work together for a book to succeed and that everything in publishing takes far longer than one imagines. Trust and communication are truly essential. How wonderful that all of my clients are dream clients.

How and why did you become an agent: When I left New York, I knew that I wanted to stay in publishing. However, editorial work was not sufficiently satisfying by itself. I knew I could acquire and develop salable properties and that my background gave me expertise in sales and running a company. I wanted to work with people long term and not just on a single project or phase of one. Plus, I had an entrepreneurial temperament and experience negotiating big money deals from raising venture capital for high-tech firms. When I developed literary projects for other agents that did not sell, I knew I could sell them myself, so I did. I've never regretted that decision. Agenting combined my love of books, my affinity for deal-making, and my preference for trusting my own intuition. I sold 28 books the first year the agency was in business and have sold over 900 personally since then.

What can writers do to increase the odds that they will get you to be their agent: A client who is willing to listen, learn, and work hard to succeed. If there are writing problems I will get this author help to produce a salable proposal. I have worked with some writers six months or more before their novel or proposal was in top-notch shape to sell it. I am looking for talent and commitment and if I feel it is a good match, I make a commitment to that writer in return.

In nonfiction, the author's passionate belief in the subject as well as expertise and a defined audience are appealing. A strong platform is a must today.

In fiction, a wonderful, fresh authorial voice, a page-turning plot that really does keep me up at night, well-structured chapters and imaginative prose, with everything tied to the premise. A writer who can pull me into another point of view and another world I don't want to leave. In fiction, the writing is everything. We are glad to encourage promising writers who still need to master some aspects of craft if they are willing to work with me or an editor.

How would you actually describe to someone from another planet what you do for a living: Unpublished writers often think an agent's job is only sales and negotiations. Of course, every writer wants a sale and to see the book in print. However, an agent's job goes far beyond just deal-making because building a career and helping a writer to earn a living from writing requires a long-term strategy and often a complex chess game of moving from one house or genre to another. I am often involved in a book's development from the initial concept through preparation of a proposal, editorial advice, selection of appropriate editors, submissions, negotiations and contract changes to final signature. Then troubleshooting publication problems begins from editorial issues to cover problems, title changes, reviewing jacket blurbs and the myriad of things that arise in the course of publication; troubleshooting marketing problems including reviewing publicity planning, press kits and releases, working on cross-promotions and product placement, distribution concerns, suggestions about creating a website and working with private publicists. Since I represent writers who, for the most part, want a writing career and not just a one-book deal after the first book has been turned in, work begins on a follow-up, fulfilling option clauses (and making sure they do not restrict an author's ability to write whatever she wishes), long-term career planning and strategies and often multi-book deals. Of course, handling an author's financial affairs is paramount, including auditing royalty statements, collecting unpaid monies, providing tax documents like 1099s and foreign tax forms, etc. In addition, I handle legal issues of many kinds from reversion of rights to their allocation; subsidiary sales including foreign rights, film rights, audio, video and other rights; handling career crises or conflicts with publishers; assisting writers with career transitions or when problems arise like their book being "orphaned"; providing expertise at writers conferences; educating clients about the publishing industry and its vicissitudes; keeping in touch with editors and their acquisitions interest or concerns about clients; attending industry events like Book Expo; consulting with writing groups—I am currently on the Board of the Faith, Hope and Love Chapter of RWA; meeting personally with clients, editors and others in the industry; traveling to New York and Hollywood several times each year; answering hundreds of emails each week; reviewing queries and partials; talking on the phone a lot; reading the work of clients and prospective clients and keeping up with trends; working with office staff and upgrading corporate procedures and technical support; supervising bookkeeper and accountant; articles and interviews for trade publications, etc. It's a long day.

What do you think about editors and publishers: Editors are indispensable and every writer should be blessed with a good one. It is one of my primary goals to match each client with the editor who is perfect for him or her. I often succeed and the result is magical like all great collaborations: Fred Astaire and Ginger Rogers;

Maxwell Perkins and Thomas Wolfe; Gilbert & Sullivan. Writers are more successful in great partnerships. No one can be objective about their own work or realistically expect to recognize all flaws. Most artistic endeavors require a coach—a voice coach, a dance teacher, a master painter. Writing is no exception. There are gifted editors, both private editors and those at publishing houses, who can turn a strong manuscript into a great one, a gifted author into a bestselling one. I want all my clients to have that opportunity. Publishers are going to have some interesting times ahead in the volatile new world of publishing, with challenges at every turn. Developing new talent and valuing the writers who are creating their long-term success would seem to be prerequisites for meeting these challenges. We keep up with changes in the industry like e-books and POD [print on demand], and also work with new emerging presses and imprints as well as major publishers. We can help authors to understand the publisher's point of view (and vice versa) in all situations so a win-win deal will result.

On a personal level, what do you think people like about you and dislike about you: I think I am liked for my authenticity and honesty, even when I have to tell a writer her material needs more work or a concept isn't salable. It is entirely possible I may be disliked for my bluntness as well. However, I feel it is a disservice to writers to fail to be clear with them. My passion for the books I represent and the fact that I deeply care about my clients and their success is an asset as well as my industry knowledge and professionalism. My clients appreciate it that I go the extra mile for them to ensure their success. I hate to give up on anything I undertake so I usually do succeed in achieving my goals and can help my clients to do the same. Even though I have strong opinions, I am also interested in learning new things from the experts—one of the joys of my job.

You're welcome to share your thoughts and sentiments about the business of writing and publishing: Believe in yourself and your own gifts. Keep in mind that the challenge for every writer is twofold—to have something to say and to have the mastery of the craft to say it well. Study and practice plotting, pacing, point of view, etc. so you can express exactly what you want to say. Nothing is more important than being true to your own artistic vision and understanding the requirements of the medium you have chosen to express it, whether you are writing a symphony, a haiku, or a novel. Keep in mind that in imitating other writers you can only be second-rate at being them. Expressing your own inner thoughts, feelings, and stories in your own way is the only path to real success. Your world, your history, your experiences, your insights cannot be duplicated by anyone else. Bring us in to share your vision, your imagination. No one can do it better than you can because the truth of your uniqueness is what you are here to offer everyone else. It is what moves us and takes us outside of our own lives when we read what you have written.

Please list representative titles you have sold: *The Inheritance*, Tamera Alexander (Thomas Nelson); *The Winds of Sonoma*, Niki Arana (Baker); *The Secret Life of God*, David Aaron (Shambhala); *One Bite Stand*, Nina Bangs (Leisure); *Adam's Tongue*, Derek Bickerton (Farrar, Straus); *Up Pops the Devil*, Angela Benson (HarperCollins); *Critical Care*, Candace Calvert (Tyndale House); *Unlawful*

Contact, Pamela Clare (Berkley); *Hope Is the Thing with Feathers*, Christopher Cokinos (Tarcher); *Cutting Loose*, Nadine Dajani (Tor); *Body by Night*, Zuri Day (Kensington); *Girlwood*, Claire Dean (Houghton Mifflin); *Ruby's Slippers*, Leanna Ellis (B&H); *Whiskey Gulf*, Clyde Ford, (Vanguard); *The Perfect Life*, Robing Lee Hatcher (Thomas Nelson); *The Ecological Garden*, Toby Hemenway (Chelsea Green); *How to Tame a Modern Rogue*, Diana Holquist (Hachette); *The Quiet Game*, Greg Iles (Putnam-Penguin); *Salty Like Blood*, Harry Kraus (Howard S&S); *Scent of Sake*, Joyce Lebra (Morrow); *A Passion Redeemed*, Julie Lessman (Revell); *A Texan's Honor*, Harold Lowry (Leisure); *A Preacher's Passion*, Lutishia Lovely (Dafina); *The Prince of Pleasure*, Connie Mason (Leisure); *A Reason to Believe*, Maureen McCade (Berkley); *Skull Mantra*, Eliot Pattison (St. Martin's); *Bone Rattler*, Eliot Pattison (Counterpoint); *Sucker for Love*, Kimberly Raye (Ballantine); *Gift from the Sea*, Anna Schmidt (Steeple Hill); *The Lady and Libertine*, Bonnie Vanak (Leisure); *The Secret Lives of the Sushi Club*, Christy Yorke (Berkley).

THE KNIGHT AGENCY

www.KnightAgency.net   email: submissions@knightagency.net

Agents' names: Deidre Knight, Pamela Harty, Lucienne Diver, Elaine Spencer, Nephele Tempest, Melissa Jeglinski

The following information pertains to Deidre Knight.

Born: July 12.

Hobbies and special personal interests: My first true passion is the written word: Beyond reading I have also always been an avid writer, penning my first story when I was seven years old for the *Atlanta Journal-Constitution*. This humble beginning was the start of many great writing adventures, leading me to a love of fan fiction and consequently, my ultimate dream come true, my own publishing contract with Penguin Putnam. I am also passionate about spending time with my family, photography, kayaking, international travel, science-fiction television, the spa and great music.

Subjects and categories you like to agent: I am probably most known for my clients within the romance and women's fiction genre (all spectrums) but my tastes are much more broad. I also have a love for great literary fiction, young-adult material, all things paranormal, anything with a Southern flair and great special-interest nonfiction titles.

Subjects and categories writers shouldn't bother pitching to you: Our agency is very diverse and between our five agents, if you have a great story there is a chance we can find the right agent for your novel. However, despite this diversity we aren't interested in children's or picture books, poetry, screenplays, short story collections, biographies, military titles, or anything with gratuitous violence.

What might you be doing if you weren't agenting: I am an entrepreneur at heart, so if I hadn't started the Knight Agency I'm not sure specifically what I would be doing, but I have little doubt I would be running some other business. I'm a natural visionary and a free spirit, so really the possibilities are endless.

What's the most effective ways for writers to grab your attention: I am easily swayed by enthusiasm and passion. I myself am a very "excitable" person, and so if I can feel your energy in your story I'm instantly hooked.

Do you charge fees separate from your commission, or offer non-agenting fee-based services: The Knight Agency doesn't charge any fees for anything related to the publishing process beyond the 15 percent commission we take off of a completed sale.

What do you like best about your clients, and the editors and publishers you work with: I think that this industry is one of the greatest businesses out there, hence the reason I have tied myself into it in so many different capacities. It's exciting, dynamic, and it keeps us each on our toes since every day is a new journey. I can think of few other professions where you are blessed enough to meet as many fascinating individuals and cross paths with so many brilliant minds. I'm proud to not only be a associated with the publishing business but a strong contributing force; we are lucky at the end of the day to look at the shelf, see a book and say, "I did that."

What are representative titles you have sold to publishers: *Intertwined* (Harlequin) by Gena Showalter, *Rampant* (Harper Teen) by Diana Peterfreund, *Heart Quest* (Berkley) by Robin Owens, *Edge of Hunger* (Harlequin) by Rhyannon Byrd, *Christmas Miracles* (St. Martin's) by Cecil Murphey and Marley Gibson.

The following information pertains to Pamela Harty.

Born: July; Atlanta, Georgia.

Career story: I started at The Knight Agency after the birth of my second child. I was eager to work with my sister Deidre Knight after leaving a successful sales career. That was almost nine years ago!

Hobbies and special personal interests: I am a runner and cyclist. I love to paint and of course…read.

Subjects and categories you like to agent: I am interested in romance, of course, including historical, suspense and paranormal, as well as young-adult and women's commercial fiction. I'm also interested in some nonfiction, including health, narrative nonfiction, relationships and pop culture.

What might you be doing if you weren't agenting: Painting and cycling in France.

The following information pertains to Lucienne Diver.

Born: April 27, 1971; Baltimore, Maryland.

Education: Graduated *summa cum laude* from The State University of New York at Potsdam.

Career story: I spent 15 years at Spectrum Literary Agency before moving in 2008 to The Knight Agency.

Hobbies and special personal interests: Writing, forensics, theater, beading, scrapbooking, yoga, photography.

Subjects and categories you like to agent: Fantasy, romance, romantica, thrillers, mystery/suspense, young adult.

Subjects and categories writers shouldn't bother pitching to you: Nonfiction, children's books.

What might you be doing if you weren't agenting: I can't imagine doing anything else.

What's the most effective ways for writers to grab your attention: Be brilliant. Come up with wonderful ideas in an original voice and keep the pace pounding.

What are representative titles you have sold to publishers: *The Pawn* (Baker/NAL) by Steven James, *The Girl She Used to Be* (Grand Central), by Dave Cristofano, *Up at the College* (Grand Central) by Michelle Andrea Bowen, *The Sister's Eight* (Houghton Mifflin) by Lauren Baratz-Logsted, *Something Happened* (Simon Pulse) by Greg Logsted.

What are your favorite books, movies, TV shows, and why: I love anything by Joss Whedon. He's got a talent for perfectly melding dark and light, a well-developed sense of the absurd, an amazing flair for dialogue and wonderful characters. That's what I look for in the books I represent as well.

Will our business exist as we know it in ten years or so: Absolutely! Books—good stories that challenge our minds and imaginations—are eternal.

The following information pertains to Elaine Spencer.

Born: January 7, Toledo, Ohio.

Hobbies and special personal interests: When I'm not reading I love spending time outdoors and in the water, working out, cooking, shopping, traveling, dining out and cheering on my beloved Georgia Bulldogs.

Subjects and categories you like to agent: My tastes really run the gamut; I love most anything that has a strong distinctive voice and vivid heartfelt emotional stakes. I am looking for diverse women's fiction and romance, original young-adult and middle-grade stories, edge-of-the-seat suspense, interesting and high-platform nonfiction and straight commercial and literary fiction.

Subjects and categories writers shouldn't bother pitching to you: I am wide open to most genres but obviously don't handle those that aren't represented by the agency as a whole. I'm also not the sci-fi gal at the agency, nor am I typically into any boundary-pushing erotica.

What might you be doing if you weren't agenting: I would be a personal shopper. I love to shop, whether it's for me or for someone else—tell me what you need and I'm your gal.

What's the most effective ways for writers to grab your attention: One of the sure-fire ways to impress me is to wow me with your knowledge of the market and your craft right off the bat. I am always inclined to continue reading when I can tell the author is treating their writing life as a career and proceeding as a professional.

What do you like best about your clients, and the editors and publishers you work with: I have a very personal and unique relationship with each of my clients. I love that I can relate to each of them on a professional yet individual level. I truly believe that one of the bedrocks of a strong relationship is communication, and I adore the one-on-one tie I have to each of my authors.

What are some representative titles you have sold: *Soul of a Highlander* (Pocket) by Melissa Mayhue, *Stonegate Investigation Agency* (Harlequin) by Candace Havens, *Death by Denim* (Puffin) by Linda Gerber, *Accidentally Demonic* (Berkley) by Dakota Cassidy

The following information pertains to Nephele Tempest.

Education: The University of Chicago, BA in English language and literature.

Hobbies and special personal interests: Reading (naturally), film, theater, music, traveling, photography and cooking.

Subjects and categories you like to agent: Fiction only; commercial literary, women's fiction, urban fantasy, romantic suspense, historical fiction, science fiction/fantasy and young adult.

Subjects and categories writers shouldn't bother pitching to you: No mysteries, inspirational or nonfiction, please.

What's the most effective ways for writers to grab your attention: Please follow our submissions guidelines. Nothing turns me off faster than someone trying to be "clever and original" by ignoring our requests regarding how to submit materials. Beyond that, polish your book to the very best of your abilities, and then give it one more edit before submitting. The extra effort will definitely show.

What are representative titles you have sold to publishers: *No Regrets* by Shannon K. Butcher (Grand Central Publishing); *Slave to Sensation* by Nalini Singh (Berkley); *Angels' Blood* by Nalini Singh (Berkley); *Mayhem in High Heels* by Gemma Halliday (Dorchester); *According to Jane: A Novel about Pride, Prejudice and the Pursuit of the Perfect Guy* by Marilyn Brant (Kensington); *Burning Alive* by Shannon K. Butcher (NAL); *Major Crush* by Jennifer Echols (Simon Pulse).

What do you like best about your clients, and the editors and publishers you work with: I love that I work with a wide range of very different and interesting people, all of whom share my love of books. It makes for a wonderful workday, knowing that at any moment someone might call me with a great new book idea or a recommendation for something fabulous they think I should read. It's a business of kindred spirits.

The following applies to Melissa Jeginsky.

Born: January 11, Pittsburgh, Pennsylvania.

Career Story: I worked at Harlequin Enterprises for seventeen years as an editor before moving to the The Knight Agency in September 2008.

Hobbies and special personal interests: I am a rabid crafter: scrapbooking, card making, crocheting, quilting.

Subjects and categories you like to agent: Romance first and foremost: contemporary, historical, erotica, suspense, inspirational and category. Young adult, both contemporary and historical. Women's fiction, from humorous to heart-wrenching.

What's the most effective way for writers to grab your attention: When a writer has really done their research about our agency and about the marketplace for their work. This shows me they are serious about their craft and that finding an agent and getting published are important to them.

LINDA KONNER LITERARY AGENCY

210 West 15th Street, Suite 1918, New York, NY 10011

email: ldkonner@cs.com

Agent's name: Linda Konner

Born: Brooklyn, New York.

Education: BA, Brooklyn College; MA, Fordham University.

Career history: Editor, *Seventeen* Magazine (1976–1981); Managing editor, *Weight Watchers* Magazine (1981–1983); editor-in-chief, *Weight Watchers* Magazine (1983–1985); entertainment editor, *Redbook* Magazine (1985–1986); entertainment editor, *Woman's World* (1986–1993); founding editor, Richard Simmons Newsletter (1993–1998); literary agent (1996–present); freelance writer, author of eight books.

Categories/subjects that you are most enthusiastic about agenting: Practical nonfiction (self-help, how-to, popular psychology, health, diet and fitness, relationships, parenting, career, personal finance, business)—all written by or with top experts in their fields, with a national platform.

What you don't want to agent: Fiction, children's. No nonfiction unless written by/with a top expert.

If you were not an agent, what might you be doing instead: Writing (with my honey) the book no one wants to publish: *Apartners: Living Apart and Loving It.*

What's the best way for writers to solicit your interest: Send a brief query with a brief bio by mail (with SASE) or email.

Do you charge reading or management fees: No reading fees.

Can you provide an approximation by percent of what you tend to represent by category: Practical nonfiction: 95 percent, narrative nonfiction, including celebrity autobiographies: 5 percent.

What are the most common mistakes writers make when pitching you: Not being/partnering with a top expert with a good platform.

How would you describe the perfect client: Follows through. Meets my deadlines. Is master of the brief phone call.

How and why did you ever become an agent: Ran out of things to be after having been an author, freelance writer, and magazine editor.

What, if anything, can a writer do to increase the odds of your becoming his or her agent: Have (or write with someone who has) a major platform. Have a good sales record with previously published books.

Do you have any favorite (current) TV shows, films, or books that you especially like and how come: *Law & Order, What Not to Wear, Ebert & Roeper.*

Please list representative titles you have sold: *The Winner's Brain* by Jeff Brown, PsyD, Mark Fenske, PhD, and Liz Neporent and the Editors of Harvard Health Publications (Da Capo/Perseus, spring 2010). *Your Successful Preschooler* by Ann Densmore, EdD and Margaret Bauman (Jossey-Bass, spring 2010), *A Baby at Last!* by Zev Rosenwaks, MD, Marc Goldstein, MD with Mark Fuerst (Touchstone Fireside/S&S, summer 2010), *Saying Goodbye* by Barbara Okun, PhD, Joseph Nowinski, PhD and the Editors of Harvard Health Publications (Berkley/Penguin, fall 2010), *Work Smart Play Hard: How to Make Your First Million by the Time You Turn 30* by Nick Friedman, Omar Soliman with Daylle Deanna Schwartz (Three Rivers Press, spring 2010).

KRAAS LITERARY AGENCY

281-870-9770

email: irenekraas@sbcglobal.net

Agent's name: Irene W. Kraas, Principal
Born: Are you kidding??? New York, New York.
Education: MEd University of Rochester.
Career history: Too long to enumerate: A sample: Beltway bandit (DC consultant); career counselor; agent.
Hobbies/personal interests: Reading, walking, eating and enjoying life.
Subjects and categories you are interested in agenting, including fiction and nonfiction: I am looking for psychological thrillers. NO mysteries, please. Think James Patterson, less Patricia Cornwell. In terms of young-adult/juvenile fiction, I am only acquiring those works that show a unique situation (preferably in history) through the eyes of a child or young adult. I am also, especially, looking for innovative middle-grade material. I am stilling looking for quality adult historical fiction such as *The Courtier's Secret, The Red Tent* and *The Girl with the Pearl Earring.*

What you don't want to agent: Please see above.

If you were not an agent, what might you be doing instead: I've done what I've wanted all along and this is the ultimate. However, if I had to choose, I would be a rich publisher and publish all those great books that I've had rejected.

What's the best way for fiction writers to solicit your interest: Please send an email query to me at irenekraas@sbcglobal.net. After that initial correspondence, I will let you know if we wish to see additional material.

What's the best way for nonfiction writers to solicit your interest: Same as above.

Do you charge reading or any upfront fees: Under no circumstances do we require an upfront reading fee! We never charge a reading fee. With pdf documents there are no other fees except those described in my contract that pertain to normal commissions.

What are the most common mistakes writers make when pitching you: Not following my submission guidelines.

How would you describe the client from hell: I'll take the fifth, thanks.

How would you describe the perfect client: Great writers who trust me to do the very best for them.

How and why did you ever become an agent: I went from 20 years in business consulting to being the great American writer to agenting. I love using my business acumen in helping first-time authors get a break and helping established authors break out.

What, if anything, can a writer do to increase the odds of your becoming his or her agent: Be extremely talented—it's a tight market, so understand that it's very competitive and make sure that your manuscript is ready to go when you submit it to me. Also, make sure that what you send me is a genre that I'm actually interested in representing.

How would you describe to someone (or something) from another planet what it is that you do as an agent: I read, read, read. Then I sell, sell, sell.

How do you feel about editors and publishers: Mostly editors are top-notch people interested in good writing. Regarding publishers, well, let's just say that they don't always see the big picture as clearly as we'd like and they don't necessarily have the author's best interests in mind. But, that's why there are agents!

How do you feel about writers: Would I be in this business if I didn't like them? Of course one has to sort between those who have talent and those that don't.

What do see in the near future for book publishing: I think it will remain pretty much as is. People who read still want to hold a book. Of course there will be a few changes regarding electronic editions and print on demand.

What are your favorite books, movies, TV shows, and why: *24, The Sopranos,* you get the idea. I now have to add *Deadwood.* I absolutely love it. I love great ensemble work and high-quality acting and innovative story lines. I don't like comedy.

In your opinion, what do editors think of you: I'm pretty sure they think well of me. After all you don't stay in this business for 18 years as a very small agency (just me these days), if you don't try to match editors with submissions. When I send something out, they are always ready to read.

On a personal non-professional level, what do you think people think of you: Wow that's a toughie. I assume some like me and some don't. Is there more to be said?

Please list representative titles you have sold: Authors include Hilari Bell, Janet Lee Carey, Mark Terry, Chelsea Quinn Yarbro, and Richard Uhlig. We have sold far too many books to list here, but please feel free to look at our website (www.kraasliteraryagency.com) or email me.

EDITE KROLL LITERARY AGENCY INC.

20 Cross Street, Saco, ME 04072

207-283-8797   fax 207-283-8799

email: ekroll@maine.rr.com

Individual agent's name: Edite Kroll

Location of birth: Germany.

Education: Germany and UK.

Career Story: Have run my independent literary agency in New York City and Maine for over 25 years. A former editor in London and New York, I represent a small list of adult and children's book writers, as well as artists who write their own books. I have also translated a number of books from German into English.

Hobbies and special personal interests: Learning languages, travel.

Subjects and categories you like to agent: Women writing about their lives in different countries; humor, both narrative and illustrative, for adults and children; fiction for children (middle grade through YA) and limited literary fiction for adults; issue-oriented nonfiction beyond self-help.

Subjects and categories writers shouldn't bother pitching to you: Genre, e.g., romantic fiction, mystery/suspense, cookbooks. No diet books, photographic books, poetry. No single projects—writers only.

What might you be doing if you weren't agenting: Running a publishing company, restaurant or bookstore. Coaching. Translating more books.

What's the most effective ways for writers to grab your attention: A brief letter outlining book and credentials, limited to subjects and areas I am interested in, or an introduction from other clients.

Do you charge fees separate from your commission, or offer non-agenting fee-based services: I only charge legal fees (previously agreed on) and copying large manuscripts. Offer no non-agented fee-based services.

What are representative titles you have sold to publishers: *Dreams of Trespass* by Fatema Mernissi, Perseus; *All I Know I Learned from My Cat* by Suzy Becker, Workman; *Work in Progress* by Brett McCarthy, Knopf; *If the Buddha Dated* books by Charlotte Kasl, Penguin; *Benny & Penny* books by Geoffrey Hayes, Raw Jr; *Who Wants a Cheap Rhinoceros?* by Shel Silverstein.

Why did you become an agent, and how did you become one: After a short stint in marketing (working with a new book division at L'eggs), publishers only offered me jobs to RUN divisions, and I wanted to work directly with authors and artists. Having started out in subsidiary rights and contracts in the UK (Chatto & Windus), I felt I had a good basic understanding of the business side.

How do you feel about writers and artists: I love their (sometimes hidden) passions and like helping them translate that passion into books.

What do you tell entities from other planets and dimensions about your job: I am a salesperson, an intermediary between writers and publishers, I represent the writer not the publisher, and I work on commission only.

What do you like best about your clients, and the editors and publishers you work with: Honest dialogue without game playing.

Finally, will our business exist as we know it in ten years or so: Being the eternal optimist, I believe books will continue to exist and be read, though the majority may not continue to be available primarily in printed form.

KT PUBLIC RELATIONS & LITERARY SERVICES

1905 Cricklewood Cove, Fogelsville, PA 18051

610-395-6298

www.ktpublicrelations.com

Visit our new blog: www.newliteraryagents.blogspot.com

Agents' names: Kae Tienstra, kae@ktpublicrelations.com, Jon Tienstra, jon@kt publicrelations.com

The following information pertains to Kae Tienstra.

Born: Denver, Colorado on June 3.

Education: BA in speech/drama, minor in English.

Career story: I stayed at home for 13 years to raise our three children, letting my husband Jon do the hunting and gathering in the corporate world. To save my sanity and bring in a bit of my own money I began a freelance writing career. I wrote articles for publications like *The Mother Earth News*, *Organic Gardening*, and our local newspaper and magazines. I also ghost-wrote a local history and photography book and penned a one-act play. When Jon quit his job to go back to school, I was hired by Rodale, Inc. as publicity assistant. I moved up quickly to director of publicity for the book division and stayed at Rodale in that capacity for 13 years. I left Rodale to launch my own publicity firm, KT Public Relations, in 1993. (Jon joined the firm a few years after that.) Over the years we've represented large publishers such as Random House, Putnam, HarperCollins, and John Wiley and Sons, as well as smaller publishers and authors. We launched our literary agency in 2006 and changed the name of our company to reflect our two businesses—KT Public Relations and Literary Services.

Hobbies and special personal interests: I'm an avid reader, which is no surprise. Gardening is a passion, especially perennials and herbs. Jon and I spend much of our down time cooking and love to sample great wines. We walk two miles every morning, travel when we can, and try to spend as much time as possible with our grandsons Rob and Max.

Subjects and categories you like to agent: Women's fiction, quirky, contemporary fantasy, mysteries, YA. Nonfiction: Gardening, health, cookbooks, narrative nonfiction, animals, nature, parenting, psychology, relationships.

Subjects and categories writers shouldn't bother pitching to you: Christian, "swords and dragons" fantasy, erotica, children's, poetry, political, inspirational/New Age.

What might you be doing if you weren't agenting: I'd be writing my own books.

What's the most effective ways for writers to grab your attention: In your query letter by describing in the first sentence the essence of your book. In the next sentence, tell me its genre and word count. Then give me the best written paragraph you can craft about why this book is the cat's pajamas. Then, wind things up by giving me a few sentences about you as a writer. (Don't bother to tell me where you live or who you married.) Then, stop already! If you have done your job, I should want to see some chapters.

Do you charge fees separate from your commission, or offer non-agenting fee-based services: We don't charge any up-front fees. Our commission is the standard 15 percent and, if the book is sold, we subtract postage and copy fees from the advance. We are publicists as well as agents, but we don't publicize our agenting clients' books. We provide publicity/marketing counsel and guidance to our authors as part of our agenting job.

What are representative titles you have sold to publishers: *Town in a Blueberry Jam* by Alex Haywood (Prime Crime); *The Red Gold Bridge* by Patrice Sarath (Ace); *Gordath Wood* by Patrice Sarath (Ace); *Are You Ready for Lasting Love?* by Paddy S. Welles (Marlowe & Company); *100 Recipes You Can't Eat* by Alexa Lett (Putnam).

Why did you become an agent, and how did you become one: I brought two books to the attention of an agent friend who encouraged me (and Jon) to consider becoming agents ourselves. It seemed the right time to use our knowledge of publishing and publicity to create an agency grounded by this foundation.

How do you feel about writers: I really love writers who know their business. I love writers who are talented, but understand that talent will only get them so far. I love writers who study the publishing business, go to writer's conferences, ask questions, and READ, READ, READ. I love writers who read their favorite authors, read out of their comfort zone, and read books, blogs, magazines, websites and newsletters about book publishing. I love writers who have a sense of humor and who don't take themselves too seriously.

What do you tell entities from other planets and dimensions about your job: I tell them I am a detective searching for the next great book.

What are your favorite books, movies, TV shows, and why: Anything by John Steinbeck because of his compassion; *Babbitt* by Sinclair Lewis, because of its setting and sense of satire; *The Jump Off Creek* by Molly Gloss because it reminds me what toughness and will can accomplish; *The Naked and the Dead* by Norman Mailer which I just began reading recently—amazing; *Madame Bovary* by Flaubert—I don't really know why. I don't like Emma Bovary, but this book is perfect. *The Great Gatsby* because no one writes like F. Scott Fitzgerald. Favorite movies: Anything done by Christopher Guest, particularly *Best in Show* because the humor is just my style. Guilty pleasures: Old movies on TBS, especially Fred Astaire when I'm in a bad mood. TV shows: HBO only, especially *Six Feet Under*. (OK, I'll admit to watching *What Not to Wear* on TLC.)

How would you describe the writer from hell: Knows nothing about the industry, does not intend to learn and is sure she/he has the next big book that editors will "buy in a heartbeat." AND, this author cannot write her way out of a paper bag.

How would you describe the publisher and/or editor from hell: My "editor/publisher from hell" does not exist—yet. So far they have all been helpful, kind and generous to us. It's true! I just remembered one exception, the subsidy publisher who did not come clean about how he works. (But we should have done our homework earlier!)

What do you like best about your clients, and the editors and publishers you work with: I like clients who become partners in the process of finding a publisher for their books. These clients don't call, they email. They don't demand, they request. They have good ideas which they share and they also share our enthusiasm for the process. We like the editors and publishers who are open and friendly and who look to us as resources. Some editors tell us where we've gone wrong and we really appreciate it, being new to this side of the business. Other editors give us hints and tips which are so useful.

Will our business exist as we know it in ten years or so: Everything changes. That's the one true thing. The book business is changing under our feet. In ten years? Who knows? All we can do is hold on for the ride and try to innovate, not duplicate.

The following information pertains to Jon Tienstra.

Born: Born in Harvey, Illinois, January 5.

Education: BA in English literature; master's in library science.

Career story: After graduating college I worked at Alpo Pet Foods as director of product quality control, then for ten years as director of environmental control. I spent another decade at a competing pet food company because the kids needed shoes. Finally, I was able to leave pet food behind and go back to school where I took a master's degree in library science. I spent two years at the Rodale Experimental Farm as the organic vegetable gardener before I joined KT Public Relations as an unpaid intern.

Hobbies and special personal interests: I'm an avid reader of most everything. I collect old vegetable gardening books and love car racing of almost all types. You'll find me in the kitchen cooking/creating during off hours. I wish I had more time to paint, but stacks of chapters are always the priority.

Subjects and categories you like to agent: Fiction: Science fiction/fantasy, mysteries, YA, literary fiction, police/detective. Nonfiction: Gardening, military.

Subjects and categories writers shouldn't bother pitching to you: Christian, "swords and dragons" fantasy, erotica, children's, poetry, political, inspirational/New Age, short stories, novellas.

What might you be doing if you weren't agenting: My whole life has led me to this point.

What's the most effective ways for writers to grab your attention: Do your homework and make your query pitch-perfect.

Do you charge fees separate from your commission, or offer non-agenting fee-based services: We don't charge any up-front fees. Our commission is the standard 15 percent and, if the book is sold, we subtract postage and copy fees from the advance. We are publicists as well as agents, but we don't publicize our agenting clients' books. We provide publicity/marketing counsel and guidance to our authors as part of our agenting job.

What are representative titles you have sold to publishers: See Kae's listing above.

Why did you become an agent, and how did you become one: All the interesting and fun parts of my life have come together at this focal point.

How do you feel about writers: I really love writers but don't love lazy writers.

What do you tell entities from other planets and dimensions about your job: I tell them I am on a treasure hunt for an explanation of what it all means.

What are your favorite books, movies, TV shows, and why: Books: I can't list them all. Movies: *Blade Runner, The Fifth Element, Constantine, Matrix, Apocalypse Now, Das Boot.* TV: HBO and the Speed Channel.

Will our business exist as we know it in ten years or so: Of course not. Change is inevitable. We embrace it as much as possible.

MICHAEL LARSEN/ELIZABETH POMADA LITERARY AGENTS

1029 Jones Street, San Francisco, CA 94109

415-673-0939

www.larsenpomada.com

Agents' names: Elizabeth Pomada, Larsenpoma@aol.com. Michael Larsen, Larsenpoma@aol.com

Born: Pomada: June 12; New York, New York. Larsen: January 8; New York, New York.

Education: Pomada: Cornell '62. Larsen: CCNY '63.

Career story: Pomada: Worked at Holt, Rinehart & Winston; David McKay; and the Dial Press. Began the agency in 1972. Larsen: Worked at William Morrow, Bantam, and Pyramid (now merged with Berkley). Co-founded the agency in 1972. Member: AAR. The agency has sold hundred of books, mostly by new writers, to more than a hundred publishers. Wrote *How to Write a Book Proposal*, and *How to Get a Literary Agent*, both of which are now in their third edition. Co-authored

How to Write with a Collaborator, with Hal Zina Bennett and *Guerilla Marketing for Writers: 100 Weapons for Selling Your Work* with client Jay Conrad Levinson, author of the 25+ [book] Guerilla Marketing series; and Rick Frishman, president of Planned Television Arts.

Hobbies and special personal interests: Pomada: France, architectural color, reading, travel. Larsen: Going to the movies, listening to jazz (mostly '40s–'60s) and classical music (mostly 1685–1791), seeing plays, visiting France, reading a book without the phone ringing, bringing people together.

Subjects and categories you like to agent: Pomada: I like positive narrative nonfiction—something that will make me feel good when I've read it. I like travel narrative that makes me hunt for my passport. And I like fiction of all kinds, from very literary to very commercial, romance, mystery, thriller, etc. Something that will keep me reading past my bedtime. Larsen: I'm looking books that will change the world, that will mean something ten years from now. Books that will add to my knowledge. Nonfiction. Something new and different. Something that will help us face the future.

Subjects and categories writers shouldn't bother pitching to you: Pomada: Please do not send poetry, children's books, fantasy, sci-fi, Westerns, misery memoirs or disease-of-the-month stories. No abuse of any kind. Larsen. Please do not send books I've already read or sold, diet books, religious tomes, yesterday's news.

What might you be doing if you weren't agenting: Pomada: If I weren't agenting, I'd be reading good books. Maybe writing a few. Larsen: If I weren't agenting, I'd be publishing, or helping to publish, books that should be published.

What's the most effective ways for writers to grab your attention: The most effective way to grab our attention? Write beautifully. Craft does leap off the page. Follow the submission guidelines on our Website.

Do you charge fees separate from your commission, or offer non-agenting fee-based services: We do not charge fees separate from our commission or offer non-agenting fee-based services.

What are representative titles you have sold to publishers: *The Scalpel & The Soul* by Allan Hamilton (Tarcher); *The Solemn Lantern Maker* by Merlinda Bobis (Delta); *Shadow Isle* by Katharine Kerr (DAW); *Guerrilla Marketing* by Jay Conrad Levinson (Houghton).

Why did you become an agent, and how did you become one: Pomada: I became an agent when I moved to San Francisco and was told there were no publishing jobs for me in the city. The employment agent represented writers and artists and she said, pointing to a wall of manuscripts, "Meanwhile, people send me these things and I don't know what do to with them." I went in every Tuesday afternoon and actually found two books that were salable—so started then. Larsen: I became an agent when Patty Hearst was captured. I knew there was a book in it and ended up selling it in four phone calls. I figured being an agent was easy! And joined Elizabeth.

How do you feel about writers: It depends on when you ask. Most mean well.

But too many think the world owes them a living and don't understand that they have to do their homework and be responsible for their success.

What do you tell entities from other planets and dimensions about your job: We tell them that we're the middlemen, the matchmakers between publishers and authors.

What are your favorite books, movies, TV shows, and why: Pomada: Favorite books: *Desiree* by Annemarie Selinko because it's romance that's basically true and historical and *Gone with the Wind* by Margaret Mitchell because in the different readings from when I was a child to now, I've seen different things and learned about life. Favorite movie: *An American in Paris*. Larsen: Favorite book: *The Leopard* by G. Lampedusa: history and life and philosophy all in one. Favorite movie: *Lawrence of Arabia*—best writing, best direction, best acting, best relevance, best music, as true today as it was then.

How would you describe the writer from hell: Pomada: A noodge who thinks he knows more than I do about the business. Larsen: I wrote about that in my book, *How to Get a Literary Agent*: someone who thinks that he is my only client and only reason for living.

How would you describe the publisher and/or editor from hell: The publisher cheats on royalties and holds back an impossible reserve against returns just so the author won't get any money. The editor simply disappears and doesn't answer phone calls, emails, etc. I won't name names but I could.

What do you like best about your clients, and the editors and publishers you work with: I like clients who are genuinely interested in their writing, their careers, the business. It's also special if they are human and interested in me as a human being, too. Friends are nice. I like publishers and editors who are still interested in writers and good writing—even though commerce is important. And all should see publishing/writing as part of life, not the only reason for living.

Will our business exist as we know it in ten years or so: Our business will exist ten years or so from now, but not as we know it. Writers will still need to have people on their side, but publishing and selling will change dramatically and machines are sure to take over much of the world—including publishing and bookselling. Do we really have ten years left?

LAUNCHBOOKS LITERARY AGENCY

566 Sweet Pea Place, Encinitas, CA 92024

760-944-9909

www.launchbooks.com email: david@launchbooks.com

Agent's name: David Fugate

Born: June 11, 1969 in Richmond, Kentucky. Moved to Springfield, Ohio when I was two, and then to San Diego, California when I was eight and have been here ever since.

Education: Bachelor of Arts with honors in English/American literature from the University of California, San Diego.

Career history or story: In 1992 I began as an intern at the Margret McBride Literary Agency while still a student at UC San Diego. Upon graduation I was hired by the McBride Agency to handle submissions and focus on project development. In 1994 I moved to Waterside Productions, Inc., and over the next 11-plus years represented more than 700 book projects that generated over $10,000,000 for authors. In August of 2005 I went out on my own to form LaunchBooks Literary Agency so that I could focus more exclusively on working with authors and projects that I'm truly passionate about.

Hobbies, interests: Reading, a variety of sports (especially basketball, soccer and skiing), video games, online culture (things like Second Life, blogs, virtual communities, etc.), renewable energy, China, world affairs, new music and film (especially foreign films, drama, and the few really good sci-fi and comedies that come out each year).

Subjects and categories you are interested in agenting, including fiction and nonfiction: 95 percent of the projects I represent are nonfiction, and within that category I have a broad range of interests including history, politics, current affairs, narrative nonfiction, health, business, biography, true crime, memoir, parenting, sports, pop culture, how-to, computers and technology, reference, diet and humor. In the fiction space I'm interested in humor science fiction, thrillers, mysteries, and mainstream/topical titles.

Subjects and categories writers shouldn't even bother pitching to you: Religion, spirituality, children's, romance, horror, short stories, poetry.

What's the best way for fiction writers to solicit your interest: An email query and a synopsis. However, if an author also wants to attach the first 25–30 pages of their novel as a Word attachment, I'm often happy to read that, as well.

What's the best way for nonfiction writers to solicit your interest: An email query and a proposal.

Do you charge reading or any upfront fees: No, I don't charge any upfront or reading fees.

How can writers increase the odds that you will offer representation: It's critical these days that authors have a clear sense of where their book fits into the market and the ability to communicate why their book will sell. It has also become more and more important for an author to have a strong marketing platform. Fortunately, there are now more ways than ever for authors to develop a platform for both themselves and their books, and having one will increase both the odds that I'll offer representation and that a publisher will pick up the book.

What are some representative titles that you have sold: *The Ghost Train* by Jon Jeter (W.W. Norton); *The Making of Second Life* by Wagner James Au

(HarperCollins); *Everyday Edisons* by Louis Foreman and Jill Gilbert Welytok (Workman); *Branding Only Works on Cows* by Jonathan Baskin (Grand Central); *The Art of Deception* by Kevin Mitnick and William L. Simon (John Wiley & Sons); *Lifehacker* by Gina Trapani (John Wiley & Sons); *Transcending CSS* by Andy Clarke (Peachpit); *The Zen of CSS* by Molly Holzschlag and Jeff Zeldman (Peachpit); *U.S. Military History for Dummies* by John McManus (John Wiley & Sons).

PAUL S. LEVINE LITERARY AGENCY

1054 Superba Avenue, Venice, CA 90291

310-450-6711, 800-883-0490   fax: 310-450-0181

www.paulslevinelit.com

email: paul@paulslevinelit.com

Carrier Pigeon: Use street address; train pigeon well.

Strippergram: Must be gorgeous and have a great routine.

Agent's name: Paul S. Levine

Born: March 16, 1954; New York, NY.

Education: B. Comm., Concordia University, Montreal (1977); MBA, York University, Toronto (1978); JD, University of Southern California, Los Angeles (1981).

Career history: Attorney for more than 27 years.

Categories/subjects that you are most enthusiastic about agenting: Commercial fiction and nonfiction for adults, children and young adults.

What you don't want to agent: Science fiction, fantasy, and horror.

If you were not an agent, what might you be doing instead: Practicing entertainment law; reading good books.

What's the best way for writers to solicit your interest: Query letter ONLY by snail mail, email, fax, carrier pigeon, or strippergram.

Do you charge reading or management fees: No.

Can you provide an approximation by percent of what you tend to represent by category: Fiction: 35 percent, children's: 15 percent, nonfiction: 50 percent.

What are some of the most common mistakes writers make when pitching you: Telling me that they're writing to me because they're looking for a literary agent. Duh!

How would you describe the client from hell: One who calls, faxes, emails, or sends carrier pigeons or strippergrams every day. One who constantly needs reassurance that each rejection letter does not mean that the client's project lacks merit and that the client is an awful person.

How would you describe the perfect client: The opposite of the above.

How and why did you ever become an agent: I have loved the book business ever since I started practicing law in 1981. My first client was a major book publisher in Los Angeles.

What, if anything, can writers do to increase the odds that you will become his or her agent: Be referred by an existing client or colleague.

How would you describe to someone (or something) from another planet what it is you do as an agent: I represent writers—book authors, screenwriters, and writer-producers.

Do you have any particular opinions or impressions of editors and publishers in general: I love them.

LEVINE GREENBERG LITERARY AGENCY

307 Seventh Avenue, Suite 2407, New York, NY 10001

212-337-0934   Fax: 212-337-0948

www.levinegreenberg.com   email: James Levine: jlevine@levinegreenberg.com; Daniel Greenberg: dgreenberg@levinegreenberg.com; Stephanie Kip Rostan: srostan@levinegreenberg.com; Victoria Skurnick: vskurnick@levinegreenberg.com; Danielle Svetcov: dsvetcov@levinegreenberg.com; Elizabeth Fisher: efisher@levinegreenberg.com; Lindsay Edgecombe: ledgecombe@levinegreenberg.com; Monika Verma: mverma@levinegreenberg.com

Agents' names: James Levine, Daniel Greenberg, Stephanie Kip Rostan, Jenoyne Adams, Victoria Skurnick, Danielle Svetcov, Elizabeth Fisher, Lindsay Edgecombe, Monika Verma.

Career history or story: Founded in 1989 by author and academic entrepreneur James Levine, we have grown into a firm of 12 people with offices in New York and San Francisco. We represent fiction and nonfiction in virtually every category.

Most of our titles are published by imprints of the major houses, but we have also worked with almost fifty independent and/or university presses.

Our strong foreign rights department works internationally with a respected network of co-agents to place our titles with leading foreign publishers, and we are regular participants at the Frankfurt Book Fair and Book Expo America. Our co-agents in Hollywood handle movie and television rights with major studios and production companies.

Subjects and categories you are interested in agenting, including fiction and nonfiction: Our agents have such wide and varied preferences that our list excludes few genres. As far as fiction is concerned: commercial women's literature, literary fiction, ethnic fiction, young-adult literature, romance, and suspense have been successfully represented by a number of our agents. Additionally, LGLA is no stranger to business, self-help, humor, food, child development, pet, science, narrative nonfiction, and political titles, all of which are of interest to our agents. Our full list can be found at our website.

What's the best way for fiction writers to solicit your interest: The thorough online submission form located at our website (http://www.levinegreenberg.com), which allows for attaching proposals and sample chapters, is the best way to submit work.

Do you charge reading or any upfront fees: No.

What are some representative titles that you have sold: *Predictably Irrational* by Dan Ariely (HarperCollins); *Sex, Drugs, and Cocoa Puffs* by Chuck Klosterman (Scribner); *Love Is a Mix Tape* by Rob Sheffield (Crown); *Fifty Places to Play Golf Before You Die* by Chris Santella; *Green Eggs and Ham Cookbook* by Georgeanne Brennan (Random House); *The Five Dysfunctions of a Team: A Leadership Fable* by Patrick Lencioni (Jossey-Bass); *Queen Bees & Wannabes: Helping Your Daughter Survive Cliques, Gossip, Boyfriends & Other Realities of Adolescence* by Rosalind Wiseman (Crown); *Why Good Things Happen to Good People: The Exciting New Research that Proves the Link Between Doing Good and Living a Longer, Healthier, Happier Life* by Stephen Post, PhD, and Jill Neimark (Broadway); *Extraordinary Knowing: Science, Skepticism, and the Inexplicable Powers of the Human Mind* by Elizabeth Lloyd Mayer, PhD (Bantam); *The Spellman Files* by Lisa Lutz (Simon & Schuster); *The Insufficiency of Maps* by Nora Pierce (Atria); *Getting Warmer* by Carol Snow (Berkley).

The following information applies to **Victoria Skurnick.**

Education: BA, University of Wisconsin.

Career Story: Began in publishing as copywriter at Avon Books, assistant director of advertising and promotion at Pocket Books, director of advertising and promotion at Holt, Rinehart and Winston; went on to become senior editor, Pocket Books and St. Martin's Press, and editor-in-chief, Book-of-the-Month Club. Began at Levine Greenberg in 2007.

Hobbies and special personal interests: Writing fiction as half of pseudonymous writing team, Cynthia Victor.

Subjects and categories you like to agent: Fiction of every kind except science fiction, nonfiction including memoir, health, politics, spirituality, all narrative nonfiction.

Subjects and categories writers shouldn't bother pitching to you: Science fiction and children's.

What might you be doing if you weren't agenting: Writing.

What's the most effective ways for writers to grab your attention: Make the synopsis very short, but include the first chapter or two in the query email.

Do you charge fees separate from your commission, or offer non-agenting fee-based services: No.

What are representative titles you have sold to publishers: *Old City Hall*, by Robert Rotenberg, FSG; *Bad Things Happen*, by Harry Dolan; Amy Einhorn books at Penguin; *Following Polly*, by Karen Bergreen, St. Martin's Press; *Chaplin: A Life*, by Stephen Weissman; *Exercising Your Spirituality*, by Gary Jansen, Warner Faith; *The Unconstipated Gourmet*, by Danielle Svetcov, Sourcebooks; *I Met the*

Walrus, by Jerry Levitan, HarperCollins; *Stay Close*, by Libby Cataldi, St. Martin's Press; *Breadline USA*, by Sasha Abramsky, Poli Point Press.

Why did you become an agent, and how did you become one: I was a writer and editor for many years before I thought about becoming an agent. As the industry changed, the book clubs became less central to the process and I missed the feel of being more hands-on in the process. Being an agent was just about the only part of publishing I had not tried, and it seemed very interesting to me. It turns out to be a perfect fit for my interests and talents, and is not corporately run, which fits my temperament.

How do you feel about writers: I am a writer, which makes me sympathetic indeed. They are almost always isolated and need all the help they can get.

What are your favorite books, movies, TV shows, and why: *Pride and Prejudice, The Glass Castle, Law & Order, Friday Night Lights.* I love narrative, love great characters, and have a tiny penchant for crime—at least on the page.

How would you describe the writer from hell: I could give you a name, but it doesn't seem very nice, now does it?

How would you describe the publisher and/or editor from hell: Giver of false promises.

What do you like best about your clients, and the editors and publishers you work with: Talent and cooperation.

Finally, will our business exist as we know it in ten years or so: It will be very different indeed. If I could define exactly how, I'd be a very wealthy woman.

LITERARY SERVICES INC.

P.O. Box 888, Barnegat, NJ 08005

609-698-7162

Cynthia Zigmund: 9039 Spring Rd., Fish Creek, WI 54212

www.LiteraryServicesInc.com

Agents' names: John Willig, john@literaryservicesinc.com; Cynthia Zigmund, cindy@literaryservicesinc.com

The following information pertains to John Willig.

Born: 1954, New York, NY

Education: Brown University, 1976.

Career history or story: 33 years of publishing experience. Started working as a college "traveler" in academic publishing; became an executive editor for business books with Prentice Hall before starting the agency. I was fortunate to grow up surrounded by books and the great Irish love of authors and writing.

Hobbies, interests: Primary interest has been to be actively involved with raising my two sons (now ages 23 and 20). I enjoy athletics—tennis, swimming, and baseball—and the arts. Hoping to begin piano lessons soon and classes in the martial arts. Any day at the beach is a slice of heaven.

Subjects and categories you are interested in agenting, including fiction and nonfiction: We work primarily in nonfiction. We do not accept memoirs! Per our website, our core topic areas are in business, investing, careers, self-help, history, science, health, current events, and global issues.

Subjects and categories writers shouldn't even bother pitching to you: Children's books, science fiction, romance.

What would you do if you weren't agenting: History teacher and baseball or basketball coach. There are days though that the allure of the sea and becoming a tuna boat captain sound just right.

What's the best way for fiction writers to solicit your interest: Right now they shouldn't. While I'm very interested in narrative nonfiction, we're not yet ready to agent fiction.

What's the best way for nonfiction writers to solicit your interest: Per our company website and submission segment, an email answering a few key questions before sending proposals and chapters. I value sample chapters with a well-thought-out proposal.

Do you charge reading or any upfront fees: No reading fees. In addition to our author representation, we offer coaching services for authors who are determined (and have decided) to self-publish. This service is based on our extensive editorial, development and marketing experience working for publishers. It is not intended to be a prerequisite for representation! It is not a fee we charge to prospective clients. It is intended to help writers venturing into uncharted waters but [who] have decided that for them the best route is to self-publish. Again, the service is offered to help writers!

In your experience, what are the most common pitching mistakes writers make: Exaggerating the market size/potential; spending too much time criticizing the competition/bestsellers and not enough on their platform; arrogant tone leading to unreasonable expectations.

Describe the client from hell, even if you don't have any: Per the above, I place a high premium on the quality of the author's attitude and learning about what type of person they are and what it will be like to work with them. Publishers do not need me to bring them "jerks" to work with so I have my own set of little tests before I'm willing to take on a prospect.

What's your definition of a great client: Someone with a great learning attitude, a sense of humor and some humility. Organized, responsive, flexible, and collaborative (vs. combative).

How can writers increase the odds that you will offer representation: Passion is a given. I worry when there is not enough or too much. I'm more impressed with someone who has done their homework, researching the market, investing time and resources into the writing, and/or has been actively developing their 'community' of potential interested buyers of their book.

Why did you become an agent, and how did you become one: To work closely with writers in developing their ideas and sharing successes (making dreams a reality). I decided to become an agent in the midst of a corporate reorganization (that did not have the best interest of authors on their radar screen).

Describe to someone from another planet what you do as an agent: I work as a writer's advocate. In doing so, this involves many "hats" such as financial consultant, writing coach, legal counsel, personal advisor/cheerleader/therapist.

How do you feel about editors and publishers: Without them I'm on the tuna boat! Having been one, I know how challenging it is to produce successful books, and it is very challenging today. They deserve my respect and admiration—this does not however compromise my ability to aggressively represent my clients and their best interests.

What do you see in the near future for book publishing: "Predictions are difficult, especially when they involve the future."—Yogi Berra. And especially when they involve publishing!

What are your favorite books, TV shows, movies, and why: Books: I love historical/thriller fiction (in the tradition of *The Alienist*, C. Carr). I collect Jazz Age authors Fitzgerald, Hemingway, Wolfe, Stein. Movies: So many!

In your opinion, what do editors think of you: Professional, knowledgeable about publishing; represents high quality authors and projects; can be a good working partner.

On a personal non-professional level, what do you think people think of you: I hope as a 'good man.'

What are some representative titles that you have sold: *Don't Give Up… Don't Ever Give Up* by Justin Spizman (Sourcebooks); *Energy Trading and Investing* by Davis Edwards (McGraw-Hill); *Listen* by Lynn Robins (Globe Pequot); *When Giants Fall* by Michael Panzner (John Wiley); *The Pursuit of Elegance* by Matt May (Doubleday/Currency); *The 2020 Workplace* by Jeanne Meister (HarperCollins); *The Complete Landlord.com Series* by William Lederer (John Wiley & Sons); *Investing in the Sustainable World* by Matthew Kiernan (AMACOM); *Carve Your Own Road* by Jennifer Remling (Career Press); *Love Your Body, Live Your Dreams* by Sarah Maira Dreisbach (AdamsMedia); *Restoring Who We Are* by Martin Melaver (Chelsea Green Publishers); *The Global Talent Showdown* by Edward Gordon (Berret Koehler); *The Recycling Robot* by Robert Malone (Workman Publishers).

TONI LOPOPOLO LITERARY MANAGEMENT

8837 School House Lane, Coopersburg, PA 18036

215-679-0560 fax: 215-679-0561

email: Lopopolobooks@aol.com   Susan's email: Donnsett@verizon.net

Agents' names: Toni Lopopolo, Susan Setteducato

Born: Toni: July 18, Los Angeles, California; Susan: September 11, 1953, Newark, New Jersey.

Education: Toni: Graduate work at State University at San Francisco and UC Berkeley; Susan: Moore College of Art, Philadelphia.

Career history: 1990–Present: literary agent; 1981–1990: executive editor, St. Martin's Press; 1975–1981: executive editor, MacMillan; 1973–1975: paperback marketing manager, Houghton-Mifflin; 1970–1973: publicity associate, Bantam Books.

Hobbies/personal interests: Toni: A Jack Russell Terrier named Babbitt; my five Italian greyhounds, Sophie Jean, Harley, Kiss, Cabrini Girl, and Santini; some are rescues; starting book reading groups that really discuss the books read, and my fiction writing workshops. Susan: Painting in acrylics, sign painting, gardening, raising sheep, growing apples.

Categories/subjects that you are most enthusiastic about agenting: Toni: Mystery series set in other countries; mysteries set in USA with ethnic protagonists. Illustrated children's books; business, parenting, women's and family health, personal growth, psychology, paranormal, anything about dogs.

What you don't want to agent: Toni: Poetry, movie scripts.

If you were not an agent, what might you be doing instead: Buying, restoring, and flipping older houses. Also I'd have more dogs.

What's the best way for writers to solicit your interest: With a great query letter and a personal greeting. Also, when it's obvious to me that the writer has done his/her homework re: writing, and publishing.

Do you charge reading or management fees: No.

Can you provide an approximation by percent of what you tend to represent by category: Nonfiction: 90 percent; Fiction: 10 percent.

What are the most common mistakes writers make when pitching you: Toni: Sending mail that has to be signed for; why not include a stamped, self-addressed postcard if they are that insecure? Telling me they've written a sure-fire bestseller before I've had a chance to read their pages.

How would you describe the client from hell: The terminally insecure.

How would you describe the perfect client: The secure professional writer who trusts and believes in him or herself, and the agent they hired.

How and why did you ever become an agent: Opening a literary agency seemed a natural segue after all those years in book publishing. I also enjoy the process of working with a talented writer and managing that writer's career.

What, if anything, can a writer do to increase the odds of your becoming his or her agent: For nonfiction, submitting an excellently crafted book proposal. For fiction, mastering the skills that make up their craft plus talent as a unique storyteller. Also, have their manuscripts edited by a professional editor before submitting the novel to this agency. Writers who have done their homework and who show strong self-confidence are welcome.

How would you describe to someone (or something) from another planet what it is that you do as an agent: I trade black dots on something white called paper for $$$$.

Do you have any particular opinions or impressions of editors and publishers in general: Because I worked as an editor for many years, I am very empathetic to their workloads and plight in the machinery of a publishing house. Publishers fight to make a profit; it must be daunting.

What do you think the future holds for writers, publishers, and agents: Despite all the electronic gadgets and ways to publish electronically, people of the future will still want to read, own, and collect bound books that they can hold in their hands. The next ten years will stay essentially the same. Worthy books will be published. And many unworthy books will be published as well. Writers have to master their skills, especially novelists, and keep up with the trends and the shorter and shorter attention spans of their readers. And now that most publishers are owned by conglomerates, maybe smaller publishers will flourish and take a chance on books that might have smaller readerships. Some agents will become paperless, sell lots of electronic rights, and still worry about the next big sale.

What are your favorite books, movies, TV shows, and why: Films: *Capote*, *Walk the Line*, *The 40-Year-Old Virgin*, *Wedding Crashers*. The first two because of the excellence of the writing, the actors, and the directors. The other two because I haven't laughed that much in a long time. I'll watch anything Vince Vaughn does, and Philip Seymour Hoffman amazes me. T.V.: *The Sopranos*, though they ran out of gas this season, *Rescue Me*, which keeps getting better and better. Almost anything on HGTV because I learned all the techniques and contracting skills, which helped when I began restoring my house. *Curb Appeal* is a favorite. All the dog shows on Animal Planet, especially the ones with the cops who rescue abused and abandoned dogs. Helen Mirren and Jeremy Irons in *Elizabeth I*, on HBO.

On a personal level, what do you think people like about you and dislike about you: They are impressed with my experience and the fact that I will help them with editing. I've been in publishing since 1970 and an agent since 1991. There is a blog written by a man who called me a stupid bitch; he comes up on Google along with my other credits. I think some people are not happy with a laid-back style of working; and some people really love it. I don't mince words and some people appreciate that and some are offended.

Please list representative titles you have sold: *Do Not Go Gently* (Harper Collins); *Hoodoo Man, Green Money* (Ballantine); *Lifebank, Remote Intrusion* (Dell); *Tuesday's Child, The Reckoning* (Pocketbooks); *Legacy, Catriona* (Kensington). Nonfiction: *Organizing from the Right Side of the Brain* (St. Martin's Press); *Stein on Writing* (St. Martin's Press); *Real-Life Homeschooling* (Fireside); *Leader of the Pack* (HarperPaperbacks); *Choosing a Dog* (Berkley); *Five Simple Steps To Emotional Healing* (Simon & Schuster); *Time Management for Creative People, Career Management for Creative People, Money Management for Creative People, Self-Promotion for Creative People* (ThreeRivers Press); *The Wild Idea Club: An Innovative and Effective Way to Encourage Your Employees to Quit Complaining and Start Solving Problems* (Career Press).

JULIA LORD LITERARY MANAGEMENT

38 West 9th Street, New York, NY 10011

212-995-2333 fax: 212-995-2332

Agent's name: Julia Lord

Born: 1962.

Education: Kenyon College.

Career history or story: Actor, actor's agent, opening the literary department of Monty Silver Agency in the late '80s. Had twins. Freelance editing, opened JLLM in 1999.

Hobbies, interests: Marathons, triathlons, politics, history, music, travel.

Subjects and categories you are interested in agenting, including fiction and nonfiction: Fiction: 40 percent, nonfiction: 60 percent. History that comes alive, anything smart with a good sense of humor.

Subjects and categories writers shouldn't even bother pitching to you: NO romance, science fiction or children's.

Why did you become an agent, and how did you become one: I became an agent because I've always loved books and wanted to be an advocate for writers. I even married one!

What are some representative titles that you have sold: *The Anti-Communist Manifestos* by John V. Fleming (Norton); *Bikeman* by Thomas F. Flynn (Andrews/McMeel); *The History of Now* by Daniel Klein (Permanent); *Plato and a Platypus Walk Into a Bar…Understanding Philosophy Through Jokes* by Cathcart/Klein (Abrams); *NYPD Confidential* by Leonard Levitt (Thomas Dunne/St. Martin's); *How NOT to Write a Novel* by Howard Mittelmark and Sandra Newman (Collins); *A Common Ordinary Murder* by Donald Pfarrer (Random House).

NANCY LOVE LITERARY AGENCY

250 E. 65th St., Suite 4A, New York, NY 10065

email: nloveag@aol.com

(Note: Veteran agent Nancy Love passed away at press time.)

Agent's name: Nancy Love

Born: Philadelphia.

Education: Attended Bryn Mawr College; graduated Phi Beta Kappa, *cum laude*, University of Pennsylvania.

Career story: Worked as an editor and writer for city magazines (managing editor *Philadelphia Magazine*, editor-in-chief *Boston Magazine*), editor for *American Home Magazine*, and *CUE*. Editor of Washingtonian Books, a joint venture with *Washingtonian Magazine*. Freelance book and magazine writer and magazine consultant. I started agenting when friends suggested I stop giving away writing advice and start getting paid for it.

Subjects and categories you like to agent: What I am looking for: Nonfiction only. Please do not send fiction. I want narrative nonfiction, memoir, health, parenting, foreign affairs, expose, women's issues, biography, history, politics, crime, pop science.

What might you be doing if you weren't agenting: I love to travel, and if I weren't a literary agent, I would spend all of my time traveling and writing about it. Otherwise, if I had more time, I'd spend it reading and hanging out with friends.

What's the most effective ways for writers to grab your attention: To get my attention, have an introduction from a writer I know or write a wonderful pitch letter.

Do you charge fees separate from your commission, or offer non-agenting fee-based services: No fees.

What are representative titles you have sold to publishers: *How Your Child Learns Best* by Judy Willis, MD, EdD (Sourcebooks); *Addiction-Proof Your Child* by Stanton Peele, PhD, JD (Three Rivers Press); *All the Shah's Men* (John Wiley); *Overthrow* by Stephen Kinzer (Times Books); *Forgotten Ellis Island* by Lorie Conway (Smithsonian Books) (PBS Special); *What You Should Know About Vaccines* by Paul Offit, MD (John Wiley); *Overkill* by James Alan Fox and Jack Levin (Perseus).

What do you tell entities from other planets and dimensions about your job: My job involves being a shrink, lawyer, editor, friend, mother, and guru—and it's the best job I've ever had.

What do you like best about your clients, and the editors and publishers you work with: I guess the most important thing I get from my clients and the people I work with in publishing is a window into other worlds that they are writing about and the books they are publishing.

You're welcome to share your thoughts and sentiments about the business of writing and publishing: If I could share one piece of advice with people trying to establish themselves in the book world, it would be this: Do your research before you start trying to find an agent. You spend years writing a book, so spend a few weeks finding out as much as you can about publishing and how it works. You will be astonished at how much easier it makes everything for you.

Will our business exist as we know it in ten years or so: The book business is in a state of flux. How it will sort out, no one knows now. But publishing has always changed over the years, maybe just not this fast.

LOWENSTEIN-YOST ASSOCIATES, INC.

121 West 27th Street, Suite 601, New York, NY 10001-6262

212-206-1630

Agent's name: Nancy Yost

Education: BA comparative lit, UNLV.

Career history or story: In the publishing industry: Contracts, Random House; editor, Avon Books; now agent.

Hobbies, interests: Reading (still!), diving, opera, antiquing, theater/dance, eating.

Subjects and categories you are interested in agenting, including fiction and nonfiction: Crime/suspense/thrillers (contemporary and historical); women's fiction—upmarket and commercial, narrative nonfiction about history, natural science, culture, the arts.

Subjects and categories writers shouldn't even bother pitching to you: No textbooks, screenplays, sci-fi, poetry, political nonfiction, Westerns, children's books.

What would you do if you weren't agenting: A different answer daily, but it consistently involves diving, shopping and playing with animals...

What's the best way for fiction writers to solicit your interest: By query letter and first chapter, but not electronically! My email blocker kicks things out, [and] if I don't recognize sender, I delete the message—sorry!

What's the best way for nonfiction writers to solicit your interest: See above.

Do you charge reading or any upfront fees: No.

In your experience, what are the most common pitching mistakes writers make: Sending material that I don't represent, sending material that is in need of extensive revision/polish, saying that "this material will make a great movie" means it will make a great book.

Describe the client from hell, even if you don't have any: Bad attitude, bad manners, incomplete communication of goals and opinions, unrealistic or unvoiced expectations, unreliable work habits, phone calls at home on weekends or after hours...

What's your definition of a great client: Curious, creative, reliable, honest, dedicated to their craft and the adventure of the career. Oh, and they could currently be on the *NYT* bestseller list, and have family members in high positions at Ingrams, B&N, etc.

How can writers increase the odds that you will offer representation: Write a really good book.

Why did you become an agent, and how did you become one: I love books, and I can't write them, I like the challenge, complexity and variety of the industry, and I like the kind of people who care about books and human issues.

How do you feel about editors and publishers: Hardworking (and overworked), dedicated and smart.

What are your favorite books, TV shows, movies, and why: Couldn't possibly list them all, but movies would have to include *The Philadelphia Story* and *Silence of the Lambs*; TV this season: *The Closer*, *The Shield*, *Project Runway*, *Scrubs*, *BBC Mystery Mondays*, *30 Rock*, *Ugly Betty*.

What are some representative titles that you have sold: *Case of Lies* by Perri O'Shaughnessy (Delacorte); *In a Dark House* by Deborah Crombie (Morrow); *Seize the Night* by Sherrilyn Kenyon (St. Martin's); *What Price Love* by Stephanie Laurens (Morrow); *Flirting with Danger* by Suzanne Enoch (Avon); *Beneath a Silent Moon* by Tracy Grant (Morrow); *Assault and Pepper* by Tamar Myers (Dutton); *The Accidental Virgin* by Valerie Frankel (Harper); *Overkill* by Linda Castillo (Berkley); *Black Lace* by Beverly Jenkins (Avon); *Chosen Prey* and *Seduced by Magic* by Cheyenne McCray (St. Martin's); *House of Dark Delights* by Louisa Burton (Bantam); *A Piece of Normal* by Sandy Kahn Shelton (Crown).

THE JENNIFER LYONS LITERARY AGENCY

151 West 19th Street, 3rd Floor

New York, NY 10011

212 368 2812

www.jenniferlyonsliteraryagency.com

Agent's name and email address: Jennifer Lyons; Jenniferlyonslitagency@gmail.com

Location of birth: NYC.

Education: Sarah Lawrence College BA, Oxford University junior year abroad, Middlebury College MA, Fulbright—two years in Vienna.

Career Story: In the late '80s I met Joan Daves, who was an independent agent for 30 years and represented six Nobel Prize authors including Martin Luther King. Joan became affiliated with Writer's House and all parties wanted someone to assist her and eventually to become the director of the Joan Daves Literary Agency. Joan taught me much about the older publishing world, where lunches were long and drinks kept flowing. Given my international background, I was able to attend the Frankfurt Book Fair 18 times, the London Book Fair, and the Jerusalem Book Fair (a long way to go for a party!). Joan passed away some years after I began working with her and I became the director of her agency as well as a senior person at Writer's House. Having built a list and with 18 years of international experience, I decided to start my own company. In addition, I grew up in publishing. My father was a nonfiction editor at Crown and founded Lyons Press. He sold Lyons Press a few years ago and his own books were published by Grove Atlantic. My younger brother started Skyhorse publishers and my brother Paul is the head of the English department at the University of Hawaii and has published a novel with Algonquin.

Hobbies and special personal interests: Who has time for hobbies! Reading is my hobby.

Subjects and categories you like to agent: All kinds of fiction and nonfiction, international and multicultural books, I also have been gaining an interest in young-adult [books] and have sold many.

Subjects and categories writers shouldn't bother pitching to you: Category romance, super-right-wing books.

What might you be doing if you weren't agenting: Sleeping!

What's the most effective ways for writers to grab your attention: A great cover letter, and praise for the writers I currently represent. Flattery and talent work.

Do you charge fees separate from your commission, or offer non-agenting fee-based services (please be honest): NO.

What are representative titles you have sold to publishers: *Dark Dude*, a debut YA novel by Pulitzer Prize–winning author Oscar Hijuelos, *Beautiful Maria of My Soul* by Oscar Hijuelos, forthcoming with Hyperion, *Thoughts of Cigarettes* by Oscar Hijuelos, a memoir forthcoming with Gotham, *Hard Boiled Bad Luck* by Banana Yoshimoto from Grove, *Lake* by Banana Yoshimoto forthcoming from Melville House, *Alexander Calder: American Inventor*, exploring Calder's iconic place in the American story, by Jed Perl, forthcoming from Yale University Press, *Antoine's Alphabet* by Jed Perl, *Confessions of a Dangerous Mind* by Chuck Barris (now a Miramax film), *The Collected Works of Frank O'Conner* by Random House, *The Complete Works of Isaac Babel*, and many more including my father Nick Lyons.

Why did you become an agent, and how did you become one: My father introduced me to blockbuster agent Knox Burger, who represented Martin Cruz Smith. He decided I should become an agent given my background and languages.

How do you feel about writers: I love their great flow of ideas, and I like to help with career management, strategy, and publishing.

What do you tell entities from other planets and dimensions about your job: This job is the most wonderful and challenging fusion of tasks. It involves reading, editing, negotiating, and diplomacy. It's all about multitasking.

What are your favorite books, movies, TV shows, and why: I read high and watch low. I love *One Hundred Years of Solitude* by Gabriel García Márquez. I watch shows to relax, *Desperate Housewives*, *Grey's Anatomy*, *Brothers and Sisters*.

How would you describe the writer from hell: Needy, thinks you're his/her personal assistant rather than a professional agent. Someone who doesn't give you space to do your job.

How would you describe the publisher and/or editor from hell: Difficult to reach and communicate with, because that can take up precious time and it makes me hyperventilate!

What do you like best about your clients, and the editors and publishers you work with: I love their creativity and expertise. As one of my writers says, "Be the dumbest in the room." I like to surround myself with intelligent, interesting people with differing views on the world.

You're welcome to share your thoughts and sentiments about the business of writing and publishing: It's getting harder and harder with the economy. Writers and agents need particular stamina and positive energy to weather this, and we must think about a lifelong career rather than a hot one-shot.

Do you wish to describe who you are: A writer's advocate, and a multilinguist.

Finally, will our business exist as we know it in ten years or so: Most definitely we will still be here, but we will be well versed in multimedia. In the end there will be fewer books published, but hopefully that will mean there are only quality books published. There will only be space for the very best books.

LYONS LITERARY LLC

116 West 23rd St., Suite 500, New York, NY 10011

212-851-8428

www.lyonsliterary.com   email: info@lyonsliterary.com

Agent's name: Jonathan Lyons

Born: San Antonio, Texas.

Education: BA, Washington University in St. Louis; JD, Benjamin N. Cardozo School of Law.

Career history or story: After working briefly as a litigation attorney, Jonathan joined Curtis Brown, Ltd. Four years later Jonathan joined McIntosh & Otis, Inc., where he served as agent and rights manager. In January of 2007 Jonathan founded Lyons Literary LLC. He is a member of the Association of Authors' Representatives, The Authors Guild, American Bar Association, New York State Bar Association, and the New York State Intellectual Property Law Section.

Subjects and categories you are interested in agenting, including fiction and nonfiction: Narrative nonfiction, history, cooking/food writing, pop culture, sports, women's issues, biographies, military, science/pop science, entertainment, politics, true crime, thrillers, mysteries, women's fiction, literary fiction.

Subjects and categories writers shouldn't even bother pitching to you: Romance, picture books, short story collections.

What's the best way for fiction writers to solicit your interest: Submission via the agency website.

What's the best way for nonfiction writers to solicit your interest: Submission via the agency website.

Do you charge reading or any upfront fees: NO.

DONALD MAASS LITERARY AGENCY

121 W. 27th Street, Suite 801, New York, NY 10001

212-727-8383 ext. 11

email: sbarbara@maassagency.com

Agents' names: Stephen Barbara, Cameron McClure; cmcclure@maassagency.com, J.L. Sterner; jlsterner@maassagency.com

The following information pertains to Stephen Barbara.

Born: August 17, 1980; New Haven, Connecticut.

Education: BA '02 in English literature (with a focus on literary criticism), University of Chicago.

Career history or story: I worked briefly on the editorial side at HarperCollins, before joining the Fifi Oscard Agency as an assistant in late 2004. Then in January of 2006 I became agent and contracts director at the Donald Maass Literary Agency.

Hobbies, interests: I follow Italian soccer, enjoy traveling, and am an avid reader of business and narrative nonfiction books.

Subjects and categories you are interested in agenting, including fiction and nonfiction: YA and middle-grade novels, picture books, SF&F, literary fiction, mystery/suspense, memoir, business, narrative nonfiction, health and fitness.

Subjects and categories writers shouldn't even bother pitching to you: Romance novels and screenplays.

What would you do if you weren't agenting: Cry, gnash my teeth, pull my hair out. I love my job.

What's the best way for fiction writers to solicit your interest: Send me a one-page query letter via email with the first five pages pasted into the body of the email. Please mention any writing credits and/or endorsements from other writers.

What's the best way for nonfiction writers to solicit your interest: Send me a one-page query letter via email. Please mention relevant credentials and any info. on your platform.

Do you charge reading or any upfront fees: No.

In your experience, what are the most common pitching mistakes writers make: It's best to avoid baseless hype ("my writing has been compared to Tolstoy's") and masses of description. They smack of a lack of confidence. Be clear, succinct, and to the point.

Describe the client from hell, even if you don't have any: The client from hell is someone who's badly in need of career help, but who won't listen to advice and blames others for problems he himself has created.

What's your definition of a great client: Hardworking, ambitious, optimistic, reasonable, but most of all trusting.

How can writers increase the odds that you will offer representation: Write a smart query letter and terrific manuscript and the odds go up. Extra kudos for flattering me—if you know something about who I represent and my track record that's generally a good sign.

Why did you become an agent, and how did you become one: Edmund Wilson was probably the writer who most filled me with awe of the New York publishing world when I was growing up, and I knew even in college I wanted to enter into that world and become an editor or agent. But agenting best suited my independent, entrepreneurial instincts.

What do you see in the near future for book publishing: I think we'll see publishers pushing fewer titles with more sales potential each season. Fewer chances for authors to break out, less tolerance for mid-list sales, more and more of an emphasis on the blockbuster or runaway hit. I'm not complaining, of course; publishing is a business.

What are your favorite books, TV shows, movies, and why: Some of my favorite books include *Feed* by M.T. Anderson, *Liar's Poker* by Michael Lewis, *The Russian Debutante's Handbook* by Gary Shteyngart, *Small Is the New Big* by Seth Godin, and the Artemis Fowl series. I'm a big fan of *Curb Your Enthusiasm* and *Entourage*, for TV series.

In your opinion, what do editors think of you: They think well of me well enough to read my projects quickly, make offers on them, invite me to lunches and drink dates. And that's all very pleasing, naturally.

What are some representative titles that you have sold: *If I Should Fall* by Lauren Oliver (Bowen Press, HarperCollins); *Wish U Wr Dead* by Todd Strasser (Egmont US); *The Pillow Book of Lotus Lowenstein* by Libby Schmais (Delacorte Press); *Kindred* by Tammar Stein (Alfred Knopf); *The Little Sleep* by Paul Tremblay (Henry Holt); *The Secret of Zoom* by Lynne Jonell (Henry Holt); *The Dead Family Diaz* and a second picture book by P.J. Bracegirdle (Dial Books); *The Body Fat Solution* by Tom Venuto (Avery, division of Penguin); *The Big Splash* by Jack D. Ferraiolo (Amulet Books); *Dead Is the New Black* by Marlene Perez (Houghton Mifflin Harcourt); *Freeze Frame* by Heidi Ayarbe (Laura Geringer Books).

The following information pertains to Cameron McClure.

Born: January 5, California.

Education: BA from University of California, Santa Barbara; Major: English and Spanish; Minor: history.

Career story: I've been with the Donald Maass Literary Agency since 2004; previously I worked as an assistant agent for Curtis Brown, New York.

Hobbies and special personal interests: Bicycling, listening to music, karaoke, soccer, yoga, reading.

Subjects and categories you like to agent: Fiction: Literary mysteries and crime fiction, urban fantasy and light science fiction, speculative fiction, women's fiction, suspense, strongly plotted literary fiction, novels with a strong sense of mystery or atmosphere. Nonfiction: Narrative nonfiction, true crime, memoir, projects on emerging subcultures.

Subjects and categories writers shouldn't bother pitching to you: Picture books, poetry, and prescriptive nonfiction.

What's the most effective ways for writers to grab your attention: Email me a query letter with a short pitch of your book, any publishing credits, and your opening five pages. For nonfiction, send me the overview from your proposal. Please don't send attachments. I respond to all e-queries that are addressed to me and follow these guidelines. If sending a query by post, please include an SASE for my reply.

Do you charge fees separate from your commission, or offer non-agenting fee-based services: No, but I respond favorably to chocolate.

What are representative titles you have sold to publishers: *Mr. Shivers* by Robert Jackson Bennett (Orbit); *Queers in History* by Keith Stern (Ben Bella); *The Disillusionists* by Carolyn Crooke (Bantam Dell).

Why did you become an agent, and how did you become one: I moved to New York because I wanted to work in publishing, and I was drawn to agenting in particular because of the freedom agents have—I can sign up any type of book I fall for, as long as I believe I can sell it. I also love the diversity of the job—we are readers, editors, negotiators, peacemakers, and spend a lot of time socializing. I get a lot of satisfaction out of contributing to book culture.

What are your favorite books, movies, TV shows, and why: Some recent great reads for me have been *Sharp Objects* by Gillian Flynn, *The Spellman Files* by Lisa Lutz, *The Intuitionist* by Colson Whitehead, and some of my favorite authors are Jonathan Lethem, Dennis Lehane, Jodi Picoult, Elizabeth George, and Jeffrey Ford.

The following information pertains to J.L. Sterner.

Name: J. L. Stermer, Agent/contracts director, jlstermer@maassagency.com

Born: January 17 (Capricorn in the house!). NYC native.

Education: High School of the Performing Arts (drama), Temple University (theater), F.I.T. (fashion merchandising management). I finally received my BA from Columbia University (English).

Career story: Began as an actress (wound up paying bills by serving martinis); then I attended F.I.T. and worked in showroom sales, finally finished strong up on 116th and Broadway, got my degree and here I am.

Hobbies and special personal interests: Still a lover of fashion, anything New York City, old skool hip-hop, trying new recipes, meeting new people, laughing with my friends till my stomach hurts, volunteering (Meals On Wheels and Senior Bingo—it gets mighty serious at Bingo!), people watching, museums, comedy shows, readings, nature walks, architecture, learning something new (about myself and others).

Subjects and categories you like to agent: I am basically looking for projects that reflect my interests, which are conveniently listed above...Here's what my official bio says: fiction, memoir, narrative nonfiction, pop-culture (cooking, fashion, style, music, art), smart humor, upscale erotica/erotic memoir and multi-cultural fiction/nonfiction. I am looking for projects that I can get behind 100 percent. And I'm looking for people I can jibe with as well.

Subjects and categories writers shouldn't bother pitching to you: Not looking for: Poetry, screenplays, sci-fi, fantasy, mysteries.

What might you be doing if you weren't agenting: I feel like I've had a couple of careers already. Part of the reason I'm thrilled to be an agent is because it's challenging every single day and this career allows me to capitalize on my strengths intellectually, creatively, socially, and entrepreneurially. So, I've already filtered though lots of jobs and learned a lot about myself in the process—this one feels right and I'm here to stay.

What's the most effective way for writers to grab your attention: You can grab my attention by keeping your query letter short and sweet. By slapping me with a captivating protagonist, or a fresh and engaging concept, or a laugh-out-loud setup. Pull this together with some smooth sentences that flow so nicely that I'm surprised when your five pages are done and I say, "More please!" (Email preferred, no attachments—just a query letter and first five pages.)

Do you charge fees separate from your commission: Nope.

What do you think of writers: Writers are brave and vulnerable. As an intern (and an assistant), I'd spend day after day reading through the slush. It got frustrating at times, but when I felt myself starting to get negative I just thought: for every person who has sent in a query letter, there've got to be at least ten people who don't. At least these people have the chutzpah and confidence to get their work out there! It's not easy to send your baby out and run the risk of rejection—nobody wants to be turned down, but writers who are going for it put themselves on the line. Gotta respect that.

What are your favorite books, movies, TV shows, and why: I love pretty much any movie by David Lynch. He is able to find the sheer horror and desperation in the most seemingly mundane of circumstances. He doesn't feel the need to tie things up nice and neatly—I like to be left to draw my own conclusions. He's also got an odd sense of sexuality that I think adds depth and intrigue to his work. Definitely a fan of Woody Allen (probably got this from my mom). Both his books and his movies. I feel like it's a cultural Jewish thing: I like chopped liver, I grew up in Manhattan, I like Woody Allen.

Authors: Bret Easton Ellis/*Less Than Zero*. This work had a huge impact on me as a kid, the film and the book. It is dire, luxurious, helpless, sexy, indulgent, and it all ends tragically. Sister Souljah/*The Coldest Winter Ever*. Winter is a strong female protagonist in a gritty, honest survival story that is beautifully written with careful insight into her complex world. Ralph Ellison/*Invisible Man*. His combination of simple sentences that hold incredibly profound subtext with an epic story-line that delves into core racial issues, well, it kind of blew me away. David Rakoff/*Fraud Smart*. Biting, totally laugh-out-loud humor. I love how he intertwines snark and self-realization. He's totally unapologetic and goes for both the obvious humor as well as the more nuanced set ups and this makes for a highly enjoyable read. And

Roz Chast (cartoonist). She taps into everyday situations and illustrates the craziness that happens in our minds when we allow ourselves to get kooky and surreal. That and she's written a hilarious story about making prank phone calls that really resonated with me. Those were the days.

TV: I try not to get sucked into that crazy vortex too often. I love and feel inspired by the depth, characters, and social commentary of *Mad Men*, the hilarity of *30 Rock* and *The Office* (such great writing—rapid-fire and unrelentingly witty), and when fashion week is happening there's a local New York channel that runs almost all of the runway shows in their entirety—don't get me started…

MACGREGOR LITERARY

2373 NW 185th Ave., Suite 165, Hillsboro, OR 97124

www.macgregorliterary.com

Agents' names: Chip MacGregor, Sandra Bishop

Education: Chip graduated from Portland State University in 1979, earned an MA from Biola University in 1984, did his doctoral work at the University of Oregon, and spent time at a post-doc at Regent's Park College, Oxford University. Sandra graduated from university after Chip—she's much younger. And smarter.

Career story: Chip started a long career in publishing in 1977, when he took a job as a copy editor with *Clearing* Magazine. He made his living as a freelance writer, worked as an editor and senior editor with publishers, and served as associate publisher with Time-Warner. He began representing authors eleven years ago. Sandra has made her living as a writer and editor for years, after working as an editor with a publishing house in Oregon. She began working with authors as an agent in 2007.

Hobbies and special personal interests: Chip has authored numerous books, loves watching Shakespeare, and has served as an editor for the International Brotherhood of Magicians for several years. Sandra has strong background in marketing, and enjoys being out of doors with her husband and son.

Subjects and categories you like to agent: Commercial fiction and nonfiction. We have significant experience working with the CBA (religious) market, with both fiction and nonfiction titles—particularly self-help, Christian living, and emergent projects.

Subjects and categories writers shouldn't bother pitching to you: Sci-fi, fantasy, poetry, children's books, general-market YA, sexually explicit romance novels.

What might you be doing if you weren't agenting: Chip would be working as a card magician; Sandra would be running the government. Both wish they could be Speedo models.

What's the most effective ways for writers to grab your attention: Every agent is looking for a combination of three things: a GREAT IDEA, expressed through GREAT WRITING, by someone with a GREAT PLATFORM. But nothing trumps great writing. Much of what we see isn't bad, it's just not special. The ideas are average, the writing pedestrian. If you really want to grab out attention, come to us with a fabulous, out-of-the-box story, presented with writing that is stunning.

Do you charge fees separate from your commission, or offer non-agenting fee-based services: No.

What are representative titles you have sold to publishers: *Quaker Summer*, a novel by Lisa Samson that was named by PW as one of their "top 100 books of the year"; *Never Say Diet*, a health book by Chantel Hobbs, who appeared on *Oprah* and on the cover of *People Magazine* (Random House); *Murder, Mayhem, and a Fine Man*, by Claudia Mair Burney, which has received rave reviews (Simon & Schuster).

Why did you become an agent, and how did you become one: On a macro level, we became agents because we both love books and words and believe they can help make the world a better place. But on a real-world level, both of us became agents because it fit our skill sets. We both began our careers as writers and editors, started working with authors, and naturally moved toward helping writers create strong proposals and sell them.

How do you feel about writers: Both of us love the creative side of writers, and enjoy the process of helping focus an idea, sharpen the words, and organize the content. We've spent our lives working with writers, love hanging around with them, and particularly enjoy helping them succeed in the very difficult process of establishing careers as artists.

What do you tell entities from other planets and dimensions about your job: If you were to study the last thousand years of life on earth, you'd discover the most significant invention was the creation of movable type. It allowed mankind to move from an oral tradition to a written one, raised the level of education in the world, and helped the common person see how he or she could live a transcendent life. Writing changed the world like nothing else. As an agent, I believe I get to play a part in that world-changing process known as publishing. I meet with writers, help them focus their ideas, insist they create the best book possible, and work to help make their book succeed in the market.

What are your favorite books, movies, TV shows, and why: Favorite books include *Huckleberry Finn*, *The Ragamuffin Gospel*, *A Distant Mirror*, *Treasure Island*, *Nostromo*, *The Education of Henry Adams*, *One Hundred Years Of Solitude*. Favorite movies would be *Citizen Kane*, *Casablanca*, *The Third Man*, *Schindler's List*, *The Thin Man*, *The Wizard of Oz*, *Gone with the Wind*, *Vertigo*, *The Godfather*. All of them cause us to think about the choices we make, and how that affects us over time.

How would you describe the writer from hell: Sends me 27 emails per day, doesn't listen to advice, needs to know daily that I love him, and has mistaken me for his mother.

How would you describe the publisher and/or editor from hell: He insists on my showing him a proposal on an exclusive, then takes six months to get back to me…except he doesn't get back to me, I get back to him and he says, "Oh…did you send that?" And yes…this has happened to me. Deciphering publisher happy-talk is one of the roles of a good agent.

What do you like best about your clients, and the editors and publishers you work with: They understand books and publishing. They listen. I like them. They're easy to get along with.

You're welcome to share your thoughts and sentiments about the business of writing and publishing: We love the industry. Frankly, helping get books published in just about the most fun thing on the planet, and both of us appreciate the opportunity we have to participate in the process. I can think of books I've read that have changed me—James Agee's *A Death in the Family*, Henri Nouwen's *In the Name of Jesus*, Dostoyevsky's *Brothers Karamazov*. I was never the same after reading Pascal's *Pensées*. It's why I continue to work with books and words—in hopes of occasionally finding that book that will change me. I'm not sure I believe I'm ever going to help publish a book that will change the world, but I MUST believe I can help publish a book that can change a life. And, in seeing that happen, continue to have hope that the world can be a better place.

Do you wish to describe who you are: Chip is a 50-year-old literary agent who is a lifelong words guy. He's been working in the industry for three decades, is well known in the industry, and understands what makes a book work. He's also been married for more than a quarter-century to a very forgiving woman, and has three grown children who also love books and words. Sandra is an experienced writer and editor who knows what makes books sing. Both of them have made their living as authors, so they know how to balance the "art" of writing with the "real-world" aspect of making a living.

Will our business exist as we know it in ten years or so: Absolutely. The written word has been around since the dawn of time, and publishing has worked nicely for the last 500 years. The delivery systems may change a bit, but people still have stories to tell, and people are still looking for wisdom and the story that will change them, and books have a long-term history in the world and in our culture. In ten years, we'll still be in the book business, and still hoping to see that great book that can change our lives.

The following information pertains to Sandra Bishop only.

Education: Sandra put herself through college while serving in the Marine Corps after high school.

Career story: Sandra started in publishing in the marketing department of a major CBA house where she worked with top-name authors, crafted marketing proposals, composed material for sales and pub board meetings and kept the marketing department on its toes. When the company was sold, Sandra stayed put in her home town and worked to make a living as a writer for the next 20 years. She began working with MacGregor Literary as an agent in 2007.

Hobbies and personal interests: Sandra enjoys gardening, reading, learning to fly fish, being beat by her ten-year-old in chess, and vacationing with her husband in Hawaii and other locales where the sun promises to dry out her soggy Oregonian self.

Representative titles: Debut women's contemporary fiction *A Dandelion Day* by Carla Stewart (Hachette Book Group); *52 Things Kids Need from a Dad* by Jay K. Payleitner (Harvest House); *The Last Woman Standing*, an African American romance novel by Tia McCollars (Moody Publishers).

Favorite books, movies, TV shows: Favorite books include *Peace Like a River* by Leif Enger, *Anything* by Elisabeth Berg, *Gentle Ben* by Walt Morey, *To Own a Dragon* by Donald Miller, *The Tender Bar* by J.R. Moehringer, *Straight Man* by Richard Russo; *The Sweet Everlasting* by Judson Mitcham, *Tender Mercies* by Anne Lamott; *All the Places to Love* by Patricia MacLachlan, *Tortilla Flat* by Steinbeck.

Favorite movies include *Oh Brother Where Art Thou*, *Braveheart*, *The Black Stallion*, *The Man in the Moon*, *The Shawshank Redemption*, *3:10 to Yuma*. Each of these quest stories is emotionally moving and uses well chosen, artful language. I don't watch much TV as my favorite shows always get cancelled—*I'll Fly Away* and *Pushing Daisies* were two of my all-time favorites.

MANUS & ASSOCIATES LITERARY AGENCY

425 Sherman Avenue, Suite 200, Palo Alto, CA 94306

650-470-5151   fax: 650-470-5159

www.ManusLit.com   email: SLEE@ManusLit.com

Agents' name: Jillian Manus, Stephanie Lee, Dena Fischer, Jandy Nelson, Penny Nelson

The following information pertains to Jillian Manus.

Born: April 26, New York.

Education: BA from New York University.

Career history: Ms. Manus has been a television agent at International Creative Management, director of development at Warner Brothers and Universal Studios, vice president of media acquisitions at Trender AG, and an associate publisher of two national magazines covering entertainment and technology. Because of this remarkably comprehensive background, she is a much sought-after speaker on writing, women in business and motherhood, politics, and the media industry.

Hobbies/personal interests: Ms. Manus lends her time to professional, artistic, and political endeavors. She serves on several local and national boards including the Board of Trustees for New York University, the Dean's Council for the Tisch School of the Arts, the board for the W.I.S.H. List (Women in the Senate and House), the board of College Track, and the Advisory Board for Stanford Hospital's Cancer Center. She is also the Chair for the Governor and First Lady's Conference for Women and Families and serves on the board of the California Museum for History, Women and the Arts. In addition Ms. Manus has served on Governor Schwarzenegger's transition team and is presently involved in his economic recovery team. Ms. Manus also remains very active in the development efforts of numerous literacy and mentoring programs across the country including serving on the Leadership Advisory Council for Save the Children.

Categories/subjects that you are most enthusiastic about agenting: Ms. Manus is known for paying special attention to books that empower people physically, psychologically and spiritually. She brings to her work extensive knowledge of the marketplace and editorial sensitivity that has been acquired in the course of a distinguished and multifaceted career. Literary fiction, multicultural fiction, women's fiction, southern fiction, narrative nonfiction, memoir, health, popular science, politics, popular culture, women's issues, history, sophisticated self-help.

What you don't want to agent: Poetry, children's, science fiction, fantasy, Westerns, romance, cookbooks.

If you were not an agent, what might you be doing instead: Teaching, climbing Everest, being a rock star!

What's the best way for writers to solicit your interest: Write a captivating pitch letter and send with: for fiction: the first 30 pages of a novel; for nonfiction: a proposal. Always include an SASE for response.

Do you charge reading or management fees: No.

Can you provide an approximation by percent of what you tend to represent by category: Nonfiction: 60 percent, fiction: 40 percent.

What are the most common mistakes writers make when pitching you: Calling instead of writing, submitting work before it's ready.

What, if anything, can a writer do to increase the odds of your becoming his or her agent: Write a STRONG book or proposal!

Please list representative titles you have sold: *One-Minute Millionaire; Cracking the Millionaire Code; Unbreakable Laws of Success; GO LONG; Be Inspired, Be Humble, and Make a Total Commitment to Life; Words of Wisdom; God, Can You Hear Me?; The Secret Language of Girlfriends; Space Between the Stars; Yoga Journal Magazine; Yoga as Medicine; Yoga Escapes; Red Cross.* Some of her *New York Times* bestsellers have been *Cane River, Gettysburg, One Minute Millionaire, All the President's Children,* and *Missed Fortune.*

This information pertains to Stephanie Lee.

Born: August 6, 1976, Palo Alto, California.

Education: BA in English/creative writing (fiction) from Stanford University.

Career history: I started interning here at Manus & Associates in college and never left!

Hobbies/personal interests: Crafting, crocheting, kitsch, obsessive blog-reading, eBay, pop culture in general.

Categories/subjects that you are most enthusiastic about agenting: I like prescriptive nonfiction including women's issues, Gen X/Gen Y issues, dating/relationships, and smart self-help served with humor, and narrative nonfiction, intriguing memoirs, popular science, popular culture, and young adult. Fiction interests include commercial literary fiction, women's fiction, chick lit, multi-cultural fiction, edgy thrillers, young adult, and new voices.

What you don't want to agent: Poetry, science fiction, fantasy, romance, children's books.

If you were not an agent, what might you be doing instead: Running a magazine, or designing knitwear.

What's the best way for writers to solicit your interest: Write a killer query letter and sample/proposal that I just can't say no to. Also, do your research and make sure the agent you are submitting to accepts the type of book you are pitching.

Do you charge reading or management fees: No.

Can you provide an approximation by percent of what you tend to represent by category: Nonfiction: 70 percent, fiction: 30 percent.

What are the most common mistakes writers make when pitching you: They forget to include their contact information and SASE, forget to include the title of their book, send me material that I don't represent, send full unsolicited manuscripts, provide too much or too little information in a query letter (you don't want to just give us a long, drawn-out, boring plot re-hash or a page with just one sentence on it, but you want to give us a concise and compelling pitch or teaser for your book).

How would you describe the client from hell: Someone who can't respect/accept the fact that we have more than just one client :), someone who isn't a hard worker and just hopes that their book will magically succeed, someone who constantly fights the system instead of trying to work with it.

How would you describe the perfect client: Creative, professional, prolific, flexible, deadline-oriented, and NICE! Sending chocolate on Valentine's Day is also a plus.

How and why did you ever become an agent: Because I am completely and utterly addicted to books, and because I got lucky and found myself working for an awesome company.

What, if anything, can a writer do to increase the odds of your becoming his or her agent: Fiction: Write the best book you can, hone your craft, really polish those opening pages, and create a mind-blowing query letter. If short stories are in your blood, get published in journals! Do what you can to get your name out there. Nonfiction: Do your research and make sure there is a market for your book, that your book fills a need, and that you are the best person in the world to write this book. Also do what you can to develop your platform and get your name out there, as an expert, a speaker, a columnist, anything.

How would you describe to someone (or something) from another planet what it is that you do as an agent: I used to say that agenting was like treasure-hunting, but now it seems a little more like gardening. You set out to find a remarkable seedling, water it, prune it, talk to it, find the most ideal location for its kind and plant it there, and hopefully see it grow into something beautiful. Sometimes you find a fabulous tree that needs a nudge or a new sunny spot, sometimes you fall in love with a tiny seed and nurture it from the very beginning. This extended metaphor is getting a little crazy.

Do you have any particular opinions or impressions of editors and publishers in general: Publishing is a very business-minded arena, so more creative people can sometimes be surprised by this. A good agent will help guide you through.

What do you think the future holds for writers, publishers, and agents: Robots writing e-books about robots. I'm not sure. I would love to see more support for first fiction and short stories.

What are your favorite books, movies, TV shows, and why: I've only recently gotten cable TV. I'm a low-brow junkie, apparently. I'm often watching/listening to Bravo, E!, and the Food Network. I know. Nobody will respect me now! I am very entertained and intrigued by the humor of human nature. I love films by Charlie Kauffman and Wes Anderson. They are about very quirky people and very quirky circumstances, yet so well-done and so engaging.

Please list representative titles you have sold: *Why You're Still Single* (Plume); *Tales from the Scale: Real Women Weigh in on Thunder Thighs, Cheese Fries, and Feeling Good…At Any Size* (Adams Media); *Avoiding Prison and Other Noble Vacation Goals: Adventures in Love and Danger* (Three Rivers Press); *I Can't Believe I'm Buying This Book: A Commonsense Guide to Successful Internet Dating* (Ten Speed Press); *Love Like That* (Red Dress Ink); *Want Some Get Some* plus untitled second novel (Kensington); *Guerilla War for Extra Credit* (Dutton Children's).

This information pertains to Dena Fischer.

Born: 4/24/??; New York, NY.

Education: BA, English lit., UCLA, 1987.

Career history: Formerly a development/production executive in the film business in Los Angeles.

Categories/subjects that you are most enthusiastic about agenting: Literary fiction, mainstream fiction, narrative nonfiction, selected practical nonfiction in areas such as health, parenting, pop culture, social commentary, current events.

What you don't want to agent: Genre fiction, science fiction, romance, Westerns, techno-thrillers, horror, fantasy, young adult.

What's the best way for writers to solicit your interest: An irresistible cover letter.

Do you charge reading or management fees: No.

Can you provide an approximation by percent of what you tend to represent by category: Fiction: 50 percent, nonfiction: 50 percent.

Please list representative titles you have sold: *Lifeguarding: A Memoir of Secrets, Swimming and the South* (Harmony Books); *Baby Lists* (Adams Media); *Scream Free Parenting: The Revolutionary Approach to Raising Your Kids by Keeping Your Cool* (Broadway Books); *Beauty & the Brain: The Doctors' Prescription for Inner & Outer Beauty* (Contemporary Books).

This information pertains to Jandy Nelson.

Born: November 25, 1965, New York.

Education: Cornell University BA; Brown University MFA.

Career history: I worked in the theater and academia before becoming a literary agent.

Hobbies/personal interests: Poetry, film, theater, travel, cooking, running, hiking, festivity.

Categories/subjects that you are most enthusiastic about agenting: Literary fiction, multi-cultural fiction, women's fiction, southern fiction, narrative nonfiction, memoir, health, popular science, politics, popular culture, women's issues, history, sophisticated self help.

What you don't want to agent: Children's, genre fiction, cookbooks.

If you were not an agent, what might you be doing instead: Teaching, climbing Everest, being a rock star!

What's the best way for writers to solicit your interest: Write a captivating pitch letter and send with: for fiction: the first 30 pages of a novel; for nonfiction: send a proposal. Always include an SASE for response.

Do you charge reading or management fees: No.

Can you provide an approximation by percent of what you tend to represent by category: Nonfiction: 60 percent, fiction: 40 percent.

What are the most common mistakes writers make when pitching you: Calling instead of writing, submitting work before it's ready.

How and why did you ever become an agent: I badgered Jillian Manus until she hired me. I became an agent to work with writers and to help bring books into the world that will move, enrich, inspire and delight.

What, if anything, can a writer do to increase the odds of your becoming his or her agent: Write a kickass book or proposal!

Do you have any particular opinions or impressions of editors and publishers in general: They are the wizards behind the curtains.

Please list representative titles you have sold: *Catfish & Mandala* (FSG); *The Mercy of Thin Air* (Atria); *Anything You Say Can and Will Be Used Against You* (Harper Collins); *Lily Dale* (HarperSF); *The New Menopause Book* (Avery); *Geisha: A Life* (Atria); *The Territory of Men* (Random House); *The World of Normal Boys* (Kensington).

This information pertains to Penny Nelson.

Career history: I have had a varied career that has included science research and years in public radio as a producer and host. Now I have combined my interests and experience to become an literary agent representing nonfiction work.

Hobbies/personal interests: Martial arts, pop culture, and following socio-political trends.

Categories/subjects that you are most enthusiastic about agenting: I represent only nonfiction at this time, with a strong interest in current affairs/politics, social trends, and lifestyle/self-help topics. It is very helpful if the author has strong professional credentials related to the material being presented. And, for self-help material, it is important that the author has an established platform.

What's the best way for writers to solicit your interest: Send a well-written query letter that clearly expresses the topic and the author's credentials.

Do you charge reading or management fees: No.

Please list representative titles you have sold: *The Jesus Machine* (St. Martin's Press); *The Fine Art of Small Talk* (Hyperion); *Where War Lives* (McClelland and Stewart); *The Best New York Sports Arguments* (Sourcebooks, Inc); *Confusing Love with Obsession* (Hazelden); *Se Habla Dinero: The Everyday Guide to Financial Success* (Wiley).

MARCH TENTH, INC.

4 Myrtle Street, Haworth, NJ 07641

201-387-6551 fax: 201-387-6552

email: schoron@aol.com

Agent's name: Sandra Choron

Education: BA, Lehman College.

Career history: Editor, Hawthorn Books, 1971–1979; editor, Dell Publishing, 1979–1981; founded March Tenth, Inc. in 1981.

Hobbies/personal interests: Reading, needlework, traveling.

Categories/subjects that you are most enthusiastic about agenting: Pop culture, especially music and leisure subjects; general nonfiction; literary fiction.

What you don't want to agent: Genre fiction, cookbooks, children's books, science.

If you were not an agent, what might you be doing instead: I would be a writer, of course.

What's the best way for writers to solicit your interest: Send me a nuts-and-bolts description of your work via email or snail mail.

Do you charge reading or management fees: No.

Can you provide an approximation by percent of what you tend to represent by category: Nonfiction: 90 percent, fiction: 10 percent.

What are the most common mistakes writers make when pitching you: They hype their books by making unrealistic claims.

How would you describe the client from hell: One who simply isn't ready for the realities of book publishing.

How would you describe the perfect client: Tall, dark…

How and why did you ever become an agent: As an editor, I felt limited by the tastes of the one publisher for whom I worked. Agenting allows me to pursue a wide range of subjects and books. I am a kid in a candy store!

What, if anything, can a writer do to increase the odds of your becoming his or her agent: Nothing, really; the work must speak for itself. But being responsive to guidance always helps.

How would you describe to someone (or something) from another planet what it is that you do as an agent: To quote a famous predecessor: "I dash hopes."

Do you have any particular opinions or impressions of editors and publishers in general: Editors? Put four of 'em in a room and you'll get five opinions. Happily, no two are alike.

What do you think the future holds for writers, publishers, and agents: Technological advances have made publishing a far more democratic industry in recent years. It will become more and more difficult to separate the wheat from the chaff, which makes agenting all the more interesting and challenging. I look forward to it.

What are your favorite books, movies, TV shows, and why: I like reality TV, mostly for the live angst.

On a personal level, what do you think people like about you and dislike about you: People respond to my enthusiasm and to the fact that I believe that books should be fun to assemble. I'm sure there are people out there who don't like me; I have no idea what their problem is.

Please list representative titles you have sold: *Bruce Springsteen on Tour* (Bloomsbury); *The Art of Woody Guthrie* (Rizzoli); *The Annotated Grateful Dead Lyrics* (Dodd, Trist); *The 100 Simple Secrets* (series) (Harper San Francisco); *The Appalachians* (Random House).

DENISE MARCIL LITERARY AGENCY, INC.

156 Fifth Ave, Suite 625, New York, NY 10010

www.denisemarcilagency.com

Agents: Denise Marcil, Anne Marie O'Farrell; amof86@aol.com
The following information pertains to Denise Marcil.
Agent: Denise Marcil
Born: February 14—Valentine's Day, Troy, New York.
Education: Skidmore College, BA English, with honors.
Career history: Avon Books, editorial assistant, Simon & Schuster, Inc., assistant editor, Denise Marcil Literary Agency, Inc., President.
Hobbies/personal interests: Ballroom dancing, theater, attending dance performances from contemporary to classic ballet, art history, travel, outdoor adventures, fly fishing.
Categories/subjects that you are most enthusiastic about agenting: Fiction: Women's fiction, thrillers, suspense. Nonfiction: Self-help, popular reference, business.
What you don't want to agent: Memoirs, sci-fi, children's books, political fiction or nonfiction, science.

If you were not an agent, what might you be doing instead: I can't imagine I'd ever find anything else I could feel so passionately about, but if I had to choose another career, I'd be a dancer or art history teacher.

What's the best way for writers to solicit your interest: With a well-written and compelling one-page query letter and SASE.

Do you charge reading or management fees: No.

Do you require any kind of upfront payments from your clients: No.

Can you provide an approximation by percent of what you tend to represent by category: Fiction: 80 percent—Women's fiction: 80 percent , suspense: 10 percent, Children's 0 percent; Nonfiction: 20 percent—Self-help: 10 percent, business 10 percent.

What are the most common mistakes writers make when pitching you: Never make a cold call, demand to speak with me, and pester my associate after [being] informed of the proper procedure. Never assume you are an exception to the rule. The most common mistake is not thoroughly researching the type of works an agent represents and not submitting work in the form agents request in profiles such as this or on their websites.

How would you describe the client from hell: This person is unprofessional, unwilling to learn, unable to take constructive criticism and refuses to adjust unrealistic expectations of the industry.

How would you describe the perfect client: He or she is appreciative of the work my staff and I do on his or her behalf. A dream client is professional, enthusiastic, constantly at work refining his or her craft, and, most importantly, a talented and creative writer. Such authors promote their books and take responsibility for the success of their work.

How and why did you ever become an agent: A book lover and avid reader since childhood, I majored in English in college and pursued a publishing career. Following a few years working for publishers, a job offer by an agent opened that side of the business to me. I discovered I enjoyed selling, which coincided with my talent for persuasion. Combined with my editorial skills, I discovered a career that became a passion and successful business.

What, if anything, can a writer do to increase the odds of your becoming his or her agent: We want to represent strong writers with fresh ideas. People who are professional, well-mannered, and polite always have a better chance of getting my attention. Do your homework to assure that I represent your type of book. Demonstrate that you can publicize and sell your work.

How would you actually describe what you do for a living: I'm the author's business partner who guides, develops, and manages his/her writing career. I'm the advocate and cheerleader for the author and the liaison between the author and the publisher. I balance the author's expectations with the realities of the publishing industry.

What are your favorite books, movies, TV shows, and why: Books: *The Great Gatsby* and *Huckleberry Finn*; Film (recent): *Wall-E*.

What do you think the future holds for writers, publishers, and agents: Like most businesses, publishing constantly changes as new technologies and new means of distribution evolve. The changes offer all stakeholders both opportunities and challenges. Authors will have more ways to self-publish their work; publishers will have to address how to protect authors' copyrights with the availability of books on the Internet, including e-books and downloadable audios, and online retailers' read-aloud functions. Agents, authors, and publishers should work together to ensure the longevity of book publishing.

Do you have any particular opinions or impressions of editors and publishers in general: There's nothing equal to an enthusiastic editor who cheerleads for the author inside the publisher. I love working with those editors and their marketing and sales teams.

On a personal level, what do you think people like about you and dislike about you: I think people like my generosity of spirit and my direct, honest, straightforward manner. Perhaps some don't like my direct, straightforward manner!

Please list representative titles you have sold: *The Inn at Eagle Point* by Sherryl Woods (Mira); *The Yellow House* by Patricia Falvey (Center Street); *Love on the Line* by Laura Castoro (Avon); *Red Cat* by Peter Spiegelman (Knopf); *The Baby Book* by Dr. William Sears, Martha Sears, RN, Dr. Robert Sears, and Dr. James Sears (Little, Brown); *The N.D.D. Book* by Dr. William Sears, Martha Sears, RN; *The Vaccine Book* by Dr. Robert Sears (Little, Brown); *The 10-Minute Total Body Makeover* by Sean Foyand Nellie Sabin with Mike Smolinksi (Workman).

The following information pertains to Anne Marie O'Farrell.

Agent: Anne Marie O'Farrell

email address: amof86@aol.com

Education: BA, Queens College.

Career History: Agent, Denise Marcil Literary Agency, Inc. since 1986; director, Westwinds Learning Center; executive producer, New York Dinner Theater. All of my positions have involved facilitating writers, educators or actors in the creation and marketing of their work.

Hobbies/personal interests: Biking, yoga, traveling, reading, tennis, personal growth.

Categories/subjects that you are most enthusiastic about agenting: Business, psychology, personal growth, health and fitness, cook books, how-to, spirituality/New Age and sports.

Best way for writers to solicit your interest: One-page query letter and SASE with any other relevant credentials sent directly to my office at Anne Marie O'Farrell, 86 Dennis Street, Manhasset, NY 11030. Make sure that your phone number and email address are included.

Reading fees: No.

If you were not an agent, what might you be doing instead: Psychologist.

Representative titles: *Ten-Minute Body Breakthrough* by Sean Foy (Workman Publishing); *Breaking into the Boys' Club* by Molly Shepard, Jane Stimmler, Peter

Dean, PhD (Taylor Trade); *Seth Speaks* and *The Nature of Personal Reality* by Jane Roberts (New World Library); *Hell Yes—Two Little Words for a Simpler, Happier Life* by Elizabeth Baskin (Andrews McMeel); *Think Confident, Be Confident* by Drs. Leslie Sokol and Marci Fox (Perigee); *The Yellow House* by Patricia Falvey (Center Street); *Twinkle, Twinkle Little Star* by Iza Trapani (Charlesbridge).

What do you like best about your clients, and the editors and publishers you work with: I love to work with people who are passionate and knowledgeable about their ideas, who think outside the box, and enjoy brainstorming.

What, if anything, can a writer do to increase the odds of your becoming his or her agent? For a nonfiction title, I find it helpful if the author has given thought to the current competition in his or her subject area and can persuasively defend the need for their book.

Why did I become an agent? I find it extremely fulfilling to help bring new ideas, information and creativity into the world that helps improve and expand humanity's understanding and quality of life.

MARTIN LITERARY MANAGEMENT

321 High School Road NE, Suite D-3, #316, Bainbridge, WA 98110

206-201-3504   206-201-3506 (fax on request only, please—save a tree)

17328 Ventura Blvd., Suite 138, Encino, CA 91316

818-595-1130   fax: on request only

www.MartinLiteraryManagement.com

Agents' names: Sharlene L. Martin, Sharlene@MartinLiteraryManagement.com; Ginny Weissman

The following information pertains to Sharlene Martin.

Born: Feb 8—I'm an Aquarius; New Haven, Connecticut.

Education: BA, University of Bridgeport, UCLA School of Entertainment.

Career history or story: I've always been highly eclectic and entrepreneurial. And although I began working for American Airlines right out of college (I had wanderlust), I became one of 12 nationwide recruiters for flight attendants and was pleased to hire the first males there. I had a great office in the Chrysler Building in NYC and enjoyed giving people a chance to change their lives at 35,000 feet.

I left AAL to start the nation's first American Nanny Agency—Helping Hands, Inc. The universe seemed to pat that endeavor on the back; I won "Entrepreneur of the Year" from *Entrepreneur Magazine*, and Small Businessperson of the Year from the Chamber of Commerce.

In 1989 I sold the company to a competitor, and moved to California. I started a production company with a former network journalist/broadcaster, and was an independent producer for a number of years, in addition to doing freelance casting for independent and feature films. Because of that experience, I was invited to join a reality television production company and spent time doing acquisitions and talent management. It was there that I realized my love of the "business" wasn't about show business—it was about working with passionate and skilled writers. I soon left to start Martin Literary Management. The lovely success that has followed seems a natural result of the fact that I've never been happier in any line of work.

Hobbies, interests: Reading novels on weekends (I read nonfiction all day for work), hiking, visiting my grown kids in Seattle (eight miles across Puget Sound by ferry), great food and occasional travel, provided that it's First Class and Four Stars! Yes, I am a material girl. You will catch me camping out on the same day that you…oh, forget it. It's not going to happen.

Subjects and categories you are interested in agenting, including fiction and nonfiction: Nonfiction ONLY. I love great, narrative nonfiction that is adaptable to film. Within that category, I do meaningful memoirs, fun pop culture subjects, true crime books, business books, how-to books along with self-help (prescriptive) books provided that they are original in tone and do not re-hash familiar material. And of course, I love doing celebrity bios. My New York agent, Ronnie Gramazio, handles all of our fiction work, and Ginny Weissman is our mind, body, and spirit agent.

Subjects and categories writers shouldn't even bother pitching to you: NO Fiction for me—only nonfiction. Also, for similar reasons: NO art books, poetry, essays, or short stories. I regret having to say this, and know that it is discouraging to some writers. You must not give up your work, or your search for representation, if you work in the long forms. However, if you do articles, essays or short stories, I strongly advise you to represent yourself. Just use a clear and concise query letter to editors whom you address by name after learning something of their past work. Impeccable manners help you, even when you are not aware of it. Trust them. People who convince writers to "stand out" by being confrontational or self-pitying in their presentation are giving terrible advice.

Most of all: I don't want anything to do with a neurotic author. If you are crazy, that's not necessarily a problem, just try to hide it. You don't need to fix your problems before I will represent your work, but you do have to keep them away from me. I run a considerate agency with a mandate to treat people as we would wish to be treated, but I draw the line at tolerating any author who tries to put me in a position of fixing his or her life. There are a disappointing number of such people. Professionalism, like the use of good manners, helps you in ways you may never even see, but which are real.

What would you do if you weren't agenting: Sorry, no time to think about it!

What's the best way for nonfiction writers to solicit your interest: Send me an email (no hard-copy letters) with a great query letter. You must learn *how to write* a query letter if you want to be taken seriously. There are plenty of good books on the market that will tell you how. Put all of your query into the *body* of the email (no attachments due to virus risk). If your query is compelling, we will quickly respond with a request for the manuscript or book proposal. Please, no hard copies. We're only dealing electronically these days. If you don't have a computer, you can't be a writer in the 21st century. Electronic writing is essential—especially when editing your book with a publisher.

Do you charge reading or any upfront fees: No.

In your experience, what are the most common pitching mistakes writers make: Biggest mistake: Calling to pitch over the phone. No! "Just wanted to see if you have any interest first…" No! I can't tell how well you write by the sound of your voice. When you take the time to do it right, that sends the signal that you can read and follow directions, which will be of utmost importance to your publishing editor if you're lucky enough to land one. *Hate it* when authors send unsolicited attachments that take forever to download. Failure to address me personally in your query: what, I'm supposed to respect your spam? And finally: If you have not run spellcheck, then you have just told me to turn and run away from you, no matter what words you use in your letter.

Describe the client from hell, even if you don't have any: I really don't have any (anymore), which the testimonials on my website will support. But I suppose it could manifest in any form wherein a writer becomes an energy vortex and attempts to suck time and energy from you when you are already working at capacity. I don't know what can be done with such clueless and self-absorbed people except to cut and run, because in my experience it makes no difference how many times you explain it to them, they always think that their concerns and their problems are exceptions to the rule.

What's your definition of a great client: The writer who understands that my time is valuable and does not waste it. The writer is willing to spend money on a professional editor if needed, or a publicist to ensure the best outcome of our team effort. This person knows that I won't send anything out for submission until it is absolutely ready, and this writer understands that the policy is in *their* own best interest, whether or not it pleases their desire for instant gratification. That ideal writer has a reasonable sense of gratitude to their editor and publisher for giving them the chance to shine in a highly competitive arena, and hopefully to me, after I secure them a book deal.

How can writers increase the odds that you will offer representation: *Do your research.* Invest the time in checking the sites of any agent who will receive your query. Spamming is for idiots. If you have checked it out and know that your work is within the parameters of the things I represent, just write that great query letter I keep mentioning. It *will* be received, it *will* be read, and my agency *will* respond to you. If we are interested, we respond right away. If the work is wrong for us, you will know within a few weeks, at the worst, and usually much less. And finally, *do not call* me on the phone to pitch me—I'm busy selling my clients' work!

Why did you become an agent, and how did you become one: The "why" is simple: I love the written word. Although I was editor of my high school literary magazine, I never realized my passion for books until later in my career. My mate, Anthony Flacco, was already a published author when we met. I fell in love with him—sight unseen—over his written words. We met 15 years ago when I optioned one of his screenplays during my time as an independent producer. After learning a few of his past horror stories with slippery agents, I vowed to be the agent he never had, and to be the same for all my other clients as well. And by the way, I've sold three books for him in the past three years! I want to make a difference in writers' lives by helping them realize their dreams. It's how I realize my own, and this is the path that gets me to that place.

Describe to someone from another planet what you do as an agent: I represent wonderful writers and help to make their literary dreams come true. I do lots of reading, plenty of persuasive selling, and creative career counseling.

How do you feel about editors and publishers: I have always believed that if you cannot love and admire them, then you should please get out of the publishing game. I cannot imagine how they keep up with their workloads, and most of the ones that I've worked with are really smart, curious and interesting people.

How do you feel about writers: I stand in awe of the abilities of the finest among them, people who conjure wonderful phrases and weave imaginative tapestries that most of us would be baffled in attempting to do. The lengths to which they are will to go in order to advance their work can be astonishing. With those writers who deserve the title "author," I take inspiration from their love of the written word when they will pour countless hours and sometimes many years in the quest to perfect their craft. I find it easy to work long and hard for such people.

What do you see in the near future for book publishing: The great unanswered question revolves around self-publishing for the Internet, and the truth is that nobody knows. So far, what we can confirm is that self-publishing is certainly not the albatross around a book's neck that it once was. The term "vanity press" is going out of style. I myself have taken on clients who have self-published, met with moderate success online, and wanted to "go mainstream." One got a book contract for six figures. Now, I do not believe that self-publishing can ever take the place of a mainstream publishing industry, because SOMEBODY has to slog through the avalanche of self-serving nonsense that many people put out in hopes of gaining a lucrative contract with minimal effort. The mainstream publishing business has industry readers to do that. Believe me, you don't want that task dumped on an unsuspecting public.

What are your favorite books, TV shows, movies, and why: TV: *Grey's Anatomy, Entourage, Medium, The Riches*, and almost anything on the Discovery Channel. Books: *The Glass Castle*, by Jeanette Walls, *The Devil Wears Prada*, by Lauren Weisberger, *The Devil in the White City*, by Erik Larson, *The Kite Runner*, by Khaled Hosseini, and *The Last Nightingale*, by Anthony Flacco.

In your opinion, what do editors think of you: I KNOW that they consider me someone who respects their commitment and their boundaries, and who will not approach them with a manuscript or proposal unless I have carefully determined that they would be a good publishing house for that particular piece of work! And, they know when they get a proposal from me, it's a polished, well crafted piece of writing.

On a personal non-professional level, what do you think people think of you:

If they like supportive people who make their own dreams come true by making the dreams of others their concern, then I think that they generally like me just fine. Most say my middle name is "Tenacious."

What are some representative titles that you have sold: *Tiny Dancer* by Anthony Flacco (St. Martin's); *But You Knew That Already* by Dougall Fraser (Rodale); *Front of the Class* by Brad Cohen (VanderWyck & Burnham); *Success Within* by Felicia Wysocky (Champion Press); *You'll Never Nanny in This Town Again* by Suzanne Hansen (Crown, Random House); *Secrets of Voice-Over Success* by Joan Baker (Sentient); *Take Command* by Kelly Perdew (Regnery); *Shopportunity* by Kate Newlin (Collins Business); *Everybody Wants Your Money* by David Latko (Collins Business); *A Place to Go, a Place to Grow* by Lou Dantzler (Rodale); *The Tabloid Prodigy* by Marlise Kast (Running Press); *The Last Nightingale* by Anthony Flacco (Ballantine); *Seven Myths of Modern Judaism* by Rabbi Art Blecher (Palgrave); *Making the Connection* by Leslie Sanchez (Palgrave); *Winning Nice* by Dawna Stone (Center Street); *Getting Sober* by Kelly Madigan (McGraw-Hill); *My Horse, My Partner* by Lisa Wysocky (Lyons Press); *Secret Cyber Lives* by Candice Kelsey (Marlowe); *An Unfinished Canvas* by Phyllis Gobbell and Mike Glasgow (Berkley Publishing); *Stop the Misery* by Dr. Stan Kapuchinski (HCI); *Smotherhood* by Amanda Lamb (Globe Pequot/SKIRT); *Low Carb Reading* by John Heath and Lisa Adams (Sourcebooks); *Hot Flashes with a Cool Beat* by Janet Horn and Robin Miller (New Harbinger); *Humble Little Condom* by Anne Morriss (Prometheus); *Prince of Darkness* by Alan Weisman (Sterling); *Truth at Last* by Lyndon Barsten and John Larry Ray (Lyons Press); *Fur Shui* by Paula Brown (Lyons Press); *Deadly Dose* by Amanda Lamb (Berkley/Penguin); *Street Guide to Scholarships* by Kimberly Ann Stezala (AMACOM); *Metaphysics of Fat* by Catherine Poole (Llewellyn); *Face It* by Babak Azizzadeh and Doug Hamilton (Wiley); *River of No Return* by Jeffrey Ford (Cumberland); *The Bridge* by Michael Glasgow (Thomas Nelson); *If I Did It* by Goldman Family (Beaufort); *Passion Brands* by Kate Newlin (Prometheus); *Smart Mama's Green Guide* by Jennifer Taggert (Center Street); *Crossroads* by Martin Cheek (AMACOM); *I'm Sorry I Missed, Mr. President* by Geri Spieler (Palgrave); *Happily Ever After* by Jessica Bram (HCI); *The Break-Up Chronicles* by Lisa Steadman (Adams Media); *Changing the Odds* by Susan Neuman (Praeger); *Of Wicked Intention* by Kevin Flynn (New Horizon); *The Hidden Man* by Anthony Flacco (Ballantine).

The following information pertains to Ginny Weissman: Mind, Body, Spirit Division.

Born: Nov. 17—I'm a Scorpio. Chicago, Illinois.

Education: Northeastern Illinois University.

Career history or story: Ginny Weissman began her career as a journalist at the *Chicago Tribune*. During her eleven-year tenure at the *Tribune*, she held a variety of management positions including editor of the *TV Week* magazine (circulation 1.2 million). She interviewed hundreds of celebrities and wrote personality profiles and articles about the importance of family programming. She is the author of two critically acclaimed, bestselling books, *The Dick Van Dyke Show, Anatomy of a*

Classic (St. Martin's Press) and *Champagne Music, The Lawrence Welk Show* (St. Martin's Press). As an adjunct professor at Northwestern University, Ginny taught writing for film and television. She believed that the future of the entertainment industry would be determined by the work of today's students and taught ethics and responsibility along with technique. Her numerous television credits include *Investigative Reports, American Justice*, and *The Unexplained* for A&E, *Wrath of God* for The History Channel, *Chicago's Lifeline* for The Discovery Health Channel and *Highway to Heaven* starring Michael Landon for NBC. Ginny was the Supervising Producer and Director for two Emmy Award-winning children's PBS specials and music videos featuring Gaia who sings while performing American Sign Language. She also wrote and produced an Emmy-nominated documentary, *Magic by the Lake: The Edgewater Beach Hotel*, for the PBS series, *Chicago Stories*. In addition, she was a producer for the PBS magazine series, *Chicago Tomorrow*.

Humanitarian work plays a large part in Ginny's life. After the terrorist attacks on September 11, Ginny organized fundraisers for the ASPCA Disaster Fund and Canine Rescue effort. After a trip to Peru, she organized a Christmas toy drive for the children living in poverty near the mountains of Machu Picchu. She is known for her valued, long-time commitment to nonprofit organizations such as the Easter Seal Society and served as co-host for their annual telethons for fifteen years. The Easter Seal Society honored her with the "Communications Award" for outstanding public service supporting the needs and rights of persons with disabilities. She was honored again by The Easter Seal Society with the "Outstanding Service Award" for fifteen years of dedication and service. Ginny also was the recipient of the Mother Theodore Guerin High School McManus Alumna Award which honors an outstanding graduate who has "distinguished herself in service to the community and achievement in her career." Ginny served for eight years on the Board of Governors for the Chicago/Midwest Chapter of the National Academy of Television Arts & Sciences and was elected second vice-president. She has served as a judge for the Emmy Awards, the Humanitas Prize, a prestigious national award for television writing, and Script, a film writing competition held by the Illinois and Chicago Film Offices. She co-founded Windy City West and hosted ten annual parties for transplanted Chicagoans working in the Hollywood entertainment industry, and produced a television special about Windy City West for NBC 5 in Chicago.

Hobbies, interests: I am an animal advocate. I rescue cats and find them good homes. I like to watch movies, mostly romantic comedies, especially about time travel. I exercise every day. My work leaves me very little time for anything but catching up on my reading.

Subjects and categories you are interested in agenting, including fiction and nonfiction: Nonfiction ONLY. I head up the Mind, Body, Spirit Division, which is my favorite genre to read. I am looking for authors who have had life-changing experiences, have a strong platform and want to make a difference in the world.

Subjects and categories writers shouldn't even bother pitching to you: NO fiction. I don't represent novels or children's books, even if they are spiritually based. MOST OF ALL: I am not looking for authors who are trying to publish their journals after years of therapy.

What would you do if you weren't agenting: Producing documentaries (my previous career), volunteering at an animal shelter, or sitting under a palm tree in Maui.

What's the best way for fiction writers to solicit your interest: Ronnie Gramazio, in our NYC office, handles fiction for MLM.

What's the best way for nonfiction writers to solicit your interest: Send me an email with a great query letter. You must learn *how to write* a query letter if you want to be taken seriously. There are plenty of good books on the market that will tell you how. Put all of your query into the *body* of the email—no attachments (virus risk). If your query is compelling, we will quickly respond with a request for the book proposal.

Do you charge reading or any upfront fees: No.

In your experience, what are the most common pitching mistakes writers make: Calling to pitch over the phone. No! "Just wanted to see if you have any interest first…" No! Please take the time to do it right. That sends the signal that you can read and follow directions, which will be of utmost importance to your publishing editor, if you're lucky enough to land one. *Hate it* when authors send unsolicited attachments. I will not download them. Failure to address me personally in your query or include me in a mass mailing. And finally: If you have not run spellcheck, you have told me to turn and run, no matter what words you use in your letter.

Describe the client from hell, even if you don't have any: I have fired two clients who have lied to me and misrepresented themselves. I will NOT tolerate anything but full disclosure and complete honesty in a working relationship.

What's your definition of a great client: That writer understands that my time is valuable and does not waste it. The writer is willing to spend money on a professional editor if needed, or a publicist to ensure the best outcome of our team effort. This person knows that I won't send anything out for submission until it is absolutely ready, and this writer understands that the policy is in *their* own best interest, whether or not it pleases their desire for instant gratification. That ideal writer has a reasonable sense of gratitude to their editor and publisher for giving them the chance to shine in a highly competitive arena, and hopefully to me, after I secure them a book deal. Also, the writer must be willing to work as hard at writing and promoting the book as I do to sell it.

How can writers increase the odds that you will offer representation: *Do your research.* Invest the time in checking out our website before you send your query letter (by email only) and be sure that you know what genre I represent. I am not going to read your query for your novel or children's book or an "idea you are thinking of writing about." And finally, *do not* call me on the phone to pitch me—I'm busy selling my clients' work! We will respond to your query letter by email.

Why did you become an agent, and how did you become one: Sharlene Martin and I have known each other for over 15 years. We have similar backgrounds as TV producers. In November, 2007, she asked me to join Martin Literary Management as the Head of the new Mind, Body, Spirit Division. I had been managing an author and thought it was a perfect fit to take on additional clients. I also like that we are a management company as well, which means we don't stop after selling our client's book. We help our clients continue to build their platform for promoting their book and look for opportunities for film and TV, speaking engagements and future books.

Describe to someone from another planet what you do as an agent: I take someone who has a compelling life experience or a professional background that makes them an expert in a certain field and help them translate that information into a book and platform that will be of interest to a publisher.

How do you feel about editors and publishers: I have found them to be accessible and courteous and willing to give feedback about what the like and don't like in our client's proposal, and also what subjects they are interested in for their own "lists."

How do you feel about writers: I started my career as a writer and editor for the *Chicago Tribune* and have written throughout my career including for television. I also have two published books with St. Martin's Press, *The Dick Van Dyke Show* and *Champagne Music* so they are "my people."

What do you see in the near future for book publishing: I think at this time on the planet when information travels around the world in seconds, traditional publishing seems behind the times. It is difficult to keep a nonfiction book timely when it will not get published for twelve to eighteen months after it is written. I hope that print-on-demand technology and innovative marketing can speed up that process.

What are your favorite books, TV shows, movies, and why: TV: My guilty pleasures are *Desperate Housewives, Dancing with the Stars, Ugly Betty* and *Deal or No Deal*. Books: *Eat, Pray, Love* by Elizabeth Gilbert, *Living an Uncommon Life* by John St. Augustine and anything by Shirley MacLaine or Julia Cameron or Wayne Dyer. Movies: *It's a Wonderful Life, The Way We Were, Hairspray,* and most romantic comedies and time-travel movies. I love to cry and fall in love with the characters. I have no interest in today's silly comedies or high-tech movies.

In your opinion, what do editors think of you: I am fortunate that I have Sharlene Martin's reputation preceding me since she is so well liked and respected, so I am fortunate that some of that spills over on to me.

On a personal non-professional level, what do you think people think of you: I have always made friends easily and have many life-long friendships. I also still keep in touch with colleagues who I have worked with decades ago so I think I can safely say I am easy to get along with and well liked.

E. J. MCCARTHY AGENCY

E. J. McCarthy Agency

1104 Shelter Bay Ave. Mill Valley, CA 94941

212-832-3428 fax: 212-829-9610

Individual agent's name: Mr. E. J. McCarthy

Education: Fairfield College Preparatory School, Fairfield, CT; Fordham University, New York, NY, Bachelor of Arts degree in English.

Career history: Started as editorial assistant in 1988 at Doubleday Book Clubs, editor at Dell Publishing; former executive editor, Presidio Press (Ballantine/Random House). Currently owner of E. J. McCarthy Agency.

Hobbies/personal interests: Media matters, politics and public policy, books, newspapers, magazines, talk radio and sports radio, music of all kinds, television, movies (mostly documentaries), travel, hiking, running, tennis, golf, baseball fan (Giants, A's, and Mets).

Subjects that you would most love to agent: Serious nonfiction, military history, politics, history, biography, memoir, media, sports, literary fiction.

Subjects that you definitely never want to agent: Science fiction, horror, romance, young adult.

If you were not an agent, what would you be doing: I would like to own and operate a publishing house.

What's the best way for unsolicited writers to pitch you: Send an email query to ejmagency@gmail.com.

Do you charge reading fees or try to sell non-agent services (if yes, please describe): No.

Do you require any kind of upfront payments from your clients: No.

Percentage of representation by category: Fiction: 5 percent. Children's: 0 percent. Non-Fiction: 95 percent.

Approximate number of titles sold during the past year: Twelve.

Approximately what percentage of all the submissions you receive do you reject: 99.9 percent.

What are some of the most common mistakes writers make when pitching you: Not getting right to the point having to do with what their book is about. Those who don't know the audience or market for their book ("anyone who reads" doesn't cut it). Neglect to tell me that the project has already been submitted to other agents or to publishers. Expect a response within a day or two. Forget to tell me about author's unique credentials or key contacts.

How would you describe your client from hell: An author who expects miracles as far as publisher promotion; one who has an unrealistic sense of what an agent can do to get a publisher to promote and market their book. An author with an overblown ego. One who sends angry emails, or too many emails (sometimes a friendly phone call will work wonders). An author who asks "Is it my job or your job" questions, for example: "Why should I solicit author blurbs, isn't that the agent's job?"

How would you describe your dream client: Someone who is kind, responsible, hard working, patient, humorous, grateful for how well things are going (and if they're not, gentle suggestions on how to improve things), polite, responsive, friendly, and especially, willing to do whatever it takes to help the book project in any way. A sense of humor is good. And one who refers other promising authors to me—probably the best compliment of all.

How and way did you become an agent: I wanted to be an agent for many years, beginning when I started my career in book publishing. I believed that I would be a good agent because I loved working with authors. I was a passionate advocate for authors when I was an editor. I knew I would enjoy the independence of being an agent. I was confident in my ability to reach a variety of editorial boards at many different publishing houses. In June 2003 I felt the time had come: I believed that I was knowledgeable about the book publishing business, and I couldn't imagine doing anything else with my life. I was lucky that I knew many excellent agents and book publishing people—I met and consulted with several of them before I officially opened shop.

What can writers do to increase the odds that they will get you to be their agent: Follow up the initial submission in about a week or ten days with a polite email. If you don't hear from me quickly, please don't worry—I get several thousand queries each year. An occasional nudge is most welcomed. Please consult books and websites dedicated to writing book proposals (such as Jeff Herman's *Write the Perfect Book Proposal*) before you send anything out. Know your audience, the market, know other successful titles in your subject area. Make sure you communicate to me what your credentials are, and if you know any famous or noted authors, respected public figures, or experts in your field who might provide you with a prepublication endorsement. Have realistic expectations.

How would you actually describe what you do for a living: I work with authors to find the right editor and publisher for their books. I endeavor to ensure that all goes well regarding contracts, payments, royalties, and any important issues regarding the author and publisher. I also spend a lot of time reading and rejecting material.

What do you think about editors and publishers: I respect and admire them. I was an editor for many years; I know it is a demanding job with modest financial compensation. But it has great rewards: i.e., playing an integral role in the editing and publishing of a great book is a wonderful feeling, one you won't forget for the rest of your life. We wouldn't have great books without great editors and great publishers.

Please list representative titles you have sold: *One Bullet Away* by Nathaniel Fick, Houghton Mifflin Harcourt; *The Sling and the Stone* by Thomas X. Hammes, Zenith Press; *Rage Company* by Thomas Daly, John Wiley & Sons, *The Unforgiving Minute* by Craig Mullaney, Penguin Press, *An Angel from Hell* by Ryan A. Conklin, Caliber/Berkley; *A Nightmare's Prayer* by Michael Franzak, Threshold/Simon & Schuster; *Lincoln's Counsel* by Arthur L. Rizer, ABA Books, *The Heart and the Fist* by Eric Greitens, Houghton Mifflin Harcourt.

GERARD MCCAULEY AGENCY

PO Box 844, Katonah, NY 10536.

Phone: 914-232-5700   fax: 914-232-1506

Email: gerrymccauley@@earthlink.net

Agency history: Agency began in September 1970.

Education: University of Pittsburgh; Columbia University (graduate study).

Career history: College textbook sales. Prentice Hall, Inc: Editor. College Department, Alfred A. Knopf., Inc.: Trade Editor. Little, Brown & Company. Literary Agent, Curtis Brown, Ltd. Started own literary agency in 1970.

What categories do you like to agent: General nonfiction and history.

What categories should writers not bother pitching to you: Fiction and children's books

What is the most effective way for writers to grab your attention: Demonstrate narrative talent.

Do you charge fees separate from your commission, or offer non-agenting fee-based services: No fees other than commission.

What are representative titles you have sold to publishers: *The Civil War, Baseball* and *Jazz* by Ken Burns, publisher Alfred A. Knopf; *A World History* and *The Human Web* by William H. McNeill, publisher Oxford and Norton; *Tragedy of American Diplomacy* by William Appleman Williams, publisher Norton; *Polio* by David Oshinsky, publisher Oxford; several nonfiction books and poetry by Donald Hall, publisher Houghton Mifflin.

Why did you become an agent: I prefer literary agents and authors over publishers.

How do you feel about writers: I respect them for their literary talent and intellect.

Finally, will our business exist as we know it in ten years or so: It will not exist they way it has been, and will change as much as it has during the past ten years.

THE MCGILL AGENCY LLC

10000 N. Central Expressway, Suite 400

Dallas, Texas 75231

214-390-5970 info.mcgillagency@gmail.com

Member agents: Jack Bollinger; Amy Cohn

Contact: Query with SASE or email. No phone calls, attachments, or faxes,

Education: Bollinger, MA University of California, Berkley.

Cohn: BA, Boston College, MFA, University of North Carolina.

Career Story: Bollinger: Prior to becoming an agent I worked as a film editor.

Cohn: Prior to becoming an agent, I worked as an editorial director for a regional magazine. From there, I worked several years as the creative director for a medium sized ad agency.

Hobbies and special interests: Bollinger: Golf, tennis, hiking and reading a good book.

Cohn: Travel, jogging, theater, and film.

Subjects and categories: 15 percent commission domestic sales; 20 percent commission foreign sales.

Bollinger: I have eclectic taste in both nonfiction and fiction. I love books as long as they are well-written. [I do] not want to see science fiction, fantasy, erotica.

Cohn: Nonfiction: Women's issues, gay/lesbian, ethnic/cultural issues, memoirs, true crime. Fiction: mystery/suspense/thriller. [I do] not want to see children's books, young-adult, textbooks. For fiction: [I do] not want to see horror, fantasy, science fiction.

Most effective way to grab our attention: Make sure your query letter is brief, compelling, and hard-hitting. For nonfiction: In addition to query letter, include synopsis, sample chapters, biography, qualifications you have for writing book, and a description of marketing platform.

For fiction: In addition to query letter, craft a one-sentence log line that implies what the story is about, synopsis, first three chapters, and brief bio. Query with SASE. No attachments with email queries. Include required query information in body of email.

Fees: We do not charge reading or editorial fees. Charge for photocopying, after accepting someone as a client.

Representative titles: We are a new agency looking for published and unpublished writers with potential.

Writer from hell is someone who has nothing to learn, does not accept advice, and defends their mistakes.

Ten years from now, the publishing industry will have undergone a tremendous upheaval. Younger people who are accustomed to reading off computers, iPods, or book-readers will download their books.

The days of enjoying a glass of wine, while sitting in an easy chair, and reading a good book will be in the province of the elderly.

MENDEL MEDIA GROUP LLC

115 West 30th Street, Suite 800, New York, NY 10001

646-239-9896 fax: 212-695-4717

www.mendelmedia.com email: scott@mendelmedia.com

Agent's name: Scott Mendel, Managing Partner

Born: New York.

Education: AB, Bowdoin College (Brunswick, Maine), MA, University of Chicago, PhD (ABD), University of Chicago.

Career history: With a background in academia, Scott Mendel has worked in publishing since the early 1990s, first as a magazine editor and freelance technical writer and then as an associate and, ultimately, the vice president and director of the late Jane Jordan Browne's Chicago-based literary agency. In November 2002, he opened the Mendel Media Group in New York. Scott holds a bachelor's degree, *summa cum laude*, from Bowdoin College in Brunswick, Maine. He earned a master's degree in English language and literature from the University of Chicago, and is completing his PhD at that institution, with a doctoral dissertation on American Yiddish literature and the meaning of the category "American literature." Scott has taught literature, English, and Yiddish at a number of institutions, including the Choate-Rosemary Hall Preparatory School in Connecticut, the Hyde Park Cluster of Theological Seminaries in Chicago, Bowdoin College, the University of Chicago, and the University of Illinois at Chicago, where he most recently held an appointment as lecturer in Jewish studies. He wrote the book *A Prosecutor's Guide to Hate Crime*, which was published through a grant from the U.S. Department of Justice, and which has been in print in new editions for several years. He has been the managing editor of a monthly and quarterly health care magazine, *Positively Aware*, and editor of the Maine literary journal, *The Quill*, which began publishing in 1897. Scott has written a produced play, several works of fiction, and many book columns, news articles, and opinion pieces. He is a member of the Association of Authors' Representatives, the Author's Guild, the Mystery Writers of America, the Romance Writers of America, the Society of Children's Book Writers & Illustrators, the Modern Language Association, and the American Association of University Professors.

Categories/subjects that you are most enthusiastic about agenting: History, narrative nonfiction, current affairs, biography, politics, popular culture. Smart literary and commercial fiction.

If you were not an agent, what might you be doing instead: I was a college instructor for a number of years before becoming an agent. I'd still be doing that.

What's the best way for writers to solicit your interest: Please follow the procedure below. If we want to read more, we'll ask for it by email or phone. If you would like a response, in the event we can't take on your project or don't want to read more, you should include a pre-addressed return mailer with sufficient return postage already affixed for the return of your materials—or just include a standard self-addressed stamped envelope, in which case we'll respond with a note but discard the submitted materials. Please do not send inquiries by email or fax. Fiction queries: If you have a novel you would like to submit, please send the first twenty pages and a synopsis by regular post to the address above, along with a detailed letter about your publication history and the history of the project, if it has been submitted previously to publishers or other agents. Nonfiction queries: If you have a completed nonfiction book proposal and sample chapters, you should mail those by regular post to the address above, along with a detailed letter about your publication history and the history of the project, if it has been submitted previously to publishers or other agents.

Do you charge reading or management fees: No.

Can you provide an approximation by percent of what you tend to represent by category: My literary agency's clientele includes both fiction writers and nonfiction writers, the latter group comprised mainly of professional journalists and very senior academics writing for the broadest possible trade readership and author-experts writing prescriptive books. On the nonfiction side, I am usually interested in compelling works on history, current events, Jewish topics, personal finance and economics, show business, health, mass culture, sports, politics, science and biography that I believe will find both a wide readership and critical admiration. I represent a number of people who work in the media, generally in the news business.

What are the most common mistakes writers make when pitching you: Instead of going to www.mendelmedia.com/FAQ, they call to ask questions about how to send a query. A surprising number of aspiring writers pitch projects that have been unsuccessfully shopped to numerous houses already, so I always ask if a project has already been submitted to and rejected by publishers. Also, we are pitched projects every day by authors who have work we can't help them with: the agency does not represent children's picture books, cozy mystery novels, poetry, drama, screenplays, or any prescriptive nonfiction projects for which the author does not have established professional expertise and/or media credentials.

How would you describe the perfect client: There are as many "dream" clients as there are writers, I think. I like working for clients who are focused on practical career-related matters. Nothing is less impressive to me than a lack of clear focus on goals and expectations, so my dream clients are clear with me and with themselves about what they want to accomplish. I want to be challenged by my clients' work, by their writing, and not by the drama of everyday life.

Please list representative titles you have sold: First-time novelist Wade Rubenstein, *Gullboy* (Counterpoint Press/Perseus); comedian/screenwriter/novelist Adam Felber, *Schrödinger's Ball* (Villard/Random House); World Trade Center and Jewish Museum Berlin master architect Daniel Libeskind, *Breaking Ground: Adventures in Life and Architecture* (Riverhead/Penguin and numerous publishers around the world); Hoover Institution Senior Fellow and Stanford University professor Larry Diamond, *Squandered Victory: The Story of the Bungled U.S. Attempt to Build Democracy in Iraq* (Times Books/Henry Holt) and Universal Democracy

(Times Books/Henry Holt); University of Chicago Professor Robert A. Pape, *Dying to Win: The Strategic Logic of Suicide Terrorism* (Random House); Dovid Katz, PhD, *Words on Fire: The Unfinished Story of Yiddish* (Basic Books); Behzad Yaghmaian, PhD, *Embracing the Infidel: Stories of Muslim Migrants on the Journey West* (Delacorte/Bantam Dell); National Public Radio national news anchor Nora Raum, *Surviving Personal Bankruptcy* (Gotham/Penguin); Annie Sprinkle, PhD, *Dr. Sprinkle's Spectacular Sex: Make Over Your Love Life with One of the World's Great Experts on Sex* (Tarcher/Penguin; Goldmann/Random House); Active Parenting founder Michael Popkin, PhD, *Parenting the Spirited Child* (Touchstone Fireside/Simon & Schuster); Anne-Marie Cusac, the George Polk and Project Censored Award-winning longtime investigative journalist at *The Progressive* magazine, *Cruel & Unusual: Punishment in America* (Yale University Press); June Skinner Sawyers, *The Beatles: Alone and Together* (Penguin); Bestselling celebrity biographer Mark Bego, *Piano Man: The Life and Times of Billy Joel* (Chamberlain Bros./Penguin); Lisa Rogak, *The Man Behind the DaVinci Code: An Unauthorized Biography of Dan Brown* (Andrews McMeel in the U.S., and many other publishers around the world); *Dr. Robert Atkins: The True Story of the Man Behind the War on Carbohydrates* (Chamberlain Bros./Penguin; UK, Robson Books; Spanish, Random House Mondadori Mexico); and *No Happy Endings: The Life of Shel Silverstein* (St. Martin's Press); Dave DeWitt, the bestselling cookbook author, *The Spicy Food Lover's Bible* (Stewart Tabori & Chang); Ray "Dr. BBQ" Lampe, *Dr. BBQ's Big Time Barbeque: Recipes, Secrets and Tall Tales of a BBQ Champion* (St. Martin's Press); long-time *Kiplinger's Personal Finance* real estate writer Elizabeth Razzi, *The Fearless Home Buyer* and *The Fearless Home Seller* (Stewart Tabori & Chang); novelty and gift book packager Ray Strobel of Strobooks LLC, *The Panda Principles: A Black Eye Isn't the End of the World* (Andrews McMeel); Paulette Wolf & Jodi Wolf, proprietors of the top-shelf event planning firm PWE-E, *Event Planning Made Easy: 7 Simple Steps to Making Your Business or Private Event a Huge Success* (McGraw-Hill); Joanne Jacobs, longtime education writer at the *San Jose Mercury News*, *Our School* (Palgrave Macmillan).

THE MENZA-BARRON AGENCY

511 Avenue of the Americas, #51 New York, NY 10011

212-889-6850

Agents' names: Claudia Menza, Manie Barron

Categories/subjects that you are most enthusiastic about agenting: Menza: African American fiction (literary or commercial), and African American non-fiction. Barron: African American fiction, especially thrillers and paranormal fiction, and African American narrative nonfiction.

What's the best way for writers to solicit your interest: Menza: Query letter with SASE, by snail mail. Barron: Query letter with SASE and a two-chapter sample by snail mail.

Do you charge reading or management fees: No.

THE SCOTT MEREDITH LITERARY AGENCY

200 West 57th Street, Suite 904, New York, NY 10019

646-274-1970

www.scottmeredith.com   info@scottmeredith.com

Agents' names: Arthur Klebanoff

Education: Yale, BA, Harvard Law School, LLB.

Career Story: Co-founder, Morton Janklow Associates; head of publishing for International Management Group; purchased Scott Meredith Literary Agency in 1993; founder, RosettaBooks, an e-book publisher.

Subjects and categories you like to agent: Category leaders in nonfiction.

Subjects and categories writers shouldn't bother pitching to you: First fiction.

Do you charge fees separate from your commission, or offer non-agenting fee-based services: No.

What are representative titles you have sold to publishers (book title, author, publisher): *The Conscience of a Liberal* by Paul Krugman (Norton); *The New American Story* by Bill Bradley (Random House); *10* by Sheila Lukins (Workman); Roger Tory Peterson, *Field Guide to North America* (Houghton Mifflin); *Mayo Clinic Book of Alternative Medicine* (Time Inc. Home Entertainment); *Janson's History of Art* (Prentice Hall).

MEWS BOOKS, LTD.

20 Bluewater Hill. Westport, CT 06880

203 227-1836 fax: 203 227-1144

email: rnewsbooks@aol.com

Agents' names: Sidney B. Kramer; Valerie Seiling Jacobs (Attorney), Associate; Fran Pollak, Associate.

Education: New York University, Brooklyn Law Schoold. St. Lawrence University, JO.

Career history: One of three founders of Bantam Books: Senior vice president (twenty-two years), founder and managing director of Bantam's London subsidiary, Corgi Books; president, New American Library (formerly Penguin Books); consultant and manager. Cassell and Collier MacMillan, London; president and owner of Remarkable Book Shop, Westport. CT: president of Mews Books Ltd.; literary agents and attorney (NY and CT Bar specializing in literary matters).

Categories/subjects that you are most enthusiastic about agenting: Children's books, all ages, that are creative, charming, [with] self-sufficient prose suited to a stated age group. Adult books: Medical and scientific nonfiction, technical and for the layman; cookery; parenting; reference works; nonfiction all subjects. Fiction: All categories but must be outstanding in their genre for plot and writing.

What you don't want to agent: All subjects badly written.

What's the best way for writers to solicit your interest: Must have an outline of the work in a page or two in enough detail (but not too much) so that an editor can pick up the story at any point in the manuscript. No cliffhangers like "The readers will be delighted with the new turn of events, everything turns out well." Don't ask us for editorial advice. We want professional work even from first-timers. Give your background and accreditation and market platform in a separate statement. Send all material by snail mail, not email. Do not send manuscript unless requested. SASE. Queries should be less than a page. We want to know if the work has been submitted elsewhere and with what results. We ask for an exclusive while reading so that we don't spin our wheels and duplicate efforts by others (occasional exceptions for established authors). Tell us what else is out there that's comparable. Tell us if you have been published. Pending contracts will be reviewed and negotiated by an attorney.

Do you charge reading or management fees: No reading fees. If we accept your work we do charge for duplication and some direct office overhead incurred in processing, usually less than $100.

Can you provide an approximation by percent of what you tend to represent by category: Fiction: 20 percent, children's: 40 percent, nonfiction: 20 percent, other: 20 percent.

What are the most common mistakes writers make when pitching you: Unfocused presentations; misspellings: poor grammar in letter. Presentation should be capable of forwarding to an editor.

How would you describe the client from hell: We have none. A disruptive client is invited elsewhere.

How would you describe the perfect client: All our clients are patient and understanding of the publishing process and understand that editors take their time.

How and why did you ever become an agent: A perfect fit for a person with my background; a former publisher and an experienced attorney.

Do you have any particular opinions or impressions of editors and publishers in general: Nice people who are overwhelmed by the flood of unpublishable material and the changing marketplace.

Please list representative titles you have sold: Richard Scarry's children's books (some bilingual); *Susan Love's Breast Books*; *Hotter than Hell* and other cookery titles, Jane Butel; *Overcoming Impotence*, Dr. J. Stephen Jones; Tom Wolsky technical media computer books; math series, Debra Ross; *When Bad Grammar Happens to Good People*, Ann Batko; Dr. Gilbert Rose's psychiatry books; Marsha Temlock's *Your Child's Divorce: What to Expect—What You Can Do*; Steve Elman and Alan Tolz's *Burning Up the Air*; Bill Littlefield's *Prospect*, novel and film option.

NELSON LITERARY AGENCY, LLC

1732 Wazee Street, Suite 207, Denver, CO 80202

www.nelsonagency.com

Visit our website before submitting. Email queries and electronic submissions only. Member: Association of Authors' Representatives, Romance Writers of America, Science Fiction & Fantasy Writers of America, SCBWI.

Agent's name: Kristin Nelson (president and senior literary agent), Sara Megibow (associate literary agent).

The following applies to Kristen Nelson.

Education: BA University of Missouri—Columbia; MA Purdue University.

Career history or story: The Nelson Agency was established in 2002. Before that, founding literary agent Kristin Nelson worked for Jody Rein Books. She went on her own to represent all types of fiction—including genre fiction like SF&F and romance.

Subjects and categories you are interested in agenting, including fiction and nonfiction: The Nelson Literary Agency represents primarily fiction works in the genres of romance (all subgenres except category and inspirational), science fiction, fantasy, young adult, middle grade, women's fiction, chick lit (including mysteries), commercial and literary fiction. We also represent some memoir. We are looking for a unique concept and outstanding writing.

Subjects and categories writers shouldn't even bother pitching to you: We don't represent thrillers, nonfiction (except memoir), gift books, cookbooks, picture books or mysteries (except chick lit).

What's the best way for fiction writers to solicit your interest: We do not accept any queries by snail mail, phone or in person. We are a paper-free office. Please visit our website first and then send us an email query letter. If we are interested in your material, we'll email detailed instructions on how to upload your sample pages or proposal to our secure electronic submissions database. We do not accept any queries or materials by snail mail. All materials sent by snail mail will be returned unread.

What's the best way for nonfiction writers to solicit your interest: See above.

Do you charge reading or any upfront fees: No. Any reimbursed expenses are after a work has sold and [are] deducted from a publisher payment.

In your experience, what are the most common pitching mistakes writers make: Mistakes: 1) Not nailing the pitch blurb in the query letter (or not having a clear story hook); 2) Describing a work as every genre under the sun. What that signals is that you don't have an understanding of your work's place in the market; 3) Antagonistic or whining queries.

Describe the client from hell, even if you don't have any: We've been lucky. We truly enjoy all our clients. However, a client from hell would be one who is not Internet- or tech-savvy (and refuses to work at becoming so).

What's your definition of a great client: Someone who is serious about the business of writing and publishing, who is tech-savvy, and is willing to go the distance to promote his or her work. And, he or she writes like a dream and is fast—at least a book a year.

How can writers increase the odds that you will offer representation: Write a terrific novel.

Describe to someone from another planet what you do as an agent: We represent and advocate for authors by placing their materials in front of publishers, negotiating the deal (and watching out for the author's interests), trouble-shooting during the publishing process, and then guiding that author's career.

What are your favorite books, TV shows, movies, and why: A&E's *Pride and Prejudice, Almost Famous, Casablanca, Clueless, Age of Innocence, Enchanted April, Undercover Brother, Star Wars, Lord of the Rings*, any Doris Day movie.

In your opinion, what do editors think of you: Nice but one tough negotiator.

What are some representative titles that you have sold: *Hotel on the Corner of Bitter and Sweet* by Jamie Ford (Ballantine); *Demon's Lexicon* by Sarah Rees Brennan (Simon & Schuster); *Soulless* by Gail Carriger (Orbit); *The Shifter* by Janice Hardy (HarperCollins); *I'd Tell You I Love You But Then I'd Have to Kill You* and *Cross My Heart and Hope to Spy* by Ally Carter (Hyperion Books for Children); *Enchanted Inc., Once Upon Stilettos* and *Damsel Under Stress* by Shanna Swendson (Ballantine); *Code of Love* and *The Winter Prince* by Cheryl Sawyer (New American Library); *Finders Keepers, Gabriel's Ghost, An Accidental Goddess, Games of Command* by Linnea Sinclair (Bantam Spectra); *No Place Safe* by Kim Reid (Kensington); *Prime Time* by Hank Phillippi Ryan (Harlequin); *Magic Lost, Trouble Found* by Lisa Shearin (Ace, Berkley); *Rumble on the Bayou* by Jana Deleon.

NORTHERN LIGHTS LITERARY SERVICES LLC

11248 North Boyer Avenue, Sandpoint, Idaho 83864

888-558-4354

www.northernlightsls.com

Agent's name: Sammie Justesen, sammie@northernlightsls.com

Born: Born in Bedford, Indiana. Let's forget the year!

Education: Purdue University, Indiana University, Harvard (one great year).

Career story: I worked as a registered nurse for over twenty years, but couldn't stay away from writing. I became a clinical editor for Mosby, then worked as a freelance editor and writer for other medical publishers. I edited fiction for several years until several clients asked me to represent them with publishers. I opened Northern Lights Literary Services in 2004 and began selling books. Though we left the east coast and moved to northern Idaho, the Internet allows us to compete with New York agencies.

Hobbies and special personal interests: Reading (of course), watercolor painting, photography, swimming, and watching wildlife from our office in northern Idaho (moose, bear, elk, turkey, and eagles).

Subjects and categories you like to agent: We accept fiction and nonfiction in almost any category, as long as it's well written and marketable.

Subjects and categories writers shouldn't bother pitching to you: We don't accept erotica, fantasy, poetry, horror, or children's and young-adult books.

What might you be doing if you weren't agenting: I'd try and make a living with my artwork, which is even harder than succeeding as a writer. I must be a masochist.

What's the most effective ways for writers to grab your attention: I prefer email queries, well written and to the point. Write your query with a confident voice; don't run yourself down, but don't oversell your book either. Let the writing speak for itself.

Do you charge fees separate from your commission, or offer non-agenting fee-based services: No.

What are representative titles you have sold to publishers: *Intuitive Parenting* by Debra Snyder PhD (Beyond Words); *The Happiness Trap Pocketbook* by Russ Harris MD (Exisle); *The Confidence Trap* by Russ Harris MD (Penguin Australia); *The Never Cold Call Again Toolkit* by Frank Rumbauskas Jr. (Wiley); *Over-the-Counter Natural Cures* by Shane Ellison (Sourcebooks); *Carry a Chicken in Your Lap* by Bruce Johnson and William Ayres (St. Martin's Press); *The Road to Fruition: Recipes from the Smokey Mountains* by Joan Aller (Andrews McMeel); *Kentucky Moon* by Elizabeth Lee (NorlightsPress.com).

Why did you become an agent, and how did you become one: I became an agent because I love discovering new projects and bringing authors and editors together. I crave those moments when I call an author and say, "I have an offer for your book!"

How do you feel about writers: My best friends are writers! I'm a writer! I love writers!

What do you tell entities from other planets and dimensions about your job: On this planet, millions of beings torture themselves by creating books they hope other humans will read. I try and sell those books to harried editors who hope the public will open their wallets. Beam me up, Scottie!

What are your favorite books, movies, TV shows, and why: I'm a junkie for self-help books and also love mysteries, memoirs, and biographies. I probably own every how-to-paint watercolor book ever written. I don't watch much television, but I like movies that are cerebral enough to hold my interest. No comic book derivatives, please! My favorite media provides entertainment, teaches me something, and inspires me.

How would you describe the writer from hell: Writers from hell go ballistic when I respond to a query with helpful suggestions. Their friends love the book, so it's perfect. Clients from hell expect to hear from me every other day and don't trust me to do my job. Luckily I don't encounter many of these folks. Most writers are great.

How would you describe the publisher and/or editor from hell: Editors and publishers are wonderful; often overworked and underpaid. I mutter and complain when they hold manuscripts for months without responding, but I understand why that happens.

What do you like best about your clients, and the editors and publishers you work with: The camaraderie of working together to create books people fall in love with.

Will our business exist as we know it in ten years or so: The Internet will continue changing the world, but I hope people will never stop reading.

ALLEN O'SHEA LITERARY AGENCY

615 Westover Road, Stamford, CT 06902

203-359-9965   fax: 203-357-9909

www.allenoshea.com

www.publishersmarketplace.com/members/AllenOShea

email: marilyn@allenoshea.com

Agent's name: Marilyn Allen
Education: Trained as an English teacher.
Career history: I worked for many years on the publishing side in senior sales and marketing positions for Warner, Penguin, Simon & Schuster, and HarperCollins.
Hobbies/personal interests: Travel, reading, tennis.

Categories/subjects that you are most enthusiastic about agenting: Non-fiction: Health, parenting, business, cooking, lifestyle, history, narrative nonfiction.

Subjects and categories writers shouldn't even bother pitching to you: Poetry, children's, fiction, memoirs.

If you were not an agent, what might you be doing instead: Running marketing department for a publisher or teaching literature.

What's the best way for fiction writers to solicit your interest: Not my area of interest.

What's the best way for nonfiction writers to solicit your interest: Email me.

Do you charge reading or any upfront fees: Never.

What are the most common mistakes writers make when pitching you: Failure to research competition and no marketing plans.

Describe the client from hell, even if you don't have any: A client who has unreasonable expectations about the industry; expects things like a quick sale to a publisher, a large advance, extensive marketing and book reviews.

What's your definition of a great client: A great client is a writer who creates a smart proposal, understands his audience and the marketplace and works collaboratively with me. Love writers who are experts in their field and have cutting-edge research.

How and why did you ever become an agent: I became an agent because I like to work with writers. I started my agency after a long publishing career.

What, if anything, can a writer do to increase the odds of your becoming his or her agent: Send me a good proposal with a fresh new idea. I love submissions that are complete and well thought out. Remember, this is a business, so act professionally.

How would you describe to someone (or something) from another planet what it is that you do as an agent: I help writers shape their book projects, then find them a publishing home and do everything in between.

How do you feel about editors and publishers: Really love working with most of them.

How do you feel about writers: Really love working with most of them.

What do you see in the near future for book publishing: Fewer books being published. E-book sales increasing.

What are your favorite books, movies, TV shows, and why: I have so many favorite books. I just finished *The Story of Edgar Sawtelle* by David Wroblewski and loved it. I look forward to vacation so that I can select books I want to read for pleasure. I enjoy the History Channel and Travel Channel.

In your opinion, what do editors think of you: They trust me and like to work with me. I have a marketing background and they often look to me for ideas. I solve problems for them.

On a personal non-professional level, what do you think people think of you: They think I'm fun and collegial.

Please list representative titles you have sold: Many books sold. Please check our Web page.

THE PARK LITERARY GROUP, LLC

270 Lafayette Street, Suite 1504, New York, NY 10012

212-691-3500   fax: 212-691-3540

www.parkliterary.com

The Park Literary Group was founded in January 2005, when Theresa Park and several colleagues left the venerable literary agency, Sanford J. Greenburger Associates. Theresa had been an agent at Greenburger for more than ten years, but at the age of 37 was eager to try building a new venture. A full-service literary agency, The Park Literary Group represents fiction and nonfiction with a boutique approach: an emphasis on servicing a relatively small number of clients, with the highest professional standards and focused personal attention. With a full-time foreign rights director and excellent relationships with film and television co-agents in Los Angeles, the agency brings to bear excellent resources and a wealth of experience in exploiting all rights associated with an author's work.

Agents' names: Theresa Park, Abigail Koons, Amanda Cardinale.

Education: Theresa Park: BA, University of Santa Cruz; JD, Harvard Law School. Abigail: BA, Boston University. Amanda: BA, Barnard College. Emily Sweet: Denison University; JD, University of Maryland.

Career history:

The following information pertains to Theresa Park.

Theresa began her career as a literary agent at Sanford J. Greenburger Associates in 1994. (Prior to that, she was an attorney at Cooley Godward, a Silicon Valley law firm.) She represents a mixture of plot-driven fiction and serious nonfiction. Some of her clients include Nicholas Sparks, Debbie Macomber, Emily Giffin, Laura Zigman, Janice Y. K. Lee, Juliette Fay, Linda Nichols, Robert Whitaker, Lee Silver, B.R. Myers, and Thomas Levenson. A graduate of U.C. Santa Cruz and Harvard Law School, she is married to Greg Irikura, a photographer, and has two children.

The following information pertains to Abagail Koons.

Eager to work with emerging and established talent, Abigail is currently looking to add to her list of diverse and engaging authors. Her passion for travel makes her a natural fit for adventure and travel narrative nonfiction, and she is also seeking projects about popular science, history, politics, current events and art. She is also interested in working with commercial fiction. As the Foreign Rights Director, she continues to build on her prior experience with agent Nicholas Ellison, as well as her time with EF Education, a multinational corporation based in Sweden. Abigail is a graduate of Boston University.

The following information pertains to Amanda Cardinale.

Amanda joined the Park Literary Group in early 2008. She is interested in representing a wide range of fiction and nonfiction from talented new voices. Her fiction interests include commercial, literary, and international fiction. She also seeks provocative nonfiction in the areas of popular culture, entertainment, art, and journalism that focuses on human issues. Drawing on her love of cuisine, Amanda is also interested in food narratives. Amanda graduated from Barnard College with BA in European history. Prior to joining the Park Literary Group, she worked at International Creative Management and Sterling Lord Literistic.

The following information pertains to Emily Sweet.

After five and a half years practicing law at King & Spalding in Washington DC, Emily joined the Park Literary Group as the director of business affairs in early 2009. While she does not represent clients, Emily provides legal and business support to the agency, and serves as the liaison to the film and media industries with the goal of helping our clients fully develop their careers. An avid reader of both nonfiction and fiction, particularly biographies, mysteries, and historical and contemporary fiction, she enjoys working in a creative industry. After receiving a BA in political science and women's studies from Denison University in Granville, Ohio, Emily later earned her JD from the University of Maryland School of Law.

Categories/subjects you are most enthusiastic about agenting: Theresa: Commercial fiction (thrillers, love stories, historical novels, etc.) and serious nonfiction (including narrative history, science, memoir, serious psychology, history and biography.) Abigail: Commercial fiction (thrillers and quirky comedies) and nonfiction (science, political science, art and art history, and business). Amanda: Commercial, literary, and international fiction; and nonfiction (popular culture, entertainment, art, and journalism).

What you don't want to agent: Theresa: Cookbooks, diet books, fitness, children's books, humor. Abigail: Young adult, psychology, romance, Westerns. Amanda: Young adult, children's, science fiction/fantasy, self-help.

If you were not an agent, what might you be doing instead: Theresa: I can't imagine doing anything else—I really love being an agent, and feel privileged to be able to follow my passion. Shannon: This is my career of choice and I'm thrilled to be doing it. Abigail: In that fantasy world where no one has a full-time job, I would spend my days traveling and reading. This is the next best thing.

What's the best way for writers to solicit your interest: A one-page letter, brief synopsis, and one to three chapters, snail-mailed (NOT emailed), with an SASE.

Do you charge reading or management fees: No—never.

Can you provide an approximation by percent of what you tend to represent by category: Fiction: 50 percent, nonfiction: 50 percent.

What are the most common mistakes writers make when pitching you: Poor grammar and spelling in written materials. Gimmicky attempts to attract attention through means other than a professional query. Overly aggressive or unprofessional behavior.

How would you describe the perfect client: Professional, disciplined, hardworking, emotionally stable, great people skills and social judgment, down-to-earth, direct.

How and why did you ever become an agent: Theresa: I love books, I love to work with people, and I love to do deals! Also, given my background as a transactional lawyer, it seemed like the right area of publishing for me. One of the best things about being a lawyer was having clients—I enjoy getting to know people and working closely with them on their manuscripts and proposals; the personal rewards of watching a client's career blossom are the best part of my job. Shannon: As an agent, I have the opportunity not only to do all of the things I would gladly do for free (reading, writing, editing) but also work with extremely talented and creative people—authors, editors, publishers. The idea of finding something relatively raw and working with the author and the project through publication remains both a thrill and a great privilege. Abigail: After dabbling in law and international economics, I decided that my career needed a healthy dose of creativity to balance out the business aspects. Being an agent allows me to utilize my business and organizational skills while working with truly wonderful clients and fascinating projects every day.

What, if anything, can a writer do to increase the odds of your becoming his or her agent: Be professional; send concise, effective query letters.

How would you describe to someone (or something) from another planet what it is that you do as an agent: We are advocates for and advisors to writers—in addition to each acting as a salesperson, negotiator and long-term strategist.

Do you have any particular opinions or impressions of editors and publishers in general: Their quality and commitment to authors varies widely—it is impossible to generalize.

Please list representative titles you have sold: Theresa: *The Notebook, Message in a Bottle, A Walk to Remember, The Rescue, A Bend in the Road, Nights in Rodanthe, The Guardian, The Wedding, Three Weeks With My Brother, True Believer, At First Sight, Dear John, The Choice* (Warner Books); *Piece of Work* (Warner Books); *Inamorata* (Viking); *Handyman* (Delacorte), *Not a Sparrow Falls, If I Gained The World, At the Scent of Water, In Search of Eden* (Bethany House); *Doomed Queens* (Broadway); *Challenging Nature: The Clash of Science and Spirituality at the New Frontiers of Life* (Ecco); *The Lost Men: The Harrowing Saga Of Shackleton's Ross Sea Party* (Viking); *A Reader's Manifesto* (Melville House); *Remember Me: A Lively Tour of the New American Way of Death* (Collins). Shannon: *I Like Food, Food Tastes Good: In the Kitchen With Your Favorite Bands* (Hyperion). Abagail: *Shop Naked: The History of Catalogs* (Princeton Architectural Press).

THE RICHARD PARKS AGENCY

The Richard Parks Agency, P.O. Box 693, Salem, NY 12865

518-854-9466

www.richardparksagency.com

Individual agent name: Richard Parks

Date and location of birth: Jacksonville, Florida.

Education: BA Duke University, MA University of North Carolina.

Career Story: I stumbled into the agency business when I took a part-time summer job at Curtis Brown, Ltd. By the end of the summer, I was hooked. I was at CB for nine years, then left to spend several years working in the movie business, first as an executive at United Artists and then as an independent producer. I produced two movies for HBO, but didn't much like it and decided to return to New York and the agency business. I opened my own agency there in 1989. Two years ago, thanks to technology, I shifted my headquarters to the village upstate where I've had a second home for quite some time. I now spend two days a week in New York and five upstate.

Hobbies and special personal interests: Gardening while listening to recorded books.

Subjects and categories you like to agent: Literary and commercial fiction (including mystery, thrillers and suspense), narrative nonfiction, biography, memoir, history, travel narratives, popular science, parenting, light business, some prescriptive nonfiction.

Subjects and categories writers shouldn't bother pitching to you: Romance fiction, Western fiction. Highly technical business or science.

What might you be doing if you weren't agenting: Teaching.

What's the most effective ways for writers to grab your attention: I read mostly by referral, but a really good query letter will sometimes catch my eye.

Do you charge fees separate from your commission, or offer non-agenting fee-based services: I only ask clients to reimburse me for special expenses that I've incurred on their behalf, such as if they ask me to send something to them by Fed Ex. I do not charge reading fees or any other kinds of fees.

What are representative titles you have sold to publishers: *Chronic City*, Jonathan Lethem, Doubleday; *The Ballad of West 10th Street*, Marjorie Kernan, HarperPerennial; *A Million Nightingales*, Susan Straight, Pantheon; *The Ghost in Love*, Jonathan Carroll, Sarah Crichton Books/FSG; *The Gerbil Farmer's Daughter, A Memoir*, Holly Robinson, Harmony Books; *7 Steps to Raising a Bilingual Child*, Naomi Steiner, MD, AMACOM; *The Age of Dreaming*, Nina Revoyr, Akashic Books; *South by South Bronx*, Abraham Rodriguez, Akashic Books; *What Ever Happened to Orson Welles?*, Joseph McBride, The University Press of Kentucky; *Deep Focus*, Sean Howe, editor, Soft Skull Press.

Why did you become an agent, and how did you become one: See #5 above for how. I became an agent because, once I discovered the business, I loved working with writers. And I've always been an avid reader.

How do you feel about writers: They enhance our lives, giving us insight and knowledge, and showing us the world from perspectives other than our own.

What do you tell entities from other planets and dimensions about your job: I don't have conversations with entities from other planets!

What are your favorite books, movies, TV shows, and why: There are so many books I love that it's hard to list favorites. I like movies with some substance, not the big action adventure stuff or date comedies. I'm not much of a television watcher at all.

How would you describe the writer from hell: Fortunately, I've rarely encountered one.

How would you describe the publisher and/or editor from hell: Again, perhaps I've been lucky, but I haven't encountered many. Most of the publishers and editors I've dealt with are bright, professional people. I do dislike editors who don't respond to legitimate phone calls, emails, or submissions, and I have encountered a few of those.

What do you like best about your clients, and the editors and publishers you work with: The fact that they are bright, interesting people who enliven my life.

You're welcome to share your thoughts and sentiments about the business of writing and publishing: As we all know, we're going through a difficult time in publishing, along with difficult times in general. But it's not a business that's going to go away. It will evolve and continue to provide readers with entertainment and enlightenment.

Do you wish to describe who you are: I'm a steady, easy-going person who loves his work and the friends he has made through it.

Finally, will our business exist as we know it in ten years or so: Some aspects of our business will remain the same, but it's going to change dramatically as electronic publishing continues to grow.

PMA LITERARY AND FILM MANAGEMENT, INC.

45 W. 21st St., 4th Floor, New York, NY 10010

212-929-1222   fax: 212-206-0238

Agent's name: Peter Miller
Born: Atlantic City, New Jersey.
Education: BA, Monmouth University.
Career story: Known as the "Literary Lion," Peter Miller has been an extraordinarily active literary and film manager for more than thirty years. He is President

of PMA Literary and Film Management, Inc. and Millenium Lion, Inc.; he and his company have successfully managed over 1,000 books worldwide as well as dozens of motion picture and television properties. These works include sixteen *New York Times* bestsellers, and fifteen produced films that Miller has managed or executive produced. Three of those films have been nominated for a total of seven Emmy Awards: *Goodbye, Miss Fourth of July* (The Disney Channel, four nominations); *A Gift of Love* (Showtime, two nominations); and *Helter Skelter* (CBS, one nomination). In addition, Miller has a number of film and television projects currently in active development, with some nearing production, in association with Warner Bros. Features, Sony Pictures Television, Warner Bros. Television, DreamWorks and many other producers and production companies.

Hobbies and special personal interests: I collect statues and images of lions, which have been celebrated by man since the beginning of time. I also enjoy traveling, films, wine and adventure.

Subjects and categories you like to agent: Quality fiction and narrative nonfiction with global marketing and motion picture and television production potential.

Subjects and categories writers shouldn't bother pitching to you: Poetry, pornography or anything low- or mid-list.

What might you be doing if you weren't agenting: I would probably be an antique dealer.

What's the most effective ways for writers to grab your attention: By writing a powerful, succinct, and perfect email or pitch letter.

Do you charge fees separate from your commission, or offer non-agenting fee-based services: No.

What are representative titles you have sold to publishers: Nonfiction: *The Element* by Sir Ken Robinson and Lou Aronica (Viking); *Strategic Acceleration* by Tony Jeary (Vanguard Press/Perseus Book Group); *Ten Prayers God Always Says Yes To* by Anthony DeStefano (Doubleday Religion); *Nathan Hale* by M. William Phelps (Thomas Dunne Books/St. Martin's Press). Fiction: *The Christmas Cookie Club* by Ann Pearlman (Atria/Simon & Schuster); *The Compass* by Tammy Kling and John Spencer Ellis (Vanguard Press/Perseus Book Group); *No More Good* by Angela Winters (Dafina/Kensington); *A Twisted Ladder* by Rhodi Hawk (Tor); *Perfect Victim* by Jay Bonansinga (Kensington); *Where There's a Witch* (Bewitching Mysteries #5) by Madelyn Alt (Berkeley/Penguin).

Why did you become an agent, and how did you become one: When I moved to New York many moons ago, I was producing an off-off-Broadway production. I then met a Broadway producer and we decided to start a literary agency. I never looked back.

How do you feel about writers: I have the utmost respect for writers, as they are the true geniuses in society.

What do you tell entities from other planets and dimensions about your job: I would tell them to write something special so I could be the literary manager of the first alien to get published in America.

What are your favorite books, movies, TV shows: *Being There* by Jerzy

Kosinski and *Steppenwolf* by Hermann Hesse; Movies: *Dr. Zhivago, The Godfather, Austin Powers, Juno* and *The Departed*; TV shows: *Boston Legal, Entourage,* and *The Sopranos.*

How would you describe the writer from hell: One that doesn't know how to communicate but doesn't stop trying to communicate with us.

How would you describe the publisher and/or editor from hell: One that makes an offer during an auction and then disappears.

What do you like best about your clients, and the editors and publishers you work with: I like the truly talented authors that we manage that just allow me to do my job and the publishers that do everything they say they're going to do.

You're welcome to share your thoughts and sentiments about the business of writing and publishing: Fortunately, having spent 30 years in the industry, I've learned how to grow with ever-constant sea changes like the one we are presently experiencing in the digital delivery of content.

Do you wish to describe who you are: I'm a passionate intellectual-property developer who loves to get six-figure advances for his clients. My favorite two words are "bidding war."

Will our business exist as we know it in ten years or so: Absolutely.

THE AARON PRIEST AGENCY

708 3rd Avenue, 23rd Floor, New York, NY 10017

212-818-0344   fax: 212-573-9417

www.aaronpriest.com

Agency history: Established in 1974. Member of AAR. Handles about 75 percent fiction and 25 percent nonfiction.

Agents' names: Aaron Priest, Lisa Erbach Vance, Lucy Childs, Nicole Kenealy

Categories/subjects that you are most enthusiastic about agenting: Aaron Priest: Thrillers, commercial fiction, biographies.

Lisa Erbach Vance: General fiction, international fiction, thrillers, upmarket women's fiction, historical fiction, narrative nonfiction, memoir.

Lucy Childs: Literary and commercial fiction, memoir, edgy women's fiction.

Nicole Kenealy: Young-adult fiction, nonfiction (narrative, how-to, political, and pop culture), literary and commercial fiction (specifically dealing with social and cultural issues).

For all four agents: No poetry, no screenplays, and no sci-fi.

What's the best way for writers to solicit your interest: How to contact: Email a query to one of our agents using the email address listed below. Please do not submit to more than one agent at this agency. (We urge you to check our website and consider each agent's emphasis before submitting.) Your query letter should be about one page long, and describe your work as well as your background. You may also paste the first chapter of your work in the body of the email. Do not send attachments. We will respond within three weeks, but only if interested.

Aaron Priest: querypriest@aaronpriest.com
Lisa Erbach Vance: queryvance@aaronpriest.com
Lucy Childs: querychilds@aaronpriest.com
Nicole Kenealy: querykenealy@aaronpriest.com
Do you charge reading or management fees: No.
Recent sales: *Divine Justice* by David Baldacci, *The White Mary* by Kira Salak, *Long Lost* by Harlan Coben, *An Accidental Light* by Elizabeth Diamond, *Trust No One* by Gregg Hurwitz, *Power Down* by Ben Coes.

SUSAN ANN PROTTER, LITERARY AGENT

110 West 40th Street, Suite 1408, New York, NY 10018

212-840-0480

Agent's name: Susan Ann Protter

Career history: Associate director, Subsidiary Right Department, Harper & Row Publishers, Inc.; founded Susan Ann Protter Agency in 1971.

Hobbies/personal interests: Sailing, opera, travel, languages, dogs and pets, tennis.

Categories/subjects that you are most enthusiastic about agenting: Fiction: Suspense including mysteries and thrillers; women's fiction; commercial science fiction and fantasy. Nonfiction by recognized experts only in the following areas: General and women's health; parenting; how-to; popular science and medicine; memoir; biography; history; Middle Eastern subjects; books by established journalists.

What you don't want to agent: Romance, Westerns, children's books, high fantasy, horror, and textbooks.

What's the best way for writers to solicit your interest: One-page query letter with SASE (no email), which gives overview, brief synopsis, author's background. If interested, we will request first thirty pages and outline with SASE. No reply without SASE.

Do you charge reading or management fees: No reading fee.

Can you provide an approximation by percent of what you tend to represent by category: Nonfiction: 45 percent, fiction: 55 percent.

What are the most common mistakes writers make when pitching you: They do not do their homework.

What, if anything, can a writer do to increase the odds of your becoming his or her agent: As an agent, I am looking for writers who genuinely care about their craft but understand current commercial trends as well. It is important that we share the same visions and goals regarding their work.

Please list representative titles you have sold: *20 Teachable Virtues* (Perigree); *Einstein for Dummies* (Wiley); *Understanding Islam* (Plume/Penguin); *Flowers: How They Changed the World* (Prometheus Books); *Getting Organized* and *The Organized Executive* (Warner Books); *Growing and Changing* (Perigree); *House of Storms* (Ace); *The House of God* (St. Martin's/Delta); *The Last Secret* (Midnight Ink/Llewellyn); *Mass Hate* (Perseus); *Mad Professor* (Thunders Mouth Press); *Night Falls on Damascus* (Thomas Dunne Books); *Operation Solomon: The Evacuation of the Ethiopian Jews to Israel* (Oxford); *The Real Vitamin and Mineral Book* (Avery/Penguin); *The Space Opera Renaissance* (Tor).

THE QUADRIVIUM GROUP

7512 Dr. Phillips Boulevard, Suite #50-229, Orlando, FL 32819

407-516-1857

www.TheQuadriviumGroup.com

Agent's name: Steve Blount, SteveBlount@TheQuadriviumGroup.com
Born: Waycross, GA.
Education: BBA, The University of Georgia; MBA, Thunderbird School of Global Management.
Career history: After ten years in banking (profitability analyst, strategic planner, mergers and acquisitions), I made the jump into Christian publishing and retail (LifeWay), starting out on the corporate side doing strategic planning, but soon getting into product development, marketing, and sales for the core publishing business. After a successful decade there, I became COO of a faith-based marketing firm that represented major ministry clients such as Billy Graham, Joyce Meyer, Joel Osteen, T. D. Jakes, and more. I've always enjoyed helping those with a compelling message to reach their audiences, whether as their publisher, book marketer, media consultant, or agent.
Categories/subjects that you are most enthusiastic about agenting: Christian nonfiction, Christian/inspirational fiction, crossover books.
What you don't want to agent: Poetry.
If you were not an agent, what might you be doing instead: I'd find some other way to help people with compelling life stories or other great messages to reach their audiences.
What, if anything, can a writer do to increase the odds that you will become his or her agent: A great proposal, including a powerful hook.
Do you charge fees separate from your commission, or offer non-agenting fee-based services : Only extraordinary costs with client's permission; no reading fees.
How and why did you ever become an agent: After leaving publishing, a

number of my authors and publishing colleagues encouraged me to become an agent. There seemed to be a need for someone who understood the inner workings of the business to help authors with compelling life stories and ideas to navigate through the often difficult publishing process.

QUICKSILVER BOOKS LITERARY AGENTS

508 Central Park Avenue, #5101, Scarsdale, NY 10583

tel/fax: 914-722-4664

www.quicksilverbooks.com   email: quickbooks@optonline.net

Agent's name: Bob Silverstein, President
Born: October 3, 1936; New York, New York.
Education: BA, City College of New York.
Career history: Bob Silverstein is president of Quicksilver Books, a literary agency and former book packaging and publishing firm established in 1973. QB is responsible for the creation of many national and international bestsellers, including novelized versions of such highly acclaimed films as *The Last Tango in Paris, Shampoo,* and *Chariots of Fire.* All of these titles were published in the U.S. and Canada as Dell/Quicksilver paperbacks. For more than 35 years, Mr. Silverstein has successfully divided his career between books and movies. After graduation from the City College of New York and post-graduate work in comparative literature at the City University of New York (Hunter College), he entered publishing as an associate editor with Gold Medal Books and later became an editor of the Crest and Premier divisions of Fawcett Publications. Between 1962 and 1965, Mr. Silverstein served as managing editor of Dell Books and as senior editor of the newly formed Delacorte Press. In 1965 he joined Anthony Quinn Productions as associate producer and story editor, assisting the actor in preparing his autobiography as well as shaping screenplays for production in the U.S. and Europe. From 1967 to 1970, Mr. Silverstein was senior unit publicist for United Artists and MGM on major motion pictures filmed on location throughout Europe. In this capacity he worked closely with producers Carlo Ponti, David Wolper, Harry Belafonte, and others. Mr. Silverstein has also co-produced several independent documentary and feature films, as well as a number of television commercials for the Ogilvy & Mather ad agency. In 1971 he returned to publishing as senior projects editor for Bantam Books. Among his acquisitions were such cutting-edge titles as *Gestalt Therapy, Verbatim,* and *In and Out of the Garbage Pail* by Frits Perls.

After several years he left to start his own company. Quicksilver Books, Inc. and since then has collaborated with writers in producing many popular works of fiction and nonfiction, including the previously mentioned movie tie-ins. Other

Quicksilver projects, many still in print, include books inspired by new therapies and holistic healing techniques such as Gestalt, Transactional Analysis, Rolfing, etc. Among them are *The Body Reveals* (HarperCollins, four editions, 12 printings); *Own Your Own Life* (McKay/Bantam), *Psychology Today* Book Club (main section); *Chalk Talks on Alcohol* (HarperSanFrancisco, 15 printings); the international bestseller *Children Learn What They Live* (Workman); and recent bestsellers by Dr. Lois P. Frankel *Nice Girls Don't Get the Corner Office* and *Nice Girls Don't Get Rich* (Warner Books). As a literary agency (founded in 1987), Quicksilver Books is primarily interested in mainstreaming adult fiction, with special emphasis on commercial and literary novels. Nonfiction categories include narrative adventure, self-help, psychology, environmental issues, nutrition, health, cooking, healing, alternative therapies, music, New Age, science, medicine, reference, biography, and inspirational memoirs.

Hobbies/personal interests: Painting, tennis, international travel, spending time with my wife and children.

Categories/subjects that you are most enthusiastic about agenting: Inspirational classics, blockbuster literary novels, bestselling narrative nonfiction, great memoirs and biographies, outstanding cookbooks, meaningful self-help. Books that uplift the spirit and that can make a positive difference in people's lives.

What you don't want to agent: Fantasy, science fiction.

If you were not an agent, what might you be doing instead: Painting, traveling, meditating, writing/collaborating on books and movies.

What's the best way for writers to solicit your interest: By query letter or email.

Do you charge reading or management fees: No.

Can you provide an approximation by percent of what you tend to represent by category: Fiction (literary fiction, women's novels, suspense thrillers): 15 percent, nonfiction: 85 percent.

What are the most common mistakes writers make when pitching you: They say nothing about themselves. Their letters are full of spelling mistakes. They tell but they don't sell.

How would you describe the client from hell: Full of ego, demanding, unaware of their part in the marketing process.

How would you describe the perfect client: Objective, intelligent, sympathetic, humble, emotionally and spiritually attuned.

How and why did you ever become an agent: Initially I was an editor, then a packager/publisher. When the markets changed in the '80s I went with the flow and became an agent.

What, if anything, can a writer do to increase the odds that you will become his or her agent: 1.) Have something original to offer; 2.) Be aware of market needs and categories; 3.) Present it professionally; 4.) Have a platform to help market the book.

How would you describe to someone (or something) from another planet what it is that you do as an agent: I consider myself an alchemist/healer-helper to turn lead into gold.

Do you have any particular opinions or impressions of editors and

publishers in general: I come from their ranks. Some stand taller than others. All have a job to do and, for the most part, I respect their efforts. Occasionally, I'm even impressed.

Do you have any favorite (current) TV shows, films, or books that you especially like and how come: I like cooking shows, *This Old House*, *The Sopranos*, *24*, Discovery and History channels, an occasional movie—no sitcoms.

Please list representative titles you have sold: *Jefferson's Great Gamble* and *Young Patriots* (Sourcebooks); *Look Great Naked* (Penguin); *Sculpting Her Body Perfect* (Human Kinetics); *The Inextinguishable Symphony* (Wiley); *Nice Girls Don't Get the Corner Office* and *Nice Girls Don't Get Rich* (Warner); *The National Public Radio Guide to Building a Classical CD Library* (Workman); *Children Learn What They Live* (Workman); *The Complete Books of Vinyasa Yoga* (Marlowe & Co.); *The Pump Energy Food* (Hyperion); *Real Food Daily Cookbook* (Ten Speed Press); *Help Me to Heal* (Hay House); *The National Public Radio Listener's Encyclopedia of Classical Music* (Workman); *The Complete Book of Ayurvedic Home Remedies* (Harmony); *Dinner at Mr. Jefferson's* (Wiley); *Indian Vegan Cooking* (Perigee); *Macrobiotics for Dummies* (Wiley); *Simply Mexican* (Ten Speed Press).

RAINES & RAINES

103 Kenyon Road, Medusa, NY 12120

518-239-8311   fax: 518-239-6029

Agents' names: Theron Raines, Joan Raines, Keith Korman
Education: T. Raines: Columbia, Oxford.
What's the best way for writers to solicit your interest: One-page letter.
Please list representative titles you have sold: *Deliverance* by James Dickey; *Forrest Gump* by Winston Groom; *Die Hard* by Roderick Thorp; *Ball Four* by Bouton and Shecter; *The Destruction of the European Jews* by Raul Hilberg; *The Man Who Walked Between the Towers* by Mordicai Gerstein (Caldecott winner); *My Dog Skip* by Willie Morris; *Brain Quest* by Chris Welles Feder; *Legacy* by Rich Lowry; *The Contender* by Robert Lipsyte; *Active Faith* by Ralph Reed; *The Glory of Their Times* by Lawrence Ritter; *How to Eat Fried Worms* by Thomas Rockwell; *The Uses of Enchantment* by Bruce Bettelheim; *Silhousette Against the Sky: A Daughter Remembers Orson Welles* (tentative title) by Chris Welles Feder (Algonquin).

RED SOFA LITERARY

2163 Grand Avenue Suite 2, Saint Paul, MN 55105

651-224-6670

www.redsofaliterary.com   email: dawn@redsofaliterary.com

Agent's name: Dawn Frederick, owner and literary agent.

Born: March 2, Atlanta, Georgia.

Education: I attended the University of Tennessee, earning a bachelor's degree in human ecology, and master's degree in information sciences from the School of Information Sciences (an ALA accredited institution).

Career story: I bring experience from the bookstore frontlines, independent publishing, and the library field, over 15 years of experience to be precise. It was pure coincidence (and part fate) my path crossed with Laurie Harper (of Sebastian Literary Agency) in 2002. Over the next five years, I learned the ins and outs of being a literary agent, with marked success. In 2008, I decided to branch out, launching Red Sofa Literary. And yes, I do own a big, red couch.

Hobbies and special personal interests: Where do we start? I am a natural risk-taker, and it's very much reflected in my personal life. There are the sports I avidly participate in: Roller derby (Rolling Ref for the Minnesota Rollergirls, known as Mani-Ax), broomball (on three teams now), currently women's lacrosse (taking MN by storm it seems), and bicycling (a much calmer outlet for the energy). Plus, I am a fan of all things quirky, which is a foundation for Red Sofa Literary. So, you should never be surprised if I attend an eclectic event/show/movie, as those are things that always appealing.

Subjects and categories you like to agent: Biography—historical, media-related, political—NO PERSONAL MEMOIRS; creative nonfiction—it needs to be smart, with noticeable platform, and highly commercial; history; humor; popular culture, especially Americana, and anything quirky; social issues/current affairs—women's studies; sports—less mainstream, more extreme sport, e.g., Roller Derby; women's narratives—chick-lit nonfiction, Latina, African American, and more; young-adult—nonfiction. My list is 99 percent nonfiction.

Subjects and categories writers shouldn't bother pitching to you: I cannot emphasize enough that I will NOT represent any personal memoirs, romances, science fiction, Westerns, parenting, and/or religious books. I sadly get multiple queries in this category daily, and end up rejecting all of them.

What might you be doing if you weren't agenting: Going to law school, more than likely.

What's the most effective ways for writers to grab your attention: I love a smart, narrative voice from a writer, and even more so when he/she has done her figurative homework on Red Sofa Literary. That kind of work stands out significantly.

Do you charge fees separate from your commission, or offer non-agenting

fee-based services: I would only in the event the accepted publisher deal is for an advance of less than $15,000. Red Sofa Literary may charge back a one-time U.S. $100 fee for partial reimbursement for the postage and phone expenses incurred prior to securing the publishing deal. The majority of the time, I never have to worry about this.

What are representative titles you have sold to publishers: *The Secrets of Skinny Chicks* (McGraw-Hill); *Finding Betty Crocker: The Secret Life of America's First Lady of Food* by Susan Marks (HarperCollins); *Stuck on You: The Indispensable History of Band-Aid Brand Bandages* by Susan Marks (Collector's Press).

What are your favorite books, movies, TV shows, and why: I have lots of favorite things, however if you cornered me and I had to list my Top Ten TV shows, they would be (in no particular order): *Buffy the Vampire Slayer, Six Feet Under, Sopranos, Alias, 24, Pushing Daisies, Queer as Folk, Sex in the City, L Word,* and *Freaks & Geeks.* Books, that's a hard question, it all depends on my mood and what I'm currently reading. Just know I have lots of favorites, that I'm well-read, and I'm always up for recommendations.

How would you describe the writer from hell: Anyone who doesn't promote him/herself, thereby making it difficult to sell the person's platform, which makes the agent's job more difficult. In addition, too many emails/phone calls in a short period of time. I always try to answer them quickly, but if an author has contacted me without giving me time to respond, and does this consistently, it tries my patience.

What do you like best about your clients, and the editors and publishers you work with: I absolutely love that we all carry a passion for books, good ideas, and our constant desire to find forums to discuss these topics.

HELEN REES LITERARY AGENCY

376 North Street, Boston, MA 02113

617-227-9014

WE DO NOT ACCEPT ELECTRONIC SUBMISSIONS.

Agents' names: Lorin Rees; lorin@reesagency.com, Ann Collette; Agent10702@aol.com

The following information applies to Lorin Rees.

Education: BA, Bard College; MBA, Boston University.

Career story: After many years trying to change the world by working in non-profit organizations and with socially responsible enterprises, I became a literary agent. My journey has exposed me to incredibly diverse and wonderful experiences that inspire me everyday. In no particular order, I've worked with underprivileged children, been a park ranger at a national park, advocated for the homeless, consulted small businesses, led the marketing efforts for an innovative food service company and worked at as line cook. Now, I am dedicated to making an impact through books. I cherish my work and feel extremely fortunate and blessed be a literary agent.

Subjects and categories you like to agent: Business, history, self-help, literary fiction, popular culture, narrative nonfiction, mystery.

Subjects and categories writers shouldn't bother pitching to you: Romance, fantasy, sci-fi, poetry.

What might you be doing if you weren't agenting: That's hard to imagine.

What's the most effective ways for writers to grab your attention: Just present your work. There're no gimmicks or tricks here.

Do you charge fees separate from your commission, or offer non-agenting fee-based services: None.

What are representative titles you have sold to publishers: *Words That Work*, and *What Americans Really Want…Really* by Frank Luntz (Hyperion); *Blood Makes the Grass Grow Green* and *The Border Crosser* by Johnny Rico (Random House); *Travel Writing* by Pete Ferry (Harcourt); *Primal Health: Stone Age Secrets to Health and Happiness* by Dr. William Meller (Perigee); *It Pays to Be Civil* by Christine Pearson and Christine Porath (Portfolio); *Brandsimple* by Allen Adamson (Palgrave Macmillan); *Who: Solve Your #1 Problem* by Geoff Smart and Randy Street (Random House).

Why did you become an agent, and how did you become one: It was destiny. The clouds parted, the stars aligned, and the moon shone brightly. (I'm not kidding.)

What do you tell entities from other planets and dimensions about your job: I read a lot.

What are your favorite books, movies, TV shows, and why: I love too many wonderful books and movies to list.

How would you describe the writer from hell: That's a difficult question to answer because I wouldn't work with a "writer from hell." I not only admire the people I work with, I like them on a personal level and consider many my friends.

How would you describe the publisher and/or editor from hell: Are you trying to get me in trouble?

What do you like best about your clients, and the editors and publishers you work with: There is nothing more satisfying than being part of a successful creative collaboration.

You're welcome to share your thoughts and sentiments about the business of writing and publishing: This is a fair business that requires patience and perseverance. While some terrible books are successful, in the end, truly great books and authors stand the test of time and get, in most cases, the recognition they deserve.

Do you wish to describe who you are: I'm about 6', 190 lbs with a shaved head.

Will our business exist as we know it in ten years or so: Mostly. There will be many differences due to technology and changing demographics, but the elements of publishing will remain the same. Writers will always need a publisher, and publishers will always need writers. And somewhere in the middle there is a literary agent.

The following information pertains to Ann Collette:

Date and location of birth: February 11, 1952, Boston, MA.

Career Story: Worked as a freelance editor and writer for over 15 years before becoming an associate at the Rees Agency almost ten years ago.

Hobbies and special personal interests: Opera, cats, beading, martial arts movies, and ZZ Top.

Subjects and categories you like to agent: Fiction: Mystery, thriller, suspense, literary fiction, women's, horror, vampire.

Nonfiction: Military, war, Southeast Asia, historical.

Subjects and categories writers shouldn't bother pitching to you: Children's, YA, middle-grade, sci-fi, fantasy, and anything to do with banking or finances.

What might you be doing if you weren't agenting: Editing for a big commercial house.

What's the most effective ways for writers to grab your attention: Write a strong, tight, well-focused query letter.

Do you charge fees separate from your commission, or offer non-agenting services: I continue to work as a freelance editor, but I never agent anyone who's paid me to edit their work. These are two distinct careers.

What are representative titles you have sold to publishers: Steve Sidor, *Skin River, Bone Factory, The Mirror's Edge*, St. Martin's; Vicki Lane, *Signs in the Blood, Art's Blood, Old Wounds, In a Dark Season*, Bantam.

Why did you become an agent, and how did you become one: Helen Rees hired me to evaluate manuscripts for her. She liked my work so much she asked me to become an agent.

How do you feel about writers: I worship the good ones; I try to avoid the pretentious ones.

What are your favorite books, movies, TV shows, and why: I love Chekhov, the poetry of Raymond Carver, Dennis Lehane, Tom Perrotta, Darrin Strauss, Elizabeth McCracken, Ken Bruen, and Steve McCauley. I love action films, particularly Hong Kong martial arts. I think my favorite film of all time is Sam Peckinpah's *The Wild Bunch*. Unfortunately, as I confessed in a previous interview for this guide, I am still enamored of *American Idol*.

How would you describe the writer from hell: Somebody who emails me a dozen times a day, who doesn't value my time.

How would you describe the publisher and/or editor from hell: One who never gets back in touch with me about a book they initially were eager to see.

What do you like best about your clients, and the editors and publishers you work with: When we all work together as a team because we have a common goal: publishing the best book possible.

You're welcome to share your thoughts and sentiments about the business of writing and publishing: I can't imagine a world without books. But I think publishers need to re-evaluate huge advances, especially for celebrity books, and the need for fiction writers to have a platform.

Do you wish to describe who you are: I'm an outgoing, informal woman with a good sense of humor, but I like my solitude.

Finally, will our business exist as we know it in ten years or so: No, we'll be doing far more e-books.

JODIE RHODES LITERARY AGENCY

8840 Villa La Jolla Drive, Suite 315 , La Jolla, CA 92037

www.jodierhodesliterary.com

Agents' names: Jodie Rhodes, President; Clark McCutcheon, fiction editor at large; Bob McCarter, nonfiction editor at large; Jill Hughes, foreign rights; Contact for all queries, Jodie Rhodes.

Born: Montreal, Canada.

Education: BA Ohio Wesleyan University. Pursued MA at Ohio State concurrently with my husband pursuing his PhD at Ohio State but ended up doing his research and writing his papers instead of my own.

Career history or story: A year out of college, I worked as an editor at McGraw-Hill for their school division based in Columbus, Ohio. Left that for a job as a copywriter at a small agency, also in Columbus, Ohio. Then moved to W. B. Doner in Detroit, where I was told no woman could be a copywriter because either directly or indirectly every account was connected to the auto industry and "everyone knew women didn't understand anything about cars," so I became a media buyer. I grew up in Detroit and was eager to leave and see the world, so I took off for San Francisco (what a magical city!) and started my own business there, an upscale employment agency titled simply Rhodes Personnel Agency. At that time, the city was flooded with young women emigrating from Britain. I shall always remember the one who wrote, in the space listing work experience, "general dogsbody." When Hoeffer, Dietrich and Brown in San Francisco called my agency, looking for a media buyer, I placed myself with them and sold the business.

A large regional agency in LA, that handled Mattel Toys among other big accounts, recruited me for twice the money and I moved down there. Had a brief stint as marketing director for Wham-O Toys. They invented the Hula Hoop. Then joined N.W. Ayer and was promoted to VP media director a few years later. Quit to pursue a writing career and sold two novels: one to Bantam and one to Putnam—the latter made the *LA Times* bestseller list its first week in print. Could not sell a third novel and grudgingly went back to advertising but only as a consultant. Here's a story to pop your eyes. The agency I consulted for was supposed to be the new Mary Wells. It had Suzuki when Suzuki was hot. It also had a technology company. I only met the president of it once but was blown away by him. Then I heard the agency dropped the account because they felt this president was too dense to understand their creative strategy. "Are you nuts?" I cried. "This is one of the most brilliant, creative human beings I've ever met." They just sneered at me—after all I was just a media person. Well, the president's name was Bill Gates and the tech company Microsoft.

Hobbies, interests: A hobby that grew into a vice was option trading. I was an active trader in the market for many years, concurrent with my positions in advertising. The day I realized I was in trouble was when I had so much money rolling in from option trades that I began regarding my salary as chump change. I now only hold stocks that pay strong dividends. Love bridge and am a Life Master. Am a passionate but rather inept tennis player. Have always loved horses and riding. Bike regularly. If you'd asked about passions, I would include my deep personal concern with the "throwaway children" in both this country and worldwide. Before I became an agent, I served as a guardian ad litem for the San Diego Juvenile Court Systems and worked (freely, as a volunteer) for Voices for Children. A recent sale, *Chloe Doe* by Suzanne Phillips, is the story of a 17-year-old girl who fled from a brutalizing home at age 12 and has been supporting herself by selling her body on the streets of LA since she was 12. I was determined to get this book published and contacted 29 editors simultaneously in the U.S. and UK. Targeted to the YA market, it scared many publishers, but I am happy to say we made a big sale and it's created a worldwide buzz.

Subjects and categories you are interested in agenting, including fiction and nonfiction: What's really hot today are edgy, literary YA/teen novels and if you're a truly gifted writer who has a strong story idea for one, I'd love to see it. These books are outselling adult fiction three to one. Editors who used to handle only adult trade novels are now acquiring these books. To give you an idea of just how hot they are, editors tend to disappear before major holidays and it's normally impossible to reach them. But the Friday before Thanksgiving I fell madly in love with a YA/teen novel I read nonstop from the moment I opened it to the last page, immediately offered the author representation and was so excited I spent the weekend writing the pitch letter, mailed it to fourteen editors on Monday, on Tuesday twelve of them asked to see the complete manuscript (many emailing from their home or their family's home), on Wednesday, Editorial Director Phoebe Yeh at HarperCollins called me with a pre-emptive offer of $200,000.

Multicultural literature, both fiction and nonfiction, makes my eyes light up. Books that have something important to say and characters with substance. Voice is everything to me in a novel. I'm fascinated by science and have sold many books by a variety of scientists and academics. Mainstream fiction, memoirs, biography, history, literary novels, those rare thrillers and mysteries that are truly original and gripping, world literature, politics, military, international affairs, women's issues, parenting, health, medicine. I am rightly known as an agent who welcomes new writers and the vast majority of books I've sold have been authored by new writers.

Subjects and categories writers shouldn't even bother pitching to you: No romances, religious, spiritual or inspirational books, no children's books, no erotic works, no science fiction, fantasy or horror.

What might you do if you weren't agenting: Writing. As most writers know, once the writing bug bites you, it's hard to get over. I was fortunate to have sold two novels to major New York houses but a writer always wants to do more. I am seriously considering writing a nonfiction book titled *Making It* which should be an interesting insider look at the publishing business from someone who started out as an outsider and had to battle their way inside, just like most of you reading this are doing.

What's the best way for fiction writers to solicit your interest: Be a gifted writer and a fantastic storyteller. Most literary fiction is focused on language and style. There's no compelling story. That's the main reason they get rejected. Sadly, most of the writers who come up with truly interesting plots don't write well enough for their books to sell.

What's the best way for nonfiction writers to solicit your interest: First, have a truly exciting story to tell that either hasn't been written about before or offers exciting new information on the subject. I expect every writer to have thoroughly researched the subject matter and to have a "platform." Publishers want writers with outstanding credentials which will attract reviewers and get media attention. The author should also have a well-planned marketing and promotion strategy of their own which they'll use to generate sales.

Do you charge reading or any upfront fees: I do not charge any fees, upfront or later (not even submission fees).

Can you provide an approximation by percent of what you tend to represent by category: 50 percent nonfiction, 35 percent YA/teen, 15 percent fiction. I might add this is not my choice. I would prefer 70 percent fiction and 30 percent the rest. The magic of fiction is that the author creates life. I love my brilliant scientists, doctors, and academics but a truly great novel is my passion. Commission structure: 15 percent in all cases except 20 percent for foreign sales or film/TV if it's placed through a sub agent. Number of titles sold last year: 45. Rejection rate: 99.5 percent.

In your experience, what are the most common pitching mistakes writers make: They don't think before they write. They just let it pour out. The result is illogical plots, inconsistent characters, clichéd, superficial writing and a bored agent. A writer should spend at least two hours of research for every hour of writing. They should know their characters as well as they know their secret thoughts. They should know everything about the situations they put their characters in, including what the streets they walk on look like.

Also, you're always off on the wrong foot when you get our name wrong. Form letters addressed to "agent" are sure losers. Query letters with misspelled words and bad grammar are instant rejects. But the most common mistake writers make is telling us how wonderful their book is. Never, ever try to sell us. Experience has taught us that the more modest the writer, the greater the talent, and vice versa. One of the funniest such letters I recently received informed me, "My book is a brilliant, compelling modern-day version of Holden Caulfield's *Catcher in the Wheat*." Writers are told to keep their query letters short but one can overdo this as per the following: "Dear Agent, A woman takes her 12 year old daughter out of school and isolates her from the world. The novel is called Elizabeth. Sincerely,..." We do need more information than this. I invite writers to send along the opening 30–50 pages of their book with their query letter. This allows me to get a sense of the writing and the voice and greatly increases the author's chance of interesting me.

Describe the client from hell, even if you don't have any: A client who emails or calls you every week after the first round of submissions has been mailed out—who falls apart emotionally when the first rejections come in—who acts as though they're the only client you have—who repeatedly asks what you're going to do after every rejection—who tries to make you feel you and only you are responsible for selling the book—the actual book they wrote has nothing to do with it.

What's your definition of a great client: Intelligent, appreciative, patient, a genuine grown-up who realizes a good agent works as hard as a writer and has enormous demands on their time from many areas.

How can writers increase the odds that you will offer representation: NEVER CALL ME ON THE PHONE WHEN I'VE NEVER HEARD OF YOU NOR SEEN ANY OF YOUR WRITING. Be honest, be professional, do your homework before you contact me, research your book, hone your writing craft, don't write for the market (meaning if you're written a book motivated simply by the desire to sell a book, go to some other agent). Write because you had to—because your story, fiction or nonfiction, was that important to you. If you've written a novel and not once during the time you wrote it did you feel excitement, fear, desire, hope, desperation, curiosity, determination—if you never laughed or cried, then you never got inside your book. If you felt nothing, the reader will feel nothing.

Give me a bio that will get editors' attention. I cannot begin to tell you how many MSs I've requested based solely on the bio info in the query letter. Here's an example: "The first chapter was a finalist in the Harcourt Brace Best New Voices in American Fiction 2007 contest and won the Katie O'Brien Scholarship for Fiction. I was subsequently awarded the Writer-in-Residence at the Footpaths to Creativity Center in the Azores Island. I've worked for ten years as a wildlife biologist." However, nothing beats an opening description of the book that hooks me.

Why did you become an agent, and how did you become one: One of these days, I may really level and tell you why. Suffice it to say, I knew going in that I had absolutely no chance whatsoever of ever being successful. The odds were just so totally against me. In fact, I never expected a writer to actually contact me since none of the guidebooks responded to the listing I sent in. I had an ulterior motive. Then one day, to my shock, I found a MS in my mailbox. *Guide to Literary Agents* had listed me without telling me. I've always been cursed with an overdeveloped sense of responsibility and that lone MS forced me to actually try and become a real agent. How I did it was through more work than I ever thought I was capable of. Most everything in my life has come easy to me. When I started my agency in late 1998, I was (and still am) living in La Jolla, California, 3,000 miles from the heart of the publishing business. I didn't have a single writer or know a single editor. I'd never worked as an editor in a New York trade house. I knew nobody and nobody knew me. For the first six months I received nothing but the most ghastly imaginable MSs, all of which I rejected. So the first step I took was to write advice columns for writers and convince some regional and national writers' magazines to publish them, in hopes of getting the attention of decent writers. Then I wrote the head of every major New York house (at this time I didn't even have a computer) and said I'd like to interview their editors. I will be grateful all my life to Sally Richardson at St. Martin's and Emily Bestler at Simon & Schuster who out of the kindness of their hearts personally called me on the phone and offered me five or six of their editors. After that, everybody was willing to give me interviews.

The other thing I did was make what I hoped would be a short-term sacrifice for a long-term benefit. There are about 3000 people who call themselves agents in this country, and I started out 3,001. Major, talented, polished writers were not querying me. So I took the best of the raw talent and revised, edited and rewrote their MSs into salable books. There are a multitude of books out there with my writing sprinkled throughout them. Above all, I owe my success to New York editors, and I'm talking major editors for their unbelievable kindness. I had several writers who told me their previous agents never received a single response from editors when they sent submissions. That was the fate I feared. So I introduced myself. I wrote them about myself. They were so gracious! I'll never forget Jane Von Mehren, past VP Editor-in-Chief of Viking Penguin, now at Random House, calling me one day simply to ask how I was doing.

Carolyn Marino is a saint. She has cheered me on for years, never letting the fact she has yet to take one of my books deter her from encouraging me to keep sending. The brilliant editor of Ecco Press, Dan Halpren, has taken the time to write notes like, "I'm sorry this one won't work for Ecco but I remain hopeful." Michael Pietsch, Brian Tart and Wendy Lamb wrote wonderful recommendation letters to LMP so I could get listed with them (LMP only lists agents who are recommended by major editors), and I'd never even come close to selling them a book. I probably shouldn't start naming editors because there are so many others who reached out a helping hand. I founded my business on unpublished writers, the majority of whom had been rejected by everyone else for years. Now of course I'm also selling published writers but almost all are writers whose first books I sold and we're now placing their second and third books.

Describe to someone from another planet what you do as an agent: I make people's dreams come true.

How do you feel about editors and publishers: There's a common belief that editors don't really edit these days—they just acquire books. Nothing could be more wrong. Good editors (and most are) do enormous editing. When Robin Desser at Knopf bought *Train to Trieste*, it had gone through five edits—three by me, one by the world-famous author Sandra Cisneros and one by her personal editor. So what did Robin Desser do? She had the author rewrite the entire book from page one six times! I'd done so much editing on it that I knew the book by heart, but when I read it after Robin's editing, I was blown away. She made it extraordinary.

When Phoebe Yeh at HarperCollins bought *The Ghosts of War*, she sent me a copy of her first edit. There wasn't a single page and hardly a single line without her comments and changes. And this was a full MS! Since she does this with every book she buys, I can't imagine how she finds time to eat, sleep or have any personal life (and she's married with children). I hope every writer who reads this begins to see why they keep getting rejected. You can't just write a book and send it out. If it's worth anything at all, you need to rework and hone it time after time until it comes to life and glows. And when it's reached that stage, it will still be only halfway there but now professionals will take over and bring it to fruition. With rare exceptions, I love editors. They are so bright. Have gained so much knowledge (from their writers, actually), most really deeply care about books and they're all under such pressure all the time—they work enormously long hours and have demands on them writers can't even begin to imagine—yet they will always give new writers a chance. Regarding publishers: It saddens me that making money is so important to them that they'll publish really bad books because there's a celebrity attached or the writer has a *National Observer*–type story. I guess to stay in the business, they have to. But it didn't used to be that way before all the mergers and acquisitions with their companies going public and becoming beholden to Wall Street. I wish they'd reward writers who make money for them by considerably more generous royalties—they know what their break-even point is—after that why not let the author share more fairly in the profits?

How do you feel about writers: My writers are all very special people to me. I consider them my friends. They share their personal life with me and I care about what happens to them. With the enormously gifted fiction writers in particular, I feel a sense of awe at their talent and great thankfulness that they chose me as their agent. As for the brilliant scientists I represent, I am in total awe of their knowledge and expertise. One of the greatest gifts being an agent has brought me is the chance to know such brilliant gifted people.

What do you see in the near future for book publishing: Most of us are very concerned about what's happening to the printed word. Newspapers have lost more than half their circulation. The Internet is the new media and it becomes more powerful all the time. Kids don't read anymore. We may all end up representing bloggers.

What are your favorite books, TV shows, movies, and why: I work 15 hours a day, seven days a week, and before I became an agent, I read a minimum of ten books a week and saw a movie at least once a week. Now I never see movies and never get to read real books. It's horrible, because I need to know what's out there. Thank God for *Publisher's Weekly* and editors who send me their writers' books so I can at least scan them. However, like most people, I am utterly fascinated by the presidential race and tape MSNBC and CNN during the day (do not care for FOX News), then sit up until one a.m. watching. As for dramatic TV, I will watch anything Helen Mirren is in.

In your opinion, what do editors think of you: I'd rather let the editors tell you. From: Judith Gurewich at Other Press: "Dear Jodie, Please send us more manuscripts. I can see you understand my love for good writing and heartfelt stories." From Amy Gash at Algonquin: "Jodie, Your books are always so fascinating. I'm interested in this topic and would love to see the proposal. I'm so glad you keep sending projects my way!" From John Aherne at McGraw-Hill: "Hi Jodie, Boy, am I glad I asked to see this. My colleagues and I really liked and responded to this proposal. We all thought it was great! Thanks again for sending this wonderful proposal my way." From Bob Pigeon at Perseus Books: "Dear Jodie, Your query letter has certainly aroused my curiosity and kindled my interest. Please do send this proposal and sample chapter as soon as convenient. Please send it to me via email attachment. Have you sent the proposal to any other imprint in the Perseus Books Group? Looking forward to receiving the material."

On a personal level, what do you think people like about you and dislike about you: They are enormously grateful that I take chances on them as new and previously rejected writers, that I edit their material, that I continue to market it to multiple publishers after numerous rejections, knowing that I will probably never earn a penny from my work. They like knowing they can trust me and that selling their books is always more important to me than making money. This past year I sold books after 60, 72, 87 rejections and that's just for starters. I sold a book, *3 Minutes on Love*, after representing it and fighting for it three years and recently sold it after 217 rejections. A debut novel by a Romanian author I took on two years ago, which received 132 rejections, was just pre-empted by Robin Desser at Knopf, won at auction by Doubleday in the UK with translation rights already sold to Italy, Germany, France, Holland, Greece, Serbia and Israel. It's currently at auction in Romania. I've had a few books that sell instantly but the majority of books I sell have gone through a minimum of 50 rejections. No wonder I have tendinitis. On the negative side, writers often find it hard to take my blunt criticisms. I don't have time to be polite and beat around the bush. If their writing sucks, I tell them. I also demand they be instantly available when I'm marketing their work and ready to provide editors with any and all material they request.

What are some representative titles that you have sold:
The Goodby Cousins by Maggie Martin (Bantam); *Black Boy—White School* by Brian Walker (HarperCollins); *Lies, Damn Lies and Science* by Sherry Seethaler, (Prentice Hall); *Stranded* by Jeanne Dutton (HarperCollins); *The Intelligence Wars* by Steven O'Hern (Prometheus); *How to Survive a Natural Disaster* by Margaret Hawkins (Permanent Press); *Murder at Gravely* by Daniel Craig (Midnight Ink Five Star Mystery); *The Broken Blue Line* by Constance Dial (Permanent Press); *The Make or Break Moment—Physical Science vs. Economists* by Robert and Ed Ayres (Prentice Hall); *The New Biology* by Joseph Panno (Facts on File); *Bacteria—Rulers of the World* by Anne Maczulak (Prentice Hall); *Science Through the Ages* by Julie Casper (Facts on File); *Freaked* by Jeanne Dutton (HarperCollins); *The Red Flag in American Bathrooms* by Dr. Wesley Jones (Penguin); *Diagnosis of Love* by Maggie Martin (Bantam); *Murder at Hotel Cinema* by Daniel Craig (Midnight Ink Five Star Mystery); *The Ring* by Kavita Daswani (HarperCollins); *Right Decisions* by Jim Stein (McGraw-Hill); *Choosing the Gender of Your Child* by Daniel Potter and Jennifer Thompson (Prometheus Books); *Messed Up* by Janet Lynch (Holiday House); *A Child's Journey Out of Darkness* by Leeann Whiffen (Sourcebooks); *The Ghosts of War* by Ryan Smithson (HarperCollins); *Seducing*

the Spirits by Louise Young (The Permanent Press); *A Year With Cats and Dogs* by Margaret Hawkins (Permanent Press); *Internal Affairs* by Connie Dial (Permanent Press); *The Archivist* by M.F. Bloxan (Permanent Press); *Does Israel Have a Future* by Connie Hilliard (Potomac Books); *Lessons from Baghdad* by Stephen O'Hern (Prometheus Books); *Hoodwinked* by Sherry Seethaler (Prentice Hall's Zoon's Trade Imprint); *America's Covert Military: The Inside Story of Private Contractors* by Shawn Engbrecht (Potomac); *The Truth about Our Energy Crisis* by Jim Mahaffey (Pegasus Books); *The Five Second Rule* by Anne Maczulak (Perseus/Da Capo); *How Math Can Save Your Life* by James Stein (John Wiley & Sons); *Murder at the Universe* by Daniel Craig (Midnight Ink Five Star Mystery); *The Root of Thought* by Andrew Koob (Prentice Hall's Zoon's Trade Imprint); *Pictures of the Mind* by Miriam-Boleyn Fitzgerald (Prentice Hall's Zoon's Trade Imprint); *A Matter of Gravity* by John Moffat (HarperCollins); *Salaam, Paris* by Kavita Daswanit (Putnam); *Mind Mapping* by Jamie Nast (John Wiley & Sons); *Inside the Crips* by Colton Simpson and Ann Pearlman (St. Martin's); *Green Planet* by Stanley Rice (Rutgers University Press); *Critical Components of J.R.R. Tolkien* by Jay Ruud (Facts on File); *Understanding Biodiversity* by Julie Casper (Facts on File); *Computers, Internet and Society* by Robert Plotkin (Facts on File); *Makers of Modern Science: Chien-Shiung Wu* by Richard Hammond (Facts on File); *The Unknown Universe* by Richard Hammond (Career Press/New Page Books); *Microscopy* by Suzanne Bell (Taylor and Francis).

THE ANGELA RINALDI LITERARY AGENCY

P.O. Box 7877, Beverly Hills, CA 90212-7877

310-842-7665   fax: 310-837-3143

www.rinaldiliterary.com   email: amr@RinaldiLiterary.com

Agent's name: Angela Rinaldi

Career history or story: Executive editor, NAL/Signet; senior editor, Pocket Books; executive editor, Bantam Books; manager of book publishing for the *Los Angeles Times*. Taught publishing programs at UCLA. Member of the Literature Panel for the California Arts Council, AAR and PEN.

Subjects and categories you are interested in agenting, including fiction and nonfiction: Fiction: Mainstream and literary fiction, upmarket contemporary women's fiction, suspense, mysteries, thrillers, historical fiction. Nonfiction: Narrative nonfiction like *Blink* or *Freakonomics*—books that present a quirky aspect of the usual, memoir, women's issues/studies, current issues, cultural and social history, biography, psychology, popular reference, prescriptive and proactive self-help, health books that address specific issues, business, career, personal finance and books written by journalists, academics, doctors and therapists, motivational, children's, and young adult.

Subjects and categories writers shouldn't even bother pitching to you: Humor, techno thrillers, KGB/CIA espionage, drug thrillers, category romances, science fiction, fantasy, horror, Westerns, cookbooks, poetry, film scripts, magazine articles, religion, gift, how-to, Christian, religious, celebrity bios or tell-alls.

What would you do if you weren't agenting: Editorial consultant/freelance editor.

What's the best way for fiction writers to solicit your interest: Brief synopsis and the first three chapters. Do not send the entire MS, unless requested. Do not query by phone or fax. Email inquiries; please be brief, no attachments. Please tell me if I have your work exclusively or if it is a multiple submission. Include SASE. No metered mail or certified mail. UPS and FedEx will not deliver to a post office box. Please allow four weeks for response.

What's the best way for nonfiction writers to solicit your interest: Queries with detailed covering letter or proposal. Do not query by phone or fax. Email inquiries; please be brief, no attachments. Please tell me if I have your work exclusively or if it is a multiple submission. Include SASE. No metered mail or certified mail. UPS and FedEx will not deliver to a post office box. Please allow four weeks for response.

Do you charge reading or any upfront fees: No.

In your experience, what are the most common pitching mistakes writers make: Not knowing the genre they are writing in. Not researching the marketplace for similar titles. Pitching a novel that isn't finished and asking the agent to read incrementally. Pitching an undeveloped proposal. Pitching ideas that have been done many times over. Pitching more than one book at a time. Pitching novels and nonfiction at the same time. Not knowing the type of book I represent. Pitching to more than one agent and not letting each agent know. Mentioning that their previous agent died or is sick.

How can writers increase the odds that you will offer representation: Having a strong platform and knowing what that means. Being an expert in their field. Having stories published in journals. Big ideas, original ideas or noticing trends. Having ideas that explain the way we live. Having a "brand." Being able to get endorsements. Lovely writing. Good storytelling. Distinct voice. Writing a novel that combines literary writing with a commercial hook.

What are some representative titles that you have sold: *Who Moved My Cheese?* by Dr. Spencer Johnson; *Zen Golf: Mastering the Mental Game* by Dr. Joseph Parent (Doubleday); *Zen Putting: Mastering the Mental Game on the Greens* by Dr. Joseph Parent (Gotham Books); *Calling in "The One"* by Katherine Woodward Thomas (Three Rivers); *Welcome to the Real World* by Stacy Kravetz (Norton); *My First Crush* by Linda Kaplan (The Lyons Press); *Bone Lake* by Drusilla Campbell (Bookspan); *Blood Orange* by Drusilla Campbell (Kensington); *Rescue Me* by Megan Clark (Kensington); *The Starlite Drive-in* by Marjorie Reynolds (Morrow); *Blind Spot, Quiet Time* by Stephanie Kane (Bantam); *TWINS! Pregnancy, Birth and The First Year of Life* by Dr. Connie Agnew, Dr. Alan H. Klein and Jill Alison Ganon (HarperCollins); *The Thyroid Solution* by Dr. Ridha Arem (Ballantine); *Before Your Pregnancy* by Amy Ogle, MS, RD and Dr. Lisa Mazzullo.

ANN RITTENBERG LITERARY AGENCY INC.

30 Bond Street, New York, NY 10012

212-684-6936 fax: 212-684-6929

www.rittlit.com

Agents' names: Ann Rittenberg, ann@rittlit.com, Penn Whaling, penn@rittlit.com
Location of birth: AR: New York.
PW: North Carolina.
Education: AR: BA comparative literature, Eckerd College 1979.
PW: BA in poetry writing, University of Virginia 2004.
Career Story: AR: After graduating and working briefly at the *St. Petersburg Times*, I moved to New York and joined Atheneum Publishers as an editorial assistant. Worked my way up to editor, then joined the Julian Bach Agency as an agent. Opened my own agency in 1992.

PW: After attending the NYU Summer Publishing Institute, I interned for the publisher of *The Paris Review* and read for *Open City* magazine. I then worked part-time at two other agencies before joining the Ann Rittenberg Agency in 2005.

Subjects and categories you like to agent: AR: Upmarket suspense, thrillers, mysteries, and women's fiction (i.e., those with very strong writing, characterizations, and plot); literary fiction; cultural and social history.

PW: Literary fiction, narrative nonfiction, anything with a strong voice.

Subjects and categories writers shouldn't bother pitching to you: AR: Poetry, sci-fi, genre fiction, how-to, gift books.

PW: Chick lit, poetry, how-to, anything about the Civil War.

What might you be doing if you weren't agenting: AR: Traveling, studying French and getting a graduate degree in literature, volunteering for non-political causes such as literacy, women's health and safety, teaching life skills to teenagers, and preserving urban green spaces.

What's the most effective ways for writers to grab your attention: AR: Write me a brief, cogent letter.

Do you charge fees separate from your commission, or offer non-agenting fee-based services: NO!

What are representative titles you have sold to publishers: *Where On Earth*, Doug Magee (Simon & Schuster, 2010); *The Poacher's Son*, Paul Doiron (St. Martin's Press); *Mystic River*, Dennis Lehane (William Morrow & Co.); *House and Home*, Kathy McCleary (Hyperion); *Afterimage*, Kathleen George (St. Martin's Press); *The Cure for Grief*, Nellie Herrmann (Scribner).

Why did you become an agent, and how did you become one: AR: I became an agent not only because I wanted to discover wonderful new writers and see them get published, but because I wanted to advocate for writers. Having worked in a publishing house, I saw how hard it was for every writer on a publisher's list to get equal attention, and I thought that if I worked on the side of the author, I'd be able to help them get the attention they deserved.

How do you feel about writers: AR: I think they're crucially important members of our society. We need storytellers to make sense of a chaotic world.

What do you tell entities from other planets and dimensions about your job: AR: I tell them I help writers find publishers. If they need a more detailed explanation, I tell them to read the book I co-wrote with my client Laura Whitcomb, *Your First Novel*. It explains the entire publishing process in a way that has helped many people.

What are your favorite books, movies, TV shows, and why:

AR: *Great Expectations*, because it's heavenly on every page; *Gone with the Wind*, because Scarlett helped me get where I am; *All About Eve*, because I love Bette Davis and because it depicts an industry's behind-the-scenes in a fresh and compelling manner; the short stories of Katherine Mansfield, because they are simply the best; *Lost*, because it's like a novel on TV.

How would you describe the writer from hell: Only gets in touch to complain.

How would you describe the publisher and/or editor from hell: Never returns calls, hates to work collaboratively, withholds information.

What do you like best about your clients, and the editors and publishers you work with: AR: They're smart and creative and they surprise me constantly with their wonderful ideas and passion.

You're welcome to share your thoughts and sentiments about the business of writing and publishing: AR: I did this extensively in the book I co-wrote with Laura Whitcomb, *Your First Novel*.

Finally, will our business exist as we know it in ten years or so: AR: It will exist, and it will be recognizable, but I hope it will have embraced all sorts of new technologies while retaining printed books.

RIVERSIDE LITERARY AGENCY

41 Simon Keets Road, Leyden, MA 01337

www.riversideliteraryagency.com   email: rivlit@sover.net

Agent's name: Susan Lee Cohen
Born: New York, New York.

Career story: I have been a literary agent for almost 30 years. I began my publishing career at Viking Penguin, and subsequently worked as a literary agent at Richard Curtis Associates and Sterling Lord Literistic before founding Riverside Literary Agency in 1990.

Subjects and categories writers shouldn't bother pitching to you: Genre fiction (romance, science fiction/fantasy, Westerns), children's books, poetry.

Do you charge fees separate from your commission, or offer non-agenting fee-based services: No.

What are representative titles you have sold to publishers: *The Myth of Sanity* (Viking), *The Sociopath Next Door* (Broadway), and *The Paranoia Switch* (Farrar Straus & Giroux) by Martha Stout; *Reviving Ophelia* (Putnam/Ballantine); *The Shelter of Each Other* (Putnam/Ballantine); *Another Country* (Putnam/Ballantine); *The Middle of Everywhere* (Harcourt); *Letters to a Young Therapist* (Basic Books); *Writing to Change the World* (Riverhead) and *Seeking Peace* (Riverhead) by Mary Pipher; *Pawprints of Katrina* by Cathy Scott (Wiley); *Right, Wrong and Risky* by Mark Davidson (Norton); *The Secret Magdalene* by Ki Longfellow (Crown); *Please Kill Me* by Legs McNeil and Gillian McCain (Grove/Atlantic); *Stop Running from Love* by Dusty Miller (New Harbinger); *Buddha Is as Buddha Does* (HarperOne); *The Big Questions* (Rodale); *Awakening to the Sacred* (Doubleday); *Awakening the Buddhist Heart, Letting Go of the Person You Used to Be* (Doubleday); and *The Mind Is Mightier than the Sword* (Doubleday) by Lama Surya Das.

RLR ASSOCIATES, LTD.

7 West 51st Street, New York, NY 10019

212-541-8641   fax: 212-541-6052

www.rlrliterary.net   email: sgould@rlrassociates.net

Agent's name: Scott Gould; sgould@rlrassociates.net
Born: Baltimore, Maryland.
Education: New York University.
Career story: I began my career in the editorial department at *Playboy* Magazine, and later, handling rights at another agency before building my client list at RLR.

Subjects and categories you like to agent: I represent and am always on the look out for literary and commercial fiction (including genre fiction) and all kinds of well-written, narrative nonfiction, from history to pop science to humor.

Subjects and categories writers shouldn't bother pitching to you: I don't represent poetry or screenplays.

What's the most effective ways for writers to grab your attention: The best way to stand out is to email (or snail mail) a query letter that tells me everything about the project and you in an interesting and professional way, along with a few pages or more of the manuscript. Creativity counts, but in the end the book stands for itself, so don't kill yourself over a query letter.

Do you charge fees separate from your commission, or offer non-agenting fee-based services: We follow the AAR guidelines and do not charge any reading or other fees.

What are representative titles you have sold to publishers: *Cash from Chaos: Creating and Building a Successful Gen X/Y Brand* by Eric Boyd and Sean Murphy (Prentice Hall/Pearson); *The Greatest Yankees Myths* by Peter Handrinos (Triumph Books); *Nathanael Greene: A Biography of the American Revolution* by Gerald Carbone (Palgrave Macmillan).

Why did you become an agent, and how did you become one: I became an agent because I love seeking out talent and making good books happen.

What are your favorite books, movies, TV shows, and why: Books: *Confederacy of Dunces, Jesus' Son, Lolita, Andy Kaufman Revealed!, Fear and Loathing in Las Vegas*. Movies and TV: *The Big Lebowski, The Wire, The Sopranos*.

You're welcome to share your thoughts and sentiments about the business of writing and publishing: This really is a business of relationships, which is generally a good thing because book people tend to be interesting people.

RITA ROSENKRANZ LITERARY AGENCY

440 West End Avenue, Suite 15D, New York, NY 10024-5358

212-873-6333

www.ritarosenkranzliteraryagency.com

Agent's name: Rita Rosenkranz; rrosenkranz@mindspring.com

Career history: Editor at various major New York publishing houses before becoming an agent in 1990. Member of AAR, Authors Guild, IWWG.

Categories/subjects that you are most enthusiastic about agenting: Animals; anthropology/archaeology; art/architecture/design; biography/autobiography; business/economics; child guidance/parenting; computers/electronic; cooking/foods/nutrition; crafts/hobbies; current affairs; ethnic/cultural interests; gay/lesbian issues; government/politics/law; health/medicine; history; how-to; humor/satire; interior design/decorating; language/literature/criticism; military/war; money/finance; music/dance; nature/environment; New Age/metaphysics; photography; popular culture; psychology; religious/inspirational; science/technology; self-help/personal improvement; sports; theater/film; women's issues/studies.

This agency focuses on adult nonfiction, stresses strong editorial development and refinement before submitting to publishers, and brainstorms ideas with authors. Actively seeking authors who are well paired with their subject, either for professional or personal reasons.

What you don't want to agent: Fiction, children's books, and poetry.

What's the best way for writers to solicit your interest: Send query letter only (no proposal) via regular mail or email. Submit proposal package with SASE only on request. No fax queries. Considers simultaneous queries. Responds in two weeks to queries.

Can you provide an approximation by percent of what you tend to represent by category: Nonfiction: 100 percent.

Please list representative titles you have sold: *Get Known Before the Book Deal: Use Your Personal Strengths to Grow an Author Platform* by Christina Katz (Writer's Digest Books); *29 Gifts* by Cami Walker (DaCapo Press); *See Me After Class: Experienced Teachers Share the Lessons They Learned the Hard Way* (Kaplan); *Twenty Strengths Adoptive Parents Need to Succeed* by Sherrie Eldridge (Bantam Dell); *Lifelines: The Black Book of Proverbs* by Askhari Johnson Hodari and Yvonne McCalla Sobers (Broadway Books); *Encyclopedia of Jewish Food* by Gil Marks (Wiley).

Tips: Identify the current competition for your project to make sure the project is valid. A strong cover letter is very important.

ANDY ROSS LITERARY AGENCY

767 Santa Ray Avenue, Oakland, Ca. 94610

510-238-8965

andyrossagency@hotmail.com

Date and location of birth: Dallas Texas, 1946.

Education: BA, political science, Brandeis University, MA, European history, University of Oregon.

Career Story: I was the owner of Cody's Books in Berkeley, California for 30 years from 1977–2007. Cody's was one of America's great independent book stores. It was three blocks from the University of California. We were well-known for our breadth of stock, particularly of intellectual subjects. Over the years, we had the world's greatest writers speaking at the store. It was a wonderful experience. I left Cody's in 2007. Sadly, Cody's closed its doors for the last time in 2008, the victim of history and changing buying habits. I opened my agency in 2008. Buying books for Cody's for so many years, getting pitched about 50,000 titles, talking to real book buyers, and doing returns of the books that didn't sell gave me a different perspective than many other agents.

Hobbies and special personal interests: Reading (of course). Photography. Fooling around with my kids.

Subjects and categories you like to agent: Politics, history, current events, narrative nonfiction, books by scholars, humor, books that change the world.

Subjects and categories writers shouldn't bother pitching to you: Fiction, personal memoir, poetry, children's books.

What might you be doing if you weren't agenting: I would be wishing I was agenting. I love it.

What's the most effective ways for writers to grab your attention: If they were a Nobel laureate, I would try to take their query over the transom with consideration. Seriously, though, I am just looking for subjects that are of interest to me and writers who speak with some authority on what they write about. I don't believe in clever pitches.

Do you charge fees separate from your commission, or offer non-agenting fee-based services: No.

What are representative titles you have sold to publishers: *The Dog Who Never Stopped Loving*, Jeffrey Masson (HarperCollins); *Christ the Jew*, Dr. Daniel Boyarin (New Press); *God and His Demons*, Michael Parenti (Prometheus Books).

Why did you become an agent, and how did you become one: I became an agent after I left Cody's. After 30 years in the retail book business, I was concerned that my future might lie in bagging groceries at Safeway. But I woke up one night and realized that I wanted to work with authors at the other end of the book food chain. It was the right decision. Fortunately most people in the book business knew about Cody's and they were very welcoming and encouraging.

How do you feel about writers: I love working with my writers and feel triumphant when I can get a book I believe in published.

What do you tell entities from other planets and dimensions about your job: I would be delighted to represent a space man or a person from an alternative universe, as long as they had an impressive "platform."

What are your favorite books, movies, TV shows, and why: My favorite book was *War and Peace* because I like epics and I didn't want it to end and it didn't. My favorite movie is *The Seventh Seal* because it, too, is an epic. I also like *Casablanca*, because everyone likes *Casablanca*. The movie I have seen the most is *High School Musical*, because I have a seven-year-old. I don't watch television.

How would you describe the writer from hell: He expects me to get him a $200,000 advance for his book on *The Idea of Nature in Kant's Metaphysical Writings*. When I submit it to publishers, it turns out that it has already gone around New York. He thinks his book is perfect as is and won't listen to his agent and his publisher. He thinks he will be on *Oprah*.

How would you describe the publisher and/or editor from hell: Since business has been so bad in publishing, most publishers and editors are in hell, not from hell. They are, as a group, pretty good.

What do you like best about your clients, and the editors and publishers you work with: Some of my clients are trying to change the world through their writing. Some are just trying to have fun. I admire how much spirit they put into their work, the risks they take doing it. I feel as if the editors and publishers are all in this together with me. The publishers I have enjoyed working with are committed book lovers.

Finally, will our business exist as we know it in ten years or so: Nothing stays the same in this world. I suspect that books will become digital eventually. The future of bookstores, particular independent stores, is in doubt. This is not what I would hope, but it is what I would expect. But people still read, and a digital book is still a book. The Internet has, sadly, created a society with Attention Deficit Disorder. Books require patience and commitment. Texting and Twittering [are] very bad news for those who believe in a literate society.

CAROL SUSAN ROTH LITERARY & CREATIVE

1824 Oak Creek Drive #416, Palo Alto, CA 94304

650-323-3795

email: carol@authorsbest.com

Agent's name: Carol Susan Roth
Born: New Brunswick, New Jersey.
Education: BA, New York University, MA counseling and psychotherapy, California Institute of Integral Studies, Professional Publishing Program, Stanford University, MegaBookMarketing Universities, Mark Victor Hansen.

Career history: Trained as a psychotherapist specializing in motivational seminars. More than a decade producing and promoting public events with the "who's who" in personal growth, spirituality and health (bestselling authors including John Gray, Scott Peck, Bernie Siegal, Elizabeth Kubler-Ross, Thomas Moore). In 1987, produced the first business and spirituality conference, The Heart of Business, with Stanford University Graduate School of Business, Michael Ray. Literary agent since 1996.

Hobbies/personal interests: Horse whispering, yoga, hiking, warm water sailing, meditation, the Dalai Lama.

Categories/subjects that you are most enthusiastic about agenting: 100 percent nonfiction. Pop culture, humor, health/fitness, business, science, history, herstory, spirituality, self-help. Also, books (in series) or gifts that can be developed as a "brand."

What you don't want to agent: Sorry, no fiction/no channeling or book written by an author without credentials, groundbreaking new content, charisma and dedication to making it a bestseller.

If you were not an agent, what might you be doing instead: Book/gift product development and packaging. I enjoy working with bright, creative, caring people who want to make an important contribution by inspiring and empowering others. Raising and riding Arabian horses.

What's the best way for writers to solicit your interest: Send an email, pitch your idea, credentials and platform (please no files) to me (carol@authorsbest.com). I'll get back to you immediately to request a proposal or not.

Do you charge any reading or management fees: No.

Can you provide an approximation by percent of what you tend to represent by category: Fiction: 0 percent; children's: 0 percent; nonfiction: 90 percent pop culture, health, business, science, spirituality, self-help; other: gift/audio 10 percent.

What are the most common mistakes writers make when pitching you: Not doing their homework on what an agent needs and wants to see in terms of pitch, query and proposal. (Please read Jeff Herman's *Write the Perfect Book Proposal*.)

How would you describe the client from hell: Lack of integrity, lack of responsibility, lack of loyalty. I avoid them like the plague!

How would you describe the perfect client: My clients! Brilliant, big hearted, creative, cooperative, enthusiastic, hard-working, honest and loyal.

How would you describe to someone (or something) from another planet what it is you do as an agent: As an agent, I work with experts to bring out the most valuable qualities in their work, the best way to position and then help sell their work from initial idea to the bestseller book lists. Many times experts come to me with a book concept and together we make it even more appealing and marketable. I'm a visionary, confidante, coach, cheerleader, marketeer and matchmaker. I study the world of information/entertainment products to see what company is doing what. Prep and position my authors to have the greatest appeal to those who can compensate and promote them best.

Do you have any particular opinions or impressions about editors and publishers in general: They are the hearts and minds of the publishing industry. I admire great editors and enjoy their friendship and respect.

What do you think the future holds for writers, publishers and agents: This is the most challenging time I have seen for authors in the last twenty years. I also see it as the most promising time for new authors. I enjoy working with wonderful, brilliant, fun, creative experts to "break the code" to success in making their books bestsellers. The secret is knowing your audience and using all the most cost-effective ways to reach them. All my authors actively market online, do traditional publicity (broadcast, cable and print). I also work with some of my authors to develop and produce PBS-TV programming.

Do you have any favorite (current) TV shows, films, or books that you especially like and how come: I enjoy "reality" TV; *The Apprentice, American Idol*, and *Survivor. Dr. Phil*. I loved *Wedding Crashers* and *Kundun*. The IMAX film *Everest*. I read lots of marketing, Tibetan Buddhism, biz, science, health books. I browse all sorts of books to find new ideas for my authors.

On a personal level, what do you think people like about you and dislike about you: Here are some of my favorite quotes: "Congratulations! Your agency has made it onto our Top 25 Agents list—Christine Mersch, Assistant Editor, *Writer's Digest*; "Carol, You have such an amazing instinct for finding important commercial books!"—Jacqueline Murphy, Senior Editor, Harvard Business School Publishing; "I have a wonderful agent, Carol Susan Roth, who helped me develop my latest book, find a great publisher and secure an outstanding advance. I have worked with other agents in the past (one who is considered The Dean of Agents!), but Carol stands head and shoulders above them all."—Michael Ray, Banc One Chair of Creativity, Stanford Business School and author, *The Highest Goal*; "I look forward to considering your future projects in personal growth, spirituality and holistic health."—Jackie Merri Meyer, Vice President, Warner Books; "Your marketing plan for Don Maruska's proposal is the BEST I have ever seen!"—Adrienne Hickey, Editorial Director, AMACOM (American Management Association Publishing).

What are representative titles you have sold to publishers: *Confessions of an Alien Hunter* and *The Immortals* (National Geographic Books); *Origins* (University of California Press); *God in the Wilderness* (Doubleday); *Glimpses of Heaven* (Revell/Baker Books); *Living Wisdom with the Dalai Lama* (Soundstrue); *Healing Zen* (Viking/Penguin); *Yoga Rx* (Broadway Books); *Yoga Gems Calendar 2003–4* (Andrews McMeel); *The Chiropractic Way* (Bantam); *Heart Smart!* (John Wiley & Sons); *Pilates Fusion Book & Deck* (Chronicle Books); *Seasons of Change* (Conari/Red Wheel/Weiser); *Feng Shui for Dummies* (John Wiley & Sons); *Snooze or Lose!* (Joseph Henry Press/National Academies Press); *The Infertility Cure* (Little, Brown); *Bird Signs* (New World Library); *The Highest Goal* (Berrett/Koehler); *How Great Decisions Get Made!* (AMACOM); *Investing in Biotech* (Perseus); *Changewave Investing 2.0* (Currency/Doubleday); *Make It Big!!!* (John Wiley & Sons); *The Internship Advantage* (Perigee/Prentice-Hall/Penguin); *10 Discoveries That Rewrote History* (Plume/Penguin); *Seven Stones That Rocked the World* (University of California Press); *Hannibal* (Simon & Schuster).

REGINA RYAN PUBLISHING ENTERPRISES, INC.

251 Central Park West, New York, NY 10024

212-787-5589

www.publishersmarketplace.com/members/reginaryanbooks

email: reginaryanbooks at rcn.com

queries: queryreginaryanbooks at rcn.com

Agent's name: Regina Ryan

Born: New York, New York.

Education: BA Trinity College, Washington DC; graduate work NYU and New School.

Career history: Editor: Alfred A. Knopf, Inc.; editor-in-chief, Macmillan Adult Books; founded firm as a book packaging and literary agency in 1977. Now, we are a literary agency only.

Hobbies/personal interests: Birding, mushroom hunting, wildflowers, cooking, gardening, ballet, modern dance, opera, reading, fine art.

Categories/subjects that you are most enthusiastic about agenting: Books that can change things for the better and/or open our eyes to something new and exciting. Areas of special interest include true adventure, memoir and well-written narrative nonfiction; also architecture, history, natural history (especially birds and wildflowers), politics, science, the environment, women's issues, parenting, cooking, psychology, health, wellness, diet, fitness, lifestyle, home improvement and design, business, popular reference, leisure activities including sports, travel, gardening.

What you don't want to agent: No fiction or children's literature (other than those by clients I already represent), no poetry, movie scripts, or celebrity tell-alls, or anything that involves vampires and/or demons or conspiracy theories.

If you were not an agent, what might you be doing instead: I would love to be a park ranger, a botanist, or an ornithologist but I suspect that in the real world I'd be a lawyer.

What's the best way for nonfiction writers to solicit your interest: I prefer a brief email query or snail mail (with SASE) query describing the project, explaining why it is needed, an evaluation of the competition, and what[the writer's] qualifications are. No telephone queries and no faxes. Please don't send by a method that requires a signature.

Do you charge reading or management fees: No.

What are the most common mistakes writers make when pitching you: They don't get to the point but deliver too much preamble. They don't understand how to analyze the competition by explaining why their books are different and better. They misunderstand the market for their books and often wildly exaggerate the possibilities to the point where it's useless.

How would you describe the client from hell: A client from hell can take several forms. There is the person who doesn't do what is asked of him or her; the person who turns in sloppy work; the person who calls on the phone for no real reason and/or talks endlessly; and finally the person who is never, ever satisfied.

How would you describe the perfect client: A great client is a really good writer who is a smart, hardworking pro who understands the business and who writes and promotes accordingly. My dream client is also polite, respectful and understands and appreciates what we've accomplished on his or her behalf.

How and why did you ever become an agent: I had been a book editor in publishing houses for many years before I went on my own, first as an out-of-house editor, then as a packager and agent. It was hard to do both packaging and agenting so I concentrated for some years on packaging. However, as a packager, most of my ideas came from my own head. I missed the variety of people and ideas that an editor is exposed to daily. Now, as a full-time agent, I delight in the interesting people and ideas that come my way nearly every single day.

What, if anything, can a writer do to increase the odds of your becoming his or her agent: A great title and a good selling sentence that defines the book really helps. A writer should convince me that first of all, he or she is a really good writer. Then, the writer must show me that the subject is important, that there is a real need for it and a significant market for it. I want to be convinced that the book hasn't been done before and that the author has a good, strong platform.

How would you describe to someone (or something) from another planet what it is that you do as an agent: The first thing I do is to find book projects to represent. This means I either read submissions or approach people who I'd like to see write a book. Once I've committed to a project, I guide the author in shaping a selling proposal using my strong editorial background and my understanding of the marketplace gained over my many years in the business. When the proposal is ready, I bring it to the attention of the editors and publishers I think would be best for it. When a publisher makes an offer, I negotiate terms and review the contract. Then, once it is sold, I exploit whatever other rights are salable. I hover over the publishing process to help the book and author succeed out in the world in whatever way I can.

How do you feel about editors and publishers: I like editors and I respect them. They are usually overworked book lovers, just as I am. They work very hard in a very difficult, often frustrating publishing environment. Publishers—the "suits"— can be the cause of a lot of the above-mentioned frustration—with their sometimes short-sighted view of the possibilities of some of my books, but in general, they too work hard and love books and try to do their best.

How do you feel about writers: I like writers. They are usually hard-working, creative, interesting and smart people. I know because I was married to one for 33 years.

What do you think the future holds for book publishing: I think it's going to get harder and harder to place books with the large publishers, unless nonfiction writers have a golden platform.

What are your favorite books, movies, TV shows, and why: I read fiction for my pleasure and recently I have developed a passion for Vladimir Nabokov *Pale Fire*. Also, Nikolai Bulgakov's *The Master and Margarita*. My favorite movie of late is *Little Miss Sunshine*. I also loved *March of the Penguins* and *The Devil Wears Prada*. On TV I like *Washington Week in Review, Book TV, Dog Whisperer, Top Chef, Project Runway, Nature, Nova, Antiques Road Show, Mystery,* and good movies on TV. Actually my favorite entertainment is listening to shows on WNYC, our local NPR talk radio station. I always learn something.

In your opinion what do editors think of you: I think they think of me as a pro, who understands the business and who represents quality projects.

On a personal non-professional level, what do you think people think of you: I think people think I'm fun, smart, a straight shooter and a caring and loyal friend.

Please list representative titles you have sold: *Gilded Mansions: The Stately Homes of America's First Millionaire Society*, Wayne Craven, W.W. Norton; *Chronicle: The 750-Year History of an Eastern European Jewish Family*, Michael Karpin, John Wiley; *Return to the Middle Kingdom: One Family, Three Revolutionaries, and the Birth of Modern China*, Yuan-tsung Chen, Union Square Press; *Rain Before Rainbows: How Successful People Failed at First in Their Chosen Fields*, Darcy Andries, Sellers Publishing; *The Legacy: The Rockefellers and Their Museums*, Suzanne Loebl, Smithsonian Press; *Escaping Toxic Guilt: Five Proven Steps to Free Yourself from Guilt for Good*, Susan Carrell, McGraw-Hill; *Mortality Bites: Living with Cancer in Your 20s and 30s*, Kairol Rosenthal, John Wiley; *Great Smoky National Park and Acadia National Park: FalconGuide Primers*, Randi Minetor, Globe Pequot Press; *151 Quick Ideas for Great Advertising on a Shoestring*, Jean Joachim, Career Press; *The Serotonin Power Diet: A Scientifically Proven Weight Loss Program That Uses Your Brain's Ability to Stop Your Overeating* by Judith Wurtman, PhD and Nina Marquis, MD, Rodale; *The Bomb in the Basement: How Israel Got Its Nuclear Option* *and What It Means for the World*, Michael Karpin, Simon & Schuster; *Anatomy of a Suicidal Mind* by Edwin Shneidman with an introduction by Judy Collins, Oxford University Press; *Escape from Saigon*, Andrea Warren; a Melanie Kroupa Book, Farrar, Straus and Giroux; *What Babies Say Before They Can Talk*, Paul Holinger, MD with Kalia Doner, Fireside Books. *The Altruist*, Walter Keady, MacAdam/Cage; *American Art: History and Culture*, Wayne Craven, McGraw-Hill; *Beyond the Bake Sale: The Ultimate School Fund Raising Book*, Jean Joachim, St. Martin's Press; *Lost in the Mirror: Borderline Personality Disorder*, Richard Moskovitz, MD, Taylor Publishing; *Surviving Hitler: A Teenager in the Nazi Death Camps*, Andrea Warren, HarperCollins Junior Books; *The Garden Primer*, Barbara Damrosch, Workman Publishing; *Thomas Eakins* by William Innes Homer, Abbeville Press; *Organize Your Office!* Ronni Eisenberg and Kate Kelly, Hyperion; *Pickups: Classic American Trucks* by Harry Moses, photographs by William Bennett Seitz, Random House; *Wildflowers in Your Garden*, Viki Ferreniea, Random House; *Living in Style Without Losing Your Mind*, Marco Pasanella, Simon & Schuster; *The Art of the Table: Table Settings, Table Manners, Table Ware* by the Baronness Suzanne von Drachenfels, Simon & Schuster; *The Last Childhood: A Family's Memories of Alzheimer's*, Carrie Knowles, Three Rivers Press.

VICTORIA SANDERS AND ASSOCIATES, LLC

241 Avenue of the Americas, Suite 11H, New York, NY 10014

www.victoriasanders.com

Agent Name: Victoria Sanders

Date and location of birth (some people skip the year): Los Angeles, California.

Education: BFA, Tisch School of the Arts at New York University and JD from Benjamin N. Cardozo School of Law.

Career Story: WNET/Channel 13, Simon & Schuster, Carol Mann Agency, Charlotte Sheedy Agency.

Hobbies and special personal interests: Architecture, reading, art, film.

Subjects and categories you like to agent: All things that are great reads and teach me something in some way.

Subjects and categories writers shouldn't bother pitching to you: Sadly, I am the wrong person for science and math, my own failing.

What might you be doing if you weren't agenting: Furniture design.

What's the most effective ways for writers to grab your attention: A terrific query letter.

Do you charge fees separate from your commission, or offer non-agenting fee-based services: No.

What are representative titles you have sold to publishers: *Fractured* by Karin

Slaughter (Bantam); *Undone* by Karin Slaughter (Bantam); *Can't Stop Won't Stop: a History of the Hip-Hop Generation* by Jeff Chang (winner of the American Book Award, St. Martin's Press); *Who We Be: The Colorization of America* by Jeff Chang (St. Martin's Press); *100 Young Americans* by Michael Franzini (Collins Design/HarperCollins); *So Happy Together* by Maryann McFadden (Hyperion); *Hold Love Strong* by Matthew Goodman (Touchstone/Fireside); *What Doesn't Kill You* by Virginia DeBerry and Donna Grant (Touchstone/Fireside); *Flow* by Elissa Stein and Susan Kim (St. Martin's Press); *Sisters and Husbands* by Connie Briscoe (Grand Central); *Never Make the Same Mistake Twice: Straight Talk on Love and Life from a Real Housewife* by NeNe Leakes and Denene Millner (Touchstone/Fireside); *The Invisible Mountain* by Carolina De Robertis (Knopf); *The Journey Home* by Sejal Ravani (Putnam); *The Opposite of Me* by Sarah Pekkanen (Atria); *Damaged* by Kia Dupree (Grand Central).

Why did you become an agent, and how did you become one: Simply, books. They have always been critically important to me. I grew up with my nose stuck in one, and I learned very early on that most authors are underappreciated.

What do you tell entities from other planets and dimensions about your job: I am a writer's advocate.

What are your favorite books, movies, TV shows, and why: *Ugly Betty, Entourage, CBS Sunday Morning* (it's all about Nancy Giles), *Good Morning America* (Robin and Diane!).

How would you describe the writer from hell: All clients are nervous, and that's normal. However, someone who, once signed, needs to go off and finish the project but likes to give daily updates or even weekly—that's too much, unless we're working closely together editorially and it's crunch time.

How would you describe the publisher and/or editor from hell: Someone who is non-responsive. Just rip the Band-Aid and tell me the truth. Don't ignore calls or emails.

What do you like best about your clients, and the editors and publishers you work with: I love it when we all get jazzed on the work.

You're welcome to share your thoughts and sentiments about the business of writing and publishing: Everything is cyclical. Good books will still be published, and those who work hard and are passionate will survive.

SCHIAVONE LITERARY AGENCY, INC.

Corporate Offices:
236 Trails End, West Palm Beach, FL 33413-2135
561-966-9294
email: profschia@aol.com

Jennifer DuVall: 3671 Hudson Manor Terrace, #11H, Bronx, NY 10463-1139
718-548-5332   email: jendu77@aol.com
Kevin McAdams: 400 East 11th Street #7, New York, NY 10009
email: kvn.mcadams@yahoo.com
www.publishersmarketplace.com/members/profschia

Agents' names: James Schiavone, EdD, CEO; Jennifer DuVall, President; Kevin McAdams, Executive VP.

Born: New York, New York.

Education: BS, MA, New York University; EdD Nova University; Professional Diploma, Columbia University; Advanced studies: University of Rome, Italy.

Career history: Director of reading, Monroe County (FL) Public Schools; professor emeritus of developmental skills at the City University of New York; literary agent.

Categories/subjects that you are most enthusiastic about agenting: Celebrity biography, autobiography and memoirs, general fiction, mystery, romance, fantasy/science fiction, business/investing/finance, history, religious, mind/body/spirit, health, travel, lifestyle, children's (no picture books), African American, Latino, ethnic, science.

What you don't want to agent: Poetry, short stories, anthologies, or children's picture books. No scripts or screenplays. We handle film rights, options, and screenplays only for books we have agented.

If you were not an agent, what might you be doing instead: Teaching graduate courses in the psychology of reading, writing nonfiction.

What's the best way for writers to solicit your interest: Query letters only, one-page preferred (no phone or fax). For fastest response (usually same or next day) email queries are acceptable and encouraged. For queries by post include SASE. No response without SASE. Do not send large envelopes with proposals, synopsis, sample chapters, etc., unless specifically requested. Queries must be sent to the main office in West Palm Beach, except for those directed to Jennifer DuVall at the New York City branch office or those addressed to Kevin McAdams in Manhattan.

Do you charge reading or management fees: No reading fee.

Can you provide an approximation by percent of what you tend to represent by category: Nonfiction: 51 percent, fiction: 41 percent, children's: 5 percent, textbooks: 3 percent.

What are the most common mistakes writers make when pitching you: Make initial contact via phone/fax; failure to query first before sending proposals, synopsis, etc.

How would you describe the perfect client: A published author who remains loyal to the author/agent partnership.

How and why did you ever become an agent: I have enjoyed a lifetime love of books and reading. I served as a reading specialist in schools and colleges and authored five trade books and three textbooks. I enjoy representing creative people and successfully working with them as partners in achieving and augmenting their career goals.

What, if anything, can a writer do to increase the odds of your becoming his or her agent: If a request is made for additional material, the author should prepare an outstanding, professionally written proposal along with sample chapters. For fiction, a brief well-stated synopsis accompanied by compelling initial chapters can make the difference in an offer of representation.

How would you describe to someone (or something) from another planet what it is that you do as an agent: Sell creative work of authors/clients to major publishing houses; negotiate contracts; handle business details—enabling authors to concentrate on the craft of writing.

Do you have any particular opinions or impressions of editors and publishers in general: I have been fortunate in working with the best editors in the industry. Generally, they are conscientious, indefatigable, and sincere in bringing an author's work to press. Agenting would be impossible without them. Publishers are the backbone of the industry. I am grateful for the serious consideration they give to my highly selective submissions.

What do you think the future holds for writers, publishers, and agents: The future holds unlimited opportunities for all, especially the reading public.

On a personal level, what do you think people like about you and dislike about you: My clients tell me that they appreciate the unlimited contact they have with me. I am always available to discuss their need and concerns as writers. The editors I work with have always appreciated the time, care, and consideration I put into my submissions to them. While dislikes may exist, they haven't been expressed to me.

Please list representative titles you have sold: *A Brother's Journey* (Warner); *A Teenager's Journey* (Warner); *Inside: Life Behind Bars in America* (St. Martin's); *Bedlam South* (State Street Press/Borders).

WENDY SCHMALZ AGENCY

Box 831, Hudson, NY 12534

518-672-7697   fax: 518-672-7662

email: wendy@schmalzagency.com

Agent's name: Wendy Schmalz
Born: Willow Grove, Pennsylvania.
Education: BA, Barnard College.
Career history or story: I started right out of college in the film department of Curtis Brown, Ltd. After a year, I went to Harold Ober Associates, where I

continued to handle film rights, but also built my own list and represented the estates of F. Scott Fitzgerald and Langston Hughes. I opened my own agency in 2002.

Hobbies, interests: Woodworking, history.

Subjects and categories you are interested in agenting, including fiction and nonfiction: I represent adult and children's fiction and nonfiction.

Subjects and categories writers shouldn't even bother pitching to you: I don't represent genre fiction such as sci-fi, romance or fantasy. I'm not looking for books for very young children and I'm not interested in taking on any new picture-book writers. I don't handle self-help or Christian books.

What would you do if you weren't agenting: Forensic pathology.

What's the best way for fiction writers to solicit your interest: When I get a submission letter, I want to know the writer wants me specifically to represent him or her—that she isn't just fishing for an agent. I want the sense that they know what I represent and want me to represent them because they think I'd be right for the kind of writing they do.

What's the best way for nonfiction writers to solicit your interest: Same as above.

Do you charge reading or any upfront fees: No.

In your experience, what are the most common pitching mistakes writers make: In children's books everyone compares their books to *Harry Potter*. With adult books, too many authors describe their characters as being on a journey of self-discovery. Avoid clichés.

Why did you become an agent, and how did you become one: When I was a teenager I read Tennessee Williams's autobiography. He went on and on and how great his agent was. Before that, I didn't know what an agent was, but it sounded like a cool way to make a living.

What are some representative titles that you have sold: *Rage* (Knopf) and *By the Time You Read This I'll Be Dead* (Hyperion) by National Book Award finalist Julie Anne Peters, *Snapshot* (Holt) by Edgar Award winner Robin MacCready, *Shadows Walking Backward* (Holt) by April Henry, *Carolina Clay* (Norton) by Leonard Todd, *Revealers* and *Devoured* (SimonPulse) by Amanda Marrone, *Fallon Urban Rescue* series (Knopf) by Sue Stauffacher. *Flat Iron* (Thomas Donne Books) by Alice Alexiou.

SCOVIL CHICHAK GALEN LITERARY AGENCY, INC

276 Fifth Avenue, Suite 708, New York, NY 10001

212-679-8686   fax: 646-349-1868

www.scglit.com   email: annaghosh@scglit.com

Agent's name: Anna Ghosh

Born: Bristol, United Kingdom.

Education: New School for Social Research, New York; Hampshire College, Massachusetts; Woodstock International School, India.

Career history: Agent at SCG since 1995.

Categories/subjects that you are most enthusiastic about agenting: Literary nonfiction, current affairs, investigative journalism, history, science, social and cultural issues, travel and adventure.

What's the best way for writers to solicit your interest: Send a well-written and thoughtful query letter.

Do you charge reading or management fees: No.

Can you provide an approximation by percent of what you tend to represent by category: Nonfiction: 70 percent, fiction: 30 percent.

Please list representative titles you have sold: *Last True Story I'll Ever Tell: An Accidental Soldier's Account of the War in Iraq* (Riverhead); *Ambitious Brew: The Story of American Beer* (Harcourt); *Living Cosmos* (Random House); *Churchill's Choice: Empire, War and the Great Bengal Famine* (Basic); *Reading Claudius* (Dial Press); *All Is Change: The Two Thousand Year Journey of Buddhism to the West* (Little Brown); *Is Gluten Making Me Ill?* (Rodale); *Art of War for Women* (Doubleday).

SEBASTIAN LITERARY AGENCY

1043 Grand Avenue #557, St. Paul, MN 55105

651-298-0076

www.sebastianagency.com

Agent's name: Laurie Harper; laurie@sebastianagency.com

Born: September 1954.

Education: Business and finance, pre-law studies, Stanford Publishing Course.

Career story: I founded the Agency in 1985 in San Francisco, after closing my regional publishing company. I have authored two published books over the years, so I have been on many sides of the business. In 2000 I moved to Minneapolis to be near my family, and have never regretted it. I use my 25-plus years of publishing experience and network in both the agency work and my consulting work for Author Biz Consulting.

Hobbies and special personal interests: Motorcycling (Suzuki Boulevard), sailing, movies, and almost any form of play. And of course, reading.

Subjects and categories you like to agent: Note: See the website for more specifics. Business and finance (management, business narratives, financial); health/medicine/nutrition (narratives from the field by professionals, leading-edge research, disease/immunology/aging, nutrition guides); women's issues (personal growth, research and studies—across fields like communications, education, family and relationships, mental health, physical health, work and careers, aging, spiritual well-being); psychology/sociology/personal growth (this is for professionals writing from their private practices or client-based work, for the general trade audience, across a broad arena).

Subjects and categories writers shouldn't bother pitching to you: First novels, short story collections, poetry, screenplays, children's or YA books, scholarly [books] or textbooks, personal autobiographies, or personal-story books about overcoming a particular disease or abuse.

What might you be doing if you weren't agenting: I would still happily work for the Authors Guild, and continue doing the consulting work I already do for writers. I enjoy it very much.

What's the most effective ways for writers to grab your attention: By email with no attachment, or snail mail—to tell me about your book and why you are the one to write it, as well as how you can market it once it is published.

Do you charge fees separate from your commission, or offer non-agenting fee-based services: I do not offer any editing or critique services and if a project is not ready to go to publishers or to sell, I do not take it on. There are no reading fees, and I do not charge back U.S. postage or phone.

What are representative titles you have sold to publishers: *Fathers and Daughters* by Linda Nielsen (Cumberland House); *Stunned: The New Generation of Women Having Babies, Getting Angry, and Creating a New Women's Movement* by Karen Bridson (HCI); *Toxic Workplace: Managing Toxic Personalities and Their Systems of Power* by Mitch Kusy and Elizabeth Holloway (Jossey-Bass); *Secret Codebook of the High Achievers* by Sandra Naiman (Jist Publishing); *Career Chronicles* by Mike Glasgow (New World Library); *Money, Sex and Kids* by Tina Tessina (Adams Media); *The Warren Buffett Way*, 2nd Edition by Robert Hagstrom (John Wiley); *More Than You Know* by Michael Mauboussin (Columbia University Press); *Port in a Storm: How to Make a Medical Decision and Live to Tell About It* by Dr. Cole Giller (Lifelong Press/Regnery).

Why did you become an agent, and how did you become one: I was helping a couple of writers find publishers when I could not publish their books, way back when, and that is how it happened. When I sold their books for them, I knew I had found the right work and the right place for me in this industry.

How would you describe the writer from hell: One who expects to be paid a large advance before he or she has done the work to warrant it, which indicates a pattern of thinking and behavior that will sabotage everyone's efforts. It also shows a lack of knowledge or understanding about publishing. I also cannot work with an author who cannot or will not promote him or herself and market the book…This pretty much kills any possibilities for the author and the book.

What do you like best about your clients, and the editors and publishers you work with: The qualities I like best are: Intelligence, commitment, creativity, hard-working, good communicators, imagination, fascinating ideas, strong language skills, and good team players. It takes a strong and talented team to get the right book out in the right way and to have all the elements work successfully to accomplish its goals.

LYNN SELIGMAN, LITERARY AGENT

400 Highland Avenue, Upper Montclair, NJ 07043

973-783-3631

Agent's name: Lynn Seligman

Born: February 25, 1947 in New York City, New York.

Education: BA, 1967, Goucher College; MA, 1968, Columbia University (French literature); graduate work for PhD in French literature except thesis, Columbia University.

Career history: Independent literary agent since 1985. Previously agent at Julian Bach Literary Agency, Inc. (1980–1985). Various subsidiary rights positions (1971–1980) at Simon & Schuster (associate director; serial rights director), Doubleday (foreign rights associate; serial rights manager) and Thomas Y. Crowell. Books editor at East/West Network (airline magazine group) in 1975.

Hobbies/personal interests: Reading, ballet, art, hiking and walking.

Categories/subjects that you are most enthusiastic about agenting: Nonfiction—memoir, psychology, health, medicine, science, women's issues and business. Fiction: literary, women's books and romance, horror, science fiction and fantasy.

What you don't want to agent: Children's books, with the exception of young-adult.

If you were not an agent, what might you be doing instead: International law? Veterinary medicine? These were areas I considered before I entered publishing, but I am very happy doing what I do. It lends itself to great change and adaptation within the field. And I am never bored.

What's the best way for fiction writers to solicit your interest: Write a great solicitation letter (no email, and with SASE enclosed), including something about your background and interests. Include a sample of the book (about 10–20 pages), and a synopsis or summary so I can get a feel for the writing and story, if desired.

What's the best way for nonfiction writers to solicit your interest: Same as fiction, although the author's background and experience is more important here. Less important to have writing sample, except for memoir or narrative nonfiction.

Do you charge reading or management fees: No.

Can you provide an approximation by percent of what you tend to represent

by category: Nonfiction: 70 percent (primarily parenting, health, medicine, psychology, memoir). Fiction: 30 percent (romance and women's fiction, horror, science fiction and fantasy, literary).

What are the most common mistakes writers make when pitching you: The most common mistake I can think of is telling me how much other editors, publishers, best friends, other writers, etc. loved the book. The latter two are not usually objective, and if the former ones loved it so much, it would have been bought before it landed on my desk.

How would you describe the client from hell: I really cannot tolerate lying or verbal abuse, but I generally do not have these kinds of clients. I have a very small list and am pretty good at figuring out the people I can work with.

How would you describe the perfect client: Imaginative, intelligent, responsible, responsive and communicative.

How and why did you ever become an agent: I started out as an ESL teacher in the public schools. I loved the kids and hated teaching. But I know I loved publishing, so I began in editorial, then moved to subsidiary rights. Since I had gone about as far as I could in that area, I chose agenting, which combined my love of being close to the creative process with selling, which I also loved.

What, if anything, can a writer do to increase the odds of your becoming his or her agent: Write a great book that interests me!

How would you describe to someone (or something) from another planet what it is that you do as an agent: I have no idea how to answer this question. Isn't what we do already being on another planet?

Do you have any particular opinions or impressions of editors and publishers in general: I think we all see how much harder it is to market books, and this trickles down to the publishers' and editors' behavior: the cult of the bestseller, the emphasis on platforms, the lack of support for a "smaller" book, etc. This issue is one for all retail businesses now, which publishing is, but when it involves creative people, it becomes more problematic for everyone to deal with. I think editors work very hard now to buy and sell books, and a lot less time on developing writers, so that job falls more and more to the agent.

How do you feel about writers: If I didn't love and respect writers and what they accomplish, I wouldn't be in this business.

What do you think the future holds for writers, publishers, and agents: Some of this answer is actually above, but I think the agent becomes even more important in the writer's career than ever before. The agent fills part of the role that the editor and publisher did. I also think that electronic publishing will be part of our future, in some kind of form, and I only hope that the rights of the creator will be protected. That role will be the responsibility of the agent as well.

What are your favorite books, movies, TV shows, and why: I have very eclectic tastes, in all respects. Two of my favorite TV shows are *24*, for its excitement and unpredictability, and *Desperate Housewives*, for its biting sarcasm. Two of my favorite books are *Truth and Beauty* by Ann Patchett, which is phenomenal view of friendship, insanity and the creative life, and *The Kite Runner*, which was beautifully written and gave a fascinating picture of another world. I love small quirky movies, mostly foreign, such as *The Class* and *The Reader*.

In your opinion, what do editors think of you: I really don't know exactly, but I think they pay attention when I send them projects, so it is a positive opinion for the most part.

On a personal level, what do you think people like about you and dislike about you: I think I am very honest and open (both a positive and negative trait!), sympathetic and caring about people close to me. On the negative side, I can be indecisive (seeing all sides at once—very Pisces) and try too hard to please everyone.

Please list representative titles you have sold: *Morbid Curiosity* by Deborah Le Blanc (Leisure Books); *Sinful under the Sheets* by Barbara Pierce (St. Martin's); *My Father Before Me: How Fathers and Sons Influence Each Other Throughout Their Lives* by Dr. Michael Diamond (Norton); *Raising a Thinking Child* by Dr. Myrna Shure (Simon & Schuster/Pocket Books); *The New Professional Image* by Susan Bixler (Adams Media); *The Red Magician* by Lisa Goldstein (Tor Books, Starscape).

THE SEYMOUR AGENCY

475 Miner Street Road, Canton, NY 13617

315-386-1831

www.theseymouragency.com   email: marysue@twcny.rr.com

Agent's name: Mary Sue Seymour, AAR

Born: September 21, New York.

Education: BS from State University of New York plus thirty graduate hours mostly in education, hold New York State teacher's certificate.

Career story: Began agency in 1992.

Hobbies and special personal interests: Hiking in the Adirondacks, walking my golden retriever, watching *American Idol* and *Walker, Texas Ranger*, going to church, reading my Bible, baking apple pies and homemade cinnamon rolls, traveling to writers conferences, and presenting workshops.

Subjects and categories you like to agent: Christian books of any type, especially historical Christian romance, category romance, and any type of secular romance.

Subjects and categories writers shouldn't bother pitching to you: Fantasy romance, sci-fi romance, erotica, short stories, poetry, general novels.

What might you be doing if you weren't agenting: Teaching art.

What's the most effective way for writers to grab your attention: A great query letter describing the project to a T—show me you can write.

Do you charge fees separate from your commission, or offer non-agenting fee-based services: No.

What are representative titles you have sold to publishers: Amy Clipton's multi-book deal to Zondervan, Beth Wiseman's multi-book deal to Thomas Nelson, Don Reid's (of the Statler Brothers) second multi-book deal to Crole Communications Ministries, Shelley Sabga's multi-book deal to HarperCollins and Harlequin American, Barbara Cameron's and Beth Wiseman's novellas to Thomas Nelson.

Why did you become an agent, and how did you become one: I was writing while teaching school. I had three agents—a couple of them were pretty bad and I wondered if I could be a successful agent. The first book I sent out sold a four-book deal to Bantam so I believe it was meant to be. I quit teaching.

How do you feel about writers: I sympathize with them. There is a lot of room for error when you write a book, yet writers have to have them perfect, and editors are so selective these days. Also the economy isn't that good and editors are buying more conservatively. It's a tough life and I have nothing but the greatest respect for authors. The key to being a happy author is to have other things you do simultaneously that you're good at. Then you will always have success in your life.

What are your favorite books, movies, TV shows and why: I absolutely love *Walker, Texas Ranger* on the Hallmark Channel and I watch it whenever I can. It's so funny in some ways and of course the good guys always win. There are certain Christian undertones in the show that I like as well.

How would you describe the writer from hell: I have never had one.

How would you describe the publisher and/or editor from hell: I have never dealt with one. Editors are always professional or they wouldn't be editors.

What do you like best about your clients, and the editors and publishers you work with: They're nice, real people just like I try to be.

Do you wish to describe who you are: I love to travel to conferences and meet writers; I do about one conference a month. Conferences I plan to attend this year include a Christian conference in Asheville, NC, RWA National in Washington DC, WOW in Las Vegas, Put Your Heart in a Book in New Jersey, Central Florida Writer's Conference, Space Coast Writer's Conference in Cocoa Beach, FL.

Will our business exist as we know it in ten years or so: The advent of DVDs [is] taking over writing a little bit. I am anxious to see where the book industry will be in ten years.

KEN SHERMAN & ASSOCIATES

9507 Santa Monica Blvd., Suite 211, Beverly Hills, CA 90210

Agents' names: Ken Sherman, President

Born: Sherman: Los Angeles, September 19.

Education: BS, psychology, Berkeley.

Career Story: Reader at Columbia Pictures, then training and becoming an agent at the William Morris Agency/Los Angeles for four and a half years, then the Lantz/LA office of NY-based company, then the Paul Koehner Agency and then my own company starting 1989.

Hobbies and special personal interests: Books, film, making art.

Subjects and categories you like to agent: All.

What might you be doing if you weren't agenting: Drawing.

What's the most effective ways for writers to grab your attention: A good connection through someone I know.

Do you charge fees separate from your commission, or offer non-agenting fee-based services: No.

What are representative titles you have sold to publishers (book title, author, publisher): A few of my clients are Anne Perry, Tawni O'Dell, the estate of John Updike, Starhawk, the John Hersey estate, Mike Carey (graphic novelist), the Luis Bunuel estate, Louis Begley, etc. Many of my authors are for film and television rights as well as book rights.

Why did you become an agent, and how did you become one: By accident. Books were always a comfort zone and films a passion so I was always looking and reading and it seems natural to become involved in writer's professional lives.

How do you feel about writers: I love them and sometimes their work even more.

What do you tell entities from other planets and dimensions about your job: I don't. They already know.

How would you describe the writer from hell: Someone who lacks respect for the agent/author relationship.

How would you describe the publisher and/or editor from hell: The irrational ones who won't let me have my way.

What do you like best about your clients, and the editors and publishers you work with: Their intelligence and thoughtfulness and ability to tailor each situation as needed.

Finally, will our business exist as we know it in ten years or so: I hope so, but it will morph like the rest of the world.

WENDY SHERMAN ASSOCIATES, INC.

450 Seventh Avenue, Suite 2307, New York, NY 10123

212-279-9027   fax: 212-279-8863

Agents' names: Wendy Sherman, Michelle Brower

Born: Sherman: New York, New York; Brower: Berlin, New Jersey.

Education: Sherman: University of Hartford, bachelor's in special education; Alspaugh: BA 1998, Sarah Lawrence College.; Brower: The College of NJ, BA, and New York University, MA.

Career history or story: Sherman: Opened this agency in 1999, was previously with the Aaron Priest Agency. Vice president, executive director at Henry Holt, vice president, associate publisher at Owl Books. Vice president, sales and subsidiary rights (1998–1999). Also worked at Simon & Schuster and McMillan.

Hobbies, interests: Sherman: Reading, traveling. Brower: Crafting, cooking, film, animals.

Subjects and categories you are interested in agenting, including fiction and nonfiction: Sherman: Quality fiction, women's fiction, suspense, narrative nonfiction, psychology/self-help. Brower: Pop culture, music, humor, crafting, commercial fiction, thriller, literary fiction, narrative nonfiction, YA, and graphic novels. Books with elements of horror, fantasy, or science fiction that are for a mainstream audience.

Subjects and categories writers shouldn't even bother pitching to you: Science fiction, fantasy, horror, mysteries, and children's books. Brower: Cozies, children's picture books, category romance.

What would you do if you weren't agenting: Sherman: I could be back in corporate publishing, but choose not to pursue that career path. Brower: I would probably be working in editorial.

What's the best way for fiction writers to solicit your interest: Query letter via regular mail to the agency, with a first chapter. Brower: Query and first chapter, by email or regular mail.

What's the best way for nonfiction writers to solicit your interest: Query letter via regular mail describing their book and credentials.

Do you charge reading or any upfront fees: No.

In your experience, what are the most common pitching mistakes writers make: The most common mistakes are not targeting the right agent and being unclear about your book in your query letter. Writers should do their research and find an agent who is a good fit for their material.

Describe the client from hell, even if you don't have any: The client from hell is unreasonably demanding and doesn't trust our judgment and experience.

What's your definition of a great client: The perfect collaboration between agent and author is one of mutual goals and respect.

How can writers increase the odds that you will offer representation: Have a fully polished book or proposal that's timely and well done.

Why did you become an agent, and how did you become one: Sherman: After leaving Henry Holt, I had the opportunity to work for the Aaron Priest Agency. I had thought about agenting for some time, and it seemed like the perfect way to make the change from working for a publisher to becoming an agent. Brower: I started with Wendy Sherman Associates in 2004 after receiving my master's degree in literature, and I love working with clients to develop their ideas, shape their proposals, and take their fiction to the next level.

Describe to someone from another planet what you do as an agent: We bring writers to the attention of the best possible/most enthusiastic editor and publisher. We then do our best to ensure the book is published with the utmost enthusiasm. Alspaugh: I represent my clients' interests to a publisher. I work with them to hone their manuscripts and proposals, and I sell their work for the most I can get, then negotiate their contracts. I follow up with publishers for timely payments and marketing efforts. I protect my clients' rights to consult on book jacket art and other matters. I support, guide, and advise my clients, and help them to develop their careers.

How do you feel about editors and publishers: More than ever, editors have a very tough job. They not only have to find manuscripts they want to publish, but then convince in-house colleagues in editorial, marketing, and sales to support the acquisitions.

How do you feel about writers: We love writers, they are why we became agents. The best writers bring an immense amount of talent to the table and take direction well.

What are your favorite books, TV shows, movies, and why: *Watership Down* by Richard Adams; *A Tree Grows in Brooklyn* by Betty Smith; *The Glass Castle* by Jeannette Walls; all of Jane Austen and George Eliot; *Middlesex* by Jeffrey Eugenides. And so many more.

What are some representative titles that you have sold: Fiction: *Love in 90 Days* by Dr. Diana Kirschner (Center Street); *Kockroach* by Tyler Knox (William Morrow); *Marked Man* by William Lashner (William Morrow); *Souvenir* by Therese Fowler (Random House); *The Cloud Atlas* by Liam Callanan (Delacorte); *The Judas Field* by Howard Bahr (Henry Holt); *The Vanishing Point* by Mary Sharratt (Houghton Mifflin); *The Ice Chorus* by Sarah Stonich (Little, Brown); *Crawling at Night* by Nani Power (Atlantic Monthly Press). Nonfiction: *My First Five Husbands* by Rue McClanahan (Broadway); *Confessions of a Prep School Mommy Handler* by Wade Rouse (Harmony); *Why Men Fall Out of Love* by Michael French (Ballantine); *Cash In on Your Passion* by Jonathan Fields (Broadway); *Real Love* by Greg Baer (Gotham); *Feed the Hungry* by Nani Power (Free Press). Brower: *Oh, The Humanity!* by Jason Roeder (TOW Books); *Gag Reflex: A Paternity Memoir* by Cori Crooks (Seal Press). Brower: *Farm City: The Education of an Urban Farmer* by Novella Carpenter (Penguin Press); *Breathers: A Zombie's Lament* by S. G. Browne (Broadway Books); *Mixed Animal* by Richard Martin (MacAdam/Cage); *Slanted and Enchanted: Indie Culture in America* by Kaya Oakes (Henry Holt & Co).

THE ROBERT E. SHEPARD AGENCY

1608 Dwight Way, Berkeley, CA 94703-1804

510-849-3999

email: mail@shepardagency.com

www.shepardagency.com

Agent' name: Robert Shepard

Education: BA, MA in English, University of Pennsylvania.

Career history: In 2009, my agency celebrated its 15th anniversary, and I marked my 25th year in the publishing world. Much has changed since I started out in the trade division of Addison-Wesley, a respected publisher that has since passed into history. But my background on the editorial, sales, and marketing sides gave me a good understanding of the "business" of publishing, including managing millions of dollars in sales and establishing excellent working relationships with scores of acquisitions editors. I bring all of that, a passion for nonfiction, and a healthy skepticism about the state of the publishing industry to bear in working with my clients. I enjoy helping them craft their proposals, sharing ideas with them as they write their books, helping them decide on the topics for their future works, and working with them to build their writing careers. I also enjoy the process of actually selling their books, and celebrating with my clients when the contract is signed and the advance check issued. The role of agents in the work of authors has become ever more critical. I'm proud of the close rapport I've established with authors and remain committed to the idea that books are the foundation of our culture; everything else springs from them. Since I love nonfiction, it's especially gratifying to see literary nonfiction works enjoying renewed success. This is an excellent time to be a nonfiction author, and I believe the works on my list have played a role in that.

Hobbies/personal interests: Hiking, biking, trains, raptors, and diagramming sentences.

Subjects that you would most love to agent: I represent only nonfiction, and under that heading I've cultivated two separate categories of books. The first consists of works driven by an exceptionally strong, unified literary narrative—books intended to make complex ideas accessible to a wider public; to shed new light on aspects of history, society, or popular culture; or to provide fresh insights into people, places, or concepts we may think of as commonplace. On this side of the practice, my subject headings include history, contemporary affairs and politics, science for laypeople, and topics in culture, sexuality, urbanism, and sports. The other general category of books I represent tends to be driven less by narrative and more by hard information; on this side, I have core interests in business, health, parenting, some topics in self-help, and occasional series-oriented works in such areas as music, science, and general reference. It's safe to say that I'm interested in neither the most commercial nor the most abstruse kinds of books, and that I'm rarely interested in works in spirituality or the metaphysical. On either side of the list, I'm happy to represent works that inform, that may change readers' minds, that may require a somewhat more intellectually curious audience, or about which someone might say "I never thought this would be an interesting subject, but I really loved reading this book." And I regularly digress. Sometimes, I represent a book simply because I think it will be fun.

Subjects that you definitely never want to agent: I never handle fiction, poetry, screenplays, or textbooks, and in general I'm not interested in memoirs, although occasionally books on my list may be written in the first person or have an autobiographical component, especially when they relate to my regular categories. Robert E. Shepard Agency titles are usually aimed at a broad audience, so that highly specialized works (such as ones that examine religious writings in detail, or whose intended readers are mainly in a single profession) are not appropriate. As a general rule, I'm also not interested in spirituality (although historical works with some kind of religious overlay might be of interest), metaphysical subjects, or recovery.

If you were not an agent, what would you be doing: I'd probably be doing a lot more bicycling, preferably in Italy, conducting a symphony orchestra (after belatedly studying to do so for a couple of decades), or riding trains while on sabbatical from my job as the publisher of a distinguished literary nonfiction house. I'm not picky.

What's the best way for fiction writers to solicit your interest: I'm afraid they shouldn't—I don't represent fiction.

What's the best way for unsolicited writers to pitch you: Never call or fax; neither will speed consideration of your proposal. I encourage authors to mail a query letter or proposal, or to email a relatively brief query describing the proposed work, its intended audience, and the author's own credentials and reasons for writing on this subject. Don't just refer me to a website; I want to see how you present your ideas in the succinct form demanded by a query letter, whether by mail or email. Please do not attach any computer files to email messages; for security purposes, they'll be deleted. If you use regular mail, always enclose a postage-paid return envelope capable of holding everything you sent me, without which you will not receive a reply.

Do you charge reading fees or try to sell non-agent services: No.

Do you require any kind of upfront payments from your clients: No.

Client representation by category: Nonfiction: 100 percent.

Number of titles sold last year: Ten. I've deliberately kept the practice small in order to devote time to my clients. I'm happy to see proposals from new authors, or from authors whose previous works may have been in genres other than general nonfiction. However, your credentials and expertise should be suited to the kind of book you're proposing.

Common mistakes writers make when pitching you: A big one is failing to share your proposal with a friend or another writer before you send it out. Authors who work in a vacuum risk losing perspective. In the many months you've been working on your book proposal—and very often they really do take that long to write—has your focus shifted inadvertently? Have you failed to discuss some aspect of your topic that an agent or editor might find fascinating—simply because you're too immersed in writing to realize you'd missed it? Have you made the strongest possible case that the audience for your book really exists, is large enough to interest publishers, and hasn't been inundated with competing books? Have you cited a date or name incorrectly, making yourself look careless even though you really do know your facts? A trusted adviser, particularly one with experience in writing books, can help you improve your proposal or even catch mistakes before you send it to agents. Not to sound like the English teacher I sometimes think I should have been, but bad spelling and grammar often guarantee rejection slips, too. Proofread your work, and if you don't trust your proofreading skills, find someone you do trust to help you. I also counsel authors to avoid proposal clichés. A big one is "there's no competition for my book." You should always try to find works that others might consider competitive, and then describe what's new, different, and better about yours. Another cliché is saying that you look forward to "partnering" with your publisher without saying, in detail, what you can do to help market your book. An author's "platform" is ever more important—critical, really, to the acquisitions process. Try to build up your portfolio. Send articles to op-ed pages and magazines, so you can include copies in your proposal packet. If you have experience on radio or television, or speaking in front of large audiences, cite it; if you don't, try to get some. Finally, there are two important housekeeping issues: Always enclose a return envelope large enough to hold your material, with the proper postage (without which you won't get a response); and always provide your return address!

Your description of the client from hell: One with a great idea but without the inclination to write a super proposal, let alone a super book. Writing is tough and an agent wants to be your ally and work hard for you and for your book. But the hardest work of all must be yours.

How would you describe your dream client: Those who are passionate about writing, passionate about their subjects, and appreciative when things go right.

How can writers increase the odds that you will offer representation: Pay attention to other books, know how to differentiate your own from others, and take steps to build up your résumé as a writer before you query. Write (and publish) articles and op-ed pieces. Try to get yourself in front of audiences if appropriate and on television and radio if possible—you don't have to be famous to be published, but you do have to be "marketable." And write a really outstanding query letter or proposal; it's critical to do your homework.

Why did you become an agent, and how did you become one: I love books and believe they can and should be central to our cultural life, even in an era when they're being joined by new sources of entertainment and information all the time. But the consolidations of leading publishers during the 1990s resulted in the loss of many editors, the very people who traditionally worked the closest with authors, helped them craft better books, and made sure that the marketing got done. The vast majority of today's editors are as talented and dedicated as ever, but find themselves with more books to edit and less time to spend with authors. So although authors create the intellectual property that fuels our culture, they can feel lost in the publishing shuffle, confused by business aspects of their writing careers, and even disillusioned by the paradoxical demand of publishers to write "fresh" books that nonetheless don't deviate much from the constraints of established categories. I see my role as an agent as that of a mentor and advocate for my clients and their work, as a diplomat who can moderate the author-publisher relationship, as a business adviser who watches over royalty statements, and, in the end, as someone who helps authors feel good about the writing experience, so they can write more books in the future. The bad news, unfortunately, is that an agent still spends a good part of his or her day saying "no." The good news is that, when everything works as it should, the wealth of media outlets available to us in the Internet age means books can be more rather than less influential.

Please list representative titles you have sold: *A Few Seconds of Panic* by Stefan Fatsis (Penguin Press), also the author of the bestselling *Word Freak* (Houghton Mifflin hardcover, Penguin paperback); *Night Draws Near* (Henry Holt & Co.), a *Los Angeles Times* Book Prize–winning work by Pulitzer Prize winner Anthony Shadid, whose next book about Lebanon will be published by Holt; *The Foie Gras Wars* by Mark Caro (Simon & Schuster); *American Band* by Kristen Laine (Gotham); *Find Your Focus Zone* by Lucy Jo Palladino, PhD (Free Press); *Your Symptoms Are Real* by Benjamin H. Natelson, MD (Wiley); *The Exhaustion Cure* by Laura Stack (Broadway Books), also the author of *Leave the Office Earlier* and *Find More Time*, both also from Broadway Books; *Champagne* by Don and Petie Kladstrup (William Morrow), also the authors of *Wine and War* (Broadway Books), an international bestseller published in ten languages; *Women of Valor* by Ellen Hampton (Palgrave-MacMillan); *The Governmental Manual for New Superheroes* by Matthew David Brozik and Jacob Sager Weinstein (Andrews McMeel), also the authors of two other books in this series; *Coal: A Human History* by Barbara Freese (Perseus hardcover, Penguin paperback), a bestseller in the U.S. and published in several editions abroad; *The Rough Guide to Climate Change* by Robert Henson (Rough Guides/Penguin).

SIMENAUER & GREENE LITERARY AGENCY

P.O. Box 770968, Naples, FL 34107-0968

239-597-9877 (Jacqueline Simenauer)

239-594-1484 (Carole J. Greene)

Agents' names: Jacqueline Simenauer, jsliteraryagent@gmail.com; Carole J. Greene, cjgliteraryagent@gmail.com

The following information pertains to Jacqueline Simenauer.

Born: New York, New York.

Education: Fordham University.

Career story: After working as an articles editor for a national publication, I decided to start my own literary agency, and as a result of this, I coauthored a number of books with my clients. Some of the six books that I was involved with include the bestselling *Beyond the Male Myth*, which was featured on *Oprah*; *Husbands and Wives, Singles: The New Americans*, which gained the attention of the White House; and *Not Tonight Dear*. They went on to sell over 200,000 copies. My work has also been featured in most of the nation's magazines and newspapers including *Time*, *Readers Digest*, *Ladies Home Journal*, *The New York Times*, and *The Washington Post*. In addition, I have appeared in 100 radio/TV showings, including *Good Morning America* and the *Today Show*.

Hobbies and special personal interests: I have always worked so hard that I never found time to even think about a hobby. However, I do love classical concerts. I am a member of a wine society; I love the Broadway theater and great fiction.

Subjects and categories you like to agent: I like a wide range of strong commercial nonfiction books that include medical, health, nutrition, popular psychology, how-to/self-help, parenting, women's issues, spirituality, men's issues, relationships, social sciences, beauty, controversial subjects.

Subjects and categories writers shouldn't bother pitching to you: This agency doesn't handle crafts, poetry, and children's books.

What might you be doing if you weren't agenting: You would probably find me cruising around the world.

What's the most effective ways for writers to grab your attention: Please write a really good query letter. This is so important. If you can't get your idea across effectively, then you've lost the agent.

Do you charge fees separate from your commission, or offer non-agenting fee-based services: We do not charge a reading fee. The agency can draw on professionals to do book doctoring when requested, and the fee for that is currently $2.50 per page. In rare instances, we also offer ghostwriting services (utilizing published writers on a contract basis). This represents a small part of our business—probably in the range of 5 percent or less.

What are representative titles you have sold to publishers: *The Insulin Resistance Diet* by Dr. Cheryle Hart and Mary Kay Grossman, RD (McGraw-Hill); *The Thyroid Guide* by Dr. Beth Ann Ditkoff and Dr. Paul Lo Gerfo (Harper); *Overcoming Anxiety without Tranquilizers* by Dr. Edward H. Drummond (Dutton); *The Feel Good Diet* by Dr. Cheryle Hart and Mary K. Grossman, RD (McGraw-Hill); *Endometriosis Sourcebook* by Mary Lou Wallweg (Contemporary); *Decoding the Secret Language of Your Body* by Dr. Martin Rush (Fireside/Simon & Schuster); *Fasting and Eating for Health* by Dr. Joel Fuhrman (St. Martin's Press); *What to Do After You Say I Do* by Dr. Marcus J. Goldman and Lori Goldman (Prima); *Why Did It Happen?* by Janice Cohn, DSW (Morrow); *The Mind Factor* by Dr. Jean Rosenbaum (Prentice Hall);

Bride's Guide to Emotional Survival by Rita Bigel-Casher, PhD (Prima); *Money Secrets the Pros Don't Want You to Know* by Stephanie Gallagher (AMACOM); *What Is Fear?* by Dr. Jean Rosenbaum (Prentice Hall); *Husbands and Wives* by Dr. Anthony Pietropinto; *The Healing Mind* by Eileen F. Oster (Prima); *Singles: The New Americans* (Simon & Schuster); *How to Avoid Divorce* by Dr. Jean Rosenbaum (Harper); *Biotypes* (Times Books); *The Joy of Fatherhood* by Dr. Marcus Goldman (Prima); *The Yankee Encyclopedia* by Mark Gallagher (Sagamore); *Every Woman's Guide to Investing* by Francie Prince and Douglas Pi (Prima); *Brave New You* by Mary Valentis, PhD (New Harbinger Publications); *Beyond the Male Myth* by Dr. Anthony Pietropinto; *The Real Truth About Mutual Funds* by Herbert Rongold (American Management); *The Single Woman's Travel Guide* by Doris Walfield (Citadel Press); *Conquering Loneliness* by Dr. Jean Rosenbaum; *The Clinic* by Dr. Anthony Pietropinto; *Reengineering Yourself* by Dr. Daniel L. Araoz and Dr. William S. Sutton (Adams Media); *The Dream Girl* by Dr. Anthony Pietropinto (Adams Media); *Kleptomania* by Dr. Marcus Goldman (New Horizon); *Is Your Volkawagon a Sex Symbol?* by Dr. Jean Rosenbaum; *How I Sold a Million Copies of My Software* by Herbert R. Kraft (Adams Media); *Single's Guide to Cruise Vacations* (Prima).

Why did you become an agent, and how did you become one: I seemed to have always been involved with the publishing world, in one way or another. I had worked for a national publication as an articles editor, I was a freelance writer and coauthor. Agenting seemed the likely next step so I opened an agency. At first I was the only one. Then I was joined by my colleague Carole Greene, who has now become my partner.

How do you feel about writers: I think my background as a freelance writer and coauthor makes me even more sympathetic to struggling writers. I understand what it feels like to see your name on a book jacket and appear on a major TV show, and if I can help you achieve your dream, then it becomes mine as well. But understand that it takes a great deal of perseverance to go from an idea to a proposal strong enough to get the attention of the publishing world.

How would you describe the writer from hell: I agree with and stand with Carole. See below.

The following information pertains to Carole J. Greene.

Born: Anderson, IN, October 14, making me a Libra; yep, I'm balanced.

Education: Two degrees from Ball State University, Muncie Indiana; BA and MA in English.

Career story: After a decade as a high school and college educator focusing primarily on composition and creative writing, I became a full-time independent journalist. I wrote more than 1,000 articles for national and regional magazines on a wide range of topics including medical, business, finance, lifestyle, home improvement, community development, real estate, and golf. I also wrote a humor column for a monthly newspaper. I created award-winning marketing materials—advertising copy, brochures, newsletters, video scripts—for private clients. I then turned my attention to book projects, as a ghostwriter, coauthor, and author of numerous books, and editor of a couple dozen more (so far), both for private clients and publishers. Since 1985, I've belonged to the same writers group (all members have been published), where each week we lovingly critique one another's works in progress. After teaching, freelancing, ghosting, editing, and critiquing, the next logical step was agenting. Ta-da!

Hobbies and special personal interests: In addition to traveling the world with my hubby, I enjoy theater, movies, fine dining, music, golf, bridge, and reading. Lots of reading. Mostly before publication.

Subjects and categories you like to agent: I find my tastes are quite eclectic, almost anything that is well written and has a chance of being salable. Fiction attracts me more than nonfiction. Query me about an intriguing story beautifully told that demonstrates expert use of the English language. But if it needs a little polish to make it shine, I have a red pen and I'm not afraid to use it!

Subjects and categories writers shouldn't bother pitching to you: Arts and crafts, poetry, children's books, horror, or fantasy.

What might you be doing if you weren't agenting: When I'm not working with/for my clients, I am writing SOMETHING—from pro bono materials for groups I support to grocery lists. I'm still tinkering with a novel I began several years ago…who knows, maybe this is the year I'll finish it. Probably not.

What's the most effective ways for writers to grab your attention: The most effective way is to write a query letter that demonstrates their grasp of language skills and their commitment to delivering their message in an interesting professional manner. Just owning a computer and a word processing program is not enough to make you a writer, so forget the stylized graphics for your cover and concentrate on making that query letter so enticing that I salivate to see more of your material.

Do you charge fees separate from your commission, or offer non-agenting fee-based services: NO.

How do you feel about writers: I am totally supportive of the creative life. If you love to mess around with words and have a story to tell that would benefit others, I'll be the wind beneath your wings. The best writers through the ages have made the world a better place. If you aspire to that lofty goal, I would love to help you get your message out.

How would you describe the writer from hell: I wouldn't describe any writer, editor or publisher as "from hell" as long as they put forth sincere effort to produce a book that people will be glad they read. That applies to agents too, so don't bug me if you're my client. I'm putting forth sincere effort even if you don't hear from me for weeks!

You're welcome to share your thoughts and sentiments about the business of writing and publishing: One of my writing group friends once said, "Writing is the hardest work I ever loved." It IS difficult, much harder than nonwriters comprehend. Getting your FIRST book published can be daunting; however, every successful author has that FIRST book. Don't ever let fear of rejection stand in your way of attaining the goal of publishing your work. Changes in the publishing industry occur so fast that the wisest sage would be unable to foresee the future.

Will we continue to read books? Absolutely; it's in our DNA. The method of delivery will continue to evolve, with e-books and Kindle right now and, who knows, maybe a micro chip inserted directly into our bodies that will auto-download books as they're being published. It's an exciting industry and I'm thrilled to fulfill my role in it—until someone has to pry that red pen out of my cold, still fingers.

MICHAEL SNELL LITERARY AGENCY

P.O. Box 1206, Truro, MA 02666

508-349-3718

email: snell.patricia@gmail.com

Agents' names: Michael Snell, Patricia Snell, Vice-President

Born: Michael: August 14, 1965, Denver, Colorado; Patricia: 1951, Boston, Massachusetts.

Education: Michael: BA, Phi Beta Kappa, DePauw University; Patricia: FIT and Pratt Institute, New York.

Career history: Michael: Thirteen years as editor and executive editor for Wadsworth Publishing Company and Addison-Wesley (science, economics, English, computer science, business college textbooks); Patricia: Design offices in New York City's garment district and in Manhattan art galleries and museums. Twelve years as partner in the Michael Snell Literary Agency.

Hobbies/personal interests: Michael: Golf, tennis, landscaping, shell fishing; Patricia: Gardening; landscaping; cooking; tennis; anything involving water (I'm a Pisces): swimming, surfing, fishing, shell fishing; movies, and all areas of design.

Categories/subjects that you are most enthusiastic about agenting: Michael: Any subject that lends itself to practical self-help and how-to presentation, especially business, management, leadership, entrepreneurship. Also health, fitness, psychology, relationships, parenting, pets, women's issues. Literary fiction. Science fiction, New Age, memoirs, children's books. Patricia: I have broad interests, from the practical to the sublime. Subjects that have the power to solve problems, enhance living, or transform lives gain my attention.

If you were not an agent, what might you be doing instead: Michael: Teaching. Patricia: Any number of things in design and the visual arts.

What's the best way for writers to solicit your interest: Michael: Write an enticing one-page query letter (with SASE), pitching your book/subject and establishing your credentials in the area. We'll tell you what we want to review (proposal, etc.). Patricia: Write a brief, one-page query letter. Get to the point right away. Always include sufficient SASE.

Do you charge reading or management fees: Michael: No, though we do at times offer collaborative developmental and rewriting services, for which we charge additional commission points. We also represent a number of professional editors, rewriters, ghostwriters and developmental editors who can help content specialists bring their books to market. Patricia: No. But I may negotiate a higher commission on projects on which I agree to collaborate as developmental editor.

Can you provide an approximation by percent of what you tend to represent by category: Michael: Adult nonfiction: 95 percent, literary fiction: 5 percent. Patricia: Adult nonfiction: 100 percent, mostly practical how-to and self-help.

What are the most common mistakes writers make when pitching you: Michael: A boring or lengthy query that does not get to the point quickly, identifying the subject and the author's credentials in a compelling way. Many new authors oversell their book, when their query letter should achieve one goal: to prompt the agent to ask to see a proposal or material. Also, too many new authors let their egos get in their way, selling too hard with too little humility. Since we only consider new clients on an exclusive basis, authors who have embarked on a fishing expedition, contacting and submitting material to many agents, put us off. Authors forget they're looking for a marriage partner, not a plumber or electrician. Tiny envelopes with insufficient postage create SASEs that will not accommodate feedback or our brochure on "How to write a book proposal" or our flyer offering a "Model proposal." Patricia: Wasting my time with long, boring self-congratulatory letters. Failure to provide the proper return postage. I refuse to waste my time (and money) on those who cannot follow simple, clear directions.

How would you describe the client from hell: Michael: Editors and agents avoid "high maintenance" authors, those who require constant communication, hand-holding, and reassurance. While agents do form strong bonds with their clients, they run a business that requires efficient, professional, respectful relationships. The worst clients can't see around their own egos: because they know everything about one thing (their subject), they think they know everything about everything. Poor students make poor clients; bad listeners make bad clients impatient people who want the publishing process to move quickly make agents' and editors' lives miserable. This is a slow way to make a fast buck: people in a hurry make too many mistakes. Patricia: Wasting my time, failing to follow directions, being a poor student in the long process of getting publishes, trying to rush what is an essentially slow process, failing to value my contribution or, worst of all, acting rudely (thankfully a rare occurrence).

How would you describe the perfect client: Michael: The ideal client possesses all the qualities of a good friend and business partner: knowledgeable, patient, humble, respectful, prompt, reliable, professional, perseverant, and funny. Nothing smoothes over the rough patches better than a sense of humor. The agent-author relationship is unique. Because the work involves a certain amount of "art," it engages strong emotions. The best clients don't let their passion for their work undermine a respectful and caring professional relationship with the people who will help them make their dreams come true: their agent and their editor. The quality of the relationship depends on trust: the ideal client trusts her agent's professionalism and listens carefully to guidance and advice. This becomes so crucial to the author-publisher relationship later on, the more an author develops trust with her agent, the better for everyone—not to mention the book's sales—later on; Patricia: The mirror opposite of the client from hell. Those who behave professionally, valuing their time and mine. Those who show enthusiasm and express gratitude. Those who follow directions. Those who work hard throughout the whole process and realize that it is a long process with a long learning curve. Those who bring a good disposition and good manners to the work at hand, honoring the most important rule: We build a relationship before we build a book.

How and why did you ever become an agent: Michael: Having learned the art of book development as an editor for a book publisher, and having helped create dozens of bestsellers, I decided I'd rather make 15 percent commission on sales than keep taking home the measly salary publishers pay. I also got weary of the fact that editors were becoming less and less involved in the actual task of development (helping writers turn good ideas into great books). As an agent you can work closely with authors on their manuscripts, when necessary, and you can choose the people and projects that most attract you. I try to honor the same principles I coach my clients to practice: patience, perseverance, and professionalism. To those I'd add passion. I love books, have spent a lifetime overseeing their publication, and can think of no greater joy than opening that brand-new baby book and smelling the ink on its pages. Patricia: I married into the business and, well, married my love of books with the opportunity to help create them.

What, if anything, can a writer do to increase the odds of your becoming his or her agent: Michael: Read this listing carefully and approach us with what you've learned about us in mind. When communicating with us, remember Pascal's apology: "I would have made it shorter, if I'd had the time." Time is priceless: don't waste it on long-winded queries and constant phone calls demanding a faster response. By the same token, take your time, pay attention to details when preparing submissions, and slow down. Nothing can kill an emerging relationship faster than hastily assembled material that arrives in our office incomplete and poorly organized. Did I mention patience? Did I mention approaching us like a good student? You can also request, with SASE, our brochure "How to write a book proposal"; you can read Michael Snell's book *From Book Idea to Bestseller*. And you can ask for information on how to buy a "Model proposal." Patricia: Read all that I (and Michael) have said here, and take it all to heart.

How would you describe to someone (or something) from another planet what it is that you do as an agent: We develop book ideas into bestsellers.

Do you have any particular opinions or impressions of editors and publishers in general: We love them. They pay our bills and help pay college tuition for our clients' children.

What do you think the future holds for writers, publishers, and agents: The market for good ideas, valuable information, and graceful communication will keep growing, no matter the form in which it gets packaged. Every ten years experts predict the death of the book, and every ten years the market has expanded.

Do you have any favorite (current) TV shows, films, or books that you especially like and how come: *The Sopranos, Rescue Me, 24, Capote, Crash,* and anything written by David James Duncan, or David Foster Wallace.

On a personal level, what do you think people like about you and dislike about you: They like our honesty; they dislike our blunt criticism. They like our humor; they dislike our bad jokes. They like the money we make for them; they dislike the fact that we don't make them more.

Please list representative titles you have sold: *How Did That Happen?: Holding People Accountable the Positive, Principled Way* by Roger Connors and Tom Smith (Viking/Portfolio); *Recovering the Lost River: Rewilding Salmon, Recivilizing Humans, Removing Dams* by Steve Hawley (Beacon Press); *You, Him, and Her: Coping with Infidelity in Your Marriage* by Dr. Paul Coleman (Adams Media); *Strategic Customer Service* by John Goodman (AMACOM Books); *The Complete Idiot's Guide to the Financial Crisis* by Tom Gorman (Alpha Books); *Gen Y on Board: Managing the New Millenials* by Nicole Lipkin (Career Press); *The Inside Scoop on Business Schools* by David Petersam (Jist Publications); *Introduction to Business Ethics* by Martin Sandby (Prentice-Hall).

STEELE-PERKINS LITERARY AGENCY

26 Island Lane, Canandaigua, NY 14424

585-396-9290

email: pattiesp@aol.com

Agent's name: Pattie Steele-Perkins

Career history: Prior to becoming an agent Pattie Steele-Perkins was creative director for a Television Production Company. Prior to that she was a producer/director.

Categories/subjects that you are most enthusiastic about agenting: Romance and women's fiction.

What you don't want to agent: Nonfiction.

What's the best way for writers to solicit your interest: A brief email query that includes a synopsis.

Do you charge reading or management fees: No.

Can you provide an approximation by percent of what you tend to represent by category: Romance and women's fiction: 100 percent.

What are the most common mistakes writers make when pitching you: They don't research what I handle or they do research and pitch the story as if it were romance even though it isn't.

How would you describe the client from hell: Clients that use foul language rather than just "stet" on copy edits. Clients that rant and rave online about their editor or publishing house.

How would you describe the perfect client: Someone who loves to write and has stories to tell.

Do you have any particular opinions or impressions of editors and publishers in general: They are the smartest people I have ever met and they love books.

THE STEINBERG AGENCY, INC.

47 East 19th Street, 3rd Floor, New York, NY 10003

212-213-9120

www.steinbergagency.com

Date and location of birth: April 23, Queens, NY

Education: BFA in film production at New York University's film school.

Career Story: After graduating from film school I was temping at HarperCollins (to pay the bills) while focusing my energy on writing screenplays, and realized—much to my own surprise—that I really enjoyed the world of publishing. At that time, there was an as an assistant opening at a prestigious (although I didn't know it at the time) boutique literary agency called Donadio & Ashworth (now called Donadio & Olson) and I got the job, fell in love with being a literary agent, and I've been an agent ever since. And in the fall of 2007 I opened my own shop, which has been extraordinarily fulfilling.

Hobbies and special personal interests: Spending time with my wife and kids.

Subjects and categories you like to agent: A broad range of novels and short story collections and the occasional YA title. Nonfiction interests include memoir, humor, biography, history, pop culture, fitness and narrative nonfiction.

Subjects and categories writers shouldn't bother pitching to you: Screenplays, poetry, romance.

What might you be doing if you weren't agenting: In the movie business in some creative capacity.

What's the most effective ways for writers to grab your attention: Great writing in combination with a referral.

Do you charge fees separate from your commission, or offer non-agenting fee-based services: Absolutely none.

What are representative titles you have sold to publishers: *Angels of Destruction*, Keith Donohue, Shaye Areheart Books (Crown); *Gossip of the Starlings*, Nina de Gramont (Algonquin); *Are You Ready!*, Bob Harper (Broadway Books); *Eden's Outcasts*, John Matteson (W.W. Norton); *The Expeditions*, Karl Iagnemma (The Dial Press); *I'm a Lebowski, You're a Lebowski* by Lebowskifest (Bloomsbury);

Towelhead, Alicia Erian (Simon & Schuster); *Jars of Glass*, Brad Barkley and Hepler Hepler (Dutton Children); *The Post-War Dream*, Mitch Cullin, Nan A Talese Books (Doubleday); *The Heaven of Mercury*, Brad Watson (W.W. Norton); *The 351 Books of Irma Arcuri*, David Bajo, Viking; *Comeback Season*, Cathy Day (Free Press); *The Affected Provincial's Companion*, Lord Whimsy (Bloomsbury); *Don't Make Me Stop Now*, Michael Parker (Algonquin); *Identical Strangers*, Paula Bernstein and Elyse Schein (Random House).

Why did you become an agent, and how did you become one: See "Career story."

How do you feel about writers: I love interacting with writers on a daily basis. It's why I do what I do.

What do you tell entities from other planets and dimensions about your job: I would tell them I have a love/hate relationship with email.

STIMOLA LITERARY STUDIO

306 Chase Court, Edgewater, NJ 07020

voice/fax: 201-945-9353

www.stimolaliterarystudio.com   email: info@stimolaliterarystudio.com

Agent's name: Rosemary B. Stimola

Born: November 6, 1952; Queens, New York.

Education: BA in Elementary Education/theoretical linguistics, Queens college; MA in applied linguistics, NYU; PhD in linguistic/educational psychology, NYU.

Career history or story: Professor of Language and Literature, children's bookseller, freelance editor, education consultant, literary agent.

Hobbies/personal interests: Beach combing, Latin dance, cockapoos.

Subjects and categories you are most enthusiastic about agenting: Preschool through young-adult fiction/nonfiction; concept cookbooks.

What you don't want to agent: Adult fiction.

If you were not an agent, what might you be doing instead: Working in publishing, editorial, or marketing.

What's the best way for writers to solicit your interest: Referral through editors, clients, or agent colleagues always helps. See SUBMISSION GUIDELINES on website. Prefer email queries, but no attachments please!

Do you charge reading or any upfront fees: No.

How do you feel about writers: I am in awe of good writers, and admire those less talented for their efforts.

How would you describe the writer from hell: Desperate for money, has unrealistic expectations and a major ego, resistant to editor guidance and revision.

How would you describe the publisher or editor from hell: Does not answer calls or respond to emails. Late with paperwork. Does not deliver what is promised in time or production.

Why did you become an agent, and how did you become one: It was an evolving state, allowing me to put the literary aesthetics I developed as an educator and the publishing knowledge I acquired as a bookseller to use in one role.

How would you describe to someone (or something) from another planet what it is that you do as an agent: In the space between authors and publishing personnel, I serve as an advocate, facilitator, champion and troubleshooter all in the service of making the best possible book, one that I can then bring to foreign and film markets.

What do you like best about your clients, and the editors and publishers you work with: We are all lovers of story, dazzled by well-crafted written words and their ability to touch head and heart.

Will our business exist as we know it ten years from now: Our business will certainly exist, but with world and technological changes, we must change as well. I couldn't say what the face of publishing will look like in future, but I would stake my life on its being an important force.

What are your favorite books, TV shows, movies, and why: *Harold and the Purple Crayon* (the perfect children's book); *Now, Voyager* (Bette Davis at her best!); *The Shawshank Redemption* (love this tale of friendship and triumph of spirit); *To Kill a Mockingbird* (read at 12 years of age, a life changing book for me); *Fried Green Tomatoes* (words and characters pull at my heart strings); *Starman* (attracted to the human element in this sci-fi tale); *Sophie's Choice* (a perfect novel); *Cider House Rules* (characters to die for).

What are some representative titles that you have sold: The *Hunger Games Trilogy* by Suzanne Collins (Scholastic); *The Haunting of Charles Dickens* by Lewis Buzbee (Feiwel and Friends); *Boys, Bears, and a Serious Pair of Hiking Boots* by Abby McDonald (Candlewick Press); *The Miles Between* by Mary E. Pearson (Holt); *Past Perfect* by Siobahn Vivian (Scholastic, Push); *Amy and Roger Discover America* by Morgan Matson (Simon & Schuster); *Barbie, for Better or Worse* by Tanya Lee Stone (Viking); *Felicity Rose and Cordelia Bean* by Lisa Jahn-Claugh (FSG); *The Flying Beaver Brothers* by Maxwell Eaton III (Knopf).

LES STOBBE

300 Doubleday Road, Tryon, NC 28782

828-808-7127   fax: 978-945-0517

email: lstobbe@alltel.net

Agent's name: Les Stobbe

Career history or story: 1962–1970: *Business* magazine editor; 1970–1978: editorial director, Moody Press; 1978–1982: VP and editorial director, Christian Herald Books and Book Club; 1982–1985: editor and director, Here's Life Publishing; 1985–1992: president, Here's Life Publishing; 1993–1996: managing editor, Scripture Press Curriculum; 1996–2001: VP of communications, Vision New England; 1993–present: literary agent; 2001–present: editor-in-chief, Jerry B. Jenkins Christian Writers Guild.

Hobbies, interests: Boston Red Sox.

Subjects and categories you are interested in agenting, including fiction and nonfiction: Adult Christian fiction and nonfiction.

Subjects and categories writers shouldn't even bother pitching to you: New Age humanistic, children's books, young-adult fiction.

What would you do if you weren't agenting: Writing books.

What's the best way for fiction writers to solicit your interest: Get editors at Christian Writers Guild conference to say, "Send me a proposal."

What's the best way for nonfiction writers to solicit your interest: See above.

Do you charge reading or any upfront fees: No.

In your experience, what are the most common pitching mistakes writers make: Sending documents with typos and grammatical mistakes.

What's your definition of a great client: One whose proposal is professionally prepared but is willing to improve the pitch.

How can writers increase the odds that you will offer representation: Attend a Christian writers conference and talk to editors.

Why did you become an agent, and how did you become one: Author friends insisted I represent them.

Describe to someone from another planet what you do as an agent: I open doors for clients at publishing houses.

How do you feel about editors and publishers: I was one of them.

How do you feel about writers: I love writers.

What do you see in the near future for book publishing: More consolidations, fewer titles.

In your opinion, what do editors think of you: I have a good reputation.

On a personal non-professional level, what do you think people think of you: A caring professional.

What are some representative titles that you have sold: *Hearing God's Voice* by Vern Heidebrecht (David C. Cook); *The Evidence* by Austin Boyd (Navpress); *Petticoat Ranch* by Mary Connealy (Barbour Publishing); *The Great American Supper Swap* by Trish Berg (David C. Cook); *Rolling Thunder* by Mark Mynheir (Multnomah-Waterbrook); *Pray Big* by Will Davis Jr. (Baker/Revell); *The 21 Most Effective Prayers of the Bible* by Dave Earley (Barbour Publishing); *From Jihad to Jesus* by Jerry Rassamni (AMG Publishing).

ROBIN STRAUS AGENCY, INC.

229 East 79th Street, Suite 5A, New York, NY 10075

212-472-3282   fax: 212-472-3833

www.robinstrausagency.com

email: info@robinstrausagency.com

Agents' names: Robin Straus (president and primary agent)

Education: Wellesley BA, NYU School of Business MBA.

Career history: Started at publishing houses, doing editorial work at Little, Brown and subsidiary rights at Doubleday and Random House; VP Wallace & Sheil Agency for four years and started Robin Straus Agency, Inc. in 1983.

Categories/subjects that you are most enthusiastic about agenting: High-quality literary fiction and nonfiction. Subject is of less importance than fine writing and research.

What you don't want to agent: Genre fiction such as science fiction, horror, romance, Westerns; poetry; no screenplays or plays.

If you were not an agent, what might you be doing instead: Traveling the world; raising horses and dogs; going to medical school.

What's the best way for writers to solicit your interest: A great query letter and sample material that speaks for itself. Caution: We are a very small agency and unable to take on more than a few clients per year, so we would have to be completely smitten.

Do you charge reading or management fees: No.

Can you provide an approximation by percent of what you tend to represent by category: Nonfiction: 60 percent (history, social science, psychology, women's interest, education, travel, biography, art history and many other fields); fiction: 40 percent.

What are the most common mistakes writers make when pitching you: Bad grammar in letters, clichés, overstating claims for book being revolutionary. Asking us to download queries and manuscripts.

How would you describe the client from hell: Being awakened every morning by a client's phone call.

How would you describe the perfect client: A captivating writer who can make any subject interesting; receptive to suggestions on how to improve work; appreciative that the publishing process is a collaborative effort; imaginative about ways to market self and books.

How and why did you ever become an agent: I started out my career working on manuscripts, but discovered I also liked the business end of publishing and moved into rights. Agenting seemed the best way to combine editorial and selling activities and be a strong advocate for authors.

What, if anything, can a writer do to increase the odds of your becoming his

or her agent: Convince me with your arguments. Dazzle me with your prose. Make me fall in love with your characters.

How would you describe to someone (or something) from another planet what it is that you do as an agent: When I want to represent an author, I work with him/her to help shape proposals and manuscripts to entice editors to make an offer. I submit material to publishers, negotiate contracts, vet royalty statements, sell translation, serial, film and audio rights on behalf of client. I generally act as the business manager for the author and intercede whenever necessary throughout the entire publishing process. I view my relationship with my clients as a continuum that extends over many books.

Do you have any particular opinions or impressions of editors and publishers in general: They do less editing than they used to, probably because they are under more pressure.

What do you think the future holds for writers, publishers, and agents: Even with all the competition for our time, books will always have an important place and publishers will continue to exist and figure out ways to stay central. With the rise of the Internet and other electronic media, there is a huge need for content and authors increasingly will find other venues and audiences for their work beyond paper over board volumes. The challenge will be in finding fair ways to compensate the writers while simultaneously protecting their work.

Please list representative titles you have sold: Fiction such as *The No. 1 Ladies Detective Agency* and other series (Pantheon/Anchor); *The Ivy Chronicles* (Viking); *The Fall of Berlin* (Viking); *Coma* (Riverhead); *The Year of the French* (NY Review); *Budapest Noir* (HarperCollins); *Miss America* (Houghton Harcourt); *Becoming Jane Eyre* (Penguin); *Who Do You Think You Are* (Touchstone); *The Time of Their Lives* (St. Martin's); *The Rose Labyrinth* (Atria). Nonfiction such as *Ideas* (HarperCollins); *Outfoxing Fear* (Norton); *Character Matters* (Touchstone); *A Writer at War* (Pantheon); *Mismatch* (Scribner); *Transatlantic* (HarperCollins); *Fishface* (Phaidon); *The Program* (Atria); *Polar Obsession* (National Geographic); *Simple Skin Beauty* (Atria).

STROTHMAN AGENCY

6 Beacon Street, Suite 810, Boston, MA 02108

www.thestrothmanagency.com   email: info@strothmanagency.com

Agents' names: Wendy Strothman, Dan O'Connell, Lauren MacLeod

Career story: Wendy Strothman, who led the turnarounds of two venerable Boston publishers, Beacon Press and Houghton Mifflin's Trade & Reference Division, has thirty years of publishing experience.

As executive vice president and head of Houghton Mifflin's Trade & Reference

Division from 1996 through July 2002, she turned an unprofitable division into one of the most profitable in the industry. Strothman's efforts to publish books at the highest standards led the company to receive more literary awards than at any time in its history: two Pulitzer Prizes, one National Book Award, three Caldecott Medals, and two Newbery Medals, among many other honors.

At Houghton Mifflin, Strothman also acquired and edited books by key authors, including James Carroll (*An American Requiem*, winner of the National Book Award; *Constantine's Sword*, *New York Times* bestseller), Philip Roth (four novels, including *American Pastoral*, winner of the Pulitzer Prize, and *The Human Stain*, *New York Times* bestseller), John Kenneth Galbraith, Arthur M. Schlesinger Jr. (*A Life in the Twentieth Century*), and Paul Theroux. She vigorously pursued the defense in the lawsuit brought by the Margaret Mitchell estate to block publication of Alice Randall's *The Wind Done Gone*, a parody of *Gone with the Wind*.

From 1983 to 1995, Strothman headed Beacon Press, a Boston publisher founded in 1854. She led Beacon to new prominence, publishing two *New York Times* bestsellers (*The Measure of Our Success* by Marian Wright Edelman and *Race Matters* by Cornel West) and one National Book Award winner, Mary Oliver's *New and Selected Poems*. Strothman began her career in 1973 at the University of Chicago Press, where she launched the *Critical Edition of the Works of Giuseppe Verdi*.

Strothman was the Senior Fellow and the Secretary of the Brown University Corporation; at Brown she has funded the annual Wendy J. Strothman Faculty Research Award in the Humanities to facilitate research planned for publication. She has served on of the Board of Governors of Yale University Press and the Board of Trustees of the Cantata Singers in Boston, and now serves as a trustee of Deerfield Academy and on the board of 826 Boston, and affiliate of 826 Valencia.

She has served as an expert witness on publishing matters and provides business consulting services to small nonprofit publishers. In addition, she has led workshops in publishing for the American Academy of Arts and Sciences, the Nieman Foundation at Harvard University, and other institutions.

Known as an advocate for authors and freedom of expression and as a friend to independent booksellers, Ms. Strothman has received numerous awards, including the Publisher of the Year Award from the New England Booksellers Association, the Person of the Year Award for "permanent and significant contributions to the book industry" from the Literary Market Place, the 1994 PEN New England "Friend to Writers" Award, and a Doctor of Humane Letters from Meadville Lombard Theological School in Chicago and a Doctor of Human Letters from Brown. She is a frequent speaker at industry, library, and university events.

Career story: Dan O'Connell has devised and executed marketing and publicity campaigns for small presses, mid-sized publishers, and trade houses.

As assistant publicity director at Houghton Mifflin's Trade & Reference Division, he worked with a range of distinguished authors including PEN Faulkner Award winner John Edgar Wideman (*Hoop Roots*), Harvard psychologist Daniel

Schacter (*Seven Sins of Memory*), NBA finalist and science writer Steve Olson (*Mapping Human History, Count Down*), National Book Award winner James Carroll (*Secret Father*), and award-winning psychologist Pumla Gobodo-Madikizela of the University of Cape Town (*A Human Being Died That Night*). O'Connell devised brand-building campaigns for two of Houghton's most significant lines— *The American Heritage*® line of dictionaries and *The Peterson Field Guides*.

As assistant marketing director at Beacon Press, O'Connell managed publicity campaigns for two national bestsellers, Cornel West's *Race Matters* and Marian Wright Edelman's *The Measure of Our Success*.

Before joining Beacon, O'Connell was Marketing Manager at Alyson Publications, the leading publisher of books for gay and lesbian readers. He began working in book publishing at The Brookings Institution in Washington, DC, where he handled subsidiary rights, among other marketing duties.

Career Story: Lauren MacLeod joined the Strothman Agency after graduating *cum laude* from Emerson College with a BFA in writing, literature, and publishing. Lauren is drawn to highly polished literary fiction. Her specialties include young adult and middle-grade fiction and nonfiction of all types.

Subjects and categories you like to agent: We specialize in narrative nonfiction, memoir, history, science and nature, arts and culture, literary travel, current affairs, and some business. We have a highly selective practice in fiction and young-adult literature.

Subjects and categories writers shouldn't bother pitching to you: We do not handle romance, science fiction, picture books, gift books, poetry, or self-help.

What's the most effective ways for writers to grab your attention: Fiction: Send a synopsis and two or three chapters of your work, with a self-addressed stamped envelope. Nonfiction: We specialize in nonfiction. Send a query letter outlining your qualifications and experience, along with a synopsis of your work, and a self-addressed stamped envelope. We are now accepting submissions via email. Please see our website for more information and the submission email address.

Do you charge fees separate from your commission, or offer non-agenting fee-based services: We do not charge any upfront fees.

What are representative titles you have sold to publishers: A book of advice on "etiquette, ethics, and everything in between" by Robin Abrahams (Times Books); *The Sound of Freedom: Marion Anderson, the Lincoln Memorial, and the Democratic Imagination* by Ray Aresenault (Bloomsbury Press); *The Weeping Time: Anatomy of a Slave Auction* by Anne Bailey (HarperCollins); *Choke: What the Secrets of the Brain Reveal about Success and Failure at Work and at Play* by Sian Beilock (Simon & Schuster); *A Slave No More* by David W. Blight (Harcourt); *The Problem of Slavery in the Age of Emancipation* by David Brion Davis (Knopf); *Columbus and the Quest for Jerusalem* by Carol Delaney (Free Press); *The Race Card* by Richard T. Ford (Farrar, Straus & Giroux); *A Patent Lie* and *Errors* and *Omissions* by Paul Goldstein (Doubleday); *Addled: A Novel* by JoeAnn Hart (Little, Brown); *New Boy* by Julian Houston (Houghton Mifflin); *Kaufman Field Guide* series and *Flights against the Sunset* by Kenn Kaufman (Houghton Mifflin); *High Crimes: The Fate* *of Everest in an Age of Greed* by Michael Kodas (Hyperion); *Education's End: Why Our Colleges and Universities Have Given Up on the Meaning of Life* by Anthony T. Kronman (Yale); *Freedom for the Thought That We Hate: Biography of the First Amendment* by Anthony Lewis (Basic Books); *Stranger from Abroad: Hannah Arendt, Martin Heidegger and the Experience of Germans and Jews in the 20th Century* by Daniel Maier-Katkin (Norton); *Snow Falling in Spring: Coming of Age in China During the Cultural Revolution* by Moying Li (Farrar, Straus and Giroux); *Attack on the Liberty* by James Scott (Simon & Schuster); *Poisoned Profits: The Toxic Assault on Our Children* by Philip and Alice Shabecoff (Random House); *Sun & Shade: Three American Families Journey from Black to White* by Daniel Sharfstein (Penguin Press); *The Book of Getting Even* and *Tales Out of School* by Benjamin Taylor (Steerforth Press); *Backcast: Fly Fishing, Fatherhood, and a River Journey through the Heart of Alaska* by Lou Ureneck (St. Martin's); *Shell Game: Rogues, Smugglers, and the Hunt for Nature's Bounty* by Craig Welch (HarperCollins); *Skipjack: Tracking the Last Sailing Oystermen* by Chris White (St. Martin's Press); *Riddled with Life: Friendly Worms, Ladybug Sex, and the Parasites that Make Us Who We Are* by Marlene Zuk (Harcourt).

THE TALBOT FORTUNE AGENCY, LLC.

John Talbot is located at: 180 E. Prospect Ave. #188, Mamaroneck, NY 10543

Gail Fortune is located at: 980 Broadway, Suite 664, Thornwood, NY 10594

www.talbotfortuneagency.com   email: queries@talbotfortuneagency.com

Agents' names: John Talbot, Gail Fortune
The following information pertains to John Talbot.
Education: BA, DePauw University.
Career history: John Talbot is a literary agent and former book editor with twenty-four years of publishing experience. Prior to becoming an agent he spent seven years with Putnam Berkley (now part of Penguin USA), where he rose to the rank of senior editor and worked with such major bestselling authors as Tom Clancy, W.E.B. Griffin, and Jack Higgins, as well as rising literary stars such as Tom Perrotta. He published national bestsellers in hardcover, trade paperback, and mass market paperback, along with five *New York Times* Notable Books. He began his editorial career at Simon & Schuster.
Categories/subjects that you are most enthusiastic about agenting: I am most enthusiastic about representing narrative nonfiction of all types, thrillers, commercial women's fiction, and literary fiction. Narrative nonfiction can cover almost any subject, but history, current events, participatory journalism, sports, pop culture, business, and Christian spirituality are particular interests of mine. Newspaper and magazine experience is helpful; many books are generated from concepts first tried

out in articles. A marketing platform, i.e., a website or blog with a fan base in the tens of thousands or a list of corporate clients and customers, and a track record of speaking engagements and media appearances can be the deciding factor in getting a nonfiction sale.

In fiction, I'm keenly interested in well-crafted thrillers with new or unusual hooks, and good genre fiction in growth categories. I am also looking for the fresh and occasionally edgy voice, no matter the subject or genre. Writers with minority backgrounds and unusual experiences and perspectives interest me, as do writers of what Sue Miller calls domestic realism. Previous publication in literary journals and magazines is a plus.

What you don't want to agent: I do not represent children's books, science fiction, fantasy, Westerns, poetry, or screenplays.

What's the best way for writers to solicit your interest: Query via email only. Please see SUBMISSIONS GUIDELINES page [of the agency website].

Do you charge reading or management fees: We do not charge reading fees.

Can you provide an approximation by percent of what you tend to represent by category: 50 percent fiction, 50 percent nonfiction.

What are the most common mistakes writers make when pitching you: Not following submission guidelines. Pitching multiple projects in one query letter. Sending queries that ramble. Using pressure tactics. Knocking published authors. Not trusting us or the business in general. Thinking someone's going to steal their idea. Relaying incomplete representation, submission, or publishing histories. Not being truthful or straightforward.

How would you describe the client from hell: The client from hell doesn't respect our time. They fail to recognize the publisher's justly proprietary attitude towards marketing, book design, and other facets of publication. They won't take suggestions for change, no matter how minor or well reasoned. They complain about writing and treat being published as a right instead of the opportunity and privilege it is.

How would you describe the perfect client: The perfect client respects our personal and professional lives. They trust us. They are open to input from their editor. They love to read and they love to write. They are enthusiastic about their ideas and about what they do.

How and why did you ever become an agent: Becoming an agent was a natural progression from being editors. The work is similar but we're able to spend less time in meetings and more time working with authors. We can also handle a more eclectic range of material, and we get to work with editors throughout the industry who share our passions and enthusiasms.

What, if anything, can a writer do to increase the odds of your becoming his or her agent: Please respect our time. Make sure your query is clear and succinct, and includes all of your contact information. Make sure your proposal (for nonfiction) or manuscript (for fiction) is complete and ready to go if we're interested. In general, approach publishing as a business and try to be as professional as possible right from the start. Of course, having a great project that's well researched and well executed goes a long way toward the above.

Do you have any particular opinions or impressions of editors and publishers in general: Editors are without a doubt the hardest working and most idealistic people in book publishing. Publishers represent the best opportunity for gifted writers to get wide distribution, readership, and money in what is often a difficult business.

Please list representative titles you have sold: Fiction: *Tom Clacy's Endwar* (Berkley); *24 Declassified: Vanishing Point* (HarperEntertainment); *Becoming Finola* (Pocket Books); *Under Darkness* (Signet Eclipse); *The Brothers Bishop* (Kensington); *If Wishing Made It So* (Signet Eclipse); *CSI: Nevada Rose* (Pocket Books); *Forgive the Moon* (NAL Accent); *French Pressed: A Coffeehouse Mystery* (Berkley Prime Crime). Nonfiction: *All Hands Down: The True Story of the Soviet Attack on the USS Scorpion* (Simon & Schuster); *Sundays in America: A Yearlong Road Trip in Search of Christian Faith* (Beacon); *While Europe Slept: How Radical Islam is Destroying the West from Within* (Doubleday); *Last Flag Down: A Civil War Saga of Honor, Piracy and Redemption on the High Seas* (Crown).

The following information pertains to Gail Fortune.

Education: BS, Northwestern University (Medill School of Journalism).

Career history or story: Gail Fortune is a literary agent and former book editor with eighteen years of publishing experience. Prior to becoming an agent she spent sixteen years at Putnam Berkley (now part of Penguin Group (USA)), where she rose from assistant to the editor-in-chief to executive editor. Her authors won six RITAs, and were nominated for Edgar and Anthony Awards. She published two *Publishers Weekly* Books of the Year. She edited many other national bestsellers in romance, mystery and narrative nonfiction.

Subjects and categories you are interested in agenting, including fiction and nonfiction: I am most enthusiastic about representing narrative nonfiction, commercial women's fiction, historical fiction, and romance novels. Narrative nonfiction can cover almost any subject, but history, food, travel and Christian spirituality are particular interests of mine. Newspaper and magazine experience is helpful; many books are generated from concepts first tried out in articles. In fiction, I am looking for a voice that grabs me and a narrative that keeps me turning the pages. I like original voices.

Subjects and categories writers shouldn't even bother pitching to you: I do not represent children's books, science fiction, fantasy, Westerns, poetry, prescriptive nonfiction or screenplays.

What's the best way for fiction writers to solicit your interest: Query via email only. Please see SUBMISSION GUIDELINES page.

What's the best way for nonfiction writers to solicit your interest: Query via email only. Please see SUBMISSION GUIDELINES page.

Do you charge reading or any upfront fees: We do not charge any reading fees.

In your experience, what are the most common pitching mistakes writers make: Not following the submission guidelines. Pitching multiple projects in one query letter. Sending queries that ramble. Using pressure tactics. Knocking published authors. Not trusting us or the business in general. Thinking someone's going to steal their idea. Relaying incomplete representation, submission, or publishing histories. Not being truthful or straightforward.

Describe the client from hell, even if you don't have any: The client from hell doesn't respect our time. They fail to recognize the publisher's justly proprietary attitude towards marketing, book design, and other facets of publication. They won't take suggestions for change, no matter how minor or well reasoned. They complain about writing and treat being published as a right instead of the opportunity and privilege it is.

What's your definition of a great client: The perfect client respects our personal and professional lives. They trust us. They are open to input from their editor. They love to read and they love to write. They are enthusiastic about their ideas and about what they do.

How can writers increase the odds that you will offer representation: Please respect our time. Make sure your query is clear and succinct, and includes all of your contact information. Make sure your proposal (for nonfiction) or manuscript (for fiction) is complete and ready to go if we're interested. In general, approach publishing as a business and try to be as professional as possible right from the start. Of course, having a great project that's well researched and well executed goes a long way toward the above.

Why did you become an agent, and how did you become one: Becoming an agent was a natural progression from being editors. The work is similar, but we're able to spend less time in meetings and more time working with authors. We can also handle a more eclectic range of material, and we get to work with editors throughout the industry who share our passions and enthusiasms.

How do you feel about editors and publishers: Editors are without a doubt the hardest working and most idealistic people in book publishing. Publishers represent the best opportunity for gifted writers to get wide distribution, readership, and money in what is an often difficult business.

What are some representative titles that you have sold: *The Great Swim* by Gavin Mortimer (Walker Books); *Texas Princess* by Jodi Thomas (Berkley); *Twisted Creek* by Jodi Thomas (Berkley); *Married in Black* by Christina Cordaire (Madison Park Press); *A Notorious Woman* by Amanda McCabe (Mills & Boon/ Harlequin Historicals).

TALCOTT NOTCH LITERARY

276 Forest Rd., Milford, CT 06461

203-877-1146   fax: 203-876-9517

www.talcottnotch.net

Agent's name: Gina Panettieri, gpanettieri@talcottnotch.net

Born: June 8, 1960, Peekskill, New York.

Education: Long Island University Southampton, University of Virginia (double major writing/pre-med).

Career story: I came into agenting through one of the less common routes, by way of writing. I began as a freelance writer while still in college, writing anything from confession stories for *Modern Romance* to consumer protection and health articles. Later, I ran an ever-expanding critique group out of my home, and became very involved with writer support groups and organizations, and was represented myself by two well-known agents who taught me a great deal both about writing and about the business. But it was after assisting a number of writers in negotiating their own contracts that I became an agent myself and found my true calling. Within the last few years, I've begun writing again in addition to agenting, and am the author of *The Single Mother's Guide to Raising Remarkable Boys* (Adams Media 2008) and *Honey, We're Spoiling the Kids* (Adams Media 2009). Since most agents who write themselves either write about publishing, or write novels, I suppose in becoming a parenting author I'm still sticking to the less common career routes!

Hobbies and special personal interests: I enjoy gardening (mind you, I didn't say I was particularly good at it, but the survival rate is improving), old movies (think *Royal Wedding* or *Arsenic and Old Lace*, NOT *Ferris Bueller's Day Off*), collecting cobalt glass and miniatures (houses, furniture, animals. I'm looking for a miniature cow if anyone knows a breeder). I love decorating for the holidays (Halloween is particularly fun). Researching for my own books keeps me reading a lot of psych, education and child development journals, which I actually enjoy. Finally, my own kids are a constant source of amusement and a limitless source of material for my books, to their great embarrassment.

Subjects and categories you like to agent: I primarily handle nonfiction, and my tastes are quite eclectic. I do a great deal of parenting, relationship, self-help, health, business/career, cooking, "green" works, memoir and current events, as well as children's nonfiction. I'm not limited to those areas, though, and writers shouldn't hesitate to query me on nearly any nonfiction project. In fiction, I work mostly with mystery/suspense/thrillers and women's fiction, but I'll also do a bit of young-adult and middle grade and some fantasy, action-adventure and science fiction.

Subjects and categories writers shouldn't bother pitching to you: Picture and board books, early readers, poetry, short stories.

What might you be doing if you weren't agenting: Probably writing full-time and continuing to be very involved in writing organizations.

What's the most effective ways for writers to grab your attention: Show you understand the market for your work, what's already been written on the subject and how your own work fills an existing need. Don't just use links to websites in lieu of writing a real query.

Do you charge fees separate from your commission, or offer non-agenting fee-based services: No, never.

What are representative titles you have sold to publishers: *Fall* by Ron Franscell, winner of the 2007 Ippy for True Crime and the 2007 *Foreword Magazine* Book of the Year Award in True Crime (New Horizon, released in paper as *The Darkest Night* by St. Martin's Press); *The Connected Child* by Dr. Karyn Purvis, Dr. David Cross and Wendy Lyons Sunshine (McGraw-Hill); *Breaking the Co-Sleeping Habit* by Dr. Valerie Levine (Adams Media); *The Essential Supervisor's Handbook* by Brette and Terrence Sember (Career Press).

Why did you become an agent, and how did you become one: (The second half of this question was answered in an earlier question.) I love being an agent because it allows me to read so many fascinating works. I feel like I'm constantly learning. Agenting's an unending education. It's also terribly exciting to find something truly wonderful, important and meaningful, and be instrumental in bringing it to the world.

How do you feel about writers: I certainly respect what they do, and because I write myself, I can relate to many of their issues. I think that helps me present constructive criticism in ways that are more easily accepted, and also gives me a deeper perspective into the craft of writing. I also love their creative energy and the generosity of spirit of many writers. This is one industry where so many successful practitioners eagerly help new hopefuls.

What do you tell entities from other planets and dimensions about your job: I find new works that will help to enlighten people, enrich lives, and that entertain, comfort or possibly provoke the readers. Books make life vastly more interesting. I help bring those books to the people.

What are your favorite books, movies, TV shows, and why: I find reality programs like *The Deadliest Catch* and *Ice Road Truckers* to be interesting (for a while) because they make you aware of a different way of life, and also because they feature people who have not yet spurned the idea of a real challenge, hard work, testing their own limits, understanding self-sacrifice. Perhaps for the same reason, I love old movies and shorts, since they're often time capsules of earlier ways of life. I listen to old radio shows on CD (the most fascinating are the World War II–era broadcasts), as well. In diving into what life was in America sixty years or seventy or even eighty years ago, again, you're learning, but this time about ourselves, and where we came from. It gives a new perspective on the present, on social roles, on the evolution of culture, on what's gone right, and wrong. With books, my tastes are eclectic and voracious, but again, I want to learn.

How would you describe the writer from hell: Someone who has completely unrealistic expectations, such as instant success or that worrying about such trivial issues as spelling and grammar is "what the editor is for," or someone who is unreasonably demanding of my time, since that would mean they're not respecting the time I must give to others.

How would you describe the publisher and/or editor from hell: Someone who pulls out all the stops to acquire a project and then loses steam afterward and doesn't continue to shepherd the project zealously. In those cases, everybody loses.

What do you like best about your clients, and the editors and publishers you work with: The exchange of ideas and energy.

You're welcome to share your thoughts and sentiments about the business of writing and publishing: This is an exciting, but challenging, time to work in publishing. The industry continues to meet new demands and pressures. From finding ways to "go green" in what's traditionally been a huge-carbon-footprint business, to exploring new ways to promote and publicize works, to looking ahead to predict the needs of consumers in a changing economy, publishing is stimulating, stressful, joyous, frustrating, rewarding and exhausting. Never a dull moment.

Do you wish to describe who you are: Mom/agent/activist/tree-hugger/writer/helpmate/friend.

Will our business exist as we know it in ten years or so: Yes, it will. It will continue to change to meet new demands and embrace new technology, but those things will occur in tandem and as a complement to the business as we know it today.

TESSLER LITERARY AGENCY, LLC

27 West 20th Street, Suite 1003, New York, NY 10011

www.tessleragency.com

Agent's name: Michelle Tessler

Education: Master's degree in English literature and member of the Association of Authors' Representatives.

Career history or story: Before forming her own agency, Michelle Tessler worked as an agent at Carlisle & Company, now part of InkWell Management. She also worked at the William Morris Agency and at the Elaine Markson Literary Agency. In addition to her agenting experience, Michelle worked as an executive of business development and marketing in the Internet industry. In 1994, just as the Internet was becoming a mainstream medium, she was hired by bestselling author James Gleick to help launch The Pipeline. She then went on to serve as Vice President of New Media at Jupiter Communications, and later at ScreamingMedia, before returning to traditional publishing. Her experience marketing content, products and services to appeal to both general and niche audiences is of great benefit to her authors as they look for creative and effective ways to get the word out on their books and grow their readerships.

Subjects and categories you are interested in agenting, including fiction and nonfiction: The Tessler Literary Agency is a full-service boutique agency. We represent writers of quality nonfiction and literary and commercial fiction. Our nonfiction list includes popular science, reportage, memoir, history, biography, psychology, business and travel. Committed to developing careers and building the readerships of the authors we represent, our agency offers personalized attention at every stage of the publishing process. Sharp editorial focus is given to clients before their work is submitted, and marketing support is provided along the way, as publishers begin to position the book in the marketplace through catalog copy, jacket designs, and marketing, promotion and launch strategies. We handle all domestic, foreign and subsidiary rights for our clients, working with a network of dedicated co-agents who specialize in film and translation rights.

What's the best way for fiction writers to solicit your interest: Please submit initial queries via the webform at www.tessleragency.com.

What's the best way for nonfiction writers to solicit your interest: See above.

What are some representative titles that you have sold: *Flower Confidential* by Amy Stewart—a *New York Times* bestseller (Algonquin); *Body Clutter* by Marla Cilley (aka The Flylady) and Leanne Ely (aka The Dinner Diva) a *New York Times* bestseller (Touchstone); *Presidential Doodles* from the creators of *Cabinet* Magazine (Basic); *A Sense of the World* and *The Extraordinary Journeys of James Holman* by Jason Roberts—finalist for the National Book Critics' Circle Award (HarperCollins); *Sixpence House: Lost in a Town of Books* by Paul Collins—a *Booksense* Bestseller (Bloomsbury); *How to be Lost* by Amanda Eyre Ward (Macadam Cage/Ballantine); *Saving Dinner* by Leanne Ely (Ballantine); *The Mommy Brain: How Motherhood Makes You Smarter* by Katherine Ellison (Basic); *Our Inner Ape: The Past and Future of Human Nature* by Frans De Waal—a *New York Times* Notable Book (Riverhead); *Mediated* by Thomas De Zengotita (Bloomsbury); *Defining the Wind: The Beaufort Scale and How a 19th-Century Admiral Turned Science into Poetry* by Scott Huler (Crown); *Sink Reflections* by Marla Cilley (aka The Flylady) (Bantam); *Suburban Safari: A Year on the Lawn* by Hannah Holmes (Bloomsbury); *Forgive Me* by Amanda Eyre Ward (Random House); *In the Furnace of the Nation-Empires* by Michael Knox Beran (Free Press); *A Mid-Sized and Immodest Mammal: A Natural History of Myself* by Hannah Holmes (Random House); *The Fruit Hunters: Inside the Fruit Underworld* by Adam Gollner (Scribners); *The Miracle: The Epic Story of Asia's Quest for Wealth* by Michael Schuman (HarperBusiness); *A Nuclear Family Vacation: Travels in the World of Atomic Weaponry* by Sharon Weinberger and Nathan Hodge (Bloomsbury); *Vatican II: A People's History* by Colleen McDannell (Basic); *Bottomfeeder: An Ethical Eater's Adventures in a World of Vanishing Seafood* by Taras Grescoe (Bloomsbury); *The Day We Lost the H-Bomb: The True Story of a Missing Bomb and the Race to Find It* by Barbara Moran (Presidio).

THOUGHT LEADERS INTL./INTELLECTUAL PROPERTY MANAGEMENT

109 Barbaree Way, Tiburon, CA 94920

415-789-9040

www.thoughtleadersintl.com

Agent name: Leanne Sindell, lsindell@thoughtleadersintl.com

Born: Near Seattle, WA.

Education: Bible College in Sweden, England and Seattle, WA. Liberal arts studies in Kuopio, Finland, Stockholm University, Sorbonne University and American University in Paris. Degree in fashion design and illustration from Studio Bercot, Paris. Securities and Commodities/Futures licensed from 1984–2005.

Professional story: Financial sales in the securities and managed futures industry for twenty plus years. Took a three-year hiatus to study fashion design in Paris and designed in NYC for a year. Commercial illustrator and artist. In 2007, I started my own literary agency.

Personal interests/hobbies: Painting, reading, cooking, films, travel, learning languages, classical/jazz/world music.

Subjects and categories you like to agent: Business books, memoir.

Subjects and categories writers shouldn't bother pitching to you: Fiction, poetry, diet books, health/fitness, New Age/spiritual.

Do you charge fees or offer fee-based services: No.

What representative titles you have sold to publishers: *The Econosphere,* by Craig Thomas (FT Press); *The Genius Machine, The 11 Steps That Turn Raw Ideas Into Brilliance,* by Gerald Sindell (New World Library); *The Art of Managing Professional Services,* by Maureen Broderick (Wharton School Publishing); *The Yahoo! Style Guide, The Ultimate Sourcebook for Writing, Editing, and Creating Content for the Digital World,* by Cris Barr and the Senior Editors at Yahoo! (St. Martin's Press); *Genereux ou egoiste? Etes-vous de ceux qui prennent ou de ceux qui donnent?* by Cris Evatt and Bruce Feld (Payot et Rivages).

Why did you choose to become an agent and how did it happen: I decided to use my love of books and ideas and combine it with my knowledge of business and sales skills.

How do you feel about writers: I love writers and have a great respect for them.

Describe yourself: Curious, ethical, funny, serious, open minded, artistic, fair, impatient, opinionated, empathetic.

What are your preferred ways for writers to pitch you: Email query letter is the best way to start a conversation.

Do you think e-readers and similar devices will significantly change the

publishing business: I think it already has and continues to do so. I imagine there will be many new forms of a book in the future.

Are you optimistic, pessimistic, neutral, or catatonic about the book business into the knowable future: Mostly optimistic.

SCOTT TREIMEL NY

434 Lafayette Street, New York, NY 10003

212-505-8353

www.scotttreimelny.com

Agents' names: Scott Treimel; John M. Cusick, Assistant
Born: San Diego, California.
Education: BA Antioch College, American history.
Career history or story: Curtis Brown, Ltd. (trained by Marilyn Marlow); Scholastic; United Features Syndicate; HarperCollins Children's Books; founding director of Warner Bros. Worldwide Publishing.
Hobbies, interests: Theater, square dancing, dogs, politics, entertaining, history, good deeds.
Subjects and categories you are interested in agenting, including fiction and nonfiction: We handle all categories of children's books, from board books through teen novels. No adult projects; no toy-only projects, no screenplays.
Subjects and categories writers shouldn't even bother pitching to you: Religious/evangelical.
What would you do if you weren't agenting: Theatrical producer or beach bum.
What's the best way for fiction writers to solicit your interest: Via website only.
What's the best way for nonfiction writers to solicit your interest: Via website only.
Do you charge reading or any upfront fees: We do not charge a reading fee or any upfront fees.
In your experience, what are the most common pitching mistakes writers make: 1) Explaining the market to me; 2) Overselling themselves, not allowing their work to speak for itself, 3) Infusing their pitch with gimmicks.
Describe the client from hell, even if you don't have any: One with unreasonable expectations, who is impatient with matters I can't control, and will not listen to advice, from me or an editor. One who sends revised manuscripts in rapid succession and confuses our submissions to editors. One who writes "Have you heard from…" emails suggesting that we do not *religiously* inform clients of all goings-on as they happen.
What's your definition of a great client: Consistent, productive, passionate

about craft, able to work well with the variety of personalities that contribute to making and marketing books. And a client who actively promotes his or her books.

How can writers increase the odds that you will offer representation: It is 99.9 percent about the content of the work. Therefore, to increase the odds, be original and write brilliantly. One key problem we see with new writers is derivative storylines and too-familiar characters. I advocate imaginative boldness. That'll do it.

Why did you become an agent, and how did you become one: I worked on both sides, buying and selling intellectual property, and then I wanted to be closer to the key ingredient to the whole process: the creator. I am not beholden to corporate oversight and am able to advocate for the people who make the first and greatest contribution—the creators.

How do you feel about editors and publishers: We have many talented editors. I worry their publishers put so much pressure on them that they are unable to take chances, try new things. I like independent vision, which the present committee-style publishing discourages. It is also true that editors are editing less these days, and publishers have off-loaded services they once provided.

What do you see in the near future for book publishing: 1) More focus on fewer titles; and 2) The increasing development of electronic distribution of literary work.

What are your favorite books, TV shows, movies, and why: I like cartoons, not the animated movies that wink at the adults in the audience, but cartoons on television. The old-style *Looney Tunes* and *Tom and Jerry* gag fests have been replaced with well-plotted storytelling—often solidly structured. I also dig the high visual style and experimenting. I watch *South Park* and *Sponge Bob*, but also *Camp Lazlo, Foster's Home for Imaginary Friends, The Grim Adventures of Bill and Mandy, Pokemon, Dexter's Laboratory, Robot Chicken, The Powerpuff Girls, Squidbilly*. Writers for children can do well to tune in and discover the level of social sophistication and cultural references cartoon characters resource. My greatest dislike is a sentimentalized recollection of childhood. Cartoons source a more authentic point of view. Going way way back, I love Monty Python. Favorite book: *Middlemarch*, of course!

In your opinion, what do editors think of you: They think I am honest, direct, reasonable but not a softie. I believe they also think I have good taste and interesting projects.

On a personal non-professional level, what do you think people think of you: Straightforward, energetic, earnest, funny.

What are some representative titles that you have sold: *Shotgun Serenade* by Gail Giles (Little, Brown); *The Hunchback Assignments* (series) by Arthur Slade (HarperCollins Canada and Random House/Wendy Lamb Books); *The First Five Fourths* by Pat Hughs (Viking); *Me & Death* by Richard Scrimger (Tundra); *The P.S. Brothers* by Maribeth Boelts (Harcourt); *Laundry Day* by Maurie Manning (Clarion); *Haunted* by Barbara Haworth-Attard (HarperCollins Canada); *Dear Canada* by Barbara Haworth-Attard (Scholastic Canada); *Roawr!* by Barbara

Joosse (Philomel); *Backlist* by Cyndy Szekeres (Sterling); *Soccer Dreams* by Maribeth Boelts (Candlewick); *Ends by David Ward* (Abrams); *Frankie Goes to School*, illustrations by Keven Atteberry; *Cakes and Miracles* by Barbara Golden (Marshall Cavendsih).

John's first sale: *The Blending Time* by Michael Kinch (Flux).

TRIADAUS LITERARY AGENCY

P.O. Box 561, Sewickley, PA 15143

http://www.triadaus.com

Agent's name: Uwe Stender; uwe@triadaus.com

Born: Germany.

Education: PhD, German literature.

Career Story: Literary Agent (since 2004), University Lecturer (Writing, German), Teacher.

Hobbies: Soccer (Runner-Up National High School Coach of the Year 2007), playing squash, reading.

Subjects and categories you like to agent: I am open to pretty much anything.

What might you be doing if you weren't agenting: I might be in the music industry as a producer.

What's the most effective way for writers to grab your attention: Send me a well written and error-free email query.

Do you charge fees separate from your commission, or offer non-agenting fee-based services: No.

What are representative titles you have sold to publishers: *86'd* by Dan Fante (Harper Perennial); *Covert* by Bob Delaney with Dave Scheiber (Union Square Press/Sterling); *The Equation* by Omar Tyree (Wiley); *Lost's Buried Treasures* by David Lavery and Lynnette Porter (Sourcebooks); *What's Possible* by Daryn Kagan (Meredith).

Why did you become an agent, and how did you become one: I have always been interested in literature (PhD and taught at universities) and after years of researching the field from a publishing perspective, I decided to become an agent (with a lot of guidance and mentoring from several well-connected publishing insiders). I love the thrill of discovering a GREAT book.

How do you feel about writers: Without them, I would not be doing my dream job.

What do you tell entities from other planets and dimensions about your job: It's like discovering new planets every day!

What are your favorite books, movies, TV shows, and why: Love things that move me on an emotional level. All of the following do:

Books: *The Little Prince*, St. Exupery; *The Tin Drum*, Grass; *Huckleberry Finn*, Mark Twain.

Films: *Cinema Paradiso, Goodbye Lenin, It's a Wonderful Life.*

TV shows: *Bonanza, Life on Mars* (British Version), *Seinfeld.*

What do you like best about your clients, and the editors and publishers you work with: These folks are hard-working, smart, and committed to making dreams come true.

TRIDENT MEDIA GROUP

41 Madison Ave., New York, NY 10010

email: JBent@tridentmediagroup.com

Agent's name: Jenny Bent

Born: November 23, 1969, New York, New York.

Education: BA, MA, English literature with Highest Honors from Cambridge University, U.K.

Career history: Joined Trident three years ago after working at a variety of agencies. Began career as an assistant to top agent Raphael Sagalyn in DC.

Hobbies/personal interests: Yoga, bad television, my dogs, animal rescue.

Categories/subjects that you are most enthusiastic about agenting: High-concept commercial women's fiction, quirky or funny literary fiction, high-concept young adult, exceptional memoir, humor, fun women's lifestyle.

What you don't want to agent: Political books, New Age, health/fitness, mysteries.

If you were not an agent, what might you be doing instead: Standing on the unemployment line.

What's the best way for writers to solicit your interest: Write a great, catchy query letter. See www.jennybent.com for an example.

Do you charge reading or management fees: No.

Can you provide an approximation by percent of what you tend to represent by category: Commercial fiction (women's): 50 percent, young Adult: 20 percent, literary fiction/memoir: 10 percent, humor: 10 percent, lifestyle: 10 percent.

What are the most common mistakes writers make when pitching you: Being boring and long-winded. Also pitching books in a genre I don't represent.

How would you describe the client from hell: Anyone who is nasty or abusive or refuses to communicate via email.

How would you describe the perfect client: Prolific, low-maintenance, fun, talented.

How and why did you ever become an agent: Too long and boring to go into, but I couldn't really imagine doing anything else.

What, if anything, can a writer do to increase the odds of your becoming his or her agent: Have good credentials and write a great book.

What are your favorite books, movies, TV shows, and why: I love all kinds of trashy television—it's my guilty pleasure.

Please list representative titles you have sold: *Freshman* by Brent Crawford (Hyperion) (Young Adult); *Stop Dressing Your Six-Year-Old Like a Skank* by Celia Rivenbark (St. Martin's); *There's a (Slight) Chance I Might be Going to Hell* by Laurie Notaro (Random House); *How to be Cool* by Johanna Edwards (Berkley); *The Sweet Potato Queen's First Big-Ass Novel* by Jill Conner Browne with Karin Gillespie (Simon & Schuster); *Yellowcake* by Ann Cummins (Houghton Mifflin).

VERITAS LITERARY AGENCY

601 Van Ness Avenue, Opera Plaza Suite E, San Francisco, CA 94102

415-647-6964   fax: 415-647-6965

www.veritasliterary.com

Agents' names: Katherine Boyle, Katherine@veritasliterary.com; Megan O'Patry, Megan@veritasliterary.com

The following information pertains to Katherine Boyle.

Born: June 16 (Bloomsday!) 1969, Stanford, California.

Education: BA, English and psychology, Stanford University.

Career story: After graduation I worked at a variety of Bay Area independent presses and agencies while pursuing a publishing certificate at Berkeley. Veritas was established in 1995, and thereafter I joined the AAR and the Authors Guild.

Hobbies and special personal interests: Music and visual art addiction, foreign films, running, hiking, chapbook making, pet adoration, eating.

Subjects and categories you like to agent: Literary fiction, multicultural fiction, historical fiction, new fabulist and literary speculative fiction, southern fiction, literary thrillers and mysteries, narrative nonfiction, reportage, memoir, popular science, popular culture, natural history, current events and politics, women's issues, art and music-related biography.

Subjects and categories writers shouldn't bother pitching to you: New Age, romance, military history, Westerns.

What might you be doing if you weren't agenting: It's a toss-up between whale scientist or London stage actress.

What's the most effective ways for writers to grab your attention: Well-written, concise queries.

Do you charge fees separate from your commission, or offer non-agenting fee-based services: No.

What are representative titles you have sold to publishers: *Hedwig and Berti* by Frieda Arkin (St. Martin's); *Sickened* by Julie Gregory (Bantam); *If I Am Missing or Dead* by Janine Latus (Simon & Schuster/Random House U.K.); *Free Burning* by Bayo Ojikutu (Crown); *I Was a Teenage Gumby* by Jean Gonick (Hyperion); *Sometimes the Soul* by Gioia Timpanelli (W.W. Norton/Vintage); *Deliberate Acts of Kindness* by Meredith Gould (Doubleday); *The Nature of Music* by Maureen McCarthy Draper (Riverhead/Putnam); *American Sideshow* by Marc Hartzman (Tarcher/Penguin); *65 Successful Harvard Business School Application Essays* by The Harbus (St. Martin's); *The Essential Nostradamus* by Richard Smoley (Tarcher/Penguin); *The Twins of Tribeca* by Rachel Pine (Miramax); *The Creative Writing MFA Handbook* by Tom Kealey (Continuum).

Why did you become an agent, and how did you become one: I've always loved books and great writing but I'm too fond of social interaction to thrive as a librarian. I couldn't ask for a better career to satisfy the introverted/extroverted poles of a Gemini personality.

How do you feel about writers: I adore them. It's a tough job and they're certainly doing more than their share to keep the culture on life support, generally earning a fraction of what video game designers make.

What do you tell entities from other planets and dimensions about your job: Storytelling is an ancient and universal art. Since dreams probably come from these other planes, it shouldn't be too hard to explain the field to an interested entity. All beings likely share the intuition that there's more wisdom embedded in a story than we'll ever know.

What are your favorite books, movies, TV shows, and why: Books: *Housekeeping*, *The Sea*, *The Restraint of Beasts*, and anything by Alice Munro, William Maxwell, and Italo Calvino. All of these authors can shift a reader's level of perception almost instantaneously. Movies: *I'm Not Scared, Dreams, The 400 Blows, Nights of Cabiria, The After Life*: all strange, beautiful, life-affirming. TV: *Flight of the Conchords* and *Prime Suspect*, because hilarity and Helen Mirren are also important.

How would you describe the writer from hell: Someone who calls to pitch a "great idea" on the phone before they've even written a word.

How would you describe the publisher and/or editor from hell: Luckily I've been spared that circle so far.

What do you like best about your clients, and the editors and publishers you work with: I couldn't ask for a better cadre of kindred spirits. There's no greater rush than celebrating a book's success with a brilliant author and a wonderfully committed editor. Of course they're all individuals, but on the whole it's so reassuring to be surrounded by so many sane, thoughtful, intellectually curious, passionate, witty and good-natured people. I just wish that they weren't spread so far apart—we could throw some great parties.

Do you wish to describe who you are: "Trying to define yourself is like trying to bite your own teeth."—Alan Watts

Will our business exist as we know it in ten years or so: While the tectonic plates are certainly shifting, books will always be beloved and necessary in this world. To sustain authors, however, it may be increasingly important to pursue alternate subrights arenas—pitching a historical-fiction series to a video game producer, for example. A protean instinct will serve both authors and agents well, but the importance of craft, originality, and excellence will never disappear.

The following information pertains to Megan O'Patry.

Born: San Diego, California; 1984.

Education: BA in pre- and early-modern literature, UC Santa Cruz; MFA in creative writing, San Francisco State University.

Career story: A long time ago when the earth was green and there were more kinds of animals than you've ever seen...

Hobbies and special personal interests: Playwriting, black and white movies, teaching infants to swim.

Subjects and categories you like to agent: Literary fiction, narrative nonfiction, mainstream fiction, YA, to name a few.

Subjects and categories writers shouldn't bother pitching to you: Self-help, guide books.

What might you be doing if you weren't agenting: Working in Elmore Leonard's coffee shop.

What's the most effective ways for writers to grab your attention: A well-written query. Don't sell try to sell me a used car. I don't need a car, I live in the city. Please don't drop me into the middle of your story with aggressive adverbs; be honest and to the point. Always spellcheck.

Do you charge fees separate from your commission, or offer non-agenting fee-based services: No.

Why did you become an agent, and how did you become one: It was a stage of evolution, more or less. I followed Katherine Boyle home one day and lived under the dining room table for a while, next to a slush pile. The rest, as they say, is in development.

How do you feel about writers: Writers are like M&M's. They come in a variety of colors and you stuff them in your mouth, hoping for a hallucinatory effect. And sometimes you wake up on the side of the road in your underwear. I love writers!

What do you tell entities from other planets and dimensions about your job: I'm very tight-lipped. I communicate with bumper stickers. I pass on and receive a lot of intergalactic wisdom this way, such as: Go North for the cold beer.

What are your favorite books, movies, TV shows, and why: *A Hero of Our Time, The House of Leaves, Lolita, The West Wing, Deadwood, Weeds, The Last Unicorn, The Seven Faces of Dr. Lao*, because of the writing, my friends, the writing!

How would you describe the writer from hell: Someone who is unrealistic in their expectations, resistant to constructive criticism, and unacquainted with courtesies like *please* and *thank you*.

How would you describe the publisher and/or editor from hell: They love what they do and they come into any project with an open mind. We extend them the same necessity. At the end of the day, we may want different things but by the end of the week, we're all lined up.

What do you like best about your clients, and the editors and publishers you work with: They love what they do and they come into any project with an open mind. We extend them the same necessity. At the end of the day, we may want different things but by the end of the week, we're all lined up.

Will our business exist as we know it in ten years or so: I have a bumper sticker somewhere that addresses this very issue…

MARY JACK WALD ASSOCIATES, INC.

111 East 14th Street, New York, NY 10003

Agent's name: Mary Jack Wald.

Born: Manhattan, New York.

Education: BA, Union College.

Career history or story: Fourth grade teacher; permissions correspondent, Random House; editor, Random House; direct marketing, Random House, Western Publishing; managing editor, Golden Books, Western Publishing; Tori Mendez Agency.

Subjects and categories you are interested in agenting, including fiction and nonfiction: Not accepting new clients.

Subjects and categories writers shouldn't even bother pitching to you: Not accepting new clients.

What would you do if you weren't agenting: Write.

Do you charge reading or any upfront fees: No.

In your experience, what are the most common pitching mistakes writers make: Telling me how much their children, husband, friends loved their manuscript.

Describe the client from hell, even if you don't have any: Calls every day or worse; calls the editor you submitted to every day.

What's your definition of a great client: Talented, helpful, sense of humor.

Why did you become an agent, and how did you become one: Wanted to work directly with the author.

Describe to someone from another planet what you do as an agent: Try to find the right editor and publisher for the author. Then handle contract, royalty, reversion of rights.

What do you see in the near future for book publishing: More independent publishing houses.

In your opinion, what do editors think of you: Honest and understanding.

What are some representative titles that you have sold: Christopher Bahjalian, first three books (Carroll & Graf); Baxter Black (Crown Publishers); Yale

Strom—too many to list; John Peel—too many to list; Denise Lewis Patrick—too many to list; Richie Tankerskey Cusick—too many to list; Gregg Loomis (Dorchester Publishing); Neil Johnson—too many to list.

WALES LITERARY AGENCY, INC.

P.O. Box 9428, Seattle, Washington 98109-0428

(For deliveries by UPS, DHL, FedEx, all door-to-door couriers, contact the agency for the office street address.)

206-284-7114

www.waleslit.com   email: waleslit@waleslit.com

Agents' names: Elizabeth Wales, President; Neal Swain, Assistant Agent
The following information pertains to Elizabeth Wales.
Born: March 30, 1952.
Education: BA, Smith College; graduate work in English and American Literature, Columbia University.
Career story: Worked in the trade sales departments at Oxford University Press and Viking Penguin; worked in city government and served a term on the Seattle school board; also worked as a bookseller and publisher's representative.

Subjects and categories you like to agent: A wide range of narrative nonfiction and literary fiction. Especially interested in nonfiction projects that could have a progressive cultural or political impact. In fiction, looking for talented mainstream storytellers, both new and established. Occasionally interested in well-crafted psychological thrillers and speculative fiction. Especially interested in writers from the Northwest, Alaska, the West Coast, and what have become known as the Pacific Rim countries.

Subjects and categories writers shouldn't bother pitching to you: Children's books, how-to, self-help, and almost all genre projects (romance, true crime, horror, action/adventure, most science fiction/fantasy, techno thrillers).

Do you charge fees separate from your commission, or offer non-agenting fee-based services: No reading fees.

What are representative titles you have sold to publishers: *Flotsametrics and the Floating World,* by Curtis Ebbesmeyer and Eric Scigliano (Smithsonian Books/HarperCollins, 2009); *Cold: An Untold Story in a Warming World* by Bill Streever (Little, Brown, 2009); *Unterzakhn: a Graphic Novel and Story of the Lower East Side* by Leela Corman (Schocken/Pantheon, 2010); *Wisdom of the Last Farmer* by David Mas Masumoto (The Free Press, 2009).

Why did you become an agent, and how did you become one: For the adventure and the challenge; also, I am a generalist—interested in variety.

JOHN A. WARE LITERARY AGENCY

392 Central Park West, New York, NY 10025

Agent's name: John A. Ware

Education: AB in philosophy, Cornell University, graduate work in English and American literature, Northwestern University.

Career history: Editor, eight years, Doubleday; agent, one year, James Brown Associates/Curtis Brown Ltd.; founded John A. Ware Literary Agency.

Hobbies/personal interests: Running, mentoring, classical music and blues, Italy and Spain.

Categories/subjects that you are most enthusiastic about agenting: Biography and history, investigative journalism, social commentary and contemporary affairs, "bird's eye" views of phenomena, nature and Americana, literary and suspense fiction.

What you don't want to agent: Technothrillers and women's romance, men's action-adventures, guidebooks and cookbooks, science fiction, reference, young-adult and children's books, personal memoirs.

If you were not an agent, what might you be doing instead: Teaching philosophy, working as a sportswriter, or in some position in race relations.

What's the best way for writers to solicit your interest: Succinct query letter (only), with SASE.

Do you charge reading or management fees: No.

Can you provide an approximation by percent of what you tend to represent by category: Fiction: 20 percent, Nonfiction: 80 percent.

What are the most common mistakes writers make when pitching you: Overselling, instead of simply describing work, sending unasked-for sample material.

How would you describe the client from hell: Untrusting, discourteous, humorless.

How would you describe the perfect client: Professional about their writerly responsibilities, trusting, courteous, possesses a sense of humor.

How and why did you ever become an agent: I enjoy working with words, writers, and editors, and believe strongly in the permanent importance of the written word.

What, if anything, can a writer do to increase the odds of your becoming his or her agent: Covered above!

How would you describe to someone (or something) from another planet what it is that you do as an agent: I try to do skilled, imaginative things with words and the writers who render them.

Do you have any particular opinions or impressions of editors and publishers in general: Smart, professional and, for the most part, prompt and courteous.

What are your favorite books, movies, TV shows, and why: *BBC News*, not much of a moviegoer, more, well, a reader.

Please list representative titles you have sold: *Where Men Win Glory: The Odyssey of Pat Tillman*, by Jon Krakauer (Doubleday); *Abundance of Valor* (military history), by Will Irwin (Random House); *Velva Jean Learns to Drive*, a novel, by Jennifer Niven (Plume); *The Art of the Game* (on basketball), by Chris Ballard (SportsIllustrated/Simon & Schuster); *The Aquanet Diaries: Big Hair, Big Dreams, Small Town* (a memoir of high school), by Jennifer Niven (Simon Spotlight Entertainment); *Spent* (a memoir of shopaholism), by Avis Cardella (Little, Brown); *To Kill a Page* (a memoir of becoming literate), by Travis Hugh Culley (Random House); *The Pledge* (of Allegiance), by Jeffrey Jones and Peter Mayer, (Thomas Dunne/St. Martin's Press).

TED WEINSTEIN LITERARY MANAGEMENT

307 Seventh Avenue, Suite 2407, New York, NY 10001

www.twliterary.com

(Agency accepts email submissions only)

Agent's name: Ted Weinstein, AAR

Education: Bachelor's degree in philosophy from Yale College, master's degree in public and private management from Yale School of Management.

Career history: Ted Weinstein has broad experience on both the business and editorial sides of publishing. Before founding the agency he held senior publishing positions in licensing, marketing, publicity and business development. Also a widely published author, Ted has been the music critic for NPR's "All Things Considered" and a commentator for the *San Francisco Chronicle* and many other publications.

Hobbies/personal interests: Politics, music, hiking, visual arts.

Categories/subjects that you are most enthusiastic about agenting: Wide range of intelligent nonfiction, especially narrative nonfiction, popular science, biography and history, current affairs and politics, business, health and medicine, food and cooking, pop culture and quirky reference books.

What you don't want to agent: Fiction, stage plays, screenplays, poetry, or books for children or young adults.

If you were not an agent, what might you be doing instead: I have so much fun as an agent that I can't imagine doing anything else. Whenever I retire (many decades from now) the only change will be I'll have time to read more fiction.

What's the best way for writers to solicit your interest: Best is by referral from someone I know and respect, but I also take on many clients who approach me unsolicited. For unsolicited queries, email only—query or full proposal. See website for detailed submission guidelines.

Do you charge reading or management fees: NEVER! I'm an AAR member.

Can you provide an approximation by percent of what you tend to represent by category : Nonfiction: 100 percent.

What are the most common mistakes writers make when pitching you: Submitting a proposal for a type of work I do not represent. Sending a proposal that isn't polished, professional and typo-free. Telephoning the agency to query. Sending a mass email cc-ing me and every other agent in the business.

How would you describe the client from hell: Someone who doesn't act like a professional—missing deadlines, personalizing business issues. Publishing is a business and success is always more likely to come to those who are disciplined and hard-working and who treat the people they work with respectfully.

How would you describe the perfect client: Talented, professional, hard working—someone who treats his or her writing like a career (even if it isn't their only career).

How and why did you ever become an agent: Before becoming an agent I spent many years in different areas of publishing—editorial, marketing, business development, licensing—and agenting is an endlessly fun, fascinating and rewarding combination of all these areas.

What, if anything, can a writer do to increase the odds of your becoming his or her agent: Treat your writing as a long-term career, not just a one-book opportunity. Constantly improve your writing by getting feedback from writing groups, editors and other thoughtful coaches. Increase your public profile by publishing your words and ideas via newspapers, magazines and radio.

How would you describe to someone (or something) from another planet what it is that you do as an agent: I'm a combination of editor, cheerleader, advocate, negotiator, marketing consultant, lawyer, accountant, career coach and therapist, in varying proportions depending on what each client needs from me to help them succeed.

Do you have any particular opinions or impressions of editors and publishers in general: They are smart businesspeople, without whom talented authors are unlikely to reach the audience they deserve, and they are some of the smartest readers anywhere. My clients and I carefully review every comment we receive from editors. No two editors will have the same reaction to any proposal, but the insights from each one are enormously valuable in helping my clients improve their work.

What do you think the future holds for writers, publishers, and agents: Authors increasingly need to think of themselves as CEOs of their own multimedia empires, promoting and publicizing themselves and their talents in every possible venue and looking to enhance and exploit the value of their insights and writing in every possible medium.

What are your favorite books, movies, TV shows, and why: I don't have enough time to read all the great books that are published every year, and I don't even own a TV.

On a personal level, what do you think people like about you and dislike about you: Professionalism-with-a-sense-of-humor, wide-ranging insights and creativity, forthrightness and integrity.

What are representative titles you have sold to publishers: *Inside Steve's Brain: The Leadership Secrets of Steve Jobs* by Leander Kahney (Penguin/Portfolio); *The Body Toxic* by Susanne Antonetta (Farrar Straus & Giroux); *The Unfinished*

Game: Pascal, Fermat and the Birth of Probability Theory by Keith Devlin (Perseus/ Basic); *Blank Spots on the Map: State Secrets, Hidden Landscapres, and the Pentagon's Black World* by Trevor Paglen (Penguin/Dutton); *The Autobiographer's Handbook: The 826 Valencia Guide to Writing a Memoir* (Holt); *The New New Deal* (Penguin/ Portfolio); *American Nightingale: The Story of Frances Stanger, Forgotten Heroine of Normandy* by Bob Welch (Simon & Schuster/Atria); *Ancient Wisdom, Modern Kitchen: Recipes from the East for Health, Healing and Long Life* (Perseus/Da Capo); *More than Human: How Biotechnology Is Transforming Us and Why We Should Embrace It* (Random House/Broadway); *One-Letter Words: A Dictionary* by Craig Conley (HarperCollins); *American Chestnut: The Life, Death and Rebirth of a Perfect Tree* by Susan Freinkel (University of California Press); *Momma Zen: Walking the Crooked Path of Motherhood* by Karen Miller (Shambhala); *The Probiotics Revolution* by Sarah Wernick and Gary B. Huffnagle (Random House/Bantam).

WRITERS HOUSE

21 West 26th Street, New York, NY 10010

3368 Governor Dr, #224F, San Diego, CA 92122

www.writershouse.com

Agents' names: Albert Zuckerman; Dan Lazar; Steven Malk, smalk@ writershouse.com; Kenneth Wright; Josh Getzler, jgetzler@writershouse.com, Amy Berkower, Susan Finiburg, Robin Rue, Jodi Reamer, Merrilee Heifetz, Susan Cohen, Michele Rubin, Simon Lipskar, Dan Conowax, Rebecca Sherman, Maya Rock.

The following information pertains to Albert Zuckerman.

Born: Bronx, New York.

Education: AB, Princeton; D.F.A. Yale Drama.

Career history or story: Naval officer; foreign services officer; assistant professor of playwriting and dramatic literature at Yale, winner of Stanley Drama Award for best play by a new American playwright; author of two novels published by Doubleday and Dell; writer for three daytime TV series, Broadway producer; founded Writers House in 1974; author of *Writing the Blockbuster Novel*.

Hobbies, interests: Tennis, movies, plays, reading wonderful books, working with talented writers.

Subjects and categories you are interested in agenting, including fiction and nonfiction: Great storytelling, fiction or nonfiction. Especially open to published novelists who are eager to move up a notch or several notches.

Subjects and categories writers shouldn't even bother pitching to you: Please, no how-to books.

What's the best way for fiction writers to solicit your interest: Write me an engaging and compelling letter. I suggest one page in three paragraphs. 1) What is fascinating and unusual about your book? How does it differ from others in its category? 2) What is it about? Its story, theme, characters, special features. 3) What is your writing experience and why are you the most qualified person to write it?

What's the best way for nonfiction writers to solicit your interest: Same as above.

Do you charge reading or any upfront fees: No.

What's your definition of a great client: Someone who has talent and craft but who also is willing to keep on revising until his or her work reaches its optimum condition.

Why did you become an agent, and how did you become one: I thought I could help writers more than the agents who had represented me. And I have.

How do you feel about editors and publishers: They have a tough job, and most of them do it well.

How do you feel about writers: Most of them are a great joy.

What do you see in the near future for book publishing: It will be with us as long as we're around.

In your opinion, what do editors think of you: I get the impression that I am liked and respected.

What are some representative titles that you have sold: *A Brief History of Time* by Stephen Hawking (Bantam); *The First Wives Club* by Olivia Goldsmith (Simon & Schuster); *The Pillars of the Earth* by Ken Follett (William Morrow); *Moneyball* by Michael Lewis (Norton); *The Religion* by Tim Willocks (Farrar Straus); *The Blue Day Book* by Bradley Trevor and Greive (Andrews McMeel).

The following information pertains to Dan Lazar.

Born: Jerusalem, Israel.

Career story: I started as an intern and worked my way up to senior agent.

Subjects and categories you like to agent: Literary and commercial fiction, women's fiction, historical fiction, thrillers, mysteries, gay and lesbian, young-adult, middle-grade, graphic novels or memoirs, Judaica, memoir, narrative nonfiction, pop-culture, humor.

Subjects and categories writers shouldn't bother pitching to you: Romance, picture books, cookbooks.

What's the most effective ways for writers to grab your attention: A great query letter and the first five pages of their manuscript.

Do you charge fees separate from your commission, or offer non-agenting fee-based services: No fees.

What are representative titles you have sold to publishers: *Island of Lost Girls* by Jennifer McMahon (Harper); *Final Theory* by Mark Alpert (Touchstone); *Eve* by Elissa Aliott (Bantam); *Savvy* by Ingrid Law (Dial/Walden); *The Last Invisible Boy* (Ginee Seo/Atheneum); *Haiku Mama* (Quirk Books).

Why did you become an agent, and how did you become one: I loved books and reading. I applied for an internship at both publishers and agencies—Writers House hired me for the summer, and happily so! I've been here ever since.

What do you tell entities from other planets and dimensions about your job: You don't go to court without a lawyer, or buy a house without a real estate agent. Same for publishing—we're the author's champion and partner. Ideally (and more and more realistically) we're the one constant in the author's career, since editors move jobs and publishers are changing constantly.

What are your favorite books, movies, TV shows, and why: Favorite movies: *The Incredibles, Monsters Inc.* Favorite TV shows: *The Daily Show, Will & Grace, DirtySexyMoney, Frasier, Freaks & Geeks.*

What do you like best about your clients, and the editors and publishers you work with: I love their books, and I admire their persistence and passion. Different tastes are what make this business tough and rewarding all at once, but we're all in it ultimately for the same reason.

Will our business exist as we know it in ten years or so: The business as we know it changes every day! But it's not going anywhere.

The following information pertains to **Steven Malk.**

Born: Johannesburg, South Africa.

Education: BA, political science and BA, history, University of California San Diego.

Career story: Opened a West Coast office for Writers House in 1998. Worked for the Sandra Dijkstra Literary Agency prior to that.

Subjects and categories you like to agent: Books for children, middle-grade readers, and young adults.

Subjects and categories writers shouldn't bother pitching to you: Books that aren't intended for children, middle-grade readers, or young adults.

What might you be doing if you weren't agenting: Playing center field for the San Diego Padres (not really, but it's a nice thought).

What's the most effective ways for writers to grab your attention: Write a carefully thought-out, focused query that demonstrates a strong command of your work, and also explains why you're querying me, specifically.

Do you charge fees separate from your commission, or offer non-agenting fee-based services: No.

What are representative titles you have sold to publishers: *The True Meaning of Smekday* by Adam Rex (Hyperion); *Clementine* by Sara Pennypacker, illustrated by Marla Frazee (Hyperion); *King Dork* by Frank Portman (Delacorte Press); *Your Own, Sylvia: A Verse Portrait of Sylvia Plath* by Stephanie Hemphill (Knopf); *John, Paul, George, and Ben* by Lane Smith (Hyperion); *Repossesed* by A. M. Jenkins (HarperCollins); *Collect Raindrops: The Seasons Gathered* by Nikki McClure (Abrams); *Knucklehead: Tall Tales and Almost True Stories of Growing Up Scieszka* by Jon Scieszka (Viking); *The Secret Order of the Gumm Street Girls* by Elise Primavera (HarperCollins); *We Are the Ship: The Story of Negro League Baseball* by Kadir Nelson (Hyperion).

Why did you become an agent, and how did you become one: It allowed me to be involved in both the creative and business sides of the industry, and to work closely with and on behalf of authors I greatly admire. It was also the perfect outgrowth of bookselling for me, as I was able to apply everything I'd learned as a third-generation bookseller to my work as an agent.

What are your favorite books, movies, TV shows, and why: Books (not including books that I've represented, obviously): Anything by Barbara Cooney or Roald Dahl. Also *The Westing Game* by Ellen Raskin, *I'll Fix Anthony* by Judith Viorst, *The Carrot Seed* by Ruth Krauss, *Dear Genius: The Letters of Ursula Nordstrom* by Leonard Marcus, and many, many more. Movies: *Hoosiers, Rushmore, Ghost World, Election, The Straight Story.*

The following information pertains to Kenneth Wright.

Education: BA, University of Colorado, Boulder; MA, Boston College.

Career story: Editor through publisher positions at Oxford University Press, Simon & Schuster, HarperCollins, Henry Holt, and Scholastic.

Subjects and categories you like to agent: Adult fiction and nonfiction; children's middle-grade and YA fiction and nonfiction.

Subjects and categories writers shouldn't bother pitching to you: Fantasy. Romance. Genre. Picture books.

What's the most effective ways for writers to grab your attention: Make me laugh. Keep it short. Know your readers.

Do you charge fees separate from your commission, or offer non-agenting fee-based services: No. Honest.

What are representative titles you have sold to publishers: David Macaulay (Roaring Brook/MacMillan); *The Lost Girls* by Amanda Pressner, Jennifer Baggett, and Holly Corbett (HarperCollins); *Why Santa Teleports* by Greg Mone (Bloomsbury).

The following information pertains to Josh Getzler.

Born: May 4, 1968, New York City.

Education: BA, University of Pennsylvania, 1990; Radcliffe Publishing Course, 1990; MBA, Columbia Business School, 1995.

Career story: Started in editorial at Harcourt in 1991, then left to go to business school, expecting to get back into publishing after. Instead, I ended up owning and operating a minor league baseball team for 12 years (Staten Island Yankees), before selling in 2006 and returning to the world of books on the agency side. Apprenticed under Simon Lipskar and Dan Lazar, and now am also building a client list.

Subjects and categories you like to agent: Procedural mysteries (particularly, though by no means exclusively, period and foreign), thrillers, literary and commercial fiction, religion (not spiritual guidance—books about religious history or philosophy), sports, music.

Subjects and categories writers shouldn't bother pitching to you: Romance, picture books, religious fiction.

What might you be doing if you weren't agenting: Sports marketing, working on the business side of a publishing house, editing.

What's the most effective ways for writers to grab your attention: Clearly and concisely email a letter that tells me quickly what kind of book you are pitching. I want to know the genre; I want to know salient details about the story. I don't want to know that you think your book is important and groundbreaking, hilarious and a must-read. I want you to offer it up for evaluation, and I will respect your willingness to put it out there.

Do you charge fees separate from your commission, or offer non-agenting fee-based services: NO.

What are representative titles you have sold to publishers: *Devil's Trill* by Gerald Elias (St. Martin's Press).

Why did you become an agent, and how did you become one: When I was selling the baseball team, I was having a conversation with my wife, who told me that it was clear I needed to work in books again. Having thirteen years of experience making deals and looking at contracts, I realized I could be suited to agenting. I decided to target existing agencies, rather than start a new one, and got lucky with timing that a position with Simon Lipskar and Dan Lazar at Writers House opened up.

What are your favorite books, movies, TV shows, and why: *Absalom, Absalom, The Caine Mutiny, The Day of the Jackal, The Tattooed Potato and Other Clues, O Jerusalem, Sherlock Holmes* (any of them, really). Movies: *Inherit the Wind, Bull Durham, My Cousin Vinny, Murder on the Orient Express, The Great Dictator.* TV Shows: *Taxi, Black Adder, Law and Order* (original), *MASH, Prime Suspect.*

Will our business exist as we know it in ten years or so: Yes, I think so, although there will be a much greater emphasis on electronic rights. We will be even more in the business of representing intellectual property.

SUSAN ZECKENDORF ASSOCIATES, INC.

171 West 57th Street, New York, NY

Agent's name: Susan Zeckendorf

Born: New York.

Education: BA, Wellesley College; MEd Teacher's College Columbia.

Career history: Formerly counseling psychologist. Member of the AAR.

Hobbies/personal interests: Music, exercise.

Subjects and categories you are interested in agenting, including fiction and nonfiction: Literary fiction, historical fiction, mysteries, music, biography.

Subjects and categories writers shouldn't even bother pitching to you: Science fiction, fantasy, spiritual works.

What would you do if you weren't agenting: Psychologist.

What's the best way for fiction writers to solicit your interest: Query letter with SASE.

What's the best way for nonfiction writers to solicit your interest: Short, clear query letter with SASE.

Do you charge reading or any upfront fees: No.

In your experience, what are the most common pitching mistakes writers make: Sending complete manuscript unsolicited. Pitch too long.

Describe the client from hell, even if you don't have any: Hostile, demanding.

What's your definition of a great client: Patient.

How can writers increase the odds that you will offer representation: Endorsements from well-known people.

Why did you become an agent, and how did you become one: I love books. Joined an agency.

Describe to someone from another planet what you do as an agent: Read, edit moderately, find appropriate publisher.

How do you feel about editors and publishers: Fine.

How do you feel about writers: Depends on the writer.

What do you see in the near future for book publishing: People will continue to read books.

What are your favorite books, TV shows, movies, and why: *The House of Mirth* by Edith Wharton.

In your opinion, what do editors think of you: Have no idea.

On a personal non-professional level, what do you think people think of you: They like me.

What are some representative titles that you have sold: *The Hardscrabble Chronicles* by Laurie Morrow (Berkley); *How to Write a Damn Good Novel* Series by James W. Frey (St. Martin's); *The True Life Story of Isobel Roundtree* (Pocket Books).

HELEN ZIMMERMANN LITERARY AGENCY

3 Emmy Lane, New Paltz, NY 12561

845-256-0977   fax: 845-256-0979

www.zimmermannliterary.com   email: Helen@zimmagency.com

Agent's name: Helen Zimmermann

Born: 1964, Bronxville, New York.

Education: BA in English and psychology, State University of New York, Buffalo.

Career history: 12 years in book publishing, most of them at Random House, then five years at an independent bookstore. I founded my agency in 2004.

Hobbies/personal interests: Climbing the 46 High Peaks in the Adirondacks (18 down, 28 to go), skiing, being an EMT, oh, and reading!

Categories/subjects that you are most enthusiastic about agenting: Memoir, pop-culture, women's issues, humor, nature, sports, accessible literary fiction, mysteries.

What you don't want to agent: Science fiction, horror, tales of male drinking habits, Westerns, poetry, picture books.

What's the best way for writers to solicit your interest: By email. Please just send a detailed query letter to start. I will be in touch within three weeks (or sooner) if I want to see more material.

Do you charge reading or management fees: No.

Can you provide an approximation by percent of what you tend to represent by category: Nonfiction: 80 percent, fiction: 20 percent.

What are the most common mistakes writers make when pitching you: Sending material that is sloppy or half-baked. If it's obvious you haven't done your homework, I won't be interested.

How and why did you ever become an agent: Working as the events director for an independent bookstore put me in contact with many aspiring writers. They would always ask, "How do I get published?" My answer was always "You need an agent." After about the 30th inquiry, I decided to become one myself.

How would you describe to someone (or something) from another planet what it is that you do as an agent: If I met someone from another planet I would ask them if they needed an agent.

Do you have any particular opinions or impressions of editors and publishers in general: They are smart, hard-working folks in search of projects they deem worthy and [that they believe] will sell well. Never a good idea to forget that publishing is first and foremost a business.

What are your favorite books, movies, TV shows, and why: One of my all-time favorite books is *The River Why* by David James Duncan.

Please list representative titles you have sold: *Saddled,* by Susan Richards (Houghton Mifflin Harcourt); *Final Target,* by Steven Gore (HarperPerennial); *She Bets Her Life: Women and Compulsive Gambling,* by Mary Sojourner (Seal Press); *Seeds: One Man's Quest to Preserve the Trees from Famous Americans' Childhood Homes,* by Rick Horan (HarperCollins); *Captain Freedom: A Superhero's Quest to Find the Celebrity He So Richly Deserves* by G. Xavier Robillard (HarperCollins); *My Private War: A WWII POW Memoir* by Normal Bussel (Pegasus Books); *Chosen by a Horse* by Susan Richards (Soho Press); *The First Season: An NBA History* by Charley Rosen (McGraw-Hill).

ADVICE FOR WRITERS

Dear Reader,

The purpose of the Essay Section is to provide knowledge, and maybe even some wisdom. To most effectively utilize all the raw data in this book, I highly recommend that you fortify yourself with proven road maps. Eventually, your own experiences will serve as your best teacher. Until then, you will need to draw from what others might share.

Whenever I teach about how to get published, I ask my students to listen to everything I say and then forget it. Why? Because within anarchy can be found holiness. Information can be either empowering or entrapping. The human mind will "see," "feel" and "hear" whatever the environment "tells" it. It is difficult to re-direct the way an individual or an entire society perceives its reality. It has been said that the best way to hide something as outlandish as extraterrestrials would be to simply put them in the middle of Times Square, because the vast majority of people would "refuse" to perceive what "cannot" be there. Some people might report that they saw something quite odd, but most of them would probably be talked out of it by the non-silent majority that relies upon reason and good sense. In the end, some unsubstantiated and inconsistent rumors might filter into the supermarket tabloids about an ET invasion in Times Square. Once that happens, nobody who ever wants to be taken seriously again will admit to seeing anything out of the ordi-nary, and would likely convince themselves that it was all perfectly explainable. Of course, Times Square is a strange place anyway.

The greatest measure of everlasting success tends to belong to those who create something new and enduring. It could be an intangible idea that somehow alters the course of history. Or it could be a physical thing or process that makes humanity more capable of manipulating time and space (like the wheel, which was presumably invented by Mrs. Wheel). People who innovate are in a way the ultimate liberators and rule breakers. It's their frustration, hunger and lack of passive complacency that moves them to focus their energies for the purpose of changing what is. By nature, they are expansive. It's safe to assume that such individuals face tremendous opposition from the status quo. The vast majority of people are understandably threatened when confronted by the requirement to change, even when it is best for them to do so. All of us are capable of think-ing beyond what already exists, and that approach to life will tend to be an asset when seeking to become a published writer. However, the risk of failure and rejection is always real, and can stand tall as the personal executioner of our dreams. To be eligible for success, a writer must be willing to endure all the pain that there might be.

Our nation's Puritan founders were fond of saying: *God is no respecter of per-sons.* That sentiment fit their belief system that human choices were mere mani-festations of a pre-ordained universe. If you accept that as your truth, then it will be pointless to resist what your heart and soul ask of you. If you don't accept such a paradigm, then there is no excuse for you not to pursue what you see as your truthful path. There is also a middle ground, which is to accept that reality is indeed pre-determined, and yet live as if it is entirely your own free will that will bring you to tomorrow.

Writing, and the effort to become published, may at times resemble a dead end surrounded by the walls of a brutal confinement. But even then there is a path, and where there is a path there is a way. I hope that these essays will serve to strengthen you.

Jeff Herman

THE BATTLE OF THE "UNS"

(UNAGENTED/UNSOLICITED SUBMISSIONS)

JEFF HERMAN

Most major publishing houses claim to have policies that prevent them from even considering unagented/unsolicited submissions. "Unagented" means that a literary agent did not make the submission. "Unsolicited" means that no one at the publisher asked for the submission.

It's possible that you, or people you know, have already run into this frustrating roadblock. You may also be familiar with the rumor that it's more difficult to get an agent than it is to get a publisher—or that no agent will even consider your work until you have a publisher. On the surface, these negatives make it seem that you would have a better shot at becoming a starting pitcher for the Yankees or living out whatever your favorite improbable fantasy might be.

But, as you will soon learn, these so-called policies and practices are often more false than true, especially if you develop creative ways to circumvent them.

I have dubbed the previous obstacle course the Battle of the "UNs."

If you're presently unagented/unsolicited, you're one of the UNs.

Welcome! You're in good company.

Nobody is born published. There is no published author who wasn't at one time an UN. Thousands of new books are published each year, and thousands of people are needed to write them. You can be one of them.

In this chapter I'll show you how to win the Battle of the UNs. But first let me clarify an important distinction. When I use the word "win" here, I don't mean to say that you'll necessarily get your work published. What I mean is: You'll gain reasonable access to the powers that be for your work, and you'll learn how to increase the odds—dramatically—that your work will in fact be acquired.

Please be realistic. For every published writer, there are, at minimum, several thousand waiting in line to get published. "Many are called, but few are chosen."

It's completely within your power to maximize your chances of getting published. It's also within your power to minimize those chances. There are reasons why some highly talented people habitually underachieve, and those reasons can often be found within them. If you fail, fail, and fail, you should look within yourself for possible answers. What can you do to turn it around? If you find some answers, then you haven't failed at all, and the lessons you allow yourself to learn will lay the groundwork for success in this and in other endeavors.

Having an agent greatly increases the likelihood that you will be published. For one thing, on the procedural level, established agents can usually obtain relatively rapid (and serious) consideration for their clients. One basic reason for this is that editors view agents as a valuable screening mechanism—that is, when a project crosses the editor's desk under an agent's letterhead, the editor knows it's undergone vetting from someone in the industry who is familiar with the applicable standards of quality and market considerations.

I usually recommend that unpublished writers first make every attempt to get an agent before they start going directly to the publishers.

It's significantly easier to get an agent than it is to get a publisher—not the other way around. Most agents I know are always on the lookout for fresh talent. Finding and nurturing tomorrow's stars are two of our functions.

However, one of my reasons for writing and researching this book is to reveal to you that as a potential author, not having an agent does not necessarily disqualify you from the game automatically. Before I show you ways to win the Battle of the UNs, I'd like you to have a fuller understanding of the system.

YOU ARE THE EDITOR

Imagine that you're an acquisitions editor at one of America's largest publishing firms in New York City. You have a master's degree from an Ivy League college and you, at least, think you're smarter than most other people. Yet you're earning a lot less money than most of the people who graduated with you. Your classmates have become lawyers, accountants, bankers, and so forth, and they all seem to own large, well-appointed apartments or homes—whereas you, if you fall out of bed, might land in the bathtub of your minuscule New York flat.

On the other hand, you love your job. For you, working in publishing is a dream come true. As in other industries and professions, much of your satisfaction comes from advancement—getting ahead.

To move up the career ladder, you'll have to acquire at least a few successful titles each year. To find these few good titles, you'll be competing with many editors from other publishers and perhaps even with fellow editors within your own firm. As in any other business, the people who make the most money for the company will get the choice promotions and the highest salaries. Those who perform less impressively will tend to be passed over. (Of course, being a good editor and playing politics well are also important.)

There are two tried-and-true sources for the titles that publishers acquire: literary agents and direct solicitations.

LITERARY AGENTS

As an editor on the move, you'll cultivate relationships with many established literary agents. You'll want them to know what you like and what you don't like. And, by showing these agents you're disposed to acquiring new titles to build your position in the company, you'll encourage them to send you projects they think are right for you.

When you receive material from agents, you usually give it relatively fast consideration—especially if it's been submitted simultaneously to editors at other houses, which is usually the case.

When something comes in from an agent, you know it's been screened and maybe even perfected. Established agents rarely waste your time with shoddy or inappropriate material. They couldn't make a living that way because they'd quickly lose credibility with editors.

DIRECT SOLICITATIONS

If you're an ambitious editor, you won't just sit back passively and wait to see what the agents might bless you with. When you're resourceful, the opportunities are endless. Perhaps you'll contact your old American history professor and ask her to do a book showcasing her unique perspectives on the Civil War.

Or maybe you'll contact that young, fresh fiction writer whose short story you just read in a leading literary journal. You might even try reaching that veteran United States senator who just got censured for sleeping with his young aides.

One place you'll tend not to use is the "slush pile." This is the room (more like a warehouse) where all the unagented/unsolicited submissions end up.

Looking through the slush pile isn't a smart use of your limited time and energy. The chances that anything decent will be found there are much less than 1 percent. You have less-than-fond memories of your first year in the publishing business, when, as an editorial assistant (which was basically an underpaid secretarial job), one of your tasks was to shovel through the slush. Once in a great while, something promising could be found; but most of the stuff wasn't even close. At first, you were surprised by how unprofessional many of the submissions were. Many weren't addressed to anyone in particular; some looked as if they had been run over by Mack trucks; others were so poorly printed they were too painful for tired eyes to decipher—the list of failings is long.

No, the slush pile is the last place—or perhaps no place—to find titles for your list.

Now you can stop being an editor and go back to being whoever you really are. I wanted to show you why the system has evolved the way it has. Yes, though it's rational, it's cold and unfair, but these qualities aren't unique to publishing.

You're probably still wondering when I'm going to get to that promised modus operandi for winning the Battle of the UNs. Okay, we're there.

OUT OF THE SLUSH

The following steps are intended to keep you out of the infamous slush pile. Falling into the slush is like ending up in jail for contempt of court; it's like being an untouchable in India; it's like being Frank Burns on *M*A*S*H*. My point is that nobody likes the Slushables. They're everyone's scapegoat and nobody's ally.

Once your work is assigned to the slush pile, it's highly unlikely that it will receive effective access. Without access, there can be no acquisition. Without acquisition, there's no book.

Let's pretend that getting published is a board game. However, in this game you can control the dice. Here are several ways to play.

GET THE NAMES!

If you submit to nobody, it will go to nobody. Sending it to "The Editors," "Gentlemen," or the CEO of a $100-million publishing house equals sending it to no one.

Use the directory in this book to get the names of the suitable contacts.

In addition to using this directory, there are two other proven ways to discover who the right editors may be:

1. Visit bookstores and seek out recent books that are in your category. Check the acknowledgments section of each one. Many authors like to thank their editors here (and their agents). If the editor is acknowledged, you now have the name of someone who edits books like yours. (Remember to call to confirm that the editor still works at that publishing house.)

2. Simply call the publisher and ask for the editorial department. More often than not, a young junior editor will answer the phone with something like, "Editorial." Like people who answer phones everywhere, these people may sound as if they are asleep, or they may sound harried, or even as if they're making the most important declaration of their lives. Luckily for you, publishers plant few real secretaries or receptionists in their editorial departments, since it's constantly reconfirmed that rookie editors will do all that stuff for everyone else—and for a lot less money! Hence, real editors (although low in rank) can immediately be accessed.

Returning to the true point of this—once someone answers the phone, simply ask, "Who edits your business books?" (Or whatever your category is.)

You can also ask who edited a specific and recent book that's similar to yours. Such easy but vital questions will bring forth quick and valuable answers. Ask enough times and you can build a list of contacts that competes with this book.

DON'T SEND MANUSCRIPTS UNLESS INVITED TO DO SO!

Now that you're armed with these editors' names, don't abuse protocol (editors yell at me when you do—especially when they know where you've gotten their names). Initiate contact by sending a letter describing your work and encouraging the editor to request it.

This letter, commonly referred to as a query letter, is in reality a sales pitch or door-opener. (Please see the following chapter in this book about query letters for a full overview of this important procedure.) In brief, the letter should be short (less than $1\frac{1}{2}$ pages), easy to read and to the point, personalized, and well printed on good professional stationery. Say what you have, why it's hot, why you're a good prospect, and what's available for review upon request.

In addition to the letter, it's okay to include a résumé/bio that highlights any writing credits or relevant professional credentials; a brief summary (two to three pages) if the book is nonfiction, or a brief synopsis if it's fiction; a photo, if you have a flattering one; and promotional materials. Be careful: At this stage your aim is merely to whet the editor's appetite; you don't want to cause information overload. Less is more.

Also include a self-addressed stamped envelope (SASE). This is an important courtesy; without it, you increase your chances of getting no response. Editors receive dozens of these letters every week. Having to address envelopes for all of them would be very time-consuming. And at 44 cents a pop, it's not worth doing.

The SASE is generally intended to facilitate a response in the event of a negative decision. If the editor is intrigued by your letter, he may overlook the missing SASE and request to see your work—but don't count on it.

You may be wondering: If I have the editor's name, why not just send her my entire manuscript? Because you're flirting with the slush pile if you do. Even though you have the editor's previously secret name, you're still an UN, and UNs aren't treated kindly. An editor is inundated with reams of submissions, and her problem is finding good stuff to publish. If you send an unsolicited manuscript, you'll just be perceived as part of that problem. She'll assume you're just another slushy UN who needs to be sorted out of the way so she can go on looking for good stuff.

A bad day for an editor is receiving a few trees' worth of UN manuscripts; it deepens her occupational neurosis.

On the other hand, a professional letter is quite manageable. It is, at least, likely to be read. It may be screened initially by the editor's assistant, but will probably be passed upstairs if it shows promise.

If the editor is at all intrigued by your letter, she will request to see more material, and you will have earned the rank of being solicited.

Even if your work is not ultimately acquired by this editor, you will have at least challenged and defeated the UNs' obstacle course by achieving quality consideration. Remember: Many people get published each year without the benefits of being agented or initially solicited.

It's okay, even smart, to query several editors simultaneously. This makes sense because some editors may take a very long time to respond or, indeed, may never respond. Querying editors one at a time might take years.

If more than one editor subsequently requests and begins considering your work, let each one know that it's not an exclusive. If an editor requests an exclusive, that's fine—but give him a time limit (four weeks is fair).

Don't sell your work to a publisher before consulting everyone who's considering it and seeing if they're interested. If you do sell it, be sure to give immediate written and oral notification to everyone who's considering it that it's no longer available.

The query-letter stage isn't considered a submission. You only need to have follow-up communications with editors who have gone beyond the query stage, meaning those who have requested and received your work for acquisition consideration. If you don't hear back from an editor within six weeks of sending her your letter, it's safe to assume she's not interested in your work.

If you send multiple queries, don't send them to more than one editor at the same house at the same time. If you don't hear back from a particular editor within 6 weeks of your submission, it's probably safe to query another editor at that house. One editor's reject is another's paradise; that's how both good and bad books get published.

We've just covered a lot of important procedural ground, so don't be embarrassed if you think you've forgotten all of it. This book won't self-destruct (and now, presumably, you won't either).

COLD CALLS BREED COLD HEARTS

One more thing: It's best not to cold-call these editors. Don't call them to try to sell them your work. Don't call them to follow up on query letters or submissions. Don't call them to try to change their minds.

Why? Do you like it when someone calls you in the middle of your favorite video to sell you land in the Nevada desert, near a popular nuclear test site?

Few people like uninvited and unscheduled sales calls. In some businesses, such as public relations, calling contacts is a necessary part of the process—but not in publishing. Furthermore, this business is based on hard copy. You may be the greatest oral storyteller since Uncle Remus, but if you can't write it effectively and engagingly, nobody will care. You'll end up soliciting their hostility. Of course, once they are interested in you on the basis of your hard copy, your oral and physical attributes may be of great importance to them.

On the other hand, some people are so skilled on the telephone that it's a lost opportunity for them not to make maximum use of it as a selling method. If you're one of these extremely rare and talented people, you should absolutely make use of whatever tools have proved to work best for you.

Everything I've said is my opinion. This is a subjective industry, so it's likely—no, it's for certain—that others will tell you differently. It's to your advantage to educate yourself to the fullest extent possible (read books, attend workshops, and so forth)—and in the end, to use your own best instincts about how to proceed.

I'm confident that my suggestions are safe and sound, but I don't consider them to be the beginning and the end. The more you know, the simpler things become; the less you know, the more complex and confusing they are.

BREAKING THE RULES

Taken as a whole, this book provides a structure that can be considered a set of guidelines, if not hard-and-fast rules. Some people owe their success to breaking the rules and swimming upstream—and I can certainly respect that. Often such people don't even know they're breaking the rules; they're just naturally following their own unique orbits (and you'll find a few illustrations of this very phenomenon elsewhere in these essays). Trying to regulate such people can often be their downfall.

On one hand, most of us tend to run afoul when we stray from established norms of doing business; on the other hand, a few of us can't succeed any other way (Einstein could have written an essay about that).

If you're one of those few, hats off to you! Perhaps we'll all learn something from your example.

Keep reading!

THE LITERARY AGENCY FROM A TO Z

HOW LITERARY AGENTS WORK

JEFF HERMAN

Literary agents are like stockbrokers and real estate agents. They bring buyers and sellers together, help formulate successful deals, and receive a piece of the action (against the seller's end) for facilitating the partnership.

Specifically, literary agents look for talented writers, unearth marketable non-fiction book concepts, and discover superior fiction manuscripts to represent. Simultaneously, agents cultivate their relationships with publishers.

When an agent detects material she thinks she can sell to a publisher, she signs the writer as a client, perhaps works on the material with the writer to maximize its chances of selling, and then submits it to one or more appropriate editorial contacts.

HOW AGENTS WORK FOR THEIR CLIENTS

A dynamic agent achieves the maximum exposure possible for the writer's material, which greatly enhances the odds that the material will be published.

Having an agent gives the writer's material the type of access to the powers that be that it might otherwise never obtain. Publishers assume that material submitted by an agent has been screened and is much more likely to fit their needs than the random material swimming in the slush pile.

If and when a publisher makes an offer to publish the material, the agent acts on the author's behalf and negotiates the advance (the money paid up front), royalties, control of subsidiary rights, and many other important and marginal contract clauses that may prove to be important down the line. The agent acts as the writer's advocate with the publisher for as long as the book remains in print or licensing opportunities exist.

The agent knows the most effective methods for negotiating the best advance and other contract terms and is likely to have more leverage with the publisher than an unagented writer does.

There's more to a book contract than the advance-and-royalty schedule. There are several key clauses that you, the writer, may know little or nothing about, but would accept with a cursory perusal in order to expedite the deal. Striving to close any kind of agreement can be intimidating if you don't know much about the territory; ignorance is a great disadvantage during a negotiation. An agent understands every detail of the contract and knows where and how it should be modified or expanded in your favor.

Where appropriate, an agent acts to sell subsidiary rights after the book is sold to a publisher. These rights can include serial rights, foreign rights, dramatic and movie rights, audio and video rights, and a range of syndication and licensing possibilities.

THE AGENT'S PERSPECTIVE

No agent sells every project she represents. Even though authors are signed on the basis of their work's marketability, agents know from experience that some projects with excellent potential are not necessarily quick-and-easy big-money sales. And, yes, each and every agent has at least on occasion been as bewildered as the author when a particularly promising package receives no takers. Some projects, especially fiction, may be marketed for a long time before a publisher is found (if ever).

THE AUTHOR'S EXPECTATIONS

What's most important is that you, the author, feel sure the agent continues to believe in the project and is actively trying to sell it.

For his work, the agent receives a commission (usually 15 percent) against the writer's advance and all subsequent income relevant to the sold project.

Although this is an appreciable chunk of your work's income, the agent's involvement should end up netting you much more than you would have earned otherwise. The agent's power to round up several interested publishers to consider your work opens up the possibility that more than one house will make an offer for it, which means you'll be more likely to get a higher advance and also have more leverage regarding the various other contractual clauses.

The writer-agent relationship can become a rewarding business partnership. An agent can advise you objectively on the direction your writing career should take. Also, through her contacts, an agent may be able to get you book-writing assignments you would never have been offered on your own.

WHO'S THE BEST AGENT FOR YOU

There are many ways to get an agent. The best way to gain access to potential agents is by networking with fellow writers. Maybe some of your colleagues can introduce you to their agents or at least allow you to drop their names when contacting their agents. Most agents will be receptive to a writer who has been referred by a current and valued client.

This book features a directory of literary agencies, including their addresses, the names of specific agents, and their specialty areas, along with some personal remarks and examples of recent titles sold to publishers.

QUERY FIRST

The universally accepted way to establish initial contact with an agent is to send a query letter. Agents tend to be less interested in—if not completely put off by— oral presentations. Be sure the letter is personalized: Nobody likes generic, photo-copied letters that look like they're being sent to everyone.

Think of the query as a sales pitch. Describe the nature of your project and offer to send additional material—and enclose a self-addressed stamped envelope (SASE). Include all relevant information about yourself—along with a résumé if it's applicable. When querying about a nonfiction project, many agents won't mind receiving a complete proposal. But you might prefer to wait and see how the agent responds to the concept before sending the full proposal.

For queries about fiction projects, most agents prefer to receive story-concept sheets, plot synopses, or both; if they like what they see, they'll request sample chapters or ask you to send the complete manuscript. Most agents won't consider manuscripts for incomplete works of fiction, essentially because few publishers are willing to do so.

If you enclose an SASE, most agents will respond to you, one way or another, within a reasonable period of time. If the agent asks to see your material, submit it promptly with a polite note stating that you'd like a response within four weeks on a nonfiction proposal, or eight weeks on fiction material. If you haven't heard from the agent by that time, write or call to find out the status of your submission.

CIRCULATE WITH THE FLOW

You're entitled to circulate your material to more than one agent at a time, but you're obligated to let each agent know that such is the case. If and when you do sign with an agent, immediately notify other agents still considering your work that it's no longer available.

At least 200 literary agents are active in America, and their individual perceptions of what is and isn't marketable will vary widely—which is why a few or many rejections should never deter writers who believe in themselves.

BUYER AND SELLER REVERSAL

When an agent eventually seeks to represent your work, it's time for her to begin selling herself to you. When you're seeking employment, you don't necessarily have to accept the first job offer you receive; likewise, you do not have to sign immediately with the first agent who wants you.

Do some checking before agreeing to work with a particular agent. If possible, meet the agent in person. A lot can be learned from in-person meetings that can't be gathered from telephone conversations. See what positive or negative information you can find out about the agent through your writers' network. Ask the agent for a client list and permission to call certain clients. Find out the agent's specialties.

Ask for a copy of the agent's standard contract. Most agents today will want to codify your relationship with a written agreement; this should protect both parties equally. Make sure you're comfortable with everything in the agreement before signing it. Again, talking with fellow writers and reading books on the subject are excellent ways to deepen your understanding of industry practices.

When choosing an agent, follow your best instincts. Don't settle for anyone you don't perceive to be on the level, or who doesn't seem to be genuinely enthusiastic about you and your work.

SELF-REPRESENTATION: A FOOL FOR A CLIENT?

Agents aren't for everyone. In some instances, you may be better off on your own. Perhaps you actually do have sufficient editorial contacts and industry savvy to cut good deals by yourself. If so, what incentive do you have to share your income with an agent?

Of course, having an agent might provide you the intangible benefits of added prestige, save you the hassles of making submissions and negotiating deals, or act as a buffer through whom you can negotiate indirectly for tactical reasons.

You might also consider representing yourself if your books are so specialized that only a few publishers are potential candidates for them. Your contacts at such houses might be much stronger than any agent's could be.

ATTORNEYS: LITERARY AND OTHERWISE

Some entertainment/publishing attorneys can do everything an agent does, though there's no reason to believe they can necessarily do more. A major difference between the two is that the lawyer may charge you a set hourly fee or retainer, or any negotiated combination thereof, instead of an agency-type commission. In rare instances, writer-publisher disputes might need to be settled in a court of law, and a lawyer familiar with the industry then becomes a necessity.

BOTTOM-LINE CALCULATIONS

The pluses and minuses of having an agent should be calculated like any other business service you might retain—it should benefit you more than it costs you. Generally speaking, the only real cost of using an agent is the commission. Of course, using the wrong agent may end up causing you more deficits than benefits, but even then you may at least learn a valuable lesson for next time.

Your challenge is to seek and retain an agent who's right for you. You're 100 percent responsible for getting yourself represented and at least 50 percent responsible for making the relationship work for both of you.

AN ALTERNATIVE INTRODUCTION TO LITERARY AGENTS

JEFF HERMAN

The title of this essay may be puzzling. I hope so, because it's meant to be. Let me explain. I wrote the essay preceding this one, also about agents, 20 years ago and have not changed it since. *Writer's Digest* magazine paid me $200 in 1987 to write that essay, and I have recycled it in this book through all 18 of its previous editions. My rationale was/is: *If it ain't broke, don't fix it.*

So is that essay broken? No, it's okay. Except it was written by a 20-something guy. Two decades since, that guy has morphed into me. What agents are and what we do has not changed too much over time, but I have. That's simply not the essay I would write today for numerous reasons. The number-one reason is that I am struggling every day to forget what I know, or at least pretend that I don't know it. What am I talking about?

At 27 I had a few years under my belt as a diversified publicist. I understood how to use the media to promote products, people and ideas. I had learned how to buy and wear a suit; how to keep my hair and face neat; how to function in an office; how to interact with other humans for the purpose of getting tasks done; how to work for jerks; and how to talk on a phone. I of course learned other things as well, but I have to stop the list somewhere.

A constellation of choices and circumstances brought me to the book business. Sensing that I had little to lose and an adventure to gain, I rented some office space and appointed myself a literary agent. It was the second half of the 1980s, disco was dead, and New York was still recovering from the humiliations of the '70s. I only had nominal experience and knowledge about the occupation that I had hired myself for, and I made the mistakes to prove it. Fortunately, the errors were to my own detriment and no one else's. But it was exciting. I was creating something and having fresh experiences along the way. I liked observing peoples' personalities and egos, and learning about their histories and the directions they chose. I was surprised to see how some of the most successful people were so clearly scared and self-doubting. And I was annoyed by the way some very gifted people could be so self-destructive and unwilling to own any accountability for their actions. I was especially intrigued by the way some people were able to make things happen for themselves and those who were with them. Native intelligence and formal education did not seem to matter as much as I expected. In the unstructured free-for-all entrepreneurial ways that are the emblem of our nation, those who may have spent their student careers in Special Ed classes could emerge from secret telephone booths as Masters of the Universe. People could be very interesting.

The passage of time and raw experience taught me what I know about the book business, and about people. Sometime in the mid-1990s I fell into a routine. My workload and commitments mushroomed. I would make decisions on the basis of other peoples' advice or the bottom-line calculations. The more visceral messages from my heart and gut lost their traditional primacy in the constitution of my life. I continued to succeed on the basis of hard work and intellect, and by riding the momentum that my earlier years established. But it was not so much of an adventure as it was a job. And that was changing me.

The changes were subtle. Looking back, I recall that I felt the urge to watch more TV; to eat more; to go out less; to be more fixed in my routines. I was inclined to think more and feel less. My time and energy belonged to the mounting tasks that my success generated. I was employed by what had to get done. I had essentially abdicated being the Master of my Domain. Of course, once I had a family to support, it could no longer be just about me. I didn't need much, but a family does. Like many people before me and since, I transitioned from being an explorer into being an expert. Explorers keep moving, looking, touching, consuming and discovering. Experts stand still and cultivate their crops. Each harvest is likely to follow the same template as the ones before, though the goal is to expand the bounty by making better use of the available resources. No accident that the root word for *husband* means "farmer." A responsible farmer does not leave his land; he roots himself into the soil with every seed he sows, and conjures the earth's power to make food out of dirt, water and light.

Without experts, we'd all be nomads like our pre-historic ancestors. No steady homes; no security; no nuclear families; no settlements; no growers of wheat and barley, and no commerce between them. To this day, we would be herds of two-legged entities chasing after herds of the four-legged kind. But without the explorers our cars would have square tires. Without the explorers we might have nothing. In fact, we might be nothing. The experts probably held their ground as the fury of serial floods, droughts and ice ages swatted them into oblivion. To the contrary, the explorers instinctively shrugged off what was left behind, and discovered the future; our future. And that's still what they do every day. It is good for a society to have different kinds of people. Perhaps it's equally as good for each of us to embrace vast differences within our own beings, no matter how conflicted that may seem. Self-directed rejection and repression leads to decades of quiet desperation. Your bills may get paid, but you will owe yourself a fortune.

I digress. If you're still with me, let's talk about literary agents.

Actually, everything I said 20 years ago is still valid. Just read the essay that precedes this one. I did make a few revisions to reflect contemporary conditions.

WRITE THE PERFECT QUERY LETTER

DEBORAH LEVINE HERMAN
JEFF HERMAN

The query is a short letter of introduction to publishers or agents, encouraging them to request to see your fiction manuscript or nonfiction book proposal. It is a vital tool, often neglected by writers. If done correctly, it can help you to avoid endless frustration and wasted effort. The query is the first hurdle of your individual marketing strategy. If you can leap over it successfully, you're well on your way to a sale.

The query letter is your calling card. For every book that makes it to the shelves, thousands of worthy manuscripts, proposals, and ideas are knocked out of the running by poor presentation or inadequate marketing strategies. Don't forget that the book you want to sell is a product that must be packaged correctly to stand above the competition.

A query letter asks the prospective publisher or agent if she would like to see more about the proposed idea. If your book is fiction, you should indicate that a manuscript or sample chapters are available on request. If nonfiction, you should offer to send a proposal and, if you have them, sample chapters.

The query is your first contact with the prospective buyer of your book. To ensure that it's not your last, avoid common mistakes. The letter should be concise and well written. You shouldn't try to impress the reader with your mastery of all words over three syllables. Instead, concentrate on a clear and to-the-point presentation with no fluff.

Think of the letter as an advertisement. You want to make a sale of a product, and you have very limited space and time in which to reach this goal.

The letter should be only one page long, if possible. It will form the basis of a query package that will include supporting materials. Don't waste words in the letter describing material that can be included separately. Your goal is to pique the interest of an editor who has very little time and probably very little patience. You want to entice her to keep reading and ask you for more.

The query package can include a short résumé, media clippings, or other favorable documents. Do not get carried away, or your package will quickly come to resemble junk mail. Include a self-addressed stamped envelope (SASE) with enough postage to return your entire package. This will be particularly appreciated by smaller publishing houses and independent agents.

For fiction writers, a short (one- to five-page), double-spaced synopsis of the manuscript will be helpful and appropriate.

Do not waste money and defeat the purpose of the query by sending an unsolicited manuscript. Agents and editors may be turned off by receiving manuscripts of 1,000-plus pages that were uninvited and that are not even remotely relevant to what they do.

The query follows a simple format (which can be reworked according to your individual preferences):

1. lead;

2. supporting material/persuasion;

3. biography; and

4. conclusion/pitch.

YOUR LEAD IS YOUR HOOK

The lead can either catch the editor's attention or turn him off completely. Some writers think getting someone's attention in a short space means having to do something dramatic. Editors appreciate cleverness, but too much contrived writing can work against you. Opt instead for clear conveyance of thoroughly developed ideas and get right to the point.

Of course, you don't want to be boring and stuffy in the interest of factual presentation. You'll need to determine what is most important about the book you're trying to sell, and write your letter accordingly.

You can begin with a lead similar to what you'd use to grab the reader in an article or a book chapter. You can use an anecdote, a statement of facts, a question, a comparison, or whatever you believe will be most powerful.

You may want to rely on the journalistic technique of the inverted pyramid. This means that you begin with the strongest material and save the details for later in the letter. Don't start slowly and expect to pick up momentum as you proceed. It will be too late.

Do not begin a query letter like this: "I have sent this idea to 20 agents/publishers, none of whom think it will work. I just know you'll be different, enlightened, and insightful, and will give it full consideration." There is no room for negatives in a sales pitch. Focus only on positives—unless you can turn negatives to your advantage.

Some writers make the mistake of writing about the book's potential in the first paragraph without ever stating its actual idea or theme. Remember, your letter may never be read beyond the lead, so make that first paragraph your hook.

Avoid bad jokes, clichés, unsubstantiated claims, and dictionary definitions. Don't be condescending; editors have egos, too, and have power over your destiny as a writer.

SUPPORTING MATERIAL: BE PERSUASIVE

If you are selling a nonfiction book, you may want to include a brief summary of hard evidence, gleaned from research, that will support the merit of your idea. This is where you convince the editor that your book should exist. This is more important for nonfiction than it is for fiction, where the style and storytelling ability are paramount. Nonfiction writers must focus on selling their topic and their credentials.

You should include a few lines showing the editor what the publishing house will gain from the project. Publishers are not charitable institutions; they want to know how they can get the greatest return on their investment. If you have brilliant marketing ideas or know of a well-defined market for your book where sales will be guaranteed, include this rather than other descriptive material.

In rereading your letter, make sure you have shown that you understand your own idea thoroughly. If it appears half-baked, the editors won't want to invest time fleshing out your thoughts. Exude confidence so that the editor will have faith in your ability to carry out the job.

In nonfiction queries, you can include a separate table of contents and brief chapter abstracts. Otherwise, it can wait for the book proposal.

YOUR BIOGRAPHY: NO PLACE FOR MODESTY

In the biographical portion of your letter, toot your own horn, but in a carefully calculated, persuasive fashion. Your story of winning the third-grade writing competition (it was then that you knew you wanted to be a world-famous writer!) should be saved for the documentary done on your life after you reach your goal.

In the query, all you want to include are the most important and relevant credentials that will support the sale of your book. You can include, as a separate part of the package, a résumé or biography that will elaborate further.

The separate résumé should list all relevant and recent experiences that support your ability to write the book. Unless you're fairly young, your listing of academic accomplishments should start after high school. Don't overlook hobbies or non-job-related activities if they correspond to your book story or topic. Those experiences are often more valuable than academic achievements.

Other information to include: any impressive print clippings about you; a list of your broadcast interviews and speaking appearances; and copies of articles and reviews about any books you may have written. This information can never hurt your chances and could make the difference in your favor.

There is no room for humility or modesty in the query letter and résumé. When corporations sell toothpaste, they list the product's best attributes and create excitement about the product. If you can't find some way to make yourself exciting as an author, you'd better rethink your career.

HERE'S THE PITCH

At the close of your letter, ask for the sale. This requires a positive and confident conclusion with such phrases as "I look forward to your speedy response." Such phrases as "I hope" and "I think you will like my book" sound too insecure. This is the part of the letter where you go for the kill.

Be sure to thank the reader for his or her attention in your final sentence.

FINISHING TOUCHES

When you're finished, reread and edit your query letter. Cut out any extraneous information that dilutes the strength of your arguments. Make the letter as polished as possible so that the editor will be impressed with you, as well as with your idea. Don't ruin your chances by appearing careless; make certain your letter is not peppered with typos and misspellings. If you don't show pride in your work, you'll create a self-fulfilling prophecy; the editor will take you no more seriously than you take yourself.

Aesthetics are important. If you were pitching a business deal to a corporation, you would want to present yourself in conservative dress, with an air of professionalism. In the writing business, you may never have face-to-face contact with the people who will determine your future. Therefore, your query package is your representative.

If editors receive a query letter on yellowed paper that looks as if it's been lying around for 20 years, they will wonder if the person sending the letter is a has-been or a never-was.

You should invest in a state-of-the-art letterhead—with a logo!—to create an impression of pride, confidence, and professionalism. White, cream, and ivory paper are all acceptable, but you should use only black ink for printing the letter. Anything else looks amateurish.

Don't sabotage yourself by letting your need for instant approval get the best of you. Don't call editors. You have invited them to respond, so be patient. Then prepare yourself for possible rejection. It often takes many nos to get a yes.

One more note: This is a tough business for anyone—and it's especially so for greenhorns. Hang in there.

QUERY TIPS

If you have spent any time at all in this business, the term *query letter* is probably as familiar to you as the back of your hand. Yet no matter how many courses you've attended and books you've read about this important part of the process, you may still feel inadequate when you try to write one that sizzles. If it's any consolation, you're far from being alone in your uncertainties. The purpose of the query letter is to formally introduce your work and yourself to potential agents and editors. The immediate goal is to motivate them to promptly request a look at your work, or at least a portion of it.

In effect, the letter serves as the writer's first hurdle. It's a relatively painless way for agents and editors to screen out unwanted submissions without the added burden of having to manhandle a deluge of unwanted manuscripts. They are more relaxed if their in-boxes are filled with 50 unanswered queries, as opposed to 50 uninvited 1,000-page manuscripts. The query is a very effective way to control the quality and quantity of the manuscripts that get into the office. And that's why you have to write good ones.

The term *query letter* is part of the lexicon and jargon of the publishing business. This term isn't used in any other industry. I assume it has ancient origins. I can conjure up the image of an English gentleman with a fluffy quill pen composing a most civilized letter to a prospective publisher for the purpose of asking for his work to be read and, perchance, published. Our environments may change, but the nature of our ambitions remains the same.

Let's get contemporary. Whenever you hear the term *query letter*, you should say to yourself "pitch" or "sales" letter. Because that's what it is. You need the letter to sell.

QUERY LETTER TIPS

+ *Don't be long-winded.* Agents/editors receive lots of these things, and they want to mow through them as swiftly as possible. Ideally, the letter should be a single page with short paragraphs. (I must admit I've seen good ones that are longer than a page.) If you lose your reader, you've lost your opportunity.

+ *Get to the point; don't pontificate.* Too many letters go off on irrelevant detours, which makes it difficult for the agent/editor to determine what's actually for sale—other than the writer's soapbox.

+ *Make your letter attractive.* When making a first impression, the subliminal impact of aesthetics cannot be overestimated. Use high-quality stationery and typeface. The essence of your words is paramount, but cheap paper and poor print quality will only diminish your impact.

- *Don't say anything negative about yourself or your attempts to get published.* Everyone appreciates victims when it's time to make charitable donations, but not when it's time to make a profit. It's better if you can make editors/agents think that you have to fight them off.

WHY NOT SIMPLY SUBMIT MY MANUSCRIPT?

Q: Why can't I bypass the query hurdle by simply submitting my manuscript?
A: You may—and no one can litigate against you. But if you submit an unsolicited manuscript to a publisher, it's more likely to end up in the so-called slush pile and may never get a fair reading. If it's sent to an agent, nothing negative may come of it. However, most agents prefer to receive a query first.

Sending unsolicited nonfiction book proposals is in the gray zone. Proposals are much more manageable than entire manuscripts, so editors/agents may not particularly mind.

But you may want to avoid the expense of sending unwanted proposals. After all, the query is also an opportunity for you to screen out those who clearly have no interest in your subject.

Also, you shouldn't be overly loose with your ideas and concepts.

These pointers, in combination with the other good information in this book and all the other available resources, should at least give you a solid background for creating a query letter that sizzles.

THE KNOCKOUT NONFICTION BOOK PROPOSAL

JEFF HERMAN

ADVICE FOR WRITERS

The quality of your nonfiction book proposal will invariably make the difference between success and failure. Before agents and publishers will accept a work of fiction (especially from a newer writer), they require a complete manuscript. But nonfiction projects are different: A proposal alone can do the trick. This is what makes nonfiction writing a much less speculative and often more lucrative endeavor (relatively speaking) than fiction writing.

You may devote five years of long evenings to writing a 1,000-page fiction manuscript, only to receive a thick pile of computer-generated rejections. Clearly, writing nonfiction doesn't entail the same risks.

On the other hand, writing fiction is often an emotionally driven endeavor in which rewards are gained though the act of writing and are not necessarily based on rational, practical considerations. Interestingly, many successful nonfiction writers fantasize about being fiction writers.

As you'll learn, the proposal's structure, contents, and size can vary substantially, and it's up to you to decide the best format for your purposes. Still, the guidelines given here serve as excellent general parameters.

An excellent model proposal is featured later in this chapter.

APPEARANCE COUNTS

+ Your proposal should be printed in black ink on clean, letter-sized (8½" x 11"), white paper.

+ Letter-quality printing is by far the best. Make sure the ribbon or toner or ink cartridge is fresh and that all photocopies are dark and clear enough to be read easily. Publishing is an image-driven business, and you will be judged, perhaps unconsciously, on the physical and aesthetic merits of your submission.

+ Always double-space, or you can virtually guarantee reader antagonism— eyestrain makes people cranky.

- Make sure your proposal appears fresh and new and hasn't been dog-eared, marked-up, and abused by previous readers. No editor will be favorably disposed if she thinks that everyone else on the block has already sent you packing. You want editors to suppose that you have lots of other places you can go, not nowhere else to go.

- Contrary to common practice in other industries, editors prefer not to receive bound proposals. If an editor likes your proposal, she will want to photocopy it for her colleagues, and your binding will only be in the way. If you want to keep the material together and neat, use a binder clip; if it's a lengthy proposal, clip each section together separately. Don't email or send CDs unless the agent or editor consents to receiving that way.

THE TITLE PAGE

The title page should be the easiest part, but it can also be the most important, since, like your face when you meet someone, it's what is seen first.

Try to think of a title that's attractive and effectively communicates your book's concept. A descriptive subtitle, following a catchy title, can help to achieve both goals.

It's very important that your title and subtitle relate to the book's subject, or an editor might make an inaccurate judgment about your book's focus and automatically dismiss it.

For instance, if you're proposing a book about gardening, don't title it *The Greening of America*.

Examples of titles that have worked very well are:

How to Win Friends and Influence People by Dale Carnegie
Think and Grow Rich by Napoleon Hill
Baby and Child Care by Dr. Benjamin Spock
How to Swim with the Sharks Without Being Eaten Alive by Harvey Mackay

And, yes, there are notable exceptions: An improbable title that went on to become a perennial success is *What Color Is Your Parachute?* by Richard Bolles. Sure, you may gain freedom and confidence from such exceptional instances. By all means let your imagination graze during the brainstorming stage.

However, don't bet on the success of an arbitrarily conceived title that has nothing at all to do with the book's essential concept or reader appeal.

A title should be stimulating and, when appropriate, upbeat and optimistic. If your subject is an important historic or current event, the title should be dramatic. If a biography, the title should capture something personal (or even controversial) about the subject. Many good books have been handicapped by poorly conceived titles, and many poor books have been catapulted to success by good titles. A good title is good advertising. Procter & Gamble, for instance, spends thousands of worker-hours creating seductive names for its endless array of soap-based products.

The title you choose is referred to as the "working title."

Most likely, the book will have a different title when published. There are two reasons for this:

1. A more appropriate or arresting title (or both) may evolve with time; and

2. The publisher has final contractual discretion over the title (as well as over a lot of other things).

The title page should contain only the title; your name, address, and telephone number—and the name, address, and phone number of your agent, if you have one. The title page should be neatly and attractively spaced. Eye-catching and tasteful computer graphics and display-type fonts can contribute to the overall aesthetic appeal.

OVERVIEW

The overview portion of the proposal is a terse statement (one to three pages) of your overall concept and mission. It sets the stage for what's to follow. Short, concise paragraphs are usually best.

BIOGRAPHICAL SECTION

This is where you sell yourself. This section tells who you are and why you're the ideal person to write this book. You should highlight all your relevant experience, including media and public-speaking appearances, and list previous books, articles, or both, published by or about you. Self-flattery is appropriate—so long as you're telling the truth. Many writers prefer to slip into the third person here, to avoid the appearance of egomania.

MARKETING SECTION

This is where you justify the book's existence from a commercial perspective. Who will buy it? For instance, if you're proposing a book on sales, state the number of people who earn their livings through sales; point out that thousands of large and small companies are sales-dependent and spend large sums on sales training, and that all sales professionals are perpetually hungry for fresh, innovative sales books.

Don't just say something like "My book is for adult women and there are more than 50 million adult women in America." You have to be much more demographically sophisticated than that.

COMPETITION SECTION

To the uninitiated, this section may appear to be a set-up to self-destruction. However, if handled strategically, and assuming you have a fresh concept, this section wins you points rather than undermines your case.

The competition section is where you describe major published titles with concepts comparable to yours. If you're familiar with your subject, you'll probably know those titles by heart; you may have even read most or all of them. If you're not certain, check *Books in Print*—available in virtually every library—which catalogues all titles in print in every category under the sun.

Don't list everything published on your subject—that could require a book in itself. Just describe the leading half-dozen titles or so (backlist classics, as well as recent books) and *explain why yours will be different.*

Getting back to the sales-book example, there is no shortage of good sales books. There's a reason for that—a big market exists for sales books. You can turn that to your advantage by emphasizing the public's substantial, insatiable demand for sales books. Your book will feed that demand with its unique and innovative sales-success program. Salespeople and companies dependent on sales are always looking for new ways to enhance sales skills (it's okay to reiterate key points).

PROMOTION SECTION

Here you suggest possible ways to promote and market the book. Sometimes this section is unnecessary. It depends on your subject and on what, if any, realistic promotional prospects exist.

If you're proposing a specialized academic book such as *The Mating Habits of Octopi*, the market is a relatively limited one, and elaborate promotions would be wasteful.

But if you're proposing a popularly oriented relationship book along the lines of *The Endless Orgasm in One Easy Lesson*, the promotional possibilities are also endless. They would include most major electronic broadcast and print media outlets, advertising, maybe even some weird contests.

You want to guide the publisher toward seeing realistic ways to publicize the book.

CHAPTER OUTLINE

This is the meat of the proposal. Here's where you finally tell what's going to be in the book. Each chapter should be tentatively titled and clearly abstracted.

Some successful proposals have fewer than 100 words per abstracted chapter; others have several hundred words per chapter. Sometimes the length varies from chapter to chapter. There are no hard-and-fast rules here; it's the dealer's choice.

Sometimes less is more; at other times a too-brief outline inadequately represents the project.

At their best, the chapter abstracts read like mini-chapters—as opposed to stating "I will do…and I will show…" Visualize the trailer for a forthcoming movie; that's the tantalizing effect you want to create.

Also, it's a good idea to preface the outline with a table of contents. This way, the editor can see your entire road map at the outset.

SAMPLE CHAPTERS

Sample chapters are optional. A strong, well-developed proposal will often be enough. However, especially if you're a first-time writer, one or more sample chapters will give you an opportunity to show your stuff and will help dissolve an editor's concerns about your ability to actually write the book, thereby increasing the odds that you'll receive an offer—and you'll probably increase the size of the advance, too.

Nonfiction writers are often wary of investing time to write sample chapters since they view the proposal as a way of avoiding speculative writing. This can be a shortsighted position, however, for a single sample chapter can make the difference between selling and not selling a marginal proposal. Occasionally, a publisher will request that one or two sample chapters be written before he makes a decision about a particular project. If the publisher seems to have a real interest, writing the sample material is definitely worth the author's time, and the full package can then be shown to additional prospects, too.

Many editors say that they look for reasons to reject books and that being on the fence is a valid reason for rejecting a project. To be sure, there are cases where sample chapters have tilted a proposal on the verge of rejection right back onto the playing field!

Keep in mind that the publisher is speculating that you can and will write the book upon contract. A sample chapter will go far to reduce the publisher's concerns about your ability to deliver a quality work beyond the proposal stage.

WHAT ELSE?

There are a variety of materials you may wish to attach to the proposal to further bolster your cause. These include:

+ Laudatory letters and comments about you

+ Laudatory publicity about you

+ A headshot (but not if you look like the Fly, unless you're proposing a humor book or a nature book)

+ Copies of published articles you've written

+ Videos of TV or speaking appearances

+ Any and all information that builds you up in a relevant way, but be organized about it—don't create a disheveled, unruly package.

LENGTH

The average proposal is probably between 15 and 30 double-spaced pages, and the typical sample chapter an additional 10 to 20 double-spaced pages. But sometimes proposals reach 100 pages, and sometimes they're 5 pages total. Extensive proposals are not a handicap.

Whatever it takes!

MODEL SUCCESSFUL NONFICTION BOOK PROPOSAL

What follows is a genuine proposal that won a healthy book contract. It's excerpted from *Write the Perfect Book Proposal* by Jeff Herman and Deborah Adams (John Wiley & Sons) and includes an extensive critique of its strongest and weakest points. All in all, it's an excellent proposal and serves as a strong model.

The book is titled *Heart and Soul: A Psychological and Spiritual Guide to Preventing and Healing Heart Disease* and is written by Bruno Cortis, MD. This project was sold to the Villard Books division of Random House.

Every editor who saw this proposal offered sincere praise. Ironically, several of these editors regretted not being able to seek the book's acquisition. From the outset I was aware this might happen. The past few years have given us numerous unconventional health and healing books—many of which are excellent. Most publishers I approached felt that their health/spirituality quota was already full and that they would wind up competing with themselves if they acquired any more such titles.

Experienced agents and writers are familiar with the market-glut problem. In many popular categories it's almost endemic. If you're prepared for this reality from the outset, there are ways to pave your own road and bypass the competition. Dedicated agents, editors, and writers want to see important books published, regardless of what the publishers' lists dictate.

Furthermore, it is not necessary for every publisher to want your book (though that is the proven way to maximize the advance).

In the end, you need only the right publisher and a reasonable deal.

Let's look first at the title page from the book proposal.

HEART AND SOUL

(This is a good title. It conjures up dramatic images similar to a soulful blues melody. And it has everything to do with what this proposal is about. The subtitle is scientific and provides a clear direction for the patients.)

Psychological and Spiritual Guide to Preventing and Healing Heart Disease
by
Bruno Cortis, MD
Book Proposal

The Jeff Herman Agency

(The title page is sufficient overall. But it would have been better if the software had been available to create a more striking cover sheet. To a large degree, everything does initially get judged by its cover.)

OVERVIEW

(One minor improvement here would have been to shift the word "Overview" to the center of the page—or otherwise styling the typeface for such headings and subheadings throughout the proposal to make them stand out from the body text.)

Heart disease is the number-one killer of Americans over the age of 40. The very words can sound like a death sentence. Our heart, the most intimate part of our body, is under siege. Until now, most experts have advised victims of the disease, as well as those who would avoid it, to change avoidable risk factors, like smoking, and begin a Spartan regimen of diet and exercise. But new research shows that risk factors and lifestyle are only part of the answer. In fact, it is becoming clear that for many patients, emotional, psychological, and even spiritual factors are at least as important, both in preventing disease and in healing an already damaged heart.

(This is a powerful lead paragraph. The author knows a lot of books are out there about heart disease. The first paragraph of the overview immediately distinguishes this book proposal and draws attention to "new research." Anything that is potentially cutting edge is going to catch the eye of a prospective publisher.)

Like *Love, Medicine, and Miracles* by Bernie Siegel, which showed cancer patients how to take charge of their own disease and life, *Heart and Soul* will show potential and actual heart patients how to use inner resources to form a healthy relationship with their heart, actually healing circulatory disorders and preventing further damage.

(The preceding paragraph contains the central thesis for the project, and it is profoundly important. In retrospect, this could have worked exceedingly well as the first paragraph of the proposal, thereby immediately setting the stage. This is a clever comparison to a highly successful book. It indicates an untapped market that has already proved itself in a similar arena. Instead of merely making unsubstantiated claims based on the success of Dr. Siegel's work, the author shows what this book will do to merit the same type of attention.)

The author, Bruno Cortis, MD, is a renowned cardiologist whose experience with hundreds of "exceptional heart patients" has taught him that there is much more to medicine than operations and pills.

(It is good to bring the author's credentials into the overview at this juncture. A comparison has been made with a highly successful and marketable doctor/author—which will immediately raise questions as to whether this author has similar potential. The author anticipates this line of editorial reasoning and here makes some strong statements.)

Dr. Cortis identifies three types of heart patients:

+ Passive Patients, who are unwilling or unable to take responsibility for their condition. Instead, these patients blame outside forces, withdraw from social contacts, and bewail their fate. They may become deeply depressed and tend to die very soon.

+ Obedient Consumers, who are the "A" students of modern medicine. Following doctors' orders to the letter, these patients behave exactly as they are supposed to, placing their fates in the hands of the experts. These patients tend to die exactly when medicine predicts they will.

+ Exceptional Heart Patients, who regard a diagnosis of heart disease as a challenge. Although they may have realistic fears for the future, these patients take full responsibility for their situation and actively contribute to their own recovery. While they may or may not follow doctors' orders, these patients tend to choose the therapy or combination of therapies that is best for them. They often live far beyond medical predictions.

(This is an exceptional overview—especially where it defines the three patient types.)

It is Dr. Cortis's aim in this book to show readers how to become exceptional heart patients, empowering them to take responsibility for their own health and well-being.

(The remaining paragraphs of this overview section show a highly focused and well-thought-out plan for the book. The writing collaborator on this project had to condense and assimilate boxes and boxes of material to produce this concise and to-the-point overview that leaves no questions unanswered. Although it took a great deal of effort for the writer to write such a good proposal, there is no struggle for the editor to understand exactly what is being proposed and what the book is going to be about.)

Although Dr. Cortis acknowledges the importance of exercise, stress management, and proper nutrition—the standard staples of cardiac treatment—he stresses that there is an even deeper level of human experience that is necessary in order to produce wellness. Unlike other books on heart disease, *Heart and Soul* does not prescribe the same strict diet and exercise program for everyone. Instead it takes a flexible approach, urging readers to create their own unique health plan by employing psychological and spiritual practices in combination with a variety of more traditional diet and exercise regimens.

While seemingly revolutionary, Dr. Cortis's message is simple: You can do much more for the health of your heart than you think you can. This is true whether you have no symptoms or risk factors whatsoever, if you have some symptoms or risk factors, or if you actually already have heart disease.

MARKET ANALYSIS

Heart and Soul could not be more timely. Of the 1.5 million heart attacks suffered by Americans each year, nearly half occur between the ages of 40 and 65. Three-fifths of these heart attacks are fatal. While these precise statistics may not be familiar to the millions of baby boomers now entering middle age, the national obsession with oat bran, low-fat foods, and exercising for health shows that the members of the boomer generation are becoming increasingly aware of their own mortality.

(The writer would be well advised to ease off the use of the term baby boomer. It is so often used in book proposals that many editors are undoubtedly sick of it. It might have been better merely to describe the exceptional number of people in this pertinent age bracket—without attempting to sound trendy. Good use of facts, trends, and the public's receptivity to what some would characterize as an unorthodox treatment approach.)

This awareness of growing older, coupled with a widespread loss of faith in doctors and fear of overtechnologized medicine, combine to produce a market that is ready for a book emphasizing the spiritual component in healing, especially in reference to heart disease.

Most existing books on the market approach the subject from the physician's point of view, urging readers to follow doctor's orders to attain a healthy heart. There is very little emphasis in these books on the patient's own responsibility for wellness or the inner changes that must be made for the prescribed regimens to work. Among the best known recent books are:

(Not a big deal in this instance—but ordinarily it would be better to have identified this portion of the proposal as the competition section, set it off under a separate heading.)

Healing Your Heart, by Herman Hellerstein, MD, and Paul Perry (Simon & Schuster, 1990). Although this book, like most of the others, advocates proper nutrition, exercise, cessation of smoking, and stress reduction as the road to a healthy heart, it fails to provide the motivation necessary to attain such changes in the reader's lifestyle. Without changes in thinking and behavior, readers of this and similar books will find it difficult, if not impossible, to follow the strict diet and exercise program recommended.

In *Heart Talk: Preventing and Coping with Silent and Painful Heart Disease* (Harcourt Brace Jovanovich, 1987), Dr. Peter F. Cohn and Dr. Joan K. Cohn address the dangers of "silent" (symptomless) heart disease. While informative, the book emphasizes only one manifestation of heart disease and does not empower readers with the motivational tools needed to combat that disease.

(This section is termed the market analysis, which in this proposal actually departs from the approach of the typical marketing section of most proposals. Instead of telling the publisher how to sell the book, the writing collaborator [see the About the Authors section further on] shows special insight into the target audience. The key is that this analysis is not merely a statement of the obvious. This type of in-depth analysis of the potential reader can be very persuasive.)

The Trusting Heart, by Redford Williams, MD (Times Books, 1989), demonstrates how hostility and anger can lead to heart disease, while trust and forgiveness can contribute to wellness. While these are important points, the holistic treatment of heart disease must encompass other approaches as well. The author also fails to provide sufficient motivation for behavioral changes in the readers.

(The author does a good job of demonstrating the invaluable uniqueness of this particular project—especially important when compared with the strong list of competitors.)

The best book on preventing and curing heart disease is Dr. Dean Ornish's *Program for Reversing Heart Disease* (Random House, 1990). This highly successful book prescribes a very strict diet and exercise program for actually reversing certain types of coronary artery disease. This still-controversial approach is by far the best on the market; unfortunately, the material is presented in a dense, academic style not easily accessible to the lay reader. It also focuses on Dr. Ornish's program as the "only way to manage heart disease," excluding other, more synergistic methods.

(The writer collaborator directly analyzed the competition, highlighting the most relevant books on the market without listing each one directly. Although you do not want to present the editor with any unnecessary surprises, if there are too many similar books out in your particular subject area, you might want to use this approach. The writer confronts the heaviest competition directly by finding specific distinguishing factors that support the strength of his proposed project.)

APPROACH

Heart and Soul will be a 60,000- to 70,000-word book targeted to health-conscious members of the baby boom generation. Unlike other books on heart disease, it will focus on the "facts of the connection between the mind and the body as it relates to heart disease, showing readers how to use that connection to heal the heart." The book will be written in an informal but authoritative style, in Dr. Cortis's voice. It will begin with a discussion of heart disease and show how traditional medicine fails to prevent or cure it. Subsequent chapters will deal with the mind-body connection, and the role in healing of social support systems, self-esteem, and faith. In order to help readers reduce stress in their lives, Dr. Cortis shows how they can create their own "daily practice" that combines exercise, relaxation, meditation, and use of positive imagery. Throughout the book, he will present anecdotes that demonstrate how other Exceptional Heart Patients have overcome their disease and gone on to lead healthy and productive lives.

In addition to a thorough discussion of the causes and outcomes of coronary artery disease, the book will include tests and checklists that readers may use to gauge their progress, and exercises, ranging from the cerebral to the physical, that strengthen and help heal the heart. At the end of each chapter readers will be introduced to an essential "Heartskill" that will enable them to put the advice of the chapter into immediate practice.

Through example and encouragement *Heart and Soul* will offer readers a variety of strategies for coping with heart disease, to be taken at once or used in combination. Above all an accessible, practical book, *Heart and Soul* will present readers with a workable program for controlling their own heart disease and forming a healthy relationship with their hearts.

(This is a good summary statement of the book.)

ABOUT THE AUTHORS

Bruno Cortis, MD, is an internationally trained cardiologist with more than 30 years' experience in research and practice. A pioneer of cardiovascular applications of lasers and angioscopy, a Diplomate of the American Board of Cardiology, contributor of more than 70 published professional papers, Dr. Cortis has long advocated the need for new dimensions of awareness in health and the healing arts. As a practicing physician and researcher, his open acknowledgment of individual spirituality as the core of health puts him on the cutting edge of those in traditional medicine who are beginning to create the medical arts practices of the future.

(This is a very good description of the author. The writing collaborator establishes Dr. Cortis as both an expert in his field and a compelling personality. All of this material is relevant to the ultimate success of the book.)

Dr. Cortis has been a speaker at conferences in South America, Japan, and Australia, as well as in Europe and the United States. His firm, Mind Your Health, is dedicated to the prevention of heart attack through the development of human potential. Dr. Cortis is the cofounder of the Exceptional Heart Patients program. The successful changes he has made in his own medical practice prove he is a man not only of vision and deeds, but an author whose beliefs spring from the truths of daily living.

(A formal vita follows in this proposal. It is best to lead off with a journalistic-style biography and follow up with a complete and formal résumé—assuming, as in this case, the author's professional credentials are inseparable from the book.)

Kathryn Lance is the author of more than 30 books of nonfiction and fiction (see attached publications list for details). Her first book, *Running for Health and Beauty* (1976), the first mass-market book on running for women, sold half a million copies. *The Setpoint Diet* (1985), ghosted for Dr. Gilbert A. Leveille, reached the *New York Times* bestseller list for several weeks. Ms. Lance has written widely on fitness, health, diet, and medicine.

(Though she wasn't mentioned on the title page, Lance is the collaborator. This brief bio and the following résumé reveal a writer with virtually impeccable experience. Her participation served to ensure the editors that they could count on the delivery of a high-quality manuscript. Her bio sketch is also strong in its simplicity. Her writing credits are voluminous, but she does not use up space here with a comprehensive listing. Instead she showcases only credits that are relevant to the success of this particular project. Comprehensive author résumés were also attached as addenda to the proposal package.)

HEART AND SOUL
by
Bruno Cortis, MD
Chapter Outline

(Creating a separate page [or pages] for the entire table of contents is a useful and easy technique to enable the editor to gain a holistic vision for the book before delving into the chapter abstracts. In retrospect, we should have had one here.)

(The following is an exceptional outline because it goes well beyond the lazy and stingy telegraph approach that many writers use, often to their own detriment. [Telegrams once were a popular means of communication that required the sender to pay by the word.] Here each abstract reads like a miniature sample chapter unto itself. It proves that the writers have a genuine command of their subject, a well-organized agenda, and superior skills for writing about it. Together they are a darn good team. Whatever legitimate reasons a publisher may have had for rejecting this proposal, it had nothing to do with its manifest editorial and conceptual merits. Some writers are reluctant to go this editorial distance on spec. However, if you believe in your project's viability and you want to maximize acquisition interest and the ultimate advance, you'll give the proposal everything you've got.)

Contents

Introduction: Beating the Odds: Exceptional Heart Patients
(See sample chapter.)

Chapter 1
YOU AND YOUR HEART
Traditional medicine doesn't and can't "cure" heart disease. The recurrence rate of arterial blockage after angioplasty is 25–35 percent, while a bypass operation only bypasses the problem, but does not cure it. The author proposes a new way of looking at heart disease, one in which patients become responsible for the care and well-being of their hearts, in partnership with their physicians. Following a brief, understandable discussion of the physiology of heart disease and heart attack, further topics covered in this chapter include:

(This is a good technique for a chapter abstract. The writer organizes the structure as a listing of chapter topics and elaborates with a sample of the substance and writing approach that will be incorporated into the book. The editor cannot, of course, be expected to be an expert on the subject, but after reading this abstract will come away with a good sense of the quality of the chapter and the depth of its coverage.)

Heart disease as a message from your body. Many of us go through life neglecting our bodies' signals, ignoring symptoms until a crisis occurs. But the body talks to us and it is up to us to listen and try to understand the message. The heart bears the load of all our physical activity as well as our mental activity. Stress can affect the heart as well as any other body system. This section explores the warning signs of heart disease as "messages" we may receive from our hearts, what these messages may mean, and what we can do in response to these messages.

Why medical tests and treatments are not enough. You, the patient, are ultimately responsible for your own health. Placing all faith in a doctor is a way of abdicating that responsibility. The physician is not a healer; rather, he or she sets the stage for the patient's body to heal itself. Disease is actually a manifestation of an imbalance within the body. Medical procedures can help temporarily, but the real solution lies in the patient's becoming aware of his own responsibility for health. This may involve changing diet, stopping smoking, learning to control the inner life.

(Although the abstracts are directed to the editor who reviews the proposal, the writer incorporates the voice to be used in the book by speaking directly to the reader. This is an effective way to incorporate her writing style into the chapter-by-chapter outline.)

Getting the best (while avoiding the worst) of modern medicine. In the author's view, the most important aspect of medicine is not the medication but the patient/physician relationship. Unfortunately, this relationship is often cold, superficial, professional. The patient goes into the medical pipeline, endures a number of tests, then comes out the other end with a diagnosis, which is like a flag he has to carry for life. This view of disease ignores the patient as the main component of the healing process. Readers are advised to work with their doctors to learn their own blood pressure, blood sugar, cholesterol level, and what these numbers mean. They are further advised how to enlist a team of support people to increase their own knowledge of the disease and learn to discover the self-healing mechanisms within.

How to assess your doctor. Ten questions a patient needs to ask in order to assure the best patient-doctor relationship.

Taking charge of your own medical care. Rather than being passive patients, readers are urged to directly confront their illness and the reasons for it, asking themselves: How can I find a cause at the deepest level? What have I learned from this disease? What is good about it? What have I learned about myself? Exceptional heart patients don't allow themselves to be overwhelmed by the disease; rather, they realize that it is most likely a temporary problem, most of the time self-limited, and that they have a power within to overcome it.

Seven keys to a healthy heart. Whether presently healthy or already ill of heart disease, there is a great deal readers can do to improve and maintain the health of their hearts. The most important component of such a plan is to have a commitment to a healthy heart. The author offers the following seven keys to a healthy heart: respect your body; take time to relax every day; accept, respect, and appreciate yourself; share your deepest feelings; establish life goals; nourish your spiritual self; love yourself and others unconditionally. Each of these aspects of heart care will be examined in detail in later chapters.

Heartskill #1: *Learning to take your own pulse.* The pulse is a wave of blood sent through the arteries each time the heart contracts; pulse rate therefore provides important information about cardiac function. The easiest place to measure the pulse is the wrist: place your index and middle finger over the underside of the opposite wrist. Press gently and firmly until you locate your pulse. Don't use your thumb to feel the pulse, because the thumb has a pulse of its own. Count the number of pulse beats in fifteen seconds, then multiply that by four for your heart rate.

This exercise will include charts so that readers can track and learn their own normal pulse range for resting and exercising, and be alerted to irregularities and changes that may require medical attention.

(The inclusion of this technique shows how specific and practical information will be included in the book—important for a nonfiction book proposal. Editors look for what are called the program aspects of a book, because they can be used in promotional settings—and may also be the basis for serial-rights sales to magazines.)

Chapter 2
YOUR MIND AND YOUR HEART

This chapter begins to explore the connection between mind and body as it relates to heart disease. Early in the chapter readers will meet three Exceptional Heart Patients who overcame crushing diagnoses. These include Van, who overcame a heart attack (at age 48), two open-heart surgeries, and "terminal" lung cancer. Through visualization techniques given him by the author, Van has fully recovered and is living a healthy and satisfying life. Goran, who had a family history of cardiomyopathy, drew on the support and love of his family to survive a heart transplant and has since gone on to win several championships in an Olympics contest for transplant patients. Elaine, who overcame both childhood cancer and severe heart disease, is, at the age of 24, happily married and a mother. The techniques used by these Exceptional Heart Patients will be discussed in the context of the mind-body connection.

(The authors do not save the good stuff for the book. If you have interesting case studies or anecdotes, include them here: The more stimulating material you can include, the more you can intrigue your editor. In general, this chapter-by-chapter synopsis is exceptionally detailed in a simplified fashion, which is important for this type of book.)

How your doctor views heart disease: Risk factors v. symptoms. Traditional medicine views the risk factors for heart disease (smoking, high blood cholesterol, high blood pressure, diabetes, obesity, sedentary lifestyle, family history of heart disease, use of oral contraceptives) as indicators of the likelihood of developing illness. In contrast, the author presents these risk factors as *symptoms* of an underlying disease, and discusses ways to change them. Smoking, for example, is not the root of the problem, which is, rather, fear, tension, and stress. Smoking is just an outlet that the patient uses to get rid of these basic elements, which he or she believes are uncontrollable. Likewise high cholesterol, which is viewed by the medical establishment as largely caused by poor diet, is also affected by stress. (In a study of rabbits on a high-cholesterol diet, narrowing of arteries was less in rabbits that were petted, even if the diet remained unhealthful.) Other elements besides the traditional "risk factors," such as hostility, have been shown to lead to high rates of heart disease.

A mind/body model of heart disease. It is not uncommon to hear stories like this: They were a very happy couple, married 52 years. Then, suddenly, the wife developed breast cancer and died. The husband, who had no previous symptoms of heart disease, had a heart attack and died two months later. All too often there is a very close relationship between a traumatic event and serious illness. Likewise, patients may often become depressed and literally will themselves to die. The other side of the coin is the innumerable patients who use a variety of techniques to enlist the mind-body connection in helping to overcome and even cure serious illnesses, including heart disease.

Rethinking your negative beliefs about heart disease. The first step in using the mind to help to heal the body is to rethink negative beliefs about heart disease. Modern studies have shown that stress plays a most important role in the creation of heart disease, influencing all of the "risk factors." Heart disease is actually a disease of self, caused by self, and is made worse by the belief that we are its "victims." Another negative and incorrect belief is that the possibilities for recovery are limited. The author asserts that these beliefs are untrue, and that for patients willing to learn from the experience, heart disease can be a path to recovery, self-improvement, and growth.

The healing personality: tapping into your body's healing powers. Although the notion of a "healing personality" may sound contradictory, the power of healing is awareness, which can be achieved by anyone. The author describes his own discovery of spirituality in medicine and the realization that ultimately the origin of disease is in the mind. This is why treating disease with medicine and surgery alone does not heal: because these methods ignore the natural healing powers of the body/mind. How does one develop a "healing personality"? The starting point is awareness of the spiritual power within. As the author states, in order to become healthy, one must become spiritual.

Writing your own script for a healthy heart. Before writing any script, one must set the stage, and in this case readers are urged to see a cardiologist or physician and have a thorough checkup. This checkup will evaluate the presence or absence of the "risk factors" and assess the health of other body organs as well. Once the scene is set, it is time to add in the other elements of a healthy heart, all of which will be explored in detail in the coming chapters.

Making a contract with your heart. We see obstacles only when we lose sight of our goals. How to make (either mentally or on paper) a contract with one's heart that promises to take care of the heart. Each individual reader's contract will be somewhat different; for example, someone who is overweight might include in the contract the desire that in six months she would weigh so much. The point is to set realistic, achievable goals. Guidelines are provided for breaking larger goals down into small, easily achievable steps. Creating goals for the future makes them a part of the present in the sense that it is today that we start pursuing them.

What to say when you talk to yourself. In the view of the author, the greatest source of stress in life is negative conversations we have with ourselves. These "conversations," which go on all the time without our even being aware of them, often include such negative suggestions as "When are you going to learn?" "Oh, no, you stupid idiot, you did it again!" When we put ourselves down, we reinforce feelings of unworthiness and inadequacy, which leads to stress and illness. Guidelines are given for replacing such negative self-conversation with more positive self-talk, including messages of love and healing.

Heartskill #2: *Sending healing energy to your heart.* In this exercise, readers learn a simple meditation technique that will help them get in touch with their natural healing powers and begin to heal their hearts.

Chapter 3
THE FRIENDSHIP FACTOR:
PLUGGING INTO YOUR SOCIAL SUPPORT SYSTEM

Heart disease is not an isolated event, and the heart patient is not an isolated human being. Among the less medically obvious "risk factors" involved in coronary disease are social isolation. In this chapter the author discusses the importance of maintaining and strengthening all the social support aspects of the patient's life, including family, friendship, community, and sex. He shows how intimacy and connection can be used not just for comfort but also as actual healing tools.

Sexual intimacy: the healing touch. Following a heart attack, many patients may lose confidence due to a fear of loss of attractiveness or fear of death. Citing recent studies, the author points out that there is a difference between making sex and making love. The desire for sex is a human need and is not limited to healthy people. Anybody who has had a heart problem still has sexual needs and ignoring them may be an additional cause of stress. Guidelines for when and how to resume sexual activity are offered. Other topics covered in this chapter include:

Keeping your loved ones healthy, and letting them keep you healthy
How you may be unwittingly pushing others out of your life
The art of nondefensive, nonreactive communication
Accepting your loved ones' feelings and your own
How to enlist the support of family and friends
Joining or starting your own support group

Heartskill #3: *Mapping your social support system*

Chapter 4
OPENING YOUR HEART:
LEARNING TO MAKE FRIENDS WITH YOURSELF

In addition to enlisting the support of others, for complete healing it is necessary for the patient to literally become a friend to himself or herself. This may entail changing old ways of thinking and responding, as well as developing new, healthier ways of relating to time and other external stresses. In this chapter the author explores ways of changing Type A behavior, as well as proven techniques for dealing with life's daily hassles and upsets. An important section of the chapter shows readers how to love and cherish the "inner child," that part of the personality that needs to be loved, to be acknowledged, and to have fun. Equally important is the guilt that each of us carries within, and that can lead not only to unhealthy behaviors but also to actual stress. The author gives exercises for learning to discover and absolve the hidden guilts that keep each of us from realizing our true healthy potential. Topics covered in this chapter include:

A positive approach to negative emotions
Checking yourself out on Type A behavior: a self-test
Being assertive without being angry
Keeping your balance in the face of daily hassles and major setbacks
Making a friend of time
Identifying and healing your old childhood hurts
Letting go of hurts, regrets, resentments, and guilt
Forgiving yourself and making a new start
The trusting heart

Heartskill #4: *Forgiveness exercise*

Chapter 5
IDENTIFYING AND ELIMINATING STRESS IN YOUR LIFE

The science of psychoneuroimmunology is beginning to prove that the mind and body are not only connected, but also inseparable. It has been demonstrated that changes in life often precede disease. Lab studies have shown that the amount of stress experienced by experimental animals can induce rapid growth of a tumor that would ordinarily be rejected. For heart patients, the fact of disease itself can become another inner stress factor that may worsen the disease and the quality of life. One out of five healthy persons is a "heart reactor," who has strong responses under stress that induce such unhealthful physiological changes as narrowing of the coronary arteries, hypertrophy of the heart muscle, and high blood pressure. In this chapter the author shows readers how to change stress-producing negative beliefs into constructive, rational beliefs that reduce stress. Included are guidelines to the five keys for controlling stress: diet, rest, exercise, attitude, and self-discipline.

Why you feel so stressed out
Where does emotional stress come from and how does it affect your heart?
Your stress signal checklist
Staying in control
Calculating your heart-stress level at home and on the job
Stress management

Heartskill #5: *Mapping your stress hotspots*

Chapter 6
YOUR FAITH AND YOUR HEART

As the author points out, there are few studies in the field of spirituality and medicine, because physicians, like most scientists, shy away from what is called "soft data." Soft data are anything outside the realm of physics, mathematics, etc.: the "exact sciences." As a physician, the author has grown ever more convinced of the body's natural healing power, which is evoked through mind and spirit. No matter how "spirit" is defined, whether in traditional religious terms or as a component of mind or personality, the truth is that in order to become healthy, it is necessary to become spiritual.

In a ten-month study of 393 coronary patients at San Francisco General Hospital, it was proven that the group who received outside prayer in addition to standard medical treatment did far better than those who received medical treatment alone. Those in the experimental group suffered fewer problems with congestive heart failure, pneumonia, cardiac arrests, and had a significantly lower mortality rate. This chapter explores the possible reasons for this startling result and illuminates the connection between spirit and health.

The difference between spirituality and religion. A discussion of the differences between traditional views of spirituality and the new holistic approach that sees mind, body, and spirit as intimately connected and interdependent.

Faith and heart disease. The healing personality is that of a person who takes care of his own body. He may also use such other "paramedical" means to get well as physical exercise, a proper diet, prayer, meditation, positive affirmations, and visualization techniques. The author surveys these techniques that have been used for centuries to contribute to the healing of a wide variety of diseases. Other topics exploring the connection between faith and a healthy heart include:

> *Tapping into your personal mythology*
> *Forgiving yourself for heart disease*
> *Keeping a psychological-spiritual journal*

Heartskill #6: *Consulting your inner adviser*

Chapter 7
PUTTING IT ALL TOGETHER:
HOW TO DEVELOP YOUR OWN DAILY
PRACTICE FOR A HEALTHY HEART

Daily Practice as defined by the author is a personalized program in which readers will choose from among the techniques offered in the book to create their own unique combination of mental and physical healing exercises. Each component of the daily practice is fully explained. The techniques range from the familiar—healthful diet and exercise—to the more spiritual, including prayer, meditation, and visualization. Included are examples of use of each of these techniques as practiced by Exceptional Heart Patients.

> *The benefits of daily practice*
> *Meditation: how to do it your way*
> *Stretching, yoga, and sensory awareness*
> *Hearing with the mind's ear, seeing with the mind's eye*
> *The psychological benefits of exercise*
> *Healthy eating as a meditative practice*
> *The healing powers of silent prayer*
> *Creating your own visualization exercises*
> *Creating your own guided-imagery tapes*
> *Using other types of positive imagery*

Heartskill #7: *Picking a practice that makes sense to you*

Chapter 8
LEARNING TO SMELL THE FLOWERS

In our society, pleasure is often regarded as a selfish pursuit. We tend to feel that it is not as important as work. And yet the key element in health is not blood pressure, or cholesterol, or blood sugar; instead it is peace of mind and the ability to enjoy life. Indeed, this ability has been proven to prevent illness. In this chapter the author focuses on the ability to live in the moment, savoring all that life has to offer, from the simple physical pleasures of massage to the more profound pleasures of the spirit. Topics covered in this chapter include a discussion of Type B behavior, which can be learned. The secrets of this type of behavior include self-assurance, self-motivation, and the ability to relax in the face of pressures. The author shows how even the most confirmed Type A heart patient can, through self-knowledge, change outer-directed goals for inner ones, thus achieving the emotional and physical benefits of a Type B lifestyle. Other topics discussed in this chapter include:

Getting the most out of the present moment
Taking an inventory of life's pleasures
Counting down to relaxation
Hot baths, hot showers, hot tubs, and saunas
Touching; feeding the skin's hunger for human touch
Pets, plants, and gardens as healing helpers

Heartskill #8: *Building islands of peace into your life*

Chapter 9
CREATING YOUR FUTURE

The heart may be viewed in many different ways: as a mechanical pump, as the center of circulation, as the source of life. The author suggests viewing the heart above all as a spiritual organ, the center of love, and learning to figuratively fill it with love and peace. A positive result of heart disease is the sudden knowledge that one is not immortal, and the opportunity to plan for a more worthwhile, fulfilling life in the future. In this final chapter, Dr. Cortis offers guidelines for setting and achieving goals for health—of mind, body, and spirit. For each reader the goals, and the means to achieve them, will be different. But as the author points out, this is a journey that everyone must take, patients as well as doctors, readers as well as the author. No matter how different the paths we choose, we must realize that truly "our hearts are the same."

The Art of Happiness
Choosing your own path to contentment
Goals chosen by other exceptional heart patients

Developing specific action steps
Reinforcing and rethinking your life goals
Finding your own meaning in life and death

Heartskill #9: *Helping others to heal their hearts*

Recommended Reading

Appendix I
FOR FRIENDS AND FAMILY:
HOW TO SUPPORT AN EXCEPTIONAL HEART PATIENT

Appendix II
ON FINDING OR STARTING A SELF-HELP GROUP

Appendix III
ABOUT THE EXCEPTIONAL HEART PATIENT PROJECT

Authors' Notes

Acknowledgments

Index

(Appendices are always a valuable bonus.)

(It is great to be able to include an actual endorsement in your proposal package. Quite often, writers state those from whom they intend to request endorsements—but do not actually have them lined up. Perhaps unnecessary to say, but valuable to reiterate, is that editors and agents are not overly impressed by such assertions. They do, however, nod with respect to those authors who demonstrate that they can deliver on their claims. The inclusion of at least one such blurb creates tremendous credibility.)

GERALD G. JAMPOLSKY, MD
Practice Limited to Psychiatry
Adults and Children

April 1, 1998

Mr. Jeff Herman
The Jeff Herman Agency, Inc.
140 Charles Street, Suite 15A
New York, NY 10014

Dear Jeff:
You may use the following quote for Bruno's book:

"Dr. Bruno Cortis writes from the heart—for the heart. This is a much-needed and very important book."

Gerald Jampolsky, MD
Coauthor of *Love Is the Answer*

With love and peace,
Jerry
Gerald Jampolsky, MD

(The author, Dr. Cortis, is very well connected in his field. He solicited promises from several prominent persons to provide cover endorsements like this one. Having these promises to provide such blurbs at the time I marketed the proposal further enhanced the agency's sales position.)

PROFOUND QUESTIONS AND HUMBLE ANSWERS

JEFF HERMAN

In the course of my ongoing participation in publishing workshops, seminar presentations, and panels at writers' conferences, certain questions arise time and again. Many of these requests for information go straight to the heart of the world of book publishing.

The following questions are asked from the gut and replied to in kind. In order to be of value to the author who wishes to benefit from an insider view, I answer these serious queries in unvarnished terms, dispensing with the usual sugarcoating in order to emphasize the message of openness and candor.

Q: I have been at this for a long time, and can't get published. How come?
Well, your stuff may not be good. That's the easy answer, which probably applies to most of what gets written and, frankly, to some of what actually gets published. After all, books get published for many reasons, including the possibility that they are of high quality. But lack of quality is not, never has been, and never will be the only factor as to why books do or don't get published. That said, it's good to make your product the best it can be.

It's safe to say that everyone who works in publishing will agree that countless works of excellence don't make it to publication. That's unfortunate. But is it unfair? Who's to say?

Many works get published because the writer managed to get them to the right people at the right time. How and why did that happen?

Other fine works fail to "connect," in spite of the diligent efforts made by the writer to sell them. Why? I don't know. Why are some people very pretty, while others are very ugly? I don't know. Some consequences can be logically traced backwards to a cause or causes, or a lack of necessary acts.

But sometimes there is no apparent pathology behind what does and doesn't happen. And that's when we must simply surrender. There's an ancient Jewish saying, "Man plans, God laughs." Some things are left to our discretion and control, whereas other things obviously are not. It's possible that that may be why you did not sell your manuscript. But I don't know.

Q: Why are memoirs and autobiographies hard to sell?

Because the vast majority of us lead lives of quiet desperation that would bore even a 300-year-old turtle. None of us ever truly listen to each other. That's why a lot of us pay strangers $90 or more an hour to listen to us. Or at least we think they're listening.

So why should someone actually pay you to read about your life? If you can effectively answer that question, you may be qualified to write a book about YOU.

Now, there are ways to maneuver around this conundrum. For instance, you can place your life within the context of fascinating events. People do connect to events and situations that mirror their own lives and feelings right back at them.

You can think ahead by doing something notable or outrageous for the sole purpose of having a platform for writing about yourself. A lot of us do ridiculous things anyway, so why not do them in a planned conscious way? It's said that we all write our own script in life. So, if you are the designer of your own life, who do you have to blame for leading a boring life? Think about your life as a feature film, and start living it within that context. Pre-empt the cutting room floor whenever possible. Become someone that other people will pay to watch, read about, and listen to.

Even if you don't get anything sold, you may still end up with more friends.

Q: Why do editors, agents and some writers seem so snobby?

Because maybe they are. Why should you care? Because you want validation and snobs counter that. A long time ago, when I was young and a bit more stupid, I told a snobby editor to come clean my bathroom for me. He didn't. Neither did I; I hired a housekeeper. To this day I enjoy foiling people who think they are better then the rest. Sometimes, I think I'm better than the rest. But my better angels take care of that by hiding my car in a parking lot, or causing me to wash my mouth with shampoo. My list of due personal humiliations is infinite, and appreciated.

Snobbery is a burden, and a punishment unto itself. Let the snobs have their burden, and keep writing.

Q: Is it more difficult to get an agent than it is to get a publisher?

I believe it's substantially easier to get an agent than it is to get a publisher.

The primary reason for this is that no agent expects to sell 100 percent of the projects she chooses to represent. Not because any of these projects lack merit (though some of them may), but because only so many titles are published per year—and many excellent ones just won't make the cut. This is especially true for fiction by unknown or unpublished writers, or for nonfiction in saturated categories. As a result, many titles will be agented but never published.

Naturally, a successful agent prefers to represent projects that she feels are hot and that publishers will trample each other to acquire. But few, if any, agents have the luxury of representing such sure-bet projects exclusively. In fact, the majority of their projects may be less than "acquisition-guaranteed," even though they are of acquisition quality.

The agent assumes that many of these projects will eventually be sold profitably, but probably doesn't expect all of them to be. Every experienced agent knows that some of the best cash cows were not easily sold.

Make no mistake—it's not easy to get a reputable agent. Most agents reject 98 percent of the opportunities that cross their desks. They accept for representation only material they believe can be sold to a publisher. That is, after all, the only way for them to earn income and maintain credibility with publishers. If an agent consistently represents what a publisher considers garbage, that will become her professional signature—and her undoing as an agent.

But don't despair. This is a subjective business, composed of autonomous human beings. One agent's reject can be another's gold mine. That's why even a large accumulation of rejections should never deter you as a writer.

Some people get married young, and some get married later!

Q: Is there anything I can do to increase my odds of getting an agent?
Yes.

First consider the odds quoted in the previous answer. The typical agent is rejecting 98 percent of everything he sees. That means he's hungry for the hard-to-find 2 percent that keeps him in business.

If you're not part of that 2 percent, he'll probably have no use for you or your project. Your challenge is to convince him that you're part of that select 2 percent.

Q: What do agents and editors want? What do they look for in a writer? What can I do to become that kind of writer?
Let's back up a step or two and figure out why agents want to represent certain projects and why editors want to buy them. This industry preference has little to do with quality of writing as such.

Many highly talented writers never get published. Many mediocre writers do get published—and a number of them make a lot of money at it. There are reasons for this. The mediocre writers are doing things that more than compensate for their less-than-splendid writing. And the exceptional writers who underachieve in the publishing arena are (regardless of their talents) most likely doing things that undermine them.

In other words, being a good writer is just part of a complex equation. Despite all the criticism the educational system in the United States has received, America is exceedingly literate and has a motherlode of college graduates and postgraduates. Good, knowledgeable writers are a dime a dozen in this country.

Profitable writers, however, are a rare species. And agents and editors obviously value them the most. Once more: Being an excellent writer and a financially successful writer don't necessarily coincide. Ideally, of course, you want to be both.

To maximize your success as a writer, you must do more than hone your ability to write; you must also learn the qualifiers and the disqualifiers for success. Obviously, you wish to employ the former and avoid the latter. Publishing is a business, and agents tend to be the most acutely business-oriented of all the players. That's why they took the risk of going into business for themselves (most agents are self-employed).

If you wish, wear your artist's hat while you write. But you'd better acquire a business hat and wear it when it's time to sell. This subtle ability to change hats separates the minority of writers who get rich from the majority who do not.

In my opinion, rich writers didn't get rich from their writing (no matter how good it is); they got rich by being good at business.

Many good but not-so-wealthy writers blame various internal or external factors for their self-perceived stagnation. My answer to them is: Don't blame anyone, especially yourself. To lay blame is an abdication of power. In effect, when you blame, you become a car with an empty gas tank, left to the elements. The remedy is to fill the tank yourself.

Learn to view mistakes, whether they be yours or those of the people you relied upon, as inconvenient potholes—learning to move around them will make you an even better driver. Remember the old credo: Only a poor workman blames his tools.

Observe all you can about those who are successful—not just in writing, but in all fields—and make their skills your skills. This is not to insist that making money is or should be your first priority. Your priorities, whatever they are, belong to you. But money is a widely acknowledged and sought-after emblem of success.

If an emphasis on personal gain turns you off, you may, of course, pursue other goals. Many successful people in business find the motivation to achieve their goals by focusing on altruistic concepts—such as creating maximum value for as many people as possible. Like magic, money often follows value even if it wasn't specifically sought. If you're unfortunate enough to make money you don't want, there's no need to despair: There are many worthy parties (including charities) that will gladly relieve you of this burden.

Here are specific ways to maximize your ability to get the agent you want:

+ *Don't start off by asking what the agent can do for you.* You're a noncitizen until the agent has reason to believe that you may belong to that exclusive 2 percent club the agent wants to represent. It's a mistake to expect the agent to do anything to sell herself to you during that initial contact. You must first persuade her that you're someone who's going to make good money for her business. Once you've accomplished that, and the agent offers you representation, you're entitled to have the agent sell herself to you.

+ *Act like a business.* As you're urged elsewhere in this book, get yourself a professional letterhead and state-of-the-art office equipment. While rarely fatal, cheap paper and poor-looking type will do nothing to help you—and in this business you need all the help you can give yourself.

    Virtually anyone—especially someone intellectually arrogant—is apt to be strongly affected on a subliminal level by a product's packaging. People pay for the sizzle, not the steak. There is a reason why American companies spend billions packaging, naming, and advertising such seemingly simple products as soap. We would all save money if every bar of soap were put into a plain paper box and just labeled "Soap." In fact, the no-frills section does sell soap that way—for a lot less. But few people choose to buy it that way. Understand this human principle, without judging it, and use it when packaging yourself.

- *Learn industry protocol.* I never insist that people follow all the rules. As Thomas Jefferson wisely suggested, a revolution every so often can be a good thing. But you should at least know the rules before you break them—or before you do anything.

  For instance: Most agents say they don't like cold calls. I can't say I blame them. If my rejection rate is 98 percent, I'm not going to be enthusiastic about having my ear talked off by someone who is more than likely part of that 98 percent. Just like you, agents want to use their time as productively as possible. Too often, cold calls are verbal junk mail. This is especially true if you are a writer selling fiction; your hard copy is the foot you want to get through the door.

  Speaking for myself, most cold calls have a neutral effect on me (a few turn me off, and a few rouse my enthusiasm). I try to be courteous, because that's how I would want to be treated. I will allow the caller to say whatever he wants for about one minute before I take over to find out what, if anything, the person has in the way of hard copy. If he has some, I invite him to send it with an SASE. If he doesn't have any, I advise him to write some and then send it. Usually, I don't remember much about what he said on the phone; I may not even remember that he called. But that doesn't matter; it's the hard copy that concerns me at first. This is the way it works with most agents. We produce books, not talk.

  An agent's time is an agent's money (and therefore his clients' money). So don't expect any quality access until the agent has reason to believe you're a potential 2 percenter. If you're the CEO of General Motors, for instance, and you want to write a book, then all you need to do is call the agent(s) of your choice and identify yourself; red carpets will quickly appear. But the vast majority of writers have to learn and follow the more formalized procedures.

- *As explained elsewhere in this book, view the query letter as a sales brochure.* The best ones are rarely more than $1^1/_2$–2 pages long and state their case as briefly and efficiently as possible.

Here are the most common query mistakes:

1. Long, unfocused paragraphs.

2. Pontificating about irrelevancies (at least, matters that are irrelevant from the agent's perspective).

3. Complaining about your tribulations as a writer. We all know it's a tough business, but nobody likes losers—least of all, shrewd agents. Always be a winner when you're selling yourself, and you'll be more likely to win.

Most agents are hungry for that golden 2 percent, and they dedicate a great deal of time shoveling through mounds of material looking for it. You must be the first to believe that you are a 2 percenter, and then you must portray yourself that way to others. Reality begins in your own head and is manifested primarily through your own actions—or lack thereof.

Every agent and editor has the power to reject your writing. But only you have the power to be—or not to be—a writer.

Q: Should I query only one agent at a time?
Some of my colleagues disagree with me here, but I recommend querying five to ten agents simultaneously, unless you already have your foot in the door with one. I suggest this because some agents will respond within ten days, while others may take much longer or never respond at all. Going agent by agent can eat up several months of valuable time before a relationship is consummated. And then your work still has to be sold to a publisher.

To speed up this process, it's smart to solicit several agents at a time, though you should be completely upfront about it. If you go the multiple-submissions route, be sure to mention in your query letters to each agent that you are indeed making multiple submissions (though you needn't supply your agent list).

When an agent responds affirmatively to your query by requesting your proposal or manuscript, it's fine then to give the agent an exclusive reading. However, you should impose a reasonable time frame—for instance, two weeks for a nonfiction proposal and four weeks for a large manuscript. If it's a nonexclusive reading, make sure each agent knows that's what you want. And don't sign with an agent before talking to all the agents who are reading your work. (You have no obligation to communicate further with agents who do not respond affirmatively to your initial query.)

Most agents make multiple submissions to publishers, so they should be sensitive and respectful when writers have reason to use the same strategy agents have used with success.

Q: How do I know if my agent is working effectively for me? When might it be time to change agents?
As I remarked earlier, agents don't necessarily sell everything they represent, no matter how persistent and assertive they may be. In other words, the fact that your work is unsold doesn't automatically mean that your agent isn't doing his job. To the contrary, he may be doing the best job possible, and it may be incumbent upon you to be grateful for these speculative and uncompensated efforts.

Let's say 90 days pass and your work remains unsold. What you need to assess next is whether your agent is making active and proper attempts to sell your work.

Are you receiving copies of publisher rejection letters regarding your work? Generally, when an editor rejects projects submitted by an agent, the work will be returned within a few weeks, along with some brief comments explaining why the project was declined. (In case you're wondering, the agent doesn't have to include an SASE; the editors want agent submissions.) Copies of these rejection letters should be sent to you on a regular basis as the agent receives them. While no one expects you to enjoy these letters, they at least document that your agent is circulating your work.

If you have received many such rejection letters within these 90 days, it's hard to claim that your agent isn't trying. If you've received few or none, you might well call the agent for a status report. You should inquire as to where and when your work has been submitted, and what, if anything, the results of those submissions have been. In the end, you will have to use your own best judgment as to whether your agent is performing capably or giving you the run-around.

If it ever becomes obvious that your agent is no longer seriously trying to sell your work (or perhaps never was), you should initiate a frank discussion with the agent about what comes next. If the agent did go to bat for you, you should consider the strong possibility that your work is presently unmarketable and act to preserve the agent relationship for your next project. Remember, if your work remains unsold, your agent has lost valuable time and has made no money.

If the evidence clearly shows that your agent has been nonperforming from day one, then your work has not been tested. You should consider withdrawing it and seek new representation.

Agent-hopping by authors is not rampant, but it's not uncommon either. Often the agent is just as eager as you—or more so—for the break-up to happen. One veteran colleague once told me that when he notices he hates to receive a certain client's phone calls, then it's time to find a graceful way to end the relationship.

The wisdom of agent-jumping must be assessed on a case-by-case basis. The evidence shows that many writers have prospered after switching, while others have entered limbo or even fallen far off their previous pace.

Before you decide to switch agents, you should focus on why you are unhappy with your current situation. It may be that if you appeal to your agent to discuss your specific frustrations—preferably in person, or at least by phone—many or all of them can be resolved, and your relationship will be given a fresh and prosperous start.

Agents are not mind readers. You only have one agent, but your agent has many clients. It is therefore mostly your responsibility as a writer client to communicate your concerns and expectations effectively to your agent. Your relationship may require only occasional adjustments, as opposed to a complete break-up.

Q: Who do agents really work for?
Themselves! Always have and always will.

True, agents serve their clients, but their own needs and interests always come first. Of course, this is the way it is in any business relationship (and in too many personal ones). You should never expect your lawyer, accountant, or stockbroker (and so on) to throw themselves into traffic to shield you from getting hit.

As long as the interests of the agent and the writer are in harmony, everything should work out well. However, on occasion the writer may have expectations that could be detrimental to the agent's own agenda (not to mention state of mind).

Writers must never lose sight of the truth that publishers are the agent's most important customers. Only a foolish agent would intentionally do serious damage to her relationships with individual editors and publishing houses. It should be further noted that there is, therefore, a fine line that an agent will not cross when advocating for her clients.

Q: What do agents find unattractive about some clients?
Agents are individuals, so each will have his own intense dislikes. But, generally speaking, a certain range of qualities can hamper any and all aspects of an agent's professional association with a client—qualities that often have similarly negative effects in realms other than publishing. Here's a litany of displeasing client types and their characteristics.

- The Pest. Nobody likes a nag, whether at home or at the office. A squeaky wheel may sometimes get the grease—not that anyone likes the effect—but more often this person gets the shaft.

- The Complainer. Some people can never be satisfied, only dissatisfied. It seems to be their mission in life to pass along their displeasure to others. These folks are never any fun—unless you're an ironic observer.

- The BS Artist. These clients believe everything even remotely connected with themselves is the greatest—for example, their fleeting ideas for books should win them millions of dollars up front. Of course, if they actually produce the goods, then the BS part of the term doesn't apply to them.

- The Screw-Up. These clients miss trains, planes, and deadlines. Their blunders can create major hassles for those who count on them.

- The Sun God. Some people believe they are more equal than others and will behave accordingly. It's a real pleasure to see Sun Gods humbled.

- The Liar. Need I say more?

Sometimes these wicked traits combine, overlap, and reinforce themselves in one individual to create what an agent may rate as a veritable client from hell. Enough said on this subject for now, except that I would be remiss if I did not insist that no trade or professional class is immune to this nefarious syndrome—not even literary agents.

Q: How does someone become an agent?
For better or worse, anyone in America can declare himself an agent—at any time. But what people say and what they do are different things. Legitimate literary agents earn most or all of their income from commissions. The less-than-legitimate agencies most often depend on reading and management fees for their cash, with few, if any, actual book sales to their credit.

Most agents earn their stripes by working as editors for publishers. But that is by no means the only route, nor is it necessarily the most effective training ground. Good agents have emerged from a variety of environments and offer a broad range of exceptional credentials. What's most important is the mix of skills they bring to their agenting careers, such as:

1. Strong relationship skills—the ability to connect with people and earn their confidence.

2. Sales and marketing skills—the ability to get people to buy from them.

3. Persuasion and negotiating skills—the ability to get good results in their dealings.

4. An understanding of the book market and of what publishers are buying.

5. An ability to manage many clients and projects at the same time.

Q: Who owns book publishing?
Many decades ago, book-publishing entities were customarily founded by individuals who had a passion for books. Though they obviously had to have business skills to make their houses survive and thrive, money was not necessarily their primary drive (at least, not in the beginning), or they would have chosen more lucrative endeavors.

The vestiges of these pioneers can be found in the family names still extant in the corporate designations of most of today's publishing giants. But apart from the human-sounding names, these are very different companies today. Much of the industry is owned by multinational, multibillion-dollar conglomerates that have priorities other than the mere publication of books. The revenues from book operations are barely noticeable when compared with such mass-market endeavors as movies, TV/cable, music, magazines, sports teams, and character licensing. Stock prices must rise, and shareholders must be optimally satisfied for these firms to feel in any way stable.

Q: How does this type of ownership affect editors and the editorial-acquisition process?
This rampant corporate ownership translates into an environment in which book editors are pressured to make profitable choices if their careers are to prosper. At first look, that doesn't sound radical or wrongheaded, but a downside has indeed developed—editors are discouraged from taking risks for literary or artistic rationales that are ahead of the market curve or even with an eye toward longer-term development and growth of a particular writer's readership.

The bottom line must be immediately appeased by every acquisition, or the nonperforming editor's career will crumble. The editor who acquires blockbusters that the culturally elite disdain is an editor who is a success. The editor whose books lose money but are universally praised by critics is an editor who has failed.

Of course, the previous comparison is extreme. Most editors are not single-minded money-grubbers and do their best to acquire meaningful books that also make commercial sense. Where the cut becomes most noticeable is for the thousands of talented fiction writers who will never write big money-makers. While slots still exist for them, large publishers are increasingly reluctant to subsidize and nurture these marginally profitable writers' careers. Commercially speaking, there are better ways to invest the firm's resources.

Q: What, if any, are a writer's alternatives?
Yes, the big kids are dominant on their own turf and intend to extend their claim to as much of book country as they can. But this isn't the end of the story. The heroes are the thousands of privately owned "Mom and Pop" presses from Maine to Alaska who only need to answer to themselves. Every year, small presses, new and old, make an important contribution to literate culture with books that large publishers won't touch. It's not uncommon for some of these books to become bestsellers. University presses also pump out important (and salesworthy) books that would not have been published in a rigidly commercial environment.

Q: Is there anything positive to say about the current situation?
I don't mean to imply that the corporate ownership of the bulk of the book industry is absolutely bad. Indeed, it has brought many benefits. Publishers are learning to take better advantage of state-of-the-art marketing techniques and technologies and have more capital with which to do it. The parent entertainment and communications firms enable the mainstream commercial publishers to cash in on popular frenzies, as with dinosaur mania, the latest and most salacious scandals, fresh interest in the environment or fitness, or celebrity and other pop-culture tie-ins, such as Gump and Madonna books.

The emergence of superstores enables more books to be sold. The stores create very appealing environments that draw much more traffic than conventional old-style bookstores. Many people who hang out at the superstores were never before motivated to go book shopping. But once they're in one of these well-stocked stores—whether at the bookshelves, ensconced in a reading seat, or perched by a steaming mug at an in-store cafe—they're likely to start spending.

The unfortunate part is that many small independent bookshops cannot compete with these new venues. However, many others are finding clever ways to hang on, by accenting special reader-interest areas or offering their own individual style of hospitality.

Q: How profitable is publishing?
One way to measure an industry's profitability is to look at the fortunes of those who work in it. By such a measure, the book business isn't very profitable, especially when compared to its twentieth-century sisters in entertainment and information industries: movies, television, music, advertising, and computers. Most book editors

require a two-income family if they wish to raise children comfortably in New York or buy a nice home. The vast majority of published authors rely upon their day jobs or spouse's earnings. A handful of authors make annual incomes in the six and seven figures, but it's often the movie tie-ins that get them there and in turn push even more book sales.

A fraction of book editors will climb the ranks to the point at which they can command six-figure incomes, but most never attain this plateau. Almost all of those writers just starting in the business earn barely above the poverty level for their initial publishing endeavors—if that.

A well-established literary agent can make a lot of money. The trick is to build a number of backlist books that cumulatively pay off healthy commissions twice a year, while constantly panning for the elusive big-advance books that promise short-term (and perhaps long-term) windfalls.

In many ways, the agents are the players best positioned to make the most money. As sole proprietors, they're not constrained by committees and can move like lightning. When everything aligns just right, the agent holds all the cards by controlling access to the author (product) and the publisher (producer).

The publishing companies themselves appear at least adequately profitable, averaging about 5 to 10 percent return on revenues (according to their public balance sheets). The larger companies show revenues of between $1 billion and $2 billion, sometimes nudging higher.

These are not sums to sneeze at. But most of those sales derive from high-priced nonbookstore products like textbooks and professional books. Large and midsize publishers alike are dependent upon their cash-cow backlist books for much of their retail sales. These books entail virtually no risk or investment, since their customer base is essentially locked in for an indefinite period, and the publisher has long ago recouped the initial investment. Many backlist books are legacies from editors and business dynamics that current employees may know nothing about.

The real risk for the current regime is their frontlist, which is the current season's crop. Large houses invest tens of millions of dollars to acquire, manufacture, market, and distribute anywhere from 50 to a few hundred "new" books. A small number of big-ticket individual titles will by themselves represent millions of dollars at risk. Most titles will represent less than $50,000 in risk on a pro-rata basis.

In practice, most of these frontlist titles will fail. The publisher will not recoup its investment and the title will not graduate to the exalted backlist status. But like the fate of those innumerable turtle eggs laid in the sand, it's expected that enough spawn will survive to generate an overall profit and significant backlist annuities well into the future.

In the fairness of a broader picture, it is known that most motion pictures and television shows fail, as do most new consumer products (such as soap or soft drinks) that have engendered enormous research-and-development costs. It's the ones that hit—and hit big—that make the odds worth enduring for any industry.

Q: What about attending writers' conferences?

Over the past 15 years I must have attended more than 100 writers' conferences in my role as an agent. I've gone to small towns, big cities, and luxury resorts. In all of them, I have discovered one common denominator: Writers' conferences are for writers what fertilizer is for crops.

It's invaluable for a writer to enter into communion with others of a like mind, at least once a year. The various classes about the usual subjects and the abundant networking opportunities are worthwhile bonuses. But the real benefit is what is received "between the lines." When does someone who writes actually become a writer? What is the initiation process? Most people who write can easily fall into an isolation zone. Family members and friends may at best be indifferent about the person's passion for writing. At worst, they may belittle it as a wasteful self-indulgence that will never mean anything. Of course, once the writer starts accumulating impressive bylines or has a book published, or best of all starts making a lot of money from writing, people may show more respect. But at any given moment most writers have not yet penetrated the ceiling that takes them into the world of actual publication, and those are the writers who need the most support and comfort. Writers' conferences are that special place where struggling writers can connect with fellow travelers, and meet those who have been "there" and suffered the same way before they arrived at greener pastures. A good conference experience will empower writers to be firmer in their identity and more determined to achieve their goals.

There are hundreds of writers' conferences each year and they are well spread out. Chances are there is at least one being given during the next 12 months within 150 miles from where you live. They are usually scheduled on weekends and sponsored by nonprofit community-based writers' clubs. The tuition is often quite modest and only intended to recoup expenses. Ask your librarian or check the Internet for information about writers' clubs and conferences near you.

Q: Is there "ageism" in book publishing?

I have only been asked about racism in publishing once or twice. Each time I answered that I have neither witnessed it nor practiced it, but that does not mean that racism does not exist beyond my limited view. But there is a related question that I hear more frequently, which is: *Do book editors discriminate against elderly writers?* That question makes me uncomfortable because I have mixed feelings about how to answer it.

I can absolutely say that there is no organized program of discrimination against writers of a certain age. That said, there is the evidence of what does and does not get published, and the more subtle evidence of what agents and editors say to each other off the record. Now here I am going out on a limb, and I have not scientifically researched the facts. Nevertheless, I am suggesting that when it comes to fiction, that young unpublished writers have an edge over elderly unpublished writers. I do not believe that the same can be said for nonfiction. Why is this? Introducing new writers to the reading public is a tricky and risky business. The primary target market for new fiction tends to consist of younger readers who have not yet formed strong ties to existing authors. Because of their relative youth, they will be most attracted to themes and styles that they can personally relate to. We also see this emphasis on youth with new films, television shows, and consumer products. It follows that writers who look like and talk like the readers who are being targeted, will be the writers who are offered contracts. If you accept that this is the case, then yes, elderly writers are discriminated against, and to say otherwise is to be disingenuous or blindfolded.

Assuming the above situation is a fact, is it a valid or immoral condition? Frankly, I don't know how to assess the morality of it for one big reason: The marketplace has its own morality. Look, the new fiction writer is as much a part of the product as anything that goes between the pages. Is it reasonable to expect that younger readers will gravitate to new fiction written by people who remind them of their parents or grandparents? Now I'll step aside and let other people pick up the debate, assuming anyone has even read this deeply into the essay section of this book.

However, writers who are of a certain age should avoid making certain mistakes. For instance, when I read a query letter or author bio section, there usually is no reason why I need to be told how old the writers is, unless their age is somehow relevant to the material. Once writers start broadcasting how old they are, certain impressions will be formed in the eye of the reader, which can range from the positive to the negative. Why? Because that's what humans do, we form impressions, which get recalled by the information we are given. If your age is a variable of no consequence in the context of what you have written, then just keep it to yourself.

Q: Should I email my query letters to agents?
I think you should, because I think that material that gets electronically delivered is easier to review and process then the submissions that get sent via hard copy. But like a lot of what I say, this is merely my impression. I have not scientifically evaluated what delivery methods are likely to achieve enhanced access, and I would also assume that a lot of it depends upon the preferences of the individual agent.

Q: What about agency fees?
Not that stupid question again. It keeps popping up wherever I meet writers. Clearly intelligent people describe the ridiculous abuses they get drawn into by people who claimed to be agents. If you pay a fee, especially to someone who has no documented track record of actually selling books to publishers, then you are making it possible for publishing scams to sustain and surpass the $50 million annual level that the FBI estimated several years ago.

THE AUTHOR-AGENCY CONTRACT

JEFF HERMAN

The author-agent relationship is first and foremost a business partnership. Like any business relationship, it is best to carefully and lucidly document what each party's respective responsibilities and due benefits are. Memories are short, but the written word is forever, assuming you don't lose the paperwork. If there is ever a disagreement or simple confusion about what's what, all you need to do is refer to the contract. A good contract that anticipates all reasonably plausible circumstances is the ultimate arbitrator, and will cost you no additional fees or aggravation.

Below is my agency's standard client contract. I consider it to be fair and liberal, and have had very few complaints about it over the years. To my knowledge, most agencies use contracts that are similar in content.

The key aspects to look for in the agency contract are as follows.

1. COMMISSIONS

Most agencies will charge a 15 percent commission against all advances and royalties they generate for the client. International and dramatization deals often require the agent to retain a co-agent, who has the necessary relationships in each respective country where a foreign rights deal might be made, or who has the requisite expertise to deal with the Hollywood jungle. When a co-agent is used, the two agents will evenly split the total commission, but this will require the overall commission to be increased to as much as 30 percent.

2. SCOPE OF REPRESENTATION

The contract should be clear about what properties are being represented at the current time, and perhaps into the future. The most liberal arrangement from the author's perspective will be to limit the scope only to the project "in hand." It's best for the author to keep his options open regarding future books. Exceptions to this may be next works that are clearly derived from the first work, or an ongoing series.

3. DURATION OF CONTRACT

This is an area of variance for agency contracts. Some clearly state a six-month or longer term; others are completely open-ended. I prefer the latter. I believe that the agent or writer should be at liberty to end the whole thing whenever they feel compelled to do so. Obviously, the author will still be charged any due commissions that were earned prior to the termination, including any deals that result from the agent's pitches, even if consummated post-breakup.

4. FEES AND/OR REIMBURSABLE EXPENSES

As has been stated elsewhere in this book, a legitimate agent will only make money from the client if a book deal is entered into, thereby paying the agency its due commission. If the agency contract is structured in a way that enables the agency to show a profit even if the work is not sold to a publisher, then the author needs to be concerned. The ways this might show up include large upfront "management fees" or "retainers for expenses." If a so-called agency were to collect $500 five times a week, and never did anything to actually sell any of these works, it would be a very profitable scam, which is much more common than it ought to be. It is perfectly legitimate for an agency to track certain out-of-pocket expenses such as photocopying and shipping, and request reimbursement from the client at some point at cost.

5. REVIEWING AND NEGOTIATING THE AGENCY CONTRACT

It's the author's responsibility to understand and be comfortable with the contract before signing it. The author should not feel awkward about asking the agent to clarify items in the contract, and it is acceptable for the author to request that some reasonable revisions get made. Some authors prefer to have all their contracts vetted by their attorney. This is okay as long as the attorney understands the customs and protocols of the book publishing business. Otherwise, the attorney may go after certain provisions that are generally left alone, and end up wrecking the relationship before it can get off the ground. Assuming that the attorney does have some legitimate points for discussion, then the author should be willing to deal directly with the agency about them, and not turn the attorney lose on the agent.

SAMPLE LETTER OF AGREEMENT

This Letter of Agreement (Agreement) between The Jeff Herman Agency, LLC (Agency), and WILLIAM SHAKESPEARE (Author), issued on JANUARY 2, 1625, will put into effect the following terms and conditions when signed by all parties to it.

REPRESENTATION

+ The Agency is exclusively authorized to seek a publisher for the Author's work, referred to as the "Project," on a per-Project basis. The terms and conditions of this Agreement will pertain to all current and future Projects the Author explicitly authorizes the Agency to represent through written expression. Separate Agreements will not be required for future Projects, unless the terms and conditions differ from this Agreement and/or the

Author requests a separate Agreement in each instance. The Agency cannot legally bind the Author to any Publisher contracts.

COMMISSION

+ If the Agency sells the Project to a publisher, the Agency will be the Agent-of-Record for the Project's income-producing duration with the publisher, and will irrevocably receive and keep 15 percent of the Author's advance and royalty income relevant to sold Project received from the publisher. Unless otherwise stated, the Agency commission will also pertain to the Project's subsidiary rights, which commonly means dramatic, foreign, audio, video, merchandising and electronic adaptations of the primary Project. If the Agency uses a subagent to sell foreign or film rights, and the subagent is due a commission, the Agency commission for such will be 10 percent and the subagent's commission will not be more than 10 percent. The Agency will not be required to return any legitimately received commissions in the event the Author-Publisher contract is terminated due to the Author's breach of contract, nor will the Agency bear any responsibility for errors and breaches committed by the Author. There will be an "Agency Clause" included in the body of the Author-Publisher contract memorializing the Agency's standing as a "third-party beneficiary," and providing for the Agency to receive due commission payments directly from the publisher and for the Author to receive due payments minus the commission directly from the publisher, the exact wording for which shall be subject to Author approval. These terms will be binding on the Author's estate in the event of his/her demise. If the Author's Project is placed with a publisher by the Agency, the Agency's status herein will extend to any subsequent contracts between Author and Publisher that pertain to a subsequent edition or revision of the Project, or are clearly derivative of the Project.

EXPENSES

+ The Agency will be entitled to receive reimbursement from the Author for the following out-of-pocket expenses (at actual cost): Manuscript/proposal copying; necessary overnight deliveries; postage for submission of materials to publishers; foreign shipping and communications. An itemized accounting and records of such items will be maintained by the Agency and shown to the Author. No expense events in excess of $75.00 will be incurred without the Author's prior knowledge and consent.

PROJECT STATUS

- The Agency will forward to the Author copies of correspondence and documents received from Publishers in reference to the Author's Project(s).

REVISIONS

- This Agreement can be amended through written expression signed by all parties to the Agreement.

TERMINATION

- Any party to this Agreement can terminate it at any time following its execution by notifying the other parties in writing to that effect. However, the Agency shall remain entitled to all due commissions which may result from successful Agency efforts implemented prior to the termination, and the Agency's existing standing as a third-party beneficiary in any existing Author-Publisher contract cannot be revoked without the Agency's expressed written consent. Termination of the Agency's representation of one or more Author Projects will not imply termination of this entire Agreement, unless such is specifically stated in writing.

Signatures below by the parties named in this Agreement will indicate that all parties concur with the terms and conditions of this Agreement, and will honor their respective responsibilities in good faith.

THE JEFF HERMAN AGENCY, LLC, JEFFREY H. HERMAN, PRESIDENT

——————————————————————————————————

Author's name: WILLIAM SHAKESPEARE

Signature:_____

Specific Project(s) represented at this time ("working" or tentative title): *101 Ways to Please a Wench*

SECRETS OF GHOSTWRITING AND COLLABORATION SUCCESS

TONI ROBINO

Thousands of people in the world have valuable information to share or incredible stories to tell. But only a few of them have the ability or the time to write their own books. That's where you—the professional writer—come into the picture. If you're a strong, clear writer, have the ability to organize thoughts and ideas into a logical order, and can put your ego in the back seat, you may have what it takes to be a successful ghostwriter or collaborator.

The life of a professional writer has its share of pains, but it also has an ample amount of perks. To begin with, it provides a means of escape from the Monday through Friday, 9-to-5 grind. The pay is good, and as you improve your skills and broaden your network, it gets better. In addition to being paid to learn and write about interesting people, philosophies, and methods, being a professional writer puts you in touch with a wide array of fascinating people.

I've had the chance to interview some of the planet's most brilliant people and to explore the work of trendsetters and pioneers in the fields of business, psychology, health, fitness, relationship building, astrology, and metaphysics. I have been flown to Paris to meet with leaders in the field of innovation, wined and dined at some of New York's most exclusive restaurants, and collected agates on the Oregon coast, all in the name of "work." If this sounds appealing, keep reading.

WHAT'S THE DIFFERENCE BETWEEN GHOSTWRITING AND COLLABORATING?

One of the most common questions I'm asked is "What's the difference between a ghostwriter and a collaborator?" The answer can vary from project to project. But, typically, a ghostwriter gathers the author's original materials and research and turns them into a book, based on the author's specifications (if the book will be self-published) or the publisher's specifications (if the book has been sold through the proposal process.) Theoretically, although ghostwriters do conduct interviews and undertake additional research, they do not contribute their own thoughts or ideas to the content of the book.

In reality, the boundaries of the ghostwriter are not always so clear. As a ghost-writer, I have created 80 percent of the exercises in a number of self-help books, provided many original ideas for content, and "given away" plenty of great title ideas. I don't regret these choices because they felt right and, in the cases mentioned, I was being fairly paid for my ideas, as well as for my services. My being generous with my contributions also made my clients happy and helped to build the foundation of my business. But don't take this too far. For one thing, it's not always a wise choice—particularly if you're giving away original ideas that are perfect for your own book. For another thing, the author you're working with may not appreciate this type of input from you. Do not overstep your boundaries as a ghostwriter by adding your own thoughts to a book, unless the author specifically asks you to do this.

In my more naïve days, and following two glasses of Chardonnay, I made the mistake of sharing my unsolicited input with the author of a health book that I was ghostwriting. In the midst of my enthusiasm, I started brainstorming ideas that she might use to illustrate some of the book's major points. Suddenly, she sprung out of her chair, pointed at me, and declared, "Let's get something straight. This is MY book!" Ouch! I was offering ideas without being asked, but on the other hand, I was only suggesting. Even so, take the word of an initiate and tread softly on your client's turf.

Nowadays, if an author wants me to contribute my own ideas and create original material to support the book, I work with that person as a collaborator and generally receive a coauthor credit, either on the cover or on the title page. Getting credit isn't the most important thing when you're starting out, but if you want to publish your own books in the future, stringing together a list of credits can give you a considerable advantage.

If a book cover says "by John Doe and Jane Smith," they were probably equal collaborators. That can mean:

+ they're both experts and one or both of them wrote the book,

+ they're both experts and they hired a ghostwriter to write the book, or

+ the first author is the expert and the second is a professional writer.

If a book cover says "by John Doe with Jane Smith," Jane probably wrote the book. It could also mean that Jane was a contributor to the book.

Whether you will be serving as a ghostwriter or a collaborator should be clarified up front. Which way to go depends on the project and the people involved. Some of my clients want me to be a "ghost" because they want exclusive cover credit, or they want people to think they wrote their own book. (If this bothers you, now would be a good time to bail out.) Other clients say, "I'm not a writer. This is my material, but I don't want to pretend I wrote this book," or "You deserve credit for what you're doing." On the flip side of the coin, you may be willing to write some books that you don't want your name on. Let's hope this is not because you haven't done a good job! Perhaps you're trying to establish yourself in a particular field of writing and may not want to be linked with projects outside of your target area. That's a judgment call, and you're the best one to make it.

BEING "INVISIBLE" HAS ITS ADVANTAGES

Years ago, after signing my first contract to ghostwrite a book about personal development, I called a friend to share the great news. But instead of being happy for me, she said, "That's not fair. Why should you write a book and not get any credit for it? You teach that stuff in your seminars. Why don't you write the book yourself?" She was also upset that I wouldn't divulge the name of the "mystery author."

She had no way of knowing how challenging it can be to publish your first book flying solo. The author whom I was writing for was well-known and regularly spoke to huge crowds of people all around the world. He had created the perfect platform for this book and was in the prime position to make it a success. He had been previously published and his depth of knowledge in this topic was far greater than my own.

For me, it was a chance to learn more about one of my favorite topics from one of the best sources available. It was also a chance to slip into the publishing world through the back door. I dashed in and never looked back. Once I completed that book, the author referred me to a friend who hired me to write a book about her spiritual journey. She, in turn, introduced me to a professional speaker who wanted to self-publish a book on personal coaching, but could never find the time to write it. And so it goes. If you do a good job, one book can easily lead to the next.

Besides that, being invisible has its advantages. I can zip into the grocery store in purple sweatpants, hair in a ponytail on top of my head, and not a stitch of make-up, and nobody notices or cares! I can kiss my husband in public without camera flashes going off around us, and nobody shows up at my door uninvited, except my mother-in-law.

WHEN CREDIT IS DUE

After you've ghostwritten your first book or two, you'll have more confidence in yourself and your abilities. You will probably start fantasizing (if you haven't already) about seeing your name on the cover, instead of tucked into the acknowledgments section—if that! My name didn't even appear in the first few books that I wrote. Beginning with the fourth book, I asked for a credit in the acknowledgments. Since then, I've been thanked for being a wordsmith, editorial adviser, writing coach, editor, and a "great friend." At least, that was a step in the right direction. However, as much as I relish my anonymity, I also look forward to the day when I'm writing more of my own books than other people's! For that reason, most of the professional writing that I do now is as a collaborator/coauthor.

TEN STEPS TO SUCCEEDING AS A PROFESSIONAL WRITER

There are a number of things to consider before quitting your job and striking out as a professional writer. Writing is a constant process and no matter how good a writer may be, that individual can always get better. Another point to consider is that being a great writer doesn't ensure your success. Writing is a business, and the more you learn about running a business, the better off you'll be. If you're stagnating in a job you abhor, reframe your situation so that you see it as an opportunity to continue earning an income while you make the transition to your writing career. Meanwhile, focus on polishing your writing and interpersonal skills and learn as much about operating a business as you can. The more you learn now, the fewer mistakes you'll make later.

1. ASSESS YOUR WRITING SKILLS

Now is the time to be as objective about your writing as possible. Regardless of where you believe you could or should be along your writing path, what counts at the moment is where you are right now. What writing experience do you have? Have you taken any writing courses? Does your writing flow from one thought logically to the next, or does it need to be better organized? Is your writing smooth and conversational, or does it sound stiff or overly academic? What sorts of positive and negative comments have you received about your writing? Have you had anything published? If not, get going!

If you're too close to your writing to be objective, hire an editor, book doctor, or writing coach to give you some forthright feedback. This assessment will help you to learn where you excel and where you should focus your efforts for improvements. The good news is that there's a market for writers at all points on the professional spectrum. You may not be ready to take on your first book, but you could be qualified to ghostwrite an article, collaborate on a chapter, or polish someone else's work. Begin at your current skill level and commit to a path of improvement. By doing this, you will increase your abilities and your income.

2. MAKE YOUR FIRST LIST

Everyone knows at least a few experts. Whether the experts in your life are doctors, professors, psychologists, interior decorators, photographers, archaeologists, or magicians, chances are that some of them have a goal to write a book. Unless these people are good writers and have a lot of free time, which very few experts have, their book will remain on their "wish list" until someone like you shows up to help them. So begin to make a "potential author" list by answering the following questions. For each question, list as many names as you can think of.

Do you know people who are pioneers or experts in their field?
Do you know people who are famous, either in general or in their area of expertise?
Who are the experts, celebrities, or trendsetters whom your friends or associates know?

Once you've made your list, number the names, starting with number one for the person you would most like to work with. Resist the urge to contact these people until you have professionally prepared for your meeting, by learning more about them and taking Steps 3 and 4.

3. PREPARE A PROFESSIONAL PACKAGE

Put together a promotional package for yourself, or hire a professional to help you do it. This package should include your résumé or bio, the services you offer, and a variety of writing samples, showing different styles and topics. You might also insert a page of testimonials from people you have helped with your writing skills or from teachers and coaches who can attest to your abilities. If you've been published, include clean copies of a few of your best clips. If you haven't, enclose a few essays that demonstrate your ability to write clearly and deliver a message effectively.

When you send out your promotional package, enclose a personal pitch letter. Basically, you are telling people what you believe they have to offer the world through their experience or expertise. You're also telling them why you are the perfect person to write the article, manuscript, or book proposal.

4. SET YOUR RATES

Some writers enclose a rate sheet in their promotional package, but I don't recommend it. I do recommend that you make a rate sheet for your own reference. This will be your guide when you are deciding what to charge your clients. Since every project is a little different, don't commit to a price until you estimate how much time and money it will take for you to do the job well.

Calculate how fast you can write final copy, by keeping track of the actual hours spent writing, editing, and proofreading an article or sample chapter. When the piece is completed to your satisfaction, follow this formula:

Total number of words in final copy
Divided by
Total number of hours to complete final copy
Equals:
Your average speed per hour

The idea isn't to race. This exercise is designed to give you a reality check. If you don't know your average speed for producing final copy, you won't be able to create realistic deadline schedules and you'll have no idea how much you're earning for a day of work.

While you may be able to speed through a first draft, the chapter isn't finished until you've edited, polished, and proofread it.

In addition to estimating your actual writing time, build in time for research, interviews, and meetings with the author. You should also estimate the amount of postage, phone charges, faxes, audio tapes, transcription services, and anything else that will be money out of your pocket. Once you've done your homework, you can present the client with a Letter of Agreement (see Step 7) that includes what you will charge and what they will get for your fee.

Writers' rates vary wildly. I was paid $10,000 for the first few books that I ghostwrote, and this is still a great starter rate for a nonfiction book ranging from 70,000 to about 85,000 words. You may not be able to charge this much the first time or two, but with each publication that you add to your list, you can inch up your price. When you reach the point where you are earning $15,000 or more on a book, you will be in the company of some of the most successful ghostwriters. The average fee to write a book proposal can range from $1,000 up to $8,000 or more. When you turn writing into a full-time adventure and write several proposals and books each year, while perhaps editing others, you'll be well on your way to ongoing financial and publishing success!

Many times, if you are working as a "writer for hire," you are paid a flat fee and do not receive royalties from book sales. If you are ghostwriting the book, you may be able to negotiate for royalties. (Royalties for ghostwriting can range from 10 percent of the author's royalties to 50 percent.) If you're a collaborator, in most cases you're entitled to a percentage of the book sales. However, many contracts state that the writer does not begin to receive royalties until the publisher has recouped the initial advance for the book. In some cases, the writer's royalties do not begin until the author has recouped the amount invested in the writer. The bottom line is that most ghostwriters don't receive a dime in royalties until thousands of books have been sold. I suggest that you charge what you're worth up front and think of royalties as icing on the cake.

5. POLISH YOUR INTERPERSONAL SKILLS

Unfortunately, some of the best writers are not comfortable talking to people or selling themselves to potential clients. If you see this as a possible pitfall in building your business, make it a priority to develop your interpersonal skills. Plenty of books, tapes, and seminars address personal development, communication skills, networking, and conflict resolution. Devote yourself to learning how to be more comfortable and effective in your interactions with others.

Practice listening closely to what your client is saying, without interrupting. Growing up in an Italian family with everyone talking at once, I had no problem paying attention to what my clients were saying. (If you can listen to three people at once, you can easily hear one at a time!) However, mastering the discipline to keep my mouth shut until it was my turn to talk was another matter entirely. While interjecting and simultaneous talking is considered par for the course in some settings, many people are offended by interruptions and consider them rude. If you have an exciting idea or pertinent question on the tip of your tongue, jot it down, and wait until your clients complete their thoughts, before chiming in.

Learn how to communicate with your clients in a way that is open and caring. For example, rather than telling an author that the file of notes she sent you was so disorganized that dealing with it was like "stumbling blindfolded through a maze," tell her you appreciate her ability to think of so many things at once. Then tell her what you want her to do. "Please put all of your notes under specific category headings, so I can keep all of your great ideas organized." The rule is to think before you speak. There are usually better ways to communicate a thought than the first words that pop into your head or out of your mouth!

Another skill that is essential for a ghostwriter and important for a collaborator is learning how to keep your ego in check. It's not uncommon for a writer to start feeling attached to a project and have a desire for greater freedom or control of the content or writing style. Remind yourself that this book is not yours. Your day will come, and working as a professional writer is paving the way for that to happen.

One of the surest ways to nip your ghostwriting career in the bud is to break the code of confidentiality that you have with the author of the book. Degrees of "invisibility" differ by project, but if the author doesn't want anyone to know you are writing the book, zip your lips. Other than perhaps your spouse, there is no one, and I mean no one, that you should tell. You can say you're writing a book, and you can divulge the general topic, but that has to be the end of the conversation. To this day, my best friends have no idea who I've ghostwritten books for—except in the cases where the authors have publicly acknowledged me for my participation.

Finally, one of the most beneficial interpersonal skills that a writer or anyone else can possess is a sense of humor. Things are bound to go wrong somewhere along the way, and being able to laugh together with your client will ease tension and stress and make the project a whole lot more fun. It's also valuable to learn to laugh at yourself. My father always said, "If you can look at yourself in the mirror at the end of the day and laugh, you'll make it in life." Oftentimes, when I write a book I create a blooper file, just for my own entertainment. This file contains all of the funny, startling, and obscene typos that I find when I proofread my work.

Keep in mind that there are scores of great writers in the world. Why would an author choose to work with someone who's cranky, arrogant, or self-absorbed if it's possible to work with someone equally talented who is also pleasant, down to earth, and fun?

6. KNOW WHEN TO RUN!

Some day, in the not too distant future, you will have a chance to write a book that you know in your gut is not a good match. This might be because it's a topic that bores your pants off, the point of view is in direct opposition to your own beliefs, or the material is leagues away from your scope of knowledge, experience, or ability for comprehension. In spite of all this, you may be tempted to leap into this "opportunity." Maybe your rent is due, the phone company is threatening to disconnect you, or maybe you just can't wait any longer to write your first book. Before you rationalize this decision or override your instincts, take a step back and think about it for at least two days before you commit. For instance, I should have failed algebra class, but my professor gifted me with the lowest passing grade. Even so, when I was offered a chance to ghostwrite *Understanding the Intrigue of Calculus*, I was tempted to do it. Fortunately, two bounced check notices (caused by my math errors) snapped me back to reality, and I graciously declined the offer.

Aside from making a good match with a topic, it is imperative that you feel good about the book's author. It usually takes about nine months to write a book and doing it with someone else can be compared to having a baby together—minus the sex. If you like each other, it can be a wonderful journey filled with creative energy. If you don't like each other, it can be a recurring nightmare that doesn't go away when you wake up.

Years ago, I took on the daunting task of "saving a book." The complete manuscript was due in three months and the author's writing team had mysteriously jumped ship. When I spoke with author for the first time, she was both friendly and enthusiastic, but she also seemed a little desperate. I ignored my instincts, and two days later I was sitting in her apartment discussing the book. Several things happened that day, and each one of them should have set off warning flares in my mind. To begin with, the author's materials were in complete disarray. (No problem, I told myself. I'm a great organizer.) Second, in between telling me how important it is to speak to our mates with respect, she was berating her husband for his lack of photocopying abilities and sundry other things that he couldn't do right to save his life. (She's just stressed out, I justified.) And third, as I leafed through the disheveled stacks of unnumbered pages, I came across a few very cryptic and angry-sounding notes from the writing team that had bailed out. (I reassured myself that even if others had failed, I would not.)

These rationalizations would soon come back to bite me. And not just once. As it turned out, nine writers had attempted to complete this manuscript before I was contacted. Four writers quit, one writer had a nervous breakdown, three of them disappeared into thin air, and another had his phone disconnected. Ironically, the week the book was released, I had the pleasure of meeting one of the writers who had wisely run for her life. We traded our "Crazy-Author Horror Stories" over steaming plates of fried rice and laughed until tears streamed down our cheeks. At that point it was funny, but not a moment before! If you connect with an author who enters the scene waving red flags, run for your life!

7. CLOSE THE DEAL

Verbal agreements are not enough. If you're working with a publishing house, the author or the author's agent will usually have a contract for you to sign. Make sure you understand this agreement before you sign it. Don't be afraid to ask questions. These contracts are written in "legalese" and can be daunting the first time you encounter one. If you're working with an author who plans to self-publish, create a "letter of agreement" that specifies exactly what services you are providing, the fees involved, the date of delivery, and any other considerations that should be put into writing. This document should be signed by both you and the author; it will help to prevent assumptions or other misunderstandings concerning your business agreement.

8. CAPTURE THE AUTHOR'S VOICE

Whether you're working as a ghostwriter or a collaborator, one of your jobs is to capture the voice of the author. Simply put, you want to write in a way that makes it sound like the author is talking. It shouldn't sound like another author whose style you admire, and it most certainly should not sound like you!

Practice reading a few paragraphs from a favorite book, and then write a few of your own, mimicking the author's voice. Do this with a wide variety of authors, and over time, you will develop an "ear" for others' voices.

One of the best ways to write in the author's voice is to conduct taped interviews with the author and have them transcribed onto computer disk. You can cut and paste the pertinent information into each chapter, in the author's own words, and then smooth it out and expand it as needed.

9. CREATE AND KEEP DEADLINES

There are nearly as many methods of meeting deadlines as there are writers. I tend to take a very methodical approach, dividing up the work into equal parts, circling my "days off," and carefully penciling each chapter deadline on my desk calendar. (I can't help it, I was born this way.) Other writers would go mad with this approach. One of the best writers I know creates 10 percent of the book the week she signs the contract and the other 90 percent the month before the manuscript is due. I couldn't even conceive of this approach and would never have believed it could be done if I hadn't witnessed it personally. The secret is to find out what works best for you. But don't kid yourself. Very few writers can write a great book in less than six months. At least until you settle into your own rhythm, pace yourself. Set reasonable deadlines and find a way to stay accountable to those dates.

Staying accountable to my own deadline schedule was initially much harder than I thought it would be. (There are so many tempting diversions in life!) Frequently, when I was supposed to be writing, I was toying with an art project, combing the forest floor in search of gourmet mushrooms, or just staring out the window. My sense of urgency wasn't ignited until my cash flow began to dwindle. That was when I discovered my motivation. Food, shelter, electricity. It may sound like common sense, but for me it was an "aha" moment. I do have some built-in motivation, but it's keeping my cash flow going that moves me from the sunroom to my office each day.

Linking your productivity with your payments works very well. Ask for one-third of your fee up front. This assures you that the author is serious and provides income so you can focus on the book. Schedule your second payment of one-third to coincide with turning in 50 percent of the manuscript. The final one-third is slated for the date you deliver the final manuscript to the author. If you feel you need more deadlines, divide your fee into four or more payments, each contingent on completing a certain amount of work.

I don't have a business card that says "writer." I don't advertise my writing or editing services, and networking requires an hour's drive from the sanctuary of my forest home into the nearest city—which translates into: I rarely do it. By all sensible accounts, I shouldn't be making it as a ghostwriter. And yet I am, and have been for more than a decade. The secret to my success is word-of-mouth marketing. My clients are happy with my work and me, so they hire me again. They also tell their friends and associates about me, and the wheel continues to spin, seemingly of its own volition.

I know there are many more approaches to marketing, but I've learned that personal referrals usually provide clients whom I want to work with. It's possible for a satisfied client to refer you to an author whom you'd rather eat glass than work with, but most of the time, personal referrals increase your chances of connecting with authors and projects that are interesting and appealing.

When you've completed your work and satisfied your client, ask for referrals. If you've delivered the goods, they'll be happy to brag about you to their friends and associates who "just can't seem to find the right writer."

MAINTAIN YOUR BRIDGES

After the manuscript is complete, the author will be busy with promotional plans and getting back to regular business. You will be focusing on your next project. It's easy to get caught up in the day-to-day happenings and neglect to maintain the bridges that you've already built.

Make it a point to connect with satisfied clients from time to time. Hearing from you will help them think of you for future projects and will increase the likelihood that they'll remember to refer you to someone else. Every couple of months, send a card, a funny email, or an upbeat fax. I phone previous clients only on occasion, and when I do, I call them at their office and keep it short. You want to be the person they look forward to hearing from, not the one who won't go away!

COLLABORATION AGREEMENT

This Collaboration Agreement ("Agreement") entered into on [Date], 2010, by and between ("Author") and ("Writer"), will put the following terms and conditions into effect when signed by both parties.

1. The Author and Writer agree to work together in writing a book about ("Concept").

2. The Writer in consultation with the Author will write a nonfiction book proposal ("Proposal") for the purpose of soliciting and obtaining a book publishing contract. The Proposal will consist of the customary elements as per industry standards and as explained in the book, *Write the Perfect Book Proposal* (John Wiley & Sons), and will include one sample chapter. The Author will make available to the Writer necessary access to herself and other relevant sources and materials for the purpose of generating the Proposal. The Proposal will not be deemed as complete and ready for showing to prospective publishers until the Author accepts it as such.

3. The Writer promises to complete a first draft of the proposal and chapter by [Date], 2010, assuming the Writer receives necessary cooperation from the Author and other necessary sources.

4. If a publisher's contract is entered into, both parties will be signatories to it and equally subject to it, unless otherwise stated. The Writer will proceed to write the manuscript to the publisher's satisfaction as per the terms and conditions of the publisher's contract, in collaboration with the Author.

5. The Writer will not submit the manuscript or any portion of it without the Author's consent. Only the Author will be permitted to accept or reject editorial suggestions made by the publisher, though the Writer will be consulted.

6. The Author will be the book's sole spokesperson, and the Author's name will appear before and in bigger print than the Writer's name in all instances. The word "With" will precede the Writer's name.

7. The Author and Writer will jointly own the book's copyright. The Author will retain sole ownership of original material used in the book to which she already possesses ownership, and no assignments of such ownership are included or implied beyond said usage in the book.

8. The Author agrees to indemnify the Writer against any damages the Writer suffers due to the publication of any material in the book provided by the Author. The Author will bear sole responsibility for confirming the veracity

and legally unencumbered nature of all material and information that is provided by the Author, including the acquisition of necessary permissions, and will be held solely responsible for paying the costs and possible damages from any libel suits resulting from the book's publication.

9. If the Proposal is used to generate a deal from a publisher, but the Writer no longer wishes to write the manuscript, or the Author does not want the Writer to do so, the Writer will be entitled to a one-time "kill-fee" in the amount of $, to be paid within 30 days of the Author's receipt of first-proceeds from the publisher, in consideration of the Writer's generating the Proposal that generated the book contract. Upon termination, the Writer will automatically relinquish any rights whatsoever to any other payments or any ownership of the material in the proposal, and agrees not to ever use the material or other proprietary information in any fashion whatsoever, and will promptly return to the Author any notes, documents, photos or audios relevant to the book.

10. If the Writer fails to generate a Proposal that is acceptable to the Author, then this Agreement will terminate and the Author will be prevented from using any of the written expression generated by the Writer for any purposes whatsoever, and the Writer will promptly return all materials in his possession provided by the Author and will be proscribed from using any information or material provided by the Author for any purposes whatsoever.

11. If no publishing offers are received by [date], 2010, this Agreement will automatically terminate, unless renewed through written expression attached hereto. The Writer will be proscribed from using the proposal or anything in it provided by the Author without the Author's expressed consent, and will promptly return all items as stated above. If the Author uses the Proposal to secure a publishing deal at a later point, then the Writer will be entitled to the "Kill fee" stated above. Otherwise, the Writer will not be due any compensation apart from due reimbursements.

12. If after entering into a publisher's contract, the publisher refuses to accept the manuscript for editorial purposes and demands reimbursement of some or all of advance payments made to the Author and Publisher as per the terms of the publisher's contract, then both Author and Writer will be separately responsible for returning their portions to the publisher. Any such publisher rejection and termination will also cause this Agreement to automatically terminate as per the terms and conditions stated in Paragraph 11, unless both parties choose to extend it through written expression attached hereto.

13. This Agreement will remain binding upon both parties' estates.

14. Neither party can assign or transfer their obligations herein without the written consent of the other party attached hereto.

15. This Agreement can be amended upon the expressed written consent of both parties attached hereto.

16. All advance and/or royalty revenues derived from the book's publication shall be divided as follows between the parties: Fifty-fifty, 50 percent-50 percent.

17. All revenues derived from any movie/TV/Dramatization licenses or options based upon the book will be divided as follows: 80 percent to the Author, 20 percent to the Writer.

18. The Writer will not receive any revenues received by the Author from the following activities: Appearances, speaking, endorsements, interviews.

19. Expenses relevant to writing the Proposal and the manuscript shall be divided as follows: 50 percent Author, 50 percent Writer. The accounts shall be balanced from first-proceeds received from a Publisher. Otherwise, the party who is due reimbursement will be promptly reimbursed by the other party. Neither party will spend more than $50 without the expressed email consent of the other following an expressed email description of what the spending is for. All expenses must be documented in order to be reimbursed.

(signatures follow)

WHEN THE DEAL IS DONE

HOW TO THRIVE AFTER SIGNING A PUBLISHING CONTRACT

JEFF HERMAN

ADVICE FOR WRITERS

Congratulations! You've sold your book to an established publishing house. You've gained entry to the elite club of published authors. You'll discover that your personal credibility is enhanced whenever this achievement is made known to others. It may also prove a powerful marketing vehicle for your business or professional practice.

Smell the roses while you can. Then wake up and smell the coffee. If your experience is like that of numerous other writers, once your book is actually published, there's a better-than-even chance you'll feel a bit of chagrin. Some of these doubts are apt to be outward expressions of your own inner uncertainties. Others are not self-inflicted misgivings—they are most assuredly ticked off by outside circumstances.

Among the most common author complaints are: 1) Neither you nor anyone you know can find the book anywhere. 2) The publisher doesn't appear to be doing anything to market the book. 3) You detest the title and the jacket. 4) No one at the publishing house is listening to you. In fact, you may feel that you don't even exist for them.

As a literary agent, I live through these frustrations with my clients every day, and I try to explain to them at the outset what the realities of the business are. But I never advocate abdication or pessimism. There are ways for every author to substantially remedy these endemic problems. In many cases this means first taking a deep breath, relaxing, and reaching down deep inside yourself to sort out the true source of your emotions. When this has been accomplished, it's time to breathe out, move out, and take charge.

What follows are practical means by which each of these four most common failures can be preempted. I'm not suggesting that you can compensate entirely for what may be a publisher's defaults; it's a tall order to remake a clinker after the fact. However, with lots of smarts and a little luck you can accomplish a great deal.

A PHILOSOPHY TO WRITE BY

Let me introduce a bit of philosophy that applies to the writer's life, as well as it does to the lives of those who are not published. Many of you may be familiar with the themes popularized by psychotherapists, self-awareness gurus, and business motivators that assert the following: To be a victim is to be powerless—which means you don't have the ability to improve your situation. With that in mind, avoid becoming merely an author who only complains and who remains forever bitter.

No matter how seriously you believe your publisher is screwing up, don't fall into the victim trap. Instead, find positive ways to affect what is or is not happening for you.

Your publisher is like an indispensable employee whom you are not at liberty to fire. You don't have to work with this publisher the next time, but this time it's the only one you've got.

There are a handful of perennially bestselling writers, such as John Grisham, Anne Rice, Mary Higgins Clark, and Michael Crichton, whose book sales cover a large part of their publisher's expense sheet. These writers have perhaps earned the luxury of being very difficult, if they so choose (most of them are reportedly quite the opposite).

But the other 99.98 percent of writers are not so fortunately invested with the power to arbitrate. No matter how justified your stance and methods may be, if you become an author with whom everyone at the publishing house dreads to speak, you've lost the game.

The editors, publicists, and marketing personnel still have their jobs, and they see no reason to have you in their face. In other words: Always seek what's legitimately yours, but always try to do it in a way that might work for you, as opposed to making yourself *persona non grata* till the end of time.

ATTACKING PROBLEM NO. 1: NEITHER YOU NOR ANYONE YOU KNOW CAN FIND THE BOOK ANYWHERE

This can be the most painful failure. After all, what was the point of writing the book and going through the whole megillah of getting it published if it's virtually invisible?

Trade book distribution is a mysterious process, even for people in the business. Most bookstore sales are dominated by the large national and regional chains, such as Waldenbooks, B. Dalton, Barnes & Noble, and Borders. No shopping mall is complete without at least one of these stores. Publishers always have the chain stores in mind when they determine what to publish. Thankfully, there are also a few thousand independently owned shops throughout the country.

Thousands of new titles are published each year, and these books are added to the seemingly infinite number that are already in print. Considering the limitations of the existing retail channels, it should be no surprise that only a small fraction of all these books achieves a significant and enduring bookstore presence.

Each bookstore will dedicate most of its visual space to displaying healthy quantities of the titles it feels are safe sells: books by celebrities and well-established authors, or books that are being given extra-large printings and marketing budgets by their publishers, thereby promising to create demand.

The rest of the store will generally provide a liberal mix of titles, organized by subject or category. This is where the backlist titles reside and the lower-profile newer releases try to stake their claims. For instance, the business section will probably offer two dozen or so sales books. Most of the displayed titles will be by the biggest names in the genre, and their month-to-month sales probably remain strong, even if the book was first published several years ago.

In other words, probably hundreds of other sales books were written in recent years that, as far as retail distribution is concerned, barely made it out of the womb. You see, the stores aren't out there to do you any favors. They are going to stock whatever titles they feel they can sell the most of. There are too many titles chasing too little space.

It's the job of the publisher's sales representative to lobby the chain and store buyers individually about the merits of her publisher's respective list. But here, too, the numbers can be numbing. The large houses publish many books each season, and it's not possible for the rep to do justice to each of them. Priority will be given to the relatively few titles that get the exceptional advances.

Because most advances are modest, and since the average book costs about $20,000 to produce, some publishers can afford to simply sow a large field of books and observe passively as some of them sprout. The many that don't bloom are soon forgotten, as a new harvest dominates the bureaucracy's energy. Every season, many very fine books are terminated by the publishing reaper. The wisdom and magic these books may have offered are thus sealed away, disclosed only to the few.

I have just covered a complicated process in a brief fashion. Nonetheless, the overall consequences for your book are in essence the same. Here, now, are a few things you may attempt in order to override such a stacked situation. However, these methods will not appeal to the shy or passive:

+ Make direct contact with the publisher's sales representatives. Do to them what they do to the store buyers—sell 'em! Get them to like you and your book. Take the reps near you to lunch and ballgames. If you travel, do the same for local reps wherever you go.

+ Make direct contact with the buyers at the national chains. If you're good enough to actually get this kind of access, you don't need to be told what to do next.

+ Organize a national marketing program aimed at local bookstores throughout the country.

There's no law that says only your publisher has the right to market your book to the stores. (Of course, except in special cases, all orders must go through your publisher.) For the usual reasons, your publisher's first reaction may be "What the hell are you doing?" But that's okay; make the publisher happy by showing her that your efforts work. It would be wise, however, to let the publisher in on your scheme up front.

If your publisher objects—which she may—you might choose to interpret those remarks simply as the admonitions they are, and then proceed to make money for all. This last observation leads to ways you can address the next question.

ATTACKING PROBLEM NO. 2: THE PUBLISHER DOESN'T APPEAR TO BE DOING ANYTHING TO MARKET THE BOOK

If it looks as if your publisher is doing nothing to promote your book, then it's probably true. Your mistake is being surprised and unprepared.

The vast majority of published titles receive little or no marketing attention from the publisher beyond catalog listings. The titles that get big advances are likely to get some support, since the publisher would like to justify the advance by creating a good seller.

Compared to those in other Fortune 500 industries, publishers' in-house marketing departments tend to be woefully understaffed, undertrained, and underpaid. Companies like Procter & Gamble will tap the finest business schools, pay competitive salaries, and strive to nurture marketing superstars. Book publishers don't do this.

As a result, adult trade book publishing has never been especially profitable, and countless sales probably go unmade. The sales volumes and profits for large, diversified publishers are mostly due to the lucrative—and captive—textbook trade. Adult trade sales aren't the reason that companies like Random House can generate more than $1 billion in annual revenues.

Here's What You Can Do

Hire your own public relations firm to promote you and your book. Your publisher is likely to be grateful and cooperative. But you must communicate carefully with your publishing house.

Once your manuscript is completed, you should request a group meeting with your editor and people from the marketing, sales, and publicity departments. You should focus on what their marketing agenda will be. If you've decided to retain your own PR firm, this is the time to impress the people at your publishing house with your commitment and pressure them to help pay for it. At the very least, the publisher should provide plenty of free books.

Beware of this common problem: Even if you do a national TV show, your book may not be abundantly available in bookstores that day—at least, not everywhere. An obvious answer is setting up 800 numbers to fill orders, and it baffles me that publishers don't make wider use of them. There are many people watching *Oprah* who won't ever make it to the bookstore, but who would be willing to order then and there with a credit card. Infomercials have proved this.

Not all talk or interview shows will cooperate, but whenever possible you should try to have your publisher's 800 number (or yours) displayed as a purchasing method, in addition to the neighborhood bookstore. If you use your own number, make sure you can handle a potential flood.

If retaining a PR firm isn't realistic for you, then do your own media promotions. There are many good books in print about how to do your own PR. (A selection of relevant titles may be found in this volume's "Suggested Resources" section.)

ATTACKING PROBLEM NO. 3: YOU DETEST THE TITLE AND JACKET

Almost always, your publisher will have final contractual discretion over title, jacket design, and jacket copy. But that doesn't mean you can't be actively involved. In my opinion, you had better be. Once your final manuscript is submitted, make it clear to your editor that you expect to see all prospective covers and titles. But simply trying to veto what the publisher comes up with won't be enough. You should try to counter the negatives with positive alternatives. You might even want to go as far as having your own prospective covers professionally created. If the publisher were to actually choose your version, the house might reimburse you.

At any rate, don't wait until it's after the fact to decide you don't like your cover, title, and so forth. It's like voting: Participate or shut up.

ATTACKING PROBLEM NO. 4: NO ONE AT THE PUBLISHING HOUSE SEEMS TO BE LISTENING TO YOU

This happens a lot—though I bet it happens to certain people in everything they do. The primary reasons for this situation are either 1) that the people you're trying to access are incompetent; 2) that you're not a priority for them; or 3) that they simply hate talking to you.

Here are a few things you might try to do about it:

+ If the contact person is incompetent, what can that person really accomplish for you anyway? It's probably best to find a way to work around this person, even if he begins to return your calls before you place them.

+ The people you want access to may be just too busy to give you time. Screaming may be a temporary remedy, but eventually, they'll go deaf again. Obviously, their time is being spent somewhere. Thinking logically, how can you make it worthwhile for these people to spend more time on you? If being a pain in the neck is your best card, then perhaps you should play it. But there's no leverage like being valuable. In fact, it's likely that the somewhere else they're spending their time is with a very valuable author.

+ Maybe someone just hates talking to you. That may be this person's problem. But, as many wise men and women have taught, allies are better than adversaries. And to convert an adversary is invaluable. Do it.

CONCLUSION

This essay may come across as cynical. But I want you to be realistic and be prepared. Many publishing success stories are out there, and many of them happened because the authors made them happen.

For every manuscript that is published, probably a few thousand were rejected. To be published is a great accomplishment—and a great asset. If well tended, it can pay tremendous dividends.

Regardless of your publisher's commitment at the outset, if you can somehow generate sales momentum, the publisher will most likely join your march to success and allocate a substantial investment to ensure it. In turn, the publisher may even assume all the credit. But so what? It's to your benefit.

FICTION DICTIONARY

JAMIE M. FORBES

In book publishing, people describe works of fiction as they relate to categories, genres, and other market concepts, which, coming from the mouths of renowned industry figures, can make it sound as if there's a real system to what is actually a set of arbitrary terminology. Categories are customarily viewed as reflecting broad sectors of readership interest. Genres are either subcategories (classifications within categories) or types of stories that can pop up within more than one category—though genre and category are sometimes used interchangeably.

For instance, suspense fiction (as a broad category) includes the jeopardy story genre (typified by a particular premise that can just as easily turn up in a supernatural horror story). Or, again within the suspense fiction category, there's the police procedural (a subcategory of detective fiction, which is itself a subcategory of suspense that is often spoken of as a separate category). The police procedural can be discussed as a distinct genre with its own special attributes; and there are particular procedural genre types, such as those set in the small towns of the American plains or in a gritty urban environment. As a genre-story type, tales of small-town American life also surface in the context of categories as disparate as literary fiction, horror stories, Westerns, and contemporary and historical romance.

As we can see, all of this yackety-yak is an attempt to impose a sense of order onto what is certainly a muddy creative playing field.

The following listing of commonly used fiction descriptives gives an indication of the varieties of writing found within each category. This is not meant to be a strict taxonomy. Nor is it exhaustive. The definitions associated with each category or genre are fluid and personalized in usage and can seem to vary with each author interview or critical treatise, with each spate of advertising copy or press release, or they can shift during the course of a single editorial conference. One writer's "mystery" may be a particular editor's "suspense," which is then marketed to the public as a "thriller."

Then, too, individual authors do come up with grand, original ideas that demand publication and thereby create new categories or decline to submit to any such designation. But that's another story—maybe yours.

ACTION-ADVENTURE

The action-oriented adventure novel is best typified in terms of premise and scenario trajectory. These stories often involve the orchestration of a journey that is essentially exploratory, revelatory, and (para)military. There is a quest element—a search for a treasure in whatever guise—in addition to a sense of pursuit that crosses over into thrillerdom. From one perspective, the action-adventure tale, in story concept if not explicit content, traces its descent from epic-heroic tradition.

In modern action-adventure we are in the territory of freebooters, commandos, and mercenaries—as well as suburbanites whose yen for experience of the good life, and whose very unawareness in the outback, takes them down dangerous trails. Some stories are stocked with an array of international terrorists, arms-smugglers, drug-dealers, and techno-pirates. Favorite settings include jungles, deserts, swamps, and mountains—any sort of badlands (don't rule out an urban environment) that can echo the perils that resound through the story's human dimension.

There can be two or more cadres with competing aims going for the supreme prize—and be sure to watch out for lots of betrayal and conflict among friends, as well as the hitherto unsuspected schemer among the amiably bonded crew.

Action-adventures were once thought of as exclusively men's stories. No more. Writers invented new ways to do it, and the field is now open.

COMMERCIAL FICTION

Commercial fiction is defined by sales figures—either projected (prior to publication, even before acquisition) or backhandedly through actual performance. Commercial properties are frontlist titles, featured prominently in a publisher's catalog and given good doses of publicity and promotion.

An agent or editor says a manuscript is commercial, and the question in response is apt to be: How so? Many books in different genres achieve bestseller potential after an author has established a broad-based readership and is provided marketing support from all resources the publisher commands.

Commercial fiction is not strictly defined by content or style; it is perhaps comparative, rather than absolute. Commercial fiction is often glitzier, more stylishly of the mode in premise and setting; its characters strike the readers as more assuredly glamorous (regardless of how highbrow or lowlife).

A commercial work offers the publisher a special marketing angle, which changes from book to book or season to season—this year's kinky kick is next year's ho-hum. For a new writer in particular, to think commercially is to think ahead of the pack and not jump on the tail-end of a bandwagon that's already passed. If your premise has already played as a television miniseries, you're way too late.

Commercial works sometimes show elements of different categories, such as detective fiction or thrillers, and may cut across or combine genres to reach out toward a vast readership. Cross-genre books may thus have enticing hooks for the reading public at large; at the same time, when they defy category conventions they may not satisfy genre aficionados. If commercial fiction is appointed by vote of sales, most popular mysteries are commercial works, as are sophisticated bestselling sex-and-shopping oh-so-shocking wish-it-were-me escapades.

CRIME FICTION

Related to detective fiction and suspense novels, in subject matter and ambiance, are stories centered on criminal enterprise. Crime fiction includes lighthearted capers that are vehicles in story form for the portrayal of amusingly devious aspirations at the core of the human norm. Crime stories can also be dark, black, noir, showing the primeval essence of tooth-and-nail that brews in more than a few souls.

Some of the players in crime stories may well be cops of one sort or another (and they are often as corrupt as the other characters), but detection per se is not necessarily the story's strong suit. It is just as likely that in the hands of one of the genre's masters, the reader's lot will be cast (emotionally, at least) in support of the outlaw characters' designs.

DETECTIVE FICTION

Varieties of detective fiction include police procedurals (with the focus on formal investigatory teamwork); hard-boiled, poached, or soft-boiled (not quite so tough as hard-boiled); and the cozy (a.k.a. tea-cozy mysteries, manners mysteries, manor house mysteries).

Detectives are typically private or public pros; related professionals whose public image, at least, involves digging under the surface (reporters, journalists, computer hackers, art experts, psychotherapists, and university academics, including archaeologists); or they may be rank amateurs who are interested or threatened via an initial plot turn that provides them with an opportunity (or the necessity) to assume an investigatory role.

The key here is that the detective story involves an ongoing process of discovery that forms the plot. Active pursuit of interlocking clues and other leads is essential—though sometimes an initial happenstance disclosure will do in order to kick off an otherwise tightly woven story.

The manifold denominations of modern detective fiction (also called mysteries, or stories or novels of detection) are widely considered to stem from the detective tales composed by the nineteenth-century American writer Edgar

Allan Poe. Though mysterious tracks of atmosphere and imagery can be traced in the writings of French symbolists (Charles Baudelaire was a big fan of Poe), the first flowering of the form was in Britain, including such luminaries as Arthur Conan Doyle, Agatha Christie, and Dorothy L. Sayers. Indeed, in one common usage, a traditional mystery (or cozy) is a story in the mode initially established by British authors.

The other major tradition is the American-grown hard-boiled detective story, with roots in the tabloid culture of America's industrial growth and the associated institutions of yellow journalism, inspirational profiles of the gangster-tycoon lifestyle, and social-action exposés.

The field continues to expand with infusions of such elements as existentialist character conceits, the lucidity and lushness of magic-realists, and the ever-shifting sociopolitical insights that accrue from the growing global cultural exchange.

Occasionally, detective fiction involves circumstances in which, strictly speaking, no crime has been committed. The plot revolves around parsing out events or situations that may be construed as strange, immoral, or unethical (and are certainly mysterious), but which are by no means considered illegal in all jurisdictions.

FANTASY FICTION

The category of fantasy fiction covers many of the story elements encountered in fables, folktales, and legends; the best of these works obtain the sweep of the epic and are touched by the power of myth. Some successful fantasy series are set within recognizable museum-quality frames, such as those of ancient Egypt or the Celtic world. Another strain of fantasy fiction takes place in almost-but-not-quite archaeologically verifiable regions of the past or future, with barbarians, nomads, and jewel-like cities scattered across stretches of continent-sized domains of the author's imagination.

Fair game in this realm are romance, magic, and talking animals. Stories are for the most part adventurous, filled with passion, honor, vengeance—and action. A self-explanatory subgenre of fantasy fiction is termed sword-and-sorcery.

HORROR

Horror has been described as the simultaneous sense of fascination and terror, a basic attribute that can cover significant literary scope. Some successful horror writers are admired more for their portrayal of atmosphere than for attention to plot or character development. Other writers do well with the carefully paced zinger—that is, the threat-and-delivery of gore; in the hands of skilled practitioners, sometimes not much more is needed to produce truly terrifying effects.

The horror genre has undergone changes—there is, overall, less reliance on the religiously oriented supernatural, more utilization of medical and psychological concepts, more sociopolitical and cultural overtones, and a general recognition on the part of publishers that many horror aficionados seek more than slash-and-gore. Not that the readers aren't bloodthirsty—it is just that in order to satisfy the cravings of a discerning audience, a writer must create an augmented reading experience.

The horror itself can be supernatural in nature, psychological, paranormal, or techno (sometimes given a medical-biological slant that verges on sci-fi), or can embody personified occult/cultic entities. In addition to tales of vampires, were-creatures, demons, and ghosts, horror has featured such characters as the elemental slasher/stalker (conceived with or without mythic content), a variety of psychologically tormented souls, and just plain folks given over to splatterhouse pastimes. Whatever the source of the horror, the tale is inherently more gripping and more profound when the horrific beast, force, or human foe has a mission, is a character with its own meaningful designs and insights—when something besides single-minded bloodlust is at play.

At times, the horror premise is analogous to a story of detection (especially in the initial setup); often the horror plot assumes the outlines of the thriller (particularly where there is a complex chase near the end); and sometimes the horror-story scenario ascribes to action-adventure elements. However, rather than delineating a detailed process of discovery (as in a typical mystery) or a protracted hunt throughout (as in the thriller), the horror plot typically sets up a final fight to the finish (until the sequel) that, for all its pyrotechnics and chills, turns on something other than brute force.

LITERARY FICTION

The term *literary* describes works that feature the writer's art expressed at its most refined levels; *literary fiction* describes works of literature in such forms as the novel, novella, novelette, short story, and short-shorts (also known as flash fiction). In addition to these fictional formats, literary works include poetry, essays, letters, dramatic works, and superior writing in all nonfiction varieties, covering such areas as travel, food, history, current affairs, and all sorts of narrative nonfiction, as well as reference works.

Literary fiction can adhere to the confines of any and all genres and categories, or suit no such designation. A work of fiction that is depicted as literary can (and should) offer the reader a multidimensional experience. *Literary* can designate word selection and imagery that is careful or inspired or that affects an articulated slovenliness. A literary character may be one who is examined in depth or is sparsely sketched to trenchant effect. Literature can postulate philosophical or cultural insights and portray fresh ideas in action. Literary works can feature exquisitely detailed texture or complete lack of sensory ambiance.

Structurally, literary fiction favors story and plot elements that are individualistic or astonishingly new, rather than tried-and-true. In some cases the plot as such does not appear important, but beware of quick judgment in this regard: Plotting may be subtle, as in picking at underlying psychology or revelation of character. And the plot movement may take place in the reader's head, as the progressive emotional or intellectual response to the story, rather than demonstrated in external events portrayed on paper.

To say that a work is literary can imply seriousness. Nonetheless, many serious works are not particularly sober, and literary reading should be a dynamic experience—pleasurably challenging, insightful, riveting, fun. A work that is stodgy and boring may not be literary at all, for it has not achieved the all-important aim of being fine reading.

Obviously, a book that is lacking with respect to engaging characters, consciousness of pace, and story development, but that features fancy wordplay and three-page sentences, is hardly exemplary of literary mastery. Though such a work may serve as a guidepost of advanced writing techniques for a specialized professional audience, it is perhaps a more limited artifice than is a slice-and-dice strip-and-whip piece that successfully depicts human passion and offers a well-honed story.

Commercial literature, like commercial fiction in general, is essentially a back-definition; *commercial literature* indicates works of outstanding quality written by authors who sell well, as opposed to just plain *literature*, which includes writers and works whose readership appeal has not yet expanded beyond a small core. Noncommercial literary works are staples of the academic press and specialized houses, as well as of selected imprints of major trade publishers.

When a literary author attracts a large readership or manages to switch from the list of a tiny publisher to a mammoth house, the publisher might decide a particular project is ripe for a shot at the big time and slate the writer for substantial attention, accompanied by a grand advance. If you look closely, you'll note that literary authors who enter the commercial ranks are usually not just good writers: Commercial literary works tap into the cultural pulse, which surges through the editorial avenues into marketing, promotion, and sales support.

In day-to-day commercial publishing discourse, to call a piece of work literary simply means it is well written. As a category designation, literary fiction implies that a particular book does not truly abide by provisos of other market sectors—though if the work under discussion does flash some category hooks, it might be referred to in such catch-terms as a *literary thriller* or *literary suspense*.

MAINSTREAM FICTION

A mainstream work is one that can be expected to be at least reasonably popular to a fairly wide readership. In a whim of industry parlance, to various people in publishing the label *mainstream* signifies a work that is not particularly noteworthy on any count—it's a work of fiction that's not literary, according to circumscribed tastes, and not something easily categorized with a targeted, predictable base of readership. Maybe not particularly profitable, either, especially if the publishing house is bent on creating bestsellers. A mainstream work may therefore be seen as a risky proposition, rather than a relatively safe bet.

Let this be a cautionary note: In some publishing minds, a plain-and-simple mainstream book signifies midlist, which equals no sale. In a lot of publishing houses, midlist fiction, even if it's published, gets lost; many commercial trade houses won't publish titles they see as midlist (see Midlist Fiction).

A mainstream work may be a good read—but if that's all you can say about it, that's a mark against its prospects in the competitive arena. When a story is just a good story, the publisher doesn't have much of a sales slant to work with; in publishing terms that makes for a dismal enough prognosis for an editor or agent to pass.

If a manuscript has to sell on storytelling merits or general interest alone, it most likely won't sell to a major publisher at all. If mainstream fiction is what you've got, you, the writer, are advised to return to the workshop and turn the opus into a polished piece with a stunning attitude that can be regarded as commercial, or redesign the story line into a category format such as mystery, suspense, or thriller. A mainstream mystery or mainstream thriller may contain characters who aren't too wacko and milieus that aren't overly esoteric. Such works are eminently marketable, but you might suppress the mainstream designation in your query and just call your work by its category or genre moniker.

If you've got the gifts and perseverance to complete a solid story, and you find yourself about to say it's a mainstream book and no more, you'll be farther along faster if you work to avoid the midlist designation. Think commercially and write intrepidly.

Please note: Many editors and agents use the term *mainstream fiction* more or less synonymously with *commercial fiction* (see Commercial Fiction).

MIDLIST FICTION

Midlist books are essentially those that do not turn a more-than-marginal profit. That they show a profit at all might testify to how low the author's advance was (usually set so the publisher can show a profit based on projected sales). Midlist books may be category titles, literary works, or mainstream books that someone, somewhere believed had commercial potential (yet to be achieved).

The midlist is where no one wants to be: You get little if any promotion, few reviews, and no respect. Why publish this kind of book at all? Few publishers do. A midlist book was most likely not intended as such; the status is unacceptable unless the writer is being prepped for something bigger and is expected to break through soon. When a writer or series stays midlist too long, they're gone—the publishers move on to a more profitable use of their resources.

If the publishers don't want you, and the readers can't find you, you're better off going somewhere else, too. (See Commercial Fiction or any of the other category designations.)

MYSTERY

Many people use the term *mystery* to refer to the detective story (see Detective Fiction). When folks speak of traditional mysteries, they often mean a story in the British cozy mold, which can be characterized—but not strictly defined—by an amateur sleuth (often female) as protagonist, a solve-the-puzzle story line, minimal body count (with all violence performed offstage), and a restrained approach to language and tone. Sometimes, however, a reference to traditional mysteries implies not only cozies, but also includes stories of the American hard-boiled school, which are typified by a private eye (or a rogue cop), up-front violence as well as sex, and vernacular diction.

On the other hand, mysteries are seen by some to include all suspense fiction categories, thereby encompassing police procedurals, crime capers, thrillers, and even going so far afield as horror and some fantasy fiction.

In the interests of clarity, if not precision, here we'll say simply that a mystery is a story in which something of utmost importance to the tale is unknown or covert at the outset and must be uncovered, solved, or revealed along the way. (See Crime Fiction, Detective Fiction, Fantasy Fiction, Horror, Suspense Fiction, and Thriller.)

ROMANCE FICTION

The power of love has always been a central theme in literature, as it has in all arts, in all life. For all its importance to the love story genre, the term *romance* does not pertain strictly to the love element. The field can trace its roots through European medieval romances that depicted knights-errant and women in distress, which were as much tales of spiritual quest, politics, and action as love stories. The Romantic movement of the nineteenth century was at its heart emblematic of the heightened energy lent to all elements of a story, from human passion, to setting, to material objects, to psychological ramifications of simple acts.

Thanks to the writers and readers of modern romances, they've come a long way from the days of unadulterated heart-stopping bodice-rippers with pampered, egocentric heroines who long for salvation through a man. Today's romance most often depicts an independent, full-blooded female figure in full partnership with her intended mate.

Modern romance fiction is most assuredly in essence a love story, fueled by the dynamics of human relationships. From this core, writers explore motifs of career and family, topical social concerns, detective work, psychological suspense, espionage, and horror, as well as historical period pieces (including European medieval, Regency, and romances set in the American West) and futuristic tales. Romance scenarios with same-sex lovers are highlighted throughout the ranks of vanguard and literary houses, though this theme is not a priority market at most trade publishers or romance-specialist presses.

Among commercial lead titles tapped for bestseller potential are those books that accentuate the appeal of romance within the larger tapestry of a fully orchestrated work. (See also Women's Fiction.)

SCIENCE FICTION

Take humankind's age-old longings for knowledge and enlightenment and add a huge helping of emergent technology, with the twist that science represents a metaphysical quest—there you have the setup for science fiction. Though the basic science fiction plot may resemble that of action-adventure tales, thrillers, or horror stories, the attraction for the reader is likely to be the intellectual or philosophical questions posed, in tandem with the space-age glitter within which it's set. In terms of character interaction, the storyline should be strong enough to stand alone when stripped of its technological trimmings.

In the future fiction genre, the elements of science fiction are all in place, but the science tends to be soft-pedaled, and the story as a whole is character-based. In a further variation, the post-apocalyptic vision presents the aftermath of a cataclysm (either engendered by technology or natural in origin) that sets the survivors loose on a new course that demonstrates the often-disturbing vicissitudes of social and scientific evolution. Such scenarios are generally set in the not-too-distant future, are usually Earth-based, or are barely interstellar, with recognizable (but perhaps advanced) technology as the norm.

Purity of genre is at times fruitless to maintain or define. Is Mary Shelley's *Frankenstein* a science fiction tale or a horror story, or is it primarily a literary work? Is Jules Verne's *20,000 Leagues under the Sea* science fiction or a technothriller—or a futuristic action-adventure?

Stories of extraterrestrial exploration, intergalactic warfare, and other exobiological encounters are almost certain to be placed within the science fiction category, until the day when such endeavors are considered elements of realism.

SUSPENSE FICTION

Suspense fiction embraces many literary idioms, with a wide range of genres and subdivisions categorized under the general rubric of suspense. Indeed, in broad terms, all novels contain suspense—that is, if the writer means for the reader to keep reading and reading, and reading on…way into the evening and beyond.

Suspense fiction has no precise formula that specifies certain character types tied to a particular plot template. It is perhaps most applicable for a writer to think of suspense as a story concept that stems from a basic premise of situational uncertainty. That is: Something horrible is going to happen! Let's read! Within suspense there is considerable latitude regarding conventions of style, voice, and structure. From new suspense writers, editors look for originality and invention and new literary terrain, rather than a copycat version of last season's breakout work.

However, that said, writers should note that editors and readers are looking for works in which virtually every word, every scene, every blip of dialog serves to heighten suspense. This means that all imagery—from the weather to social setting, to the food ingested by the characters—is chosen by the writer to induce a sense of unease. Each scene (save maybe the last one) is constructed to raise questions or leave something unresolved. Every sentence or paragraph contains a possible pitfall. A given conversational exchange demonstrates edgy elementals of interpersonal tension. Everything looks rosy in one scene? Gotcha! It's a setup to reveal later what hell lurks underneath. Tell me some good news? Characters often do just that, as a prelude to showing just how wrong things can get.

The jeopardy story (or, as is often the case, a woman-in-jeopardy story) reflects a premise, rather than being a genre per se. A tale of jeopardy—a character under continuous, increasing threat and (often) eventual entrapment—can incorporate what is otherwise a psychological suspense novel, a medical thriller, an investigatory trajectory, or a slasher-stalker spree.

Additional subdivisions here include romantic suspense, in which a love relationship plays an essential or dominant role (see Romance Fiction); erotic suspense, which is not necessarily identical to neurotic suspense; and psychological suspense (see immediately following).

SUSPENSE/PSYCHOLOGICAL

When drifts of character, family history, or other psychodynamics are central to a suspense story's progress and resolution, the tale may aptly be typified as psychological. Sometimes superficial shticks or gimmicks suffice (such as when a person of a certain gender turns out to be cross-dressed—surprise!), but such spins work best when the suspense is tied to crucial issues the writer evokes in the characters' and readers' heads and then orchestrates skillfully throughout the storyline.

There are, obviously, crossover elements at play here, and whether a particular work is presented as suspense, psychological suspense, or erotic suspense can be more of an advertising-copywriting decision than a determination on the part of editor or author.

THRILLER

The thriller category is exemplified more by plot structure than by attributes of character, content, or story milieu. A thriller embodies what is essentially an extended game of pursuit—a hunt, a chase, a flight worked fugue-like through endless variations.

At one point in the history of narrative art, thrillers were almost invariably spy stories, with international casts and locales, often set in a theater of war (hot or cold). With shifts in political agendas and technical achievement in the real world, the thriller formula has likewise evolved. Today's thriller may well involve espionage, which can be industrial or political, domestic or international. There are also thrillers that favor settings in the realms of medicine, the law, the natural environs, the human soul, and the laboratory; this trend has given rise to the respective genres of legal thriller, medical thriller, environmental thriller, thrillers with spiritual and mystical themes, and the technothriller—assuredly there are more to come.

The thriller story line can encompass elements of detection or romance and certainly should be full of suspense, but these genre-specific sequences are customarily expositional devices or may be one of many ambient factors employed to accentuate tension within the central thriller plot. When you see a dust jacket blurb that depicts a book as a mystery thriller, it likely connotes a work with a thriller plot trajectory that uses an investigatory or detective-work premise to prepare for the chase.

WESTERN FICTION

The tradition of Western fiction is characterized as much by its vision of the individualist ethic as it is by its conventional settings in the frontier milieu of the American West during the period from the 1860s to the 1890s, sometimes extending into the early 1900s. Though the image of the lone, free-spirited cowpoke with an internalized code of justice has been passed down along the pulp-paper trail, it has long been appreciated by historians that the life of the average itinerant ranchhand of the day was anything but glamorous, anything but independent.

Whatever the historical record, editors by and large believe readers don't want to hear about the lackluster aspects of saddle tramps and dust-busting ruffians. Nevertheless, there have been inroads by books that display the historically accurate notions that a good chunk of the Western scene was inhabited by women and men of African American heritage, by those with Latino cultural affinities, by Asian expatriates, and by European immigrants for whom English was a second language, as well as by a diversity of native peoples.

Apart from the traditional genre Western, authors are equipped for a resurgence in a variety of novels with Western settings, most notably in the fields of mystery, crime, action-adventure, suspense, and future fiction. Among the newer

Western novels are those replete with offbeat, unheroic, and downright antiheroic protagonists; and the standardized big-sky landscape has been superseded by backdrops that go against the grain.

Family sagas have long included at least a generation or two who drift, fight, and homestead through the Western Frontier. In addition, a popular genre of historical romance is set in the American West (see Romance Fiction).

Many contemporary commercial novels are set in the Western United States, often featuring plush resorts, urban and suburban terrain, as well as the remaining wide country. The wide variety of project ideas generated by writers, as well as the reader response to several successful ongoing mystery series with Western elements, indicates a lively interest out there.

WOMEN'S FICTION

When book publishers speak of women's fiction, they're not referring to a particular genre or story concept (even if they think they are). This category—if it is one—is basically a nod to the prevalence of fiction readers who are women. Women's fiction is a marketing concept. As an informal designation, women's fiction as a matter of course can be expected to feature strong female characters and, frequently, stories offered from a woman's perspective.

As for the writers of books in this category—many (if not most) are women, but certainly not all of them are; the same observation applies to readers. Men can and do read these works, too—and many professional male writers calculate potential readership demographics (including gender) as they work out details of story and plot.

In essence, what we've got is storytelling that can appeal to a broad range of readers, but may be promoted principally to the women's market. It makes it easier to focus the promotion and to pass along tips to the publisher's sales representatives.

Many women writers consider their work in abstract compositional terms, regardless of whom it is marketed to. Other women writers may be publicized as cultural pundits, perhaps as feminists, though they don't necessarily see their message as solely women-oriented. Are they women writers or simply writers? So long as sales go well, they may not even care.

Some women writers adopt the genderless pose of the literary renegade as they claw their way through dangerous domains of unseemly characterization, engage in breakthrough storytelling techniques, and explore emergent modes of love. (After all, how can a force of nature be characterized by sex?) Any and all of these female wordsmiths may find themselves publicized as women authors.

Romantic fiction constitutes one large sector of the women's market, for many of the conventions of romance tap into culturally significant areas of the love relationship of proven interest to women bookbuyers.

Descriptive genre phrases pop in and out of usage; some of them trip glibly from the tongue and are gone forevermore, while others represent established literary norms that endure: kitchen fiction, mom novels, family sagas, domestic dramas, historical romances, chick lit, lipstick fiction, erotic thrillers. When these popular titles are written, promoted, or both, in ways intended to pique the interest of women readers, whatever else they may be, they're automatically women's fiction.

SELF-PUBLISHING

JEFF HERMAN

Many books in print have sold hundreds of thousands of copies but will never appear on any lists, nor will they ever be seen in a bookstore, nor will the authors ever care. Why? Because these authors are self-publishers and make as much as a 90 percent profit margin on each copy they sell.

Their initial one-time start-up cost to get each of their titles produced may have been $15,000, but after that, each 5,000-copy print run of a hardcover edition costs about $1.25 per unit. The authors sell them for $25 each. When they do a high-volume corporate sale, they're happy to discount the books 20 percent or more off the $25 list price.

Now, we said that no bookstores are in the picture. Then how and where are the authors selling their books? The answer to this question is also the answer to whether it makes sense for you to self-publish. Here's what these authors do:

1. A well-linked website designed to sell and upsell.

2. A well-oiled corporate network, which translates into frequent high-volume orders by companies that distribute the book in-house as an educational tool or distribute them at large as a sales vehicle (customized printings are no problem).

3. Frequent public speaking events where backroom sales happen.

4. Frequent and self-generated publicity that's designed to promote the books and leads people to the website, a toll-free number, or both.

Obviously, most of us don't have this kind of in-house infrastructure, which brings us back to the most important question: How will you sell copies of your self-published book? If you don't have a realistic answer in place, then self-publishing may not be a viable option after all, or at least your initial expectations have to be reoriented.

Why can self-publishers make so much money? Because they get to keep it. Here's how a conventional book publisher's deal gets divided up:

+ Start with a trade paperback listed at $20.

+ $10 goes to the retailer.

- $1.50 goes to the author.

- The first $15,000 goes to set the book up.

- $1.00 goes to printing each copy.

- $? Corporate overhead. (If the publisher overpaid on the advance, then this number goes higher.)

- $?? Publisher's profit. (This is a real wild card. If a publisher is an inefficient operation, than any profit may be out of reach. If too few books sell, there are only losses, no matter how lean and mean the publisher may be.)

A secondary source of no-overhead revenues for both publishers and self-publishers is ancillary rights, which include exports, translations, and audio editions.

What's clear is that the published author makes a tiny fraction of the per-unit sale versus what the self-publisher makes. But the publisher also absorbs all the risks. And then there's the distribution factor...

WHAT'S DISTRIBUTION?

AND WHY DO SELF-PUBLISHERS HAVE A TOUGH TIME WITH IT?

Because everyone else does, too. Distribution is the process that gets books onto shelves, theoretically. Strong distribution does not ensure that bookstores will elect to stock the title. Too many books are published, compared to the quantity and quality of shelf space to accommodate them. You can have a big-name publisher and an invisible book. Distribution only generates the potential for the book to be available in stores, and nonexistent distribution deletes that potential.

All established book publishers have proven distribution channels in place, consisting of warehouses, fulfillment and billing operations, and traveling or regional salespeople who pitch the stores.

Smaller-sized presses may not be able to afford all of that, so they'll pay a 15 percent commission to a large house to handle it for them, or they will retain an independent distributor that does nothing but distribute for small presses.

Brick-and-mortar bookstores are not eager to open accounts with self-publishers. It's too much of a hassle. Same goes for independent distributors.

Several brilliant self-publishing consultants have devised ways to bypass these distribution obstacles. Look for their books in the "Suggested Resources" section of this book.

Vanity publishing is for morons. I don't mean to be insulting. It's just that you end up spending so much more than necessary, all for the illusion that you've been published in the conventional sense. In truth, the only thing you'll get out of the deal are boxes of expensive books that were probably not edited or well produced.

Hiring qualified editors, consultants, and so on, to help you make the best self-published book possible does not fall under the *vanity* label.

CAN SELF-PUBLISHERS SELL THEIR BOOKS TO CONVENTIONAL PUBLISHERS? SHOULD THEY WANT TO?

THE ANSWERS TO THE ABOVE QUESTIONS ARE: "YES" AND "MAYBE."

For the sake of clarity, a "conventional" publisher is a house that publishes books that are written by other people, as opposed to having been written by the same people who own or run the house. From here on, I'll refrain from having to use the word *conventional*.

A self-published book may have sold as many as one million copies (a few actually have), but publishers may still deem the book as virtually unpublished. Why? Because publishers essentially focus on retail sales, and within retail sales, most of their focus is on bookstores. Few publishers have the capacity or mandate to sell books in other ways. Large non-store sales frequently happen, but generally because the buyers have come to the publisher to purchase or co-market the title in question, not because the publisher has been especially aggressive or innovative about generating such deals.

It follows that self-published books that have not penetrated bookstore shelves in any meaningful way can still be seen as virgin meat by publishers, even if sales have been tremendous beyond the stores. As publishers see it, the bookstore represents an entirely new population of potential consumers who have not yet been tapped by whatever other sales activities the author has in place. Interestingly, consumers who purchase their books in stores are different then consumers who purchase books in other ways.

What's also interesting is just because a book is very successful outside the stores, does not necessarily mean that it will achieve the same or any success in the stores. The reverse is also true. Why? The answer should be obvious in a general sense: Consumers who buy books through infomercials, websites, SPAMs, direct mail and at public events, may never go to bookstores. Conversely, consumers who go to bookstores may not be nearly as reachable through these other channels.

At a minimum, publishers evaluate self-published books as if they are untested raw manuscripts, and all consideration will be based upon the publisher's sense of the work's salability in bookstores. At a maximum, the publisher will take into consideration the self-published book's sales history and the author's ability to manifest those results. If it's believed that the author can duplicate her proven capacity to sell books once the product makes it into the stores, then that will add leverage to the kind of deal the author can make with a publisher.

Even if a self-published book did not sell very many copies, a publisher may still be very happy to pick it up if they can see that it has unfulfilled potential once it has distribution behind it. Publishers do not have any expectations that self-publishers can or should be able to succeed by themselves. But once again, even a successful self-publisher may not be able to interest a publisher, if the publisher does not think that the success can be transferred to bookstores.

Why would a successful self-publisher even want to give up his rights to a publisher? After all, the per-copy profit margin greatly surpasses the per-copy royalty. However, there are several good reasons why going over to the "other side" can be a shrewd move. Basically, the self-publisher would want to achieve the best of both worlds. She would want to be able to buy copies of the book from her publisher at a very high discount, so that she can still sell the copies through non-bookstore channels at an excellent margin. At the same time, the publisher would be selling the book in her behalf through bookstores, something she was unable to do by herself, thereby generating new revenues that would not have been earned otherwise.

If one of the self-published author's goals is to use the book as a medium for selling additional goods and services, then maximizing distribution may actually be more crucial than the per-copy profits, and bookstores are a wonderful way to "meet" quality consumers.

What all of this reveals is that self-publishers have to develop a flexible form of logic when it comes to understanding who buys books, and who conventional publishers know how to sell books to. Pretty much everyone buys certain kinds of food and clothing in predictable ways. But until you immerse yourself into the "laws" of the book market, you may be confused at what first appears to be the relative randomness of what books people buy, and how and where they get bought. If you are able to accept the apparent nonsense of it all, and open your mind to seeing through the dissonance into the way the book universe functions, then 2 + 2 will again equal 4, and you will also end up being a bit smarter than you were before.

THE AMAZON FACTOR

Over the last couple of years, many self-publishers have discovered clever ways for their books to reach the top 100 ranking on Amazon; a few have even managed to hit the #1 spot. The same is also true for some conventionally published authors.

Several highly paid consultants have made it their specialty to teach authors how to manipulate Amazon sales. It basically comes down to getting as many people as possible to buy the book from Amazon on a given day, which artificially spikes its ranking. Due to the growing prevalence of this strategy, it's not uncommon for an obscure book to abruptly become an Amazon Bestseller for a single day, and then revert to its natural stratospheric ranking.

The Amazon sales probably have nil impact on brick-and-mortar sales, and the marketing costs to drive the sales probably eat whatever extra revenues are generated.

So why do it? There are many valid reasons, such as: 1) Even fleeting visibility generated by a high ranking might attract lasting momentum and attention. 2) It's valuable and feels good to say and document that you were an Amazon Bestseller. 3) It might achieve specific professional benefits that go beyond simply selling a book.

THE GOOGLE FACTOR

Not only can none of us ever hide, but we can also make sure people find what we want them to.

Google has become the dominant search engine, to the extent that people now routinely say, "Google me/yourself/it/them." That could change, by the way. A few decades ago we used to say, "Make me a Xerox." I can't recall the last time I've seen a Xerox machine in person. Whatever the brand, search engines are obviously here to stay, and will become progressively more precise and invasive.

Like the Amazon Factor, many consultants have emerged who charge top dollar to help people achieve top Google rankings. You can also just pay Google a lot of money for high visibility. One common formula is to pay every time you get a "hit." However, this has been a big mistake for some entrepreneurs who ended up owing a lot of money for a huge surge of hits that failed to generate any actual sales. Everything has a learning curve, and we all try not to be the ones who get smashed into the curve while taking calculated risks. The bottom-line is that search engines, and the Internet in general, are still relatively new frontiers for creative "small fries," which includes self-publishers, to score outsized results.

THE WRITER'S JOURNEY

THE PATH OF THE SPIRITUAL MESSENGER

DEBORAH LEVINE HERMAN

If you have decided to pursue writing as a career instead of as a longing or a dream, you might find yourself focusing on the goal instead of the process. When you have a great book idea, you may envision yourself on a book-signing tour or as a guest on a talk show before you've written a single word.

It's human nature to look into your own future, but too much projection can get in the way of what the writing experience is all about. The process of writing is like a wondrous journey that can help you cross a bridge to the treasures hidden within your own soul. It is a way for you to link with God and the collective storehouse of all wisdom and truth, as it has existed since the beginning of time.

Many methods of writing bring their own rewards. Some people can produce exceptional prose by using their intellect and their mastery of the writing craft. They use research and analytical skills to help them produce works of great importance and merit.

Then there are those who have learned to tap into the wellspring from which all genius flows. They are the inspired ones who write with the intensity of an impassioned lover. They are the spiritual writers who write because they have to. They may not want to, they may not know how to, but something inside them is begging to be let out. It gnaws away at them until they find a way to set it free. Although they may not realize it, spiritual writers are engaged in a larger spiritual journey toward ultimate self-mastery and unification with God.

Spiritual writers often feel as if they're taking dictation. Spiritual writing has an otherworldly feeling and can teach writers things they would otherwise not have known. It is not uncommon to read something after a session in "the zone," and question if indeed you had written it.

Writing opens you up to new perspectives, much like self-induced psychotherapy. Although journals are the most direct route for self-evaluation, fiction and nonfiction also serve as vehicles for a writer's growth. Writing helps the mind expand to the limits of the imagination.

Anyone can become a spiritual writer, and there are many benefits to doing so, not the least of which is the development of your soul. On a more practical level, it is much less difficult to write with flow and fervor than it is to be bound by the limitations of logic and analysis. If you tap into the universal source, there is no end to your potential creativity.

The greatest barrier to becoming a spiritual writer is the human ego. We treat our words as if they were our children—only we tend to be neurotic parents. Children are not owned by parents, but rather must be loved, guided, and nurtured until they can carry on, on their own.

The same is true for our words. If we try to own and control them like property, they will be limited by our vision for them. We will overprotect them and will not be able to see when we may be taking them in the wrong direction for their ultimate wellbeing. Another ego problem that creates a barrier to creativity is our need for constant approval and our tendency toward perfectionism. We may feel the tug toward free expression, but will erect blockades to ensure appropriate style and structure. We write with a "schoolmarm" hanging over our shoulders, waiting to tell us what we are doing wrong.

Style and structure are important to ultimate presentation, but that is what editing is for. Ideas and concepts need to flow like water in a running stream. The best way to become a spiritual writer is to relax and have fun. If you are relaxed and pray for guidance, you'll be open to intuition and higher truth. However, writers tend to take themselves too seriously, which causes anxiety, which exacerbates fear, which causes insecurity, which diminishes our self-confidence and leads ultimately to mounds of crumpled papers and lost inspiration. You are worthy. Do not let insecurity prevent you from getting started and following through.

If you have faith in a Supreme Being, the best way to begin a spiritual writing session is with the following writer's prayer:

Almighty God (Jesus, Allah, Great Spirit, etc.), Creator of the Universe, help me to become a vehicle for your wisdom so that what I write is of the highest purpose and will serve the greatest good. I humbly place my (pen/keyboard/Dictaphone) in your hands so that you may guide me.

Prayer helps to connect you to the universal source. It empties the mind of trash, noise, and potential writer's blocks. If you are not comfortable with formal prayer, a few minutes of meditation will serve the same purpose. Spiritual writing as a process does not necessarily lead to a sale. The fact is that some people have more commercial potential than others. Knowledge of the business of writing will help you make a career of it. If you combine this with the spiritual process, it can also bring you gratification and inner peace. If you trust the process of writing and make room for the journey, you will grow and achieve far beyond your expectations.

Keep in mind that you are not merely a conduit. You are to be commended and should take pride in the fact that you allow yourself to be used as a vessel for the Divine. You are the one who is taking the difficult steps in a world full of obstacles and challenges. You are the one who is sometimes so pushed to the edge that you have no idea how you go on. But you do. You maintain your faith and you know that there is a reason for everything. You may not have a clue what it is...but you have an innate sense that all of your experiences are part of some bigger plan. At minimum they create good material for your book.

In order to be a messenger of the Divine you have to be a vessel willing to get out of the way. You need to be courageous and steadfast in your beliefs because God's truth is your truth. When you find that your inner truth does not match that of other people, you need to be strong enough to stay true to yourself. Your soul, that inner spark that connects you to all creation is your only reliable guide. You will receive pressure from everywhere. But your relationship with your creator is as personal as your DNA. You will be a house divided if you accept things other people tell you to please them while sensing that it does not resonate with your spirit.

When you do find your inner truth your next challenge is to make sure that you do not become the person that tries to tell everyone else what to believe. When a spiritual writer touches that moment of epiphany it is easy to become God-intoxicated. There is no greater bliss than to be transformed by a connection to source of all Creation. It is not something that can be described. It is individual. This is why it is important for a spiritual writer to protect this experience for another seeker. The role of a spiritual messenger who manifests his or her mission through the written word, is to guide a person to the threshold of awakening. Bring them to the gate but allow God to take them the rest of the way. Your job is to make the introduction. From there the relationship is no longer your responsibility. Your task is to shine the light brightly for some other seeker to find it.

It is difficult to believe so strongly in something while feeling unable to find anyone to listen to you. If you try too hard you might find that there are others who will drain your energy and life force, while giving nothing in return. They may ridicule you and cause you to step away from your path. You do not have to change the world by yourself. You need to do your part. Whether it is visible or as simple as helping someone know you care, you are participating in elevating the world for the better. Some people like it exactly as it is. There are those who thrive on chaos and the diseases of the soul. Your job as a spiritual writer is to protect your spirit as you would your own child. Do not give away your energy; make it available for those who truly want it and will appreciate it. When you write, expect nothing in return. While following the protocols of the business world, do not set your goal too high as needing to transform people's souls. If you do, you will elevate your responsibility beyond the capability of simple humans. If you do the groundwork, God will do the rest.

The world of the spiritual writer can be a very lonely place. It is easier to love God, creation and humanity than it is to feel worthy of receiving the love in return. Those of us who devote our energy to wanting to make a difference through our writing forget that God has given us this gift as a reward for our goodness, faith and love. It is a two-way street. What we give we can also receive. It maintains the balance. It replenishes our energy so we can continue to grow and fulfill our individual destiny. We are all loved unconditionally. God knows everything we have ever thought, done or even thought about doing. We judge ourselves far more harshly than God ever would. We come into this world to learn and to fix our "miss" takes. We only learn through object lessons. We have free will. Sometimes we have to burn our hands on the stove several times before we learn that it is too hot to handle. I personally have lived my life with the two-by-four-on-the-head method. While not recommended, it is the only way I have been able to learn some of my more difficult lessons. I have often considered wearing a helmet.

When we connect with our inner truth we can become intoxicated with our own greatness. It is a very heady thing to write, especially if we are able to see our name in print. If we have people listening to what we have to say, we can believe that we are the message and forget that we are merely the messenger. Spiritual writers need to start every day praying for humility. If we don't, and there is danger that we are going to put ourselves before the purity of Divine truth, we will not be able to be the pure vessel that we had hoped to become. The universe has methods of protecting itself. We will experience humiliation to knock us down a few pegs to give us the opportunity to get over ourselves. I have experienced many instances of humorous humiliation such as feeling amazed with myself, only to literally splat on my face by tripping over air. No injury, except to my inflated pride. God has a sense of humor.

On a more serious note, spiritual messengers who are taken in by their own egos are vulnerable to negativity. The information they convey becomes deceiving and can help take people off their paths. This is why spiritual writers should always begin each session with a prayer to be a vessel for the highest of the high and for the greater good. While readers have the choice to discern the wheat from the chaff, in this time of rapid spiritual growth, it is important to help seekers stay as close to their paths as possible. There is no time for major detours. We all have a lot of work to do.

We are all here to improve the lives of each other. We are blessed with living in an information age where we can communicate quickly and clearly with one another. However, technology also serves to make us separate. We all cling to our ideas without respecting the paths of one another. We are all headed to the same place, the center of the maze, where there is nothing and everything all at once. We are all headed for the place of pure love that binds all of us to one another. We don't want to get caught up with trivial arguments about who is right and who is wrong. Our goal right now needs to be how to foster everyone's path to his or her own higher truth. We share what we have so others can find it, without wasting time arguing the point to win them to our side. Too many battles have been fought over who is the most right. We all come from the same source.

When it comes down to it, spiritual writers are the prophets of today. You are here to give God direct access to our world in ways that we as human beings can understand. We need to listen to the essence of the message rather than focusing on who is the greater prophet. In the business of writing, there is no sin in profit. But in the mission of writing, one must not forget that we all answer to the same boss and serve the same master.

You are also a messenger. When you agree to be a spiritual writer, you are also agreeing to bring light into the world. This is no small commitment. Remember to keep your ego out of it. While it is important to learn to promote and support your work, you must not forget that you are the messenger and not the message. If you keep this at the center of your heart and remember that you serve the greater good, you are a true spiritual writer who is honoring the call. May God bless you and guide you always.

REJECTED...AGAIN

THE PROCESS AND THE ART OF PERSEVERANCE

JEFF HERMAN

Trying to sell your writing is in many ways similar to perpetually applying for employment, and it's likely you will run into many walls. That can hurt. But even the Great Wall of China has a beginning and an end—for it's simply an external barrier erected for strategic purposes. In my experience, the most insurmountable walls are the ones in our heads. Anything that is artificially crafted can and will be overcome by people who are resourceful and determined enough to do it.

Naturally, the reality of rejection cannot be completely circumvented. It is, however, constructive to envision each wall as a friendly challenge to your resourcefulness, determination, and strength. There are many people who got through the old Berlin Wall because for them it was a challenge and a symbol—a place to begin, not stop.

The world of publishing is a potentially hostile environment, especially for the writer. Our deepest aspirations can be put to rest without our having achieved peace or satisfaction. But it is within each of us to learn about this special soil and blossom to our fullest. No rejection is fatal until the writer walks away from the battle, leaving the written work behind, undefended and unwanted.

WHY MOST REJECTION LETTERS ARE SO EMPTY

What may be most frustrating are the generic word-processed letters that say something like: "not right for us." Did the sender read any of your work? Did that person have any personal opinions about it? Could she not have spared a few moments to share her thoughts?

As an agent, it's part of my job to reject the vast majority of the submissions I receive. And with each rejection, I know I'm not making someone happy. On the other hand, I don't see spreading happiness as my exclusionary purpose. Like other agents and editors, I make liberal use of the generic rejection letter.

Here's why: Too much to do, too little time. There just isn't sufficient time to write customized, personal rejection letters. To be blunt about it, the rejection process isn't a profit center; it does consume valuable time that otherwise could be used to make profits. The exceptions to this rule are the excessive-fee-charging operations that make a handsome profit with each rejection.

In most instances, the rejection process is "giveaway" time for agents and editors since it takes us away from our essential responsibilities. Even if no personal comments are provided with the rejections, it can require many hours a week to process an ongoing stream of rejections. An understaffed literary agency or publishing house may feel that it's sufficiently generous simply to assign a paid employee the job of returning material as opposed to throwing it away. (And some publishers and literary agencies do in practice simply toss the greater portion of their unsolicited correspondence.) Agents and editors aren't Dear Abby, though many of us wish we had the time to be.

Therefore, your generic rejection means no more and no less than that particular agent/editor doesn't want to represent/publish you and (due to the volume of office correspondence and other pressing duties) is relaying this information to you in an automated, impersonal way. The contents of the letter alone will virtually never reveal any deeper meanings or secrets. To expect or demand more than this might be perceived as unfair by the agent/editor.

KNOW WHEN TO HOLD, KNOW WHEN TO FOLD

It's your job to persevere. It's your mission to proceed undaunted. Regardless of how many books about publishing you've read, or how many writers' conferences you've attended, it's up to no one but you to figure out how and when to change your strategy if you want to win at the book-publishing game.

If your initial query results are blanket rejects, then it may be time to back off, reflect, and revamp your query presentation or overall approach. If there are still no takers, you may be advised to reconceive your project in light of its less-than-glorious track record. Indeed, there might even come a time for you to use your experience and newfound knowledge of what does and doesn't grab attention from editors and agents—and move on to that bolder, more innovative idea you've been nurturing in the back of your brain.

AN AUTHENTIC SUCCESS STORY

Several years ago, two very successful, though unpublished, gentlemen came to see me with a nonfiction book project. My hunch was that it would make a lot of money. The writers were professional speakers and highly skilled salespeople, so I arranged for them to meet personally with several publishers, but to no avail.

All told, we got more than 20 rejections—the dominant reason being that editors thought the concept and material weak. Not ones to give up, and with a strong belief in their work and confidence in their ability to promote, the authors were ultimately able to sell the book for a nominal advance to a small Florida publishing house—and it was out there at last, published and in the marketplace.

As of this writing, *Chicken Soup for the Soul*, by Jack Canfield and Mark Victor Hansen, has sold millions of copies and has been a *New York Times* bestseller for several years straight. Furthermore, this initial success has generated many bestselling sequels.

We all make mistakes, and the book rascals in New York are definitely no exception. Most important, Canfield and Hansen didn't take no for an answer. They instinctively understood that all those rejections were simply an uncomfortable part of a process that would eventually get them where they wanted to be. And that's the way it happened.

A RELENTLESS APPROACH TO SELLING YOUR BOOK

I once heard a very telling story about Jack Kerouac, one from which we can all learn something. Kerouac was a notorious literary figure who reached his professional peak in the 1950s. He's one of the icons of the Beat Generation and is perhaps best remembered for his irreverent and manic travel-memoir-as-novel *On the Road*.

SALES TALES FROM THE BEAT GENERATION

The story begins when Kerouac was a young and struggling writer, ambitiously seeking to win his day in the sun. He was a charismatic man and had acquired many influential friends. One day Kerouac approached a friend who had access to a powerful publishing executive. Kerouac asked the friend to hand-deliver his new manuscript to the executive, with the advice that it be given prompt and careful consideration.

When the friend handed the manuscript to the executive, the executive took one glance and began to laugh. The executive explained that two other people had hand-delivered the very same manuscript to him within the last few weeks.

What this reveals is that Kerouac was a master operator. Not only did he manage to get his work into the right face, but also he reinforced his odds by doing it redundantly. Some might say he was a manipulator, but his works were successfully published, and he did attain a measure of fame in his own day, which even now retains its luster.

I will now share a very different and more recent story. It starts in the 1940s, when a bestselling and Pulitzer Prize–winning young-adult book was published. Titled *The Yearling*, this work was made into an excellent movie starring Gregory Peck. The book continues to be a good backlist seller.

In the 1990s, a writer in Florida, where *The Yearling*'s story takes place, performed an experiment. He converted the book into a raw double-spaced manuscript and changed the title and author's name—but the book's contents were not touched. He then submitted the entire manuscript to about 20 publishers on an unagented/unsolicited basis. I don't believe the submissions were addressed to any specific editors by name.

Eventually, this writer received many form rejections, including one from the book's actual publisher. Several publishers never even responded. A small house in Florida did offer to publish the book.

What is glaringly revealed by this story? That even a Pulitzer Prize–winning novel will never see the light of day if the writer doesn't use his brain when it's time to sell the work.

HOW TO BEAT YOURSELF—AND HOW NOT TO

People who are overly aggressive do get a bad rap. As an agent and as a person, I don't like being hounded by salespeople—whether they're hustling manuscripts or insurance policies. But there are effective ways to be heard and seen without being resented. Virtually anyone can scream loud enough to hurt people's ears. Only an artist understands the true magic of how to sell without abusing those who might buy. And we all have the gift to become artists in our own ways.

Here's an example of what not to do:

It's late in the day and snowing. I'm at my desk, feeling a lot of work-related tension. I answer the phone. It's a first-time fiction writer. He's unflinchingly determined to speak endlessly about his work, which I have not yet read.

I interrupt his meaningless flow to explain courteously that while I will read his work, it's not a good time for me to talk to him. But he will not let me go; he's relentless. Which forces me to be rude and cold as I say "Bye" and hang up.

I then resent the thoughtless intrusion upon my space and time. And I may feel bad about being inhospitable to a stranger, whatever the provocation.

Clearly, the previous scenario does not demonstrate a good way to initiate a deal. I'm already prejudiced against this writer before reading his work.

Here's a more effective scenario:

Same conditions as before. I answer the telephone. The caller acknowledges that I must be busy and asks for only 30 seconds of my time. I grant them. He then begins to compliment me; he's heard I'm one of the best, and so forth. I'm starting to like this conversation; I stop counting the seconds.

Now he explains that he has an excellent manuscript that he is willing to give me the opportunity to read and would be happy to send it right over. He then thanks me for my time and says good-bye.

I hang up, feeling fine about the man; I'll give his manuscript some extra consideration.

In conclusion, relentless assertiveness is better than relentless passivity. But you want your style to be like Julie Andrews's singing voice in *The Sound of Music*, as opposed to a 100-decibel boom box on a stone floor.

TRIBULATIONS OF THE UNKNOWN WRITER (AND POSSIBLE REMEDIES)

JEFF HERMAN

Many nations have memorials that pay homage to the remains of their soldiers who died in battle and cannot be identified. In a way, it seems that the legions of unpublished writers are the *Unknown Writers*. As has been expressed elsewhere in this book, it cannot be assumed that the unknown writer and her unknown work are of any lesser quality than those works that achieve public exposure and consumption, any more than those soldiers who died were less adept than those who got to go home. To the contrary, perhaps they were more adept, or at least more daring, and therefore paid the ultimate price.

No warrior aspires to become an unknown soldier, let alone a dead soldier. Every soldier prefers to believe that her remains would be known; would perhaps even explain what happened towards the end, and would be presented to her loved ones for final and proper farewells. It is much the same for the writer. No writer worth her ink wants to believe that her legacy of expression will be forever unknown. Even if her other accomplishments in life are magnificent, it is still those words on the pages that she wants revealed, preferably while she's still around to experience and enjoy it.

Obviously, in life and beyond, there are many unknown writers. That's just the way it is.

It may just be that the fear of living and dying as an unknown writer is the extra push you need to bring your work to the first step on the road to publication—getting your work noticed by a publishing professional, be it agent or editor. If you are still reading this essay, then it is absolutely true that you are willing to try harder to reach that goal. In recognition and respect for your aspirations and determination, I will provide additional insights and strategies to help you help yourself avoid the fate of the unknown writer.

But let's make sure that your goals, at least in the early stages of your publishing life, are reasonably measured. It is suitable to imagine yourself one day at the top of the publishing food chain. Why not? Genuine humans have to be there at any given moment, so why not you? However, it is improbable that you will arrive there in one step. Your odds will be enhanced through your dedication to learning, calculating, and paying the necessary dues. For the purposes of the lesson at hand, I will encourage you to focus on the more humble goal of simply transitioning to the realm of being a published writer. For sure, there is more to do after that, but we will leave those lessons for other places in this book, and for other books.

WAYS TO BE SEEN IN A CROWD

Established literary agencies, including yours truly's, are inundated with unsolicited query letters (both hard-copy and digital), proposals, pieces of manuscripts, and entire manuscripts. This stream of relentless *intake* easily runs from 50 to 150 uninvited submissions per week, depending on how visible the agency in question is to the world of writers at large. These numbers do not account for the many works that the agency has requested or were expecting from existing clients. Frankly, many successful agents are simply not hungry for more than what they already have, and make efforts to be as invisible and unavailable as possible.

The above scenario only tells of the agencies. It's likely that the publishers, both big and small, are receiving the same in even greater volumes, which is of dubious value since many publishers will simply not consider anything that is unsolicited or unrepresented, period.

How can your work go from being an unseen face in the crowd to a jack-in-the-box whose presence cannot be denied? Here are some suggested steps.

1. Don't merely do what everyone else is already doing. That doesn't mean that you should entirely refrain from doing what's conventional or recommended. After all, the beaten track is beaten for a reason: It has worked before and it will work again. But be open to the possibility of pursuing specific detours along the way. Look upon these excursions as a form of calculated wildcatting. If nothing happens, or if you end up puncturing the equivalent of someone's septic tank, then just take it as a lesson learned.

2. Make yourself be seen. A pile of No. 10 envelopes is simply that, and none of the component envelopes that form the pile are seen. Someone once sent me a letter shaped like a circle. It could not be grouped with that day's quota of query letters; it demanded to be seen and touched and dealt with, immediately. Another time I received a box designed as a treasure chest, which contained an unsolicited proposal. I did not appreciate receiving a bag of white powder with a certain proposal. The powder was flushed down the toilet and the manuscript returned without being read.

3. Be generous. Most submissions are actually a demand for time, attention and energy. During a long day in the middle of a stressful week in the throes of a month in hell, none of those submissions will be seen as good

faith opportunities from honorable people. To the contrary, they will feel like innumerable nuisances springing forth from the armpits of manic brain-eating zombies, with drool and odor. I can recall opening a package to find a handwritten card from a stranger telling me how much he appreciated my wonderful contributions to the business and how much I have helped him and others, etc., etc. I always remember those kinds of things; wouldn't you?

4. Don't be a nag, be a gift. Everyone likes gifts, and nobody likes nags. So why do so many aspiring writers (and others) act out like nags? It's counterintuitive. Of course, nature teaches us from the moment we are born that the noisy baby gets the tit. Passivity invites neglect. Noise attracts attention. What an interesting conundrum. Nagging is bad. Passivity leads to death. Noise can't be ignored. Well, all of that is equally valid, and none of it disqualifies the original point that you are a gift, so act like one.

5. Keep knocking, even after the door is opened. That does not make sense, and it might not be appreciated. But if someone were to keep knocking on my door even after I opened it, I would simply have to ask that person why he or she is doing that, and therein is the beginning of a conversation. Of course, it may all go downhill from there, but then it may not. What happens next depends on the nature of the conversation that has just been launched, regardless of its weird genesis.

6. Don't ask for anything, but offer whatever you can. If that is the energy projected throughout your communications, you will attract due wealth. However, the word *due* is rather crucial in this context. A well-intentioned worm may end up on the end of a fish hook, and a nasty frog may be well-fed all summer. Too often people stop at just being nice, and then they become prey. Is it fair that they are eaten for doing nothing at all? Actually, that's exactly what they asked for, to end up nourishing the needs of others. We must all serve a purpose, and we must all consume to survive. If you don't wish to be consumed, then don't present yourself for that. The universe is a layered place of lessons and challenges, and being a writer is just one of many ways to play the game. Don't just give yourself away, any more than you would throw yourself away. If you value the gems you wish to share, you will discern with whom to grant them, and simply refuse to participate with others.

7. Know your gifts and appreciate them. I can tell right away when I am reading a query letter from a writer who believes in herself and the quality of her product, and I can see those who are not so sure that they should even be trying. Sometimes the writer is apologetic, or even goes as far as asking me if they should be trying. Ironically, the writer's quality as a writer cannot be predicted by their native sense of self-worth. In fact, great

literature has emerged from the hearts of those who are seemingly committed to a life of losing. But there is a logical explanation for that: To each writer is assigned a muse. Some writers may hate themselves while loving their muse, and it shows.

WHEN NOTHING HAPPENS TO GOOD (OR BAD) WRITERS
AKA IGNORED WRITER SYNDROME (IWS)

JEFF HERMAN

I will not be ignored!" screams Alex Forrest, the book editor played by Glenn Close, to her philandering lover played by Michael Douglas in the classic film, *Fatal Attraction*.

What perfect karma, a book editor being ignored, even though her job was not relevant to the conflict. Too bad about the rabbit, though.

It's an inalienable truth that any writer who aggressively pitches his or her work will encounter abundant rejections along the way. You know that. But what you may not have been prepared for was the big-loud-deafening nothing at all. You followed the given protocols; have been gracious, humble and appreciative; and have done nothing egregious. And you would never boil a rabbit. So what's your reward? Absolutely nothing; you have been ignored.

A document stating that your work has been rejected, even if clearly generic, may be a much more welcome outcome than the silence of an empty universe. At least that formal rejection letter reflects that you are part of a genuine process. True, you have been turned away at the gate, but it still seems that you belong to a fraternity of sorts. It's like you're an understudy, or simply wait-listed. Your existence is acknowledged even if un-welcomed, whereas to be ignored is proof of nothing. Nature abhors a vacuum, and any writer with nerve endings will understand why soon enough, if not already.

I write this essay because of the frequent feedback I receive from readers complaining about the non-responsiveness of editors and agents. I have carefully considered this phenomenon and how it must negatively affect the morale and stamina of those who are endeavoring in good faith to be published. I have decided that to be ignored deserves its own category in the travails of writing, and that it inflicts even more pain and frustration than the proverbial rejection. I shall designate it with a logical term: Ignored.

Why are so many writers ignored by editors and agents? I will respond to that with questions of my own. Why are so many children ignored? Why are so many of the poor and needy ignored? Why are so many social problems ignored? I could ask this question in countless ways, and the primary universal answer would essentially remain the same: It's far easier to do nothing.

Let's get back to our specific context. Agents and editors have demanding, often tedious, workloads that overwhelm the typical 40-hour work week (they tend to put in way more hours than that, even though they can rarely bill by the hour or receive extra pay). They are rewarded for generating tangible results, which is most often measured in the form of monetary revenues. Taking the time to respond to writers, even in a purely perfunctory manner, might be the courteous thing to do, but neither their businesses nor their bosses will reward their kindness. You may feel such inaction is a misguided and shortsighted "policy," and you might be right, but it doesn't change the facts as they are.

Does being ignored mean that you have actually been read and rejected? This question can't be answered, because you're being ignored. It's possible that someone did read your work and rejected it, and then threw it out even if an SASE was attached. Why would someone do that? Because it's much easier to and they can't justify the time it would take to answer as many as 100 submissions per week. It's also possible that your submission has not been read and may never be read, because nobody is available to screen the "incoming" in any organized fashion. It's not out of the question that submissions will accumulate in numerous piles and boxes for several years before they are simply discarded, never to be opened. Does this strike you as harsh or ridiculous? Whatever; it is the way it is.

What is certain is that if your work is read and accepted, you will hear about it.

In closing, my message to you is that you not allow being ignored to diminish your dreams and goals. It's simply a part of the process and part of the emotional overhead you might encounter on your road to success. It's also a crucial reason why you should not put all of your manuscripts in one basket. To do so may be tantamount to placing your entire career into a bottomless pit. Making multiple submissions is reasonable and wise if you consider the possible consequences of granting an exclusive without any deadline or two-way communications. Please refer to the other essays and words of advice in this book to keep yourself from becoming a victim of Ignored Writer Syndrome (IWS).

POST-PUBLICATION DEPRESSION SYNDROME (PPDS)

JEFF HERMAN

If you're struggling to get published, then this essay isn't for you, yet. If you're currently under contract, now is a good time to read this. If you have already been published and experienced what the above title indicates, then hopefully this essay will help you heal and realize you are far from alone.

You don't need to be reminded how much passion, fortitude and raw energy goes into crafting your work, followed by the grueling process of getting it published. What you're probably not prepared for is the possibility of post-publication blues.

No one directly discusses or recognizes this genuine condition because newly published authors are expected to be overjoyed and grateful for the achievement of being published. After all, each published author is amongst the fortunate "one-out-of-a-thousand" struggling writers who make it to the Big Show. In reality, people who reach the pinnacle of success in any field of endeavor will often feel an emotional letdown in the wake of their accomplishment. The feelings can be comparable to a state of mourning, as the thrill of chasing the goal instantly evaporates and is replaced by nothing. Writers are especially prone to wallowing alone, as theirs is a solitary process by design, and only other writers who have been through the same cavern can be truly empathetic.

Emotional let downs happen when results don't fulfill expectations. Everything preceding the point of publication involves drama, excitement and anticipation. Butterflies flutter in the belly and endorphins soar through the brain. One day the writer's goal will be manifested in the body of a published book, and the self-constructed dreams will be displaced by a reality that seems to lack sizzle. What follows might feel sad and un-nourishing. No matter how much is achieved, something crucial might feel left behind.

Achieving awesome goals is a reward unto itself, but it may not be enough to satisfy what's needed. The writer's imagination may have drawn fantastic pictures of glamorous celebrity parties, profound talk-show appearances, instantaneous fame and goblets of money. But just as the explosive passions and idealized assumptions of first love might experience an anticlimatic consummation, finally receiving the bound book in hand might prove to be surprisingly uneventful.

Sometimes the publication is everything the writer hoped for, which of course is a wonderful outcome. But for many it feels like nothing much happened at all.

The media isn't calling; few people show up for signings/readings, and perhaps most upsetting of all, friends and relatives report that the book can't be found. Meanwhile, no one from the publisher is calling anymore and they act like their job is done. In truth, most of the publishing team is probably absorbed with publishing the endless flow of new books, whereas what's already been published is quickly relegated to "yesterday's list." A chirpy in-house publicist may be available, but he/she may not appear to be doing or accomplishing much while adeptly saying imprecise things in a glib patronizing manner.

There's abundant information available about how to be a proactive author and successfully compensate for the universal marketing deficits endemic to the book publishing business. But that's not the purpose of this essay. For sure, it's constructive to take practical steps for mitigating disappointments and solving existential problems, but such activities may also distract the troubled writer from the tender places crying somewhere inside. These feelings must be recognized and soothed separate from business-oriented solutions. It's good to sell as many copies as possible, but unwise to turn away from needs radiating beneath the skin.

Seeking or initiating communities of "published writers in pain" should be what the doctor ordered. If done right, such personal connections will help level the loneliness and despair that defines post-publication depression. However, the community must consciously dedicate itself to a positive process. Nothing useful will be accomplished by reinforcing anger, resentment or sense of victimhood. Even worse is unsupportive competitiveness or negativity that pushes people down. And as can happen in any inbred community, distortions, misinformation and poor advice might circulate with a bogus badge of credibility.

Life is rarely a clear trail. If it looks to be, then unexpected destinations are likely to prevail. Writers will eat dirt and wear thorns in exchange for self-compassion and self-discovery. Pain isn't punishment but a consequence that expands the writer's integrity, authenticity and relevance. Post-publication depression is an item on a menu in a script written by the writer for the writer. Never fear the pain, just be prepared to live through it and learn it, and to help others do the same.

WRITING & PUBLISHING IN 2013 & BEYOND

JEFF HERMAN

Writing is innately immune from transformation because the need to communicate, learn and be entertained is organically human, and not provoked or hindered by technology. Computers can process many kinds of information faster and more reliably than the human brain, but they are unable to purely create, imagine, dream, emote, or be a fulfilling social companion for most of us. As long as people have hearts and minds, there will be writers, readers and other kinds of humans.

Electromagnetic energy isn't a human creation, but humans are rapidly mastering the ability to manipulate it. Digital information can be produced in infinite quantities and immediately distributed to all people with current hardware and digital connections. You or I could instantaneously distribute, or advertise, our "unpublished" manuscript(s) to every existing email address on Earth. There are services that can penetrate state-of-the-art spam catchers or stealthily hack away at any website without constraint. You know this because you get unwanted email, and perhaps your account has been "possessed" by parties unknown who used your base to unilaterally "communicate" with everyone you've ever emailed with.

There's no reason to believe that digital security will ever outpace digital porosity. Anything that flows through the digital stream becomes as public as the molecules in the air we breathe. We can and do make laws declaring some data to be propriety, but laws are only for those who either choose to obey them or lack the skills to do otherwise.

Literary agents and publishers receive countless unsolicited digital manuscripts that are simultaneously distributed to ALL of us. The digital age has enabled the pace and volume of random submissions to surge like never before. Cheap copy machines, printers and PCs were huge production and distribution accelerators, but barely a warm-up for what's happening now. The ability to massively distribute content makes the avoidance of massive dismissal the real challenge.

Once upon a time manuscripts and documents required steady hands, smooth stones or nonperishable animal skins. In-person encounters were the primary method for expressing and delivering information. The staggered introductions of paper, ink, printing presses, postal systems, telegraphs and codes, telephones, motorized transportation and radio transmissions, carried Western societies ever deeper into the Modern Age. Communications became progressively less personal, less intimate and more officious. Family and communal relationships became much less binding. It became much easier for different peoples to discover each other, which triggered new economic opportunities and the blending of diverse cultures. But it also manifested unprecedented opportunities for stronger societies to exploit weaker ones, and that tendency hasn't dissipated.

As we become even more digitally connected and reliant, we risk becoming increasingly lonely and socially alienated. Online "relationships" are just that, and can't substitute for the real thing. Physical and emotional distance from others is inherently un-human. Much of the developed world's social chaos and self-destructive behavior is attributable to the breakdown of the undeniable human need to be genuinely intimate and communal. We won't succeed at digitally faking out what DNA demands.

Unfortunately, technology hasn't been an equal-opportunity benefit, and won't be as long as current dynamics prevail. The gulf between rich and poor is unnecessarily growing, not contracting. The vast majority of people in undeveloped countries, and large pockets of people in developed countries, are left behind. Social elites (which presumably includes the writer and readers of this essay) are emotionally insulated from the way disadvantaged people live, and are intellectually deceived about the underlying currents. Elites are conditioned to believe that poor people are envious, covetous, perhaps less worthy, and eager to steal what they want in ruthless ways. This provokes fear, defensiveness, isolation and an unnecessary sense of scarcity. Instead of generosity, we end up with a sense of cold competiveness, besiegement and antipathy towards others.

The media sometimes makes a dramatic show of the world's abundant misery and injustice, which elicits rivers of donations and genuine compassion, though many donors ensure that their names are visibly attached to their deeds. However, there's an absence of discussion about the underlying causes of the world's miseries. The victims are implicitly blamed for not being able to cultivate functional societies, or for being unable to thrive within wealthy countries. It's rarely stated that poverty could be universally phased out everywhere if power, wealth and opportunities were equitably and justly distributed. The dying majority would be remade into valuable contributors to themselves and the world at large. But elites are locked in to not seeing how their societies are systematically exploiting the mineral resources and cheap/slave labor impoverished countries richly possess.

Americans refer to its domestic restless hordes as ignorant rednecks or urban hooligans, and refer to third-world malcontents as incorrigibly hateful of what America "stands for." The word *terrorist* is a catch-all for anyone who aggressively seeks to turn the status quo upside-down. There are many psychopathic bad seeds sowing destruction in the name of justice, but many other so-called terrorists are using the only leverage available to confront truly unjust circumstances. In turn, defenders of the status quo often use ruthless tactics in the name of law and order.

Misguided violence erupts by design when deliberate fallacies about racial, cultural and religious conflicts are deployed to confuse and exploit valid grievances.

People are easily distracted from recognizing the real reasons for their own and other people's pain. As a result, kindred interests are frequently divided against each other through the infusion of calculated lies, and fail to take a united stand against the real reasons for their shared plight.

Violence, regardless of its alleged cause or purpose, becomes the apparent problem and everything shifts to both promoting and confronting it at the expense of constructive solutions. Those who possess the cherished throne of power will assume a self-righteous posture, and claim to be defending a just system against agents of chaos. It's easier to erase those who oppose you for religious, racial or political reasons, and not because they simply want you to re-slice the proverbial pie.

None of the above necessarily represents this writer's point of view, but all of it is germane to this essay and a plausible portrayal of current/future events. Chaos is a consequence of injustice. Power and wealth needs to be evenly disbursed if only for the simple reason that nature abhors disequilibrium, and will invariably seek balance. People can try to obstruct natural laws, but the costs will multiply until the structure either corrects or eliminates itself. Man plans, nature laughs.

Research is underway to combine human attributes and biology with man-made technology. It will be convenient to run a vacuum cleaner or lawn mower with our thoughts instead of our muscles. It will be thrilling to immediately know French by the painless insertion of a "stick" into the tiny piercings (ports) leading into our brains. Eventually, humans could become so physically and mentally enmeshed with high-tech components, that infants will receive "post-partum construction" in addition to any vestigial forms of upbringing that might still exist. The dreaded day may arrive when factions of our species are in conflict with the existence of souls. But as long as there are writers who see and express the truth, there will be hope for positive choices and outcomes.

At their best, writers deliver reality and universal values. Sometimes they may only impress a few, or their words may be dormant for generations before suddenly blooming when needed. Movements and revolutions are shaped, and humans are formed, by what's written. The past is documented and understood on the basis of what's written, which provides a context for future choices. History becomes a guessing game once we go beyond the written record. Memories and oral accounts rarely match the range of feelings and impressions written when events happen.

A steamy romance novel, a practical how-to book or profound treatise, are all equal because each is written to benefit those who need or want them. With obvious exceptions, no writer should judge the merits of what they or others are called to write. The most seemingly basic forms of entertainment or mundane self-help/how-to guides can make very significant differences in people's lives, and the future won't take that away.

Traditional commercial publishing models may not survive into the near future. Today's dominant publishing institutions are burdened with obsolete infrastructures unsuitable for the digital age. They will either fail or be radically restructured. Jobs will be lost but new ones created. Large sums of money will be lost but large capital investments will flow. The dominant brick-and-mortar book chains may lose their purpose for existing, but the mom-and-pop stores and independent presses will be poised to successfully adapt and survive, and will continue generating decent revenues for many years by doing things the old fashioned way for Baby Boomers and volitional luddites.

Book publishers aren't bringing the digital future, they're being dragged into it kicking and screaming. They are being forced to comply with technology and marketplace preferences. Yes, writers who are published by the large houses will be collateral passengers on the roller coaster, as will their agents. But writers have always been the most versatile tool in the shed, and only need the air to breathe and some bread to eat to keep writing. As per the old saying, "And agents tend to take care of themselves as well."

THE INDEPENDENT EDITORS

Over the past few years, independent editors (aka "Book Doctors") have become much more numerous and are more frequently an important part of the publishing process. This relatively new and potentially indispensable utility player has earned a section all their own.

Simply stated, an independent editor is someone who is retained by a writer at a negotiated fee, for the purpose of helping to make the writer's proposal, pitch letter, marketing materials, story summary, chapters, entire manuscript, or any combination thereof, as professionally perfect as possible. These services are not to be confused with ghostwriting, collaborating or co-authoring, as it is not the editor's function to actually write anything, but to merely help the writer reach her best potential.

In-house editors may recognize an unpublished writer's rich potential, but lack the time or incentive to help chisel the raw product into a publishable form, and therefore reject it. In some cases the editor will conditionally reject it with the generous suggestion that if the writer can somehow make it better, he's welcome to re-submit it, which in turn opens the door for an independent editor. It's not uncommon for agents to do the same. Some writers decide to preempt or reduce the chance of rejection by retaining editorial support prior to pitching anything to anyone.

A significant trend, which has hopefully peaked, is the endemic downsizing that has plagued corporate publishing for more than a dozen years. Many excellent veteran editors were granted the proverbial "golden parachute" for the purpose of eliminating overhead. For obvious reasons, this brain drain hasn't been good for in-house quality, but that's for another essay. This displaced talent pool includes more than a few who have edited the most important and successful books that have been published over the past generation. These same editors are now available to help eligible writers reach their full potentials, for fees that are modest when compared to unrelated professional services.

The community of downsized and retired editors lent itself to mutual support and combined marketing efforts. For instance, those who are best suited for memoirs can make referrals to those who specialize in romance. It can be inefficient and lonely to be an isolated freelancer, so forming loosely organized groups came naturally to those who had spent years in offices working with others. The initial groups didn't want to become too crowded or structured, so several new groups have been spawned to absorb the increasing supply of independent editors.

Presented here is verbatim information presented by each of the groups and their respective members. While I endorse the concept of using an independent editor when appropriate, and have confidence in the veracity and quality of everyone listed here, I do not specifically endorse any of them. In future editions, I hope to expand this section by including qualified independent editors who are not affiliated with a group. If you are one of them, feel free to contact me.

Jeff Herman

SCAMS AND BOOK DOCTORS

IN THAT ORDER

JEFF HERMAN

Publishing scams have become an epidemic. I read somewhere that writers are getting ripped off for more than $50 million a year, and some scam artists have even gone to jail.

Let's start by looking at ethics. I don't like ethics. They're like organized religion—prone to promoting arrogance, subjective judgment, and hypocrisy. I do like honesty. Honesty's best defense is the fast and consistent enforcement of consequences against those people who harm others.

The best defense is not to be a victim in the first place. Without becoming a paranoid lunatic, you must accept that bad deeds are hovering around waiting to happen. Sometimes, you may be tempted into being a perpetrator. That's why houses have glass windows and why the universe can't stay angry, or else we'd all have to go to hell. It's more likely, however, that you'll be a victim, not a doer, on any given day; though it's hoped you'll be neither. Both extremes may be mostly, or completely, within your power to be or not to be. For instance, I'll never understand why women jog by themselves in Central Park when it's dark out. And I'll never understand why writers send fat checks to virtual strangers.

To what extent should society protect its citizens from making stupid choices? I've seen smart men and women date and marry morons, with predictably disastrous results. I've done enough stupid things in my life to qualify for the Infra-Mensa society many times over. How about you? Should someone have stopped us? And if we were stopped, might we not have been even more stupid the next time?

Basically, I'm praising stupidity as a natural right and gift. It's unnatural to overly protect people from themselves. We all see what happens to individuals who are excessively parented or to entire communities that are enabled to subsist in perpetual poverty and social decay.

So what about writers who get scammed? Well, they should stop doing it.

+ They should stop sending money to get people to "read" their work, since there are several hundred real agents who will do that for free.

+ They should stop smoking and stop eating other fat mammals.

- They should stop giving money to unproven strangers who promise to get them published, since there are several hundred real agents who will do that on a contingency.

- They should wear seatbelts, especially when in New York taxis.

- They should stop giving money to unproven strangers who promise to "fix" the work, especially since there are at least dozens of real former book editors who can genuinely fix your work.

- They should stop maintaining balances on their credit cards.

- They should always ask for evidence of ability whenever asked for money.

If we, as writers, walk the previous line, then parasitic acts could not exist and thrive. We would not need more laws, more people working for government, or any ethics. Such things only exist in the absence of honesty and in the dissonance that follows.

As a service, I have attached information about specific "Book Doctor" organizations and individuals that I'm familiar with and trust. These are people who either have deep experience working as real editors at real publishers, have "doctored" many manuscripts to the point of publication, or both. Retaining their skills will often make the difference between getting a deal or being a "close call."

I endorse none of these people or the expectations they might create. I simply want you to have a safe place to turn if you need help and are ready to receive.

The following is an actual pitch letter from a fee-charging agency, with only the names and other identifying information changed. Such correspondence is typical of the alluring invitations writers often receive in response to their agent submissions.

If a writer chooses to explore this route, I strongly advise following these preliminary steps:

1. Ask for references. You're being asked to shell out hundreds of dollars to a virtual stranger. Get to know those who would eat your money.

2. Ask for a list of titles sold. Find out whether the so-called agency actually has an agenting track record. Or is this particular operation just a high-priced reading service with an agency façade?

3. Better yet, call or write to non–fee-charging agents and ask them to recommend book doctors, collaborative writers, or editorial freelancers whom they use to shape and develop their own clients' works, or see the "Book Doctor" section in this book. This may be a better place to spend your money.

BEWARE OF SHARKS!

The following correspondence is genuine, though all names and titles have been altered. My purpose for exposing these ever-so-slightly personalized form letters isn't to condemn or ridicule anyone. I simply wish to show how some subsidy publishers hook their clients.

SHARK HOUSE PUBLISHERS

Mr. Bourne Bate
Brooklyn Bridge
East River, NY 00000

Dear Mr. Bate:

Your manuscript *A Fish's Life* is written from an unusual perspective and an urgent one. In these trying economic times that have created despair and anguish, one must give thought to opportunities, and this upbeat and enthusiastic book makes us realize that those opportunities are out there! My capsule critique: Meticulous aim! With a surgeon's precision we're taught how to work through everything from raising money to targeting areas. There is a sharp eye here for all of the nuances, studded with pointers and reasoning, making it a crucial blueprint.

What can I say about a book like this? It stopped me in my tracks. I guess all I can do is thank you for letting me have the opportunity to read it.

The editors who read this had a spontaneous tendency to feel that it was imbued with some very, very good electricity and would be something very special for our list and saw such potential with it that it was given top priority and pushed ahead of every other book in house. The further problem is that publishing being an extremely rugged business, editorial decisions have to be based on hard facts, which sometimes hurt publishers as much as authors. Unfortunately, we just bought several new nonfiction pieces...yet I hate to let this one get away. Publishing economics shouldn't have anything to do with a decision, but unfortunately, it does and I was overruled at the editorial meeting.

Still I want you to know that this is a particularly viable book and one that I really would love to have for our list. Furthermore, this might be picked up for magazine serialization or by book clubs because it is so different. Our book *Enraptured* was serialized six times in *International Inquirer* and sold to Andorra. *The Devil Decided* sold well over 150,000 copies, and we have a movie option on it. *Far Away*, serialized in *Places* magazine and *Cure Yourself*, was taken by a major book club.

I really want this book for our list because it will fit into all the areas that we're active in. Therefore, I'm going to make a proposition for you to involve yourself with us. What would you think of the idea of doing this on a cooperative basis? Like many New York publishers these days, we find that sometimes investors are interested in the acquisition of literary properties through a technique that might be advantageous under our tax laws. There is no reason that the partial investor cannot be the writer, if that person so chooses. Tax advantages may accrue.

I'd be a liar if I promised you a bestseller, but I can guarantee that nobody works as hard promoting a book as we do: We nag paperback, book clubs, magazines, and foreign publishers with our zeal and enthusiasm. We do our PR work and take it seriously because this is where we're going to make the money in the long run. One of our authors hired a top publicist on his own for $50,000. He came limping back to us, saying they didn't do the job that we did, and which we don't charge for. This made our office feel very proud of all our efforts.

I feel that your book deserves our efforts because it is something very special. Think about what I've written to you, and I will hold the manuscript until I hear from you. I truly hope that we can get together because I really love this book and believe it is something we can generate some good action for vis-à-vis book clubs, foreign rights, etc., because it is outstanding and has tremendous potential.

Sincerely,

Eda U. Live

Eda U. Live
Executive Editor

The writer of *A Fish's Life* wrote back to Shark House (all names have been changed) and informed the vanity press that he did not want to pay any money to the publisher to have his book published.

The vanity house responded with the following letter.

(This publisher has probably learned from experience that some exhausted writers will return to them with open wallets after fruitless pursuit of a conventional commercial publishing arrangement.)

SHARK HOUSE PUBLISHERS

Mr. Bourne Bate
Brooklyn Bridge
East River, NY 00000

Dear Mr. Bate:

I have your letter in front of me and I want you to know that I think very highly of the book. Before I go any further, I want to tell you that it is a topnotch book and it hits the reader.

In order for us to do a proper job with a book, there is a great deal of PR work involved and this is very costly. To hire an outside agent to do a crackerjack job would cost you upward of $50,000. Yet here we do not charge for it because it is part of our promotion to propel a book into the marketplace, and it is imperative that this be done. The author has to be booked on radio and TV, stores have to be notified, rights here and abroad have to be worked on, reviewers contacted, autograph parties arranged, and myriad details taken care of.

In view of this, why did I ask you to help with the project? I think the above is self-explanatory, especially when we are in the midst of a revolution between books and television. Publishers are gamblers vying for the same audience. Just because a publisher loves a book is no guarantee that the public is going to love it. In times when bookstores are more selective in the number of books they order, the best of us tremble at the thought of the money that we must put out in order to make a good book a reality.

Be that as it may, I have just come from another editorial meeting where I tried to re-open the case for us, but unfortunately, the earlier decision stands.

As a result, I have no choice but to return the manuscript with this letter. I would also like to tell you that you must do what the successful writers do. Keep sending it out. Someone will like it and someone will buy it.

I wish you every success. Live long and prosper.

Sincerely,

Eda U. Live

Eda U. Live
Executive Editor

NINE SIGNS OF A SCAM BOOK DOCTOR

JERRY GROSS

Working with an expert, ethical book doctor can often make the difference between being published or remaining unpublished. Conversely, working with an unqualified, unethical book doctor can often be hazardous—even fatal—to your career.

You've worked hard to save the money to hire a book doctor. Make sure that the book doctor you hire will turn out to be a good investment. Here are nine signs that someone who claims to be a professional book doctor may be trying to scam you.

1. **A scam book doctor states that you can't get published unless you hire a book doctor.**

   You may hear that editors and publishers demand that a manuscript be professionally edited before they will consider it for publication, or that agents won't take on a client unless the writer first works with a book doctor to polish the manuscript.

   Not true. Agents and editors still take on manuscripts that need a lot of work, but, to be candid, they don't do it too often because they are usually overworked and overwhelmed by the volume of material submitted to them. That's why working with a good book doctor can at least improve your odds of being accepted by an agent and an editor.

2. **A scam book doctor guarantees, or at least implies, that his editing will get you accepted by an agent.**

   Not true! No reputable book doctor can make this statement because no book doctor can persuade an agent to represent a project that the agent does not like, believe in, or see as commercially viable. Beauty is in the eye of the beholder, and editors and agents often see a manuscript's potential through very different eyes.

3. **A scam book doctor guarantees, or strongly implies, that once she's edited your manuscript, an agent will definitely be able to sell it.**

   Not true. The vagaries, shifts of taste, and trends in the publishing marketplace are such that agents themselves cannot be sure which manuscripts will be salable.

4. **A scam book doctor admits (or you discover) that he has a "financial**

arrangement" with the person or company who referred you to him. In plain English, this means that he kicks back part of his fee for the referral.

This is inarguably unethical. There should be no financial relationship between the book doctor and the referring party. If one exists, it can adversely affect the honesty and integrity of his evaluation of your manuscript, or both.

5. **A scam book doctor does not guarantee that she will edit your manuscript personally.**

   Since you are hiring the editor for her specific expertise, insist that she guarantee in writing that she will edit the manuscript herself. If she won't do this, look elsewhere for an editor.

6. **A scam book doctor tells you that he can't take on your project, but will subcontract it.**

   However, he won't tell you who will edit it, and he won't provide you with that editor's background, samples of that editor's work, or any references. And he does not give you the right to accept or refuse the editor he suggests.

   If you do decide to work with another editor because the one you wanted is overbooked or otherwise unavailable, then you have every right to know as much about the person recommended by him as you know about the editor making the recommendation. You also have every right to decide whether you want to work with the editor whom he recommends.

7. **A scam book doctor won't provide references from authors or agents she's worked with.**

   Obviously, the editor won't provide you with names of dissatisfied clients, but you can learn a lot by gauging the enthusiasm (or lack of it) with which the client discusses working with the book doctor. Ask questions: "Was she easy and friendly to work with?"; "Was she receptive to ideas?"; "Was she available to discuss her approach to line-editing, critique of the manuscript, or both?"; "Did you feel that you got good value for your money?"

8. **A scam book doctor won't provide samples of his editing or critiques.**

   Engaging in a book doctor without seeing how he line-edits or addresses problems in a manuscript is akin to buying oceanfront property in Arizona from a real estate salesman on the phone or on the Web. Talk is cheap, but good editing is expensive. Make sure you are buying the expertise you need; demand to see samples of the editor's work. If he balks, hang up the phone!

9. **A scam book doctor sends you an incomplete Letter of Agreement that does not specify all the costs you will incur, what she will do for each of her fees, a schedule of payment, and a due date for delivery of the edited or critiqued manuscript.**

Every one of your contractual obligations to each other should be spelled out clearly in the Letter of Agreement before you sign it. If changes are agreed upon during the course of the author-editor relationship, these changes should either be incorporated into a new Letter of Agreement that both parties sign or be expressed in rider clauses added to the Agreement that are initialed by both editor and author. There should be no hidden or "surprise" costs at the time of the final payment to the book doctor.

A final caution: Be convinced that you are hiring the right book doctor before signing the Letter of Agreement. Not only your money, but also your career is at stake!

Jerry Gross has been a fiction and nonfiction editor for many years, the last nineteen as a freelance editor/book doctor. He is editor of the standard work on trade-book editing *Editors on Editing: What Writers Need to Know About What Editors Do*. He also creates and presents workshops and panels on editing and writing at writers' conferences. He can be reached at 63 Grand Street, Croton-on-Hudson, NY 10520-2518 and at jgross@bookdocs.com.

AN EDITOR OF ONE'S OWN

BY THE EDITORS OF WORDS INTO PRINT   (WWW.WORDSINTOPRINT.ORG)

A re book doctors really worth it? What do they do that agents and in-house editors might not? With all the help a writer can get on the journey from manuscript to published book, why hire an editor of one's own?

Before the Age of the Independent Editor, literary agents and publishing staff were the first publishing insiders to read a proposal or manuscript. Today, however, the focus on business interests is so demanding and the volume of submissions so great—agents alone take in hundreds of query letters a month—that a writer's work has to be white-hot before receiving serious consideration. In light of these developments, a writer may turn to an independent editor as the first expert reader in the world of publishing's gatekeepers.

WHAT ELSE DO INDEPENDENT EDITORS DO, AND HOW MUCH DO THEY CHARGE?

Services. Not every writer and project will call for the services of an independent editor. However, if you are looking for the kind of personalized and extensive professional guidance beyond that gained from workshops, fellow writers, online sources, magazines, and books, hiring an editor may well be worth the investment. An editor of your own can provide a professional assessment of whether or not your project is ready to submit, and to whom you should submit it; expert assistance to make your manuscript or book proposal as good as it should be; help with preparing a convincing submissions package; and an advocate's voice and influence to guide you in your efforts toward publication.

Another key role an independent editor plays is to protect writers from querying their prospects before their material is irresistible. Premature submissions cause writers needless disappointment and frustration. Your editor can zero in on the thematic core, central idea, or storyline that needs to be conveyed in a way that is most likely to attract an agent and a publisher. In short, an editor of your own can identify the most appealing, salable aspects of you and your work.

Rates. "Good editing is expensive," our venerable colleague Jerry Gross prudently notes. What kind of editing is good editing and how expensive is it? The Internet and other sources quote a wide range of rates from a variety of editors.

THE INDEPENDENT EDITORS

The numbers are not necessarily accurate or reliable. We've seen hourly rates ranging from about $25 to well above $200. Several factors account for this spread: the type of editing, the editor's level of experience, and the publishing venue. For example, rates for copyediting are lower than those for substantive editing. Moreover, standards in book publishing are particularly rigorous because books are long, expensive to produce, made to last, and vulnerable to the long-term impact of reviewer criticism.

Process. Book editors are specialists. Every book project arrives on the desk of an independent editor at a certain level of readiness, and the first task is to determine what the project needs. A deep book edit is typically a painstaking, time-consuming process that may move at the pace of only three or four manuscript pages per hour—or, when less intensive, eight to twelve pages per hour. Occasionally a manuscript received by an independent is fully developed, needs only a light copy-edit, and may well be ready to submit as is. In other cases, the editorial process may require one or more rounds of revisions. If you are hiring an editor to critique your work, you should be aware that reading the material takes considerably more time than writing the critique. Sometimes a flat fee, rather than an hourly rate, may be appropriate to the project. Sometimes an editor will offer a brief initial consultation at no charge. A reputable independent book editor will be able recommend a course of action that may or may not include one or more types of editorial services, and give you a reliable estimate of the time and fees involved.

BUT WON'T THE IN-HOUSE EDITOR FIX MY BOOK?

Sometimes. Maybe. To an extent. Independents and in-house editors are, in many ways, different creatures. For starters, in-house editors spend much of the day preparing for and going to meetings. Marketing meetings. Sales meetings. Editorial meetings. Production meetings. The mandate for most of these in-house editors is to acquire new book projects and to shepherd those that are already in the pipeline. With so many extended activities cutting into the business hours, the time for actually working on a manuscript can be short.

Many in-house editors have incoming manuscripts screened by an already overworked assistant. (The days of staff readers are long gone.) The only quiet time the editor has for reading might be evenings and weekends. We have known editors to take a week off from work just to edit a book and be accessible to their authors. These days, too, the acquiring editor may not do any substantive work on a book project under contract, leaving that task to a junior editor. There is also a distinct possibility the acquiring editor may leave the job before that book is published, and this can occur with the next editor, too, and the next, threatening the continuity of the project. All of which doesn't mean that there aren't a lot of hard-working people at the publishing house; it means that editors have more to do than ever before and must devote at least as much time to crunching numbers as to focusing on the writer and the book.

Independent editors, on the other hand, spend most of their business days working exclusively with authors and their texts. They typically handle only a few manuscripts at a time and are free from marketing and production obligations. An independent editor's primary interest is in helping you to get your book polished and published. An editor of your own will see your project through—and often your next book, too.

WHAT DO AGENTS SAY ABOUT INDEPENDENT EDITORS?

"As the book market gets tougher for selling both fiction and nonfiction it is imperative that all submissions be polished, edited, almost ready for the printer. Like many other agents I do as much as possible to provide editorial input for the author but there are time constraints. So independent editors provide a very valuable service these days in getting the manuscript or proposal in the best shape possible to increase the chances of impressing an editor and getting a sale with the best possible terms." —Bill Contardi

"Agents work diligently for our clients, but there are situations in which outside help is necessary. Perhaps a manuscript has been worked on so intensively that objectivity is lacking, or perhaps the particular skill required to do a job properly is not one of an agent's strong suits. Maybe more time is required than an agent can offer. Fortunately, agents and authors are able to tap into the talent and experience of an outside editor. The outside editors I've worked with offer invaluable support during the editing process itself and for the duration of a project. Their involvement can make the difference between an author getting a publishing contract or having to put a project aside, or the difference between a less- or more-desirable contract."—Victoria Pryor

"The right editor or book doctor can make all the difference in whether a manuscript gets sold. A debut novelist, for example, may have a manuscript that is almost there, but not quite. With the input of a good editor, the novel can reach its full potential and be an attractive prospect to a potential publisher. Similarly, someone writing a memoir may have had a fascinating life but may not really have the God-given writing talent that will turn that life into a compelling and readable book. An editor can take that person's rough-hewn words and thoughts and turn them into a memoir that really sings on the printed page." —Eric Myers

"Occasionally a novel will land on my desk that I feel has talent or a good concept behind it but for whatever reason (the writing, the pacing) needs an inordinate amount of work. Instead of just rejecting it flat-out I may then refer the author to a freelance editor, someone who has the time and expertise to help the author further shape and perfect their work." —Nina Collins

"I have had several occasions to use the help of freelance editors, and think they provide incalculable good service to the profession. In these competitive times, a manuscript has to be as polished and clean as possible to garner a good sale to a publisher. If it needs work, it simply provides an editor with a reason to turn it down. My job is to not give them any excuses. I do not have either the time or the ability to do the editorial work that may be required to make the manuscript salable. Paying a freelance professional to help shape a book into its most commercially viable form ultimately more than pays for itself." —Deborah Schneider

SO, HOW CAN I FIND THE RIGHT EDITOR?

You've searched online. You've looked in annual directories such as this one. You've asked around. A personal recommendation from a published writer-friend who has used an independent editor may or may not do the trick. Every author has different needs, every author-editor dynamic a different chemistry.

Although sometimes an author and editor "click" very quickly, many editors offer free consultations, and it's fine to contact more than one editor at this stage. A gratis consult may involve an editor's short take, by phone or in writing, on sample material the editor asked you to send. But how to distinguish among the many independent editors?

Some editorial groups are huge, and they are open to all who designate themselves as editors; it might take some additional research to identify the members who are most reputable and best suited to your work. The smaller groups consist of editors who have been nominated, vetted, and elected, which ensures the high quality of the individual professionals. They meet with regularity, share referrals, and discuss industry developments. Your consultation, references offered, and the terms of any subsequent agreement can tell the rest.

Another way to find the right editor is to prepare your manuscript to its best advantage—structurally, stylistically, and mechanically. Jeff Herman's annual guide, for example, is filled with directions on manuscript preparation, and it is a good idea to follow them. Asking the opinion of one or more impartial readers—that is, not limiting your initial reviewers to friends and relatives—is a great strategy as well. If you have the benefit of a disinterested reader, you may be able to make some significant changes before sending an excerpt to an independent editor. One more element to consider: editors often will take your own personality and initial written inquiry into account as carefully as they do your writing. Seasoned independents do not take on every project that appears on the desk; they can pick and choose—and, working solo, they must.

TALES FROM THE TRENCHES

We hope we've given you a sense of what an editor of your own can do for you and where we fit into the publishing picture. But next to firsthand experience, perhaps nothing communicates quite as sharply as an anecdote. Here are a few of ours:

"An in-house editor called me with an unusual problem. He had signed up an acclaimed author for a new book project. She had written a number of stories—nonfiction narratives about her life in an exotic land. The problem was this: some of the stories had already been published in book form in England, and that collection had its own integrity in terms of theme and chronology; now she had written another set of stories, plus a diary of her travels. How could the published stories and the new ones be made into one book?

"I decided to disregard the structure of the published book altogether. As I reexamined each story according to theme, emotional quality, geographical location, and people involved, I kept looking for ways in which they might relate to each other. Eventually, I sensed a new and logical way in which to arrange them. I touched not one word of the author's prose. I did the same thing I always try to do when editing—imagine myself inside the skin of the writer. A prominent trade book review had this to say about the result: 'One story flows into the next...' " — Alice Rosengard

"A writer had hired me to help with his first book after his agent had sold it to a publisher because he wanted to expedite the revisions and final approval of his manuscript. As a result of our work together, the book came out sooner than anticipated; it also won an award and the author was interviewed on a major TV news program. The same author hired me a year later for his second book, purchased by a larger publisher, and this book, too, entailed some significant developmental editing. At that point we learned the in-house editor had left the publisher and a new one had come aboard. This editor not only objected strongly to one whole section of the book, she also gave the author a choice: revise the section in one week or put the project on hold for at least six more months.

"From halfway across the world, the writer called me on a Friday to explain his publishing crisis, which was also coinciding with a personal crisis, and asked if we could collaborate closely on the fifty pages in question over the weekend. I agreed, cancelled my weekend plans, and we camped out at each end of the telephone and emailboxes almost nonstop for three days. He resubmitted the book on Tuesday, the book received all requisite signatures in-house, and a month later it went into production. This hands-on and sometimes unpredictable kind of collaboration with writers helps illustrate the special nature of independent editing." —Katharine Turok

"In August of 2005, a young woman who had just been fired from her very first job contacted me. She wanted my help writing a book about her experience. I asked if she'd written much before and I suppressed my groan when she said she hadn't, but what she lacked in credentials she made up for in energy and enthusiasm. She told me she had graduated at the top of her Ivy League college class and done everything right—good grades, great internships—to land a plum job at a consulting firm, but when she got there she quickly discovered that she didn't know how to have a job—she lacked the tools to deal with sexist bosses; she hadn't mastered PowerPoint; she believed her female coworkers would be supportive, not catty. She was determined to share what she'd learned to help other young women.

"As we worked together on her proposal, we not only structured her book but found ways to use her youth and inexperience in her favor—especially in terms of marketing. She built up her platform by writing for neighborhood papers, national newspapers, and eventually high-profile websites. All the pieces added up, the timing was right and she landed a great agent who secured a two-book deal." — Alice Peck

"My work on a book about a near-extinct species of birds was greatly enhanced when the author gave me a tour of a California estuary. Guided by his passion and on-site expertise, I was able to spot exquisite birds, hear bird-watching lingo, and see his high-end scope in action. Now I understood the thrill of what he was writing about, and was better able to help him communicate it.

"One of my most challenging assignments was to add action scenes to a memoir by an Olympic fencing champion. Here was a subject I knew nothing about. I tried to bone up in advance through reading, but my author had a better idea. Working his way across my living room floor, he sparred with an invisible opponent, demonstrating what he wished to describe in his book. I wrote down what I saw.

"As an independent editor, I have the time and freedom to work 'outside the book,' to literally enter the worlds my authors are writing about." —Ruth Greenstein

YOUR BOOK MAY BE BETTER THAN YOU (AND THEY) THINK

BY THE EDITORS OF THE CREATIVE LITERARY ALLIANCE   (WWW.CREATIVELITERARYALLIANCE.COM)

As independent editors, we are often approached by writers who are "stuck." They may have spent a great deal of time crafting their manuscript or book proposal, only to find their energy and confidence waning. Some have received repeated rejections from literary agents or publishers. Others may be grappling with confusing feedback from writing workshops, or well-meaning but indiscriminate praise from family members or friends. Suddenly—or gradually—these authors have come to feel that it just may not be worth the effort.

They may even be wondering, "Is my book really that bad?"

Perhaps it's not.

We've all heard stories about bestselling authors who were rejected by virtually every publisher before finally selling their work. Luckily for these writers, they didn't give up in despair. But you can bet they asked themselves whether their work was any good, and if anyone would find it worth publishing.

The truth is, agents and in-house editors are so overworked that few of them have time to tell a writer precisely why they are passing on his work, and what he needs to do to fix it. In fact, many of them don't read far enough into a manuscript or proposal to know for sure whether it has any value. They know that they'll have to reject a large portion of submissions, and so any of a number of fixable issues may trigger their rejection—freeing them to move on to the next in the pile.

This is where a good independent editor can help. She will look at your manuscript or proposal the way industry professionals would view it, if they had the time. She can show you exactly where the weak points are, help you formulate a plan to address them, and guide you along the way. She can help you answer such common questions as:

Why have I received so many rejection letters?

You may get dozens of rejections without knowing why, and what you can do about it. If there are personalized comments in those rejection letters, an independent editor might discern some common thread in them that would help you understand why. In addition, your editor will know the sort of material agents and publishers are looking for, and can help you bring out the elements of your work that are most likely to sell. She can also guide you in defining your market. It may be that with some shift of language or perspective, your book would appeal to a broader or very different group of people than you originally had in mind.

My family and friends love my book, so why can't I get an agent?

Thank goodness for supportive family and friends—where would we all be without them? Yet the fact is that because they are so close to you, they can't possibly be objective about your work. Even a relative who is a published, successful author may not be the best person to critique your book. Enjoy the compliments, but put your trust in an independent editor who understands the publishing business and has your best interests at heart.

How do I make sense of all the conflicting feedback I've received in writing workshops?

Unfortunately, workshops are not always helpful. The group members are not publishing professionals; they may be too kind, failing to point out your book's flaws, or too critical, because they are competitive or simply not knowledgeable. Plenty of good manuscripts have permanently ended up in bottom drawers because their authors received discouraging workshop feedback. An independent editor, on the other hand, can be like a breath of fresh air. He knows publishing from the inside out, and has no agenda but helping you to make your book the best it can be.

I'm really nervous about sending my manuscript out. It's my baby. What if an agent or house editor "rips it to shreds"?

If you're sitting on a manuscript because you are afraid to let it out into the world, to possibly to exposed to harsh scrutiny, relax. An independent editor can be an excellent first reader. She will emphasize your manuscript's strong points, while gently showing you how it can be improved. She wants you to succeed, and understands the complicated emotions authors may feel. She has had years of experience in communicating with writers in ways that they can understand and use.

What kind of publishing is best for my work?

Are you aiming for traditional (commercial) publication, self-publishing, or an e-book? Would you be happy with a limited edition, privately printed for friends, family or clients? Do you see your book as part of an overall media strategy, in conjunction with a website or online marketplace? Perhaps you want publication to help further your career, or even as a stepping stone to a new career. An independent editor can help you define your publication goals.

I've gone over my work countless times and I've done as much as I can on my own. But how do I really know if it's ready for submission?

Working together, you and your independent editor will review your manuscript or proposal, looking for anything that might need improvement. If your work is fiction or a memoir, your editor will be looking at such aspects as character development, point of view, plot, structure, tone, dialogue, theme, pacing, and originality. If you're writing a nonfiction book or proposal, your editor will evaluate your basic concept and idea development, your planned approach and writing style, your platform, and the market for your book.

It's very possible that with the proper guidance and some reworking, you will find your manuscript or proposal is not just better than you thought, but a work you can be proud of and one that will catch the attention of agents and publishers.

(The Creative Literary Alliance, www.creativeliteraryalliance.com, is a group of expert independent editors and publishing consultants who work with authors, literary agents and publishers.)

WORDS INTO PRINT

www.wordsintoprint.org

Words into Print is one of New York's top networks of independent book editors, writers, and publishing consultants. Founded in 1998, WiP is a professional alliance whose members provide editorial services to publishers, literary agents, and book packagers, as well as to individual writers. Members of WiP have extensive industry experience, averaging twenty years as executives and editors with leading trade book publishers. As active independent professionals, members meet individually and as a group with agents and other publishing colleagues; participate in conventions, conferences, panels, and workshops; and maintain affiliations with organizations that include PEN, AWP, the Author's Guild, the Women's National Book Association, the Modern Language Association, and the Academy of American Poets.

The consultants at Words into Print are committed to helping established and new writers develop, revise, and polish their work. They also guide clients through the publishing process by helping them find the most promising route to publication. WiP's editors and writers provide:

- Detailed analyses and critiques of proposals and manuscripts

- Editing, cowriting, and ghostwriting

- Expert advice, ideas, and techniques for making a writer's project the best it can be

- Assistance in developing query letters and synopses for literary agents and publishers

- Referrals to literary agents, publishers, book packagers, and other publishing services

- Guidance in developing publicity and marketing strategies

- Project management—from conception through production

- Inside information writers need to make their way successfully through the publishing world

Words into Print's editors offer top-tier assistance at competitive rates. Brief profiles appear below. For more information, please visit www.wordsintoprint.org.

Marlene Adelstein
email: madelstein@aol.com

Thorough, constructive critiques, editing, advice on material's commercial potential and agent referrals when appropriate. Over twenty years' experience in publishing and feature film development. Specializes in commercial and literary fiction: mysteries, thrillers; women's fiction, romance, historical; young adult; memoir; nonfiction proposals; screenplays.

Linda Carbone
email: lindacarbone@optonline.net

Twenty-five years of experience editing nonfiction for publishers, agents, and authors. Former senior developmental editor with Basic Books. Has worked with Stephen Carter, Alice Miller, Seth Godin, Herbert Simon, Schmuley Boteach, and Paul Bloom. Concentrations: health, psychology, parenting, self-help, business, memoir, and biography. Offers proposal and manuscript evaluations, rewriting, and developmental, substantive, and line editing.

Ruth Greenstein
email: rg@greenlinepublishing.com

Over twenty years' experience with literary fiction, biography/memoir, social issues, cultural criticism, arts, travel, nature, health, psychology, religion/spirituality, poetry, photography, media companions, reference. Cofounder of WiP; formerly with Harcourt and Ecco. Has worked with Anita Shreve, Erica Jong, John Ashbery, Gary Paulsen, and Dennis Lehane. Offers a full range of editorial services, including synopsis writing, submissions guidance, and career advice.

Melanie Kroupa
email: mkroupa@verizon.net

Thirty-five years of editing literature for children and young adults, including two National Book Award finalists and a Caldecott Honor Book, most recently at Farrar, Straus and Giroux/Melanie Kroupa Books. Manuscript and proposal evaluation, developmental, substantive, and line editing on picture books, fiction, nonfiction, and memoir. Authors include Phillip Hoose, Marc Brown, Tim Wynne-Jones, Ibtisam Barakat, Cari Best, and Martha Brooks.

Alice Peck
email: alicepeck@alicepeck.com

Edits, evaluates, and rewrites memoir, narrative, religion, spirituality, and fiction (especially first novels); writes and edits proposals. Acquired books and developed them into scripts for film and television (David Brown to MTV) before shifting her focus to editing in 1998. Authors include Elaine Brown, Tim Cockey (Richard Hawke), Carmen Flowers and Sue Bailey, Laurence Klavan, Slim Lambright, Susan McBride, Kim Powers, Jack Ross, and Hannah Seligson.

Alice Rosengard
email: arosengard1@yahoo.com

Manuscript and proposal evaluation; developmental, substantive, and line editing on books published by HarperCollins, Palgrave Macmillan, Doubleday, Basic Books, St. Martin's, and Bantam, among others. Concentrations: literary and mainstream fiction, history, memoir, biography, science, international affairs, cookbooks, poetry. Over thirty-five years of experience guiding new and established writers. Authors worked with include Stephen Mitchell, Martha Rose Shulman, Larry Sloman, Bette Bao Lord, John Ehle, and George C. Daughan.

Katharine Turok
email: kturok@gmail.com

Manuscript evaluation; developmental, substantive, and line editing; rewriting; condensing. Literary and mainstream fiction, autobiography/memoir, biography, contemporary issues, film, history, nature, poetry, psychology, popular reference, theater, travel, visual arts, women's issues, translations. Over twenty years' international experience acquiring and editing works from new and established writers and published by major houses including Bloomsbury, Dutton, Folger Shakespeare Library, Scribner, and independent presses.

Michael Wilde
email: michaelwildeeditorial@earthlink.net

Provides first-time and experienced authors with all manner of editorial services and help with writing. More than twenty years' experience working with leading authors and publishers in subjects ranging from scholarly and professional books to popular culture, literary and mainstream fiction, children's books, and young-adult novels. Can assist in finding an agent when appropriate.

INDEPENDENT EDITORS GROUP

www.bookdocs.com

The Independent Editors Group is a professional affiliation of highly select, diverse, experienced freelance editors/book doctors who work with writers, editors, and agents in trade book publishing. They are: Sally Arteseros, Maureen Baron, Harriet Bell, Susan Dalsimer, Paul De Angelis, Michael Denneny, Joyce Engelson, Jerry Gross, Susan Leon, Richard Marek, James O'Shea Wade, Betty Sargent, and Genevieve Young.

Years of distinguished tenure at major publishing houses made them eminently qualified to provide the following editorial services on fiction and nonfiction manuscripts.

- In-depth evaluations and detailed critiques

- Problem-solving

- Plot restructure

- Developmental and line editing

- Reorganization, revision, and rewriting

- Book proposals and development

- Ghostwriting and collaboration

If any editor is unavailable, referrals will be made to other appropriate IEG members. Inquiries are welcomed; please do not send manuscripts. Fees, references, and résumés are available from editors on request.

Whenever you have a project calling for freelance editorial expertise, get in touch with the best editors in trade book publishing today to solve your manuscript problems.

Sally Arteseros
email: SArteseros@cs.com
Edits all kinds of fiction; literary, commercial, women's, historical, contemporary, inspirational. A specialist in short stories. And in nonfiction: biography, autobiography, memoir, psychology, anthropology, business, regional books, and academic books. Editor at Doubleday for more than twenty-five years.

Maureen Baron
150 West 87th Street, #6C

New York, NY 10024
212-787-6260
Former vice president/editor-in-chief of NAL/Signet Books continues to work with established and developing writers in all areas of mainstream fiction and nonfiction. Specialties: medical novels and thrillers; women's issues; health matters; African American fiction; biography; memoirs. Knows the market and has good contacts. Book club consultant.

Harriet Bell
315 E. 68th Street
New York, NY 10065
email: harrietbell@verizon.net
www.bellbookandhandle.com
www.bookdocs.com
More than 25 years as editor and publisher at leading trade houses. Areas of interest and expertise: Nonfiction including business, cooking, crafts, diet, fitness, health and lifestyle, how-to, gastronomy, illustrated books, memoir, nonfiction narrative, popular psychology, reference and wine.

Susan Dalsimer
Editorial Consultant
320 West 86th Street
New York, NY 10024-3139
212-496-9164   fax: 212-501-0439
email: SDalsimer124@aol.com
Edits fiction and nonfiction. In fiction edits literary and commercial fiction as well as young-adult fiction. In nonfiction interests include the areas of memoir, spirituality, psychology, self-help, biography, theater, film and television. Authors worked with include Paul Auster, Fredric Dannen, Thomas Farber, Annette Insdorf, Iris Krasnow, Padma Lakshmi, D.J. Levien, Anthony Minghella, John Pierson, Martin Scorsese, and Veronica Webb.

Paul De Angelis Book Development
273 Town Street
West Cornwall CT 06796
860-672-6882
email: pdeangelis@bookdocs.com
www.bookdocs.com
Manuscript evaluations, rewriting or ghostwriting, and editing. Thirty years' experience in key positions at St. Martin's Press, E. P. Dutton, and Kodansha America. Special expertise in history, current affairs, music, biography, literature, translations, popular science. Authors worked with: Delany sisters, Mike Royko, Peter Guralnick, Barbara Pym, Alexander Dubcek.

Michael Denneny
459 Columbus Ave. Box 204
New York, NY 10024
212-362-3241
email: MLDenneny@aol.com
Thirty-four years' editorial experience at the University of Chicago Press, the Macmillan Company, St. Martin's Press and Crown Publishing. Works on both fiction and nonfiction manuscripts for publishers, literary agents and authors, doing editorial evaluations, structural work on manuscripts, and complete line editing, as well as helping with the preparation of book proposals. Published, among others, Ntozake Shange, Buckminster Fuller, G. Gordon Liddy, Linda Barnes, Joan Hess and Steven Saylor. Has won the Lambda Literary Award for Editing (1993), the Literary Market Place Editor of the Year Award (1994) and the Publishing Triangle Editor's Award (2002).

Joyce Engelson
1160 Fifth Avenue, #402
New York, NY 10029
Sympathetic, hands-on editing; goal: commercial publication. Forty years' experience. Concentrations: Thrillers, mysteries, literary and first novels; health, psychology, mind/body, women's issues, American history, pop culture, sports, comedy ("best sense of humor in the biz"—try me!). Authors include Richard Condon, Norman Cousins, Gael Greene. And me.

Jerry Gross
63 Grand Street
Croton-on-Hudson, NY 10520-2518
email: GrosAssoc@aol.com
More than forty years of specific, problem-solving critiquing, line editing, restructuring, and rewriting of mainstream and literary fiction and nonfiction manuscripts and proposals. Specialties: Male-oriented escape fiction, popular psychology, and pop culture. My goal is to make the manuscript as effective and salable as possible.

Susan Leon
21 Howell Avenue
Larchmont, NY 10538
fax: 914-833-1429
Editor specializing in preparation of book proposals and collaborations, including two *New York Times* bestsellers. Fiction: All areas—commercial, literary, historical, and women's topics. Nonfiction: History, biography, memoir, autobiography, women's issues, family, lifestyle, design, travel, food. Also, law, education, information, and reference guides.

Richard Marek
240 Hillspoint Road
Westport, CT 06880
203-341-8607
Former President and Publisher of E. P. Dutton specializes in editing and ghost-writing. Edited Robert Ludlum's first nine books, James Baldwin's last five, and Thomas Harris's *Silence of the Lambs*. As ghostwriter, collaborated on six books, among them a novel that sold 225,000 copies in hardcover and more than 2 million in paperback.

James O'Shea Wade
1565 Baptist Church Road
Yorktown Heights, NY 10598
voice/fax: 914-962-4619
With 30 years' experience as Editor-in-Chief and Executive Editor for major publishers, including Crown/Random House, Macmillan, Dell, and Rawson-Wade, I edit and ghostwrite in all nonfiction areas and specialize in business, science, history, biography, and military. Also edit all types of fiction, prepare book proposals, and evaluate manuscripts.

Betty Kelly Sargent
212-486-1531   fax: 212-759-3933
email: bsargent@earthlink.net
Betty Kelly Sargent is a veteran book and magazine editor with over 30 years of experience in the publishing business. Most recently she was editor-in-chief of William Morrow and before that books and fiction editor at *Cosmopolitan Magazine*. She has been an executive editor at large at HarperCollins and executive editor of Delacorte Press, and started out as a senior editor at Dell Books. Now a writer and freelance editor, she is co-author of *Beautiful Bones Without Hormones* with Leon Root, MD, *What Every Daughter Wants Her Mother to Know* and *What Every Daughter Wants Her Father to Know* with Betsy Perry. She specializes in women's fiction as well as memoir, diet, health, lifestyle, self-help and general nonfiction.

Genevieve Young
30 Park Avenue
New York, NY 10016
fax: 212-683-9780
Detailed analysis of manuscripts, including structure, development, and line editing. Areas of special interest include biography, autobiography, medicine, animals, modern Chinese history, and all works with a storyline, whether fiction or nonfiction.

THE CONSULTING EDITORS ALLIANCE

The Consulting Editors Alliance is a group of highly skilled independent book editors, each with a minimum of 15 years' New York publishing experience.

We offer a broad range of services, in both fiction and nonfiction areas. These services include development of book proposals, in-depth evaluation of manuscripts; project development; line editing and rewriting; "book doctoring"; and collaboration and ghostwriting.

We work with writers both published and unpublished, literary agents, packagers and editors at major publishers and at small presses across the country.

Arnold Dolin
212-874-3419   fax: 212-580-2312
email: abdolin@consulting-editors.com
Specialties: Contemporary issues/politics, popular psychology, business, memoir/biography, literary fiction, gay fiction, theater, films, music. Arnold Dolin has held various editorial and executive positions during his nearly five decades in publishing. Most recently he was senior vice-president and associate publisher at Dutton Plume. He has edited a wide range of fiction and nonfiction, including *The Cause Is Mankind* by Hubert Humphrey, *On Escalation* by Herman Kahn, *Martha Graham: A Biography* by Don McDonagh, *With Child* by Phyllis Chesler, *Parachutes and Kisses* by Erica Jong, several books by Leonard Maltin, *Cures* and *Stonewall* by Martin Duberman, *Inside Intel* by Tim Jackson, *Defending the Spirit* by Randall Robinson, and *RFK* by C. David Heymann. His services are available as an editor and a consultant.

Moira Duggan
914-234-7937   fax: 914-234-7937-*51
email: mduggan@consulting-editors.com
Specialties: Self-help, health, sports (especially equestrian), travel, nature, architecture, illustrated books, biography. Moira Duggan offers critique and solutions in all phases of adult nonfiction book development: concept, presentation, writing style, factual soundness. Whether as an editor, collaborator or ghost, she aims for excellence of content and peak marketability in every project. Before turning freelance, she was managing editor at The Ridge Press, which conceived and produced quality illustrated books. She has written eight nonfiction titles, including *Family Connections: Parenting Your Grown Children* (coauthor), *The Golden Guide to Horses*, and *New York*. Her editorial philosophy: Respect and guide the writer; be committed, tactful and reliable; deliver on time.

Sandi Gelles-Cole
914-679-7630

email: sgelles-cole@consulting-editors.com

Specialties: Commercial fiction and nonfiction. Other: First novels; "wellness" issues for women; general fiction or nonfiction on behalf of nonwriter experts or celebrities. Sandi Gelles-Cole founded Gelles-Cole Literary Enterprises in 1983, after eleven years as an acquisitions editor for major New York publishers. Strong points include: developing concept and integrating for fiction and nonfiction, concretizing concept and integrating it throughout the work; for fiction: structuring plot, developing subplot, deepening characterization, collaboration, rewriting, preparing proposals. Some authors Sandi Gelles-Cole has worked with: Danielle Steel, Alan Dershowitz, Victoria Gotti, Christiane Northrup, Rita (Mrs. Patrick) Ewing, and Chris Gilson, whose first novel, *Crazy for Cornelia*, was sold in an overnight preemptive sale as a major hardcover and became a *Los Angeles Times* bestseller.

David Groff

212-645-8910

email: dgroff@consulting-editors.com

Specialties: Fiction, biography/memoir, science, current affairs. David Groff is a poet, writer, and independent editor focusing on narrative. For the last eleven years, he has worked with literary and popular novelists, memorists, journalists, and scientists whose books have been published by Atria, Bantam, HarperCollins, Hyperion, Little Brown, Miramax, Putnam, St. Martin's, Wiley, and other publishers. For twelve years he was an editor at Crown, publishing books by humorist Dave Barry, novelists Colin Harrison and Paul Monette, and journalists Patrice Gaines, Michael D'Antonio, and Frank Browning. He co-authored *The Crisis of Desire: AIDS and the Fate of Gay Brotherhood* by Robin Hardy, and *An American Family*, with Jon and Michael Galluccio. David's book *Theory of Devolution* was published in 2002 as part of the National Poetry Series.

Hilary Hinzmann

212-942-0771

email: hhinzmann@consulting-editors.com

Specialties: History, science, technology, business, sports, music, political/social issues, biography/memoir and fiction. Formerly an editor at W.W. Norton, Hilary Hinzmann has edited *New York Times Book Review* Notable Books of the Year in both fiction and nonfiction. Books he has worked on include *Winfield: A Player's Life* by Dave Winfield and Tom Parker (a *New York Times* bestseller), *Marsalis on Music* by Wynton Marsalis, *Virgil Thomson: Composer on the Aisle* by Anthony Tommasini, *The Perez Family* by Christine Bell, the Kevin Kerney mystery series by Michael McGarrity and *The Symbolic Species: The Coevolution of Language and the Brain* by Terrence W. Deacon. He is now assisting fiction and nonfiction writers with development of their work, editing manuscripts for publishers, ghostwriting and cowriting.

Judith Kern

212-249-5871   fax: 212-249-4954

email: kernjt@aol.com

Specialties: Self-help, spirituality, lifestyle, food, health and diet. Other: Mysteries, women's fiction. Judith Kern was an in-house editor for more than twenty-five years, most recently a senior editor at Doubleday, before becoming an independent editor and writer. She has worked with well-known fiction writers including Charlotte Vale Allen, Jon Hassler, Bette Pesetsky, and Patricia Volk, and Edgar award-winning mystery writers Mary Willis Walker and John Morgan Wilson. Her bestselling and award-winning cookbook authors include Alfred Portale, Pino Luongo, Michael Lomonaco, and Madeleine Kamman. She has collaborated with Jennifer Workman on *Stop Your Cravings* (The Free Press); with Joe Caruso on *The Power of Losing Control* (Gotham); and with Dr. Jane Greer on *The Afterlife Connection* (St. Martin's Press). She also worked with Alan Morinis on *Climbing Jacob's Ladder* (Broadway); Dr. Arlene Churn on *The End Is Just the Beginning* (Doubleday/Harlem Moon); and Ivan Richmond on *Growing Up Zen in America* (Atria). She is a member of the Author's Guild, The James Beard Society, and the International Association of Culinary Professionals.

Danelle McCafferty

212-877-9416   fax: 212-877-9486

email: dmccafferty@consulting-editors.com

Specialties: Thrillers, mysteries, women's contemporary and historical fiction, romances and inspirational novels. Other: Self-help, religion/spirituality, theater and true crime. A former senior editor at Bantam Books, Danelle McCafferty started her own editorial services business in 1990. She works on all stages of a manuscript, from outline and plot development to line editing and/or rewriting. Over the past twenty-five years, she has edited bestselling novels by Tom Robbins, Dana Fuller Ross, Peter Clement, Frank Perretti, Nora Roberts, Patricia Matthews and Janelle Taylor, among others. Nonfiction authors include Bill Ury (negotiating), Ed Jablonski (theater), and Eileen MacNamara (true crime). As editorial director for a packager, she oversaw six highly successful mystery series. The author of two nonfiction books and numerous articles, she is a member of the American Society of Journalists and Authors and the Editorial Freelancers Association.

Nancy Nicholas

email: nnicholas@consulting-editors.com

Specialties: Fiction, including first novels, historical fiction, and mysteries; biographies and autobiographies, history, theater, hobbies, and gay issues. Nancy Nicholas has worked at three book publishers and three magazines in a variety of roles. In eighteen years at Knopf, she worked on literary and popular fiction, serious nonfiction, and translations. At Simon & Schuster, she edited fiction and nonfiction by a number of celebrities, including Joan Collins, Marlene Dietrich's daughter Maria Riva, Jerry Falwell, Jesse Jackson, Shirley Conran, and Shelley Winters. At

Doubleday, she worked on the revised Amy Vanderbilt etiquette book. She was also a senior editor at *Vogue*, *Mirabella*, and *Connoisseur* magazines. Since becoming a freelancer, Nicholas has handled projects for many publishers, from editing Nick Malgieri's baking books and Michael Lee West's "Crazy Lady" Southern fiction to riding herd on the project that became Bill Gates's *The Road Ahead* and writing *Cooking for Madam* with Marta Sgubin, Jacqueline Kennedy Onassis's cook.

Joan B. Sanger

voice/fax: 212-501-9352

email: jsanger@consulting-editors.com

Specialties: Mainstream commercial fiction, primarily legal and medical thrillers, mysteries, contemporary women's fiction. Other: Structuring nonfiction proposals, biography and autobiography. Joan Sanger has been an independent editorial consultant for over ten years, primarily developing and editing commercial fiction. Her referrals come from agents, publishers and private clients. Her authors, who are published by Berkeley, Warner Books, HarperCollins, and Simon & Schuster, include Gary Birken, MD, an author of medical thrillers who is working on his fourth novel, James Grippando, and Bonnie Comfort. Prior to setting up her consultancy she was a senior editor for fifteen years at Simon & Schuster, founder, vice-president and editor-in-chief of the hardcover division of New American Library, and vice-president and senior editor at G.P. Putnam. Among her best-selling authors are Irving Wallace, Kitty Kelley, Anne Tolstoi Wallach, Henry Fonda, and Arthur Ashe. She has been a member of the Women's Media Group for twenty years.

Carol Southern

email: csouthern@consulting-editors.com

Specialties: Personal growth, relationships, spiritual/inspirational, health/beauty, women's issues, biography, memoir, lifestyle. Carol Southern is a consultant, editor, book doctor, and ghostwriter. Prior to starting her own business in 1998, she held editorial and executive positions at Crown and Random House, where she was publisher of her own imprint, Carol Southern Books. She has edited many successful authors, including Donald Kauffman, *Color*; Ron Chin, *Feng Shui Revealed*; Sonia Choquette, *The Psychic Pathway*; biographer Carol Brightman; and Pulitzer Prize winners Naifeh and Smith (*Jackson Pollock*), as well as bestselling lifestyle authors Martha Stewart, Lee Bailey, and Chris Madden.

Karl Weber

voice/fax: 914-238-6929

email: kweber@consulting-editors.com

Specialties: Business, including management, personal finance and business narratives; also current affairs, politics, popular reference, and religious/spiritual. Karl Weber is a writer, book developer and editor specializing in nonfiction, with a focus on business-related topics. In fifteen years as an editor and publisher with McGraw-Hill, the American Management Association, John Wiley & Sons and Times Business/Random House, Weber edited many bestsellers in fields such as management, investing, careers, business narratives and memoirs. He helped to create Wiley's acclaimed *Portable MBA* book series, and, when *Worth* magazine in 1997 selected the fifteen best investment books of the past 150 years, two were titles edited by Weber. He also edited three bestselling books by former President Jimmy Carter, *Living Faith*, *Sources of Strength*, and *An Hour Before Daylight*.

THE EDITORS CIRCLE

www.theeditorscircle.com

We are a group of independent book editors with more than 100 years of collective experience on staff with major New York book publishers. We have come together to offer our skills and experience to writers who need help bringing their book projects from ideas or finished manuscripts to well-published books.

As publishing consultants (or "book doctors"), we offer a variety of editorial services that include defining and positioning manuscripts in the marketplace; evaluating and critiquing complete or partial manuscripts and book proposals; editing, ghostwriting, or collaborating on manuscripts and proposals; offering referrals to agents and publishers; helping authors develop platforms and query letters; and consulting on publicity and marketing.

So if you need help refining your book idea, editing or restructuring your manuscript, or defining and positioning your project in the marketplace, the book publishing professionals of The Editors Circle can offer you the editorial services you seek, a successful track record of projects placed and published, and the behind-the-scenes, hands-on experience that can help you take your idea or manuscript wherever you want it to go.

The editorial professionals of The Editors Circle include:

Bonny V. Fetterman
Editing and consulting: Academic and popular nonfiction, with special expertise in Judaica and books of Jewish interest (Jewish history, literature, religion, culture, and Bible); general nonfiction (history, biography, memoirs); works of scholarship (social sciences). Currently based: Jamaica, New York. Previous on-staff experience: senior editor of Schocken Books (15 years). Currently literary editor of *Reform Judaism* magazine.

Rob Kaplan

Editing, ghostwriting, and collaborating on nonfiction books and book proposals, including business, self-help, popular psychology, parenting, history, and other subjects. Currently based: Cortlandt Manor, New York. Previous on-staff experience: AMACOM Books (American Management Association), Macmillan, Prentice Hall, HarperCollins.

Beth Lieberman

Editing, collaborating, and proposal preparation: Parenting, psychology/motivational, women's issues, Los Angeles–interest, memoir, Judaica; commercial women's fiction, general fiction. Currently based: Los Angeles, California. Previous on-staff experience: New American Library (NAL), Warner Books, Kensington Publishing, Dove Books and Audio, NewStar Press.

John Paine

Commercial and literary fiction, including thrillers, women's suspense, historical, African American, and mystery. Trade nonfiction, including adventure, memoirs, true crime, history, and sports. Currently based: Montclair, New Jersey. Previous on-staff experience: Dutton, New American Library, Prentice Hall.

Susan A. Schwartz

Ghostwriting: fitness, memoirs, other nonfiction subjects. Nonfiction editing: Popular health, parenting, business, relationships, memoirs; popular reference books (all subjects); book proposals, assessments, and evaluations; corporate marketing publications (histories, biographies, conference materials); website content. Fiction editing: Women's fiction; medical, legal, and political thrillers; general categories. Currently based: New York, New York. Previous on-staff experience: Random House, Doubleday, Facts on File, NTC/Contemporary Books.

THE CREATIVE LITERARY ALLIANCE

www.creativeliteraryalliance.com

The Creative Literary Alliance is a group of independent New York City publishing professionals, offering clients worldwide a broad range of writing and editorial services. Each of us has at least 20 years' experience in the field, working with authors, literary agents and every major publisher. We are specialists in both fiction and nonfiction, and are accessible via telephone, email and/or in person.

Members of the Creative Literary Alliance can help you with:

+ A detailed evaluation and critique of your manuscript or proposal

- Idea development

- Substantive editing, rewriting, and polishing of any written material

- Book collaboration, co-authoring, and ghostwriting

- Assistance with query letters and book synopses

- Coaching throughout the writing process

- Project management, from conception through production

- Guidance on self-publishing

- Advice on platform development and marketing strategies

- Referrals to literary agents, publishers, and other literary services

- Advice on all aspects of the publishing process

You may contact us collectively through our website, or any of us individually via email. We have helped many authors maximize their potential...we can help you!

Penelope Franklin
email: penfrank@yahoo.com
Specialties—Nonfiction: Animals/pets, art/architecture, biography/memoir/ oral history, food/entertaining, health/fitness/nutrition, history/social sciences, humor, illustrated books, narrative nonfiction, natural history, paranormal, popular science, self-help/popular psychology, travel, women's issues/feminism.

Penelope Franklin is a versatile editor and writer with over 30 years of publishing experience. She has been associated with major publishers, including Reader's Digest Books, Columbia University, the United Nations, Oxford University Press, *American Heritage* magazine and *Current Biography* magazine. She has assisted many writers who use English as a second language. She works skillfully with first-time authors, as well as established ones, with an emphasis on preserving a client's unique voice throughout the writing process.

Janet Spencer King
email: janet.s.king@verizon.net
Specialities—Nonfiction: Health/fitness/nutrition, medical, narrative nonfiction, self-help/popular psychology, spirituality/New Age, travel, women's issues/feminism. Fiction: commercial/mainstream.

Janet Spencer King has been an editor and writer for more than 25 years. She was editor-in-chief and founding editor of three national magazines as well as the author or co-author of four books with major publishers. Janet has written hundreds of magazine articles and was for several years a book agent, placing both nonfiction and fiction with key publishing houses. Janet is also a certified holistic health counselor.

Diane O'Connell

email: doconnell@nyc.rr.com

Specialties—Fiction: Commercial/mainstream, thrillers/mysteries/suspense, young adult. Nonfiction: Biography/memoirs, business, health/fitness/nutrition, social sciences, narrative nonfiction, self-help/popular psychology, spirituality/New Age, true crime.

An award-winning writer and editor with 25 years' experience, Diane O'Connell has worked as an editor at Random House and Sesame Workshop, and is the author or co-author of five books, including the groundbreaking *Divorced Dads: Shattering the Myths* (Tarcher/Putnam), which was the subject of a *20/20* report. As editor, collaborator, and writing coach, Diane's approach helps authors find their voice and articulate their visions in published form. She specializes in working with first-time authors and those who are looking to take their career to the next level.

Olga Vezeris

email: OVerzeris@aol.com

Specialties—Fiction: Commercial/mainstream in areas of adventure, historical, sagas, thriller/mysteries/suspense, women's market. Nonfiction: adventure, animals/pets, art/architecture, business, crafts/hobbies, food/entertaining, gift books, health/fitness/nutrition, illustrated books, lifestyle/decorating, narrative nonfiction, self-help/popular psychology, spirituality/New Age, travel, true crime.

Olga Vezeris has some of the most extensive experience in the publishing industry, having had senior editorial and subsidiary rights positions in companies including Simon & Schuster, Grand Central Publishing (Warner Books), Workman, HarperCollins and the Bertelsmann Book Club group, where she has acquired, edited or licensed many commercial fiction and nonfiction titles.

THE ELEVEN ESSENTIAL QUESTIONS FOR EVERY NONFICTION AUTHOR

GERALD SINDELL

When I work with authors, as part of the book development process I have eleven basic questions that need to be addressed. Once we've worked through all of them authors can be fairly well assured they've reached the heart of their material, and that if the book is a success, it will be the success they actually want.

1. **Distinctions.** *What is new here? What are the new distinctions you have made that no one has seen before?*

   All new ideas are the result of making new distinctions. When we see something that no one else has seen, we are truly thinking and creating. The fundamental work of authors is making new distinctions and sharing those with their readers so that the reader, too, can see what is new.

2. **Identity.** *Who am I?*

   Each of us is inherently unique—we couldn't be like anyone else even if we spent our entire lives trying. I happen to believe that if anyone can get to the truth of who they are and get it written, they will have made a valuable contribution to the human condition.

   Before we can write authentically, we must understand who we are. We must discover our identity, the part of us that is immutable, the fingerprint of our soul. We can express our identity by asking ourselves, "What am I driven to do in this world?"

3. **Implications.** *Where do your ideas lead if taken to their extreme? In other words, what are their implications? Do your ideas agree with each other, forming a coherent whole, or is there conflict between your ideas? Can that conflict be resolved?*

   Even ideas that appear simple on the surface will have implications if applied elsewhere. Only by testing our ideas in a wide range of contexts can we discover if they are really what we mean, or whether we must continue to refine our thinking. For instance, if we express the notion that everyone should always obey the law, how do we justify the American Revolution?

And if we discover there are exceptions to our beliefs, those exceptions can help us refine what we actually believe.

4. **Testing.** *What would prove your theories wrong? If you can describe the right test, your thinking and writing will be more readily accepted.*

We are, of course, free to assert anything we want. Our readers, though, will often ask for some reasonable validation that what we are asserting is also true. The adoption of ideas will be greatly advanced if we can also offer the appropriate test that would show whether our assertions are true, or not. For instance, if we assert that high school students don't learn well until after 11:00 a.m., it would be valuable if we would also show how this has already been proven in the past, or could be tested in the future. If we can't figure out a convincing test, our ideas will be relegated to the scrapheap of pure conjecture.

5. **Precedent.** *Which writers and what ideas are your precedents? Are you clear how you fit into the great conversation of ideas?*

Mortimer Adler described the history of thought in Western Civilization as being a Great Conversation. When we write nonfiction, we are automatically entering into dialogue with all of those who preceded us whether we are aware of it or not, so it would be valuable to find the leading writers both currently and in previous generations that have addressed the challenges that we are addressing. If we don't, we are risking appearing to be not well-informed. If we do discover our precedents, we will be much clearer about what is unique in our own thinking.

6. **Need.** *Who needs your knowledge? If you are writing to solve the problems of a small group, can you find others who would benefit from the same solutions? The second group might be larger than your initial target readership.*

Most of us write to address our immediate audience that we know has a clear urgent need for what we have to say. It is frequently worthwhile to step back for a moment and ask if our work would benefit a wider group of people than just our core imagined readers. If it turns out that we have a much larger potential audience that would benefit from our work, it might be worthwhile to include their needs as we write. Our publisher will have a greater incentive to publish our book if we are writing for our largest prospective audience.

7. **Foundation.** *Is your thinking so new that it might represent a new body of law that can stand alone? If so, can you identify your underlying principles, and how they work together?*

Not every book can or ought to re-order the universe, but once in a while we might realize that we are defining a new field or a completely new way of organizing some area of thought. If we can discover the core underlying principles in our work we might add great value for our readers.

8. **Completion.** *Have you decided what the boundaries of your book are, and what it will take to be complete in and of itself?*

   Whether you are addressing your reader's desire to build a stone wall or understand the history of the Civil War, it is generally preferable to provide your reader with a single source solution for their needs—your book. If you cannot cover everything they will need to know, then you should consider providing the smallest possible list of the essential sources they will need.

9. **Connection.** *Once you know your target readers, have you thought about what voice will make it easiest for them to hear you? Have you structured your book in a way that will make it most easily grasped by your reader, as opposed to the way you might logically organize your ideas?*

   Most of us start out developing our books focused on what we have discovered and what we want to say. Our readers, generally, want to add to their knowledge and will benefit from a voice that seems to anticipate their questions and needs. It is helpful if authors can imagine several of their typical readers, and write with each of them in mind.

10. **Impact.** *Three years from now, if your book is successful, what will have changed in the world because of your work?*

    This question gets to the heart of why you're writing a book in the first place. Another way of getting to the same core question is asking yourself—if you had never lived, and what you knew to be true had never been heard by the world, what would have been lost? The answer to this question often takes the form of, "I want people to know that..." and whatever follows contains the essential part of your message, or your contribution.

    We can also ask ourselves, is there in existence a book that says what I want to say in pretty much the same fashion that I would want to say it? If so, we don't yet have a compelling reason for writing our book. If it would require a stack of books to pull together what it is we want to say, then we know we really need to write our own book.

11. **Advocacy.** *At first, only you can be a brilliant advocate for what you are creating. Have you crafted the language, metaphors, stories, and endorsements that will help others quickly and accurately understand the significance of what you have created?*

    If we ask others to take the first pass at defining us we run the overwhelming risk that they will get it wrong. We need to be brilliant at characterizing what we have created, so that others can easily grasp the value of what is new here. Great authors are also great advocates for their work, which enhances the likelihood of reaching the audience that will benefit from it.

Gerald Sindell is an independent publishing consultant who works with his clients from the initial inception of their nonfiction books, to develop their strategy, and align that strategy with their business and personal goals. Sindell develops the book proposal with the author, supports the sale of the book with various agents, provides editorial support if required as the book is written. Sindell then coordinates the efforts of the author, publisher, and independent PR services in order to achieve the goals for success that were defined at inception. He can be reached at ThoughtLeadersINTL., www.thoughtleadersintl.com, 415-789-9040, 158 Saint Thomas Way, Tiburon, CA 94920.

THE INDEPENDENT EDITORS

RESOURCES FOR WRITERS

WEBSITES FOR AUTHORS

One of the most valuable aspects of the World Wide Web for writers is that it provides the opportunity to explore the world of publishing. This annotated list of websites offers descriptions of some of the most useful sites for writers.

Now more than ever there's an infinite amount of resources available for writers on the Internet in anything from membership/subscription sites to personal websites of authors who also list agents of the same genre.

The trend of blogging has spread among publishers—it is now common for trade and university publishers to keep a blog, or even separate blogs for different imprints. Publishing bloggers keep things mixed up with guest pieces by house authors, book reviews, interviews, links, industry news, current events, videos, and more. Publishers use blogs to keep the public aware of new releases, establish goodwill between press, authors, and customers, and as an outlet for interesting topical content related to their books.

Not only publishers keep blogs, though. The blogging trend has spread across the whole spectrum of the book world. Many literary agents keep blogs that give writers invaluable advice, critique mistakes, and lend crucial insights into their individual preferences and personalities. Writers keep blogs chronicling their own publishing experiences and hurdles. And others, from critics to businessmen, printers, and engineers, lend their own unique and valuable opinions about the publishing world.

We are aware that blogs sprout up quickly, and while a fairly large list has been gathered, it is far from comprehensive. Follow links, sample, and explore and you will learn much about what people are thinking and how to approach them.

Below is a sampling of what's available on the Web, grouped according to the following categories:

+ Anthology Resources

+ Blogging Resources

  - Literary/Industry Blogs

  - Literary Agent Blogs

  - Publisher Blogs

  - University Press Blogs

- Children's Literature Resources

- E-Publishing Resources

- Funding Resources

- Horror Resources

- Mystery Resources

- Poetry Resources

- Romance Resources

- Science Fiction Resources

- Screenwriting Resources

- Western Resources

- General Resource Sites

ANTHOLOGY RESOURCES

ANTHOLOGIESONLINE

http://www.AnthologiesOnline.com

Writers will find more than great articles and frequent postings of calls for manuscripts. From *Chicken Soup* to Horror, anthology publishers post their calls for writers. Subscribers have advance notice of calls for manuscripts and may apply for a free promotional page.

The site has a comprehensive, up-to-date list of paying markets for writers of science fiction, fantasy, horror, and slipstream. One page lists all markets; other pages break out markets by pro, semi-pro, anthologies, and contests, as well as by print and electronic formats. Listings include summaries of guidelines and indications of markets' "aliveness," plus website URLs.

LITERARY/INDUSTRY BLOGS

BLOG OF A BOOKSLUT

http://www.bookslut.com/blog

Bookslut, the alias of eminent litblogger Jessa Crispin, features prolific magazine and book reviews, columns, interviews, essays, news, unusual links, history, book society, and much more.

BOOKDWARF

http://www.bookdwarf.com

The blog of Megan Sullivan, one of the frontlist buyers at the Harvard Book Store. She writes on books, reading reports, publishing news, film adaptations, humor, and opinion.

BOOKENDS, LLC

http://bookendslitagency.blogspot.com

Bookends is a literary agency focusing on fiction and nonfiction books for adult audiences. Their blog features publishing advice, views from the agent's perspective, industry opinions, book reviews, and inspiration.

BOOKNINJA

http://www.bookninja.com

Founded by Canadian editor and publisher George Murray, Bookninja is the premier Canadian literary site and is frequented by thousands of people from around the globe. It posts unusual publishing-related stories, hearsay, industry news, humor, and technology.

BOOKSQUARE

http://www.booksquare.com

The primary blog of Kassia Krozser. Honest, entertaining, and often hilarious writing on the publishing industry, technology, the Internet, markets, and writers.

CHEKHOV'S MISTRESS

http://www.checkovsmistress.com

Chekhov's Mistress, written by Web developer, writer, and online publisher Bud Parr, is dedicated to discussing literature. Bud is also the organizer of Metaxucafe, the network "blog of literary blogs." Essays discuss literary classics, links, blogworld news, and literary history. Bud also runs an online Don Quixote discussion group, 400 Windmills (http://400windmills.com).

CONFESSIONS OF AN IDIOSYNCRATIC MIND

http://www.sarahweinman.com

Confessions of an Idiosyncratic Mind is the blog of Sarah Weinman, the *Baltimore Sun*'s crime fiction columnist and writer of "Dark Passages," a monthly mystery and suspense column for the *Los Angeles Times Book Review*. It provides commentary on crime and mystery fiction, industry links, and genre news.

CONVERSATIONAL READING

http://esposito.typepad.com/con_read/

The blog of Scott Esposito, member of the National Book Critics Circle, reviewer and essayist, has been singled out by the *New York Times*, *The Village Voice*, and *Variety*, among others. It features literary news, interviews, reviews, rants, opinions, links, and more.

DEAR AUTHOR...

http://dearauthor.com/wordpress/

Six devoted readers serve up fiction book reviews (primarily romance and fantasy with some non fiction and manga thrown in) and provide honest commentary on the Romance genre and publishing industry.

THE ELEGANT VARIATION

http://www.marksarvas.blogs.com/

According to Fowler's, "The Elegant Variation" is a term for the inept writer's pained efforts at freshness or vividness of expression. The acclaimed blog itself is the work of Mark Sarvas, writer, book reviewer, screenwriter, and newspaper editor. The posts feature quotes, marginalia, book reviews, contests, interviews, publishing news, book giveaways, and videos.

GALLEYCAT

http://www.mediabistro.com/galleycat/

Galleycat is an all-purpose literary weblog that features updates in the writing world, announcements, profiles, essays, interviews, events, industry and bookseller news, multimedia,

GOLDEN RULE JONES

http://goldenrulejones.com

This blog was started to cover literary events in Chicago, specifically fiction, poetry, and literary nonfiction.

LAILA LALAMI

http://www.lailalalami.com/blog

The blog of Laila Lalami, Moroccan-born writer, novelist, Fulbright fellow, and professor. It features journal entries, news, commentary, links, photographs, and opinions.

LITBLOG CO-OP

http://www.lbc.typepad.com

The Litblog Co-Op is made up of a coalition of bloggers for the purpose of drawing attention to the best of contemporary fiction, authors, and presses. A variety of participating bloggers post their opinions about fiction, publishing news, reviews, and podcasts.

THE LITERARY SALOON

http://www.complete-review.com/saloon

The Literary Saloon offers opinionated commentary on literary matters, news, links, and tirades. Updated daily, it offers plenty on commentary and updates on the industry, both at home and internationally.

RESOURCES FOR WRITERS

MAUD NEWTON

http://www.maudnewton.com

Brooklyn editor and writer Maud Newton's entertaining blog has been widely praised by publications as various as the *New York Times Book Review*, *Forbes*, *New York Magazine*, the *Washington Post*, and *Entertainment Weekly*. It features literary links, politics, humor, rants, recipes, essays, complaints, gossip, and more.

METAXUCAFÉ

http://www.metaxucafe.com

Metaxucafe aims to highlight the best content from the community of bloggers who write about books. Posts include litblog headlines—the 30 most recent posts from the "litblogosphere," member-posted content, editors choice section, a Flickr group, forums, and a blog-finding tool.

PUBLISHING FRONTIER

http://pubfrontier.com/about/

Started by Peter Brantley, the director of the Digital Library Federation, Publishing Frontier aims to conduct provocative public discussion of the publishing revolution and how it affects readers, society, economics, and fundamental values such as privacy. Posts follow on technology, popular culture, book printing, publishing practice, business, science, gadgets, and more.

PUBLISHING INSIDER

http://www.publishinginsider.typepad.com/publishinginsider

Written by Carl Lennertz of HarperCollins Publishers, Publishing Insider reflects a fascination with how and why books sell. Movies, music, and museums are also explored as he studies how word of mouth operates in larger society. Posts on style, songs, bestsellers, reissues, and marketing.

SLUSHPILE

http://www.slushpile.net

SlushPile features interviews, reviews of nonfiction, essays on publishing, advice for writers, industry news and commentary, pop-culture, and celebrity nonfiction.

THREE PERCENT

http://www.rochester.edu/College/translation/threepercent

Three Percent has the goal of becoming a destination for readers, editors, and translators interested in finding out about modern and contemporary international literature. The title is taken from the fact that only 3 percent of books published in the United States are works in translation (and for poetry and fiction the number is closer to 0.7 percent). The site is a part of the University of Rochester's translation program. It posts on translation exercises, international book series, reviews, magazines, international events, and publishing.

WOULDN'T YOU LIKE TO KNOW?

http://isabelswift.blogspot.com

The blog of Isabel Swift, a member of Harlequin's New Business Development team, it offers posts about publishing, editing, business, relationships, romance, and storytelling in the 21st century.

LITERARY AGENT BLOGS

AGENT IN THE MIDDLE

http://agentinthemiddle.blogspot.com

The blog of NY-based literary agent Lori Perkins, AITM focuses on horror, social science fiction, dark fantasy, erotica, and pop culture. She posts on conventions, titles-I'd-like-to-see, erotica, romance, advice for writers, and agenting stories.

BG LITERARY

http://bgliterary.livejournal.com

Children's book agent Barry Goldblatt writes about books he loves, books he's sold, events in children's publishing, and details in the life of an agent.

BOOKENDS, LLC

http://bookendslitagency.blogspot.com

Literary agent Jessica Faust posts on out-of-control clients, writing, submissions, frustrations, working with agents, reviews, revisions, genre, and breaking the "rules."

DHS LITERARY SHOW + TELL

http://dhsliterary.blogspot.com

The blog of DHS Literary (short for David Hale Smith Literary) releases information on new releases, deals, best-of lists, and industry buzz.

DYSTEL AND GODERICH LITERARY MANAGEMENT

http://knightagency.blogspot.com

The excellent Dystel and Goderich blog has posts on advances, insider publishing information, opinions, the business of writing, conferences, pitching, do's and don'ts, publicity, and essays.

ET IN ARCAEDIA, EGO

http://arcaedia.livejournal.com

The blog of Jennifer Jackson, agent at the Donald Mass Literary Agency. Jennifer writes "letters from the query wars," chronicling the war-torn battlefield of query submission and rejection, observations, links, lists, and small essays on writer-agent relations.

THE EVIL EDITOR

http://www.evileditor.blogspot.com

The Evil Editor's blog features writing exercises, cartoons, fill-in-the-captions, feedback, horror, science fiction, obituaries, and plots.

FULLCIRCLELIT

http://fullcirclelit.blogspot.com

The blog of Full Circle Literary is chock-full of literary links and excerpts culled from all corners of the Web.

THE KNIGHT AGENCY

http://knightagency.blogspot.com

The blog of the Knight Agency features member blogs, book reviews, news, recent deals, and manuscript submission.

LIT AGENT X

http://raleva31.livejournal.com

The blog of literary agent Rachel Vater, with Folio Literary Management. She posts on inspirational author tales, announcements, queries, blogs, websites, publicity, deals, and rejections.

LIT SOUP

http://litsoup.blogspot.com/

The blog of Jenny Rappaport, literary agent at the L. Perkins Agency. Posts on upcoming events, query rejections, interns, cat tales, advice for writers, and titles.

JANET REID, LITERARY AGENT

http://jereidliterary.blogspot.com/

Janet Reid is an agent with FinePrint Literary management and specializes in crime fiction. She writes on recent titles, advice for writers, funny experiences, crankiness, events, book covers, procrastination, and the more irreverent side of book agenting.

THE REJECTER

http://rejecter.blogspot.com/

This is the anonymous blog of an assistant at a literary agency. S/he writes: "On average I reject 95 percent of the letters immediately and put the other 5 percent on the 'maybe' pile. Here, I'll talk about my work." He posts on vanity presses, Amazon, podcasts, fiction, blogs, platforms, writer advice, and genres.

MISS SNARK

http://misssnark.blogspot.com

Although discontinued in May 2007 after receiving over 2.5 million hits, the archives of Miss Snark, the Literary Agent, are definitely worth perusing, especially for the writer who wants an extremely candid view of how poor submissions are received. Writers ask questions about the various details of the submission process, courting an agent, how queries should be structured etc., and Miss Snark provides her very meticulous, professional, and uncensored opinions on what writers can do better.

NADIA CORNIER

http://agentobvious.livejournal.com

Nadia Cornier is founder and agent at Firebrand Literary. Her blog is more reflective and personal. It gives a closer look at what it's like to be an agent beyond just queries and proposals.

NATHAN BRANSFORD (OF CURTIS BROWN LTD.)

http://nathanbransford.blogspot.com

Nathan's excellent and regularly updated blog sports lengthy posts that give writing tips, critiques, and his opinions on publishing. His blog also has a thriving message board community, regularly garnering 75–100+ comments on each post. Read for advice on queries, submitting, and what goes on in the mind of an agent.

PUB RANTS

http://pubrants.blogspot.com

The blog of Denver-based literary agent Kristin, PubRants features advice for writers, opinions on details of query structuring, beginning-writer mistakes, videos, journal entries, and music updates.

PUBLISHER BLOGS

THE ABBEVILLE MANUAL OF STYLE

http://www.abbeville.wordpress.com

The blog of Abbeville press, producer of fine art and illustrated books. Their posts feature interviews, photography, news, reviews, contests, videos, and opinions.

ADDENDA & ERRATA

http://www.ivpress.com/blogs/addenda-errata/

Addenda and Errata is a blog from the editors of InterVarsity Press and brings readers up to date on issues, trends, and news related to evangelical publishing program of IVP Academic.

ALYSON BOOKS

http://www.alyson.com

Alyson Book's website doubles as a blog with posts on new books, podcasts, a bookstore, submission calls, event announcements, literary awards, links, excerpts, and reviews.

AMISTAD CONFIDENTIAL

http://www.amistadconfidential.blogspot.com

An imprint of HarperCollins, Amistad Confidential publishes book by and for the people of the African Diaspora. Posts on writers, upcoming books, African and African American issues in publishing, and more.

ANDREWS MCMEEL PUBLISHING, LLC NEWS

http://andrewsmcmeelpublishing.blogspot.com

The Andrews McMeel blog has book reviews, print and YouTube interviews, publishing news, author press, and links.

BANTAM DELL NEWS

http://www.randomhouse.com/bantamdell/news

The Bantam Dell blog features free excerpts, links to audio readings, author awards, sweepstakes info, podcasts, and event announcements.

THE BEST WORDS IN THE BEST ORDER

http://www.fsgpoetry.com

The venerable publishing house Farrar, Straus, and Giroux has an excellent poetry blog that features giveaways, audio poetry readings, posts by FSG poets, reviews, and poetry links.

CHELSEA GREEN

http://www.chelseagreen.com

The front page of Chelsea Green's website doubles as a blog with posts on environmental news, new books, international events, podcasts, video interviews, YouTube, environmental events, profiles, green tips, and recipes.

CHRONICLE BOOKS BLOG

http://www.chroniclebooks.com/blog

The Chronicle Books blog's mission is to let visitors know "what we're reading, what we're publishing, what makes us laugh, and what excites us." It features giveaways, book release info, event announcements, design ideas, photographs, tips, and television reviews.

THE CONTEXT BLOG

http://www.dalkeyarchive.com/blogs/

The Dalkey Archive blogspace provides a place where the staff and friends of the Dalkey Archive can post about current issues in the literary (or non-literary) world.

DAVID R. GODINE, PUBLISHER

http://www.drgodine.blogspot.com/

The blog of David R. Godine, Publisher, and Black Sparrow Books features upcoming titles, book reviews, articles, literary links, translations, blogs, bookstores, announcements, eulogies, and interviews.

ECO-COMPASS BLOG

http://www.blog.islandpress.org

The blog of environmentally oriented Island Press features posts by Island Press authors on current environmental issues, observations, opinions, essays, economics, public transportation, history, forests, fish, global warming, sustainability, and wildlife.

FALCON GUIDES

http://www.falcon.com/blog

Falcon Guides, an imprint of Globe Pequot, features blogs of travel logs, articles, book tours via kayak, news items, essays by travelers, expert blogs, and tips from experienced travelers.

FLOG!

http://www.fantagraphics.com/index.php?option=com_myblog

FLOG!, the blog of Fantagraphics, publisher of comic and art books, features doodles, art scans, convention coverage, cartoons, podcasts, interviews, sales, author and artist spotlights, and signings.

HAMPTON ROADS PUBLISHING INSIGHTS BLOG

http://www.hamptonroadspub.com/blog/

The blog of spiritual publisher Hampton Roads features posts on book reviews, novels, prizes, spiritualism, points of view from the editors, links, and op-eds.

HARLEQUIN'S PARANORMAL ROMANCE BLOG

http://paranormalromanceblog.wordpress.com/

This blog features frequent posts by Harlequin Paranormal Romance authors, talking about their books, writing experiences, inspirations, and personal stories. There are also interviews, and convention updates.

HARLEQUIN HISTORICAL AUTHORS BLOG

http://harlequinhistoricalauthors.blogspot.com/

Harlequin Historical authors discuss new releases, book excerpts, writing, and offers and promotions.

HARLEQUIN AMERICAN ROMANCE AUTHORS

http://harauthors.blogspot.com

The blog of authors who write Harlequin American Romance, the HAR blog features journal-style entries by authors on writing strategies and experiences, new releases, recipes, families, and pets.

HIPPOCRENE BOOKS LANGUAGE AND TRAVEL BLOG

http://hippocrenebooks.blogspot.com

This very interesting blog features free samples of language learning programs, travel writing, vocabulary, and language.

HOUSE/WORK BLOG

http://blogs.thomasnelson.com/thenelsonbuzz.do

This is the central blog hub of Thomas Nelson Publishers, housing the blogs of several Thomas Nelson editors, authors, and businessmen.

INTRIGUE AUTHORS BLOG

http://www.intrigueauthors.com/blog

Harlequin Intrigue authors write about romance, writing, sexy books, journal-style experiences, and new releases.

LONELY PLANET TRAVEL BLOG

http://www.lonelyplanet.com/blogs/travel_blog

Lonely Planet's 326 authors and 400 travel-loving staff use their blog network to bring the best in travel blogging—buzzword events, breaking news, tough travel, odd corners, and the world's craziest kitsch.

THE MAC BLOG

http://www.foundry01.com/macmillan/

The blog of Macmillan family of publishers and imprints is written by a number of executives and influencers across the board, including adult trade, children's, college and academic, and magazine publishing.

NOLO BLOGS

http://www.nolo.com/blogs.cfm

The hub of Nolo legal publishing, it features numerous blogs on legal economics, divorce, estate planning, real estate, fundraising, patents, LLCs, law reform, and bankruptcy.

THE OLIVE READER

http://olivereader.com

The Olive Reader is the weblog of the Harper Perennial imprint of HarperCollins. It features posts on movies, a literary quote generator, info on books, the book world, event coverage and announcements, up-and-coming writers, amusing anecdotes, tattoos, pictures, and T-shirts.

ONE MISSION BLOG

http://blogs.augsburgfortress.com

The blog of Augsburg fortress contains "reflections on the ministry of publishing," worship, opinion, observations, announcements, book news, event information, and technology.

ORBIT BOOKS

http://www.orbitbooks.net

Orbit is a UK-based leading publisher of science fiction and fantasy, recently established in the United States as an imprint of the Hachette Book Group USA. Their blog features items on Orbit books, info on author appearances, interviews, links, sci-fi–related news, and movies.

O'REILLY RADAR

http://radar.oreilly.com

The O'Reilly Radar features tech reviews and laments, guest bloggers, Internet, social networks, updates on the press, new books, statistical charts, and computer networks.

PANTHEON GRAPHIC NOVELS NEWS

http://www.randomhouse.com/pantheon/graphicnovels/news/

The blog of the Random House Graphic Novel imprint has updates on author appearances, comic book news, animated movies, reviews, event announcements, awards, and upcoming publications.

ROWMAN AND LITTLEFIELD PUBLISHERS BLOG

http://romanblog.typepad.com

The Rowman and Littlefield blog features lengthy, high-quality articles and opinion by R&L authors, current events, political science, economics, literary updates, and education.

PENGUIN BLOG (USA)

http://www.us.penguingroup.com/static/html/blogs/

Reveals what life is like for Penguin editors, articles by Penguin authors and guest bloggers, podcasts, Penguin imprint news, and upcoming books.

SIMON & SCHUSTER CANADA

http://canada.simonsaysblogs.com/

This eclectic blog features YouTube posts, new books, scandals, appearances, recipes, photographs, author appearances, contests, book expos, and technology.

GIBBS SMITH BOOKS BLOG

http://gibbs-smithbooks.blogspot.com/

Lifestyle and design publisher Gibbs Smith's blog has posts on new releases, author events, pictures, YouTube videos, kitchen tips, design tips, and interviews.

AN INDEPENDENT VISION

http://www.sourcebooks.com/independentvision/index.php

An Independent Vision provides the latest Sourcebooks news on their books and authors, conferences, and other activities.

SOFT SKULL

http://www.softskull.com/news

New York's premier alternative press. Features reviews, links to articles, video posts, art shows, publishing gossip, and technology.

THE TYNDALE BLOG

http://www.tyndale.com/articles/blog/

The Tyndale Blog offers a closer look at Tyndale's products and its authors, including upcoming media interviews, information about publishing trends, and Tyndale corporate initiatives.

THE WINGED ELEPHANT

http://theoverlookpress.blogspot.com/

The book blog and book vlog of The Overlook Press, the Winged Elephant has posts on book reviews, new releases, literary essays, author profiles, and announcements.

ZONDERVAN BLOG

http://zondervan.typepad.com/zondervan

Zondervan's mission is to express the current evangelical POV as manifested in author commentary, book excerpts, interviews, trends analysis, stimulating links, news from behind the scenes, and user comments.

UNIVERSITY PRESS BLOGS

BEACON BROADSIDE

http://www.beaconbroadside.com

Beacon Press's blog features political writing, articles by Beacon authors, book updates, political links, opinion essays, interviews, and news.

BOOKMARK

http://www.uapress.blogspot.com

Bookmark, the blog of The University of Arkansas Press, has reviews, announcements, links to UA author press, event info, and new books.

BROOKINGS PRESS BLOG

http://brookingspress.typepad.com/

The blog of The Brookings Institution has new and featured books, excerpts from Brookings Press authors, essays, links, and politics.

THE CHICAGO BLOG

http://pressblog.uchicago.edu/

The blog of the University of Chicago Press includes posts on author essays, interviews, excerpts, documentaries, book reviews, recent releases, current events, opinion, magazines, and links.

COLUMBIA UNIVERSITY PRESS BLOG

http://www.cupblog.org

The Columbia University Press Blog features posts on CUP titles, current events, reviews, politics, interesting books, posts by CUP authors, radio, and press.

DUKE UNIVERSITY PRESS

http://www.dukeupress.typepad.com

News from Duke University Press includes posts on current events, recent releases, videos, guest posts, reviews, and contests.

HARVARD UNIVERSITY PRESS PUBLICITY

http://www.harvardpress.typepad.com

HUP's blog features posts on book news and reviews, event notifications, current events, author interviews, and links.

ILLINOIS PRESS BOOK BLOG

http://www.press.uillinois.edu/wordpress/

As the tagline puts it, the UIP blog brings "author appreciation, broadcast bulletins, event ephemera, and recent reviews from the University of Illinois Press." Publishing news and links, trivia, amusements, and reviews.

INDIANA UNIVERSITY PRESS BLOG

http://iupress.typepad.com/blog/

The Indiana University Press blog features book reviews, feeds, history, Indiana-related material, choice links, catalogs, and Twitter updates.

LSU PRESS

http://lsupress.typepad.com/lsu_press_blog/

The Louisiana State University Press blog features interviews, release info, literature news, amusing videos, author events, essays, and photography.

MITPRESSLOG

http://mitpress.typepad.com/mitpresslog/

MIT Press features posts on technology, video games, international relations, academic news, environment, music, video, award news, the Internet, blog watches, author links, architecture, math, philosophy, and more.

NEWS FROM THE UNIVERSITY OF GEORGIA PRESS

http://ugapress.blogspot.com/

The University of Georgia Press blog features book news, reviews, awards, press news, and info on UGA Press authors.

OUPBLOG

http://blog.oup.com

The blog of Oxford University Press USA features links, publishing updates, pop-culture articles, curious facts, words of the week, short biography, and much more eclectic material.

SAGE HOUSE NEWS

http://cornellpress.wordpress.com

Sage House News, the blog of the Cornell University Press, features author interviews, recent releases, links to articles, a Publicity Roundup, current events, blog reviews, podcasts, author news, and science.

THERE'S A HOLE IN THE BUCKET

http://holeinthebucket.wordpress.com/

The blog for The University of Alberta Press features posts by the editors, new books, reviews, event reports, awards, announcements, many photographs, info for authors, and links.

UNIVERSITY OF CALIFORNIA PRESS WEBLOG

http://uspress.typepad.com/ucpresslog/

The University of California Press Weblog features posts on book reviews, science, author posts, excerpts, press news, photographs, interviews, wine, podcasts, poetry, websites, awards, and current events.

UNIVERSITY OF HAWAI`I PRESS LOG

http://uhpress.wordpress.com

One the most respected publishers of Asian and Pacific studies in the world, the UHP blog includes posts on awards, recent releases, reviews, articles on Asian and Pacific history and current events, and Hawai`ian book event announcements.

UNIVERSITY OF NEBRASKA PRESS BLOG

http://www.nebraskapress.typepad.com/

This blog has info on new releases, Tuesday trivia, history, UNP author guest blogs, reviews, interviews, and event announcements.

UNIVERSITY OF PENNSYLVANIA PRESS LOG

http://pennpress.typepad.com/pennpresslog/

The UPenn Press blog features posts on new and forthcoming titles, excerpts, previews, interviews, links, current events, publishing updates, and commentary.

UNC PRESS BLOG

http://uncpressblog.com

The University of North Carolina Press blog has reviews, new releases, a Today in History feature, roadtrip journals, audio links, history, blogosphere updates, awards, and event reports.

UNIVERSITY OF WASHINGTON PRESS BLOG

http://uwashingtonpress.wordpress.com

Billing itself as a "forum for the exploration of Western and Environmental History," this press blog features podcasts, reviews, author info, book awards, and links to articles.

YALE PRESS LOG

http://yalepress.typepad.com/yalepresslog/

The Yale Press blog features recent releases, Yale Press author opinion, photo contests, podcasts, video, awards, eulogies, and summer reading lists.

CHILDREN'S LITERATURE RESOURCES

CHILDREN'S WRITING RESOURCE CENTER

http://www.write4kids.com/

"Whether you're published, a beginner, or just someone who's always dreamt of writing for kids," here you'll find a free library of how-to information, opportunities to chat with other children's writers and illustrators, links to research databases, articles, tips for beginners, secrets for success as a children's writer, message boards, a children's writing survey, the chance to ask questions of known authors, and the opportunity to register in the website's guestbook to receive free email updates filled with news and tips. The site also features a listing of favorite books, Newberry Medal winners, Caldecott Award winners, current bestsellers, and a link to its own children's bookshop.

THE CHILDREN'S BOOK COUNCIL

http://www.cbcbooks.org/

"CBC Online is the website of the Children's Book Council—encouraging reading since 1945." It provides a listing of articles geared toward publishers, teachers, librarians, booksellers, parents, authors, and illustrators—all those who are interested in the children's book field.

THE SOCIETY OF CHILDREN'S BOOK WRITERS AND ILLUSTRATORS

http://www.scbwi.org/

This website "has a dual purpose: It exists as a service to our members, as well as offering information about the children's publishing industry and our organization to nonmembers." It features a listing of events, awards and grants, publications, information for members, information on how to become a member, and a site map.

VERLA KAY'S WEBSITE FOR CHILDREN'S WRITERS

http://www.verlakay.com

This site is packed with information to assist writers of children's stories. Whether you are a beginner or a multi-published writer, there is something here for you. A chat room with nightly chats with other children's writers, online workshops and transcripts of past workshops, a Getting Started page, and a Published Writers page are just some of the features of this award-winning website.

E-PUBLISHING RESOURCES

E-BOOKS CAFÉ

http://www.topzone.com/ebookscafe/

E-books Café is dedicated to helping fellow writers reach out and touch the world through words. It provides an assortment of books to the public in the e-book and POD format in all genres of fiction, as well as nonfiction. It also offers authors worldwide the opportunity to promote and sell their e-books and POD books for free at its site.

FUNDING RESOURCES

THE ART DEADLINE

http://custwww.xensei.com/adl/

The Art Deadline is a "monthly newsletter providing information about juried exhibitions and competitions, call for entries/proposals/papers, poetry and other writing contests, jobs, internships, scholarships, residencies, fellowships, casting calls, auditions, tryouts, grants, festivals, funding, financial aid, and other opportunities for artists, art educators, and art students of all ages. Some events take place on the Internet."

THE AT-A-GLANCE GUIDE TO GRANTS

http://www.adjunctadvocate.com/

The At-a-Glance Guide to Grants offers information about grants, including a glossary of terms in grant forms, sample contracts, links to grant-related sites, a database of funding opportunities, and related agencies, foundations, and organizations. The site also includes a tutorial section with information on how to write a proposal and how to win a grant.

THE FOUNDATION CENTER

http://fdncenter.org/

The Foundation Center website is dedicated to assisting writers in finding grants. It offers "over 200 cooperating sites available in cities throughout the United States. Of particular note is its large online library, with a wonderful interactive orientation to grant seeking. You'll even find application forms for several funding sources here."

FUNDS FOR WRITERS

http://www.fundsforwriters.com and
http://www.chopeclark.com/fundsforwriters.htm

Funds for Writers specializes in leading writers to grants, awards, contests, fellowships, markets, and jobs. The two websites and three newsletters provide a weekly abundance of sources for writers to reference and put checks in the bank. The other sites teach you how to write. Funds for Writers tells you where to make a living doing it.

MICHIGAN STATE GRANT INDEX FOR WRITERS

http://www.lib.msu.edu/harris23/grants/3writing.htm

This index includes a list of websites containing information on poetry grants, award programs, science writing, screenwriting, contests, scholarships, fellowships, reference, and student writing. The website is divided into categories for easy browsing.

NATIONAL FOUNDATION FOR THE ARTS

http://www.nea.gov/grants/apply/Lit.html

The National Foundation for the Arts believes that through literature, a nation express its hopes and fears and tell its stories to its citizens and to the world. Their website includes information on grants for arts projects, literature fellowships, radio and television programs, and more.

NATIONAL WRITERS UNION

http://www.nwu.org/

The union for freelance writers working in U.S. markets offers grievance resolution, industry campaigns, contract advice, health and dental plans, member education, job banks, networking, social events, and much more.

SOUTHERN ARTS FEDERATION

http://southarts.org

The Southern Arts Federation, a nonprofit regional arts organization founded in 1975, creates partnerships and collaborations; assists in the development of artists, arts professionals and arts organizations; presents, promotes and produces Southern arts and cultural programming; and advocates for the arts and arts education.

WESTERN STATES ARTS FEDERATION

http://www.westaf.org/

The WSAF is a "nonprofit arts service organization dedicated to the creative advancement and preservation of the arts. Focused on serving the state arts agencies, arts organizations, and artists of the West, WSAF fulfills its mission by engaging in innovative approaches to the provision of programs and services and focuses its efforts on strengthening the financial, organizational, and policy infrastructure of the arts in the West."

HORROR RESOURCES

DARK ECHO HORROR

http://www.darkecho.com/darkecho/index.html

Dark Echo Horror features interviews, reviews, a writers' workshop, dark links, and a newsletter. Articles relate to topics such as the perception and psychology of the horror writer, the "best" horror, and reviews of dark erotica. The site also offers information and links to fantasy writing.

HORROR WRITERS ASSOCIATION

http://www.horror.org/

The Horror Writers Association (HWA) was formed to "bring writers and others with a professional interest in horror together, and to foster a greater appreciation of dark fiction in general." Bestower of the Bram Stoker Awards, HWA offers a newsletter, late-breaking market news, informational email bulletins, writers' groups, agents, FAQ, and links.

MASTERS OF TERROR

http://www.horrorworld.org

Masters of Terror offers information about horror fiction, book reviews, new authors, horror movies, author message boards, HorrorNet chat room, and a reference guide and critique of horror fiction that features some 500 authors and 2,500 novels. The site also includes exclusive author interviews, book and chapbook reviews, and horror news.

MYSTERY RESOURCES

CLUELASS HOME PAGE

http://www.cluelass.com

The ClueLass Home Page offers awards for mystery fiction and nonfiction, information about conferences and conventions, and mystery groups for writers and fans. It includes information about markets, other contests, reference material, and online support, as well as listings of mystery magazines and newsletters, an international directory of mystery booksellers and publishers, and factual links about crime, forensics, and investigation.

MYSTERY WRITERS OF AMERICA

http://www.mysterywriters.org

Mystery Writers of America "helps to negotiate contracts, watches development in legislation and tax law, sponsors symposia and mystery conferences, and publishes books." The site includes mystery links, awards, a calendar of events, writers' discussions, and a new online mystery every day. It was established to promote and protect "the interests and welfare of mystery writers and to increase the esteem and the literary recognition given to the genre."

SHORT MYSTERY FICTION SOCIETY

http://www.shortmystery.net

The Short Mystery Fiction Society "seeks to actively recognize writers and readers who promote and support the creative art form of short mysteries in the press, in other mystery organizations, and through awards." The site offers a newsletter and other resources.

SISTERS IN CRIME

http://www.sinc-ic.org

Sisters in Crime is a website that vows to "combat discrimination against women in the mystery field, educate publishers and the general public as to inequities in the treatment of female authors, raise awareness of their contribution to the field, and promote the professional advancement of women who write mysteries." The site includes information about local chapters of Sisters in Crime and offers mystery links and online bookstores.

POETRY RESOURCES

ACADEMY OF AMERICAN POETS

http://www.poets.org/index.cfm

The Academy of American Poets website offers news regarding contest opportunities and winners, an online poetry classroom, the first-ever poetry book club, events calendars, and a search feature to find a specific poet or poem. Users can also listen to an author read a poem in RealAudio. The "My Notebook" feature allows visitors to keep a file of favorite poems or readings from the site. There are also discussion group and literary links sections.

ELECTRONIC POETRY CENTER

http://wings.buffalo.edu/epc/

There are perhaps more poetry websites online than for any other literary genre, so picking one representative site is really quite pointless. But we do recommend the Electronic Poetry Center at the University of New York at Buffalo, which is the heart of the contemporary poetry community online, having been around since the early days of gopher space—practically the Dark Ages in computer time. Of particular note are the active and well-respected poetics mailing list, the large collection of audio files, and an extensive listing of small press poetry publishers.

POETRY SOCIETY OF AMERICA

http://www.poetrysociety.org/

The Poetry Society of America website includes information about the newest developments in the Poetry in Motion project, which posts poetry to seven million subway and bus riders in New York City, Chicago, Baltimore, Portland, and Boston. It also includes news about poetry awards, seminars, the tributes in libraries program, the poetry in public program, and poetry festivals.

POETS & WRITERS

http://www.pw.org/

Poets & Writers is an online resource for creative writers that includes publishing advice, message forums, contests, a directory of writers, literary links, information on grants and awards, news from the writing world, trivia, and workshops.

THE INTERNATIONAL LIBRARY OF POETRY

http://www.poetry.com

The International Library of Poetry website offers information about its writing competitions, which focus on "awarding large prizes to poets who have never before won any type of writing competition." The site also includes Internet links, a list of past winners, anthologies of winning poems, and chat rooms.

ROMANCE RESOURCES

ROMANCE WRITERS OF AMERICA

http://www.rwanational.org

Romance Writers of America (RWA) is a national nonprofit genre writers' association—the largest of its kind in the world. It provides networking and support to individuals seriously pursuing a career in romance fiction.

SCIENCE FICTION RESOURCES

CRITTERS WRITER'S WORKSHOP

http://www.critters.org

Critters is a free online workshop/critique group for writers of science fiction, fantasy, and horror. Writers interested in having their work dissected send short stories or chapters to the submission queue, whereupon members read it and deliver a critique in a week. Critters has several thousand members and has handled thousands of manuscripts. There is also a system in place for evaluating full novels.

ONLINE WRITING WORKSHOP FOR SCIENCE FICTION, FANTASY, AND HORROR

http://sff.onlinewritingworkshop.com

At this writing workshop members submit, review, rate, and improve their manuscripts. There are dozens of reviews and submissions each day and links to other workshop resources, such as critique guides. It is free the first month and afterwards membership costs $49.

SCIENCE FICTION AND FANTASY WRITERS OF AMERICA

http://www.sfwa.org

The official website of the Science Fiction and Fantasy Writers of America offers information about the organization, its members, affiliated publications, an art gallery, and various awards.

SFNOVELIST

http://www.sfnovelist.com/index.htm

SFNovelist is "an online writing group dedicated to novelists who write 'hard science' SF." It is a highly structured and organized system of the exchange of science fiction manuscripts for consideration by other writers. Its goals are to "become in the marketplace a premier source of novelists who write believable/hard science" SF; garner the attention of SF publishers, SFWA, and other writers' organizations for SF novelists; and develop a cadre of strong novelists, most of whom become published. Behind every great writer is usually a group of fellow writers who are equally serious about their writing, establish a presence at major SF writer conferences and conventions, and provide services and information to members that will help them in their search for self-improvement and in getting published. This includes contacts with other known writers and publishers and sources of distribution and marketing.

STORYPILOT'S SCIENCE FICTION AND FANTASY MARKET ENGINE

http://www.storypilot.com

StoryPilot is a search engine that allows writers to search for paying markets, customizable to fit their needs. Science fiction and fantasy writers can search by genre, pay rate, experience required, dates, and format.

SCREENWRITING RESOURCES

THE HOLLYWOOD CREATIVE DIRECTORY

www.hcdonline.com

The Hollywood Creative Directory's mission is to be the preferred and preeminent source of professional and educational information to, for, and about the entertainment industry, not only to the current entertainment industry professional community, but to aspiring professionals as well. HCD publishes the *Producers Directory*, "the phone book to Hollywood," a must-have directory for screenwriters. HCD offers screenwriter and film directories in an online subscription database. The website maintains one of the best entertainment job boards for the industry. HCD also publishes many how-to screenwriting books under the imprint of Lone Eagle Publishing, including the bestselling *Elements of Style for Screenwriters* and *How Not to Write a Screenplay*.

HOLLYWOOD SCRIPTWRITER

http://www.hollywoodscriptwriter.com

Hollywood Scriptwriter is an international newsletter that offers articles on craft and business "to give screenwriters the information they need to work at their careers." The site includes low-budget and indie markets available for finished screenplays, as well as a listing of agencies that are currently accepting submissions from readers of Hollywood Scriptwriter. According to Hollywood Scriptwriter, "people like Harold Ramis, Francis Ford Coppola, and Larry Gelbart have generously given of their time, knowledge, and experiences to share with HS's readers."

SCREENWRITER'S RESOURCE CENTER

http://www.screenwriting.com

The Screenwriters Resource Center aims to "provide links to products and services for screenwriters, compiled by the staff at the National Creative Registry." It includes links to many screenwriting sites and offers advice and copyright words of warning for writers posting original work on the Internet.

SCREENWRITER'S UTOPIA

http://www.screenwritersutopia.com/

Screenwriter's Utopia includes "helpful hints for getting screenplays produced, script development services, and contest information." The site includes a screenwriters' work station, tool kit, agent listings, and creative screenwriting magazines. Interviews with the screenwriters of *Sleepless in Seattle*, *Blade*, and *The Crow: City of Angels* are featured, and other interviews are archived. The site also includes chat rooms, message boards, a writer's directory, and a free newsletter.

WESTERN RESOURCES

WESTERN WRITERS OF AMERICA, INC.

http://www.westernwriters.org

"WWA was founded in 1953 to promote the literature of the American West and bestow Spur Awards for distinguished writing in the Western field." The site offers information about Old West topics, a listing of past Spur Award winners, and opportunities to learn about WWA and the Spur Award, to apply for membership in WWA, to subscribe to *Roundup Magazine*, or to contact Western authors whose work interests you.

GENERAL RESOURCE SITES

1001 WAYS TO MARKET YOUR BOOKS

http://www.bookmarket.com/1001bio.html

1001 Ways to Market Your Books is a site that offers a book marketing newsletter, consulting services, and book marketing updates. Other topics include success letters, author bios, sample chapters, and tables of contents.

3AM MAGAZINE

http://www.3ammagazine.com

3am is a webzine dedicated to countercultural, radical, and the cutting edge of fiction, poetry, and nonfiction. It features author profiles, interviews, links, and samples of poetry and fiction.

ABSOLUTE WRITE

http://www.absolutewrite.com/

Absolute Write is the "one-stop Web home for professional writers." It offers specific resources for freelance writing, screenwriting, playwriting, writing novels, nonfiction, comic book writing, greeting cards, poetry, songwriting, and more. The site also features interviews, articles, announcements, and a newsletter.

AGENT QUERY

http://www.agentquery.com

Agent Query is meant to be the one-stop writer's resource on the Web about literary agents and publishing. It aims to help writers navigate through the arcane world of book publishing and offers a free searchable database of over 900 agents and profile information.

AMERICAN BOOKSELLERS ASSOCIATION

http://www.bookweb.org

The American Booksellers Association is a trade association representing independent bookstores nationwide. The site links members to recent articles about the industry and features Idea Exchange discussion forums.

AMERICAN DIALECT SOCIETY

http://www.americandialect.org/

The American Dialect Society website offers discussion lists, a newsletter, and a contacts list. Writers will find the "Dialect in Literature Bibliography" useful, as well as CD-ROM dictionaries and style and grammar guides.

AMERICAN SOCIETY OF JOURNALISTS AND AUTHORS

http://www.asja.org/

The American Society of Journalists and Authors is "the nation's leading organization of independent nonfiction writers." It offers its members professional development aids, such as confidential market information, an exclusive referral service, seminars and workshops, and networking opportunities. The site offers all visitors a newsletter, legal updates from the publishing world, and professional links.

AMERICAN JOURNALISM REVIEW

http://www.ajr.org/

This redeveloped site includes more editorial content, updated links to news industry sites, an improved job search function called "The Employment Section," and other interactive features.

THE ASSOCIATED WRITING PROGRAMS

http://www.awpwriter.org/

The Associated Writing Programs website offers information about the AWP annual conference, a list of writers' conferences, a list of AWP member schools, articles and information on writing and writing programs, and a sample of articles and news from the AWP magazine *The Writer's Chronicle*. Members of AWP enjoy an online conferencing system, career advice, career placement service, a subscription to *The Writer's Chronicle*, and notice of contests and awards.

AUTHOR NETWORK

http://www.author-network.com

Author Network is a flourishing international community for writers. The site includes articles, monthly columns, a newsletter, message board, discussion group, critique service, and thousands of links to other writing sites. The writer in residence, Paul Saevig, provides a regular supply of instructional essays that may help new writers or even established authors. Other material and articles are provided by regular contributors, who are generally published authors themselves. Author Network promotes individual writers and other sites of interest to writers, as well as competitions, conferences, and courses.

AUTHOR'S GUILD, THE

http://www.authorsguild.org/

For more than 80 years the Guild has been the authoritative voice of American writers...its strength is the foundation of the U.S. literary community. This site features contract advice, a legal search, information on electronic rights and how to join the organization, a bulletin index, publishers' row, a listing of board members, and current articles regarding the publishing field. There is also a link for Back-in-print.com, an online bookstore featuring out-of-print editions made available by their authors.

AUTHORLINK

http://www.authorlink.com/

This information service for editors, literary agents, and writers boasts more than 165,000 loyal readers per year. Features include a "Manuscript Showcase" that contains 500-plus ready-to-publish, evaluated manuscripts.

BLACK WRITERS ALLIANCE

http://www.blackwriters.org/

The Black Writers Alliance is the "first literary arts organization to utilize the power of the online medium to educate, inform, support and empower aspiring and published black writers. The Black Writers Alliance (BWA) is dedicated to providing information, news, resources, and support to black writers, while promoting the Internet as a tool for research and fellowship among the cultural writing community." The site offers users access to its media kit, a forum, a directory of speakers, a photo album, mailing lists, and chat rooms. The Black Writers Alliance is the first online community that has hosted an annual conference for its members.

BOOKLIST

http://www.ala.org/booklist/index.html

Booklist is a "digital counterpart of the American Library Association's *Booklist* magazine." In the site is a current selection of reviews, feature articles, and a searchable cumulative index. Review topics include books for youth, adult books, media, and reference materials. The site also includes press releases, the Best Books list, and subscription information.

BOOKTALK

http://www.booktalk.com/

Want to find out how to click with the people who talk books? Booktalk is a site where writers and readers learn more about the publishing industry. Besides an extensive literary agent list, there are articles about how to get published, writing tips from authors, and a bulletin board. The host for many author home pages, Booktalk allows readers to interact with bestselling authors, learn about new releases, read book excerpts, and see what's upcoming. A slushpile section lists conferences and publishing links.

BOOKWIRE

http://www.bookwire.com/

Partners with *Publishers Weekly, Literary Market Place*, and the *Library Journal*, among others, BookWire is a site that offers book industry news, reviews, original fiction, author interviews, and guides to literary events. The site features publicity and marketing opportunities for publishers, authors, booksellers, and publicists, and it includes a list of the latest BookWire press releases.

THE BURRY MAN WRITERS CENTER

http://www.burryman.com/

With members and visitors in 104 countries, the Burry Man truly is "a worldwide community of writers." Working professionals and beginning writers find exclusive articles on the craft and business of writing, an extensive list of freelance job resources, a vast section focusing on Scotland, and links to more than 3,000 primary sources of information, giving writers the chance to speak to one another and use the Internet to hone their skills.

THE ECLECTIC WRITER

http://www.eclectics.com/writing/writing.html

This site is an information source for those interested in crime, romance, horror, children's, technical, screen, science fiction, fantasy, mystery, and poetry writing. It features articles, a fiction writer's character chart, resources by genre, reference materials, research, general writing resources, online magazines and journals, writing scams, awards, and a writing-related fun page.

THE EDITORIAL EYE

http://www.eei-alex.com

The Editorial Eye website consists of a sampler of articles originally printed in the newsletter by the same name. The articles discuss techniques for writing, editing, design, and typography, as well as information on industry trends and employment. *The Eye* has been providing information to publication professionals for 18 years.

GRANTA

http://www.granta.com/

The *Granta* website offers information about the most current issue of this highly regarded literary journal. The introduction is an explanation and background info about the topic around which the issue is based. The contents of the issue are listed, and visitors to the site may read a sample from the issue, as well as obtain subscription and ordering information. It also offers similar information about back issues and a readers' survey.

HELIUM

http://www.helium.com

Helium is a community of writers who share expert information on virtually any topic. Helium welcomes essays and articles on subjects as diverse as cooking, traveling, and computers, rated and classified by the user community itself. Helium also features a Marketplace for Freelance Writers section where publishers advertise assignments and writers can submit their material.

HOLLYLISLE.COM

http://hollylisle.com/

HollyLisle.com offers a community of supportive writers helping each other reach their writing goals. Led by full-time novelist Holly Lisle, the community includes crit circles, discussion and research boards, workshops, free real-time writing classes with professional writers and people who can offer their expertise in areas of interest to writers, writing articles, free writing e-books and the award-winning free e-zine *Vision: A Resource for Writers*, plus chapters, cover art, works in progress, and surprises for readers.

LITERARY MARKET PLACE

http://www.literarymarketplace.com/

The Literary Market Place website offers information about publishers, which are categorized by U.S. book publishers, Canadian book publishers, and small presses, as well as literary agents, including illustration and lecture agents. The site also offers trade services and resources.

THE MARKET LIST

http://marketlist.com

The Market List was started in 1994 as an e-zine on AOL and Compuserve. The first comprehensive writers market guidelines online.

MIDWEST BOOK REVIEW

http://www.midwestbookreview.com

Responsible for *Bookwatch*, a weekly television program that reviews books, videos, music, CD-ROMs, and computer software, as well as five monthly newsletters for community and academic library systems and much more, the Midwest Book Review was founded in 1980. This site features its reviews.

NATIONAL ASSOCIATION OF WOMEN WRITERS—NAWW

http://www.naww.org/

The National Association of Women Writers—NAWW was founded to support, encourage, entertain, motivate, and inspire women writers. NAWW offers a *free* weekly inspirational/how-to e-magazine, an online Member Portfolio, a Member Publications page, a quarterly member publication (*"The NAWW Writer's Guide"*), a Discussion List, a Member-Only Online Critique Group, Daily Inspiration, a Writer's Resource Library, and much more. The NAWW site was voted one of the Top Ten "Best Sites" by *Writer's Digest* for 2001.

THE NATIONAL WRITERS UNION

http://www.nwu.org/

The National Writers Union is the trade union for freelance writers of all genres. The website provides links to various service of the union, including grievance resolution, insurance, job information, and databases.

PARA PUBLISHING

http://www.parapublishing.com/

The Para Publishing Book Publishing Resources page offers "the industry's largest resources/publications guide," a customized book writing/publishing/promoting information kit, as well as current and back issues of its newsletter. The site also includes research links, a listing of suppliers, and mailing lists.

PEN AMERICAN CENTER

http://www.pen.org/

PEN is an international "membership organization of prominent literary writers and editors. As a major voice of the literary community, the organization seeks to defend the freedom of expression wherever it may be threatened, and to promote and encourage the recognition and reading of contemporary literature." The site links to information about several PEN-sponsored initiatives, including literary awards.

PUBLISHER'S LUNCH

http://publisherslunch.com/

Publisher's Lunch is the publishing industry's "daily essential read," read by more than 30,000 publishing people every day. It gathers together stories from all over the Web and print media of interest to the professional trade book community, along with original reporting, perspective, and wisecracking.

PUBLISHER'S MARKETPLACE

http://publishersmarketplace.com/

Publishers Marketplace shares a brand with and is run by the same people as Publisher's Lunch, but is a different service. For a registration fee, Publishers Marketplace provides real-time information on book deals, profiles of agents and publishers, a publishing industry Job Board, Publisher's Lunch Deluxe and reviews.

PUBLISHERS WEEKLY ONLINE

http://publishersweekly.com/

Publishers Weekly Online offers news about the writing industry, as well as special features about reading and writing in general and genre writing. The site also includes news on children's books, book-selling, interviews, international book industry news, and industry updates.

PUT IT IN INK

http://www.putitinink.com

Put It In Ink brings you articles, tips, books, software, and information about the craft of writing and getting published. Find information about newsletters (both print and online), e-zines, self-publishing and traditional publishing, freelancing, freelance jobs/markets, marketing tips, article writing, ideas to write about, and more.

R. R. BOWKER

http://www.bowker.com/

R. R. Bowker is a site that offers a listing of books in print on the Web, books out of print, an online directory of the book publishing industry, a data collection center for R. R. Bowker publications, and a directory of vendors to the publishing community.

SHARPWRITER.COM

http://www.sharpwriter.com/

SharpWriter.Com is a practical resources page for writers of all types—a "writer's handy virtual desktop." Reference materials include style sheets, dictionaries, quotations, and job information. The Office Peacemaker offers to resolve grammar disputes in the workplace.

UNITED STATES COPYRIGHT OFFICE

www.copyright.gov

The United States Copyright Office site allows the user to find valuable information about copyright procedures and other basics. In addition, the user can download publications and forms, then link to information about international copyright laws.

WOMEN WHO WRITE

http://members.aol.com/jfavetti/womenww/www.html

Women Who Write is a "collage of women based all over the United States with a passion for writing." The site provides useful links and a large dose of encouragement to women writers of all experience levels.

WOODEN HORSE PUBLISHING

http://www.woodenhorsepub.com/

Wooden Horse Publishing is a complete news and resource site for article writers. Visitors get news about markets, including planned, new, and folding magazines; editor assignments; and editorial changes. The site features a searchable market database of over 3,000 U.S. and Canadian consumer and trade magazines. Entries include full contact information, writer's guidelines, and—only at Wooden Horse—reader demographics and editorial calendars. Newsletter describes new markets and industry trends.

WRITE FROM HOME

http://www.writefromhome.com/

Whether you're a freelance writer, author, or writing from home but employed by a publication, this site strives to offer work-at-home writers tips, information, and resources to help you balance your writing career and children under one roof. You'll also find lots of writing and marketing resources to help you achieve the success you desire. It features a chat room, email discussion list, and a monthly e-zine, featuring articles, markets, guidelines, tips, and more.

WRITER'S MANUAL

http://www.writersmanual.com/

Writer's Manual is an online writer-related information warehouse. It receives information from writers, publishers, and agents worldwide, which includes links, announcements, articles, book reviews, press releases, and more. The site features free writer-related articles, links and resources, recommended books, and a vast job board that lists jobs for traditional and online publishing markets, syndication markets, publishers, grants/fellowships, and contests. The site hosts contests on a monthly basis, including the Writer Critique Contest, in which a published author edits and critiques the writing of one winner.

WRITERS CENTER, THE

http://www.writer.org

The Writers Center is a Maryland-based nonprofit that "encourages the creation and distribution of contemporary literature." The website provides information on the organization's 200-plus yearly workshops and links to its publication *Poet Lore and Writer's Carousel*.

WRITERS GUILD OF AMERICA

http://www.wga.org/

The WGA West site provides information about the Guild and its services, such as script registration. Other links to writing resources are provided as well.

WRITERS NET

http://www.writers.net/

Writers Net is a site that "helps build relationships between writers, publishers, editors, and literary agents." It consists of two main sections, "The Internet Directory of Published Writers," which includes a list of published works and a biographical statement for each writer, and "The Internet Directory of Literary Agents," which lists areas of specialization and a description of the agency. Both are searchable and include contact information. It is a free service that hopes to "become an important, comprehensive matchmaking resource for writers, editors, publishers, and literary agents on the Internet."

WRITERS ON THE NET

http://www.writers.com/

"Writers on the Net is a group of published writers and experienced writing teachers building an online community and resource for writers and aspiring writers." A subscription to the mailing list provides a description and schedule of classes offered by the site and a monthly newsletter.

WRITERS WRITE

http://www.writerswrite.com/

This "mega-site" provides myriad resources, including a searchable database of online and print publications in need of submissions. The Writers Write chat room is open 24 hours a day for live discussion.

WRITERS-EDITORS NETWORK

http://www.writers-editors.com/

The Writers-Editors Network has been "linking professional writers with those who need content and editorial services since 1982." The site features agent listings, articles on marketing tools, and a database of over 10,000 email addresses of editors and book publishers. The site also links to fabulous how-to e-books of dream jobs for writers.

WRITERSPACE

http://www.writerspace.com/

"Writerspace specializes in the design and hosting of websites for authors. We also provide Web services for those who may already have websites but wish to include more interactivity in the way of bulletin boards, chat rooms, contests, and email newsletters." The site features an author spotlight, contests, workshops, mailing lists, bulletin boards, chat rooms, romance links, a guestbook, information on adding your link, Web design, Web hosting, its clients, and rates.

WRITERSWEEKLY.COM

http://www.writersweekly.com/

This is the home of the most current paying markets to be found online. WritersWeekly publishes a free weekly e-zine featuring new paying markets and freelance job listings. Serving more readers than any other freelance writing e-zine (60K, as of December 2001), it is dedicated to teaching writers how to make more money writing.

WRITING CORNER

http://www.writingcorner.com/

Writing Corner is dedicated to the reader and writer alike, providing a one-stop place for author sites, chats, and giveaways, along with articles on all aspects of writing. The weekly "JumpStart" newsletter is designed to motivate writers at every level, while the "Author's Corner" newsletter keeps readers apprised of author events. The site features market information, resource listings, book reviews, and vast archives of writing information for fiction, nonfiction, and corporate writers.

YOUCANWRITE

http://www.youcanwrite.com/

YouCanWrite is one of *Writer's Digest's* 101 Best Sites for Writers and is the brainchild of two long-time publishing professionals who know the business from the inside out. Aspiring nonfiction writers can get the real story on what agents and editors look for in a salable manuscript. The site offers a wealth of free information, and its Insider Guides are practical, fun to read e-books that cover all the bases— from agents to books proposals to contracts.

WRITERS FREE REFERENCE

http://www.writers-free-reference.com

Writers Free Reference is a very unique resource site with many eclectic features and links. Its most outstanding asset is a continuously updated list of literary agents and their email addresses.

WRITING.ORG

http://www.writing.org

Writing.org is a very simple but very useful website. It includes links to articles and interviews with agents, tips on finding an agent, tips on avoiding scam artists, and other "no-nonsense" tips on being an aspiring writer. This site's creator is a published author, former editor, former agent, and has been helping writers online for almost ten years.

SUGGESTED RESOURCES

SUGGESTED RESOURCES

SELF-PUBLISHING RESOURCES

Aiming at Amazon: The New Business of Self-Publishing, or, How to Publish Books for Profit with Print on Demand
by Lightning Source
and *Book Marketing on Amazon.com*
by Aaron Shepard (Shepard Publications, 2007)
www.shepardpub.com

Business and Legal Forms for Authors and Self-Publishers
by Tad Crawford (Allworth Press, 2005)
10 East 23rd Street, Suite 210, New York, NY 10010
212-777-8395

The Business of Writing for Children: An Award-Winning Author's Tips on Writing Children's Books and Publishing Them
by Aaron Shepard (Shepard Publications, 2000)
www.shepardpub.com

The Complete Guide to Self-Publishing: Everything You Need to Know to Write, Publish, Promote and Sell Your Own Book
by Tom Ross, Marilyn J. Ross (Writer's Digest Books, 2002)
4700 E. Galbraith Road, Cincinnati, OH 45236
512-531-2690

The Complete Guide to Successful Publishing
by Avery Cardoza (Cardoza Pub, 2003)
132 Hastings Street, Brooklyn, NY 11235
800-577-WINS, 718-743-5229; fax: 718-743-8284
email: cardozapub@aol.com

Dan Poynter's Book Publishing Encyclopedia
by Dan Poynter (Para Publishing, 2006)
PO Box 8206-240, Santa Barbara, CA 93118-8206
805-968-7277; fax: 805-968-1379; cellular: 805-680-2298
email: DanPoynter@aol.com, 75031.3534@compuserve.com

The Fine Print of Self-Publishing: The Contracts and Services of 45 Self-Publishing Companies Analyzed, Ranked, and Exposed
by Mark Levine (Bascom Hill Publishing Group, 2008)
212 3rd Ave. North, Suite 570, Minneapolis, MN 55401

How to Self-Publish & Market Your Own Book: A Simple Guide for Aspiring Writers
by Mark E. Smith, Sara Freeman Smith (U R Gems Group, 2006)
PO Box 440341, Houston, TX 77244-0341
281-596-8330

How to Self-Publish Your Book with Little or No Money!
A Complete Guide to Self-Publishing at a Profit!
by Bettie E. Tucker, Wayne Brumagin (Rainbow's End Company, 2000)
354 Golden Grove Road, Baden, PA 15005 US
724-266-2346; fax: 724-266-2346

Indie Publishing: How to Design and Publish Your Own Book
by Ellen Lupton (Princeton Architectural Press, 2008)
37 E. 7th Street, New York, NY 10003
212-995-9620; email: editorial@papress.com

Make Money Self-Publishing: Learn How from Fourteen Successful Small Publishers
by Suzanne P. Thomas (Gemstone House Publishing, 2000)
PO Box 19948, Boulder, CO 80308
800-324-6415

Perfect Pages: How to Avoid High-Priced Page Layout Programs or Book Design Fees and Produce Fine Books in MS Word for Desktop Publishing and Print-on-Demand
by Aaron Shepard (Shepard Publications, 2006)
www.shepardpub.com

Print-on-Demand Book Publishing: A New Approach to Printing and Marketing Books for Publishers and Self-Publishing Authors
by Morris Rosenthal (Foner Books, 2008)
www.fonerbooks.com

Self-Publishing for Dummies
by Jason R. Rich (Wiley)
111 River Street, Hoboken, NJ 07030-5774
201-748-6000

The Self-Publishing Manual: How to Write, Print & Sell Your Own Book
by Dan Poynter (Para Publishing, 2007)
PO Box 8206-240, Santa Barbara, CA 93118-8206
805-968-7277; fax: 805-968-1379; cellular: 805-680-2298
email: DanPoynter@aol.com, 75031.3534@compuserve.com

Sell Your Book on Amazon: Book Marketing Coach Reveals Top-Secret "How-To"
Tips Guaranteed to Increase Sales for Print-on-Demand and Self-Publishing Writers
by Brent Sampson and Dan Poynter (Outskirts Press, 2007)
10940 S. Parker Rd., PO Box 515, Parker, CO 80134

Top Self-Publishing Firms: How Writers Get Published, Sell More Books, and
Rise to the Top
by Stacie Vander Pol (CreateSpace, 2008)
100 Enterprise Way, Suite A200, Scotts Valley, CA 95066
email: info@createspace.com

The Well-Fed Self-Publisher: How to Turn One Book into a Full-Time Living
by Peter Bowerman (Fanove Publishing, 2006)
3713 Stonewall Circle, Atlanta, GA
770-438-7200

INDUSTRY RESOURCES

30 Steps to Becoming a Writer and Getting Published: The Complete Starter Kit
for Aspiring Writers
by Scott Edelstein (Writer's Digest Books, 1993)
4700 E. Galbraith Road, Cincinnati, OH 45236
512-531-2690

1,818 Ways to Write Better & Get Published
by Scott Edelstein (Writer's Digest Books, 1997)
4700 E. Galbraith Road, Cincinnati, OH 45236
512-531-2690

2010 Children's Writer's & Illustrator's Market
by Alice Pope (Writer's Digest Books, 2009)
4700 E. Galbraith Road, Cincinnati, OH 45236
512-531-2690

2010 Guide to Literary Agents
by Chuck Sambuchino (Writer's Digest Books, 2009)
4700 E. Galbraith Road, Cincinnati, OH 45236
512-531-2690

2010 Novel & Short-Story Writer's Market
by Rachel McDonald (Writer's Digest Books, 2009)
4700 E. Galbraith Road, Cincinnati, OH 45236
512-531-2690

2010 Poet's Market
by Nancy Breen, Editor (Writer's Digest Books, 2009)
4700 E. Galbraith Road, Cincinnati, OH 45236
512-531-2690

2010 Screenwriter's and Playwright's Market
by Chuck Sambuchino (Writer's Digest Books, 2009)
4700 E. Galbraith Road, Cincinnati, OH 45236
512-531-2690

2010 Writer's Market
by Robert Brewer (Writer's Digest Books, 2009)
4700 E. Galbraith Road, Cincinnati, OH 45236
512-531-2690

Advice to Writers: A Compendium of Quotes, Anecdotes, and Writerly Wisdom from a Dazzling Array of Literary Lights
by John Winoker, Compiler (Vintage Books, 2000)
299 Park Avenue, New York, NY 10171
212-751-2600

Alchemy with Words: The Complete Guide to Writing Fantasy, vol. 1
by Darin Park and Tom Dullemond (Dragon Moon Press, 2008)

The American Directory of Writer's Guidelines: More Than 1,700 Magazine Editors and Book Publishers Explain What They Are Looking for from Freelancers
by Steven Blake Mettee, Michelle Doland, and Doris Hall (Quill Driver Books, 2006)
1831 Industrial Way, #101, Sanger, CA 93657
fax: 559-876-2170; email: sbm12@csufresno.edu

The Art of the Book Proposal
by Eric Maisel, PhD (Tarcher, 2004)
375 Hudson Street, New York, NY 10014-3657

The Autobiographer's Handbook: The 826 National Guide to Writing Your Memoir
by Jennifer Traig (Holt Paperbacks, 2008)
175 Fifth Avenue, New York, NY 10010
646-307-5151

Book Business: Publishing: Past, Present, and Future
by Jason Epstein (W.W. Norton & Company, 2002)
500 Fifth Avenue, New York, NY 10110
212-354-5500; fax: 212-869-0856

Book Proposals That Sell: 21 Secrets to Speed Your Success
by W. Terry Whalin (WriteNow Publications, 2005)
The Stables, Priory Hill, Dartford, Kent, DA1 2ER
01322 286386

Business and Legal Forms for Authors and Self-Publishers
by Tad Crawford (Allworth Press, 2005)
10 East 23rd Street, New York, NY 10010
fax: 212-777-8261; email: groberts@allworth.com

The Business of Writing for Children: An Award-Winning Author's Tips on Writing Children's Books and Publishing Them
by Aaron Shepard (Shepard Publications, 2000)

The Career Novelist: A Literary Agent Offers Strategies for Success
by Donald Maass (Heinemann, 1996)
22 Salmon Street, Port Melbourne, Victoria 3207, Australia
email: customer@hi.com.au

The Case of Peter Rabbit: Changing Conditions of Literature for Children
by Margaret MacKey (Garland Publishing, 1999)
29 W. 35th Street, New York, NY 10001-2299
212-216-7800; fax: 212-564-7854; email: info@taylorandfrancis.com

Christian Writer's Market Guide 2009: The Essential Reference Tool for the Christian Writer
by Sally Stuart (WaterBrook Press, 2009)
12265 Oracle Blvd., Suite 200
Colorado Springs, CO 80921
719-590-4999

The Complete Guide to Book Marketing
by David Cole (Allworth Press, 2004)
10 East 23rd Street, New York, NY 10010
212-777-8395

The Complete Guide to Book Publicity
by Jodee Blanco (Allworth Press, 2004)
10 East 23rd Street, Suite 210, New York, NY 10010
212-777-8395

The Complete Guide to Writer's Groups, Conferences, and Workshops
by Eileen Malone (John Wiley & Sons, 1996)
605 Third Avenue, New York, NY 10158-0012
212-850-6000; fax: 212-850-6088; email: info@wiley.com

The Complete Guide to Writing and Selling the Christian Novel
by Barbara Kipfer (Writer's Digest Books, 1998)
4700 E. Galbraith Road, Cincinnati, OH 45236
512-531-2690

A Complete Guide to Writing for Publication
by Susan Titus Osborn, Editor (ACW Press, 2001)
5501 N. 7th Ave., # 502, Phoenix, AZ 85013
877-868-9673; email: editor@acwpress.com

The Complete Idiot's Guide to Getting Published, 4th Edition
by Sheree Bykofsky, Jennifer Basye Sander (Alpha Books, 2006)
201 West 103rd Street, Indianapolis, IN 46290
317-581-3500

The Complete Idiot's Guide to Getting Your Romance Published
by Julie Beard (Alpha Books, 2000)
357 Hudson Street, New York, NY 10014
212-366-2000

The Complete Idiot's Guide to Publishing Children's Books, 3rd Edition
by Harold D. Underdown et al (Alpha Books, 2008)
357 Hudson Street, New York, NY 10014
212-366-2000

The Complete Idiot's Guide to Writing Christian Fiction
by Ron Benrey (Alpha Books, 2007)
357 Hudson Street, New York, NY 10014
212-366-2000

The Copyright Permission and Libel Handbook:
A Step-by-Step Guide for Writers, Editors, and Publishers
by Lloyd J. Jassin, Steve C. Schecter (John Wiley & Sons, 1998)
605 Third Avenue, New York, NY 10158-0012
212-850-6000; fax: 212-850-6088; email: info@wiley.com

The Craft and Business of Writing: Essential Tools for Writing Success
by Robert Brewer and the Editors of Writer's Digest Books (Writer's Digest Books, 2008)
4700 E. Galbraith Road, Cincinnati, OH 45236
512-531-2690

Directory of Small Press/Magazine Editors & Publishers: 2008–2009
by Len Fulton, Editor (Dustbooks, 2008)
PO Box 100, Paradise, CA 95967
530-877-6110, 800-477-6110; fax: 530-877-0222

Directory of Poetry Publishers 2007–2008
by Len Fulton (Dustbooks, 2007)
PO Box 100, Paradise, CA 95967
530-877-6110, 800-477-6110

Editors on Editing: What Writers Need to Know about What Editors Do
by Gerald Gross, Editor (Grove Press, 1994)
841 Broadway, New York, NY 10003
212-614-7850

The Fast Track Course on How to Write a Nonfiction Book Proposal
by Stephen Blake Mettee (Quill Driver Books, 2008)
1254 Commerce Ave, Sanger, CA 93657
559-876-2170; fax: 559-876-2180

The First Five Pages: A Writer's Guide to Staying Out of the Rejection Pile
by Noah T. Lukeman (Fireside, 2005)
1230 Avenue of the Americas, New York, NY 10020
212-698-7000

Formatting & Submitting Your Manuscript (Writer's Market Library Series)
by Jack Neff (Writer's Digest Books, 2004)
4700 E. Galbraith Road, Cincinnati, OH 45236
512-531-2690

Get Known Before the Book Deal: Use Your Personal Strengths to Grow an Author Platform
by Christina Katz (Writer's Digest Books, 2008)
4700 E. Galbraith Road, Cincinnati, OH 45236
512-531-2690

Getting It Published: A Guide for Scholars and Anyone Else Serious about Serious Books
by William Germano (University of Chicago Press, 2008)
1427 East 60th Street, Chicago, IL 60637
773-702-7700; fax: 773-702-9756

Get Your First Book Published: And Make It a Success
by Jason Shinder, Jeff Herman, Amy Holman (Career Press, 2001)
3 Tice Road, PO Box 687, Franklin Lakes, NJ 07417
201-848-0310

Guerilla Marketing for Writers: 100 Weapons to Help You Sell Your Work
by Jay Conrad Levinson, Rick Frishman, and Michael Larsen (Writer's Digest Books, 2000)
4700 E. Galbraith Road, Cincinnati, OH 45236
512-531-2690

Hooked: Write Fiction That Grabs Readers at Page One & Never Lets Them Go
by Les Edgerton (Writer's Digest Books, 2007)
4700 E. Galbraith Road, Cincinnati, OH 45236
512-531-2690

How to Be Your Own Literary Agent: The Business of Getting a Book Published
by Richard Curtis (Houghton Mifflin Company, 2003)
222 Berkeley Street, Boston, MA 02116-3764
617-351-5000

How to Do Biography: A Primer
by Nigel Hamilton (Harvard University Press, 2008)
79 Garden Street, Cambridge, Massachusetts 02138
800-405-1619

How to Write a Book Proposal
by Michael Larsen (Writer's Digest Books, 2004)
4700 E. Galbraith Road, Cincinnati, OH 45236
512-531-2690

How to Write a Damn Good Mystery: A Practical Step-by-Step Guide from Inspiration to Finished Manuscript
by James N. Frey (St. Martin's Press, 2004)
175 Fifth Avenue, New York, NY 10010
212-674-5151

How to Write a Damn Good Novel
by James N. Frey (St. Martin's Press, 1987)
175 Fifth Avenue, New York, NY 10010
212-674-5151

How to Write a Damn Good Novel II: Advanced Techniques for Dramatic Storytelling
by James N. Frey (St. Martin's Press, 1994)
175 Fifth Avenue, New York, NY 10010
212-674-5151

How to Write Irresistible Query Letters
by Lisa Collier Cool (Writer's Digest Books, 2002)
4700 E. Galbraith Road, Cincinnati, OH 45236
512-531-2690

How to Write Killer Fiction
by Carolyn Wheat (Perseverance Press, 2003)
PO Box 2790, McKinleyville, CA 95519
707-839-3495

Immediate Fiction: A Complete Writing Course
by Jerry Cleaver (St. Martin's Press, 2005)
175 Fifth Avenue, New York, NY 10010

Inside Book Publishing
by Giles Clark (Routledge, 2008)
270 Madison Avenue, New York, NY 10016
212-216-7800   fax: 212-563-2269

The Joy of Publishing: Fascinating Facts, Anecdotes, Curiosities, and Historic Origins about Books and Authors
by Nat G. Bodian (Open Horizons, 1996)
PO Box 205, Fairfield, IA 52556

Jump Start Your Book Sales: A Money-Making Guide for Authors, Independent Publishers and Small Presses
by Marilyn Ross, Tom Ross (Writer's Digest Books, 1999)
4700 E. Galbraith Road, Cincinnati, OH 45236
512-531-2690

*Keep It Real: Everything You Need to Know About Researching and
Writing Creative Nonfiction*
by Lee Gutkind (W. W. Norton, 2009)
500 Fifth Avenue, New York, NY 10110
212-354-5500   fax: 212-869-0856

Kirsch's Guide to the Book Contract: For Authors, Publishers, Editors and Agents
by Jonathan Kirsch (Acrobat Books, 1998)
PO Box 870, Venice, CA 90294
fax: 310-823-8447

Kirsch's Handbook of Publishing Law: For Authors, Publishers, Editors and Agents
by Jonathan Kirsch (Acrobat Books, 1994)
PO Box 870, Venice, CA 90294
fax: 310-823-8447

Literary Agents: A Writer's Introduction
by John F. Baker (IDG Books Worldwide, Inc., 1999)
919 E. Hillsdale Boulevard, Suite 400, Foster City, CA 94404-2112
800-762-2974

*Literary Marketplace 2009: The Directory of the American Book Publishing Industry with
Industry Yellow Pages*
by Karen Hallard, Mary-Anne Lutter, and Vivian Sposobiec (Information Today)
630 Central Avenue, New Providence, NJ 07974
888-269-5372; email: info@bowker.com

Making the Perfect Pitch: How to Catch a Literary Agent's Eye
by Katherine Sands (Watson-Guptill, 2004)
770 Broadway, New York, NY 10003
email: info@watsonguptill.com

Make a Real Living as a Freelance Writer: How to Win Top Writing Assignments
by Jenna Glatzer (Nomad Press, 2004)

Negotiating a Book Contract: A Guide for Authors, Agents and Lawyers
by Mark L. Levine (Moyer Bell Ltd., 1988)
Kymbolde Way, Wakefield, RI 02879
401-789-0074, 888-789-1945; fax: 401-789-3793
email: sales@moyerbell.com

Nonfiction Book Proposals Anybody Can Write: How to Get a Contract and Advance Before Writing Your Book
by Elizabeth Lyon (Blue Heron Pub, 2000)
1234 SW Stark Street, Suite 1, Portland, OR 97205
fax: 503-223-9474; email: bhp@teleport.com

The Plot Thickens: 8 Ways to Bring Fiction to Life
by Noah Lukeman (St. Martin's Press, 2003)
175 Fifth Avenue, New York, NY 10010
212-674-5151

Plug Your Book! Online Book Marketing for Authors, Book Publicity through Social Networking
by Steve Weber (Weber Books)
www.weberbooks.com

The Portable Writers' Conference: Your Guide to Getting and Staying Published
by Stephen Blake Mettee, Editor (Word Dancer Press, 2007)
1831 Industrial Way, #101, Sanger, CA 93657
559-876-2170; email: sbm12@csufresno.edu

Publicize Your Book: An Insider's Guide to Getting Your Book the Attention It Deserves
by Jacqueline Deval (Perigee Trade, 2008)
375 Hudson Street, New York, NY 10014
212-366-2000

Secrets of a Freelance Writer: How to Make $85,000 a Year
by Robert W. Bly (Henry Holt, 1997)
115 West 18th Street, New York, NY 10011
212-886-9200; fax: 212-633-0748; email: publicity@hholt.com

Self-Editing for Fiction Writers
by Renni Browne, Dave King (HarperCollins, 2004)
10 East 53rd Street, New York, NY 10022-5299
212-207-7000

A Simple Guide to Marketing Your Book: What an Author and Publisher Can Do to Sell More Books
by Mark Ortman (Wise Owl Books, 2001)
24425 Fieldmont Place, West Hills, CA 91307
818-716-9076; email: apweis@pacbell.net

The Shortest Distance Between You and a Published Book
by Susan Page (Broadway Books, 1997)
841 Broadway, New York, NY 10003
212-614-7850

Telling Lies for Fun & Profit
by Lawrence Block, Sue Grafton (Introduction); (William Morrow & Company, 1994)
1350 Avenue of the Americas, New York, NY 10019
212-261-6500

This Business of Books: A Complete Overview of the Industry from Concept Through Sales
by Claudia Suzanne, Carol Amato & Thelma Sansoucie, Editors (Wambtac, 2004)
17300 17th Street, #J276, Tustin, CA 92780
800-641-3936; fax: 714-954-0793; email: bookdoc@wambtac

The Well-Fed Writer: Financial Self-Sufficiency as a Freelance Writer in Six Months or Less
by Peter Bowerman (Fanove Publishing, 2000)
3713 Stonewall Circle, Atlanta, GA 30339
770-438-7200

Writer Tells All: Insider Secrets to Getting Your Book Published
by Robert Masello (Holt Paperbacks, 2001)
115 West 18th Street, New York, NY 10010
212-886-9200

Write the Perfect Book Proposal: 10 Proposals That Sold and Why
by Jeff Herman, Deborah M. Adams (John Wiley & Sons, 2001)
605 Third Avenue, New York, NY 10158-0012
212-850-6000; fax: 212-850-6088; email: info@wiley.com

The Writer's Market Companion
by Joe Feiertag, Mary Carmen Cupito (Writer's Digest Books, 2004)
1507 Dana Avenue, Cincinnati, OH 45207
513-531-2222; fax: 531-531-4744

Writer's & Illustrator's Guide to Children's Book Publishers and Agents
by Ellen R. Shapiro (Prima Publishing, 2003)
3000 Lava Ridge Court, Roseville, CA 95661

The Writer's Legal Companion: The Complete Handbook for the Working Writer
by Brad Bunnin, Peter Beren (Perseus Press, 1998)
11 Cambridge Center, Cambridge, MA 02142
email: info@perseuspublishing.com

The Writer's Legal Guide (2nd ed.)
by Tad Crawford, Tony Lyons (Allworth Press, 2002)
10 East 23rd Street, Suite 210, New York, NY 10010
212-777-8395

The Writer's Little Instruction Book: 385 Secrets for Writing Well and Getting Published
by Paul Raymond Martin, Polly Keener (Writer's World Press, 2005)
35 N. Chillecothe Road, Suite D, Aurora, OH 44202
330-562-6667; fax: 330-562-1216; email: Writersworld@juno.com

Writing the Breakout Novel
by Donald Maass (Writer's Digest Books, 2002)
4700 E. Galbraith Road, Cincinnati, Ohio 45236
513-531-2690

Writing the Breakout Novel Workbook
by Donald Maass (Writer's Digest Books, 2004)
4700 E. Galbraith Road, Cincinnati, Ohio 45236
513-531-2690

Writing Down the Bones: Freeing the Writer Within
by Natalie Goldberg (Shambhala Publications, 2005)
PO Box 308, Boston, MA 02117
617-424-0030; fax: 617-236-1563

Writing Fiction: The Practical Guide from New York's Acclaimed Creative Writing School
by Gotham Writers' Workshop (Bloomsbury USA, 2003)
175 5th Ave., 8th floor, New York, NY 10010
212-780-0115

Writing Life Stories: How to Make Memories into Memoirs, Ideas into Essays, and Life into Literature
by Bill Roorbach (Writer's Digest Books, 2008)
4700 E. Galbraith Road, Cincinnati, Ohio 45236
513-531-2690

Writing Successful Self-Help and How-To Books
by Jean Marie Stine (John Wiley & Sons, 1997)
605 Third Avenue, New York, NY 10158-0012
212-850-6000; fax: 212-850-6088; email: info@wiley.com

Writing the Nonfiction Book
by Eva Shaw, PhD (Rodgers & Nelsen Publishing Company, 1999)
PO Box 700, Loveland, CO 80537
970-593-9557

You Can Make It Big Writing Books: A Top Agent Shows How to Develop a Million-Dollar Bestseller
by Jeff Herman, Deborah Levine Herman, Julia DeVillers (Prima Publishing, 1999)
3000 Lava Ridge Court, Roseville, CA 95661

Your Novel Proposal: From Creation to Contract: The Complete Guide to Writing Query Letters, Synopses and Proposals for Agents and Editors
by Blythe Camenson (Writer's Digest Books, 1999)
4700 E. Galbraith Road, Cincinnati, OH 45236
512-531-2690

E-PUBLISHING RESOURCES

Electronic Publishing: Avoiding the Output Blues
by Taz Tally (Prentice Hall, 2001)

Electronic Publishing: The Definitive Guide
by Karen S. Wiesner (Avid Press, 2003)
5470 Red Fox Drive, Brighton, MI 48114
810-801-1177; email: cgs@avidpress.com

ePublishing for Dummies
by Victoria Rosenborg (Hungry Minds, Inc., 2000)
909 Third Avenue, New York, NY 10022

From Entrepreneur to Infopreneur: Make Money with Books, E-Books, and Information Products
by Stephanie Chandler (Wiley, 2006)
111 River Street, Hoboken, NJ 07030-5774
201-748-6000

How to Publish and Promote Online
by M. J. Rose, Angela Adair-Hoy (Griffin Trade Paperback, 2001)
175 Fifth Avenue, New York, NY 10010
212-647-5151

How to Write a "How-to" Book (Or eBook): Make Money Writing About Your Favorite Hobby, Interest, or Activity
by Shaun Fawcett (Final Draft!, 2006)
803-746-4675

How to Write and Publish Your Own eBook in as Little as 7 Days
by Jim Edwards and Joe Vitale (Morgan James Publishing, 2007)
1225 Franklin Avenue, Suite 325, Garden City, New York, 11530
516-620-2528

Self-Publishing EBooks and PODS: One Step at a Time
by Timothy Sean Sykes (The Forager, 2006)

Write Your eBook or Other Short Book—Fast!
by Judy Cullins, Dan Poynter, and Marshall Masters (Your Own World Books, 2005)
P.O. Box 67061, Scotts Valley, CA 95067
775-546-1472

Writing.Com: Creative Internet Strategies to Advance Your Writing Career
by Moira Anderson Allen (Allworth Press, 2003)
10 East 23rd Street, Suite 210, New York, NY 10010
212-777-8395

GLOSSARY

GLOSSARY

A

abstract   A brief sequential profile of chapters in a nonfiction book proposal (also called a **synopsis**); a point-by-point summary of an article or essay. In academic and technical journals, abstracts often appear with (and may serve to preface) the articles themselves.

adaptation   A rewrite or reworking of a piece for another medium, such as the adaptation of a novel for the screen. (*See also* **screenplay**.)

advance   Money paid (usually in installments) to an author by a publisher prior to publication. The advance is paid against royalties: If an author is given a $5,000 advance, for instance, the author will collect royalties only after the royalty moneys due exceed $5,000. A good contract protects the advance if it should exceed the royalties ultimately due from sales.

advance orders   Orders received before a book's official publication date, and sometimes before actual completion of the book's production and manufacture.

agent   The person who acts on behalf of the author to handle the sale of the author's literary properties. Good literary agents are as valuable to publishers as they are to writers; they select and present manuscripts appropriate for particular houses or of interest to particular acquisitions editors. Agents are paid on a percentage basis from the moneys due their author clients.

American Booksellers Association (ABA)   The major trade organization for retail booksellers, chain and independent. The annual ABA convention and trade show offers a chance for publishers and distributors to display their wares to the industry at large and provides an incomparable networking forum for booksellers, editors, agents, publicists, and authors.

American Society of Journalists and Authors (ASJA)   A membership organization for professional writers. ASJA provides a forum for information exchange among writers and others in the publishing community, as well as networking opportunities. (*See also* **Dial-a-Writer**.)

anthology   A collection of stories, poems, essays and/or selections from larger works (and so forth), usually carrying a unifying theme or concept; these selections may be written by different authors or by a single author. Anthologies are compiled as opposed to written; their editors (as opposed to authors) are responsible for securing the needed reprint rights for the material used, as well as supplying (or providing authors for) pertinent introductory or supplementary material and/or commentary.

attitude   A contemporary colloquialism used to describe a characteristic temperament common among individuals who consider themselves superior. Attitude is rarely an esteemed attribute, whether in publishing or elsewhere.

auction Manuscripts a literary agent believes to be hot properties (such as possible bestsellers with strong subsidiary rights potential) will be offered for confidential bidding from multiple publishing houses. Likewise, the reprint, film, and other rights to a successful book may be auctioned off by the original publisher's subsidiary rights department or by the author's agent.

audio books Works produced for distribution on audio media, typically audiotape cassette or audio compact disc (CD). Audio books are usually spoken-word adaptations of works originally created and produced in print; these works sometimes feature the author's own voice; many are given dramatic readings by one or more actors, at times embellished with sound effects.

authorized biography A history of a person's life written with the authorization, cooperation, and, at times, participation of the subject or the subject's heirs.

author's copies/author's discount Author's copies are the free copies of their books the authors receive from the publisher; the exact number is stipulated in the contract, but it is usually at least ten hardcovers. The author will be able to purchase additional copies of the book (usually at 40 percent discount from the retail price) and resell them at readings, lectures, and other public engagements. In cases where large quantities of books are bought, author discounts can go as high as 70 percent.

author tour A series of travel and promotional appearances by an author on behalf of the author's book.

autobiography A history of a person's life written by that same person, or, as is typical, composed conjointly with a collaborative writer ("as told to" or "with"; *see also* **coauthor; collaboration**) or ghostwriter. Autobiographies by definition entail the authorization, cooperation, participation, and ultimate approval of the subject.

B

backlist The backlist comprises books published prior to the current season and still in print. Traditionally, at some publishing houses, such backlist titles represent the publisher's cash flow mainstays. Some backlist books continue to sell briskly; some remain bestsellers over several successive seasons; others sell slowly but surely through the years. Although many backlist titles may be difficult to find in bookstores that stock primarily current lists, they can be ordered either through a local bookseller or directly from the publisher.

backmatter Elements of a book that follow the text proper. Backmatter may include the appendix, notes, glossary, bibliography and other references, lists of resources, index, author biography, offerings of the author's and/or publisher's additional books and other related merchandise, and colophon.

bestseller Based on sales or orders by bookstores, wholesalers, and distributors, bestsellers are those titles that move the largest quantities. List of bestselling books can be local (as in metropolitan newspapers), regional (typically in geographically keyed trade or consumer periodicals), or national (as in *USA Today, Publishers Weekly,* or the *New York Times*), as well as international. Fiction and nonfiction are usually listed separately, as are hardcover and paperback classifications. Depending on the list's purview, additional industry-sector designations are used (such as how-to/self-improvement, religion and spirituality, business and finance); in addition, bestseller lists can be keyed to particular genre or specialty fields (such as bestseller lists for mysteries, science fiction, or romance novels, and for historical works, biography, or popular science titles)—and virtually any other marketing category at the discretion of whoever issues the bestseller list (for instance African American interests, lesbian and gay topics, youth market).

bibliography   A list of books, articles, and other sources, that have been used in the writing of the text in which the bibliography appears. Complex works may break the bibliography down into discrete subject areas or source categories, such as General History, Military History, War in the Twentieth Century, or Unionism and Pacifism.

binding   The materials that hold a book together (including the cover). Bindings are generally denoted as hardcover (featuring heavy cardboard covered with durable cloth and/or paper, and occasionally other materials) or paperback (using a pliable, resilient grade of paper, sometimes infused or laminated with other substances such as plastic). In the days when cloth was used lavishly, hardcover volumes were conventionally known as clothbound; and in the very old days, hardcover bindings sometimes featured tooled leather, silk, precious stones, and gold and silver leaf ornamentation.

biography   A history of a person's life. (*See also* **authorized biography; autobiography; unauthorized biography.**)

blues (or **bluelines**)   Photographic proofs of the printing plates for a book. Blues are reviewed as a means to inspect the set type, layout, and design of the book's pages before it goes to press.

blurb   A piece of written copy or extracted quotation used for publicity and promotional purposes, as on a flyer, in a catalog, or in an advertisement (*See also* **cover blurbs**).

book club   A book club is a book-marketing operation that ships selected titles to subscribing members on a regular basis, sometimes at greatly reduced prices. Sales of a work to book clubs are negotiated through the publisher's subsidiary rights department (in the case of a bestseller or other work that has gained acclaim, these rights can be auctioned off). Terms vary, but the split of royalties between author and publisher is often 50 percent/50 percent. Book club sales are seen as blessed events by author, agent, and publisher alike.

book contract   A legally binding document between author and publisher that sets the terms for the advance, royalties, subsidiary rights, advertising, promotion, publicity—plus a host of other contingencies and responsibilities. Writers should therefore be thoroughly familiar with the concepts and terminology of the standard book-publishing contract.

book distribution   The method of getting books from the publisher's warehouse into the reader's hands. Distribution is traditionally through bookstores but can include such means as telemarketing and mail-order sales, as well as sales through a variety of special-interest outlets such as health-food or New Age venues, sports and fitness emporiums, or sex shops. Publishers use their own sales forces as well as independent salespeople, wholesalers, and distributors. Many large and some small publishers distribute for other publishers, which can be a good source of income. A publisher's distribution network is extremely important, because it not only makes possible the vast sales of a bestseller but also affects the visibility of the publisher's entire list of books.

book jacket (*See* **dust jacket.**)

book producer or **book packager** An individual or company that can assume many of the roles in the publishing process. A book packager or producer may conceive the idea for a book (most often nonfiction) or series, bring together the professionals (including the writer) needed to produce the book(s), sell the individual manuscript or series project to a publisher, take the project through to manufactured product—or perform any selection of those functions, as commissioned by the publisher or other client (such as a corporation producing a corporate history as a premium or giveaway for employees and customers). The book producer may negotiate separate contracts with the publisher and with the writers, editors, and illustrators who contribute to the book.

book review A critical appraisal of a book (often reflecting a reviewer's personal opinion or recommendation) that evaluates such aspects as organization and writing style, possible market appeal, and cultural, political, or literary significance. Before the public reads book reviews in the local and national print media, important reviews have been published in such respected book-trade journals as *Publishers Weekly*, *Kirkus Reviews*, *Library Journal*, and *Booklist*. A gushing review from one of these journals will encourage booksellers to order the book; copies of these raves will be used for promotion and publicity purposes by the publisher and will encourage other book reviewers nationwide to review the book.

Books in Print Listings, published by R. R. Bowker, of books currently in print; these yearly volumes (along with periodic supplements such as *Forthcoming Books in Print*) provide ordering information, including titles, authors, ISBN numbers, prices, whether the book is available in hardcover or paperback, and publisher names. Intended for use by the book trade, *Books in Print* is also of great value to writers who are researching and market-researching their projects. Listings are provided alphabetically by author, title, and subject area.

bound galleys Copies of uncorrected typesetter's page proofs or printouts of electronically produced mechanicals that are bound together as advance copies of the book (compare **galleys**). Bound galleys are sent to trade journals (*see* **book review**) as well as to a limited number of reviewers who work under long lead times.

bulk sales The sale at a set discount of many copies of a single title (the greater the number of books, the larger the discount).

byline The name of the author of a given piece, indicating credit for having written a book or article. Ghostwriters, by definition, do not receive bylines.

C

casing Alternate term for binding (*see* **binding**).

category fiction Also known as genre fiction. Category fiction falls into an established (or newly originated) marketing category (which can then be subdivided for more precise target marketing). Fiction categories include action-adventure (with such further designations as military, paramilitary, law enforcement, romantic, and martial arts); crime novels (with points of view that range from deadpan cool to visionary, including humorous capers as well as gritty urban sagas); mysteries or detective fiction (hard-boiled, soft-boiled, procedurals, cozies); romances (including historicals as well as contemporaries); horror (supernatural, psychological, or technological); thrillers (tales of espionage, crisis, and the chase), Westerns, science fiction, and fantasy. (*See also* **fantasy**, **horror**, **romance fiction**, **science fiction**, **suspense fiction**, and **thriller**.)

CD or **computer CD** High-capacity compact discs for use by readers via computer technology. CD-ROM is a particular variety; the term is somewhere between an acronym and an abbreviation. (CD-ROMs are compact computer discs with read-only memory, meaning the reader is not able to modify or duplicate the contents.) Many CDs are issued with a variety of audiovisual as well as textual components. When produced by publishers, these are sometimes characterized as books in electronic format. (*See also* **multimedia**.)

children's books Books for children. As defined by the book-publishing industry, children are generally readers aged 17 and younger; many houses adhere to a fine but firm editorial distinction between titles intended for younger readers (under 12) and young adults (generally aged 12 to 17). Children's books (also called juveniles) are produced according to a number of categories (often typified by age ranges), each with particular requisites regarding such elements as readability ratings, length, and inclusion of graphic elements. Picture books are often for very young readers, with such designations as toddlers (who do not themselves read) and preschoolers (who may have some reading ability). Other classifications include easy storybooks (for younger school children), middle-grade books (for elementary to junior high school students), and young adult (abbreviated YA, for readers through age 17).

coauthor One who shares authorship of a work. Coauthors all have bylines. Coauthors share royalties based on their contributions to the book. (Compare **ghostwriter**.)

collaboration Writers can collaborate with professionals in any number of fields. Often a writer can collaborate in order to produce books outside the writer's own areas of formally credentialed expertise (for example, a writer with an interest in exercise and nutrition may collaborate with a sports doctor on a health book). Though the writer may be billed as a coauthor (*see* **coauthor**), the writer does not necessarily receive a byline (in which case the writer is a **ghostwriter**). Royalties are shared, based on respective contributions to the book (including expertise or promotional abilities as well as the actual writing).

colophon Strictly speaking, a colophon is a publisher's logo; in bookmaking, the term may also refer to a listing of the materials used, as well as credits for the design, composition, and production of the book. Such colophons are sometimes included in the **backmatter** or as part of the copyright page.

commercial fiction Fiction written to appeal to as broad-based a readership as possible.

concept A general statement of the idea behind a book.

cool A modern colloquial expression that indicates satisfaction or approval, or may signify the maintenance of calm within a whirlwind. A fat contract for a new author is definitely cool.

cooperative advertising (co-op) An agreement between a publisher and a bookstore. The publisher's book is featured in an ad for the bookstore (sometimes in conjunction with an author appearance or other special book promotion); the publisher contributes to the cost of the ad, which is billed at a lower (retail advertising) rate.

copublishing Joint publishing of a book, usually by a publisher and another corporate entity such as a foundation, a museum, or a smaller publisher. An author can copublish with the publisher by sharing the costs and decision making and, ultimately, the profits.

copyeditor An editor, responsible for the final polishing of a manuscript, who reads primarily in terms of appropriate word usage and grammatical expression, with an eye toward clarity and coherence of the material as presented, factual errors and inconsistencies, spelling, and punctuation. (*See also* **editor.**)

copyright The legal proprietary right to reproduce, have reproduced, publish, and sell copies of literary, musical, and other artistic works. The rights to literary properties reside in the author from the time the work is produced—regardless of whether a formal copyright registration is obtained. However, for legal recourse in the event of plagiarism or other infringement, the work must be registered with the U.S. Copyright Office, and all copies of the work must bear the copyright notice. (*See also* **work-for-hire.**)

cover blurbs Favorable quotes from other writers, celebrities, or experts in a book's subject area, which appear on the dust jacket and are used to enhance the book's point-of-purchase appeal to the potential book-buying public.

crash Coarse gauze fabric used in bookbinding to strengthen the spine and joints of a book.

curriculum vitae (abbreviated **CV**) Latin expression meaning "course of life"—in other words, the **résumé.**

D

deadline In book publishing, this not-so-subtle synonym is used for the author's due date for delivery of the completed manuscript to the publisher. The deadline can be as much as a full year before official publication date, unless the book is being produced quickly to coincide with or follow up a particular event.

delivery Submission of the completed manuscript to the editor or publisher.

Dial-a-Writer Members of the American Society of Journalists and Authors may be listed with the organization's project-referral service, Dial-a-Writer, which can provide accomplished writers in most specialty fields and subjects.

direct marketing Advertising that involves a "direct response" (which is an equivalent term) from a consumer—for instance, an order form or coupon in a book-review section or in the back of a book or mailings (direct-mail advertising) to a group presumed to hold a special interest in a particular book.

display titles Books that are produced to be eye-catching to the casual shopper in a bookstore setting. Often rich with flamboyant cover art, these publications are intended to pique bookbuyer excitement about the store's stock in general. Many display titles are stacked on their own freestanding racks; sometimes broad tables are laden with these items. A book shelved with its front cover showing on racks along with diverse other titles is technically a display title. Promotional or **premium** titles are likely to be display items, as are mass-market paperbacks and hardbacks with enormous bestseller potential. (Check your local bookstore and find a copy of this edition of this *Guide*—if not already racked in "display" manner, please adjust the bookshelf so that the front cover is displayed poster-like to catch the browser's eye—that's what we do routinely.)

distributor An agent or business that buys books from a publisher to resell, at a higher cost, to wholesalers, retailers, or individuals. Distribution houses are often excellent marketing enterprises, with their own roster of sales representatives, publicity and promotion personnel, and house catalogs. Skillful use of distribution networks can give a small publisher considerable national visibility.

dramatic rights Legal permission to adapt a work for the stage. These rights initially belong to the author but can be sold or assigned to another party by the author.

dust jacket (also **dustcover** or **book jacket**) The wrapper that covers the binding of hardcover books, designed especially for the book by either the publisher's art department or a freelance artist. Dust jackets were originally conceived to protect the book during shipping, but now their function is primarily promotional—to entice the browser to actually reach out and pick up the volume (and maybe even open it up for a taste before buying) by means of attractive graphics and sizzling promotional copy.

dust-jacket copy Descriptions of books printed on the dust-jacket flaps. Dust-jacket copy may be written by the book's editor but is often either recast or written by in-house copywriters or freelance specialists. Editors send advance copies (*see also* **bound galleys**) to other writers, experts, and celebrities to solicit quotable praise that will also appear on the jacket. (*See also* **cover blurb**.)

E

editor Editorial responsibilities and titles vary from house to house (often being less strictly defined in smaller houses). In general, the duties of the editor-in-chief or executive editor are primarily administrative: managing personnel, scheduling, budgeting, and defining the editorial personality of the firm or imprint. Senior editors and acquisitions editors acquire manuscripts (and authors), conceive project ideas and find writers to carry them out, and may oversee the writing and rewriting of manuscripts. Managing editors have editorial and production responsibilities, coordinating and scheduling the book through the various phases of production. Associate and assistant editors edit; they are involved in much of the rewriting and reshaping of the manuscript and may also have acquisitions duties. Copyeditors read the manuscript and style its punctuation, grammar, spelling, headings and subheadings, and so forth. Editorial assistants, laden with extensive clerical duties and general office work, perform some editorial duties as well—often as springboards to senior editorial positions.

Editorial Freelancers Association (EFA)   This organization of independent professionals offers a referral service, through both its annotated membership directory and its job phone line, as a means for authors and publishers to connect with writers, collaborators, researchers, and a wide range of editorial experts covering virtually all general and specialist fields.

el-hi   Books for elementary and/or high schools.

endnotes   Explanatory notes and/or source citations that appear either at the end of individual chapters or at the end of a book's text; used primarily in scholarly or academically oriented works.

epilogue   The final segment of a book, which comes "after the end." In both fiction and nonfiction, an epilogue offers commentary or further information but does not bear directly on the book's central design.

F

fantasy   Fantasy is fiction that features elements of magic, wizardry, supernatural feats, and entities that suspend conventions of realism in the literary arts. Fantasy can resemble prose versions of epics and rhymes or it may be informed by mythic cycles or folkloric material derived from cultures worldwide. Fantasy fiction may be guided primarily by the author's own distinctive imagery and personalized archetypes. Fantasies that involve heroic-erotic roundelays of the death-dance are often referred to as the sword-and-sorcery subgenre.

film rights   Like **dramatic rights**, these belong to the author, who may sell or option them to someone in the film industry—a producer or director, for example (or sometimes a specialist broker of such properties)—who will then try to gather the other professionals and secure the financial backing needed to convert the book into a film. (*See also* **screenplay**.)

footbands   (*See* **headbands**.)

footnotes   Explanatory notes and/or source citations that appear at the bottom of a page. Footnotes are rare in general-interest books, the preferred style being either to work such information into the text or to list informational sources in the bibliography.

foreign agents   Persons who work with their United States counterparts to acquire rights for books from the U.S. for publication abroad. They can also represent U.S. publishers directly.

foreign market Any foreign entity—a publisher, broadcast medium, etc.—in a position to buy rights. Authors share royalties with whoever negotiates the deal or keep 100 percent if they do their own negotiating.

foreign rights Translation or reprint rights that can be sold abroad. Foreign rights belong to the author but can be sold either country-by-country or en masse as world rights. Often the U.S. publisher will own world rights, and the author will be entitled to anywhere from 50 percent to 85 percent of these revenues.

foreword An introductory piece written by the author or by an expert in the given field (*see* **introduction**). A foreword by a celebrity or well-respected authority is a strong selling point for a prospective author or, after publication, for the book itself.

Frankfurt Book Fair The largest international publishing exhibition—with five hundred years of tradition behind it. The fair takes place every October in Frankfurt, Germany. Thousands of publishers, agents, and writers from all over the world negotiate, network, and buy and sell rights.

Freedom of Information Act Ensures the protection of the public's right to access public records—except in cases violating the right to privacy, national security, or certain other instances. A related law, the Government in the Sunshine Act, stipulates that certain government agencies announce and open their meetings to the public.

freight passthrough The bookseller's freight cost (the cost of getting the book from the publisher to the bookseller). It is added to the basic invoice price charged the bookseller by the publisher.

frontlist New titles published in a given season by a publisher. Frontlist titles customarily receive priority exposure in the front of the sales catalog—as opposed to backlist titles (usually found at the back of the catalog), which are previously published titles still in print.

frontmatter The frontmatter of a book includes the elements that precede the text of the work, such as the title page, copyright page, dedication, epigraph, table of contents, foreword, preface, acknowledgments, and introduction.

fulfillment house A firm commissioned to fulfill orders for a publisher—services may include warehousing, shipping, receiving returns, and mail-order and direct-marketing functions. Although more common for magazine publishers, fulfillment houses also serve book publishers.

G

galleys Printer's proofs (or copies of proofs) on sheets of paper, or printouts of the electronically produced setup of the book's interior—the author's last chance to check for typos and make (usually minimal) revisions or additions to the copy (*see* **bound galleys**).

genre fiction (*See* **category fiction**.)

ghostwriter (or **ghost**) A writer without a byline, often without the remuneration and recognition that credited authors receive. Ghostwriters often get flat fees for their work, but even without royalties, experienced ghosts can receive quite respectable sums.

glossary An alphabetical listing of special terms as they are used in a particular subject area, often with more in-depth explanations than would customarily be provided by dictionary definitions.

H

hardcover Books bound in a format that uses thick, sturdy, relatively stiff binding boards and a cover composed (usually) of a cloth spine and finished binding paper. Hardcover books are conventionally wrapped in a dust jacket. (*See also* **binding**; **dust jacket**.)

headbands Thin strips of cloth (often colored or patterned) that adorn the top of a book's spine where the signatures are held together. The headbands conceal the glue or other binding materials and are said to offer some protection against accumulation of dust (when properly attached). Such bands, placed at the bottom of the spine, are known as footbands.

hook A term denoting the distinctive concept or theme of a work that sets it apart as being fresh, new, or different from others in its field. A hook can be an author's special point of view, often encapsulated in a catchy or provocative phrase intended to attract or pique the interest of a reader, editor, or agent. One specialized function of a hook is to articulate what might otherwise be seen as dry albeit significant subject matter (academic or scientific topics; number-crunching drudgery such as home bookkeeping) into an exciting, commercially attractive package.

horror The horror classification denotes works that traffic in the bizarre, awful, and scary in order to entertain as well as explicate the darkness at the heart of the reader's soul. Horror subgenres may be typified according to the appearance of were-creatures, vampires, human-induced monsters, or naturally occurring life forms and spirit entities—or absence thereof. Horror fiction traditionally makes imaginative literary use of paranormal phenomena, occult elements, and psychological motifs. (*See* **category fiction**; **suspense fiction**.)

how-to books An immensely popular category of books ranging from purely instructional (arts and crafts, for example) to motivational (popular psychology, self-awareness, self-improvement, inspirational) to get-rich-quick (such as in real estate or personal investment).

hypertext Works in hypertext are meant to be more than words and other images. These productions (ingrained magnetically on computer diskette or CD) are conceived to take advantage of readers' and writers' propensities to seek out twists in narrative trajectories and to bushwhack from the main path of multifaceted reference topics. Hypertext books incorporate documents, graphics, sounds, and even blank slates upon which readers may compose their own variations on the authored components. The computer's capacities to afford such diversions can bring reader and hypertext literature so close as to gain entry to each other's mind-sets—which is what good books have always done.

imprint A separate line of product within a publishing house. Imprints run the gamut of complexity, from those composed of one or two series to those offering full-fledged and diversified lists. Imprints also enjoy different gradations of autonomy from the parent company. An imprint may have its own editorial department (perhaps consisting of only one editor), or house acquisitions editors may assign particular titles for release on appropriate specialized imprints. An imprint may publish a certain kind of book (juvenile or paperback or travel books) or have its own personality (such as a literary or contemporary tone). An individual imprint's categories often overlap with other imprints or with the publisher's core list, but some imprints maintain a small-house feel within an otherwise enormous conglomerate. The imprint can offer the distinct advantages of a personalized editorial approach, while availing itself of the larger company's production, publicity, marketing, sales, and advertising resources.

index An alphabetical directory at the end of a book that references names and subjects discussed in the book and the pages where such mentions can be found.

instant book A book produced quickly to appear in bookstores as soon as possible after (for instance) a newsworthy event to which it is relevant.

international copyright Rights secured for countries that are members of the International Copyright Convention (*see* **International Copyright Convention**) and that respect the authority of the international copyright symbol, ©.

International Copyright Convention Countries that are signatories to the various international copyright treaties. Some treaties are contingent upon certain conditions being met at the time of publication, so an author should, before publication, inquire into a particular country's laws.

introduction Preliminary remarks pertaining to a piece. Like a foreword, an introduction can be written by the author or an appropriate authority on the subject. If a book has both a foreword and an introduction, the foreword will be written by someone other than the author; the introduction will be more closely tied to the text and will be written by the book's author. (*See also* **foreword**.)

ISBN (International Standard Book Number) A ten-digit number that is linked to and identifies the title and publisher of a book. It is used for ordering and cataloging books and appears on all dust jackets, on the back cover of the book, and on the copyright page.

ISSN (International Standard Serial Number) An eight-digit cataloging and ordering number that identifies all U.S. and foreign periodicals.

J

juveniles (*See* **children's books**.)

K

kill fee A fee paid by a magazine when it cancels a commissioned article. The fee is only a certain percentage of the agreed-on payment for the assignment (no more than 50 percent). Not all publishers pay kill fees; a writer should make sure to formalize such an arrangement in advance. Kill fees are sometimes involved in work-for-hire projects in book publishing.

L

lead The crucial first few sentences, phrases, or words of anything—be it a query letter, book proposal, novel, news release, advertisement, or sales tip sheet. A successful lead immediately hooks the reader, consumer, editor, or agent.

lead title A frontlist book featured by the publisher during a given season—one the publisher believes should do extremely well commercially. Lead titles are usually those given the publisher's maximum promotional push.

letterhead Business stationery and envelopes imprinted with the company's (or, in such a case, the writer's) name, address, and logo—a convenience as well as an impressive asset for a freelance writer.

letterpress A form of printing in which set type is inked, then impressed directly onto the printing surface. Now used primarily for limited-run books-as-fine-art projects. (*See also* **offset**.)

libel Defamation of an individual or individuals in a published work, with malice aforethought. In litigation, the falsity of the libelous statements or representations, as well as the intention of malice, has to be proved for there to be libel; in addition, financial damages to the parties so libeled must be incurred as a result of the material in question for there to be an assessment of the amount of damages to be awarded to a claimant. This is contrasted to slander, which is defamation through the spoken word.

Library of Congress (LOC) The largest library in the world is in Washington, DC. As part of its many services, the LOC will supply a writer with up-to-date sources and bibliographies in all fields, from arts and humanities to science and technology. For details, write to the Library of Congress, Central Services Division, Washington, DC 20540.

Library of Congress Catalog Card Number An identifying number issued by the Library of Congress to books it has accepted for its collection. The publication of those books, which are submitted by the publisher, are announced by the Library of Congress to libraries, which use Library of Congress numbers for their own ordering and cataloging purposes.

Literary Market Place (LMP) An annual directory of the publishing industry that contains a comprehensive list of publishers, alphabetically and by category, with their addresses, phone numbers, some personnel, and the types of books they publish. Also included are various publishing-allied listings, such as literary agencies, writer's conferences and competitions, and editorial and distribution services. LMP is published by Information Today and is available in most public libraries.

literature Written works of fiction and nonfiction in which compositional excellence and advancement in the art of writing are higher priorities than are considerations of profit or commercial appeal.

logo A company or product identifier—for example, a representation of a company's initials or a drawing that is the exclusive property of that company. In publishing usage, a virtual equivalent to the trademark.

M

mainstream fiction Nongenre fiction, excluding literary or avant-garde fiction, that appeals to a general readership.

marketing plan The entire strategy for selling a book: its publicity, promotion, sales, and advertising.

mass-market paperback Less-expensive smaller-format paperbacks that are sold from racks (in such venues as supermarkets, variety stores, drugstores, and specialty shops) as well as in bookstores. Also referred to as rack (or rack-sized) editions.

mechanicals Typeset copy and art mounted on boards to be photocopied and printed. Also referred to as pasteups.

midlist books Generally mainstream fiction and nonfiction books that traditionally formed the bulk of a publisher's list (nowadays often by default rather than intent). Midlist books are expected to be commercially viable but not explosive bestsellers—nor are they viewed as distinguished, critically respected books that can be scheduled for small print runs and aimed at select readerships. Agents may view such projects as a poor return for the effort, since they generally garner a low-end advance; editors and publishers (especially the sales force) may decry midlist works as being hard to market; prospective readers often find midlist books hard to buy in bookstores (they have short shelf lives). Hint for writers: Don't present your work as a midlist item.

multimedia Presentations of sound and light, words in magnetically graven image—and any known combination thereof as well as nuances yet to come. Though computer CD is the dominant wrapper for these works, technological innovation is the hallmark of the electronic-publishing arena, and new formats will expand the creative and market potential. Multimedia books are publishing events; their advent suggests alternative avenues for authors as well as adaptational tie-ins with the world of print. Meanwhile, please stay tuned for virtual reality, artificial intelligence, and electronic end-user distribution of product.

multiple contract A book contract that includes a provisional agreement for a future book or books. (*See also* **option clause/right of first refusal.**)

mystery stories or **mysteries** (*See* **suspense fiction.**)

net receipts   The amount of money a publisher actually receives for sales of a book: the retail price minus the bookseller's discount and/or other discount. The number of returned copies is factored in, bringing down even further the net amount received per book. Royalties are sometimes figured on these lower amounts rather than on the retail price of the book.

New Age   An eclectic category that encompasses health, medicine, philosophy, religion, and the occult—presented from an alternative or multicultural perspective. Although the term has achieved currency relatively recently, some publishers have been producing serious books in these categories for decades.

novella   A work of fiction falling in length between a short story and a novel.

O

offset (offset lithography)   A printing process that involves the transfer of wet ink from a (usually photosensitized) printing plate onto an intermediate surface (such as a rubber-coated cylinder) and then onto the paper. For commercial purposes, this method has replaced letterpress, whereby books were printed via direct impression of inked type on paper.

option clause/right of first refusal   In a book contract, a clause that stipulates that the publisher will have the exclusive right to consider and make an offer for the author's next book. However, the publisher is under no obligation to publish the book, and in most variations of the clause the author may, under certain circumstances, opt for publication elsewhere. (*See also* **multiple contract.**)

outline   Used for both a book proposal and the actual writing and structuring of a book, an outline is a hierarchical listing of topics that provides the writer (and the proposal reader) with an overview of the ideas in a book in the order in which they are to be presented.

out-of-print books   Books no longer available from the publisher; rights usually revert to the author.

P

package   The package is the actual book; the physical product.

packager   (*See* **book producer.**)

page proof   The final typeset copy of the book, in page-layout form, before printing.

paperback   Books bound with a flexible, stress-resistant, paper covering material. (*See also* **binding.**)

paperback originals   Books published, generally, in paperback editions only; sometimes the term refers to those books published simultaneously in hardcover and paperback. These books are often mass-market genre fiction (romances, Westerns, Gothics, mysteries, horror, and so forth) as well as contemporary literary fiction, cookbooks, humor, career books, self-improvement, and how-to books—the categories continue to expand.

pasteups (*See* **mechanicals.**)

permissions The right to quote or reprint published material, obtained by the author from the copyright holder.

picture book A copiously illustrated book, often with very simple, limited text, intended for preschoolers and very young children.

plagiarism The false presentation of someone else's writing as one's own. In the case of copyrighted work, plagiarism is illegal.

preface An element of a book's frontmatter. In the preface, the author may discuss the purpose behind the format of the book, the type of research upon which it is based, its genesis, or underlying philosophy.

premium Books sold at a reduced price as part of a special promotion. Premiums can thus be sold to a bookseller, who in turn sells them to the bookbuyer (as with a line of modestly priced art books). Alternately, such books may be produced as part of a broader marketing package. For instance, an organization may acquire a number of books (such as its own corporate history or biography of its founder) for use in personnel training and as giveaways to clients; or a nutrition/recipe book may be displayed along with a company's diet foods in non-bookstore outlets. (*See also* **special sales.**)

press agent (*See* **publicist.**)

press kit A promotional package that includes a press release, tip sheet, author biography and photograph, reviews, and other pertinent information. The press kit can be put together by the publisher's publicity department or an independent publicist and sent with a review copy of the book to potential reviewers and to media professionals responsible for booking author appearances.

price There are several prices pertaining to a single book: The invoice price is the amount the publisher charges the bookseller; the retail, cover, or list price is what the consumer pays.

printer's error (**PE**) A typographical error made by the printer or typesetting facility, not by the publisher's staff. PEs are corrected at the printer's expense.

printing plate A surface that bears a reproduction of the set type and artwork of a book, from which the pages are printed.

producer (*See* **book producer.**)

proposal A detailed presentation of the book's concept, used to gain the interest and services of an agent and to sell the project to a publisher.

public domain Material that is uncopyrighted, whose copyright has expired, or that is uncopyrightable. The last includes government publications, jokes, titles—and, it should be remembered, ideas.

publication date (or **pub date**)   A book's official date of publication, customarily set by the publisher to fall six weeks after completed bound books are delivered to the warehouse. The publication date is used to focus the promotional activities on behalf of the title—so that books will have had time to be ordered, shipped, and be available in the stores to coincide with the appearance of advertising and publicity.

publicist (press agent)   The publicity professional who handles the press releases for new books and arranges the author's publicity tours and other promotional venues (such as interviews, speaking engagements, and book signings).

publisher's catalog   A seasonal sales catalog that lists and describes a publisher's new books; it is sent to all potential buyers, including individuals who request one. Catalogs range from the basic to the glitzy and often include information on the author, on print quantity, and on the amount of money slated to be spent on publicity and promotion.

publisher's discount   The percentage by which a publisher discounts the retail price of a book to a bookseller, often based in part on the number of copies purchased.

Publishers' Trade List Annual   A collection of current and backlist catalogs arranged alphabetically by publisher, available in many libraries.

Publishers Weekly (PW)   The publishing industry's chief trade journal. *PW* carries announcements of upcoming books, respected book reviews, interviews with authors and publishing-industry professionals, special reports on various book categories, and trade news (such as mergers, rights sales, and personnel changes).

Q

quality   In publishing parlance, the word "quality" in reference to a book category (such as quality fiction) or format (quality paperback) is a term of art—individual works or lines so described are presented as outstanding products.

query letter   A brief written presentation to an agent or editor designed to pitch both the writer and the book idea.

R

remainders   Unsold book stock. Remainders can include titles that have not sold as well as anticipated, in addition to unsold copies of later printings of bestsellers. These volumes are often remaindered—that is, remaining stock is purchased from the publisher at a huge discount and resold to the public.

reprint   A subsequent edition of material that is already in print, especially publication in a different format—the paperback reprint of a hardcover, for example.

résumé   A summary of an individual's career experience and education. When a résumé is sent to prospective agents or publishers, it should contain the author's vital publishing credits, specialty credentials, and pertinent personal experience. Also referred to as the **curriculum vitae** or, more simply, vita.

returns Unsold books returned to a publisher by a bookstore, for which the store may receive full or partial credit (depending on the publisher's policy, the age of the book, and so on).

reversion-of-rights clause In the book contract, a clause that states that if the book goes out of print or the publisher fails to reprint the book within a stipulated length of time, all rights revert to the author.

review copy A free copy of a (usually) new book sent to electronic and print media that review books for their audiences.

romance fiction or **romance novels** Modern or period love stories, always with happy endings, which range from the tepid to the torrid. Except for certain erotic specialty lines, romances do not feature graphic sex. Often mistakenly pigeonholed by those who do not read them, romances and romance writers have been influential in the movement away from passive and coddled female fictional characters to the strong, active modern woman in a tale that reflects areas of topical social concern.

royalty The percentage of the retail cost of a book that is paid to the author for each copy sold after the author's advance has been recouped. Some publishers structure royalties as a percentage payment against net receipts.

S

sales conference A meeting of a publisher's editorial and sales departments and senior promotion and publicity staff members. A sales conference covers the upcoming season's new books, and marketing strategies are discussed. Sometimes sales conferences are the basis upon which proposed titles are bought or not.

sales representative (sales rep) A member of the publisher's sales force or an independent contractor who, armed with a book catalog and order forms, visits bookstores in a certain territory to sell books to retailers.

SASE (self-addressed stamped envelope) It is customary for an author to enclose SASEs with query letters, with proposals, and with manuscript submissions. Many editors and agents do not reply if a writer has neglected to enclose an SASE with correspondence or submitted materials.

satisfactory clause In book contracts, a publisher will reserve the right to refuse publication of a manuscript that is not deemed satisfactory. Because the author may be forced to pay back the publisher's advance if the complete work is found to be unsatisfactory, the specific criteria for publisher satisfaction should be set forth in the contract to protect the author.

science fiction Science fiction includes the hardcore, imaginatively embellished technological/scientific novel as well as fiction that is even slightly futuristic (often with an after-the-holocaust milieu—nuclear, environmental, extraterrestrial, genocidal). An element much valued by editors who acquire for the literary expression of this cross-media genre is the ability of the author to introduce elements that transcend and extend conventional insight.

science fiction/fantasy   A category fiction designation that actually collapses two genres into one (for bookseller-marketing reference, of course—though it drives some devotees of these separate fields of writing nuts). In addition, many editors and publishers specialize in both these genres and thus categorize their interests with catchphrases such as sci-fi/fantasy.

screenplay   A film script—either original or one based on material published previously in another form, such as a television docudrama based on a nonfiction book or a movie thriller based on a suspense novel. (Compare with **teleplay**.)

self-publishing   A publishing project wherein an author pays for the costs of manufacturing and selling his or her own book and retains all money from the book's sale. This is a risky venture but one that can be immensely profitable (especially when combined with an author's speaking engagements or imaginative marketing techniques); in addition, if successful, self-publication can lead to distribution or publication by a commercial publisher. (Compare with **subsidy publishing**.)

self-syndication   Management by writers or journalists of functions that are otherwise performed by syndicates specializing in such services. In self-syndication, it is the writer who manages copyrights, negotiates fees, and handles sales, billing, and other tasks involved in circulating journalistic pieces through newspapers, magazines, or other periodicals that pick up the author's column or run a series of articles.

serial rights   Reprint rights sold to periodicals. First serial rights include the right to publish the material before anyone else (generally before the book is released, or coinciding with the book's official publication)—either for the U.S., a specific country, or for a wider territory. Second serial rights cover material already published, either in a book or another periodical.

serialization   The reprinting of a book or part of a book in a newspaper or magazine. Serialization before (or perhaps simultaneously with) the publication of the book is called *first serial*. The first reprint after publication (either as a book or by another periodical) is called *second serial*.

series   Books published as a group either because of their related subject matter (such as a biographical series on modern artists or on World War II aircraft) and/or single authorship (a set of works by Djuna Barnes, a group of books about science and society, or a series of titles geared to a particular diet-and-fitness program). Special series lines can offer a ready-made niche for an industrious author or compiler/editor who is up to date on a publisher's program and has a brace of pertinent qualifications and/or contacts. In contemporary fiction, some genre works are published in series form (such as family sagas, detective series, fantasy cycles).

shelf life   The amount of time an unsold book remains on the bookstore shelf before the store manager pulls it to make room for newer incoming stock with greater (or at least untested) sales potential.

short story   A brief piece of fiction that is more pointed and more economically detailed as to character, situation, and plot than a novel. Published collections of short stories—whether by one or several authors—often revolve around a single theme, express related outlooks, or comprise variations within a genre.

signature A group of book pages that have been printed together on one large sheet of paper that is then folded and cut in preparation for being bound, along with the book's other signatures, into the final volume.

simultaneous publication The issuing at the same time of more than one edition of a work, such as in hardcover and trade paperback. Simultaneous releases can be expanded to include (though rarely) deluxe gift editions of a book as well as mass-market paper versions. Audio versions of books are most often timed to coincide with the release of the first print edition.

simultaneous (or multiple) submissions The submission of the same material to more than one publisher at the same time. Although simultaneous submission is a common practice, publishers should always be made aware that it is being done. Multiple submissions by an author to several agents is, on the other hand, a practice that is sometimes not regarded with great favor by the agent.

slush pile The morass of unsolicited manuscripts at a publishing house or literary agency, which may fester indefinitely awaiting (perhaps perfunctory) review. Some publishers or agencies do not maintain slush piles per se—unsolicited manuscripts are slated for instant or eventual return without review (if an SASE is included) or may otherwise be literally or figuratively pitched to the wind. Querying a targeted publisher or agent before submitting a manuscript is an excellent way of avoiding, or at least minimizing the possibility of, such an ignoble fate.

software Programs that run on a computer. Word-processing software includes programs that enable writers to compose, edit, store, and print material. Professional-quality software packages incorporate such amenities as databases that can feed the results of research electronically into the final manuscript, alphabetization and indexing functions, and capabilities for constructing tables and charts and adding graphics to the body of the manuscript. Software should be appropriate to both the demands of the work at hand and the requirements of the publisher (which may contract for a manuscript suitable for on-disk editing and electronic design, composition, and typesetting).

special sales Sales of a book to appropriate retailers other than bookstores (for example, wine guides to liquor stores). This classification also includes books sold as premiums (for example, to a convention group or a corporation) or for other promotional purposes. Depending on volume, per-unit costs can be very low, and the book can be custom-designed. (*See also* **premium.**)

spine That portion of the book's casing (or binding) that backs the bound page signatures and is visible when the volume is aligned on a bookshelf among other volumes.

stamping In book publishing, the stamp is the impression of ornamental type and images (such as a logo or monogram) on the book's binding. The stamping process involves using a die with a raised or intaglioed surface to apply ink stamping or metallic-leaf stamping.

subsidiary rights The reprint, serial, movie and television, and audiotape and video-tape rights deriving from a book. The division of profits between publisher and author from the sales of these rights is determined through negotiation. In more elaborately commercial projects, further details such as syndication of related articles and licensing of characters may ultimately be involved.

subsidy publishing   A mode of publication wherein the author pays a publishing company to produce his or her work, which may thus appear superficially to have been published conventionally. Subsidy publishing (alias vanity publishing) is generally more expensive than self-publishing, because a successful subsidy house makes a profit on all its contracted functions, charging fees well beyond the publisher's basic costs for production and services.

suspense fiction   Fiction within a number of genre categories that emphasize suspense as well as the usual (and sometimes unusual) literary techniques to keep the reader engaged. Suspense fiction encompasses novels of crime and detection (regularly referred to as mysteries. These include English-style cozies, American-style hard-boiled detective stories), dispassionate law-enforcement procedurals, crime stories, action-adventure, espionage novels, technothrillers, tales of psychological suspense, and horror. A celebrated aspect of suspense fiction's popular appeal—one that surely accounts for much of this broad category's sustained market vigor—is the interactive element: The reader may choose to challenge the tale itself by attempting to outwit the author and solve a crime before detectives do, figure out how best to defeat an all-powerful foe before the hero does, or parse out the elements of a conspiracy before the writer reveals the whole story.

syndicated column   Material published simultaneously in a number of newspapers or magazines. The author shares the income from syndication with the syndicate that negotiates the sale. (*See also* **self-syndication.**)

syndication rights   (*See also* **self-syndication; subsidiary rights.**)

synopsis   A summary in paragraph form, rather than in outline format. The synopsis is an important part of a book proposal. For fiction, the synopsis portrays the high points of story line and plot, succinctly and dramatically. In a nonfiction book proposal, the synopsis describes the thrust and content of the successive chapters (and/or parts) of the manuscript.

T

table of contents   A listing of a book's chapters and other sections (such as the front matter, appendix, index, and bibliography) or of a magazine's articles and columns, in the order in which they appear; in published versions, the table of contents indicates the respective beginning page numbers.

tabloid   A smaller-than-standard-size newspaper (daily, weekly, or monthly). Traditionally, certain tabloids are distinguished by sensationalism of approach and content rather than by straightforward reportage of newsworthy events. In common parlance, "tabloid" is used to describe works in various media (including books) that cater to immoderate tastes (for example, tabloid exposé, tabloid television; the tabloidization of popular culture).

teleplay A **screenplay** geared toward television production. Similar in overall concept to screenplays for the cinema, teleplays are nonetheless inherently concerned with such TV-loaded provisions as the physical dimensions of the smaller screen, and formal elements of pacing and structure keyed to stipulated program length and the placement of commercial advertising. Attention to these myriad television-specific demands are fundamental to the viability of a project.

terms The financial conditions agreed to in a book contract.

theme A general term for the underlying concept of a book. (*See also* **hook**.)

thriller A thriller is a novel of suspense with a plot structure that reinforces the elements of gamesmanship and the chase, with a sense of the hunt being paramount. Thrillers can be spy novels, tales of geopolitical crisis, legal thrillers, medical thrillers, technothrillers, domestic thrillers. The common thread is a growing sense of threat and the excitement of pursuit.

tip sheet An information sheet on a single book that presents general publication information (publication date, editor, ISBN, etc.), a brief synopsis of the book, information on relevant other books (sometimes competing titles), and other pertinent marketing data such as author profile and advance blurbs. The tip sheet is given to the sales and publicity departments; a version of the tip sheet is also included in press kits.

title page The page at the front of a book that lists the title, subtitle, author (and other contributors, such as translator or illustrator), as well as the publishing house and sometimes its logo.

trade books Books distributed through the book trade—meaning bookstores and major book clubs—as opposed to, for example, mass-market paperbacks, which are often sold at magazine racks, newsstands, and supermarkets as well.

trade discount The discount from the cover or list price that a publisher gives the bookseller. It is usually proportional to the number of books ordered (the larger the order, the greater the discount), and typically varies between 40 percent and 50 percent.

trade list A catalog of all of a publisher's books in print, with ISBNs and order information. The trade list sometimes includes descriptions of the current season's new books.

trade (quality) paperbacks Reprints or original titles published in paperback format, larger in dimension than mass-market paperbacks, and distributed through regular retail book channels. Trade paperbacks tend to be in the neighborhood of twice the price of an equivalent mass-market paperback version and about half to two-thirds the price of hardcover editions.

trade publishers Publishers of books for a general readership—that is, nonprofessional, nonacademic books that are distributed primarily through bookstores.

translation rights Rights sold either to a foreign agent or directly to a foreign publisher, either by the author's agent or by the original publisher.

treatment In screenwriting, a full narrative description of the story, including sample dialogue.

U

unauthorized biography   A history of a person's life written without the consent or collaboration of the subject or the subject's survivors.

university press   A publishing house affiliated with a sponsoring university. The university press is generally nonprofit and subsidized by the respective university. Generally, university presses publish noncommercial scholarly nonfiction books written by academics, and their lists may include literary fiction, criticism, and poetry. Some university presses also specialize in titles of regional interest, and many acquire projects intended for commercial book-trade distribution.

unsolicited manuscript   A manuscript sent to an editor or agent without being requested by the editor/agent.

V

vanity press   A publisher that publishes books only at an author's expense—and will generally agree to publish virtually anything that is submitted and paid for. (*See also* **subsidy publishing**.)

vita   Latin word for "life." A shortened equivalent term for *curriculum vitae* (*see also* **résumé**).

W

word count   The number of words in a given document. When noted on a manuscript, the word count is usually rounded off to the nearest 100 words.

work-for-hire   Writing done for an employer, or writing commissioned by a publisher or book packager who retains ownership of, and all rights pertaining to, the written material.

Y

young-adult (YA) books   Books for readers generally between the ages of 12 and 17. Young-adult fiction often deals with issues of concern to contemporary teens.

young readers or **younger readers**   Publishing terminology for the range of publications that address the earliest readers. Sometimes a particular house's young-readers program typifies books for those who do not yet read, which means these books have to hook the caretakers and parents who actually buy them. In certain quirky turns of everyday publishing parlance, *young readers* can mean anyone from embryos through young adults (and "young" means *you* when you want it to). This part may be confusing (as is often the case with publishing usage): Sometimes *younger adult* means only that the readership is allegedly hip, including those who would eschew kid's books as being inherently lame and those who are excruciatingly tapped into the current cultural pulse, regardless of cerebral or life-span quotient.

Z

zombie (or **zombi**) In idiomatic usage, a zombie is a person whose conduct approximates that of an automaton. Harking back to the term's origins as a figure of speech for the resurrected dead or a reanimated cadaver, such folks are not customarily expected to exhibit an especially snazzy personality or be aware of too many things going on around them; hence some people in book-publishing circles may be characterized as zombies.

INDEX

INDEX

PUBLISHERS AND IMPRINTS

INDEX

AGENTS AND AGENCIES

PUBLISHERS AND
IMPRINTS BY SUBJECT

PUBLISHERS AND IMPRINTS BY SUBJECT

ADULT NONFICTION

INDEX

BOOKS FOR CHILDREN/TEENS

COOKING

CRAFTS

FANTASY/SCIENCE FICTION

ROMANCE